HOSPITAL ADMINISTRATION HANDBOOK

Edited by
Howard S. Rowland
and
Beatrice L. Rowland

AN ASPEN PUBLICATION®
Aspen Systems Corporation
Rockville, Maryland
Royal Tunbridge Wells
1984

Library of Congress Cataloging in Publication Data

Rowland, Howard S.
Hospital administration handbook.

"An Aspen publication."
Includes bibliographical references and index.
1. Hospitals—Administration—Handbooks, manuals, etc.
I. Rowland, Beatrice L.   II. Title. [DNLM: 1. Hospital
administration. 2. Leadership.   WX 150 R883h]
RA971.R66   1984   362.1'1'068   83-9236
ISBN: 0-89443-941-3

Publisher: John Marozsan
Executive Managing Editor: Margot Raphael
Editorial Services: Eileen Higgins
Printing and Manufacturing: Debbie Collins

Copyright © 1984 by Aspen Systems Corporation

All rights reserved. This book, or parts thereof, may not be
reproduced in any form or by any means, electronic or
mechanical, including photocopy, recording, or any
information storage and retrieval system now known or
to be invented, without written permission from the
publisher, except in the case of brief quotations embodied
in critical articles or reviews. For information, address
Aspen Systems Corporation, 1600 Research Boulevard,
Rockville, Maryland 20850.

Library of Congress Catalog Card Number: 83-9236
ISBN: 0-89443-941-3

Printed in the United States of America

To the hospital administrator,

who, from the "eye of the hurricane," provides steady direction for the most complex and effective health care delivery system in the world.

CONTENTS

PART I—MANAGEMENT 1

Chapter 1—The Hospital Administrator 3
    Specific Duties of the Administrator 3
    Managing 6
    The Creative Executive 11
    Self-Evaluation 14
    Management Stress 16
    How a CEO Changes Jobs 19

Chapter 2—Leadership 21
    Styles of Leadership 21
    The Administrator as Power Broker 23
    Leadership Tests 25

Chapter 3—Participatory Management 34
    The MBO Method 34
    The Delphi Technique 40

Chapter 4—Management Control 46
    Overview 46
    Internal Auditing 47
    Program Evaluation 49
    The Hospital Manual 51

Chapter 5—Managing Subordinates 58
    Sound Practices 58
    Problem Managers 60

Chapter 6—Problems, Change, and Decisions 71
    Problem Solving 71
    Managing Change 73
    Decision Making 75

Chapter 7—Delegation and Time Management 79
        Delegation 79
        Work Planning 82
        Time Management 84

Chapter 8—Managing Outsiders 95
        Consultants 95
        Evaluators 96

PART II—ORGANIZATION 99

Chapter 9—A Primer on Organization 101

Chapter 10—Using Committees 109
        What Makes Committees Work? 109

Chapter 11—Hospital Systems 116
        Overview 116
        Contract Management 123
        Everything You've Wanted To Know about Hospital Chains 125
        Multihospital Systems 128

PART III—PLANNING 135

Chapter 12—Organizing for Planning 137
        Overview 137
        Strategic Planning 143
        Systems Engineering 151
        The Hospital Long Range Plan: A Model Outline 152
        Forecasting 154

Chapter 13—Strategies for Growth 158
        Gaining More Business 158
        Diversification 160
        Developing New Health Services 162
        Primary Medical Care 166
        The Emergicare Center 172
        Health Facilities Conversion: Strategies 174

Chapter 14—Marketing 179
        Overview 179
        Organizing for Marketing 188
        P.R. and Advertising 204

PART IV—FINANCIAL MANAGEMENT 207

Chapter 15—Operations 214
        Financial Planning 214
        Profitability for Hospitals 218
        Capital Formation 219
        Cost Finding 220
        Effective Cash Management 223

Internal Financial Auditing: A List of Checkpoints 227
The "Troubled Hospital Syndrome" 233

Chapter 16—Budgeting.. 235
    Overview.. 235
    The Budget Process.. 236
    Budgeting Approaches 240
    Types of Budget Documents 246
    Interpreting and Acting upon Budget Reports 247
    Cost Benefit/Cost Effectiveness Analyses 253
    Cost Analysis Concepts Applicable to Department Management 258
    Internal Audit Checklist for Planning and Budgeting........................ 261

Chapter 17—Cost Containment 265
    Overview.. 265
    Cost Containment Strategies 269
    Case Study of a Hospital's Cost Containment Efforts 271

Chapter 18—Reimbursement and Rate Setting 281
    Overview.. 281
    Medicaid 281
    Medicare Hospital Insurance... 282
    The Provider Reimbursement Review Board (PRRB) 292
    Reimbursement—Other Services Covered and Uncovered 295
    Rate Setting... 295
    Prospective Rate Setting 303

Chapter 19—All You Need To Know about Gifts, Trusts, and Taxes 308
    Overview.. 308
    Types of Gifts... 309
    Setting up a Foundation 311

PART V—CAPITAL FORMATION, EXPENDITURES, AND CONSTRUCTION......... 313

Chapter 20—Capital Formation 315
    Overview.. 315
    Long Term Debt Financing 319
    Short and Intermediate Term Financing.................................... 325
    The Full Cost of Borrowing.. 327
    Capital Investment and Reimbursement Penalties 329

Chapter 21—Capital Expenditures.. 331
    Capital Expenditure Requests... 331
    An Example of Capital Expenditure Planning 333
    Cost Finding for New Hospital Services or Equipment 335
    Equipment Leasing 338

Chapter 22—Construction 345
    The Master Plan.. 345
    How To Organize for the Planning Process 347
    A Step-by-Step Schedule of Activities for the Planning Team 350
    Contracts for Services with Consultants and Contractors................ 358
    Project Management Techniques 361

Key Factors 364
Capital Cost Minimization 367

PART VI—INFORMATION MANAGEMENT: COMPUTERS, HOSPITAL INFORMATION SYSTEMS, WORD PROCESSORS 375

Chapter 23—Computers 377
How Hospitals Use Computers 377
Pointers on Purchasing 383
Main Frame vs. Mini-Computer 389
Shared Systems vs. In-House Systems 395

Chapter 24—Hospital Information Systems (HIS) 404
Overview 404
Six Critical Issues 407
Planning an HIS 412
Establishing an HIS 420

Chapter 25—Patient Management: Computerized Information Systems ... 426
Overview 426

Chapter 26—Word Processing 434

PART VII—HUMAN RESOURCES MANAGEMENT 437

Chapter 27—Communications 442
Improving Communications 442
Communication Targets 444
Communication Techniques 449
Scoring 451
Developing Personnel Policies 455

Chapter 28—Recruitment, Interviewing, and Orientation 458
Recruitment 458
Interviewing Techniques 460
Orientation 463

Chapter 29—Troubled and Troublesome Employees 466
Troubled Employees 466
Problem Employees 468
Dead-End Employees 474

Chapter 30—Motivation and Job Enrichment 475
Motivation 475
Motivation Theory 477
Job Enrichment 483

Chapter 31—Absenteeism and Turnover 487
Overview 487
Absenteeism 489
Turnover 492

Contents ix

Chapter 32—Criticizing, Disciplining, and Handling Grievances **499**
    Criticizing 499
    Disciplining 501
    Handling Grievances 504

Chapter 33—Employee Salaries **508**
    Salary Policies 508
    Administering Salaries of Hospital Managers 515

Chapter 34—Employee Benefits (Pension, Disability, Medical, and Death Benefits) **518**
    Overview 518
    Retirement Benefits 524
    Death Benefits 526
    Disability Benefits 527
    Medical Benefits 528
    Current Practices and Trends 530

Chapter 35—Employee Performance Appraisal **536**
    Appraisal Methods 536
    Bars and MBO 540
    Common Appraisal Problems 541
    Standards for Evaluating Employees 541
    The Appraisal Interview 545

Chapter 36—Productivity **552**
    Overview 552
    Developing Work Standards 554
    Work Simplification 562
    Productivity Improvement Programs 567
    Flexible Staffing Approaches 586
    Employee Incentives 589

Chapter 37—Unions **592**
    Why Employees Join Unions 592
    The Organizing Campaign 594
    Management Strategies To Oppose Unions 600
    Collective Bargaining 608
    The Strike 621

PART VIII—QUALITY ASSURANCE AND SAFETY **625**

Chapter 38—Quality Assurance **627**
    Overview 627
    Organizing for Quality Assurance (QA) 630
    Identifying Issues/Concerns/Problems in QA Investigation 635
    Quality Assessment Techniques 637
    Setting Criteria for Quality of Care 638
    Data Collection 640
    Three Specific Techniques 642
    JCAH Quality Assurance Standard 651
    Medical Audit 653
    Utilization Review 655
    CLTR (A Retrospective Utilization Review) 657

Chapter 39—Disaster, Fire, Infection, and Occupational Health 664
    Handling Disasters 664
    Fire 669
    Management of Infection Control 669
    Occupational Health and Safety in Hospitals 672

PART IX—THE HOSPITAL AND THE LAW 679

Chapter 40—Hospital Liability 681
    Overview 681
    Areas of High Liability Risk 682
    Torts 689

Chapter 41—Informed Consent 692
    Overview 692
    Medical Experimentation and Research 693
    Consent Forms 694
    Refusal of Consent 697

Chapter 42—Medical Records and the Law 703
    Maintaining Records 703
    Access to Medical Record Information 705

Chapter 43—Licensure and Permits 715

Chapter 44—Trustees/Administrators and the Law 723
    Trustees 723
    The Hospital Administrator 725
    Administrator's Preparation for Litigation 726

Index 729

PART I
MANAGEMENT

Chapter 1—The Hospital Administrator

The administrator of a charitable hospital is the executive officer directly in charge of the hospital, responsible only to the governing board. He is the general supervisor of all the operations of the hospital. The governing board delegates powers to the administrator whereby he is able to fulfill this responsibility. Although he may in turn delegate specific areas of responsibility to various subordinate supervisors, the administrator is primarily responsible for the efficient and orderly management of the hospital. He is the employee or agent of the governing board and subject to its authority.

The administrator of a proprietary hospital, however, may have a different relationship. He may be one of several people owning the hospital, and will have two functions: one as the supervisor and the other as an owner. As supervisor, he is the group's agent and must carry out the policy as determined by the group, whether or not he is personally in accord with that policy. As an owner, he has stature equal to that of other owners of the organization and a voice in determining hospital policy proportionate to his share of ownership. Difficulties may arise in keeping these functions distinct. If the administrator is not part-owner, he has but one function: that of supervisor.

In governmental hospitals the administrator is usually an appointed public official. Whether he is a public official or a hired supervisor like the administrator of a charitable hospital, he is directly responsible to the federal, state or local body which controls the health facility. In some instances, his actions may be governed by the civil service laws.*

SPECIFIC DUTIES OF THE ADMINISTRATOR*

The administrator has only those duties delegated to him by the hospital's governing board. Legal responsibility for the conduct of the hospital is vested in the governing board; and, to fulfill this responsibility, the board appoints an administrator and charges him with certain general duties in the management of the hospital. In addition, by resolution, bylaw or order, the board may fix specific duties upon the administrator and grant authority to him to discharge these duties. The delegation of authority to the administrator may be broad or narrow, depending upon the policy of the board.

Following are examples of the administrator's general and specific duties delegated to him by the board.

The administrator has the general duty to oversee every activity taking place in the hospital. He must carry out the policies of the board by implementing these policies in the various departments of the hospital through the transmission and interpretation of the board's policy to medical staff and other personnel. The admin-

---

*Source: Reprinted from *Hospital Law Manual,* Vol. I, Health Law Center, with permission of Aspen Systems Corporation, © March 1979.

istrator must ensure that all patients, visitors, private-duty nurses, hospital personnel and members of the medical staff are informed and comply with all hospital rules formulated by the board or the administrator. He must take appropriate disciplinary action where noncompliance with hospital rules occurs, except in cases where disciplinary authority has been retained by the board or the medical staff. He also has the general duty to make periodic reports to the board indicating the nature of the hospital's operations.

Normally, the administrator will be authorized to select or recommend selection of administrative department heads. He then delegates to department heads the authority to select their assistants, but reserves the authority to coordinate the overall operation of the departments. In addition, the administrator is usually responsible for employment in the hospital and, within budgetary limits, can fix individual salaries and wages.

The administrator is also generally responsible for the care and treatment of patients. He must ensure that proper admission and discharge procedures are formulated and carried out, and that adequate cooperation with the medical staff in the maintenance of satisfactory standards of medical care are maintained. The administrator must also insure that departments directly concerned with patient care work in complete coordination with the attending physician, and that the various adjunct facilities used in diagnosis and treatment are properly functioning.

Despite the fact that administrative authority may be delegated to subordinates, ultimate responsibility still rests with the administrator since it is he, in the final analysis, who must answer to the board for the operation of the hospital; and it is the board which has the ultimate legal responsibility for the hospital.

In addition to those duties specifically or impliedly delegated by the governing board, the administrator may also be responsible for duties imposed by state statutes, regulations, or by municipal ordinances. To determine if a regulation is valid, the hospital attorney should be consulted. If the administrator feels that the regulation may have been amended, he should consult the appropriate department or board to obtain a current version of the regulation in question.

The administrator should also be familiar with the regulations of his state. In addition to these duties, most states require those in charge of hospitals and related institutions to report vital statistics information to health authorities. In several states, communicable disease reports must be made, as well as reports on the treatment of persons with gunshot wounds.

Finally, hospitals that wish to receive reimbursement as health providers under the Medicare and Medicaid programs must comply with federal regulations, known as *Conditions of Participation*. These standards, in addition to many other things, set forth duties that must be undertaken by hospital administrators:

The administrator acts as the executive officer of the governing body, is responsible for the management of the hospital, and provides liaison among the governing body, medical staff, nursing staff, and other departments of the hospital. The factors explaining the standard are as follows:

1. In discharging his duties, the administrator keeps the governing body fully informed of the conduct of the hospital through annual, monthly, or written reports and by attendance at meetings of the governing body.

2. The administrator organizes the day-to-day functions of the hospital through appropriate departmentalization and delegation of duties.

3. The administrator establishes formal means of accountability on the part of subordinates to whom he has assigned duties.

4. To maintain sufficient liaison between the governing body, medical and nursing staffs and other departments, the administrator holds inter-departmental and departmental meetings, where appropriate, attends or is represented at such meetings on a regular basis, and reports to such departments as well as the governing body the pertinent activities of the hospital.

5. The administrator has sufficient freedom from other responsibilities to permit adequate attention to the management and administration of the hospital.

An ACHA List*

To clarify the responsibilities of the chief executive the American College of Hospital Administrators (ACHA) offers a list of duties.

The chief executive:

1. establishes an organizational climate in which problems are viewed as challenges and encourages a willingness to undertake difficult assignments;

2. initiates proposals as to what the mission of the hospital should be and what the priority mix and time schedule of programs should be to achieve it;

3. anticipates public expectations for the institution and exercises judgment as to what its response should be, both at present and in the future;

4. initiates proposals on the information system so board members can understand and use the data to control program effectiveness and financial position;

5. initiates proposals for policy changes in response to changing conditions and trends;

6. seeks acceptance of key individuals and groups from both inside and outside the hospital for the approved goals of the institution;

7. plans the course of the organization so it remains financially and otherwise viable, while responding to public needs and expectations; and

8. provides leadership in orchestrating the human resources inside and outside the organization, including the board members, administrative staff, professional staff, and employees, to develop and execute the organization's mission and programs.

In exercising these responsibilities the chief executive faces new challenges and public expectations. The planning requirements of his role have become formalized through the establishment of the National Health Planning Resources and Development Act.

---

*Source: Reprinted from *Principles of Appointment and Tenure of Executive Officers*, by ACHA Task Force V, with permission of the American College of Hospital Administrators, © 1973.

A State Government's List*

The Executive Officer shall:

a. Maintain an organizational structure which defines and makes known the authority and responsibility of various positions and their relationships and employ sufficient trained personnel to adequately man the facility.

b. Develop, with the assistance of hospital personnel and the Medical Staff, a program of patient care and hospital operation in line with goals of hospital and needs of patients served.

c. Measure the effectiveness of the hospital operation in terms of goals and the expected results of patient care.

d. Maintain long-range plans to provide for the continuous improvement of the hospital.

e. Consult with representatives of the organized Medical Staff on matters which are of concern to the Medical Staff in its hospital work.

f. Designate an administrative officer for the facility to serve during the administrator's absence.

g. Provide induction and follow-up training programs for all hospital personnel.

h. Provide for department head staff meetings to achieve effective communications and coordination of activities of the various elements of the hospital.

i. Maintain a written record of all business transactions, committee activities, and patient services rendered and submit reports on same to the governing authority.

j. Establish and maintain a functioning hospital safety committee.

k. Require pre-employment and subsequent physical examinations, chest X-rays, laboratory tests, and immunization, as deemed necessary by the Medical Staff, of all personnel coming in direct or indirect contact with patients. Supervisors shall continually observe their personnel for signs of communicable disease and encourage their personnel to promptly report any illnesses in themselves. An ac-

---

*Source: Indiana: *Regulations for General and Special Hospitals (HHL 42)*, effective Dec. 18, 1977 (State Board of Health).

ceptable test for tuberculosis may be given in lieu of the chest X-ray, as long as the test remains negative, and shall be repeated each year. If the test converts to positive, a chest X-ray, a physical, and a laboratory examination shall be made, and the employee must be deemed free of active tuberculosis before resuming duties.

l. Periodic surveillance of patients and personnel in hemodialysis units for HBV (hepatitis B virus) infection shall be carried out at intervals to be determined by the Medical Staff.

m. Maintain and periodically test a plan for emergency operation of the hospital to provide for the safety and well-being of patients and personnel in event of fire, explosion, or other internal disaster and for the provision of care to casualties from an outside disaster.

n. Be responsible for formulating a written dress code for all personnel to prevent possible outside contamination.

MANAGING

Characteristics of Managerial Work*

1. Because of the open-ended nature of his job, the manager feels compelled to perform a great quantity of work at an unrelenting pace. Little free time is available and breaks are rare. Senior managers, in particular, cannot escape from their jobs after hours, because of the work they take home and because their minds tend to be on their jobs during much of their "free" time.

2. In contrast to activities performed by most nonmanagers, those of the manager are characterized by brevity, variety, and fragmentation. The vast majority are of brief duration. The variety of activities to be performed is great, and the lack of pattern among subsequent activities, with the trivial interspersed with the consequential, requires that the manager shift moods quickly and frequently. In general, managerial work is fragmented and interruptions are commonplace.

3. The manager actually appears to prefer brevity and interruption in his work. He becomes conditioned by his workload; he develops an appreciation for the opportunity cost of his own time; and he lives continuously with an awareness of what else might or must be done at any time. Superficiality is an occupational hazard of the manager's job.

4. The manager gravitates to the more active elements of his work—the current, the specific, the well-defined, the non-routine activities. Very current information (gossip, hearsay, speculation) is favored; routine reports are not. Time scheduling reflects a concern with the definite and the concrete, and activities tend to focus on specific rather than general issues. The pressure of the job does not encourage the development of a planner, but of an adaptive information manipulator who works in a stimulus-response environment and who favors live action.

5. Verbal and written contacts are the manager's work and his prime tools are five media—mail (documented), telephone (purely verbal), unscheduled meetings (informal face-to-face), scheduled meetings (formal face-to-face), and tour (observational). The manager clearly favors the three verbal media, spending most of his time in verbal contact.

6. Mail receives cursory treatment, although it must be processed regularly. The mail contains much general data and lengthy documents (reports, periodicals, and so on) and numbers of formal communications and inconsequential requests that must, nevertheless, be answered. The manager generates much less mail than he receives, most of it necessary responses to input mail.

7. The informal media (telephone and unscheduled meeting) are generally used by the manager for brief contacts when the parties are well known to each other, and when information or requests must be transmitted quickly.

8. The scheduled meeting consumes more of the manager's time than any other me-

---

* Source: From *The Nature of Managerial Work* by Henry Mintzberg. "Propositions About Managerial Work Characteristics" (pp. 51–53) Copyright © 1973 by Henry Mintzberg. Reprinted by permission of Harper & Row Publishers, Inc.

dium. It allows for contacts of long duration of a formal nature, with large groups of people, and away from the department. Activities for the purposes of ceremony, strategy-making, and negotiation generally take place at scheduled meetings. Of special interest in scheduled meetings is the general discussion at the beginning and end of each, which frequently involves the flow of important information.

9. Tours provide the manager with the opportunity to observe activity informally without prearrangement. But the manager spends little of his time in open-ended touring.

10. The manager may be likened to the neck of an hourglass, standing between his own organization and a network of outside contacts, linking them in a variety of ways. External contacts generally consume one-third to one-half of the manager's contact time. These are of great variety and include suppliers, associates, peers, and others. These people serve, in effect, as a network of informers. Nonline relationships are a significant and complex component of the manager's job.

11. Subordinates generally consume one-third to one-half of the manager's contact time, most often for purposes of making requests, of sending or receiving information, and of making strategy. The manager interacts freely with a wide variety of subordinates, bypassing formal channels of communication to do so.

12. The manager spends relatively little of his time with his superior—generally on the order of 10 percent.

13. The manager's job reflects a blend of duties and rights. Although superficial study of manager's activities suggests that they often control little of what they do, closer analysis suggests that the manager can exert self control in two important ways. The manager is responsible for many initial commitments, which then lock him into a set of ongoing activities; and the manager can take advantage of his obligations by extracting information, by exercising his leadership, and in many other ways.

Manager Roles*

Managerial activities may be divided into three groups—those that are concerned primarily with interpersonal relationships, those that deal primarily with the transfer of information and those that essentially involve decision-making. (See Table 1-1.)

General Functions of Management**

The duties common to all managers are most often referred to as functions of management. They include planning, organizing, directing, coordinating, and controlling.

Planning

The planning process is largely one of forecasting and decision-making. Forecasting provides the manager with information and messages about the future. By combining the forecast with other data related to the past and present, a manager can then select those courses which appear to be most appropriate in terms of forecasting conditions. Yet, while a manager can be assisted in the planning process by various staff groups, it should be noted by each manager that the ultimate responsibility for planning rests with him alone.

Since planning is always future oriented, it can be further characterized as the process whereby the management of an organization bridges the time span between where it is at present and where it wants to be at some point in the future. In doing so, planning involves the choice of objectives along with the policies, strategies, programs, procedures, and rules that are necessary for their accomplishment. In this sense, planning directs our thinking toward *what* we expect to do, *why* it will be done, *where* it will be done, *when* we expect to do it, *how* it will be done, and *who* is going to do it.

Organizing

Basically, the function of organization is concerned with establishing a chain of command

---

*Source: From *The Nature of Managerial Work* by Henry Mintzberg, an adaptation of Table 2, "Summary of Ten Roles," (pp. 92–93) Copyright © 1973 by Henry Mintzberg. Reprinted by permission of Harper & Row Publishers, Inc.

**Source: Reprinted from *The Tools of Managing* by M. Gene Newport, Copyright © 1972 by permission of Addison-Wesley Publishing Co., Reading, MA.

Table 1-1 Summary of Managerial Roles

Role	Description	Identifiable Activities
Interpersonal		
Figurehead	Symbolic head; obliged to perform a number of routine duties of a legal or social nature	Ceremony, status requests, solicitations
Leader	Responsible for the motivation and activation of subordinates; responsible for staffing, training, and associated duties	Virtually all managerial activities involving subordinates
Liaison	Maintains self-development network of outside contacts and informers who provide favors and information	Interdepartmental relations and other activities involving outsiders
Informational		
Monitor	Seeks and receives wide variety of special information (much of it current) to develop thorough understanding of organization and environment; emerges as nerve center of internal and external information of the organization	Handling all contacts categorized as concerned primarily with receiving information (e.g., periodical news, observational tours)
Disseminator	Transmits information received from outsiders or from other subordinates to members of the organization; some information factual, some involving interpretation and integration of diverse value positions of organizational influencers	Forwarding mail into organization for information purposes, verbal contacts involving information flow to subordinates (e.g., review sessions, instant communication flows)
Spokesman	Transmits information to outsiders on organization's plans, policies, actions, results, etc.; serves as expert on organization's industry	Department meetings; handling contacts involving transmission of information to outsiders
Decisional		
Enterpreneur	Searches organization and its environment for opportunities and initiates "improvement projects" to bring about change; supervises design of certain projects as well	Strategy and review sessions involving initiation or design of improvement projects
Disturbance Handler	Responsible for corrective action when organization faces important, unexpected disturbances	Strategy and review sessions involving disturbances and crises
Resource Allocator	Responsible for the allocation of organizational resources of all kinds—in effect the making or approval of all significant organizational decisions	Scheduling; requests for authorization; any activity involving budgeting and the programming of subordinates' work
Negotiator	Responsible for representing the organization at major negotiations	Negotiation

and a division of labor. To accomplish these ends, organizing involves the identification of duties to be performed; a grouping of these duties to indicate division, unit, section, or departmental arrangements; and an assignment of authority according to the line, staff, or functional relationships that will exist between individual jobs and total organizational units.

The steps outlined above can, of course, be applied to either the initial design of an organization structure or to the maintenance of the structure once it has been established. In either case, the process is indispensable since it combines human and material resources into an orderly and systematic arrangement which provides the basic ingredients necessary for a coordination of effort.

Directing

While planning can determine what will be done, organizing can combine the necessary resources for doing the job, coordination can maintain harmony among the resources, and control can monitor performance, it is direction that initiates and maintains action toward desired objectives. Direction is, therefore, closely interrelated with leadership in that a manager's style of leadership is determined by the manner in which he exercises his authority in the direction of subordinates.

Success in carrying out this function depends on many factors. Among the most important, however, are delegation, communication, training, and motivation. Through delegation, subordinates receive the authority required in fulfilling their responsibilities. Communication provides individuals with the information needed in performing their jobs and allows for feedback of results related to their performance. Training is involved with the initial orientation of employees in addition to the continued direction of learning once an individual is on the job. Finally, motivation is concerned with assisting individuals in satisfying their needs in such a way that they continue to exhibit behavior that is consistent with their potential.

Coordinating

A coordination of effort involves the synchronization of activities toward established goals. If all employees are given the right to do a job in their own way, each is usually guided by his own ideas of what should be done. And even though these individuals may be quite willing to cooperate, the end result could well be a waste of time, effort, and money, since there is no meaningful direction to guide their efforts. Consequently, coordination is required and becomes a major responsibility of all managers.

To reiterate, we must consider coordination as something different from cooperation. While the latter may arise spontaneously among the members of a group, coordination occurs only through effective leadership. As with a tug-of-war, the manager can make a great contribution by learning when and how to let go of the rope, so to speak, in order to call the cadence that causes his team to pull together. In this sense, coordination is the means of concentrating and applying cooperative effort to accomplish a task with economy and effectiveness. Therefore, it becomes the very essence of management and results from good planning, organizing, directing, and controlling.

Controlling

The purpose of control is to see that actual performance corresponds to that which is called for in various plans. All managers exercise control by: (1) knowing or establishing the standards that relate to a particular course of action; (2) measuring actual performance against the standards; and (3) correcting deviations from standards, when necessary.

Leadership is also essential to control since inanimate objects are really not controlled, per se. People operate machines, use equipment, follow procedures, and, in fact, bring an organization to life. Thus control focuses on the direction of human behavior, but leadership is needed to cause persons to perform in a desired manner.

Each of the functions and activities identified here is performed by every *professional* manager at every level. The differences are ones of magnitude and frequency. Figure 1-1 shows the variation in the percentage of effort devoted to each of the five functions at three levels of management.

As is readily apparent from the illustration, the biggest variation in proportionate effort is in the directing function. The closer the manager is to production activity, the larger is the proportion of effort he is likely to devote to the directing function. Conversely, the further away from production he gets, the less time and effort he should devote to directing and the more attention he should give to the other functions. Obviously, the actual mix of the various functions will not be as smooth as in the illustration, and will be influenced by other factors as well. Nevertheless, the marked change in the mix as a manager proceeds up the management ladder is inescapable. Therefore, a highly successful first-line supervisor will not necessarily make a good middle manager. Nor, on the other hand, will a middle manager who possesses the necessary skills to perform effectively at that level be a guaranteed success as a first-line supervisor.

How Not To Manage*

The application of the following principles will result in disunity, distrust, lack of commitment, and chaos.

---

*Source: Reprinted from "A Long-Range Model for Organizational Chaos At Any Level," *Personnel Journal* (July) by Larry B. Meares with permission of the publisher, © 1979. All rights reserved.

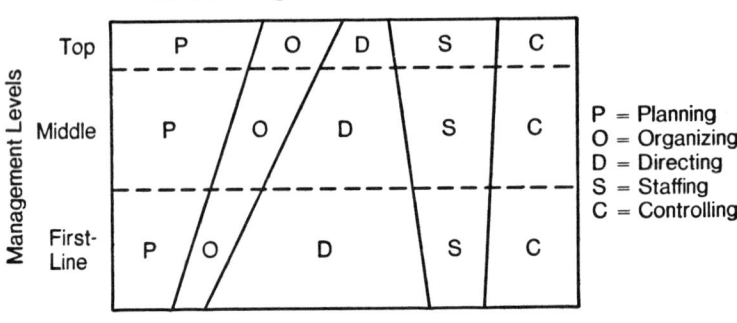

Figure 1-1   Proportion of management effort devoted to planning, organizing, directing, staffing, and controlling

*Source: Reprinted from *The Tools of Managing* by M. Gene Newport, Copyright © 1972 by permission of Addison-Wesley Publishing Co., Reading, MA.

1. Create distinct and visible status symbols which make everyone sensitive to the "haves" and "have nots" at various levels of the organization.
2. Refrain from installing any type of formal promotion and transfer procedure.
3. At lower levels of the organization's hierarchy, ignore seniority completely when contemplating any work-related promotion, transfer, or other reward considerations, except where required for vacation accrual or pension vesting.
4. Communicate only mundane and elementary information.
5. Title people with levels of visible difference, e.g., the hourly or factory subordinate, as opposed to the salaried, exempt manager, and refer to them by these titles instead of by their names.
6. Deliberately refrain from the installation of position descriptions, authority parameters, or any other semblance of a performance appraisal system.
7. Encourage favoritism wherever possible.
8. Make it a public practice to discharge errant persons without employing a system of progressive consultation.
9. Provide nothing which resembles a system permitting persons to air their complaints, problems, questions, or suggestions.
10. Provide no management development or training for members of supervision and other management personnel.
11. Retain only managers who are mechanically and technically competent, but managerially deficient.
12. Establish written rules and regulations for every conceivable infraction, and impose them without flexibility on the group for whom they are intended.
13. Encourage each member of management to hire and staff all vacancies under their jurisdiction, without providing any assistance or training in how to perform such activities.
14. Maintain benefits and pay levels below the average of the competitive marketplace.
15. Follow a policy of affixing individual blame when mistakes or errors occur, and especially stress punitive measures.
16. Discourage socializing, whether on or off the job.
17. Attempt to avoid any formalized approach to planning and forecasting, since it often leads to a more stable work group, with too many participants aware of too much information.
18. Always attempt to visibly show disrespect for the dignity of the people you want to disturb or upset.
19. Make it a routine practice to promise people whatever they need or want and then conveniently forget to live up to your word.
20. It is always helpful to arrange for managers and supervisors to be caught telling

untruths to each other and their employees, so take care to always plant at least one or two "whoppers" that will be naturally discovered in the course of daily events.
21. Never provide advance notice when overtime work is necessary.
22. If you have the unfortunate tendency to be outgoing and friendly, you must overcome it!
23. Always take credit for the contributions of others, and make sure they find out.
24. Do a lot of monotonous lecturing about everything.
25. Criticize everyone to everyone else.

THE CREATIVE EXECUTIVE*

To start with, the creative executive has more energy, is more impulsive, and is more responsive to emotions and feelings than the less creative manager. Creative executives can generate large numbers of ideas rapidly, choose and investigate a wide variety of approaches to problems, discard one frame of reference for another, change approaches, and adapt quickly to new developments.

Your less creative colleague probably suffers from "hardening of the categories," which is a lack of flexibility that often results from overfamiliarity with objects or ideas. The really creative executive allows his thoughts to mill about without categorizing.

Youthful Curiosity

Creativity is contingent upon how much of our innate curiosity and youthful sense of wonder has remained intact. Unfortunately, these attributes are educated out of most of us by the pressures of conformity and conservatism. Very few adults retain them, but the creative executive holds on to an intense curiosity about everything. An interested, expectant, responsive attitude toward life keeps the creative mind well stocked with all kinds of information that can be drawn on when engaged in creative activity. Creative executives are not content just to see how something works, but they delve into the whys, the cause-and-effect relationships of what they see and perceive. Their curiosity is not centered just on their own fields; their spectrum of interest embraces disparate areas and generates spontaneous enthusiasm toward almost any puzzling problem.

Originality and Openness

Originality in thought is another trait of the creative executive. He or she can think of unusual solutions and can see remote relationships between phenomena. Such persons are likely to perceive the unexpected, the novel, and the fresh in everything they encounter.

The creative individual's openness to unusual ideas sometimes extends to the point of gullibility. Such managers are usually quite ready to entertain bizarre or crackpot ideas and frequently play around with them seriously before discarding them. New perspective, new concepts, and venturesome ideas offer an endless source of mental exercise.

Sensitivity to Problems

The creative executive not only finds fresh approaches to problems, he also detects problems. The ability to see need areas or to be aware of the odd or promising allows this manager to note gaps in his department's organization or services.

Such executives can also see the significance or possibility in situations that a less sensitive manager might overlook. They are acutely aware of peoples' needs and of the unrealized potential of their staffs. Always interested in improving upon existing products or situations, these managers are like the Socratic philosopher with a "thorn in his flesh"—perpetually disturbed by something. For the creative executive, there is hardly a situation free of problems: this happy state of dissatisfaction keeps his ever-present problem-orientation alive.

Confidence To Dare

Daring to transcend accepted patterns of thinking and to stick to convictions in the face of possible discouragement or censure is very necessary in creative work. Rare indeed, however, is the established creative executive, and even rarer, the novice who can maintain complete detachment from criticism.

---

*Source: Reprinted, by permission of the publisher, from "Are You a Creative Executive?" Eugene Raudsepp, *Management Review*, February 1978, © 1978 by AMACOM, a division of American Management Associations. All rights reserved.

Self-confidence is an important attribute that can be developed only through experience and exercise. It has been said that nothing breeds success like success, and this is probably true; but the corollary that failure breeds failure need not also be true. Though fear of making a mistake is a devastating emotional block to creativity, executives should realize that progress is made through failure as well as through success.

Since most executives' career orientations are governed by the premise of success, the specter of failure looms large. In the risk-taking enterprise of creativity and innovation, however, failures do occur. Failure should be regarded as a situation from which new or improved ideas may arise. In reality the greatest failure is not to attempt a new idea at all.

The fear of failure prevents many executives from daring anything really creative, especially when the element of risk taking is considerable. So the young executive needs encouragement and recognition in order to develop the confidence that he or she will eventually come through, no matter how many failures there are.

High Motivation vs. "Success"

Some executives, however, blunt their effectiveness by excessive motivation or the desire to succeed too quickly. The overmotivated executive may narrow his field of observation, looking for and using only clues that provide a quick solution to a problem. This person frequently passes up leads to novel or better solutions by picking the first workable solution rather than considering alternatives.

Overmotivation can also result in excessively ambitious goals. Some executives want to tackle only very big and complex problems. Failure to solve such complex problems successfully can undermine confidence to tackle problems well within their capabilities.

A lack of persistence or a feeling of flagging interest is often a signal to get away from a problem and relax for a while. Many creative executives turn to another problem because they find they function best when involved in several undertakings simultaneously, each at a different stage and each affording the chance to "relax" when necessary.

During the creative process, however, the creative executive maintains an uninterrupted rapport with the "proposals" that emerge from his subconscious as he forms them into something that makes daylight sense. This requires great self-discipline.

Toying with Ideas

There is often a seemingly light side to the creative executive's involvement in work. He may seem to be lost in an irresponsible play of ideas, relationships, and concepts, which he shapes into all kinds of ostensibly incongruous combinations. However, this apparently purposeless exercise strengthens and, at the same time, loosens the "muscles" of imagination. It enables the person to come up with more unique solutions to problems.

Creative executives have often found that playful sketching and shaping of ideas helps them come upon really valuable ones. Furthermore, this toying serves to get them in a proper mood to start ideas flowing. These quasi-serious exercises relax the ever-present critical and conservative orientation of the conscious. By putting this watchful censor to sleep, they can set the stage for the emergence of novel ideas and solutions.

Tolerance of Ambiguity and Complexity

One reason for the lack of creative ideas among many executives is their strong preference for predictability and order. Many immediately reject ideas that either do not fit into an established pattern or are too elusive for immediate comprehension and categorization.

On the other hand, creative executives can tolerate a high degree of ambiguity. They are actually suspicious of any pat explanations and have developed a healthy respect for groping around and for the unknown during the creative process. Creative persons can perceive a variety of possibilities and are able to simultaneously consider and balance different, even conflicting and contradictory frames of reference and concepts.

Selectivity

Likewise, creative executives differ from the less creative or noncreative in the quality they show in the selection of elements when confronting a problem. They are able to choose more fundamental aspects and cast the superfluous aside. In creative problem solving, it is, as a rule, not necessarily the executive who is highly fluent with the problem who shows the highest degree of creativity. Whether fluent in thinking or not, the executive who can grasp the heart of the matter frequently shows the highest degree of creativity. In creative thinking, it is quality that counts, not necessarily the quantity of ideas.

Creative Memory

The subconscious is a storehouse of facts, observations, impressions, and other memories. While the creative executive's mind is always richly stocked with these memories, this does not in itself indicate creativity. As a matter of fact, a prodigious memory can act as a deterrent to creativity.

What makes memory creative is the dynamic mobility of the components. Where the uncreative memory files its data and impressions within neat and independent cubicles, the creative memory's boundaries are permeable. All kinds of related and unrelated data and ideas can always be cross-indexed and interrelated.

The creative mind is continuously rearranging, pruning, discarding, relating, and refining these data and ideas. In such a permeably structured memory there is the ever-present possibility for new configurations and combinations.

Creativity requires exact, recallable observations and discriminating use of the senses. Try this simple test: In the margin of this page, draw the face of your watch—without first looking at it.

This test illustrates the effect of overfamiliarity. We look at our watches so often we cease "seeing" them. That's what happens when behaviors become automatic and when we take objects too much for granted.

Incubation

There comes a time when thinking becomes clogged, when errors pile up, and when no significant insights occur. At this point, the creative executive stops working on that particular problem and turns to something entirely different. According to Dr. A. Schlien of the University of Chicago, "Although he has confidence in his ability, the creative individual also has an attitude of respect for the problem and admits the limits of his conscious power in forcing the problem to solution. At some point, called 'incubation' by many who have reported the process, he treats the problem as if it had a life of its own, which will, in its time and in its relation to his subliminal or autonomous thought processes, come to solution."

The creative executive also likes to contemplate, reflect, meditate, or just "chew the mental cud." During these periods he often gets some of his best ideas.

Some managers tackle problems with a dogged effort. Although commendable, keeping busy without time for relaxation or change of activity frequently serves as an effective barrier to novel solutions. The executive who knows when persistence with a recalcitrant problem begins to result in diminishing returns, and who then drops it for a while, frequently finds that on returning to it a fresh approach comes with greater ease.

There is a popular but fallacious notion that the creative individual relies on effortless insight and unforced spontaneity. True creativity requires a great deal of self-discipline and old-fashioned effort.

The majority of creative executives do not know the meaning of an eight-hour workday. Their preoccupation with problems is incessant. Creativity, in whatever field, is generated by hard thinking, prolonged reflection, and concentrated hard work. But creative persons have their moments of joy when ideas start flowing after a disrupting hitch.

Frequently, however, the intense struggle with problems is useless. But these efforts, futile as they seem to be, are not necessarily wasted because they activate the subconscious processes of cerebration and incubation. Without preparatory work, the subconscious can be notoriously unproductive.

Whatever the field, creation is a product of hard thinking, prolonged reflection, and concentrated toil. There is a continuous assimilation of data and observations, a continuing pondering on the causes of regularly met difficulties, and a sorting out of hunches and ideas that flash across the firmament of consciousness.

Creative executives develop a retrospective awareness of when they have solved problems creatively. They take note of the methods that have succeeded and failed. They try to learn "why" by retracing as far as possible the routes followed and those avoided.

Creative individuals schedule their creative thinking periods for times when they have their most favorable mental set for producing ideas. They are aware of their personal rhythms of output. By keeping a record of their most creative periods during a day, they can establish a pattern and plan ahead, reserving peak periods for concentration, contemplation, and uninhibited thinking, and using the less productive times for reading or routine tasks. But even without a time sheet of productive periods, the creative executive develops a sensitivity to moods that promise good returns—and knows when these moods are approaching.

A Creativity Checklist

The creative executive has distinct characteristics that set him apart from less creative colleagues. However, there is no perfect example, because no one executive could have all the attributes of creativity to a uniformly high degree. Thus there are many gradations of attributes and skill levels among creative persons, but all such executives have some measure of these characteristics in common.

The following checklist of behavioral and personality attributes offers further insight into the makeup of the creative executive. It was adapted from a listing by Dr. Ross L. Mooney of Ohio State University, a leading researcher in the field of creativity.

The creative executive:

— Is willing to give up immediate gain or comfort to reach long-range goals.
— Is determined to finish work even under conditions of frustration.
— Has a great amount of energy, which is channeled into productive effort.
— Perseveres despite obstacles and opposition.
— Has the ability to examine his or her own ideas objectively.
— Has great initiative.
— Is irritated by the status quo and refuses to be restricted by habit and environment.
— Has many hobbies, skills, and interests.
— Can open up to experiences and abandon defenses.
— Feels he or she has untapped potentials.
— Criticizes him or herself more than others do.
— Is not afraid to ask questions that show ignorance.
— Likes ventures involving calculated risks.
— Believes, even after repeated failures, that he or she can solve a problem.
— Has the confidence to meet new problems, find out new things, and do original things.
— Is willing to stand alone if integrity demands it.
— Does not blame others or make excuses for errors or failures.
— Competes with self rather than others.
— Has neither fear nor resentment toward authority, and is nonauthoritarian.
— Is open and direct with people and respects their rights.
— Wants to examine things from another's viewpoint.
— Knows how to give inspiration and encouragement.
— Is governed by inner stimulus rather than outer command and has a rising level of aspiration.
— Gets the greatest pleasures from creative activities.
— Believes that fantasy and daydreaming are not a waste of time.
— Has an inherent desire and respect for perfection.
— Wants to integrate utility with the aesthetic.
— Moves toward solutions using intuition.
— Knows that getting stuck on a problem is frequently because of asking the wrong question.
— Is alert to new perspectives and knows that much depends on the angle from which a problem is seen.
— Is willing to listen to every suggestion, but judges for him or herself.
— Always has more problems and work than time to deal with them.

SELF-EVALUATION

How Do You Rate Your Skills?*

There are many different sets of categories management experts have developed that represent executive skills. The one used below represents twenty-one job-oriented areas of executive ac-

---

*Source: From *The Executive Deskbook,* 2nd edition, by Auren Uris, © 1970 by Van Nostrand Reinhold Company. Reprinted with permission of the publisher.

tivity. Taken together in this quick quiz form, they give you a chance to rate your executive performance. You'll find an interpretation of your score following the items. To answer, ask yourself, "How do I rate my past performance in the given area?" (See Table 1-2.)

Assessments and Skills Improvement

Some executives feel that after making an overall assessment of their abilities, the next step is to concentrate on the weak spots.

This may be best. But note suggestions concerning your ratings in each of the three columns:

- **Skills rated "high."** The items marked "high" are the ones in which you have the strongest natural proficiency. There's a tendency to pass over these. "Why bother doing anything about them?" the reasoning goes. There are some good reasons:

Table 1-2 Skills Rating Chart

	Low	Medium	High
1. *Using the expert*—getting information, opinions, ideas from well-informed people inside or outside your department.	☐	☐	☐
2. *Building reputation*—making yourself known; developing a favorable name for yourself in the hospital.	☐	☐	☐
3. *Activating*—getting your people to understand and follow your instructions.	☐	☐	☐
4. *Imparting information*—making yourself understood by subordinates or superiors.	☐	☐	☐
5. *Judging people*—gauging individuals so as to be able to establish good relations and increase job satisfaction.	☐	☐	☐
6. *Working with subordinates*—establishing cordial and effective relationships with those who work for you.	☐	☐	☐
7. *Interviewing*—talking with people face-to-face.	☐	☐	☐
8. *Listening*—learning from the words of others how they think and feel.	☐	☐	☐
9. *Getting cooperation*—motivating people to join you in accomplishing departmental goals.	☐	☐	☐
10. *Maintaining good relations with your superior*—being both friendly and businesslike in your dealings up the line.	☐	☐	☐
11. *Using working time effectively*—being able to get 60 minutes of work out of every hour.	☐	☐	☐
12. *Decision-making*—arriving at a logical conclusion and sticking to it.	☐	☐	☐
13. *Planning*—developing a course of action to accomplish a definite objective.	☐	☐	☐
14. *Controlling paper work*—maintaining the flow of inter-department communications, reports, and the like, to and from your desk.	☐	☐	☐
15. *Getting information*—uncovering the facts you need to advance your work.	☐	☐	☐
16. *Delegation*—making subordinates responsible for some of your activities, while retaining control.	☐	☐	☐
17. *Problem-solving*—licking the tough situations that interfere with efficiency.	☐	☐	☐
18. *Pacing your energy expenditures*—conserving yourself so as to be able to complete the day without undue fatigue.	☐	☐	☐
19. *Concentration*—being able to to stick with a given task.	☐	☐	☐
20. *Memory*—remembering events, incidents, ideas, plans, or promises.	☐	☐	☐
21. *Self-scheduling*—accomplishing the objectives of your job by efficient allotment of your time.	☐	☐	☐

1. *Locating fertile ground.* Since these "highs" are likely to represent natural strong points, you may find that with only slight effort they can be made outstanding.
2. *Magnifying your strong points.* The parts of your job in which you've already been doing well may prove to be the best areas to work in. You are likely to be at an advantage and you put yourself in a position to extend past successes.

Say you have a knack for "getting information" (#15 in Table 1-2). By concentrating on this item, you may win special assignments from your superior, involving trouble shooting or analytical inquiries, for example.

- **Skills rated "medium."** These may be your real danger areas. In some cases the tip-off to trouble lies in the thought, "Let well enough alone."

  Look over each item you've rated in the "medium" column. Supply actual working situations involving these skills. For example, if you've rated "imparting information" (#4 in Table 1-2) in this column, visualize the handicaps you've run into as a result. Ask yourself this question:

  Do your instructions fail to get across, causing an assistant to fail to correctly carry out an assignment? An affirmative reply can set you on the road to new insight and remedy.

- **Skills rated "low."** These may be the toughest items to work on. Chances are that they are the areas in which you have least natural proficiency or experience.

Face that fact frankly. That means improvement in these areas may require an uphill battle. You may have to go all out for a comparatively moderate gain. Yet, if the skill involved is a key to the objective you've set for yourself, it may be well worth the effort involved.

In general, selecting the skills to improve should be guided by these additional considerations:

Which do you use most?
Which play the most important role in the operation of your department?

And finally, the key question that takes your personal objectives into account:

Which are the most important in helping you advance toward your specific goal?

Educational Needs of Hospital Administrators*

In a major study by the University of Missouri, hospital administrators were asked about the content of continuing education programs that schools of hospital and health services administration should offer to hospital administrators. The results of the study are shown in Table 1-3.

MANAGEMENT STRESS**

Trying to survive in the organizational jungle of a large governing board, a suspicious medical staff, restrictive third party reimbursement, and inappropriate decisions from the local HSA requires of a hospital administrator the hide of a rhinoceros and the single-minded determination of a bulldog. Intellectual skills need to be blended with emotional maturity.

Analytical abilities are now superseded in importance by a sense of humor, a state of optimism, an ability to absorb unwarranted criticism, an understanding of group dynamics, stubbornness and perseverance in the face of unreasonable odds, and an ability to anticipate questions and answer them before they are even asked. Obviously, this is a set of performance requirements difficult to fulfill.

Chief executives of hospitals live with a great deal of organizational uncertainty because of the peculiar organizational relationship of the medical staff. They may find themselves in a dilemma; the governing board expects vigilance about the quality of patient care, but, at the same time, expects cooperation with the medical staff. If administrative steps need to be taken that affect physicians, the hospital CEOs accept

---

*Source: Reprinted from *Continuing Education in the Health Professions* by Robert Boissoneau with permission of Aspen Systems Corporation, © 1980.

**Source: Reprinted from *Hospitals in Transition* by Everett A. Johnson and Richard L. Johnson with permission of Aspen Systems Corporation, © 1982.

Table 1-3 Views of Health Professionals re the Content of Continuing Education Programs

The question: "What content would you suggest for continuing education programs offered by schools of hospital and health services administration?"

Category	Administrators Frequency	Administrators Rank	Chiefs of staff Frequency	Chiefs of staff Rank	Board chairmen Frequency	Board chairmen Rank	Executives Frequency	Executives Rank	Freq. Totals	Rank
1. Financial management	128	1	45	1	74	1	82	1	329	1
2. Governmental regulations	66	2	31	3	41	2	18	3	156	2
3. Personnel management	39	3	23	4	27	3	11	4	100	3
4. Administrator-physician relationship	21	7	41	2	22	4	10	5	94	5
5. Public relations	11	11	12	5	17	6	9	7	49	8
6. Planning	18	8	5	12	13	9	60	2	96	4
7. Legal affairs	38	4	10	6	22	4	10	5	80	6
8. Budgeting	24	6	6	9	15	7	8	10	53	7
9. Computer science	6	17	8	8	1	18	2	20	17	16
10. Current issues in hospital administration	11	11	6	9	6	11	1	22	24	11
11. Management theory	10	13	0	21	0	22	3	16	13	17
12. Management by objectives	8	16	1	15	2	15	8	10	19	15
13. Professional Standards Review Organizations	12	10	6	9	3	13	3	16	24	11
14. Practical problems	18	8	0	21	3	13	2	20	23	13
15. Labor relations	25	5	1	15	14	8	9	7	49	8
16. Systems approach	3	20	0	21	1	18	9	7	13	17
17. Construction management	6	17	2	14	2	15	0	23	10	19
18. Shared services	1	21	1	15	0	22	7	12	9	21
19. Public health	0	25	1	15	1	18	3	16	5	23
20. Occupational Safety and Health Act	1	21	0	21	0	22	0	24	1	25
21. Health Maintenance Organizations	9	15	4	13	2	15	5	13	20	14
22. Organizational theory	4	19	1	15	1	18	0	25	6	22
23. Education for boards of trustees	1	21	1	15	4	12	4	15	10	19
24. Marketing	0	25	0	21	0	22	0	26	0	26
25. Decision making	1	21	0	21	0	22	3	16	4	24
26. Current health legislation	10	13	9	7	11	10	5	14	35	10
27. Miscellaneous	140	*	112	*	84	*	116	*	452	*

*Not applicable.

Source: Boissoneau, Robert. "The Influence of Mandatory Continuing Education on Perceived Effectiveness of Hospital Administrators." Ph.D. Dissertation, The Ohio State University, 1974.

the fact that they are creating a stressful situation for themselves.

Chief executives cannot exercise direct control over a medical staff, the governing board, or the external factors that operate on the hospital; however, in the board's mind, they remain fully accountable for the total hospital. This level of accountability severely restricts their ability to adjust, even if they are competent, secure executives. Their frustration arises out of their awareness that they see the need to respond to changing conditions, recognize the organizational steps needed to be taken, but can't get persons who need to agree to the changes to see the necessity of doing so. This is compounded by demands on their time.

At the core of the stresses that now affect them are three factors:

1. Their organizational relationship to the medical staff is clouded in ambiguity.
2. They are accountable to a governing board that cannot meaningfully measure their organizational performance.
3. They function at the apex of an organizational structure that requires participation in many activities that cannot be delegated to others in the administrative structure. Stated another way, their ability to manage their own time is severely restricted because of the expectations of those they cannot control about what they should be doing.

Collectively, these three factors severely limit CEOs' abilities to exercise a full range of coping mechanisms. Even though they have the ability and willingness to put themselves in other people's shoes—be it board member, physician, agency official, or consumer—they cannot effectively respond to all of them. Their time is too limited because of the perceptions of others about their role and others' demands on their personal participation. The fact that the others may be unrealistic goes unrecognized. The problem is not that hospital executives fail to see these pressures, but rather in knowing how to extricate themselves from these constraints.

Symptoms of Stress

Symptoms of too much stress on administrative staffs abound. Its manifestations vary according to the personalities of individuals and the characteristics of the institutions. Overstress in an individual is difficult to identify because any one act is not usually sufficient to cause concern; rather, a set of behavior manifestations collectively become significant.

These behavior changes are usually quickly noticed by the hospital staff because of their daily interactions with the administrative staff. When reimbursement restrictions increase from third party payers, and as a medical staff simultaneously pressures the administration to increase the quality or number of hospital staff members, while trustees are insisting on a reduction in a contemplated rate increase, administrative organizational behavior may change.

Withdrawal from decision making is a commonly used behavior adjustment to cope with unmanageable situations. An administrator may begin to find reasons for being away from the hospital in order to avoid being asked to grapple with current management problems. A variation of withdrawal behavior is to remain at the hospital, but, when a management problem is discussed, to either ask the person presenting it to suggest an answer that is immediately accepted or to project an attitude that any suggestion is acceptable since the larger institutional problems are unmanageable anyway.

Another withdrawal coping behavior is to increase the delegation of authority to associates at lower levels in the organization to avoid requests for direction. At times, this kind of behavior is often preceded by an effort to increase centralization of decision-making authority. When this fails, the administrator may suddenly and unpredictably shift authority for decision making to lower levels in the organization.

A similar type of behavior may occur with the board of trustees and the medical staff. An administrator may either initiate increased use of the committees in the organization, in order to let them make decisions rather than have to make a decision, or reduce the number of committee meetings to avoid facing problems and pressures and, instead, ask the hospital administrative staff to make the necessary decisions without his or her participation.

In order either to avoid confrontation with medical staff or to buy their support, administrative efforts to control clinical activities may be reduced or stopped. In addition, administrative supervision of the hospital staff may be tightened beyond a reasonable level to meet the demands of the medical staff for improved performance of hospital personnel, even when these demands are unreasonable.

Essentially, the administrative response to a limited authority and increased accountability is to stop leading the institution and to make decisions only when consensus from institutional power groups has been achieved, which is basically riskless decision making.

Along with these changes in administrative leader behavior, personal behavior in the institution may also shift. Interpersonal relationships may be altered from an even-handed tolerance and good humor to behavior that is abrupt and abrasive.

The overall effect of these changes may have serious organizational consequences. Decision making will be slower than usual.

The morale of the institution will also be lowered because of attempts to shift blame for apparent administrative inadequacies to other personnel. Prolonged pressures that are not relieved will ultimately decrease management levels of performance, and the institutional quality of care to patients will slowly deteriorate.

A sense of isolation and lonesomeness aggravates administrators' deteriorating mental health status. They feel increasingly trapped as institutional pressures rise, and there is no place to turn to for help without telegraphing the message that they are no longer invincible.

HOW A CEO CHANGES JOBS*

There is a great shortage of leaders in health care management; yet when a top manager decides that he or she should make a move, it is often difficult to locate the right opportunity.

Luck Plays a Role

Luck sometimes has a great deal to do with obtaining a good position in management. One hospital, for example, hired as a CEO a man with few credentials in management. The hospital was looking for a nonthreatening person, one who would have little power in dealing with the board and medical staff. The person hired may not last long in the position in his present hospital, but his chances of finding another CEO position are good. Many boards are willing to hire an individual because he or she "has been there," not because the individual has the appropriate background and professional manner.

Being in the right place at the right time often lands high-level positions. In one suburban hospital the board and medical staff had some strong personal and philosophical differences. Various issues had been festering for several years. The only thing the board and medical staff could agree on was that they should not look for a qualified executive director outside the hospital because the overall objectives of the hospital were obscure. So they decided to promote a young assistant hospital director to the position—an individual in whom neither side had faith.

Although luck can play a large part in finding a CEO or other key position, by and large people make their own business breaks. A tenacious individual who suffers from some bad luck early in his or her career will eventually make it to the top if he or she has the talent and the motivation.

Where To Look

The first place to start looking for a job—providing you have the appropriate relationship with your supervisor in the present position—is to approach your immediate supervisor or in the case of a CEO, the Board of Trustees, and discuss the matter. Whenever possible, this should be the first step, both for ethical reasons and for ease in investigating new opportunities.

Next you should contact trusted acquaintances and friends in the field and let them know of your availability.

There are several reputable executive recruiting firms who should be contacted. In dealing with these firms you can be assured that they will talk to you first about any opportunity before talking to a client about you. You should remember, however, that an executive recruiting firm's job is to find an individual to meet the client's needs, not the other way around.

Four reliable executive recruiting firms with an active practice in health care are:

- Witt & Dolan Associates Inc., Oak Brook, Illinois

---

*Source: Reprinted from "Finding a New Financial Position: Some Basics," *Topics in Health Care Financing,* Vol. 7:1 (Fall) by Richard C. Dolan with permission of Aspen Systems Corporation, © 1980.

- A. T. Kearney, Inc., Chicago, Illinois (and other cities)
- Heidrick & Struggles, Inc., Chicago, Illinois (and other cities)
- Spencer, Stewart and Associates, Chicago, Illinois (and other cities)

Some of the Big 8 public accounting firms also become involved in this kind of activity in some regions of the country and are worth checking into.

Many people find good positions in management through classified advertisements, especially advertisements in health care journals. You may also want to contact the school you previously attended or educators you are acquainted with; however, the higher up you are in the career pyramid, the less likely these people will be of help. Another possible source is individuals in state hospital associations and professional associations.

Many well-educated and professionally competent people assume an interview situation involves a friendly chit-chat and needs no preliminary plan. The interview, however, is a crucial aspect of the recruiting process, and the impression created by the interviewee can be the factor that determines whether or not the candidate is hired. Therefore it is essential that a person seeking a new career be prepared for the interview.

Assessing Your Strengths and Weaknesses

The biggest single problem in planning career goals is the failure of individuals to identify their own weak points. Conversely, these same people often overestimate their strengths.

Some common weak points include: the inability or refusal to delegate properly; the tendency to become overly involved with favorite interests; the reluctance to discipline or fire employees when necessary; the inability to balance work with family or outside activities; the tendency to either procrastinate or make snap decisions and thus damage the decision-making process relative to meeting the objectives for the position.

Many weak points can be improved. Once they are identified, an individual can develop a plan to try to overcome them. The solution should be approached by setting realistic objectives with time frames established for each step in the plan. Check points with periodic followup are essential to successfully overcoming a weak point in one's performance.

Two Character Types That Are Avoided

Two character types that are often avoided when prospects are being considered for health care management are the "one-institution person" and the "job hopper." The one-institution person is one who has spent his or her entire career in a single institution. Job hoppers are those who change positions more than five times after the age of 28, or three times after age 40. Few employers in the health care field will hire either type of individual.

Chapter 2—Leadership

In theory, leaders are capable of independent thought and decisions. They exude self-confidence and emotional stability. They bring order out of chaos and demonstrate sensitivity to needs and feelings of subordinates.

They act to help groups attain their objectives with maximum application of the groups' capabilities, but they never lose their own identities. They are a combination of two main factors: personality and the power vested in them by the organization. They must be responsive to the needs of the organization. They lose their effectiveness if their decisions are not approved or they are not given enough authority. To be effective they have to have authority, and they have to demonstrate personal fortitude and ability to motivate others to produce.

Some leaders are charismatic. Their subordinates tend to associate and identify with them. It is personal charm and magnetism that binds the followers in a way that transcends the limits of formal authority and reason. This charisma is the result of a combination of qualities, such as appearance, competence, character, and attractiveness of personality.

STYLES OF LEADERSHIP*

Various terms such as "autocratic"–"democratic" have been attached to the decision-making behavior vis-à-vis the manager and the subordinates. These labels are traditionally called "styles of leader decision authority" and can be displayed on a continuum. In addition, terms such as "employee centered" and "work centered" have been used to describe various supervisory styles used by the manager in overseeing work activity. Rather than being a continuum, they represent opposites characterizing the way in which the manager interacts with subordinates.

Autocratic

In the continuum of leader authority presented in Figure 2-1 the "autocratic" end represents the manager who makes decisions and announces them to the group. The use of the autocratic style means that the manager has made a decision pertaining to what the purpose of the group activity is, how the group activity is to be structured, and who is to be assigned to what specific tasks. The total interacting relationship and the work setting have been decided by the manager. The role of subordinates is to carry out orders without having any opportunity to materially alter the decisions that have been made. The manager provides little opportunity for a subordinate to participate in making decisions.

In health care settings, we seldom see the pure form of the autocratic leader decision authority style exercised by administrative personnel. It is often the physician who adopts this style as the individual responsible for the activities required for patient care. Out of necessity, the physician must make decisions that no one else

---

*Source: Reprinted from *Managing Health Care Organizations* by J. Rakich, B. Longest, and T. O'Donovan with permission of W.B. Saunders and Company, © 1977.

22 HOSPITAL ADMINISTRATION HANDBOOK

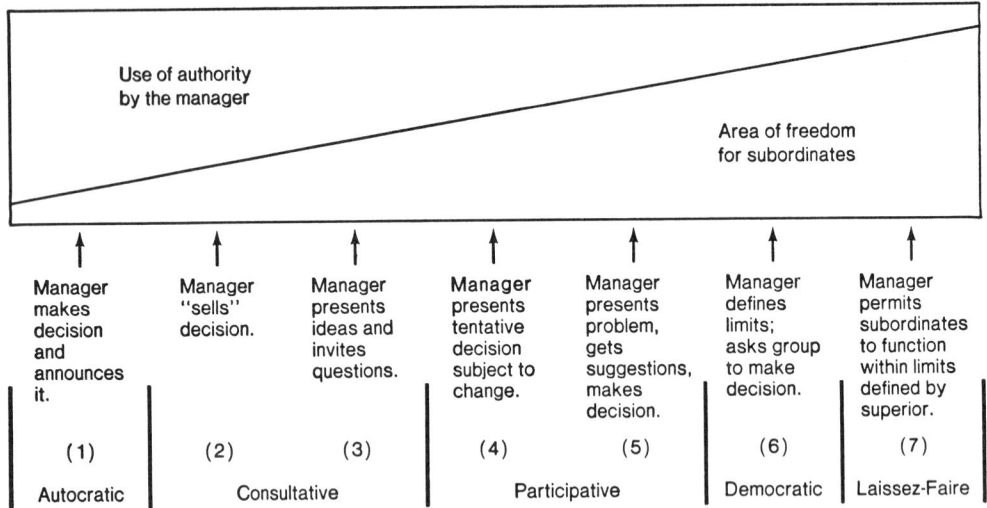

Figure 2-1 Continuum of leader decision-making authority*

*Source: Reprinted by permission of the *Harvard Business Review*. Exhibit from "How To Choose a Leadership Pattern" by Robert Tannenbaum and Warren H. Schmidt, May–June 1973, Copyright © 1973 by the President and Fellows of Harvard College; all rights reserved.

can. Consequently, he or she will make decisions and announce them to other personnel, such as nurses and technicians, who will be expected to carry out the activities without deviation.

Consultative

The "consultative" style appears to the right of "autocratic." In this situation, the manager "sells" the decision or presents ideas and invites questions from subordinates, or both. Specifically, the manager makes decisions concerning the work activity to be carried out, its purpose, how it is to be done, when, and by whom, and attempts to sell the subordinates on the decisions. The manager may recognize the possibility of some resistance and invite questions: however, unless overwhelming reasons cause a change in the decisions made, they stand.

Participative

If the manager presents a tentative decision which is subject to change or presents the problem to the subordinates, gets suggestions, and then makes the decision, we are dealing with a "participative" style. The manager identifies the purposes, the problems, and the means by which the activities should be carried out; presents a tentative decision already made or seeks subordinate opinion; then, makes the decision. In this instance the "area of decision freedom for subordinates" is much greater and the "use of authority by the manager" is much smaller than with the autocratic and consultative styles.

Participative management is a very powerful motivator in enabling employees to have some measure of influence and control over work-related activities. The work group can influence the decisions made concerning work activities and their purpose.

Democratic

Within a "democratic" style the manager defines the limits of the situation and the problem to be solved and asks the group to make decisions. The subordinates have a relatively large "area of decision freedom," as indicated in Figure 2-1. The boundaries of activity are set by the manager, who permits the group to make decisions within those restrictions. For example, a nurse supervisor allows only RN's to give medication, but permits them to decide among themselves who will give the medication and who will perform other tasks that must be done.

Laissez-faire

The term "laissez-faire" was originally coined for the doctrine that government should not interfere with commerce. It is sometimes called "free rein." Under such leadership subordinates are permitted to function within the limits set by the manager's own superior. There is no interference within the group by the manager, who, although participating in the decision-making, attempts to do so with no more influence than any other member of the group. The subordinates basically have complete freedom in making decisions, with minimum participation by the manager. The manager is merely a figurehead. This style of leader decision authority is rarely found in health care organizations.

THE ADMINISTRATOR AS POWER BROKER*

The gap between responsibility and authority may lead hospital executives into an administrative style that becomes a life of leverages and of using tonal qualities, facial expressions, and body language to buttress their skills in carefully controlling information, agendas, and timing. They need skills of persuasion in one-on-one situations, but they also need to appreciate how such conversations fit into an overall plan to solve multifaceted, complex problems. This is a unique set of skills that can be acquired only by repeated exposure and frequent mistakes.

The hospital is an ideal organizational structure for a power broker because of the multiplicity of hospital departments and clinical services. It is difficult to trace the ill-defined decision-making process accurately. Chief executives may be the only common thread among the hospital's committees and governing board. This provides them with an opportunity to wield real power by reporting information to the various groups in a manner most advantageous to the course of action they desire.

---
*Source: Reprinted from "The Power Broker—Prototype of the Hospital Chief Executive?" *Health Care Management Review* by Richard L. Johnson with permission of Aspen Systems Corporation, © 1978.

Characteristics of a Power Broker

1. Probing for New Information

Power brokers, because they possess long and sensitive organizational antennae, are constantly probing for new information and listening to informal channels of conversation. Not only do they want to know what is being said in various circles, but who is saying it.

This goes on in almost every contact that is made. Though concealed by a smile, or a joke, or an arm around the shoulder, or a verbal pat on the back, the intent is constant—to disarm other people so they will say whatever is on their minds. In effect, the other person is dealing with a warm, friendly, information-processing system that has its radar screen constantly in use, sweeping the organizational structure.

2. Anticipating Behavior

A second characteristic is the ability to anticipate the individual behavior of those involved in the decision-making ladder. Because of their understanding of behavior patterns, chief executives may read a situation as the prelude to a gale while all others may see the unfolding events as a whispering breeze. Recognizing where the problem is headed may lead them into vigorous action and a flurry of telephone calls.

By concentrating their efforts at the onset of the problem, chief executives avoid spending large chunks of their time later in committee meetings. In addition, they stand the best chance of working out a solution to their liking because opposition has not had an opportunity to organize.

3. Focusing Attention on the Problem

A third characteristic of power brokers is their ability to keep their attention riveted on the problem. Once they know their preferred solution and have it clearly in mind, they will devote their time to planning how to overcome any potential objections. Being single-minded, power brokers are not distracted by how well people dress, how much wealth they may possess, how charming they are as conversationalists; their eyes see all the decision-making participants as parts of a jigsaw puzzle that must be fitted together to bring about the desired results. Because their own time must be rationed among competing priorities, they single out those elements they consider most likely to interfere with their decision and devote their time and talents to those aspects.

4. Controlling Information

A fourth characteristic of power brokers is that they have access to more information than the other participants and are in a position to be the controller of how and when it is dispensed. While they cannot hold the information to themselves for prolonged periods of time, they can withhold it for limited periods.

The ability to withhold information permits the stage to be set for its reception. For example, chief executives may walk through the emergency room suite, glance into the cast room as they go by and observe a technician casting a patient with no physician in attendance. Not only have they observed a poor medical practice, but they have gleaned a useful piece of information that can be tucked away in their mind until they decide to use it at an appropriate time.

Using Meetings

Power brokers are interested in ferreting out any strong viewpoints prior to a meeting to discuss a sensitive matter. Instinctively, they will take a head count. If they determine the group is likely to reach a stalemate or not be able to cope with the issue, they will search for an alternative route to follow. If they feel it is warranted, they may delay the call of a meeting in order to provide a cooling-off period. Chief executives also will make an effort to determine which persons involved in the decision-making ladder will or will not be present at the scheduled meetings. By carefully reviewing the discussion that is likely to occur, they can determine the order of items placed on the agenda.

The core of a power broker's influence rests in having an information base that is wider and deeper than that of any other organizational participant.

The ability to deal adroitly with finance, nursing, personnel, organization, medical care, radiology, materials management, reimbursement, fire codes and building maintenance leads to substantial respect up and down the organizational chain.

Effective power brokers may use their authority as chief executives to grant exceptions to institutional policies or reward cooperation by providing needed equipment or space. They may use horse-trading ability to achieve institutional goals.

As governmental intervention in hospital affairs has increased, the number of regulations and bulletins has rapidly multiplied. This is a ready-made situation for power brokers. Being the first to read and cite those bulletins enhances the power broker's role as the major source of important information. First knowledge of a new regulation or a change in a government formula increases the dependency of others on chief executives for guidance. The wider the gap they can create, the more effective they can become as power brokers.

Dealing with the Governing Board

Governing boards lack knowledge about medical care and tend to listen more carefully to medical staff recommendations about diagnostic and treatment needs than they do to administrative recommendations on the same subject. Lacking some credibility in this arena, administrators often feel compelled to resort to power broker techniques.

When hospital administrators state that they see no advantage in being a formal member of the governing authority, what they may really mean is that they have so adapted to the role of power broker that they are satisfied with their influence on board decisions. By not becoming board members, they may believe their actions are less observable to others. They can also find benefits in being able to say that they are not part of the governing structure.

Dealing with the Medical Staff

Medical staff members are an organizational aspect unique to hospitals. They are both part of the hospital and apart from its functioning. They are surrogate customers on behalf of their patients. New administrators quickly learn that physicians may talk quite openly in the privacy of the chief executive's office, but that this is no indication of their willingness to say the same things in an open forum, even if the group is composed entirely of physicians. Usually private talks center on the issues of quality of care and the exercise of professional judgment.

These are matters of considerable importance to the institution, but they are also of a very personal nature because they involve the reputation of the physician under discussion.

Experienced professional administrators appreciate that this kind of knowledge gained in confidence cannot be divulged in a straightforward manner, but that the stage must be carefully set and the matter engineered with sensitivity and caution on their part.

This requires that they carefully think through a scenario that permits enough information to be reported to appropriate persons without labeling the source.

Chief executives must concern themselves with who to tell, how much of what they know to tell, under what circumstances to tell, how to tell it to achieve the result required and, finally, how to sequence the decision-making process from committee to committee to governing authority.

The power broker method of dealing with physicians does not go unnoticed. Trustees appreciate it because it minimizes the risks of any confrontations between the governing board and medical staff. They are anxious to avoid quality of care problems in which they might have to make decisions on their intuitive judgment, and would much prefer the problem reach the board room table with a proposed solution that has the backing of the leadership of the medical staff.

On the other hand, individual medical staff members may ascribe personal ambition or a hunger for power as the power broker's motivating force, rather than the pursuit of worthy institutional goals.

Dealing with Sensitive Personal Matters

Exercising the role of power broker in a hospital is relatively easy because of the multiplicity of information channels that converge at the door of the administrator. In addition to the financial statements and operating statistics, administrators are often alerted to sensitive problems through conversations with people in and out of the organization. These can include nursing personnel, pharmacists, pathologists, leaders of the medical staff, orderlies, nurse's aides, trustees, police chiefs, reporters, federal agents, as well as friends and neighbors. In nearly all cases, the information transmitted will be verbal and in confidence, and no written records are available. The subjects usually covered are drug addiction, unexpected pregnancies, alcoholism, discovery of terminal diseases, conflicts of interest, rapes, acute psychotic episodes, and involvements with local police. Administrators find out about such problems as criminal activity, serious social maladjustments, or other potentially embarrassing situations.

They come to understand their role as being helpful and sensitive when confronted with these events, and they learn to forget the events as quickly as possible after they have been resolved. Physicians, trustees, and community leaders who experience serious personal or family problems come to appreciate that executives can be trusted to be discreet and to never use such knowledge for their own benefit. This tends to build a strong reservoir of support and goodwill for their administrative decisions.

One of the dangers of using the power broker style is that it may be used when it is not needed. Without meaning to, they apply this technique to all their managerial problems. Instead of using a direct, straightforward approach in their relationships with hospital department directors and assistant administrators, they continue to use the tools of manipulation.

This can be disconcerting to the directors and assistant administrators who see no need for the power broker approach. Until they become totally familiar with the motives, value systems, and adherence to solid performance of the chief executive, the directors and assistant administrators may remain wary of him and uncomfortable with this style of management.

LEADERSHIP TESTS

Emphasis of Leadership*

This is not a test with right or wrong answers. It is a questionnaire designed to describe some of your attitudes about leadership. It contains ten statements about situations. After each state-

---

*Source: Reprinted from *Effective Communication in Health Care* by Harry E. Munn, Jr. and Norman Metzger with permission of Aspen Systems Corporation, © 1981.

ment, there are three possible behaviors or actions indicated that you might take.

Place a number 3 beside the position you would *most likely* take, a number 2 beside the position you would *next likely* take, and a number 1 beside the position you would *least likely* take.

1. *In leading a meeting it is important to:*
   - keep the focus on the agenda at hand .... (1) _____
   - focus on each individual's feelings and help people express their emotional reactions to the issue .... (2) _____
   - focus on the differing perceptions people have and how they deal with each other .... (3) _____

2. *A primary objective of a leader is:*
   - to maintain an organizational climate in which learning and accomplishment can take place .... (4) _____
   - to maintain the efficient operation of the organization (5) _____
   - to help members of the organization find themselves and be more aware of who they are .... (6) _____

3. *When strong disagreement occurs between a leader and a group member about work to be done, the leader should:*
   - listen to the person and try to discover how that person might have misunderstood the task .... (7) _____
   - try to get other people to express their views in order to involve them in the issues . (8) _____
   - support the group member for raising the question or disagreement .... (9) _____

4. *In evaluating a group member's performance, the leader should:*
   - involve the entire group in setting goals and in evaluating one another's performance .... (10) _____
   - try to make an objective assessment of each person's accomplishments and effectiveness .... (11) _____
   - allow individual members to be involved in determining their own goals and performance standards .... (12) _____

5. *When two group members get into an argument, it is best to:*
   - help them deal with their feelings as a means of resolving the argument .... (13) _____
   - encourage other members to respond to the argument and to try to help resolve it .... (14) _____
   - allow some time for expression of both sides, but keep in focus the relevant subject matter and the task at hand (15) _____

6. *The best way to motivate group members who are not performing up to the best of their ability is to:*
   - point out to them the importance of the job to be done and their role in it .... (16) _____
   - try to get to know them better so you can understand why they are not realizing their potential .... (17) _____
   - show them how their lack of motivation is affecting other people .... (18) _____

7. *The most important element in judging group members' performance is:*
   - their technical skill and ability .... (19) _____
   - how they get along with their peers and how they help others learn and get the work done .... (20) _____
   - their success in meeting the goals they set for themselves (21) _____

8. *In dealing with minority group issues, a leader should:*
   - deal with such issues as they

threaten to disturb the atmosphere of the work group ... (22) _____
- be sure that all group members understand the history of racial and ethnic minorities in the community and country .... (23) _____
- help group members to achieve an understanding of their own attitudes toward people of other races and cultures .... (24) _____

9. *A leader's goal should be to:*

- make sure that all group members have a solid foundation of knowledge and skills that will help them become productive and effective people .... (25) _____
- help people to learn to work effectively in groups, to use the resources of the group, and to understand their relationships with one another as people .... (26) _____
- help group members become responsible for their own education and effectiveness .. (27) _____

10. *The trouble with leadership responsibilities is that:*

- they make it very difficult to cover adequately all the details that must be attended to (28) _____
- they keep a leader from really getting to know group members as individuals .... (29) _____
- they make it difficult for the leader to keep in touch with the climate and pulse of the group .... (30) _____

Testing Your Leadership Knowledge*

For each statement, answer *True* or *False.*

1. Leaders are born not made.

---

*Source: Reprinted from *Effective Communication in Health Care* by Harry E. Munn, Jr. and Norman Metzger with permission of Aspen Systems Corporation, © 1981.

2. Leadership should be a reward for loyalty or length of service.
3. Only extroverts can be effective leaders.
4. You can tell leaders by their neat appearances.
5. The more automatic and habitual the thinking and action of leaders, the more democratic their leadership will become.
6. Effective leaders often forget about a problem for a while in order to solve it.
7. A leader with a deep interest in people will normally be more effective than a leader who is interested only in getting the job done.
8. Leaders are best suited to select future leaders.
9. In most cases, how people behaved in the past will determine their future behavior.
10. Leadership effectiveness is dependent upon the situation.

Answers

1. FALSE. Research indicates that environmental factors and proper training play a significant role in the development of leadership abilities.
2. FALSE. Only the most sincere, energetic, and capable individuals who have a desire to serve should be appointed to positions of leadership. Loyalty is important, but leadership requires more than just loyalty.
3. FALSE. To be a leader, one must have visibility. However, many reserved and quiet people exhibit tremendous leadership ability when given the opportunity to express themselves.
4. FALSE. We should be more interested in what leaders do when they are leading. Their ideas, their attitudes, their ability to motivate others are more important than the first impressions they make.
5. FALSE. Automatic and habitual reactions portray highly directive, autocratic leadership.
6. TRUE. Sometimes it is best to walk away from a problem for a while. This gives the leader the opportunity to look at the problem and examine it from many different points of view.

Figure 2-2 Scoring

Note that, in scoring the questionnaire, the scoring columns are not in the usual sequential order.

SCORING COLUMNS

INSTRUCTIONS

	TASK	INDIVIDUAL	CLIMATE
	(1)___	(2)___	(3)___
	(5)___	(6)___	(4)___
	(7)___	(9)___	(8)___
	(11)___	(12)___	(10)___
	(15)___	(13)___	(14)___
	(16)___	(17)___	(18)___
	(19)___	(21)___	(20)___
	(23)___	(24)___	(22)___
	(25)___	(27)___	(26)___
	(28)___	(29)___	(30)___
	TOTAL___	TOTAL___	TOTAL___

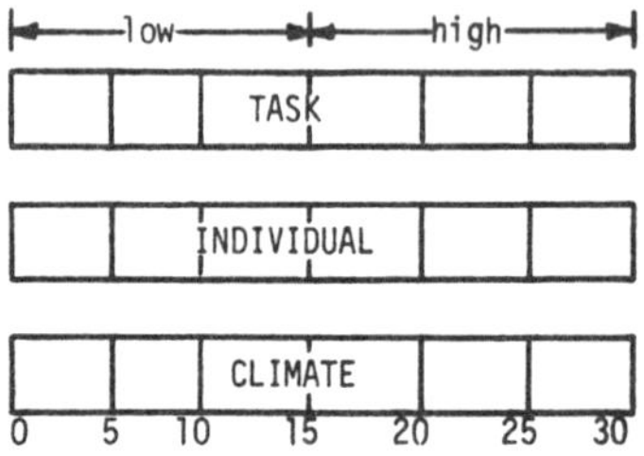

1. Transfer your answers from the Leadership Style Questionnaire to the scoring columns at right, placing a 1, 2, or 3 beside each question number.
2. Add up your totals for each column. The three totals combined should equal 60.
3. Mark your score for each dimension on the bar graph below. Blacken in the bar from the left to your score on each dimension.
4. The completed bars represent your leadership profile at this moment in time.

|←—low—→|←—high—→|

[bar graph with TASK, INDIVIDUAL, CLIMATE rows]
0 5 10 15 20 25 30

HOW TO INTERPRET YOUR LEADERSHIP PROFILE

1. Three bars of similar length (within variations of two or three points) indicate that you try to balance your concerns for task, feelings, and climate.
2. The longest bar tends to symbolize your characteristic leadership style in most situations. This style is probably functional for you most of the time, but it may be overused.
3. The shortest bar indicates an area you may tend to overlook. You might improve the situation by placing more emphasis on the leadership style represented by that bar.
4. You will improve your leadership the fastest by attending to issues symbolized by the shorter bars.

7. TRUE. Leadership does depend upon the situation, but a leader with a deep interest in people will be better able to get the job done time and time again. A leader interested only in the job may get that particular job done, but what about the next job?
8. FALSE. Research has shown that leaders should be selected by how well they work

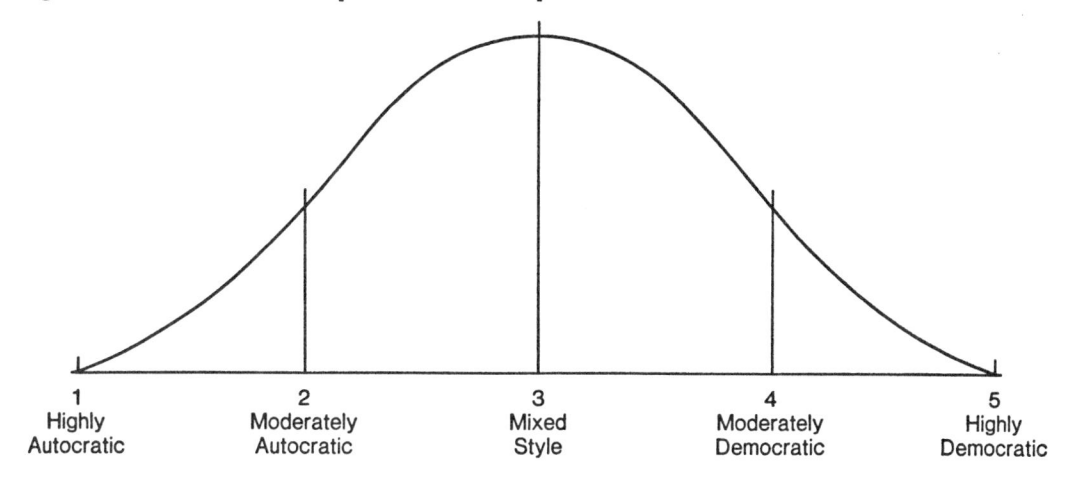

Figure 2-3 The leadership or followership continuum

1	2	3	4	5
Highly Autocratic	Moderately Autocratic	Mixed Style	Moderately Democratic	Highly Democratic

and interact with the people they are to lead. Appointed leaders may work well with the person who appointed them, but how do they work with the people they are to lead? A leader must have followers, for without followers there is no need for a leader.

9. TRUE. Remember, the statement applies to *most cases* and does not mean to suggest that a person cannot ever change. On the other hand, if a person has been a hard worker and reliable and conscientious over a long period of time, the chances that that person will stay that way are pretty good.

10. TRUE. A leader cannot always respond to everyone in the same way. The behavior of leaders will be determined to a large extent by the attitudes and training of their followers.

If you scored nine or ten of the statements correctly, you are going in the right direction and have an excellent awareness of the meaning of leadership. If you scored seven or eight correctly, you are at times uncertain about the way to go, and you have some misconceptions about leadership that may limit your ability to lead effectively. If you scored less than seven correctly, you need to work on your leadership awareness and capabilities.

Self-Evaluation: Leadership or Followership*

This Leadership-Followership-Style instrument measures two different dimensions of organizational importance:

1. Leadership style, or the idealized approach that a person would prefer to take to supervising
2. Followership style, or the kind of leadership patterns which would be preferred by an individual in his/her boss

Each dimension is conceptualized as existing on a five point scale as shown in Figure 2-3.

A number "4" leader, for example, would be a person whose natural approach to leadership would be moderately democratic, and a number "4" follower is a person whose preference would be a boss whose leadership style is moderately democratic.

Test

Following are two tests and a scoring chart to determine your leadership and followership styles. (See Tables 2-1, 2-2, and 2-3.)

---

*Source: Reprinted for "A Long Range Model for Organizational Chaos At Any Level," *Personnel Journal* (July) by Larry B. Meares with permission of the publisher, © 1979. All rights reserved.

Table 2-1 Structural Leadership Profile

The following twenty statements relate to your ideal image of leadership. We ask that as you respond to them, you imagine yourself to be a leader and then answer the questions in a way that would reflect your particular style of leadership. It makes no difference what kind of leadership experience, if any, you have had or are currently involved in. The purpose here is to establish your ideal preference for relating with subordinates.

The format includes a five point scale ranging from strongly agree to strongly disagree for each statement. Please select one point on each scale and mark it as you read the twenty statements relating to leadership. You may omit answers to questions which are confusing or to questions that you feel you cannot answer.

	Strongly Agree	Agree	Mixed Feelings	Disagree	Strongly Disagree
1. When I tell a subordinate to do something I expect him/her to do it with no questions asked. After all, I am responsible for what he/she will do, not the subordinate.	(1)	(2)	(3)	(4)	(5)
2. Tight control by a leader usually does more harm than good. People will generally do the best job when they are allowed to exercise self control.	(5)	(4)	(3)	(2)	(1)
3. Although discipline is important in an organization, the effective leader should mediate the use of disciplinary procedures with his/her knowledge of the people and the situation.	(1)	(2)	(3)	(4)	(5)
4. A leader must make every effort to subdivide the tasks of the people to the greatest possible extent.	(1)	(2)	(3)	(4)	(5)
5. Shared leadership or truly democratic process in a group can only work when there is a recognized leader who assists the process.	(1)	(2)	(3)	(4)	(5)
6. As a leader I am ultimately responsible for all of the actions of my group. If our activities result in benefits for the organization I should be rewarded accordingly.	(1)	(2)	(3)	(4)	(5)
7. Most persons require only minimum direction on the part of their leader in order to do a good job.	(5)	(4)	(3)	(2)	(1)
8. One's subordinates usually require the control of a strict leader.	(1)	(2)	(3)	(4)	(5)
9. Leadership might be shared among participants of a group so that at any one time there could be two or more leaders.	(5)	(4)	(3)	(2)	(1)

Table 2-1 continued

	Strongly Agree	Agree	Mixed Feelings	Disagree	Strongly Disagree
10. Leadership should generally come from the top, but there are some logical exceptions to this rule.	(5)	(4)	(3)	(2)	(1)
11. The disciplinary function of the leader is simply to seek democratic opinions regarding problems as they arise.	(5)	(4)	(3)	(2)	(1)
12. The engineering problems, the management time, and the worker frustration caused by the division of labor are hardly ever worth the savings. In most cases, workers could do the best job of determining their own job content.	(5)	(4)	(3)	(2)	(1)
13. The leader ought to be the group member who the other members elect to coordinate their activities and to represent the group to the rest of the organization.	(5)	(4)	(3)	(2)	(1)
14. A leader needs to exercise some control over his/her people.	(1)	(2)	(3)	(4)	(5)
15. There must be one and only one recognized leader in a group.	(1)	(2)	(3)	(4)	(5)
16. A good leader must establish and strictly enforce an impersonal system of discipline.	(1)	(2)	(3)	(4)	(5)
17. Discipline codes should be flexible and they should allow for individual decisions by the leader given each particular situation.	(5)	(4)	(3)	(2)	(1)
18. Basically, people are responsible for themselves and no one else. Thus a leader cannot be blamed for or take credit for the work of subordinates.	(5)	(4)	(3)	(2)	(1)
19. The job of the leader is to relate to subordinates the task to be done, to ask them for the ways in which it can best be accomplished, and then to help arrive at a consensus plan of attack.	(5)	(4)	(3)	(2)	(1)
20. A position of leadership implies the general superiority of its incumbent over his/her workers.	(1)	(2)	(3)	(4)	(5)

Table 2-2 Structural Followership Profile

This section of the questionnaire includes statements about the type of boss which you prefer. Imagine yourself to be in a subordinate position of some kind and use your responses to indicate your preference for the way in which a leader might relate with you. The format will be identical to that within the previous section.

	Strongly Agree	Agree	Mixed Feelings	Disagree	Strongly Disagree
1. I expect my job to be very explicitly outlined for me.	(1)	(2)	(3)	(4)	(5)
2. When the boss says to do something, I do it. After all he/she is the boss.	(1)	(2)	(3)	(4)	(5)
3. Rigid rules and regulations usually cause me to become frustrated and inefficient.	(5)	(4)	(3)	(2)	(1)
4. I am ultimately responsible for and capable of self-discipline based upon my contacts with the people around me.	(5)	(4)	(3)	(2)	(1)
5. My jobs should be made as short in duration as possible, so that I can achieve efficiency through repetition.	(1)	(2)	(3)	(4)	(5)
6. Within reasonable limits I will try to accommodate requests from persons who are not my boss since these requests are typically in the best interest of the company anyhow.	(5)	(4)	(3)	(2)	(1)
7. When the boss tells me to do something which is the wrong thing to do, it is his/her fault, not mine when I do it.	(1)	(2)	(3)	(4)	(5)
8. It is up to my leader to provide a set of rules by which I can measure my performance.	(1)	(2)	(3)	(4)	(5)
9. The boss is the boss. And the fact of that promotion suggests that he/she has something on the ball.	(1)	(2)	(3)	(4)	(5)
10. I only accept orders from my boss.	(1)	(2)	(3)	(4)	(5)
11. I would prefer for my boss to give me general objectives and guidelines and then allow me to do the job my way.	(5)	(4)	(3)	(2)	(1)
12. If I do something which is not right it is my own fault, even if my supervisor told me to do it.	(5)	(4)	(3)	(2)	(1)
13. I prefer jobs which are not repetitious, the kind of task which is new and different each time.	(5)	(4)	(3)	(2)	(1)

Table 2-2 continued

	Strongly Agree	Agree	Mixed Feelings	Disagree	Strongly Disagree
14. My supervisor is in no way superior to me by virtue of position. He/she simply does a different kind of job, one which includes a lot of managing and coordinating.	(5)	(4)	(3)	(2)	(1)
15. I expect my leader to give me disciplinary guidelines.	(1)	(2)	(3)	(4)	(5)
16. I prefer to tell my supervisor what I will or at least should be doing. It is I who is ultimately responsible for my own work.	(5)	(4)	(3)	(2)	(1)

Table 2-3 Scoring and Interpretation*

You may score your own leadership and followership styles by simply averaging the numbers which are included in parenthesis below your answers to the individual items. For example, if you scored item number one strongly agree you will find the point value of "1" below that answer (Leadership Profile). To obtain your overall leadership style add all the numerical values which are associated with the twenty leadership items and divide by twenty. The resulting average is your leadership style. Followership is measured the same way, using the sixteen items contained within Part II of the instrument.

INTERPRETATIONS

Score	Description	Leadership Style	Followership Style
Less than 1.9	Very Autocratic	Boss decides and announces decisions, rules, orientation.	Can't function well without programs and procedures. Needs feedback.
2.0-2.4	Moderately Autocratic	Announces decisions but asks for questions, makes exceptions to rules.	Needs solid structure and feedback but can also carry on independently.
2.5-3.4	Mixed	Boss suggests ideas and consults group, many exceptions to regulations.	Mixture of above and below.
3.5-4.0	Moderately Participative	Group decides on basis of bosses' suggestions, rules are few, group proceeds as they see fit.	Independent worker, doesn't need close supervision, just a bit of feedback.
4.1 & up	Very Democratic	Group is in charge of decisions; boss is co-ordinator, group makes any rules.	Self-starter, likes to challenge new things by him/herself.

*It should be noted that scores on this instrument will vary depending upon mood and circumstances. Your leadership or followership style is best described by the range of scores from several different test times.

Chapter 3—Participatory Management

THE MBO METHOD*

To get all levels of managers really behind a newly instituted management by objectives (MBO) program, it is advisable to create a little stir at the time of the announcement. Some hospitals have set aside a section of their main bulletin board (near the time-card clock, or in the employees' cafeteria), clearly marking it for MBO news, to stimulate hospitalwide interest.

The use of these efforts goes a long way toward creating an environment in which "objectives" and "my MBOs" become a part of daily conversation among all workers.

The decision to install the program should also consider how *deeply* into the organization the program will go initially (as opposed to how *broadly*). Some administrators find it more effective to limit the formal preparation and discussion of goals to the administrative team and the department head levels the first time through. After these two levels of management have had a year's experience with the system, they usually feel a little more comfortable with the whole program and can take a more affirmative role in implementing it at lower levels of management within each department.

Top Management Training

Who should be included in the top management level? While it is recognized that the administrator and his/her associate and/or assistant administrators will be the ones most involved in using MBO as a daily management tool, it is strongly urged that the entire board of directors (trustees) participate in the initial learning experience.

It is also a good idea to include representatives of the medical staff in the top administrative team when possible. The chief of staff or executive committee can often lend much-needed support in implementing objectives later if they are invited to participate in setting priorities in the MBO program.

Long Range and Medium Range Goals

The administrative team should review and/or prepare statements of goals that go beyond a single year's operation. Sometimes it is helpful to distinguish between long range goals and medium range goals. The former are most often understood today to encompass anything that might take five years or more to accomplish. (See Table 3-1.)

Medium range goals incorporate results that take longer than one year to achieve but less than five years. It is not always necessary to have these two groups of goals separately stated. But recognition should be given to the fact that although some results will not be accomplished in the present operational period, some effort will be required in the present period if the goal is to be ultimately achieved. (See Table 3-2.)

---

*Source: Reprinted from *Management By Objectives* by Arthur X. Deegan II with permission of Aspen Systems Corporation, © 1977.

Table 3-1 MBO: Sample Long Range Goals

- Establishment of this hospital as not only an acute care facility, but also a medical center for this metropolitan area, with consequent emphasis on medical education and research.
- Consolidation of our services with those of other hospitals in our Area Planning District so that we do not duplicate services (and expenses) unnecessarily.
- Establishment of a long range statistical data base (population figures, economic data, highway plans, etc.) to enable the hospital to always have realistic and up-to-date long range plans.
- Gradual implementation of a policy of having the chief of each medical department (Medicine, Surgery, OB-Gyn, etc.) be paid hospital employees.
- Relocation of the hospital to a new location available to the people we serve where we can provide _____ more beds and _____ new services.
- Merger of our hospital with _____ Hospital to provide one comprehensive health care facility for the people of this community with lower combined operating costs.
- Implementation of the "holding company" concept under which we join four smaller hospitals in providing one central administration for five institutions.
- From operations, funding 50 percent of depreciation for long term capital development.
- Generation of 3 to 5 percent net gain as a percentage of gross revenue.
- Reduction of operating deficit of our Clinic to $_____ by the development of outside sources of funds for support of this program.
- Development of a community relations program aimed at providing as many services for the community as are identified by community representatives and offering no services that are not seen by them as appropriate.

Table 3-2 MBO: Sample Medium Range Goals

- Phasing out of our OB department in favor of _____ hospital, while they phase out their pediatric facilities in favor of us.
- Revised budget system to involve all department heads in the preparation of their budgets (capital and operating) with consequent financial information being shared with them.
- Development of a total management information system, using latest computer system and comparison with appropriate comparable hospitals, as a basis for tracking our own performance against our own objectives.
- Orderly transition into new building upon its completion.
- Establishment of administrative connection with nearby nursing homes to insure place to transfer our patients when appropriate.
- Participation in feasibility study of centralized laundry facility.
- Erection of a 400-car parking structure on our property.
- Completion of a building fund drive to net $_____ within the next 36 months.
- Acquisition of grant from the federal government to permit implementation of at least two paramedical training programs.
- Initiation of construction of medical office building adjacent to our hospital, with ownership of same vested in someone else.
- Completion of a skills inventory of all management staff in the several hospitals included in our corporation, to identify the quantity, quality and marketability of our personnel and the areas where back-up people are needed.
- Completion of micro-filming of all charts not on unit-record system.

MBO Implementation Plan

The hospital administrator must give directions to his/her subordinates and not preempt their decision-making prerogatives. How can one do this?

The following sequence of events has been found helpful in some hospitals as a way of involving department heads in determining the hospital goals so they are not imposed from above, yet they truly can give the direction called for.

1. The hospital administrator identifies what he/she believes to be the Key Results Areas, which should be included on the hospital list of goals. He/she might arrive at this list by a Needs Analysis tool, by consulting a checklist of top management concerns (e.g., as found in Peter Drucker, *The Practice of Management*), by calling to mind points covered in board meetings, by reviewing results of the last visit of the Joint Commission on Accreditation, etc. He/she gives this list to key managers at the department head level with an invitation to join in a discussion of the indicators of success and specific numbers appropriate for the ensuing year. He/she is pointing to areas of concern without prejudging how much progress can be made in these areas and without consultation with those who will have to accomplish the results.

2. The hospital administrator conducts a meeting with major department heads and the top management team. The list might include: chairman of the board, hospital administrator, two to three associate or assistant administrators, nursing service or patient care director, controller, personnel manager, chief of medical staff, director of laboratories, radiologist, director of development/public relations, director of buildings and grounds. The purpose of this meeting is to respond to the list of Key Results Areas: to suggest indicators of success, to recommend specific levels of achievement to be aimed at, and to offer additions or deletions from the list—all based on what the entire group believes to be realistic in the knowledge they have to implement the list. The dynamics of such a meeting often involve such things as:

    a. one or another manager will learn how important it is to others for him/her to raise or lower sights on a target of performance in his/her own department;
    b. one or another manager will find that some pet project simply is not considered high priority on a hospitalwide basis;
    c. one or another manager learns how strongly others are counting on him/her to achieve some goal because of its implications on other departments;
    d. all managers begin to start thinking like the head of the organization by broadening their perspective.

3. The hospital administrator reflects on the recommendations given and does his/her best to reconcile these with other sources of information/pressures available. He/she considers demands and advice of the board, of third-party payors, of regulatory agencies, of community representatives and area planning councils, of financial backers and lenders, of professional groups, physicians, patients, and countless other sources. He/she does what is possible to blend all these (sometimes) conflicting inputs to the planning process and finalizes the goals to which he/she wishes to commit the institution. These are *his/her* goals!

4. The hospital administrator communicates the finalized list of hospital goals to the board and to the staff. In some cases he/she has to convince the board to be more realistic in what it can expect. In other cases it's a matter of selling the staff on the importance of raising their sights and inviting them to respond to a challenge they might not have recommended but which has become necessary for such and such reasons. Here the important thing is to give the reasons for any changes in the recommendations given. This is best done in a meeting, rather than by written memo only. The finalized list ought to be distributed to all participants in the MBO system and explained in person to all department heads.

Table 3-3 illustrates the three categories of hospital annual goals. Here it will be seen that the institution's objectives must be as precisely measurable as anyone else's.

Departmental Implementation

Training for Department Heads

The principal work of department heads is in the formulation of their own departmental goals, so their training ought to focus more immediately on setting goals at that level. The complete preparation recommended for department heads includes formal training, practice on their own, and an opportunity for critiquing of their initial

Table 3-3 Sample Hospital Annual Goals

Result Area	Indicator of Success	Minimum Acceptable (worst)	Expected Average	Maximum Probable (best)
Daily discharges	Percent accomplished by 11 a.m. daily	90%	92%	95%
Inventory of expendable supplies	Percent of previous year's on hand each department	90%	85%	80%
Maintenance of standards for accreditation	Number of departments meeting or exceeding those set by Joint Commission (out of 24)	18	20	22
Operating costs	Percent reduction across all departments over last year	5%	6%	7%
Personnel administration	Turnover of full time equivalents	40%	35%	30%
	Number of departments completing review of job descriptions (out of 24)	20	22	24
Productivity	Total number patient days divided by total number of FTEs	11.0	11.6	12.1
	Average patient stay (number of days)	8.6	8.4	8.2
Occupancy rate	All in-patient beds	91%	93%	94%
Accounts receivable	Outstanding by end of fiscal year	$700M	$600M	$550M
	Percent aged 6 months	8%	6%	4%
Establishment of MBO program	Number of departments completing goals inverviews and monthly reports all year	20	22	24
New residency in pediatrics	Date opened	Feb 1	Jan 1	Dec 1
	Increased occupancy by year end	20%	25%	30%

efforts. Most hospital managers are accustomed to a type of in-service which includes input → practice → demonstration. They will respond positively to a method of training that explains how to set goals, gives them a chance to experiment on their own "where it doesn't really count," and then reinforces the practice by personal assistance and tutoring during a critique session.

Drafting Departmental Goals

The department head should respond to the hospital list the way anyone reacts to a challenge.

The hospital goals define the ideal of a well-managed institution. The department head should begin by asking "Are there any goals on the hospital list I am primarily responsible for?" (It is hoped that the earlier discussion meeting regarding hospital goals flagged all such goals for each department head, so they would not miss any cue meant for them.) "Are there any goals on the hospital list which call upon me to contribute some portion of the results?"

Taking Table 3-3 as the goals of a hypothetical hospital, the controller or business office manager would undoubtedly see the item referring to accounts receivable and would recognize that this must become a high priority item on his list, since it obviously falls within his area of responsibility. He would also see the item concerning operating costs, calling on all departments to make a reduction; and he would know this must also be on his list somewhere, as he must make a contribution to this goal along with all other department heads. (There are others on the same list.)

But this is only the start of the list. Now the department head must ask as regards his/her department the same kind of questions the hospital administrator asked himself about the entire hospital. Within the department, he/she is responsible for routine operations, for solving problems, and for improving performance by innovation. He/she should then make a list of Key Results Areas and choose for each indicators of success and statements of results expected in all three categories.

To check the completeness of this list of goals, the department head might examine these points:

1. If I were the hospital administrator, which Key Results Areas in this department would I wish to monitor on an ongoing basis to be sure the department was under control?
2. As department head, have I given all my key people something on which to hang their hat? Can they find their cue in the list of departmental goals? If not, perhaps the goals are not broad enough.
3. Before I go to the administrator and commit my department to these goals, have I checked out what I plan to do with my key people? Do I have their ideas? It will be embarrassing to set a goal with the administrator and then find out my people cannot accomplish it.

The department head might wish within his/her department to use the same approach recommended to the hospital administrator for the hospital annual goals. That is, he/she may wish to feed his/her people some Key Results Areas and invite their response as to the indicators of success and the actual numbers (results) before finalizing the draft for discussion with the administrator. He/she should avoid, however, the approach of *simply* getting the goals of his/her people one by one, tying a rubber band around all, and bringing the package to the administrator as department goals.

Department Goal-Setting Interviews

Next comes the one-on-one goal-setting interviews between each department head and his/her administrative superior.

A schedule for these interviews should be prepared in such a way that they are all accomplished in a relatively short span of time, say one calendar week. They only take about one hour each and, depending on the span of control, should not tie down any top management person for too many hours. A department head meeting should be held shortly thereafter for the purpose of acquainting all departments with the goals of each department and thus reinforce the need for mutual assistance.

The final step relative to departmental goals is providing copies of them to all subordinates within a given department.

Supervisor Level Implementation

Drafting Goals

Supervisors are next invited by their respective department heads to prepare a draft of a statement of goals to which they wish to commit themselves as a part of implementing hospital and departmental goals. They should have copies of common goals from which to take their cue.

They should start putting together their list as the department head did. They should begin with whatever they can see of the common goals that fall to them directly or jointly with someone else. Such items are always high in priority on their list. But the list should not stop there. The supervisor goes on to identify other results areas for which he is responsible.

What is happening in the whole organization is the building of a pyramid of goals, where the base becomes quite broad by the time firstline supervision is reached. The original fifteen or so hospital goals can become several hundred as each department head finds the 1 or 2 hospital goals involving him and adding until he has maybe 10-15, and then each supervisor begins with the 1 or 2 involving him and adding until he has 6-8.

Supervisor Goal-Setting Interviews

Next should come another round of one-on-one goal-setting interviews between each supervisor and his department head.

The output of such interviews should be written goals, commitments between each superior-subordinate matched pair. Normally, copies of these goals are not channeled above the department level. To do so invites supervisors to begin to deal directly with top management and short-circuit the chain of command, which may sound stuffy and archaic, but is still good organization theory if delegation of authority to department heads is to mean anything.

Monthly Reports

At this point the system is installed, and all that remains is its maintenance. It was mentioned earlier that feedback or constant monitoring of progress toward accomplishing goals was as essential a part of MBO as the original setting of goals. Yet many programs in hospitals and elsewhere get a great kick-off and then are left to die for lack of follow-up.

The first kind of follow-up recommended is a management information system, which automatically provides information for the manager to monitor progress and report that progress to others. Most hospitals already have a routine of monthly statistical reports indicating procedures performed, meals served, laundry washed, and the like. It has been found feasible for department heads to add a small section to this monthly report entitled "Progress on Other Objectives" to report, using the exception principle, on matters not covered in the basic statistics. This information can then be collected and summarized in monthly statements to help top management keep track of progress on hospital goals or departmental goals, as needs warrant.

A second kind of follow-up about accomplishment of goals can best be handled by the appointment of a coordinator of MBO, a part-time assignment for someone on the administrative team of a hospital. This is not a position of decision-making authority, but more of a staff job to "bird-dog" and remind people of their responsibilities under the MBO program when a deadline for something is near. This would include such things as putting together the schedule for one-on-one interviews, designing monthly report forms, calling managers to see if they have done what they said they would do by promised dates, and so on.

Evaluation

The word evaluation here refers to the whole system of MBO, as well as to the performance of each manager in meeting goals. An MBO program should meet its goals or be discarded. After the hospital has been using MBO for a reasonable length of time (two to three years) and assuming implementation at all levels of management, it should be formally evaluated. Such an event not only revitalizes the program but also uncovers a host of feelings about the management of the organization.

Q & A on Implementation

How Long Will It Take To Get Various Levels of Managers in Our Hospital Actually Working under an Objectives System?

If a formal commitment is made, starting with the administrator and executive committee, and the sequence of events is scheduled, a three-month period of concentrated effort can launch the system very effectively. The first month would be spent by the administration in reviewing the mission statement, updating the long range plan, doing a needs analysis, and writing the hospitalwide objectives. The second month would be used for training of department heads, preparation of their departmental goals, and negotiating their goals with administration. The third month would repeat the same for supervisors within each department.

Is It Necessary To Commit the Entire Hospital to This System from the Outset?

While some recommend total immersion, there is also the possible strategy of implementing more gradually. A pilot project is often a beginning step. You might wish to set goals only at the administrative level first, or only down through department heads, and only if it proves worthwhile to go further down in the organization.

Or, you could take a vertical slice of the organization: that is, implement first only in fiscal affairs, or in nursing service, or some other group of departments—but involving all levels of management. Then, if the pilot proves worthwhile, other departments will be anxious to do the same.

If We Choose the Piecemeal Approach, How Do We Know Which Areas To Involve First?

This is another important strategy. Some will choose to work first with those managers who seem to be most anxious, most supportive, most interested in making it work. Others will choose those areas where it is easier to measure results, such as the business office or clinical departments with readily identifiable work units like radiology or the laboratory.

Annual Goals. Is That the Only Time Frame Used?

What a manager can accomplish by way of results is normally dependent on available resources. Resources are normally allocated on some sort of a budgetary cycle, typically twelve months (or thirteen four-week periods in some organizations). It makes sense then to have the time you covered by goals coincide with the time span covered by the budget. And many institutions now begin considering next year's goals when they start putting together next year's budget. (See Table 3-4 for a summary of the MBO cycle.)

THE DELPHI TECHNIQUE*

The Delphi technique is a simple and efficient method of assuring participatory decision making, policy setting, and planning. This technique was developed over a decade ago at the Rand Corporation by Olaf Helner as a way of predicting future events and was dubbed "Delphi" after the famous oracle of that ancient city.

One advantage of the Delphi approach is that each individual's major concerns receive equal attention; those with narrow or parochial outlooks as well as those with broad managerial views can be heard, and their problems considered equally by their peers. Because it involves the respondents in the continual redesign of the plan, the Delphi technique enhances motivation. Another benefit of the Delphi method is that, if the statements of the issues are truly reflective of the members' concerns, they will, almost as a whole, commit themselves to implementing the plan.

Essentially, the Delphi method uses a questionnaire to determine the views and attitudes of committee (or groups) concerning the task before them and to delineate the areas of concern to the committee. Since the questionnaire is completed anonymously, a higher number of frank answers is likely especially where identification of the opinion holder would result in reduced creativity, biased estimates or constrained suggestions.

Usually the first round of questioning encourages the generation of new or additional problem statements, issues, or alternatives from the committee members. After sufficient discussion to insure that all participants understand what is being sought, each member receives a questionnaire. The participants are asked to respond to the questionnaire and to comment on the phrasing of the questions, whether they are important to them or not, and to add further questions that they regard as significant. This is valuable in two respects. First, the rephrasing may translate the issues from a technical jargon to the normal vocabulary of the committee, and second, the priorities of the individuals involved are reflected. The members are also asked to rate their responses according to the need for particular information.

Between each round of questionnaires the latest opinions of the members are analyzed, compiled, and pooled. Answers may be quantitative or qualitative. The wording of the responses may be changed as similar responses are melded into a single statement for resubmission, and collation of the results shows where consensus exists and where there is a difference of opinion. Qualitative responses are generally typed out and listed.

On successive rounds the altered questionnaires are resubmitted to the committee who evaluate the revised results in an attempt to find general agreement in those areas where opinion is only slightly divided. They are asked to choose the questions, objectives, or criteria

---

*Source: Reprinted from *Evaluating Quality of Care* by M. Clinton Miller, III and Rebecca Grant Knapp with permission of Aspen Systems Corporation, © 1979.

Table 3-4 Summary of MBO Cycle*

Phase	Key activities	Participants
Planning phase	1. Identifies and defines key organizational goals 2. Identifies and defines key departmental goals that result from overall goals 3. Identifies and defines performance measures (operational goals) for employees	Manager
	4. Formulates and proposes goals for own specific job 5. Formulates and proposes measures for own specific job	Subordinate
	6. Participate in management conferences 7. Achieve joint agreement on individual objectives and individual performance 8. Set up timetable for periodic meetings for performance review	Manager and Subordinates
Performance review	1. Continue to participate in periodic management conferences 2. Adjust and refine objectives based on feedback, new constraints, and new inputs 3. Eliminate inappropriate goals 4. Readjust timetable as needed 5. Maintain continuing comparison of proposed timetable and actual performance through use of control monitoring devices such as visible control charts	Manager and subordinates
Feedback to new planning stage	1. Reviews overall organizational and departmental goals for next planning period, such as for next fiscal year	Manager

*Source: Reprinted from *Managing Health Records* by Joan Gratto Liebler with permission of Aspen Systems Corporation, © 1980.

which seem most appropriate and to add their comments. They may also add other items if none of those offered seem likely to be effective, point out items that are particularly inappropriate, and state why. For areas of considerable divergence, each member is asked to reexamine his premises and to discuss with others the bases of these premises. Verbal discussions can spur

Table 3-5 Current Problems/Issues Reported on Second Round Questionnaire

A. Organizational Structure

1. a) Inadequacy of the participatory management system to deal with the increasing complexity and diversification of the Center. (6)
   b) The Committee structure is too large and causes duplication of effort: it unnecessarily involves staff who do not have the responsibility to direct.
   c) Minority concerns being carried directly to the Administrator instead of being incorporated as minority concerns in the report of the Joint Advisory Committees.
2. Absence of strategic planning to anticipate the future, to attempt to mold it and balance short and long-range goals.
3. a) The present situation of staff being responsible to the Department Heads and the Program Directors being responsible for patient care and for program development should be replaced by a more integrated approach.
   b) Lack of cooperation between the Departments/Services. (4)
   c) No clear definition of authority, responsibility and complementarity between Department Heads and Program Directors.
   d) Since the Services remain in separate buildings, there is a feeling of autonomy and decreased interest in functioning among personnel. The physical separation of staff of the same discipline has given rise to these feelings.
4. Improper use of the decision-making prerogative given to clinical staff causing delays in the process.
5. Inadequate staffing standards for clinical staff to assess individual staff members and substantiate complaints.
6. Lack of motivation among staff since:
   a) upward mobility at the Center is slow,
   b) seniority and the state personnel system make dismissal difficult.
7. a) Lack of strong leadership at the Center since no one wants to take responsibility for decision-making, so little gets done.
   b) The experience of unilateral decision-making, changing of programs and policy with no regard to the effect on the total system.
   c) Isolationist policies in many areas — i.e., power building, ego trips, etc.
   d) Disregard for existing policy in many areas.
   e) Managers who seem to operate in isolation, not accepting committee decisions and who therefore cause extra energy to be spent correcting actions, which lowers staff morale.
8. To finalize the Disaster Plan of the Center and ensure that all staff are aware of their roles.
9. a) The problem of the Nursing Department reporting to the Administrator rather than the Medical Director.
   b) To clarify the role and function of the Director of Nursing.
10. Inadequate passing on of information from day to evening or weekend staff.
11. Support Services have grown enormously in recent years, costing the taxpayer millions of dollars, with no compensatory increase in efficiency.

B. Facility Utilization

1. To avoid duplication of facilities and provide necessary additional service by clearly defining the role of

the Center *vis-a-vis* other psychiatric facilities serving the same population.
2. The extreme difficulty in transferring patients from one unit to another. Thus duplication of staff programs and facilities occurs and patients miss appropriate treatment.
3. The mezzanines of the patient dining area continue to offer an invitation to potential suicides.

C. Standards for Patient Care

1. a) Discharge of patients "too soon" without adequate follow-up often leading to patients returning with loss of faith in the efficacy of the treatment.
   b) Need for improvement in housing of discharged patients.
2. Patients of indeterminate category begging and accosting the general public on the streets adjacent to the hospital, creating irritation and raising doubts about care at the Center.
3. The treatment of the mentally ill is still modelled after the physical diseases model, leading to inappropriate treatment and rehabilitation programs for patients.

D. Outpatient and Inpatient Treatment Programs

1. Inadequate assessment of patients admitted after "working hours" since one duty doctor has to report on all calls.

E. Program Evaluation

1. Less than optimum usage of staff or hours because of inability or reluctance of those responsible, such as program directors and department heads, to evaluate performance and work loads and rearrange staff usage or numbers as warranted.

F. Staff Development

1. Inability of staff to develop useful educational programs since they do not feel confident to direct a student or flunk another, fearing that this may make them unpopular.
2. Lack of adequate orientation programs for staff at all levels.

G. Other Problems

1. Communication
   a) To evolve a more effective means of communication to the lower ranks so that they are aware of decision-making and developments at the Center.
   b) There is an overabundance of written communications, sometimes where oral ones will do.
2. Support Services
   a) Insufficient security personnel, especially on weekends. Public has direct access to ward areas through elevator in front lobby. Recreational equipment has been stolen.
   b) Delay in receipt of keys for new staff after a requisition is made to the Maintenance Department.
3. Turnover Rate
   a) Frequent turnover of staff disrupts committee work and planning. (5)
4. Safety
   a) A way of controlling people at a fire area is needed.
5. Funding
   a) Due to the uncertainty related to funding, there is considerable difficulty in developing and trying to establish new programs at this Center.

Table 3-6 Second and Third Round Responses

Issue: Inadequacy of participatory management system, committee structure and minority concerns going directly to the Administrator.

Solutions:

1. Problems should be dealt with and decisions made by those people having the knowledge and authority, thus decreasing size and perhaps the numbers of committees. People should be doing what they are employed to do, managers to manage and others to perform within the context of their classifications. Strong and informed leadership backed by a small administrative committee consisting of staff trained and skilled in administration. (4 responses)
2. Review the committee structure completely and indicate clearly the responsibilities of each committee. Also clearly delineate the responsibilities of each department head and service chief.
3. Complete revision of the committee structure with agreement of members that they abide by the recommendations of the committee. If there is disagreement, then minority concern should be incorporated with the report. (3 responses)
4. Assemble a management team to decide the purpose of the Center and develop objectives to achieve this purpose, then identify the key result activities and design the organization structure around them.
5. Dissolve all committees for a period of two months and allow departments and programs to carry on normal procedures and consult with each other as the problems arise.
6. Impart management procedures knowledge to the staff and reduce number on committees by having only members whose participation is *essential*, and have service chiefs/department heads do their own jobs, checked by the Administrator. (3 responses)
7. Reduce the number of standing committees and number of committees attended by the same personnel, i.e. department heads and service chiefs.
8. Have a forum of monthly meetings, (or some system like Delphi with a selected managerial staff) to get the attitudes of staff who work directly with patients to get some feedback as to the course of action to be adopted in improving the participatory management system.
9. Fewer participants in the management system but participants who reflect the views of sub-groups.
10. a) Management should assure its role and responsibility in the area of decision-making.
    b) I. Have Joint Advisory Committee reduce committee structure.
       II. Review the structure of all other committees with an eye to reducing membership and eliminating duplication.
       III. Elimination of existing members without line or departmental authority.
       IV. Establish the Management Committee as the senior committee.
    c) I. Follow the organization chart lines of authority and channels of communication, and have the Administrator establish and enforce these criteria.
       II. Minority concerns should be handled at the supervisory level and not go beyond department head level.

Favored solutions in Round 3:

1 — 33%	Combinations suggested	
2 — 10%	1 and 10	
3 — 15%	1, 3 and 6	
6 — 10%	1 and 6	
7 — 5%	1, 6, and 10c (II)	
	1, 4, and 10	
	1, 2, 3, 9, 10c (II) and 10c (I)	

reevaluation and lead to a shifting of positions.

The process of recirculating the questionnaire for review and revised opinions is repeated until a consensus is reached. Each round should reduce the set of issues since the members will have deleted some of their concerns and will have combined others. Within relatively few rounds opinions will generally converge to a point where either a consensus is obtained on all decisions, or if total agreement is not reached, the divergence is so small that a compromise or average of all opinions is acceptable.

The Process: An Illustration*

After the first round of questionnaires is processed, only those items classed as very urgent and significant or urgent and significant are fed back to participants. Those items suggested by more than two participants are also identified as such. In one case the administrator of a large urban health center announced the start of a Delphi study and asked each of the 45 senior staff members to:

> "Suggest three problems requiring clarification at the Center or in its operational environment," and indicate on a scale of 1 to 3 the urgency they associated with arriving at a solution to this problem. Anonymity was guaranteed and a return envelope was provided.

---

*Source: Curtis R. McLaughlin, Alan Sheldon, R. C. Hansen and Brian A. McIver, "Management Uses of the Delphi," *Health Care Management Review*, Spring 1976.

Table 3-5 lists the items reported back to the employees on the second round of questionnaires.

Table 3-5 shows that the process of employee participation is a mixed blessing; there is a mixture of "ants and elephants" here. Daily operational problems rub shoulders with broader questions of policy. But one advantage of the Delphi approach is that each individual's major concerns are paid attention to on an equal footing; those with narrow or parochial outlooks as well as those with broad managerial views can be heard, their problems considered equally by their peers.

If the senior managers are committed to implementation, they also may welcome some relatively simple and easily-dealt-with "ants" on the list. Then some immediate actions are assured.

For the third questionnaire the solutions suggested by the staff were culled and then resubmitted to the participants for their evaluation. They were asked to choose the solution which seemed most appropriate and add their comments. They also could add another solution, if none of those offered seemed likely to be effective, and to point out those solutions that were particularly inappropriate and to say why.

Table 3-6 presents the second and third round responses for selected problems. They list the alternative solutions presented and the votes taken on them.

In Round 4 the initial votes and comments were reported back and the participants were asked to vote again on a reduced set of solutions and on some combinations thereof as suggested in Round 3 responses.

Chapter 4—Management Control

OVERVIEW*

Controlling is the management function in which performance is measured and corrective action is taken to ensure the accomplishment of organizational goals. In controlling, the manager evaluates performance by pointing out errors and weaknesses and rectifying the situation to prevent recurrence. It is the policing operation in management, although the manager seeks to create a climate of positive control so that the process is acceptable as part of routine activity. Controlling also is a forward-looking process in that the manager seeks to anticipate deviation and therefore prevent it.

The Basic Control Process

The control process involves three phases that are cyclic: establishing standards, measuring performance, and correcting deviation. In the first step, specific units of measure are determined for monitoring. The basic standard could be stated as staff hours per activity, speed and time limits, and number of errors or rejects permitted. The definition and characteristics of acceptable work would be delineated. The second step in the control process, measuring performance, involves comparing the work or the service provided against the standard. Employee evaluation is one of the aspects of this measurement. In the third step, correcting deviation, remedial action is taken, including retraining employees.

Characteristics of Adequate Controls

Control processes and tools should be characterized by several features that are necessary to ensure their adequacy, including the following:

- Timeliness: the control device should reflect deviations from the standard promptly, at an early stage, so there is only a small time lag between detection and the beginning of corrective action.
- Economy: if possible, control devices should involve routine, normal processes rather than the development of special inspection routines at additional costs. The control devices also must be worth their cost.
- Comprehensiveness: the controls should be directed at the major phases of the work rather than extensive monitoring at a later level or step in the process.
- Specificity and appropriateness: the control process should reflect the nature of the activity. Laboratory inspection methods will differ from the financial audit, for example.
- Objectivity: the processes should be grounded in fact and standards should be known and verifiable.
- Responsibility: controls should reflect the authority-responsibility pattern. As far as possible, the worker and the immediate su-

---

*Source: Reprinted from *Managing Health Records* by Joan Gratto Liebler with permission of Aspen Systems Corporation, © 1980.

pervisor should be involved in the monitoring and correction process.
- Understandability: control devices, charts, graphs, and reports that are too complicated or cumbersome will not be used.

Tools of Control

Certain tools of control may be combined with the planning process. Management by objectives, the budget, the Gantt chart, and the PERT Network are examples of tools used both for planning and controlling. The flow chart, the flow process chart, the work distribution chart, and work sampling, all may be used in planning workflow or assessing a proposed change in plan or procedure (see Part III, Planning). They also may be adapted for specific control use, such as when the flow chart is employed to audit the way in which work is done, as compared to the original plan. Some control tools are directed at employee performance, such as the principle of requalification. Specific, quantifiable output measures may be recorded and monitored through a variety of visible control charts. In addition to these specific tools, the manager exercises control through the assessment and limitation of conflict, through the communication process, and through active motivating of employees.

INTERNAL AUDITING*

Administrators are responsible for managing the hospital through internal control systems they specifically designed for their institution. Internal control is the product of good managerial organization that provides constant measuring and evaluation of: (1) the representativeness and accuracy of data and reports, (2) the overall efficiency of the organization, and (3) the degree to which organizational participants follow policies and procedures.

The nature of the control process encompasses seven steps. First, top management must select and communicate the hospital's objectives. The entire staff should understand these objectives and, ideally, agree with them. Top management also should provide performance standards to guide all staff members on a job-to-job and day-to-day basis. Second, assuming the objectives have been stated in measurable terms, management must assess current performance. Third, performance results then must be compared with the objectives. Fourth, causes for variance above or below the objectives must be analyzed. Fifth, top management must determine what corrective action is in order. It must make two basic managerial decisions: after searching for the causes of the variance and determining possible avenues for improvement, it may decide (1) the objective cannot be reached and lower it, or raise it if performance has been above expectation; or (2) management may choose a course of action to solve the problem and continue to seek to fulfill the objective. Sixth, management must implement the new course of action and take the time to supervise it. And seventh, the results of the new action must be reappraised constantly, based on the measurement of results.

The Internal Auditor

The internal auditor has an important role in ensuring that top management has provided a good control system and in assuring the administration the system is working well. The auditor must:

- determine whether management has provided adequately defined and measurable objectives and that the objectives are realistic and oriented toward the control of the most important resources and activities of the hospital.
- explore the nature of the control system to determine whether the measurement processes are accurate and timely and place reports of performance results into the right hands and, in instances of variances, see to it that the administration responds to the reports.

Internal auditors can fulfill this function for the hospital because of their professional expertise, independence, and objectivity. They rely on an understanding of general management and hospital administration and the ability to cross and recross operational areas while tracking down all components of control systems. The ability to evaluate findings objectively is the in-

---

*Source: Reprinted from *Internal Auditing for Hospitals* by Seth Allcorn with permission of Aspen Systems Corporation, © 1979.

ternal auditors' key contribution in evaluating hospital control systems.

Internal auditors serve the hospital by acting as an extension of management. In doing so, they identify and report problems. They do more than search and report; they recommend improvements. Depending on the numbers and types of problems they encounter, they may present many cost savings and income-generating recommendations for management's consideration.

Information Management

Internal auditors must have a firm grasp of hospital administrative functions and responsibilities to be able to assist administrators in controlling the hospital, must be prepared to review all of the institution's activities with management perspective. One of the more important aspects of internal auditing is appraising the overall quality of the information management receives for use in performing its control function. If the information management receives through the formal reporting systems or from subordinates is unreliable, lacks essential facts, or is otherwise misleading, management works with less than perfect knowledge, and probably will not find out about a problem until it is too late. If management cannot rely on what it sees or hears as being accurate and as fairly representing reality, how then can its information be validated as accurate?

The internal auditor breaks the cycle of questionable information flows by analyzing data gathering techniques and data processing procedures (whether manual or electronic) and by observing the information's flow to top management. Unsound and biasing procedures will be found and reported. As the auditor conducts the information appraisal, a second equally important assessment will be going on. Here enters the strongest application of the management perspective. The auditor must decide whether the information received by management, if accurate, is meaningful. Perhaps information is received routinely that is of no use to management, or is formatted poorly, or is untimely. Equally possible would be the discovery that important operational units of the hospital were providing inadequate or even no performance information to management. Regardless of the situation, the internal auditor has as a goal ensuring that top management receives accurate, timely, comprehensive, and meaningful information.

Benefits

Internal auditing can benefit hospitals of all sizes regardless of whether it is available in the form of an internal auditing staff, as a staff shared with other hospitals, or by the use of existing staff members who have been trained to audit departments and functions other than their own.

The benefits hospitals can expect are the same as those that large corporations already experience with internal auditors. These include:

1. appraising the soundness, adequacy, and application of accounting, financial, and operating internal controls, and promoting effective control at the least cost
2. appraising the extent to which employees comply with established hospital policies and procedures
3. appraising the accountability and safety of hospital assets
4. appraising the reliability of management information systems
5. appraising personnel performance
6. appraising all phases of management performance
7. recommending operating improvements

General Checkpoints

Internal auditing has many practical applications in hospitals and most of them share common checkpoints. A checkpoint is a specific matter of interest regarding a particular subject that internal auditors should review during an audit. Since internal audit programs appraise elements that exist in most departments and functions, such as written procedures or physical facilities, auditors are obliged to review the same checkpoints again and again. A listing of the more frequent audit checkpoints used in hospital departments appears below.

Organization and Internal Control

1. Who does the administrator of the department report to? Is this the right person to report to? How often are reports made and in what form? Are they clear, accurate, representative, and timely?
2. How is the department organized? Is there an organizational chart? Does it provide for good internal controls? Are areas of au-

thority and responsibility indicated clearly? Is it centralized or decentralized and to what advantage?
3. How is the department's work coordinated with the rest of the hospital? Are the interdepartmental organizational relationships clear and satisfactory?
4. What internal controls are used? Where needed, do they accomplish their purpose economically?
5. What records are generated by the department? Do they promote efficient work accomplishment?

Policies and Procedures

1. Are all departmental policies and procedures committed to writing? Who prepared them and were they approved by the governing board? Are they followed?
2. Are the policies and procedures kept complete and current? Are they adequate? Do they deal effectively with patient care needs?
3. Are departmental policies and procedures in harmony with those of the hospital?
4. Are there too many or too few policies and procedures? Are there procedures for handling all routine work decisions? How are nonroutine decisions made?
5. Have all policies and procedures been communicated clearly to employees and patients? Are they aware of the policies and procedures?

Goals, Objectives, and Planning

1. Have clear goals and objectives been established for the department? Are they in writing?
2. Are the goals and objectives measurable and achievable? Are they in harmony with those of the hospital?
3. Are departmental plans committed to writing? Is there sufficient planning and how is it integrated with the overall planning process of the hospital?

Staffing

1. Are employee interviewing and screening procedures adequate?
2. Are employees properly certified?
3. What provisions are made for daily supervision and training?

4. Are employees routinely moved about when there is not enough work available to keep everyone fully employed?
5. Are there adequate job descriptions? Are there adequate productivity measures?
6. How good is employee morale? What is the employee turnover rate? How are breaks and absences handled and with what impact on internal control?
7. Is the area staffed properly with adequate numbers of employees who are qualified and capable of performing at expected levels?

Facilities

1. Does the department's location contribute to accomplishing its goals?
2. Is the department adequately equipped? Is the equipment modern and in good operating order?
3. Does the department have good communication systems? In particular, are there effective uses of telephone communication capabilities?
4. Is there enough space for employees and patients? Does the area and arrangement of space promote efficiency?
5. Is the environment of the area safe and does it promote efficiency? Is it clean, well lighted, and temperature controlled?
6. What security measures exist to safeguard the space, equipment, employees, and patients from crime?

Specific Department

Operations auditing may be applied to virtually any patient care area of the hospital. Internal auditors eventually must evaluate the entire hospital to be certain all departments and operating areas are contributing to the institution's goals.

PROGRAM EVALUATION*

Informal and Formal Evaluations

Examples of informal evaluations are easily identified in most health care settings. These ac-

---

*Source: Reprinted from "Program Evaluation: Resource for Decision Making," *Health Care Management Review* (Summer), by Marie E. Michnich, Stephen Shortell, and William C. Richardson with permission of Aspen Systems Corporation, © 1981.

tivities include evaluating employee performance, periodic review of various departmental functions, most budget review processes, evaluation of the performance of a new billing system, and the typical "keeping-a-finger-on-the-pulse" activities characteristic of good management practice. In these evaluations, implicit standards and criteria for determination of acceptable performance originate from independent professional judgment and experience or commonly available guidelines from accrediting agencies, procedure manuals, consultants and professional associations.

Formal program evaluation may be distinguished from informal or other types of evaluation activities by its application of the scientific method to augment professional judgment. Through the use of research methods, it seeks to discover the congruence between performance, i.e., what is taking or has taken place, and objectives, i.e., what was supposed to occur. It further attempts to identify the reason or *cause* of a particular event or outcome, thus offering a more explicit basis for selecting among possible options for future action.

The distinction between formal program evaluation and what is considered research is not the methods employed but rather the way the results are used. The former is designed to supplement "real world" decision making; the latter, to add to disciplinary knowledge.

Internal versus External Evaluation

It will also be useful to draw a distinction between internally initiated and externally imposed evaluation. Internally initiated evaluations serve the needs of the organization's decision makers. The evaluator is employed to answer their concerns. Thus the administrator will be instrumental in posing the key evaluation questions. Externally imposed evaluation is usually linked with federal or other outside funding sources. In these instances, the funding agency requires information about program performance to fulfill some very basic decision-making needs of its own. Consequently, the role of the evaluator is to provide them with information as well as to work with management and program staff.

Again, some very large health care organizations employ formally trained evaluators. While this has become more common in state health agencies, local health departments, prepaid health plans as well as major medical centers, most often formal program evaluators are based outside the organization, typically at universities and other research centers.

Internal evaluators have the advantage of intimate knowledge of the organization, the program, the data sources, the people and the needs of the decision makers. Because they are part of the organization, they may be perceived as "one of us" and thus move freely in and out of program activities without creating much notice. They may have the benefit of being called in early in the program planning stages and the ability to build in evaluation data bases before the program develops. However, they can be more susceptible to organizational politics, even if they are isolated from direct program pressures. Some organizational structures are set up so that the evaluation team is peripheral to the main hierarchy, reporting only to the chief executive officer or the governing board. However, there may be a potential to discount or give lighter weight to internally generated evaluation reports to make them fit in with other organizational plans.

The external evaluator is usually accompanied by the prestige factor associated with outside expert consultants. Often, this person is a well-known researcher, thus more likely to have an ego involvement in the validity and objectivity of the evaluation design. Efforts will be made to broaden the scope and the implications of the evaluation. Similarly, the external expert's reputation may increase the weight given to evaluation findings. However, the organization, particularly the program staff, may feel a need to "look their best." As a result, some information may be concealed and the program staff may dispute evaluation methods and findings as "irrelevant" because the outside person does not really "know how things are around here."

The Administrator's Role in Formal Program Evaluation

Initiation

At the initiation stage the administrator is essentially involved in determining whether the following criteria have been met:

- Is the program well defined?
- Is the program description acceptable to

those policy makers and managers interested in the evaluation results?
- Does the program description validly represent the activities to be carried out?
- Are the expected results plausible given the program activity?
- Is the evidence required to support the program reliable and economical?
- Are management's expected uses of evaluation information plausible?

Facilitation

Most often, the administrator is charged with the responsibility of ensuring that the evaluator receives whatever is necessary from the organization to get the job done. This may include people, ideas, data, space and authority to work within the organization. Introductions need to be made, meetings need to be held, data sources need to be available and interpreted. The administrator, in essence, "paves the way" for the evaluator.

Perhaps the most important area where the administrator may facilitate the evaluation is in the area of formulating program objectives. Through an understanding of the needs of the evaluation and the function of the program, it may be that the administrator is the best person to take a lead role in objective setting.

Mediation

The relationship between program staff and evaluators is sometimes less than mutually supportive. While some degree of anticipation and planning may minimize the need for mediation, conflicts can occur and may compromise the performance of both.

Often, it is the manager who introduces the evaluation team to the program staff. The way that team is presented may be critical to the eventual program receptivity to the evaluation effort. Managers can minimize conflicts by (1) ensuring that time be allocated for discussions and the development of mutual understanding, and (2) if conflicts do arise, engaging in conflict resolution as swiftly and equitably as possible.

Implementation

Health care organizations and funding agencies expend considerable resources to produce formal program evaluations to augment their decision-making abilities. (Evaluation results are intended to be used; however, the full impact of the efforts is often diluted.)

An administrator who works closely with the evaluator can shape the form of the evaluation to be sure the key questions are answered and reported in a manner that makes sense to the intended audience. Evaluation reports that are difficult to wade through will not be read. Many evaluators have recognized these problems and will provide executive summaries to allow for broader review of the findings.

THE HOSPITAL MANUAL*

In a hospital setting, manuals provide standardized operational guidelines and present a clear picture for employee understanding of the institution's philosophy and goals. The hospital, while remaining open-minded to new methods and change, must be in control of its practices.

Medical advances, frequency of changes in both the professional and nonprofessional hospital staff population, and pressure from regulatory agencies demand a constant review and updating of existing policies and procedures and the development of new ones.

Decision making within the total framework of the facility is diversified and produces a multiplicity of methods that must be communicated interdepartmentally.

It should not be assumed that experienced hospital personnel are well-versed in every detail of all of its policies, procedures, and activities; even the best-informed persons require refresher courses occasionally. New employees on any level must know proper policy and procedure to meet the institution's expectations and to accomplish specific tasks.

Licensing bodies, accreditation agencies, and third party payers rely heavily on documentation as well as on personal observations for indications of the quality of care provided by the institution. Both the Joint Commission on Accreditation of Hospitals and Medicare stipulate as conditions of participation that hospitals must

---

*Source: Reprinted from *Hospital Manuals: A Guide to Development and Maintenance* by Reba Douglass Grubb with permission of Aspen Systems Corporation, © 1981.

develop and maintain written policy and procedure manuals to meet responsibilities and achieve goals.

Multiple Uses for Manuals

Effective manuals serve users according to their needs. Depending upon a user's personal objectives, a manual may:

1. Serve as a frame of reference for communication. All departments and services should have a common understanding of hospitalwide policies, procedures, and activities.
2. Increase quality of performance and avoid confusion. Quality and quantity of work may be reduced if all staff members perform the tasks their own way. Manuals are especially useful in on-the-job training.
3. Serve as resource material for research projects or surveys.
4. Keep users in touch with new developments in technology or new supplies in the health care field.
5. Educate new employees. Manuals are used during orientation to introduce new workers to departmental policies and procedures. Repetition in learning is important. After new employees have completed orientation in the classroom, they may use manuals to review and enforce that learning.
6. Orient experienced new employees to the hospital's accepted methods of operation. Regardless of how much experience individuals may have in a particular area, they still must learn how the employing agency functions.
7. Promote cost savings by eliminating unnecessary function duplication or overlapping. Procedures may be evaluated before they are approved for distribution.
8. Reduce error and confusion in decision making by defining essential steps, in writing. Oral instructions promote trusting to memory, thus increasing the probability of error.
9. Ensure that proper sequential steps are taken. Procedures are written in logical sequence.
10. Assist the personnel office and educators in training new employees or transferring experienced individuals interdepartmentally or intradepartmentally. Manuals are especially helpful to new staff physicians and administrative personnel.
11. Promote confidence that administrative directives will be followed. Manuals contain established principles of management, the philosophy of the hospital, and its goals.
12. Establish lines of authority for delegating responsibility and provide support when there is staff conflict.
13. Support evaluations of employee performance.
14. Provide a means of comparing competent practice to the written approved descriptions of procedures.
15. Serve as legal protection in hospital malpractice actions involving standards of care.
16. Respond to needs on a 24-hour basis. Hospitals function around the clock and manuals serve to tie the three shifts together for continuity of patient care.
17. Promote teamwork among all employees.
18. Serve as a reference for inspection agencies.
19. Provide basic subjects for inservice programs.
20. Orient private duty nurses or medical pool employees to hospital procedures. Manuals may be made available to nurse or medical pool registries for advance information on the hospital's operation.
21. Serve as reference materials for nursing schools.
22. Ensure compliance with equal opportunity laws.
23. Provide guidelines for interagency transactions. Agencies often work together to provide better care and reduce costs—centralized purchasing, lending and borrowing equipment and supplies, patient transfers.
24. Review procedures that are not used routinely.

Development Process

Developing manuals follows a definite pattern:

1. initiating
2. proposing

3. gathering data
4. analyzing data
5. setting content priorities
6. delegating responsibilities
7. selecting format
8. organizing materials
9. outlining topics
10. writing
11. checking facts
12. reviewing rough draft
13. rewriting
14. evaluating
15. typing final draft
16. proofreading
17. numbering pages
18. indexing
19. printing
20. binding
21. distributing
22. utilizing
23. maintaining, and
24. revising.

Hospitalwide Manual Coordinator

Effective manual development is a specialized priority function, not an afterthought. The person who writes the manuals should have a positive working relationship with employees at all levels, writing talent and experience, organizational ability, time to devote to the project, and the sanction and support of administration. The logical step in filling this position is to employ a manual coordinator responsible directly to administration. This gives the management sanction and support that is so crucial to success of the project.

Depending on the way the hospital is organized, the manual coordinator has direct or indirect responsibilities to do the following:

1. Prepare, issue, and implement original policies and procedures.
2. Revise and reissue existing policies and procedures.
3. Maintain a master file of all manuals.
4. Initiate methods for evaluation and approval of policies and procedures.
5. Contact consultants as needed.
6. Keep in close touch with committee members.
7. Edit and write as necessity requires and time allows.
8. Obtain necessary assistance when priority needs develop.
9. Assign tasks to members of the committee when they relate to that individual's department.
10. Initiate discussion for selection of standardized policies and procedures formats.
11. Appoint subcommittees.

Guidelines for the Manual Committee

In creating the manual committee, hospital administration should:

1. Select the coordinator.
2. Select the committee members.
3. Develop a method whereby the committee is able to work together effectively. A project of this type is not simple; internal struggles, personal conflicts, emotional situations, and misunderstandings can cause problems. Change always is difficult and radical change can be disruptive and anxiety producing. Ground rules must be established and the effort should be kept productive. Bylaws are the most accepted method for control.
4. Originate a process for developing policies and procedures.
5. Establish an evaluation subcommittee to review policies and procedures and to make decisions when the committee cannot reach agreements.
6. Establish the coordinator's responsibilities.
7. Decide committee member responsibilities.
8. Decide how often the committee will meet.
9. Write bylaws.

Committee members are representatives from administration and all departments or services in the hospital. One member may be appointed by each department head or selected by the coordinator, subject to the department head's approval. The department head may opt to serve on the committee.

Each committee member is responsible for that individual's departmental manual. In meeting this responsibility, each member should:

1. Collect data and analyze it for content.
2. Review and revise existing departmental policies and procedures.

3. Prepare and issue original departmental policies and procedures.
4. Request assistance of other department members, the manual coordinator, or consultants.
5. Assist in hospitalwide manual development as necessary.

Manual Content

Selection

The selection of topics for manuals begins with a tentative table of contents. One method for researching topics for the list is to review thoroughly all job descriptions and list all tasks in the department. Another method is for each department to list a full day's routine plus special or emergency tasks it has performed in the past, along with any anticipated for the future. Tables of contents in existing policy and procedure manuals or in other manuals such as federal, state, or city codes also may be reviewed.

The content list grows as individual listings are combined. Organizing begins as topics are sorted into broad categories. A tentative content list must remain open-ended to allow for later additions.

Basic Content

Front matter, or introductory material, and a core of information pertaining to all departments usually is included in both general and orientation manuals.

Front Matter

Front matter includes the title page, welcome from the administrator, table of contents, preface, foreword or introduction, and a brief history of the hospital or department. Some definitions and examples of front matter are included here.

Table of Contents. The table of contents is not an index. It lists content by main headings and major subheadings in their order of appearance in the manual.

Preface. The preface is the author's statement of the purpose of the manual, suggested reader use, and some pertinent data on the content. It usually is short, followed by acknowledgments, and is signed by the author.

Introduction. The introduction in a hospital manual provides general information on the publication's content or serves as a user's guide. Although optional, it should be included if it adds something to the manual that would not be appropriate in the preface.

Foreword. The foreword generally is written by a prominent person who is familiar with the subject. It contains a general discussion of the field covered by the manual and a brief mention of how the author treated or approached the subject. It is not essential and is used only if the material would enhance prestige or understanding of the manual.

History of the Hospital. The history of the hospital is of special interest to new employees because it gives them background information on the employing institution. It should be brief but comprehensive. A similar history of the department or a fact sheet is an interesting addition to the departmental manual.

Core Material

Core material consists of information that pertains to all departments in the hospital. Much of this is basic content in orientation manuals and, with other introductory material, is included in all hospital manuals.

Core material consists of the following:

Organizational chart (hospital and/or departmental)
Physical layout of department
Philosophy of department
Objectives of department
Philosophy of patient care (usually found in administrative and nursing service manuals)
Ethics
Medicolegal considerations
Job descriptions
Delineation of skills
Departmental relations (relationship of the department to other departments or services of the hospital)
Standards of Joint Commission on Accreditation of Hospitals (for individual department)
Forms used in the department
Work area duties
Medical terminology and abbreviations
General hospitalwide rules and regulations, pertinent to all departments
Reference materials
Employment practices

The Writing of Policies

Purposeful policies are not achieved by accident. They are the result of careful planning and systematic analysis of needs as they relate to job performance or patient care.

Each policy should be written in explicit language, clearly stated to convey what is meant, to prevent individual interpretations. Policies should be revised to meet new or changing situations.

General policies usually are broad in scope; they guide, rather than direct. Specific policies carry the obligation of exact compliance.

Written policies become the accepted authority. They state the official position of the hospital on purpose and practice.

Following is a list of guidelines for policy development:

1. Authentic sources of information should be used as references for policy development.
2. Policies must not be in conflict with legal aspects of hospital operations.
3. General policies are established by management to deal with everyday situations that affect hospital functions. They set forth guiding principles for all personnel.
4. Departmental policies are written to meet the needs of the department. They must not conflict with general policies; they must be in harmony with other departmental policies.
5. Policies are written positively, dated, enforceable, and have the support of administration.
6. Policies serve as guides to decision and action.
7. Some policies may be written as one broad statement as long as interpretations are clear and cannot be contradicted.
8. Although the elements of policies and procedures are interrelated, they should not be combined; rather, they should be parallel, with procedures stated for each policy.
9. Some policies are so specific that detailed procedures are unnecessary.
10. Policies may be in a separate policy manual, in a special division of a policy and procedure manual, or stated at the beginning of each procedure in a policy and procedure manual and interrelated in the teaching manual.
11. A policy may stand alone: "No visitors will be allowed."
12. One policy may be stated broadly and require as many as 100 procedures to fulfill it. For example:

    Central service will prepare, store, and distribute medical and surgical equipment used by hospital personnel in the care and treatment of patients. This includes receiving, sorting, cleaning, disinfecting, inspecting, assembling, testing, packing, labeling, sterilizing, dating, controlling, and distributing.

    Procedures must be written for each step in the process from receiving through distribution of both disposable and reusable products and equipment.
13. Each department head should review and approve all administrative policies concerning the department. Procedures for fulfilling some of the policies often are judgments by supervisors or other personnel as to the best method of implementation.
14. Some policies will require more time for approval than others. This includes those concerned with compliance (consents); other legal considerations; insurance aspects (benefits); medical treatment; federal, state, and local codes; controversial topics; and outside agency involvement.
15. Departmental policies affecting more than one department must be coordinated and authorized properly before they can become effective.
16. Questions regarding policies should be referred to the manual coordinator or a person assigned this authority.
17. A policy statement in existing manuals or reference books may be adapted for use in the hospital.

Distribution Lists

The distribution of departmental manuals depends on the nature of the content and the size of the department. For example:

- The personnel handbook is issued to all employees.

- The personnel manual is issued to all departments and services.
- The administration manual is issued to all departments and services.
- The business office manual is issued to administration, education, and medical records; selected portions go to departments as they relate to those particular areas.
- The nuclear medicine manual is issued to administration and education; portions on preparing patients for treatments and how to transport them are sent to the nursing units.
- Nursing service on the other hand needs to issue manuals to each nursing unit, administration, education, and all ancillary services concerned with patient care.

Limiting distribution of manuals has both advantages and disadvantages. It is difficult to keep all copies of widely distributed manuals up to date. On the other hand, issuing departmental manuals for management use only may cause resentment from personnel at other levels and encourage a belief that line staff are not important enough to help in decision making. If limitation is necessary, it is recommended that manuals issued to department heads be placed where the entire staff will have access to them.

Master Distribution Lists

A master distribution list should be compiled for each manual in the hospital. The list should include every department or individual who receives a copy, the date of what is issued, and to whom.

Supplements to the manual, revised pages, and memorandums concerning certain subjects also are entered on the distribution list according to date of issue.

Memorandums are included because they usually announce changes in policies or procedures that eventually will be written into format and approved for inclusion in the manual.

The master list is reviewed periodically and memorandums are kept in an active file until they become either a part of a manual or obsolete.

Implementation of Manuals

A new manual or revised individual policies and procedures bring about changes, sometimes suddenly. If personnel are not prepared for these changes, discord, confusion, and resentment may result.

The channel of communication between the hospital manual committee and personnel should be open and dependable. It would be difficult to believe that personnel are totally unaware that a new or revised policy or procedure is in the works if they have been included in the process.

1. Distribute new or revised policies and procedures to the entire staff at the same time. Ask every person to read and demonstrate that they understand and can perform them. Their signing that they have read and do understand the information places the responsibility on them. Learning hasn't taken place until the knowledge and skill are developed and put into practice.

2. Hold a conference or meeting in small departments to discuss and demonstrate new policies and procedures. This can be done as a part of regular meetings that are held weekly or monthly.

3. Have a procedure demonstration day. If a number of hospitalwide or large departments such as nursing have distributed several policies and procedures at the same time, it is difficult to be sure all employees have read all of the new information and can perform the procedures. A procedure demonstration day should be held to acquaint employees with this new information. The time should be convenient to most employees. Two or more sessions may be required before all shifts are instructed. The largest conference room or auditorium available should be used, to allow for a larger number of participants, and room for demonstrations. Extra sessions may be held on consecutive days or weeks, depending on the departmental work schedule and availability of demonstrators.

All participants are given a copy of the procedures so they can follow along as demonstrations are made. Return demonstrations from the group also are used to reinforce learning.

Each participant is given an unsigned posttest, including a few questions from each procedure. At the close of the session, these are analyzed and the questions that were answered incorrectly are emphasized in the next sessions. If too many questions were missed on one procedure, this indicates that further instruction is needed or that the procedure needs to be rewritten.

Personnel who were unable to attend the regular sessions should be scheduled to attend another or work the "buddy system" with one who is experienced in the procedure. Released time for this education program is provided for each employee. Refreshments are served and prizes may be given.

4. Place the complete manual on each unit. Discuss one or two revised or new policies and/or procedures at each conference or departmental meeting until the manual has been reviewed by all employees. This would be difficult for a large department or if the manual is large.
5. Send out notices implying a mystery, or that something unusual will be going on. Curiosity is an inducement for learning. The program must be interesting to support the advertisement. One surprise could be a demonstration of a procedure by a well-known former employee who no one expected to be available.
6. Observe various personnel on the unit performing new or revised procedures and praise them for a good performance. Recognition leads to the urge to repeat the experience and helps to promote self-confidence.
7. Cut a procedure into unnumbered steps, with action separated from the rationale. Give a set to each participant or a group and ask them to assemble the procedure in correct order.
8. To promote familiarity with the manual, cut a copy of the manual's table of contents into individual policy or procedure titles, with no page numbers visible. Distribute a number of slips to all participants and ask them to find the policy or procedure in the manual. This could be a contest (group or single person) activity with a time limit for completion of the assignment.
9. Plan the learning session with the entire group. Cooperative endeavors or contributions to activities will lead to better acceptance and satisfaction in participation.
10. Ask personnel of one nursing unit to demonstrate a procedure to another unit; that unit then demonstrates the procedure to another unit; this continues until all units have participated in a learning session.
11. Have three employees demonstrate a procedure, but only one do it correctly. Other participants must discover which demonstrator's performance is correct and point out the others' mistakes. In a large group, a panel of four or five persons could be delegated to the task of selecting the correct performance. The roles may then be reversed with the panel performing a procedure and the previous performers becoming the critics.
12. Arrange a special session for employees who seem unhappy at being forced to attend a session and for those who appear unable to learn well in a regular group session. Learning readiness is important since some persons need more preparation for learning than others.
13. Train the trainer. Set the climate by being well prepared in advance: have all tools ready and workable, have handouts prepared and enough copies for all participants, and most important, be sure that those teaching or demonstrating for the session have practiced ahead of time.
14. Videotape a procedure and hand out written copies of the process. Let the personnel follow the videotaped action. The tape may be shown as often as necessary.
15. Plan a cooperative group learning session. Divide the participants into small groups and let each team demonstrate the procedure. Cooperative efforts give people a sense of worth and of belonging.
16. Use outside resource people. Recognition that the learning session is important enough to bring in outside experts points up the fact that management is interested in the learning session.
17. Present a case study of a patient who has received treatment according to a specific procedure. This makes the information less abstract and easier to visualize.

Chapter 5—Managing Subordinates*

SOUND PRACTICES*

Promotions to Management

In evaluating applicants for top and middle level positions various types of structural formats are employed including performance appraisals and potential assessment centers, merit systems, psychological, intelligence and motivation tests, interviews, in-basket tests, managerial grid, transactional analysis, etc.

However, there are ten traits, skills or attributes that distinguish the very successful manager from those who do not quite reach that level of performance. Thus, whatever selection or evaluation devices are used, the goal should be to identify those candidates who have a proven track record and/or high potential in regard to the items listed below.

To use this list as a scoring device, place different weights on each of these I factors. Some of the I's might have a weight of 1, others 1.25 and others 1.50 or some other weighing system. Thus, one could score individuals on a 1–10 scale, multiply by the weights involved, and then come up with a reasonably accurate differentiation among candidates.

---

*Source: Reprinted from "The 'I' Test—Evaluating Executive Talent and Potential" (April), *Personnel Journal* by Sigmund G. Ginsburg with permission of the publisher, © 1976. All rights reserved.

The I-Factor Test—What To Look For in Managers

Intelligence. How has he demonstrated both broad and specific knowledge, understanding, and perception; quick grasp of the general as well as technical details; knows what information he needs and how to use it; sharpness and clarity of thought and written and oral expression; creative solutions to difficult problems; flexibility in the face of changing times and needs; ability to pose penetrating questions and deal with the main issues; ability to learn from the past, deal with the present, anticipate the future; ability to plan, organize resources to meet the plan, supervise and control.

Individual Confidence and Self-knowledge. Trust and confidence in one's own ability to handle the ordinary as well as the new, future or extraordinary demands of the position without ending up as an egotist; understanding of one's own strengths and weaknesses and ability to build on the strengths, improve on the weaknesses or to shore up the weaknesses; ability to know when one doesn't know enough or even anything about a problem and to take steps to acquire the knowledge either personally or through staff assistance; ability to handle defeats and bounce back with confidence in oneself.

Intestinal Fortitude. Ability and courage to make tough decisions, to be decisive, to stick one's neck out to take sides if needed, to do the unpopular but necessary before the crisis stage is reached—yet at the same time be willing to reverse time honored practices, precedents and policies and one's previous decisions; courage to be bold, to take a chance, to be unpopular, to be wrong.

Integrity. The individual's word and promises are good; he is fair, trustworthy and unbiased in action; holds to high standards of truth, conduct, honesty, ethics—and expects it of others.

Interpersonal Relations. Ability to communicate and relate to people as well as problems; understands social and human dynamics, the effect of actions on individuals and the various psychological, emotional and ego needs of individuals at various levels; ability to sympathize and empathize; to supervise and set high standards while earning respect and support.

Innovation. Ability to think beyond the traditional or pedestrian—to see new opportunities, better approaches and ways of doing things—a willingness to "dream things that never were, and say, why not"; possesses a healthy dissatisfaction with the status quo, is creative.

Intensity. Ability to handle a wide variety of problems, both as to scope and magnitude; to bear up under pressure; possesses the physical, mental and emotional stamina to meet the every day as well as crisis pressures of management responsibility. Ability to see the tough, often long and grinding tasks accomplished.

Implementation. A concern for seeing to it that plans, policies and programs are carried through on a timely basis with modifications as necessary—a concern for the details involved in bringing about successful implementation; an ability to make things happen.

Identification. Willingness and ability to identify with the goals and aspirations of the department; to support and represent it with other departments; to identify with the hopes, aspirations and needs of the staff of the organization; to be loyal to the organizations and to supervisors, subordinates and peers commensurate with integrity.

Influence-Inspire. He is able by word, action, interpersonal relations, achievements, standards of conduct, by how he carries out all the other 9 "I's" to influence all levels of the organization and inspire others to meet his high standards and expectations, motivate others to develop fully their own potential.

Using Subordinate Leaders*

Providing Assistance

How your subordinate leaders perform is a reflection of your own leadership.

You may find it relatively easier to modify your subordinates' leadership situations than your own, once you determine the types of situations in which they perform best. You are in an excellent position to counsel them on the types of leadership situations in which they appear to perform well.

There are many different ways in which you can help match your subordinate leaders' job situation with their abilities. You can assign the leader to harmonious or to more conflicting groups, and gradually change the composition of the group to make it more harmonious or more challenging as a problem in personnel administration. You can assign to one leader highly structured tasks, or give highly detailed and specific instructions on how the task is accomplished. You can assign to another leader the problems and tasks which are naturally more vague and nebulous, or you can give your instructions in a less specific manner and imply that the leader and his/her group are to develop their own procedures in dealing with the problem.

You can shore up the leader's authority by providing a great deal of support and backing, by assuring that all the organizational information is channeled through the leader, and by extending greater authority to reward and punish or by letting everyone know that you will almost certainly accept the leader's recommendations.

You can give leaders close emotional support by making yourself available to them for guid-

---

*Source: *Improving Leadership Effectiveness,* Fred Fiedler et al. © 1976 John Wiley & Sons, Inc. Reprinted with permission of John Wiley & Sons, Inc.

ance and advice, by being as nonthreatening as possible, and by giving them assurance that you stand behind them. Alternatively, you can take a more aloof evaluative stance, implying that subordinate leaders are on their own, and that it is up to them to find the right methods and to develop the appropriate policies to deal with their problems. While this latter way of dealing with your subordinate leaders might appear cold, certain types of leaders are better able to perform in this type of climate than in a warmer, more accepting atmosphere.

Selection and Placement

Knowing the personality of your subordinates, and the nature of the task, you can select the leader who will excel at the beginning, or the type of leader who will gradually mature into a great performer.

You may require that certain leaders obtain intensive training, knowing that others may perform just as well with little or no training (remembering that all leaders must have minimum qualifications in order to be considered for a leadership position).

You should insure that leaders are either placed in a position in which they can perform well or that the situation is modified so that their leadership potential is used to the fullest.

Consider the options which are open to you in selecting subordinate leaders for maximum performance. The recommendations which might guide your procedures are indicated in Table 5-1.

Appraising Supervisory Personnel

For sample forms used to appraise supervisory personnel see Figures 5-1 and 5-2.

Subordinate Self-Evaluation*

Administrators with assistants reporting to them may want a performance checklist that these subordinates can use to show how they're doing in a given time period—quarterly, semiannually, and so on. Here are the kinds of items that form the basis of such a performance review, and the ratings that can pinpoint areas requiring consultation with you. (See Table 5-2.)

PROBLEM MANAGERS

Abrasive Managers*

Unfortunately, organizations reward and support individuals who are overly aggressive and even abrasive based upon a results-oriented reward system. The abrasive manager occupies an interesting role as a stress agent in such an organization. These individuals often occupy solid managerial positions and usually are considered to be bright. They are perfectionists, need to be always accurate, and push themselves extremely hard. They usually will achieve what they had planned in an excellent manner. They want to do the job themselves and find it difficult to work in groups. This is a problem when they are in managerial positions since it is difficult for them to delegate. They are analytical and are capable of cutting clearly through muddled issues to the core of the problem, but with their need for high achievement, they become impatient with those who cannot move as quickly as they can on this level. Their ability to analyze problems usually is not matched by others in the organization. Their intense rivalry leads them to undercut others, which also increases the general tension level in the organization. When they are involved with groups, they tend to dominate and treat any differences of opinion as challenges that must be argued and resolved only in their favor.

Checkpoints**

There are 13 questions that individuals may want to ask themselves to determine whether they have an abrasive personality. These indices may be an insightful beginning for managers trying to cope with this type of problem:

---

*Source: From the *The Executive Deskbook* by Auren Uris, Copyright © 1970 by Van Nostrand Reinhold Company. Reprinted with permission of the publisher.

*Source: Reprinted from *Stress Management for Health Care Professionals* by Steven H. Appelbaum, with permission of Aspen Systems Corporation, © 1980.

**Source: Reprinted by permission of the *Harvard Business Review*. "The Abrasive Personality" by Harry Levinson (May/June 1978). Copyright © 1978 by the President and Fellows of Harvard College; all rights reserved.

Table 5-1 Guide for Assigning Subordinate Leaders

If the situation for the experienced leader is:	The situation for the inexperienced leader is:	Leadership styles	To obtain best Long-Range Performance, proceed as follows:	To obtain best Short-Run Performance proceed as follows:
High Control	Moderate Control	Task-motivated	Train leader Structure task Increase position power Support leader	If possible, do not select If selected, train Structure task Provide position power
		Relationship-motivated	Do not increase leader control Rotate eventually	Select if possible Do not train Keep task structure low
Moderate Control	Low Control	Task-motivated	Do not increase leader control	Select if possible Do not train or structure task more than necessary
		Relationship-motivated	Train leader Structure task Support leader Increase position power to move situation to moderate as quickly as possible	If possible, do not select If selected, train intensively, support, structure task
Low Control	Very Low Control	Task-motivated	Support leader Structure task	Select if possible
		Relationship-motivated	Increase position power Train leader	Do not select

Explanation of Terms

Kinds of Leadership Styles

1. *Relationship-motivated*: concerned with maintaining good interpersonal relations, sometimes even to the point of letting the task suffer.
2. *Task-motivated*: emphasis on task performance. These leaders are the no-nonsense people who tend to work best from guidelines and specific directions.

Kinds of Leadership Situations

1. *High control* situations allow the leader a great deal of control and influence and a predictable environment in which to direct the work of others.
2. *Moderate control* situations present mixed problems—either good relations with subordinates but an unstructured task and low position-power, or the reverse,
3. *Low control* situations offer the leader relatively low control and influence, where the group does not support the leader and neither the task nor his position-power gives him much influence.

Source: Improving Leadership Effectiveness, Fred Fiedler et al. © 1976 John Wiley & Sons, Inc. Reprinted with permission of John Wiley & Sons, Inc.

1. Are you condescendingly critical? When you talk of others in the organization, do you speak of straightening them out or whipping them into shape?
2. Do you need to be in full control? Does almost everything need to be cleared with you?
3. In meetings, do your comments take a disproportionate amount of time?
4. Are you quick to rise to the attack, to challenge?
5. Do you have a need to debate? Do discussions quickly become arguments?
6. Are people reluctant to discuss things with you? When someone does, are their statements inane?
7. Are you preoccupied with acquiring symbols of status and power?

Figure 5-1 Management appraisal of supervisory personnel[*]

APPRAISAL OF SUPERVISORY PERSONNEL

Name_____ Department _____

Appraisal for Period Ended _____

Prepared by_____

INSTRUCTIONS FOR USE

This form is intended as an aid to formulating a carefully considered and fair appraisal of a supervisory employee's job performance, and potentiality for greater responsibilities.

Although the masculine pronoun is used throughout, the form is equally applicable to the feminine gender.

Such appraisals are important, not only to the individuals concerned, but to the hospital in its program for developing management personnel. The report should therefore be prepared with great care, in order that it will be fair and accurate.

Thoroughly familiarize yourself with the entire form before attempting to use it, noting that for each factor or characteristic there are five different degrees, one of which should be selected as the one most applicable to the person under consideration.

Read the definition and thought-provoking questions of each characteristic before selecting the degree which, in your considered judgment, best describes the extent to which that characteristic is displayed by the individul being appraised.

Consider the individual's performance in his present position. Keep in mind his results, his methods, and his manner.

Any inappropriate words or phrases which appear in the selected paragraph should be crossed out or modified as necessary. On the other hand, if words or phrases appear in another paragraph which aptly describe the person, such words or phrases should be underscored.

Your attention should be devoted to a single characteristic at a time, and do not let your rating on one characteristic influence your rating on other characteristics.

After completing the appraisal, a personal interview should be held with the individual who has been appraised. The purpose of this interview is to give the individual appropriate praise, suggestions, and constructive criticism where needed.

Proper preparation for the interview should be made by the appraiser with the prime purpose of encouraging and improving the performance of the employee.

In the discussion of this appraisal with the individual being evaluated:

1. Give the individual recognition of his outstanding performance.
2. Let him know exactly where he stands.
3. Show him where it is felt he can improve himself.
4. Explain why it is to his advantage to undertake improvement.

*Source: Reprinted from *Health Care Labor Manual* by Martin E. Skoler with permission of Aspen Systems Corporation, © 1981.

Figure 5-1 continued

1. ACCEPTABILITY—Ability to get along with others and to maintain their respect and confidence.

   Review in your mind the individual's performance in relation to the following questions:

   Can you say that the employee has the confidence of his associates? Their respect? Is he successful in developing a first impression into increasing respect in successive contacts? Does he arouse opposition because he is too blunt and abrupt in expressing his ideas? Do others feel at ease in discussing matters with him? Is he stand-offish? Insincere? Not always straightforward? Does he have the respect of those in capacities lower than his own? Of those in positions above him? Is he inclined to be egotistical? Domineering? Vindictive?

   Check one of the following which most accurately describes the individual:

   ☐ People really like him. Adapts self very well without sacrificing standards. Always doing the "extra something" to promote team effort.
   ☐ Willing and eager to please. Works in harmony with others. Adaptable and tactful.

   ☐ Generally adapts self to persons and situations. Reasonably tactful and acceptable.
   ☐ Has difficulty in establishing satisfactory relationships with some peope.
   ☐ Poor mixer. Has difficulty getting along with people.

2. ANALYZING—Obtaining and evaluating facts, and from a consideration of all facts, thinking out a conclusion.

   Review in your mind the individual's performance in relation to the following questions:

   Does the employee get all he facts when considering a given problem? Does he reach a conclusion and then try to interpret the facts to justify the conclusion? Does he fail to put his finger on the more important facts of a problem? Does he fail to recognize the meaning of the facts? Does he present complete factual data in support of his opinions? Is he inclined to accept things at face value rather than to seek more conclusive proof of his own?

   Check one of the following which most accurately describes the individual:

   ☐ Fails to obtain facts. Judgments premature.
   ☐ Rarely obtains facts and limited in evaluating them.
   ☐ Usually obtains and considers facts—generally evaluates properly.
   ☐ Alert in seeking all facts, picks out important elements and generally arrives at sound conclusions
   ☐ Highly analytical. Keen searching mentality. Judgments very sound.

3. LEADERSHIP—Inspiring others to great determination and unity of purpose.

   Review in your mind the individual's performance in relation to the following questions:

   Is he successful in winning acceptance for hospital policies from his people? Does he encourage those working under him to figure things out for themselves and to take action? Does he give credit to others where credit is due? Does he leave others with the feeling that their cooperation, opinions and interest are important? Does he get the cooperation of his employees and associates? Is he considerate of others?

   Check one of the following which most accurately describes the individual:

   ☐ Commands high respect and gets excellent teamwork. Knows how to criticize and when to praise. Expresses self effectively and has high inspirational qualities.
   ☐ Stimulates others. Employees enjoy working with him. Has a "following".
   ☐ Conventional in manner, spirit and enthusiasm. Conveys ideas but does not motivate entire group. Average leader.
   ☐ Limited in leadership qualities. Employees feel they are working for him.
   ☐ Poor leader. Lacks enthusiasm. Constant dissension within his sphere.

Figure 5-1 continued

4. MAKING DECISIONS—Willingness and ability to arrive at a conclusion on a course of action.

   Review in your mind the individual's performance in relation to the following questions:

   Does he appear to be hesitant and reluctant about making a decision? Are his decisions based on prejudices and personal feelings? Does he put off making a decision even though he has all the facts on which to act? When he is convinced his decisions are sound, does he defend them rather than to reverse himself merely because others take a strong contrary position? If new facts are presented, is he sufficiently open-minded to give serious consideration to them even though it means changing his decisions?

   Check one of the following which most accurately describes the individual:

   ☐ Slow, fussy, vacillating and unreliable. Usually "on the fence".
   ☐ Slow in reaching decisions. Without strength of conviction. Easily influenced by others' thinking.
   ☐ Generally sound and accurate on problems of routine nature, otherwise hesitant and cautious.
   ☐ Usually decisive in difficult problems. Generally prompt in giving answers. Faces facts squarely with conviction.
   ☐ Entirely self-confident. Makes prompt decisions and backs them up.

5. ORGANIZING ABILITY—Ability to arrange for the accomplishment of his job responsibility in an orderly, efficient manner.

   Review in your mind the individual's performance in relation to the following questions:

   Has he divided his work into the different tasks which make up his total job responsibility? Does he concentrate on one or two parts of his responsibility so that little is accomplished on the rest of his job? Does he show that he is willing to delegate responsibility and authority? Does he give responsibility to others but fail to give them authority to carry it out? Does he feel that if the job is to be done right he must do it himself? Does he control the activity without destroying the initiative of those who work under him?

   Check one of the following that most accurately describes the individual:

   ☐ Delegates authority very effectively. Recognizes broad objectives clearly and arranges for most effective accomplishment.
   ☐ Successful in apportioning work load effectively. Needs little guidance in coordinating major efforts.
   ☐ Some attempt at delegation on normal, routine affairs. Needs guidance on major changes.
   ☐ Little organized approach by delegation. Overburdens self with details.
   ☐ Poorly organized. Tries to do everything himself.

6. RESPONSIBILITY—Willingness to assume and conscientiously discharge the obligation of his job.

   Review in your mind the individual's performance in relation to the following questions:

   Is he the sort of person who will follow through on an assignment? If something goes wrong, does he "pass the buck"? When things bog down is he the sort of person who has a ready excuse? Having discussed an assignment with him, do you have to follow him up to keep it moving? Does he seek added responsibilities? Does he avoid added responsibilities?

   Check one of the following that most accurately describes the individual:

   ☐ Avoids responsibility. Needs constant supervision.
   ☐ Reluctant to accept responsibility. Follow-up often required.
   ☐ Generally accepts and discharges responsibility willingly. Requires only general supervision.
   ☐ Willingly accepts obligations. Requires only minimum follow-up. Sticks with problem to satisfactory conclusion.
   ☐ Seeks additional responsibility and authority. Manages functions in an outstanding manner. Unruffled in the face of consequences.

Figure 5-1 continued

MERIT RATING

Appraisal Summary

In the light of the appraisal on the preceding pages, what are the individual's STRONG CHARACTERISTICS? _____

_____
_____
_____
_____
_____

Areas where Supervisory or Administrative Ability could be IMPROVED:

_____
_____
_____
_____

Are there any limiting factors such as health, habits, character or personality that would impede his results in carrying out administrative or supervisory responsibilities? _____

If "Yes", explain: _____

_____
_____

DEVELOPMENT PLANS

To improve the individual in his present assignment or for advancement, what SPECIFIC training recommendation do you have? _____

_____
_____

What is he doing to improve himself both personally and in relation to his present position? _____

_____
_____

As a result of your discussion, list the immediate steps or plans you have agreed upon for the individual's improvement: _____

_____
_____

Discussed with the
Individual   by_____ Title _____ Date _____

Employee Signature _____ Date _____

Figure 5-2 Management performance appraisal

THE _____ HOSPITAL MEDICAL CENTER   Please print – DO NOT use typewriter

NAME	DATE
DEPARTMENT	AREA NUMBER	JOB TITLE
REASON FOR REVIEW: ☐ END OF TRIAL PERIOD ☐ PROMOTION/TRANSFER ☐ MERIT/ANNUAL REVIEW ☐ OTHER _____	JOB CODE AND GRADE

CATEGORY I – FUNCTIONAL RESPONSIBILITIES

   A. ACCOMPLISHING ORGANIZATIONAL OBJECTIVES: CONSIDER ABILITY TO RECOGNIZE OBJECTIVES AND CONCENTRATE ON THEM AS OPPOSED TO THE STRICT MECHANICS OF THE JOB.

   B. DECISION MAKING: CONSIDER ABILITY TO UNDERSTAND BASIC PROBLEMS, GATHER PERTINENT DATA, ANALYZE ALTERNATIVE COURSES OF ACTION, AND MAKE AND CARRY OUT INTELLIGENT DECISIONS ON OWN INITIATIVE WITHOUT UNDUE DELAY.

   C. WORK PLANNING: CONSIDER ABILITY TO DETERMINE WORK PRIORITIES, AND TO PLAN AND SCHEDULE WORK TO MAXIMIZE OVERALL EFFECTIVENESS OF THE FUNCTION.

   D. FISCAL RESPONSIBILITIES: CONSIDER COST CONSCIOUSNESS AND CONCERN FOR BUDGETARY IMPLICATIONS OF DECISIONS; (I.E., USE OF OVERTIME AND REQUESTS FOR PERSONNEL AND EXPENSE ITEMS).

   E. METHODS IMPROVEMENT: CONSIDER ABILITY TO DEVELOP AND IMPLEMENT IMPROVEMENTS TO WORK METHODS, SYSTEMS AND PROCEDURES.

CATEGORY II – SUPERVISORY RESPONSIBILITIES

   F. UTILIZATION OF PERSONNEL: CONSIDER ABILITY TO MAXIMIZE CONTRIBUTIONS OF ALL PERSONNEL AND MINIMIZE MANPOWER REQUIREMENTS.

   G. MOTIVATING SUBORDINATES: CONSIDER EFFECTIVENESS IN MOTIVATING CONSTRUCTIVE BEHAVIOR BY EMPLOYEES, USE SUCH INDICATORS AS TEAMWORK IN OPERATIONS, TERMINAL AND TRANSFER RATE, QUALITY OF APPRAISALS, JUDGMENT IN HANDLING DISCIPLINE, EMPLOYEE COMPLAINTS, AND HIS/HER GENERAL RAPPORT WITH EMPLOYEES.

   H. COMMUNICATIONS: CONSIDER ABILITY TO ARTICULATE AND GAIN POSITIVE RESPONSE TO INSTRUCTIONS AND DIRECTIVES, THE DEGREE TO WHICH PERSON UNDERSTANDS NEEDS AND REACTIONS OF EMPLOYEES, AND THE DEGREE TO WHICH EMPLOYEES LOOK TO PERSON FOR GUIDANCE.

   I. SELECTION, TRAINING AND DEVELOPMENT: CONSIDER ABILITY TO SELECT COMPETENT EMPLOYEES; ALSO THE SPEED IN WHICH AND DEGREE TO WHICH EMPLOYEES BECOME PROFICIENT IN THEIR WORK AND THAT OF OTHERS, AND THE EXTENT TO WHICH THEY BECOME PROMOTABLE.

          (RANK CATEGORIES I AND II BELOW "COMMENTS" SECTION)

CATEGORY III – PROFESSIONAL RESPONSIBILITIES (USE OPTIONAL)

   J. CONSIDER SUCH FACTORS AS QUALITY OF JUDGMENT, RELATIONSHIP TO PEERS, SIGNIFICANT RECENT PROFESSIONAL ACCOMPLISHMENTS, AND INITIATIVES IN SELF-DEVELOPMENT.

CATEGORY IV – GENERAL COMMENTS (USE OPTIONAL)

   K. FOR ANY SUMMARY – TYPE COMMENTS WITH PARTICULAR EMPHASIS ON MANAGER/SUPERVISOR DEVELOPMENT.

APPRAISAL REVIEWED WITH:

_____ (DATE) _____
(NAME)   (SIGNATURE)

Source: Reprinted from *Health Care Labor Manual* by Martin E. Skoler with permission of Aspen Systems Corporation, © 1981.

Table 5-2 Performance Review Checklist for Subordinates

	Excellent	Satisfactory	Requires Att'n	Top Priority
1. Holding cost line	☐	☐	☐	☐
2. Cooperation from work group	☐	☐	☐	☐
3. Suggestions and ideas from work group	☐	☐	☐	☐
4. Ability to handle rush or emergency tasks	☐	☐	☐	☐
5. Keeping up with work	☐	☐	☐	☐
6. Flexibility of work group	☐	☐	☐	☐
7. Improving employee skills (Training, job rotation, etc.)	☐	☐	☐	☐
8. Relations with line departments	☐	☐	☐	☐
9. Relations with staff and service departments	☐	☐	☐	☐
10. Staying on top of personal workload	☐	☐	☐	☐
11. Equipment maintenance and performance	☐	☐	☐	☐
12. Self-improvement, updating of management skills	☐	☐	☐	☐
13. Other (add your own)	☐	☐	☐	☐

8. Do you weasel out of responsibilities?
9. Are you reluctant to let others have the same privileges or perquisites as yourself?
10. When you talk about your activities, do you use the word "I" disproportionately?
11. Do your subordinates admire you because you are so strong and capable, or because in your organization they feel so strong and capable and supported?
12. To your amazement, do people speak of you as cold and distant when you really want them to like you?
13. Do you regard yourself as more competent than your peers? Than the boss? Does your behavior let them know that?

Neurotic Managers*

Neurotic managers can function in an effective manner in an organization. On the surface they appear to be quite normal because some of the manifestations of their behavior are congruent with the mission of the organization. Generally they are extremely ambitious and unusually competitive. They can produce both quantitatively and qualitatively and are totally devoted to their jobs. This attracts the attention of top management, which moves these individuals on to higher responsibilities. These people are workaholics, are willing to travel, and often devote their life to the job. Involvement over the weekend and lack of family life appear to be no problem in their quest for achievement. They frequently are persons who are basically insecure and frustrated but who appear on the surface to be very dynamic and self-confident.

This conflict of internal turmoil and external facade is a source of anxiety and stress for these managers. They have a strong need to deny these characteristics and will initiate a campaign against individuals who they feel are in competition with them by demonstrating rivalry, resentment, and even overt hatred in an extremely aggressive manner. When they are promoted to demanding positions, their own deficiencies become apparent and they feel threatened since their inadequacies may be exposed, thus creating more pressure that illuminates their limitations and weakness. To compensate for this anxious state of affairs, they work even harder at their jobs, thus plunging deeper into their own anxieties.

This managerial neurosis is an extreme problem for many organizations because executives who demonstrate some of these patterns usually do not have these inadequacies and limitations recognized by top management until after they have been placed in positions where they are highly visible and in control.

---

*Source: Reprinted from *Stress Management for Health Care Professionals* by Steven H. Appelbaum with permission of Aspen Systems Corporation, © 1980.

Executives who are well equipped to handle management jobs usually are emotionally mature and have high emotional and physiological energy levels. The extent of individuals' emotional maturity depends upon their early training, background, and experiences and how their talent capabilities have been developed. The most important qualities are self-reliance, the ability to receive as well as to give, to deal with other people, to develop self-discipline, to be intrinsically motivated, and to be a long-range thinker. Neurotic executives do not possess these essential qualities and often create a negative environment by resorting to an authoritarian, autocratic style that is terribly frustrating for subordinates. The subordinates at that point, realizing they cannot control this counterproductive environment, basically give up on the job. As a rule, they become very passive and dependent or will even psychologically sabotage the operation.

Neurotic managers will try to eliminate any subordinates who do not support their troubled behavior pattern by firing, demoting, or transferring them. They have a difficult time in dealing with most people, accepting personal responsibility, and cooperating with peers. They may become suspicious of other managers and peers with whom they are working and ultimately develop emotionally defensive attitudes toward anyone who questions their policies.

These managers become hypercritical and have a tendency to replace individuals who question their decisions with other subordinates who appear to support them. In many organizations, this group is not very difficult to find. In the more tragic cases, neurotic managers stay on the job indefinitely and find it essential to develop "flight behavior" in which they avoid all the responsibilities of the job and take a great deal of time off. This may occur in the form of attending many professional seminars in which they abdicate their decision-making role to others by their absence or become heavily involved in alcohol and drugs, preventing them from performing effectively.

One of the major issues to address at this juncture is the identification of this troubled individual within the organization. It is clear that the reduction of stress and altering the nature of the work is a primary step. The person may be transferred from a pressure-packed line position to a staff position or moved to a status position as an internal consultant where the pressure and stressors are kept at a minimum. The organization can involve this distressed individual in counseling sessions where the employer assumes responsibility for the situation and is truly concerned with the manager's welfare.

Most of these managers attempt to mask their inadequacies by avoiding the painful reality that they are not superhumans, are not totally self-reliant, and are not as capable as they feel they should be. They spend a tremendous amount of energy and time attempting to camouflage their deficiencies and to present an unrealistic profile for others who they hope will view them in a much more positive way than they view themselves. It is most interesting that with all the pressures and stress, high-ranking managerial positions are very appealing to individuals who possess this personality profile. This is one of the dangers and problems to be found in organizations since these managers' expectations are not realistic. They give little thought to the prerequisites, trade-offs, and stress associated with the position and instead think of the power and glamour the position seems to project. It is common to discover that managers who are improperly placed in positions and who actually should not be managers or executives demonstrate this neurotic pattern.

It is important that today nearly all promotions to top management positions are based on such obvious factors as the amount and type of the individuals' education and technical training, the level of their intelligence, and length and character of their experience.

A better approach would be to carefully review past performance of personnel being considered for moves into managerial positions. In general, they must at least have demonstrated on previous assignments:

1. the ability to accept heavy responsibility without undue anxiety
2. the capacity to make sound judgments under pressure without panic or undue aggressiveness
3. an active, creative, dynamic orientation toward the job environment; that is, must not merely have adapted passively to it, but have shaped and molded it to meet their needs

Burned-Out Managers*

Consider the manager who is winding up his or her spring too tightly. The overstressed manager puts in very long hours on the job, has almost no time for recreation, accumulates unused vacation time, tries to keep a hand on everything, usually bogs down with details, tries too hard to please everyone, finds it difficult to complete projects on time and to make decisions, tends to lose his or her temper more than ever before (particularly at home), has few if any close friends because he or she is too busy to cultivate friendships (and friendship needs cultivation), finds it more difficult to really communicate with family members, is physically tired much of the time and thus becomes run down, is uneasy or uncertain about the future, and even experiences moments of panic.

Have you ever experienced any of these symptoms? Are we all the outgoing, confident people we seem to be to each other? Do we have our stress under control?

Stress is that factor which, when harnessed productively, will produce innovation and vitality; when left unchecked, it will destroy and cripple both physical and spiritual growth.

Most of us consider stress a negative influence. Stress, if described, would include words such as fear, anger, insecurity, poor health, financial pressure, sexual incompatibility, and so on. But stress can be described as highly desirable if described as love, children, success, financial independence, sailing a perfect race, or climbing a mountain. Attainment of these accomplishments also requires some stress. Almost all of the good things that take place in life result from some form of stress.

Administrative Burnout

Hospital and clinic administrators, department heads, and managers face the most stressful, ongoing circumstances.

"Burned out" is a street expression that became popular in the Haight-Ashbury era and referred to the drug users who became hopelessly addicted. "Burnout" can occur in administration when a person operates at full throttle for too long without appreciating the energy drain taking place until almost too late. It is as if the individual was running in a never-ending marathon race. After a while the individual does not have the extra energy to cope with new challenges and as a result begins to buckle down for the long, slow run with gradually diminishing strength. Instead of leaping over obstacles, the individual approaches them slowly and too carefully. To the burned-out executive the race track ahead looks both tedious and dangerous, repetitive yet unpredictable, and just plain painful.

The difference between burned-out managers and those who flourish under stress is that the latter can recharge their batteries with a little rest or a break in routine, and will return to the job with renewed enthusiasm and vigor. Burned-out executives, however, find only temporary respite in being away and very quickly run out of gas upon returning to the job.

Subtle changes can be spotted in those becoming overstressed. Individuals who are burning out often begin to take an easy way out in decision making. They show only superficial enthusiasm for the job and tend to be too willing to agree with others. They are willing to let others make decisions and do not like to take risks. The anger they feel, because the world is beginning to pass them by, is directed first at themselves and then at their families.

Burned-out managers begin to promote job security and resist innovation by subordinates. Alcohol at the end of the day becomes essential rather than optional. A shift takes place in working habits. Burned-out executives, already workaholics, will either work harder but feel progressively less capable or will shorten job-related activities but will not succeed in recharging their batteries.

Whenever individuals become overcommitted to a job, their interest and participation wane in other aspects of their lives—perhaps at home. Because of the drain of energy associated with always being on top of things at the office, there is little time left to develop compensating factors at home. The cumulative drain at work steals energy from other activities until literally the individual burns out.

Then comes the extra crunch or bump, a new crisis at work or home, the final confrontation, and there is nothing left to fall back on. As if in

---

*Source: Reprinted from "Managing Executive Stress and Other Related Subjects," *The Journal of Ambulatory Care Management* (November) with permission of Aspen Systems Corporation, © 1980.

war, strategic reserves have been totally depleted and there is nothing left with which to fight.

When To Quit

One particular problem facing each individual is knowing when to quit and move on to another position or even to another field. Sensitive executives will be able to pinpoint signposts along their career paths and assess whether they are really accomplishing their goals and, more basically, whether their accomplishments were worth the effort. A number of individuals in their forties and fifties even change career paths entirely.

Little has been written about the question of how to decide when to quit. Following are four questions that might provide clues as to whether it is time to move.

1. When you go to work in the morning, do you look forward to work or is it a continual drag? In other words, do you view your work as a challenge or as an anchor?

2. Are you so comfortable in your setting that you can predict what your colleagues, physicians, or others are thinking? Are you so comfortable that you use these predictions to make decisions? If so, you are well on your way to becoming lazy in problem solving. This in turn places you in a high-risk category. Your alleged extraordinary level of ESP will soon be resented by those with whom you work who are not provided with the courtesy of full involvement. If the challenge is out of your work to the point where you begin to act on assumptions rather than on communication of fact, your decision as to whether it is time to quit may soon be out of your hands.

3. Are you in a deficit position in terms of your good-will bank? Every manager must operate with a good-will bank. This bank is something a manager develops over a period of time in terms of personal credibility, integrity, and competence. Every time you make an appropriate decision, solve a problem, or contribute toward organizational goals, someone at some level of the organization will make a deposit to your good-will bank on your behalf. However, as you make poor decisions, or even if they are correct but unpopular, people are equally willing to make a withdrawal from your good-will bank. Your good-will bank can be wiped out, and you might be forced to operate in a "deficit position." As a manager, to get things done, you need a surplus of good will. When you overdraw too frequently on your good-will account, realistically you may need to consider whether it is time to quit and move on. If you are operating in a deficit mode, but continue to have enthusiasm for your job, you can rebuild your good-will bank. But if your level of enthusiasm and vitality also happens to be in a deficit mode, you should begin to think seriously about where you are heading.

4. Are your principles intact or are they badly compromised? This is a basic question. Professional managers cannot survive long where their principles are being compromised. I am referring to your philosophy and approach toward problem solving. For example, if a number of individuals, managers or others, are violating accepted company policy and procedure, and the organizational structure is unwilling to act to correct this, then this is the type of an issue that, if not solved, will ultimately destroy your peace of mind and require a change for you to survive.

Chapter 6—Problems, Change, and Decisions

PROBLEM SOLVING

Problem Indicators*

Following is a list of conditions that may indicate a problem that needs further study.

- *Backlog* of unfinished work in any operation.
- *Delays and Interruptions* in the performance of a function or service.
- *Overtime* which is needed repeatedly in the carrying out of an activity.
- *Waste* of effort, equipment, material, personnel, time or space.
- *Complaints* from patients, personnel or visitors.
- *Costs* of the function appear to be unduly high.
- *Absenteeism* or *Turnover* occurring continually in any hospital area.
- *Loss* or *Damage* of hospital supplies or equipment; also injury to employees and others.
- *Congestion* or *Disorderliness* of a work area involving one or more individuals.
- *Excessive time* being devoted to an activity in proportion to the actual end result.
- *Location* of an object in an out-of-the-way place.
- *Fatigue* due to walking, bending, reaching or other nonproductive or tiresome work motions.

Typical Problem Situation*

- an inadequate or outdated policy is interpreted differently by individuals or groups
- job performance expectations are unclear
- territorial rights are misused
- individual selfish motives cause someone to obtain an increased amount of formal or informal power
- discrepancies exist between priorities of the boss and subordinate
- grapevine hearsay is interpreted as factual
- someone reports to more than one boss
- established channels of communication are bypassed
- an individual does not have the authority needed to carry out the job responsibilities
- people do not respect or trust their coworkers or superiors.

Selecting a Problem for Study**

As a first step in the process of selecting a problem for study, attempt to develop a complete

---

*Source: Reprinted from *Methods Improvement in Hospitals* by A.C. Bennett, with permission of J.B. Lippincott, © 1964.

*Source: Reprinted from *Time Management for Health Care Professionals* by Steven H. Appelbaum and Walter F. Rohrs with permission of Aspen Systems Corporation, © 1981.

**Source: Reprinted from *Methods Improvement in Hospitals* by A.C. Bennett, with permission of J.B. Lippincott, © 1964.

listing of all work situations which may offer improvement possibilities. This listing should be kept current by adding to it any newly identified problem situations as they come to mind.

Then establish an order of study priority with respect to the various work problems which have been identified. In ranking the relative importance of each of the listed problems, certain factors should be considered in making a decision. Some of these relevant factors are listed below in the form of questions which should, of course, be adapted to the needs of the specific problem situation involved.

1. Which problem situation is causing the most difficulty?
2. How soon must a solution be found to the problem situation?
3. Is the problem situation in question really the one to be solved, or is it simply a part of a still larger problem which requires study?
4. What is the status of the job in question? Is it temporary in nature? If not, what will be the future demands?
5. Is the timing for study appropriate from the standpoint of employee turnover, absenteeism, work demands and personalities presently involved in the job situation?
6. Is there a good chance of achieving success in the way of improvement?
7. How soon can discernible results be attained? What may be the extent and the nature of the benefits to be achieved?
8. How long has it been since any changes were introduced on the job in question? What were the experiences with these changes?
9. What are the attitudes of personnel toward the existing process or procedure? How much employee resistance or resentment may be anticipated?
10. Are there any management policies or professional requirements that might limit changes in the existing situation?
11. Are there any management plans presently underway that might either eliminate the problem situation or have some effect on the nature of the problem?

Developing Problem-Solving Skills*

Following are six methods of developing problem-solving skills paraphrased in part from *Use Your Head*, by Aaron Levenstein.

- The Classification Method
    1. What class does my problem fall into?
    2. How is it like other problems in this class?
    3. How does it differ from other problems in this class?
    4. What are the usual solutions for this class of problem?

- Panoramic Method
    1. What are the basic alternatives?
    2. What data are relevant?
    3. Have I listed all the alternatives?
    4. How accurate are my predictions?

- Critical Factor Method
    1. Is there a critical factor?
    2. What must I put in or take out of the situation?
    3. Am I generating additional problems?
    4. What is the most important aspect of my problem?

- Adaptation Method
    1. How might I adapt previous solutions?
    2. Could I adapt a general principle?
    3. How can I use past experience?
    4. How can I draw from different elements?

- The Innovation Method
    1. How can I change cause and effect?
    2. What if my basic beliefs are inaccurate?
    3. What would happen if the problem extended to its extreme?
    4. How could I alter the limiting factor?

- Brain Storming Method
    1. Create an informal but enthusiastic environment.
    2. Have a tape recorder, pads, and blackboard at hand.

*Source: Reprinted from *Hospital Crisis Management* by A. Brent Garber, Leroy Sparks, and Aaron Korngold with permission of Aspen Systems Corporation, © 1978.

3. Keep pushing for solutions with an attitude that there are never too many alternatives.
4. As leader, have your own list of solutions to add to the discussion whenever the session slows down.
5. Immediately inform all participants of any action taken as a result of the session.

Dealing with Complex Problems*

1. How long has this been a problematic area? The best way to answer this question is to ask others at the grass roots level of the work group. Try to include those who are long-term employees and who have historical insight into the area involved. If there have been similar situations in the past involving the same categories of people, then it is likely to be a complex situation.
2. How many people or work groups are involved? The involvement of three or more work groups, either intra- or interdependent, indicates complexity.
3. To what degree has the situation interfered with work group activity? Ask the people affected by the turbulence to tell you how much time they are spending to cope with the situation. Then make a determination about the appropriateness of the time expenditure. An unreasonable amount of time means there is an underlying, complex situation.
4. How much of your management time is being focused on the symptoms? Also, how much time have you spent in this area? Are other areas getting shortchanged because of the amount of attention paid to this situation? If the presenting symptoms are repeatedly throwing your workday out of balance, then the situation is complex.
5. To what extent will the people involved have to change established behaviors to implement an acceptable solution? To what degree will the success of any solution depend upon the support of others? If the answer is "a great deal" to either of these questions, then you will need to involve other people in the solution-seeking process. When you have to build a support system to ensure a solution you have a complex situation.

MANAGING CHANGE

56 Reasons Why "It" Can't Be Done*

1. It's been done this way for 15 years, why change now?
2. I don't like it.
3. I know it won't work.
4. That's Mike's job, not mine.
5. We don't have enough time for it.
6. It's not practical.
7. It costs too much.
8. We can't pay for the needed tools/equipment/supplies/labor.
9. It's been tried before.
10. It leaves me cold.
11. It's against hospital policy.
12. Our hospital is different.
13. We don't do it that way.
14. We can't do it that way.
15. It won't work in a small hospital.
16. It won't work in a medium-sized hospital.
17. It won't work in a large hospital.
18. It won't work in any hospital.
19. Another hospital tried it once.
20. No other hospital is doing it.
21. It's never been done before.
22. The boss will never allow it.
23. We can't phase it in.
24. It's too late now to make changes.
25. Even if it will work, it won't be approved.
26. We can't stop for that now.
27. It's too much trouble to change.
28. This isn't the right time for it.
29. We haven't the time to go into the details now.
30. Let someone else try it first.
31. Let's think about it some more.
32. We're over the budget already.

---

*Source: Reprinted from *Creative Problem Solving for Health Care Professionals* by Cecelia K. Golightly with permission of Aspen Systems Corporation, © 1981.

*Source: Compiled by Eugene Burger, assistant administrator, Mount Sinai Hospital Services, City Hospital Center at Elmhurst, Elmhurst, N.Y. *Modern Hospital,* September 1970.

33. We're happy with it this way.
34. We'll come back to it later.
35. It's too visionary.
36. It's too radical.
37. It will obsolete other procedures being followed.
38. We can't take the chance.
39. It needs more committee study.
40. The patient won't like it.
41. The patient likes it this way.
42. The doctor won't like it.
43. The nurse won't like it.
44. The floor clerk won't like it.
45. The therapist won't like it.
46. The social worker won't like it.
47. The technician won't like it.
48. The housekeeper won't like it.
49. The engineer won't like it.
50. The dietitian won't like it.
51. The accountant won't like it.
52. The administrator won't like it.
53. The trustees won't like it.
54. It's impossible.
55. We're not ready for it yet; this is only 1983.
56. Don't bother me with facts; my mind's made up.

Approaches*

Change doesn't simply happen; it is brought about by forces within the organization. There are various organizational approaches used to introduce change. At one extreme is the *unilateral* approach where authoritative decisions are made at the top of the power-structure and handed downward. At the other extreme is the *delegated* approach where subordinate levels hold the responsibility for new solutions to identified problems. In between is the *shared power approach,* the most successful means of arranging change, where higher-level authority interacts with lower-level decision groups. Each of these approaches takes several forms.

I. Unilateral Approach:

- *By Decree*—an impersonal announcement handed down by the top echelon, a "one-way" declaration of intention usually phrased in a memo, policy statement or lecture. The assumption is that automatic compliance with authority will produce changed behavior and anticipated improvements.
- *By Replacement*—a singling out of strategically located key positions, to be filled more effectively by new personnel. This is a device used when the decree approach is insufficient but rests on the same assumptions that upper authority control and mandate are necessary to bring about change at the bottom organizational rungs.
- *By Structure*—a relatively formal mechanism for change that relies on a redesign of the organizational pattern, with the assumption that the creation of new or different slots will result in improved performance. If the arrangement is not adjusted to the informal authority lines evident in current practices, it will be ineffective, becoming merely an exercise in logic on paper.

II. Shared Power

- *By Group Decision-Making*—a two-phase approach where upper-authority identifies the problem but subordinates debate and select the most appropriate solution for stimulating change. The assumption is that participation in the change-decision increases support and commitment.
- *By Group Problem-Solving*—the two functions of problem identification and solution are faced by the subordinate discussion group, in recognition of their practical experience and knowledge of the issue at hand.

III. Delegated Power

- *By Case Discussion*—a generalized discussion of a situation aimed at developing problem solving skills which can then be applied by personnel to carry out changes.
- *By Sensitivity Sessions*—a psychologically-oriented method which doesn't deal with task-oriented problems or changes but instead places emphasis on social, interpersonal processes. Led by a professional trainer, the members of the group develop a means toward self-awareness and insight into the attitudes of others. This increased understanding is expected to lead to infor-

---

*Source: Reprinted by permission of the *Harvard Business Review.* "Patterns of Organization Change" by L.E. Greiner (May/June 1967). Copyright © 1967 by the President and Fellows of Harvard College; all rights reserved.

mal and self-initiated change. Customarily used for top management, the method has been used in nursing services, working with an entire staff of an individual unit.

Making Change More Acceptable*

Ralph Besse, a highly successful chief executive, has ten conditions under which change can be made *more* acceptable:

when it is understood than when it is not.
when it does not threaten security than when it does.
when those affected have helped to create it than when it has been externally imposed.
when it results from an application of previously established impersonal principles than it is when it is dictated by personal order.
when it follows a series of successful changes than it is when it follows a series of failures.
when it is inaugurated after prior change has been assimilated than when it is inaugurated during the confusion of other major change.
if it has been planned than it is if it is experimental.
with people new on the job than people old on the job.
with people who share in the benefits of change than those who do not.
if the organization has been trained to plan for improvement than it is if the organization is accustomed to static procedures.

DECISION MAKING

As a tool of management, decision making permits the best selection among alternatives for the efficient, effective allocation of limited human and other resources.

Decision making is most often identified with problem situations. To start any discussion on decision making, one must arrive at the proper identification of the problem—being as specific as possible. Obviously, it is difficult to make a decision about something unless we understand the exact nature of the problem.

A manager's responsibilities are (1) to have clear objectives; (2) to be able to see variations among paths that lead to these objectives; (3) to be able to identify alternatives for correcting the deviations involved; and (4) to look at the implications of these alternatives before making the final decision. Once this process is complete, he then decides.

When Decisions Go Sour*

Executives—using one method or another—somehow manage to make decisions. But only a small percentage of decision-makers know how to proceed when a decision goes wrong. And remember, even the most carefully considered, well-planned decision can turn sour. Five positive moves may save the day.

Recognizing

This move is a "must" prelude to all the others. Clear-headed, honest recognition of the fact that, on this particular decision, you have come up with a clinker. It may not be your fault at all. Other people, other forces, other events may be wholly or partially responsible. But whatever the cause, there is nothing to be gained by clinging to a losing situation. Executives who don't—or won't—recognize the inevitable, who are determined to make a decision work, to stick it out come what may, are only compounding wrong. *Your* lead: to accept the losses, analyze the causes, try to recoup what you can.

Reversing

Many a decision is the result of a multi-step process. From Step A to Step B to Step C . . . and on and on till the final stage is reached. Somewhere along the line you may have tripped. Can you, after thinking things out, retrace your steps to the point where the misstep occurred? Backtrack from E to B, for instance? Then revising B, begin a subsequent series of steps, this time in the right direction? If so, you're halfway home.

---

*Source: R. Besse, "Company Planning Must Be Planned," *Dun's Review and Modern Industry* 69, no. 4, April 1957.

*Source: From *The Executive Deskbook*, 2nd edition, by Auren Uris, © 1970 by Litton Educational Publishing Inc. Reprinted by permission of Van Nostrand Reinhold Company.

Replacing

There will be times when you have a decision that looks great—on paper. You've followed all the proper procedures, made all the right moves, said all the right things. Then, in execution, up pops a weak link. And trouble. Does this mean that your idea is not workable? Not at all.

The weak link should be replaced, the decision can look good again—on paper and in execution.

Revising

In some instances, of course, a decision-turned-bad can't be remedied by simply replacing or retracing. Accordingly, major surgery is called for, a complete revision of the original plan. Now's the time to ask yourself, "Do I have an alternative? Is there a workable Plan B that I can substitute for unworkable Plan A?" Undoubtedly, in arriving at Plan A you had considered other ways, other means of achieving your objective. Can one, or a combination of these, with additions, subtractions, amendments, successfully serve your purpose? Possibly it can.

This stage, incidentally, may call for consultations up, down, and along the line.

Reviewing

Results are the proof of the decision-making pudding. When they go wrong, analyzing when, why, how can teach you a great deal. About your own decision-making ability. About techniques that need sharpening. About pitfalls to be avoided. About planning, performance, people. Failure often triggers more knowledge than success.

The Creative Decision-Making Process

The search for alternative solutions and their consequences may be approached through what has been labeled the creative decision-making process, which involves the following five steps:*

1. *saturation:* becoming thoroughly familiar with a problem as well as ideas and activities akin to the problem;
2. *deliberation:* mulling over these ideas, analyzing them, challenging them, rearranging them and evaluating them from several viewpoints;
3. *incubation:* relaxing, turning off the conscious and purposeful search and letting the subconscious mind work;
4. *illumination:* receiving a sudden insight or bright idea which appears to have promise for solving the problem;
5. *accommodation:* clarifying the idea, putting it on paper, getting the reaction of others and reframing and adopting it.

Types of Decisions*

1. Considered Decisions

Considered decisions are usually those of great magnitude—that is, they tend to be complicated and call for considerable reflection. In addition to a lot of personal thought, they require interaction with others, because the perceptions and ideas of other people often provide multiple alternatives that help in approaching the problem situation.

In seeking this kind of help, we ask associates for their opinions, we sound out their feelings, we identify what they know about the subject.

Obviously, a considered decision requires time—time to find alternatives, to seek other opinions, to get dissent, to determine implementation problems. Incorporating these elements in a decision-making situation leads to appropriate decisions that can be implemented with minimum trouble and maximum probability of success.

2. Operational Decisions

Operational decisions are those we make practically every day. Some of these decisions, in fact, may be made at approximately the same time each day, and they may prevent problems as well as solve them.

From a management development point of view, operational decisions give subordinates an

---

*Source: W.H. Newman and C.E. Summer, *The Process of Management,* Prentice-Hall, Inc., 1964, p. 280.

*Source: Reprinted by permission of the publisher, from "How to Make Different Kinds of Decisions," Peter G. Kirby, *Supervisory Management,* February 1977, © 1977 by AMACOM, a division of American Management Associations. All rights reserved.

excellent opportunity to practice decision making. A subordinate, for instance, may draw up a needs plan. After the projections are verified and discussed between manager and subordinate, the decision is implemented.

Subordinates can eventually make decisions by themselves. Periodic reviews and later discussions reinforce good decisions and reveal areas in which other directions might have been appropriate.

3. Swallow-Hard Decisions

Swallow-hard decisions are ones that are often personally uncomfortable to make because they may result in discomfort or uneasiness for subordinates or others. These can be generally classified as decisions impacting interpersonal relationships—that is, decisions affecting relationships among people in an organization. But although this kind of decision makes us feel uncomfortable, it is a kind of decision that is necessary—the kind that managers are paid to make.

Consider a decision on changing the way employees are scheduled. Say that a manager's boss looks at the schedule and decides that scheduling should be done in a different manner. Because of the subordinate manager's personal knowledge of the organization and its people, he may feel that this new approach would be disastrous to morale.

A swallow-hard decision is called for. As subordinate in the boss-subordinate relationship, the manager has the obligation to tell his boss that the new plan is not a good one and to give specific reasons why. If his opinions and ideas are then rejected the manager again has the obligation to swallow hard and carry out the decision as outlined by his boss.

4. Ten-Second Decisions

Ten-second decisions are ones we make during daily operation. They are the decisions that bring our operation together, keep it ready, alive and running well. The overriding factor in a ten-second decision is the pressure to make it quickly.

Before we make a ten-second decision, we must first determine whether the situation really requires one. Basically, we are asking, "I know this person wants the answer now—but is the answer potentially of such a consequence that I should delay answering the request?" Too many times the precedents we set—and the rules and guidelines we inherit—result from ten-second decisions that perhaps should have been considered or operational decisions.

Second, if we do decide to make a ten-second decision, then we should determine the major objective of that decision. Before we leap in and "solve the problem," we should first determine what we are trying to accomplish.

Table 6-1 Characteristics of Four Main Types of Decisions

Considered	*Major—affecting overall operation*
	Has heavy impact.
	Requires data gathering—facts and opinions of others.
	Proceeds from multiple alternatives, with implementation of each considered.
	Seeks dissent as method of winnowing alternatives.
	Allows extended time to decide.
Operational	*Day-to-day*
	Has immediate and intermediate impact.
	Ensures smooth flow of operations.
	Is continuing, often daily.
Swallow-hard	*Interpersonal relationships*
	Makes decision maker uncomfortable.
	Usually affects others in organization.
	Is difficult / necessary.
Ten-second	*Time compression—now*
	Is made alone.
	Requires quick thought.
	Sets potential precedent.
	Is frequent decision, with short time frame.

Source: Reprinted, by permission of the publisher, from "How to Make Different Kinds of Decisions," Peter G. Kirby, *Supervisory Management*, February 1977, © 1977 by AMACOM, a division of American Management Associations. All rights reserved.

Third, once we have identified our objectives, we must determine what alternatives are available.

Fourth, once we have considered alternatives, the last question concerns implications. That is, what could go wrong in the future if we pursue a given course of action?

Consider these four areas when responding to problem situations that require quick decisions. If we do this automatically, we can shift from making snap decisions to making sound ten-second decisions. (See Table 6-1 for a summary of types of decisions.)

Factors To Consider*

Within each organization there are decision-making constraints. Some of the things to consider when determining the best acceptable alternatives are:

- Timing—What else is going on within the institution or within work groups; what will be happening to work groups at the time the solution will be implemented?
- Budget—What cost factors are directly or indirectly related to implementation of the solution; will the solution require adding employees or purchasing new equipment and/or supplies?
- History—How have changes comparable to this one been accepted in the past; are circumstances different now that would make accepting a change easier or more difficult?
- External Factors—What is happening outside of the organization that might influence the implementation of the solution?
- Mission Statement, Philosophy, Policies—How compatible is the solution with basic beliefs, current practices, long- and short-range goals of the institution?
- Interdepartmental Impact—Which departments will be affected by a solution; would the solution be compatible with the capabilities and limitations of other work groups?
- Health Care Trends—Does the solution represent a step backwards or is it progressive; which direction is most in keeping with the posture of the institution?

---

*Source: Reprinted from *Creative Problem Solving for Health Care Professionals* by Cecelia K. Golightly, with permission of Aspen Systems Corporation, © 1981.

Chapter 7—Delegation and Time Management

DELEGATION

Five Areas To Delegate*

Here are five areas to consider for delegation:

1. *Routine tasks.* Screening mail, preliminary interviewing of job applicants, handling minor scheduling problems—activities like these may be parceled out to subordinates when you're not inclined to do them yourself.
2. *Tasks for which you don't have time.* There's another group of activities, not necessarily routine, but of comparatively low priority. When you have time for these, you prefer to do them yourself. But when more urgent matters occupy your attention, these may be passed along to a capable subordinate.
3. *Problem-solving.* Some executives properly turn over a problem situation to a subordinate. This is usually of a low or medium priority area; and actually there may be one or more of your subordinates with a particular knowledge or skill in the area that qualifies him to take on the task. In addition, he will be motivated to give it special attention, since it will represent a challenge for her.
4. *Changes in your own job emphasis.* For the average executive, job content changes over the years, slowly in some cases, rapidly in others. As executives become aware of these changes in emphasis, they understand that new elements in their activity require more of their time. To "make" the time, the executive must, as a practical matter, delegate "old" aspects of her responsibility to subordinates.
5. *Capability building.* Last but not least, delegation may be used to increase the capability of individual subordinates and your staff as a group. Properly managed, delegation becomes the means by which you train and develop the skills of subordinates.

When Not To Delegate

Just as there are situations for which delegation is a solution, there are circumstances which make it inadvisable.

Delegation can cause trouble if the wrong duties are handed over. Some of your responsibilities are yours for keeps:

1. *The power to discipline.* This is the backbone of executive authority.
2. *Responsibility for maintaining morale.* You may call upon others to help carry out assignments that will improve morale. You cannot ask anybody else to maintain it.
3. *Overall control.* No matter how extensive are the delegations, ultimate responsibility for final performance rests on your shoulders.
4. *The hot potato.* Don't ever make the mis-

---

*Source: From *The Executive Deskbook,* 2nd edition, by Auren Uris © 1970 by Van Nostrand Reinhold. Reprinted with permission of the publisher.

take of passing one along, just to take yourself off the spot.

Some jobs must be retained. It's best to hang on to them, if:

5. *They are too technical.* Staff scheduling or annual budgeting may be routine to you—but completely beyond a subordinate's skill.
6. *The duty involves a trust or confidence.* For instance, handling confidential department information or dealing with the personal affairs of one of your staff.

How To Delegate*

Select and Organize the Task

Managerial activities lend themselves to partial delegation. For instance, you may obtain staff input and assistance in planning, scheduling, budgeting, purchasing, and other such activities, but the authority to approve, recommend, or implement still calls for the exercise of your supervisory authority.

Take the time to make a list of duties you perform that could reasonably be delegated. If you consider each workday for a period of weeks, noting down each such task whenever one occurs, you may be surprised at the significant amount of work falling into the category of tasks that can be delegated. Preparing routine reports, answering routine correspondence, preparing service schedules, serving on certain committees, and many other activities may present themselves as candidates for delegation. List them all, and rank them according to two criteria: the amount of your time they require and their importance to the institution. In short, establish a priority order of tasks for delegation.

Do not, however, attempt to delegate all these nonmanagerial duties at once.

Pick *one* task to begin with, preferably that which is either of most importance to the institution or takes the largest part of your time or both. You should plan on delegating a single function, or as much of one as possible, to a single person and thus avoid the situation in which a function is so broken up that no one person is able to develop a sense of the whole job. Also, in considering activities to delegate, concentrate on ongoing functions, on jobs that regularly recur. There is little to be gained by delegating a one-shot activity if you can do it faster and better by yourself.

Determine the specific authority you will have to provide the person to whom you delegate an activity. Plan also on defining the limits of that authority. In all cases the authority given should be consistent with the responsibility assigned.

Generally, you should consider delegating as much of your technical task authority as possible. Even some of the routine portions of a few of your managerial tasks can be delegated. For example, you can delegate much of the numerical work involved in preparing a budget as long as you maintain final decision-making authority over the complete budget.

Select the Appropriate Person

Pick the employee you will delegate to by matching the qualifications of available employees with the requirements of the task to be delegated.

Beware of either overdelegating or underdelegating. When you overdelegate, the employee to whom you give a task is clearly not ready to handle it. While a modest amount of challenge is certainly desirable, too much challenge can be overwhelming to the employee. Overdelegation frequently leads to an employee's failure in a first attempt at handling increased responsibility, a harsh beginning that is not easily overcome. On the other hand, underdelegation—assigning a task to an employee who is overqualified and can obviously handle it with the greatest of ease—can be fully as damaging. Underdelegation is a waste of an employee's capabilities and often results in that employee's boredom and stagnation. Ideally, delegation should provide a modest amount of challenge, modest but recognizable opportunity for growth, and the opportunity for diversification and expanded usefulness. Also, the employee must be able to see the importance of the delegated task.

You must also be reasonably convinced that the employee you have in mind has the time available to handle the delegated task. Even if person and task are properly matched you can create a hardship by assigning more work to someone who is already fully occupied.

---

*Source: Reprinted from *The Effective Health Care Supervisor* by Charles R. McConnell with permission of Aspen Systems Corporation, © 1982.

Instruct and Motivate the Person

One of the most common errors in delegation is turning an employee loose on a task with inadequate preparation. It is at this point that the pressure of time can set the stage for delegation failure. If the task you are delegating is one you have previously done yourself, and very often this is the case, there may be few instructions, procedures, or guidelines existing in writing. It may be that the only available instructions are those in your mind. In gathering the information you need to turn over a job, it may be necessary for you to put those instructions in writing as well as prepare to personally teach the employee how to do the job.

When you are completely ready to turn a task over to an employee, you should be able to provide satisfactory answers to the following questions:

- Am I prepared to give the reasons for the task, fully explaining why it is important and why it must be done?
- Am I giving the employee sufficient authority to accomplish the results I require?
- Are all the details of the assignment completely clear in my mind?
- If necessary, can I adapt all the instructions and procedural details to the level of the employee's knowledge and understanding?
- Does the assignment include sufficient growth opportunity to appropriately motivate the employee?
- Does the employee have the training, experience, and skills necessary to accomplish the task?
- Are the instructions or procedures sufficiently involved that they should be put in writing?

Assuming you can answer the foregoing questions satisfactorily, turning a task over to an employee then becomes a critical exercise in two-way communication. When meeting to make the actual assignment, encourage the employee to ask questions. If questions are not readily forthcoming, ask the employee to restate your instructions. Whenever possible, demonstrate those parts of the activity that lend themselves to demonstration and have the employee perform those operations to your satisfaction.

Last in the process of turning over a task, but extremely important, is the necessity for you and the employee to achieve agreement on the results you expect.

Maintain Reasonable Control

Control of delegation is largely a matter of communication between supervisor and employee. The frequency and intensity of this communication will depend significantly on your assessment of the individual. You should know your employees well enough to be able to judge who needs what degree of control and assistance. Overcontrol can destroy the effects of delegation. The employee will not develop a sense of responsibility, and you may remain as actively concerned with the task as though you had never delegated it at all. Undercontrol is also hazardous in that the employee may drift significantly in unproductive directions or perhaps make costly or time-consuming errors that you could have helped to avoid.

Set reasonable deadlines for task completion, or for the completion of portions of the task, and prepare to follow up as those deadlines arrive. Give the employee plenty of time to do the job, including, if possible, extra time for contingencies. However, when a deadline arrives and you have not been presented with results, take the initiative and go to the employee. If you let only a few deadlines slide by unmentioned, some employees will automatically adapt to this pattern of behavior and assume that the deadlines you impose are unimportant. On the other hand, if you make it a habit to always follow-up on deadlines your employees will pick up on this pattern and expect you to look for timely results.

Throughout the entire delegation process, try to avoid being a crutch for the employee. Regardless of how much guidance and assistance you are called on to provide, try to avoid solving problems for your employees. Rather, focus on showing your employees *how to solve* their own problems.

In most instances of delegation failure the responsibility rests with the supervisor, not with the employee.

Self-assessment

To keep failures to a minimum you should regularly assess your performance with the following questions:

- Did I assign a task only to take it away

before the employee could truly demonstrate any competence at the task?
- Did I maintain too much or too little control?
- Did I split up an activity such that no single person with some authority could develop a sense for the whole?
- Was I overly severe with an employee who made a mistake?
- Am I giving proper credit to the employee for getting the job done?
- Am I keeping the more interesting tasks for myself, delegating only the mundane or unchallenging activities?
- Have I slacked off in my own work as I delegated certain activities away, or have I used the time saved to increase my emphasis on managerial activities?

Barriers to Delegation*

Barriers in the Delegator

1. Preference for operating oneself.
2. Demand that everyone "know all the details"
3. "I can do it better myself" fallacy
4. Lack of experience in the job or in delegating
5. Insecurity
6. Fear of being disliked
7. Refusal to allow mistakes
8. Lack of confidence in subordinates
9. Perfectionism, leading to overcontrol
10. Lack of organizational skill in balancing workloads
11. Failure to delegate authority commensurate with responsibility
12. Uncertainty over tasks and inability to explain
13. Disinclination to develop subordinates
14. Failure to establish effective controls and to followup

Barriers in the Delegatee

1. Lack of experience
2. Lack of competence
3. Avoidance of responsibility

4. Overdependence on the boss
5. Disorganization
6. Overload of work
7. Immersion in trivia

Barriers in the Situation

1. One-man-show policy
2. No toleration of mistakes
3. Criticality of decisions
4. Urgency, leaving no time to explain (crisis management)
5. Confusion in responsibilities and authority
6. Understaffing

One theorist [David Brown] says the most difficult part of learning to delegate is learning to accommodate differences. It is easy to accept the idea that people are not the same; it is much harder to accept its application. There can be immense variations not only in the quality and quantity of work performed but also in the ways it is done. The manager must be prepared to accept and live with his subordinates' methods and decisions. It may be a very big order, but he cannot reap the benefits of delegation unless he is willing to accept the risks. Delegation is a calculated risk and we must expect that over time the gains will offset the losses.

WORK PLANNING*

The work planning and review process consists of periodic meetings between subordinate and supervisor. The meetings are oriented toward the daily work and result in mutual planning of the job, a review of progress, and mutual solving of problems that arise in the course of getting it done. The process does not involve formal ratings; rather, it provides the basis for the employee and manager to sit down informally, discuss the job to be done, and then (1) agree on a plan and (2) review progress.

The process was designed to take advantage of known principles that relate to certain conditions necessary for subordinate motivation and job growth. They are not exhaustive but do in-

---

*Source: Reprinted, by permission of the publisher, from *The Time Trap*, R. Alec Mackenzie, © 1972 by AMACOM, a division of American Management Associations, pp. 133–134. All rights reserved.

*Source: Reprinted from "Management by Objectives," *Handbook of Health Care Human Resources Management*, by Theodore W. Kessler, ed. Norman Metzger, with permission of Aspen Systems Corporation, © 1981.

clude the essential ingredients that must be present for best personnel utilization. The three basic motivational principles are:

1. An employee needs to know what is expected on the job.
2. An employee needs to know what individual progress is being made.
3. An employee needs to be able to obtain assistance when and as needed.

Some Do's and Don'ts

Do:

- Ensure supervisor-subordinate agreement on major plans and tasks.
- Make plans specific rather than general.
- Relate work plans to business needs.
- Change work plans to conform with changing business needs.
- Have subordinates develop their own work plans when capable.
- Keep it as informal as is practicable; jot down work plans rather than have multiple carbons made.

Don't:

- Try to set work goals too far in advance.
- Make activities, responsibilities, or tasks too broad.
- Become overinvolved in completing forms; instead, concentrate on mutual understanding.
- Be inflexible about changing work plans in response to need.

The Job Well Done

Identification of the specific goals, tasks, or activities is only the first part of implementing the principle of "knowledge of what is expected." The second part is to develop achievement measures or success criteria.

These measures help both parties to determine when a job is done well and to outline areas where improvement seems needed. They must be outlined in advance so that both participants can agree with them. Developing achievement measures is easier said than done. They must be designed carefully to answer the question for supervisor and subordinate, "How will we both know whether the job has been done well?"

The yardsticks, or success measures, should be specific to the task and should be as objective as possible. However, good judgmental, subjective measurements are better than poor objective measures. Time deadlines, of course, are one type of measurement, but they should be used alone only when they are the sole factor of job success. If subordinates develop their own work plans, they should develop the results measures at the same time.

Do:

- Be sure the measures cover the whole project.
- Make certain that achievement criteria are spelled out clearly before the employee starts the task.
- Make sure that supervisor and subordinate agree on the yardsticks before the job is started.
- Make measures as specific as possible.
- Make measures as objective as possible.
- Be willing to change measures if the task or conditions change.
- Approach from a positive, rather than negative, direction.
- Identify factors that can be used to improve job performance.

Don't:

- Use time deadlines only; they are only part of a job well done.
- Develop the measures as a way of "trapping" the subordinate.
- Make the yardsticks too broad or general.
- Become overinvolved in completing forms; instead, concentrate on mutual understanding of what is expected.

In summary, the steps in work planning are:

1. Have the employee develop a set of work goals and measurements; supervisors who wish to do this alone may omit this step.
2. Schedule a planning session.
3. Ensure that supervisor and subordinate come to a mutual agreement during the planning discussion on tasks, due dates, and measurements of achievement.
4. Write down the finally agreed-upon goals and yardsticks after the planning session: the supervisor then should keep one copy and give the other to the employee.

TIME MANAGEMENT

Checklist*

Health care managers have at their disposal the following five time-use checklists that can yield insights about individual style and concern with time so that corrections can be made that will lead to a more effective and efficient operation.

Analysis One:

- Do I know how much time I allot to each type of task? _____
- Do I make sure important information is passed on and used as soon as possible? _____
- Do I minimize written reports? _____
- Do I skim reading material? _____
- Do I have a system to rapidly process incoming communications? _____
- Do I effectively use subordinates, assistants or coworkers to get better control of my time? _____
- Do I allocate my prime time to do important tasks? _____
- Do I force myself to make decisions systematically and as quickly as possible? _____
- Have I worked at writing rapidly and clearly? _____

Analysis Two:

- Do I have a clearly defined set of long-range goals? _____
- Do I have a detailed set of goals for the next three months? _____
- Have I done something yesterday and do I plan something today to move me closer to my long-range and short-range goals? _____
- Do I periodically question my objectives and reassess my priorities? _____
- Do I have a systematic method for setting my top priorities and for determining the necessary programmed steps to accomplish these top priorities? _____

Analysis Three:

- Do I make a detailed schedule for each day? _____
- Do I make a conscious effort to compress tasks? _____
- Do I concentrate on high-priority items when I schedule my day, staying aware of the posteriorities I am establishing? _____
- Am I aware of what I want to accomplish next week? _____
- Do I have a method to remember postponed tasks? _____
- Do I have a way to make sure I take time to plan? _____

Analysis Four:

- Do I have a checklist for my major daily activities? _____
- Do I review my progress at the end of each day? _____
- Do I set deadlines for myself and my subordinates? _____
- Do I make a daily measurement of my personal effectiveness? _____
- Do I have a journal to record ideas, results of meetings, assignments? _____

Analysis Five:

- Do I keep my desk clear? _____
- Do I have a system to handle incoming, outgoing communications? _____
- Am I really in control of my time? Do I determine my activities or are they dominated by crises and the priorities of other people? _____
- Do I try to prevent unneeded information from reaching me? _____
- Am I taking steps to prevent recurring crises? _____
- Have I stopped any noneffective routine recently? _____
- Do I take things with me to work on during lulls? _____

---

*Source: Reprinted from *Time Management for Health Care Professionals* by Steven H. Appelbaum and Walter F. Rohrs with permission of Aspen Systems Corporation, © 1981.

- Do I have an effective plan to update my skills? _____
- Do I analyze situations for time conservation possibilities? _____

Paradoxes*

Open-door paradox—By leaving a door open in hope of improving communication, managers tend to increase the wrong kind of communication, that of a trivial or socializing nature. This multiplies interruptions and distracts them from more important tasks. The "open door" was originally intended to mean "accessible" not physically open.

Planning paradox—Managers often fail to plan because of the time required, thus failing to recognize that effective planning saves time in the end and achieves better results.

Tyranny-of-the-urgent paradox—Managers tend to respond to the urgent rather than the important matters. Thus long-range priorities are neglected, thereby ensuring future crises.

Crisis paradox—Managers tend to over-respond to crises, thereby making them worse.

Meeting paradox—By waiting for latecomers before starting a meeting, we penalize those who came on time and reward those who came late. So next time those who were on time will come late, and those who were late will come later.

Delegation paradox—A manager tends not to delegate to inexperienced subordinates due to lack of confidence. Yet subordinates can win the manager's confidence only by gaining the experience that only comes through delegated authority.

Cluttered-desk paradox—Managers leave things on their desks so they won't forget them. Then they either get lost or, as intended, attract attention every time they are seen, thus providing continual distractions from whatever the manager should be doing.

Telephone paradox—By insisting on talking to the boss instead of his secretary, a caller may delay getting information he urgently needs.

Long-hours paradox—The longer hours a manager works, the more fatigued he becomes and the longer he assumes he has to complete tasks. For both reasons he slows down necessitating still longer hours.

Activity-vs.-results paradox—Managers tend to confuse activity with results, motion with accomplishment. Thus, as they gradually lose sight of their real objectives, they concentrate increasingly on staying busy. Finally, their objective becomes to stay busy, and they have become confirmed "workaholics."

Efficiency vs. effectiveness—Managers tend to confuse efficiency with effectiveness. They will be more concerned about doing the job right than doing the right job. No matter how efficiently a job is done, if it is the wrong job, it will not be effective.

Paradox of time—No one has enough, yet everyone has all there is.

Time Management Techniques*

1. The Gantt Chart—Monitoring Work Time

This management technique can be applied as a control mechanism to initially plan and then monitor work time. As an added feature, it also provides an early warning system when slippage occurs, indicating what and how much additional time is or can possibly be made available.

In brief, a Gantt Chart allows observation and evaluation of progress toward the completion of established objectives as measured against a previously determined time schedule. Actually, this is something like setting up a realistic budget and then comparing actual expenditures, in this case time instead of money, with what was previously planned.

Figure 7-1 is a simplified version of a Gantt Chart which illustrates only the major duties for a person in charge of a materials management department. The inevitable and numerous office

---

*Source: Reprinted from "Time Management Strategy for Women," *Management Review* by E.B. Schwartz and R.A. Mackenzie (September) with permission of Aspen Systems Corporation, © 1977.

*Source: Reprinted from *Time Management for Health Care Professionals*, by Steven H. Appelbaum and Walter F. Rohrs with permission of Aspen Systems Corporation, © 1981.

Table 7-1 Time Wasters: Causes and Solutions

Time Waster	Possible Causes	Solutions
Lack of planning	Failure to see the benefit	Recognize that planning takes time but saves time in the end.
	Action orientation	Emphasize results, not activity.
	Success without it	Recognize that success is often in spite of, not because of, methods.
Lack of priorities	Lack of goals and objectives	Write down goals and objectives. Discuss priorities with subordinates.
Overcommitment	Broad interests	Say no.
	Confusion in priorities	Put first things first.
	Failure to set priorities	Develop a personal philosophy of time. Relate priorities to a schedule of events.
Management by crisis	Lack of planning	Apply the same solutions as for lack of planning.
	Unrealistic time estimates	Allow more time. Allow for interruptions.
	Problem orientation	Be opportunity-oriented.
	Reluctance of subordinates to break bad news	Encourage fast transmission of information as essential for timely corrective action.
Haste	Impatience with detail	Take time to get it right. Save the time of doing it over.
	Responding to the urgent	Distinguish between the urgent and the important.
	Lack of planning ahead	Take time to plan. It repays itself many times over.
	Attempting too much in too little time	Attempt less. Delegate more.
Paperwork and reading	Knowledge explosion	Read selectively. Learn speed reading.
	Computeritis	Manage computer data by exception.
	Failure to screen	Remember the Pareto principle. Delegate reading to subordinates.
Indecision	Lack of confidence in the facts	Improve fact-finding and validating procedures.
	Insistence on all the facts—paralysis of analysis	Accept risks as inevitable. Decide without all facts.
	Fear of the consequences of a mistake	Delegate the right to be wrong. Use mistakes as a learning process.
	Lack of a rational decision-making process	Get facts, set goals, investigate alternatives and negative consequences, make the decision, and implement it.
Lack of delegation	Fear of subordinates' inadequacy	Train. Allow mistakes. Replace if necessary.
	Fear of subordinates' competence	Delegate fully. Give credit. Insure corporate growth to maintain challenge.
	Work overload on subordinates	Balance the workload. Staff up. Reorder priorities.
Routine and trivia	Lack of priorities	Set and concentrate on goals. Delegate nonessentials.
	Oversurveillance of subordinates	Delegate; then give subordinates their head. Look to results, not details or methods.
	Refusal to delegate; feeling of greater security dealing with operating detail	Recognize that without delegation it is impossible to get anything done through others.

Table 7-1 continued

Time Waster	Possible Causes	Solutions
Visitors	Enjoyment of socializing	Do it elsewhere. Meet visitors outside. Suggest lunch if necessary. Hold stand-up conferences.
	Inability to say no	Screen. Say no. Be unavailable. Modify the open-door policy.
Telephone	Lack of self-discipline	Screen and group calls. Be brief.
	Desire to be informed and involved	Stay uninvolved with all but essentials. Manage by exception.
Meetings	Fear of responsibility for decisions	Make decisions without meetings.
	Indecision	Make decisions even when some facts are missing.
	Overcommunication	Discourage unnecessary meetings. Convene only those needed.
	Poor leadership	Use agendas. Stick to the subject. Prepare concise minutes as soon as possible.

Source: Reprinted, by permission of the publisher, from *The Time Trap*, R. Alec Mackenzie, © 1972 by AMACOM, a division of American Management Associations, pp. 173–176. All rights reserved.

routines are omitted. A brief explanation may generate interest and encouragement in using the chart as a means of planning and controlling what you want to do when it has to be done. In this illustration, the chart highlights an eight-hour, five-day work week plus the first three days of the succeeding week. The planned and expected duties and activities are listed vertically along the left margin of the diagram.

The symbols on the chart which resemble a staple, or a ⌐ ¬, are used to indicate the time planned to perform each major job duty or activity. Solid lines directly below show how much of the task was actually accomplished during the specified time period. For example, the job "write report" was planned for Tuesday morning, with the afternoon set aside for a meeting to "negotiate contract A." As it turned out, however, the report was not finished Tuesday morning (indicated by a shortened solid line underneath the "work planned" symbol), and further work on it had to be postponed because of the negotiating meeting scheduled for the afternoon.

The advantages of using a Gantt Chart as a technique for planning, scheduling, and controlling are readily apparent. It is unique in that it provides an overall visible means for setting goals and then scheduling time use in order to attain those goals. In addition, it permits observations of accomplishments and a more effective reassignment of time to take care of unexpected contingencies and demands. A Gantt Chart is also helpful in situations where an unexpected delay causes a period of unplanned waiting time. An inspection of the chart shows possible readjustments to fill the time vacuum created by being trapped in an unexpected holding pattern. If a meeting is cancelled, be sure some alternate activity can be readily implemented as a backup task to save that precious resource—time.

The opportunity to conveniently shift time allocations and to reorder priorities can help identify the immediately required time in periods of severe time constraints, while still preserving possible alternatives to fulfill previously planned objectives. It thus becomes an adjustable timetable for rescheduling time priorities to fulfill objectives.

A few suggestions that should prove useful in devising and implementing your own Gantt Chart follow in the checklist.

One final note: Some people in attempting to cope with a difficult problem may see or consider only one alternate solution or option. The Gantt Chart visibly displays an individual's entire time schedule, showing sequences and interdependencies of events and activities, and thus permits a broader view; it should therefore help in seeking and finding the most desirable of a number of possible solutions.

Figure 7-1 Gantt chart

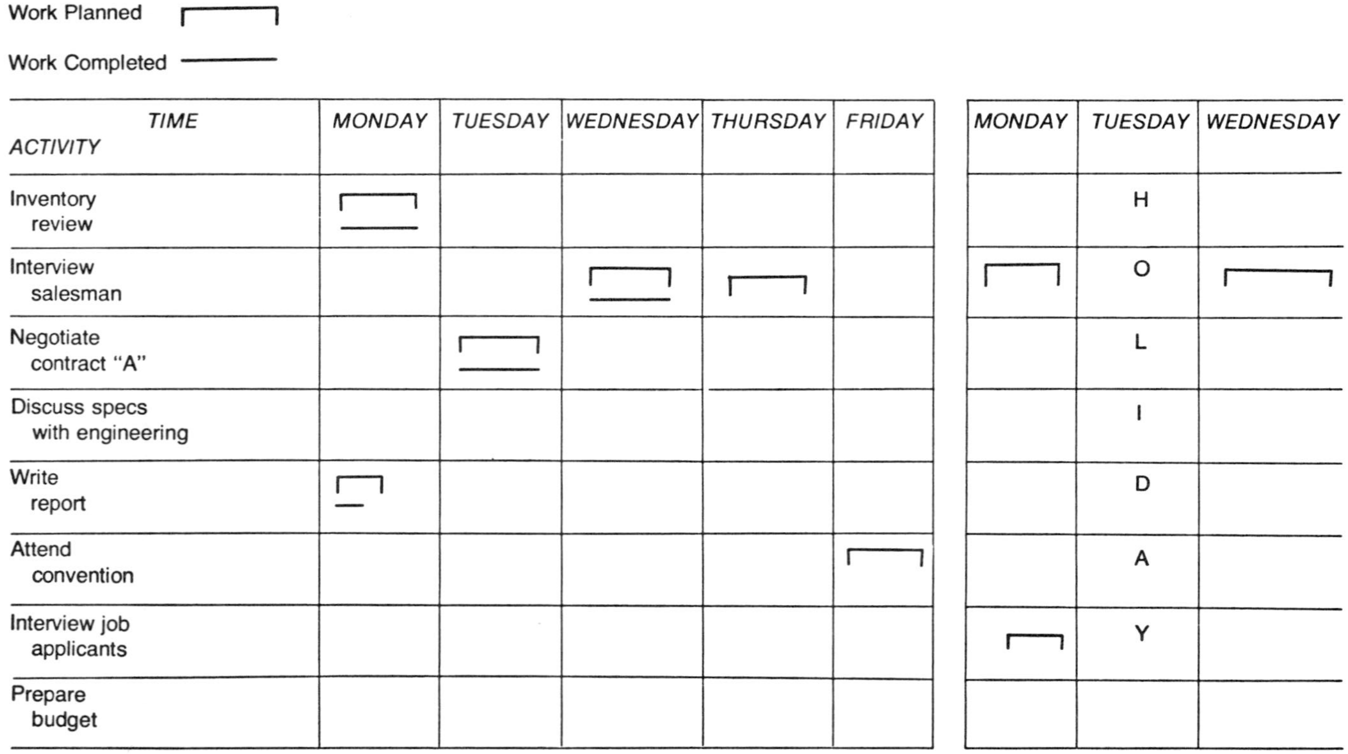

Work Planned [ ]
Work Completed ———

ACTIVITY \ TIME	MONDAY	TUESDAY	WEDNESDAY	THURSDAY	FRIDAY	MONDAY	TUESDAY	WEDNESDAY
Inventory review	[ ]						H	
Interview salesman			[ ]	[		[	O	[
Negotiate contract "A"		[ ]					L	
Discuss specs with engineering	[						I	
Write report							D	
Attend convention					[		A	
Interview job applicants						[	Y	
Prepare budget								

Checklist for Using a Gantt Chart for Time Management

1. Consider the Gantt Chart as a budget—plan your time carefully.
2. Be realistic and practical about using your time. Plan what is possible.
3. List only major time-consuming events, activities, and duties of a recurring and nonrecurring nature.
4. Plan and schedule on at least a weekly basis.
5. Build in occasional discretionary time for surprises and emergencies.
6. Have backup activities for unexpected vacuums.
7. If necessary, use reserves of time—hours in excess of a normal work period.
8. Plan changes of pace and subject matter.
9. Give yourself *short* breaks for reflection and relaxation.
10. Set time limits for the duration of meetings, interviews, lunches, visits, and telephone calls.
11. Plan for interruptions when activities exceed time limitations.
12. When required, be unreachable—allow no interruptions by spending day at home, having a "do not disturb sign" at office, or not taking telephone calls.
13. Under duress, delegate—send a surrogate to meetings or to perform a specific duty.
14. Be flexible; reschedule time when and if possible.
15. Evaluate and review your performance on a daily basis.
16. Keep on schedule.
17. Be wary of nibblers—people who frequently ask for "a minute" and then take ten—or more.

2. Program Evaluation Review Technique (PERT)

PERT as a management technique evolved from the basic concepts contained in the Gantt Chart. This technique utilized statistical probability theory to furnish three-time estimates (pessimistic, most probable, and optimistic) and added events to the graphing of activities. Briefly, the PERT concept requires:

- setting of objectives,
- designating sequences of events or activities to attain goals,
- organizing and coordinating people, materials, and equipment,
- exercising control over the progress of the entire project to ensure completion as scheduled.

It is a planning, scheduling, organizing, coordinating, and controlling technique. PERT, as a management technique, makes a number of important assumptions which form the basis for its successful adoption:

1. Some activities must occur or be completed before others can start. Before putting a roof on a new facility, the walls must be in place.
2. Some activities take longer to accomplish than others and therefore should start sooner. It may take longer to get delivery of an EKG system than operating room equipment.
3. Some activities can occur concurrently. Doors and windows can be installed at the same time.
4. It is possible to reallocate or reassign some resources from one activity to another in order to avoid postponing the projected completion date. One worker can be sent to pick up needed supplies rather than waiting for a delivery next week.

Figure 7-2 is a representation of a PERT network which was prepared for planning a recognition banquet for health care personnel with ten years of service. Customarily a PERT diagram is read from left to right. In this example each step in the process is indicated by the circled letters, A through I. A first thing to do, quite logically, is to announce the start of the project. Once that is accomplished, a number of other separate sequential tasks can be planned—as shown by the three tracks, A-B-C-D-I, C-E-I, and A-F-G-H-I. The numbers that appear between the lettered steps represent the estimated time it will take to complete each separate task along that particular track. For example, the number 2 between A and B means that 2 weeks are allocated for selecting a time and site from the starting date of the project. Mailing announcements should be completed in 3 weeks, in moving along from B to C. Because the track A through I takes 12 weeks and thus more time than A-F-G-H-I (10 weeks), or A-B-C-E-I (8 weeks), it is called the "critical path." Any delay along this longest track will cause a postponement of the banquet, (I). For

Figure 7-2 Program evaluation and review technique (PERT)

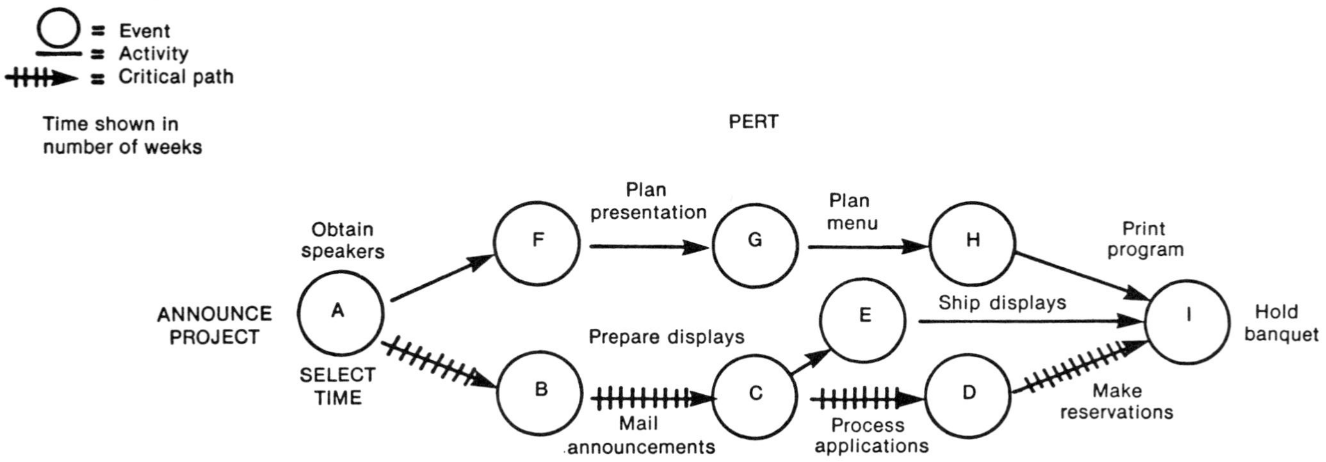

◯ = Event
— = Activity
⊢⊢⊢⊢⊣ = Critical path

Time shown in number of weeks

PERT

Planning a Banquet

Source: Reprinted from *Time Management for Health Care Professionals* by Steven H. Appelbaum and Walter F. Rohrs with permission of Aspen Systems Corporation, © 1981.

instance, assuming the estimated times as being accurate, if the announcements are sent out the fourth, rather than the third week, the whole project will be delayed one week. Thus, in order to keep on schedule, the announcements must be mailed during the third week. As noted above, A-F-G-H-I requires only 10 weeks and therefore two extra weeks, called slack, are available along this track. This means the activities along this route or network can be delayed by as much as two weeks without affecting the date originally set for the banquet. Similarly H, which is scheduled for the seventh week, need not begin until the ninth week. The flexibility or rescheduling capability for this PERT is shown on Table 7-2. By subtracting the "latest start time" from the "scheduled time," the amount of slack time is determined. Figure 7-3 is a variance of PERT using a systems approach to chart organizational activities through the medium of time.

One other important aspect of PERT should be mentioned. In the event that a blockage causes a delay along the critical path, or for that matter any other track, it is not necessary to accept the condition and announce a new later completion date, or go into a crisis situation by attempting to adhere to the original schedule and hiring new resources or authorizing double or triple overtime pay. It may be quite possible to transfer or shift existing resources from a network having slack to the one experiencing difficulty. This procedure assumes that the resources are mobile and capable of performing the required functions. This kind of action includes moving people or equipment or both.

Where a PERT system is developed with a great many long-range and sophisticated networks, probability theory is used for estimating the chance of achieving specific completion dates and the entire plan is computerized.

To summarize, the following benefits accrue from using a PERT as a time management tool:

- Provides logical and visible sequences of activities.
- Schedules activities in accordance with a predetermined completion date.
- Communicates the present status of a project and thus allows for evaluation and necessary remedial actions.
- Indicates the existence of available slack time, which allows shifting rather than employing additional resources.
- Allows for the coordination and integration of a number of activities toward attaining a common objective.
- Pinpoints responsibility and problems.

Finally, a few caveats are worth noting:

- A PERT does not guarantee that either the individual activities or the entire project will be completed as planned. This technique is subject to many uncontrollable

Table 7-2 PERT Activity Chart

	Activity	Scheduled time Start	End	Latest time Start	End	Slack time
A-B	Select sites	0	2	0	2	0
B-C	Mail announcements	2	5	2	5	0
C-D	Process applications	5	10	5	10	0
D-I	Make reservations	10	12	10	12	0
A-F	Obtain speakers	0	2	2	4	2
F-G	Plan special presentation	2	4	4	6	2
G-H	Plan menu	4	7	6	9	2
H-I	Print program	7	10	9	12	2
C-E	Prepare displays	5	6	9	10	4
E-I	Ship displays	6	8	10	12	4

Source: Reprinted from *Time Management for Health Care Professionals* by Steven H. Appelbaum and Walter F. Rohrs with permission of Aspen Systems Corporation, © 1981.

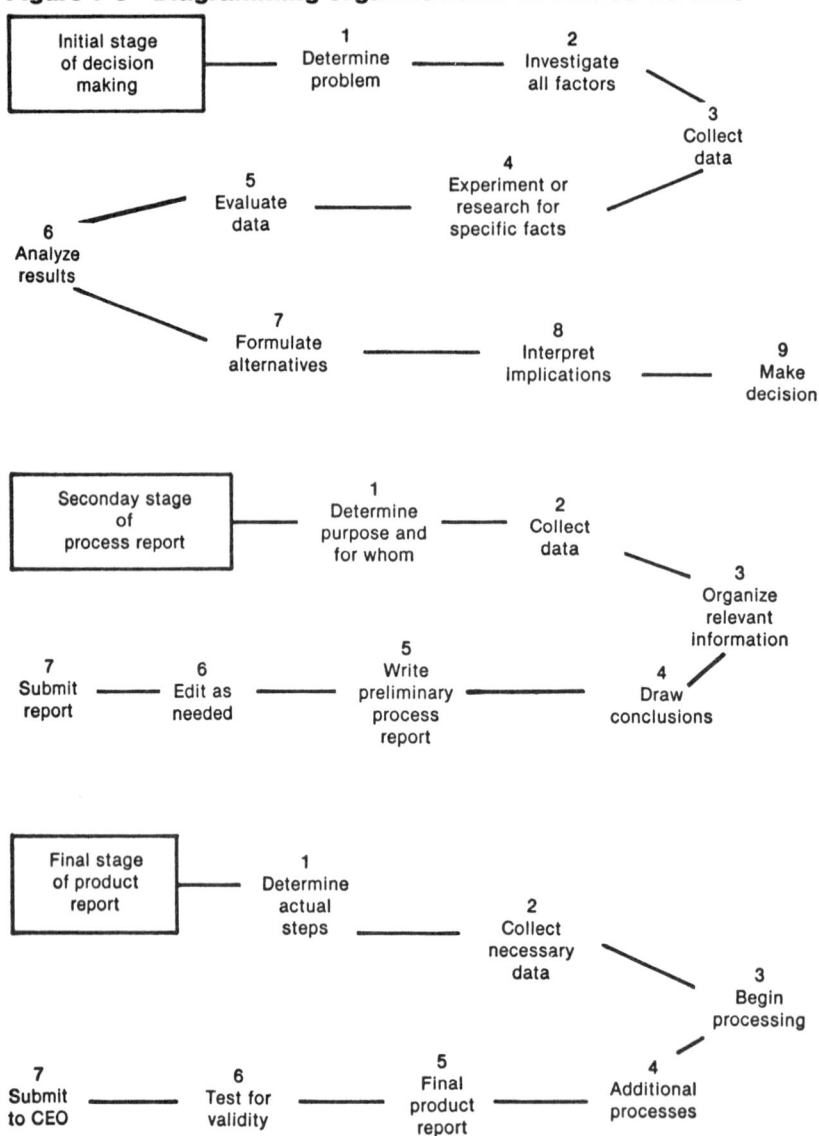

Figure 7-3 Diagramming organizational activities via time

Initial stage of decision making → 1 Determine problem → 2 Investigate all factors → 3 Collect data → 4 Experiment or research for specific facts → 5 Evaluate data → 6 Analyze results → 7 Formulate alternatives → 8 Interpret Implications → 9 Make decision

Seconday stage of process report → 1 Determine purpose and for whom → 2 Collect data → 3 Organize relevant information → 4 Draw conclusions → 5 Write preliminary process report → 6 Edit as needed → 7 Submit report

Final stage of product report → 1 Determine actual steps → 2 Collect necessary data → 3 Begin processing → 4 Additional processes → 5 Final product report → 6 Test for validity → 7 Submit to CEO

Source: Reprinted from *Time Management for Health Care Professionals* by Steven H. Appelbaum and Walter F. Rohrs with permission of Aspen Systems Corporation, © 1981.

variables, including the unpredictable vagaries of human beings.
- The available resources may not be adaptable or transferable because of the need to hold costs to a minimum while maintaining the original schedule.
- Any plan is only as good as the ability of the person or persons who devise it. It is based on human judgment and, therefore, is subject to human error.

3. Systems Approach

Systems activity is concerned with the review, evaluation, and improvement of the methods and procedures by which input units of work are processed so as to produce a satisfactory output. There are a number of opportunities available to the health care manager for developing changes in systems activity that will provide more effective and efficient ways of processing work in the work unit.

In the management of a health care organization, the systems approach is often applied to complex problems that are connected with macro systems and that cannot be examined independently of their environment. The importance of the systems view is that it can usually increase insight and understanding for the decision maker in need of a total view of his organization and allows the administrator to:

- evaluate existing conditions,
- change and improve the current state of the process,
- design and add something new to the process to stimulate performance to a more optimum level.

No matter what the problem is or what the desired form of the solution, the systems approach may be identified as containing the same four basic steps: problem formulation, modeling, analysis and optimization, and implementation.

1. *Problem formulation* is the first and most difficult step, usually requiring about three quarters of the total effort expanded in the analysis. It requires a deep understanding of the total problem in the form of verbal descriptions that permit quantification of the significant features. If we wanted to study the outcome of the delivery of health service to a particular segment of the population, we would have to perform these tasks:
   a. identify all involved decision makers
   b. determine the decision makers' range of alternative actions
   c. determine the consequences of each action in terms of the goals and value structure of the decision maker
   d. include the influence of the total environment within which the decision process occurs
2. *Modeling* refers to the process by which the investigator goes from the real world where the problem has been defined to the abstract world of the model where the analysis will be accomplished. The model is a representation of reality and can be manipulated in ways the actual entities and situations cannot. Model formation is based on maintaining a sensitive balance between inclusion of only the essential reality aspects in the model and limitation of model complexity by the practical considerations of existing theoretical tools, computation time, and data availability.
3. In *analysis and optimization* the model is analyzed with a suitable set of tools in order to find the best strategy for resolving the research problem within the domain of the model. The most common options are analytical techniques or a computer simulation.
4. The final step, *implementation,* is the procedure by which the results determined from the model are translated as a set of actions and transported to the real world.

These four steps of the systems approach, in effect, answer the following five questions in a way that is more specific about the tasks to be accomplished.

1. What is the state of things? Here we are required to select entities of the system, list their attributes, identify activities that can cause changes, and then gather data that provides the attributes' values and defines the relationship involved in the activities. No evaluation is involved.
2. What is the status of things? To answer this question we must utilize an evaluation methodology, and system performance must be measured against some visible, generally accepted standard.
3. What is wrong (or right) with the system? We will answer this question by doing some form of analysis to isolate the difficulties or, if the evaluation was positive, to isolate the critical factors contributing to the success.
4. What can we do about it? To resolve any troubles in the system, we must make a series of recommendations cast in a useful form for the person or agency that has the power to act upon them.
5. How can we promote or advocate our results? The answer to this last question suggests that the investigator should be

willing to take responsibility for injecting himself into the policy making process. The implication for scientists is that they leave their traditional role of neutrality. The intention of this step is that the collaboration of resource people doing the work will make a commitment for positive utilization of their results.

4. Gaming

This decision-making technique is a systematic method to deal with complexity. It permits reality-oriented interaction to occur within a simulated organizational environment in which controls can be exercised by the participants. The settings are unstructured and the process of planning is encouraged for the participants. This simulation also saves time usually lost by poor planning during the initial investment in the technique.

The steps required to construct a game are similar to the basic steps of the systems approach.

1. There must be significant understanding of the phenomenon being investigated.
2. With the information of step 1, a model must be constructed that can be controlled, manipulated, and analyzed.
3. The model of step 2 must be stored in a digital computer.
4. Suitable experiments for the game must be designed and the output arranged so that the game results can be appropriately displayed.

Chapter 8—Managing Outsiders

CONSULTANTS*

In general, consultants can be classified into four categories: (1) the individual entrepreneur consultant (the one-person show), (2) the health care consulting firm, (3) the general consulting organizations, and (4) the major national accounting and consulting firms.

The *individual entrepreneur* is a person who by reason of experience, expertise, glibness, or position is able to hang out a consultant's shingle and obtain clients. Oftentimes, such a person has developed a very narrow specialty and thus is invaluable to an organization having specific problems in that area.

These consultants have some important strengths. An obvious advantage is that the client is always dealing with the top person in the consulting organization and the very same person who will be doing the study and writing the report. Therefore, the client can continually monitor and evaluate the consultant's progress and, if necessary, the consultant can be redirected or fired. Perhaps even more important, it is easier to evaluate the expertise of an individual consultant than that of a firm prior to an engagement. A list of former clients and a check of those references, perhaps including a review of other reports prepared by the consultant, should indicate whether this is the person who should be engaged.

Of course, there are problems, too. First, there is no depth in a one-person organization. If the project's complexity is such that it requires additional expertise that the consultant does not possess, then this type of consultant either does a second-rate job on that component of the project or hires a "subcontractor" who may or may not satisfy the client. The second problem can come about when the organization is dealing with one of the "superstar" consultants or academic consultants and must share the consultant with other clients—which leads to the third problem. Academics who consult are also notorious for missing deadlines. If deadlines are important, then the individual's time commitments become an important factor in the selection.

The first generation of *specialty consulting firms* in the health care field was populated by former administrators (usually hospital administrators) who had established reputations for excellence. In general, they tackled a wide range of consulting type problems, and many of them established themselves as excellent "general practitioner" consultants. Because of their size, which often was in the area of 10 or 15 professionals, they offered a considerable breadth of services. To offset their weaknesses in depth, most of these firms have enough affiliations with independent consultants and sometimes academics so that special problems can be "subcontracted" with relative ease. Perhaps their major strength is their concentration on the health field; these firms are totally involved in the range of activities within health care. Their solutions, or recommendations, to most problems can be

---

*Source: Reprinted from *Health Care Management* by Seth B. Goldsmith with permission of Aspen Systems Corporation, © 1981.

expected to have the value of field trial, since they seldom work from theoretical models but rather have a pragmatic orientation based on experience.

The large national consulting firms have a depth of experience in the private and government sectors that can often be translated into solutions or recommendations for the health care industry. Also, because of their large size, they have a depth of knowledge that is simply not present in smaller firms.

It could be said that the *public accounting firms* probably have the greatest strength in terms of work that is heavily financially oriented, the management consulting groups shine most in studies involving general management, and the health consulting groups are strongest in those areas where an in-depth understanding of the inner workings of a health care organization is required.

The critical points for the clients to remember are that they should not be defining the consulting problem or problems for themselves. Second, they should interview as many as possible of the consultants and consulting firms which have expertise in their area of concern. Third, they should carefully check references and review the previous work of the consultants. Fourth, they should find out as much as possible about the experience and expertise of those individuals who will be actually working on the job. Firms often send out their "top guns" to make the presentation and then have the actual work executed by much more junior and often inexperienced staff. Since most consultants are expensive, it is rather important to find out specifically who will be working on the project. Finally, the client should be prepared to give serious consideration to the consultant's findings—not necessarily adopt them automatically, but at least give them a fair chance.

EVALUATORS*

Periodic surveys by national accrediting or federal/state regulatory bodies are a fact of life in most hospitals in the United States. Although

---

*Source: Reprinted from "How To Manage Yourself and the Surveyor," *Health Care Management Review* (Summer), by Morgan D. Martin with permission of Aspen Systems Corporation, © 1980.

surveys sometimes strain the patience of hospital staff, there are ways to minimize their ill effects and in fact make them constructive experiences.

The hospital survey is more than a mere licensing inspection. It presents the hospital with a vital gift—an outside opinion. It covers programs, plant and personnel—the full gamut of hospital activity. The surveyors, often vastly experienced observers, can be a useful source of new ideas and an impetus for change.

The behavior of hospital personnel during a survey depends on an awareness of the survey's benefits as well as its pitfalls. Identifying the benefits can increase staff tolerance of the survey as well as help in the management of its hazards.

Accenting the Positive

Hospital surveys have four positive aspects:

Preparation for a survey involves getting records, files and minutes in order. It means a myriad of meetings during which the hospital group develops special cohesiveness and increased morale as it gathers together in the face of the outside threat. Also, there are the healthy aspects of having a deadline. Jobs that have hung fire for a long time suddenly get done. Even the most reluctant contributors to program descriptions and medical records succumb to pressure and get things in shape.

The second positive aspect, feedback, consists of useful suggestions and ideas from the surveyors. These are presented not only during the formal wrap-up but also during tours, interviews and informal conversation. Surveyors have personal and, in some cases, charismatic authority as well as the weight lent to the pronouncements of those who have been many places and seen many things. They exert considerable influence on staff. A survey is an inexpensive, effective way of getting new ideas and new ways into a hospital. They can, in a brief time, produce considerable change in how things are perceived and done.

The third positive feature, the repercussions of being found out of compliance, is dramatic. Where previously a facility has been unable to justify its needs to the home office, the legislature or whoever controls its funding, now, with the threat of loss of approval of the overseer body—and the ensuing loss of money, training programs and recruitment effectiveness—the previously unmoved begin to move. Funds are found for increasing staff, remodeling the physical plant and meeting other demands of the overseers. This is a formidable payoff and an important raison d'etre for surveys.

Finally, there are the satisfactions and the reassurance from identification by the surveyors of positive features of the hospital's program and personnel. It is seldom that a hospital is told about the good things it is doing and the good people doing them. Programs and people may have been appreciated before the survey, but when surveyors point out that something or someone is outstanding, this has real impact on morale.

Dealing with Dangers

But the survey remains a threat and as the instrument of a body committed to development, the surveyor betokens change. Surveyors and surveyees alike may enjoy the ideas of progress, but when this progress is on terms dictated by just one of the parties, the changes demanded may seem threatening, especially to hospitals lacking the necessary human and material resources.

Since the first purpose of any organization is to survive, the threatening aspects of a survey will stimulate resistance. Instead of a healthy reaction to survey stress, there may be something akin to an organism's foreign-body reaction, with the surveyors being walled off like a sliver in a finger. Thus the administration must carefully orient hospital staff so that they can benefit from the survey, behave appropriately and avoid undue damage to the hospital's image in the surveyors' eyes.

Control Offhand Remarks

If hospital people are too honest or let their hair down, they simply show the surveyor their weaknesses. Yet this happens again and again. Why? The reason is that department or program heads, frustrated in attempts to get their needs supplied by the administration, turn to the surveyor in the mistaken belief that the surveyor will be able to get them what they have wanted all along. This is nonsense; the surveyor cannot change the allocation of hospital resources.

Use Sincerity as a Weapon

Surveyors rely heavily on impressions. Conversations influence them and if one projects sincerity, the surveyor may be convinced in the first 20 minutes that things are going well with the hospital.

One should show that the survey body's standards are familiar and understood. The surveyee should demonstrate a tight grasp of the findings of past surveys and mention, in passing, progress in correcting deficiencies. The message is: We're not as good as we want to be, but we're making progress.

Hospitality Helps

The provision of amenities is a good tactic. These amenities include a pleasant room with privacy, coffee, etc., and what may be called cheerful people.

Two important people are the administrator's secretary and the medical records librarian. The boss's secretary is important because this particular person can do almost anything: orient surveyors, schedule their appointments and make all manner of arrangements, including those for transportation and accommodations if necessary.

The medical records librarian is indispensable to the surveyors, helping them to locate material they might not otherwise find.

Because surveyors spend many long hours in the medical records room, wading through charts, the records librarian may well spend more time with surveyors than does the administrator.

Keep Up the Guard

Even survey-wise hospitals let down their defenses after the first, tight day of the survey. It is then that they are most vulnerable because the surveyors return after a night of preparing questions based on first-day observations and impressions. Now is the time the hospital staff must be especially on guard.

Despite preparation of staff, department and program heads are certain to answer before understanding the surveyor's question, to miss the implications of some questions, to answer too frankly and to try too hard. Administrators can be expected to offer gratuitous comment—particularly as fatigue sets in from being on stage and from touring—and to fail to stick to their guns when questioned closely about something in which they really believe. Staff must remind themselves that they are still in the midst of adversarial encounters and that continuing tactical maneuvers are necessary.

Tactics for the latter part of the survey come easily to those who are survey-wise rather than survey-weary.

PART II
ORGANIZATION

Chapter 9—A Primer on Organization*

Organizing is the process of grouping the necessary responsibilities and activities into workable units, determining the lines of authority and communication, and developing patterns of coordination. It is the conscious development of role structures of superior and subordinate, line and staff. The organizational process stems from the underlying premises associated with formal institutions: that there should be a common goal toward which work effort is directed, that the goal is spelled out in detailed plans, that there is need for clear authority-responsibility relationships, that power and authority factors need to be reconciled so individual interactions within the organization are productive and goal directed, that conflict is inevitable but may be reduced through clarity of organizational relationship, that individual needs must be reconciled with and subordinated to the organizational needs, that unity of command must prevail, and that authority must be delegated.

Fundamental Concepts on Authority

Hierarchy refers to the arrangement of individuals into a graded series of superiors and subordinates. A pyramidal shaped organization tends to result from the development of hierarchy (Figure 9-1).

Individual workers are placed in a specific authority relationship to a superior whose authority can be traced from the next level of authority, on up to the top level of the hierarchy. This flow of authority and responsibility constitutes a distinct chain of command, also referred to as the scalar principle: the chain of direct authority from superior to subordinate. A companion expectation is that unity of command will prevail. Unity of command is the uninterrupted line of authority from superior to subordinate so that each individual reports to one, and only one, superior. A clear chain of command shows who reports to whom, who is responsible for the actions of an individual, who has authority over the worker.

The authority delegation given to any individual must be equal to the responsibility assigned. This principle of parity—that responsibility cannot be greater than the authority given—assures that the individual given an assignment can carry it out without provoking conflict over the person's right and duty to do so. At the same time, no managers can so completely delegate authority that they themselves have no responsibility. This is stated in the principle of the absoluteness of responsibility: that authority may (and must) be delegated, but ultimate responsibility is retained. The superior who delegates authority ultimately remains responsible for the actions of the subordinate. It is from this same concept that the manager receives the right to exercise the necessary controls and require accountability. Because work must be coordinated and because there are necessary limits on each manager's authority, splintered authority sometimes occurs.

---

*Source: Reprinted from *Managing Health Records* by Joan Gratto Liebler with permission of Aspen Systems Corporation, © 1980.

Figure 9-1 Pyramidal hierarchy

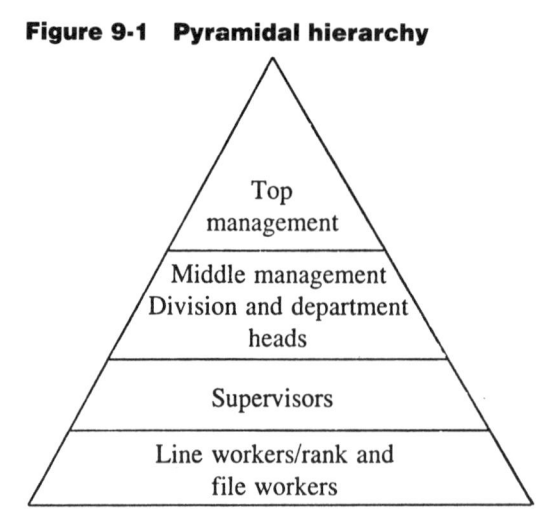

```
              /\
             /  \
            / Top \
           /management\
          /------------\
         / Middle management \
        / Division and department \
       /        heads              \
      /----------------------------\
     /        Supervisors            \
    /--------------------------------\
   /    Line workers/rank and         \
  /          file workers              \
 /--------------------------------------\
```

It is overcome in three ways. In the first, the managers simply pool their authority and make the decision or solve the problem. In the second, the problem is referred to a higher level of authority until it is resolved by one manager with sufficient authority. A third approach is that of reorganizing so that situations of splintered authority that tend to recur are eliminated. Such recurring situations sometimes are signs of poor organization.

Concurring authority sometimes is given to related departments to assure uniformity of practice. For example, when a data processing division manager in a health care setting must approve any forms design changes, although this is the primary responsibility of the medical record practitioner, concurring authority is needed.

The Span of Management

If the authority delegation is to be made effectively, consideration must be given to the span of management. The essential focus of this concept is the recognition that there is a limit to the number of individuals whose activities can be coordinated and controlled effectively by one manager. The factors that shape the appropriate span of management for any superior-subordinate relationship are:

1. The type of work: routine, repetitive, homogeneous work allows a greater or larger span of management.
2. The degree of training of the worker: those who are well trained and well motivated do not need as much supervision as a trainee group; the more highly trained the group, the larger the span of management may be.
3. Organizational stability: when the organization climate as a whole, and within a specific department, is stable, the span of control can be wider; when there is rapid change, high turnover, and general organizational instability, there may be need for closer supervision with a resulting closer or narrower span of control.
4. Geographical location: the physical location of the work units must be considered; when they are dispersed over a scattered physical layout, even one involving separate geographic locations, there is need for closer supervision to effect the necessary control and coordination of the work.
5. Flow of work: the degree of interrelationships must be considered; if much coordination is needed, there is a companion need for greater supervision, a narrow span of control.
6. Supervisor's qualifications: the degree of training and amount of experience for a supervisor is a factor; as these increase, the span of control for that supervisor also may increase.
7. Availability of staff specialists: when the manager has available staff specialists and selected support services, such as a training or personnel department, the span of management may be widened.

8. The value system of the organization: in highly coercive organizations, an individual may be placed over many others since there is a pervasive control system to help ensure conformity; in a highly normative organization, there may be an emphasis on participation in planning and decision making and a resultant complexity in the communication process; a smaller span of management may be indicated in such an organization.

Line and Staff as Authority Relationship

The original usage of the term "staff" evolved in the military. The military developed the staff assistant pattern as a means of relieving commanders of details that could be handled by others. The concept of the "assistant to" is the sense in which the term was used, and this assistant was an extension of line authority. The staff assistant or specialist provides advice and counsel or technical support to the line manager who has the right to command others to act.

The essence of line authority is this direct chain of command or line from top level of authority through each successive level of the organization. A manager with line authority has direct authority and responsibility for the work of a unit, while a staff assistant provides advice, counsel, or technical support that may be accepted, altered, or rejected by the line officer.

A final note concerning the authority mandate of a staff officer or manager: such an individual may hold a staff position, that is, be the designated officer in charge of a staff department such as legal counsel or personnel; yet this manager also may have charge of one or several workers within the unit and would exercise line authority within that unit. Organizational charts, job descriptions, and similar documents should contain clear statements as to the nature of each position: line or staff, kind of authority, and area of responsibility. (See Table 9-1.)

Dual Pyramid of Organization

Health care institutions are characterized by a dual pyramid of organization because of the traditional relationship of the medical staff to the administrative component. The ultimate authority and responsibility is vested in the governing board. That board, in accordance with the stipulations of licensure and accrediting agencies, appoints a chief executive officer (administrator) and a chief of medical staff, resulting in two lines of authority. The chief executive officer is charged with the responsibility of effectively managing the administrative components of the institution. This administrative official in turn delegates authority to each department head in the administrative component. In this sense, there is a typical pyramidal organization, with a unified chain of command within the administrative units.

A second organizational pyramid results from this organization of the medical staff into clinical services, with each having a chief of service who reports to the chief of staff.

In an effort to consolidate authority and clarify responsibility, the top administrative levels of a health care organization may be expanded to include some central officer to whom both the administrator and the chief of medical staff report. In some institutions there may not be a permanent medical staff position that is the opposite number of the administrator on the organizational chart. The elected president of the medical staff may fill a role similar to the medical director or chief of staff when there is no organizational slot for a medical director *per se*. It is important to determine the precise meaning of titles as they are used in a specific health care setting. Titles may include:

- chief of staff: an officer of the medical staff to whom the chief of services reports; appointed by the governing board
- chief of service: physician director of specific clinical service; line officer for physicians who are appointed to the specific service; example: chief of surgery
- chairman of department: physician director of specific clinical service in an academic institution such as a teaching hospital; this title may be used as an alternative to chief of service in this type of setting; example: chairman of the department of neurosurgery
- medical director: sometimes used to refer to a full-time position in line authority structure; may be seen as the counterpart of the chief executive officer for the medical staff
- president of the medical staff: the elected position as presiding officer for the medical

Table 9-1 Seven Basic Line–Staff Relationships Compared*

No. Type	Relationship of staff unit employees to head of operating unit.	Relationship of head of operating unit to staff unit and members of staff unit working in his department.	Relationship of staff unit to employees of operating unit.
1. Advisory	May only volunteer suggestions . . . but may not necessarily have to wait to be invited.	May or may not have to avail himself of suggestions.	Do not give or receive instructions.
2. Service as requested	Similar to (1) but involves services, and the staff unit must be invited into the department.	Same as toward any outside contractor. The "boss" of the staff personnel is their own staff unit head.	Through operating unit's supervisors issue such requests as required to make service effective.
3. Staff services supplied on a programmed basis	Somewhat stronger than (2). Services are rendered on a programmed basis approved by higher authority and cannot be refused by operating head.	The direct chain of command of the staff personnel is to the staff unit head. Operating unit head must work through head of staff unit if dissatisfied with mode of operations.	Same as (2).
4. Auxiliary services routinely supplied	Services are a routine part of operations, not on an "invited" or specially programmed basis.	Same as (3).	Staff-service personnel can insist on regular procedures' being followed. Routine communications flow directly between staff and operating personnel except in cases of sharp disagreement.

5. Central staff and counterpart staff unit in operating department	Advisory and suggestive only ... but does not have to wait to be invited.	May or may not have to avail himself of advice and suggestions of central staff unit. Through his own chain of command, head of operating unit is "boss" of the staff unit in his department.	"Functional" relationship between central unit and employees of staff unit in operating department ... on matters of professional standards, mode of operation, etc., "suggestions" from central unit have strong force and are to be disregarded only under special circumstances and with approval of head of operating unit.
6. Personnel assigned to operating unit by staff unit	Assigned personnel are under administrative command of head of operating unit as to deployment on job, discipline, hours of works, etc., but their "boss" is the head of the staff unit.	In administrative command of the assigned personnel ... head of staff unit may, with notice to head of operating unit, withdraw them from the job if he can supply replacements	Relationships are those of any employees under direct supervision of head of operating unit. They carry on their own activities and work through normal channels within department.
7. A staff unit which is part of an operating organization unit	Supply information and advise and recommend ... Decisions are made by operating head, and he issues instructions to operating personnel.	Direct relationship, through chain of command.	Same as (6). Staff personnel do not issue direct instructions to operating personnel except under unusual circumstances (e.g., a safety man or quality inspector shutting down an operation where emergency does not permit normal working through channels).

*Source: From *The Encyclopedia of Management*, 2nd edition, edited by Carl Heyel. © 1973, by Van Nostrand Reinhold Company, p. 657. Reprinted by permission of the publisher.

staff, usually for a year; in the absence of a full-time medical director, this individual fills the role of coordinating officer for the medical staff

Although all authority flows from the governing board, there are two distinct chains of command, one in the administrative sector and one in the medical staff sector. In matters of direct patient care, the physician exercises professional authority; thus, a particular employee (such as nurse) may be subject to more than one line of authority. Line officers in the administrative units may find that their authority is limited in some areas because of the specific jurisdiction of the medical staff committees, such as the pharmacy and therapeutics committee of the medical records committee. Because of the dual pyramid structure much coordination is needed. This is achieved through the extensive use of committees to bridge the gap.

The Organization Chart

The organization chart is a diagrammatical form, a visual arrangement, that depicts the following aspects of an institution:

1. major functions, usually by departments
2. the respective relationships of functions or departments
3. channels of supervision
4. lines of authority and of communication
5. positions (by job title) within departments or units

Advantages and Reasons for Use

There are numerous advantages and reasons for using organization charts, including the following:

- Since such a chart maps major lines of decision making and of authority, managers can review it to determine any inconsistencies and complexities in the organizational structure. The diagrammatic representation permits greater ease in determining and correcting these complexities and inconsistencies.
- An organization chart may be used to orient employees, since it shows where each job fits in relation to supervisors and to other jobs in the department. It shows the relationship of the department to the organization as a whole.
- The chart is a useful tool in managerial audit: managers can review such factors as the span of control, mixed lines of authority, and splintered authority; they also can look for individual job titles that are not clearly on the chart, that is, when it is not evident to whom the employee reports. Managers can assess current practice with the original plan of job assignment and determine where discrepancies now exist.
- The chart conveys information about the chain of command, supervisory relationships, channels of communication, and lines of decision making.

Limitations

However, there are certain limitations inherent in the rather static structure presented by the organization chart, including the following:

- Only formal lines of authority and communication are shown.
- Important lines of informal communication and significant informal relationships cannot be shown.
- The chart may become obsolete easily if not updated—at least once a year, and more frequently if there is a major change in organizational pattern.
- There is a tendency to confuse authority relationships with status: individuals higher up in the organization as depicted in the chart may be perceived as having authority over individuals lower on the chart.

The Master Chart

There are two major kinds of organizational charts: master and the supplementary. The former depicts the entire organization, although not in great detail and normally shows all departments and major positions of authority. The latter depicts some section, department, or unit, giving specific details for the organizational pattern for the section. A supplementary chart for a department usually refers to the master chart, and makes clear the linkage of authority by showing the direct chain of command from highest authority to that derived by the department chief. An organization would have as many supplementary charts as there are departments or

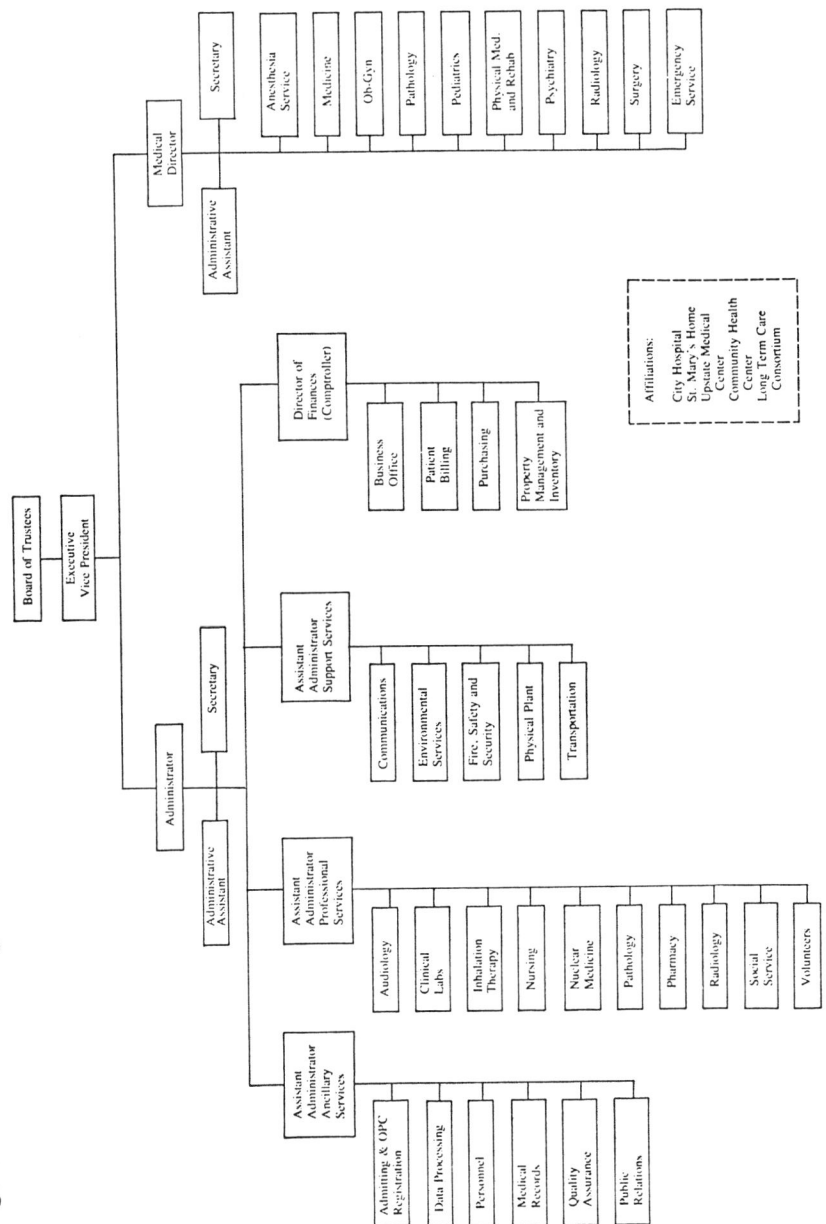

Figure 9-2 Master organization chart

units. The master chart of the organization or department usually shows the major functions while the supplementary charts depict each individual job title and the number of positions in each section, as well as full-time or part-time status. Additional information such as cost centers, major codes, or similar identifying information sometimes appears on the charts.

Arrangements

The conventional organization chart is a line or scalar chart showing each layer of the organization in sequence. (See Figure 9-2.)

Mechanics and General Conventions

In drawing the organization chart, certain general conventions tend to be followed. Ordinarily *line* authority and *line* relationships are indicated by solid lines and *staff* positions by broken or dotted lines.

Occasionally, a special relationship is indicated by surrounding an entire unit or even another organization with broken lines. This remains unconnected to any line or staff unit and is included to call attention to the existence of a related, auxiliary, or affiliated organization.

Chapter 10—Using Committees

The reason usually offered for setting up and using committees is the belief that a group's multiple perspectives, talents, and areas of expertise brought to bear in solving problems, setting goals, establishing policies, and carrying out projects or activities result in a superior product.

However there are other reasons that should be appreciated. Among them is the well-known fact that people are more inclined to accept and implement decisions that they or their representatives have helped develop, than those imposed on them.

Still another reason for favoring group decision-making deals with the diffusion of responsibility. Spreading of responsibility may appear very attractive when a good decision calls for actions that are unpopular, unpleasant, or risky. A single person may not be inclined to pursue a course of action because he or she alone will be held accountable for any negative consequences, whereas a group may decide to go on with an unpleasant, or risky, action because responsibility is shared among its members. The group may function, in effect, as a superindividual entity, in which members can achieve some degree of anonymity.

WHAT MAKES COMMITTEES WORK?

Committees work when they are formally organized; have assigned jobs to do; have a leader; keep written records of their deliberations for future reference; and know results are expected.

Committees fail when they are not wisely constituted; when their purpose is vague or is lost sight of; when members are not well oriented and are not convinced that the results will be worth the effort; when they meet only for the sake of meeting; or when the preparation for their meetings is inadequate.

Checklist

1. *Purpose.* The charge to the committee should be clearly defined, and its responsibilities, duties and objectives should be spelled out. The choice of chairman and members and the willingness of individuals to serve largely depend on the committee's purpose.
2. *Need.* Is the committee the best technique for accomplishing the purpose that has been defined? If so, should a new committee be formed or can an existing committee do the job? Or would a conference of one or two sessions do it just as well?
3. *Functions.* What kind of committee is this going to be? Is it to be administrative, assigned a definite action responsibility such as that for the development of policies and procedures? Or is it to be advisory, set up to explore, to communicate, and to coordinate?
4. *Organization.* How many members will it have, and how will they and the chairman be selected and appointed? Will there be ex officio members and will they have votes? To whom will the committee report? How

often will it meet? Who will call special meetings? Who should receive copies of the minutes? Will the committee spend money, and how much? Who will be responsible for arrangements and agenda?

5. *Selecting the Leader.** First, would the prospective leader be *optimistic* about the committee's task? The leader's attitudes have a very definite influence on the group.

Second, would the prospective leader be able to *organize* the committee into a tightly-knit task-oriented group? A clue as to whether a potential leader would be able to organize the group efficiently might be found by looking at the employee's daily work patterns. An employee who is conscientious, organized, and efficient would probably bring those same patterns to the committee.

Third, would the prospective leader be able to ask pertinent questions and to listen and comprehend the answers which are received?

6. *Committee Members.* A sensitive administrator will carefully select individuals who can comfortably work with other individuals. The following questions might be asked of potential committee members. If the answer is "yes" to most of these questions, the chances are good that he will be a productive member of the group.

   1. Has this individual worked on committees before? If yes, was his input constructive?
   2. In general, does he relate well to his peers within the hospital?
   3. When there is conflict, can this individual look at the underlying causes of the problem?
   4. Does this individual think critically?
   5. Can this individual look past his vested interests in order to examine all sides of an issue?

7. *Feedback.* When an administrator lets a committee know that he is pleased with the work which they are doing; when he gives suggestions on how they could do their work better; when he is available as a resource person, he is providing a healthy impetus for the committee.

   An administrator cannot afford to set up committees and let them flounder. He must keep track of what is going on within the committees and give encouragement and support.

8. *Committee Recommendations.* Taking the suggestions of the committee seriously does not necessarily mean always agreeing to what a committee has recommended. It does mean, however, that the administrator will carefully look at the suggestions, meet with the committee to understand the logic behind the recommendations, and then respond to the output of the committee.

The Committee Chairman*

The manager who finds himself in the position of running a large meeting has several strikes against him. In the first place, if there are eight or more people in the meeting, the network of intercommunication becomes so complex that the expression of individual feelings and points of view is inhibited unless the group is accustomed to working together. Second, if the chairman is not perceptive about the needs of the group, there is the danger that he may act either too arbitrarily or too permissively, producing resentment on the one hand or frustration on the other. Third, if communications bog down and the group feels resentment or frustration, the only way the chairman can hope to reach a committee decision is by a "democratic" majority vote. In such a situation the minority group will eventually be forced to go along with the majority, but it will resent this, too, because its members will feel that their views have not been given adequate consideration. In these circumstances, they can hardly be expected to be wholeheartedly committed to the final decision.

Skill in group leadership is necessary if the chairman is to steer clear of these negative developments.

---

*Source: Items 5 through 8 are adapted from Robert Veninga, "Applying Hospital Control to Hospital Committees," *Hospital Topics*, June 1974.

*Source: Reprinted by permission of the publisher, from "Fewer Camels, More Horses: Where Committees Go," Hensleigh C. Wedgwood, *Personnel*, July/August 1967, © 1967 by AMACOM, a division of American Management Associations. All rights reserved.

If the chairman of the meeting is the superior of the other members, he can use his position of authority to control the meeting. This may be all very well in the case of an informational kind of meeting, where the chairman makes most of the contributions to the subject under discussion; he is the prime source of information, and his job is essentially that of a briefer. This arrangement may also work, but with less chance of success, in the instructional type of meeting where, again, the chairman has the information to give to the group, but where, in addition, the members are expected to participate, ask questions, and make their own contributions.

In a developmental or problem-solving meeting, however, the chairman would be unwise indeed to impose his views on the members of the group, because here he must depend on the maximum of participation if something constructive is to come out of the meeting. In this case, a nondirective approach creates a climate in which the individual can express his views without fear of reprisal or of being put in his place.

Types of Hospital Committees

There may be as many as one hundred committees within the entire hospital complex. For example, listed below are just a few of the medical staff committees. Other committees would include those related to pharmacy, therapeutics, etc.

Medical Staff Committees*

1. *Executive Committee.* The Executive Committee acts on behalf of the staff and serves as a sort of program director. It receives reports from other committees and takes action on them. It coordinates activities and sets general policies for all committees and the medical staff as a whole.
2. *Joint Conference Committee.* The Joint Conference Committee acts when there's need of medical and nonmedical consideration. It provides liaison between medical staff and governing board.
3. *Credentials Committee.* Credentials Committee members consider qualifications of education, experience, interests, and other pertinent information before giving medical staff endorsement. Prospective appointees are ultimately approved by the governing board.
4. *Utilization Review Committee.* Members of the Utilization Review Committee are mainly concerned with making optimum use of the hospital's resources. Criteria for effective operation are constantly reviewed and evaluated.
5. *Infection Committee.* The Infection Committee is responsible for the education and re-education of hospital personnel in ways of investigating and dealing with infection within the hospital.
6. *Medical Record Committee.* The Medical Record Committee works through the medical record administrator, who is responsible for the actual clerical procedures. The committee acts as judge of clinical care based on what has been documented.
7. *Tissue Committee.* The function of the Tissue Committee is to: Examine and code tissues removed in surgery, insure quality control of surgery, and judge the overall performance of the medical staff.

Running a Committee

How To Get More from Committee Meetings*

Before

1. Explore alternatives to meeting.

    a. A decision by the responsible party often eliminates the need for group action.
    b. Postpone the meeting. Consolidate the agenda with that of a later meeting.
    c. Cancel the meeting. Ask yourself, "Is this meeting necessary?"
    d. Send a representative. This gives a subordinate experience and saves your time.

2. Limit your attendance. Attend only for

---

*Source: *Orientation to Hospital Operation,* DHEW Pub. No. (HRA) 75-4009.

*Source: Reprinted by permission of the publisher, from *The Time Trap,* R. Alec Mackenzie, © 1972 by AMACOM, a division of American Management Associations, pp. 110–112. All rights reserved.

the time needed to make your contribution.
3. Keep the participants to a minimum. Only those needed should attend.
4. Choose an appropriate time. The necessary facts and people should be available.
5. Choose an appropriate place. Accessibility of location, availability of equipment, size of the room, and so forth are all important.
6. Define the purpose clearly in your own mind before calling the meeting.
7. Distribute the agenda in advance. This helps the participants prepare—or at least forewarns them.
8. Compute the cost per minute of meeting by figuring the total salaries per minute, adding perhaps 35 percent for fringes. Assess the cost of starting late and of the time allocated to the topics on the agenda.
9. Time-limit the meeting and the agenda. Allocate a time to each subject proportional to its relative importance.

During

10. Start on time. Give warning; then do it. There is no substitute.
11. Assign timekeeping and minutes responsibilities. Keep posted on the time remaining and the amount behind schedule if any.
12. Hold a stand-up meeting if appropriate. This speeds deliberations. Try it on drop-in visitors.
13. Start with and stick to the agenda. "We're here to . . . . The purpose of this meeting is . . . . The next point to be decided is . . . ."
14. Control interruptions. Allow interruptions for emergency purposes only.
15. Accomplish your purpose. What was the specific purpose of the meeting—to analyze a problem, to generate creative alternatives, to arrive at a decision, to inform, to coordinate? *Was it accomplished?*
16. Restate conclusions and assignments to insure agreement and to provide reinforcement or a reminder.
17. End of time. Adjourn the meeting as scheduled so that participants can manage their own time. Placing the most important items at the start of the agenda insures that only the least important will be left unfinished.
18. Use a meeting evaluation checklist as an occasional spot check. Questions should be answered by each participant before leaving. Was the purpose of the meeting clear? Was the agenda received in advance? Were any materials essential for preparation also received in advance? Did the meeting start on time? If not, why not? Was the agenda followed adequately, or was the meeting allowed to wander from it unnecessarily? Was the purpose achieved? Were assignments and deadlines fixed where appropriate? Of the total meeting time, what percentage was not effectively utilized? Why? The evaluations, unsigned, should be collected for the chairman's immediate review.

After

19. Expedite the preparation of the minutes. Concise minutes should be completed and distributed within 24 hours if possible or 48 hours at the outside. Minutes are a reminder and a useful followup tool, as shown in the next suggestion.
20. Insure that progress reports are made and decisions executed. Provide followup to insure the implementation of decisions and checks on progress where warranted. Uncompleted actions should be listed under "Unfinished Business" on the next meeting's agenda.
21. Make a committee inventory. Survey all committees, investigating whether their objectives have been achieved and if not when they can be expected to be. Abolish those that have accomplished their intended purpose.

Groupthink*

Most of us know that obvious factors, such as embarrassment and fear of reprisal, tend to restrict free expression of ideas in groups. How-

---

*Source: Reprinted, by permission of the publisher, from "Groupthink: When Too Many Heads Spoil the Decision," C.W. Von Bergen, Jr. and R.J. Kirk, *Management Review,* March 1978, © 1978 by AMACOM, a division of American Management Associations. All rights reserved.

ever, other more subtle restrictive factors, such as high regard for unanimity sought by members of groups, also are at work.

The danger is not that each will fail to reveal his strong objections to a proposal, but that each will think the proposal is a good one without even attempting to carry out a critical scrutiny that could reveal grounds for strong objections.

As a group becomes excessively close knit groupthink develops. The process is characterized by a marked decrease in the exchange of potentially conflicting data and by an unwillingness to conscientiously examine such data when they surface.

Groupthink Symptoms

1. Illusion of unanimity regarding the viewpoint held by the majority in the group and an emphasis on team play.
2. A view of the opposition as generally inept, incompetent, and incapable of countering effectively any action by the group, no matter how risky the decision or how high the odds are against the plan of action succeeding.
3. Self-censorship of group members in which overt disagreements are avoided, facts that might reduce support for the emerging majority view are suppressed, faulty assumptions are not questioned, and personal doubts are suppressed in the form of group harmony.
4. Collective rationalization to comfort one another in order to discount warnings that the agreed-upon plan is either unworkable or highly unlikely to succeed.
5. Self-appointed mindguards within the group that function to prevent anyone from undermining its apparent unanimity and to protect its members from unwelcome ideas and adverse information that may threaten consensus.
6. Reinforcement of consensus and direct pressure on any dissenting group member who expresses strong reservations or challenges, or argues against the apparent unanimity of the group.
7. An expression of self-righteousness that leads members to believe their actions are moral and ethical, thus inclining them to disregard any ethical or moral objections to their behavior.
8. A shared feeling of unassailability marked by a high degree of esprit de corps, by implicit faith in the wisdom of the group, and by an inordinate optimism that disposes members to take excessive risks.

Preventing Groupthink

1. *Leader encouragement.* The leader should encourage free expression of minority viewpoints, do all he or she can to protect individuals who are attacked, and create opportunities for them to clarify their views.
2. *Diversity of viewpoints.* Attempt to structure the group so that there are different viewpoints. Diverse input will tend to point out nonobvious risks, drawbacks, and advantages that might not have been considered by a more homogeneous group.
3. *Legitimized disagreement.* Voicing objections and doubts should be subordinated to fears about "rocking the boat" or reluctance to "blow the whistle." Each member should take on the additional role of a critical evaluator and should be encouraged by the leader and other members to air reservations.
4. *Idea generation vs. idea evaluation.* The tendency to evaluate suggested solutions as they appear, instead of waiting until all suggestions are in, inhibits the expressing of opinions, tends to restrict freedom of thinking and prevents others from profiting from different ideas.
5. *Advantages and disadvantages of each solution.* The group should try to explore the merits and demerits of each alternative. This process of listing the sides of a question forces discussion to oscillate from one side of the issue to the other. As a result, the positive and negative aspects of each strategy are brought out into the open and may become the foundation for a new idea with all its merits and few of its weaknesses.
6. *New approaches and new people.* In many cases, thinking about the problem by oneself or discussing it with an outside associate can result in refreshing new perspectives.

7. *Examination of group processes.* A group should periodically examine the processes it uses to assess how its members are working together.

Roles Committee Members Play*

Group Blocking Roles

The Aggressor

- deflates status of others in group
- disagrees with others aggressively
- criticizes others in group

The Blocker

- stubbornly disagrees and rejects others' views
- cites unrelated personal experiences
- returns to topics already resolved

The Withdrawer

- will not participate
- is a "wool gatherer"
- carries on private conversations within group
- is a self-appointed taker of notes

The Recognition Seeker

- tries to show his importance through boasting and excessive talking
- is overly conscious of his status

The Topic Jumper

- continually changes the subject

The Dominator

- tries to take over the meeting
- tries to assert authority
- tries to manipulate group

The Special Interest Pleader

- uses the group's time to draw attention to his own concerns

The Playboy

- wastes the group's time in showing off, telling funny stories, and the like
- acts with nonchalance or cynicism

The Self-Confessor

- talks irrelevantly about his own feelings and insights

The Devil's Advocate

- when he is more devil than advocate

Group Building Roles

The Initiator

- suggests new or different ideas for discussion
- proposes new or different approaches to problems

The Opinion Giver

- states pertinent beliefs about what group is considering and others' suggestions

The Elaborator

- elaborates or builds on suggestions made by others

The Clarifier

- gives relevant examples
- offers rationales
- probes for meaning and understanding of matters under discussion
- restates problems

The Tester

- raises questions to "test out" whether group is ready to come to a decision

The Summarizer

- tries to pull together or reviews the discussion content

Group Maintenance Roles

The Tension Reliever

- uses humor at appropriate times to draw off negative feelings

---

*Source: Reprinted, by permission of the publisher, from "Fewer Camels, More Horses: Where Committees Go," Hensleigh C. Wedgwood, *Personnel*, July/August 1967, © 1967 by AMACOM, a division of American Management Associations. All rights reserved.

- calls for a break at appropriate times

The Compromiser
- does not stick stubbornly to his point of view, but is willing to yield when necessary for the progress of group

The Harmonizer
- mediates differences of opinion
- reconciles points of view

The Encourager
- praises and supports others in their contributions
- is friendly and encouraging

The Gate Keeper
- keeps communications open
- creates opportunities to encourage participation by others

Chapter 11—Hospital Systems

OVERVIEW

The U.S. health service industry, particularly hospitals, is in the middle of a wide-scale, serious debate about how health care institutions should be structured and managed. Cost constraints, reimbursement strategies, tax policy and the continuing rapid changes evolving in medical technologies lead many observers to question the viability of the single free-standing separately managed hospital. Some people question the viability of single small hospitals but recognize that a wide range of organizational strategies exist to help the needed and necessary hospital which finds it difficult to cope in today's harsh marketplace. While some providers cannot develop multihospital systems and shared services fast enough, others wonder why federal regulatory, purchasing and taxing power seems lined up in favor of eliminating the individually managed voluntary community hospital from the health care scene.

Are U.S. health services, particularly hospitals, moving toward a more integrated system? Is the performance of the more integrated hospital and health services superior to that of less well integrated single units? Is there potential for further improvements in performance in the more integrated multiunit hospital system and for the formation of other such organizations? The general answer to these questions seems to be yes.

Organizational Arrangements for Systems Integration*

A variety of organizational arrangements are being developed to facilitate systems integration. Among these are shared services, condominiums, consortia, mergers, regional multiunit hospital systems and national chains.

Some preliminary distinctions among this range of arrangements are needed.

Three Basic Configurations

Within the broad rubric of multiunit systems, there are three basic configurations which should be separated for discussion. First, shared services, affiliations for service and education, and similar arrangements deal with subsystems of existing corporations. Some other arrangements called consortia attempt to coordinate and jointly plan for both subsystems of existing corporations and the overall collective destiny of the group. Ownership and basic management and policy remain essentially intact.

The chain organization represents a second major category of relationships: the ownership and management of more than one hospital with

---

*Source: Reprinted from "Systems Development: Trends, Issues and Implications," *Health Care Management Review*, (Winter) by Montague Brown, with permission of Aspen Systems Corporation, © 1979.

none or few of the owned hospitals having any medical staff or patient populations in common. Investor-owned chains represent the fastest growing sector of the industry with chains owning, operating or managing about 11 percent of the industry and more than 55 percent of the investor-owned sector. Religious orders and church-related chains constitute the other most important sector of the group. The religious chains have been around for some time. What is changing among these groups, however, is that they are adopting the corporate management approaches of the investor-owned chains.

The third major arrangement is the regional multiunit health care organization which does and/or can share physicians and provide different levels of care to the same or overlapping patient populations. These regional systems most resemble the classical regional health care system. More organizations aspire to this type of configuration than succeed, but the bulk of the interest in multiunit systems in this country applies to this configuration.

Table 11-1 Eight Most Frequently Shared Services in Community Hospitals

Service	1970 or earlier	1971 to present	Overall Percent Sharing
Purchasing	11.9	26.0	37.9
Electronic Data Processing	8.3	12.6	20.9
Blood Banks	12.6	7.5	20.1
Education and Training	6.2	12.6	18.8
Laboratory	8.4	9.1	17.5
Laundry	5.7	8.5	14.2
Insurance	6.6	7.0	13.6
Management Engineering	2.8	7.5	10.3

Source: From special survey on Selected Hospital Topics, September 1975. Preliminary data analysis supplied by Elworth Taylor, Staff Specialist, Department of Health Planning and Delivery, American Hospital Association, Chicago, July 12, 1976.

Shared Services

Sharing involves two or more organizations joining together to produce and/or use the same service for the member institutions. This ranges from the joint use of computers, laundries and laboratories to purchasing and specialized clinical services. A variety of organizational arrangements have been developed to handle shared services among organizations including new corporations, existing hospital associations, contractual agreements among institutions and the outright sale of services from one (usually large) institution to others in need of the service.

The AHA lists about 180 shared service organizations and periodically surveys the field to determine the extent of shared activities. Services shared by over ten percent of the 4,729 community hospitals reporting (95.2 percent responded) appear in Table 11-1.

This survey suggests that sharing occurs most easily in administrative and nondirect patient service areas of the institution. Over 63 percent of the responding hospitals engage in one or more shared services. Less than 3 percent report sharing of intensive care, cardiac intensive care, open heart surgery, pediatrics or obstetrics. While sharing of high-cost medical services can produce highly significant savings, the only available research reports that the typical administrative sharing programs contribute only one to two percent of the hospital's budget.

While the direct savings from such programs may be low, some successes and even some failures of such efforts may be contributing to a climate of cooperation on other more significant organizational changes such as consortia, condominiums, mergers and multiunit systems under single management.

Consortia

Consortia of hospitals, often including medical schools, are membership organizations with full-time staff devoted to joint planning and programming. Agreements usually include criteria for the size of investment which can be made by individual member institutions without efforts to plan the program jointly and/or share the service. Early case studies of these efforts, mostly in urban areas, suggest that they are beginning to tackle the most difficult but potentially most promising areas of sharing, namely medical services.

The consortia seek to get agreement on which institution should specialize in each major clinical service. This will help to limit major investment to fewer institutions and to improve utilization patterns and thus may help to ensure efficient and quality services. To avoid pressures for duplicative programs, medical staff privileges are usually extended to all physicians of the medical staff of a system of hospitals and not merely of hospital "X."

Condominium Hospitals

In a private condominium, multiple owners have unique and shared space. For the individual, having a condominium allows one to retain social control over one's personal space while sharing the ownership and use of common space and services. The same holds true for commercial condominiums.

What makes a condominium attractive to individuals and families? Control, cost and more comprehensive services seem to be available in all types of condominium arrangements.

A variety of common law types of condominium development exist in the hospital world.

In Texas, the Texas Medical Center (TMC) hosts 23 separate organizations sharing grounds, power, parking, buildings, services and a multitude of other things. St. Luke's Episcopal Hospital, Texas Children's Hospital and the Texas Heart Institute reside on the Texas Medical Center campus, share a condominium type set of plants and services, have one administration to manage the complex but three separate and distinct boards of trustees. In Minneapolis, the Metropolitan Medical Center, a 774-bed general nonprofit hospital, and the Hennepin County Medical Center, a 438-bed general governmental-controlled hospital, have separate bed towers but share a major common diagnostic service area.

Mergers

Some of the early consortia have contributed to the complete merger of some or all of the institutions involved.

Unfortunately, when one studies cost associated with the merged entity, it is difficult to compare the surviving entity with the cost which might have been associated with the continued growth, expansion and technological enrichment of separate institutions. In a number of cases institutions which merged claimed that the number of total beds in the newly merged organizations was significantly less than would have been necessary for the two organizations if they had not merged.

Multiunit Organizations under Single Management

Multiunit organization development has been stimulated by a variety of factors. Satellite hospitals have allowed existing organizations to follow physicians and patients to the suburbs. Mergers often bring together organizations that are short on capital, serve overlapping markets and face pressures for program expansion or elaboration. Increasingly, hospitals and multiunit systems have decided that economies of scale are sufficient to justify their going into new markets or joining with others to insure sufficient size to deal both with exploding costs of technological demands and with the politics of regional planning.

Some communities, mostly those with small hospitals, have chosen to lease their operation to an outside organization thus retaining the long-term option of regaining total operational control. Still others have retained ownership and control while hiring larger multiunit systems to supply the key management teams for the operation.

Researchers have identified a number of factors associated with proprietary hospital systems:

- savings in construction;
- volume purchasing;
- ability to afford specialized management talent;
- standardization of supplies and equipment;
- sufficient breadth and diversity to attract capital.

Others point out benefits in cost effectiveness, comprehensiveness of care, availability of care, organization and management and acceptance of voluntary not-for-profit systems. The evidence suggests that not-for-profit multiple unit systems are more efficient than similar units operating independently. Specifically, reports of multiunit systems effectiveness show:

- slower growth in case cost;
- lower levels of average case cost;
- lower price levels;

- lower growth in prices;
- higher outputs;
- comparable services with other hospitals;
- lower average lengths of stay (suggesting stronger management—tighter control of medical practice patterns);
- higher wage rates but not high labor costs;
- slower growth in labor hours per case.

Effects on Individual Hospital Management*

Protection and support of institutional integrity will be more likely with multihospital systems than with the current situation where board members may not have the will to stand strongly behind policies in the face of local indifference or concern.

At the individual hospital level:

- Local boards will be worked with primarily by the local administrator but within corporate guidelines for procedures for approaching capital decisions, using corporate control systems and procedures, and involving the corporate office whenever the local board tends to go in a direction which might seem adverse for the overall system.
- The local administrator will have a peer review system within the overall corporate structure. This adds a new and potentially favorable dimension to management. Key decisions and plans will be reviewed not just by the local board but by a host of experts from the corporate office. Defense of plans will be among other experts, not just a lay board.
- Fewer management specialists will be in each unit. When truly outstanding persons exist in local units their expertise will be brought to bear at the system level by either transferring them to the corporate office or having them serve as consultants from their local base of operations.
- Local units will tend to have implementors aboard with planners, systems specialists and outstanding experts going to corporate functions.
- All local administrators will have between 10 and 30 management specialists backing them up in the management triangle of the hospital power structure. This represents an historic shift of power towards the professional manager.

Health administrators face changes in their work place. For instance, they will continue to be generalists and can now choose whether to remain as "plant" managers or to become corporate level generalists. Administrators prepared in programs without a good grounding in such subjects as economics, information systems, accounting, finance, marketing, regional planning, law and politics will need to broaden their preparation for corporate roles. For many of the corporate roles, preparation in hospital and/or health administration may not be a requirement, but such preparation would provide a decided competitive edge for the individual who had a good grasp of health administration and some corporate specialty preparation.

Governance and Management Structure of Hospital Systems*

What are the emerging characteristics of the governance and management structure of hospital systems? The typical elements, and their differences from an individual hospital structure, include the following:

- **A corporate or system board of directors.** This governing body has the responsibility for system-wide governance separate and apart from individual institution governance.
- **Individual hospital boards of governors.** These local hospital boards have most of the responsibilities of the freestanding hospital board of trustees, but now govern their individual hospital within the broader structure of a multi-unit corporation.
- **Representation, in some manner, from the individual hospital boards to the corporate board of directors.** The larger the system, the less structured or equal is the representation.
- **Assets of the entire system are controlled, although in differing fashions, by the corpo-**

---

*Source: Reprinted from "Systems Development: Trends, Issues and Implications," *Health Care Management Review,* (Winter) by Montague Brown with permission of Aspen Systems Corporation, © 1979.

*Source: Reprinted from "From Hospital to Health Care System," *Health Care Management Review,* (Winter) by Donald C. Wegmiller with permission of Aspen Systems Corporation, © 1978.

rate board of directors. A central element to governance of the hospital system is the management of the assets of the system.
- **A corporate management staff, usually somewhat specialist in nature, responsible for management of the system.** In some of the emerging hospital systems there may be a sharing of the staff with individual hospital responsibilities. As the system matures, the separation of individual hospital administrations and corporate management staff becomes more clear and distinct.
- **Individual hospital administrative staffs.** Usually given most of the management responsibilities and accountabilities of a freestanding hospital administration, but with the added responsibility of coordination with and supervision by the system management staff.
- **Some common services among the hospitals,** usually varying by the willingness to relinquish or not add a service, rather than a conscious effort to share a service.
- **Medical staffs of the individual hospitals usually separate and distinct from each other.** What little interlocking occurs takes the form of some reciprocity in privileges.
- **Little, if any, sharing of clinical services.** The sharing in clinical services usually occurs through an agreement of one hospital to initiate a new service with the cooperation of another hospital in the system not to initiate the same service for a period of time. Therefore, the characteristic may be more accurately described as an avoidance of duplication of clinical services rather than a sharing.

Operational Characteristics

Operational characteristics of today's emerging hospital systems include:

- **Finances, both operational and capital, are controlled** and directed to a large degree by the corporate management and board of directors.
- **System-wide planning is directed and coordinated centrally,** having an impact on the individual planning efforts of the local hospitals.
- **There are very few, if any, medical staff relationships** at the corporate level of management or governance. The medical staff relationships and authorities are retained in the individual hospital unit.
- **Local administration is quite controlling** in the areas of physical plant, budget development, personnel relations, local board relations, medical staff relations and community relations.
- Increasing numbers of **services are provided centrally** by the system, such as management engineering, data processing and education.
- Attention to the systems image and visibility had caused the **addition of public relations specialists** to the corporate staff.

Over the past few years the form of ownership by the hospital system of its local units has changed somewhat. The pure ownership of assets by the ownership group is giving way to leasing of assets and operation of facilities from other owners, such as governmental bodies with the actual ownership of the assets being retained in the previous operators. Contract management, particularly in the investor-owned sector, is another form of system development which is growing rapidly. In some cases this is a mere stepping stone to a form of ownership, such as lease-purchase or outright purchase of the assets.

Stages in Inter-Institutional Organization*

Once an inter-institutional organization is established, it must go through a number of developmental stages.

Stage One—Deciding Who Should Join

Why should an individual organization join? What benefits will that organization receive? The question involves the issues of equality, respect, strength and competence. Institutions are concerned that their particular strengths be respected by other institutions in the system and that they not be singled out for special treatment because of resources they have or do not have. It is important to consider who should join in

---

*Source: Reprinted from "The Janus Principle," *Health Care Management Review,* (Spring) by Alan Sheldon and Diana Barrett with permission of Aspen Systems Corporation, © 1977.

terms of relative strength or weakness. If an institution joins out of weakness, whether one of competence or finances, it will become a burden to the group. Smaller regional hospitals may wish to join not because of a positive sense of purpose but out of a fear that by not joining they might eventually suffer. Once they have joined, moreover, they may feel that their competence is not respected.

In Stage One, political arbitration is the key. The leader must deal competently and discreetly with the various constituencies that interact with the institution. More important, he must be able to represent both his own organization and the inter-institutional organization, attending with equal incisiveness to the interests of both. At times, the leader may have to make decisions that involve conflict of interest. Unless he has given some thought to the problem of dual roles, and has established relationships of trust and power with his own constituencies at home, the inter-institutional organization will begin to crumble.

Stage Two—Becoming a Member

How does an institution become a member of an inter-institutional organization? Is a new organization created? The key issues involved in working through this stage of membership and organization include:

- Working out goals.
- Developing an appropriate and effective decision-making mechanism.
- Dealing with competitive roles.

Joining an organization out of fear of being excluded is not the best way to become involved. Membership requires an overriding sense of purpose, one that is more than empty rhetoric. This must be translated into a decision-making mechanism that allows the purpose to be achieved and a set of actions developed that will further the purpose. (See Stage Three.) The importance of a sense of purpose is that it is something with which all member institutions can identify; thus, it enables them to transcend their differences in terms of needs and disparate facilities, while at the same time taking these differences into account. In Stage Two, the leader, as administrator, must understand the need for purpose and must be able to fashion decision-making alternatives and mechanisms. The leader must be able to confront conflict, rather than attempting to smooth it over, or force decisions through. He must bring key issues to the surface, so they can be dealt with effectively and the inter-institutional organization can progress to Stage Three.

Stage Three—Getting Things Done

An inter-institutional organization exists to get things done. From all the possible activities, the leader must help participants to select a subset in which priorities reflect the overall purposes of the inter-institutional organization. These activities must be backed by commitment. The member institution must act according to those priorities and be willing to sanction those members who do not. This commitment may take the form of backing up difficult actions, of committing resources, or of committing time. It may also include securing stability by means of obtaining long-term funding—another form of commitment. Certainly, it requires reviewing and monitoring. The quality and mechanism of decision-making will be reflected in the quality of the action. At this stage, leadership issues are those of consistency, trust and commitment.

Stage Four—Growing

In this stage, there are five distinct issues:

- Whether to pursue more of the same activities (as in Stage Three).
- Whether to add activities of a different kind.
- Whether to add more members of the same kind.
- Whether to add members of a different kind.
- When to add additional members or activities.

The key consideration in addressing the issue of sequence is how each decision affects the ultimate purpose of the inter-institutional organization. This sense of purpose will determine who belongs. As the purpose changes over time, considerations of membership will also change.

Opportunities for Sharing*

There are many problems which can be tackled by sharing resources, including management, plant operations, and medical expertise. Problems of rural and urban access to services offer opportunities for sharing.

Rural Areas

Rural areas suffer a general lack of medical resources. Small operations find it difficult to attract capital, medical manpower, and management talent. When coupled, as it often is, with poverty, the problems are compounded. Access and distance may prevent rural shared laundries, but common management services can be moved easily over very long distances. Many rural hospitals today operate as satellites or affiliates of larger institutions in nearby and sometimes remote cities. Clinics and other health agencies in rural areas could benefit from similar arrangements.

Urban Areas

In urban areas with geographic proximity, sharing can be extended to almost every service in the institution. Talented, expert managerial personnel, especially financial, labor relations, and hotel services, can manage more than one institution simultaneously, while less experienced personnel carry out systematized tasks under their direction. Such sharing arrangements can provide a necessary challenge to high-quality personnel whose talents are underutilized in the single institution—especially the finance officer. Laundries, computer services, collections, laboratories, and a host of other services can be shared with benefits to both the most poorly situated hospital and the most affluent.

By joining together for sharing, the services of several institutions can be made more accessible to the people being served by all of the institutions. When medical staffs operate under a common organization, it becomes easier to transfer patients with less cost and less time consumed. It also makes it more likely that patients will be admitted to the most appropriate institution in the first instance, obviating later transfers.

Quality of Care

Quality of care can also be improved when institutions share services which must operate at a fairly high volume in order to keep specialized personnel at a high peak of efficiency. More specialized personnel can be afforded as the clinical base for their services is expanded. Laboratories can conduct more quality determination, use more specialized equipment, and engage in improved educational programs when larger numbers of institutions engage in common services.

By linking up institutions through sharing arrangements, the comprehensiveness of care offered to the respective patient and physician groups can be economically expanded. Social workers, physical therapists and many other disciplines can contribute their expertise to more than one organization at a time.

Economies of Scale

Finally and most frequently cited, economies of scale derived from sharing can reduce the resources utilized to deliver services. While sharing will not reduce all costs in every instance, it seems reasonable to assert that the opportunities for effective sharing have hardly been tapped.

Medical Services

Medical services sharing probably offers the most dramatic opportunities for more effective use of resources. High energy therapy, open heart surgery, specialized laboratories, and the like require a high degree of manpower specialization, capital equipment, and a constant volume of patients to operate economically. Long-term changes in birthrates, shifting population needs, highway system changes, and other related factors make it necessary to modify the roles of place-bound institutions.

Coping with Reimbursement

One group of very large hospitals considers as a high priority a shared service to keep them fully up to date on reimbursement rules and frequent audits for effective approaches. Many voluntary

---

*Source: Reprinted from "Sharing: An Overview," *Topics in Health Care Financing*, (Summer) by Montague Brown with permission of Aspen Systems Corporation, © 1976.

hospital administrators consider the talent to do this job well to be a major advantage of the investor-owned hospital chains.

Capital Financing

In a recent incident involving the contract management of a small hospital by a large city-based medical center, the ability of the contracting organization to develop a strategy to refinance the smaller one kept the hospital from failure. Many mergers, consolidations, and acquisitions by successful organizations require, and benefit greatly from, expertise in capital financing. As grants and endowments level off along with growth in capital needs for new construction, replacement, and expensive technology, greater capital financing expertise will be required.

Resource Utilization

Trustees are increasingly asking if there is some way to reduce the upward spiral of demands, to utilize resources more efficiently, and to avoid the now almost universally acknowledged duplication of services. Shared services provide some of the answers to these questions while mergers, consortia, and closings answer others.

CONTRACT MANAGEMENT*

Investor-owned hospital management corporations, not-for-profit hospital systems, and other health care management corporations are actively seeking hospitals that wish to hire not a single administrator, but a total management team and its management systems. The growth of hospital and health facility contract management in both the investor-owned and not-for-profit sector in recent years has been well documented. In 1980, 493 hospitals were managed under contract, an increase of 17 percent over 1979. Of this total, 342 are investor owned and 151 are in the not-for-profit sector and increased by 14 and 24 percent respectively between 1979 and 1980.

A management contract usually contains the following elements:

---

*Source: Montague Brown and William H. Money, "Contract Management for Health Care Facilities." Reprinted, with permission, from *Trustee*, published by the American Hospital Publishing, Inc., copyright February 1976, Vol. 29, No. 2.

1. The board of directors of the managed hospital controls policy and retains legal responsibility for and ownership of the facility.
2. The managing organization appoints an administrator, subject to board approval, and pays the administrator's salary (this may be reimbursed to the managing organization).
3. The administrator manages the operation of the facility under a budget approved by the board of directors and obtains approval of key decisions from the board.
4. Specialized services and personnel are provided to the managed hospital by the managing corporation. The administrator may implement new management systems, perform feasibility studies, suggest changes in services, and take daily management responsibility for the institution. All major changes in operations or activities are typically performed with the approval of the board of directors.

In some instances, the management corporation also employs the director of finance and, on occasion, the director of nursing. These positions appear to be crucial to effective management performance.

In the precontract exploration phase, the contractor will identify priority areas for managerial emphasis. These will be confirmed or modified when the resident administrator begins his full-time service with the hospital. Generally, he will have the option, with board approval, of initiating special studies or modifications of existing practice. Orchestrating and directing changes become the primary responsibility of the onsite administrator once initial operations begin. Consultants from the parent organization visit the hospital at his request and serve primarily to assist him in his task, not to supplant his leadership. The hospital's operational data is monitored by the contracting organization and processed according to its procedures. The use of such control data to monitor performance represents a major step forward in the management of many.

Reasons for Seeking Assistance

Why are some hospitals turning to management contracts? Many of the 150 hospitals visited in a recent survey received the assistance outlined below when they were having difficulty in one or more areas.

Financial difficulties. In hospitals with short-term cash flow problems, good business practice and loans sponsored by the managing organization have relieved most of the problem. Loan payments and/or guarantees of payment are made a part of the contract. In institutions with capital shortages, managing organizations have assisted in gaining access to money markets, insurance companies, and banks. The promise of improved management has apparently strengthened the hospital's borrowing power.

Management problems. Boards that have been unable to find a suitable or acceptable hospital administrator in some instances have accepted the managing corporation's representative. Small hospital size, which has made it virtually impossible to hire and retain sufficient specialized management talent or consulting assistance, has provided no obstacle to management corporations as of this date.

Inability to attract medical staff. A stable, successful management team provides attraction for medical staff.

Internal conflict among the medical staff, management, and the board, which has to be corrected or mediated by the managing organization.

The need to obtain specialized talent and management expertise because of increased regulation. The management organization shares this expertise. The hospitals turned to contract management when their problems (licensing, capital financing, occupancy, reimbursement, medical staff-board relations) became so acute that administrative and board personnel viewed the obstacles as insurmountable.

Advantages of Contract Management

The backup resources of the contracting organization and the security and status of belonging to a larger and more successful organization apparently make it less difficult to find competent administrators. In a similar fashion, boards and medical staffs tend to impute greater powers and knowledge to the administrator because of his organizational backup and support. Also, they tend to be more confident that if one administrator leaves or proves to be unacceptable, an acceptable replacement will be found quickly.

Improved financial management is cited as the most important advantage derived from corporate assistance. By being up-to-date on ways of allocating cost for reimbursement, by allocating charges properly, by instituting effective credit and collection procedures, and by taking advantage of discounts, hospitals frequently are able to realize large savings and significant increases in income. The new administrators usually find ways to reduce costs by applying control statistics to staffing patterns and using cost data from similar operations elsewhere. Because most contractors use comparative statistics derived from similar operations, the local hospital, often for the first time, has some standards by which to assess local performance.

Other potentially beneficial management activities depend upon the needs of the particular institution. Many institutions can benefit from better purchase prices available through group purchasing. Some can benefit from new wage and salary programs, physician recruitment programs, or simply an old-fashioned cleanup and new paint.

Models of Contract Management*

The recent proliferation of hospital and health care facility contract management has resulted in three basic structural models or forms of the arrangement: (1) the operating division model, (2) the wholly owned subsidiary model and (3) the shared or joint management model.

Operating Division Model

The most prevalent model of contract management in the health field is the operating division model, representing well over 90 percent of the hospital and health care facility contract management market. The key feature of the operating division model is that the contract management activity typically functions as a department of the managing organization.

The operating division model is achieved using two distinct approaches. Under the *centralized approach* hospital management is administered through the central corporate headquarters. Some of the larger firms have regional or even district personnel responsible for

---

*Source: Reprinted from "Contract Management of Health Care Facilities," *Health Care Management Review*, (Fall) with permission of Aspen Systems Corporation, © 1981.

one or more managed hospitals. These managers are typically employees of the corporate office rather than employees of one of the owned or affiliated hospitals of the system.

Relatively fewer hospitals are managed via the *decentralized approach*. In this approach, member hospitals of a hospital chain or system serve as the managing organization for hospitals and health care facilities in their geographic area. Direct supervision of managed facilities is the responsibility of a member hospital within a corporate chain, and the management contract is signed between a member hospital and the managed institution. In the centralized approach the management agreement is signed between the managed facility and the hospital corporation.

Wholly Owned Subsidiary Model

Some nonprofit hospitals and hospital systems have established wholly owned for-profit subsidiaries to handle the management contract and shared service business of the organization. The wholly owned subsidiary is typically governed by members of the board of trustees and management team of the sponsoring organization. Any "profit" from the subsidiary's activities is used exclusively for the benefit of the not-for-profit corporation.

Shared Or Joint Management Model

These management arrangements are usually achieved between hospitals or health care facilities that are considered "equals," in that they do not necessarily involve a larger managing hospital or corporation and the usually smaller, rural managed hospital or health facility.

The area-wide management corporation, either an investor-owned or not-for-profit entity, is established when hospitals and other health care facilities in a region join together to sponsor a management organization that will, in turn, manage each of the participating institutions. Participating institutions appoint members to the governing board of the management corporation and purchase management services under contract from that organization.

The condominium concept brings together two or more autonomous health institutions either on the same campus (horizontal condominium) or in the same building (vertical condominium). "Condominium management" would occur when separately governed health care institutions come together on the same campus (or building) and agree to share management services.

Another variation of the shared or joint management model is the "law office partnership." Under this concept, administrators from participating institutions would form a partnership for the provision of several specific management functions. Under this arrangement, each administrator would remain an employee of his or her institution while relying centrally on one or more of his or her partners for various specific management services (e.g., finance, planning, labor relations, etc.). The partnership would be reimbursed by the participating hospitals for the specific corporate services rendered.

EVERYTHING YOU'VE WANTED TO KNOW ABOUT HOSPITAL CHAINS

There were 32 investor-owned hospital chains listed in the Federation of American Hospitals' *Directory of Investor-Owned Hospitals and Hospital Management Companies 1975*. Each corporation owned or managed from three to 70 hospitals. A total of 378, or 35.7 percent, of the 1060 investor-owned hospitals in the country were owned by such management companies.

The hospital chains have been using hospital management contracts to facilitate their expansion plans. This is expected to continue. Under a typical hospital contract, the investor-owned chain takes over management of an independent hospital and handles all operations for a fixed fee, alleviating the problem of large capital investment for the chain.

What Hospital Chains Do*

All 32 investor-owned hospital corporations that own or manage over three hospitals were contacted in a 1976 survey and twenty-one or 65.7 percent answered the questionnaire. Nineteen of these 21 corporations own hospitals and 16 of the 21 presently have contracts for the management of hospitals.

*Source: "Management Policies in Investor-Owned Hospitals," *Health Care Management Review*, (Summer) by David D. Springate and Melissa Craig McNeil with permission of Aspen Systems Corporation, © 1977.

For services sometimes provided at the corporate level, corporations are split almost 50-50 with respect to each of the following:

- Purchasing over half the dollar value of medical, administrative and housekeeping supplies,
- Drafting of annual operating budgets, and
- Compilation of income and expense data.

The compilation of daily census statistics, however, is done at the corporate level for only six of the 21 respondents. Obviously services in hospital chains are not greatly centralized.

Training programs are, in general, supported by the responding corporations. Twelve out of 21 corporations provide intern and resident training at some of their hospitals, although only two of the 21 offer programs in the majority of their hospitals. Approximately 70 percent of the respondents provide educational training for nursing students and allied health personnel in some of their hospitals. Eight of the 21 and nine of the 21 provide education for nurses and allied health personnel, respectively, at the majority of their hospitals.

The decision-making process was studied in relation to the level in which a decision was originated and finalized, and to the factor which predominates the basis for the decision. In the latter series of questions factors in decision making were ranked in order of importance. These questions focused on four areas.

- Decisions on services to be offered originated with the individual hospital administrator in 40 percent of the cases and are finalized by the corporation head or staff in 57 percent of the cases. The chief factors forming the basis for the decisions vary among corporations, but included the desire of the individual hospital's chief of service (40 percent), the availability of similar services nearby (29 percent) and the desire of the individual hospital administrator (19 percent). Clearly there are multiple answers to the question of which services to offer. They reflect the blend of desire for service and desire for profit.
- Decisions on prices charged originate with the hospital administrator in 76 percent of the cases. Forty-eight percent of the corporations responded that decisions are finalized at the corporate level, 29 percent that decisions are finalized at the individual hospital administrator level, and 24 percent responded that the pattern varied across hospitals. The local average charge for a service is the most important factor noted in pricing decisions for 62 percent of the 21 corporations with another 29 percent indicating that cost plus a percentage is the primary factor in these decisions. Most chains appear not to be price leaders in the communities they serve.
- Origination and finalization of decisions on types of patients admitted vary, although 11 of the 21 respondents noted the individual hospital administrator originates the decision, and nine of the 21 indicated that individual administrators finalize the decision. Community need ranks highest with 48 percent of the respondents indicating it as the most important factor in the decision. Average length of stay of a diagnosis is the factor ranked as second most important (19 percent).
- Asset expansion decisions appear to have no clear point of origin, but are finalized by 80 percent of the corporations at the corporate level. Community needs and projection of cost to profit were each indicated as primary factors in the decision by ten of the 20 corporations which responded.

The setting of standards and review of actual results compared to these standards is carried out by the majority of corporations. The percentage of corporations where standards are determined by the company varies for different concerns:

Level of supplies on hand	76%
Utilization rate for equipment	33%
Dollar amount of earnings	90%
Ratio of number of beds set up and staffed to number of patients	81%
Ratio of number of medical staff to number of patients	43%
Ratio of number of nurses to number of patients	76%
Number of total personnel to number of patients	86%

Monthly and weekly are the most common periods after which results are compared to standards. Initial comparison of actual results to standard appears split. Comparisons are usually made by a member of the hospital staff or jointly with a member of the corporate staff. Corporate staff alone do not provide many initial comparisons. Most remedies, if variances are noted, are determined jointly by hospital and corporate staff.

Questions regarding incentives reveal a majority of the corporations use varied techniques to attempt to stimulate the performance of top administrative management in their hospitals. Eighty-one percent of the respondents conduct in-house training programs to encourage promotion within the hospital's administrative management structure. Seventy-six percent of the corporations base top management salary increases on merit determined by review at the end of a period. Seventy-one percent of the corporations provided added monetary bonuses based on merit or accomplishment of a predetermined target for the hospital's top management. Corporations are divided, however, on offering a stock option plan to top administrative personnel at the hospitals, with 12 of the 21 respondents making the offer.

Data on financial and accounting policies of the corporations were collected. In terms of accounting policies:

- Sixteen of the 21 corporations depreciate buildings and major equipment on the straight line method for financial reporting purposes.
- For tax reporting purposes 76 percent of the corporations depreciate the maximum amount permitted by tax authority.
- Seventy-six percent of the corporations use different methods of depreciation for financial and tax reporting purposes.
- Inventory valuation methods vary. Most common (62 percent) is to use the FIFO method for valuation of supplies.

The questions asked relating to financial policies focused on debt and on methods of financing, with the following results:

- Sixty-two percent of the corporations set specific limits on the amount of long-term debt the corporation can use.
- Less than 20 percent of the corporations allow individual hospitals to borrow for their own purposes and on their own authority. Three of four corporations do require review of the borrowing level of each hospital by the corporate staff.
- Eighty-six of the responding corporations actively seek new alternatives for financing asset expansion and acquisition as opposed to the use of a set method of financing.
- Eighty-six percent of the responding corporations lease some of their major equipment or medical facilities.
- Just over 80 percent of the corporations have publicly traded common stock, while only 24 percent of them have outstanding preferred stock. Forty-three percent have outstanding convertible securities and warrants.

Administrator Job Opportunities in Management Corporations[*]

Hospital management corporations have significantly expanded the options generally available to health care personnel by creating the new environment of multifacility management.

Administrators who have mastered the role of chief executive of a hospital may seek even greater challenges in multifacility management. Further steps of group, division and corporation management are available to the administrator who chooses a vertical career path in corporate business management. The administrator may choose to pursue vertical growth as a hospital administrator, if that best accommodates his or her interests, values and life style.

Yet these vertical paths are not the only ones available to the administrator. Other areas, such as marketing, education, planning, consulting and development may prove to be more satisfying.

The hospital controller and other financial personnel have more flexibility in career pathing. Having risen to the position of chief financial officer in the hospital, the controller may pursue vertical progression by moving from a small facility to a large facility or into group, division and corporate executive positions. There is also the option of internal consulting in financial areas ranging from reimbursement to investment analysis. Within hospital management corporations the hospital controller can switch from financial management to hospital administration and continue to have the same

---

[*]Source: Reprinted from "Career Planning in Hospital Management Corporations," *Topics in Health Care Financing,* (Summer) with permission of Aspen Systems Corporation, © 1980.

career options as the person who began in the administrator's position.

All these mobility and career options are supported by other corporate systems that make the career pathing even more attractive. These support systems include such benefits as relocation management and reimbursement, continuity of benefits and seniority within the organization.

As Figure 11-1 indicates, career planning is an ongoing cycle of activities. The content of the cycle varies greatly, and the process, which remains intact, ensures that new and effective human resource designs and activities will be generated. Career development, then, is a vital system that encourages organizational growth and renewal.

The manner in which career development is implemented in corporations varies, ranging from complex assessment centers to workshops, workbooks and simple written instructions.

MULTIHOSPITAL SYSTEMS*

Benefits

- centralization of administrative and support services, thereby securing economies of scale through specialization and reducing unit costs by the shared application of advanced technology;
- greater management capability to cope with internal problems and weaknesses as well as with the external environment;
- larger capital bases providing additional financial stability;
- a central focus for assigning priority to financially realistic program and resource decisions; and
- an opportunity to bring medical staffs into a rational management structure that recognizes the need for their input in key management activities such as planning and evaluation.

Free-Standing Hospitals Versus Hospital Systems

The primary difference between the free-standing hospital and the hospital system is the imposition of the corporate management staff between the hospital and the governing body in the hospital system.

In the free-standing hospital, the governing body is generally involved with the operation of a set of services that supports the hospital's and medical staff's patients. The board interacts with the hospital's management staff, while the medical staff members vie for development of services that will benefit their own patients and practices. The board's attention frequently centers around operations, facilities development and other financial decisions because management is primarily occupied with day-to-day operations. This is the garden variety hospital.

In the hospital system, the governing body often has a much wider focus. With the imposition of a corporate management staff, the board is once removed from the various hospitals' managements and medical staffs, so the board can concentrate on the system as a whole. It need not focus on the specific programs and finances of any one hospital *except* as they relate to the system. The board's attention is generally on the growth and financial strength of the entire system with particular emphasis on new lines of business, acquisitions and capital planning strategies. While concern for program development is still evident, it is the job of corporate management to deal with variances in performance among the hospitals in providing services and producing financial results.

Depending on the degree of centralization of authority in the hospital system, the role of medical staffs can vary from business-as-usual in the traditional mode of hospital operations, to a feeling of helpless frustration in trying to deal with a distant corporate management and board, to intensive interaction with hospital management in planning and operating the specific hospital as an integral part of the larger corporation.

Finally, the system's larger size, in comparison to the free-standing hospital, enables it to spread central overhead over a broader operating base and affords a much greater opportunity for securing high calibre board members and corporate managers.

Variations in Hospital System Organization

There are four types of structures: the consortium model, the overlapping institutional board

---

*Source: Reprinted from "The Organization of Not-for-Profit Hospital Systems," *Health Care Management Review*, (Summer) by James Reynolds and Ann E. Stunden with permission of Aspen Systems Corporation, © 1978.

Figure 11-1 Business goals and objectives

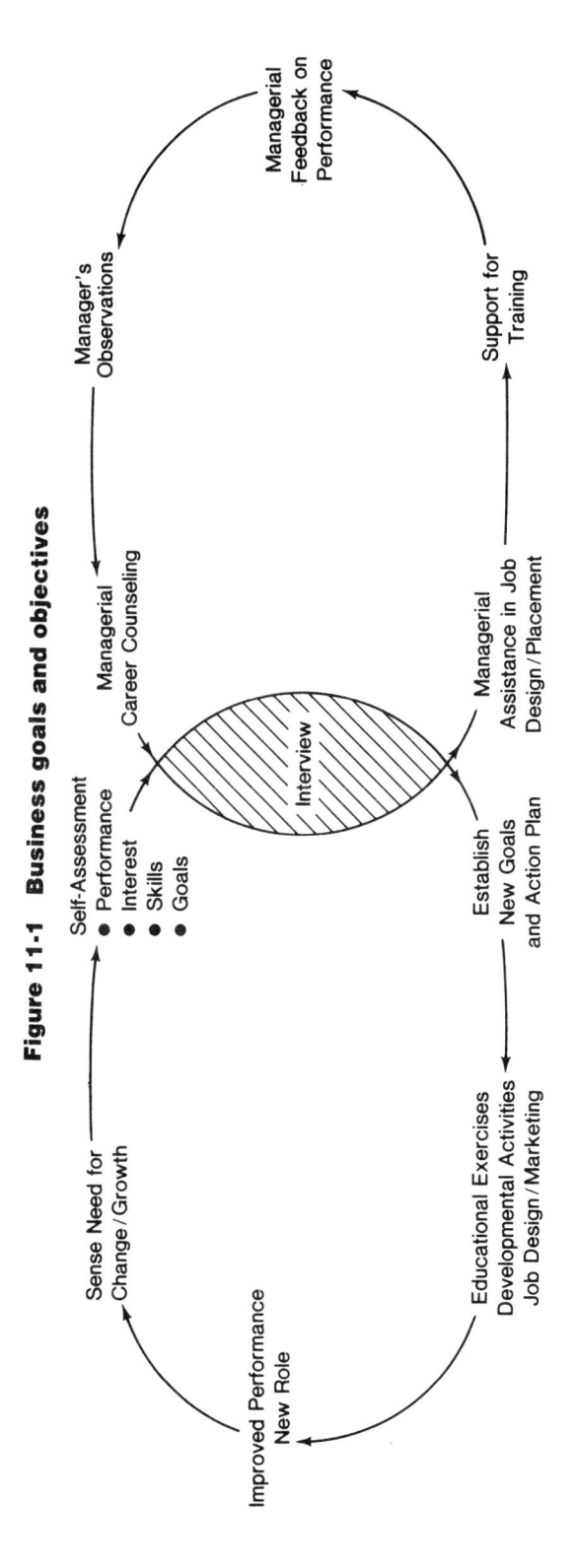

Self-Assessment
- Performance
- Interest
- Skills
- Goals

Managerial Career Counseling

Manager's Observations

Managerial Feedback on Performance

Support for Training

Managerial Assistance in Job Design/Placement

Establish New Goals and Action Plan

Interview

Sense Need for Change/Growth

Educational Exercises
Developmental Activities
Job Design/Marketing

Improved Performance
New Role

membership model, the holding company model and the corporate model.

The **consortium model** is frequently a tentative first step toward the development of a system. Here each hospital maintains its own identity and governing body, which works with a coordinating body responsible for the activities in which the individual hospitals are venturing jointly—usually lobbying, planning and/or shared services. The coordinating body, often dependent on a consensus, is powerless outside its specific domain, and often has little power within. The real power remains with each hospital. Examples of such arrangements include the Quadrangle hospitals in Detroit and the Maryland Health Care System in Baltimore.

The **overlapping institutional board membership model** can result from a consortium model or from a merger process. This structure is used most often among medical schools and affiliated hospitals, such as Mount Sinai in New York, but is also relevant to hospital systems as a transitional arrangement leading to the corporate model. This structure has equivalent memberships for each of the merging boards so that the business of each component is handled sequentially at board meetings. One or more individuals can serve as the chief executive officer (CEO) for each hospital.

The **holding company model** develops from a consortium or through a merger/acquisition process. It can take at least two forms: (1) that in which the hospital boards report through the corporate management staff; or (2) a structure in which the hospital boards are relatively autonomous, circumventing corporate management by reporting directly to the corporate board—a situation that often results in conflict. Hospital management and the trustees generally have the authority for developing program and financial plans for their hospital within a set of corporate guidelines, subject to the corporate board's approval. The Intermountain and Fairview systems utilize this kind of arrangement.

The **corporate model** often evolves from the natural growth of a single hospital (the Greenville Hospital System is such a case), but can also develop from a consolidation of any one of the other models (for example, The Sisters of Mercy Health Care Corporation based in Detroit). Here, the corporate management and governing body have maximum control in guiding the direction of the system and its component hospitals. In some instances, advisory boards have been developed to relate to each hospital and represent the interests of local markets.

Working within a Hospital System Today

The key issue in most voluntary hospital systems today is the extent of autonomy for each component hospital, particularly in setting its own direction for program development, resource acquisition and control of the resources necessary for its day-to-day operations. This relates to two other questions: (1) Which program and resource variables within what limits are to be controlled at each management level? (2) Which services should be provided centrally and how can their responsiveness to hospital management be assured?

Hospital Administrators

Hospital administrators within the systems have many of the classic problems that beset freestanding hospitals. Prime concerns are assuring that operations run smoothly and that the hospital stays within its approved budget. Patient-, personnel- and expense-related issues are their principal domain.

While the hospital administrators in a system are routinely responsible for controlling expenses, there is often confusion about their role in revenue control. Whether the corporation regards each hospital as a cost or profit center depends on the attitude of the board and the CEO's management style. (The manager of a profit center should have authority to participate in pricing decisions and to develop and implement strategies to increase service volumes, while a cost center manager needs authority only to control resource acquisition and allocation as variations in service volumes occur.) Even when the CEO regards the hospitals as profit centers, administrators are often frustrated in managing to the bottom line. This occurs because prices are frequently set at the corporate level, allocations are not under the control of the administrators and adjustments are often made to the hospital's monthly operating statements by the corporate financial staff.

If goals and objectives are set by the individual hospitals, they are frequently isolated from the system's goals. In addition, few systems require that administrators tie their objectives to a formal planning *and* budgeting process.

The level of medical staff relationships maintained by administrators generally depends on the extent of their autonomy. While administrators generally relate to medical staff on day-to-day matters, there are systems in which administrators do not attend joint conference committee meetings.

Obviously, interfacing with corporate administrative and support services can be a serious problem for administrators. Problems often relate to services not performed in the hospital, such as finance and personnel. In these situations a frequent complaint is that the corporation does not understand hospital operations. Among corporate support services provided in the hospitals, such as maintenance, engineering or security, administrators are frequently frustrated by not having line control of personnel actually working or needed in their hospitals. This frustration usually has to do with setting priorities, scheduling and having authority to discipline personnel.

Medical Staff

The medical staff within a system's hospital can be guided by bylaws either that they have adopted or that have been imposed by a joint medical staff committee operating at the corporate level. Although many systems allow development of individual bylaws for each medical staff, there is currently some movement to develop a single set of systemwide bylaws that umbrella all component hospital bylaws. Regardless of the level at which bylaws are set, medical staffs find themselves responsible for implementing bylaws as well as policies that may be set by system-wide departments and committees.

In instances where both large and small hospitals comprise a single system in a geographically concentrated area, the size differential and, therefore, power of the larger medical staffs leaves staffs of the smaller hospitals believing there is an imbalance and possibly bias on the part of system-wide groups that decide how to respond to their requests for service development and allocation of resources. Further, they often feel that system-wide departmental and committee policies are imposed on them by the staffs of the larger hospitals.

In all instances, medical staffs find themselves with an additional level of management to cope with, and confusion often ensues as to which matters should be addressed to which level of management.

Corporate Management

Corporate management staffs frequently find that most of their efforts focus on finance. Some of this focus is on system-wide issues relating to the bottom line, but there is also significant focus on each component hospital. Where formal planning and evaluation methods do not exist, which is true in most cases, the emphasis on the bottom-line financial performance of each hospital represents the corporation's only real means for holding hospital administrators accountable.

The corporate managements of some systems have developed good management control systems for day-to-day operations. Data processing services generate reports allowing monitoring of revenue and expenses, manpower control and patient utilization. Such control systems, however, generally do not deal with strategic matters related to the overall direction of the system or to performance of each hospital against program goals.

Currently, there is a trend towards the development of a corporate planning staff. Emphasis is shifting away from facilities planning towards program planning, based on environmental assessment and system resources. A few sophisticated systems (Fairview, for example) have developed or are developing comprehensive, integrated planning services at the corporate level.

Corporate Services

Corporate finance appears to be the strongest corporate service. Corporate finance is routinely responsible for assets management, capital financing, budgeting and accounting functions. (Sometimes this unit includes data processing services.) The division of responsibility in patient accounting functions between corporate financial services and the hospitals often varies. Where corporate financial services has total responsibility for patient accounting there is almost routinely some conflict between the corporate staff and the hospital administrators. This usually relates to the hospital's collecting sufficient and accurate billing information at admission and complete and timely collection of charge data during the stay. It also relates to corporate finance's collection efforts and its impact on each hospital's bottom line.

The centralization of other services varies with the system's size and whether it is geographically dispersed or concentrated. Human resource divisions are being developed. While these divisions still retain the classic personnel functions, there is new emphasis on management development, incentive compensation, succession planning and especially on educational services relating to career ladders. In concentrated environments, functions such as materials management also tend to be centralized. Levels of centralization of support services (maintenance, laundry, and so forth) vary widely from system to system. Although centralization of administrative and support services allows systems to achieve economies of scale, these services often generate conflicts with hospital administrators who do not have line control.

Corporate Board

The board structure varies among hospital systems:

- All boards have a finance committee.
- Most boards have a joint conference committee.
- Some boards have a planning committee.
- Many boards have other committees, such as audit, personnel, education or community relations.

The presence of many committees tends to involve board members more with operational issues and to result in overlapping committee functions.

Boards generally recognize their responsibility for management performance and for the quality of patient care. Board members, however, struggle with the manner in which they can hold management and the medical staff accountable. Most boards hold the CEO accountable principally for the system's financial performance. With goals and objectives development in its infancy, corporate management is seldom measured in terms of performance against plans, which include key aspects of system structure, process and outcome.

Multi-Hospital Constraints*

The Health Planning and Resources Development Act of 1974, PL 93-641, provides specific encouragement for integration among hospitals. Of the ten priorities offered as guidelines to HSA, several are directed toward the development of multi-institutional arrangements:

- the development of multi-institutional systems for coordination or consolidation of institutional services (including obstetric, pediatric, emergency medical, intensive and coronary care and radiation therapy services);
- the development of multi-institutional arrangements for sharing support services necessary to all health service institutions;
- the development by health service institutions of the capacity to provide various levels of care (including intensive care, acute general care and extended care) on a geographically integrated basis; and
- the adoption of uniform cost accounting, simplified reimbursement and utilization reporting systems and improved management procedures for health service institutions.

Forces from within the hospital industry clearly have been joined by national legislation, notably PL 93-641, to encourage the formation and development of multiple hospital systems. Such systems are expected to aid in rationalizing the delivery of medical care services and will contribute to capital and operating efficiencies. Yet despite this effort, we find countervailing forces. Within the legal arena, particularly antitrust and tax laws, and in the financial arena, notably in reimbursement systems, a number of developments appear to be countering the intent in the planning area and may serve as constraints to interinstitutional arrangements.

Antitrust Constraints

The hospital industry has not been exempted from the application of antitrust laws; a series of recent court actions has clearly established that

---

*Source: Reprinted from "Legal and Financial Constraints on the Development and Growth of Multiple Hospital Arrangements," *Health Care Management Review*, (Winter) by Robert A. Vraciu and Howard S. Zuckerman with permission of Aspen Systems Corporation, © 1979.

hospitals are subject to the restrictions of the antitrust laws. Many actions of multiple hospital systems could be said to constitute anticompetitive behavior. The current feeling is that prosecution is possible, regardless of the motive. Examples of activities where hospitals and multiple hospital systems are vulnerable are:

1. The merger of hospitals which "substantially lessens competition or creates a monopoly" may be in violation of Section VII of the Clayton Act. Thus hospitals in a close geographical area which are contemplating merger as the means of integration (regardless of the intent) face possible civil suits.
2. The sharing of budgets and discussions of prices by hospitals under separate corporate ownership could constitute price fixing prohibited under the Sherman Act.
3. "Cooperative attempts" by hospitals to divide markets through the allocation of customers among themselves could be illegal under the Sherman Act. Thus attempts to reduce duplication of services and match the capacity of hospitals with the expected demand might be considered illegal.
4. Certain types of multiple hospital system arrangements, such as the consortium, which represent a substantial portion of providers in a particular geographical area might be charged with conspiring to restrict the supply of hospital services in a noncompetitive way or with attempting to obtain monopoly power. Attempts to prevent outsiders from establishing themselves in the market—a conspiracy to delay and, if possible, prevent the issuance of a CON by means other than furnishing testimony in open hearings—could be viewed as violations of the Sherman Act.

The encouragement of multiple hospital systems in PL 93-641 is based on the belief that integration of management functions in hospitals will lead to an improved system, that the current form of competition in the hospital industry is dysfunctional. The antitrust laws are based on the notion that monopolistic behavior is inherently bad and competition is inherently good. The dichotomy begs the question of whether competition in the health field, with all its market imperfections, is better for the public interest than collusive or cooperative behavior.

Federal Tax Law Constraints

Federal tax laws do not directly prohibit organizational forms or activities as do the antitrust laws. Rather, they penalize certain organizational forms or behavior by taxing income. For the most part the federal tax laws interfere with multiple hospital systems in the area of shared services between "separate ownership" forms. For example:

1. The types of services eligible for sharing are restricted. For example, a shared service organization established as a Section 501(e) organization—both tax exempt and eligible for tax deductible donations—is limited to providing certain enumerated services. Laundry services are clearly omitted from this list.
2. Restrictions on the membership of a shared services organization can prevent such an organization from operating to its maximum potential. Shared service organizations established under S.501(e) can provide services only to governmental hospitals and to other nonprofit organizations established under S.501(c)(3). Thus, investor-owned hospitals and tax-exempt nursing homes could not receive services from S.501(e) organizations.

Restrictions on tax-exempt status, types of services and hospitals eligible for sharing, payout provisions and the taxability of specific categories of income, act as impediments to the development and desirability of shared services. The Internal Revenue Code and IRS do not prevent the development but rather pose obstacles which appear to be inconsistent with the mandate of PL 93-641.

Reimbursement Constraints

Medicare reimbursement fails to encourage multiple hospital systems as the amount paid is generally less than "total financial requirements" for all tax-exempt organizational forms. While this problem is not unique for multiple hospital systems, the impact can be greater because of the larger fiscal demands for a developing or growing system. The two principal financial areas where reimbursement consequences are greatest are in the accumulation of capital and the reimbursement for operating expenses.

Area of Capital Requirements: Many types of the multiple hospital system arrangements include growth in assets of one or more entities:

- When one organization purchases another, it increases the book value of its assets.
- When two or more deteriorated and financially troubled hospitals merge to form a new organization, capital for a new facility is generally necessary.
- Shared services organizations set up as separate corporations often require start-up and expansion capital.

Thus the development and expansion of multiple hospital systems often require significant amounts of funds to finance their activities.

Medicare's reimbursement formula does not allow a contribution to capital (i.e., an accounting profit) for nonprofit hospitals.

Area of Operating Expenses: There are at least two areas where multiple hospital systems are adversely affected by reimbursement for operating expenses. The first is that of the "payout provision" for a shared services organization established under S.501(e). Such an organization must distribute the net earnings to its patrons. Similarly, shared services organizations established under subchapter T must pay income tax on any undistributed earnings. Since the shared services organization is likely to require capital of its own, it will in many instances make this distribution in the form of script, thus providing no cash to the hospital. The Medicare reimbursement regulations will treat the receipt of this script as an offset to the allowable costs of the purchased services. Clearly, if the scope of shared services is great and/or the hospital is in a tight cash situation, this treatment of script will decrease the hospital's liquidity position and such a shared services organization will look unattractive.

The second area is Medicare's limit of its liability to hospital routine service costs according to a hospital's relationship to a peer group determined by hospital bed size and location. For example, hospitals above the 80th percentile of their peer group are reimbursed at the 80th percentile. A single hospital within a multiple hospital system may offer a more sophisticated set of services and treat a more complex case mix than independent hospitals of the same size simply because of its ties with other hospitals in the system. Consequently, a hospital in a multiple hospital system may lie at the high end of the distribution and get penalized because of its shared clinical services arrangements.

Table 11-2 Hospitals and Beds in Multihospital Systems and as Percent of All Community Hospitals (1979)*

	Total Community Hospitals	Multi-hospital Systems	Percent in Multi-hospital Systems
No. of hospitals	5,851	1,519	26%
No. of beds	975,000	301,894	31%

*Source: Reprinted from "Trends in Multihospital Systems: A Multiyear Comparison," *Health Care Management Review,* (Fall) with permission of Aspen Systems Corporation, © 1980.

PART III
PLANNING

Chapter 12—Organizing for Planning

OVERVIEW*

The easy days of converting wishful thoughts into an actuality overnight have vanished. Planning for health care institutions has become a complex reaction to a complex situation. There are short-range plans and long-range plans to be solidified in a fluctuating economy; there are constraints and restraints, regulations and requirements, all to be met simultaneously; there are accountabilities to guidelines and criteria, whether mandatory, voluntary, internal or external; and finally, there is the increasingly urgent call for the hospital to sell itself, because standing still today means falling back. More than ever before, the hospital administrator needs to know how to look ahead.

The Administrator's Role

In his role as a planner, the hospital administrator should:

1. Organize a formal planning process involving the right people with the right information to make recommendations on the future of the institution.
2. Stimulate the effective development of formal planning among each of the divisions and departments and integrate their plans with overall institutional plans.
3. Study the institution's current programs of service, the nature of the communities served by those programs, and their relationship to the programs of other health care institutions serving the same area.
4. Identify community gaps in service and opportunities for program innovations, and recommend allocations of institutional resources for new or existing programs.
5. Establish planning links with other health institutions and agencies, and identify and evaluate opportunities for joint or shared programs of service.
6. Continually survey evolving trends in economic, political, and social characteristics of the community served and recommend actions to advance the institution's ability to be responsive to community needs.
7. Guide an organized process of institutional goal evaluation and development, and coordinate the development of strategies for achieving the institution's objectives.
8. Maintain an appropriate follow-up program of progress made on decisions resulting from planning activities.

Different Approaches

Planning usually takes one of the following forms:

1. No formal planning program exists at all. Planning is done by each line manager in conjunction with the annual budgeting cycle or as needed for new projects. In the case of modernization or expansion proj-

---

*Source: Except where noted, the "Overview" consists of excerpts from Martin S. Perlin, *Managing Institutional Planning,* Aspen Systems Corporation, © 1976. Reprinted with permission.

ects, planning might be carried out by a consultant to demonstrate feasibility and help in securing approvals by outside agencies.
2. A personal assistant to the chief executive is assigned the responsibility. His duties can include other aspects of the organization, but a major focus is on planning "staff work." This can include collecting and evaluating data, writing position papers, and providing staff assistance to planning groups. In such cases, the chief executive often is the central focal point for planning, with his assistant providing aid where needed. In some situations the staff assistant assumes greater responsibility to represent the chief executive.
3. A line manager's assignments are organized to permit him time to carry out the job. Although he can be responsible for other functional areas, a portion of his time will be spent on planning work. He might or might not serve as a planning focal point depending on the wishes of the chief executive.
4. An executive vice president or president is responsible for all planning, and an operating chief executive is responsible to him for current operations. The top planning individual usually will have staff assistance to help him carry out this function.
5. A planning executive and staff are made the central focus for all planning work, with that individual reporting to the chief executive officer. The responsibilities of this department can encompass the entire planning function, including liaison with outside agencies and project management in the case of expansion or modernization.
7. In multi-institutional systems a variation of the previous form includes a planning executive or staff in each major division or operating unit, with overall system planning the responsibility of a planning officer at central headquarters.

Planning Committees

The function of the planning committee is to study the institution's external and internal environments, evaluate alternative courses of both short range and long range action, understand the implications on those who will be affected by those actions, make recommendations to its parent organization, and establish a mechanism to evaluate continuously past plans in light of changing environments. The process is obviously cyclical, requiring a continuously functioning planning committee, well guided by clearly focused issues, appropriate information, and knowledgeable input.

By composition the board planning committee should include a membership that balances the views of the board, medical staff, administration, and other key groups both inside and outside the institution. Some of its members might be appointed by nature of their office or position, and others might be elected by their constituencies.

The individual who is responsible for the planning function should serve as staff to this committee and work closely with the chairman in the development of agenda, dissemination of material to members, presentation of position papers, provision of knowledgeable opinion, and action behind the scenes to achieve consensus. Committee meetings should be well prepared, with background materials circulated well in advance of a scheduled meeting. Because of the broad scope of subjects that will encompass the committee's charge and the divergence of opinion and perspectives of its members, lack of work structure and organization can result in endless deliberations with little substance.

The board's planning committee serves as the central focus for channeling the opinions, proposals, and suggestions of the organization and the many publics served by the institution. Appropriate mechanisms should, therefore, be structured to allow a free exchange of opinion and the opportunity for potentially useful ideas to reach the top planning body. Such ideas could emerge from the medical staff, nursing staff, other employees, community groups, other institutions, or outside agencies.

A particularly good example of this process was observed in a 300-bed community hospital in a large city in Pennsylvania. The hospital had been experimenting for about a year with the process for getting effective input into planning decisions from both internal and external groups. The medical staff had complained that historically their views had not been sought on major planning decisions that were made by an "elite group of board members."

Likewise, community groups were seeking greater involvement in health industry decisions and were getting it through federal legislation mandating their participation on the boards of comprehensive health planning agencies. To respond to these pressures for participatory planning, the hospital created a management planning committee, medical staff planning committee, and a community advisory committee to serve this function. (See Figure 12-1). These groups not only passed on their ideas and proposals to the board committee but also reviewed and commented on the conclusions or recommendations of the board with respect to planning options.

Determining the Institution's Mission

The following questions should be carefully considered by decision makers in evaluating the mission of an institution:*

What population does the institution serve? What are its present characteristics? What are its most important health needs? Are these needs being met by existing institutions and agencies? How well are they being met?

Are there any groups within this population whose health needs are not being met or who are underserved? If this is so, what are the reasons? What efforts should the institution make in this regard?

Is the present mission of the institution relevant to the present needs of the population it serves? What do the institution's various publics think of it and its service? What are the specific patient care services provided by the institution? What is the quality of each of these services? What is the volume of each service? Is the volume sufficient to achieve reasonable economies of scale? Are these programs essential to the present mission of the institution? Do they duplicate the services of neighboring institutions?

What is the role of the institution in the health care system of the area? How do the institution's existing programs and services fit into the overall health care system? What levels of health care does it provide? What arrangements exist to assure that patients requiring services not available in its own facility are referred to other organizations in the area where such services are available?

What is the quality of the institution's overall program? Does it meet or exceed generally accepted standards of the local community? of the area? of the region? of the nation?

Would the institution's patient clientele be better served if any of these services were integrated or combined with the program of another institution? Should any of these programs be dropped because of low volume, poor quality, inadequate resources or irrelevancy?

What are the scope and quality of the institution's ambulatory care services? Do they meet the needs and expectations of local residents?

Does the institution operate or use an emergency ambulance service? Is the service properly staffed with trained personnel? Is the emergency room capable of providing a satisfactory range of emergency services?

Are services provided or have arrangements been made for the care of long-term patients? drug abusers? alcoholics? the mentally ill? Is the institution willing to accept the challenge of caring for such patients if such programs seem indicated in its neighborhood or local community?

What are the educational commitments of the institution? What changes are necessary or desirable to improve them?

What educational arrangements or affiliations does the institution have with medical schools? Is the affiliation meaningful to both institutions?

What are the institution's research capabilities? Are its present research activities an important part of the institution's overall programs? Is sufficient space available for this activity?

What is the nature and extent of the institution's commitments to non-staff physicians in its neighborhood or local community?

Is the Board of Trustees supportive of the administrative leadership of the institution? Is the Board representative of the community served by the institution? What steps has it taken in recent years to seek community input and attitudes to guide in its deliberations?

Is the medical staff organized and qualified? What is the average age of the staff? Have new members been added in recent years? Is there a fulltime staff? How are they selected? What are their responsibilities? What is their contribution to the overall effectiveness of the institution?

---

*Source: N.J. State Health Planning Council, *Planning Guide for Hospital Long Range Plans* (March 21, 1975). (The original version of this list appeared in Joseph P. Peters, *Concept, Commitment, Action*, New York: United Hospital Fund of New York and the Health and Hospital Planning Council of Southern New York, Inc., 1974.)

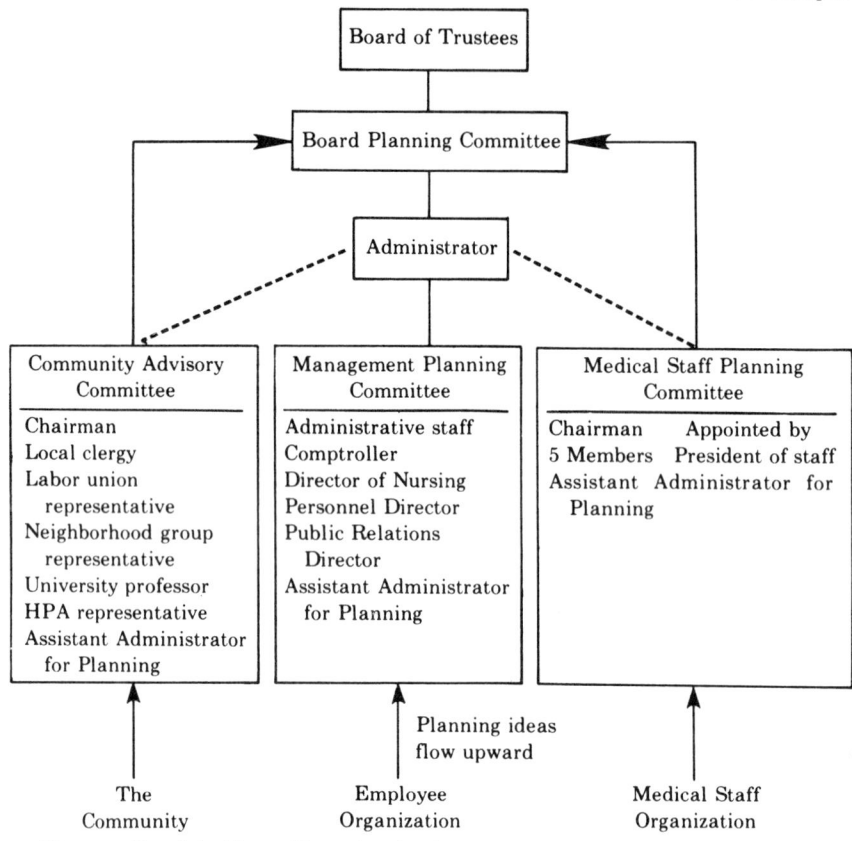

Figure 12-1 Case study: planning committees in a 300-bed hospital

```
                    Board of Trustees
                           │
                           ▼
                 Board Planning Committee
                           │
                           ▼
                     Administrator
          ┌────────────────┼────────────────┐
          ▼                ▼                ▼
```

Community Advisory Committee	Management Planning Committee	Medical Staff Planning Committee
Chairman Local clergy Labor union representative Neighborhood group representative University professor HPA representative Assistant Administrator for Planning	Administrative staff Comptroller Director of Nursing Personnel Director Public Relations Director Assistant Administrator for Planning	Chairman Appointed by 5 Members President of staff Assistant Administrator for Planning

Planning ideas flow upward

The Community — Employee Organization — Medical Staff Organization

*Source: Reprinted from *Managing Institutional Planning* by Martin S. Perlin with permission of Aspen Systems Corporation, © 1976.

Does the institution encounter any unusual difficulties in recruiting and retaining personnel?

Are the institution's financial resources and income capable of supporting its various programs and commitments in accordance with desired standards?

How does the future promise to affect these programs and commitments? Are there any anticipated external happenings which will change what the institution is doing or presently not doing? How will such events or trends affect the capability of the institution to carry out its mission or its programs? Is the institution willing to commit itself to offer new services, to extend its present services, or to reach new population groups? Is the institution prepared to make the necessary changes in structure, programs, or facilities? What "business" will the institution be engaged in five years from now? ten years from now?

Linking Objectives to Mission

The links between mission, long range objectives, and short range objectives must be established if the institution is to implement programs and actions with desired results.

One way of looking at the way objectives interlace is demonstrated in Figure 12-2. The hospital's mission clearly becomes the overriding direction for all other objectives and actions. Long range objectives (usually five to ten years) are the most general and overriding statements of how the hospital plans to carry out its mission in the long run.

Figure 12-2 Linking objectives to mission—a model

BASIC MISSION:
To provide or arrange for high quality comprehensive health care services for the population we serve with the goal of improving the health and well-being of that population, within the limits of available resources

Long Range Objectives (5-10 years)

I.	II.	III.	IV.
Develop the diagnostic and treatment services with special emphasis on early detection, rehabilitation and follow-up.	Develop a comprehensive ambulatory care program, emphasis on preventive and extended care, and increased accessibility.	Improve utilization and productivity of present facilities.	Develop manpower resources with emphasis on physician extenders.

Short Range Objectives (1 Year)
(III: UTILIZATION AND PRODUCTIVITY)

1. Strenghten the planning and coordination between services
2. Expand and improve our utilization review program
3. Initiate a management engineering study of a major service
4. Establish mechanisms for measuring productivity.

A specific set of short range objectives are then stated, which implement each of the long range objectives. Although short range objectives have a greater degree of specificity than long range objectives, they do not state exactly how they will be carried out. Implementation of short range objectives is left for the next level of goal development, namely the operating departments.

Relating Departmental to Institutional Objectives

Clearly, a health institution achieves its mission and objectives through the work accomplished by its operating departments. It is essential, therefore, that each department head establish departmental objectives consistent with institutional objectives and be encouraged to push the process down into the organization.

One of the most common errors made by health institutions is to stop the linking process at the level of institutional objectives. Department heads are given a published list of hospital objectives and asked to submit a list of departmental objectives without demonstrating the links. After the fact analysis by management often finds that some departmental objectives are not desirable, or even worse, that some institutional objectives are not being implemented by operating departments. Knowledge of the relationship between departmental objectives and institutional objectives is also essential to management when it attempts to assess departmental accomplishments and contributions.

The following "Objective Responsibility Chart" (Table 12-1) provides a convenient way to link objectives and to evaluate accomplishments. Beginning with one of the institution's

Table 12-1 Objective Responsibility Chart
Short Range Objective III-1: *Strengthen the planning and coordination between services.*

To be implemented by these departments as follows:		Target Date	Completed
Transport Department:	Correct inefficiencies in the patient transport system, demonstrating a 10 percent reduction in "down time" without sacrificing quality	7/1	
Business Office and Nursing:	Eliminate missed charges for items dispensed by nursing service	8/1	
Purchasing:	Implement an interdepartmental materials management system	6/1	
Admission:	Implement an improved bed control system	8/30	

short range objectives, the chart delineates the responsibilities of each affected department, including the expected date of project completion.

One hospital located in the southeast uses the following cycle to guide its department heads in the development of program objectives:[1]

June and July: Department heads meet with superiors and review planning program, concept of mission and objectives, the development of departmental objectives.

July and August: Department heads meet with supervisors, develop departmental objectives in written form, backed up by narrative description of program, based on planning objectives for the next budget year.

September: Department and administration hold conferences and agree on objectives and narrative description of program for the next budget year. They prepare overall hospital objectives and narrative description of hospital program for the next budget year.

September-October: Overall hospital objectives and program are prepared along with departmental objectives and program description and presented to the board for approval.

October: Approved objectives and program descriptions are shared with department heads, and budget drafts are prepared. Budgets based on objectives and program descriptions are prepared in detail in prescribed, uniform format, including staffing patterns, salary levels, alterations in space, programmed capital expenditures, etc.

At this same time, the department head prepares program objectives and descriptions for the second and third fiscal year for purposes of Section 234 capital expenditures budgeting. The capital expenditures budget for the two additional fiscal years are prepared in draft form at this time. The additional two years are more in the form of "projections" rather than specific operational instruments. The degree of specificity decreases as time extends into the future.

October: Administration prepares overall budget and program descriptions for next fiscal year for presentation to planning committee and board.

November: Planning committee reviews budget, program descriptions, and objectives for next fiscal year and makes recommendations to the board for approval, either as presented or in modified form. Board considers recommendations, reviews budget, program descriptions and objectives and takes formal action for approval.

December: Approved budget, program descriptions, and objectives are distributed to all operating department heads and become operational as of December 31 for the next fiscal year.

Quarterly intervals during budget year: Progress reports including comparative budget statements are prepared and submitted to operational department heads and the board. Variance from program and budget are responded to by department heads and reported to the board. Formal adjustments in program and operating budgets are prepared as numbered revisions and

---
[1] Vernon D. Seifert, "A Model For Institutional Planning" presented at a seminar on Institutional Planning, Tulane University, November 7–9, 1975.

approved by the board as circumstances require.

The first criteria has to do with responsibility. Perhaps the first test of whether an objective will be accomplished is if the individual responsible for achieving the desired results understands and accepts the objective statement. Importance would be attached to the creation of a climate which will develop the attitudes, perspectives, and personal commitment to make the implementation of plans feasible. One of the most effective ways to achieve this climate is by permitting employees to participate in the development of those objectives for which they will be held responsible, or for which their actions are expected to make a contribution. Those responsible for carrying out objectives should feel that they are attainable, given the time and resources available.

The second criteria has to do with the achievement of results. Objectives should be as concrete as possible and should state the results to be achieved. In other words, what outcome or behavior is anticipated as a result of the successful accomplishment of the objective? Related to this criteria is the need to specify by what measures one will be able to determine if the objective has been accomplished.

The final criteria involves the importance of delineating the time frame in which the objective is to be accomplished. Time constraints help establish work priorities and enforce accountability. When several individuals or departments are responsible for different objectives, which must be linked at some predetermined time, accountability for meeting completion deadlines can be essential.

STRATEGIC PLANNING

A Financial View*

The strategy selection process should begin with a "blue sky" discussion of alternative scenarios ten years into the future. Where would the hospital like to be in ten years? How many beds? What programs? What level of assets? What patient mix? What payer mix? How much outpatient care? What affiliations with other hospitals? What other businesses?

After a "wish list" has been developed, the focus should shift to the short run (two to three years). How does the hospital respond to threats? What opportunities are especially attractive? How does the hospital correct weaknesses? At what cost? Often a hospital will discover that it needs to "position" itself before it can take action on some of its long-range plans. For example, it may have to strengthen its financial condition before it is ready to assume more debt. It may have to correct gross physical plant deficiencies to check unfavorable demand trends. It may have to counter a competitor's certificate-of-need application. It may have to solve a short-term cash problem created by growth in patient accounts receivable or large third-party payables. It may have to institute selective cost controls because of Section 223 limitation excess.

The reason for starting with long-range time planning is to prevent it from being overshadowed by the proposed solutions to short-range problems. In fact, the strategy evaluation is likely to shift in focus several times. The outcome of this process should be a one-page document that includes:

- a description of the short-range strategies;
- a description of the long-range strategies; and
- an explanation of the reasons for selecting a particular strategy in favor of the other alternatives considered.

Borrowing Strategy

Given the level of debt capacity established in the financial assessment, should borrowing begin immediately or should it be deferred? Increasing government regulation is causing investors to perceive higher levels of business risk in the health care industry. As a consequence, interest rates go up and long-term debt capacity shrinks. These pressures are causing some financial managers to conclude that immediate borrowing is the only sure way to realize anticipated debt capacity.

Investment Strategy

How should cash be invested to maximize returns? The particular strategy selected will be a

---
*Source: Reprinted from Kenneth M. Jones, Jr., "Long Range Statistic Financial Planning," *Topics in Health Care Financing*, Summer 1981, with permission of Aspen Systems Corporation.

function of the hospital's liquidity requirements, risk preferences, investment expertise and need for nonoperating revenue to meet return on equity targets.

Pricing Strategy

Many of the new programs that hospitals are undertaking will be more price sensitive than traditional acute services have been (e.g., outpatient services). Pricing may play a vital role in the success of a new program. However, the impact of a pricing decision on overall financial returns needs to be carefully evaluated.

Financial managers often have the responsibility of evaluating the risk/return trade-offs among various strategies because they have the expertise necessary for a quantitative analysis of return on equity. This analysis must be balanced with an analysis of the risks involved in a particular strategy. It should take into account the business risk (that the expected volumes, revenues, costs and cash flows will not materialize) as well as the financial risk (that the institution would default on its debt service payments).

Case #1

A financially and operationally healthy medium-sized nonprofit, full-service community hospital is located in a small city with two other hospitals. The physical plant is old and functionally obsolete. The service area demand is growing and this hospital has had a constant 30 percent share of market over the last five years. The service area leader has had a constant 45 percent, and the third hospital has had a constant 25 percent. Management is strong but thin. The health systems agency and the state planning agency have acknowledged the need for more beds to meet the growing demand. The hospital assumes that the cost reimbursement mechanism will change in the next ten years to a flat all-inclusive rate.

The basic strategy for this hospital is to capture a better than 30 percent share of the incremental growth in demand. After a careful analysis of population trends, they determine that the growth over the next ten years will be in women of childbearing age and the elderly. Hence, the obstetrics program and the medical program are emphasized in planning for construction. Flexibility of use of the obstetrics beds is also emphasized, since at some point in the future, these beds may have to be converted to medical/surgical beds.

The hospital's short-term strategy is aimed at "positioning" itself for implementation of the long-term strategy. It increases its cash reserves. It consolidates its position in obstetrics and medicine. It acquires adjacent land. It develops a relationship with the health systems agency. It develops detailed design documents. After two years it is in a position to issue debt to finance construction of hospital replacement and remodeling as well as a free-standing medical office building/clinic for a large obstetrician group practice.

Case #2

A financially and operationally sound medium-sized nonprofit hospital is situated in an urban market. Although the county in which this hospital is located is growing rapidly, the immediate service area is not experiencing any growth. The area is badly overbedded. The physical plant and functional layout are satisfactory. The hospital's financial condition is good, with relatively low debt and high debt capacity. Management is very aggressive. In fact, they are seeking new challenges.

This hospital's strategy is one of growth through acquisition. It plans to use its managerial and financial strength to acquire and operate hospitals located in the rapidly growing area of the county. These "feeder" hospitals will be restricted to primary and secondary services, with the original hospital moving into more expensive (and profitable) specialized surgery services.

The hospital's short-term strategy is to execute two mergers and assume managerial control over the acquired hospitals. Their long-term strategy involves remodeling construction and equipment acquisition to support tertiary services at the original hospital.

The financial manager should be able to summarize the plan in the form of a 10–15-year projection of sources and applications of funds. The rate of return acquired by the projection can be compared to the financial goals established earlier.

Characteristics of Strategic Planning*

Strategic planning is not just master planning with a few additional considerations. It is a dramatically different approach to planning. Four important features of effective strategic planning as compared to master planning are: (1) a shift in orientation from producing services to marketing, (2) recognition that the mission statement is not the starting point of planning, (3) realization that planning is a political, not simply a technical, exercise and (4) understanding that planning is an integral part of management.

Marketing Orientation

The change in orientation from producing services to marketing converts the primary question from "What services do I want to deliver?" to "What services are needed?" and "Who will purchase them?" The starting point for the planning process is also changed. Instead of asking hospital personnel "What services do you want to sponsor?" planning starts with inquiries to identify consumer needs that are not currently being met.

An equally important shift in focus is also implied when strategic planning is adopted. *Production* gives way to *people and population groups* as the main units of focus. While a manufacturing approach focuses on "products we want to produce," a consumer marketing approach identifies important "people" constituencies and their needs. Hospital strategic planning addresses the multiple groups served by and related to the institution: patients, the general public, professional staff, employees, planners and board members. Improving management's ability to diagnose and be responsive to the needs of these various "market" constituencies is the main purpose of strategic planning.

Mission Statement

Traditionally, hospitals (like most complex institutions) operate on a set of implicit assumptions and beliefs that define organizational identity and relationships with the outside world. These contribute to the creation of an "organizational mythology" which underlies their perception of the organization's basic role and purpose—the mission of the organization. Unchallenged, this mythology can lead to planning for inappropriate roles in a context of unrealistic expectations.

Strategic planning, however, does not start with assumptions about institutional mission. Rather, the goal/role elements of a strategic plan are derived only after external and internal assessments are completed, and the associated mythologies fully probed and tested.

Planning As Political Exercise

Master planning has tended to be technical and heavily quantitatively oriented. The emphasis has been on facts, numbers and ratios.

This approach has frequently been inappropriate and has often led to planning efforts that failed to be responsive to social needs or even to institutional values. In a creative strategic planning process, decisions chosen from among realistic options are more likely to reflect value judgments than quantitative assessments.

In addition, an attempt to modify the perspectives of key publics (or power holders) is a legitimate political objective of strategic planning. Technical data will contribute, and contribute substantially, to strategic decision making, but that *alone* is not sufficient to ensure successful implementation. Good plans must be complemented by an emphasis on political process and negotiation.

Strategic Planning As Integral Part of Management

In the past, facility or master planning was often contracted to consultants, and a final planning document was unveiled at the end of a process. In contrast, strategic planning is fully integrated within the hospital's day-to-day management concerns.

Integrating the planning process into the institutional management system requires broad involvement and commitment. The designation of a planner or the appointment of a marketing director does not automatically ensure that the hospital will move into an effective strategic

---

*Source: The remaining material in this section on "Strategic Planning" consists of excerpts from Carl W. Thieme, Thomas E. Wilson, and Dane M. Long, "Strategic Planning for Hospitals Under Regulation," *Health Care Management Review*, Spring 1981. Reprinted with permission of Aspen Systems Corporation.

planning mode. Similarly, unless representatives of all critical hospital constituencies are appropriately involved in resource allocation decisions, strategic planning has not become an integral dimension of management.

Approach to Strategic Planning

A conceptual approach to strategic planning, incorporating the characteristics identified above, is simply illustrated in Figure 12-3.

Strategic planning begins with an external and internal analysis. The external and internal analyses lead to the identification and analysis of critical strategic issues. Strategic options emerge from the analysis of issues. The external, internal and issues analyses provide the background and inform about the development of reshaping of an institution's mission. The development of goals and objectives set institutional strategies and link organizational activities to strategies.

External Analysis

The full range of external forces affecting a particular hospital needs to be realistically identified, and the potential impact of these forces needs to be assessed. The mapping of the external environment sets the territorial boundaries for future hospital operations, defines and assesses the actual and potential markets, identifies franchise opportunities and constraints and provides the basis for assessing how the institution "stacks up" against its neighbors and competitors (not necessarily one and the same). Without an accurate "environmental assessment," a hospital may adopt unrealistic planning goals.

This external assessment leading toward strategy choices involves detailed examination of many critical interfaces between the hospital and its environment.

Demographic Forecasting

A key external variable is the characteristics of population groups potentially served by a health care facility. These groups are the market. Developing an understanding of the probable characteristics of the groups to be served provides important clues as to the types of services and the quantity of services that will be needed and demanded.

Demography is both a science and an art, best left to demographers; however, hospital planners need to approach demographic projections with a healthy skepticism. Following a few simple guidelines can sometimes avoid significant error.

- Research and develop an understanding of

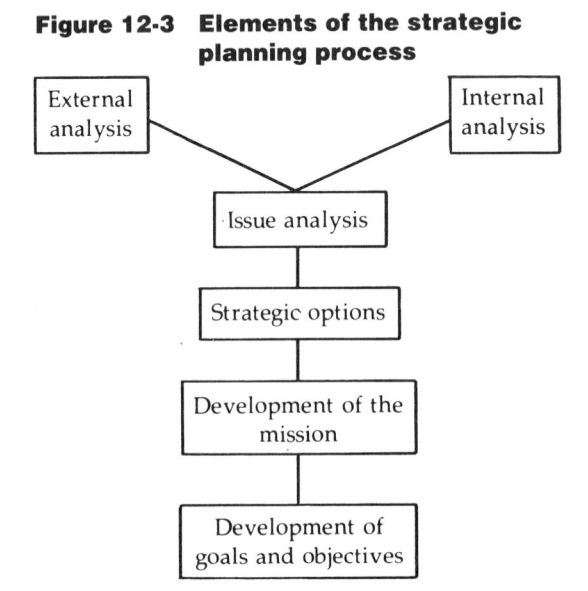

Figure 12-3 Elements of the strategic planning process

External analysis → Issue analysis ← Internal analysis

Issue analysis → Strategic options → Development of the mission → Development of goals and objectives

the methodology used to create a projection. Projections may be based on assumptions that are appropriate when applied to a state as a whole, but may not be appropriate for the local area. Adjustments may be needed.
- Search out more than one projection. Projections often have systematic biases reflecting the interest of particular agencies, e.g., political units tend to overestimate populations because state and federal funds are tied to population estimates.
- Disaggregate the data. If a hospital serves a small portion of a region, and there is real diversity within the region, regional data may mask important characteristics of the populations which are the hospital's markets.

Mapping the Regulatory Environment

Regulatory mapping involves the distillation of the impact of laws and regulations on an individual hospital. This usually can be accomplished by matrixing the law's key provisions against characteristics of the health care system.

For instance in mapping PL 93-641 (the National Health Planning Resources and Development Act) the left-hand rows of such a matrix would identify elements of the law, including the planning system, resource and development, control mechanisms, etc. Across the top of the matrix would be the elements of the health care system or institution.

The elements might include capital formation, facilities, technology, need and demand for services, access, cost, etc. In each cell of such a matrix a simple high, medium or low code can be used to identify and focus attention on key high-impact areas. Such a "map" can help institutions analyze both where and how elements of this law can impact future strategic options.

In addition, such mapping can assist the institution in targeting key committees and agencies and help identify where they should concentrate their resources and focus their attentions on developing working relationships to protect institutional interests. Analysis of such regulatory "maps" may also indicate potential threats for which the only strategic option open to the hospital is business diversification. Regulatory mapping is one of the hardest and most crucial elements to identify in the development of strategic options available to the institution.

Competitive Assessment

Analyzing the institution's key competitors, their strengths, weaknesses and future plans, and identifying from this analysis opportunities and threats is perhaps the most difficult external analysis element for most institutions to deal with in strategic plan development. The analysis involves developing information on key competitors' market positions, utilization characteristics, major changes in services and programs, examination of medical staff patterns (age, mix, etc.), administrative management capabilities, strategic plans, financial positions and resources, building needs and conditions, and other factors. These building blocks of competitive analysis must be analyzed and woven together to extract important elements of competitive advantage and disadvantage. Competitive analysis also involves identification of areas where mutual interests between institutions can be pursued.

Consumer Needs, Demands, Preferences

As the health care industry and its institutions shift from the manufacturing to the market orientation, and as understanding consumer needs and wants becomes more important, health care institutions will have to develop additional external marketing information. Consumers may be patients, physicians, employees and other key publics. By using market research techniques (physician surveys, consumer surveys, focus group techniques, etc.) hospitals are identifying how people access the system, what their preferences are, how they view the hospital vis-à-vis its competitors, and what they identify as critical competitive factors affecting consumer choices. Such research techniques are becoming a crucial element in the understanding of the hospital's external environment and in the development of viable strategic choices available to the hospital.

Program/Service Delivery Trends

Strategic planning requires monitoring and assessing the impact and importance of trends in the delivery of hospital care and health care services. These trends may be technologically based and impact a hospital's need for capital equipment, or reflect social or lifestyle changes that affect the need for a service or the way it is delivered. The recognition of changed attitudes and preferences enabled many hospitals to gain a competitive advantage in maternity care by offering birthing rooms and other amenities.

The key in carrying out an external analysis is not just to accumulate data, but to assess its impact. Analysis is thus used to transform data into relevant information. For example, population projections can be transferred into bed-need estimates. A competitive assessment can point out the needs not being met. A regulatory assessment shows where an institution might be vulnerable and incur financial penalties.

Internal Analysis

To think, however, that planning deals only with externalities creates blind spots and fosters additional misperceptions of hospital capabilities. A comprehensive, hardnosed internal assessment must also be undertaken, but is frequently overlooked (or bypassed) because of the anxieties produced. Such a self-analysis may be painful, but it may also lead to organization development initiatives which will significantly strengthen the organization. Just as the external analysis identified realistic horizons, an internal assessment is needed to purge organizational mythology and develop a balanced picture of hospital limitations, strengths and opportunities for further development.

An internal assessment requires analysis of a variety of data descriptive of an institution, including: utilization of hospital services; diagnoses treated; physician characteristics and admitting patterns; financial performance; facilities inventory; and organizational assessment. The last item, organizational assessment, is one of the most overlooked components of an internal analysis. Essentially it is an evaluation of the organization structure and an assessment of how well that structure works.

Two principles are essential in evaluating institutional data: (1) Whenever possible, the data should be compared to something external. Benchmarks which give perspective should be provided. (2) Trends and patterns should be looked for without worrying about decimal points.

Issue Analysis and Strategic Options

The external analysis and the internal analysis provide the basis for the identification of key issues; the critical challenges and opportunities confronting the institution. In-depth study of the critical issues results in the identification and evaluation of options which provides the basis for a realistic assessment of the institution's mission.

Development of Mission

Development of an institutional mission requires balancing the answers to four fundamental questions: What (services) do we want to do? (What businesses do we want to be in?) What will we be allowed to do? What do we have the resources to do? What does society need?

A mission states the overall, broad purpose and role of an institution. A mission statement has to be broad enough to allow creativity and the development of a vision; yet by its nature, it limits. It circumscribes activity and thereby provides guidance to institutional leaders.

Development of Goals and Objectives

Goals and objectives reflect and operationalize the institutional strategy. A mission statement specifies role and purpose. Goals articulate specific strategies. Objectives specify and operationalize the strategy. Objectives should have three characteristics: they should be measurable; their time for completion should be specified; and the person responsible for them should be identified.

The strength of the approach outlined in Figure 12-3 is that it suggests starting with an objective appraisal of the environment and of the organization and then reassessing the organization's mission and strategy. Starting with the identification of the mission can lead to wishful thinking, not based on reality.

Hospitals that have undertaken planning processes like that outlined above are beginning to develop innovative strategies designed to meet the challenges posed by the environment.

Emerging Strategies

The increased prominence of both regulation and competition has led some hospitals to examine and develop strategies analogous to those used by firms in other regulated yet competitive industries. Such strategies include nonprice competition and vertical and horizontal integration.

Nonprice Competition

Regulation and the current reimbursement schemes are leading hospitals to adopt a classic regulated industry strategy, that of nonprice competition.

Nonprice competition becomes an important strategic consideration when price competition is eliminated or restricted in importance but market conditions make competition likely. With the elimination of price as a competitive tactic, institutions turn their attention to service as the competitive variable. The history of the U.S. airlines industry, prior to deregulation, is a case in point. The development of special clubs, business coaches, in-flight movies, on-flight delicatessens and other amenities was a classic case of nonprice competition.

Critical to this strategy is the assurance that no competitor can or will be allowed to compete on price.

In hospitals, the nature of nonprice competition can take several forms. It can take the form of increased pressure for modern, beautiful facilities; increased efforts to make services available, accessible and acceptable to target populations; or emphasis on developing good will and positive institutional images in the consumer's mind.

One example of this trend is already evident in obstetrics services. Major institutions are providing patients with a variety of obstetrical/delivery options and packages such as 24-hour discharge plans, birthing rooms, follow-up care after discharge, guaranteed availability of desired accommodations and candlelight dinners for new parents.

Nonprice competitive strategies occur most often around those services where consumer choice can be directly affected. Variations on the nonprice competitive strategies occur when the choices among institutions are made at the professional level, physician to physician.

Vertical Integration

The second major strategy pursued by firms operating within a regulated environment is vertical integration. Vertical integration may be backward or forward.

Backward vertical integration means entering into the businesses that supply the resources needed to run the main business operation. A business example would be public utilities buying a coal or oil company or a turbine manufacturer.

In many instances, the industries into which backward integration takes place are unregulated. This often creates opportunities to improve the financial performance of the parent institution. Even using competitive transfer pricing, institutions may be able to receive a higher return on total sales or total assets than currently exists in their own industry. Such integration may also help produce cash flow needed for capital formation in the regulated component.

Hospitals have already begun to examine some of the potential opportunities in backward vertical integration. They have launched businesses in the manufacture of generic pharmaceuticals, prosthetic devices and I.V. solutions. Traditionally, hospitals have been in the laundry business, group distribution and purchasing of products, etc. The strategy concepts of backward vertical integration are starting to be implemented by health care institutions.

Forward vertical integration involves moving closer to the ultimate consumer or end user of products or services. A business example would be railroads moving into the hotel or restaurant business or an electronic component company moving into the manufacture of radio and television sets.

For health care institutions, the potential areas for forward integration are numerous and exciting. They include health maintenance organizations, health-related clinics, satellite facilities, store-front medical services and industrial medicine programs.

Moving into the above markets can in effect redefine the businesses of the institution. Health Maintenance Organizations move the institution into the organized delivery of medicine, industrial medicine into environmental health problems, and diet and smoking clinics into preventive health.

The forward-integration examples raise the question: Are you in the business of acute intervention in illness or is your business health? Your strategic choices may have a large impact on institutional perceptions of business opportunities, competitive posturing and risk diversification.

Horizontal Integration

Horizontal integration is the arena of mergers, acquisitions and consolidation of institutions providing the same or complementary services. It may take three forms: linkage of geographically dispersed institutions or of geographically proximate institutions, and combinations of acute/nonacute inpatient services. The business reasons for employing horizontal integration may be to achieve economies of scale, concentration of management talent, increased access to capital markets or more efficient management of capital resources.

Geographic integration has been the strategy of the for-profit chains and several large not-for-profit groups. They have accomplished this by acquisition or merger, or by independently building new institutions where need existed.

The horizontal integration or expansion strategy allows centralization of management services and the ability to provide key middle management support in an increasingly specialized and competitive environment. Specialized functions needed to implement political strategies in highly regulated environments (i.e., planners, lawyers, financial experts) are affordable for these geographic systems and provide important competitive advantages to them.

The financial benefits of such integration can be substantial. Ability to generate cash flow at each institution, centralize it and redistribute it to high-growth programs, services or geographic areas is one potential advantage. The lowering of overall risk, both financial and regulatory, through geographic diversification is another. This can provide access to capital on very favorable terms.

The history of increased regulation in many industries indicates that the trend toward larger, more concentrated competitors for economic, management and political reasons will continue to be a viable strategy in health care.

The last form of horizontal integration in health care is to expand into a complete spectrum of acute and nonacute institutional health services. This form of horizontal integration attempts to control patient movement throughout the inpatient system. The horizontal integration, for example, of nursing homes, post-acute rehabilitation facilities, hospices and psychiatric facilities into one organization has been a strategy for many providers in recent years. This particular strategy may be especially risky where third party payment mechanisms are not widespread or coverage is not standardized.

Lobbying the Agencies

- Contacts should be developed at many levels in the agencies: chief executive officer to chief executive officer, technical specialist to technical specialist and so on. The relationships should be cultivated on an ongoing basis, and not simply prior to institutional interaction with agency.
- Technical studies, planning committees, technical advisory groups, etc., should be initiated and participated in.
- Prior to adopting policies and procedures, agencies should be helped to understand the institutional point of view.
- If appropriate, employees should be made available to assist agencies in carrying out their responsibilities.
- Former agency employees should be hired.

These are but a few of the activities that may be critical in developing a mutual trust relationship and a better understanding between your institution and outside agencies.

Successful Strategic Planning

Successful strategic planning requires gathering together the appropriate people, providing leadership, staff support and appropriate consulting help, and developing a process that provides for meaningful involvement by key members of the organization. Characteristics for successful planning process include the following:

1. The planning process has an active planning committee composed of the influence leaders among the board, administration and medical staff. In addition to the established influence leaders, the emerging future influence leaders should be tapped.
2. The planning committee is a working committee. Involvement is the key to understanding, and ultimately, commitment.
3. Leadership is by a key trustee, perhaps the future chairman of the board, and by the administrator.
4. Staff support is provided to gather information and perform initial analysis. (When planning fails it is often because of lack of staff support.)

5. Persons with special interests and expertise are involved in task forces conducting in-depth issue analysis. This increases the quality of the analysis and gets broader involvement.
6. Third party objectivity, usually in the form of consultants, helps keep the process intellectually honest.
7. A workplan and timetable are followed. This provides people with a sense of accomplishment and results in the formulation of strategy rather than just the accumulation of information.

Implementing strategic planning requires a conceptual refocusing of the planning activity. It requires a shift from facility-oriented master planning to market-oriented strategic planning. It requires bringing together the institutional leaders and engaging them in a process of candidly assessing the hospital's present situation and future options.

By being market oriented, institutions are more likely to develop programs responsive to people's needs. By developing a healthy planning process, they are more likely to achieve a consensus and institutional commitment to implementation. When achieved, these outcomes improve a hospital's ability to survive and thrive.

SYSTEMS ENGINEERING*

Health systems engineers (frequently referred to as industrial or management engineers) are employed by hospitals and other health care institutions to study facility design and utilization, information flow, personnel utilization, and the degree to which performance objectives are being met, in the expectation that they will be of aid in reducing costs and improving the quality of and access to care.

Eleven activities summarize the majority of services provided by systems engineers:

1. The analysis, design, and improvement of work systems, work centers, and work methods.
2. The establishment of work standards for determining staffing patterns, personnel utilization, and costs.
3. The development of job descriptions, job evaluation plans, merit rating procedures, and employee motivation plans.
4. The design of physical facilities, layout and arrangement, floor space utilization, material flow, and traffic patterns.
5. The installation of systems for production control, inventory control, and quality control in the storing, handling, processing, and using of materials and supplies.
6. The economic analysis of alternative combinations of personnel, materials, and equipment, and the development of models to optimize such combinations.
7. The simplification of paperwork and the design of forms.
8. The improvement of organizational structure, authority-responsibility relationships, and patterns of communications.
9. The development of data processing procedures and management reports in order to establish information systems for managerial control on a continuing basis.
10. The generation of technical information, the forecasting of future needs and demands, and the conversion of relevant information into a form useful in managerial and administrative decision making.
11. The performance of general staff work for the administrator for his use in policy determination, fiscal budgeting, building plans, and public relations.[1]

Operations Analysis

This function is described as making a thorough analysis of an operation by dissecting it into its component parts or elements. Each part or element then is considered separately, and the study of an operation becomes a series of fairly simple problems. Systems engineers have found from experience that few established methods cannot be improved if examined sufficiently.

---

*Source: Reprinted from *Cost Containment through Systems Engineering* by David F. Johannides with permission of Aspen Systems Corporation, © 1979.

[1]From *Hospital Industrial Engineering* by Harold E. Smalley and John R. Freeman © 1966 by Van Nostrand Reinhold Company. Reprinted by permission of the publisher.

Process Analysis

Another term for a similar evaluation is process analysis. It is described as "the act of studying the process used for producing a product for the purpose of developing the lowest-cost, most efficient process which will yield products of acceptable quality." Applied to health care, the end result of a process should result in better health, although objective measurement may be difficult. When a current process is evaluated to find ways of improving it, the analysis usually is made with the aid of one or more types of process charts. The process chart is a convenient way to show the relations among operations, the steps of a process, and such factors as distance moved, working and idle time, cost, operations performed, and time standards. It permits the quick perception of a problem so that improvement can be undertaken in a logical sequence.

Systems Analysis

Another evaluation term is systems analysis. A system is defined as a network of interrelated operations joined together to perform an activity. In a sense, it is a broader application of the operation analysis definition, with key elements reviewed for their negative or positive impact on the decision points of the system.

Systems analysis requires 10 steps in which the systems engineer must:

1. define the problem
2. prepare an outline of the systems study
3. obtain general background information on the areas to be studied.
4. understand the interactions between the areas being studied
5. understand the existing system
6. define the system requirements
7. design the new system
8. prepare economic cost comparisons
9. sell the new system to management
10. provide implementation, follow-up, and re-evaluation[2]

In addition to this process, an effective system should produce the following important results:

1. the right information furnished to the right people, at the right time, and at the right cost
2. a decrease in uncertainty and improvement of decision quality
3. an increased capacity to process present and future volumes of work
4. an ability to perform profitable work that was previously impossible
5. increased productivity of employees and capital, and reduced costs.[3]

To achieve these results, one step is all-important—the design of the new system. Here the information developed earlier is combined into a synchronized approach to desired goals. It requires the recognition that alternative configurations may offer success in varying degrees, which must be assessed. It is a practical process that is limited by the availability of such resources as time, money, and personnel. It remains a key instrument for implementing decisions.

THE HOSPITAL LONG RANGE PLAN: A MODEL OUTLINE*

Though this plan should be basic to the needs of most health care institutions, individual situations might dictate additions or deletions to fit unique circumstances.

I. INTRODUCTION

Purpose of This Plan:
Defines the future role of the institution and develops a long range plan for fulfilling this role.

Approach to the Study:
Describes the rationale for the way in which the plan was developed, including its major components and how the components fit together.

---

[2]Reprinted from *Fundamentals of Systems Analysis* by John M. & Ardra F. FitzGerald by permission of John Wiley & Sons, © 1973.

[3]*Ibid.*

*Source: Reprinted from *Managing Institutional Planning* by Martin S. Perlin with permission of Aspen Systems Corporation, © 1976.

II. THE PLANNING PROCESS

Planning Philosophy:
States the basic institutional philosophy that guided the development of this plan. For example, this institution sought to develop new programs and services only after a thorough study of the community and its needs and potential relationships with other institutions. Further, the process was designed to include the impact of key individuals both inside and outside the institution.

Planning Participants:
The role of the governing body, administration, and particularly the medical staff and community should be clearly delineated as this is an important aspect of project review by planning bodies. A statement of how individual participants were selected and the methods by which their deliberations were structured would also be of value, not only giving proper acknowledgments but also understanding how the final product was derived.

Endorsements:
Provides evidence of the plan's endorsement by the board, medical staff, and key community institutions and groups. Often, letters of endorsement are attached.

III. THE COMMUNITY SERVED

Service Area:
Presents the methodologies used to identify the population groups served by the institution and describes the geographic, political, natural, or other boundaries that encompass those areas.

Service Area Characteristics:
Describes the characteristics of the population residing within the institution's service area with projections of future changes in population growth and composition. Considers future changes in the character of these communities including governmental planning and services, industrial and business development, and other factors that can affect the need for future health services.

IV. COMMUNITY HEALTH NEEDS AND RESOURCES

Forecast of Community Needs:
Presents the methodologies used to forecast the future health program needs of the areas served, considering population and community changes and the expected utilization of health services by that population. Reviews the guidelines and pronouncements of external planning bodies and either confirms or suggests revisions to forecasted area health needs.

Existing Resources and Services:
Describes the nature and scope of the area's health institutions and the services they provide to the study population. Examines the availability of physician and other health manpower.

Service Gaps or Duplications:
Compares forecasted community needs with the provision of existing services to identify present and future gaps or excesses. Describes health services not now provided by community health resources and examines service competition or program and facility duplications.

V. MISSION AND ROLE OF THE INSTITUTION

Mission Statement:
States the reason for the institution's existence and its overall purpose in the community's health care delivery system.

Roles and Relationships:
Describes the part the institution plays along with other health institutions in the community and its present or planned cooperative relationships in the provision of health services to the area's population.

VI. PROGRAMS AND SERVICES

Historical Utilization:
Describes the existing programs and services of this institution and traces their historical utilization by the population served. Identifies, where possible, the internal or external

factors responsible for past utilization patterns.

Planned Programs and Services:
Based on the stated mission and role, and considering the identified gaps and duplications in community health services, this section describes the institution's short and long range plans to carry out service programs in inpatient care, ambulatory care, diagnostic and treatment services, education, research and others that might be relevant.

Projected Utilization:
Projects future utilization of the institution's planned programs and services. Provides statistical information for future program, manpower, facility, or financial planning.

VII. FACILITY EVALUATION

Physical Facilities:
Presents a description and an evaluation of existing physical facilities and their capacity to respond to the needs of planned programs and services.

Manpower:
Examines the institutional manpower complement and its capacity to respond to planned programs and services. Provides a detailed analysis of medical staff composition and their support of the institution through patient admissions and referrals.

Operations and Finances:
Analyzes the operating statistics of the institution with particular emphasis on financial position and capacity to incur further debt.

VIII. IMPLEMENTATION PLAN

Program Priorities:
Places planned programs and services into short and long range priorities and establishes a phased plan for their implementation. Discusses the factors affecting these decisions on priorities and describes the planning assumptions that should be periodically reexamined as each phase of the plan is implemented.

Physical Facility Requirements:
Delineates the requirements for facility modernization, expansion, contraction, or relocation that might be necessitated by each phase of the program plan.

Manpower Requirements:
Describes the numbers and types of manpower needed to staff future programs. Delineates what recruitment efforts or other manpower planning will be required as each phase of the plan is implemented.

Financial Requirements:
Delineates the additional financial resources needed to implement each phase of the plan, with particular emphasis on estimated capital expenditures.

FORECASTING

Forecasting Demand*

There are two practical issues in forecasting that must be addressed as part of selecting a method or strategy for estimating the future. First, how far into the future is it necessary and appropriate to estimate? This decision determines whether short-, medium- or long-range forecasting techniques are appropriate. Second, how far into the past is it necessary and appropriate to collect data in order to make a forecast? The amount of data required, their availability and cost of acquisition will determine which forecasting technique is feasible and reasonable to use.

Future Time Requirements

The period over which a demand for health services is to be forecast is a function of two factors—lead time and duration for the decisions that are to be made based on the forecast. Lead time refers to the period of time it will take to implement a decision; the delay in response peculiar to any specific decision. Duration refers to the period of time during which the decision, once implemented, will continue to interact with demand to affect the organization's performance. Lead time indicates the beginning of the period for which a forecast is needed, and duration indicates the extent or length of the period.

---

*Source: Reprinted from Robin E. Scott MacStravic, "Forecasting Health Services Demand: Timeframes and Data Requirements," *Health Care Planning and Marketing Quarterly*, January 1982, with permission of Aspen Systems Corporation.

Lead Time

It is generally a good idea to have forecasts made as far ahead as the maximum lead time necessary for the types of responses likely to be needed. The hospital should always have its eye on what demand is likely to be five years ahead, in case a dramatic change is in sight and a major response will be needed. Otherwise, the future may sneak up on the organization with a dramatic change in demand that the organization does not have the ability to respond to promptly because of lead time.

Correction Point

For any particular decision there is likely to be a point in time between when it is made and when it is implemented that it can be reversed or modified. A decision to add temporary staff may be cancelable with 12 hours notice, for example, even though its lead time is 24 hours. A commitment to buy a new piece of equipment may be cancelable any time prior to 30 days before delivery. A decision to build a new facility may be reversible up to two years before its scheduled opening, even though its lead time is five years.

Duration

The forecast of future demand should indicate whether or not a long-duration decision is warranted. A confident expectation of continuing high utilization or greater increases in demand would justify an enduring commitment. A forecast of a short-term surge in demand followed by decline or return to normal would suggest some temporary expedient. In either case the expected general pattern of demand, over the entire period of time the decision and its consequences would be in effect, should be incorporated in making that decision.

There is a correction point with respect to duration also. Short of the expected or normal duration for a particular decision, there is likely to be a point where, if demand proves to be other than expected, the situation may be altered accordingly.

Combining lead time and duration, the key period of time for which demand should be forecast is the period from the earliest point that a decision could be implemented (current period plus lead time) to the earliest point where a decision, once implemented, could be corrected (decision point plus correction time). Demand for this period should be estimated with all reasonable care, once for making the decision, then again at the latest possible correction point before implementation. A third series of running forecasts should be made once the decision has been implemented, just far enough ahead to equal the earliest possible correction point after implementation.

Data Requirements

The amount of data about the past and present needed to make a forecast is a function of the technique to be used. Past-based, naive techniques may employ as little as one period's data, but often require from five to ten as a minimum. Since the past alone is an unreliable basis for predicting the future, especially in longer range forecasts, there is limited value in acquiring large amounts of past data, unless a time series or cyclical forecasting technique is to be used.

Future-based forecasting techniques may require no formal data if intuition and experience are used (Delphi). They may require minimal data if simple correlations are to be used, or large numbers of observations if a significant number of influential factors are to be employed. Quantity of data generally adds to knowledge about the present and past, and may not increase the accuracy of forecasts of the future.

Forecasting Utilization*

The purpose of analysis, forecasting and changing markets or market shares is to determine what the use of a specific service will be. Whether future use is passively predicted or specifically targeted for intervention, an estimate of future utilization should result. If change is expected, the factors which will cause such changes should be identified and analyzed. If change is desired, the strategies which will effect such change should be selected and implemented based on their anticipated results. If changes are feared, strategies to prevent them may have to be selected, implemented and their effectiveness estimated.

There are numerous technical approaches to forecasting future utilization. Simple estimates

---

*Source: Reprinted from Robin E. Scott MacStravic, "Resource Requirements for Health Care Organizations," *Health Care Management Review*, Fall 1979, with permission of Aspen Systems Corporation.

assuming no intervention may be made by trend extrapolation or correlation. Such techniques assume that whatever changes or relationships have existed in the past will persevere into the future. But unless the reasons for such trends are identified and understood, the trends should not be relied upon too heavily.

Complex Techniques

Complex techniques such as multiple regressions and simulations may enable the organization to deal with more factors affecting utilization. Such techniques, however, are likely to be expensive and may not always be accurate. Multivariate equations for forecasting beyond next year require estimates of future measures for all the variables used to forecast utilization. Each such estimate is only a guess, so the result may be simply a more expensive and scientific-looking wild guess.

Nevertheless, multivariate quantitative techniques can be very useful as guides to provide insight into how change occurs. When used carefully, they should identify aspects of complex situations that are sensitive to changes in certain factors. Once factors have been identified and their linkage to utilization recognized, forecasts or strategies may be developed that incorporate changes in such factors and their anticipated effects. Sophisticated analytical and forecasting models should assist rather than replace reasoned judgment.

The best forecasting of future use of health services should incorporate some recognition of at least the following:

1. changes in the numbers of people in the service population;
2. changes in the demographic characteristics of the service population (e.g., age, sex, race, income);
3. changes in the attitudes and behavior patterns of the service population (e.g., fertility rates, preference for home care or self-treatment, ambulatory versus inpatient care);
4. changes in the numbers of physicians serving the service population;
5. changes in medical practice patterns (e.g., length of stay, preference for ambulatory versus inpatient care, new technology); and
6. changes in the environment affecting utilization behavior (e.g., national health insurance, developments by competitors, employment levels).

Forecasting Manpower Needs[*]

Manpower forecasting is the prediction of needed health care and the availability of personnel to perform the needed health care functions for some future time period. Each department is expected to forecast future supply and demand, areas of expected operations and manpower needed taking into consideration expected turnover, retirements, vacation benefits, etc. by training and utilizing their personnel. The main steps in the Manpower Planning process are:

1. *Analyze the present supply situation by making an inventory of work forces:*

    - How many employees do we have?
      by department
      skill
      age
      sex
      education
      classification
      career interest
      length of service

    - Analyze present work force trends and problems:
      absences
      turnover
      vacancies
      recruiting problems
      numbers in training
      standards
      wage/salary distribution

    - Analyze organizational structure and manpower policies:
      duplications
      underutilizations
      supervision ratio
      policy problems

---

[*]Source: Reprinted from Joan Holland, "Workshop: Manpower Planning to Meet Needs," *Health Care Management Review,* Fall 1976, with permission of Aspen Systems Corporation.

2. *Analyze the demand situation—short and long term:*
   - Analyze organization plans and future priorities:
   activity changes
   types of work
   needs forecast
   budget forecast

3. *Analyze productivity trends:*
   - technological changes
   productivity experiences of the past
   governmental/environmental changes

4. *Evaluate and update the forecast:*
   - Analyze the flows and trends in the supply of manpower in relation to future needs
   - Prepare tentative manpower forecast

5. *Evaluate and update the forecast periodically:*
   - Inaugurate and evaluate related processes of recruitment, selection training, career planning and organizational development.

Chapter 13—Strategies for Growth

GAINING MORE BUSINESS*

Any hospital within an area which becomes economically healthier through increase in the number of hospital beds filled, does so usually at the expense of another. If the beds used in one hospital increase, those filled in another often decrease.

How can a hospital survive without merely redirecting the flow of patients away from the doors of its neighbor to its own doors? There are several ways to do this:

1. Extend the area of service by creating a physical facility at some distance which opens the hospital's doors to a population to which it previously did not have access. The location will determine the effect on neighboring hospitals. Often such a satellite is a vehicle for primary health care sponsored by the hospital. Depending upon local circumstances, it could increase, not simply redirect, the access to health care in a community previously denied adequate hospital facilities.
2. Provide a new hospital service which expands the hospital's role, such as an emergency room, an open-heart surgery program or a hospital-based home-care service. If this method creates access to formerly unavailable and needed health care resources, it properly creates additional sick days. But if the method undesirably duplicates resources, it is contrary to public interest.
3. Sponsor recruitment of a physician to the area in anticipation of hospital referrals in loyalty to that sponsorship. To the extent that the physician satisfies a community need, the public benefits. But the development of a new medical practice with a specific hospital allegiance in the existing patient base of an area serves only to redirect patient flow.
4. Appeal to the community in areas where the hospital renders direct health care. The health care industry increasingly sanctions advertising special services, such as an outpatient clinic, an emergency room or a drug abuse center. Such action may appropriately increase the use of the hospital's facilities by allowing the area's true but previously suppressed morbidity to express itself.

These four approaches to increasing hospital census—the new satellite area, the new hospital service, the imported physician and the direct appeal to the community—all serve to increase census by bringing persons to the hospital who need to be there and who would not otherwise have gone to any hospital. Achieving this goal without causing overuse or duplication may test the integrity of the administration's motivation. Is the move made to satisfy the community's

---

*Source: Reprinted from Wyndham B. Blanton, Jr., M.D., "The Hospital Census Problem: Ways to Fill Hospital Beds," *Health Care Management Review*, Spring 1979, with permission of Aspen Systems Corporation.

health need or the hospital's economics? Or is this an instance where the two go hand-in-hand?

The first three approaches and usually the fourth require the hospital's commitment to new goals and a large amount of cash at the beginning. What can administrators do within their own organizations to avoid or supplement such costly demand?

Increasing Census by Changing Physicians' Habits

Basically the hospital executive can (1) facilitate the increased referral of patients from outlying physicians and others to the members of the current admitting physician staff; (2) encourage local physicians to shift their allegiance to the hospital and (3) attract an increased proportion of the hospital practice of each physician on the staff who presently admits to several hospitals.

In all three of these actions, the hospital administrator is trying to change the physician's attitudes and habits. It can be done, but only if (1) the particular hospital's name and image comes to mind when a potential referring or admitting physician considers hospitalizing a patient, and (2) something makes the thought stick and the idea comfortable. Obviously, these reactions require more than creating a technically competent hospital. If physicians referred patients to only the technically best hospital, all patients would be lined up at one door. That's not often the case in the multihospital town.

What Referring Physicians Look For

But good relations with admitting physicians go beyond the administrator's own public relations efforts. Referring physicians look for many qualities in the hospital to which they send their patients.

Pleasant Physician-to-Physician Relationship

First, they want a physician to whom the patient can be referred. With obvious exceptions, referrals for hospitalization are not to hospitals, but are to specific physicians. Referring physicians are not going to be content, and the hospital will not continue to receive their referrals, unless there is a pleasant, easy and repeatable physician-to-physician relationship.

Referring physicians want to be able to pick up the telephone and say, "Bill, I have a patient on the way. He about him so yo be able to tell talked to the do They do not wa had to struggle t think your patie pital?"

Continued Communications

Second, referring physicians want continued communications. They want a report back after admission telling them that the patient did get there, reports of significant changes in the patient's progress in the hospital and a report as soon as possible after discharge.

Why do referring physicians want all this? They need the academic satisfaction of knowing, and they want to be able to deal knowledgeably with the patient's family. There is nothing worse than to have a patient's wife call up and say, "Joe got back from the hospital today. Now what do I do?" And the home physician has to say, "Darned if I know."

Comprehensive Quality Service

Third, physicians look to the hospital to which they refer for comprehensive service. They do not like to have their patients bounced between hospitals seeking complete service.

Fourth, physicians obviously must demand quality. In no way can they satisfy their own feelings of involvement and liability if they send a patient into a situation which they do not think will produce a quality result.

Finally, referring physicians seek patient satisfaction. Seldom is a referring physician more unhappy than when a patient comes back and says, "Yes, I survived, but . . . ."

Increasing Admissions from Staff

In addition to stimulating referrals to the hospital and its staff, administrators must promote more admissions from the hospital's own courtesy and active staffs.

They can do so by (1) encouraging a shift in the basic allegiance of a local physician to one hospital from another, and/or (2) stimulating further admissions from those physicians whose partial loyalty the hospital already holds.

although the hospital may desperately need the physician's contribution to the census, it only needs physicians who can deliver quality medical care, foster the total hospital objectives and work as a physician-citizen by teaching and doing committee work. Influencing allegiances is one of the most sensitive facets of the competition among hospitals, because every gain to one is a loss to another. It is far more threatening than bringing in the new physician from a different area.

DIVERSIFICATION*

Diversification can range from merely increasing the hospital's product line to engaging in various operations that are not generally associated with hospitals. Many hospitals are discovering that through diversification they can position themselves both defensively and offensively and ensure their survival for many years to come.

The motivation for hospital diversification may be more fully understood in the context of some of the new trends in the health care environment that are encouraging hospitals to diversify. Four of the most prominent trends are: (1) a marked increase in capital erosion, (2) a growth in the demands that must be addressed by the health care delivery system, (3) an increase in competition for the hospital's traditional market and (4) increased awareness by hospital managers of the need for improved business management techniques.

1. Capital Erosion

Most hospitals face the threat of capital erosion and if it is not detected and treated properly it can become a terminal illness for an organization. Growing hospital dependence on "cost payers" (who do not pay full economic costs for health services) and state rate review agencies (who often take arbitrary actions and consider only short-range objectives such as artificially reducing hospital rates in order to meet their political goals) are leading hospitals to discover that their rather fragile capital base is slowly being eroded because of insufficient revenue collection. As a result, the financing of replacement, expansion or enhancement of technology is becoming contingent on the hospital's ability to acquire capital from nonoperating sources. Diversification to other sources of revenue is one means that could result in accumulation of additional capital or at least slow the erosion of capital.

2. Health Care Service Demand

Because of increases in the costs of new technology and the emphasis on cost-effective care, hospitals are beginning to deemphasize acute care services in favor of prevention and outpatient treatment. Diversification into expanded services is not normally motivated by the goal of expanding the revenue base, but rather by the desire to satisfy public demands and improve the quality of health care in the community. Expanding or integrating multiple health services is commonly called vertical diversification.

3. Competition

Because of the increasing threat of competition through health maintenance organizations, emergency centers, birthing centers and so on hospitals are in the unfamiliar position of price and service access competition. They now have to consider offering many of the services offered by their competitors in order to retain their market share. Again, the traditional acute care hospital is forced to look beyond a singular product line of acute care services and related ancillary departments to a more comprehensive product line.

4. Improved Management

Hospital management is undergoing a transformation from management geared toward achieving idealistic goals, with little regard for cost effectiveness, to a realistic business management approach that balances the general financial welfare of the organization with the achievement of practical goals that improve a hospital's delivery of health care programs. Managers and trustees are looking beyond the confines of the hospital for diversification ventures that will increase the hospital's long-term ability to survive.

---

*Source: Reprinted from G. Rodney Wolford, "Is Diversification for You?" *Topics in Health Care Financing,* Summer 1981, with permission of Aspen Systems Corporation.

Areas of Diversification

Diversification can mean increasing the product line of an organization (related diversification) or engaging in varied operations not directly related to an original line of business (unrelated diversification). Both forms of diversification should be considered by hospitals.

Related Diversification

Related diversification can be vertical or horizontal. Under vertical diversification, the hospital may expand its product line by offering more comprehensive levels of health care through increased services. Under horizontal diversification, the hospital diversifies, usually outside its immediate geographic service area, by expanding its operations to more than one hospital or health care entity. Some of the areas that could be considered when studying the possibilities of health-related diversification are:

A. Vertical Diversification
  1. Outpatient surgical unit
  2. Birthing centers
  3. HMOs
  4. Partial hospitalization psychiatric centers
  5. Hospice care
  6. Skilled nursing facility
  7. Cardiac rehabilitation
  8. Commercial laboratory
  9. Emergency centers
  10. Ambulatory care centers
  11. Ambulance services
  12. Industrial medicine
  13. Executive fitness programs
  14. Elderly housing
B. Horizontal Diversification
  1. Hospital acquisitions
     a. Purchase (ownership)
     b. Long-term leasing
  2. Management contracts
     a. Total hospital
     b. Department management

Unrelated Diversification

Since unrelated diversification is as broad as the existing business world, it is practically unlimited. Hospitals can diversify into any type of business venture.

Example:
1. Local commercial businesses—gasoline stations, office equipment suppliers, florist shops, etc.
2. Real estate investment and speculation—undeveloped land, residential rentals, business rentals, physicians' office rentals, etc.
3. Extension of hospital support services—laundry service, computer service, business office services.

When a hospital is considering diversification, the use of marketing techniques for measuring the needs for a specific product is a necessary task in the planning and decision-making process. With the broader application of marketing techniques, a hospital may be able to identify major health-related services that are not being provided to a public that desires such services.

Financial Analysis

The decision-making process for diversification efforts requires a thorough financial feasibility study. The facts and assumptions that have been derived from the planning and market analysis process are converted into measurable financial data that are used to define capital requirements, project revenues and expenses, determine the resulting cash flow and compute the expected return on investment. The financial feasibility study is much like a summation, expressed in financial terms, of all data collected and assumptions made on a proposed diversification effort. The financial study should weigh the expected demand for a particular product against the economic cost of providing the product in concise terms.

Although the ability to obtain outside capital is becoming increasingly difficult because of continued capital erosion, the financial manager should make predictions on the alternative sources of capital that may be available, and determine the cost and appropriateness of each source.

Operating forecasts based on the predicted demand for a product and the projected expenses of providing the new product must be incorporated into a set of financial statements that project at least three years of operating results. Based on these operating results, cash flows can be determined and the rate of return on invested capital can be computed.

The objectives for the rate of return on investment for diversification efforts may vary with the purposes of the diversification. There are usually some "benevolent" services that hospitals must offer without achieving an acceptable rate of return on their investment. However, like all business concerns, hospitals must weigh their financial stability against their intended mission.

In many instances, even though health services are needed by the community, and the demand is significant, inadequate reimbursement by cost payers and other third parties may create a situation in which the return on investment is reflected as a loss. For example, hospice services, preventive medicine programs and, in many states, skilled nursing services are in demand, and could be considered cost-effective, but because of inadequate reimbursement hospitals are reluctant to consider such diversification efforts.

Risk usually increases as the hospital enters into diversification activity in non-health-related areas. Correspondingly the required rate of return on investment should be higher.

Corporate objectives regarding the rate of return on capital necessary to prevent potential capital erosion are essential to the strategic planning process.

Organizational Approaches

For some diversification efforts, organizational changes may be necessary to retain the tax-exempt status of a nonprofit hospital. For other efforts, more drastic organizational changes may have to be made, such as merging or consolidating with other hospitals to achieve a broader base of capital.

If the revenue derived from the new business might be so substantial that the tax-exempt status of the organization would be questioned, a nonprofit hospital could consider conversion to for-profit status. Conversion is also a means of positioning for the future, since for-profit status could increase the capability of obtaining necessary equity capital.

Recently many hospitals have considered and implemented for-profit entities as subsidiaries owned by the hospital organization. Ownership in these for-profit entities is most frequently held through a foundation that has been established to protect the hospital's philanthropic capital from potential government de facto appropriation.

Even more radical moves are being explored by tax-exempt multihospital systems. Forecasters have predicted that the progressive nonprofit multihospital systems would start to expand by acquiring or merging with investor-owned multihospital systems.

DEVELOPING NEW HEALTH SERVICES*

To a great extent, the "need" and potential demand for health services is virtually infinite. As inpatient and conventional medical services programs become increasingly constrained by government regulation and reimbursement, and increasingly competitive, interest inevitably will grow in opportunities for diversification. Growth is accepted as an almost universal measure of success, and in many areas, growth will be possible only through development of new programs.

Great care should be taken in examining new program alternatives. It is a common phenomenon for almost any development, even before it is tried and proved, to spawn competitors. Unless a new program can be expected to succeed against potential competition, it probably should not be attempted. Clear indication of success measures, expectations, and the actions in the market necessary to achieve success should be spelled out and analyzed relative to each opportunity.

Many development opportunities are related closely and should be considered together. If each is supportive of the other, promoting greater and more efficient use of facilities, equipment, and personnel, it may be advantageous to develop them together, even though the initial investment may be larger. Multiple development of interacting options may provide multiple avenues for success, enabling generally positive outcomes, even if parts of the program fall short.

Virtually all new program opportunities require conscious marketing analysis and effort, in contrast to more traditional programs dependent on the successful recruitment of physicians. Most can be developed with relatively little capi-

---

*Source: Reprinted from *Marketing Objectives for Hospitals* by Robin E. Scott MacStravic, with permission of Aspen Systems Corporation, © 1980.

tal investment through use of existing facilities or leasing of space. All entail some risk, however, since marketing and resources development costs are likely to be significant. Most have some promise of developing additional users of traditional services through disease detection or referral.

All these programs are susceptible to conventional though adapted marketing techniques and all require some formal approach to promotion (advertising or publicity). All are subject to some internal resistance or at least concern because they both extend the bounds of traditional medical services and border on the corporate practice of health care. All may have to be "sold" to support publics as well as potential users of specific services, both through design (product, price, place) and persuasion (promotion). (See Figure 13-1 for "Sources for Hospital Admissions.")

The following sample of developmental opportunities represents programs that have been developed successfully in at least a few settings. Each of the opportunities is sketched only briefly, with emphasis on marketing implication.

Checklist for New Services

1. Are there market segments (such as the aged) for which you could develop a new service program (e.g., day care, nutrition services, speech and hearing)?
2. Do you now have the basic capability of providing those services or would you have to start from scratch?
3. What is your present competition and what does it offer in terms of product, price, and place to that segment?
4. What other organizations have a better basic capacity to provide such services (personnel, equipment, facilities, location) and might decide to do so?
5. What can you do that is better than existing and potential competition?
6. What would be the impact on your organization if you succeeded in implementing such a program? At what levels of utilization?
7. What internal groups must be won over to the idea for it to succeed?
8. What external groups?
9. How might the program be developed so as to improve the probability that internal groups will support it?
10. Can you involve potential consumers or referral agencies in developing the program?
11. What groups or individuals might oppose the development and for what reasons?
12. Can they be won over or is it necessary to defeat them?
13. What strategies can you use for either?
14. What benefits can you promise to interested groups as a result of implementing the program and at what costs?
15. How can you communicate most effectively to the precise segments of the market most likely to use the program?
16. What message will be most likely to stir their interest?

Types of Services

Outpatient Surgery

Outpatient surgery is an already well-established alternative to traditional patterns of care. Whether freestanding or hospital-based, such programs offer distinct cost, convenience, and quality advantages. By saving an overnight stay in the hospital, recipients enjoy reduced charges and less disruption of their lives, though the former advantage may be eliminated by the vagaries of health insurance. The psychological and social advantages of outpatient surgery are considerable, as the risk tends to be perceived as very small when surgery can be done without an overnight stay.

The biggest consideration in developing an outpatient surgery program probably should be whether it represents simply an alternative approach to providing the same services to the same markets or is likely to involve new services or new markets. If a hospital's inpatient surgery program is keeping many beds full, and use of operating room facilities is optimal, switching a large number of individuals to outpatient status simply will decrease inpatient revenues and lower occupancy. If an outpatient program produces greater use of operating room facilities in a hospital where lack of beds reduced surgical workloads, or enables an organization to see more patients, the benefits are likely to be greater.

At least three markets are critical to a successful outpatient surgery program. First and foremost are surgeons and referring physicians who must accept outpatient surgery as superior or at least equal to the inpatient alternative in terms of their values: safety for the patient, income for the physician, malpractice risk, ac-

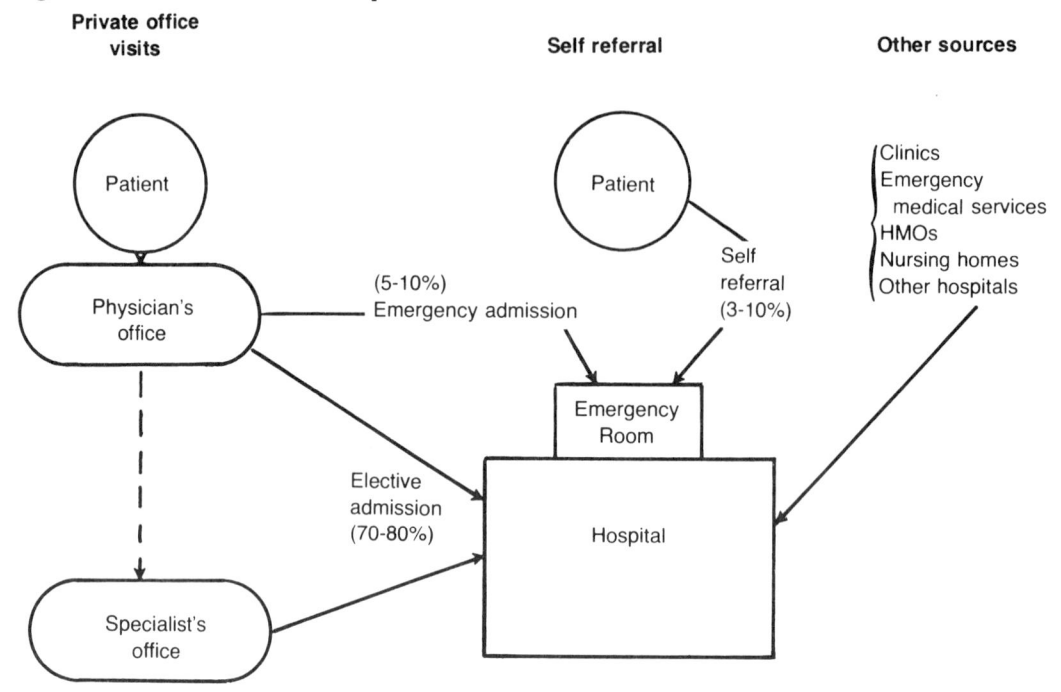

Figure 13-1 Sources for hospital admissions

Private office visits — Self referral — Other sources

- Patient → Physician's office
- Physician's office → Emergency admission (5-10%) → Emergency Room
- Physician's office ⋯ Specialist's office
- Physician's office / Specialist's office → Elective admission (70-80%) → Hospital
- Patient → Self referral (3-10%) → Emergency Room
- Emergency Room → Hospital
- Other sources (Clinics, Emergency medical services, HMOs, Nursing homes, Other hospitals) → Hospital

NOTE: Percentages are based on experience from 25 completed marketing studies by Hospital Corporation of America.

Source: Reprinted from Terence Scott, "Estimating the Market for Physician Services," *Health Care Planning & Marketing Quarterly,* July 1981, with permission of Aspen Systems Corporation.

ceptability to the family, etc. Second are the patients and families themselves, who may resist or welcome an outpatient alternative, depending on how they see themselves affected. Third are the health insurance companies whose coverage policies may discriminate inadvertently against outpatient surgery.

All three are interrelated closely, since the judgments by decisionmakers (referring physician, surgeon, patient/family) all will be affected by cost and quality perceptions.

Screening Services

Screening programs are aimed at early detection of chronic conditions that can be corrected or at least controlled through medical care, diet, etc. Effective screening programs are being carried out for diabetes, hypertension, glaucoma, blood cholesterol/triglycerides, visual, hearing, and other common but frequently undetected problems. The benefit to the community is substantial: early detection of major health threats, potential reduction in costs if early treatment prevents acute levels of need, and identification of major communitywide problems that might be dealt with preventively (e.g., lung diseases resulting from occupational or environmental pollution).

The key to screening programs is to make the product as simple as possible, a service that can be done quickly, without pain or embarrassment, yet is accurate. Moreover, screening should be done only for conditions where early intervention significantly improves the quality of results, or at least reduces the cost of care. Screening that merely promises early identification without changing the consequences is more harmful than beneficial.

Place considerations suggest locating screening services as convenient as possible to where large numbers of persons congregate: downtown parks or malls, shopping centers, etc. Such services also may be offered at the institution if a second purpose is to raise the level of community awareness of its existence, to impress individuals favorably with a new building, or similar reasons. The price normally should be free, both of out-of-pocket costs and of any discomfort.

Referral of persons with positive findings should be handled very carefully. An aggressive, competitive approach would be to refer everyone possible to the organization's own treatment programs or medical staff. Except in a one-hospital or one-clinic community, however, it may be better to refer them to their own physician if they have one, and offer the organization as a choice only to those who claim no personal physician relationship.

Promotion of screening services can be carried out legitimately through public service announcements in the news media. Schools and social service agencies often will be willing to promote screening services through announcements and posters. National organizations such as heart associations and cancer societies will be able to supply materials and assistance. Joint sponsorship with such organizations may be necessary as a *quid pro quo*, but should be well worth the price. The specific benefits to the organization of new patient referrals as well as general public relations advantages make screening for problems the institution is prepared to handle a typically rewarding option.

Sports Medicine

With increasing interest in exercise, and perhaps the likelihood that we'll all be doing more walking, running, and biking as gasoline supplies dry up, there are bound to be increasing numbers of sore muscles, joints, feet, knees, etc. As a result, there will be a growing market for sports medicine programs. While a physician's services are necessary on occasion, a physical therapist will be very useful in initiating and monitoring corrective exercise programs, hydrotherapy, flexibility conditioning, and other direct services.

Consultations by orthopedists, podiatrists, and physical medicine and rehabilitation specialists may be called for on occasion. The equipment required for a sports medicine program need not be extensive or expensive, although considerable space is needed to carry on diagnostic therapy and exercise activities on a regular basis.

The newsworthy event approach to publicity is a logical choice for sports medicine programs. If local sports heroes can be encouraged to visit, test out the facilities, etc., the "legitimacy" of the program may be established. Descriptions of services and hours should be placed in areas frequented by sports participants—Y's, community centers, tennis and racquetball clubs, and jogging areas.

Behavior Modification Programs

The general area of behavior modification programs covers a host of specific services. These include diet and nutrition programs, stop-smoking clinics, exercise promotion, phobia clinics, etc. They generally are fairly remote from traditional medical care and, in any community, are likely to be offered by a number of diverse organizations. Most include some sort of consciousness-raising together with group support and educational approaches to modifying undesirable behavior.

Individuals may enter such programs on referral from physicians and social service agencies, or on their own. Industries may encourage workers or executives to partake of specific services, such as exercise or diet clinics. Many persons are likely to be interested potentially in more than one program. The health care organization has some advantages in providing such services where linkage to medical care is useful. Medical testing and monitoring is helpful for exercise programs and diet clinics. Psychiatric backup services may be worthwhile for any behavior modification program where severe emotional problems are involved.

Health care organizations are likely to enjoy credibility advantages over unfamiliar single-purpose agencies. They also may be able to use existing facilities such as physical therapy areas for exercise. Care must be taken in assigning facility costs and overhead to such programs, lest the costs push charges above competitive levels.

The critical market factors in achieving success in such programs are likely to be place and promotion. Evening hours and local sites are likely to be essential in attracting working people to regular meetings. Schools and churches may be available as inexpensive facilities, and both are likely to have accessible parking. Price can be adjusted based on the competition and the size of groups attracted to the programs. Dieticians, physical therapists, psychologists, social workers, and other professionals already working in health organizations may be interested in staffing the programs for extra income.

Since the capital outlay for these programs is very low, all provide opportunities for toe-in-the-water approaches. Some preliminary market research as to the level of interest, attitudes toward the potential sponsoring organization, and nature of the competition still would be worthwhile, however. Where use of ancillary services is promoted (lab tests in diet programs, stress tests and EKGs for exercise services, etc.), additional revenue should be anticipated.

Birthing Centers

There is a growing interest in alternative approaches to obstetrics. The high-cost sterile institutional experience of hospital obstetric programs is being questioned increasingly. One source of objection appears to be related to feminist resistance to turning over control to predominantly male obstetricians. Another is the expensive, impersonal environment. A third comes from the feeling that birth is a natural phenomenon and ought to take place in a natural setting.

The result of these attitudes is the growth of home deliveries and freestanding birth centers. Yet, from a medical perspective, many of the clients of such alternatives are taking a dreadful risk.

Hospitals may be able to offer the advantages of the alternatives without the disadvantages. Birthing centers may be developed adjacent to or even as part of the hospital. Given the low utilization of obstetric services, hospitals may be able to offer both the traditional medical and the newer alternative approaches to obstetrics. The alternative program with its lower cost and homelike atmosphere may be used up to the point that medical intervention is deemed necessary.

Industrial Health

The general area of industrial health can include a number of specific services. At the simplest level, new employees may be given preemployment or insurance physicals, for example. Expanding further, employees in risky industries may be monitored regularly for conditions affecting their lungs, blood, etc. The working environment itself may be monitored for hazards, either of accidental injury or occupational disease, including stress from noise, employment pressure, or other occupational causes.

Marketing services to industry is a slightly different problem from marketing directly to the public. First, the advantages to the specific industry of having a health service program must be identified and designed into the program. Second, the advantages of your organization as the source of the program must be clear and real. The advantages of marketing to industry lie in the large number of patients who come with each industrial concern recruited, in contrast to direct marketing to the general public. Similarly, the large volume of use that can result should enable the organization to offer high quality services at reasonable costs.

PRIMARY MEDICAL CARE

Overview*

As family practitioners and general internists replace general practitioners, the new physicians are less likely to refer patients to other physicians for routine surgery, medical care, or obstetrics. Institutions and organizations that have relied on referrals from outside their control have seen diminished utilization and revenue.

For such organizations, the development of their own primary care programs offers two distinct advantages. First, it promotes greater use of facilities and equipment as individuals increase their use of services. Second, it creates new, internal sources of referrals for specialized services. The proximity of specialists, relationships with colleagues that develop, and mutual economic advantages tend to firm up referral patterns when the organization sponsors its own primary care programs.

These are likely to be barriers, however. Specialist groups and hospitals may resent the loss of power that comes from bringing in a number of primary practitioners. Unless the specialists yield a little on privileges related to simple surgery and obstetrics, they may be unable to attract new primary care physicians. If they do yield, they may be going counter to their own principles and automatically be decreasing the percentage of cases that will be referred. They may see the introduction of primary care services as a dilution of their specialist image, as well.

---

*Source: Reprinted from *Marketing Objectives for Hospitals* by Robin E. Scott MacStravic with permission of Aspen Systems Corporation, © 1980.

Sponsorship of primary care programs is likely to be somewhat riskier for hospitals than for medical groups. If physicians are recruited for the primary care program on the basis of salary compensation or contract, they eventually may become disenchanted with the constraints of the institutional linkage and strike out on their own. This could leave the institution holding the bag of primary care facility without patients. A medical group, in contrast, can make the primary care practitioner a full and equal participant in the group's affairs and income, making retention more likely.

Populations in truly isolated rural regions, or areas where residence turnover is high, are better prospects for new primary care programs. Care must be taken to be sure that persons in such areas are willing to change their way of dealing with primary care needs and have sufficient numbers and income to support such a program financially. The reason for any current absence of primary care physicians should be examined carefully. Perhaps these reasons will represent a problem that a sponsored program can solve, or an insurmountable barrier to successful development by anyone.

The Market for Primary Care*

The primary care market is comprised of potential patients who must be attracted directly rather than referred by physicians. Much of primary care (e.g., preventive or routine maintenance services) is perceived by most people as of marginal utility, and subject to personal choice as to whether and where to seek it. In contrast to inpatient or true emergency care, the patient is likely to have a definite notion as to what constitutes an acceptable quality of care, rather than rely on the expertise of the physician. In developing a primary care program, the hospital must attract patients directly, to make initial contact with and become regular users of primary care services.

If a hospital proposes to develop a new primary care center even in an area totally devoid of physicians, it must draw its customers from one or more of the following sources:

---
*Source: Reprinted from Robin E. MacStravic, "Marketing Health Care Services: The Challenge of Primary Care," *Health Care Management Review*, Summer 1977, with permission of Aspen Systems Corporation.

- People who now receive primary care from sources they may be willing to abandon in favor of a more accessible alternative.
- People who now use little or no primary care but would if a source were made available.
- Growth or migration which will produce more or different customers.

The easiest method of estimating the market would be to simply count noses and multiply each times some physician/population ratio. If it is assumed that there ought to be one physician per 2500 population, then a market area with 10,000 population and no physicians should presumably be able to support four physicians. A more complex calculation might include counting the population (e.g., 10,000 people), multiplying by an anticipated utilization rate (e.g., three visits per person per year) to yield total utilization (30,000 visits), then dividing by some expected productivity level per physician (e.g., 6000 visits per year) to yield physician requirements (in this case $30,000 \div 6000 = 5$ physicians).

Approaching the Market

The marketing discipline offers many potentially useful concepts and techniques for primary care program development. Because the hospital is trying to "market" a service directly to the customer (patient), the primary care situation is very much analogous to traditional marketing situations. It is likely that most, if not all the following techniques of approaching the market can be useful:

- **Identify and measure** exactly what the consumer needs from primary care. The "utilities" of such care include: relief from anxiety, relief from pain, protection from illness, etc.
- **Analyze current responses** available in the event of such needs. The "competition" may include non-medical providers such as pharmacists, chiropractors, faith healers, etc., as well as physicians in distant areas. Determine the utilities vs. costs of such responses from the consumer perspective.
- **Decide the feasibility and desirability of responding to unmet needs** given the hospital's financial, personnel and other resources.

- **Determine the potential for attracting patients** willing and able to pay (out-of-pocket, private health insurance, Medicare, Medicaid, etc.) what the hospital has determined to be requisite charges for services.
- **Identify the specific market segments** which may be particularly attractive in terms of potential utilization and payment or which may require a separate product, price, place or promotion. Characteristics such as income, education, location, ethnic identity, health status, age, etc., may suggest separate treatment in some phase of program development.
- **Design the services, locations, hours of operation, facilities, personnel, equipment, etc., most appropriate to the "markets" identified.**
- **Determine which services the organization is best suited to provide, are most likely to succeed.**
- **Decide on the "price" for such services,** including all that potential patients must go through in order to utilize them. This includes not only out-of-pocket payment but waiting for appointments, waiting to be seen, travel to the site of care, loss of time from work, type of personal handling by program staff, etc. All such "costs" must be balanced by the benefit or utilities of the services provided, and contrasted to competitive offerings.
- **Implement and adjust the program,** evaluating its results and correcting its shortcomings from both organizational and patient perspectives.

How To Establish a Primary Care Satellite*

The primary care satellite has attracted a good deal of interest among hospitals as well as physician-short communities. It provides an excellent marketing challenge because it requires attracting patients directly rather than through recruitment of their family physicians.

Checklist

a. *Capital.* The hospital requires some source of capital funding for the satellite facility and equipment. Possible sources include the hospital's own capital reserve (requiring board of trustees approval), bank loans, bond issues, donations, etc. The community in which the satellite is to be located may donate the money or an existing facility. A wealthy individual or business firm may donate sufficient funds if the satellite is given a particular name.

b. *Regulations.* The hospital will no doubt have to secure the approval of regulatory agencies. Certificate of need laws will most probably require a formal application even if no federal or other governmental funds will be used. Local government zoning boards will also insist on reviewing plans. The hospital must be prepared to supply the requested information (on need, program plans, costs, etc.) and assurances (on environmental impact, value to the community, etc.) required to secure the approval of such agencies.

In addition, effort will probably have to be expended to secure general community acceptance of the satellite and assure that zoning or other regulatory approvals are granted. The hospital may develop a community advisory board to provide local input into program planning.

c. *Staffing.* The hospital must recruit staff for the satellite. Physicians especially are likely to be hard to find for rural or urban poverty areas—that's why the problem existed in the first place. The hospital must offer physicians exchange values that weren't present in the past: controlled hours, referral network, administrative support, salary guarantees, etc. Because of the independence of physicians, each one recruited represents a possible future competitor as well, should the exchange relationship fall below a satisfactory level.

d. *Local Physicians.* The existing physicians or other sources of care serving the target community represent a major source of support (in referrals, assistance, even contributions) if relations are positive. If negative, of course, they can make life very difficult for a new organization. Moreover, potential benefits from shared services or coordinated programs may be lost if local practitioners are ignored.

e. *Internal Relations.* The administration of the hospital will require the approval of the board of trustees and the acquiescence of the medical staff and employees in developing such a new program. The medical staff might fear the loss of patients or object to "organizational practice of medicine." Arguments may arise

---

*Source: Reprinted from *Marketing Health Care* by Robin MacStravic, with permission of Aspen Systems Corporation, © 1977.

over which specialists will get how many referrals from the satellite.

f. *Clients.* The very idea of a satellite is predicated upon successfully achieving desired demand for the services the satellite is prepared to render, revenue the satellite requires to cover expenses, and sufficient referrals to the hospital. Clearly, the people in whatever target area is chosen have somehow been meeting their perceived need for primary care: self-treatment, use of quacks or charlatans, the local pharmacist, distant clinics or physicians. It is highly unlikely that a completely untapped mass of unrealized demand is just waiting for the satellite to open.

g. *Economy.* The general state of the economy can greatly affect the availability and/or price of capital funds for facility and equipment. High interest rates for loans could change the satellite from a paying to a losing proposition at the utilization levels anticipated. High employment levels and wage rates in the local community might make staff recruitment difficult and expensive. Low employment might mean that many prospective patients would be unable to pay, or it might reduce the numbers of patients, making anticipated revenue less than needed.

h. *Demographics.* The population may be adequate now to sustain the satellite but be declining, or shifting dramatically in factors affecting use of satellite services (e.g., age, sex, fertility). The people in the target community may be unusually hardy and self-reliant, suggesting low potential use rates. They may have very strong identification with their existing sources of care. On the other hand, in a rapidly expanding population, newcomers might be much more easily attracted to the satellite.

i. *Technology.* What does the current technology require for effective and high quality primary care? Is there some minimum volume of utilization necessary to include lab and x-ray services? Will foreseeable developments in technology wipe out the small clinic or solo practitioner in favor of large programs? What will keeping up with technology do to the satellite's costs and charges? Given the expected potential utilization, what kinds of services can be justified at the satellite vs. on referral to the hospital?

j. *Competition.* Given that a significant opportunity exists in some target area, why has no one else moved in? Are individual physicians, public health clinics, or even other hospital satellites capable of moving in or likely to? If the potential for successful satellite development is that great, why won't others see it? Do some competitors have an edge—such as private physicians, who don't require certificate of need approval? Are current sources of primary care in the area winding down (e.g., local physicians reducing practice or retiring due to age, planning to return to a specialized residency, etc.).

k. *Negative Markets.* If the satellite is identified with a racial, religious, or otherwise homogeneous group which is considered foreign, inimical, or simply different from the prevailing norm in a prospective area, potential constituents may have negative feelings about the new program and consciously avoid it. For postponable services such as routine office visits, or unpleasant services such as immunizations, a negative attitude may effectively keep people away, with only emergency situations generating any demand. In countering such attitudes, the hospital may:

- incorporate local citizens in the planning and development of the satellite
- name the satellite after a local citizen or hero rather than identify it with the hospital
- employ local citizens wherever possible in jobs at the satellite (perhaps even local physicians)
- implement public relations campaigns to change people's attitudes
- wait for people to try out the satellite and change their minds plus those of their neighbors

l. *Unrealized Markets.* The probability that a satellite might succeed merely by opening its doors and announcing its availability is low. Even if there are such places, they are few and diminishing in numbers.

People are coping somehow and may continue behavior they have found satisfactory in the past rather than try something new. If the actual state of the market situation can at least be estimated (e.g., via questionnaire, interviews) it should provide a better basis for developing market strategy than assuming potential patients are just waiting to come.

Market Analysis

In most cases, a market strategy for a primary care satellite will include segmenting of the potential patient population. Segments may then be analyzed separately in designing services, determining prices or developing communications and promotion strategy. The separate segments may then be managed so as to achieve overall objectives or specific objectives per segment.

Geography

The initial segment decision may well be geographic. In analyzing alternative locations, the hospital will examine areas which have sufficient populations to support the basic satellite concept, and lack readily accessible alternatives. Preference may be given to areas which:

- have had a long history of using the hospital's emergency room as a source of primary care. This suggests that their attitudes toward the hospital are receptive enough to promise success of the satellite *and* that the success of the satellite will relieve pressure on the emergency room.
- are experiencing a rapid influx of population from distant places. This suggests there will be large numbers of people with no strong ties to other local sources of primary care.
- have local physicians who commonly refer patients to the hospital or are on its medical staff. This suggests receptivity to the satellite and perhaps even the employment of local physicians and the "capture" of their patients as a base for the satellite.
- are truly remote from other sources of care. This suggests a strong probability of their switching to the satellite for care.

Service

Within the geographic area potentially served by a satellite, there are likely to be different segments based on the services anticipated for the satellite. The population of children in the area represents the segment appropriate for a pediatrician, women for an obstetrician-gynecologist, etc. Aside from these obvious service segments, there may be employment-related segments such as miners for black-lung programs, very young children for lead-screening, blacks for sickle-cell programs, etc. The numbers of people in such segments may well dictate whether services are to be offered, how frequently, etc.

Risk

For organizations with high levels of commitment to community service, especially if external funding sources are available, segments may be deliberately selected based on high risk despite lower probability of paying. The conditions which make the need for a satellite most pressing (isolation, poor populations, physician shortage, etc.) are most likely to hold in areas where per capita income is low and health insurance coverage meager. Within such areas, greatest risk may exist among those lacking personal transportation or physically unable to secure needed health services. Special efforts may have to be made to develop utilization among such populations, including outreach and transportation services.

Income

Where external sources of funding are not available, it may be necessary to identify segments which include people who can pay the charges for all care received either through personal income or insurance, so that the costs of care to nonpaying patients can be covered. The extent of unrecovered costs may be predicted as a basis for identifying what charge levels must be applied to paying patients in order to enable some level of service to nonpaying. The extent to which paying patients must pay more to cover "charitable" services must increase the burden on them and diminish the competitive position of the satellite, of course.

By identifying different income segments, such as:

—people unable to pay at all
—people who can be expected to pay 80–90% of all charges
—people who are virtually sure sources of payment through contracted services with their employer, health insurance coverage, health maintenance agreement, etc.

the organization should be able to calculate what total numbers within each represents an appropriate and desirable patient mix. The demographic, cultural, geographic, or other factors which distinguish one income segment from another may then be used to develop different marketing strategies for each so that the proper mix can be achieved.

Behavior

A further basis for segmenting prospective patients might be some specific current or desired behavior. The populations now using the hospital's emergency room may be specifically identified by name and address and consciously recruited as patients to reduce inappropriate use of the ER. The satellite may also set targets based on the numbers of patients they want to attract as family rather than individual clients, as regular rather than episodic users of its services. To achieve a desired level of regular family utilization, the satellite may have to provide a fairly comprehensive range of services, including pediatric and obstetric. Such a range may be needed even to achieve desired levels of utilization for adult, primary care services since families often prefer to use the same person or organization as a source of care where possible.

Determining and Forecasting Need and Demand

There are a number of ways to determine the level of need for services potentially offered by a satellite program and to forecast future need. A survey of the population conducted by physicians, public health or nursing personnel may be employed where a strong case for need must be made to an outside agency. To secure federal or foundation grant funds or a certificate of need, such a survey may be justified. For the hospital's own planning, however, such a survey may be unnecessary and expensive.

Perceived need may be a much more useful item of information than medically determined need. That is, the population's desire to be served is probably a better predictor of their coming to the satellite than the physician or nurse's measurement of how many *should* come. Once initial contact is made, of course, such professionals then do, in fact, determine need by diagnosing illness and prescribing treatment. The hospital must first estimate how many people might make initial contact, then calculate probable subsequent prescribed utilization based on who and how many perceive their own needs to be such that they would visit the satellite.

Some estimate of the likelihood of use may be derived from national or regional average utilization levels, adjusted for age, sex, income, and education levels where possible. Rural populations frequently tend to use fewer services per person than urban groups, for example, so some adjustment should be made for types of populations to be served. Interviews and phone or mail surveys of the population may be useful in estimating their current level of use of primary care and current sources of care.

Product Design

Based on the market segments, perceived needs, and expressed attitudes of the population, the hospital can make informed decisions about the services to be offered. If the results of population surveys indicate that pediatric, obstetric, or some specific type of care is particularly difficult to secure from available alternatives, and that perceived need for such care is great, such a service may be an appropriate basis for designing the satellite program. Getting the mother to come to the satellite will often result in adding the children as patients, and vice versa. Initial contacts may be stimulated by offering immunizations during a flu scare or screening for a condition of local concern (e.g., sickle-cell anemia). Such services may be offered on a get-acquainted basis or as a permanent part of the program.

In promoting acceptance of a new program, it may be more effective as well as more efficient to begin with limited services or even a specific service rather than a comprehensive primary care program. People frequently wait to hear from neighbors about sources of health care, and acceptance may be slow.

Price

As in most health services, the specific charge for services is by no means the only or even most important price consideration. Primary services are, however, more likely to require out-of-pocket expenditures. If the population survey identified sources of care currently being used by the target population segments, the charges made by such sources can also be identified. If the satellite is seen as offering greater convenience, higher quality, more concerned care, etc., the charge could easily be above that of other sources without reducing utilization.

The calculation of price based on target revenues, together with consideration of charges by alternative sources available may identify the probable range of money prices appropriate for the satellite's services. The other aspects of price should be determined on the basis of the organization's policy toward patient care, the cost vs. value to the community of improving such aspects, and the likely impact on future utilization. Specific alterations may be made based on the segments to be attracted. Play areas and even a baby-sitter may be provided where a large number of mothers with young children are expected. Soft-drink and even sandwich machines may ease long waiting periods or enhance the attractiveness of the satellite for appointments during meal times.

Place

The selection of a location for the satellite should be made on the basis of accessibility for the different target segments. There is no precise calculus for measuring the impact of time or distance on the likelihood of using a particular source of care. Nevertheless, for disabled segments or people lacking personal transportation, locations in their immediate vicinity may be warranted. The cost of land, accessibility to employees and medical staff, etc. will also be considerations, but location does have an effect on the "price" to be paid by prospective patients.

If previous surveys of the population have identified common travel patterns, such as to shopping or employment, this information should be useful in analyzing potential locations. It is easier for people to continue familiar travel routes in seeking health care than to change their habits. A satellite may be successful in a relatively isolated location if it is on common travel paths, where costs of land in the focus of travel is expensive or where no land is available. Locations near shopping, schools, or employment may be desirable for different segments. Mobile locations may even be offered in widely dispersed population areas.

Promotion

For them effectively to make use of its services, prospective patients must be made aware of the satellite's program and conditions of availability. Communication of information about specific services to be offered, hours of availability, etc. is a legitimate basis for general mailings, posters, or public service notices. Straightforward educational messages may be broadcast through churches, social organizations, and employers as well as newspapers and radio.

An open house is often used to encourage people to visit as well as to get newspaper coverage. Prominent citizens may be invited to attend and a famous speaker invited. In some cases, of course, if only prominent citizens show up, the specific segments whose use is desired may not. Some combination of entertainment and health education aimed at mothers and children may be useful in attracting people at least to drop by.

Outreach programs may be used, especially during initial months of operation. Volunteers or paid local citizens can visit residents in some segments and even arrange transportation where that is a problem.

Unforeseen Problems

Managers should insist on effective planning to reduce the number of "unforeseen" problems they have to deal with.

- Physicians may be hard to recruit, or leave to set up their own practice, taking satellite patients with them.
- Another source of care may move into the area, creating competition where none was anticipated.
- The staff employed may have difficulty in meeting patient needs because of communications problems, social distance, etc.
- The strength of existing patient loyalties, even to distant sources of care, may be greater than anticipated.
- Acceptance of the satellite may occur faster than anticipated, flooding it with demand before facilities and staff are available.
- The local industry may go bankrupt, altering dramatically the insurance coverage and income situation.

In such circumstances the manager must be able to adjust the program and even alter the expectations and objectives of the satellite.

THE EMERGICARE CENTER*

The emergicare center could be characterized as a free standing facility *without* licensed hospital beds that integrates the following services

---

*Source: Reprinted from James A. Rice and Gregory T. Oltvedt, "The Emergicare Center," *The Journal of Ambulatory Care Management*, August 1980, with permission of Aspen Systems Corporation.

- 16- to 24-hour emergency treatment;
- Ambulance station for emergency transportation;
- Minor diagnostic laboratory and x-ray studies;
- Pharmaceutical dispensing;
- Modular office space for private medical and dental practitioners; and
- Community health education/promotion.

This relatively new concept represents a unique facility that conceptually and architecturally falls between traditional views of the small, private medical clinic and a full-service hospital. Somewhat similar facilities were developed during the late 1960s in some inner-city areas as neighborhood or community health centers. The emergicare center, however, differs from these facilities in that it

- Emphasizes its important emergency medical treatment and ambulance base component;
- Could be designed for cost-effective, energy-conserving construction in rural areas;
- Can incorporate office space for private practitioners; and
- As a component of a multiunit health care system, could either be a free standing facility owned and operated by a local board or considered as a satellite of a distant hospital or be linked through modern telecommunication systems to an entire support system of care and management along a rural-urban continuum.

The concept is currently gaining widespread support as a bold new approach to such challenges as

- Cost containment through great reliance on outpatient care;
- Predictions that few new acute-care hospitals will be constructed in the United States;
- Some rural hospitals may need to find viable conversion models that are nonbed health facilities to which community pride can remain attached and physician morale and diagnostic support can be retained; and
- National health insurance's predicted emphasis on health promotion and treatment occurring in nontraditional health facilities to promote greater access and lower cost.

Flexible Organization Formats

As a result of these factors, the purpose of the emergicare center could be characterized as one or more of the following:

- *Option A.* To provide better accessibility to primary care services within an existing hospital's service area via satellite locations (service expansion option);
- *Option B.* To provide essential primary health care services to communities that can no longer support an acute-care hospital (role conversion option); or
- *Option C.* To provide services to a community that is expected to grow to a point where a new acute-care hospital would be required in the future (claim stake option).

Under option A an existing hospital could use this type of facility to expand its service area or improve its responsiveness to local community needs. Such an approach could broaden the service area base needed to support the hospital goals, as well as provide a more cost-effective expansion strategy than the addition of hospital beds.

Under option B, one could expect to find a rural community of 2,000 to 5,000 persons that used to have or presently has a small "marginal" hospital. Rather than force the traumatic upheavals in either community service or pride often associated with the closing of a hospital, a modern emergicare center could be developed. Telecommunication and transportation systems would link this facility with an appropriate neighboring hospital or a hospital system. Local physicians would continue to control their own practices and patients.

Under option C, the hospital would utilize such a facility to effectively "stake a claim" in another part of or in an adjacent service area. The facility could be designed to function just as described above, but more careful site planning and a larger land parcel would be required to accommodate the potentiality of a future hospital.

Management would probably rest within the existing health facility's board. Ownership of the facility could be by

- A single hospital;
- The community, leased to the hospital;
- The hospital, leasing part to physicians;
- Local physicians leasing part of the hospital;

- Joint venture between hospitals and local physicians and dentists; or
- A multiunit hospital system.

The size, design, and furnishings of each emergicare center should be tailored to meet local needs and attitudes. A modular design approach would therefore probably be used to ensure flexibility for future growth and function modifications.

HEALTH FACILITIES CONVERSION: STRATEGIES*

Conversion analysis can be an innovative way to explore new and better ways to meet a population's health service needs instead of simply closing existing "surplus" hospital beds, constructing new facilities, or expanding existing physical plants to meet newly developing demands.

The more common forms of conversion can be identified:

1. The swing bed (alternating between acute and long-term care based on needs as they change from day to day);
2. Conversion to specialized units such as alcoholism treatment and rehabilitation, long-term psychiatric, mental retardation, or drug abuse treatment and rehabilitation units;
3. Conversion to more intensive care such as hemodialysis units, intensive care units/coronary care units (ICUs/CCUs), Level II intensive neonatal care, nuclear medicine, burn care, and other uses in which operating costs are higher but needs for service may be more evident;
4. Conversion to skilled nursing facility-intermediate care facility (SNF-ICF) (based on general analysis of shortages and surpluses);
5. Possible reduction of volume occupancy by elimination of wards, limitation of semiprivate occupancy, i.e., conversion to private occupancy to reduce bed capacity;
6. Development of a rural primary health care center such as has been proposed in California under Chapter 1332, calling for diversification of small rural hospitals under a demonstration project established in 1979;
7. Establishment of clinic space in lieu of inpatient space in urban settings, particularly in connection with prepaid health care;
8. Conversion of publicly subsidized or operated facilities, in whole or in part, for ambulatory services; preventive, detective, and promotive services; congregate meals for ambulatory elderly; preparation of meals on wheels; day care for children; community centers for the aged; rehabilitation centers; hospice; emergency room expansion; and
9. Conversion related to change of ownership or operating responsibility, expecially in the case of low-occupancy, financially distressed public general hospitals.

There are also nonhealth-related uses of facilities that might be considered, such as prisons or long-term care for the criminally insane, residential facilities (motel-apartments for patients' families, congregate housing for the infirm elderly), office, or laboratory space.

Opportunities for Successful Conversion

The greatest opportunities for successful conversion include the partial-limited conversion, the multipurpose institution, and the development of a community-based study in advance of, or concurrent with, study by the provider institution considering conversion options.

The partial-limited conversion permits an institution to maintain its institutional continuity, most of its personnel, and its most financially viable current activities, with minimal disturbance of its spatial arrangements and least cost of construction. The multipurpose institution holds the key to diversity of financial base, adaptability to future needs, and identity as a community health resource that is responsive to changing demographic conditions. These two concepts fit together easily and, taken together, make it possible for HSA planners to approach underutilized facilities in a much less threatening manner.

---

*Source: Reprinted from Cyril Roseman, "Health Facilities Conversion: Innovative Community Planning to Reduce Excess Bed Capacity," *Health Care Planning and Marketing Quarterly,* April 1981.

Constraints

Two obvious constraints on conversion options are the architectural limitations and the financial restrictions regarding governmental reimbursement under Titles XVIII or XIX for nonacute inpatient care. The latter poses serious inhibitions for long-term care in an acute care facility; the former may rule out many of the more imaginative uses to which excess capacity could be put.

The difficulties of conversion have been highlighted by the language of Section 1642, especially (c)(1), which refers to the Secretary of Labor's review of the arrangements regarding protection of the "interests of employees affected by the discontinuance of service," including reassignment of affected employees, retraining programs, fringe benefits, and adequate severance pay. In addition, Section 1642 (a)(2) indicates the character of financial distress that may accompany conversion, such as liquidation of outstanding debt; costs connected with the planning, development, and delivery of the new use; and terminating pay for personnel, retraining costs, and costs of securing alternative employment.

There are of course additional costs associated with adapting the old space to the new use (which may exceed the cost of new construction) and possibly inadequate revenues under the new use to offset all the costs of the conversion. This is particularly true of the long-term care option.

In addition, an institution is not only a building physically convertible to another use; it is a complex set of working human relationships, assembled and maintained with great effort, not easily altered to another purpose. The people, especially the people in positions of prestige and control, assembled in a hospital have little identification, knowledge, or loyalty regarding possible other uses of hospital facilities. Hospital administrators want to administer hospitals; the medical staff want inpatient hospital service available and do not wish to establish new ties elsewhere; hospital nurses, and especially intensive care nurses, have a different set of technical skills than do non-hospital nurses which they do not wish to abandon; hospital boards and volunteers have devoted their efforts and identified with a hospital, not something else.

The hospital employees who can be carried over to alternative use tend to be the lowest skilled people with the least influence or authority. The remaining institutional constituencies have a vested concern in maintaining the hospital activities and will usually use every means to do so. If, after such efforts are exhausted, it becomes clear that hospital activities are no longer viable, the people, especially the key people, in these constituencies will begin to leave. These key leaders and key program people are the glue that holds the rest of the institution together. Such people are hard to find and hard to replace; they can seldom be developed from the remaining staff, especially if the institution is to convert to another purpose.*

Determining Feasibility

The feasibility of proposed conversion can be reviewed emphasizing seven factors of analysis, as follows:

1. *Economic considerations* (current low occupancy + financial distress);
2. *Community maldistribution of resources* (evidence of unmet needs, shortage of appropriate facilities);
3. *Opportunity for facility conversion* (evidence of structural soundness, appropriateness for proposed conversion, good location);
4. *Business practicality* (financial feasibility of conversion);
5. *Human resources* (potential for staffing and satisfactory treatment of unneeded personnel);
6. *Legal considerations* (elimination of legal obstacles to conversion); and
7. *General support for conversion* (institutional, community, and planning agency commitment to proposed converted use).

Each of these factors must be examined in the course of study of conversion options.

In the analysis of conversion possibilities, the limitations of the existing facility must be given priority consideration. These limitations are the location, size, age, general condition, existing capital costs (and impact on financing of new use), and special configuration (number of stories, ceiling heights, support column locations,

---

*Source: *Conversion and Other Policy Options to Reduce Excess Hospital Capacity*, Health Planning Information Series, DHEW, September 1979, Pub. No. (HRA) 79-14044.

utility locations, etc.). Because these limitations are best understood by the institution-based facility planners, they can best proceed with this analysis of options while the community-based planners concurrently can be examining space deficits in any of the proposed categories of use suggested.

Financial feasibility should involve more than consideration of cost savings passed on to the public. The hospital considering conversion must see the advantages of the modification in dollar terms. Thus all costs of the facility's operation (including amortization of its debt) under the conversion should not only be less than the anticipated revenues, but the considered conversion will not likely be adopted unless it is assumed that the hospital's financial position will be improved with the change. In addition, the conversion should be the most cost-effective approach to the new use. This type of analysis, which the health planning agencies must approve under the terms of Section 1642, can best be analyzed by means of a decision tree for financial viability of health facility conversion. (See Figure 13-2.)

Approval Strategy

Community Planners' Participation

Conversion holds out certain advantages to community planners as well as hospital-based planners. It places emphasis on existing capabilities, moves toward rationalization of facilities in relation to need and demand, fosters more effective linkage and communication between providers and community interests, identifies system responsiveness as the hallmark of facility planning rather than capacity reduction vs. expansion, builds on a cooperative rather than conflict-oriented approach to planning, and in general, strengthens the best parts of the health care delivery system while it shifts resources away from the least cost-effective elements of the system.

Community health planners should have an active role to play in developing the conversion strategy and especially in conducting the basic analytic work necessary before strategy implementation begins.

HSA and State Approvals

Before any exploration of conversion feasibility is undertaken there should be clarification of three concerns by appropriate policy planners at the state and areawide levels.

First, a general state policy should be adopted regarding the desirability of undertaking conversion analyses within the framework of the cost-containment philosophy. Health Systems Agencies, in the context of the medical facilities component of their Health Systems Plan (HSP), should identify "the extent to which existing medical facilities are in need of modernization," or conversion to other uses. State findings of inappropriateness of existing services likewise should involve a recommendation of remedial action.

Because the most likely candidates for conversion are financially marginal, older public facilities, plans for care of their often medically indigent clientele should be outlined before proceeding with conversion analysis.

Second, needs assessment for conversion uses should be undertaken as an intrinsic element of the comprehensive analysis of the area's needs for health services in the light of existing, planned, or under-construction facilities. Identification through needs assessments of surpluses; deficits; maldistributions of facilities and services; unmet needs; and under- and overutilization of services in different planning subareas should provide a list of potential targets for subsequent feasibility analysis of reuse.

The third concern is the limitation on conversion opportunities posed by third party reimbursement policy regarding settings for delivery of care. In some cases of converted use there may be little or no possibility for reimbursement for ambulatory or long-term care under Medicare-Medicaid, Blue Cross-Blue Shield, or private insurance coverage. In some cases the constraints are directed to the type of care to be offered in an acute care setting.

Conversion Analysis: Its Scope and Framework

A conversion analysis should include not only the proposed use and the need for such use, but also the staffing concerns; organizational concerns; operating (as well as construction) financial dimensions; architectural and engineering concerns; and legal, political, community, and institutional dimensions of the conversion option in question. The framework of analysis should involve criteria setting, identification of data sources, recording of data, and comparison of actual data with criteria.

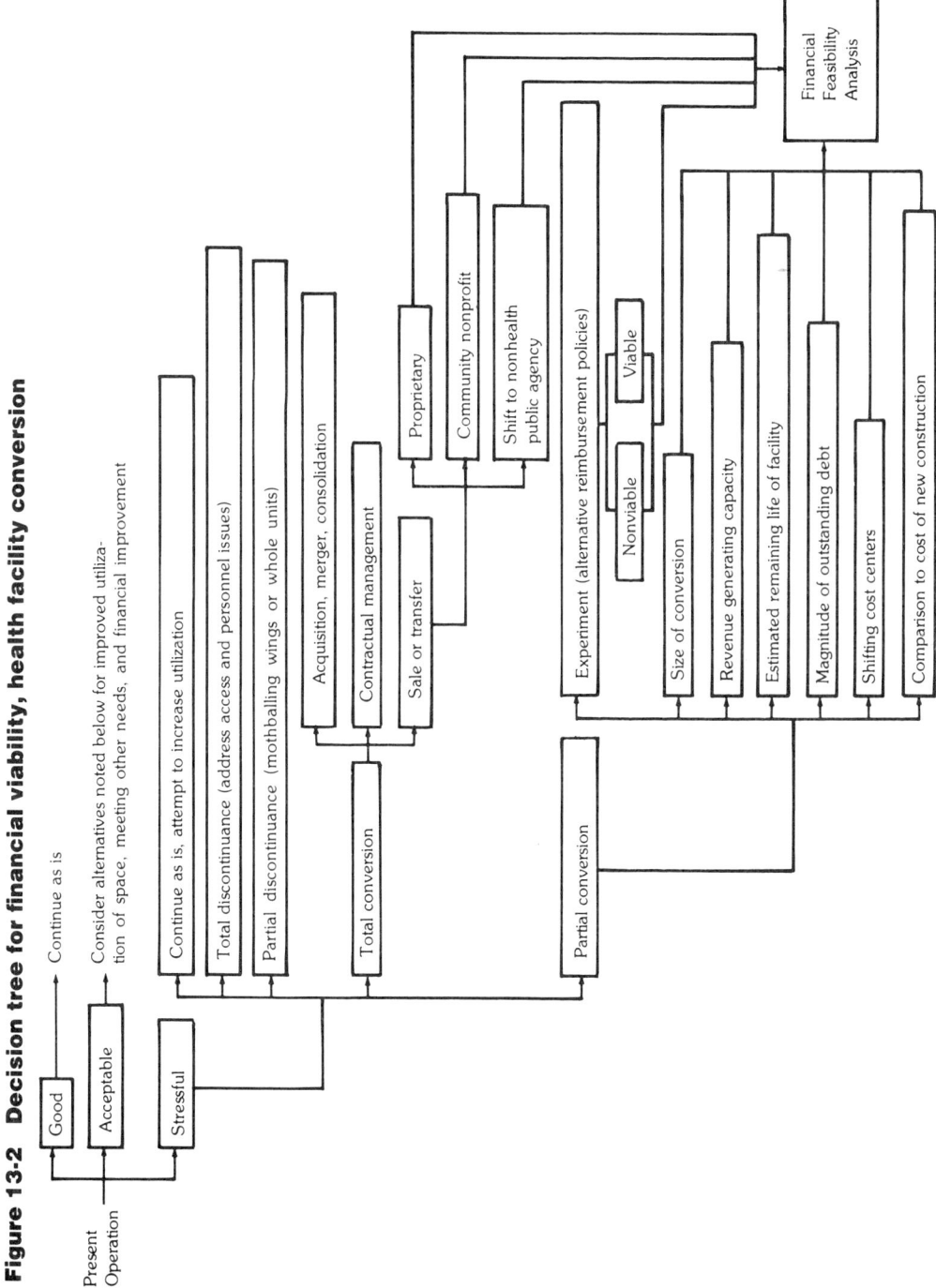

Figure 13-2 Decision tree for financial viability, health facility conversion

The following kinds of questions should be addressed:

1. Can the present staff continue to be employed after the proposed conversion?
2. If not, will there be work for displaced employees elsewhere in the area?
3. If not, is retraining necessary?
4. If new workers must be hired, will they be available in the local labor market?
5. Can the converted use be implemented with out-of-area personnel with or without retraining?
6. How will the converted use be organized and administered relative to the existing sponsoring organization?
7. Is the existing space adequate to perform all the functions necessary in relation to the converted use?
8. What modifications in facilities will have to be made to accommodate the proposed conversion?
9. Will any building codes, health codes, or regulations require special physical modernization or rehabilitation?
10. Approximately how much will it cost to convert the facility?
11. How might this cost be paid?
12. What is the probable size of the operating budget under the converted use, and how will that be paid?

In setting criteria and conducting the feasibility screening, key consultant services employed are administrative, architectural, financial, and legal.

Working with the HSA

The HSA and the sponsoring institution should establish and maintain a close working relationship, embodied in both the sharing of data and the creating and adhering to an explicit working agreement.

The institutional and political factors to be explored by the HSA include managerial capacity for new services; handling of the range of conflicts that might be generated between continuing old and proposed new services; the impact of change on philanthropic and trustee support; and the symbolic and real investments that the institution, the employees, and the public make in continuing the original purposes of the sponsoring institution.

Consultants or planning personnel employed by the sponsoring institution should be involved in the refined analysis of physical adaptability and financial feasibility. Adaptability focuses primarily on space flexibility (mobility of equipment, partitions, walls, ceilings, circulation, environment, and utility service adaptability), and construction cost of conversion options and necessary renovation. Financial feasibility should deal with both internal impact (income statement/balance sheet), including capital costs, operating costs and revenues, and external impact, including community costs, investment, expenditures, payroll, and funds flow in the health care industry. The HSA should assist in the community aspects of conversion analysis and review the institutional aspects of the conversion feasibility studies.

In plan development, a linkage between population-based planning and health care delivery system component planning should be emphasized. In addition, the conversion strategy should permit the HSA to identify a focus for implementation of the cost-containment emphasis. Conversion, moreover, is a form of resource reallocation that can be dealt with expressly in the HSP.

The most significant link to HSA functions is in terms of appropriateness review. Conversion might be given attention as a viable alternative to discontinuance or construction and placed within the context of the overall area-wide facility planning framework.

Chapter 14—Marketing

OVERVIEW*

The practice of competing with area hospitals and health service agencies for a larger part of the marketplace must be accepted. There is no intention of proposing cutthroat competition or unethical practices to achieve more patient involvement, but unless there is open competition for this market, chances for survival or for maintaining all services that currently exist will be substantially lessened. Effective competition will control costs, keep operations more efficient and allow for better fulfillment of community needs. Active competition must become both the style and the goal of a marketing program. Administrators must look at their patients as customers. This will not be unusual or difficult for many since, as with other industries, there is a product (service) and a reliance on others for use. Hospitals are similar to industry, and administrators need not feel uncomfortable using proven industrial techniques to effectively develop an appropriate market for hospital services. (See Table 14-1 for the reasons for hospital administrator interest in marketing and Table 14-2 for the issues involved.)

---

*Source: Reprinted from James K. Simon, "Marketing the Community Hospital: A Tool for the Beleaguered Administrator," *Health Care Management Review*, Spring 1978, with permission of Aspen Systems Corporation.

---

*Marketing Elements**

Marketing encompasses the analysis and management of four factors essential to the delivery of health care:

Product: the type of service to be offered—preventive, diagnostic, therapeutic, etc., especially viewed in terms of the benefits the service provides to the patient—relief from pain or anxiety, longer life, less disability, etc.

Place: how the service will be delivered to the patient—the location, hours, referral mechanism, etc., which determine the extent and mode of access to the product.

Price: not only the charge made for the service (which often isn't paid directly by the patient anyway), but everything the organization requires the patient to go through in order to utilize the service.

Promotion: how and what the prospective patient learns about the organization and the services it offers—how the patient can become aware of services offered, develop an interest in using a service, decide to use it, actually utilize it, use it regularly, recommend the organization to friends, etc.

---

*Source: Reprinted from Robin E. Scott MacStravic, "Marketing Health Care Services: The Challenge of Primary Care," *Health Care Management Review*, Summer 1977, with permission of Aspen Systems Corporation.

Table 14-1 Some Reasons for Rising Levels of Interest in Health Care Marketing*

Reason	Explanation
1. Rising costs	With rapid escalation of health care costs has come a search for methods and techniques to slow the rate of increase. Marketing may be useful to health care administrators in effecting cost containment measures.
2. Rising accountability	Legislation has created mechanisms for review of health care service providers. Providers are now required to have information to support requests for additional services and to defend the allocation of resources. Marketing techniques and concepts are useful in the development of such information.
3. Trustees and directors have placed increasing emphasis on the health care consumer's needs	Administrators must demonstrate to governing boards that health care consumers have been consulted and their needs considered in planning and operating the services offered.
4. Increase in proprietary health care services	There have been widely reported successes of such profit-making health care services as hospital management firms, proprietary hospitals, health maintenance organizations, group practices, and emergency clinics. As a result, many health care organizations believe that they must become more competitive and devote increased attention to their principal markets.
5. Underutilization viewed as waste	Marketing provides the administration with concepts and techniques to smooth irregular demand patterns, to review consumer needs, to identify and reach target markets, and to measure customer satisfaction with services offered. Thus, marketing may be useful in increasing levels of utilization without creating demand for unneeded services.
6. Duplication of services	Marketing can assist administrators to measure total demand, assess the level and quality of services offered by other health care providers, and determine which services should be offered to meet effectively the needs of the markets served by the organization. Thus, marketing can provide information to assist decision makers in their quest to achieve effective utilization of available financial, human, and equipment resources.
7. Rising sense of professionalism by staff	Increasingly, nurses, pharmacists, respiratory therapists and other staff members seek recognition for their contributions. Marketing, with its emphasis on exchange relationships with key publics, provides an approach to administrators faced with an increasingly complex set of staff needs and expectations.
8. Changing nature of patient-physician relationship	Patients have become more active participants in decisions affecting their health care. Choices with respect to where, how, and what health care services are sought are influenced increasingly by consumer awareness and knowledge. Marketing techniques are useful in development of consumer awareness and in providing information about alternative services.
9. Rising interest in prevention	While most consumers still seek health care on an episodic, curative crisis basis, there is a clear trend toward utilization of preventive health services. Preventive health services possess characteristics that are amenable to marketing efforts, and that can reduce the overall costs of health care substantially.
10. Rising consumer dissatisfaction with health care providers	Expectation levels of health care consumers are rising. Therefore, health care providers must develop better understanding of consumer expectations and satisfaction levels. Marketing provides the measurement techniques needed to determine patient expectation and satisfaction.

Table 14-1 continued

Reason	Explanation
11. Health care as a business	Many observers believe that health care possesses the elements of a business. That is, there are products and services that are offered to consumers by competitors at prices and locations that differ substantially. Effective public relations and promotional techniques also use the same principles as do business firms.

*Source: Reprinted from Larry M. Robinson and F. Brown Whittington, "Marketing as Viewed by Hospital Administrators," *Health Care Marketing: Issues and Trends,* ed. Philip D. Cooper, with permission of Aspen Systems Corporation, © 1980.

Table 14-2 Issues in Health Care Marketing*

Pro	Con
Marketing is more than advertising, selling, and public relations. It includes all activities required to plan, facilitate, and conduct voluntary exchanges to mutual benefit.	Marketing is the same thing as advertising. Marketing is the same thing as selling. Marketing is the same thing as public relations.
Health care marketing is a process of determining what health care consumers need, tailoring services to meet those needs, and then attracting patients to use these services.	Marketing is equated with "hucksterism" and manipulation.
Health care marketing recognizes that health care is a service with differentiable characteristics. Marketing techniques reduce the cost of health care by helping consumers and providers to make more rational and efficient decisions.	Active competition may force health care providers to promote, thus increasing the cost of health care to the community. To label health care a "product" is ultimately to demean it.
Health care organizations must become competitive in a variety of markets just to survive.	Active competition may lead to unnecessary utilization.
Competition is an inescapable reality. Without competition, there is little incentive for efficient and effective utilization of scarce resources.	Hospitals should not promote and expand services at the expense of other hospitals. Competition could cause hospitals to focus on filling beds rather than on providing needed services. Given extraordinary regulations that health care to which providers are subject, a true market orientation probably is not possible.
Marketing is value free. It is a set of concepts and techniques that can be used for good or for evil.	The misapplication of marketing methods can damage the service reputations of health care institutions.
It is legitimate to position a hospital as the one in the community that provides only routine inpatient services, and to thus establish a lower daily service charge than hospitals with highly specialized services.	Hospitals will be affected adversely by competitors who become known as "discount health care stores."

*Source: Reprinted from Larry M. Robinson and F. Brown Whittington, "Marketing as Viewed by Hospital Administrators," *Health Care Marketing: Issues and Trends,* ed. Philip D. Cooper, with permission of Aspen Systems Corporation, © 1980.

Consumers—Who Are They?

In the past, physicians were considered the primary consumers of health services. They admitted and discharged patients and wrote the orders for various tests. While this continues to be true, there are at least five distinct consumer groups identified for marketing purposes: (1) patients, (2) physicians, (3) employer or union groups, (4) government and regulatory agencies, and (5) employees.

Patients

Consumers are rapidly assuming much greater responsibility and interest in their own health care. Because of their improved health care "education," augmented by media coverage of various aspects of health delivery, they are now more sensitive to what happens to them when they enter a facility as a patient. Yet the consumer is still inadequately informed. Consumer education must be one of the first targets of a marketing, or competitive, health care program. Marketing requires a look beyond the user group—those with whom contact is maintained as they use health services—to include those potential users of services who will then increase the market share.

Physicians

Currently, physicians still retain a major position in managing and controlling the types of care rendered by hospitals to patients. They can control the flow of patient activities to or from a facility, private laboratory or other health care services, directly affecting the use of services within the hospital. They are also the prime source of overutilization of services and may extend the length of stay for tests or care that might be accomplished on an outpatient basis. Physicians may order a battery of laboratory tests, all of which might not be necessary or pertinent to the immediate problem facing the patient.

In the past, these particular areas of overutilization were not considered negative by the administrator, but rather were considered as additional sources of revenue to assist in the constant struggle to maintain a financially viable institution and to keep pace with the requirements for new services and equipment. However, now these activities can be the source of penalties in reimbursement and in increased dealings with regulatory agencies.

Physicians are the prime sources of information (or lack of it) for the patient consumer. Physicians also play a key role in the expansion of hospital medical staff. The larger the staff, the broader the base for referrals to the hospital for both in- and outpatient services. Physicians as consumers are probably the most complex of the five consumer groups. They can control and maintain a hospital's position in the health care market and ensure the adequate use of existing health services and facilities. Much consideration must be given to physicians in the development of a marketing program.

Employers and Labor Unions

In the past, employers or labor unions have not necessarily been of concern to individual hospitals or administrators. Hospitals have always been recipients of reimbursement for insurance paid for by either the employer or labor unions for services rendered. Now, however, these same groups are expressing concerns similar to those voiced by the public about the high cost of health, duplication of services, the need for greater accessibility and less waiting time, and even more services. Growing interest in health maintenance organizations (HMOs), freestanding health centers to provide services on a more timely and less costly basis, and surgical centers now being developed to provide one-day outpatient surgery reflect the employer-labor union's growing dissatisfaction and changing requirements. Industry is not only becoming aware of its growing liability in health premiums for employees, but is suggesting that perhaps they can do it better for less. Industry might assume a major role in providing health services to its own population. This group can no longer be considered just the payer of insurance premiums, but must be dealt with as consumers or as potential competitors.

Governmental and Regulatory Agencies

Every hospital administrator is becoming critically aware of the increasing number of regulatory agencies influencing day-to-day life. Government influence on hospital operating activities is growing. Greater restrictions are being placed on institutional and managerial decision making. Of all the target groups, agencies have the greatest potential for bringing about major and potentially disastrous changes to the health care system.

Hospitals are not the first to be subject to the growing controls of government. The experiences, both good and bad, of other industries should be used to develop a baseline of knowledge from which a marketing program can be developed for this consumer group.

Employees

Employees are a critical part of the entire marketing program. No one wishes to lose the existing market, and maintaining it becomes a strong responsibility of the hospital staff. Employee attitudes and satisfaction with their own jobs are important in passing on to patients warmth, interest, concern and quality of service. It is imperative that employee relations programs not be overlooked, since they and their members compose one of the prime consumer groups. This group is the foundation, the implementor and the primary public image to patients entering the hospital.

Market Profile

A marketing profile helps identify strengths and weaknesses in services, programs and population draw, and determines what programs should be developed or perhaps phased out. The profile identifies trends in specific areas, such as why services are not currently being used by consumers; or if being used, why these services are being obtained at other facilities and locations. This in turn is the foundation for developing marketing program goals.

Essential to any hospital administrator considering a marketing program is the recognition of the current status of the institution. Research should reveal how the hospital is perceived by competitors, the communities served and health care regulatory agencies.

Potential Markets

Actual and potential markets must be clearly identified. One approach that might be taken in this initial endeavor is a well-designed questionnaire, geared to meet specific areas of interest.

In the development of the initial market profile, one hospital produced a number of questionnaires which were used to gather specific data about the potential marketplace. Consumers, physicians and area hospitals were surveyed with a variety of questions about health care practices, needs and current marketing activities.

Preprofile plans can be affected by the thrust of population trends and the identification of attitudes expressed by patients, physicians or area hospitals. Perhaps earlier planning will become invalid because of a newly developed, more comprehensive and consumer-oriented data base.

The Changing Environment

Existing operating and planning practices will need to be modified in a changing health services environment. Specifically, this refers to the determination of when a new or expanded program should be considered as part of a health provider's role or responsibility. Frequently, motivations for new services, programs, equipment or expansion of existing activities come from influential physicians, other political interests or restricted donations. Motivation for new programs should be based on sound market research identifying need, potential market and financial viability, not emotional enthusiasm. The program itself may not be a money-maker, but may generate other avenues of revenue that may bring about a continued and longer term benefit to the total institution.

Research for Effective Marketing

Occasionally, an industry will maintain a product line that is considered a "loser." The item is maintained because the ripple effect may provide substantial or offsetting revenue, and it permits the industry to compete while providing an appropriate bottom line for the stockholders and board. As with industry, hospitals have programs that appear superficially to be a liability to the organization, but in fact add revenue and utilization potential to other services within the total structure. The emergency room in many instances does not generate sufficient bottom line revenues to offset its own operating expense. However, it *does,* through its emergency admissions and use of supportive diagnostic service, provide substantial revenue which influences the hospital balance sheet. An effective marketing program must be based on marketing research and the control of emotional enthusiasm for new programs.

The evaluation of marketing research is critical and must be carried out in an objective manner, eliminating to the best degree possible the influence of those persons who have developed an "empire" and who might resist change for the purpose of retaining services that are no longer viable or properly utilized. Commitment to the program on the part of all staff, including medical, will give an additional opportunity for success.

Channels of communication with consumers are initially opened by means of questionnaires, site visits, public or private meetings, informational mailings or advertising, or mall intercept (which offers an opportunity to meet the community in a one-to-one encounter in shopping centers). Means of maintaining these open channels of communication and dialogue should be considered. These sources of data help test and update the changing requirements of the market area and evaluate the program's effectiveness in meeting consumer needs.

In developing a program of marketing services, planning priorities established by external influences must be included, i.e., political, governmental and regulatory groups whose actions can and do influence a hospital's role and services. Preventive health care, HMOs and new legislation to provide insurance coverage for the alcoholic patient are but a few key examples of the trends and priorities that must be considered in the development of a marketing plan.

The influence of newly emerging state and local health planning agencies (HSAs) cannot be understated.

Pricing Practices

At present, most hospitals, although capable of sophisticated pricing practices, rely more on a standard markup based on a rationale of unknown origin. Or their pricing practices are based on the relationship of charges or rates compared with the hospital down the street. Frequently, the basis for this practice is confirmed by a telephone call or survey to ensure similar charges for a specific treatment or service.

Pricing Structure

A pricing structure that prevents criticism of one hospital for being out of line with its peers must be developed. An objective review of charges for services, including all the direct and indirect expenses that may be related to a specific cost center, will usually demonstrate little relationship to the actual cost of providing and maintaining these services. It is not unusual to find charges marked up in excess of 100 percent on diagnostic services such as electrocardiographs. The purported reasons are that it is necessary to profit in this service to offset a losing department or that all area hospitals charge the same. Such a situation offers an excellent opportunity to reevaluate pricing and marketing practices, to develop a means of providing the services at a lesser cost to the public and to become more competitive in the marketplace.

The greatest limitation facing hospitals in developing a well-formulated competitive pricing policy may be the third party payers. Currently, reimbursement formulas serve to penalize a hospital when cost or pricing reductions are implemented. Such cost savings would not be realized in consumers' insurance premiums. A reduction in cost to the public can be negatively received if the public feels that such actions indicate a "cut-rate" pricing of services, reflecting poorer quality. Yet despite limitations encountered when revising a pricing policy, current practices must be altered.

Advertising

Despite the present controversy, advertising has been practiced by hospitals for many years under the headings of public relations, press releases and community relations. This kind of publicity should now be expanded not only to assist in identification of services provided, but also to function as an educational and motivational tool. Such a tool should awaken the public to realities facing the health care industry today, while still attracting them to the available services. Some hospitals, specifically one in Las Vegas, Nevada, have aggressively advertised. Although there have been some cries of unethical practice and dollar wasting, at first indication these programs have been successful in improving utilization. If properly and ethically applied, advertising will become a strong tool for the health care industry in publicizing its services to consumers.

Naturally, the goal of such advertising efforts—lower costs—may restrict an effective approach. However, the per capita cost of media advertising may compare favorably with direct mailing charges, which could prove to be prohibitive when the target audience is large. Through the use of standard media, information about new services as well as cost-saving activities can be announced. This same vehicle can identify health education activities to the public, and suggest the benefits of preventive medicine.

Using appropriate advertising methods to establish identification of the hospital should be one of the marketing goals. West Jersey Hospital has advertised a unique, toll-free telephone number to bring public attention to the availability of prenatal clinics maintained for those who do not have the opportunity or the motivation to seek out their own private physician. The clinics include four outreach satellite clinics and one hospital-based clinic, and have been identified with a single, easy-to-remember telephone number, although some are located 15 miles apart. Television has carried the information as a public service.

There are, of course, many ways to acceptably use advertising to create this identification. Another technique has been the publication of a directory of health services, which clearly identifies various hospitals and health agencies, the type of service they provide, room rate structures, accreditations and all other characteristics that might provide patients a better understanding of the facility, service or agency. Hospitals need not wait for the press to pick up the story; rather, they should aggressively use marketing expertise to develop ways to introduce their own story to the press. It may be costly, but it may also be less of an expenditure and more effective than current means of providing consumer education, such as mailings.

Competition

Generally, a position of noncompetition with fellow hospitals and health agencies has been embraced, and competition is unfamiliar to hospital administrators. Competition does not imply an intent to alienate area hospitals or agencies, or to try to drive them out of business. However, hospitals and agencies must begin to sharpen their management styles and internal practices to effectively withstand any infringement by an outside agency.

Intelligence Network

Most hospitals probably are not aware of the potential market lost ("the leakage" of patients) from their service area to other facilities. A hospital needs a good "intelligence network" to understand what services are being used and where. This information should be developed from the marketing profile as it will underline an important focus of future efforts in marketing. Are the programs (i.e., pickup services, convenient service hours, accessible neighborhood centers for diagnostic care) geared to the convenience of the patient? Are they similar to what patients may be receiving through other facilities?

The long- and short-range plans of other area health facilities, the types of service they plan to provide or continue to provide, and their expansion plans should be noted. It is not essential or wise to copy everything that another area health facility or provider offers, but administrators should at least know what is available so that facilities and services can be planned more effectively.

If the existence or survival of a service between a multiple of hospitals is in question, it would be in the administrator's best interest to develop procedures to provide better service at lower cost. Consumers—patients, physicians or employers—will be attracted to such an institution. In effect, administrators will be competing to retain or establish that specific service.

It is appropriate to meet with area administrators to discuss the whole question of marketing, competition and intentions related to this new administrative philosophy. Any future concerns or disagreements that arise out of a misunderstanding of goals may be offset by such a meeting.

Meeting the Competition

Meeting the competition requires the strengthening of strong areas of services while enhancing and developing those that are weak. Not only cost, but quality, accessibility, available resources and existing referral patterns play a role in competition effectiveness. One of the hospital's greatest assets will be the availability and understanding of what can be offered, at what price and quality to consumers.

Hospitals must be more innovative and quicker to respond to the needs of the community to achieve service goals before other agencies have an opportunity to do so. Marketing expertise made available to hospitals can provide sound guidance in an approach towards this competitive mode. If candidly discussed with peers and professionally carried out in the best interests of consumers *and* the hospital, marketing becomes a very effective tool in upgrading the quality of services while reducing underutilized ones.

Marketing Targets

Patients

One approach to increase marketing potential to consumers is the "courtesy discharge" which allows patients to be discharged without stopping at the business office. Ease of entry into the health care system—by outreach clinics, family health centers, or simply reduced waiting time resulting from effective internal procedures—promotes positive consumer reactions. Consumers feel more comfortable, more wanted and more like customers.

Admission is critical to the marketing image. Preadmission forms, including letters notifying patients of their scheduled admission and assuring them of the hospital's availability to answer any questions or provide any support prior to admission, can be very reassuring. Often, patients feel a negative reception on their first contact with hospitals. Hospitals should function in a positive manner to eliminate patients' concerns. Some hospitals have established advisory boards with a complement of members from the community to serve as a liaison in information sharing.

To further share information, auxiliary members' homes may be the sites of "coffee klatches" for which auxilians extend an invitation to members of their neighborhoods for an informal discussion of health care in the hospital. Key members of the hospital staff may also attend to informally address questions raised, to encourage greater participation in the ongoing activities of the hospital and to seek support for the programs and ideas that will be in their best interest. Such approaches will serve to break down some of the barriers that currently exist between patient/consumer, hospitals and health agencies.

Consumer Health Education

The inpatient is a captive audience for closed-circuit television which can be programmed for health education related to: preventive health care; an outline of cost containment procedures and their effectiveness; energy conservation activities or other information related to the impact of current regulations. To-be-admitted patients provide the hospital with an opportunity to publicize itself through preadmission handouts and flyers which completely inform patients of the services they will receive.

Outpatient services and activities can also be publicized through leaflets. The public can be made aware of ambulatory care and its availability without an inpatient stay.

Prime-Time Care Program

More should be done to generate activities that will reduce hospital charges. A program of "prime-time care" could reduce hospital charges by identifying times during the day or week when use levels are low. Patients would then be encouraged to use services during these hours at a lesser cost than that which would be charged during prime time. Because the hospital is underutilized at certain times, a cost benefit can accrue to the patients. Many of these services can be on an outpatient basis so that direct out-of-pocket savings can be realized by a patient rather than by the insurance carrier. Attention should also be focused on the convenience of the hours that services are provided. Hospitals should be willing to innovate programs in the best interest of their customers, perhaps earlier laboratory hours for tests to be performed before commuting to work, longer evening hours or a larger scope of available services on weekends.

Target Patients

When marketing to patients, it is appropriate to be sensitive to "target market" individuals who, because of age, social standing, finances or geography, may be considered underserved or excluded from the mainstream of health care. To this end, one hospital has developed a proposal to provide a diagnostic screening program for senior citizens. The foundation of this program is based on a similar service provided by a west coast hospital to offer senior citizens a battery of diagnostic tests on a prepaid arrangement. The cost to the subscriber represents only the cost of supplies ($7 to $10) per year. The program has been expanded to offer to this target population lunch or breakfast (depending on test schedule), along with a social setting providing health education services. Such a program offers preventive health services, responds to needed health education and develops political support while enhancing the hospital's image.

Physicians

In marketing to physicians as consumers it is imperative to effectively use the marketing profile explained earlier, and to further obtain information concerning the characteristics of each individual physician's practice. One method of achieving this goal is to establish a program of medical technology forecasting, identifying how physicians currently utilize services. It is necessary to know what patterns of care they predict will change in both their practices and hospitals in the foreseeable future, as well as what type of changes are most desirable from the physician's perspective.

Categorizing Physician Needs

Records on patient activities can establish a trend of hospital use by individual physicians. Admissions can be categorized—i.e., those requiring surgery and class of admission (emergency, urgent or elective)—and assessed at six-month intervals. The information can be graphed and used to project by month the type of utilization historically practiced by specific physicians. The same type of trends can be graphed by disease category to help develop a correlation of disease by medical specialty and by frequency to assist in projecting service and physician recruitment requirements. All questionnaire and medical forecasting data can become a component of the marketing profile, to be continuously updated through hospital records and physician input.

The directions to be taken as a result of these findings will reinforce the necessity of commitment on the part of the medical staff to this new approach to planning, particularly if such activities involve the hospital directly in medical or physician recruitment activities.

Workshops, Discussions

Workshops or retreats should be initiated or continued and should include all key members of medical staff, board and administration. Such workshops or programs, held in a quiet location where interruptions will be limited, encourage candid discussion about projected programs, needs and requirements as seen by physicians, the board and management. Through this type of dialogue, one would hope to bring about a mutual understanding and willingness to support the marketing approach, particularly when it begins to identify programs that might not be totally comfortable for the medical staff. Suggested discussions might include prepaid activities such as the HMO, programs for executive physicals, and extension of the hospital's employee health service to provide similar programs to small industry in the area.

Another critical role that physicians play as consumers is in the recruitment of new staff. Frequently, additions to hospital staff offer limited extension into the marketplace, because they are members of existing practices. Physicians who start new practices are in better positions to attract new clientele to the hospital. The medical staff heavily influences the recruitment of new physicians. This can present a critical problem if the medical staff feel that facilities and services are already overcrowded or that there is not an adequate market to support new practices and that bringing in a physician without new practice threatens to reduce their own financial capabilities. Nevertheless, in the longer run of the marketing program, one of the specific objectives should be the development of a medical staff that will use facilities effectively while supporting recruitment of additional medical expertise.

Employers

Marketing to employers is an activity new to most hospitals, and it requires identification of appropriate employers to reach into the community. Patients' origins, which can be used to identify local employers, are undoubtedly already available in many hospital records.

Here, as with the consuming public, a strong program of education and involvement in hospital activities will be appropriate and can be accomplished through industrial dinner meetings to which the key members of industry or employer groups are invited. Discussions may center on the problems of the health industry and its impact on the employer, and may culminate in joint approaches to be undertaken for improvement. This same group can be an excellent focus for a marketing program providing for executive health physicals, executive spouses' physicals and employee health services. Attractive packages can offer preventive diagnostic services on a prepaid or fee-for-service per capita basis.

These programs should try to reach those not presently covered by third party insurers.

Governmental Groups

Hospitals must seize a leadership role, and present to politicians and regulatory agencies more effective programs for curtailing health care cost. Such programs will have to demonstrate a strict and disciplined regimen for hospitals if it is to be accepted by these agencies.

The hospital image to date is one of *no,* it cannot be done; *no,* it will affect the quality of health care; and *no,* you don't understand our problems. The response has been obvious in view of the increased regulations in health services. An aggressively more positive and objective approach controlled by health facilities is more desirable than the head butting which is resulting in less effective programs with greater governmental control.

All marketing activities should be packaged in a marketing program addressed to the governmental and regulatory sector. With an improved image and the support of consumer groups, with cost stabilized or reduced through competitive activities, and with the development of sound factual planning decisions, the administrators of the health care industry can participate in the formulation of health care regulations as consultants rather than adversaries.

Third Party Insurance Carriers

It is important to develop with insurance carriers a program of incentives. At present, cost containment programs and cost reduction efforts on the part of hospitals result, in most cases, in a reimbursement penalty. This holds true for consumers, who receive no visible benefit for prudent use of health services (i.e., greater use of preventive rather than curative services). Participation in innovative programs that will be mutually beneficial to insurance carrier, hospital and patient alike should be the goal for all concerned.

Marketing in the Multihospital Setting

If a hospital is to survive, it is essential that it respond to changing needs, be competitive in a variety of markets and be identified with innovative, quality and effective customer services. Multihospital or shared services arrangements offer each of these elements of survival as a key product of their system. Legislation currently exists and is being implemented by local health system agencies or planning agencies to identify as one of their goals the encouragement of multihospital and shared system arrangements. It is urged that in the development of a marketing profile and the establishment of the goals and objectives for a particular institution, consideration for the development of some type of multihospital or shared service arrangement be given for both the marketing program and the long-range goals of the institution.

ORGANIZING FOR MARKETING*

Who's in Charge?

A critical decision for the chief executive officer is the assignment of the marketing function in the management structure.

Failing the in-house availability of an administrator with a marketing background an agency or institution would do well to select an individual with a sound base in a major profession and then provide the person with experience or education in marketing. Some of the ways that this can be done include:

- taking business courses or marketing training in local or nearby universities
- attending seminars and courses in social marketing
- providing part time consultation to the marketer from universities or firms experienced in social marketing
- acquiring a library of books and articles on marketing
- participating in activities of the local professional marketing association

---

*Source: Reprinted from *Marketing Health and Human Services* by Robert Rubright and Dan MacDonald with permission of Aspen Systems Corporation, © 1981.

The organization that employs a person with marketing skill, but who is without experience in health or human services, can use the same tools in reverse; that is, expose the person most thoroughly to the workings of the agency and its dominant professions. This would include:

- orientation to daily operations of each department of the agency or institution
- participation in management meetings at all levels of the organization
- participation in appropriate inservice or staff development programs

The marketing function is sufficiently important that the person holding the position not be insulated from top administration. If not immediately below the CEO in the staff organization chart, then the marketer should report to an associate director or vice president. The important point is the availability of and access to the CEO at all times, reflecting both the desirability for close communication and the relative importance that the CEO attaches to the function.

The Outside Marketing Consultant

A consultant should have the ability to conduct research, competence in public speaking, and management skills. Ideally, the consultant should have had exposure to the health field but this is not as important as having a knowledge of marketing and its techniques.

There are several ways to use a marketing consultant:

- Ask the consultant to provide marketing training for staff and volunteers.
- Request intermittent or regular consultation with the in-house staff person responsible for marketing.
- Contract with the consultant for a specific project that requires special knowledge of the subject rather than solely of marketing.
- Ask the expert to develop marketing plans for separate projects for execution by different units or departments of the agency.

With the exception of larger firms that dominate the management and financial side of health and human services consulting, most consultants are known because of their work within a region or because they have a particular service specialty. Since much of their success in acquiring work stems from satisfaction by former clients, they become known primarily by word of mouth. There is no formal system of acquiring consultants in marketing. Trade and professional associations generally maintain lists of approved or recommended consultant firms in other fields. Consultant fees in marketing vary with firms, of course, according to the demand for service, the caliber of the specialists involved, and the work expected. Most consultants charge a per diem fee plus expenses for short-term activity. For a given project, an agency can negotiate a block fee that also covers expenses. A retainer for regular consultation is not unusual. In any event, the consultant can be expected to specify in writing the services, materials, and assistance the expert will provide and to detail expected costs and fees. Reports and written documents depend on the desire of the contracting organization.

Suggested Steps in the Marketing Process

1. Convene marketing team; discuss charge, project situation, rationale for a social marketing approach; set up ground rules and procedures, dates for regular meetings; develop checklists.
2. Review, revise, and agree on approaches recommended in initial analysis of project.
3. Define primary objective of project (which may differ from #2); detail secondary objectives; review against agency's stated objectives and current policies.
4. Identify key target dates for project.
5. Identify all possible problems and opportunities related to project. (Detail barriers and how to overcome them.)
6. Review research activities according to outline (as modified).
7. Initiate and conduct special research projects as required.
8. Concentrate on identification of targets, proper analysis of their importance, ranking and sequence to implementation of project.
9. Identify exchange and sources of influence, advocacy, leverage that are related to target organizations.
10. Review targets; place in their proper sequence for implementation of strategies.

11. Identify internal adjustments needed with agency operations: policies, staff deployment, service fees, and so forth.
12. Hold progress report meetings with management to discuss findings, key decisions to be made, and preliminary recommendations.
13. Decide on tools that must be developed and used in implementation; arrange for their production.
14. Produce written marketing plan with provision for periodic adjustments.
15. Evaluate effect of strategies at key dates; be prepared to determine measurable results.

Note: For a survey of hospital activities see Table 14-3.

The In-House Marketing Team

Criteria for the selection of individuals to serve on the marketing team include:

- knowledge or background of the specific marketing project or subject
- existing or past relationships to potential target groups in the project
- special interest in the project in addition to having knowledge that is useful to the project
- leadership qualities
- management indication of their strong potential for job advancement
- enthusiasm for working with peers and others
- innovative thinking, flexibility in approaching work

Representation from a cross section of staff will produce strong participation and prevent overprotection of special interests or fiefdoms.

Marketing Information and Market Research

Prior to undertaking any market research effort, a health care organization should collect and analyze all relevant marketing information already available within the organization or accessible to it with a limited amount of detective work. Much of this information is often already collected by the planning officer within the organization but not viewed as marketing information. If an organization can answer its marketing-related questions through analyses of these available data, it should avoid the unnecessary ex-

Table 14-3 Hospital Marketing Activities*

Activity	% of administrators who say activity should be included	% of administrators carrying out this activity in 1977	% of administrators planning this activity for future
Attitude survey of current or discharged patients	100%	70	8
Marketing research techniques to assist in feasibility studies	86	34	5
Patient-oriented advertising	52	20	8
Direct mail promotion to physicians	65	39	6
Patient demographic profile	88	46	17
Staff member with well-defined marketing responsibilities	70	4	4
Defined hospitals target market	89	59	18
Formal marketing plan	75	9	19
Seminars for medical professionals	94	71	7
Study of services offered by nearby hospitals	97	64	10
Lounges for physicians	89	77	9

NOTE: Totals may not add to 100 percent because of rounding.

*Source: Reprinted from Larry M. Robinson and F. Brown Whittington, "Marketing as Viewed by Hospital Administrators" (1980 survey of 182 hospital administrators), *Health Care Marketing: Issues and Trends,* ed. Philip D. Cooper, with permission of Aspen Systems Corporation, © 1980.

pense of original, objective, systematic (and usually professionally performed) market research.

Marketing Information*

Marketing information can be divided into internal data (about the hospital itself) and external data (about the hospital's competition, market and general operating environment). The significant advantage of this basic information is that most of it is currently available within the hospital or can be collected to a large extent by the hospital's own staff.

The challenge presented by the collection of basic marketing data is being able to look at familiar information from a new perspective. Many hospitals have a wealth of marketing information already available or easily accessible to management. The failure to use this information results primarily from a failure on the part of planning and management to recognize that the data *are* marketing information and should form part of the basic marketing analysis. Not only should this information help identify marketing problems and issues, but it should also aid in determining strategic responses.

No one problem or opportunity is likely to require the use of all the information given in Table 14-4. However, it is wise to have the information readily accessible so that it can be used when a relevant marketing problem arises.

Advantages of Marketing Information

Marketing information collected and analyzed on an ongoing basis has the following advantages:

1. It is not expensive to collect compared to the higher prices associated with market research.
2. Once the baseline marketing information is collected, it can be easily updated to allow the rapid identification of trends.
3. Marketing information can be collected and analyzed by the hospital's own staff, particularly with the involvement of the planning staff. (For the initial collection and analysis effort, it is sometimes wise to hire outside marketing experts both to aid in the analysis and to transfer the skills of the experts to the relevant hospital staff.) By keeping the collection and analysis of the marketing information within the hospital, the hospital should be able to develop and internalize the marketing skills within its staff.
4. The results of the analysis of marketing information are necessary for and invaluable in the development of marketing strategies for the hospital.

Market Research*

Market research is original, objective, systematized research. Its value lies largely in providing information that is complementary to rather than duplicative of marketing information.

Information Generated

Specifically, market research can generate information on:

1. *Perceptions*—What does the consumer (physician, potential donor, etc.) think about this hospital and its specific services? What are his or her attitudes toward the hospital? The physical facility? The nursing care?
2. *Preference*—Which hospital would the consumer prefer (or intend to use) if he or she needs to be hospitalized? Does this preference vary by service or nature of the diagnosis? Or does the consumer's preference even matter since physicians admit patients?
3. *Potential demand*—For what new services is there a demand? In other words, what unmet health care needs exist in the community? In what way should the hospital structure services to meet these needs in

---

*Source: Reprinted from Roberta M. Clarke and Linda Shyavitz, "Marketing Information and Research—Valuable Tools for Managers," *Health Care Management Review*, Winter 1981, with permission of Aspen Systems Corporation.

*Source: The material on "Market Research" consists of excerpts from two articles by Roberta M. Clarke and Linda Shyavitz: "Marketing Information and Research—Valuable Tools for Managers," *Health Care Management Review*, Winter 1981; and "Market Research: When, Why and How?" *Health Care Management Review*, Winter 1982. Reprinted with permission of Aspen Systems Corporation.

Table 14-4 General Marketing Information

Internal	External
Census—aggregate and by service	Characteristics of the hospital's service area
Admissions/discharges	age distribution
by service (medical, surgical, pediatric, etc.)	income distribution
by diagnosis within service	level of education
by physician	by religion (if applicable)
by source of payment	by culture or ethnic background (if applicable)
by patient origin by community	by medical service usage rates (inpatient, ambulatory, emergency room)
by source of referral (medical staff, emergency room, outpatient department, etc.)	market size and growth rate
by patient age	natality and mortality statistics
by average length of stay	membership in HMOs (number of members in each HMO)
Medical staff	Profile of MDs in hospital's market area
aggregate number and by department	age
by credentials	specialty
by specialty	practice setting
by age	office location
by practice plans	admission rates
by office location	affiliations
by use of ancillary services and operating room	patients' origins
by admissions by diagnosis	credentials
by other hospital affiliations and percentage use of each other hospital affiliation	
by total hospital revenue generated	
Emergency department utilization	Competitors
gross utilization	number of beds
by shift	occupancy by service
by time of year, day of week	service configuration
by source of payment	characteristics of population served
by patient origin by community	service expansion or alteration plans including major capital projects
by type of diagnosis	medical staff makeup
time in waiting area until patient treated	prices
percentage of EMS ambulance runs to emergency department	
patient origin by incidence of emergency	
by source of referral (walk-in physician, fire, police, etc.)	
percentage of emergency department patients who are admitted as inpatients	

Table 14-4 continued

Internal	External

Ambulatory medical services utilization
  gross utilization
  by service
  by diagnosis
  by patient source
  by patient origin by community
  by source of referral
  by patient age
  percentage of ambulatory patients who are admitted as inpatients
	Planning, regulatory and hospital reimbursement trends
	
	Medical (clinical) practice trends (i.e., decreasing tendency to hospitalize children, increasing use of home health care, etc.)

Financial information
  revenues by department
  expenditures by department	

Gross index of patient satisfaction with all services
  from patient cards
  from hospital ombudsmen	

terms of service policies, price (if any), location, access and promotion?

4. *Usage*—General marketing information should generate substantial usage information, but market research can complement significantly the hospital profile of its user (patient) base. It can better indicate past usage (as reported by the consumer, compared to future usage, as preference information would project) by identifying who went to which hospital for what service.

Due to its expenses, marketing research should be used only when information on specific issues is needed and such information cannot be obtained through the marketing information available internally.

Research should typically be performed with the aid of or by outside professionals with expertise in the area of market research. However, in an attempt to minimize costs, hospital managements have sometimes tried to perform their own market research through the use of internally available staff.

Typical Market Research Questions

By far, the questions most commonly addressed by market research deal with low occupancy and low utilization of services.

Other issues include patient financial mix problems ("How do we get more privately insured patients?"), patient age mix problems ("Can't we get more younger patients so that this hospital won't end up looking like a 300-bed nursing home?") and the effect of new competition ("How will Hospital A's new satellite practice affect our market share?").

Each health care provider may also have market research questions specific to that organization's situation (e.g., the effect of opening up staff privileges in a hospital with previously closed staff privileges, the impact of new reimbursement policies on the use of relevant services, the determination of appropriate locations at which to open new professional medical offices and the identification of unmet consumer health needs).

These questions may focus on the whole organization ("Why is the census declining throughout the hospital?") or on specific services ("Why is the number of pediatric staff members declining?"). Generally, when a health care organization undertakes a market research effort, it does so with the intent of answering a number of specific questions rather than just one. This is both appropriate and more efficient than creating a whole new market research effort each time a new question arises. However, addressing a variety of issues in one research effort can only be done when the research effort for all the questions is directed at the same markets (i.e., consumers and medical staff, local business and industry, or police, fire and emergency medical technicians).

Health care organizations would be unwise to go on "fishing trips." The market research effort should be focused on questions for which a thorough analysis of the hospital's marketing information cannot provide the answers. Examples of specific questions which could appropriately be addressed by market research are: How will the health maintenance organization (HMO) moving into our service area affect our census and patient mix? Who will join the HMO and therefore be drawn away from our hospital? The answer in this instance was that the HMO would attract primarily younger families from the hospital's service area. Since young families are heavy users of obstetric and pediatric services, it was in those services that the hospital would experience a census decline as a result of the expansion of the HMO.

Who Should Perform Market Research?

A health care organization should consider performing its own market research only if it has the competence to do so. At the very least, this competence includes both skill and experience in experimental versus nonexperimental designs, qualitative versus quantitative research methods, sampling procedures, questionnaire construction, interview techniques, survey management, data processing, and data analysis and interpretation methods.

What Type of Consultant?

There is not a large cadre of market research consultants who have substantial experience in health care market research. It is especially important to recognize that health care consultants in areas such as planning and public relations

---

WHAT CAN GO WRONG IN A SURVEY?

If a market survey is done by someone with insufficient skill and experience, what can go wrong? Among other things:
- The wrong questions are asked.
- The questions are worded incorrectly (insensitively, misleadingly or in an incomprehensible manner).
- The questions are ordered improperly so as to be leading, to bias the response, or to artificially raise the salience of some issue or entity.
- The sample is poorly selected.
- The market from which the sample is selected is not the appropriate market for study.
- The methodology used is incorrect, resulting in less valuable information than could have been obtained.
- The survey results are inadequately or improperly analyzed and interpreted so that the worth of the survey is diminished or negated.

---

can make no realistic claim to marketing research expertise unless they have received training in and run market research projects.

Since market research requires very specific technical skills, a health care organization faced with the choice between market researchers

---

SKILLS AND ATTRIBUTES TO LOOK FOR IN SELECTING A MARKET RESEARCH CONSULTANT

- knowledge and understanding of the purposes and applications of qualitative and quantitative market research
- expertise in a variety of research methodologies
- substantial experience in the use of qualitative research
- substantial experience in designing market research projects, including data collection instrument design
- substantial experience in managing the data collection (field study, telephone survey, one-on-one interviews) aspects of market research
- substantial experience in managing the data processing and analysis aspects of market research; strong statistical skills
- if possible, health care market research; if not, substantial experience in utilizing market research skills in a variety of industries

with no health care experience and health systems consultants with no expertise in market research would be better off selecting the market research consultant. The health care organization can supplement the market researcher's skills with its own vast knowledge of the health care field.

Top Management Involvement

Even though an outside consultant may be retained, the hospital still has responsibilities for planning, developing and implementing the market research project. Given the probability that the consultant will be expert in market research but unfamiliar with the health care industry, the execution of a role complementary to the role of the consultant is essential to the success of the project. This complementary role is usually played by top management. It is management's responsibility to identify the specific unanswered questions that the market research is intended to address, to secure resources for the project and to recruit, select and hire the consultant. Later, when the research results are fully collected and the analyses complete, it is management's responsibility to select and implement specific strategies that will best serve the organization from those that the research suggested.

In addition, management shares a number of responsibilities with the consultant, such as identifying the research target population, setting the timetable and, at times, analyzing the data for their strategic implications.

The Marketing Audit*

The marketing audit has many purposes:

- It appraises the total marketing operation.
- It centers on the evaluation of objectives and policies and the assumptions that underlie them.
- It aims for prognosis as well as diagnosis.
- It searches for opportunities and means for exploiting them as well as for weaknesses and means for their elimination.
- It practices preventive as well as curative marketing practices.

---

*Source: Reprinted from *Marketing Objectives for Hospitals* by Robin E. Scott MacStravic, with permission by Aspen Systems Corporation, © 1980.

The first step in gathering the information—the intelligence—to serve as a basis for a marketing effort is the market audit. Usually referred to as a market*ing* audit in most industries, it is essentially a data base to guide marketing decisions. Its fundamental purpose is to examine systematically how well the organization is doing in its market relations. How well things are going in your market includes both a still picture of what things are like right now and a preview of where they seem to be headed in the future.

Both the present and foreseeable future of your market relations are important. The first lets you know whether you have immediate problems or success, the second identifies possible future problems or opportunities. A market audit should enable you to identify where your intervention is required and where it will do the most good. It precedes but leads directly to action, toward achieving a desired change or preventing one you'd rather avoid. (For a list of possible elements in a marketing audit see Table 14-5. For a suggested market audit procedure see Table 14-6.)

Impact Data

There are a number of factors that should be studied for impacts on the health of the organization itself: financial factors especially, but also measures of efficiency and internal effectiveness. Traditional examples among financial measures include expenditures, revenues, and their relationship for specific programs as well as overall cash flow, receivables, debt ratios, acid tests, etc. Factors such as occupancy levels, numbers of patients turned away, delayed or rescheduled surgery, etc., will indicate internal effectiveness or efficiency. Such measures result from the interaction of your behavior with your patients' behavior but also may reflect degrees of satisfaction and reputation.

Internal measures for the most part should be available through your own records. Financial data, occupancy levels, productivity figures, and so on should be collected and analyzed routinely. Occasionally, you may wish to devote special efforts to study some aspect of your performance not routinely monitored.

Market Segments

The first step in measuring and analyzing behavior is to designate whose behavior interests you.

Table 14-5 Elements of a Marketing Audit

THE MARKET AND MARKET SEGMENTS

- How large is the territory covered by your market? How have you determined this?
- How is your market grouped?
  — Is it scattered?
  — How many important segments are there?
  — How are these segments determined (demographics, service usage, attitudinally)?
- Is the market entirely urban, or is a fair proportion of it rural?
- What percentage of your market uses third party payment?
  — What are the attitudes and operations of third parties?
  — Are they all equally profitable?
- What are the effects of the following factors on your market?
  — Age
  — Income
  — Occupation
  — Increasing population
  —
  — Decreasing birthrate
  } demographic shifting
- What proportion of potential customers are familiar with your organization, services, programs?
  — What is your image in the marketplace?
  — What are the important components of your image?

THE ORGANIZATION

- Short history of your organization:
  — When and how was it organized?
  — What has been the nature of its growth?
  — How fast and far have its markets expanded? Where do your patients come from geographically?
  — What is the basic policy of the organization? Is it on "health care," "profit"?
  — What has been the financial history of the organization?
    — How has it been capitalized?
    — Have there been any account receivable problems?
    — What is inventory investment?
  — What has been the organization's success with the various services promoted?
- How does your organization compare with the industry?
  — Is the total volume (gross revenue, utilization) increasing, decreasing?
  — Have there been any fluctuations in revenue? If so, what were they due to?
- What are the objectives and goals of the organization? How can they be expressed beyond the provision of "good health care"?
- What are the organization's present strengths and weaknesses in:
  — Medical facilities
  — Management capabilities
  — Medical staff
  — Technical facilities
  — Reputation
  — Financial capabilities
  — Image

- What is the labor environment for your organization?
  — For medical staff (nurses, physicians, etc.)?
  — For support personnel?
- How dependent is your organization upon conditions of other industries (third party payers)?
- Are weaknesses being compensated for and strengths being used? How?
- How are the following areas of your marketing function organized?
  — Structure
  — Manpower
  — Reporting relationships
  — Decision-making power
- What kinds of external controls affect your organization?
  — Local?
  — State?
  — Federal?
  — Self-regulatory?
- What are the trends in recent regulatory rulings?

COMPETITORS

- How many competitors are in your industry?
  — How do you define your competitors?
  — Has this number increased or decreased in the last four years?
- Is competition on a price or nonprice basis?
- What are the choices afforded patients?
  — In services?
  — In payment?
- What is your position in the market—size and strength—relative to competitors?

PRODUCTS AND SERVICES

- Complete a list of your organization's products and services, both present and proposed.
- What are the general outstanding characteristics of each product or service?
- What superiority or distinctiveness of products or services do you have, as compared with competing organizations?
- What is the total cost per service (in-use)? Is service over/under utilized?
- What services are most heavily used? Why?
  — What is the profile of patients/physicians who use the services?
  — Are there distinct groups of users?
- What are your organization's policies regarding:
  — Number and types of services to offer?
  — Assessing needs for service addition/deletion?
- History of products and services (complete for major products and services):
  — How many did the organization originally have?
  — How many have been added or dropped?
  — What important changes have taken place in services during the last ten years?
  — Has demand for the services increased or decreased?
  — What are the most common complaints against the service?
  — What services could be added to your organization that would make it more attractive to patients, medical staff, nonmedical personnel?

Table 14-5 continued

- What are the strongest points of your services to patients, medical staff, nonmedical personnel?
- Have you any other features that individualize your service or give you an advantage over competitors?

PRICE

- What is the pricing strategy of the organization?
  - Cost-plus
  - Return on investment
  - Stabilization
- How are prices for services determined?
  - How often are prices reviewed?
  - What factors contribute to price increase/decrease?
- What have been the price trends for the past five years?
- How are your pricing policies viewed by:
  - Patients
  - Physicians
  - Third party payers
  - Competitors
  - Regulators

PROMOTION

- What is the purpose of the organization's present promotional activities (including advertising)?
  - Protective
  - Educational
  - Search out new markets
  - Develop all markets
  - Establish a new service
- Has this purpose undergone any change in recent years?
- To whom has advertising appeal been largely directed?
  - Donors
  - Patients
    - Former or current
    - Prospective
  - Physicians
    - On staff
    - Potential
- What media have been used?
- Are the media still effective in reaching the intended audience?
- What copy appeals have been notable in terms of response?
- What methods have been used for measuring advertising effectiveness?
- What is the role of public relations?
  - Is it a separate function/department?
  - What is the scope of responsibilities?

CHANNELS OF DISTRIBUTION

- What are the trends in distribution in the industry?
  - What services are being performed on an outpatient basis?
  - What services are being provided on an at-home basis?
  - Are satellite facilities being used?
- What factors are considered in location decisions? When did you last evaluate present location?
- What distributors do you deal with? (e.g., medical supply houses, etc.)
- How large an inventory must you carry?

Source: Reprinted from Eric N. Berkowitz and William A. Flexner, "The Marketing Audit: A Tool for Health Services Organizations," *Health Care Management Review*, Fall 1978, with permission of Aspen Systems Corporation.

The community and actual patients should be divided into market segments for the purpose of analysis and strategy development. A market segment is simply a set of persons (or organizations):

- who are sufficiently alike to be treated as a homogeneous group and
- who are sufficiently different from others to be treated as a distinct group

The numbers and types of market segments you designate are purely a matter of judgment. The more there are, the more complex your analysis becomes, but the more focused your strategies can be.

Some examples of the kinds of factors that may unite a segment internally and distinguish it from other segments are the following:

Community: Patients

- age (<15, 15–44, 45–64, 65+, etc.)
- sex (combined with age cohorts)
- race
- residence
- income level
- insurance coverage
- diagnoses
- employment
- religious preference
- marital status
- physician identification

Organization: Employees

- department
- type of employee
- length of service
- union vs. nonunion
- shift
- function/service
- unit

In addition to the community and patient market, you should segment the physician and referral agency markets:

Table 14-6 Market Audit Procedure*

Step 1. Identify the specific set of market transactions you want to audit—e.g., inpatient utilization by service.

Step 2. Identify the specific behaviors you're interested in measuring: Current   Past Years
  A. Patients
     admissions
     length of stay
     average daily census (ADC)
     variability of census (standard deviation)
     ancillary service use
  B. Physicians
     number of admissions
     length of stay
     vacation timing
     ancillary service use
     numbers of physicians on staff

Step 3. Describe how you behave with respect to this market:
  A. Patients
     number of people wait-listed
     average length of wait for admission
     number of patients placed in "wrong" units
     proportion of time unit was understaffed/overstaffed
     percent of meals served hot, on time, etc.
  B. Physicians
     admitting privilege rules
     priorities
     perquisites
     percent of admissions delayed
     percent of surgeries cancelled
     emergency room coverage required
     committee responsibilities

Step 4. Evaluate current behavior and current direction of change in terms of hospital performance/success measures:
     occupancy rate
     lost patient days because of lack of beds
     total revenue this service
     total expenses this service
     total estimated lost revenue due to lost patients, if any
     revenue contributions to other services
     expenditure contributions to other services
     payments as percent of charges
     receivables rate

Step 5. Identify patient's demographic and psychographic factors of interest that might explain behavior or be focused on to change it.
  Demographic: age, sex, race, income, health insurance coverage, employment, size of family, residence, family physician, religious preference
  Psychographic: knowledge of hospital's services, attitudes toward quality, cost, personal aspects of care received, understanding of condition, feelings about doctors, nurses, hospital

*Source: Reprinted from *Marketing Objectives for Hospitals* by Robin E. Scott MacStravic, with permission of Aspen Systems Corporation, © 1980.

Physician

- location
- specialty
- size of practice
- age
- group vs. solo
- medical staff status
- privileges

Referring Agency

- location
- function/service
- community served
- funding source

The sole purpose of segmenting a population is to treat each segment differently either in your analysis or, later, your market strategy—and preferably both.

Behavior

The market audit should cover all those behaviors that are understood to lead to important impacts. For patients, the behaviors are likely to include:

- admissions rates
- length of stay
- visits per year
- whether they pay bills, what portion they pay, and how long they take to pay
- compliance with regimen or advice
- appointment keeping or breaking, or tardiness

For physicians and referral agencies, the behavior is likely to include:

- patients admitted or referred to you
- total patients admitted or referred anywhere
- length of stay or visits per patient/registrant
- diagnosis mix of admission/referrals
- patient days or visits generated
- revenue generated vs. charges
- expenditures generated vs. costs

Each behavior should be capable of being evaluated in terms of its impact upon the organization's performance. The numbers and types of physicians on a hospital's medical staff and how many of what kinds of patients they refer or admit determine a hospital's census levels, expenditures, and, ultimately, revenue.

Causal Factors

Just as each behavior should be linked to its impact(s), so, too, should it be linked to potential causal factors. The first set of causal factors may have been partially identified already in the attributes used to determine the market segments. Demographic characteristics of markets are useful in two ways:

1. in identifying segments that are distinct from each other and warrant your separate treatment
2. in explaining or predicting how different individuals or organizations behave

Demographic characteristics of patients should be useful in understanding or predicting their disease or injury patterns, what use of health services they make, how much they can or will pay for specific services, and where they will look for such services. Demographic characteristics of physicians or referral agencies should be useful in understanding or predicting how many patients they will admit or refer, of what types, how many services they will prescribe for those patients, and where they will tend to send them. Anticipating future changes in such demographic factors can help your organization predict future changes in behavior and respond to them.

Patients' demographic factors include age, sex, race, education, income, insurance coverage, religious preference, place of residence, and employment. Much of these data are available from your records on actual patients or census data for potential patients. Demographic attributes of physicians that might interest you include age, sex, race, specialty, medical school, internship and residency training, specialty board status, type of practice (single, specialty, or multispecialty group, partnership or solo), office location, and residence. Such data should be available from your records on physicians on your medical staff, from state licensing boards, or from the American Medical Association.

Such demographic factors may help you understand and predict behavior by patients and physicians, but not completely. Psychographic factors—what people know or believe and how they feel about you—also are important. Such knowledge and beliefs will fall into one of three categories that are important to your marketing strategy: product, place, and price. *Product* is defined as the benefits people believe they will derive out of doing business with you, being your patient, or becoming a member of your medical staff, for example. *Place* includes the understanding people have about how to go about doing business with you and the circumstances under which they can avail themselves of your product. *Price* is the flip side of product: the financial, physical, and psychological costs to people of doing business with you.

Product Factors:

- what services you offer to people
- what good they will do them
- what quality of care you provide
- how modern and complete is your equipment
- how modern, spacious, and clean is your facility
- how qualified and courteous is your staff
- whether staff members care about your patients as people

Note: For physicians you may try to recruit, such factors include both the benefits you offer their patients and the benefits you offer to physicians:

- surgical facility, equipment, and staff
- operating room schedules
- privileges
- perquisites such as physician lounges, dinners for spouses, guarantees of income, etc.
- prospects of responsible positions on the medical staff
- prospects of financial success in the community

Place Factors:

- hours and days of service availability
- types of people (or physicians) eligible
- types of people (or physicians) welcomed
- convenience of location
- availability of parking
- waiting time for appointments
- waiting time to be seen
- length of time to process application

Price Factors:

- out-of-pocket charges/costs to patients
- length of time allowed for payment
- pain or discomfort involved in your services
- personal indignities or psychological discomforts involved
- committee assignments and scutwork required of physicians

As psychographic factors, it matters not so much whether individuals' "knowledge" and beliefs are true but whether they perceive them to be true. The kinds of feelings you'd be interested in knowing about are likely to include:

- how people rank in importance such factors as convenience, quality, caring, and cost in deciding whether and where to seek services
- how they feel about your organization and its "image"
- what they'd like you to change about yourself
- how they think they'd behave if you did make changes
- how they feel about other organizations offering similar benefits (your competition)

Psychographic information, in contrast to demographic, seldom is likely to be available from records or other secondary sources. To find out what people believe and how they feel, you must anticipate collecting original information.

Externalities

In addition to the data you gather and analyze on your current market relations, two other categories of information are necessary in the market audit. First is the analysis of the environment, identifying what is happening out there that will affect how you and your markets interact in the future. Second is analysis of the competition, determining how it now interacts with its markets and what kinds of changes in its market relations are foreseeable or probable in the future.

Environment

Environmental factors include such direct and obvious developments as governmental regulation, planning and rate-setting agencies, educational institutions, licensing agencies, national health insurance, developments in the overall economy, changes in medical technology, or trends in health. Any such developments that might alter your behavior or that of your markets significantly should be assessed, as should the market-specific demographic and psychographic factors already discussed.

Competition

Other organizations that currently or potentially offer similar benefits (products) to similar markets also should be included in your market audit. Ideally, you would like to have a copy of their audits, telling you how they and their markets behave, what impacts such behaviors have, and what factors explain why customers choose them over you. Some of this information you can get from published data such as their annual reports, the American Hospital Association's Guide issue, and public records on data that must be furnished to governmental agencies and made available to the public.

In addition to public records, you may learn of your competitors' market relations through informal, even casual, conversations with them or through persons who have market relationships with both you and them. Physicians who are on the medical staff of more than one hospital or refer to colleagues at other institutions may be informed about what's going on there. Patients who use your services as well as theirs may describe their experiences there. Members of your governing or advisory boards may have some knowledge of what competing organizations are doing or planning.

A more formal source of information on your competitors' market relations would be a survey of the general community. By dividing responses from a community survey into persons who use the competition vs. those who use your services, you can get an idea of how the two groups behave, how they differ, and how well you're doing relative to the competition.

Audit Results

The output of the market audit should be a thorough and accurate description of how specific groups of persons behave, what characteristics might explain that behavior, and what impact this has upon the groups themselves and upon your organization. It should tell you what kinds of activities you're doing well, both in terms of their impact and in terms of how your behavior is perceived by others. It also should tell you what you're not doing so well and where you might wish to focus attention. It should help you understand why your performance—your contribution to the community and to the health of your organization—is good, bad, or indifferent.

To evaluate the data output of the market audit, it is necessary to judge, not simply collect, information. You may evaluate the facts you develop by comparing them to specific standards. You probably will have fairly precise expectations for impacts such as the health status of your target community and its satisfaction levels. Similarly, precise standards are likely for internal performance factors such as financial outcomes, occupancy, and total service. You also may have predetermined expectations for behavior, both yours and theirs, such as seeing every emergency room patient within one minute of arrival for triage, or attracting 80 percent of your target community as registrants.

Researching the Competition*

Because in health and human services, competition is not pointedly price oriented, a hospital's reputation for dependability, skill, and perhaps creativity becomes its chief promotional aid.

Through sound marketing planning, a hospital must convince potential users that its staff is experienced, skilled, knowledgeable, caring, ethical, and sensitive since it can't blatantly promote low service fees, offer guaranteed results, or conduct special sales. Also, it can't overrun its competition overnight. It must develop its reputation gradually, using rational, honest marketing strategies.

There are three ways to react to new competition: ignore it, imitate it, or adopt some of its main features.

How can new competition impact on an established human services organization? It can: (1) compete for the clients who represent the existing institution's market core; (2) compete for the attention of referring professionals or for capable volunteers to serve on its board, task forces, or committees; (3) compete for employees, especially professionals who seek better salaries, fringe benefits, or quicker advancement opportunities; (4) compete for the attention of community interests such as politicians, news media leaders, bankers, and service clubs. A new com-

---

*Source: Reprinted from *Marketing Health and Human Services* by Robert Rubright and Dan MacDonald, with permission of Aspen Systems Corporation, © 1981.

petitor may offer different services, such as extended daily or weekend coverage, new specialties, computerized billing, influence with third party payers, chain ownership, less paperwork, or better office location.

A Checklist

The established agency always will require basic information about the new agency to help it respond to its programs or promotions. To assist the established agency in organizing its knowledge about the new rival so it can formulate its revised marketing objectives, strategies, targets, and tools, the information listed in Table 14-7 should be sought.

Approaching the Competition

Gathering information and data about a new rival is bound to frustrate an established agency, but the results should be worth the effort.

The competition usually is receptive to its rival's questions. A rival's answers usually will be forthright since the competitor can learn something in turn from the interrogator; this is helpful because the newcomer usually has a need to be accepted early by established agencies. Here is one way to approach the new rival:

1. Phone the rival and extend a welcome. Share some background about your own agency; start asking some questions about the newcomer in order to feel your way.

Table 14-7 Checklist for Competitors

1. Name of competitor:_____
2. Address of competitor:_____
3. Date competitor opened for business:_____
4. Describe the nature of competitor's business:
5. Who sponsors the competitor's agency?
6. Describe competitor's financial backing, if known:
7. Name and title of competitor's chief administrative officer:
8. Previous employment of that chief administrative officer:
9. Name of competitor's chairman of the board:
10. Names and business titles of other volunteer board members:
11. Names, titles, immediate past positions of key members of competitor's administrative staff:
12. Did a community survey precede the competition's formation? ___ Yes ___ No
    If Yes, describe the survey and state who conducted it:_____
13. Did the new program facility undergo a formal project review through a community planning council or any other central planning agency or authority? ___ Yes ___ No
    If Yes, what agency and when?_____
    What were the final recommendations?
14. Is the competition's program or facility licensed? ___ Yes ___ No
    If Yes, when and by whom was the license issued?_____
    Was a license ever denied? ___ Yes ___ No
    If Yes, by whom was the license denied and for what reason?
15. Was a certificate of need (CON) issued? ___ Yes ___ No
    If Yes, when was it issued?_____
    Any unusual qualifications or conditions attached to the CON?
16. In your opinion, are clients of the competitor's program or facility being recruited from (circle one)
    your own agency's service area,   a new service area,   a combination of both?
17. Who on the new competitor's staff is the contact person with clients and referring sources in the community?
18. What services are offered by the competition?
19. Do any of the competitor's services differ from those your own agency offers? ___ Yes ___ No
    If Yes, how do they differ?_____

Table 14-7 continued

20. Does the competition have any striking features to help it attract clients? ___ Yes ___ No
 If Yes, what are those features?_____
21. What are the competition's costs and charges in comparison with your own?_____
22. What socioeconomic, psychic advantages do you think the competitor has over your own operation?_____
23. What disadvantages does the competitor face in the community?_____
24. Does the physical location of your competitor offer any advantage over your own locations? ___ Yes ___ No
 If Yes, what advantages?_____
25. What are the competitor's main marketing targets?
26. List the competitor's marketing tools and how they are used:
27. If your competitor were to make a major marketing change in the next several months, to which markets or targets would the rival shift?
28. What challenges does the competitor face from your agency?
 From other competitors in the area?_____
29. In a paragraph or two (use a separate sheet of paper if necessary) describe how the competition might characterize your own agency from a competitive viewpoint:
30. What does your organization need to do to protect itself from the new competition, both immediately and long range?

---

2. Ask for the competitor's brochure and other literature it is distributing. Tell the rival you'll send your brochure if it does not have one.
3. Determine who the competitor's key managers are, as well as their backgrounds. If the agency is small, there may only be one or two. It is not unorthodox to discuss staffing during the first visit.
4. Set up a session to get to know the newcomer better. At that point, obtain an understanding of the agency's owners, sponsors, financial angels. Though the competitor might volunteer such information by telephone, go ahead and arrange for the social meeting anyway.

- *If answers are hard to obtain:*

1. Shop the new facility as a prospective user or delegate the task to someone else.
2. Telephone the new facility's switchboard or intake section and ask appropriate questions.
3. Ask colleagues what they've heard about the newcomer.
4. If there is a known parent organization, obtain its last annual report for clues about the newcomer's objectives, goals.
5. Contact appropriate licensing agencies to determine more about the organization's origins and makeup.
6. Talk with professionals who may have had dealings with the newcomer.

- *If there are unreasonable roadblocks in your way, and there is some legitimate concern about the competition, try the following, but cautiously:*

1. Use the Freedom of Information Act to gain access to information about the competitor's ownership, financial strength, and management.
2. Contact a Better Business Bureau for information.
3. Ask an attorney to assist in gathering facts.

It may not be possible to compile a complete profile on a competitor, but if the existing agency's efforts are applied systematically, it can determine enough to reassess its own marketing strategies and strengths, estimate how the newcomer may seek entry into its core market, and calculate how successful it might be in becoming a part of the professional life of the community.

The careful study of competition, established or new, is one of the most beneficial facets of marketing. It forces the marketer's agency or clients to evaluate its own operations in the light of the strengths and weaknesses of its rival. It is likely to reveal marketplace gaps that neither agency is serving properly. It removes the tendency to grouse about the other entity and its tactics. It opens opportunities for improving or developing one's own product or service, to stay a step ahead. Sometimes it brings about a judgment or conclusion that it might be better to join 'em than fight 'em, thus leading the way to consolidation of interests and objectives that can only benefit clients or patients and the community.

P.R. AND ADVERTISING

Public Relations and Marketing: Overlapping Spheres*

Often, marketing is lumped together with the public relations function under the mistaken assumption that marketing is equivalent to public relations.

Few public relations directors are trained in developing marketing studies that can result in management changes, and it is the rare marketing director who understands the subtleties of working with the media. A positive synergistic effect can result for the hospital, with each department focusing on its unique areas of responsibilities and integrating the overlapping areas. (See Figure 14-1.)

Advertising**

Hospital advertising achieved legitimacy in 1977 when both the American Hospital Association and the Federation of American Hospitals recognized the need for hospitals to advertise their services. Since that time as many as 20 percent of the hospitals in the United States have engaged in some form of patient-oriented advertising. The content of such advertising has varied widely. The extremes in terms of message content and complexity may be represented, on the one hand, by the series of annual hospital progress reports that have been printed in local newspaper supplements and on the other hand, by the chance to win an all-expense-paid cruise for the patient entering the hospital on Friday or Saturday.

It is useful to recognize that consumers can influence the selection of a hospital in three different ways:

- recognize a problem and go directly to the hospital;
- select a physician because of the hospital that he or she is (or is not) affiliated with; or
- select a physician and then choose among hospitals with which the physician is affiliated, or switch to another physician if none of the first physician's affiliated hospitals are acceptable.

Message strategies, then, designed to reach this segment are likely to be effective if they focus on providing information related to one or more of the decision points where a consumer might influence hospital selection.

In the area of direct access to hospital services, the pro-advertising segment may include many who look toward the hospital to maintain wellness, while being prepared to treat illness.

These people believe hospitals should offer special services such as diet workshops and stop-smoking programs. Strategies in this area should be service specific, focusing on those aspects of the service that are not normally observable, differentiating the service from those available in other organizations. Emergency services may also fit into this area. Here attempts to differentiate your services from others may focus on the rapid, systematic way that care is provided or on the patient as a customer who must be satisfied with the care provided.

To encourage consumers to use physicians affiliated with your hospital, the hospital might create a physician referral service that permits a consumer to call the hospital to get the names of one or more primary or specialist physicians who are affiliated with the hospital. Advertising about the referral service might then be done through specially designed messages or as part of a more general message about the various services of the hospital.

---

*Source: Reprinted from Eric N. Berkowitz et al., "Marketing/Public Relations—A New Arena for Hospital Conflict," *Health Care Planning and Marketing*, January 1982, with permission of Aspen Systems Corporation.

**Source: Reprinted from William A. Flexner and Eric N. Berkowitz, "Media and Message Strategies: Consumer Input for Hospital Advertising," *Health Care Management Review*, Winter 1981, with permission of Aspen Systems Corporation.

Figure 14-1 Spheres of responsibility

Public relations / Marketing

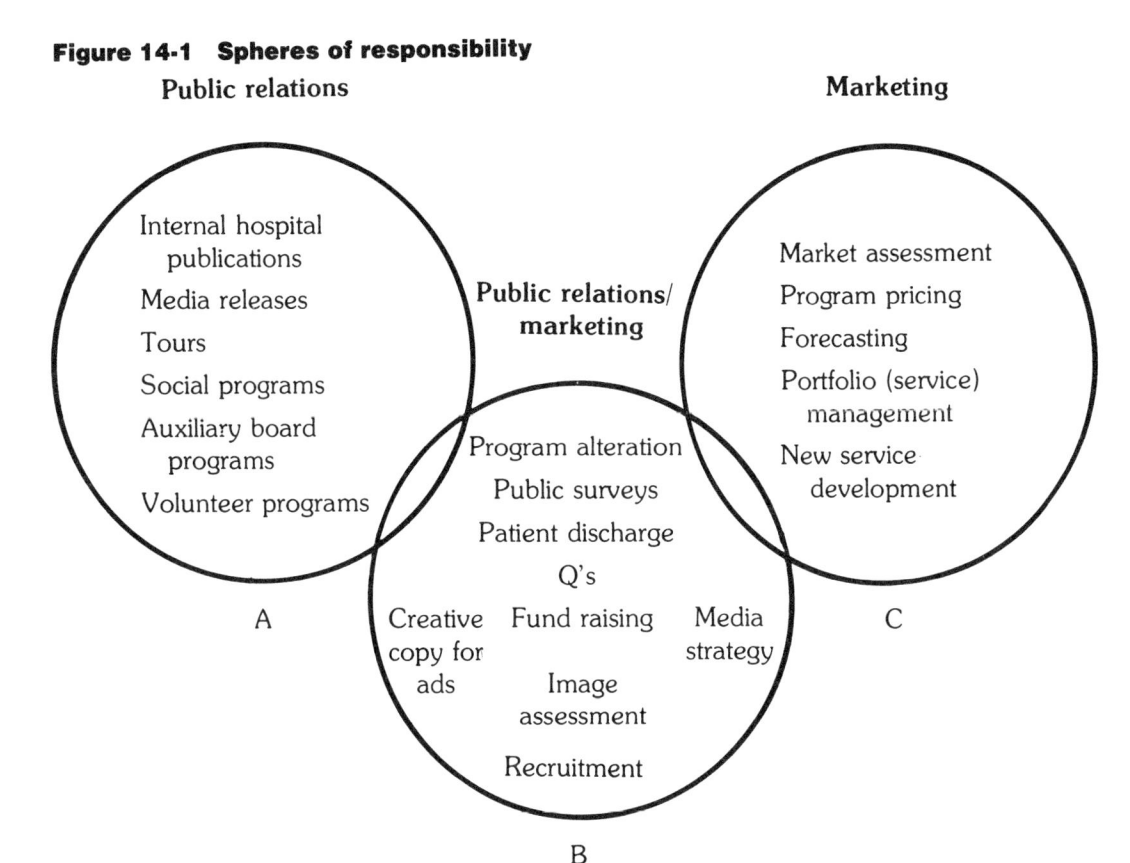

A (Public relations):
- Internal hospital publications
- Media releases
- Tours
- Social programs
- Auxiliary board programs
- Volunteer programs

B (Public relations/marketing):
- Program alteration
- Public surveys
- Patient discharge Q's
- Creative copy for ads
- Fund raising
- Media strategy
- Image assessment
- Recruitment

C (Marketing):
- Market assessment
- Program pricing
- Forecasting
- Portfolio (service) management
- New service development

Because many physicians are affiliated with more than one hospital, an advertising strategy might be developed to inform consumers that their physician often can offer a choice of hospitals, and to encourage them to make their hospital preference known to the physician. A similar strategy might also be developed for physicians, informing them that more and more patients want a choice of hospitals and listing the reasons that patients give for wanting to come to your hospital.

Finally, to position your hospital for the segment of consumers who believe advertising is appropriate, it is important to show what steps are being taken to run the place as a business. Among the areas that might be addressed are efforts to reduce costs, ways that the hospital shares services with other facilities, methods used to make the financial (billing) system more responsive to consumers, and the efforts the hospital will make to assist the consumer with getting into, through and out of the hospital smoothly.

PART IV
FINANCIAL MANAGEMENT

OVERVIEW

For the administrator, making financial decisions isn't easy. For one thing he has less power than his counterpart in the outside business world. He's the man in the middle, wedged between the trustees and medical staff. The trustees hold him responsible for the solvency of the institution, and the medical staff holds him responsible for maintaining a state of efficiency that contributes to the quality of services. As a result, he is absolutely dependent on sound reporting from his financial officer.

The financial officer's responsibility virtually parallels that of the administrator. What both are dealing with is a microworld, with as many different human and mechanical factors as are present in any community. The modern institution may have as many as 20 or 30 independently organized revenue centers; each source may have different regulations and timetables. The financial system may have to track as many as 2,000 billable items and maintain an inventory that runs to several thousand items.*

---

*Source: Reprinted from Jack C. Wood, "Financial Management Tools," *Topics in Health Care Financing,* Fall 1974, with permission of Aspen Systems Corporation.

Management Control Phases*

"Management control is a process by which managers assure that resources are obtained and used effectively and efficiently in the accomplishment of an organization's objectives."

Anthony and Herzlinger,
Management Control in Nonprofit Organizations

There are four distinct phases in management control:

1. Programming
2. Budgeting
3. Accounting
4. Analysis and reporting

Programming

Programming is the phase of management control that determines the nature and size of programs an organization will use to accomplish its stated goals and objectives. The programming phase of management control would take stated objectives and evaluate alternative programs to accomplish them.

---

*Source: Reprinted from *Essentials of Hospital Finance* by William O. Cleverley, with permission of Aspen Systems Corporation, © 1978.

Budgeting

Budgeting is a quantitative expression of a plan of action. Budgets are usually stated in monetary terms and cover a period of one year.

The budgetary phase of management control follows the determination of programs in the programming phase. In many cases, no real review of existing programs is undertaken, so the budgeting phase often builds on a prior year's budget, or actual results for existing programs. Proponents of zero base budgeting have identified this as a major shortcoming.

The budgeting phase primarily translates program decisions into terms that are meaningful for responsibility centers.

Budgeting may also change programs. More careful and accurate estimation of revenues and costs may reevaluate prior programming decisions as financially unfeasible.

Accounting

Accounting is the third phase of the management control process. Once programs have been decided on and budgets developed for these programs along responsibility center lines, operations begin. Accounting accumulates and records information on both outputs and inputs during the operating phase.

Analysis and Reporting

The last phase of management control is analysis and reporting. In this phase, differences between actual costs and budgeted costs are analyzed to determine the probable cause of the deviation and reported to the individuals who can correct it. Successful analysis and reporting rely heavily on the information provided from the accounting phase to break down the deviation into categories which suggest possible cause.

In general, there are three primary causes for differences between budgeted and actual costs:

1. Prices paid for inputs were different than budgeted prices.
2. Output level was higher or lower than budgeted.
3. Actual quantities of inputs used were different from budgeted levels.

Within each of these areas, the problem may come from budgeting or operations. A budgetary problem is usually not controllable; no operating action can be taken to correct the situation. For example, the surgi-center may have budgeted for ten RNs at $1,250 each per month. However, if there were no way to employ ten RNs at an average wage less than $1,300 per month, the budget should be adjusted to reflect this change in expectations. Alternatively, the problem may come from operations and be controllable. Perhaps the nurses of the surgi-center are more experienced and better trained than expected. If this is true, and the mix of RNs originally budgeted is still regarded as appropriate, some action should be taken to change the actual mix over time.

Chief Financial Officer (CFO)*

Functions

The chief financial officer directs the overall financial management of the institution under the direction of the CEO. [The CFO] directs the overall financial planning and analysis, accounting, data processing, treasury functions, internal audit, real estate and insurance activities for the institution; plans, organizes and analyzes the appropriate accounting and statistical data with and for all departments of the institution; coordinates all relationships (except selection) with third party auditors and third party reimbursers.

Specifically the CFO:

- Analyzes the institution's current financial position and develops mid- and long-range financial plans to ensure the present and future financial viability of the institution.
- Works closely with the CEO and the chief operations officer regarding business-related planning and problem solving for the entire institution.
- Supervises the controller in the management of the following functions: general accounting, cost accounting, accounts payable, cash management, payroll, electronic data processing, billing and collections, and reimbursement planning.

---

*Source: Reprinted from "Financial Career Opportunities," ed. Richard C. Dolan, *Topics in Health Care Financing*, Fall 1980, with permission of Aspen Systems Corporation.

- Supervises the budget director; supervises other managers and the functions of financial planning, cash planning, fiscal analysis and forecasting.
- Works closely with the finance and/or audit committee of the board of trustees; informs committee members on the business factors affecting the total health care environment; utilizes the expertise of board members in the financial planning process; makes financial presentations at board of trustees meetings.
- Acts as financial advisor to the CEO and board of trustees of the hospital.
- Advises the CEO, the chief operating officer and other key personnel about elements of financial management and accounting that are necessary to effectively carry out their responsibilities.
- Performs a variety of personnel administration tasks; educates and develops managers and other key personnel within the financial division; evaluates the performance of key personnel and oversees mechanisms to make sure other personnel are evaluated; recommends promotions, salary increases and terminations; acts as final decision maker on personnel matters within the established management guidelines of the institution within his or her jurisdiction.
- Updates the table of organization to meet the fast-changing demand of the financial division; develops a personnel plan to ensure that technical capabilities of the organization remain current.
- Oversees the production and distribution of all the institution's important financial, accounting and budgetary reports.
- Works closely with controller and department managers in the proper development of and adherence to important budgetary and accounting policies.
- Under the overall direction of the CEO, makes important financial presentations to outside bodies such as HSAs and lending institutions.
- Performs other duties as assigned by the CEO or as required to effectively meet the responsibilities for the position.

Qualifications

This position requires as much financial management, accounting and business background as is necessary to be the expert financial resource of a large complex business, professional and community enterprise. The individual must be comfortable in forecasting future needs based on a thorough background in financial analysis, treasury functions and accounting. It requires a highly intelligent, clear-thinking individual with the ability to earn the respect of executives and professionals.

The person must not only be accurate in developing financial data and materials; he or she must also be able to sell the analysis that comes from the material. This does not require an extroverted personality so much as it requires the ability to project an air of professionalism and confidence. Proven oral and written communication skills are important to be effective. Some theoretical and practical background in accounting is necessary but the person need not be a CPA or have many years of accounting experience per se if he or she meets the other qualifications mentioned. There is a relatively brief break-in period allowed for those without a health care background.

NOTE: For a representative table of organization for a hospital's department of fiscal services see Figure IV-1.

Economic Myths and the Hospital*

One of the more cherished beliefs of the American public is that hospitals are inefficient and mismanaged. They also think that because hospital costs to the patient have risen to unprecedented heights profits are enormous. These prevailing notions have caused no end of frustration in the hospital field and have periodically led to public relations programs aimed at telling the real hospital story to a disbelieving public. This meeting of fire with fire only deepens the public's mistrust—thinking "he doth protest too much".

Much of what makes for sound hospital management does not jive with public concepts of good economics based on their own sets of business and personal experiences. Against these perspectives, hospitals are inevitably going to be misunderstood. A look at a number of the eco-

---

*Source: Reprinted from Richard L. Johnson, "Hospital Economics: 19 Myths," *Healthcare Financial Management,* January 1975, with permission of Healthcare Financial Management Association.

Figure IV-1 A department of fiscal services

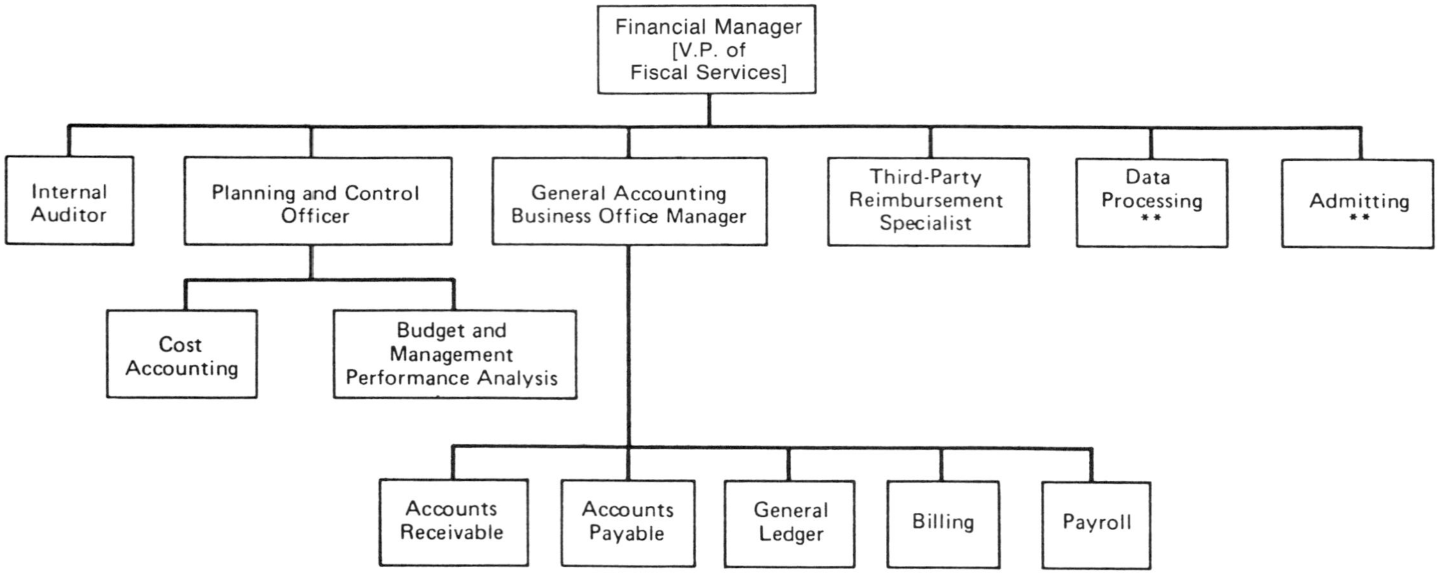

```
                        Financial Manager
                        [V.P. of
                        Fiscal Services]
        ┌───────────────┬────────────────┬───────────────────┬──────────────┬──────────────┐
   Internal      Planning and     General Accounting   Third-Party        Data           Admitting
   Auditor       Control          Business Office      Reimbursement      Processing     **
                 Officer          Manager              Specialist         **
                     │                   │
                 Budget and      ┌───────┼───────┬──────────┬──────────┐
   Cost          Management      Accounts   Accounts   General    Billing    Payroll
   Accounting    Performance     Receivable Payable    Ledger
                 Analysis
```

**Optional

NOTE: Smaller institutions might not have personnel occupying each of the listed positions, but the areas of responsibilities which are identified must be assigned to the existing complement of employees in order to establish accountability for the appropriate performance of these procedures.

Source: Reprinted from *Healthcare Financial Management*, May 1974, with permission of Healthcare Financial Management Association.

nomic myths held dear by the public shows the magnitude of the problem of trying to get them to measure hospitals against meaningful economic yardsticks.

Economic Myth #1: The larger the total volume of services produced, the lower the average unit cost of service. Unlike manufacturing, the more units produced, the higher the cost per patient day. Large hospitals have a higher average cost per day than do medium sized hospitals, which in turn have higher average costs per patient day than small hospitals. This occurs because as the size of the hospital increases, so does the range and comprehensiveness of service.

Economic Myth #2: Competition is desirable because it leads to lower prices to the customer. In hospitals the reverse occurs; the greater the competition, the higher the cost to the user of the services. Hospitals compete with each other by clinically "keeping up with the Joneses." Competition between hospitals is not on a cost basis but on a service and convenience basis. Physicians who hold multiple staff appointments do not decide where to send their patients on the basis of lower cost, but rather on the basis of the quality and range of services available for diagnosing and treating patients. Nor do patients request their physicians to admit them to the lowest cost hospital, but rather to the one where they will receive quality service and the amenities that make hospitalization comfortable.

Economic Myth #3: Payment for services rendered exceeds the cost of providing the services. Largely unknown by the public is that cost reimbursement formulas provide less than full cost revenues to a hospital. If the public knew that hospitals sign Blue Cross contracts and Medicare agreements that provide revenues at a lower level than the costs for rendering them, they would question the business judgment of a hospital for entering into such a deal. The public would be doubly perplexed about hospitals that provide their employees Blue Cross coverage under such a contract, when the hospital could provide employees with equally good coverage and be reimbursed on charges rather than by an unfavorable cost reimbursement contract.

Economic Myth #4: To the greatest extent possible, capital should be substituted for labor. Under cost reimbursement formulas, all direct labor costs related to hospital activities are 100 percent reimbursable. On the other hand, funds spent on buildings, materials handling systems, diagnostic equipment and treatment facilities are all depreciated under allowable costs on the basis of Internal Revenue Service standards which do not appropriately take into account obsolescence. If hospital administrators were to behave in a totally economically rational manner, they would follow the guideline of automating as little as possible so as to assure maximum reimbursement. To their credit, they prefer to automate in spite of its effect on reimbursement.

Economic Myth #5: An increase in operational efficiency leading to a reduction in operational expenses results in an equal increase in dollars to the bottom line of the profit and loss statement. This belief is held not only by the public, but by many trustees, physicians and hospital personnel. They tend to believe that hospitals achieve the same results from improving operational efficiencies as do other industries. They fail to recognize the penalties that occur under a cost reimbursement system of payment for services rendered. It is difficult for them to grasp that if a hospital receives 80 percent of its revenue for patient services from cost reimbursement sources and achieves an actual annual cost reduction of one million dollars that the revenue to the hospital will decrease by $800,000 and the net effect on the bottom line of the profit and loss statement is only an improvement of $200,000, not $1 million.

Economic Myth #6: The user of the services determines the amount, kind and quality of what he purchases. In a hospital the patient is usually not even asked if he wants the laboratory, X-ray, or other diagnostic or treatment procedures ordered by the attending physician. He (or his insurance company) is expected to pay for these services without questioning their value to him. It is not at all clear whether the patient is the customer of the hospital or whether it is the attending physician (who in many ways is a surrogate customer).

If in reality the attending physician is the customer, he too has many restrictions placed on his economic ability to select services for his patient. Once he admits the patient to the hospital he cannot order only selected services for the patient and have other hospitals perform needed services on that patient. Even if the other hospital is located nearby and can perform services at a lower cost, his only economic decisions are to withhold a procedure or service or to shorten the patient's stay in the hospital.

Economic Myth #7: The marketing goal of the organization is to maximize the demand for its services. Given an investment of nearly $100,000 per bed and 2.5 employees per patient day, it would seem to be just good common sense to use the facilities and available services to the greatest extent possible. This spreads the capital and operating costs across the widest possible number of units of services. Today, the emphasis is on minimizing the use of hospital services. This is the intent of the PSRO legislation where the concern is for reducing the average length of stay of a patient.

The aim of federal programs and Blue Cross plans is to keep the patient in a vertical position rather than a horizontal one. Under such circumstances a marketing program by the providers of hospital services to increase the use of inpatient services would be frowned upon by the reimbursers.

Economic Myth #8: The sharing of cost data and pricing policies among competitors in the same industry for the purpose of establishing common pricing structures is illegal. In the health field, hospitals are encouraged to share cost data and to standardize rate structures. Cost reimbursing agencies and state rate review commissions tend to establish categories of hospitals by bed size and to reimburse at the same rate for all hospitals in a category. Using variations on pricing structures in order to increase utilization of the hospital by attracting patients who might otherwise go to another nearby hospital is regarded by many health professionals as unethical. The effect of prospective reimbursement programs is to establish a nearly uniform revenue program for hospitals of similar size though not necessarily similar in terms of patient mix by clinical service, financial category or age distribution.

Economic Myth #9: The sharing of a service between two hospitals leads to a reduction in the unit cost of providing the shared service. This is perhaps the greatest current myth prevalent in the health field today. For example, it is commonly believed that if two hospitals located a few miles apart could share a laundry or dietary service, the total costs of the combined operations would be reduced. If combining the service adds a factor of transportation from one hospital to the other, the likelihood is that no savings can be effected. Experience indicates that such sharing usually requires a substantial capital investment in new equipment, renovation of space or the construction of additional space abutting the existing space. When these capital costs are taken into account in the operating statements, the usual result is to find that the cost per unit of service is higher than it was before the combining of the service.

Economic Myth #10: The board of directors' primary allegiance is to the corporation. In a for-profit enterprise, the governing board is single minded in the application of criteria for measuring its success—the profitability of the firm. All else—community responsibility, economic opportunities for the disadvantaged, environmental controls—are of secondary importance. In a hospital, the measurement of success is not as clearcut and trustees may find themselves in a different position. Many trustees regard the hospital as a quasi-public institution and believe that when the interests of the community come into conflict with those of the hospital, the community interests are primary and the hospital's secondary.

Economic Myth #11: Corporations strive for an annual surplus in order to pay dividends to stockholders, but a hospital surplus is not necessary since nonprofit corporations do not pay dividends and are therefore not concerned with a return on investment. The notion of a return on investment—so dear to the hearts of stockholders—has equal force in the nonprofit hospital. The surplus generated in the operation of the hospital is reinvested in new or expanded services for patients, and a successful hospital is one that can demonstrate a long history of adding to the comprehensiveness of available services. This is as much of a return on investment as paying dividends to stockholders. In this case, the return is in the form of services rather than dollars. Hospitals of 500 beds and larger typically run occupancy rates between 85 to 90 percent and have a cost per day that may be twice that of a rural hospital. Hospitals of under 100 beds typically have occupancy rates in the 60 percent rate even though their costs are half of the larger ones'. In hospitalization, the American public places a higher value on well being than on purchasing at the lowest possible cost.

Economic Myth #12: All profit centers in the corporation should contribute to the profitability of the firm. Unlike industry, some profit centers in hospitals never produce a net surplus of funds but continue to operate year after year because the service is needed in the community. In most hospitals, emergency room services and obstetrical services lose money. If the hospital is deeply involved in education, the expenses for a medical education program, a nursing school and paramedical training programs are all loss operations. Yet so long as the hospital as a whole breaks even, the losing profit centers are continued because they are a necessary community resource.

Economic Myth #13: The corporation is directly responsible for monitoring the quality of the services provided. In hospitals physicians are expected to accept the responsibility for controlling the quality of medical care. Yet they are not employed by the institution but are "privileged" to attend to patients if they have a medical staff appointment. Paradoxically the courts and the public do not distinguish between the roles of the physicians and the hospital corporation. In a very real sense, the private practitioner is a businessman operating his own enterprise.

Economic Myth #14: The satisfied customer is expected to reuse the services offered by the corporation. Unlike private industry, the hospital is expected to prevent persons from using their inpatient services if at all possible. When the facilities are used hospitals are expected to limit that use to the minimum amount necessary to assure a satisfactory physiological result even if a patient may be inconvenienced. Moreover, the physician and hospital are expected to answer to third party payer interests rather than those of the recipient.

Economic Myth #15: Managers are encouraged to operate profitably by payment of bonuses at year end. Private industry has long accepted the idea that year end bonuses to executives are an incentive to continued outstanding performance. Because hospitals do not generate profits but rather surpluses, key executives are expected to produce at full throttle for a predetermined salary level.

Chapter 15—Operations

FINANCIAL PLANNING

Using Financial Information*

There are five uses of financial information that may be important in decision making:

1. Financial Condition

    Evaluating an entity's financial condition is probably the most common use of financial information. Usually, an organization's financial condition is equated with its viability or capacity to continue pursuing its stated goals at a consistent level of activity.

2. Stewardship

    Historically, evaluating stewardship was the most important use of accounting and financial information systems. These systems were originally designed to prevent the loss of assets or resources through employees' malfeasance.

3. Efficiency

    Efficiency is simply the ratio of outputs to inputs, not the quality of outputs—good or not good—but the lowest possible cost of production.

4. Effectiveness

    Assessment of the effectiveness of operations is concerned with the attainment of objectives through production of outputs, not the relationship of outputs to cost. Measuring effectiveness is much more difficult than measuring efficiency because most organizations' objectives or goals are typically not stated quantitatively. Because measurement is difficult, there is a tendency to place less emphasis on effectiveness and more on efficiency. This may result in the delivery of unneeded services at an efficient cost.

5. Compliance

    Finally, financial information may be used to determine whether compliance with directives has taken place. The best example of an organization's internal directives is its budget, an agreement between two management levels regarding use of resources for a defined time period. External parties may also impose directives for the organization's adherence, many of them financial in nature. For example, rate setting or regulatory agencies may set limits on rates determined within an organization.

Making Financial Decisions*

As Figure 15-1 indicates, quantitative data may be expressed in either monetary or nonmonetary terms. During the course of a given day, the health care facility generates a considerable amount of accounting information that

---

*Source: Reprinted from *Essentials of Hospital Finance* by William O. Cleverley, with permission of Aspen Systems Corporation, © 1978.

*Source: Reprinted from *Hospital Accounting Practice*, Vol. II, by Robert W. Broyles, with permission of Aspen Systems Corporation, © 1982.

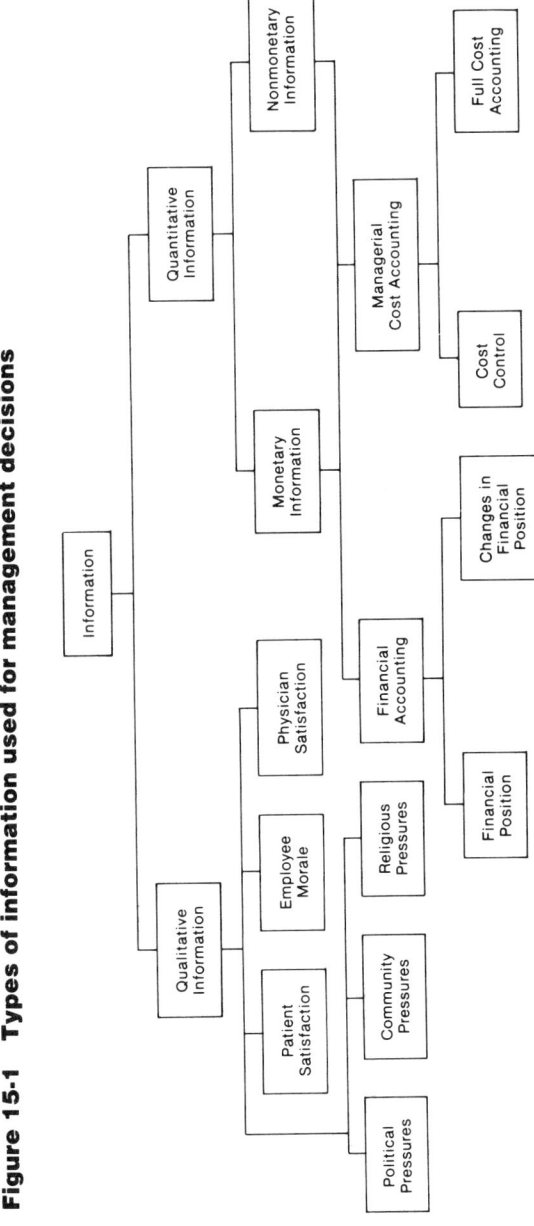

Figure 15-1 Types of information used for management decisions

frequently is incomprehensible when examined in detail. However, a greater sense of perspective may be gained by recognizing that detailed information emanates from several identifiable streams of data that reflect:

1. *The Quantity and Composition of Services:* This information originates from service logs, charge tickets, and patients' medical records.
2. *Use and Cost of Labor:* These data are derived from the payroll records that indicate the amount of labor employed in each expense center, the distribution of personnel hours by type of service, the wage rates, and the wages or salaries paid to each employee. Since each employer is required to provide the employee and the government with information on amounts earned, the payroll records of different health facilities are quite similar.
3. *Acquisition and Cost of Consumable Supplies:* This information is obtained from the records on the quantity and composition of consumable supplies ordered, received, and distributed to the facility's expense centers.
4. *Plant and Equipment:* These data indicate the cost, location, and condition of each significant item of building and equipment as well as related depreciation information.
5. *Revenues and Receivables:* These data involve revenues earned and emanate from charge tickets, service logs, discharge records, and patients' accounts. When service is provided on credit, information concerning the resulting receivable appears in subsidiary records that indicate the amount owed and the party responsible for payment.
6. *Financial Transactions:* This information is derived from several records and specifies the cash balance as well as cash receipts, cash disbursements, the payment of liabilities, and investments in marketable securities.
7. *Areas of Responsibility:* Such data depict the expenses incurred and, in the case of revenue-generating centers, the income earned during a given period.
8. *Costs:* These data detail the costs of providing service.

Using Computer Models for Financial Planning*

To meet the increasing demand for planning, the hospital administrator or financial manager will have to use financial planning techniques such as flexible budgeting, preparation of quarterly or even monthly cost reports to estimate the year-end reimbursement situation, and multiyear financial projections to analyze the long-term impact of construction programs or changes in patient mix. However, even though the need is recognized and the desire to implement these planning techniques is sincere, one of the major stumbling blocks to the success of these techniques has been the amount of time which must be incurred to perform the required calculations either initially or when changes are made to the assumptions.

The financial model is an important tool which can relieve managers and their staff from the task of performing the repetitive mathematical calculations required for thorough financial planning. Simply stated, a financial model is a computer program that simulates, either in whole or in part, the financial operations of the hospital. It can perform predetermined calculations required by a flexible budget, a cost report or most other types of financial analyses. The financial model provides its user with two distinct groups of advantages:

1. Clerical Efficiency
   - It reduces the time necessary to initially prepare or revise the financial projections.
   - It reduces the cost of preparing and revising the financial projections.
   - It eliminates the arithmetical errors of manually prepared projections.

2. Planning Improvement
   - It improves the planning process since it allows more time to be directed at analyzing the problems encountered.
   - It provides insight into hospital operations by identifying (or forcing someone

---

*Source: Reprinted from Ben I. Boldt, Jr., "Financial Modeling: A Must for Today's Hospital Management," *Health Care Management Review,* Summer 1978, with permission of Aspen Systems Corporation.

to identify) how factors within the hospital interact.
- It provides an ability to quickly try numerous alternative strategies to find or identify those that provide optimum results.

The General Model

General models include those models which provide pro forma financial statements and are not restricted to any one industry or purpose. The principal output of these models includes: an income statement, balance sheet, and statement of cash flow or change in working capital.

The general category of financial models has many applications in the area of multiyear financial projections. For example, it can be used to answer types of planning questions such as: What is the expected impact on operating costs due to the planned renovation program? Can the hospital generate the necessary cash flow to undertake a $12 million construction program? What happens to the hospital's financial position if pediatric services are phased out and a 7-percent average occupancy is lost over the next five years?

These questions are answered by changing the projection variables affected by the criteria of the question.

After identifying the known or estimated value of the variable changes, the user can input the data and run the model to reflect the effect of these changes on the income statement, balance sheet and cash flow statement.

The Industry Model

The industry category of financial models is structured and has two principal applications within the health care industry: flexible budgeting and the preparation of cost reimbursement reports.

The Budget Model

The budget model provides a hospital with the ability to develop departmental budgets based on a desired level of service and expected occupancy rate. When all department-level assumptions are input, the model executes the calculations necessary to determine each department's budget as well as consolidating all departments to obtain the budget for the total hospital.

Once the budget is established, the model provides the user with the ability to rapidly recalculate the budget to reflect varying conditions such as changes in occupancy and labor costs, increases in radiology service charges or other departmental revenue, or cost changes. Depending on the degree of sophistication used, this type of model offers to the hospital financial manager complete flexible budgeting capability.

The features that distinguish a forecasting model from a budget model are the length of time covered by the projections and the level of detail included. Typically, a budget model is designed to cover a one-year period by month and provides for totaling the months for each line item entered to obtain the budgeted amount for the year. Additionally, this type of model provides for not only revenue and expense data but operating statistics at the department level. The overall level of detail utilized in a budget model should correspond to the hospital's chart of accounts. This chart of accounts detail is desirable since it facilitates easy comparison of the actual results versus budgeted data throughout the year.

A major benefit of a budget model is the ability to develop meaningful departmental detail and be in a position to quickly analyze the impact of alternative courses of actions on the affected department(s) and the hospital in total.

The Cost Reimbursement Model

This model is specifically designed to prepare or recalculate a hospital's cost reimbursement report. The more advanced models allow for rapid recalculation and comparison of alternative allocation formula and reimbursement strategies. This capability allows the hospital financial executive to evaluate which of a number of allocation bases will provide the maximum reimbursement to the hospital or, alternatively, which is capable of answering the question, "What impact will that new Medicare regulation have on my expected reimbursement?"

Some of the capabilities provided by this type of model are:

- The model provides the user with the capability to experiment with various statistical bases, cost center composition and sequence of allocation alternatives. The effect of these alternatives on cost reimburse-

ment can be quickly and economically determined.
- A user can quickly determine the effect of audit adjustments proposed by the Medicare intermediary. This information can assist the hospital in devising a strategy for discussing the adjustments with an intermediary.
- The model simplifies the preparation of cost reports by greatly reducing manual calculations and by automatically preparing worksheets for the cost report.
- Cost reimbursement and related contractual allowances can be estimated for interim periods.
- The model assists in developing realistic budgets and forecasts by providing the capability to determine cost reimbursement and related contractual allowances using budgeted and forecasted data.
- It allows analysis of reimbursement and preparation of special reports which assist in developing an appropriate reimbursement strategy.

The Custom Model

The custom model is required when the simulation or analysis desired is so complicated or detailed that it cannot be performed by a model within the general or industry category.

In the case of a major midwest medical center, the model was designed to aid the planning process specifically in the area of projecting the cost changes resulting from a planned shared clinical service program, not only for the total medical center consortium, but at each institution within the consortium.

The model provides the planners with capability to:

- project the cost impact of a specific shared clinical service program under consideration;
- project the cost impact of alternative programs; and
- update the financial projections related to an acceptable program with each year's current cost data and patient information.

The development of a custom computer model can assist health care planners or hospital financial executives to analyze some of the financial considerations encountered during the development of a hospital's or group of hospitals' long-range plan.

PROFITABILITY FOR HOSPITALS*

Hospitals are embarrassed by almost any positive level of profit. If profits are considered too high, health care executives will feel pressure from their boards or community to reduce them through rate reductions or subsidies. If profits are too low, the long-run viability and quality of care posture of the organization is compromised. Determining and attaining a level of profitability that is both acceptable and sufficient is not an easy task.

Health care executives have a responsibility to their organizations to actively seek choices of methods for obtaining necessary levels of profit. Failure to do so can have disastrous consequences. In the short run, quality of care can be impaired seriously because of an insufficiency of resource support, both personnel and capital. In the long run, the viability of the institution may be threatened because of an inadequate capital base that will ultimately restrict the organization's ability to enter new and expanding markets.

Adequate levels of profitability are not guaranteed to any health care organization. They must be eagerly and aggressively sought. A good way to organize the search for alternative sources of profitability is to analyze the categories of the income statement. An examination of an income statement reveals the existence of five major areas for profit improvement:

1. Expansion of patient-related revenue.
2. Minimization of deductions from patient revenue.
3. Expansion of other operating revenue.
4. Control over operating costs.
5. Expansion of non-operating revenue.

Expansion of Patient-Related Revenue

There is no guarantee that expansion of revenue from patient services will necessarily result in any improved profitability. In fact, present trends indicate that possible reductions in profit-

---

*Source: Reprinted from William O. Cleverley, "Profitability in the Health Care Industry: An Overview," *Topics in Health Care Financing*, Fall 1977, with permission of Aspen Systems Corporation.

ability may result from expansion of patient service revenue because of insufficient levels of reimbursement by third party payers and/or inequitable regulation of rates. Nevertheless, this is the primary objective of most health care organizations. To remain viable in the long run, expansion of services, and therefore revenue, is essential. Expansion must be in those areas where service demands of the community are growing.

Adjustments and Allowances from Gross Revenue

Major types of allowances include charity, courtesy and contractual. Charity allowances arise largely from the treatment of indigent patients. The distinction between charity allowances and bad debts is now an extremely important one. Charity allowances may be used to satisfy the free care requirements for Hill-Burton recipients. Writeoffs for bad debts may not be used to satisfy the Hill-Burton free care provisions. Courtesy allowances represent the difference between established rates and amounts actually collected from special individuals such as employees, employee dependents, clergymen and others. Contractual allowances represent the difference between established rates and amounts received from third party payers. They may arise from third party payers who pay either on a cost or a charge basis. However, in most situations, contractual allowances result largely from the difference between rates and costs, where costs are defined by the respective third party payer. Since in many situations as much as 80 percent of a health care organization's total gross patient services revenue may be generated under third party cost formulas, this allowance category is very important.

Other Operating Revenue

Expanding other operating revenue is another potential source of improved profitability. Major sources of other operating revenue include:

- Tuition from educational programs.
- Research grants.
- Rental of space in the existing plant.
- Parking lot fees.
- Gift shop.
- Cafeteria.
- Commercial laboratory operations.

It makes good sense to utilize existing resources and management expertise to the fullest extent. However, poorly planned expansion into areas which promise increases in other operating revenue can jeopardize the nonprofit status of the health care organization.

Operating Expense

Controlling operating expenses is an important way to improve profitability. It is a management activity that the public currently demands.

Non-Operating Revenue

Non-operating revenue usually results from one of two sources: unrestricted gifts, or investment income (either from prior investments of unrestricted monies, or prior investments of monies with principal restrictions but no restrictions on income).

Philanthropic giving is important to health care organizations. It represents, in many cases, the only real source of external equity available. Sound financial structures, whether in nonprofit or profit organizations, are built on this equity base.

Few health care organizations have endowments of sufficient size to warrant a fulltime investment manager. While this may be true, many health care organizations currently have or are anticipating funds set aside for eventual plant replacement, for future losses to be incurred under self-insurance programs, for employee retirement benefit programs and for many other purposes. The importance of maximizing the investment yields for these funds cannot be overstated. A slight change of one to two percent in the investment yield rate can have a profound effect when compounded over a long period of time.

CAPITAL FORMATION

Capital formation is the process of securing long-term capital financing in the form of debt or equity, and investing this cash in expectation of an economic return. When we refer to this process we usually are thinking about how money from various sources is used in the acquisition and deployment of physical capital. However, other needs for such cash exist. Capital formation is a dynamic process involving a continual assessment of the appropriate mix of long-term financial sources and the appropriate mix of investment options.

A General Formulation of the Capital Formation Model*

A model of the capital formation process is depicted schematically in Figure 15-2. This model focuses on two major decisions (the financing decision and the investment decision) that are executed continually by health care institutions. These decisions, which in some aspects are interdependent, are made within an environmental context reflective of social, economic, political, and technological factors.

The financing decision involves setting institutional goals for the appropriate mix of various long-term money capital financing sources that will subsequently be invested in assets. Subsidiary decisions involve the establishment of profit targets, depreciation policies, leverage strategies (i.e., the appropriate mix of debt and equity), and assessment of philanthropic giving and external equity investment potential, where these are applicable to proprietary organizations.

The second major strategic decision revolves around investments in assets. In general, physicians have a lesser role in actual decision making whereas bureaucrats (administrators and trustees) play a relatively greater role. On the other hand, physician sponsorship is frequently, if not almost always, required for both types of investment. For capacity-augmenting expenditures, particularly increases in bed capacity, a principal stimulus often comes from attending physicians. Hospital-based physicians, on the other hand, are less concerned with this type of expenditure.

Hospital-based physicians frequently initiate and sponsor technology-enhancing investments, particularly those that relate to their specific specialty. In doing so, however, they often must enlist the support of attending physicians particularly, as these physicians may constitute the base of referrals for the new or enhanced service.

Hospital administration is described as always having a formal role in the decision-making process and frequently being involved in sponsoring or supporting various investment projects. Finally, trustees, in discharging their stewardship function, seldom initiate a project and rarely actively sponsor or champion a given proposal as it is being developed. Rather, because they are required to ration scarce resources, they are unable to commit themselves to projects and the necessary investment too far in advance of formal deliberation.

COST FINDING

Objectives*

The purpose of cost finding is to determine the true or total costs of operating the revenue producing departments of the health care industry. Cost finding determines the total cost for producing a department's patient services. It also informs department managers of nonrevenue producing departments of the cost of services their departments perform for other departments. Accordingly, this information should be used to establish the charge for patient services.

Some of the objectives of cost finding in a health care facility or a department are: to provide management with decision-making information:

- regarding the profitability of a specific revenue/cost center
- for establishing rates for departmental services
- for use in negotiating reimbursement
- for contracts with third party contracting agencies, i.e., Workmen's Compensation, Blue Cross, or Medicare
- for use in its public relations efforts to explain costs of health care services
- for reports to external groups such as health facility associations, commissions, and other governmental agencies.

---

*Source: James S. Emrich, "The Capital Formation Process: An Institutional Perspective" in *Health Capital Issues*, Bureau of Health Facilities, February 1980, DHHS Pub. No. (HRA) 81-14531.

*Source: Reprinted from *Understanding Hospital Financial Management* by Allen G. Herkimer, Jr., with permission of Aspen Systems Corporation, © 1978.

Figure 15-2 The capital formation (financing/investment) model

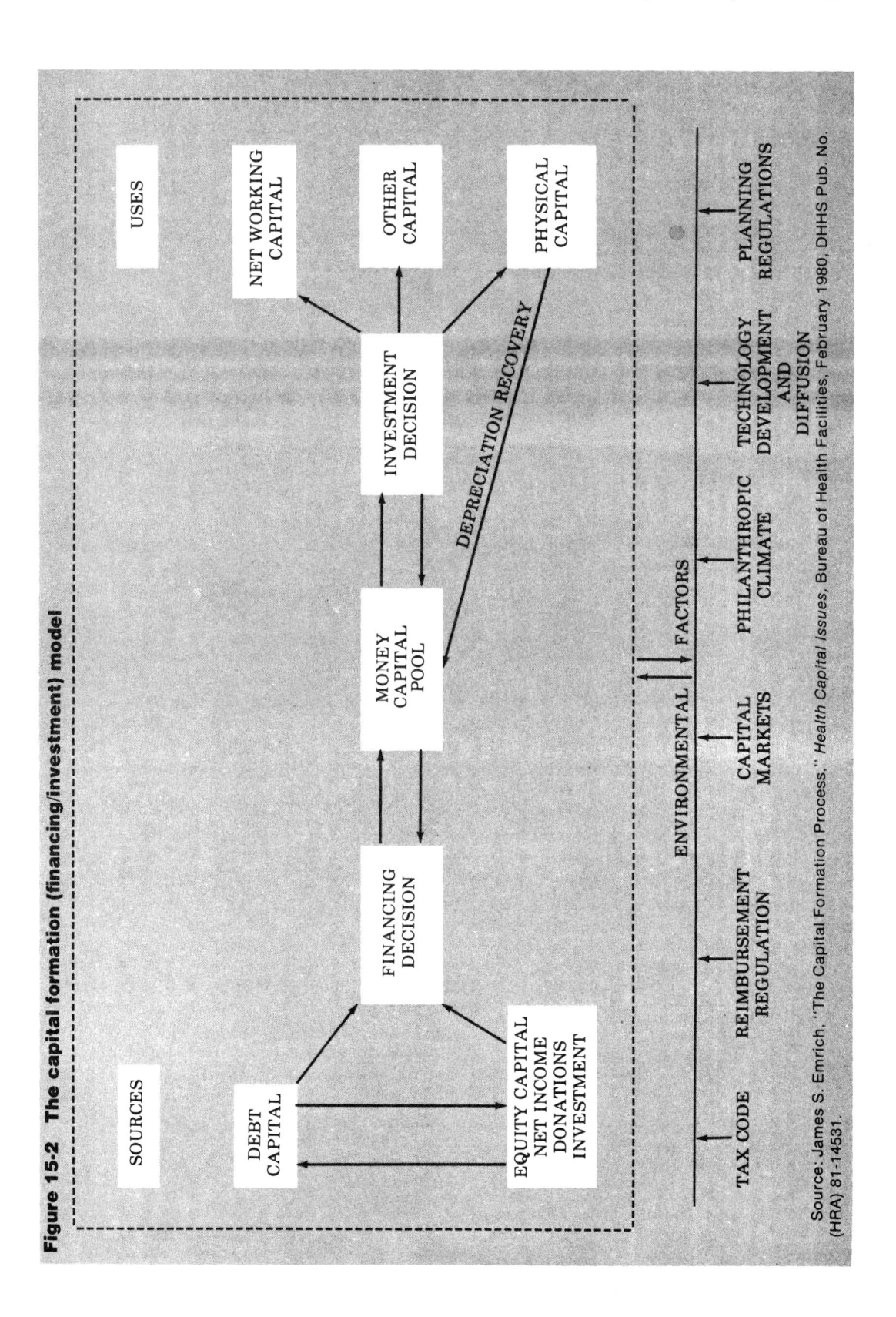

SOURCES

- DEBT CAPITAL
- EQUITY CAPITAL / NET INCOME / DONATIONS / INVESTMENT

→ FINANCING DECISION ↔ MONEY CAPITAL POOL ↔ INVESTMENT DECISION

USES
- NET WORKING CAPITAL
- OTHER CAPITAL
- PHYSICAL CAPITAL

DEPRECIATION RECOVERY (from PHYSICAL CAPITAL back to MONEY CAPITAL POOL)

ENVIRONMENTAL FACTORS:
- TAX CODE
- REIMBURSEMENT REGULATION
- CAPITAL MARKETS
- PHILANTHROPIC CLIMATE
- TECHNOLOGY DEVELOPMENT AND DIFFUSION
- PLANNING REGULATIONS

Source: James S. Emrich, "The Capital Formation Process," *Health Capital Issues*, Bureau of Health Facilities, February 1980, DHHS Pub. No. (HRA) 81-14531.

Allocating Indirect Costs to Departments*

In most cost accounting systems, costs are classified by department or responsibility center or by object of expenditure. Costs are classified primarily along departmental lines. Individual cost items are charged to the departments to which they are traceable. Costs are also classified by object of expenditure, whether the expense was for supplies, salaries, rent, insurance or other.

Departments in a health care facility can be classified generally as direct or indirect departments, based on whether they provide services directly to the patient or not. Sometimes the terms revenue and nonrevenue are substituted for direct and indirect. In the hospital industry, the following breakdown is used in general purpose financial statements.

Operating Expense Area	Type of Department
Nursing Services Area	direct/revenue
Other Professional Services	direct/revenue
General Services	indirect/nonrevenue
Fiscal Services	indirect/nonrevenue
Administrative Services	indirect/nonrevenue

Whatever the nomenclature used to describe the classification of departments, cost allocation is a fundamental need. The costs of the indirect, nonrevenue departments need to be allocated to the direct revenue departments for many decision making purposes. For example, third party payers usually reimburse on the basis of the full costs of direct departments and are interested only in the cost of indirect departments as far as they affect the calculation of the direct departments' full costs. Pricing decisions also need to be based on full costs, not just direct costs, if the costs of the indirect departments are to be covered equitably.

Equity is a key concept in allocating indirect department costs to direct departments. Ideally, the allocation should reflect as nearly as possible the actual cost incurred by indirect departments to provide services for a direct department. Department managers who receive cost reports showing indirect allocations are vitally interested in this equity argument, and for good reason. Even if indirect costs are not regarded as controllable by the department manager, the allocation of costs to a given direct department can have an important effect on a variety of management decisions. Pricing is an important one, expansion or contraction of department, purchase of new equipment and salaries of departmental managers are also affected by the allocation of indirect costs.

Costs of indirect departments are in most cases not traceable to direct departments. If they were, they could be reassigned. They must be allocated to direct departments in some systematic and rational manner.

Methods of Cost Finding*

Presently, whenever health care managers speak of cost finding, they automatically think of step-down. The step-down or the American Hospital Association's (AHA) Method Two, is the universally used cost finding process, because variations of it are mandated by Medicare and other rate setting and/or review agencies. The cost-finding formulas as prescribed by Medicare should *not* be used for internal use in allocating costs and establishing rates because they are designed specifically for the purpose of reimbursement—more specifically, for reimbursement by the federal government. Therefore, they eliminate costs which should be included for an internal management tool.

For a number of years, three basic methods of cost finding were promoted by the American Hospital Association. They were often referred to simply as Method One, Method Two, and Method Three.

Method One

Using Method One, the costs of the nonrevenue producing centers are allocated only to the revenue producing centers. Most nonrevenue producing centers render services to each other as well as to the revenue producing centers, but this fact is ignored in the mechanics of Method One. None of the costs of the nonrevenue producing centers is allocated to other nonrevenue producing centers.

---

*Source: Reprinted from *Essentials of Hospital Finance* by William O. Cleverley with permission of Aspen Systems Corporation, © 1978.

*Source: Reprinted from *Understanding Hospital Financial Management* by Allen G. Herkimer, Jr. with permission of Aspen Systems Corporation, © 1978.

Method One is the simplest of the traditional methods of cost finding, because it requires less clerical effort and fewer statistics. Under certain circumstances, the end results of Method One may not differ significantly from the end results of the more sophisticated methods. Method One, however, does not produce the full costs of the nonrevenue producing centers.

Method Two

Method Two, as mentioned above, is better known as the step-down method, and recognizes the important fact that the services rendered by certain nonrevenue producing centers are utilized by certain other nonrevenue producing centers, as well as by the revenue producing centers or departments. The accumulated costs in a nonrevenue producing center, therefore, are allocated to those nonrevenue producing centers which utilize its services, as well as to the revenue producing centers to which it renders service. The unique feature of the step-down method is that once the costs of a nonrevenue producing center have been allocated, the center is considered closed. Being closed, it will not receive any portion of the costs of the other nonrevenue producing centers, whose costs are yet to be allocated. The choice of sequence in which the nonrevenue producing centers are to be closed, therefore, is very important. To reduce the amount of cost distortion that can occur because of this feature of Method Two, careful consideration should be given to the determination of:

- the number of nonrevenue producing centers served by each center
- the amount of service rendered to other nonrevenue producing centers by each center

The closing sequence should be based upon these determinations. In other words, the first center to be closed should be the center that renders the greatest amount of service to the largest number of centers and, in turn, receives the least amount of service from the fewest number of centers. An excellent example of this type of cost center is Interest and/or Depreciation Expense.

The last center to be closed should be the center that renders the least service to the fewest nonrevenue producing centers and, in turn, receives the greatest amount of service from the largest number of centers, such as the School of Nursing.

Method Two is more difficult and time consuming than Method One, but, more importantly, it is likely to provide significantly more accurate cost information with respect to revenue producing centers. While it recognizes that certain nonrevenue producing centers render service to other nonrevenue producing centers, Method Two (like Method One) does not produce the total nonrevenue producing costs used by the revenue producing departments. Since the primary emphasis of cost finding is on determining the true or full costs of revenue producing centers, Method Two is acceptable for most purposes, including rate setting and reimbursement. (This statement is true with the condition mentioned in reference to the Medicare formula for the step-down process.) If the total costs of the nonrevenue producing centers need to be developed, the determination can be made through special cost studies.

The term step-down was adopted from Method Two's worksheet configuration, which looks like a series of steps.

Method Three

The most complex of the three original AHA methods of cost finding is Method Three, which is frequently referred to as the "double distribution" or the "double apportionment" method. This method gives greater recognition to the fact that nonrevenue producing centers render services to other nonrevenue producing centers, as well as to the revenue producing centers. Using Method Three, the nonrevenue producing centers are *not* considered permanently closed after their costs have been initially allocated (as in Method Two). Instead, they are reopened in the second apportionment process, to receive cost allocations from other nonrevenue producing centers from which services are received. After the costs of each nonrevenue producing center have been allocated once, some costs will remain in some departments, representing services received from other departments.

EFFECTIVE CASH MANAGEMENT

Cash management plays an integral role in the process by which required services are provided to the patient population. On the one hand, frequent cash shortages may jeopardize the hospital's ability to acquire the resources it needs to provide service. Moreover, should the hospital encounter frequent cash shortages, it incurs financial costs, which may take the form of a deteriorating credit rating or interest charges that must be paid to obtain a short-term loan. Consequently, frequent cash shortages may result in disruptions in the process by which care is provided as well as give rise to additional financial costs. On the other hand, idle cash earns nothing for the hospital. Indeed, during periods of inflation, excess funds that remain in idle cash balances earn a negative return—an opportunity cost that is equal to the rate of return that could have been earned by investing the funds in an interest-bearing security.

Thus, if management is to achieve the goal of providing required services at minimum costs, these considerations suggest that neither "too little" nor "too much" cash should be on hand at any given time. Techniques such as cash forecasting, cash budgeting, and probability models of cash management can provide the administrator with the information and the frame of reference with which to reach decisions concerning the desired cash balance.*

Policies and Procedures**

Effective cash management begins with policy statements. The organization must formulate policies regarding the recording and collection of cash for services rendered, recording and payment of current liabilities, preparation of the cash budget, and nature of the institution's banking relationships. If these management policies are well formulated and well executed, the periodic sources and uses of cash should be fairly predictable and, hence, manageable.

Collection of Cash for Services Rendered

Management's policy regarding the collection of cash for services rendered should attempt to minimize the time between the rendering of service and the collection of the cash from the patient or third party payer. The most desirable collection policy, from the institution's point of view, is for the patient account to be settled at the time of discharge. However, if the institution is unable or unwilling to institute and enforce a policy requiring the collection of cash for services rendered at the time of discharge, accounts receivable must be created.

Once accounts receivable have been created, three periods of time become relevant in managing these accounts: the "in-house billing float," the time the account is outstanding, and the "mail float." The in-house billing float is the period of time between rendering the service and issuing a billing invoice. This time period can be minimized by maintaining an effective information system which is coordinated with an adequate system of internal control. The time the account is outstanding or the time between mailing the billing invoice and the cash remittance by the debtor can be minimized by an aggressive collection policy. Finally, the mail float, the period of time between the debtor's remittance and the receipt of the check by the payee's bank, can often be reduced by using lock boxes (discussed in the case study in the following section). If each of these time periods can be minimized, the goal of the accounts receivable collection policy will be realized.

Case Study

The hospital currently has $15 million of accounts receivable arising from two sources—patient accounts and nonpatient accounts. Patient accounts, which are divided into inpatient and outpatient accounts, for administrative, billing, and collection purposes, comprise 95 percent of total accounts receivable. The remaining accounts receivable arise from such nonpatient accounts as cafeteria charges, television rentals, office space charges, and miscellaneous departmental billings.

More timely conversion of the patient and nonpatient accounts receivable could significantly improve the hospital's cash position.

To assist the hospital in managing its cash, Blue Cross and Medicare have recently agreed to make periodic interim payments (PIP) or automatic reimbursement payments to the hospital every two weeks, rather than as bills are received by Blue Cross and Medicare. The auto-

---

*Source: Reprinted from *The Management of Working Capital in Hospitals* by Robert W. Broyles, with permission of Aspen Systems Corporation, © 1981.

**Source: Reprinted from *Financial and Managerial Control: A Health Care Perspective* by Edward J. Lusk and Janice Gannon Lusk, with permission of Aspen Systems Corporation, © 1979.

matic reimbursement payments are estimated from prior period payments. These payments are adjusted and the estimates revised at the end of each quarter.

This new reimbursement procedure results in two major benefits. First, the short-term credit requirement of the hospital can be estimated more accurately. Second, the reduction in the average age of the Blue Cross and Medicare receivables will result in a one-time cash flow increase. If Medicaid were to participate in the PIP program, these benefits would be enhanced because cash inflows from the hospital's revenue could be estimated more accurately and an additional one-time cash benefit would be realized.

The collection of accounts receivable from payers other than the major insurers can be problematic. The differences in the policies offered by the various private insurance companies are bewildering. Each carrier specifies covered and noncovered procedures, different patient/insurance company copayment agreements, different limits of coverage and special documentation requirements. As a result, insurance coverage must be handled on a patient-by-patient basis. Furthermore, these private insurance companies tend to delay payment so that their resources can be maintained in income-producing investments as long as possible. These problems combine to make the timely collection of these accounts quite difficult.

Hence, a new billing policy was implemented by the hospital. Under this policy, private patients are billed for the entire cost of their hospital stay. The patients must then contact the appropriate insurance company so that their accounts can be paid. This policy is expected to improve the cash flow from patients covered by private insurance companies because these insurance companies could lose clients by withholding payments for substantial time periods. Hence, by converting the patient from a secondary payment source into an active collection agent for the hospital, the hospital expects to realize more timely payments from the private insurance companies.

Most of the hospital's cash is collected after the billing of accounts receivable. However, in an attempt to speed the collection of cash and to minimize the probability of bad debts, the hospital makes a collection effort (1) prior to patient admission, (2) at the time of patient admission, (3) during the patient's hospitalization, (4) at the time of the patient's discharge, and (5) after the patient has been billed. This collection cycle is diagrammed in Figure 15-3.

Payment of Current Liabilities

Management's policy regarding the payment of current liabilities should require that two time periods be maximized. The first is the time between the date an invoice is received from a vendor and the date a check is issued which qualifies for the purchase discount. The second is the time between the issuance of a check to the vendor and the date that check clears the institution's bank account. The first time period can be maximized if information regarding the date that discount will be lost is routinely generated from the accounting system. By coordinating the issuance of checks to vendors with this information, the first time period can be maximized. The second time period can be maximized by attempting to maximize the float. A common practice used to extend float is to use out-of-state checking accounts.

Forecasting and Developing the Cash Budget

An effective cash management system also requires a cash budget that records the forecasted cash inflows from various sources and also records the forecasted demands for cash. Accurate forecasting of these cash flows can alert management to the possible need for financing cash deficits or the possible opportunities to invest cash excesses.

Case Study (Continued)

The current forecasting process involves estimating the revenues and expenses for the coming fiscal year (July/June), collecting budgets from the hospital cost centers, and developing the cash budget.

Forecasting Revenues and Expenses: The revenue and expense forecasts take into account expected patient volume and anticipated inflation. Patient volume estimates are developed from past trends in patient volume, while inflation estimates are based on national trends in various hospital expense categories. The Health Care Index component of the Consumer Price Index is the primary source for these estimates,

226 HOSPITAL ADMINISTRATION HANDBOOK

Figure 15-3 The cash collection cycle

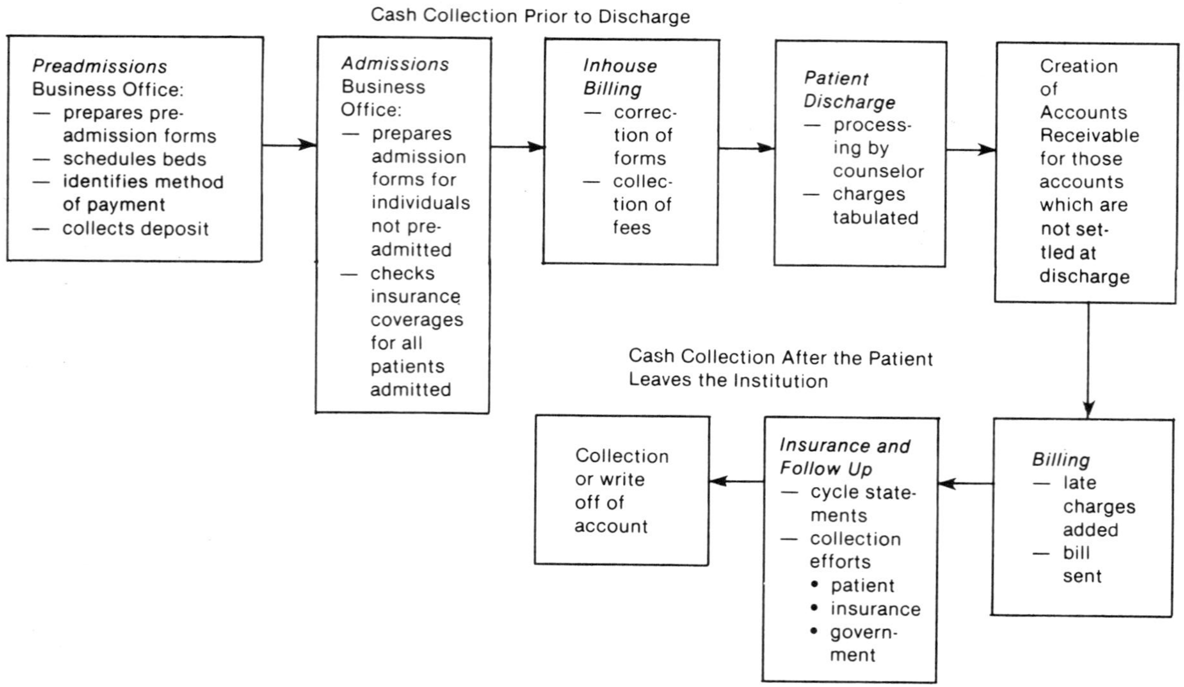

Cash Collection Prior to Discharge

Preadmissions
Business Office:
— prepares pre-admission forms
— schedules beds
— identifies method of payment
— collects deposit

↓

Admissions
Business Office:
— prepares admission forms for individuals not pre-admitted
— checks insurance coverages for all patients admitted

↓

Inhouse Billing
— correction of forms
— collection of fees

↓

Patient Discharge
— processing by counselor
— charges tabulated

↓

Creation of Accounts Receivable for those accounts which are not settled at discharge

→

Billing
— late charges added
— bill sent

↓

Cash Collection After the Patient Leaves the Institution

Insurance and Follow Up
— cycle statements
— collection efforts
  • patient
  • insurance
  • government

↓

Collection or write off of account

but inflation figures published in *Hospital Week* also are used.

Cost Centers' Proposed Budgets: Once the revenue and expense forecasts have been formulated, the comptroller's office requests a proposed budget from each cost center. These budget proposals are reviewed individually and in the aggregate. Then the appropriate budget adjustments are made so that the total sources and uses of cash in the cost center budgets are coordinated with the forecasts. All cost center budgets for the ensuing fiscal year receive final approval by the end of April.

Preparation of the Cash Budget: The cost center budgets are used to develop the capital budget and the operating expense budget. These two budgets, in conjunction with historical monthly data, are used to develop the final cash budget shown in Table 15-1. In preparing this budget, noncash transactions are eliminated from both the capital budget and the operating expense budget and the effect of changes in accounts receivable and accounts payable are considered. The variance between the budgeted and the actual sources and uses of cash provides important information useful in future cash planning activities.

Banking Relationships

Finally, the institution should have a policy regarding the nature of the relationship to be maintained with the banking community. Cooperative interaction with local banks may allow the institution to take advantage of numerous special banking services that may enable the institution to better manage its cash and may also aid in the preparation of the cash budget. The institution should maintain cash balances in several banks if these banks offer different services that may be useful to the institution.

Most banks offer two services which could benefit the hospital: a lock box service and a service that provides information to the hospital regarding anticipated changes in the banking industry which may affect the hospital's cash management system. Of course, the costs and benefits of these services must be evaluated before the hospital elects to use them.

Lock Box Service

A lock box arrangement permits the hospital to maintain a special mail depositor box, called a lock box, at a post office. The hospital's cash receipts are mailed to that lock box and collected by the bank at which the hospital maintains cash accounts. The bank immediately credits these receipts to the hospital's account and mails the results of the transaction to the hospital for posting to the hospital's records. The advantages of a lock box are that the mail float is reduced by several days and the clerical effort needed to process cash receipts is eliminated, which reduces the possibility of cash misappropriations.

Other banking services that aid hospital cash management also may be available. For example, the bank may, upon request and without charge, provide the hospital with an activity analysis of the hospital's cash account. In addition, the bank may counsel the hospital when banking changes could affect the hospital's cash management system. For example, a number of recent developments in electronic fund transfers among banks may be able to reduce the hospital's accounts receivable mail float significantly.

INTERNAL FINANCIAL AUDITING: A LIST OF CHECKPOINTS*

Financial auditing is concerned with the adequacy of the internal control of cash, accounting, assets, receipts, disbursements, payroll, billing, and any other elements that impact on hospital finances. Compliance auditing involves all activities that have written procedures. Internal auditors review the adequacy of the written procedures in terms of internal control and then assess the extent to which employees comply with them.

Closely related to financial and compliance auditing, and of concern to all hospitals is fraud. Following are the areas where effective internal and financial controls are required as safeguards against needless losses.

Accounts Payable

The purchase of supplies and equipment requires a process of financial control to assure prompt, authorized, and accurate payments are

---

*Source: Reprinted from *Internal Auditing for Hospitals* by Seth Allcorn, with permission of Aspen Systems Corporation, © 1979.

Table 15-1 1982–83 Cash Budget ($000s)

	Total	July to October Actual	Nov Budget	Nov Actual	Dec Budget	Dec Actual	Jan Budget	Jan Actual
Cash—Beginning Balance	$ 263	$ 263	$ 290	$ 290	$ 611	$ 611	$ 602	
Add: Cash Receipts								
Medicare	13,349	4,511	946	946	1,307	1,307	1,013	
Blue Cross	17,528	4,909	1,408	1,508	1,500	1,540	2,806	
Medical Assistance	6,879	2,767	371	518	500	392	530	
Patient Cash	2,508	729		311	174	382	156	
Other Insurance	11,648	2,714	1,307	962	1,007	764	1,182	
Private Outpatient	2,782	896		272	175	213	200	
Clinic Cash	2,275	810	180	205	180	145	180	
Total Accounts Receivable	$56,969	$17,336	$4,212	$4,722	$4,843	$4,743	$6,067	
Third Party Payments (Prior Years)	$ 1,695	$ 711	$ —	$ 169	$ 155	$ 155	$ —	
School of Nursing	138	63	2	1	22	1	56	
Cafeteria Sales	553	192	45	49	40	47	45	
Research Overhead	190	—	—	—	—	—	—	
Utilization Review	100	29	8	9	9	—	10	
Miscellaneous Operating	5,302	1,784	262	500	385	706	385	
Restricted Contributions	762	104	35	13	4	—	14	
Endowments	686	285	55	1	55	6	80	
University Loan	200	200	—	—	—	—	—	
Total Receipts	$66,595	$20,704	$4,619	$5,464	$5,513	$5,658	$6,657	
Less: Cash Disbursements								
Payroll	$23,592	$ 7,525	$1,535	$1,745	$2,316	$2,446	$2,227	
Employee Benefits	11,065	3,691	814	947	1,296	1,173	980	
Accounts Payable	21,360	7,905	1,815	1,855	1,657	1,640	1,674	
Interest	101	34	—	—	34	34	—	
Equipment	1,585	97	55	53	158	42	128	
Alterations and Improvements (A & I)	890	200	93	48	116	123	111	
Prior Year Equipment & A & I	412	237	132	9	22	14	25	
Long-Term Debt	151	26	9	—	65	72	9	
Third Party Payments	1,090	—	—	—	—	—	565	
University Comptroller Accounts Payable	3,823	760	357	396	381	25	737	
Working Capital	700	100	—	—	—	—	—	
Overhead (Prior Year)	817	96	90	90	90	90	90	
Equipment Advance	76	6	9	—	18	8	10	
Total Disbursements	$65,662	$20,677	$4,909	$5,143	$6,153	$5,667	$6,556	
Net Increase or (Decrease)	$ 933	$ 27	$(290)	$ 321	$ (640)	$ (9)	$ 101	
Cash Ending Balance	1,196	290	—	611	(29)	602	703	

made to vendors and that the materials paid for have been received in good order. Hospitals can lose funds to embezzlers unnecessarily by paying for materials not received. Hospitals also may expend funds unnecessarily when they do not take advantage of discounts for prompt payment. As can be seen from the ten sets of audit checkpoints below, a good accounts payable system needs many internal controls.

1. What procedures are used to control accounts payable? Are requests for purchases entered into the purchasing system at the earliest possible time? Is there a controlling ledger? Are only purchase transactions recorded? How does the system control against double payments?
2. What is the frequency with which payments are made to vendors? Is there a period of accumulation before preparing a check to pay multiple invoices or are many small checks issued at additional cost?
3. When the person authorized to approve disbursements signs the checks or vouchers, is supporting documentation available for review? Are receiving notices provided? Have all invoice prices, extensions, and footings been checked for accuracy? Are checks ever made out to employees or cash? Who mails the checks after they are signed?
4. Are vendor discounts taken advantage of? Are they paid near the last day of the discount's availability so as to permit the hospital use of the funds a few additional days?
5. How are credit memos handled? Do they become the responsibility of the accounting department? How are orders and payments controlled on blanket authorizations? How are advance payments controlled?
6. Are all accounts paid within vendor time limits? This will require preparing a schedule that ages accounts payable. Are delinquent accounts reviewed and resolved?
7. Is there a significant number of deficiencies in accounts payable? If so, the auditor should consider confirming a sample of all vendors, regardless of whether or not hospital records indicate an active accounts payable balance.
8. How are records of requisitions, orders, vouchers, and disbursements maintained? What is their retention period? Are they cross-referenced so as to permit inquiries by vendor, purchase order, or disbursement?
9. What organizational relationships exist among purchasing, receiving, accounting, and check signing? Are they independent of each other? What are the paper flows to and from each area and what are their responsibilities? For example, which area receives invoices—purchasing or accounting? Are procedures used in conformance with the governing board's guidelines?
10. Are good internal controls evident in each department or are many functions performed by a few persons in some departments?

Accounts Receivable

Good internal control is a key element in managing accounts receivable. Internal control prevents fraud and guards against errors. Accounts receivable are subject to several types of manipulation that can produce illegal benefits for employees and their friends. Balances can be reduced or unapplied payments posted to accounts either to pay off a bill or even as a refund.

1. What policies have been developed to deal with decisions on credit, referrals of patient accounts to collection agencies, and bad debts? Are they reasonable and are they followed? Who is authorized to approve these types of decisions? Are personnel responsible for approving credit denied access to cash? What policies and procedures exist for unapplied payments?
2. Does the organization of the accounts receivable section, credit department, cashier, and collection department promote good internal control? Are employees of these sections restricted from working in the other areas even during lunch breaks and absences? How are records safeguarded from unauthorized access? What provisions are there for sharing or lending records?

3. What type of controlling account or ledger is used for accounts receivable? Are the accounts receivable reconciled on a regular basis?
4. Do the types, size, and aging of accounts receivable and bad debt writeoffs resemble national averages?
5. How are cash receipts posted to individual accounts and are they reconciled to total receipts?
6. In what form are patient accounts maintained? What detail is available on charges and payments?
7. How often and in what manner are charges posted? What internal controls exist that ensure all charges are posted and correctly? Are there many late charges? Is a total bill available to the patient at departure?
8. How are credit balances controlled? What are the policies and procedures for refunding credit balances to the patient? Who authorizes the refunds? Are there enough credit balances to affect reporting of accounts receivable materially? If so, credit balances should be placed in a separate account.
9. What reports are prepared routinely and what is their distribution? Are all exceptions reported? Are accounts receivable aging schedules prepared that cover aging by date of discharge, by date of last payment, and by area of payment responsibility starting with the discharge date? What reports are prepared on unapplied payments?
10. Is confirmation of accounts receivable performed? This may be a standard step of the certified public accounting firm's annual audit. This process will help determine whether patients' payments have been applied properly to their accounts.

Payroll

Following are some checkpoints for auditing payroll procedures.

1. What records are used to control payroll? How are pay scales checked for accuracy? How are payroll calculations checked, including computations of overtime, holiday pay, and call time? How and for how long are records retained? How are payroll deductions authorized and reported to employees? What records are used to document employees' receipt of pay?
2. How are payroll checking accounts controlled? Are they regularly reconciled by employees other than payroll's? Are payroll employees properly bonded? Does the hospital use multiple payroll checking accounts to save time on reconciliations? Multiple accounts will allow reconciliations of individual payroll periods. Reconciliations can be timed to permit most, if not all, checks to be accounted for.
3. What internal controls are in evidence? Are the various payroll steps distributed among employees? Are employees rotated on jobs on a regular basis? What provisions are there to avoid using employees of one department to fill in for absences or lunch hours in other departments and thus permit possible tampering with records? Are blank payroll checks safeguarded properly? Are checks prenumbered? Who is responsible for approving or signing the payroll and the checks? Do the steps taken by the person in charge guard effectively against error and fraud?
4. What is the procedure for distributing payroll checks and cash? How are employees identified? How are unclaimed payroll checks and payments handled? Does a department other than payroll resolve the exceptions? What procedure is there for mailing out income tax statements? Does the procedure secure the statements from tampering? Who is responsible for mailing checks and statements? How are returned checks and statements handled?
5. Who is responsible for authorizing hiring, pay scales, and overtime? Are there sufficient records by employee to document hiring levels and raises? What forms must new hires complete? Are W-4 forms completed regularly?
6. What types of time records are kept? Are they accurate? Do supervisors monitor employees closely to make sure times reported are correct? What records are maintained for vacations and sick leave?

7. Do the payroll systems and procedures appear to be efficient and accomplish the function at a minimum of cost? Do they promote accuracy? Does the system handle emergency payroll situations effectively?
8. Are payroll disbursements made on time? Are all time records and other documents received on schedule from all departments? What electronic data processing applications exist?
9. How is the confidentiality of the payroll records safeguarded? Do payroll employees avoid discussing records with others? Are records disposed of in a manner that safeguards confidentiality?
10. What reports and analyses are prepared routinely of payroll matters and what is their distribution? Are quarterly tax reports prepared on time and deposits made?

Cash Receipts

Cash represents a high risk because it is vulnerable to theft. Employees taking cash need worry only about covering up its disappearance, unlike fraud in purchasing or accounts receivable in which the employee must convert transactions into cash or something of value. Accounting for cash also can be difficult unless effective operating procedures are used. Errors represent real and immediate dollar losses and problems that require resolution.

1. Is the custody of cash separated from those responsible for cash receipt records and reporting? Cashiers must be responsible only for receiving cash, not accounting for it. Are all employees properly bonded? How are new employees screened to avoid hiring persons with obvious problems in their work history?
2. Is a minimum number of employees involved with handling cash? How are absences and lunch hours covered?
3. Is cash received centrally? If not, are remote locations properly staffed, equipped, and controlled? Is cash adequately protected physically? Are daily deposits made intact?
4. Are employees required to rotate jobs and to take vacations?
5. If the hospital routinely cashes checks, is an imprest fund used? Are the procedures associated with the fund followed closely?
6. Are mail payments opened and listed by personnel other than the cashier's office or accounting? Are reports of the mail receipts provided to persons who ultimately can check the amounts deposited? Are checks restrictively endorsed at once?
7. Are cash registers used for over-the-counter payments? Is the cash drawer balanced against the internal tape? Are prenumbered receipts used? What provision is there for multiple cashiers?
8. Is the bank deposit slip returned to someone other than the cashier's office or accounting? Is an armored car service used to transfer cash?
9. How are cash receipts for interest, dividends, sale of scrap, rents, and all other nonpatient care revenues handled? Are they reported separately from patient fee revenue?
10. Does the institution receive payments for physicians and other health care professionals not paid by the hospital?

Uncollectable Patient Accounts

There is much that needs to be audited to ensure patient accounts written off as bad debts in fact are uncollectable. A secondary aspect is to analyze why the bad debts are incurred. The analysis may lead to changes in screening and admitting procedures.

1. Are accounts that are written off as bad debts adequately documented as to all efforts at collection? Are all policies and procedures followed? How rigorous are they? Do they permit an unnecessarily high level of uncollected accounts to be written off? Were the policies approved by the governing board?
2. Are bad debt write-offs authorized by a position that exercises control over the process?
3. How are bad debts reported and accounted for? How are the records maintained and for how long?
4. Is a sample of bad debts confirmed to assure that collection efforts are rigorous enough and that the debts are not abused?

5. Are uncollected accounts referred to a collection agency? Are these referrals controlled by a separate account?
6. Is the collection agency making a reasonable effort on all accounts or does it concentrate on the easier ones? What impact does the collection agency's efforts have on community relations?
7. What has been learned from the hospital's uncollectable accounts experience? Is there an indication policies and procedures need to be changed?
8. What impact does the hospital's screening procedure have on uncollectable accounts? Does the screening include verification of insurance coverage and credit? Does the hospital have adequate financial counseling for patients?
9. Are the credit, collections, and counseling areas adequately staffed by qualified personnel?
10. What is the hospital's policy on patients who return for care with account balances owed from prior visits?

Patient Billing

All billing systems have in common the compiling of an accurate and timely record of all charges for all patients. To the extent the systems fail in this or succeed at excessive cost, hospitals lose resources. Internal auditors, when designing audit programs for hospital billing systems, must be resourceful to do a thorough job without requiring an excessive amount of time. The checkpoints demonstrate how financial and compliance auditing may be blended with operations auditing.

1. Do the medical records support the charges to patients? Are there records or reports for all laboratory tests and are there physician and technician notes for all professional services rendered and billed?
2. How are business records maintained? Is the system economical and does it promote accuracy and efficiency? What use is made of microfilm? What records retention schedules have been prepared and are they reasonable? Are records retrieved quickly when requested? How secure are the records from damage, loss, and search by unauthorized personnel?
3. Are patient billings reviewed routinely for obvious problems and errors? The process used should be expected to spot obvious billing errors that appear out of the ordinary. Are there numerous late charges?
4. What procedure is used to determine hospital charges and how often are existing charges adjusted and new ones added? Are there adequate cost finding studies? Do charges comply with cost containment guidelines?
5. Are charges compiled by revenue centers so as to permit comparisons with operating costs?
6. What controls are used to assure that all chargeable supplies and services are billed to the patient? Are inventories of supplies controlled to permit accounting for sales and unexplained shrinkages? Are billing system forms designed thoughtfully and, when appropriate, controlled by prenumbering? What methods are used in batching and batch control?
7. What are the procedures for computing, checking, and entering contractual adjustments on patient accounts?
8. What is the procedure for billing the hospital room rate to the patient? Is the record used to prepare the billing reliable? Does the procedure allow for instances such as a patient transfer to an intensive care unit and return to the ward on the same day?
9. Does the billing system provide for adequate detailed and summary reporting? Are detailed reports of all charges sorted in a manner to permit inquiry? Do summary reports provide management useful information? What use is made of them?
10. Is there a continuing system for auditing at least a sample of medical records for supporting documentation for charges? This is an especially important process for hospitals that have large patient populations with Medicare and Medicaid coverage.

In addition to reducing the cost of external audits, the development and implementation of a sound internal control system will promote efficiency in the business office. It is in this regard that an internal control system reduces errors and out-of-balance situations so that daily and monthly reports are both more accurate and timely.

A sophisticated internal control system sometimes is difficult to implement in a small institution since it may not be possible to provide for an entirely satisfactory division of duties. In such a situation, increased attention must be given to the application of the other principles and procedures such as bonding, job rotation, surprise cash counts, and similar practices. The administrator should ensure that as many additional internal controls are implemented as are feasible.

THE "TROUBLED HOSPITAL SYNDROME"*

When a hospital recognizes that it is in financial trouble (i.e., its expenses begin to chronically exceed its revenues and it is unable to finance its losses) there appear to be a series of options which it attempts to ensure its survival. We observed this sequence sufficiently often that we have come to call it the "troubled hospital syndrome."

The first set of options in this series might be called "internal" actions, involving minimal change in the physical plant or governance structure. These include such steps as raising charges, cutting costs, and boosting admissions through promotion, physician recruitment and adding new services. Should these fail, the troubled hospital may attempt a major building addition, or even a completely new facility, in an effort to become more attractive than competing hospitals. Such construction or attempted construction by a hospital with low occupancy and chronic deficits is a strong indication of trouble. Should this fail, the hospital may finally begin to think about sacrificing some autonomy to join or merge with or, if all else fails, even to be acquired by a second hospital or chain. Dissolving the institution is seldom considered until all the previous actions have failed.

There are basically two sources of trouble for hospitals which might occur either independently or simultaneously. One is a situation in which new hospitals enter the area, and/or one or more hospitals in the area enhance their attractiveness by adding certain services, equipment, personnel, or by modernizing their physical plant. Under the incentive structure of the present medical care system, this will draw physicians and patients away from those institutions that do not keep up with the competitive pace, thereby weakening their financial base. (Note that the market failure in the present system creates uneconomic competition over non-price factors rather than competition over prices and efficiency.) The other basic source of trouble is patient losses and accompanying losses in revenues as a result of demographic shifts in the population surrounding a hospital. Note that in both situations the basic issue is patients. If a hospital can maintain a sufficient base of patients it can usually juggle charges and costs enough to survive. However, when patients shrink below some minimum, the juggling act becomes too difficult and the hospital begins to fail, and will fail unless patient volume can be recovered.

Other in-house measures that a hospital might take include attempting to increase its revenues and cut costs. Revenues can be increased by raising prices if this can be negotiated with major third parties or if this will not drive away too many patients who have low insurance coverage (a problem in rural and low income areas). Revenues can also be increased by fund drives. And most important, the hospital can try to attract more patients, which increases revenues and lowers unit costs by spreading them over the larger patient base. Patients can be attracted by attracting medical staff and adding new (and it is hoped, more profitable) services. Active recruitment, bonuses and guaranteed salary programs, improved equipment and facilities can help draw physicians. The added cost will be more than offset if the recruitment succeeds. The hospital may have to bring in new administration to carry out these actions successfully.

A new administrator might also try cutting expenses by making the present services more efficient or stepping up the more profitable services and decreasing or dropping the less profitable services. However, there is a potential danger that in paring or dropping some services, a hospital might ultimately decrease its attractiveness and threaten its ability to compete.

If the above actions fail, the hospital may consider constructing a new wing or building. The

---

*Source: *Conversion and Other Policy Options to Reduce Excess Hospital Capacity,* Health Planning Information Series, DHEW, September 1979, Pub. No. (HRA) 79-14044.

hope is to make the hospital more attractive to physicians and patients. However construction is expensive and a troubled hospital will usually try less extreme measures first to improve its position. Often the "troubled" hospital will fail to secure adequate financing to begin construction. (Dust-covered frame drawings and architectural models are signs of these unfulfilled efforts.) If construction is completed, it may help turn the hospital around, as hoped. But it may not, in which case the hospital may be in worse financial condition.

If these steps fail, i.e., if the hospital's financial trouble is so severe that in-house attempts are not adequate to ensure survival, the distressed hospital will usually seek some form of alliance, ranging from loose sharing agreements to formal merger with or acquisition by other institutions. This is usually the last set of options considered, because it means surrendering part or all of the hospital's autonomy. It might attempt such an alliance with one or more other weak hospitals to try to aggregate and strengthen patient and financial bases, or an alliance might be sought with another hospital whose financial position is already strong. Again, depending on the severity of the hospital's financial trouble, it will likely seek first a looser type of alliance that will allow it to preserve its institutional identity and autonomy. If a loose type of arrangement is not sufficient or possible, the only alternative short of closing its doors is formal merger or acquisition. This will ensure survival of a successor corporation which can fulfill financial and legal obligations and maintain positions for the medical and hospital staff, and so is usually more acceptable to constituents than closure. It appears then that a hospital will voluntarily close only when these measures are not successful in alleviating financial pressure or when these are simply not within the realm of possibilities.

Chapter 16—Budgeting

OVERVIEW*

The basic budget program has four objectives:

- to provide in quantitative terms a written expression of the objectives, policies and plans of the hospital;
- to provide a basis for the evaluation of financial performance in accordance with this plan;
- to provide a useful tool for the control of costs; and
- to create cost awareness throughout the organization.

These objectives interface with and incorporate the functions of planning, forecasting and controlling of activities. When the budget program is properly supervised and coordinated, it provides guidelines for future decisions as well as a basis for cost finding and rate setting in relation to financial needs.

Financial Requirements

The basic reason for the budget plan is to assist the hospital in meeting its financial requirements. These are:

- current operating needs:

    operating expenses
    education
    research
    bad debts
    charity allowances

- plant capital needs:

    preservation and replacement of existing facilities
    new technology
    expansion

- working capital or operating cash needs
- reasonable profit.

Benefits

Effective budgeting provides an institution's management with several benefits. First, it establishes realistic goals and objectives in requiring the institution to measure expenditures against revenues. Second, it requires that the activities of all departments be coordinated into the overall plan. Third, it provides a standard against which actual results can be measured, thereby becoming a basis for effective cost control, planning and allocation of people and funds.

The preparation of a budget requires coordinated teamwork. In a survey of 1,500 hospitals by Kearney Management Consultants, it was found that nearly 80 percent of administrators and department heads participate in budget preparation, while participation of board members and medical staff was limited to about 33 percent. The amount of time spent each year in budget-making activities ranged from a single

---

*Source: Reprinted from J. Keith Deisenroth, "Understanding the Budget Process," *Topics in Health Care Financing,* Summer 1979, with permission of Aspen Systems Corporation.

man-day to 2,000 man-days, with an estimated average between 200 and 300 man-days.

An effective budget is a collection of the carefully conceived financial plans of all departments. Although the methods and mechanics in processing budgets may vary, the basic steps are similar in any system.* (See Figure 16-1.)

A Budget Manual

A good budget manual can serve as the framework for the budgeting process. It delineates the scope of the process and describes the pertinent duties and lines of authority. The manual gives examples of budget forms, states the period of time to be covered, and describes approval procedures. A typical budget manual table of contents might read as follows:

- introduction;
- budget planning;
- units of service;
- staffing and payroll expenses;
- nonsalary expenses;
- capital budget;
- revenue budget;
- deductions from revenue;
- rate evaluation and rate setting;
- operating budget;
- performance reporting;
- exhibits and appendices.

THE BUDGET PROCESS**

Steps

The budget process includes the following steps:

- Prepare statistical assumptions, including, but not limited to, patient days by service, changes in building gross square feet, introduction of new services and projected dates, number of procedures for the major departments (laboratory, radiology, and so on), and number of outpatient visits.

---

*Source: Reprinted from Jack C. Wood, "Financial Management Tools," *Topics in Health Care Financing,* Fall 1974, with permission of Aspen Systems Corporation.

**Source: Reprinted from *Basic Hospital Financial Management* by Donald F. Beck, with permission of Aspen Systems Corporation, © 1980.

- Prepare economic forecasts that include salary inflation factors; fringe-benefit inflation factors; inflation factors for supplies and other nonsalary items detailed by major expense item and by department; new developments that may affect the hospital, such as additional physicians joining the staff, physicians leaving the staff, additions to other hospitals in the service area, or major clinics under construction; proposed legislation or government regulations, if they are expected to pass or be implemented; and any other factor that might affect the hospital's income or expense during the budget period.
- Distribute budget packages to department heads. These packages will include assumptions, forms, schedules, and historical data for each department. It is best to distribute the packages at a department head meeting and to have at least one hour of formal instruction in budget techniques and accounting constraints.
- Give technical assistance to department heads as they prepare the first drafts of their budget requests. Prepare budget goals and policies for the period. These will constitute an outline of the financial plan. They may include a targeted net gain or loss, a marketing strategy, third party payer strategy, or any other item that has a bearing upon the hospital's finances.
- Obtain approval of budget assumptions, goals, and policies. Depending upon the hospital, this may mean governing board approval, approval by a committee of the governing board, administrative approval, or operating budget committee approval.
- Hold departmental budget hearings. Those present should include the controller, the administrator or assistant administrator, and the department head. It is also a good idea to attempt to have a board member present during each budget hearing. This makes the department heads feel they have been heard and at the same time provides board members with an excellent opportunity to learn the intricacies of day-to-day hospital operating problems.
- Prepare typed summaries of each budget hearing. This documents promises and statements made between administration and department heads. These summaries

Figure 16-1 The budget timetable

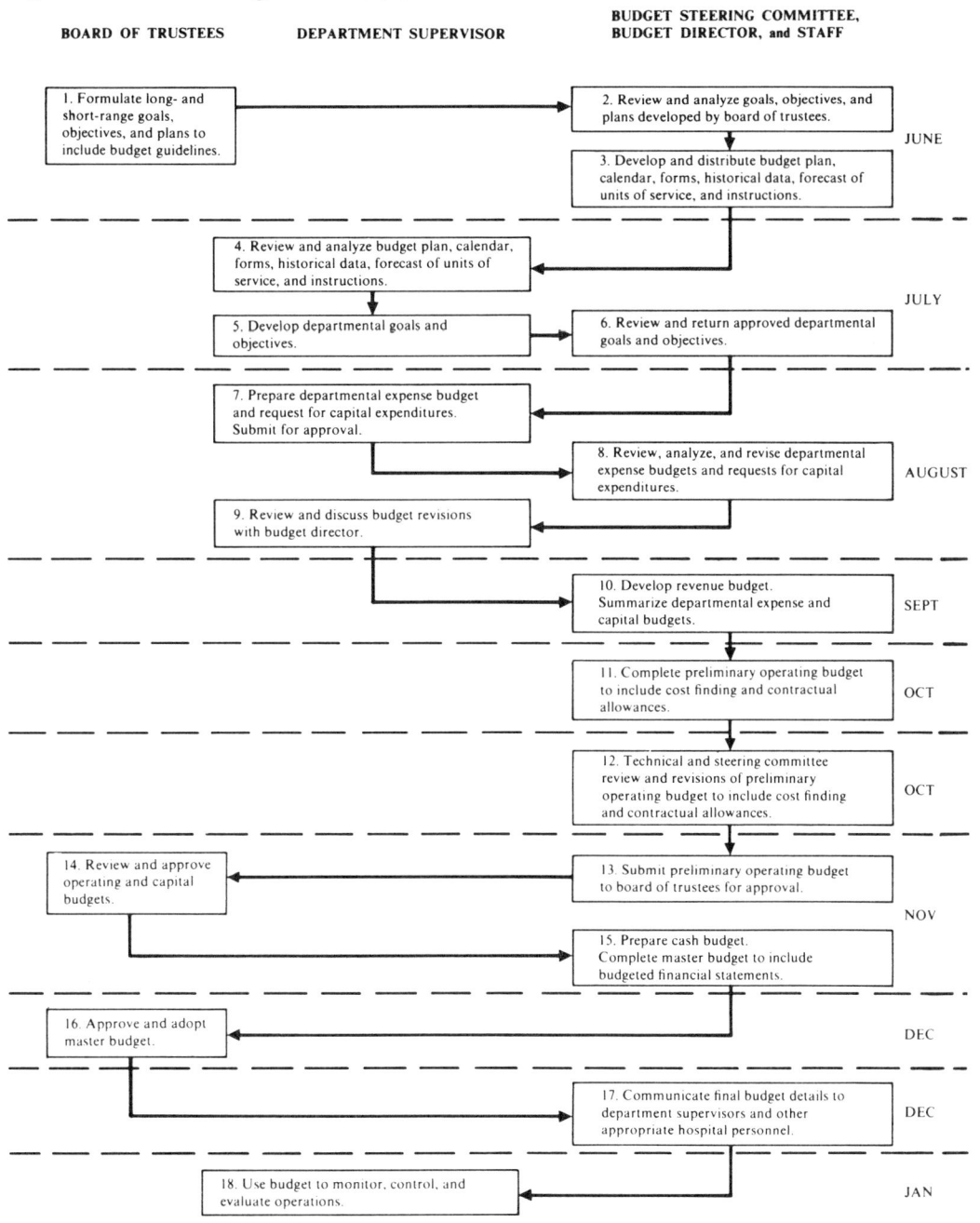

BOARD OF TRUSTEES	DEPARTMENT SUPERVISOR	BUDGET STEERING COMMITTEE, BUDGET DIRECTOR, and STAFF	
1. Formulate long- and short-range goals, objectives, and plans to include budget guidelines.		2. Review and analyze goals, objectives, and plans developed by board of trustees.	JUNE
		3. Develop and distribute budget plan, calendar, forms, historical data, forecast of units of service, and instructions.	
	4. Review and analyze budget plan, calendar, forms, historical data, forecast of units of service, and instructions.		JULY
	5. Develop departmental goals and objectives.	6. Review and return approved departmental goals and objectives.	
	7. Prepare departmental expense budget and request for capital expenditures. Submit for approval.		
		8. Review, analyze, and revise departmental expense budgets and requests for capital expenditures.	AUGUST
	9. Review and discuss budget revisions with budget director.		
		10. Develop revenue budget. Summarize departmental expense and capital budgets.	SEPT
		11. Complete preliminary operating budget to include cost finding and contractual allowances.	OCT
		12. Technical and steering committee review and revisions of preliminary operating budget to include cost finding and contractual allowances.	OCT
14. Review and approve operating and capital budgets.		13. Submit preliminary operating budget to board of trustees for approval.	NOV
		15. Prepare cash budget. Complete master budget to include budgeted financial statements.	
16. Approve and adopt master budget.			DEC
		17. Communicate final budget details to department supervisors and other appropriate hospital personnel.	DEC
	18. Use budget to monitor, control, and evaluate operations.		JAN

Source: Reprinted from *Topics in Health Care Financing,* Winter 1974, Ernst and Ernst, issue ed., with permission of Aspen Systems Corporation.

will be referred to throughout the year as budget variances are investigated. If the typed summaries include personal observations and impressions of the controller, they should be shared only with administration. If these summaries are rather formal and include only factual information, a copy of each summary can be given to the appropriate department head. The format and distribution of budget hearing summaries will depend upon the preferences of the controller and the administrator.

- Summarize the individual department budgets into a first draft of the master budget. After reviewing this for reasonableness, the controller's department summarizes the total budget into a format to be presented to the board or a committee of the board. This presentation will be enhanced by graphs, descriptive narrative, and comparative historical data.

After making revisions mandated by the governing board, the budget is submitted to any relevant outside agency for approval. Many states have a formal rate review process. Others have a required rate and budget review process by a major third party payer. In addition, Medicare intermediaries require a review of the budget and proposed rates before the start of the fiscal year.

Budget Timetable

The budget timetable (see Figure 16-1) lists the dates of each segment of the budget process, tells who is responsible for the segment, and provides a brief narrative to explain the purpose of the segment and to show how it fits into the total budget process.

The purpose of the budget timetable is to make a plan for the completion of the budget in time to meet outside constraints and to set deadlines. All personnel who have a role in the annual budget should see the entire plan so that they know how their part fits into the overall plan. They should see how missing a deadline will affect others and should know about deadlines imposed by others.

Budget Assumptions

In some hospitals, information on projected patient statistics, additional services, proposed salary increases, economic factors, hospital goals, expense policies, and other pertinent information never reaches the department heads. This is because the information is rationed rather than shared, with each department head's ration being only that information that appears to affect that department directly.

The major purpose of budget assumptions is to share as much information as possible with all departments. That way the entire hospital will be planning on the same track.

Budget assumptions should also be used as a tool to initiate cost-containment measures and to announce any new policy that directly affects expenses in either a positive or negative manner. Assumptions set the tone of the budget. The hospital may want to increase expenses in order to increase the quality of care or patient convenience. On the other hand, the hospital may want to reduce significantly the rate of increase in costs per patient day. The important point is that through budget assumptions the hospital has a choice and can directly influence the result.

Table 16-1 is an abbreviated list of assumptions for a community hospital.

An average community hospital should have a minimum of 25 assumptions, and a major medical center may have as many as 100 assumptions.

Worksheets

Nonsalary Worksheet

The nonsalary worksheets contain historical data that are used by department heads in conjunction with the budget assumptions to prepare an estimate of nonsalary expense requirements for the budget period.

The historical information provided should include at least one full year's actual expense, the

Table 16-1 Examples of a Community Hospital's Budget Assumptions

Fiscal Year Ended June 30, 1984
1. All approved budgets are subject to the availability of funds.
2. A CT body scanner will be operational in September.
3. Two family practice physicians, one pediatrician, one nephrologist, and up to four other physicians will be added to the active staff in the first six months of the year.
4. Supply costs will increase as follows: drugs six percent, medical supplies eight percent, chemicals nine percent, services eight percent, food nine percent.
5. Reimbursement for use of an employee's personal automobile will be increased from $.19 per mile to $.21 per mile.
6. Patient days will increase approximately five percent over last year.

current year's budget, and a portion of the current year's actual.

Personnel Requirements Worksheet (Position Control System)

Personnel costs in a hospital cannot be effectively budgeted or controlled without some type of formal position control system. A position control system is sometimes confused with the employee master list, which is a personnel department control tool. The position control is a budget and expense control tool. It itemizes by department all approved positions by shift and by job title. When an employee terminates, no change is made in the position control. The department head simply has a vacant approved position that can be filled. When employees are hired, they are slotted into an approved position. Administrative control is exercised over positions. Department control is exercised over employees assigned to approved positions.

The personnel requirements worksheet should be used only to request changes in the present position control. This includes planned reductions, requested additions, and planned changes in job descriptions, such as replacing registered nurses with licensed practical nurses or replacing a secretary with a clerk typist. It should be understood by department managers that if a completed worksheet is not received, it will be assumed that the present department manpower is satisfactory.

After changes in the position control are approved, the controller's department calculates budgeted salary expense by department. This calculation takes into account the cost-of-living pay increases, approved changes in the position control, the effect of any applicable union contracts, and other information that would not be available to department heads when their budgets were prepared. This calculation should consider the effect of vacation coverage, overtime pay, shift differential, on-call pay, and other factors that may affect department salary expense.

Budget Hearings

At a budget hearing those present should include the controller, the administrator or assistant administrator, and the department head. Their first task is to get all parties to agree that the overall budget request is reasonable. The controller should have Monitrend statistics, comparisons with other area hospitals, and any other comparable data that have been collected. The budget request should be negotiated between the department heads and their administrative superior with the controller acting only as a facilitator. The most difficult task of the controller will be to keep the hearing on a rational basis. The department heads will have a tendency to justify the status quo because they have a vested interest in present operations. If the administrator does not have a strong accounting background, there will be a tendency to use intuition or to rely excessively on past experience. As a facilitator, the controller will refer to documented examples, statistical data, and the parameters established by the budget assumptions.

Throughout the budget hearings, it is important for administration, the controller, and the hospital board member, if one is present, to keep in mind that the budget assumptions are based on facts known at the time the budget is being prepared. During the budget period, certain events or circumstances will occur that could not have been anticipated in advance.

Overbudgeting

Because of third party payer constraints—such as reimbursement under the lower of costs or charges and the constraints of external rate-setting processes—the hospital must guard its financial viability through deliberate overbudgeting in some expense categories. Deliberate overbudgeting must always be in expense categories that either will not be abused by department managers or that are completely controlled by administration. The following are areas in which deliberate overbudgeting can be effective: bad debt expense, contractual allowances, fringe benefits, departments where it is known that the manager will not spend more than necessary in spite of favorable budget variances, categories such as travel expense if administration can control such expense through an administrative policy (i.e., prior approval required before all hospital-reimbursed travel), utilities, insurance, and other expense areas that are not directly controlled by department heads.

The Master Budget

After the budget hearings are completed, the tentatively approved departmental requests must be summarized into the master expense budget for the hospital. The master expense budget is summarized by program or by major expense category for the entire hospital and compared to the current year's projected expense or to the current year's budget. Each line of this comparison should be examined for reasonableness.

This first draft of the consolidated expense budget should be presented to the administrator or to the budget committee with an estimate of the average price increase necessary to fund the budget and at the same time achieve the targeted net gain. If the average price increase appears reasonable as well as achievable, the controller can begin the revenue budget. If the needed price increase is not reasonable, the controller must propose areas, functions, or categories of budgeted expenses that can be cut. Although the expenses proposed to be cut will depend upon the individual hospital and on the prevailing circumstances, it should be noted that at this point in the budget process most reductions will be made either in discretionary costs or in those categories of expense that are deliberately overbudgeted.

Other Budget Items

In addition to the departmental budgets, the hospital will have several items that affect the entire hospital. These include, but are not limited to, depreciation, planned consulting fees, pension plan benefits, interest expense, and other expenses of an administrative nature. These are normally budgeted by the controller.

BUDGETING APPROACHES*

1. Program Budgeting

An internal control system should be designed to ensure that resources are used efficiently in achieving the goals and objectives of the health care facility. The institution's program structure portrays the programs that management plans to implement or operate during the budget period. For example, the structure might include programs for home dialysis, day surgery, and health education. Once the program structure has been specified, management can develop a budget for the identified activity areas and evaluate the relative costs and benefits of each.

The basic focus is on the allocation of resources to achieve the facility's common goals. Each area may consist of several subprograms and program elements. Once the components of each have been identified, management must ensure that all their goals are consistent with and contribute to the institution's objectives. Management next must determine the rates of activity needed in each program to achieve the objectives. Management then is in a position to allocate resources to achieve the goals. Program budgeting, then, is a technique for reaching strategic decisions on the composition of the institution's program structure as well as on achieving a balance between the allocation of resources and the facility's goals.

2. Zero-Base Budgeting

Zero-base budgeting complements program budgeting by examining specific expenditure alternatives within a general operational area.

Under the traditional budgeting approach, managers of established activity areas are required to justify any increased funding they seek for the fiscal period. The previous level of funding is accepted as being necessary and represents a portion of the approved expenditure for the budget period. Zero-base budgeting differs from the traditional process in that it requires managers to defend their entire budget requests. It mandates that managers develop, evaluate, and ordinally rank alternate approaches to achieving the goals of the unit for which they are responsible. Rather than assessing only the incremental changes in expenditures, zero-base budgeting forces management to evaluate total spending. Once expenditure alternatives are ordinally ranked, management can select those that yield the greatest benefit for the community.

Zero-base budgeting involves two basic steps. The first requires management to identify the objectives of the functional unit, the operational results required to achieve stated goals, alternate approaches to achieving these goals, and the outcomes and resource requirements associated with each. This first phase should be performed by the lowest level of managerial re-

---

*Budget approaches 1, 2 and 3 are excerpts reprinted from *Hospital Accounting Practice,* Vol. II, by Robert W. Broyles, with permission of Aspen Systems Corporation, © 1982.

sponsibility in the organization. Ideally, the individual who supervises each activity, operation, or task in the functional area should be responsible for developing alternate approaches, outcomes, and resource requirements.

The second step of zero-base budgeting involves an evaluation of the approaches developed earlier. Theoretically, the evaluation is accomplished by developing a rank ordering of the alternatives that is based on cost-benefit or cost-effectiveness analysis. A rank ordering is simply a list of projects arranged so that those with the most favorable cost-benefit or cost-effectiveness ratios appear at the top of the list. Once the ordinal ranking has been constructed, management uses the cost-benefit or cost-effectiveness ratios to develop funding priorities.

The initial ranking of expenditure alternatives should be developed by the managers responsible for specifying the project parameters. Subsequently, managerial personnel at successively higher levels of responsibility consolidate the rankings received from their subordinates and develop their own sets of priorities. Finally, senior management aggregates the subordinates' recommendations into the final ordinal ranking of expenditure alternatives for the institution.

3. Responsibility Center Budgeting

In a responsibility budget, the unit of analysis is a center or a series of centers for which an identifiable individual is responsible.

Responsibility budgets are developed in accordance with the chart of accounts and the organizational structure of the health care facility. An organizational structure that specifies lines of authority and responsibility, plus a satisfactory chart of accounts, are prerequisites to an effective responsibility budgeting program. When these prerequisites are satisfied, the cost of operating each responsibility center can be estimated by object of expenditure.

Control by Department Head*

Since control includes measuring actual results against plans and objectives, the accounting system must be built around the responsibility structure of the hospital. Therefore, responsibility accounting can be defined as a "system of accounting tailored to an organization so that costs are accumulated and reported by centers of responsibility within the organization." Each of these centers of responsibility is charged only with the costs for which it is responsible and over which it has control.

Responsibility normally encompasses only the controllable costs specifically identified with a cost center, which are subject to direct control of the department head, and are referred to as controllable costs (e.g., salaries and supplies). Costs not controllable at department level (e.g., administrative cost and depreciation) are referred to as noncontrollable cost. One needs to understand that a department head never has full responsibility for all direct costs, but there are many costs over which the department head exercises significant control.

The budgeting process should encourage a department head to offer the best estimate of the direct cost to operate that department. This action then justifies measuring that department head's performance against that estimate.

Expense and Revenue Budgets

An expense budget should be developed for each of the institution's responsibility centers. Similarly, revenue budgets should be developed for units that provide income-generating service.

When developing revenue budgets, it is necessary to differentiate between revenue-generating and nonrevenue-generating centers. The former offer direct patient care for which the institution earns income; conversely, the latter provide general support services that do not result directly in revenue. Since one of management's primary objectives is to ensure that total revenues are at least equal to total costs, the fee structure (and hence the revenue budget) should be based on the costs of operating both revenue and nonrevenue-generating centers.

The Expense Budget

When developing the expense budget for the responsibility center it is customary to chart separate schedules for labor and nonlabor costs.

---

*Source: Reprinted from J. Keith Deisenroth, "Understanding the Budget Process," *Topics in Health Care Financing*, Summer 1979, with permission of Aspen Systems Corporation.

The process of developing either the salary and wage budget or the supply expense budget of a responsibility center requires:

1. an estimation of the unit's workload
2. a translation of the workload into resource requirements
3. an application of factor prices to estimated resource requirements to derive the expected costs of operation

Given a projection of probable workloads, resource estimates should be developed by the managers responsible for ensuring that the organizational units operate efficiently. The translation of anticipated resource requirements into monetary or financial terms is a nonpolicy or routine task that should be performed by the fiscal services division.

The Revenue Budget

A comprehensive approach requires the development of a revenue budget that reflects the anticipated income generated by providing direct patient care, as well as other operating and nonoperating revenues.

The gross patient revenues that management expects to generate during the budget period emanate from:

1. providing stay-specific services
2. providing ancillary or other professional services to inpatients
3. providing ancillary or other professional services to outpatients

When anticipated deductions from income are subtracted from anticipated gross patient revenues, the result is an estimate of the net service revenue expected from direct patient care. When other sources of income are added to net patient service revenue, the net operating revenue anticipated during the budget period is obtained.

4. Forecast Budgeting*

A critical element in forecast budgeting is the grasp of the upside/downside concept. The upside concept reflects factors that would demonstrate growth or increased demands on services and the cost of providing them. The downside concept would indicate adverse trends or a decline in the demand for services. Forecasting requires a firm grasp of future events, conditions, and the upside/downside impacts determine the measure of budgetary adjustments to be made over previous budgets.

There are basically two types of forecasting methods to consider. These are mechanical and analytical forecasting.

1. Mechanical forecasting, also known as historic forecasting, usually involves a straight percentage increase multiplied across the board. It can be used for yearly projections on demands and services. However, it is best to go back three years as the base from which to project.
2. Analytical forecasting employs the upside/downside concepts and seeks to project realistic figures based on the impact of demands for services. Critical factors to be considered in forecasting are future events or conditions that will affect situation, people, time, and causative controls.

Examples of critical factors that affect situations in health care might be a change in patient days or in patient mix or in patient services.

Examples of critical factors impacting people might be personnel turnover rate, availability of various levels of medical record personnel.

Examples of critical factors influencing time or showing trends toward change might be trends toward more outpatient services, inservice education unionization. . . .

Examples of critical factors influencing place are: a new office building, a move to another location, an outside group moving in, sharing space or facilities with another department.

Examples of critical factors that affect controls or constraints might be new legislation; the JCAH; medical audit demands; PSRO requirements.

Management Activities

A listing of management activities performed during the forecasting phase of budget preparation would probably include the following:

- Identify the budgetary and forecasting period. This might be twelve months, eight-

---

*Source: Reprinted from *Medical Records in Health Information* by Kathleen A. Waters and Gretchen F. Murphy, with permission of Aspen Systems Corporation, © 1979.

een months, five years, or whatever period is selected.

- Identify and gather information on future events and conditions affecting people, place, trends, controls, and situations.
- Sort out information into upside/downside influences and trace these to departmental activities and services.
- Translate or convert these impacts into measurable units: hours, people, equipment needed, dollars and cents.
- Communicate to and obtain understanding and acceptance of the forecast by all affected components of your facility. (If, for example, one knows nursing service is planning to go into a heavy-scale nursing-audit activity, one can project the .5 full-time equivalent employee increase needed to do ten audits per year and obtain a signature on the justification statements. This defines the limit on the number of audits requested by nursing service and might provide half a full-time equivalent position to do the work, rather than trying to get by on existing staff.)
- Write out indirect costs debited against department budgets and check into increases in cost and activity for the future.

5. Flexible Budgeting*

Use of a flexible budget versus a forecast budget has received much discussion among health care financial people. At the present time, very few hospitals and other health care facilities use a formal system of flexible budgeting. However, flexible budgeting is a more sophisticated method of budgeting than typical forecast budgeting and is being adopted by more and more health care facilities as they become experienced in the budgetary process.

A flexible budget is a budget that adjusts targeted levels of costs for changes in volume. For example, the budget for a nursing unit operating at 95% occupancy would be different than the budget for that same unit operating at an 80% occupancy. A forecast budget would make no formal differentiation in the allowed budget between these two levels.*

Concepts

There are two underlying concepts to flexible budgeting.

1. The classification of cost into fixed and variable is possible only when the time period to which these costs are related is specified.
2. The variability of cost estimates from historical data must be adjusted for factors other than volume changes.

The flexible budget, like the forecast budget, must still provide in quantitative terms the plan of the hospital, the basis for financial evaluation and the means of controlling costs. However, flexible budgeting includes the additional requirements of analyzing cost behavior and developing more sophisticated standards. The flexible budgeting process is illustrated in Figure 16-2.

The basic difference between the two is that the forecast budget is prepared at a given level of demand, and any shift in demand necessitates making changes at the point of origin (i.e., at the budget document preparation process). The flexible budget, on the other hand, develops a model for each department and permits management to evaluate how costs vary with demand *without* having to revert to point of origin.

Cost Analysis

Cost behavior analysis enables management to determine how expenses are affected by volume. Such an analysis is dependent on a well-designed plan of attack. Cost behavior can be analyzed by reviewing historical experience. This involves segregating the cost charged to the various expense accounts into the appropriate cost classification (i.e., fixed, semivariable and variable). Another means is to use statistical analysis to determine how costs varied with the applicable unit of volume.

A flexible budget complements standard cost procedures in that it provides data for comput-

---

*Source: Reprinted from J. Keith Deisenroth, "Understanding the Budget Process," *Topics in Health Care Financing,* Summer 1979, with permission of Aspen Systems Corporation.

*Source: Reprinted from *Essentials of Hospital Finance* by William O. Cleverley, with permission of Aspen Systems Corporation, © 1978.

Figure 16-2 The flexible budgeting process

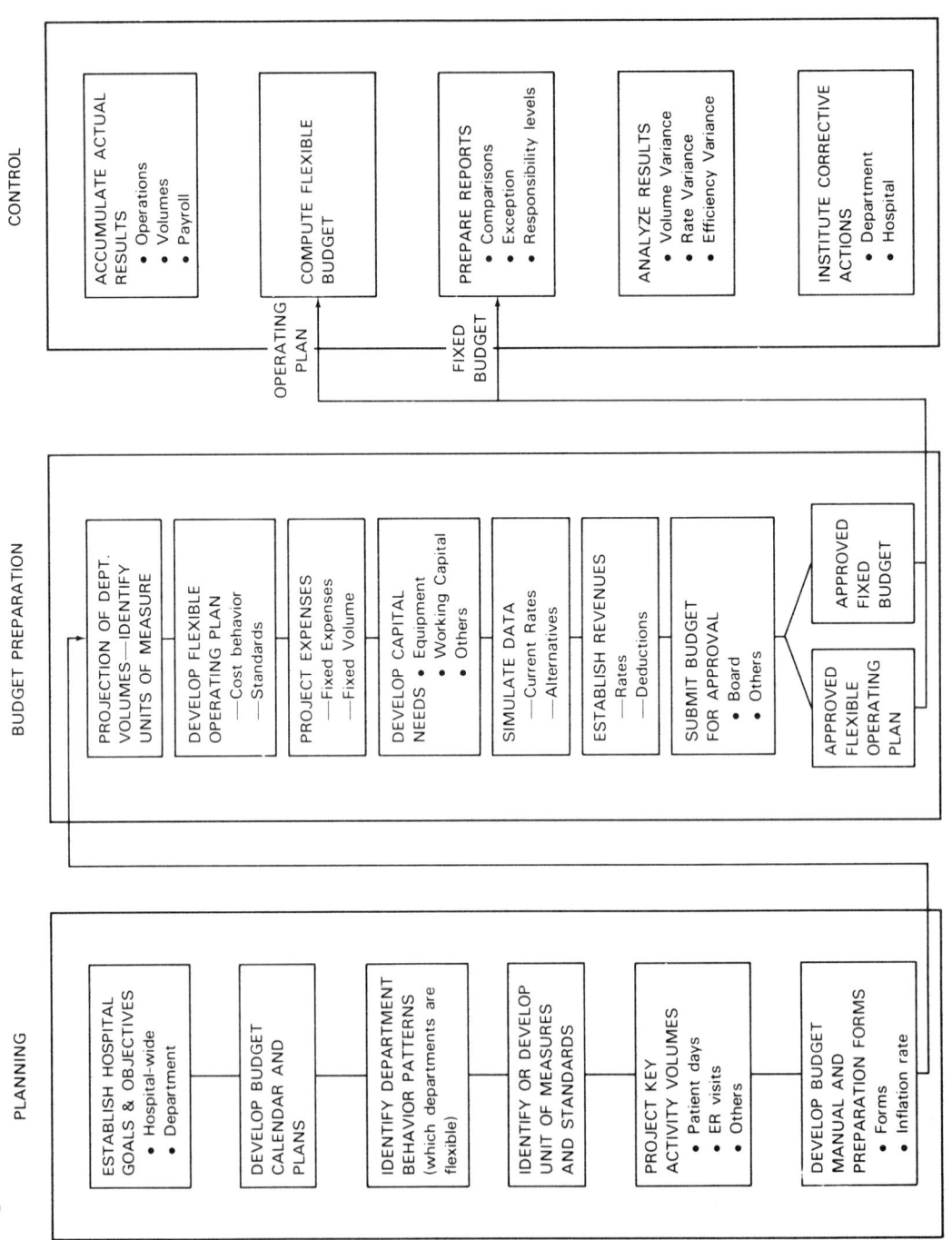

ing of cost center overhead rates and overhead variance analysis. Basically, in a standard cost accounting system, the costs *recorded* are predetermined or target costs, and the variances between them and the actual amounts incurred are recorded in separative variance accounts. The latter values are reviewed as "losses due to inefficiencies." Therefore, a standard cost system entails at the time of recording transactions a comparison process (actual compared with objectives or targets) similar to that used in budgetary control. The standard cost specification itemizes the standard cost of labor, supplies and other overhead costs. This standard cost specification generally is the culmination of the budgetary process and a series of cost analyses and engineering studies to develop reliable standards.

Before implementing a flexible budgeting system, hospital management must evaluate the advantages and disadvantages between the two budget processes. Table 16-2 summarizes some of the considerations.

Once implemented, the flexible budgeting program provides more than a month-to-month or annual evaluation of actual to budget. Rather, the program creates individual models for each cost center within the hospital. This feature permits management to create a simulation of individual cost centers or of the entire institution. Modeling allows the hospital to ask the "what if" questions—to analyze the impact of unanticipated events—and to consider the "now what" questions that may impact on the short-range and/or long-range plans of the hospital.

Is Flexible Budgeting for Your Hospital?

Although the flexible budgeting process does provide hospital management more control and more meaningful information, is flexible budgeting worth the additional time and effort? The answer depends upon the answers to other fundamental questions. For example: Is the organizational structure well documented, and is there a formalized delegation of authority? Is there an effective responsibility accounting system? Is the hospital's environment conducive to participative management?

Flexible budgeting demands effective communication among all management personnel. It cannot tolerate a "closet" approach. For output to be meaningful, the input must be accurate. This demands team effort, responsibility ac-

Table 16-2 Advantages and Disadvantages of Forecast vs. Flexible Budgeting

Forecast (Fixed) Budgeting		Flexible Budgeting	
Advantages:	**Disadvantages:**	**Advantages:**	**Disadvantages:**
Traditional approach	Difficult to adjust to actual activity levels	Can be adjusted to reflect actual activity levels	More time consuming
Easily understood			More costly to implement and monitor
Preparation and reporting time is less than with a flexible budget	Cannot readily analyze discrepancies caused by changes in volume, price and activity	Easier to obtain meaningful variance analysis	Requires additional training
Meaningful only if actual level of activity closely approximates budget	Due to inherent limitations, the approach to budget preparation and variance analysis can become haphazard and meaningless	Can serve to more adequately contain costs	Places greater demand on hospital personnel and requires more financial sophistication
		Assists management in identifying the hospital's problems before the fact thru the use of budget model applications	
		More defensible in rate review, prospective reimbursement and external price control negotiations	
		More acceptable control tool	

counting, delegation of authority, adequate support resources, and effective reporting.

Since flexible budgeting often requires greater sophistication, management may want to select one or two departments as a pilot project for flexible budgeting rather than implementing a complete flexible budget system immediately.

TYPES OF BUDGET DOCUMENTS

As a prerequisite to understanding budget concepts and practices, the following definitions are offered.*

- *Operating Budget* consists of three separate budget documents:
    1. Statistics Budget—the accumulation of the necessary statistical data needed to quantify the expense budget.
    2. Expense Budget—the conversion of statistical budget into anticipated dollar amounts of expense.
    3. Revenue Budget—the establishment of enough revenue to meet the financial requirements of the hospital.
- *Cash Budget*—a projection of cash receipts, disbursements, and balances for a given future period in time. It is designed to assist in controlling the hospital's cash position. It enables management to predict the timing and amount of future cash flows, cash balances, and cash needs and surpluses; and to examine cost implications of cash decisions.
- *Capital Budget*—the schedule of capital expenditures, capital dispositions and resources available for the budget period.

The Operating Budget**

The first budget document to be completed is the statistical budget. Its preparation involves accumulating statistical data (i.e., occasions of service, work units, and relative value units) by cost center. Although the department head is responsible for gathering these data, the actual task should be delegated to supervisory and clerical personnel.

The second budget document to be prepared is the expense budget. This involves converting the statistical budget into anticipated dollar expenses. The expense budget is segregated into two components: (1) salary and wage budget and (2) supplies and other nonsalary expenses. The salary and wage budget requires establishing staffing objectives for each cost center. Methods that may be used for this purpose are (1) management engineered standards, (2) historical experience and (3) experience of other hospitals. The nonsalary expenses are best forecasted by (1) understanding accounting practices, (2) knowledge of expense relationships to the units of service, (3) analysis of historical data, (4) realistic estimates of vendor price increases and (5) identification of technological and environmental change.

The third budget document is the revenue budget. The hospital's financial objective is to generate enough revenue to meet its financial requirements. Hospital revenues are normally generated from three sources: (1) patient revenues, (2) other operating revenues (i.e., activities incidental to patient services) and (3) nonoperating revenue (i.e., investment income, grants and donations and endowments).

Discretionary revenue may be important, especially for institutions with large endowments. Any good management control system should establish a budget for expected return on endowments. Variations from the expected level should be investigated; changes in investment management may be necessary.

The Cash Budget[1]

The cash budget is management's best indicator of the organization's expected short-run solvency. It translates all of the above budgets into a statement of cash inflows and outflows. The cash budget is usually broken down by periods within the total budget period, such as months or quarters.

---

*Source: Reprinted from J. Keith Deisenroth, "Understanding the Budget Process," *Topics in Health Care Financing*, Summer 1979, with permission of Aspen Systems Corporation.

**Source: Reprinted from *Essentials of Hospital Finance* by William O. Cleverley, with permission of Aspen Systems Corporation, © 1978.

[1]Reprinted from Robert B. Taylor, Jr., "Budget Reporting and Control," *Topics in Health Care Financing*, Summer 1979, with permission of Aspen Systems Corporation.

A poor cash budget could cause an increase in rates, a reduction in expenses, a reduction in capital expenditures, or many other changes. These changes and revisions must be made until the cash budget reflects a position of short-run solvency.

Budgeted Financial Statements[1]

The two major financial statements that are developed on a budgetary basis are the balance sheet and the statement of revenues and expenses. These two statements are indicators of both short- and long-run solvency; however, they are more important in assessing long-run solvency. Unfavorable projections in either statement might also cause changes in any of the other budgets. (For a representation of the relationship of all the budgets see Figure 16-3.)

INTERPRETING AND ACTING UPON BUDGET REPORTS

Reporting formats and the manner in which they are compiled will vary among hospitals. Developments in the area of automated data processing provide countless techniques that improve and simplify the job of reporting financial data to management.

The reports should show deviations (exceptions) from the fixed and variable performances projected in the budget. The administration should investigate any deviation from a budget projection.

A properly designed reporting system will provide the user with data to answer questions such as:[*]

- Are the variations in net departmental revenue due to a change in the level of activity, fee per procedure or mix of cost-based versus charge-based payers?
- Are the variations in labor costs due to a change in the number of workers, rate of wages or efficiency?
- Are the variations in supply costs due to changes in the quantity used or to a change in the price of the material?
- Are increases in noncontrollable costs due to waste, inaccurate budget estimates or poor supervision?

A different type of report may be required for each level of management. The closer the user is to the activity, the greater the amount of detail

---

[1]Reprinted from Robert B. Taylor, Jr., "Budget Reporting and Control," *Topics in Health Care Financing,* Summer 1979, with permission of Aspen Systems Corporation.

[*]Source: Reprinted from *Basic Hospital Financial Management* by Donald F. Beck, with permission of Aspen Systems Corporation, © 1980.

Figure 16-3 Integration of budgets

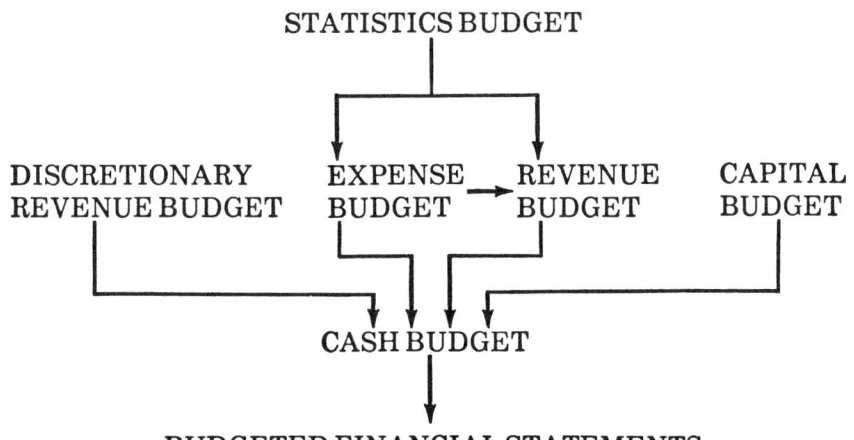

STATISTICS BUDGET
↓
DISCRETIONARY REVENUE BUDGET — EXPENSE BUDGET → REVENUE BUDGET — CAPITAL BUDGET
↓
CASH BUDGET
↓
BUDGETED FINANCIAL STATEMENTS
Balance Sheet
Revenues and Expenses

that must be provided. The user must be able to interpret, with the assistance of the reports, the actual versus budgeted results and to develop alternate strategies if necessary. Corrective action must be taken quickly after considering the interaction of specific variables.

Types of Financial Reports*

Monthly Reports: Comparisons of Actual to Budget

Every hospital should have a minimum of four sets of monthly reports comparing actual to budget. These are departmental reports, program reports, the hospital statement of income and expense, and sources of applications of cash.

Most departmental reports show actual, budget, and variance for both the current period and the fiscal year to date. These reports are used by department managers in controlling direct costs. An example of a departmental report for the outpatient clinic of a typical hospital is shown in Table 16-3.

Each budgeted departmental account should be detailed separately on the department budget reports. Revenue-producing departments should be held accountable for budgeting revenue as well as for explaining budget variances. The example shown in Table 16-3 reports revenue on the same page with expenses. Many hospitals report revenue separately by department. Although the department heads have limited control over revenue, there are two important reasons why they should be required to explain significant budget variances. First, if department heads are managing their revenue, problems with lost charges, missing charges, price increases, and other factors that prohibit the hospital from maximizing gross revenue are placed at the level of responsibility where timely corrective action can be taken. Second, if department heads are managing their revenue, the hospital will have a more accurate annual revenue forecast.

Program reports should show the same detail and be in the same format as department reports. These programs can be prepared either by reporting responsibility or by function. If reporting responsibility is used, all cost centers that report to the director of nursing would summarize in one report, all cost centers that report to an assistant administrator would summarize in another report, and so on. If the program reports summarize by function, all ancillaries would be on one page, all inpatient nursing units on another page, all outpatient nursing units on a third page, and so on.

The hospital statement of income and expense should be presented with a comparison to budget. This comparison should compare actual results to budget for every line on the hospital's regular income statement. It is especially useful to report the total hospital income statement in both whole dollars and per unit cost. The unit costs most often used are inpatient days and adjusted patient days. Adjusted patient days are equal to inpatient days plus outpatient activity expressed as equivalent patient days. Adjusted patient days can be calculated by using the following formula:

$$\text{Patient Days} \times \frac{\text{Inpatient Revenue} + \text{Outpatient Revenue}}{\text{Inpatient Revenue}} = \text{Adjusted Patient Days}$$

Some hospitals have developed an extensive income and expense budget reporting system but have failed to report the budget versus actual cash position by month. Often the controller fails to report the ending cash balance each month. It must be remembered that all purchases, liabilities, and expenses are paid out of cash. Therefore, it is important that the hospital prepare a detailed comparison of actual to budget sources and the application of cash every month.

Special Problem Reports

In addition to the four sets of monthly reports described in the previous section, many hospitals prepare supporting schedules that track special problem areas or report other information used by administration.

The month-end balance sheet is sometimes compared to the beginning of the period with a column titled net change. For example, a balance sheet may report six columns of information. For the current month, it would show beginning of period, end of period, and either net change or percentage change for each item on

---

*Source: Reprinted from *Basic Hospital Financial Management* by Donald F. Beck, with permission of Aspen Systems Corporation, © 1980.

Chapter 16—Budgeting 249

Table 16-3 A Monthly Departmental Report for an Outpatient Clinic

Department 200—Outpatient Clinic   D. Smith

		Current Month			Year to Date		
Account	Description	Actual	Budget	Variance	Actual	Budget	Variance
050	Clinic	XXX	XXX	XX	XXX	XXX	XX
060	Prof. fees	XXX	XXX	XX	XXX	XXX	XX
Total revenue		XXX	XXX	XX	XXX	XXX	XX
100	Salaries-prof.	XXX	XXX	XX	XXX	XXX	XX
150	Salaries-nursing	XXX	XXX	XX	XXX	XXX	XX
170	Salaries-other	XXX	XXX	XX	XXX	XXX	XX
200	Social security	XXX	XXX	XX	XXX	XXX	XX
210	Health insurance	XXX	XXX	XX	XXX	XXX	XX
Total personnel expense		XXX	XXX	XX	XXX	XXX	XX
310	Drugs	XXX	XXX	XX	XXX	XXX	XX
320	Medical supplies	XXX	XXX	XX	XXX	XXX	XX
330	Other supplies	XXX	XXX	XX	XXX	XXX	XX
410	Service contracts	XXX	XXX	XX	XXX	XXX	XX
420	Repairs-maintenance	XXX	XXX	XX	XXX	XXX	XX
500	Travel	XXX	XXX	XX	XXX	XXX	XX
600	Miscellaneous expense	XXX	XXX	XX	XXX	XXX	XX
Total nonpersonnel expense		XXX	XXX	XX	XXX	XXX	XX
Total expense		XXX	XXX	XX	XXX	XXX	XX
Net gain (loss)		XXX	XXX	XX	XXX	XXX	XX

the balance sheet. The report would also show beginning of period, end of period, and either net change or percentage change for the year to date.

Most hospitals that prepare supporting schedules will have at least one schedule to analyze revenue. For each revenue-producing department, revenue can be shown broken down into outpatient and inpatient, with that particular department shown as a percentage of the total.

This schedule could show revenue per patient day or per adjusted patient day rather than by each department's percentage of the total. Additional reports on the following revenue areas can be generated if the hospital has electronic data processing: total revenue by admitting physician, total revenue by nursing unit or by floor, total revenue by medical specialty, average revenue per admission or per day by admitting physician or by admitting diagnosis, and total revenue by procedure or test for the period. With electronic data processing, supporting schedules are limited only by the amount of accurate source-document information and the technical capability of the data-processing staff.

Supplies expense by department and professional fees by department are frequently used to monitor these high-dollar expenditures. Other monthly supporting schedules may include deductions from revenue, other revenue, and drug expense by department. If the hospital has a program to allocate nonrevenue-producing departments to revenue-producing departments, several performance analysis reports can be generated that will quickly identify areas needing special management attention in order to maximize third party reimbursement. A departmental performance analysis report shows gross revenue reduced by allowances and deductions, direct expense, and allocated indirect expense to arrive at an actual gain or loss. The two most common methods of allocating indirect cost (nonrevenue-producing departments) to the revenue-producing departments are stepdown and simultaneous equations.

The many different supporting schedules described provide a basis for developing many more schedules. Hospital administrators should develop an intuitive or acquired ability to determine the cost-benefit ratio of all new reports as well as ongoing reports. They need to ask if this report is worth the time and expense it will take to develop and maintain it. Will the users of the report be able to absorb and use all of the information, or would a simpler, less expensive report be just as beneficial? If the schedule does not pass this cost-benefit analysis test, it should not be prepared.

Statistical Budget Reports

In addition to supporting income and expense schedules, many hospitals find it helpful to report budgeted operating indicators. This includes the number of admissions, patient days, outpatient occasions of service, tests or procedures by department, man-hours by department, and other statistics. Operating or workload statistics can be effectively presented in graph or table form. It is especially useful to prepare a graph to illustrate a trend or trends covering several years.

For department managers, statistical budget comparisons are a more effective tool than actual dollar comparisons. Statistical budgets that break costs, hours, or other statistics down to a workload basis are much more effective than budgets that report unadjusted statistics. This is because it is easy to relate to a procedure, a patient day, or a test but difficult to relate to hundreds of procedures, patient days, or tests. Time spent breaking statistical budgets down to a lower common denominator is normally effective.

Other statistics that could be considered are procedures per patient days, salary expense per procedure, nonsalary expense per procedure, and total expense per patient day. In addition to showing current month and year to date, it may be useful to report prior-year statistics, prior-month statistics, or next month's statistics. The information presented on statistical reports should be tailored to fit the needs of the individual hospital.

Variance Analysis of Budgets

Monthly analysis of significant budget variances has a twofold purpose. First, it acts as a control by requiring managers to identify any potential problem areas. Potential problem areas, once identified, are further analyzed. Second, the reports represent a historical account of whatever creates a significant unfavorable variance. Managers as well as administration become very knowledgeable about the major spending patterns within the institution.

The hospital should have definite policies to determine responsibility for analysis-of-budget variances. The responsibility can either be centralized in the accounting department or the departments can be required to analyze and report their own variances. If the accounting department prepares the variance analysis for all departments, department heads should participate in explaining major variances to the accounting analyst. It is important to have the department heads involved as much as possible in studying budget variances.

Identification of budget variances to report each month is a judgmental matter to be decided by each hospital. In establishing parameters, the hospital should remember that one of the purposes of this report is to provide a historical account of spending patterns. It is better to have too much detail than not enough. The following can be used as a guide:

- Seldom are variances of less than one hundred dollars significant.
- The expense should be reasonable for the function of the particular department. For example, accounting should never report research supplies or drug expense.
- If a pattern of overspending occurs each month and is explainable, it should be included only occasionally in the written variance description.
- Significant variances are a function of percentage as well as of dollar amount. For example, a variance of two hundred dollars is significant for an item budgeted at one hundred dollars for the period but is not significant for an item budgeted at one hundred thousand dollars for the period.

Action To Be Taken*

Interpretation of the reported results involves not only the identification and justification of specific variances but also the interpretation of the impact that these contributing causes will have on the various levels of cost behavior. Table 16-4 has been designed to provide an understanding of the interaction between the causes of variances and the resulting impact on cost behavior.

Each of the variances will have some impact on the overall cost behavior of the hospital.

---

*Source: Reprinted from Robert B. Taylor, Jr., "Budget Reporting and Control," *Topics in Health Care Financing*, Summer 1979, with permission of Aspen Systems Corporation.

Management's key role is to identify the type of variance, the probable duration of the contributing cause and the corrective action that must be taken. The following information provides a course of action to be taken based upon specific variances.

PRICE VARIANCE (LABOR)

Management Action

- Determine reasons causing increase in wages and determine if wage increase is permanent or temporary.
- Determine if substitute for labor is acceptable *and* available.
- Determine if wage and salary framework is structured and competitive with our facilities.
- Determine impact (if any) on profitability.

Rate-Setting Action

- Increase may support increased rate adjustments (if necessary).

Reimbursement Action

- May indicate the necessity for increasing the interim per diem from cost-based reimbursers.

Department Action

- Assist personnel in identifying alternatives to current personnel disciplines.
- Closer alignment of available staffing to actual departments.

RATE VARIANCE (PATIENT REVENUE)

Management Action

- Determine reasons causing increase or decrease in rate structure and determine if change is permanent or temporary.
- Determine if change is attributable to change in patient mix, intensity of service, or change in makeup of medical staff.

Rate-Setting Action

- See recommendation under "Reimbursement Action."

Reimbursement Action

- If change-based revenue is adversely affected, shift may necessitate increase in the interim per diem from cost-based reim-

Table 16-4 Summary of Impact of Specific Types of Variances on Cost Behavior

	Variable Cost Behavior	Fixed Cost Behavior	Semivariable Cost Behavior
Price variance	If price increase (decrease) of permanent nature, variable cost will be affected permanently in direct proportion to the level of activity.	If price increase (decrease) of permanent nature, fixed cost will increase (decrease) in total and increase (decrease) per volume indicator.	If price increase (decrease) of permanent nature and affects variable component, variable cost will increase (decrease) in direct proportion to level of activity. If price increase (decrease) of permanent nature and affects fixed component, fixed cost will increase (decrease) per volume indicator.
Volume variance	If volume increase (decrease) of permanent nature, variable cost will be affected permanently in direct proportion to level of activity.	If volume increase (decrease) of permanent nature, the fixed cost per volume indicator will move in the opposite direction of the volume increase (decrease).	If volume increase (decrease) of permanent nature, variable component will increase (decrease) in proportion to volume change. If volume increase (decrease) of permanent nature, fixed component will increase (decrease) per volume indicator.
Capacity variance	If there is excess capacity, the variable cost behavior will not be affected and vice versa.	If there is excess capacity, the fixed cost will remain constant and vice versa.	Same rationale as above.

bursers. Or, determine if an increase in the charge structure is not justified. Analysis of contribution margin or actual versus budget level is prescribed.

Department Action

- Assist management in the identification of causes for rate variance.

PRICE VARIANCE (SUPPLIES)

Management Action

- Determine reasons causing price increase and if price increase is permanent or temporary.
- Determine availability of substitute supplies.
- Determine feasibility of reducing price through bidding process or other purchasing techniques.

Department Action

- Reexamine supply usage by specific volume indicator and reevaluate cost behavior trends.

EFFICIENCY VARIANCE (PRODUCTIVITY)

Management Action

- Determine reasons causing increase/decrease in labor component and assess impact of patient mix, service mix, and the like.
- Determine if labor variance is permanent and, if so, reassess impact of change as cost behavior.
- Examine fringe benefit program and other contributing reasons if variance is due to substantial incurrence of nonproductive labor.

Rate-Setting Action

- Increased labor requirements may provide support for rate adjustments.

Reimbursement Action

- With increased volume and corresponding changes in the departmental cost structure, a request for a change in the interim reimbursement rate may be in order.

Department Action

- Change in required labor component will necessitate reexamination of cost behavior.
- Determine impact, if any, on profitability.

VOLUME VARIANCE (PATIENT REVENUE)

Management Action

- Determine reasons causing increase/decrease in number of procedures and determine if volume change is permanent or temporary.
- If change is permanent, make necessary changes in staffing and supply requirements and recompute contribution margin and reassess cost behavior.
- If change is permanent, evaluate the need for changes in the fixed asset structure.
- Determine the impact, and causes thereof, if volume changes are being experienced throughout facility.

Rate-Setting Action

- Price increase may support increased rate adjustments (if necessary).

Reimbursement Action

- May indicate the necessity for increasing the interim per diem from cost-based reimbursers.

Department Action

- Assist purchasing in identifying alternate services or supplies.

CAPACITY VARIANCE

Management Action

- Determine reasons for increase/decrease in level of use and identify degree of permanence.
- If permanent increase/decrease, assess need for reallocation of resources and reexamine cost behavior.

Rate-Setting Action

- Identify impact on profitability caused by capacity variance and identify need for rate adjustments.

Reimbursement Action

- Same process as rate-setting action (see above).

Department Action

- Identify specific course of action that can be used to correct (if adverse capacity variance) or sustain (if favorable variance) change in capacity.

COST BENEFIT/COST EFFECTIVENESS ANALYSES

Distinctions*

Cost benefit and cost effectiveness analyses are primarily analytical techniques which are used by the manager in making decisions. By their use it is possible to select what is considered to be an optimal approach from a group of feasible alternatives. The cost benefit approach has been used in industry in various forms. It is not a new tool; it is only new to many hospital planners. It opens the door to a wide range of decision possibilities, both administrative and technical, which heretofore have not been taken advantage of.

In cost-benefit analysis generally one seeks to value all inputs (i.e., costs) and all outcomes (i.e., benefits) in dollars. Cost-benefit analysis can assist in setting priorities across programs with substantially different outcomes and in the process yield an estimate of the net dollar value associated with each course of action. Cost-effectiveness analysis, on the other hand, can help in choosing among alternative means of achieving a given, presumably desired, outcome possessing a single measure of effectiveness. The

---

*Source: *Analysis of New Health Technologies*. Health Planning Information Series, DHHS, 1980, Pub. No. (HRA) 80-14014.

price paid to accomplish the more powerful cost-benefit analysis, however, is high, for in valuing all benefits subjective problems arise, such as valuing human life or the quality of life in dollars. Despite the conscientious efforts of analysts to attack these issues, many decision-makers may not find such valuations palatable.

Finally, a still simpler form of economic analysis is the comparative cost analysis. In this case, the benefits from two projects are presumed or known to be indistinguishable; the choice may be made on costs alone.

Guidelines for Use of CEA/CBA*

Following are 10 principles of analysis that could be used to guide the conduct, evaluation or use of CEA/CBA studies:

1. **Define Problem.**—The problem should be clearly and explicitly defined and the relationship to health outcome or status should be stated.
2. **State Objectives.**—The objectives of the technology being assessed should be explicitly stated, and the analysis should address the degree to which the objectives are (expected to be) met.
3. **Identify Alternatives.**—Alternative means (technologies) to accomplish the objectives should be identified and subjected to analysis. When slightly different outcomes are involved, the effect this difference will have on the analysis should be examined.
4. **Analyze Benefits/Effects.**—All foreseeable benefits/effects (positive and negative outcomes) should be identified, and when possible, should be measured. When possible, and if agreement on the terms can be reached, it may be helpful to value all benefits in common terms in order to make comparisons easier.
5. **Analyze Costs.**—All expected costs should be identified, and when possible, should be measured and valued in dollars.
6. **Differentiate Perspective of Analysis.**—When private or program benefits and costs differ from social benefits and costs (and if a private or program perspective is appropriate for the analysis), the differences should be identified.
7. **Perform Discounting.**—All future costs and benefits should be discounted to their present value.
8. **Analyze Uncertainties.**—Sensitivity analysis should be conducted. Key variables should be analyzed to determine the importance of their uncertainty to the results of the analysis. A range of possible values for each variable should be examined for effects on results.
9. **Address Ethical Issues.**—Ethical issues should be identified, discussed, and placed in appropriate perspective relative to the rest of the analysis and the objectives of the technology.
10. **Discuss Results.**—The results of the analysis should be discussed in terms of validity, sensitivity to changes in assumptions, and implications for policy or decision-making.

Cost Benefit Analysis*

Cost-benefit analysis consists of five sequential steps:

1. Articulation of a clear, unambiguous statement of the decision faced and objectives sought by the health planner;
2. Identification of alternative actions or programs that satisfy stated objectives;
3. Identification separately of the costs and benefits associated with the proposed undertaking and each alternative action;
4. Quantitative evaluation of all costs incurred and benefits returned for each action;
5. Comparison of alternatives against explicit decision criteria to yield the preferred program.

Advantages

- Provides a systematic and consistent approach to the evaluation of alternative actions;
- Requires explicit (numerical) statements regarding the values of all recognized effects attributed to the various interventions,

---

*Source: *Cost Effectiveness Analysis of Medical Technology*, Office of Technology Assessment, August, 1980, Pub. No. (OTA)H-125.

*Source: *Analysis of New Health Technologies*, Health Planning Information Series, DHHS, 1980, Pub. No. (HRA) 80-14014.

thereby avoiding purely subjective judgments;
- Takes a total view of the allocation decision, as opposed to that of a dollar cost alone;
- Yields an explicit appraisement of the net value of undertaking the preferred alternative.

Cost Effectiveness Analyses*

In cost effectiveness analysis, as in cost benefit analysis, there are several basic concepts which must be considered. Among these concepts, the following three are most important:

1. There are alternative ways to accomplish an objective and we must select the optimal alternative, which may not be the least costly one.
2. There must be at least two alternative ways to accomplish a task in order to undertake cost effectiveness analysis.
3. Cost effectiveness analysis is not cost reduction; it is optimization of an approach to a specific goal or set of goals.

From a managerial standpoint cost effectiveness analysis is directed by two basic economic considerations: (1) A minimum expectation that in either social or economic terms, for the program being undertaken, there will be a dollar of return for each dollar of investment. (2) An optimal expectation that one dollar plus some additional increment of economic or social return will accrue for each dollar of investment.

A cost effectiveness analysis is ultimately reduced to a series of models. These models, which are frequently but not always complex, set out alternatives and indicate the anticipated return of each alternative relative to a given level of investment. Operationally, the procedure requires a separate set of models for each available alternative.

In undertaking cost effectiveness analysis we must consider the inputs which go into the development of the analytic models. Essentially, the same inputs are used that have always been used in decision making and planning. For example: (1) Capital—What dollars are available to do the job? (2) Labor—How many people are available to accomplish the goal? (3) Tools—What techniques, facilities, etc., are available? (4) Data—What sources of information are available?

A disciplined look is being taken in order to fully analyze information, alternatives, and problems and, where possible, take advantage of various new technological developments which are available.

The initial step is to delineate clear and specific objectives, which ask why it is necessary to do a given task and what is expected in return for the undertaking. We do not merely say we want to reduce condition X by 20 percent or build 50 new hospital beds. Rather, we ask why we should be doing this and what our real short and long range objectives are. After the objectives have been determined, the cost effectiveness approach evaluates the alternatives, asking the questions, "To attain this objective, how many alternatives and what types of alternatives are available? Do we only have one way to do the job? Are there two alternatives open to us? Are there more than two alternatives? If there are several alternatives, what specifically are they?"

After setting objectives and determining possible alternative ways to attain these objectives, it is necessary to specify what resources are required for each alternative—resources in terms of people, money, equipment, and facilities. Having thus developed objectives, alternatives, and resource needs, the analyst then prepares cost effectiveness models for each alternative and also determines the criteria to be used for the selection of the preferred alternative or alternatives.

As the cost effectiveness models are built, we are concerned with several pertinent measurements which will be used in making a decision and which form parts of the model. These include:

1. Measures of effectiveness—the criteria which indicate how well the alternative satisfies the objectives.
2. Measures of operational use—the criteria for consideration of alternatives in light of

---

*Source: Royal A. Crystal and Agnes W. Brewsterm, "Cost Benefit and Cost Effectiveness Analyses in the Health Field: An Introduction." Reprinted, with permission of the Blue Cross Association, from *Inquiry*, Vol. 3, December 1967, pp. 3–13, Copyright © 1966 by the Blue Cross Association. All rights reserved.

Table 16-5 Targets for Cost Evaluation*

1. acquisition costs
2. available funds
3. cost acceptability
4. cost advantage
5. cost containment
6. cost of administrative manhours per bed
7. cost of blood bank
8. cost of central service's supply
9. cost of clinics
10. cost of development
11. cost of direct expense per patient meal
12. cost of emergency services
13. cost of equipment
14. cost of fiscal manhours per bed
15. cost of full-time employees per bed
16. cost of full-time employees per occupied bed
17. cost of hardware
18. cost of implementation
19. cost of inhalation therapy
20. cost of inpatient laboratory services
21. cost of inpatient laboratory tests
22. cost of inpatient radiology services
23. cost of installation
24. cost of intensive and coronary care units
25. cost of IV therapy
26. cost of laboratory expenses excluding fees per test
27. cost of laboratory direct expenses excluding fees per weighted unit
28. cost of laboratory tests per admission
29. cost of laboratory tests per manhour
30. cost of laboratory weighted units per manhour
31. cost of linens per patient day
32. cost of laundry and linen per 100 pounds
33. cost of maintenance
34. cost of LPN manhours per patient day
35. expense of manhours per patient day
36. cost of manpower
37. cost of meals per patient day
38. cost of medical and surgical nursing units
39. cost of medical record manhours per discharge unit
40. cost of nursing manhours per patient day
41. cost of obstetrical suite
42. cost of operating and recovery room
43. cost of outpatient laboratory services
44. cost of outpatient laboratory tests
45. cost of outpatient radiological services
46. cost of pharmacy
47. cost of physical therapy
48. cost of present value of services
49. cost of present value of system
50. cost of procurement
51. cost of radiology procedure per admission
52. cost of radiology direct expenses per procedure excluding fee
53. cost of radiology manhours per procedure
54. cost of radiology outpatient procedures
55. cost of research
56. cost of R&D
57. cost of RN manhours per patient day
58. cost of software development
59. cost of software maintenance
60. cost of spare parts
61. cost of subsystem operations
62. cost of initial program
63. cost of system operation
64. cost of total program
65. cost of total project
66. cost of total system
67. cost of training
68. cost savings as a percent of current operations
69. cost savings as a percent of Nth year operations
70. cost savings of intangibles
71. cost savings of tangibles
72. cost savings of tangibles and intangibles
73. days of revenue in patient accounts receivable
74. debt service
75. depreciation
76. direct expenses of medical records per discharge unit
77. direct expense per patient day
78. direct expense of plant engineering per 1000 feet
79. expense of all nursing units
80. expense per length of stay
81. expense as percent of occupancy
82. funding rate
83. inpatient cost per patient day
84. inpatient cost per stay
85. inpatient revenue per patient day
86. recurring costs
87. reserve as percent of accounts receivable
88. savings in total cost of operation

*Source: Reprinted from *The Practice-Oriented Method* by Gerald S. Lang and Kenneth J. Dickie, with permission of Aspen Systems Corporation, © 1978.

the other responsibilities which must be undertaken.
3. Measures of personnel and equipment needed—the determination for each alternative of the number and kinds of people and equipment required.
4. Cost factors.
5. Measures of cost—the determination of cost for each alternative way of doing the job and the manner in which cost will be measured.

Cost Effectiveness: Targets and Criteria

For a list of possible targets for cost evaluation see Table 16-5. For a list of criteria that can be used in determining the effectiveness of a particular cost factor see Table 16-6.

Table 16-6 Criteria for Effectiveness Evaluation*

1. ability
2. acceptance
3. accomplishment
4. accuracy
5. adaptability
6. adequacy of data availability
7. adequate data capacity
8. age of data available
9. amount of power per month
10. availability
11. availability of data
12. benefits of current values
13. benefit of resale value
14. capability
15. capacity
16. compatibility
17. consumables required
18. data formatting
19. data overlay
20. data rate
21. data retrieval rate
22. degree of physician acceptance
23. dependability
24. development risk
25. ease of data entry
26. effect of breakthroughs
27. effectiveness of less than maximum operating activity
28. efficacy
29. error rate
30. failure rates
31. flexibility
32. geopolitical considerations
33. growth potential
34. growth rate
35. health value
36. inconvenience to interfacing departments
37. information retrieval rate
38. maintainability
39. maintenance-downtime
40. manhours/month
41. manpower and skills required
42. maximum number of active inpatients
43. maximum number of patients
44. mean-time-between failure (MTBF)
45. mean-time-to-repair (MTTR)
46. medical value
47. mobility
48. number of productive mandays
49. operability
50. operating effectiveness
51. operating-time-between-failures
52. operating lifetime
53. operational manpower requirements
54. peak load availability
55. performability
56. performance
57. personnel safety
58. personnel training requirements
59. privacy
60. professional acceptance
61. professional accreditation
62. professional confidence
63. professional training requirements
64. program urgency
65. psychological considerations
66. quality of displays
67. quality of outputs
68. quantity of analyses performed per unit time
69. quantity of reports per unit time
70. readiness of system
71. redundancy
72. reliability
73. remote performance capability
74. repairability
75. replicability
76. reserve capacity
77. safety
78. satisfaction with results
79. scientific information yield
80. security
81. service lifetime
82. size
83. speed of data input
84. spillover effects
85. spin-off value
86. state-of-the-art benefits
87. subsystem requirements
88. sufficiency

Table 16-6 continued

89. system response time	102. vulnerability
90. system sensitivity	103. weekend personnel requirements
91. system specificity	104. workdays of employment required for operation
92. timeliness	
93. time required for development	105. workdays of employment available in labor surplus area
94. total data available	
95. types of user data available	106. workdays of minority employment available
96. utility	
97. value of data base	107. workdays of semiskilled employment available
98. value of prestige	
100. value of new capabilities	108. workdays of unskilled employment available
101. volume	

*Source: Reprinted from *The Practice-Oriented Method* by Gerald S. Lang and Kenneth J. Dickie, with permission of Aspen Systems Corporation, © 1978.

COST ANALYSIS CONCEPTS APPLICABLE TO DEPARTMENT MANAGEMENT*

Opportunity Costs

Opportunity costs are defined as the maximum contribution that is foregone by using limited resources for a particular purpose, or the maximum alternative earning that might have been obtained if the productive good, service or capacity had been applied to some alternative use.

To illustrate opportunity costs (see Table 16-7), suppose that the alternatives under formal consideration are described as choices W, X, Y and Z and related costs and revenues are as illustrated in the table.

Table 16-7 Illustration of Opportunity Costs Alternatives (000's omitted)

	W	X	Y	Z
Revenue	$320	$280	$410	$360
Relevant Costs:				
Inventory	90	90	90	90
Labor and Overhead	260	190	275	200
Net Advantage (Disadvantage)	(30)	00	45	70

According to this analysis, alternative Z offers the most rewarding opportunity. However, if management chose alternative Y, there would

---

*Source: Reprinted from *Understanding Hospital Financial Management* by Allen G. Herkimer, Jr., with permission of Aspen Systems Corporation, © 1978.

be an opportunity cost of $25,000 as developed below:

OC—Opportunity Costs
Z—Best Alternative
Y—Selected Alternative
OC = Z − Y
OC = $70,000 − $45,000
OC = $25,000

Theoretically, health care department managers should accept only projects yielding more than their real operating and capital costs. By so doing, managers increase the department's contribution to the institution's net profit or loss. However, all enlightened and appropriate decisions need more than financial and statistical information. General accounting systems usually confine their recording to those facts that ultimately involve the actual exchanges of assets. Opportunity costs are not customarily included in the general accounting systems, since such costs represent foregone revenues and costs.

Social costs are those costs which management knowingly or unknowingly imposes upon the general or specific segment of society as a result of its decisions. For example, suppose that a health care facility's management installs a new sewage system which drains directly into a river. This new system would ultimately cause a health and environmental hazard which would eventually require a clean-up campaign. The related costs of this campaign would be classified as social costs. Occasionally, the best alternative from an opportunity or operating cost standpoint such as alternative Z in the above illustration may result in a substantial social cost. Perhaps this was the reason alternative Y was selected. In short, management decisions which impose costs, present or eventual, upon the general public are classified as social costs.

Contribution Margin

The contribution margin is the difference between the total charges to patients and the related variable expenses. The margin may be expressed either in dollars, as a ratio, or on a per unit basis. Table 16-8 illustrates the use of contribution margin for the Emergency Department, while Table 16-9 is an analysis of three laboratory sections related to the combined Laboratory Department total. The contribution margin concept identifies the amount (sales-minus-variable expenses) contributed toward covering the fixed costs of a department.

The contribution margin is utilized to compute the break-even point of a health care department or section.

Break-even Analysis

The break-even point determines the point at which total revenue equals total expense. The use of the break-even concept requires that all costs be classified, at the minimum, as either fixed or variable. Step-variable costs should be included if they can be determined. Compara-

Table 16-8 Contribution Analysis—Statement of Operation
(In Thousands of Dollars)

EMERGENCY DEPARTMENT
MEMORIAL HOSPITAL
ANYTOWN, U.S.A.

		Total	% of Charges	% Total Variable Costs
Net Charges		$200	100%	167%
Variable Labor Costs	$100			
Variable Nonlabor Costs	20	120	60	100
Contribution Margin		$ 80	40	67
Fixed Costs				
Direct	$ 30			
Allocated	40	70	35	59
Target Net Profit		$ 10	5%	8%

Table 16-9 Contribution Method—Laboratory Departmental Analysis
(In Thousands of Dollars)

MEMORIAL HOSPITAL
ANYTOWN, U.S.A.

Description	Total	Clinical Lab	Hematology	Histology
Net Charges	$3,800	$2,000	$1,600	$200
Variable Costs	2,840	1,600	1,120	120
Contribution	$ 960	$ 400	$ 480	$ 80
Contribution Margin (a)	(25%)	(20%)	(3%)	(40%)
Fixed Expenses				
Direct	$ 530	$ 300	$ 200	$ 30
Allocated	360	120	200	40
Total Fixed Expenses	$ 890	$ 420	$ 400	$ 70
Net Income	$ 70	$ (20)	$ 80	$ 10

(a) Includes salaries, depreciation, insurance, property taxes, etc. Also includes department salaries and other separable costs which could be avoided by not operating the specific department.

tively speaking, the higher the fixed costs, the higher the break-even point. Conversely, the lower the fixed costs, the lower the break-even point will be. Figure 16-4 illustrates the graphic determination of the break-even point if the following data are used:

Variable Costs	$60,000
Fixed Costs	$40,000
Charge Per Unit	$ 100

Note that the break-even charges are $100,000 or 1,000 production units.

The most common approach in computing the break-even point is the equation technique which follows:

$$B/E = \frac{\text{Total Fixed Costs} + \text{Net Profit}}{\text{Charge per Unit} - \text{Variable Cost per Unit}}$$

$$B/E = \frac{\$40,000 + 0}{\$100 - \$60}$$

$$B/E = \frac{40,000 + 0}{\$40}$$

$$B/E = 1,000 \text{ Units}$$

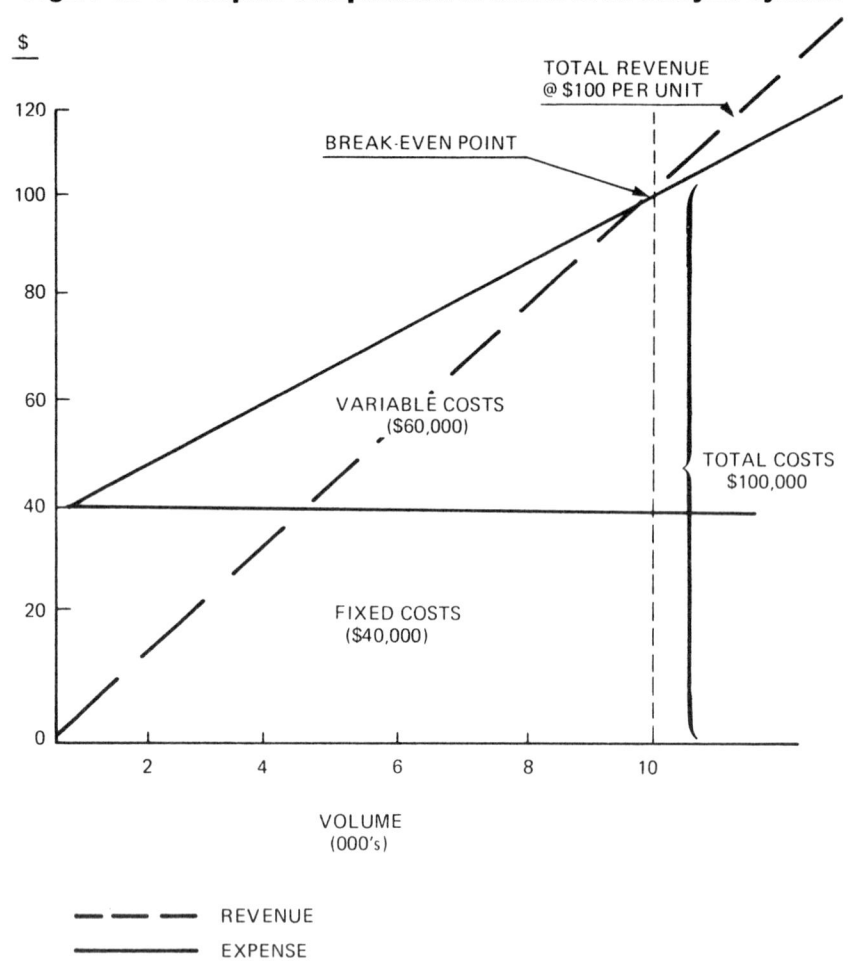

Figure 16-4 Graphic computation of break-even analysis system

Graph showing:
- Total Revenue @ $100 per unit
- Break-Even Point (at approximately 1,000 units, $100,000)
- Variable Costs ($60,000)
- Fixed Costs ($40,000)
- Total Costs $100,000
- Y-axis: $ (0 to 120)
- X-axis: Volume (000's), 0 to 10
- Dashed line: Revenue
- Solid line: Expense

In analyzing departmental costs, total departmental fixed costs stay constant over a relevant range of activity whereas the total variable departmental costs increase as volume increases. Conversely, total production unit costs decline as volume increases and total variable costs per production unit remain constant over a relevant range of activity. Another method is the arithmetic unit approach:

Unit Charge	= $100
Unit Variable Expense	= 60
Unit Contribution to fixed expenses and net profit	= $ 40

The computation in terms of percentage to dollar sales is similar:

Charges	100%
Variable Cost as a percentage of dollar charges	60%
Contribution Margin	40%

General shortcut formulas are as follows:

(a)—Break-even (B/E) volume in units

$$= \frac{\text{Fixed expenses + Net Profit}}{\text{Contribution Margin per unit}}$$

$$B/E = \frac{\$40,000 + 0}{\$40}$$

B/E = 1,000 Units

(b)—Break-even volume in dollars

$$= \frac{\text{Fixed Expenses + Net Profit}}{\text{Contribution Margin Ratio}}$$

$$\text{B/E} = \frac{\$40,000 + 0}{.40}$$

$$\text{B/E} = \$100,000$$

Note that in these samples zero net profit was calculated. Had a profit or some return on investment been desired, that amount would be used in place of the zero (break-even).

Break-even analysis provides a valuable statistical background for important planning decisions such as rate setting, staffing, and market methods.

Margin of Safety

The margin of safety is an application of the break-even concept that develops a percentage (margin of safety) drop in charges that can occur before a loss starts in the department. This percentage is a dramatic way of calling to management's attention how close their charge level is to their break-even point. The formula can be expressed in one of two ways:

$$\text{MS} = \text{Profit/Contribution}$$
$$= \text{P/C}$$

or

$$\text{MS} = (\text{Charges minus Break-Even})/\text{Sales}$$
$$= (\text{CH} - \text{BE})/\text{S}$$

Both formulas are used. The answer is expressed as a percentage. Using the following data, the total dollar contribution is:

Charges	$300,000
Contribution Margin	40%
Profit	$ 30,000
Break-Even Sales	$225,000

Charges × Contribution Margin or $300,000 × .40 = $120,000, and:

$$\text{MS} = \text{P/C}$$
$$= \$30,000/\$120,000$$
$$= 25\%$$

or

$$\text{MS} = (\text{CH} - \text{BE})/\text{S}$$
$$= (\$300,000 - \$225,000)/\$300,000$$
$$= \$75,000/\$300,000$$
$$= 25\%$$

Using this example, the department's charges could decrease twenty-five percent before losses develop. This means the department's break-even point is seventy-five percent. If the department is at the break-even volume, the margin of safety is zero.

INTERNAL AUDIT CHECKLIST FOR PLANNING AND BUDGETING*

The objectives of the auditor in reviewing this function are to ascertain that necessary, timely and accurate information is available about the amounts of resources required to fulfill hospital objectives, and that the information is being used properly to ensure that resources are available when needed.

1. Consider the need for planning beyond the immediate year (preferably three years into the future to comply with PL 92-603, Section 234) based on stated goals and assumptions.
2. Evaluate budget performance for previous years to determine if present budget plans are realistic.
3. Determine if the responsibility for budget preparation is properly assigned, and that the budget process allows time for review, adjustment, evaluation and approval.
4. Determine if estimates of revenues and expenditures take into account national and industry-wide economic trends, i.e., changes in the hospital's service area population, changes in medical staff, services offered by competing hospitals and other factors which might affect utilization.
5. Evaluate the manpower planning mechanism to see that projections are made of manpower needs for future years.
6. Evaluate the planning mechanism which projects departmental needs for additional facilities, renovation and modernization of existing facilities, installation of fixed equipment, and disposition of obso-

---

*Source: Reprinted from R. Neal Gilbert, "Operational Auditing Checks Effectiveness," *Healthcare Financial Management*, August 1977, with permission of the Healthcare Financial Management Association.

COST CONCEPT GLOSSARY*

Operating costs are the actual costs incurred by a department to generate patient services and other functions required by the department. Operating costs in the broad perspective include salaries, supplies, equipment, and other related costs. Under a financial planning and control system, these costs would be further subdivided into routine operating costs and capital expenditures.

Historical costs are either actual or budget costs for past accounting periods. Historical *actual* costs are frequently used as the basis for establishing future trends. Historical *budget* costs are usually compared to historical actual costs to evaluate the assumptions and projections made.

Current costs represent the real or actual costs spent for the present or immediate accounting period. Customarily, current costs are compared to the present account period's budgeted costs to evaluate a department's actual performance and its planned performance.

Budgeted costs are projected for the future. These are based upon historical costs—known facts of present or future events. In summary, budgeted costs represent management's best judgment of costs in future accounting periods.

Direct costs, or controllable costs, are those which are charged directly to the using department's general ledger accounts. Usually these costs are expenditures requisitioned by department managers or their designates. Since the department manager has considerable control over these costs in most budget programs, the direct costs are frequently used to evaluate the effectiveness of the department.

Indirect, or noncontrollable costs, include those allocated or overhead expenditures over which the department managers and their supervisors have little or no control. These are not usually included in the department's budgets. It is, however, useful to know how these costs occur, since some depend upon the expected or actual occupancy of the health care institution. The same costs may be direct for one department and indirect for another department. For example, housekeeping supplies are direct costs to the Housekeeping Department but indirect costs to the Physical Therapy Department.

Salary, or labor costs, include all labor-related costs such as direct salaries, wages, and fringe benefits. It is important to separate these costs into fixed, step-variable, and variable in order to properly forecast break-even points and establish staffing patterns. Labor costs for professional fees, i.e., physician, audit, and legal, are usually handled as purchased services and classified with nonlabor costs. They may also be isolated under the labor classification. One of the purposes of the breakdown is not to allow distortion in computing average labor rates and prospective labor costs.

Nonsalary, or labor costs, are all costs not included in the above classification, such as supplies, depreciation, rent, utilities, and insurance. However, it is advisable to separate nonlabor costs into categories such as direct supplies, purchased services, and depreciation. The degree of segmentation will depend upon management's requirements. Usually, capital related costs, such as depreciation, rent, and interest, are separated.

Committed costs consist largely of fixed costs which arise from the possession of plant, of equipment, and of a basic organization. Examples are depreciation, property taxes, rent, insurance, and salaries of key personnel.

Programmed costs (sometimes called managed costs), are fixed costs which arise from periodic (usually annual) appropriation decisions directly reflecting top management policies, such as public relations, training programs, and consulting fees. Programmed costs have no relationship to volume.

Capacity costs is an alternate term for fixed costs, emphasizing the fact that fixed costs are needed to provide operating facilities and an organization ready to produce and sell at a planned volume of activity.

Replacement costs are the real or estimated costs required to replace a facility's present assets. Usually, the term is used in relation to the replacement cost of a piece of equipment, i.e., computer, trash compactor, laundry washer-dryer-extractor, or x-ray machine. However, replacement costs can be computed to determine the costs required to replace a supply inventory, i.e., fuel oil, medical and surgical supplies, and food.

Inflation costs are not usually accounted for and because of economic conditions are highly unpredictable. However, they must be considered in any inflationary time—which, in most countries, means the present. Drucker tells us that inflation should be considered a genuine cost. He states that there is good reason to adopt, at least for internal purposes, a method of accounting in "constant dollars

*Sources: Term descriptions above the asterisks are reprinted from *Understanding Hospital Financial Management* by Allen G. Herkimer, Jr., with permission of Aspen Systems Corporation, © 1978. Term descriptions below the asterisks are reprinted from *Hospital Accounting Practice*, Vol. II, by Robert W. Broyles, with permission of Aspen Systems Corporation, © 1982.

. . . ." At least, Drucker concludes, such a method will force management to realize that information, rather than its own performance, underlies a good profile showing.

* * * *

Variable costs vary in direct proportion to changes in the volume of care. Thus, if the volume of care increases by, say, 15 percent, variable costs also will increase by 15 percent; as a result, unit variable costs remain constant as the volume of care is expanded. In most health institutions there is a more or less fixed relation between the use of specific resources, such as consumable supplies, and the volume of care. The corresponding expenses thus can be regarded as variable costs.

Semivariable costs may increase in discontinuous fashion as the volume of service is expanded. A semivariable cost also may increase or decrease continuously as the volume of service is increased or decreased but the percentage change in cost is less than in the level of activity. For example, if the volume of care increases by 15 percent, semivariable costs may rise by only 10 percent, and, as a result, the corresponding cost per unit of service will decline. In most health facilities, the use of labor to provide direct patient care or general support services, and the resources required to maintain the physical plant, are semivariable costs.

Fixed costs in contrast to variable and semivariable costs do not vary with changes in the volume of care. More specifically, fixed costs refer to a given time interval, called the budget period, and remain constant in response to changes in activity within a given span of activity that is called the relevant range. In most health facilities, fixed costs are associated with the very existence of the institution and must be paid even if no care is provided. For example, interest on bonded indebtedness, rental payments, a portion of the depreciation on plant and equipment, insurance premiums, and the salaries of top management and other key personnel are fixed costs.

From the perspective of controlling and planning operational activity, discretionary and committed costs are the most useful method of classifying fixed costs. *Committed costs* consist largely of fixed expenditures that relate to plant and equipment as well as to the institution's basic organization.

Discretionary costs are expenditures that may be altered at the discretion of management. As the name implies, discretionary costs pertain to items for which there is no rational method for determining the optimal amount of expense that should be incurred. In the absence of reliable criteria, the amount of cost that management is willing to accept is a matter of judgment and an issue that frequently is resolved by negotiation.

BUDGET GLOSSARY*

Hospital Budgeting is the process of estimating proposed expenditures and the means of financing these expenditures.

A Master Budget is an "over-all" budget, that is, all phases of the business are budgeted. A Master Budget would contain separate budgets such as the Operating Budget, the Plant and Equipment Budget, the Cash Budget, et cetera; these budgets would be coordinated and their results expressed in forecasted financial statements.

A Static or Forecast Budget is one prepared where income and expense remain relatively unchanged or even constant and/or can be forecast quite accurately. For example, a hospital might have an average occupancy of 85% with the range being between 82% and 88%. With such relatively fixed figures, a static budget could be prepared.

A Flexible or Sliding Scale Budget is prepared where income and expense may vary greatly throughout a year. The budget is prepared for different levels of occupancy or capacity; for example, the income and expense might be budgeted for (1) 60% occupancy, (2) 70% occupancy, and (3) 80% occupancy, or any other desired levels of occupancy. In such a budget, recognition must be given to fixed expenses, variable expenses, and semivariable expenses.

Budgetary Control exists when the budget upon adoption becomes an operational plan. The budget becomes a predetermined standard against which actual operations are measured and corrective action taken when indicated.

---

*Source: Reprinted from *HFMA* exams—made available by Exec. Dir. Robert Shelton, *Financial Management of Health Care Facilities,* ed. William O. Cleverley, with permission of Aspen Systems Corporation, © 1976.

Budget Reports provide a measurement of the effectiveness of the operational plan or budget. Generally, comparative statements in the areas of both accounting and statistics are prepared; these statements present the budget figures and the actual operational figures compared for the current month and for the year to date, and an explanation of deviations and future responsibilities is given in the budget report.

The Budget Period is merely the period of time covered by the budget. Usually, this period is the fiscal year although longer or shorter range budget forecasts may be desirable in certain areas of activity.

The Formal Budget Plan is merely a formalized plan or schedule which will be followed in the process of preparing the budget. Many steps in the process are set forth but, in essence, they will require (1) departmental estimates, (2) coordination of estimates, and (3) budget reports.

The Budget Calendar indicates the date or dates when meetings will be held to discuss and agree upon the various parts of the budget. Since budgeting entails forecasting, coordinating, and controlling, then the process of preparing, revising, and adopting the data covered by the budget should be started early; it should proceed logically and on schedule in order that the budget will be available for the ensuing budget period.

A Budget Committee is usually comprised of the administrator and/or controller (or budget officer), and the various department heads who are accountable and responsible for respective areas of control. AHA's manual "Budgeting Procedures for Hospitals" states "Employee participation in preparing the budget is a stimulant to efficient management, and employee responsibility for making it work promotes cost consciousness." At times, a Board Member or Members, external auditor, or consultant, may serve on the Budget Committee.

lete equipment, and their possible effect on the operating budget.

7. Review the accounting system to determine if timely and accurate cost and revenue data are being made available and utilized properly by administration.
8. Determine if there is periodic financial reporting which allows for the comparison of actual performance (cost, revenue, volume, etc.) with projected amounts.
9. Determine if the responsibility for maintaining budget control has been established on all appropriate levels and that amendments and revisions to the budget are held to a minimum.
10. Review the procedures for analyzing and projecting cash flows.
11. Ascertain that unallowable costs (nonreimbursable by third parties) are clearly identified and segregated in the accounting records and are excluded from revenue projections.

Chapter 17—Cost Containment

OVERVIEW

Reductions and Reactions*

Generally speaking, a manager may reduce or contain his costs in one of three major ways:

1. Reduce the physical quantity of resources utilized per output measurement unit.
2. Reduce the prices paid for resources.
3. Change the nature and volume of outputs produced.

Reductions of physical quantities of resources are usually labeled as improvements in efficiency. Certainly efficiency improvements in the health care industry are possible, as they are in all industries. However, greater care must be exercised in the implementation of efficiency moves in the health care industry because of the relatively unmeasurable relationship between quantity of input and quality of output. A patient day of care cannot be subjected to the same objective quality control standards possible in the manufacture of automobiles.

Control over prices has been and continues to be a promising area for the exercise of cost control. Typically, the greatest savings are possible when bargaining power is increased through group purchasing or shared service arrangements.

Changing the nature and volume of outputs is a decision area that is subject to manager control in the long run through programming changes. In the short run, the manager is more of a reactor to service demands as brokered by the physician than he is a change agent. Basically, two forms of cost containment are possible. One, total volume of services can be reduced, perhaps by control mechanisms such as PSRO. However, reductions in volume will raise average unit cost because of the presence of fixed cost. If average unit cost is used as a control variable for rate review, as it has, the incentive for volume reduction is clearly not present. Two, the nature or composition of outputs can be changed to produce more less costly, but equally effective outputs. Typical strategies here are home health care programs, outpatient surgery and a variety of other ambulatory or subacute programs.

Table 17-1 summarizes the types of cost containment programs hospitals have developed. The data source for this table comes from the responses to an American Hospital Association survey of cost containment projects solicited from its membership.

---

*Source: Reprinted from William O. Cleverley, "Cost Containment in the Health Care Industry," *Topics in Health Care Financing*, Spring 1977, with permission of Aspen Systems Corporation.

Table 17-1 Specific Cost Containment Proposals

Resource Reducing Projects
- staffing by patient activity
- staffing on a 12 hour shift basis
- decentralize transport service
- combine night admissions with emergency room
- close low activity departments during holidays
- replace incandescent lighting with florescent
- eliminate unit managers
- shared service arrangements
- telephone interconnect systems
- construction of joint surgical and obstetrical suites
- incinerator waste/heat recovery system
- development of accurate census forecasts
- installation of electric capacitors
- improvements in boiler efficiency
- employee incentive plan
- computerized inventory systems
- unit dose systems in pharmacy
- elimination of lost charges
- development of hospital drug formulary
- lowering thermostats in non-working areas
- evaluating service maintenance contracts

Price Reducing Projects
- group purchasing arrangements
- utilization of generic drug equivalents
- negotiating professional contracts on volume of professional work and not percentage of revenue
- rebates from State Workmen's Compensation Funds due to safety programs
- self insuring Unemployment Insurance benefits
- installing own well and water system
- mutual insurance companies for malpractice
- forming a consultative service program among hospital members to reduce need for paid outside consultants

Nature and Volume of Output Projects
- outpatient surgery
- pre admission testing
- post discharge testing
- home health care programs
- expansion of outpatient services
- meals on wheels

Other Projects
- development of sophisticated budgetary systems
- formation of systems for soliciting employee ideas on cost reduction
- development of cost containment boards
- sending patient bills to physicians to create cost awareness

Source: American Hospital Association, *Digest of Hospital Innovation*

Elements of a Cost Containment Program[*]

There are four components to a hospital-wide cost containment program:

1. *Cost Awareness*—Intensifying organizational awareness of what costs are, how they can be managed and the processes that are available to contain them. The focus is on all costs and by all individuals—from the person that sweeps the floor to the chairperson of the board.

2. *Cost Monitoring*—Providing a mechanism and the media for identifying, reporting and monitoring all costs. Analyzing the relationship between these costs and the costs of individual, functional as well as the overall organizational performance. The focus is on where, how much and why dollars are spent.

3. *Cost Management*—Establishing a responsibility and accountability system for communicating and controlling the attainment of plans, strategies, programs and objectives involving cost containment. The focus is on what can be done and will be done to contain costs, and by whom.

4. *Cost Incentives*—Maintaining incentives and compensation mechanisms that motivate continuing cost containment efforts and reward performance in proportion to cost containment contribution, individually and collectively. The focus is on when and where the effort is most appropriate.

---

[*]Source: Reprinted from Leonard B. Fox III and Howard Mintz, "A Strategy for Cost Containment—The Use of a Suggestion Plan," *Cost Containment in Hospitals*, ed. Efraim Turban, with permission of Aspen Systems Corporation, © 1980.

The Administrator's Limited Power in Cost Containment*

What a hospital is currently doing about cost containment depends on a number of factors, the three most important of which are presented here: previous emphasis, potential for saving costs, and the power to do it. The "administrator's power" refers to the administrator's perception of his/her ability to influence an action *relative* to the medical staff's influence over this action. For example, administrators feel they have maximum power over the medical staff to control investments in capital and human resources and minimal power to control the types of patients admitted (case mix).

Drawn from a recent study of hospital administrators, the data underlying the analysis of the actions taken in hospitals to control costs are shown in Table 17-2. Cost-influencing variables (CIVs), a term coined by William L. Dowling, are shown in the first column of the table. These are believed to be among the major determinants of total hospital costs. Each of these CIVs is, in turn, influenced by specific actions of the hospital. The responses of hospital administrators in this study were averaged and placed in rank order (Table 17-2).

One rarely meets the administrator who has attempted to control costs by limiting the size or specialty composition of the medical staff.

---
*Source: Reprinted from Robert F. Allison, "Prospective Reimbursement," *Topics in Health Care Financing,* Winter 1976, with permission of Aspen Systems Corporation.

Where actions are taken to control length of stay or case mix, they are usually taken to meet government regulations or to control quality rather than cost.

It seems clear that administrators now know more about controlling costs than they are able to implement because of a real or perceived lack of *power* to do so.

Variable costs are, by definition, the ones that can be controlled. By estimates, only 30 percent of all hospital costs are variable in the short run. Also, certain hospital costs are seen as being controlled more by the physicians than administration. In Table 17-3 are listed hospital administrators' perceptions of the influence of the medical staff over the CIVs. The first five CIVs *are* the major aspects of the practice of medicine in hospitals; and the sixth CIV, quality, is merely another aspect of these five. The last five CIVs are part of the administrative half of the so-called dual hierarchy in hospitals.

What Causes Increases in Hospital Expenditures?*

- The higher prices hospitals pay for the goods and services—often referred to as the "market basket"—they use in delivering care. As the costs of food, fuel, supplies, and labor increases, hospital costs also increase.
- The increasing use of hospital services. The number of hospital admissions and days of

---
*Source: *Controlling Rising Hospital Costs,* Congressional Budget Office, September 1979.

Table 17-2 Cost-Influencing Actions

CIV	Current Emphasis	Previous Emphasis	Cost-Saving Potential	Administrator's Power
Investments	1	1	10	1
Quality	2	2	3	7
Admissions	3	9	2	6
Scope of Services	4	10	7.5	8
Teaching	5	4	5	4
Length of Stay	6	6	1	5
Case Mix	7	8	9	10
Efficiency	8	5	6	3
Intensity	9	7	4	9
Input Prices	10	3	7.5	2

before prospective reimbursement

Table 17-3 Physician Control of CIVs as Perceived by the Administrator

1.	Case Mix	3.65
2.	Admissions	3.50
3.	Scope of Services	3.45
4.	Intensity	3.35
5.	Length of Stay	3.25
6.	Quality	3.05
7.	Teaching	2.65
8.	Efficiency	2.30
9.	Amenities	2.30
10.	Input Prices	2.25
11.	Investments in Resources	1.65

Notes: N = 33. Scoring key: 4 = very great influence, 3 = much influence, 2 = some influence, 1 = little influence.

hospital care have been increasing. Outpatient visits have also shown especially rapid growth.
- The changing character—often referred to as the "service intensity"—of hospital services. Hospitals continually add services and deliver existing ones (for example, lab tests and x-rays) more frequently.
- Slow productivity changes. The American economy depends on productivity gains to keep increases in product prices below increases in wages. If hospital productivity gains relative to wage increases are smaller than elsewhere in the economy, hospital prices and hence expenditures on hospital care will increase more rapidly than expenditures in other sectors.

Factors other than wage and price increases account for almost all of the portion of hospital expenditure increases that exceeded the growth in spending in the general economy. Utilization increased faster than can be explained by the growth and aging of the population.

Utilization increased at an average annual rate of 2.9 percent while population (adjusted for the higher utilization associated with the aging of the population) grew by only 1.3 percent a year.

Four major reasons have been suggested to explain why hospital expenditures have been growing more rapidly than can be accounted for by the increased price of the market basket and by population increases: a lack of competition in the market for hospital services, new technological developments, rising real incomes, and the changing health status of the population. Changing consumer tastes and preferences, while difficult to document, also affect the growth in hospital expenditures.

- *Lack of Competition.* The hospital care industry is much less competitive than other industries. Since over 90 percent of hospital bills are paid by third parties—such as Medicare, Medicaid, and private insurance companies—patients usually have little immediate stake in the cost of their care. Further, few patients or doctors have much information as to whether particular services delivered by a hospital are worth their cost, a situation probably made worse by the extensiveness of third party payment.

Health insurance raises the amounts spent on hospital care in two ways. From the perspective of the patient, hospital care costs less, so financial deterrence is reduced. For a given illness, patients are less reluctant to be hospitalized or to remain for a long stay. They are more likely to insist that their physicians employ all of the diagnostic and therapeutic procedures available. To the physician acting as the patient's agent, insurance gives parallel inducements to order additional services. It removes a deterrent to the ordering of any service that might benefit the patient regardless of cost. Indeed under the fee-for-service system of financing, insurance increases the additional income physicians may obtain from performing additional services.

Although hospitals do not have to worry much about the prices charged patients, they do worry about attracting physicians who are the source of patient admissions. Since physicians prefer to practice at hospitals that offer a full range of modern services, hospitals often duplicate each others' facilities, with wasteful excess capacity the result.

- *Technological Developments.* The adoption of new technologies has also contributed to rising expenditures on hospital care. While new technology usually benefits patients, increases hospital productivity, and lowers costs, it is often embodied in new services that are additions to, rather than replacements for, existing services. Consequently, new technology often increases the utilization and intensity of hospital care, two important factors in the growth of expenditures by hospitals.

An important issue is the relationship between the introduction of cost-increasing technology and third-party payment. Some argue that third-party payment has increased the rate of adoption of such technology. If they are correct, then much of the increase in hospital expenditures associated with new technology is another manifestation of the third-party financing system.

- *Rising Personal Income.* As people's real incomes grow, they tend to purchase more goods and services of all kinds. Some, especially the uninsured, may demand more hospital care as their incomes rise. Others may purchase more health insurance, leading in turn to increased expenditures for hospital care. With over 90 percent of hospital bills already covered by insurance, however, rising incomes have little additional potential to increase hospital expenditures.
- *Changing Health Status.* Trends in the population's health status also influence expenditures through changes in the utilization and intensity of hospital care. Consensus on the net impact of this factor does not yet exist, however. The aging of the population should increase both utilization and intensity. Changing lifestyles may also affect health status and hospital expenditures. When daily life involves more stress and poorer diets, health may decline. On the other hand, increasing education and better nonhospital medical care may improve health and reduce inpatient hospital use.

COST CONTAINMENT STRATEGIES*

1. Short-Term Amenities' Reductions and Purchase Delays

There are a number of short-term strategies to pursue for an immediate expense reduction: minor benefits to employees might be reduced, educational programs cut back, planning activities curtailed, community relations reduced, plant and equipment replacement deferred and implementation of new services and equipment purchases delayed. These short-term strategies reduce existing operating expenses, defer capital costs and may defer increases in operating expenses associated with new programs.

These types of activities do not represent a major part of a typical hospital's budget, and it is unlikely that for any group of hospitals savings are likely to exceed two to five percent.

Regardless of the amount, the savings will accrue immediately. The savings will, however, benefit the hospital only once since in subsequent years they reduce the costs used as the "base" in the percentage increase calculation.

2. Input Price Reductions

At some point where goods and services are purchased, management has some ability to affect the negotiated price. This is illustrated in the negotiation of wages and salaries where the administrator can bargain harder.

Similar savings might be expected through group purchasing (both of supplies and capital equipment) and substitution of less expensive inputs, e.g., revision of insurance programs. Substitution of less expensive capital for labor, as in the case of computerizing labor-based activities, is a more complex way to reduce expenditures.

In general, this second strategy has only limited opportunities. Better management, harder bargaining and good luck might yield a savings of one or two percentage points per year compared to present practices. While the savings associated with more effective negotiations may be incurred more than once, possible hidden costs include the likelihood that the other side will respond in turn. The savings associated with group purchasing and substitution of less expensive inputs will generally benefit the hospital only in the year of implementation.

3. Improved Production Efficiency

The typical hospital faces a wide range of opportunities to improve its internal efficiency (output divided by input) given a constant volume of services. These opportunities range from the simple—employee suggestion programs for improved methods, optimum inventory purchasing policies, etc.—to more complicated changes in

---

*Source: Reprinted from Robert A. Vraciu and John R. Griffith, "Cost Control Challenge for Hospitals," *Health Care Management Review,* Spring 1979, with permission of Aspen Systems Corporation.

the technology—setting capacity to correspond to demand via admissions scheduling, variable staffing, operating room scheduling and contracting with outside organizations to provide services which take advantage of economies of scale. The simple methods still have potential since few hospitals have done everything that can be done.

The more complex approaches are rapidly becoming more popular. Their payment is quite promising in many settings, but installation cost time lags are correspondingly high.

How much these general efficiency strategies will save, net of investment, is unclear. Although engineers are fond of citing figures in the ten- to 15-percent range for potential improvements, it is not clear that all of this potential is real and it is even less clear whether the savings could be realized in the near term. While the cost savings associated with each improvement is by itself a one-time savings, the process of searching for more efficient technologies is likely to yield additional ideas and subsequent savings.

4. Improved Market Efficiency (Volume Reduction)

Potential exists for reducing the use rate of hospital services without adversely affecting the quality of care. Further, the responsibility for achieving these lower use rates lies jointly with the physician, hospital representative and community. Analysis of the HMO and the low-use communities suggests that important decisions about organization of services that influence utilization are made by all parties, but that the hospital's commitment to making available adequate ambulatory care services and creating a milieu that encourages cost-effective clinical decisions is not only a prerequisite but an important catalyst.

Cost control programs that reduce the volume of inpatient services either shift services to a lower cost setting or reduce the total number by eliminating unnecessary services. Such programs include preadmission testing and ambulatory surgery (substitute outpatient for inpatient services), utilization review (reduce number of admissions and length of stay) and discharge planning (substitute lower-cost chronic care services). The net effect of many of these programs will be to decrease the volume of patient days. Others will eliminate unnecessary ancillary services.

However, evidence suggests that hospital administrators turn first to other cost-control strategies since the complexities of involving the medical staff slow progress. Consequently, significant changes in volume are likely to occur only after several years in a cost-control environment, reflecting long lead times before strategies are implemented and further lags before they become effective. The magnitude of the dollar savings will vary according to the hospital's willingness to curtail services and the hospital's operating conditions.

5. Involving Physicians*

[An Example from Jackson Memorial Hospital, Miami, Florida]

Specific efforts involving physicians centered about a formal program by the house staff of cost awareness, aimed at informing the doctors of the financial as well as the medical effects of their efforts. It was continually stressed that cost containment or cost effective medicine should not adversely affect, in any way, the quality of care.

Education

1. An orientation program has been designed for incoming House Staff with topics for discussion to include Cost Containment, Risk Management and Medical Records. Proper usage of the Pharmacy, Blood Bank and Medical Examiner's services are also reviewed.
2. House Staff members are issued rate and charge manuals associated with those areas of his or her concern.
3. Patient's bills are randomly placed on medical charts for review by attending physicians and House Staff.
4. Costs of tests, diagnostic studies, equipment and drugs are placed on durable sheets on the patient's medical chart.

---

*Source: Reprinted from Leon Zucker, "Cost Containment of Jackson Memorial Hospital, Miami, Florida," *Cost Containment in Hospitals,* ed. Efraim Turban, with permission of the author and Aspen Systems Corporation, © 1980.

5. Third year medical students beginning clinical rotation receive a cost containment presentation by House Staff.
6. A new House Staff newsletter, numerous memos, posters and a Cost Containment bulletin board promote cost effectiveness and awareness.
7. House Staff participate on all committees in the hospital that have an effect on patient care or cost effectiveness.
8. The House Staff Steering Committee and the Administration will enforce the policy of writing orders for discharge of patients 24-hours prior to their discharge.
9. Patient education and social service consultations in preparation for discharge should be started on the first day of admission.
10. Medical cases are presented at departmental "grand round" conferences. The format includes presentation of the actual cases, but with a discussion of the costs in addition to the results of the various tests and procedures.
11. Preventive medicine programs are emphasized to teach the patient about their own disease as well as cigarette and alcohol abuse. Education about nutrition is also focused to include information on the economics of the proper diet.
12. "What You Can Do To Hold Down Costs" is being prepared by the House Staff to be distributed to patients.
13. The House Staff Steering Committee is emphasizing to all physicians to critically review the need for specific lab tests before they are ordered.
14. Necessary admission and pre-operative laboratory test requirements are being reviewed.

CASE STUDY OF A HOSPITAL'S COST CONTAINMENT EFFORTS*

[NOTE: Illinois Masonic Medical Center—a major teaching hospital on Chicago's North Side—serves a Latino population and its share of illegal aliens. Because of its location, Illinois Masonic Medical Center provides approximately $5 million of free care and bad debts per year. Half of that amount emanates from the emergency room. Here is what the center did in one year, 1977, to contain its costs in four general areas: management, outside services, equipment and purchasing. Similar programs were conducted in 1978 and 1979.]

Management

Elimination of Positions

- The Systems Department at IMMC was eliminated and the functions absorbed by other department head level personnel. Systems analysts were replaced by a staff auditor. Total personnel dollars saved on an annual basis amount to $43,000.
- Previously budget and cost reimbursement were separate positions within the Fiscal Division. These positions were combined into one department. Due to more efficient use of personnel and increased computerization of certain tasks, one full-time equivalent position was eliminated. This saved the institution approximately $15,000 annually.

Improving Management Tools

- The Financial Division instituted a quarterly budget variance report which enables management to quickly review actual to budget comparisons for every department of the hospital and pinpoint problem areas. It is estimated that this timely management cost control aid has reduced expenses by at least $50,000 annually.

Adjustments for Low Census

- During periods when the patient census is low, nursing personnel are encouraged to take excused absences without pay. In addition, other nursing personnel are shifted to nursing units requiring more help during these periods. In some cases, entire nursing units were shut down. Such measures account for a savings of about $20,000 on an annual basis.

Automation

- The accounting activities at IMMC's 300-bed skilled nursing facility have been auto-

---
*Source: *Field Hearings before the House Sub-Committee on Health,* Committee on Ways and Means, May 27, 1980, Serial 96-98.

mated. The general ledger, payroll, accounts payable and budget have been installed using the hospital computer system. Patient accounting has been automated using an outside vendor. This conversion will cost $12,500 annually in EDP expenses. However, two clerical salaries have been saved by this computerization, so the system has paid for itself. In addition, the institution is benefiting by the wide variety of management and accounting reports now available through the new system.

Managerial Changes

- During the last two years the following managerial changes were made in Medical Transcription: 1) the paper flow within the department was streamlined; 2) a performance-based pay scale was instituted; 3) newer and more productive keyboard equipment was installed; and 4) the working environment was improved. During this same period, the department's workload increased by 244 percent. Had the above changes not been made, Medical Transcription's staff would have had to be increased from 8 to more than 19 employees to keep pace with the increased work load. Instead, the department's staff was increased to 10 with some additional money invested in equipment, remodelling and higher salaries. Net annual savings are in excess of $67,000.

Reprocessing

- Hospitals are required to keep patients' X-rays for five years. After the fifth year these films are discarded and sold by the pound to a silver reclaiming company, which performs a second process to remove the remaining silver. IMMC recovers $4,000 per year through this process.
- Every X-ray film that goes through the developing processor deposits some amount of silver in the tanks. The recovery units gather up this silver and store it. Every month the silver is weighed and sold. IMMC recovers an average of $10,000 to $12,000 a year through this process.

Quality Control

- Our Radiology Department, with assistance from the outside film company, is evaluating discarded X-ray films and analyzing departmental quality control procedures. A discarded film (repeat) represents a radiograph found unacceptable for viewing by a radiologist. The evaluation of these radiographs indicates areas where costs can be reduced and overall film quality improved. Estimated savings are about $10,000 per year.

Outside Services

Performing Services In-House Which Were Formerly Done Outside the Institution

- For years, the IMMC Dietary Department menu blanks were printed outside the hospital by a commercial printer. The total cost for printing 285,000 menu blanks was $7,000, or $24 per thousand. For an investment of $500 (perforator attachment for an offset press and art work for seven menu blanks) the IMMC print shop is now able to print its own menu blanks each year at a total cost of $2,000. This is a savings for the hospital of approximately $5,000 each year.
- The Environmental Service Department of IMMC uses 219,000 pounds of soiled dust and wet mops annually. Based on the cost of $.22 per pound (soiled weight) of an outside hospital laundry service, the Medical Center spent $49,275 for this service. In 1976, IMMC purchased an industrial washing machine and dryer to launder its own mops. The total cost of laundering its own mops is now $.04 per pound, or $8,738 annually. The savings to the institution in the first year was approximately $40,000.
- The Inpatient Business Office instituted the use of a letter service prior to placement of an account with a collection agency. Three letters are sent out under a credit bureau name to delinquent accounts at a cost of $1.50 per patient. During the first 10 months of the program, $25,000 was collected at a cost of $1,300. For this service a collection agency would have cost $8,400—hence, a savings of $7,100. This letter service will save the institution about $10,000 annually.

- Accounting schedules and analyses needed for the annual audit were previously prepared by the external auditors at a considerable expense to the hospital. Audit fees average approximately $23 per hour. Employees of the General Accounting Department were trained to prepare the various analyses and accounting schedules needed by the external auditors. This has resulted in an annual cost savings of approximately $10,000.
- The hospital Print Shop prints letter head and interoffice memo forms for every department at an annual savings of $1,000.
- Prior to September, 1976, IMMC used cover gowns from an outside laundry service. These gowns, used by surgeons and nurses to cover surgical uniforms when leaving the surgical suites, were costing the Medical Center $5,163 per year. This figure was based on a cost of $20 per day for 255 working days per year. Based on the results of a feasibility study, IMMC purchased 120 warm-up jackets for $720 and a large capacity washing machine for $300. With this equipment, the cost of laundering our own jackets is $191 per year, for a total cost of $1,211. Under this plan, first year savings were $3,952 and the savings in subsequent years will be about $5,000.

Sharing Services and Equipment

- IMMC has participated in a shared data processing service with MacNeal Memorial Hospital for six years. This arrangement saves IMMC an estimated $200,000 each year compared with comparable in-house computer costs.
- IMMC has a working relationship with St. Joseph Hospital to provide hearing testing on machines that are not owned by this hospital. This includes sound field testing for infants under three, hearing and evaluations, and acoustic impedence audiometry. If IMMC were to purchase these machines, it would cost about $50,000.
- Prior to May, 1976, only 50 percent of the Medical Assistance-No Grant applications were approved by the Department of Public Aid, and this took four to six months. Most of the denied cases ended up as bad debts for the Medical Center. IMMC entered into the Medical Assistance-No Grant Verification Project for Public Aid in cooperation with the Chicago Hospital Council. The total annual cost to the Medical Center of this program is $30,500. For the six months ended April 30, 1977, Public Aid had rendered decisions on 480 MA-NG cases, representing 5,623 patient days. Seventy-seven percent of these were approved. With a current Public Aid per-diem rate of $251, the new program will result in approximately $170,000 additional reimbursement on an annual basis. In addition, applications are now being acted upon within three months or less.

Equipment

Servicing Our Own Equipment

- Electroencephalogram machines use recording paper and require regular maintenance. EEG technicians have discovered that by reversing the recording paper half way through a record, they can utilize both sides and reduce the cost of paper by 50 percent (approximately $710 per year). In addition, the technicians clean and service each machine on a daily basis. This eliminates outside service contracts for maintenance of EEG machines of approximately $1,000 per year.
- Whenever possible, our Audio-Visual Department repairs our radio pagers instead of sending them back to the company which leases them to us. The difference between our repairman's hourly rate and the repair-per-pager rate charged by the company has resulted in a savings of approximately $600 to the hospital.
- By having our printer service all copiers, dryer and off-set printing presses, we were able to remove these machines from the service contract at an annual savings of approximately $1,200.
- By repairing our own alarm doors, the Security Services Department has saved the Medical Center charges for more than 25 service calls since December, 1976. The service call costs $25 plus $20 per hour. The average time spent to repair these doors is

one hour. Total savings through 1977 will be approximately $1,800.
- Instead of ordering new locks every time a door lock needs to be changed, the Security Services Department repins old locks to fit new keys. Within the past year, 35 locks have been repinned and installed at a cost savings of $650.
- The Security Services Department repairs the microphones on our HT-220 radios. At an average of nine radio failures per year, we are saving about $480 in service calls.

Installing New Equipment

- IMMC's Patient Accounting Department installed a Public Aid Master file inquiry terminal and printer at an annual cost of $6,696. The terminal allows instant verification of a public aid recipient's eligibility, and speeds up payment by eliminating billing errors. The Outpatient Business Office is able to confirm at least 10 visits a week on accounts which are considered bad debts. Numerous inpatient accounts are now billable which reduces our writeoffs. Annual savings are estimated at $70,000–$100,000.
- Formerly data were punched into data processing cards, which were transported to the central computer by messenger. This resulted in one-day turn-around time and a total cost of $2,500 per month. Data Processing installed new equipment to record data on magnetic diskettes which are reusable and have a life span of five years. In a matter of minutes, the data are transmitted over telephone lines directly to the computer, where they are processed, and returned over the telephone lines to our terminal for printing. At a total cost of $1,500 per month, these new data recorders are saving an estimated $12,000 annually.
- The Duplicating Center installed an electronic lock on its Xerox 4000. This allows only 1–3 copies to be made on this machine. Copying work with more than 3 copies was transferred to the larger Xerox 7000, for an estimated annual savings of $2,400. By downgrading the Xerox 4000 to a Xerox 3100, equipment rentals were reduced by an estimated $1,300 per year. In addition, a new supplier for Xerox paper was selected after placing it out for bid, at an estimated annual savings of $500. Total annual savings are approximately $4,200.

Shutting Down Electrical Equipment Not in Use

- Air handlers which condition the air in the operating rooms and in the morgue are being turned off for eight hours during the night with no detrimental effects on the daytime operations. The total annual savings attributable to this effort amount to about $22,000.
- The exhaust fan for the cafeteria kitchen is being shut off by timer from 8:00 PM to 6:00 AM for a savings of $7,200 per year.

Storage Techniques

- General Stores introduced a Data Service—Inventory Control Program at a cost of $700 per month. With this program, General Stores has been able to reduce its dollar inventory from $170,000 to $155,000—a one-time $15,000 savings. Since purchase orders are generated automatically, there is a savings of time in Purchasing of approximately $1,740 per year. Since departmental issues are automatically priced, there is a savings of time in Accounts Payable of approximately $4,360 per year, for a total annual savings of about $6,100.

Reconditioning Equipment

- Two Physical Therapy Ultra Sound machines were sent out to be rewired and reconditioned to meet UI requirements, thereby eliminating the need to purchase two new units costing approximately $3,000.

Purchasing

Buying a Less Expensive Product

- The Product Evaluation Committee of Nursing Service recommended that the hospital switch from using mercury-type (7 cents per unit) to electronic thermometers (4.1 cents per unit). Total annual savings will be approximately $12,000. In addition, this change will help standardize

product usage for taking patient temperatures.
- By switching over to 35 watt-miser fluorescent lamps in place of the 40 watt bulbs and using longer life incandescent lighting, our annual costs on lighting have been reduced by $33,000.
- Toilet tissue and paper towels were costing the Medical Center $624.80 per week. A search and evaluation of suppliers resulted in finding an outside vendor who supplies the same quantity and quality of product for $574 per week, for a savings of $2,600 per year.
- An evaluation was made of treated-paper copier vendors which service several departments throughout the Medical Center. The prime treated-paper copier vendor was changed, for an estimated annual savings of $3,000.
- By placing high dollar products and commodity lines out for competitive bids, the Purchasing Department saved approximately $30,000 in fiscal year 1976 in its purchase of forms, kits, office supplies, paper goods, examination gloves and poly bags.

Plan-Ahead Purchasing

- Early in 1977 we learned that the Chicago Hospital Council Group Purchasing Program was anticipating a 12-15 percent increase in the price of intravenous solutions. IMMC ordered a three-month supply of IV solutions before the price increase, thereby minimizing the impact of the increase and saving the Medical Center approximately $5,400.
- In February, the IMMC Purchasing Department suspected that sizeable price increases were imminent for Kodak and Dupont radiology film. IMMC ordered a three-month supply of radiology film prior to a March 4th 6 percent price increase, for a savings of $1500.
- The Purchasing Department has entered into several percentage discount agreements with outside vendors based on exclusive or near-exclusive use of a particular product. These agreements have resulted in a savings to the hospital of $37,000 during the past year.

- The Purchasing Department is currently negotiating with the Medical Center's major suppliers to combine volumes for both the hospital and the Warren N. Barr Pavilion—IMMC's 300-bed skilled nursing facility—in order to obtain the best possible price. The first of these agreements has already resulted in a savings of $1,100 for the Medical Center.
- Many of the hospital's trade vendors offer discounts of 1 to 4 percent of the invoiced amount for early payment. To meet the terms of the offered discounts, Accounts Payable set up special procedures and payment priorities to process the invoices rapidly and accurately. Vendors who did not offer discounts were informed that the hospital would pay earlier than the normal terms if a discount were offered. The hospital's purchase of goods was reduced by approximately $22,000 during the fiscal year ended Sept. 30, 1976, and it is estimated that $32,000 in cost savings will be realized in the current fiscal year.

Conclusion

The total dollar savings from these cost containment efforts at Illinois Masonic Medical Center for the current year is approximately $1,000,000. (This includes the estimated savings on equipment costs for the sound field testing machines and the Physical Therapy ultra sound machines which amounted to $53,000.) This figure represents about 2 percent of IMMC's yearly budget and a savings of $6 per patient day for each patient.

These reductions were accomplished through the use of new technology, the sharing of services and innovative management techniques. IMMC views cost containment as a continuing program and one which should maintain the critical balance between the quality and the cost of service. There is an irreducible minimum cost for every service and activity in a hospital. To reduce costs below this level lessens the quality of care.

Value Analysis (Reducing Cost, Not Quality)

The primary goal of value analysis is to provide a given service or product at less cost without affecting its quality, durability or appearance. To effectively achieve this goal certain analytical steps must be taken.

The Process*

1. Information Gathering

Basic facts need to be gathered on the work performed, its related components and the costs related to performing the service. The information is recorded from direct observation and direct measurement of the quantity of work in the service.

1. What is the function of the service?
2. What are the technical procedures required to provide the service?
3. What kinds of input are required?
4. How many days are required to provide the service?
5. What are the costs of providing the service?
6. Where is the service performed?
7. Who should perform the service?
8. Is there any duplication or overlapping of activities in performing the service?
9. What are the consequences of not providing the service?
10. Are there cost-free ways of providing the service?

These data may then be subjected to analysis.

2. Analysis of Facts

It is here that the status quo is critically questioned and challenged. This step reconsiders the purpose and function of the service, the place where it is performed, its sequences, its specific components and the means by which it is done.

3. Creative Search

The value analyst seeks answers from such diverse specialists as physicians, pharmacists, nurses, purchasers, quality control engineers, suppliers, etc., to questions such as the following:

1. Can alternative materials or other inputs be used?
2. Can the service be simplified?
3. Can alternate methods be used?
4. Can costs be reduced by turning to alternate methods or equipment?
5. Can any step be eliminated?
6. Can the duration of the service be reduced?

A Functional Value Analysis Program*

Phase I: Getting FVA Under Way

1. Deciding on Scope

The first step is to decide which parts of the hospital budget will be considered as overhead expense and included in the analysis. As a starting point all the "hotel" components of the hospital should be included: dietetics, housekeeping and plant operations. General administration, including some medical support activities such as records, would also be a prime candidate.

2. Organizing the Team

The FVA team has three principal parts: unit managers, a task force and a steering committee. Almost all the members of this team are regular line management of the hospital who take on extra FVA functions for the duration of the process. In their FVA capacities these individuals direct and monitor analysis, and actually generate and evaluate cost-reduction ideas. Implementation decisions are made through the institution's normal chain of command. Figure 17-1 illustrates the typical relationships between the FVA team and line management.

The unit managers spend from 5 to 40 percent of their time on FVA and are the most important component of the team.

A full-time task force should also be selected. The usual ratio is one task force member for every five to ten unit managers. This will mean a task force of four or five people in a large hospital. The members' task is to tailor the FVA process to the institution's specific needs—e.g.,

---

*Source: Reprinted from Ahmed Rifai, Joseph O. Pecenka and Paula J. Ford, "Value Analysis Pinpoints Costs," *Healthcare Financial Management,* July 1978, with permission of the Healthcare Financial Management Association.

*Source: Reprinted from James E. Bennett and Jacques Krasny, "Functional Value Analysis: A Technique for Reducing Hospital Overhead Costs," *Topics in Health Care Financing,* Spring 1981, with permission of Aspen Systems Corporation.

Figure 17-1 The FVA team

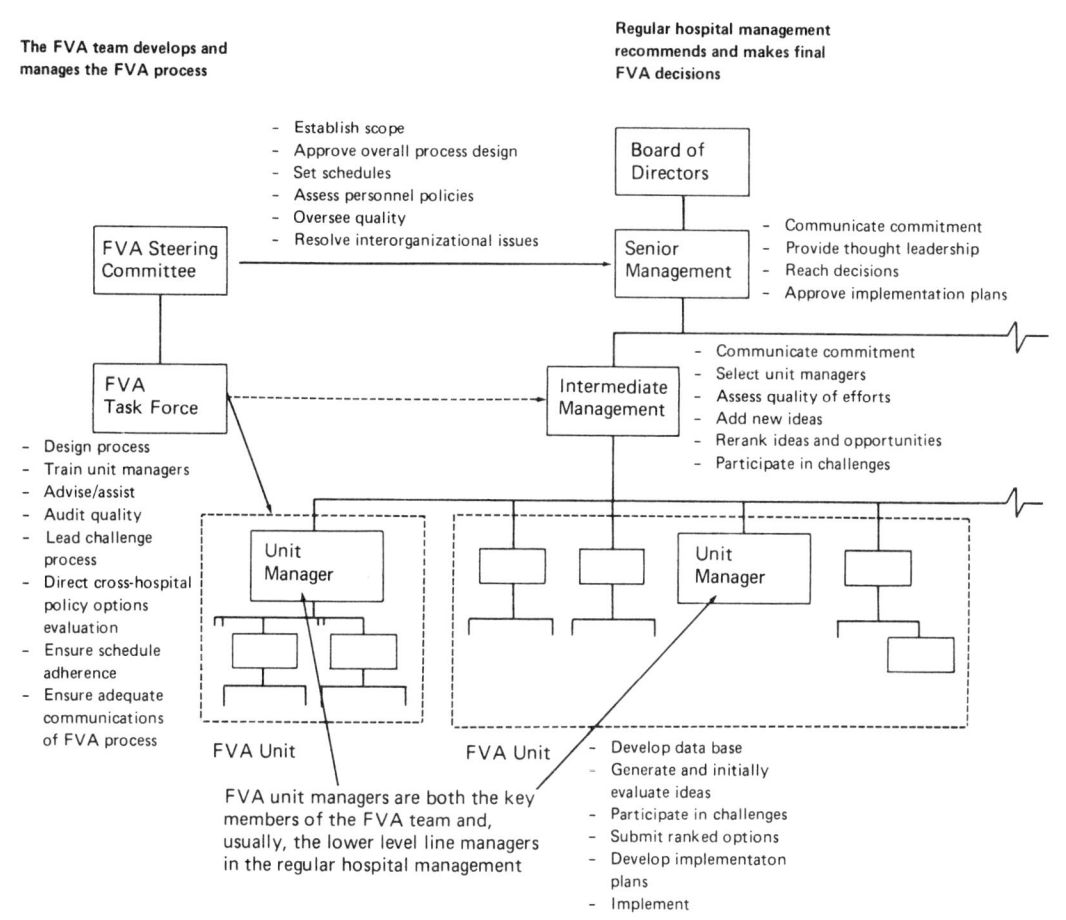

The FVA team develops and manages the FVA process

Regular hospital management recommends and makes final FVA decisions

FVA Steering Committee
- Establish scope
- Approve overall process design
- Set schedules
- Assess personnel policies
- Oversee quality
- Resolve interorganizational issues

Board of Directors

Senior Management
- Communicate commitment
- Provide thought leadership
- Reach decisions
- Approve implementation plans

FVA Task Force
- Design process
- Train unit managers
- Advise/assist
- Audit quality
- Lead challenge process
- Direct cross-hospital policy options evaluation
- Ensure schedule adherence
- Ensure adequate communications of FVA process

Intermediate Management
- Communicate commitment
- Select unit managers
- Assess quality of efforts
- Add new ideas
- Rerank ideas and opportunities
- Participate in challenges

Unit Manager / **Unit Manager**

FVA Unit / FVA Unit

FVA unit managers are both the key members of the FVA team and, usually, the lower level line managers in the regular hospital management

- Develop data base
- Generate and initially evaluate ideas
- Participate in challenges
- Submit ranked options
- Develop implementaton plans
- Implement

---

by sequencing the work and setting work schedules, and developing specific analyses and information sources. They must teach the necessary analytical techniques to the unit managers and, in a consultative capacity, assist them in carrying out the process. Task force members are typically department heads or, in the case of large departments, their assistants, intermediate-level staff (e.g., assistant director of finance), or functional heads (e.g., director of plant operations).

A four- or five-member FVA steering committee and a chairperson should be appointed from among the senior management of the hospital. This group is accountable to their colleagues as well as to the board of directors for the success of the overall program. They are additionally charged with making any FVA process decisions such as which departments should or should not be included, and how much time should be allowed for completion.

3. Establishing the Ground Rules

Once the FVA organization is established, some ground rules for carrying out the analysis should be set. Each unit that will undergo FVA must be assigned a *stretch target*, a percentage of its gross budget that becomes the target total of all its cost-reduction ideas. The purpose of this target is to stretch the thinking of unit managers by bringing forth all good ideas for discussion. The target typically used in industry is 40 percent. In the hospital environment this might be divided into 20 percent that could be implemented immediately, and an additional 20 percent that would substantially reduce the unit, but still permit it to continue its core functions.

Because a key aspect of FVA is discipline, a rigorous timetable should be established for the completion of each of the analytical and decision-making steps that make up phase II. The

278 HOSPITAL ADMINISTRATION HANDBOOK

total FVA process usually takes four to six months.

4. Developing Communications and Personnel Programs

The technique and timetable should be explained to all management and professional staff, and management's intentions should be explained to union leaders with the aim of gaining their understanding and, ideally, their cooperation. A complete communications program should also cover special interest groups.

Perhaps the most critical preplanning step is the formulation of a personnel program. Because about two-thirds of hospital operating costs are personnel related, achieving meaningful savings will at some point require personnel reductions. Given the relatively high turnover in many employee categories, it should be possible to capture most of these reductions in a reasonable time period through attrition. Nonetheless, it is prudent to develop plans for reassigning personnel whose activities have been altered or eliminated.

Phase II: Carrying Out the Process

Once the appropriate groundwork has been laid, the hospital can carry out the five main FVA steps that lead to lasting cost reductions:

1. Redefining Costs

In the first step of the FVA analytical process, each unit manager carefully analyzes exactly what his or her unit produces or does for the other parts of the hospital and determines how much this costs.

The analysis begins with the development of a three-part "function tree" for each unit consisting of the basic missions of the unit, the activities stemming directly from each mission and the end products and services resulting from these activities. (See Figure 17-2.)

Figure 17-2 The FVA function tree

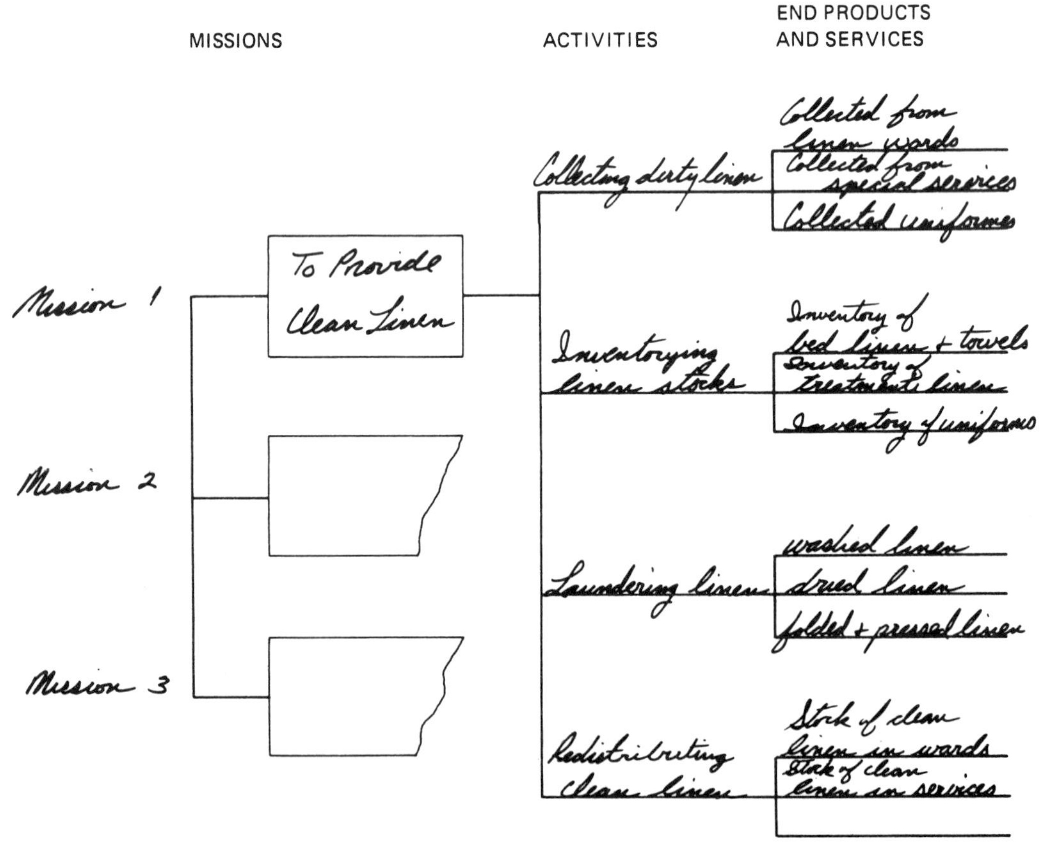

MISSIONS — ACTIVITIES — END PRODUCTS AND SERVICES

Mission 1: To Provide Clean Linen
- Collecting dirty linen: Collected from linen wards; Collected from special services; Collected uniforms
- Inventorying linen stocks: Inventory of bed linen + towels; Inventory of treatment linen; Inventory of uniforms

Mission 2
- Laundering linen: washed linen; dried linen; folded + pressed linen

Mission 3
- Redistributing clean linen: Stock of clean linen in wards; Stock of clean linen in services

To avoid unnecessary detail, a useful rule of thumb is that an end product or service should not be smaller than $2,000 or one-tenth of a staff year.

Once completed, the function tree provides a clear picture of what comprises a particular unit. It provides a concise description of a unit's missions, activities, and the end products and services produced.

With this picture in mind, the unit manager determines how much his or her operation costs the hospital—both in total and for each activity and end product or service. To determine the total the manager develops a "base line budget" for the unit. This budget includes the salaries and benefits of employees whose time is completely dedicated to the unit, and the cost of supplies the unit consumes. The base line budget must also include an estimate of the resources indirectly used by the unit, such as the cost of floor space, utilities and general building services.

After the base line budget is determined, the unit manager must allocate it against all the end products that have been defined. Because this is intended to be an exercise in judgment, accuracy of plus or minus 15 percent is acceptable. The actual allocation can be accomplished by creating a worksheet that lists all the end products and services on the vertical axis, and all the cost elements of the department (individual employees and nonpersonnel costs) on the horizontal axis. (See Figure 17-3.) This approach ensures that all the expenses of the unit are accounted for. It also enables individuals to be involved in deciding how their own time is allocated to the various end products or services that are produced.

Figure 17-3 FVA resource allocation worksheet

END PRODUCT OR SERVICE	PERSONNEL COST — Susan		Mary		Joe				Total		NON-PERSONNEL COSTS	TOTAL COST OF EACH END PRODUCT OR SERVICE
	WY*	$	WY	$	WY	$	WY	$	WY	$		
Collected linen from wards			0.3	3,200	0.5	7,000			0.8	10,200	500	$10,700
Inventory of bed linen and towels	0.2	3,000	0.1	1,070	0.1	1,400			0.4	5,470	150	$5,620

The total of any person's time must equal 1.0 WY

* WY = the fraction of one work-year spent on the end product
  $ = the dollar value (based on salary plus fringes) of the time spent

2. Generating Ideas

The task force now plays a major role because it has the responsibility of designing the best method of generating cost-reduction ideas for each unit manager. "Think sessions" are the most frequently used method in industry, but other approaches such as consultation with peers in other hospitals should be used as a supplement wherever they may yield promising suggestions.

There should be at least one think session for each unit manager. The people who attend should be carefully chosen to ensure that as many ideas as possible are generated and discussed. At a minimum, this would include the unit manager, the manager's most trusted lieutenants and at least one task force member. Any cost-reduction expert (either from within or outside the hospital) who may have something to contribute should also be invited.

This work group should consider each unit's end product or service, and each of the following possibilities for reducing demand for that service:

- reduction in amount, frequency or quality;
- outright elimination;
- combination with another activity; or
- deferral to a later point in time.

They should also consider automation (or de-automation), rebalancing the workload and changing the work flow entirely.

3. Evaluating Attractiveness

In step 3, line management and the task force evaluate the ideas that have been generated. This means weighing the potential dollar savings against the many kinds of risks involved for each idea. An approximate (plus or minus 15 percent) savings figure is measured against the idea initially.

The severity of risk (the degree to which the hospital could be adversely affected) for each idea must be rated as slight, moderate, severe or extreme. The unit manager must make a similar judgment regarding the likelihood of occurrence of the adverse consequences identified for each idea.

This overall assessment of risk can be combined with the estimated potential savings to form an overall attractiveness score. Each cost-reduction opportunity can be ranked from the most attractive (high potential savings, low risk—code A) to the least attractive (low savings, high risk—code I). This overall attractiveness ranking permits the comparison of all the ideas from the FVA units.

4. Making Decisions

To verify the judgments, every cost-reduction opportunity that involves changing a service performed for hospital personnel outside the unit in question undergoes a challenge process. Other units or individuals in the hospital who typically receive that service should have the chance to comment on the accuracy of the risk evaluation and advise management of any aspects of a particular idea that have not been adequately considered. The challenge process may lead to changes in risk evaluations and savings estimates for individual cost-reduction ideas.

After the analyses and recommendations of unit managers and the comments of the "challengers" are considered, senior hospital management decides which cost-reduction opportunities will be implemented.

5. Implementing Ideas

This step of FVA is aimed at ensuring that the cost-reduction ideas chosen by management are actually implemented and that estimated savings are in fact achieved. Management should initially ensure that every idea has one person assigned to its implementation. These individuals should be asked to develop an implementation plan that describes how and when they will achieve the cost-reduction objective. Periodic reviews to check progress serve as reinforcement for the individual, and help assure management that the projects are being implemented according to plan.

Chapter 18—Reimbursement and Rate Setting

OVERVIEW

As demands for health care have increased throughout the country, providers have become more dependent upon third party reimbursement programs, including Medicare, Medicaid, and private insurance. It is estimated that approximately 90 percent of the nation's population is covered by some form of third party health care coverage.

As a result, health care providers have become more vulnerable to cost controls imposed by third party payors, who may attempt to reduce cost increases while continually expanding coverage. Simultaneously, state and federal agencies have intensified their efforts to exert regulatory control over some or all rates or costs of hospitals. Such efforts have been particularly significant under the Medicare and Medicaid programs. One example of such an effort is the Schedule of Limits on Routine Costs adopted by Medicare. Those routine cost limits deny reimbursement to providers to the extent that they exceed arbitrarily defined cost ceilings.

In a similar vein, many states have attempted to freeze increases in reimbursement for Medicaid services. Although many of these state efforts have been ruled illegal by courts, state agencies have not been deterred from attempting to control the rising costs of health care by limiting reimbursement to providers under state-financed health programs. Moreover, many states have adopted, or are now considering the implementation of, rate review or rate-setting programs that would limit the rates that could be charged by providers.

Governmental efforts have been mirrored by the efforts of private insurers to decrease reimbursement to health care facilities without decreasing coverage to their customers. In many cases, Blue Cross plans and other private insurers have been in the forefront of efforts to limit health care spending by making prospective payment for services according to negotiated budgets.*

MEDICAID**

The program is designed to provide medical assistance to those groups or categories of people who are eligible to receive cash payments under one of the existing welfare programs established under the Social Security Act; that is, Title IV-A, the program of Aid to Families with Dependent Children (AFDC), or Title XVI, the Supplemental Security Income (SSI) program for the aged, blind, and disabled. In most cases, receipt of a welfare payment under one of these programs means automatic eligibility for Medicaid. In addition, States may provide Medicaid to the "medically needy," that is, to people (1) who fit into one of the categories of people covered by the cash assistance programs and (2) to those who have enough income to pay for their basic living expenses (and so are not recipi-

---

*Source: Reprinted from Health Law Center, *Hospital Law Manual,* Vol. I, September 1980, with permission of Aspen Systems Corporation.

**Source: *Medicare and Medicaid Data Book, 1981,* DHHS Pub. No. (HCFA) 03128, April 1982.

ents of welfare), but not enough income to pay for their medical care. As shown in Figure 18-1, the categorically needy include AFDC and SSI cash assistance recipients and may also include optional groups related to each cash assistance category. Table 18-1 indicates who is covered, by state, under AFDC.

Federal regulations mandate that certain basic services be offered to all categorically needy persons. Title XIX of the Social Security Act requires that every State Medicaid program offer: inpatient hospital services, outpatient hospital services, laboratory and X-ray services, skilled nursing facility services for individuals 21 and older, home health care services for individuals eligible for skilled nursing services, physicians' services, family planning services, rural health clinic services, and early and periodic screening, diagnosis, and treatment services for individuals under 21. In addition, States may provide a number of other services if they elect to do so, including drugs, eyeglasses, private duty nursing, intermediate care facility services, inpatient psychiatric care for the aged and persons under 21, physical therapy, and dental care. Figure 18-2 indicates the optional services covered by each State for either the categorically needy or both the categorically and the medically needy.

Medicaid operates as a vendor payment program. Payments are made directly to providers of service for care rendered to eligible individuals. Providers must accept the Medicaid reimbursement level as payment in full. In medical institutions and intermediate care facilities, individuals are required to turn over income in excess of their personal needs and maintenance needs of their spouses to help pay for their care. States may require Medicaid recipients to pay cost sharing on services but they may not require the categorically eligible to share costs for mandatory services.

States administer their Medicaid programs within broad Federal requirements and guidelines.[1] These requirements allow States considerable discretion in determining income and other resource criteria for eligibility, covered benefits, and provider payment mechanisms. As a result, the characteristics of Medicaid programs vary considerably from State to State.

MEDICARE HOSPITAL INSURANCE*

The law governing the hospital insurance program (HI) establishes limits on coverage, based on the concept of a "benefit period" (or "spell of illness"). A benefit period begins with an enrollee's first day of hospitalization and ends when the enrollee has not been a bed patient in a hospital or skilled nursing facility for at least 60 consecutive days. Although there is no limit to the number of benefit periods that an enrollee may have, there are limits on covered services within each benefit period.

The hospital insurance program covers services in a participating hospital for up to 90 days in a benefit period. After an initial deductible (applicable to each benefit period), the patient is entitled to 60 days of hospitalization with no additional cost sharing. The Secretary of DHHS is required each year to determine the deductible amount, using a formula specified by law. The HI deductible amount approximates the current cost of room and board for one day in a hospital. For each of the remaining 30 days in the benefit period, the patient is responsible for coinsurance equal to one-fourth of the deductible.

Each hospital insurance beneficiary also has a "lifetime reserve" of 60 additional hospital days which can be used at his or her option whenever the 90 days covered in a benefit period have been exhausted. Lifetime reserve days are subject to coinsurance equal to one-half the deductible.

The HI program also provides for payment to nonparticipating hospitals which administer emergency services to eligible patients. Under these provisions, the hospital may bill the program on an annual basis for all emergency services rendered. In the event this arrangement is unacceptable to the provider, the patient may pay for services received and submit a claim for reimbursement. These reimbursements are

---

[1]Medicaid is financed jointly with State and Federal funds. Federal contributions vary with States' per capita income and currently range from 50 percent to 77.55 percent of program medical expenditures. States participate in the Medicaid program at their option. All States except Arizona currently have Medicaid programs.

---

*Source: *The Medicare and Medicaid Data Book, 1981*, DHHS Pub. No. (HCFA) 03128, April 1982.

Figure 18-1 Medicaid: eligibility coverage of the categorically needy

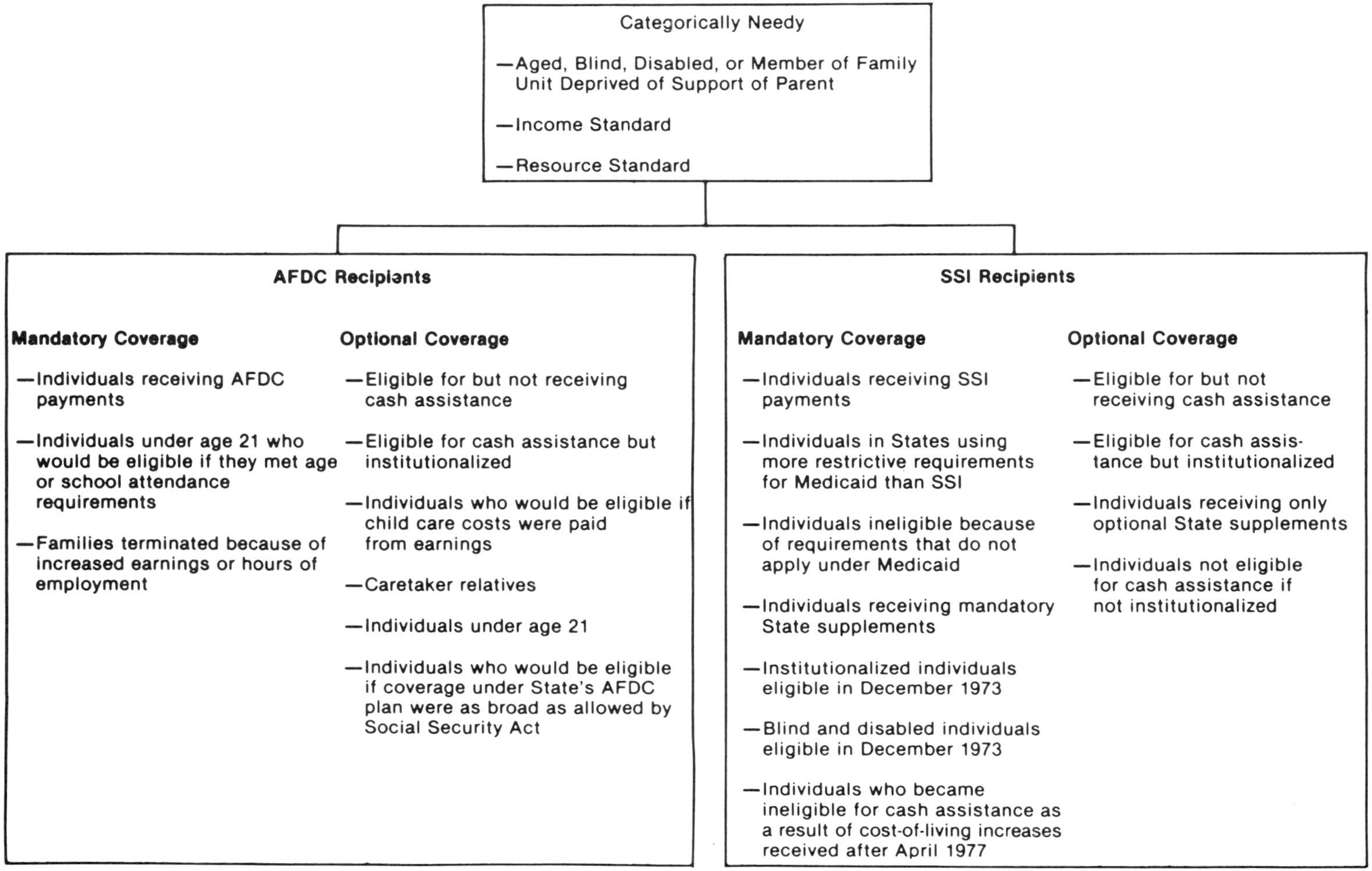

Categorically Needy
— Aged, Blind, Disabled, or Member of Family Unit Deprived of Support of Parent
— Income Standard
— Resource Standard

AFDC Recipients

Mandatory Coverage
— Individuals receiving AFDC payments
— Individuals under age 21 who would be eligible if they met age or school attendance requirements
— Families terminated because of increased earnings or hours of employment

Optional Coverage
— Eligible for but not receiving cash assistance
— Eligible for cash assistance but institutionalized
— Individuals who would be eligible if child care costs were paid from earnings
— Caretaker relatives
— Individuals under age 21
— Individuals who would be eligible if coverage under State's AFDC plan were as broad as allowed by Social Security Act

SSI Recipients

Mandatory Coverage
— Individuals receiving SSI payments
— Individuals in States using more restrictive requirements for Medicaid than SSI
— Individuals ineligible because of requirements that do not apply under Medicaid
— Individuals receiving mandatory State supplements
— Institutionalized individuals eligible in December 1973
— Blind and disabled individuals eligible in December 1973
— Individuals who became ineligible for cash assistance as a result of cost-of-living increases received after April 1977

Optional Coverage
— Eligible for but not receiving cash assistance
— Eligible for cash assistance but institutionalized
— Individuals receiving only optional State supplements
— Individuals not eligible for cash assistance if not institutionalized

Source: *The Medicare and Medicaid Data Book, 1981*, DHHS Pub. No. (HCFA) 03128, April 1982.

Table 18-1 Medicaid Coverage Under AFDC (December 1980)

Medicaid Jurisdiction	AFDC State Plan Includes			Optional Categorically Needy			
	Families with Unemployed Parents	Unborn Children	Children Age 18–21 Regularly Attending School	Caretaker Relatives	All Financially Eligible Individuals Under Age 21	Individuals Eligible But Not Receiving Aid	Individuals Eligible But In Institutions	Individuals Who Would Be Eligible If AFDC Is Broad As Social Security Act Allows	Individuals Who Would Be Eligible If Child Care Cost Paid From Earnings
Alabama		x	x		x				
Alaska			x				x		
Arkansas			x			x	x		
California	x	x	x	x	x	x	x		x
Colorado	x	x	x	x	x	x	x		
Connecticut	x	x	x	x	x	x	x		
Delaware								x	
District of Columbia	x	x	x	x	x	x	x	x	x
Florida		x					x		
Georgia	x	x	x	x	x		x		
Guam	x	x	x				x		
Hawaii	x	x	x		x x		x	x	
Idaho	x		x		x	x	x	x	
Illinois								x	
Indiana									
Iowa	x	x		x			x	x	
Kansas	x		x	x		x	x	x	
Kentucky		x	x	x	x x	x	x x	x x	
Louisiana				x	x	x x	x x		
Maine	x	x	x	x	x		x x	x x	x x
Maryland	x	x	x	x	x		x x		x x
Massachusetts	x	x	x	x	x		x x		
Michigan	x	x	x	x		x	x x	x x	x x
Minnesota									
Mississippi	x	x	x				x x		
Missouri	x		x		x	x	x x		
Montana	x		x		x	x	x x		
Nebraska		x	x				x	x	
Nevada			x	x	x x	x x	x	x	
New Hampshire	x	x	x	x	x x	x	x	x	x x
New Jersey	x	x	x	x		x		x	x x
New Mexico				x			x		
New York		x	x	x	x	x			x
North Carolina		x		x					
North Dakota			x	x					
Northern Marianas	x	x	x	x	x	x			x

Table 18-1 continued

	AFDC State Plan Includes				Optional Categorically Needy			
Medicaid Jurisdiction	Families with Unemployed Parents	Unborn Children	Children Age 18–21 Regularly Attending School	Caretaker Relatives	All Financially Eligible Individuals Under Age 21	Individuals Eligible But Not Receiving Aid	Individuals Eligible But In Institutions	Individuals Who Would Be Eligible If AFDC Is Broad As Social Security Act Allows	Individuals Who Would Be Eligible If Child Care Cost Paid From Earnings
Ohio	x	x					x	x	x
Oklahoma			x	x		x	x		x
Oregon			x	x	x	x	x	x	
Pennsylvania	x	x		x	x	x	x	x	x
Puerto Rico				x	x	x	x		
Rhode Island	x	x		x	x	x	x		
South Carolina		x	x	x	x		x		
South Dakota		x					x		
Tennessee			x		x				
Texas			x				x		
Utah	x	x	x	x	x	x	x		
Vermont	x	x	x	x	x	x	x		
Virgin Islands			x	x		x	x	x	
Virginia			x			x	x		
Washington	x	x	x		x	x	x		x
West Virginia	x	x	x			x	x		x
Wisconsin	x	x		x	x	x	x		
Wyoming		x	x				x		x

Source: State Plans Branch, Bureau of Program Operations, HCFA, *The Medicare and Medicaid Data Book, 1981*, Pub. No. HCFA 03128, April 1982.

Figure 18-2 Medicaid services

FMAP[1]	CN[2] / Both CN and MN[3] BASIC REQUIRED MEDICAID SERVICES SEE ABOVE	State	Podiatrists' Services	Optometrists Services	Chiropractors' Services	Other Practitioners' Services	Dental Services	Physical Therapy	Occupational Therapy	Speech, Hearing, and Language Disorder	Rehabilitative Services	Prescribed Drugs	Dentures	Prosthetic Devices	Eyeglasses	Screening Services	Preventive Services	Diagnostic Services	Clinic Services	Emergency Hospital Services
71	●	Alabama		●								●		●	●					●
50	●	Alaska		●					●						●			●	●
61		Arizona																		
73	+	Arkansas		+	+	+	+					+		+	+				+	+
50	+	California	+	+	+	+	+	+	+	+	+	+	+	+	+	+	+	+	+	+
53	●	Colorado	●									●		●				●	●	●
50	+	Connecticut	+	+	+	+	+	+	+	+	+	+	+	+	+	+	+	+	+	+
50	●	Delaware	●									●		●				●	●	●
50	+	D.C.	+	+		+		+			+			+	+		+	+	+	+
59	●	Florida		●		●	●		●			●	●		●					
67	●	Georgia	●			●								●					●	
50	+	Guam		+			+	+		+		+	+	+	+				+	+
50	+	Hawaii	+	+		+	+	+	+	+	+	+	+	+	+		+	+	+	+
66	●	Idaho	●	●	●			●			●								●	●
50	+	Illinois	+	+	+	+	+	+	+	+	+	+	+	+	+		+	+	+	+
57	●	Indiana	●	●		●	●		●	●		●		●		●	●	●	●	●
59	●	Iowa	●	●	●	●	●	●	●		●	●	●	●		●	●	●	●	●
54	+	Kansas	+	+	+	+	+	+	+	+	+	+	+	+	+				+	+
68	+	Kentucky		+		+		+	+	+		+		+					+	+
69	+	Louisiana			+						+	+		+					+	+
70	+	Maine	+		+	●		+	+	+	+	+		+		+	+	+	+	●
50	+	Maryland		+	+			+				+		+	+				+	+
52	+	Massachusetts	+	+		+	+	+	+	+	+	+	+	+	+	+	+	+	+	+
50	+	Michigan	+	+	+	+	+	+	+	+	+	+	+	+					+	+
56	+	Minnesota	+	+	+	+		+	+	+	+	+	+	+	+	+	+	+	+	+
78	●	Mississippi					●					●								
60	●	Missouri		●			●					●		●	●		●		●	●
64	+	Montana	+	+		+	●	+	+	+	+	+	+	+	+	●	+	+	+	+
58	+	Nebraska	+	+	+	+	+	+			+	+	+	+	+				+	+
50	●	Nevada	●	●	●	●		●	●	●	●	●	●	●	●				●	
61	+	New Hampshire	+	+	+	+		+	+	+	+	+		+	+	+	+	+	+	+
50	●	New Jersey	●	●	●	●	●	●	●	●	●	●	●	●	●	●	●	●	●	●
69	●	New Mexico	●	●		●	●	●	●	●	●	●	●	●					●	●
50	+	New York	+	+		+	+	+	+	+	+	+	+	+	+				+	+
68	+	North Carolina	+	+	+		+					+	+	+	+				+	+
51	+	North Dakota	+	+	+		+	+	+		+	+	+	+	+		+	+	+	+
50	+	N. Mariana Islands		+			+	+				+	+	+	+				+	+
55	●	Ohio	●	●	●	●	●	●	●	●		●	●	●	●				●	●
64	●	Oklahoma		+						+		●		●						
56	●	Oregon	●	●	●	●	●	●			●	●	●	●	●		●		●	●
55	+	Pennsylvania	●	+	+		●					●		●					+	+
50	+	Puerto Rico			+		+	+	+	+	+					+	+	+	+	+
58	+	Rhode Island	+	+			+					+		+	+					
71	●	South Carolina	●									●		●						●
69	●	South Dakota		●			●	●	●			●	●	●				●	●	
69	+	Tennessee										+		+					+	+
58	●	Texas	●	●	●						●	●		●	●					●
68	●	Utah	●	+			+			●		+	+	+	+				+	+
68	+	Vermont	+									+		+	+				+	+
50	●	Virgin Islands					+		+	+		+	+	+	+				+	
57	+	Virginia	+	+				+	+	+		+		+					+	+
50	+	Washington	+	+	+	+	+	+	+		+	+	+	+		+	+		+	+
67	+	West Virginia	+	+	+	+	+	+		+		+	+	+					+	+
58	+	Wisconsin	+	+	+	+	+	+	+	+	+	+	+	+	+	+	+	+	+	+
50	●	Wyoming		●				●		●		●		●						
●	20	●	14	14	10	9	11	10	7	7	11	19	11	16	12	3	4	6	12	18
+	34	+	25	27	17	20	23	26	18	23	20	33	24	30	26	13	16	17	32	28
	54	Total	39	41	27	29	34	36	25	30	31	52	35	46	38	16	20	23	44	46

[1] FMAP-Federal Medicaid Assistance Percentage: Rate of Federal financial participation in a State's medical vendor payment expenditures on behalf of individuals and families eligible under Title XIX of the Social Security Act. Percentages effective from October 1, 1979, through September 30, 1981 are rounded.
[2] Categorically Needy: People receiving federally supported financial assistance.
[3] Medically Needy: People who are eligible for medical but not for financial assistance.

Source: *The Medicare and Medicaid Data Book, 1981*, DHHS Pub. No. (HCFA) 03128, April 1982.

(Read Figure 18-2 across two pages.)

made according to a specified level, subject to deductible and coinsurance provisions.

Covered hospital services under HI include room and board in "semi-private" accommodations containing from two to four beds, nursing services (except for private duty nursing), drugs and biologicals, and other services ordinarily furnished by a hospital to its inpatients. The HI program covers the services of physicians salaried by hospitals. Other physicians' services, including those of hospital-based specialists, are covered under HI. Hospital benefits also include reimbursement for inpatient services provided by tuberculosis hospitals and psychiatric hospitals, subject to a 190-day lifetime limit.

The hospital insurance program pays hospitals the "reasonable costs" of providing services to Medicare beneficiaries. Reasonable costs

Intermediate Care Facility Services	ICF for Mentally Retarded	Inpatient Psychiatric Service for Under Age 22	SNF for Under Age 21	Personal Care Services	Private Duty Nursing	Christian Science Nurses	Christian Science Sanitoria	A Inpatient Hospital Services	B SNF Services	C ICF Services	A Inpatient Hospital Services	B SNF Services	C ICF Services	Total Additional Services	
●	●	●	●					●				●	●	12	AL
●	●	●	●								●			10	AK
															AZ
●	●		●	●				●	●	●	●	●	●	21	AR
+	+	+	+			+	+	+	+	+	+	+	+	30	CA
●	●	●	●								●	●	●	12	CO
+	+	+	+		+		+				+			24	CT
●	●		●								●			10	DE
+	●	+	+	+				+			+			19	DC
●	●	●	●				●	●			●			14	FL
●	●		●					●	●	●		●	●	13	GA
														10	GU
+	+		+										●	20	HI
●	●		●										●	12	ID
+	+	+	+		+		+	+	+	+	+	+	+	29	IL
●	●	●	●		●	●	●				●			24	IN
●	●	●	●								●			21	IA
+	+	+	+		+			+	+	+	+	+	+	26	KS
+	+	+	+					+			+	+	+	17	KY
●	●	●	●					●			●	●	●	15	LA
+	+	+	+			+	+				+	+	●	23	ME
+	+		+					+			+			15	MD
+	+	+	+	+	+	+	+	+			+	+	+	28	MA
+	+		+	+			+				+	+	+	24	MI
+	+	+	+	+	+		+	+	+	+	+	+	+	31	MN
●	●		●				●	●			●			8	MS
●	●							●						14	MO
+	+	+	+	+	+						+	+	+	26	MT
+	+	+	+	+	+						+	+	+	23	NB
●	●		●	+	●						●			20	NV
●	●		●	+	+	+	+				+		●	25	NH
●	●	●	●				●	●			●	●		27	NJ
●	●		●		●									18	NM
+	+	+	+	+	●			+	+	+	+	+	+	29	NY
+	+	+	+					+			+		+	19	NC
+		+	+		+						+			22	ND
	+	+	+	+				+	+		+	+		16	NMI
●	●	●	●		●		●				●	●	●	23	OH
+	+	+		+							+			10	OK
●	●		●	●	●		●				●			22	OR
+	+	+	●								+	+	+	16	PA
								+						13	PR
●	●		+								+			11	RI
●	●		●					●			●			11	SC
●	●		●	●								●	●	16	SD
+	+	+				+	+	+	+	+	+	+	+	14	TN
●	●		●	●				●	●					13	TX
+	+	+	+	+	+						+			18	UT
+	+		+								+			10	VT
														9	VI
+	+		+				+	+			+	+	+	17	VA
+	+	●	+		+			+	+	+	+	+		27	WA
+	+		+		+			+	+		+	+		20	WV
+	+	+	+	+	+	+	+				+			27	WI
●			●											6	WY
24	23	12	19	4	5	1	7	9	2	2	14	8	11		
26	25	22	27	12	14	5	11	17	9	7	29	17	16		
50	48	34	46	16	19	6	18	26	11	9	43	25	27		

are determined after services have been delivered, according to program regulations. The Medicare statute and regulations specify the kinds of hospital costs that Medicare will recognize or allow. Medicare does not allow the costs of private duty nursing, for example; nor does it allow costs unrelated to patient care. Once a hospital's allowable costs are determined, Medicare's hospital insurance program pays the share of those costs attributable to Medicare patients.

Maximizing Medicare Reimbursement*

To obtain the *maximum* reimbursement under the program, while staying within the confines of the Medicare law requires a working knowledge of the law itself, the regulations that promulgate

*Source: Reprinted from *Maximizing Hospital Cash Resources* by C. W. Frank, with permission of Aspen Systems Corporation, © 1978.

it, and the administrative publications that interpret it.

The Reimbursement Formula

The original Medicare law provided for the establishment of two separate trust funds to finance Medicare health care expenditures. The Part A trust fund, financed primarily by social security taxes and patient deductible and coinsurance amounts, was designed to cover the *reasonable cost* of services rendered to a covered beneficiary while hospitalized in an approved patient care facility. The Part B trust fund, financed primarily by monthly premiums and deductible and coinsurance amounts paid by the covered beneficiary, was designed to cover the *reasonable charge* of professional services rendered by a licensed physician on an inpatient or outpatient basis. In addition, Part B provides coverage for the *reasonable cost* of hospital services rendered on an outpatient basis and for certain ancillary services rendered on an inpatient basis where inpatient benefits are either nonexistent or where coverage is no longer applicable.

Since Part B of the Medicare law deals with reasonable charge, which is an element of the predetermined prevailing rate structure of a given geographical area, the maximization discussion will focus primarily on Part A, or the *reasonable cost* concept. The concept of cost-based reimbursement can be most simply described in the formula (PS/TS × AC = R − IP = S), with the elements of the formula defined as follows:

PS = program services
TS = total services
AC = allowable cost
R = reimbursement
IP = interim payments
S = settlement

The first part of the formula (PS/TS) is based on the Medicare or program utilization of the facility and can be expressed in patient days or patient revenues, depending on what aspect of the reimbursement formula is being discussed. The allowable cost (AC) portion of the formula is based on recorded expenses taken from the general ledger and adjusted for the application of the principles of Medicare reimbursement as defined in the Medicare law and its regulations. To be classified as an allowable cost, a recorded expense must be considered (1) reasonable; (2) necessary; and (3) related to patient care. The reimbursement (R) portion of the formula is simply a mathematical function of Medicare or program utilization multiplied by allowable cost. Interim payments (IP) are based on amounts received during the reporting year on either the individual claim method or the periodic interim payment method. Settlement(s) is the sum of computed reimbursement less interim payments.

Planning the Cost Report

One of the best ways to maximize reimbursement is to manipulate the cost allocation process in an attempt to move costs into areas that reflect greater Medicare utilization, and thereby provide greater reimbursement. Although maximization may be a by-product of this cost allocation manipulation, the only real argument (in theory) for choosing an allocation method different from that recommended by the program is to achieve a more *accurate* cost allocation formula. This means that the provider must honestly believe, and be prepared to document, that his method of cost allocation represents a more realistic approach to the reimbursement formula. In addition, the Medicare program has one basic rule which must be carefully considered before a change is made: once the provider elects an option that represents a more sophisticated (or more accurate) method of cost allocation, it normally may not revert back to the less sophisticated method. This forces the financial manager to view a proposed change in relation to future needs (two to five years down the road) as well as current operations.

Much of the process of Medicare maximization takes place during the planning period. In fact, without proper planning for the preparation of the cost report, there is little that can be done in the actual mathematical crunching of numbers to effect a greater reimbursement yield.

The more important aspects of the planning process are:

- Specific identification of all available cost centers and establishment of a revenue or expense account for each function within the cost center
- Direct costing of all identifiable expenses as part of the normal accounting process
- Analysis of Medicare utilization by category of service by department, in order to

determine those departments that will produce the maximum reimbursement
- Development of an effective and accurate budgetary process involving all persons with responsibility and accountability for departmental operations
- Review of the various statistical alternatives available for allocation of each overhead cost center, and establishment of procedures to ensure accurate accumulation of such information
- Determination of which basis of allocation yields the maximum reimbursement, and documentation of that statistic as a more accurate method of cost allocation
- Maintenance of an accurate and timely Medicare log that corresponds with the revenue-producing departments of the general ledger.

Specific Areas of Maximization Potential

In approaching the concept of maximizing, it is beneficial to review the flow of financial information through the reimbursement process. Figure 18-3 illustrates this information flow and designates specific areas in which direct action can be taken to maximize reimbursement.

Checklist for Maximizing Reimbursement

The following checklist has been devised so that each question should be answered in the affirmative. Any question answered negatively should be fully explained before the cost report is actually filed.

The checklist is divided into two main parts. Questions relating to the planning process should be completed before the beginning of the fiscal year. Questions relating to the preparation

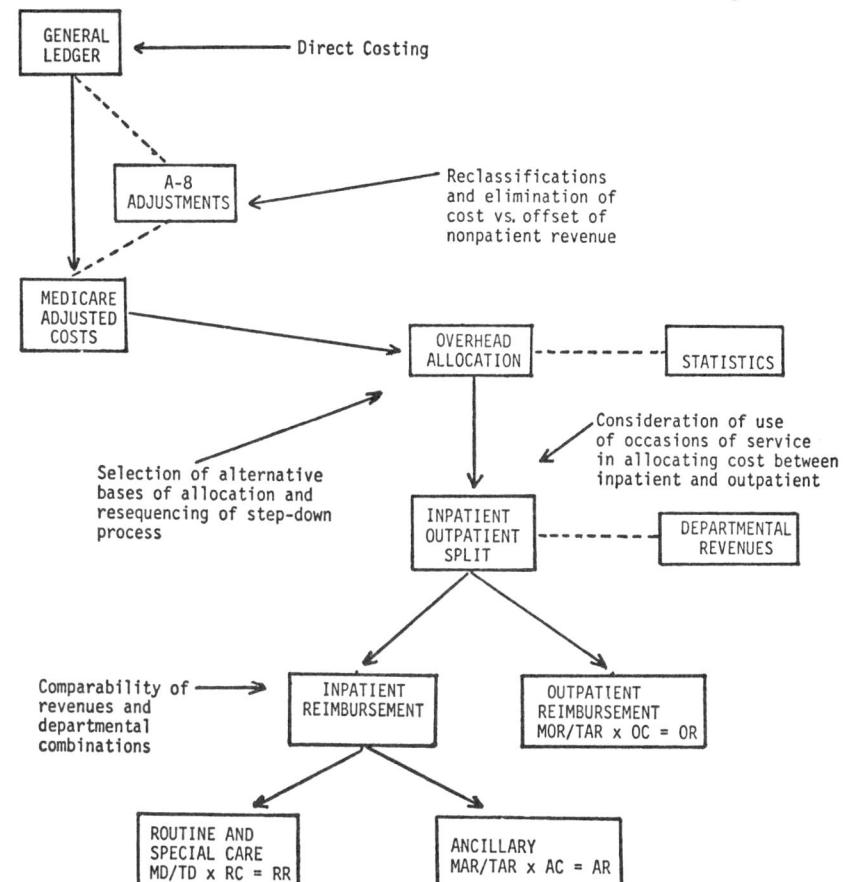

Figure 18-3 Flow of information in the Medicare cost report

```
GENERAL
LEDGER  ←───────── Direct Costing
  │  ↑
  │  │
  ↓  │
 A-8           ← Reclassifications
ADJUSTMENTS      and elimination of
  │              cost vs. offset of
  │              nonpatient revenue
  ↓
MEDICARE
ADJUSTED
COSTS ─────────→ OVERHEAD
                 ALLOCATION ─────── STATISTICS
                    │
                    │   Consideration of use
                    │   of occasions of service
                    │   in allocating cost between
                    │   inpatient and outpatient
                    ↓
Selection of alternative
bases of allocation and
resequencing of step-down
process ───────→ INPATIENT
                 OUTPATIENT ─────── DEPARTMENTAL
                 SPLIT              REVENUES
                   │
                 ┌─┴─┐
                 ↓   ↓
Comparability of → INPATIENT      OUTPATIENT
revenues and      REIMBURSEMENT   REIMBURSEMENT
departmental                      MOR/TAR x OC = OR
combinations
              ┌───┴───┐
              ↓       ↓
         ROUTINE AND    ANCILLARY
         SPECIAL CARE   MAR/TAR x AC = AR
         MD/TD x RC = RR
```

process should be completed at the time of filing the cost report.

The Planning Process

1. Has the general ledger been reviewed to determine that all possible cost centers have been established?
2. Have procedures been established to ensure direct costing of all applicable costs?
3. Has the Medicare utilization of each department been reviewed to determine the impact of moving cost from one department to another?
4. Has a schedule been prepared reflecting the percentage relationship between inpatient and outpatient services?
5. Has consideration been given to the use of occasions of service to allocate cost between inpatient and outpatient?
6. Have all available bases of allocation been reviewed for each cost center to determine the basis most beneficial in the allocation process?
7. If a basis of allocation is to be changed, has approval of the intermediary been requested before the beginning of the fiscal year?
8. Have all statistics been reviewed for reasonableness of departmental distribution?
9. Has consideration been given to alternative methods of accumulating statistics (i.e., square feet computed net or gross; laundry computed wet or dry)?
10. Has fixed equipment cost (plumbing, air conditioning, electrical wiring, kitchen equipment, elevators, mechanical equipment) been properly segregated from building cost, and has the proper life been established in accordance with AHA recommendations?
11. Has the remaining estimated useful life of all assets been challenged to determine that they are reasonable in relation to the operation of the hospital? (Consideration should be given to shortening or lengthening useful life depending on the situation.)
12. Is it practical and advantageous to segregate depreciation by building or building component and have a separate allocation (based on square footage or other acceptable basis) for each building or building component?
13. Can depreciation of fixed and/or major movable equipment be identified by the using department?
14. Has provision been made to accumulate mortgage interest separately from other interest for purposes of reclassification and allocation on the basis of square feet?
15. In developing the allocation basis for housekeeping expenses, has consideration been given to the fact that some departments are not serviced by the housekeeping department?
16. Has consideration been given to applying a weighting factor (properly supported by studies) to square feet for the allocation of building depreciation, interest, or plant maintenance and/or operation?
17. Has the sequence of allocation been challenged to determine if it is applicable to current hospital operations?
18. If a change in sequence is to be made, has approval of the intermediary been requested prior to the beginning of the fiscal year?
19. Has the accumulation of the statistical basis of allocation been tested to ensure accuracy and desired results?
20. Has a cost center been established on the Medicare log for every revenue-producing center on the general ledger?
21. Have procedures been established (through either the admitting or discharge departments, or both) to ensure that all Medicare patients admitted are included on the log?
22. Has a study of the emergency room been made to determine if the charge structure should be changed, based on some form of relative value scale?
23. Has the method of cost allocation been challenged to determine if double apportionment would be more advantageous?
24. Has consideration been given to component allocation of administrative and general expenses?
25. If there is a need to borrow money, has consideration been given to borrowing from a restricted fund?
26. Have procedures been established to keep track of an owner's time to ensure that the maximum allowance is obtained under owner compensation guidelines?

27. Has consideration been given to revision of physician contracts to exclude computation of fee on a percent or revenue basis and to provide for uncollectible accounts resulting from revenue generated by the physician?
28. Has a review been made to determine if any new construction projects require certificate of need approval?
29. Have all of the implications of contracting for therapy services been considered, and has the loss of Medicare revenue been used as a leverage point in the contract negotiations?

The Preparation Process

1. Has it been determined that all necessary reclassifications have been made?
2. Has a schedule been prepared reflecting average employee salary cost by department (after the necessary reclassifications), and are the results reasonable in relation to the personnel staffing requirements of each department?
3. Has it been determined that there is a proper allocation of emergency room revenue between inpatient and outpatient?
4. Has cost been determined and removed (rather then revenue offset) for the following nonpatient-related functions:
   a) vending machines?
   b) cot rental?
   c) TV rental?
   d) patient telephones?
   e) medical record transcripts?
   f) others as considered necessary?
5. Has a determination been made that where cost is removed, the nonpatient function is not operating at a loss?
6. Have separate cost centers been established for all special care units?
7. Has a review been made of those departments that serve more than one revenue-producing function to determine if it is more advantageous to combine or segregate revenues?
8. Has a review been made for those assets on which depreciation is being computed on an accelerated basis to determine if it is advantageous to switch to the straight-line method?
9. Has consideration been given to including Hill-Burton charity writeoffs as a cost of providing services?
10. Has an analysis been made of the "revenue deduction" accounts to determine if they include any allowable expenses (collection expenses, employee discounts, etc.)?
11. Have Medicare bad debts on deductibles and coinsurance been flagged for inclusion in the cost report?
12. Has the funding award for research grants been worded to ensure that offset against allowable cost is not required?
13. Have donors/grantors been instructed on how to word their transmittal letters so that offset is not required?
14. Has a hybrid method of cost-finding been established for removal of maintenance applicable to Sisters' service?
15. Have cash discounts been analyzed to determine if it is more advantageous to departmentalize the discount or record it in one central account?
16. Have all costs (including overhead) associated with obtaining services from a related organization been identified?
17. Have all nonpatient-related assets been reviewed to determine if they can be applied to a patient-related activity for purposes of computing return on investment?
18. Have patient days applicable to pediatric, maternity, and aged days been properly accumulated?
19. Has it been determined whether it is more advantageous to net or gross revenues for the professional component of physician fees?
20. Has the hospital recently challenged the allocation of physician time between administrative and professional?
21. If a problem exists with the routine cost limitation, has a review been made to determine if a reallocation of costs is appropriate or if the hospital meets any of the appeal situations?
22. Has it been determined at what point it is more advantageous to offset cafeteria revenue?
23. Have all accruals for vacation and sick pay been made?
24. Has a determination been made that the Medicare log is complete and that all serv-

ices are included? (This normally requires reconciliation of the log totals to the remittance advices.)
25. Has a review of the Medicare log been made to determine that departmental totals crossfoot to the amount billed to the Social Security Administration after taking into consideration noncovered charges, contractual allowance, and deductibles and coinsurance?
26. Have the percentage relationships of the current year cost report been compared with those of the prior year and any unusual variances explained?
27. Have the most recent proposed Medicare adjustments been applied in the current year, and a footnote attached for explanation if not?

THE PROVIDER REIMBURSEMENT REVIEW BOARD (PRRB)

Powers*

Congress established the Provider Reimbursement Review Board (PRRB) to handle appeals of Medicare cost reports.

The Board has the power to affirm, modify or reverse a determination of an intermediary with respect to a cost report. It may make any other modifications on matters covered by that cost report, including modifications adverse to the provider or other parties, even though such matters were not considered in the intermediary's determination.

When a request for a PRRB hearing is filed, the PRRB also has the authority to determine:

1. whether a hearing is warranted, including: the right of a provider to have a PRRB hearing, timeliness of filing the appeal, determining the "amount in controversy" and timeliness of an intermediary's determination;
2. who may be a party to the hearing; and
3. the disposition of the matter.

The PRRB has exclusive authority and complete responsibility for the conduct of the hearing and any prehearing proceedings that may be requested.

Finally, the PRRB may reopen a decision with respect to findings on matters at issue either on its own motion or at the request of the provider. The request to reopen must be made within three years of the date of notice of the final decision unless there was fraud or similar fault of any party to the decision. In the latter case, no limitation applies.

Processing PRRB Appeals*

Briefly, a request for a hearing may be made in either of two instances: (1) to disagree with the Notice of Program Reimbursement (NPR) issued by an intermediary or (2) where an intermediary has failed to issue on time an NPR after the cost report has been filed on time by a provider. (See Figure 18-4 for the timing of PRRB appeal procedures.)

The Scoreboard

Strictly in terms of numbers, providers have not fared too well, being successful in only about one-third of their appeals. However, this figure is misleading because in several instances the board was ruling on the same or similar issues.

Also, HCFA has overturned about one-half of the PRRB decisions that were in favor of providers. However, these, too, are frequently the same issues being presented by different providers.

On the more positive side, because the opportunity to appeal to the PRRB now exists, it seems that many cases are being administratively resolved in favor of the provider before the hearing. And there have been cases where the courts have overturned the HCFA's reversal of PRRB's decisions that were favorable to the provider.

Preparation for a PRRB Hearing**

The key to success is thorough preparation. Simply stated, this means *first* thinking through

---

*Source: Reprinted from Charles K. Bradford, "The PRRB: An Overview," *Topics in Health Care Financing,* Spring 1979, with permission of Aspen Systems Corporation.

*Source: Reprinted from C. K. Bradford, "An Overview," *Topics in Health Care Financing,* Spring 1979, with permission of Aspen Systems Corporation.
**Source: Reprinted from Sherwin L. Memel and Michael J. Tichon, "How to Prepare and Present an Appeal to the PRRB," *Topics in Health Care Financing,* Spring 1979, with permission of Aspen Systems Corporation.

Figure 18-4 Timing of the PRRB appeal procedures

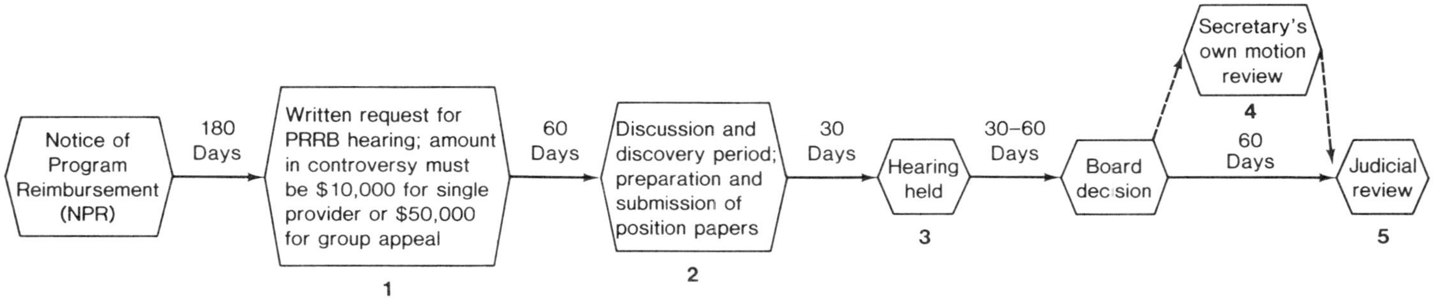

```
Notice of          Written request for         Discussion and
Program    180    PRRB hearing; amount   60   discovery period;    30    Hearing   30-60   Board
Reimbursement Days  in controversy must  Days  preparation and    Days   held      Days    decision
(NPR)              be $10,000 for single        submission of
                   provider or $50,000          position papers
                   for group appeal
     1                    2                         3                                      

                                                                      Secretary's
                                                                      own motion
                                                                      review
                                                                           4
                                                                         60
                                                                        Days
                                                                                    Judicial
                                                                                    review
                                                                                      5
```

1. If the request is deficient to determine jurisdictional aspects, the provider is given 30 days to perfect the request.
2. Parties freely exchange information via conferences, prehearing discovery such as interrogatories, etc. Detailed position papers are then submitted to the Board.
3. A Notice of Hearing is sent to parties of negotiated hearing date. Hearings may be either "live" with a full oral presentation or "on the record" based upon written submission.
4. The secretary may affirm, reverse or modify a Board decision within 60 days.
5. Judicial review is available to providers in any case decided by the PRRB. A PRRB decision is final unless the secretary of HEW reverses or modifies the decision, then such decision becomes the secretary's decision. Providers must begin judicial action within 60 days of a decision either of the PRRB or secretary. The 60-day period following PRRB decision is concurrent for both the secretary's review and for judicial review. If, however, the secretary reverses or modifies, then 60 days remain to obtain judicial review of that action.

all the elements or issues involved in the case. *Second,* the provider must determine and evaluate the weaknesses and strengths of its and the intermediary's respective positions in order to evaluate the likelihood of success in an objective manner. *Third,* the provider should anticipate how the PRRB and a court will resolve the issue.

Fourth, after considering the above elements, the provider should consider how to prove the case. A team approach using legal, accounting, administrative and, if necessary, medical input is advised. It is then necessary to decide what evidence should be accumulated and presented to the PRRB. Evidence can be documentary, such as contracts, or oral, presented through witnesses. An additional consideration with regard to the presentation of evidence is anticipating what type of case the intermediary will present.

Fifth, the provider and its authorized representative must establish a legal basis for its position. The provider should carefully review Medicare reimbursement principles and consider potential constitutional issues, administrative agency decisions which may be supportive, such as the Armed Services Board of Contract Appeals, or in some instances, Internal Revenue rulings, as well as general principles of administrative law, accounting principles or other relevant legal principles.

An appeal should be viewed as a considerable undertaking, and a cost-benefit analysis should be undertaken prior to disputing an issue. In determining the benefits of the appeal, the provider should not only consider the impact on the current cost-reporting period but should consider the impact on future cost-reporting periods as well. In considering the cost of the appeal, attention should be given not only to consultant services such as legal, accounting and expert witnesses fees, but also to the costs of the necessary internal commitment of manpower.

PRRB Jurisdiction*

A prerequisite to an appeal is a dispute stemming from a cost-report adjustment.

The PRRB will review an intermediary's decision concerning the allowability and reasonableness of costs, the portion of cost to be borne by the Medicare program and the amount owing to the provider. If the basis for review is the intermediary's failure to issue a Notice of Program Reimbursement, the PRRB will determine whether the provider is entitled to a hearing and, if necessary, then determine the amount of reimbursement owed to the provider.

However, the PRRB lacks jurisdiction when its decision would impact: a determination that services are excluded from coverage; the interim rate of reimbursement; an intermediary determination to recoup overpayments by offsetting money currently owed to the provider; and the constitutionality of regulations, or Social Security Administration (SSA) or Health Care Financing Administration (HCFA) instructions or rulings.

The provider can seek judicial review of a final decision of the PRRB. The action should be brought in the U.S. District Court in which the provider is located or in the District of Columbia, within 60 days of receipt of the decision by the PRRB or secretary.

Judicial Review*

The decision of the provider and its attorney to seek judicial review should be based at least in part on the following criteria:

1. the principle at stake;
2. whether a one-time cost report, multiple years or long-term recurring situations such as depreciation of buildings or interest on bonds is the issue;
3. the precedent of other decisions by the PRRB, the administrator of HCFA, as well as judicial decisions on the particular issue;
4. the retroactivity of a rule that has "substantive impact" (the substantive impact of a new rule or change in rule is best described in Christian Hospital of St. Louis v. Califano);
5. the degree to which the written decision of the Board or the administrator, as the case may be, is supported by substantial evidence;
6. the amount of reimbursable dollars at stake; and
7. the costs of appeal are allowable as administrative and general expenses.

---

*Source: Memel and Tichon, *op. cit.*

*Source: Reprinted from James W. Malloy, "After the PRRB: HCFA and Judicial Review," *Topics in Health Care Financing,* Spring 1979, with permission of Aspen Systems Corporation.

REIMBURSEMENT—OTHER SERVICES COVERED AND UNCOVERED*

Third party payment systems generally classify physicians' services into covered and non-covered categories. Services for which coverage is commonly excluded or specifically limited include dentistry, psychiatry, routine eye care, cosmetic surgery, and so forth. Type-of-service-based distinctions may be used independently or in conjunction with other classification systems, such as place rendered.

Further distinctions between covered and non-covered services are commonly based upon the patient's *condition* for which the service is required. Common exclusions include pre-existing conditions, alcoholism, drug abuse, and self-inflicted injuries.

Needless to say, all third party payment systems exclude coverage of services which are not *medically necessary*. Furthermore, many third party payers will not cover services which reflect a higher *level of care* than is necessitated by the patient's condition.

Allied Professionals

It is fairly common for policies to cover services rendered by certain types of allied professionals, if the allied professional is working under the supervision of a physician and if the bill for services is submitted by the physician.

While services rendered by allied professionals working independently, rather than under the direction of a physician, may clearly not be covered by a particular plan, gray areas are created as health insurance plans try to cover services rendered independently by some allied professionals, such as psychologists, while not covering those rendered independently by other allied professionals.

Ancillary Services

Ancillary services covered by third party payment mechanisms include such items as diagnostic laboratory tests, x-ray therapy, rehabilitation services, and other diagnostic and therapeutic services. As with other medical services, third party payment systems have generally distinguished between ancillary services rendered on an inpatient basis and those rendered on an ambulatory basis. Individuals are still hospitalized needlessly for diagnostic laboratory and x-ray tests because their insurance plans do not cover such services on an ambulatory basis. However, the current trend in private third party payment systems is to broaden coverage to include ancillary services rendered on an ambulatory basis, which reduces unnecessary hospitalization.

RATE SETTING

It is commonly assumed that rates should cover only the traditional direct patient care operating expenses expressed in the hospital's accounting records. However, if rates are set only to equal these expenses, the hospital will not:

1. Provide for such activities as education, research, and community health programs.
2. Accumulate any funds for expansion or improvement of services.
3. Cover the cost of services to those unable or unwilling to pay.
4. Provide for contingencies.
5. Accumulate sufficient funds for replacement of existing facilities.
6. Provide sufficient working capital (operating cash) to meet current obligations.
7. Provide a reasonable return on net equity.

These items are classified as *other financial requirements* (see AHA list of "Financial Requirements," Table 18-2) and should be considered when establishing hospital rates. Coupled with operating expenses, they make up the total financial requirements of operating a hospital.*

Mechanics of Rate Setting**

The mechanics of rate setting should include the following procedures:

1. Immediate and long-range objectives are established for the institution by first estab-

---

*Source: Reprinted from Jeffrey A. Prussin and Jack C. Wood, "Reimbursement for Physicians' Services," *Topics in Health Care Financing*, Fall 1975, with permission of Aspen Systems Corporation.

*Source: Reprinted from Robert S. Lerner and David D. Willman, "Rate Setting: A Theoretical Approach," *Topics in Health Care Financing*, Winter 1974, with permission of Aspen Systems Corporation.

**Source: Reprinted from Health Law Center, *Hospital Law Manual*, Vol. I, September 1980, with permission of Aspen Systems Corporation.

Table 18-2 AHA's Definition of Financial Requirements of Hospitals*

Current operating requirements

Current operating requirements include the following costs:

1. Patient care

    These costs include, but are not limited to, salaries and wages, employee benefits, purchased services, interest expense, supplies, insurance, maintenance, minor building modification, leases, applicable taxes, depreciation, and the monetary value assigned to services provided by members of religious orders and other organized religious groups.

2. Patients who do not pay

    It must be recognized that a portion of the total financial requirements will not be met by certain patients who:

    a. Fail to fully meet their incurred obligation for services rendered.
    b. Are relieved wholly or in part of their responsibilities because of their inability to pay for services rendered.

    Therefore, these unrecovered financial requirements must be included as a current operating requirement for those who pay.

3. Education

    Where financial needs for educational programs having appropriate approval have not been met through tuition, scholarships, grants, or other sources, all purchasers of care must assume their appropriate share of the financial requirements to meet these needs.

4. Research

    Appropriate health care services and patient-related clinical research programs are an element of the total financial requirements of an institution. The cost of these programs should be met primarily from endowment income, gifts, grants, or other sources.

Operating margin

In order to meet the total financial requirements of an institution, a margin of total operating revenue in excess of current operating requirements must be maintained. This difference will provide necessary funds for working capital and capital requirements for public and not-for-profit institutions and for a return on equity for investor-owned institutions.

Public and not-for-profit institutions

Following are the elements, together with such others as may be proper, that must be included in public and not-for-profit institutions' operating margins, and in their totality they should ensure access to the capital markets of philanthropy and borrowing:

1. Working capital requirements

    Financial stability is dependent on having sufficient cash to meet current fiscal obligations as they come due.

2. Capital requirements

    Health care institutions are expected to provide for capital needs that arise for a variety of reasons, such as population shifts, discontinuance of other existing services, and changes in the public's demand for types of services delivered. In order to be in a position to respond to these changing community needs, health care institutions must anticipate and include the related capital needs in their financial requirements. There must be assurances that adequate resources will be available to finance recognized necessary changes.

    The capital requirements of a health care institution must be evaluated and approved by its governing authority in the context of the institution's role and mission in the community's health care delivery system. Coordination among the health care institution's governing authority, administration, and medical staff and cooperation among health organizations and the appropriate areawide health planning agency are essential to this evaluation.

    a. Major renovations and repairs

        Funds must be provided for necessary major repairs of plant and equipment to ensure compliance with changing regulatory standards and codes and to finance planned and approved renovation projects.

    b. Replacement of plant and equipment

        Because of deterioration and obsolescence, assets must be replaced and modernized based on community needs for health care services. Funds that reflect changes in prices must be available for

Table 18-2 continued

the replacement and modernization of plant and equipment.

c. Expansion

Sufficient funds must be available for the acquisition of additional property, plant, and equipment when consonant with community needs.

d. New technology

Advances in medical science and advances in the technology of delivering health services often require additional expenditures. Sufficient financial resources must be available for continued additional investment in the improvement of plant and equipment, consonant with community needs, so that health care institutions can keep pace with changes in the health care delivery system.

Investor-owned institutions

Investor-owned institutions should receive a reasonable after-tax return on their owners' equity sufficient to attract and compensate equity shareholders. This return should enable these institutions to provide for capital requirements as well as dividends.

*Source: Reprinted from *Financial Requirements of Health Care Institutions* with permission of the American Hospital Association, © 1978.

lishing them for each department within the institution. Department heads should be responsible for goal setting within their individual departments, and these goals can then be considered in establishing objectives for the entire institution.

2. The objectives should then be translated into total financial requirements for the institution, as follows:

    a. An operating budget should be established setting forth total current operating needs related to patient care.
    b. A capital budget should be created setting forth total capital needs.
    c. The addition of current operating needs related to patient care and total capital needs should represent the hospital's total financial requirements.

3. Overhead must then be allocated through all revenue-producing departments within the hospital.

4. Total operating costs of each revenue-producing department or center are then calculated by adding overhead to direct costs.
5. Remaining financial requirements must then be allocated to each revenue-producing department.
6. The total of each of the previous elements is calculated to determine total financial requirements for each revenue-producing department within the hospital.
7. Each revenue-producing department's total financial requirements are allocated through the type of service rendered by that department so as to establish a basis for setting individual rates for each department.

One of the most difficult tasks in the rate-setting process is relating objectives to total financial requirements. To do so, objectives must be stated in quantitative terms that are practical, obtainable, and understandable by those responsible in the departments. In addition, the hospital must calculate its total financial requirements by way of a budget in order to forecast and control costs.

In order to calculate the total operating cost of revenue-producing departments, the direct costs of overhead departments must be allocated to revenue-producing departments on some logical basis. In hospitals, this allocation process is referred to as "cost finding." The most common method of cost finding used by hospitals is the "step down method." Under this method, overhead is allocated to the revenue-producing departments according to the amounts of service rendered to each by the overhead departments. The term *step down* simply refers to the fact that each overhead department is sequentially allocated, left to right, across an accounting worksheet, which thereby gives the visual appearance of steps.

After the total operating costs are calculated, bad debts, costs of charity cases, and capital needs must be allocated. The sum of all of these elements constitutes the total financial requirements of the hospital. The total financial requirements are then allocated to the revenue-producing departments so that the total financial requirements of each department may be calculated and departmental charge rates can be set to equal those requirements. (See Table 18-3.)

Table 18-3 Allocation of Overhead Operating Expenses to Revenue Producing Departments (Via "Step Down" Cost Finding Method)

Departments	1974 Actual Expenses	1975 Total Budgeted Direct Expenses	Other Operating Revenue	Total Financial Requirements	Depr. Bldg.	Depr. Equip.	Adm. & General	Employee Health & Welfare	Maint. of Plant	Laundry & Linen Service
Depreciation—Building	$ 48,000	$ 60,000		$ 60,000	$(60,000)					
Depreciation—Equipment	72,000	74,000		74,000		$(74,000)				
Administrative & General	486,000	517,000	$ (4,000)	513,000	2,000	3,000	$(518,000)			
Employee Health & Welfare	230,000	257,000		257,000			54,000	$(311,000)		
Maintenance of Plant	132,000	142,000		142,000	6,000	9,000	33,000	16,000	$(206,000)	
Laundry & Linen Service	49,000	56,000		56,000		1,000	12,000	9,000	1,000	$(79,000)
Housekeeping	104,000	110,000		110,000	1,000	1,000	23,000	21,000	3,000	
Dietary Raw Food	85,000	98,000		98,000			20,000			
Dietary—Other	138,000	145,000	(20,000)	125,000	3,000	5,000	28,000	25,000	15,000	1,000
Medical Supplies Overhead	25,000	27,000		27,000	1,000	1,000	6,000	11,000	4,000	
Pharmacy Overhead	35,000	37,000		37,000	1,000	1,000	8,000	8,000	2,000	
Medical Records	39,000	43,000	(6,000)	37,000		1,000	8,000	8,000	2,000	
Operating Rooms	73,000	81,000		81,000	5,000	7,000	20,000	12,000	25,000	3,000
Delivery Rooms	9,000	11,000		11,000			2,000	2,000	1,000	
Anesthesia	34,000	37,000		37,000			8,000	6,000	1,000	
X-Ray	103,000	109,000		109,000	2,000	2,000	24,000	17,000	8,000	2,000
Laboratory	215,000	232,000		232,000	1,000	1,000	49,000	21,000	4,000	
Blood Bank	25,000	26,000		26,000			5,000	3,000		
EKG & EEG	55,000	59,000		59,000			12,000	5,000	1,000	
Oxygen Therapy	25,000	25,000		25,000		1,000	6,000		4,000	
Physical Therapy	44,000	37,000		37,000	1,000	1,000	8,000	8,000	5,000	3,000
Cost of Medical Supplies Sold	47,000	50,000		50,000			10,000			
Cost of Drugs Sold	73,000	81,000		81,000			17,000			
Inpatient—Routine	580,000	616,000		616,000	35,000	37,000	143,000	120,000	123,000	69,000
Nursery	38,000	40,000		40,000	1,000	1,000	9,000	7,000	2,000	
Emergency	31,000	60,000		60,000	1,000	2,000	13,000	12,000	5,000	1,000
Total Operating Expenses	$2,795,000	$3,030,000	$(30,000)	$3,000,000	$ -0-	$ -0-	$ -0-	$ -0-	$ -0-	$ -0-

Operating cash needed $ 15,000
Plant Capital:
  Price level depreciation increment 37,000
  Expansion 99,000
  Replacement cost differential 67,000
  218,000
Bad debts and chairty losses 143,000
  361,000 ———EQUAL———

TOTAL FINANCIAL REQUIREMENTS $3,361,000 ———EQUAL———

NOTE: Allocations are rounded for simplicity of presentation.

Source: Reprinted from Robert S. Lemer and David D. Willman, "A Case Study in Determining Financial Requirements and Rate Setting," *Topics in Health Care Financing,* Winter 1974, with permission of Aspen Systems Corporation.

(*Read Table 18-3 across two pages.*)

Chapter 18—Reimbursement and Rate Setting 299

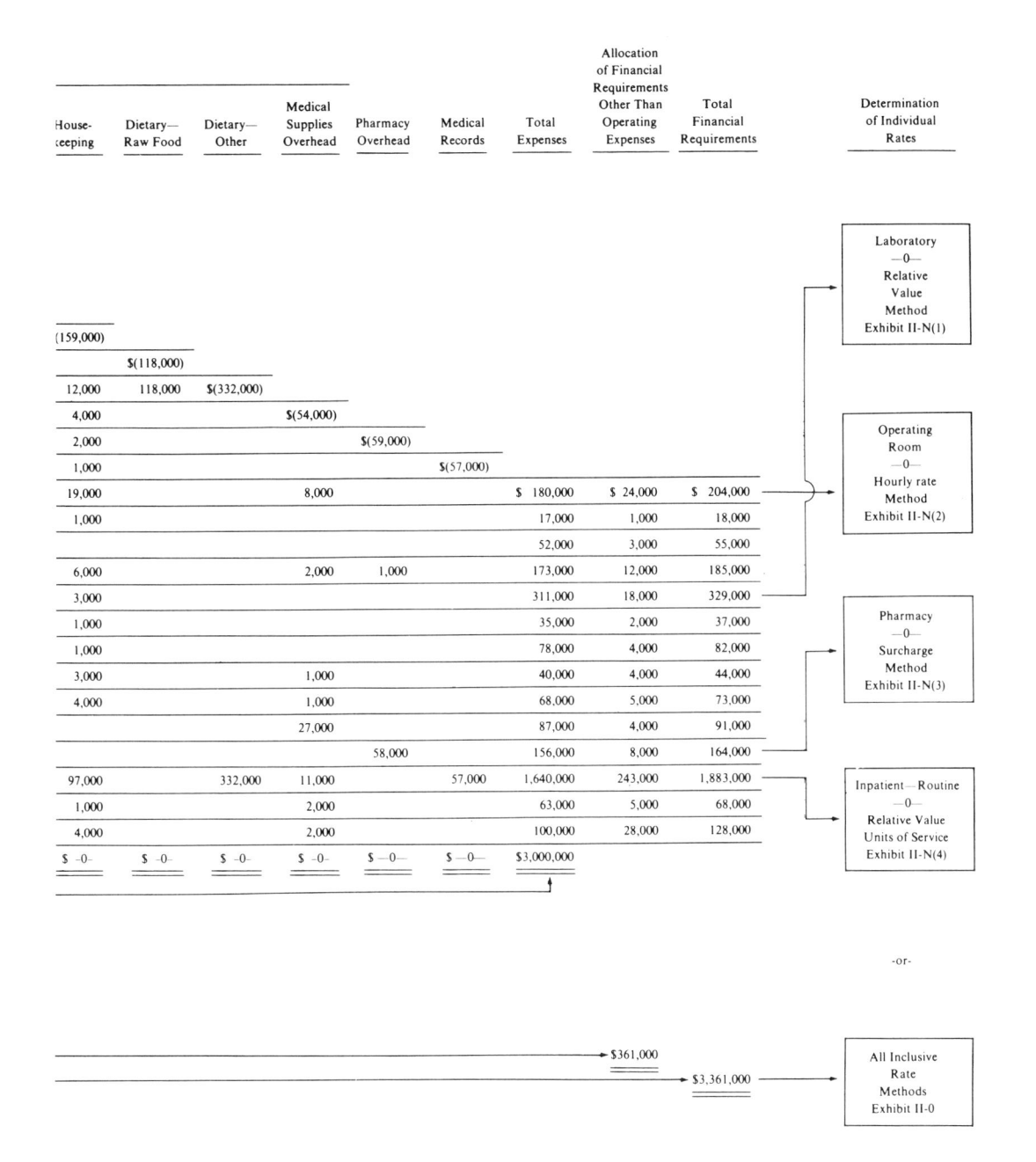

House-keeping	Dietary—Raw Food	Dietary—Other	Medical Supplies Overhead	Pharmacy Overhead	Medical Records	Total Expenses	Allocation of Financial Requirements Other Than Operating Expenses	Total Financial Requirements	Determination of Individual Rates
(159,000)									
	$(118,000)								Laboratory —0— Relative Value Method Exhibit II-N(1)
12,000	118,000	$(332,000)							
4,000			$(54,000)						
2,000				$(59,000)					
1,000					$(57,000)				
19,000			8,000			$ 180,000	$ 24,000	$ 204,000	Operating Room —0— Hourly rate Method Exhibit II-N(2)
1,000						17,000	1,000	18,000	
						52,000	3,000	55,000	
6,000			2,000	1,000		173,000	12,000	185,000	
3,000						311,000	18,000	329,000	Pharmacy —0— Surcharge Method Exhibit II-N(3)
1,000						35,000	2,000	37,000	
1,000						78,000	4,000	82,000	
3,000			1,000			40,000	4,000	44,000	
4,000			1,000			68,000	5,000	73,000	
			27,000			87,000	4,000	91,000	
					58,000	156,000	8,000	164,000	
97,000	332,000	11,000		57,000		1,640,000	243,000	1,883,000	Inpatient—Routine —0— Relative Value Units of Service Exhibit II-N(4)
1,000			2,000			63,000	5,000	68,000	
4,000			2,000			100,000	28,000	128,000	
$ -0-	$ -0-	$ -0-	$ -0-	$ -0-	$ -0-	$3,000,000			

-or-

→ $361,000

→ $3,361,000

All Inclusive Rate Methods Exhibit II-0

Methods of Rate Setting*

One of the most frequent errors in rate setting is the exclusive use of historical costs and statistics. Only budgeted or planned costs and statistics should be used to establish a published charge. Although historical data, and even competitors' charges, can serve as reference points, they should only be used as benchmarks. Published charges or prospective rates are for future services. Therefore, it is logical to base these rates on future costs and statistics.

The hospital's charge rate structure may be developed under one of two general methods: individual charges (a la carte) or inclusive rates, or some combination of these.

Individual Charges

There are a few generally used methods of establishing rates for individual departmental services:

1. Relative Values

Each departmental service or output procedure is assigned a relative value unit (RVU). This is based on the relative time and/or resources required to perform it. Each is multiplied by the number of services or outputs in the cost period to determine a weighted value. The total amount (financial requirements) to be recovered from rates, divided by total weighted values, produces the unit value. The unit value is then multiplied by the relative units for each service to provide the weighted rate per service.

2. Cost Plus a Percentage

This method of rate setting is used in merchandising-type departments, such as Pharmacy and Central Supply.

For example:

Central Supply	Direct Supply costs	Mark-Up on Cost %	$	Rate
Disposable syringe	$ 1.00	100%	$ 1.00	$ 2.00
Disposable OR Packs	$15.00	100%	$15.00	$30.00

*Source: Reprinted from *Understanding Hospital Financial Management* by Allen G. Herkimer, Jr., with permission of Aspen Systems Corporation, © 1978.

It is important to determine a method of mark-up. The percentage of mark-up can be based either on cost or on selling price.

3. Hourly or Time Rates/Routine Services

The hourly rate method is used in such departments as operating and recovery rooms, anesthesiology, physiotherapy and emergency services. There are two basic approaches: straight hourly (partial hour) or person-minute rates, and a base or set-up charge plus time. Table 18-4 illustrates four variations upon the hourly or time rate method of rate setting, to illustrate the versatility of this approach.

Routine Services

The routine service method is directly related to the type of accommodation. To calculate rates, computations are based on fixed and variable costs related to a specific type of routine service. Table 18-5 is an illustration for developing

Table 18-4 Four Variations Upon the Hourly or Time Rate Method of Rate Setting

Straight Hourly Rate		
Number of OR Minutes	90	
Rate per Hour	$150	
Total Charge per Case		$225
Ranges of Time		
30–60 minutes	$150	
61–90 minutes	$225	
Total Charge per case 90 minutes		$225
Set-up Base Plus Hourly Rate		
Fixed Set-up Charge	$150	
Rate per OR Hour	$ 50	
Charge for 90 Minute Case		
Set-up Charge	$150	
90 OR Minutes	75	
Total Charge per Case		$225
Set-up Base Plus Person-Minute Rate		
Number of OR Minutes	90	
Number of Paid OR Personnel	3	
Number of OR Person-Minutes	270	
Charge per Person-Minutes	$ .50	
Set-up Base Charge	$ 90	
Charge for 90 Minute Case		
Set-up Charge	$ 90	
270 Person-Minutes @ $.50	$135	
Total Charge per Case		$225

Table 18-5 Developing Room Rates for Routine Medical and Surgical Nursing Service

Description	Total	Private	Semiprivate	Ward
Patient Days	40,940	8,188	21,290	11,462
% Patient Days	100%	20%	52%	28%
Weighted Value	-0-	3	1.5	1
Weighted Patient Days	67,961	24,564	31,935	11,462
% Weighted Patient Days	100%	36%	47%	17%
Total Costs	$5,117,500	$1,842,300	$2,405,225	$869,975
Computer Average Cost Per Patient Day	$125.00	$225.00	$112.97	$75.90
Rounded Published Charge Per Room	$125.00	$225.00	$115.00	$80.00
Projected Gross Charge	$5,207,610	$1,842,300	$2,448,350	$916,960
Favorable Charge/Cost Variance	$90,110	none	$43,125	$46,985

room rates for routine medical and surgical nursing service, using a weighted method in which a ward patient equals 1, a semiprivate patient equals 1.5 and a private patient equals 3.

Inclusive Charges*

Inclusive charge rates usually combine into one or more overall rates the itemized (or a la carte) charges for services rendered.

Inclusive rates may be designed to apply on either a daily or a case rate (episode of stay) basis. Inclusive rates may be weighted to recognize such differentials as (1) personal characteristics of the patient such as age and (2) diagnosis; (3) category of care—medical, surgical, obstetric, pediatric, intensive care, and so on; (4) rehabilitation level—ambulant or self-care; and (5) financial characteristics—payer, income level, and so on. Daily types of inclusive rates may also be weighted to reflect a varying length of stay, since ancillary services and costs usually lessen as the stay lengthens.

Advocates of inclusive rates cite quantifiable advantages—primarily a reduction of patient billing costs.

Opponents of inclusive rates cite such disadvantages as (1) possible increased use of laboratory and X-ray examinations; (2) patients' objections to paying for someone else's bills; (3) loss of competitive advantage because the public historically correlates hospital costs with room rates, and the room rate "loss leader" practice would not be available under the inclusive rate method; and (4) difficulties which would be encountered in third-party monitoring of hospitals. At present, third parties often monitor by means of profiles of charges.

Testing the Adequacy of Charges*

Margin of Safety and Break-even

The margin of safety (MS) is the percentage drop in charges that can occur before a loss. This formula is a dramatic way of calling to management's attention how close its charge level is to the break-even point. It can be expressed in one of two ways:

$$MS = Profit/Contribution$$
$$MS = P/C$$

or

$$MS = (Gross\ charges\ minus\ break\text{-}even\ charges)/Gross\ Charges$$
$$MS = (CH - BE)/CH$$

Both formulas are used. The result (the margin of safety) is expressed as a percentage.

---

*Source: Reprinted from Robert S. Lemer and David D. Willman, "Rate Setting: A Theoretical Approach" *Topics in Health Care Financing,* Winter 1974, with permission of Aspen Systems Corporation.

*Source: Reprinted from *Understanding Hospital Financial Management* by Allen G. Herkimer, Jr., with permission of Aspen Systems Corporation, © 1978.

To illustrate the formulas:

1. Establish the break-even charges and contribution margin:

   The break-even point can be computed using the following formula:

   BE = Fixed Expenses/CM
   BE = F/CM

   The contribution margin (CM) is calculated as follows:

   CM = Gross charges minus variable expense = Gross charges
   CM = (CH − V)CH

   BE = $400,000/.40
   BE = $1,000,000

   CM = ($1,000,000 − $600,000) $1,000,000
   CM = 40%

2. Assuming:

   Gross Charges (CH) = $1,500,000
   Contribution Margin (CM) = 40%
   Contributions (C) = $600,000
   ($1,500,000 × .40)
   Profits (P) = $200,000
   Break-even Charges (BE) = $1,000,000

3. The margin of safety would be calculated as follows:

   MS = P/C
   MS = $200,000/$600,000
   MS = 33⅓%

   Or

   MS = (CH − BE)/CH
   MS = ($1,500,000 − $1,000,000)/$1,500,000
   MS = 33⅓%

In summary, the margin of safety (MS) percentage of 33⅓ percent means that gross charges to patients could drop 33⅓ percent before losses develop. Another way to look at this is that the department's break-even point is 66⅔ percent of present charges.

Simulation Analysis

Simulation analysis is another method used to test adequacy of rates. The simulation process is the formulation of a complex computer model, which is based on a series of real world logical relationships and interrelationships. This model is a statistical and monetary representation of a health care facility or department based on a set of basic assumptions. Resulting projections of the system can assist management in the decision-making process and in answering "what if" questions. This simulation or "what if" approach is fast becoming an everyday management tool for many health care managers, regardless of the size of the facility. This is made possible by the already developed simulation models from either a time-sharing computer system or a computer service bureau.

State Systems for Rate Setting[*]

As of August 1980, 17 States had legislation requiring the disclosure, review, or regulation of hospital rates or budgets. Those programs which require hospitals both to participate and comply with the results of a budget review or rate setting process are considered mandatory rate setting programs. There were eight mandatory State rate setting programs (Connecticut, Maryland, Massachusetts, New Jersey, New York, Rhode Island, Washington, and Wisconsin). The remaining programs solicit voluntary compliance with the results of the review processes or operate simply as disclosure programs.

There is a substantial amount of diversity in these programs. Some systems relate to revenues, others to costs. Some systems involve individual budget review; others use formulas and screens. Some systems constrain the level of costs through penalties, others through screens or through the application of statistical standards. Some systems constrain the rates of increase in costs through global budget approaches, others by guaranteeing inflation increases but scrutinizing all other requests in detail.

Most of the programs are revenue-based and are concerned with the total financial needs of individual hospitals. The commission programs in particular attempt to limit the total revenue collected or received by a hospital to that hospital's total financial needs. This revenue limit is largely independent of whether or not payment

---

[*]Source: *Abstracts of State Legislated Hospital Cost Containment Programs,* Health Care Financing Administration, March 1981, HCFA Pub. No. 03089.

rates are being set for all purchasers of health services.

The cost based systems are primarily concerned with establishing a reasonable payment rate for a hospital, given the cost of delivering care in the hospital (where cost is defined according to a payer's principles) and in other comparable hospitals. The cost based systems are primarily Blue Cross and Medicaid prospective reimbursement programs using very similar definitions of hospital costs. However, these programs may apply to a total hospital budget as they do in Rhode Island. Further, if the payment unit is based on charges, the cost based system in effect limits total revenue, since charges must be set consistently for all payers.

Characteristics of State Programs*

Emphasis on Refined Interhospital Comparison. The state programs place more importance on interhospital comparisons and use more sophisticated methods in doing so. There is less automatic acceptance of past levels of costs, which tends to put efficient hospitals at a disadvantage.

With the use of complex statistical techniques, large numbers of characteristics can be considered in grouping hospitals. This usually results in more homogeneous groups than those formed on the basis simply of bed-size and metropolitan/nonmetropolitan location, permitting interhospital comparisons to play a larger role in determining rates.

Some states include data on variations in case mix among hospitals, thus permitting better comparisons.

More Explicit Treatment of Fixed and Variable Components of Costs. Hospital expenditures vary in proportion to permanent changes in volume of service, but less in proportion to temporary changes in volume. State programs have done a great deal of experimentation in handling this problem, with the goal of avoiding incentives to increase volume while ensuring equitable treatment of hospitals. One technique is the corridor for volume changes. In an attempt to induce hospitals to control volume, a number of programs limit passthroughs of volume changes. Often a corridor, or range, is established for volume changes that are passed through. Hospitals with changes greater than those permitted by the corridor have their revenues increased or decreased less than in proportion to the volume change. Typically, 25 to 60 percent of the volume change is translated into a revenue change.

The theory behind such a scheme is that changes within the corridor are more likely to reflect long-term trends, while those outside the corridor are more likely to reflect temporary changes. In place of a fixed corridor, Maryland uses a staff-developed projection of volume changes as a ceiling for the passthrough.

Explicit Attention to Capital Requirements. Many state programs have separated out capital reimbursement for special treatment, for two reasons. First, most capital costs (interest, depreciation, retained funds) are based on past decisions and cannot be altered for some time by greater attention to efficiency. Second, regulation may reduce operating surpluses. As a result, careful attention must be given to a hospital's ability to finance needed facilities in the future.

State-level programs have shifted their emphasis from fair reimbursement of costs for existing facilities to the provision of adequate funding for needed facilities.

PROSPECTIVE RATE SETTING

Overview*

Prospective rate-setting (PRS) is a cost-containment strategy wherein an external authority (e.g., a Blue Cross plan or a public agency) establishes the prices that hospitals will be allowed to charge (or the charges that third parties are required to pay) for a certain set period. The key difference between prospective rate setting and conventional methods of reimbursement is that hospitals are not paid the costs they actually incur, nor are they free to unilaterally adjust their charges to cover their costs or their own interpretations of their financial requirements; rather, they are paid at rates that are determined

---

*Source: *Controlling Rising Hospital Costs,* Congressional Budget Office, September 1979.

*Source: Reprinted from William L. Dowling, "Hospital Rate Setting Programs: How, and How Well, Do They Work?" *Topics in Health Care Financing,* Fall 1979, with permission of Aspen Systems Corporation.

by another body and that are set in advance of and considered fixed for the prospective year. Although a hospital's costs are not constrained directly under PRS, it is assumed that the constraint on revenues imposed by fixing what the hospital can charge (or what third parties must pay) will cause the hospital to contain costs in order to avoid losses (or earn surpluses).

The basic elements of prospective rate setting are simple:

1. An external authority is empowered to approve or set hospital charges and/or third party payment rates (or, what amounts to the same thing, to establish a ceiling or "cap" on rates).
2. Rates are set in advance of the year during which they apply and are considered fixed for the year.
3. Patients and/or third parties pay the prospective rates rather than the costs hospitals actually incur during the year.
4. Hospitals are at risk for losses or surpluses.

It should be noted, however, that existing prospective rate-setting systems only approximate these elements in actual practice, and they vary widely in design and structure.

In 1979 about 35 prospective rate-setting systems were in operation. More than 20 Blue Cross plans operate prospective rate-review or rate-setting programs, and approximately 17 states by 1980 had enacted rate-setting laws. These PRS systems are far from uniform. They differ not only with regard to the sponsoring organization, but also with regard to the nature of the prospective rates, the method of rate setting used and the range of third party purchasers actually paying the rates.

Sponsoring Organization

The agency or organization sponsoring a prospective rate-setting system may well affect its stringency. Participation by hospitals in Blue Cross and hospital association programs is generally voluntary, whereas participation in state programs is mandatory, and many assume that voluntary programs are not likely to be very stringent. Blue Cross prospective rate-setting systems affect only what hospitals are paid for Blue Cross patients and so may not have much economic "clout." State systems, on the other hand, differ with regard to who must pay the rates set by the agency or commission. In some states, the rates apply only to patients who pay billed charges, with Blue Cross and Medicaid continuing to reimburse costs. In other states, Blue Cross and Medicaid pay the approved rates. No state, of course, has jurisdiction over the federal Medicare program, but in a few states, HEW has waived certain Medicare reimbursement regulations to allow participation in prospective rate-setting systems on an experimental basis.

Of the two state alternatives, the department of health or an independent rate-setting commission, hospitals prefer the latter, arguing that a conflict of interest exists when the agency administering the state's Medicaid program and, hence, purchasing large amounts of hospital services is also empowered to set the rates to be paid for these services.

Basis of Payment

Prospective rate-setting systems differ in terms of the basis or unit of payment for which rates are set. This feature is important because the basis of payment determines the incentives posed by the system. Four alternative bases of payment are in use at this time:

1. determination of a hospital's total budget, which is translated into a total allowable revenue figure and then apportioned to third parties based on their shares of the hospital's workload;
2. payment of per-admission or per-stay rates;
3. payment of per-diem rates; and
4. payment of specific services rates (following the traditional a la carte charge structure now used by hospitals).

It is argued that the total budget and per-stay approaches encourage hospitals to be concerned about the quantity of service they provide (i.e., how many patients are admitted, how long they stay, and how many services they receive), as well as about the cost per unit of service; whereas payment of per diem or specific services rates focuses attention on per unit costs (i.e., on the efficiency with which services are produced), but may actually encourage increases in the quantity of services provided.

Rate-setting Methods

Prospective rate-setting systems also vary in the methods they use to set rates.

The two most commonly used rate-setting methods are:
1. the application of a formula to project a hospital's past or present year costs forward into prospective rates (or to set a ceiling or cap on future rates). Such formulas typically incorporate a factor for expected inflation.
2. the review of a hospital's budget to determine the reasonableness of its proposed costs. The hospital's budget, once approved, is then translated into prospective rates sufficient to generate enough revenue to cover it.

Because normative standards of "reasonableness" are lacking, comparative standards are generally used in judging costs. Hospitals are grouped according to cost-influencing characteristics such as ownership, location, size, scope of services, teaching status, etc. Judgments about reasonableness are then made by comparing each hospital's costs with its peer group.

Much refinement of data, methods and techniques will be necessary before fair but tight rates can be set with assurance. Despite the problems, however, prospective rate setting appears to have considerable potential. Operating a hospital under a fixed budget or fixed rates is fundamentally different from operating under cost reimbursement. The use of PRS causes costs to be given more weight in decision making, and causes emphasis to be placed on better budgeting, planning, cost finding and cost control. It may make cash flow and revenue more predictable. It may provide a basis for straightening out differences in payment among different third party purchasers. Perhaps most importantly, it gives administrators and financial managers a clear mandate to attack the cost problem in their institutions.

Management Strategy for Prospective Case-Based Payment*

Prospective case-based payment systems heighten the degree of managerial responsibility, increasing the potential for either severe losses or substantial gains. The case-based aspect of such systems expands the scope of managerial responsibility, holding management accountable for operational realms beyond those areas that have traditionally been within their purview. Here are some guidelines for management.

1. Increase Cooperation and Communication among Administration Fiscal Services, Medical Records and the Medical Staff

One means of facilitating communication and cooperation among administration, fiscal services, medical records and the medical staff is the formation of a case-based payment committee (CBPC) to guide medical and administrative responses to the new payment system. In hospitals where encouraging physician involvement will require effort, the CBPC might be a committee of the medical staff with a liaison to administration. In other situations, a joint administrative-medical format, with membership from administration, fiscal services, medical records and the medical staff, might be preferable.

The CBPC should:

- review the system's dynamics and evaluate its effects on patient care and institutional revenue;
- assist the medical staff and hospital departments in the development of specific policies and procedures to respond to the system's impact; and
- serve as the coordinating body for the following strategic actions.

The chairperson may be a physician, administrator, member of fiscal services or full-time coordinator. This person must have both a technical knowledge of the system and an ability to unobtrusively educate medical and nonmedical members of the hospital community.

2. Strengthen and Coordinate Quality Assurance

A major possible deleterious effect of prospective case-based payment systems is pressure to reduce the quality of care rather than improve the efficiency of delivering it. Accordingly, there is a need for increased interinstitutional and intrainstitutional quality monitoring and safeguarding.

3. Orient the Hospital Information System

Administrative management reports should provide information on the profit/loss for each case

---

*Source: Reprinted from Robert A. Connor, "A Management Strategy for Prospective Case-based Payment," *Health Care Management Review,* Fall 1981, with permission of Aspen Systems Corporation.

category, for each department and possibly for each service. Medical management reports should provide profit/loss information (for the direct care component) of each case category, each medical specialty, each physician and possibly each service.

4. Revise Financial Planning

The most fundamental change in financial planning under case-based payment is revision of revenue forecasting. Under case-based payment, revenue will be much more sensitive to a host of factors including changes in labor and material costs, changes in occupancy levels, changes in case mix, trends in medical technology, added or deleted services, demographic trends affecting case mix and case severity, major shifts in the medical staff and changes in the payment regulations themselves.

Accordingly, if significant changes are anticipated in some of these factors, revenue forecasting should consider their impact. Also, as a strategic measure, trends that are beyond the hospital's control and are well documented may prove to be helpful considerations when rates are being set or appealed.

5. Orient Medical Records

In addition to educating medical records personnel concerning the system, steps can be taken to improve the financial functioning of medical records without compromising their role in medical care. Indeed, some of these steps may improve both financial and medical functions.

These steps include training personnel to improve the accuracy of diagnostic coding, efforts to reduce the backlog of incomplete charts (the case-based analog to accounts receivable) and proper selection of secondary diagnoses. Finally, if future systems use that diagnosis which accounts for the most resource consumption (major) rather than that diagnosis which prompted the patient's admission (principle), the medical records staff must adjust the orientation of their thinking and coding accordingly.

6. Strengthen and Direct Cost-Containment Efforts

Under a prospective incentive payment system, cost containment becomes imperative for preservation of institutional viability.

One of the ripest areas for cost containment is materials management.

Another area concerns contracted employees or professionals who receive as income a percentage of the value of services rendered in the hospital. For example, a radiologist may receive a percentage of gross departmental revenue. Such escalatory dynamics run contrary to an institution's financial incentives for lower costs per case and should be reviewed.

Another area that warrants discussion is that of information reports which guide management in focusing cost-containment efforts where they are most needed. There are two approaches to determining where they are needed. One may simply calculate the profit/loss figures for particular units (case categories, services or supplies). Those units or areas with high losses are then targeted for highest priority cost-containment efforts. Alternatively, one may calculate the marginal profitability of cost reductions in particular units (case categories, services or supplies), whether they are financial winners or losers, and concentrate cost-containment efforts on those with the highest return per dollar saved (highest MPCR).

7. Increase Cooperation and Communication with Other Providers

Cooperation and communication among providers becomes increasingly important under case-based payment in order to further cost-containment and joint planning efforts. Cost-containment efforts, as discussed in the previous section, are essential to revenue generation, and sharing of services or equipment to take advantage of economies of scale is an excellent means of reducing costs. Accordingly, trends toward multi-institutional arrangements and specialty care providers will be further encouraged by case-based payment.

8. Orient Marketing Efforts to Case-Based Incentives

Unless a hospital's cost for treatment of patients in each category is under/over the respective market average cost for each case category by the same amount, shifts in a hospital's case mix will significantly impact revenue. For example, suppose your hospital treats patients in group A at a cost which is lower than average, but patients in group B at a cost which is much higher than average. Under a case-based system, your institution is paid on the basis of those market averages. Thus if next year brings a shift in case mix, with more B and fewer A patients, then your revenue will decrease. Alternatively, if more A and fewer B patients arrive, your revenue will increase.

Appropriately, albeit perhaps frustratingly for the fiscal staff, the hospital has no control over the case mix of its patients once they arrive. It may be, however, that efforts to market hospital services can, in an ethical and profitable manner, be oriented toward those services which a hospital provides most efficiently. Special attention may be paid to provision of up-to-date equipment in these profitable areas.

The Diagnosis Related Group (DRG) Approach*

One of the newest prospective rate-setting concepts is based on the diagnosis related group (DRG). A DRG is a grouping of direct patient cost data determined by the diagnosis, treatment and age of a patient. In other words, DRG is an attempt to define a hospital's products in terms of its diagnostic patient mix.

It is claimed that the DRG concept can more realistically measure and control hospital costs. It will supposedly be possible to compare relative performance between hospitals. As a result efficient hospitals can be identified and rewarded. This incentive will encourage efficiency, which will help control hospital costs.

Probably the most threatening aspect of the DRG concept is its impact on patient care. Often many diagnoses and treatments are similar enough that a diagnostic related group can be properly defined and measured. As a result some DRGs can be standardized in terms of product quality and cost. For example, a normal delivery without surgery or a tonsillectomy could probably be reimbursed on a DRG basis.

---

*Source: Reprinted from Michael J. Haley, "What Is a DRG?" *Topics in Health Care Financing,* Summer 1980, with permission of Aspen Systems Corporation.

Many diagnoses can neither be clearly defined nor treated in a similar manner. Furthermore, if all treatments are paid at cost, where is the incentive for efficiency?

Another problem with the DRG concept is how to reimburse changing medical technology and improved treatments. A heart attack victim 30 years ago would have been treated with extensive bed care and rest. Today a recommended treatment might be open heart surgery. If the DRG reimbursement rate were defined by the less costly treatment of the past, the progress toward open heart surgery could have been slowed.

Diagnosis related groups emphasize cost control without adequately considering the issues of quality control. There is a risk that the product will be cheapened to reduce costs, which may sacrifice patient care.

Alternatives

The following approaches might represent a framework for an improved DRG:

- The concept should only be applied to diagnosis that can be clearly defined and treated in a standardized manner, such as a normal delivery without surgery.
- Patients should be allowed some freedom to pay for extra service if they perceive a health care benefit.
- Reimbursement should be based on a fixed price for each appropriate DRG admission and not on a hospital peer group comparison of the cost of an average hospital admission.
- If hospitals cannot realize a surplus at a DRG price, either the hospital should discontinue the service or receive a direct subsidy from the state. However, the surplus of efficient hospitals should not be taxed to subsidize inefficient hospitals. In other words, efficient hospitals should not be paid less simply because their costs are less.

Chapter 19—All You Need To Know about Gifts, Trusts, and Taxes[*]

OVERVIEW

Hospital executives and board members who can intelligently discuss with potential donors the tax economics of charitable giving are better able to increase the flow of donated funds to their own hospitals. Careful planning can result in properly structured donations that reduce taxes paid by the donor, increase the donor's personal cash flow and increase donations to the hospital.

Qualified Gifts

A transfer of money or other property to a hospital is not always a tax-deductible contribution. Qualified gifts must meet certain qualifications including:

- If the hospital provides something of commensurate value in return for the contribution, no deduction is allowed to the donor.
- A gift must be complete and irrevocable.
- The receipt by a hospital of a gift that requires the occurrence of some precedent event before the gift becomes effective yields a current tax deduction to the donor only in the limited case of deferred gifts discussed below.

---

[*]Source: Reprinted from Albert W. Herman, "Tax Economics of Charitable Giving: Pointers for the Hospital and Donor," *Topics in Health Care Financing,* Winter 1980, with permission of Aspen Systems Corporation.

- No deduction is allowed for a gift of services to the hospital no matter how valuable those services may be.
- A tax deduction is allowed for the gift of an income interest to a hospital only if the transfer is made through a trust.

Types of Contributions

Two general types of charitable contributions may be made to a hospital: current, or outright, contributions in which the transfer of the property to the hospital is completed in the same year the tax deduction is claimed, and deferred gifts that result in a current income tax deduction even though the receipt of the property by the hospital must await the occurrence of some future event.

Current Giving

Current contributions usually consist of cash but may include appreciated property such as stock or real estate. The donor receives a current income tax deduction resulting in income tax savings in the year of the donation and the donor probably will pay a reduced estate tax by removing the property from his or her estate. The hospital benefits immediately by receiving the property for its own use.

While cash gifts are the simplest gifts to deal with, gifts of property may offer substantial tax benefits with prior planning by the prospective donor. With a gift of property, the deductible amount to the donor may be (a) the fair market value of the property at the date of the gift, (b) the cost or the basis of the property in the hands of the donor, or (c) the donor's cost plus 60 percent of the long-term gain that would have resulted had the property been sold.

Deferred Giving

In deferred giving, a donor receives an immediate tax deduction for the transfer of a future interest in property although the actual transfer is not consummated until some time in the future. Unlike a current gift, which yields a current deduction equal to the value of the property, the value of a deferred gift is divided into two parts—an income interest that the donor retains in the form of annuity and a remainder interest that passes to the hospital at some time in the future.

The present value of the remainder interest determines the amount of current contribution deductions to the donor. The older the income beneficiary, the less the anticipated income he or she would be expected to receive as an annuity and the greater the value of the contribution deduction.

Procedures for structuring deferred gifts are quite complex. Current law provides that no charitable contribution deduction will be allowed for income, estate or gift tax purposes for the value of a remainder interest unless transferred in trust or unless the remainder interest is in a personal residence or a farm.

With careful planning and consultation between the donor and the hospital and with assistance from accounting and legal counsel, a donor may receive substantial income and estate tax benefits as well as increase cash flow by making a deferred gift to a hospital.

TYPES OF GIFTS

Charitable Remainder Annuity Trust

A taxpayer donor creates a charitable annuity trust by transferring property to the trust, reserving an annuity for his or her lifetime, for the joint lives of spouses, for the lifetime of another or for a certain term of years. The retained income interest is fixed in advance as a percentage of the value of the property at the time of the gift.

To qualify, a charitable annuity trust must meet certain requirements:

- The trust must pay a fixed sum to at least one noncharitable beneficiary, who must be living at the time the trust is created.
- The amount paid cannot be less than 5 percent of the initial net fair market value of the contributed property.
- The fixed sum must be payable, at least annually, either for a term of years (but not more than 20) or for the life or lives of the noncharitable beneficiary or beneficiaries.
- On the death of the beneficiaries, the trust corpus must be transferred to or for the use of a qualified charitable organization or retained by the trust for such use.
- No additional contributions to an annuity trust are permitted after the initial contribution.

The principal advantage of an annuity trust is that the donor receives an immediate tax benefit from the charitable deduction for a portion of the amount put in the trust but continues to enjoy income in the form of an annuity from the property contributed. The annuity income is generally taxable to the donor or other beneficiary in the year of receipt.

An annuity trust also may increase a donor's cash flow.

Charitable Remainder Unitrust

The principal difference between an annuity trust and a unitrust lies in the computation of the annual annuity. With an annuity trust, the annual income interest is based on the value of the property on the date of the gift. With a unitrust, the retained income interest is determined to be a fixed percentage of the value of the property determined annually.

Although a unitrust generally must pay a fixed percentage of the annual net fair market value of its assets to the noncharitable beneficiary, the trust can be structured to distribute only the amount of the trust income received in a year when this income is less than the payment ordinarily required.

A donor may fund an annuity trust or a unitrust with tax-exempt securities that would pass to the hospital on the death of the donor. As long as the trust held the securities, the annual annuity income distributed to the beneficiary would be tax free.

Pooled Income Fund

A pooled income fund is an investment fund maintained by a tax-exempt organization that receives contributions from many donors who retain life income interests in the property they have contributed. On the death of a particular income beneficiary, his or her pro rata share of the trust assets is distributed to the hospital but the trust remains in existence for the benefit of the remaining beneficiaries and for future donors.

To qualify, a pooled income trust must meet certain requirements:

- The donor must transfer an irrevocable remainder interest in property to or for the use of an organization qualifying for the charitable deduction and retain an income interest for the life of one or more beneficiaries.
- The property transferred must be commingled with property transferred by other donors.
- The trust may receive only amounts received from gifts that meet the requirements for pooled income funds.
- The trust must be controlled by the exempt organization for which the remainder interest is contributed and cannot have a donor or a beneficiary of an income interest as a trustee.
- The income received each year by the income beneficiary must be determined by the rate of return earned by the trust for that year.

A principal advantage of the pooled income fund is that it allows hospitals to receive deferred contributions that otherwise would be too small to economically establish a separate unitrust or annuity trust. The pooled income fund also gives the donor access to the professional investment skills of the fund's managers. A donor who is concerned with preserving the corpus of the remainder trust so that it will pass intact to the charitable beneficiary may prefer a pooled income fund for making a gift, since the fund generally distributes only the income and does not invade corpus to make distributions to the income beneficiaries.

One disadvantage of a pooled income fund is that it cannot be used to secure tax-exempt income for the income beneficiary since a pooled income is prohibited from investing in tax-exempt securities. Also, a donor who wishes to retain an income interest for a term of years cannot use the pooled income fund since a lifetime interest must be retained.

Personal Residence or Farm

The Tax Reform Act of 1969 made specific provisions for tax deductions resulting from the contribution to charity of a remainder interest in a personal residence or a farm. The regulations provide that while the interest must be in a personal residence, it does not have to be the donor's principal residence. Vacation homes may qualify for this type of contribution deduction. Farms are defined to be land and improvements used for the production of crops, fruit or other agricultural products or for the raising of livestock. In this arrangement, the taxpayer contributes a remainder interest in his or her home or farm to the hospital, retaining a life estate for donor and spouse permitting them to live in the home for the remainder of their lives. Following the death of the life beneficiaries, title to the property passes to the hospital.

Charitable Lead Trusts

Somewhat the reverse of deferred giving, a charitable lead trust involves the transfer of an immediate income interest to the hospital while the remainder interest remains with the donor or is transferred to a noncharitable donee of the donor's choice.

There are two uses of a lead trust in tax-planning programs. In the first instance, the donor receives an immediate income tax deduction for the actuarially determined value of the income stream that passes to the hospital. The donor is treated as the owner of the trust and the annual income of the trust is taxed to the donor even though it is distributed to charity. This permits a donor to realize an immediate tax deduction in high-income years with some income reportable in later years when the donor may be in a lower tax bracket. The donor may fund this type of lead trust with tax-exempt securities that would result in the same immediate tax deduction with no taxable income to be reported by the donor in the future. The gift of an income interest is for the use of a hospital and thus subject to the deduction limitation with no carryover of unused deductions to future years.

The second use of the lead trust is in a program of lifetime giving or an estate planning program in which the donor purposely avoids a current income tax deduction by structuring the trust so that he or she is not its owner. Although the donor foregoes the current income tax deduction, the future trust income is not taxable to the donor and the trust corpus is still distributed to noncharitable beneficiaries of his or her choice, typically a child or grandchild. In this case the value of the gift subject to tax or the value of a decedent's property subject to estate tax is reduced by the present value of the income stream that passes to the hospital.

Charitable Gift Annuity

With a charitable gift annuity, a donor actually sells his or her property to the hospital in exchange for a lifetime annuity. The donor receives estate tax benefits from this arrangement by removing the property from the taxable estate and by the fact that no amount of the annuity is includible in the estate since it was a lifetime interest only. The donor also receives an immediate income tax benefit from a gift annuity.

Using actuarial tables prepared by the conference on Gift Annuities for this purpose, the annuity is structured so that the value of the annuity retained by the donor is less than the value of the property transferred to the hospital. The difference in value represents a tax-deductible contribution by the donor in the year of the gift. The gain on the sale is taxed to the donor over the estimated lifetime as he collects the annuity.

SETTING UP A FOUNDATION*

Alert governing boards and managements of hospitals are turning increasingly to the charitable foundation, in a form sometimes referred to as a "hospital development foundation," organized and operating externally to a hospital but with some linkage or "relatedness" to the hospital, as a mechanism to encourage the growth of alternative financial resources to support health care delivery, and to protect those resources from erosion.

A foundation may take the form of a charitable trust, or even an unincorporated association, but increasingly foundations are organized as charitable corporations under the nonprofit corporation statutes of the state in which they are incorporated.

If a charitable foundation is to serve, or at least reasonably hope to serve, its intended purposes of attracting philanthropic support for health care, protecting contributed funds and their investment from a hospital's liabilities, and maximizing the financial benefits provided to health care by avoiding wasteful offsets in the reimbursement or rate-setting process, it must be carefully structured. If the foundation is structured so that it is clearly controlled by the hospital or has the hospital as its sole beneficiary, it will be considered "related" to the particular hospital. This relatedness may seriously affect the foundation's ability to hold its assets safe from the financial pressures discussed above.

If it is intended that the foundation be treated for all purposes as unrelated, the foundation should not solicit funds in the name of or for a particular hospital. No difficulty should result from a foundation's in fact, but without prearrangement, making most of its expenditures in such a way as to supplement the available financial resources of a particular hospital—the essential factor is genuine independence of the foundation to determine for what purpose its expenditures will be made. Disbursements should be made, when appropriate, for the benefit of other charitable organizations and activities in the community in addition to the hospital.

While the hospital may not dominate the foundation, e.g., by appointing its governing board, the foundation board may almost certainly include some (less than a majority) members or former members of the governing board of a hospital. The lesser the percentage of hospital-related board members, however, the more likely that unrelatedness will be found to exist.

If a hospital has existing investments and/or endowment funds (whether owned by the hospital or by a supporting foundation), and the hospital wishes to establish an independent foundation to realize the reimbursement and other

---

*Source: Reprinted from John J. Whitney, "Hospital Philanthropy: Strengthening the Financial Base of Nonprofit Hospitals," *Health Care Management Review,* Spring 1981, with permission of Aspen Systems Corporation.

resource protection objectives previously discussed, it should carefully consider:

- whether, if existing assets are turned over to the new "independent" foundation, such a transfer (in addition to its obvious financial reporting effects) might be deemed to demonstrate hospital control or domination to such an extent that the objectives sought will be unlikely to be achieved;
- whether a transfer of substantial hospital assets to the "independent" foundation will, under the law of the state in which the hospital and foundation exist, in fact remove such assets from potential creditor claims, or on the contrary, in the event they become mingled with other foundation assets, subject the foundation's independently generated assets to unnecessary risk;
- whether state law limitations, bond or loan agreement restrictions, or donor restrictions, will permit such a transfer, or permit it only upon express conditions;
- whether, as to investments not derived from gifts or grants, addition of such investments should preferably be made to the hospital's funded depreciation account (to the extent not already fully funded), in order to provide at least partial shelter for such assets.

In general, the greatest opportunity for obtaining favorable reimbursement and rate-setting regulation immunity for investments and endowment, as well as maximizing resource protection from other risks, lies in the establishment of a new independent development foundation, without a transfer of existing hospital assets to the foundation, except modest assets needed for start-up purposes, which should, if possible, be assets derived from gifts rather than from reimbursement sources.

PART V
CAPITAL FORMATION, EXPENDITURES, AND CONSTRUCTION

Chapter 20—Capital Formation

The procedure for borrowing funds and repaying debt has never been a simple one for hospitals. In today's climate, however, it is even more intricate, with considerable attention required for coping with the nuances. With this in mind, this chapter presents those factors which can affect the hospital's present and future capacity for financing and debt repayment—the changed direction of attitudes and trends; the policies of government intervention and rate regulation; the different nature of financial source alternatives; the actual cost of borrowing; and the technique of calculating repayment ability.

OVERVIEW*

In general, most hospitals to date have been able to obtain the capital they needed for approved hospital projects. Supporting this view are the following factors:
(a) Hospital occupancy rates in most States are at their highest level since 1960, despite the increase in average hospital size over the period.
(b) Capital financing alternatives at the State, local and Federal levels have expanded.
(c) Favorable treatment under most third-party reimbursement systems are afforded to the payment of all borrowing costs with no regard to interest rate.

(d) A generally low failure rate has prevailed in the hospital industry to date, although this may be changing in some economically depressed areas.
(e) Investors tend to view certificate of need programs as a method of protecting their investment.
(f) There has been an increase in investor interest in tax-exempt bonds as rising incomes and profitability increase the number of investors who can benefit from this form of tax sheltered income.

Problems Ahead

Despite these conditions, a number of other factors suggest that the future may not be so rosy. For one thing, hospitals may be forced to expand still further their reliance upon debt to finance construction projects. Hospitals have gradually decreased their reliance upon government grants and philanthropy while increasingly turning to debt financing. With the declining amount of Federal grant funds available, and the continuing decline in philanthropy, hospitals will be able to finance new projects only through internal operations (either by increasing the rate of depreciation or by generating a surplus over operating expenses) or through additional borrowing. Because it is unlikely that hospitals will be able to generate higher surpluses in the current and expected regulatory environment, the pressure for more borrowing and more frequent modernizations to raise depreciation levels will increase.

---

*Source: *Capital Formation in Health Care Facilities,* Health Resources Studies, DHEW, March 1979, Pub. No. (HRA) 79-14527.

A second factor is that hospital operating margins are more likely to fall rather than rise in the future because of the broader use of hospital rate regulation programs. Over two-thirds of all hospital revenues in 1976 were obtained from sources that either provide no operating margin (cost-based systems) or that regulate payments in excess of expenses (prospective rate systems). This trend is likely to continue as more States adopt these programs and as existing programs become more stringent.

A third factor is that the ability of hospitals to raise capital has become more heavily dependent upon the status of local municipal capital markets. There are several reasons for this. If local government cannot raise capital at reasonable rates, this may jeopardize State and local participation in Medicaid and other programs for indigents, thus threatening hospital revenues. State hospital authorities that issue general or special obligation bonds, or that pool hospital revenue bond issues to reduce risk, may find low acceptance for their issues if State budget deficits or low bond ratings persist. Also, States themselves may be forced to rely more heavily on municipal bonds to finance essential operation if income and property tax revenues come under increasing pressures. Thus, hospitals may have to turn to other sources of capital to obtain the long-term debt financing they require for modernization.

Sources of Capital Formation

Medicaid and Medicare reimbursement is being used to finance capital investment. These funds can be used for capital purposes in two major ways:

1. A prospective approach through accumulation of reserves to finance future investment in capital facilities; and
2. A retrospective approach through which operating funds are used to pay interest and retire debt incurred when purchasing capital. This latter method is rapidly becoming the method of choice for most hospitals.

In this latest stage of capital development, long-term debt is now equal to approximately one-fourth of the total assets of short-term hospitals. If the requirements for debt repayment are not met by the various reimbursement formulas of Medicare, Medicaid, Blue Cross, or other third-party payers, hospitals face real or potential financial trouble. The specifics of reimbursement have become vital to capital development for health facilities, as well as for operations.

Debt financing by 1976 had become the major source of funds for construction. For non-Federal, short-term hospitals, debt financing had grown from 39 percent of total construction funds in 1968 to 68 percent, an increase of 74 percent. (See Figure 20-1.)

Within the sources of debt financing, tax-exempt bonds issued by State and local bonding authorities are the largest single source of capital for construction projects. In 1976, tax-exempt bond issues provided 34 percent of the total sources of funds for hospitals according to data from the American Hospital Association.

It is interesting to note that only about 55 percent of the capital formed for a given project actually goes for construction costs. Some goes for financial reserves (usually to pay interest during construction or to retire some principal) and to meet the institution's working capital needs (these two total about 25 percent); some goes for equipment and other purchases (about 12 percent) and some goes to refinance other institutional debt (about 8 percent). (See Figure 20-2.)

While the demand for care continues to be strong and exhibits steady growth, the major growth of hospital services appears to be in the nature of specific services rather than their volume. Whether characterized as services with higher quality or greater intensity, physicians appear to be recommending (and their patients expecting) a different type of service than before, and approvals of insurance payments for these services have increased accordingly.

Trends in hospital plant assets indicate that many hospitals are increasing the capital intensity of their care. This can occur by such things as expanding outpatient facilities, upgrading the quality of intensive care service, modernizing facilities more frequently, and employing new technological innovations, with treatment rooms devoted exclusively to the new equipment purchased.

Current Federal Interventions in Capital Formation

The Federal Government has at least three major areas of influence that affect the capital fi-

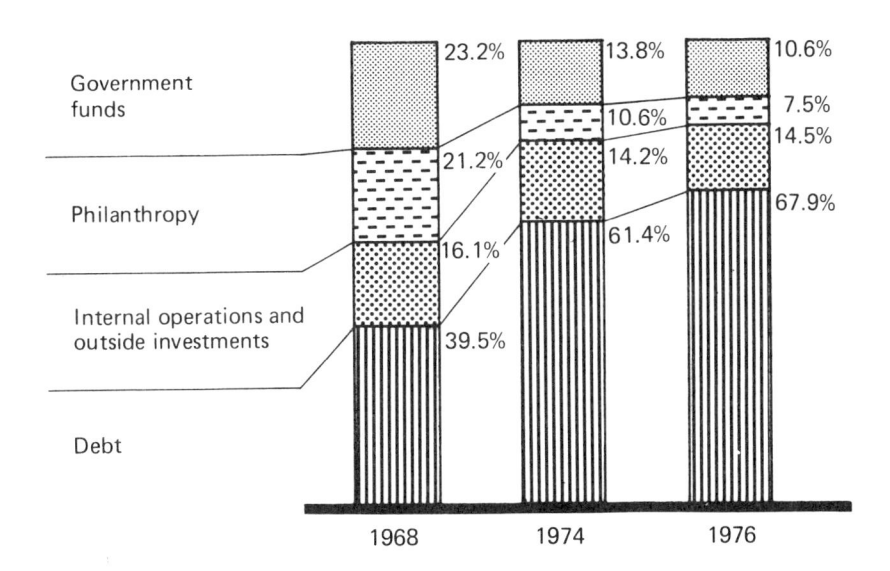

Figure 20-1 Trends of capital formation (in percentages)

	1968	1974	1976
Government funds	23.2%	13.8%	10.6%
Philanthropy		10.6%	7.5%
Internal operations and outside investments	21.2%	14.2%	14.5%
	16.1%		
Debt	39.5%	61.4%	67.9%

Figure 20-2 Uses of new capital

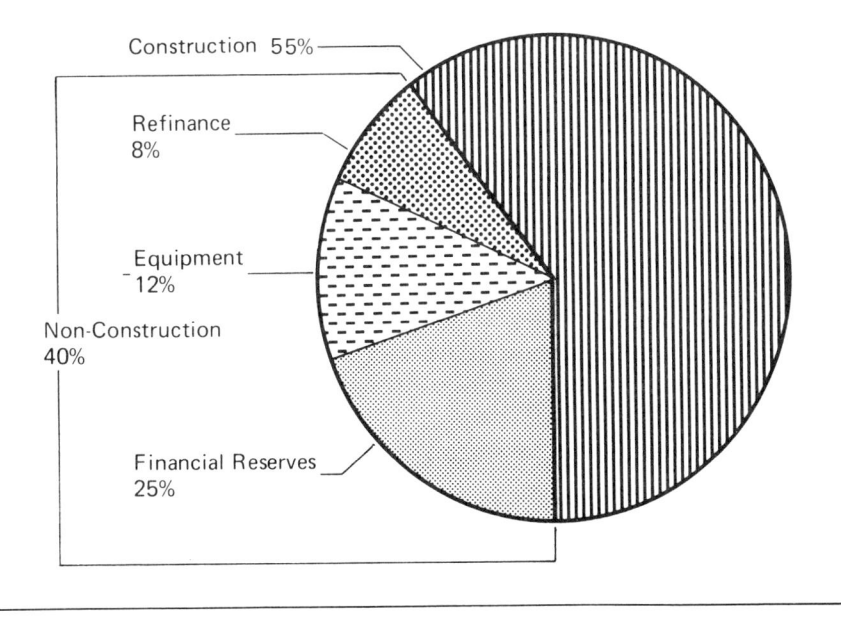

- Construction 55%
- Refinance 8%
- Equipment 12%
- Financial Reserves 25%
- Non-Construction 40%

---

nancing of health facilities: Medicare and Medicaid reimbursement policies, health planning and regulation, and health facility construction subsidies.

1. Reimbursement Policies

By providing that depreciation and interest are allowable expenses, the reimbursement system has established a mechanism whereby hospitals can use future revenues to finance capital needs, by turning to debt financing.

Guaranteed reimbursement for interest and depreciation provides hospitals with substantial security for previous capital investments. By allowing full payment for interest expenses, regardless of the interest rate, the hospital's sensitivity to interest rates in making future capital investment decisions is reduced. This is in contrast to most industries that reduce borrowing during periods of high interest rates.

Where hospitals employ level debt service arrangements for repayment of debt, cost-based reimbursement systems generally provide high rates of cash flow in the early years and low rates in the later years, creating powerful incentives for reinvestment or refinancing before the crossover point in order to increase hospital cash flow. These actions increase the total capital costs borne by the insurance system over the longer term.

From another point of view, hospital groups contend that cost-based reimbursement fails to recognize a return on equity. This form of reimbursement makes it difficult to accumulate internal reserves, and also discourages hospitals from investing equity in projects. Depreciation, computed on the basis of historical cost, is inadequate to meet the cost of replacing facilities and equipment.

Depreciation payments under Medicare/Medicaid have made a significant contribution to capital financing. According to a Bureau of Health Insurance sample of participating hospitals in 1974, about 6.9 percent of Medicaid allowable costs were represented by interest (1.5 percent) and depreciation (5.4 percent). In 1977, Medicare expenditures for hospital care were $15.5 billion. If the same proportion of expenditures continued as in the 1974 sample, Medicare would have paid $1.1 billion for depreciation and interest in 1977.

2. Health Planning and Regulation

The National Health Planning and Resources Development Act gives health planning agencies at State and local levels major responsibilities in determining the need for health facilities.

Through the certificate of need provisions of the planning law and Section 1122 (of the Social Security Act), the agencies also are to review proposals for new facilities and major capital expenditures for equipment and services to ensure that only those found to be needed are offered or developed within the State. With full designation, some of the agencies also are beginning to review existing institutional health services for appropriateness.

A recent survey by the American Health Planning Association found that the health planning agencies turned down some $1.8 billion in capital expenditure projects out of a total of $7 billion considered.

3. Federal Subsidies

While the decline of funding under the Hill-Burton program has removed a major source of Federal financing, the Federal Government continues to subsidize hospital construction through a variety of programs located outside HEW, principally in the Departments of Agriculture, Housing and Urban Development, and Commerce. HEW has worked out agreements with some of the programs, insuring that construction will be within the limits of the National Guidelines for Health Planning (specifically the 4 beds/1000 population and 80 percent occupancy rate restrictions). Other programs, however, operate independently of such requirements.

The principal Federal programs involved in health facility financing include:

- Federal Housing Administration (FHA), National Housing Act, Section 242, which provides mortgage insurance to nonprofit private and proprietary hospitals.
- FHA, National Housing Act, Section 232, which provides mortgage insurance for nursing homes.
- Farmers Home Administration (FmHA) which provides low interest direct loans for the construction of community facilities, including health facilities, to communities of less than 10,000.
- Small Business Administration, which provides direct loans and which guarantees loans for proprietary hospitals and other health care facilities.

Although most of the projects funded by these Federal assistance programs are subject to State certificate of need requirements, they may still add to excess capacity if the State CON process is not tight enough. In addition, by making capital available or less costly, they add pressure for new capital investment.

Fund Raising*

Not for profit health care facilities have long relied on contributions as a source of capital financing. Though the dollar amount of contributed capital continues to rise, contributions as a percent of total capital needs are decreasing. Yet that continues to be an important source for health care facility financing needs. Contributions, in many cases, provide the equity portion of a capital project needed before debt can be obtained (i.e., a lender may be willing to finance 80 percent of a particular project if contributed capital could supply the remaining 20 percent).

The services of a fund-raising firm should be used if warranted. Before a firm is retained, however, there should be clear understanding of the fees to be paid, the goals to be accomplished, the methodology to be employed, records to be kept, and reports to be made. A specific fee—stated in dollars, not as a percentage of funds raised—should be agreed upon. Those of the firm's expenses that are to be reimbursed by the hospital should be delineated. The timing of the payment of fees and expenses also should be established.

The special fund-raising program has four distinct phases: (1) the feasibility study, (2) the program organization, (3) the solicitation, and (4) the follow-up. A major decision to be made by the governing board is whether to use pledge forms, which are legally enforceable against the donor, rather than cards, which merely state the pledge in terms of a present intention.

Before undertaking a special purpose fund-raising program, the hospital should realize that the program will cost money and take time; that the actual solicitation will be done by volunteers such as trustees, medical staff, and others; and that consideration must be given to planning the time required for the study of feasibility, organizational activity, active solicitation, and follow-up. Follow-up alone could require from six months to several years.

LONG TERM DEBT FINANCING

Credit Rating Criteria*

There are three basic criteria used by institutional lenders to evaluate hospital credit and viability—these are debt service coverage, leverage and management. The analysis of debt service coverage is the fundamental determination of the hospital's capacity to repay the loan. The leverage is the indication of underlying equity support of the borrower, and the establishment of creditor priority. The analysis of the management is the only determining factor of the prospect the hospital has of being able to meet future challenges and repay the loan.

It may be worth noting that the combination of these factors is the most significant contributor to the credit rating of the hospital. The higher the coverage the better. The lower the debt to total capitalization ratio the better. Also the higher the debt to total capitalization ratio becomes the heavier the reliance will be on a higher coverage of debt service.

Financing Alternatives**

In the past, debt financing was not considered a viable means of obtaining the funds needed to expand the services of health care institutions because banks and other lenders considered these institutions to be highly specialized, high risk investments that would be difficult to salvage in the event of default.

In today's capital markets, however, many lenders consider health care institutions to be among the safest forms of investment. This change in attitude is due primarily to the implementation of the Medicare and Medicaid programs and, more recently, to federal health planning legislation. By significantly increasing the percentage of patient service revenues flowing to health care institutions directly from the federal government, Medicare and Medicaid have provided health care institutions with a stable

---

*Source: Reprinted from *Capital Projects for Health Care Facilities* by W. Thomas Berriman, William J. Essick, Jr., and Peter Bentivegna, with permission of Aspen Systems Corporation, © 1976.

*Source: Reprinted from Frederick R. Blume, "Hospital Debt Management," *Topics in Health Care Financing,* Fall 1976, with permission of Aspen Systems Corporation.

**Source: Reprinted from *Financial and Managerial Control: A Health Care Perspective* by Edward J. Lusk and Janice Gannon Lusk, with permission of Aspen Systems Corporation, © 1979.

and dependable revenue source that forms a basis for loan security. Federal health planning legislation has provided added security for institutional lenders by requiring approval to health care institutions before any major capital improvements are undertaken. Many investors view this planning legislation as a federal franchising program which protects the institution from future competition.

The new attitude toward health care debt financing is one of the reasons that long-term debt has become the single dominant source of capital financing in health care institutions today. A variety of debt financing alternatives are available to health care institutions, including tax-exempt revenue bonds, Federal Housing Administration (FHA) insured mortgage loans with a Government National Mortgage Association (GNMA) guarantee, conventional mortgage financing, and public taxable bonds.

Selecting the Appropriate Financing Alternative

Many factors affect the selection of the appropriate financing alternative.

The selection of the most appropriate financing alternative must be based on a detailed understanding of the institution's financial and management priorities and a knowledge of the relationship between these priorities and the available methods of financing. (See Table 20-1.)

Major Sources of Debt Financing*

Tax-Exempt Revenue Bonds

Tax-exempt revenue bonds (see Table 20-2) have two basic features: the interest payments to the bondholders are not subject to federal income taxation, and the bonds are secured by the *gross* revenues of the organization being financed. These bonds are issued on behalf of tax-exempt institutions by a state finance authority, a municipal finance authority established by a county or city government, or the institution itself, under Section 63-20 of the Internal Revenue Code. In addition to the basic features, in most states the interest income on the bonds is also exempt from state income taxation if the bondholders live in the state in which the bonds are issued. Furthermore, in many cases, the bondholders are able to maintain a first mortgage on the institution's assets as additional security.

FHA-Insured Mortgage Loans with GNMA Guarantees

FHA-insured mortgage loans with GNMA guarantees are mortgage loans that are insured primarily by the FHA and have a secondary guarantee provided by the GNMA. (See Table 20-3.) This double federal insurance lowers the risk inherent in this type of financing and aids in attracting investors who are willing to receive a lower interest rate for their funds. FHA-insured mortgage loans with GNMA guarantees may be obtained by proprietary, as well as nonprofit, institutions.

Conventional Mortgage Financing

Under a conventional mortgage, the investor (usually a savings bank) agrees to convey funds to the institution in exchange for the title to the facility (including plant, major equipment, and land) which is pledged as security until the mortgage is repaid. The expertise provided by an investment banker is extremely important in this type of financing because lending policies, interest rates, and attitudes toward health care institutions vary among institutional lenders. Although this financing technique is not designed specifically for health care institutions, the investment banker often can negotiate an agreement that makes conventional mortgages a viable debt financing alternative.

This financing alternative is generally only available to highly rated, well endowed, and well known institutions. (See Table 20-4.)

Public Taxable Bonds

Public taxable bond financing has two basic features: (1) bond indentures are issued to the public in exchange for cash, and (2) the interest payments on the bonds are subject to federal, state, and local income taxation. This type of financing traditionally was the method most widely used by health care institutions. However, the advent of new financing techniques designed specifically for health care institutions has caused a

---

*Source: Reprinted from *Financial and Managerial Control: A Health Care Perspective* by Edward J. Lusk and Janice Gannon Lusk, with permission of Aspen Systems Corporation, © 1979.

Table 20-1 Factors Affecting the Selection of Appropriate Financing Alternative

Financial Community Factors
Governmental health care policies
Financial condition of the nation's cities and municipalities
Institutional investment policies and attitudes
General supply and demand for investment funds

Requirements of the Financing Alternative (See Appendix 5-B)
Term to maturity
Interest rate
Prepayment provisions
Refinancing provisions
Default provisions
Additional debt restrictions
Working capital restrictions
Funding requirements (debt service reserve, depreciation, sinking fund, etc.)

Institutional and Management Restrictions
Board of managers' policies
Management attitudes toward government involvement in construction programs and institutional operations
Future borrowing requirements
Equity requirements

Other Financial Considerations
Institutional management
Financial position of the institution
Results of feasibility study
Results of bond ratings (see Appendix 5-A)
Availability of working capital
Availability of government grants, guarantees, and subsidies
Availability of philanthropic contributions
Size of financing

Timing Factors
Length of time required to obtain funds
Length of construction period

---

decline in the use of public taxable bonds as a means of debt financing.

The advantages of public taxable bond financing are not overwhelming. (See Table 20-5.)

Refunding Long-Term Debts[*]

Reasons To Consider Refunding

Two benefits can be gained from an early redemption of long-term indebtedness—reduced annual interest expense and relief from burdensome indenture provisions. The opportunities to effect a refunding include:

- decline in prevailing interest rate levels below the interest rate on the outstanding debt;
- improvement in hospital's creditworthiness;
- change in financing vehicle from taxable to tax-exempt bonds;
- concern over future money market conditions in light of an impending "balloon" loan payment; and
- incompatability of existing loan provisions with the planned activities of the hospital.

---

[*]Source: Reprinted from Daniel M. Cain and R. Neal Gilbert, "Refinancing and Refunding Options," *Topics in Health Care Financing,* Fall 1978, with permission of Aspen Systems Corporation.

Table 20-2 Advantages and Disadvantages of Tax-Exempt Revenue Bonds

Advantages	Disadvantages
1. Interest costs are usually 1–2½ percent lower than other methods of financing.	1. When the bonds are issued under a state or local authority, title to the facility may have to be transferred to the authority during the life of the issue.
2. The term of the loan can be as long as 30 years.	
3. Since the loan amount is determined by the ability of the facility to generate revenue, up to 100 percent of total project costs might be financed.	2. If a nonprofit institution issues its own tax-exempt bonds under a state's nonprofit corporation statute, Internal Revenue Service guidelines require that the institution pass title to a municipality at the end of the term of the bonds. (However, operational control would remain with the institution.)
4. Bond proceeds are available before construction, thus eliminating the need for interim construction financing.	
5. Interest payments can be capitalized during construction.	3. A comprehensive feasibility study executed by a recognized consulting firm is required.
6. Tax-exempt bond issues are usually structured with open-ended provisions that allow for issuance of additional bonds, provided certain levels of financial performance are maintained.	4. Financing expenses, including the feasibility study, bond counsel, other legal fees, and printing costs generally are higher than in some other methods of financing.
7. Existing debt usually can be refinanced.	
8. Tax-exempt bond issues often can be privately placed.	5. A debt-service reserve fund, usually equaling one year's average principal and interest payment may be required. (The reserve fund, however, is used to pay off the last maturing bond principal and earns interest income.)
9. Principal repayment schedules may be structured so that the principal payments in the early years of the loan are reduced. This results in the loan being tailored to the institution's ability to repay. First repayment is normally scheduled for one or two years after completion of the project.	
	6. A bond discount, typically between two and three percent, is required.
	7. Prepayment of the bonds usually cannot be made during the first ten years of the issue; thereafter, the bonds are callable at a premium decreasing from approximately 3 percent to zero in the 11th through 15th years.
	8. A bond rating usually is required. Investors require an "A" rating before accepting tax-exempt revenue bonds.

Constraints

The constraining factors to frequent refundings, however, are twofold. First, bond purchasers commit capital to long-term fixed interest rates investments only if protected against prepayment for a given time period. The specific requirement of buyers will determine their willingness to trade off higher yield for reduced refunding protection. Insurance companies may be the most demanding in terms of refunding protection while individuals tend to be more responsive to yield.

The second constraint is that refunding programs are expensive to implement. Besides fees paid to investment bankers, attorneys and various consultants, a hospital is usually required to

Table 20-3 Advantages and Disadvantages of FHA-Insured Mortgage Loans with GNMA Guarantee(s)

Advantages	Disadvantages
1. Loan-to-value ratio can be as high as 90 percent.	1. Processing of the FHA application can be time-consuming.
2. The value of the land, existing buildings, and major movable equipment may satisfy the institution's equity requirement.	2. Construction must conform to FHA/HEW standards.
3. Most preparation and application costs can be included in eligible costs.	3. Construction labor costs can be higher than under other methods of financing because of strict government regulations.
4. The full faith and credit guarantee of the U.S. government allows the institution to secure an attractive interest rate.	4. If the FHA interest rate is below current money market rates, the institution must discount the mortgage to bring the yield to the investor up to market levels.
5. The GNMA Construction Loan Certificate enables the institution to obtain both construction and permanent financing in a single package at the same interest rate.	5. The institution must pay an annual mortgage insurance premium of 0.5 percent of the unamortized principal amount.
6. If the institution is undergoing an expansion or modernization program, eligible debt can include refinancing of existing debt.	6. The institution must pay front-end inspection and filing fees totaling 0.8 percent of the principal amount.
7. The term of the loan can be as much as 25 years after completion of construction.	7. Many investment bankers involved with this program lack expertise, or are not capable, in all aspects of the FHA/GNMA program.
8. Prepayment of 15 percent of the original principal amount is permitted in a calendar year without penalty. In addition, the loan can be structured to allow for prepayment in excess of this amount at any time for a negotiated penalty.	

pay some type of early prepayment penalty on the existing debt.

Mechanics of Bond Refunding

Several options exist for refunding. Depending on money market conditions, hospitals can substitute one debt instrument for another, conduct open-market bond redemption programs or initiate a bond refunding program.

The sale of new bonds where the proceeds are applied to the redemption of outstanding debt obligations is referred to as a refunding issue. The security description would then read "Revenue Refunding Bonds" or "Mortgage Refunding Bonds." Outstanding bond issues containing provisions against early redemption to a date not yet reached (including final maturity) can also be refunded through a technique referred to as advance bond refunding. The objective of refunding the outstanding bonds prior to the first call date is usually to exploit favorable current market conditions and thus "lock in" a guaranteed savings. An advance refunding also provides the opportunity to modify indenture constraints that now or with the passage of time may adversely affect hospital management.

To effect an advance refunding generally requires the defeasance (annulment) of the existing bond indenture so that the hospital assets or revenues become available as security for the investors in the refunding bonds issue. A straight refunding merely entails notification as required under the loan agreement and payment through refunding proceeds of the outstanding obligations.

Table 20-4 Advantages and Disadvantages of Conventional Mortgage Financing

Advantages	Disadvantages
1. This method takes the shortest amount of time to implement.	1. The loan-to-value ratio usually is lower than that of other financing techniques. Therefore, the institution must contribute a high percentage of equity or utilize alternative methods of financing.
2. This method of financing allows the institution the greatest amount of flexibility to structure a financing package most suitable to its financial priorities.	2. The loan term may be shorter than the terms of alternative methods of financing.
3. The institution does not have to conform to DHEW/FHA construction standards.	3. The loan covenants usually are more restrictive than the covenants under other methods of financing.
4. Flexible interest rates obviate the need for substantial discounting.	4. The interest rate usually will be higher than the interest rates of alternative methods of financing.
5. Since the interest rate is negotiated well before closing, the institution can predict total costs more accurately and easily.	5. Funds may be difficult to obtain when money markets are tight, or if the hospital is located in an unattractive area.
6. A feasibility study frequently is not required, printing expenses are reduced or avoided, and legal fees usually are less expensive than with other alternatives.	
7. This method does not require many of the reserve funds required in a tax-exempt issue.	

Table 20-5 Advantages and Disadvantages of Public Taxable Bonds

Advantages	Disadvantages
1. Traditionally, the prepayment provisions have been more liberal than the prepayment provisions of any other financing alternative.	1. Traditionally, the loan-to-loan value ratio has been less than 60 percent. However, greater reliance on the revenue-generating capacity of the institution is affecting this ratio.
2. Generally, the stated interest rate will be lower than the interest rate associated with a private placement.	2. If high ratio financing is involved, an extensive feasibility study is required.
3. These issues normally are structured with an open-ended provision which allows for the issuance of additional debt, provided that certain financial performance levels are maintained.	3. Usually, the loan term is shorter than the terms for alternative methods of financing.
4. The effect of serialized maturities frequently reduces the net effective cost to the institution.	4. Front-end fees, including the underwriters' spread and legal and printing expenses, are substantial. As a result, the net effective cost to the institution usually is higher than alternative methods of financing.
5. The institution does not have to conform to DHEW/FHA construction standards.	5. The preparation and placement of the issue can be time consuming.
6. Bond proceeds are available before construction, alleviating the need for interim construction financing.	

SHORT AND INTERMEDIATE TERM FINANCING

The major distinction between short and intermediate term financing is obviously the maturity life of the loan. Short term financing is generally self liquidating and is retired within one year while intermediate term financing is of a longer maturity, generally one to ten years. From a balance sheet perspective, all short term financing would be included in the current liabilities section while intermediate term financing would be in the long term liabilities section.

Short-Term Financing Sources*

Short term financing has not received much attention in the health care financing literature, although the use of short term financing by health care organizations appears to be growing.

Trade credit as a source of short term financing is a topic extensively discussed in many introductory financial management texts. Interest in this subject has recently waned largely because of the decline in the number of firms selling merchandise with explicitly stated credit terms. The major topic of discussion in trade credit financing was usually the calculation of the effective interest rate. Generally speaking, the optimal payment points were (1) the last day of the discount period, (2) the due date, or (3) some later date, if the effect of delinquent payment would not adversely effect the purchaser's credit rating. Payment made later than the due date is referred to as "stretching accounts payable."

Salaries and wages or other accrued expenses is another source of short term financing that has not been frequently discussed. To the extent that employees can be paid on a monthly as opposed to a biweekly basis, a rather significant amount of short term financing could be obtained with little or no cost. For example, in a hospital with a six million dollar labor budget, the payment of wages and salaries on a monthly as opposed to a biweekly basis will create approximately 230,000 dollars in additional short term financing for the institution.

Deferred revenue shown as a current liability usually results from advance payment by patients. This is a common practice in some hospitals, especially for self-pay patients. It is a very low cost source of short term financing, but the institution must carefully weigh the social merit of such a course of action. Finally, it is possible that short term deferred revenue could result from an overpayment by one or more third party payers. If interim rates can be set at levels greater than expected costs with no adverse effects on future interim rates, this source of short term financing should be used.

Short term bank loans are probably the most important source of short term financing, not because they are necessarily the largest source of short term financing but rather because they are usually the most discretionary. As a result, management can exert greater control over both the timing and magnitude of this source of short term financing. Ideally, short term bank loan decisions should automatically flow from the cash budget. Perhaps the most common way of extending credit is via a line of credit. A line of credit is very simply an agreement between a borrower and a bank specifying the maximum amount of credit the bank will grant the borrower during a given time period, usually one year. Negotiations for a new line of credit often take place after the bank has received a new audited set of financial statements from the borrower. For example, an institution with a fiscal year end of December 31 might negotiate a new line of credit in late March. It should be stressed that a line of credit is not a binding agreement between the two parties. If the bank so chooses, it does not have to extend credit to the borrower in the amount stated in the line of credit.

Another unsecured form of short term financing is a *revolving credit agreement*. This is a binding legal commitment as contrasted with the line of credit. Under this financing agreement, the bank commits itself to loan to the borrower a maximum amount for a specified period of time; in many cases this may be more than one year. The binding nature of the agreement is linked to the consideration involved in this contract. Usually, the borrower commits himself to paying, in addition to the rate of interest on borrowed funds, a rate of interest on the unborrowed por-

---

*Source: Reprinted from "Short and Intermediate Term Financing," *Financial Management of Health Care Facilities*, ed. William O. Cleverley, with permission of Aspen Systems Corporation, © 1976.

tion. It is also commonplace for many banks to require the borrower to maintain a compensating balance with the bank to reduce the bank's risk and also raise the effective rate of interest earned by the bank. Many banks are moving away from compensating balance requirements towards full cost pricing of individual bank services.

Intermediate Term Financing

Intermediate term financing shows up in the long term debt section of the balance sheet. There are two major classes of intermediate term financing applicable to hospitals: (1) Bank Term Loans and (2) Leases.

Bank Term Loans. There is very little literature describing the utilization of bank term loans in the health care industry. What there is in the general financial management area focuses on the effective cost of restrictions imposed in the loan indenture. For example, many indentures will stipulate that certain levels of working capital are to be maintained, or that limitations on levels of capital expenditures will be imposed, or that future issues of debt financing will be subject to some restrictions.

Leasing is another source of intermediate term financing especially useful in the acquisition of capital equipment. The use of leasing in the health care industry has been growing at a rapid rate, as of late, and is widely reported on in the literature.

Leases may be characterized from an accounting perspective on the basis of ownership. If the lessee is construed to be the effective owner of the asset, the lease must be capitalized. This means that an asset and a liability are created and placed on the firm's financial statements. If the lessee is not construed to be the owner of the acquired assets, there is no need for lease capitalization, but payment patterns for the lease must be shown in the footnotes to the financial statements. The capitalization issue is important for health care organizations in two ways. First, lease capitalization will increase the proportion of total debt financing and thus have an effect on the firm's ability to acquire additional debt financing. Second, capitalization of leases can also have an important effect on the nature and amount of reimbursement obtained under many cost reimbursement formulae used in this industry.

Tax Exempt Financing*

Many hospitals have moved away from the traditional forms of financing—mortgages, government grants and philanthropy—and turned increasingly to tax-exempt bond financing. The trend toward tax-exempt financing has been accompanied by an increasingly complex legal structure to accommodate the concept of conduit financing (i.e., through a hospital finance authority). (See Table 20-6.)

The proverbial "typical" hospital used to finance its construction program with either a conventional mortgage from an institutional lender or through a note issue with an underwriting firm that would, in turn, market or "retail" the debt in small units to the public. However, tax-exempt financing requires an additional participant to endow the borrowing with tax exemption since not-for-profit hospitals do not have the power to issue tax-exempt securities. (See Figure 20-3.)

Tax-exempt hospital financing did not really begin to flower until the Connecticut Legislature created the Health and Educational Facilities Authority and empowered it to issue tax-exempt securities to finance the construction of hospitals or higher educational facilities. The concept of conduit financing, "on behalf of" private not-for-profit hospitals, began a long evolutionary process that is still being refined today.

The essence of security in tax-exempt hospital financing is the ability of the hospital to generate revenues and is not solely based upon the value of the physical assets. Accordingly, the legal instruments securing such debt are designed primarily to secure an unquestioned first lien on the hospital's revenue stream and to insulate that revenue stream from future claims.

Tax-exempt hospital financing can be accomplished through various legal arrangements: a lease, installment sale arrangement or simply a mortgage and loan transaction. (See Table 20-6.) The financing, irrespective of legal arrangements, is effected by four basic legal documents, two of which are short lived and have limited functions, and two which will endure for the life of the bond issue. The short-lived documents

---

*Source: Reprinted from Daniel M. Cain and R. Neal Gilbert, "Legal Documentation of Hospital Financing," *Topics in Health Care Financing*, Fall 1978, with permission of Aspen Systems Corporation.

Table 20-6 Principal Types of Tax-exempt Conduit Financing Arrangements

Lease	Installment Sale	Loan
User-beneficiary* conveys project title to issuer-authority.** Issuer sells bonds and leases project back to User. User pays rent sufficient to amortize bonds.	Issuer sells bonds secured by property conveyed to it by user. Issuer agrees to sell the project and improvement back to the user under an installment sale agreement.	Issuer sells bonds and agrees to loan proceeds to user. User agrees to repay loan to issuer sufficient to retire the bonds. Secured by mortgage, although not always necessary.

*User-beneficiary usually the hospital.
**Issuer-authority in state and local authority serving as conduit.

are the official statement and bond purchase agreement, and the two documents with long-term application are the bond indenture and lease (or loan agreement). There may also be various collateral agreements between the involved parties such as a mortgage, a guaranty or an escrow deposit agreement, whose primary purpose is to enhance the security provided by the two basic agreements.

THE FULL COST OF BORROWING*

There are two major categories of costs to analyze: tangible and intangible.

The Tangible Costs

In analyzing the tangible costs and the effect they have on your loan costs, it is necessary to use an analytical technique that examines both the dollar impact and the timing of such costs over the life of the loan. Not to use such a technique would give you a false reading as to the true cost of the loan.

The tangible costs can be itemized as follows:

1. interest rate
2. maturity
3. repayment schedule
4. loan fees
5. commitment fees
6. other origination or issuance costs
7. redemption premiums
8. financial reserve requirements.

---
*Source: Reprinted from Frederick R. Blume, "Hospital Debt Management," *Topics in Health Care Financing*, Fall 1976, with permission of Aspen Systems Corporation.

The interest rate is felt by many to be the most important single determining factor in selecting a financing package and/or financial agent. This should not be so; the true effective cost and the flexibility of the covenants should be of equal importance. Interest rate is a function of the hospital's credit strength, money market conditions existing at that time, and the desirability of the loan package being presented in its entirety. Interest rates also reflect the state of the economy, that is to say they are an indicator of the anticipated inflation rate.

Repayment schedule. The important thing to remember about interest charges is that they are a cost determined by amount and time; therefore, the repayment schedule and maturity have an equally important impact on costs. The repayment schedule should be designed to be a percentage of depreciation which allows sufficient cash flow still available to make ordinary replacements and invest in technological change. Hospitals should also consider the present value effect on principal repayment. The discounting of future principal payments by your "opportunity cost" of funds or the inflation rate has the effect of diminishing the size of the payment, and encouraging the use of level payments (including principal and interest). Conversely, extending the time by which the principal is outstanding does increase the absolute dollars paid in interest.

Loan fees, commitment fees, "points," and other costs of issuance incurred at the start of a credit arrangement have the effect of raising the cost of your issue since you do not receive 100% of the loan proceeds. Loan fees are typically charged to cover costs incurred in arranging or establishing the issue. Such fees should be negotiated down as an absolute percentage as the

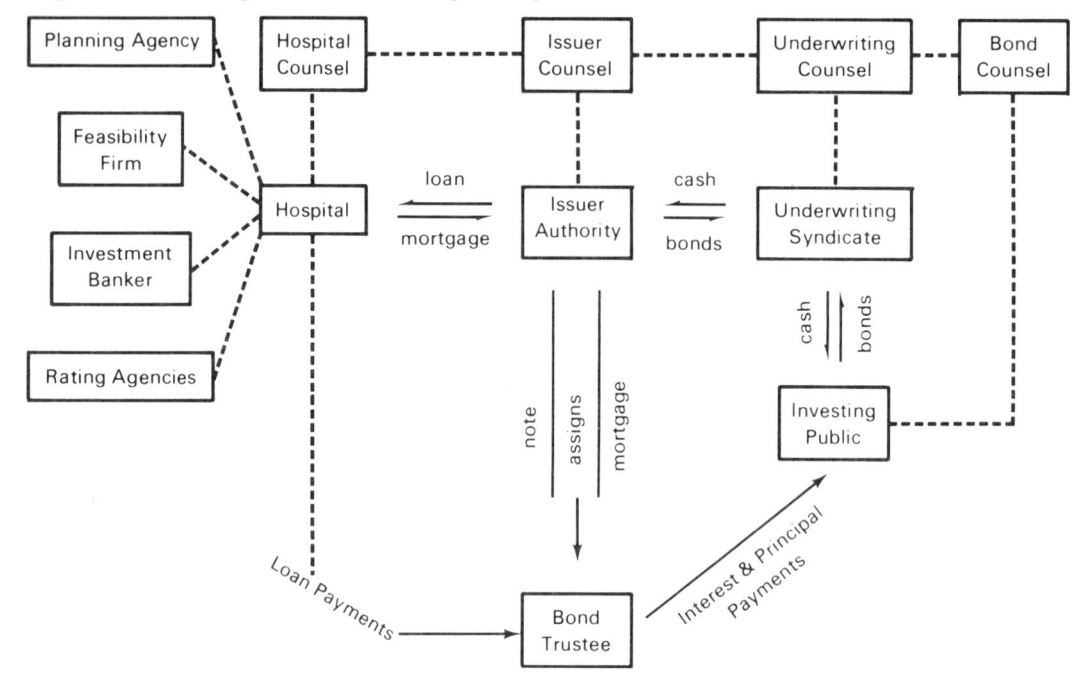

Figure 20-3 Hospital bond issue participants

size of the issue increases. Commitment fees are charged on unused but committed funds to compensate the lenders for assuming the risks of rate fluctuations over the time the funds are not utilized. The terms, loan fees and points, are virtually interchangeable. Points are simply a percentage of loan proceeds deducted by the lender. Other issuance costs including such items as legal fees, underwriters' fees, consultants' fees and printing costs are determined by the type of issue selected and also reduce the usable proceeds received thereby raising the cost.

Redemption privileges generally refer to the borrowers' rights at their own option to accelerate the payment of principal at par or with a penalty (defined as "optional prepayments without premium" or with premium). The lenders on long-term bond issues usually limit the amount of optional prepayments without premium because they want to keep their funds invested at the rates of the issue involved over the time of the issue for the purposes of keeping a known yield (rather than risk downward rate fluctuations).

Financial reserves can be either bank credit compensating deposit requirements or debt service reserves. The two are very different. Bank credit compensating deposit requirements receive no interest income and therefore have an opportunity cost. Debt service reserves, on the other hand, do accumulate interest income which may more than offset the impact of the interest expensed for maintaining such reserves.

The Intangibles

The intangible costs of a loan are those which affect flexibility of management decisions and impose controls on the future of the hospital. Among the intangible costs of a financing are the following:

1. restrictions on additional debt (closed end debt covenants)
2. prohibition against merging and/or sale or disposition of a substantial portion of assets
3. working capital controls—generally not onerous due to large receivables of hospital
4. limitations on capital expenditures
5. required amounts of insurance coverage and/or limitations on self-insuring

6. leasing restrictions
7. limits on ability to prepay the debt
8. the requirement of ownership change such as that which is experienced through an IRS 63–20 ruling financing
9. the lack of control on the funding of the issue or the timing used to enter the money market
10. the relative ease of obtaining waivers or changes to the terms after the debt is issued.

In each of the above examples, the relative value (or cost) of the covenant is determined by the unique situation of the hospital involved. In most cases some latitude exists in structuring covenants and they may be negotiated.

CAPITAL INVESTMENT AND REIMBURSEMENT PENALTIES*

What is the effect that third party reimbursement has on the investment decision process of health care institutions?

An important, if not critical, aspect of any capital budgeting decision by a hospital is the estimation of a project's future cash flows. If economic considerations are taken into account in the decision process, then the final decision that will be reached, i.e., whether to accept or reject a given project depends to a large extent on the accuracy of these estimates. The capital budgeting decision therefore will be only as good as these estimates are.

The reason that the monetary benefits of a project should be evaluated in terms of the cash flows it generates is that cash is central to all operations within a hospital. Only the cash that is actually received by the hospital can be used to pay for current expenses or new equipment, or to retire debt. Therefore it is cash and not accounting income that is important in the capital budgeting process.

One of the factors that differentiates hospitals from other economic units is that part of the hospitals' revenues are generated by cost based reimbursements. In most organizations the revenues generated from the sale of goods or services equals the quantity sold times the price per unit. This is not the case in hospitals. Since for part of the services provided the hospital will get compensated on the basis of the cost of providing the service rather than on the basis of the price charged for the service, the revenue generated by a given treatment will not equal the quantity provided times the price charged. The same applies to an investment that is aimed at reducing operating costs. While a cost saving investment reduces the total operating cost of the hospital it also reduces the cost base used in calculating reimbursements and thus it reduces the revenue generated from this source.

The following example illustrates the impact of cost base reimbursements on cash flows generated by an investment project.

Cost Saving Investment

Suppose a hospital's division is considering the purchase of equipment that will reduce labor cost in the division. The cash flow position of the division before the new equipment is described in the first column of Table 20-7. The total revenue of the division is $23,000, its operating costs are $20,000, and the annual depreciation charges of the division's existing assets is $1000. The division has a 60% cost base reimbursements rate. That is, the division gets reimbursed for 60% of its cash operating expense plus 60% of its depreciation charges. The division's cash inflow before making the investment was $3,000. Thus the new equipment although generating cost saving of $5,000 increased cash flow by only $2,900. The reason for it is that as a result of cost based reimbursement a reduction in cost also brings about a reduction in revenue. That is, the hospital does not get to keep all the benefits from a cost saving investment but rather has to share it with those third parties which pay on a cost basis. In many ways, the impact of reimbursement is similar to effects that taxes have on for-profit organizations. These effects should be taken into consideration and therefore into the evaluation of projects by hospitals; the cash flows should be estimated on a post reimbursement basis.

---
*Source: Reprinted from David A. Dittman and Aharon R. Ofer, "The Impact of Reimbursement on Hospital Cash Flow," *Topics in Health Care Financing,* Fall 1976, with permission of Aspen Systems Corporation.

Table 20-7 Cost Saving Investment

	Cost Saving Investment		
	Before the Investment	After the Investment	Change (2-1)
Revenue from Charges	$10,400	$10,400	$0
Revenue from Operating Cost Reimbursement	12,000	9,000	−3,000
Revenue from Reimbursement of Depreciation Expense	600	1,500	+900
Total	$23,000	$20,900	$−2,100
Operating Cost	20,000	15,000	+5,000
Net Cash Inflow	$ 3,000	$ 5,900	$+2,900

Impact of Rate Regulation on Debt Financing*

The impact of rate regulation agencies on the ability of health facilities to acquire debt financing is becoming an important issue in considering the role of such agencies. The importance of debt financing to hospitals has increased dramatically in recent years. A survey by Standard and Poors, one of the two agencies that provides ratings on the credit worthiness of bond issues, shows that the percentage of debt financing used in hospital capital projects rose from 12 percent in 1962 to 78 percent in 1977. To acquire debt financing, health care institutions must enter the capital markets along with other borrowers. The AHA has stated that "the overall operating margin for all institutions must be determined in consideration of the need to compete in the capital market against industries of comparable risk for available capital."

A clear reflection of the impact of regulation on the ability to compete for capital is that the two leading hospital-bond credit rating agencies,

---

*Source: *Health Capital Issues,* Bureau of Health Facilities, February 1980, DHHS Pub. No. (HRA) 81-14531.

Moody's and Standard and Poor's, tend to give lower marks to hospitals in States with rate review agencies.

Standard and Poor's key concerns regarding a State's rate review mechanism are:

- How pervasive is the agency's power?
- Does it cover all payers?
- What costs are recognized, and how are they defined?
- How will working capital be treated?
- Will depreciation be recognized as a cost?
- How are capital financings regarded?

Health care institutions face the difficulty of assuring prospective lenders that rate regulators will not impair their ability to repay.

This concern of lenders and bond credit-rating agencies has been expressed by Standard and Poor's, which has stated that regulatory uncertainty has been reflected in its ratings of hospital bonds. Over a recent period, only one hospital received an AAA rating, a few received AA ratings, and most others received A ratings or lower. The difference in interest rates between AAA and A rated bonds for a recent 12-month period ranged between 2.5 percent and 3 percent.

Chapter 21—Capital Expenditures

CAPITAL EXPENDITURE REQUESTS

Problem Areas*

A review of the capital expenditure system used by many hospital managements reveals several key reasons why optimal results are not being achieved.

1. The apparent and actual decision makers are often not clearly identified.
2. Insufficient information is available to the decision maker.
3. Management feels that medical personnel do not have a realistic appreciation of capital goods expenditures and the associated problems.
4. There is not a clear understanding of priority allocations, nor is there a clear division of classes of items according to individual item cost. Further, clear decision rules are not identified for each class and priority.
5. Purchasing responsibilities are not clearly identified and competitive bidding is often not employed where it is appropriate.
6. Sufficient contingency funds are not budgeted.
7. The useful life of equipment is not carefully considered and a computation of the cost savings or revenue produced is not made for each period.
8. There may be a subtle, but potentially serious, unresolved conflict between medical personnel and administrative personnel.

Ranking Requests*

The allocation of capital budget funds should be the responsibility of the highest authority within the organization staff. It must be based on a system which considers all capital proposals which merit corporate attention but selects only those that are expected to optimize the organization's value within the budgetary constraint.

The bulk of proposal requests originate at the department level and should be initially screened by the department head before proceeding to the administrator. Because of his experience and judgment, the administrator should be well qualified to do a more sophisticated screening of the proposals before passing them on to the corporate committee or some other final authority for capital expenditures.

From an examination of various hospital requests, the following proposal categories are suggested:

- *Category I:* Essential and/or required by legislative action (equipment that is required in order to maintain operations).
- *Category II:* Revenue-producing or cost-saving equipment (non-essential).
- *Category III:* Optional accessories for improvements (non-essential, non-revenue or

---

*Source: Reprinted from Denis T. Railhall and J. William Gotcher, "How to Rank Requests for Capital Expenditures in Your Hospital," *Healthcare Financial Management*, December 1971, with permission of Healthcare Financial Management Association.

cost-saving items that are suggested to substantially improve operations).
- *Category IV:* Miscellaneous.

In addition to the above categories, capital expenditure requests should be identified by the projected cost of the requested proposal. This can be accomplished by using a three-class system, such as Class A: under $200; Class B: $200–$1,000; and Class C: over $1,000.

In light of these categories and expenditure classes, the relevant decision-makers should be able to compare each request with a predetermined set of decision rules designed to produce an "Accept," "Reject," or "Reserve Judgment" decision.

The "Reserve Judgment" may indicate two conditions. First, it may be used when the decision-maker is unable to reach a decision without additional information. If this is the case, the request should be recycled to develop the needed information. "Reserve Judgment" may also indicate that the decision should not be made at the individual decision-maker's responsibility level, but should be passed upward.

Techniques for Evaluation*

To illustrate how four techniques for evaluating capital investment work—payback period, average rate of return, net present value and internal rate of return—let us examine a hypothetical investment.

Assume that the Scioto Valley Convalescent Center has been investigating a new potato peeler for the Dietary Department. The machine has a cost of $5,000 and a useful life of 10 years. Reductions in annual operating costs of $800 per year should be realized in each of the next 10 years. There is no expected salvage value assigned to the machine. Scioto Valley can borrow or invest funds at 10%. The percentage of cost reimbursement at Scioto Valley is currently 80% with no major changes expected over the 10 years.

The above information can be restated into expected yearly cash flows. Ignoring the effects of cost reimbursement, the expected cash flows would be $800 per year for the next 10 years. Incorporating the effects of cost reimbursement reduces this figure to $560 per year for the next 10 years. This figure was derived by multiplying the annual operating savings of $800 by .20 (the percentage of operating savings realized with 80% cost reimbursement) and adding to it the yearly depreciation reimbursed by cost payors, $400 (.80 × $5,000/10).

Payback Period

The payback period is one of the simplest, and one of the most frequently used methods for evaluating capital investments. It is simply defined as the length of time required for the cash proceeds from the investment to equal the original investment cost. The payback periods for the hypothetical investment case would be:

1. Payback—excluding effects of cost reimbursement

$$\$5,000/\$800 = 6.25 \text{ years}$$

2. Payback—incorporating effects of cost reimbursement

$$\$5,000/\$560 = 8.93 \text{ years}$$

Average Rate of Return

A measure used by many accountants is the average ratio of earnings to the book value of the investment. When this measure is used the earnings are computed after depreciation. The average rates of return for the hypothetical case would be:

1. Average Rate of Return—excluding effects of cost reimbursement

$$\frac{\$800 - \$500}{\frac{\$10,000}{2}} = .06$$

2. Average Rate of Return—incorporating effects of cost reimbursement

$$\frac{\$560 - \$500}{\frac{\$10,000}{2}} = .012$$

---

*Source: Reprinted from "An Illustration of Analytical Approaches for Capital Investment Evaluation," *Financial Management of Health Care Facilities,* ed. William O. Cleverley, with permission of Aspen Systems Corporation, © 1976.

Net Present Value

The net present value method is a discounted cash flow technique defined as the present value of the future returns discounted at the firm's relevant cost of capital minus the present value of the investment outlay. A modification of this method referred to as the *Equivalent Annual Cost* Method is very useful for projects where the monetary benefits are in excess of the expected costs. In these cases, the appropriate decision may focus upon selecting the least cost method of providing a given service. Equivalent annual cost is simply the present value of all costs, investment and operating, divided by the appropriate present value annuity factor. (Present value tables are included at the end of this paper.)

1. Net Present Value—excluding effect of cost reimbursement

    $800 × 6.45 − $5,000 = −$84

2. Net Present Value—incorporating effect of cost reimbursement

    $560 × 6.145 − $5,000 = −$1,558.80

Internal Rate of Return

The internal rate of return method is another discounted cash flow technique defined as that interest rate which equates the present value of future returns with the investment outlay (net present value equals zero).

1. Internal Rate of Return—ignoring cost reimbursement effects
    a) $800 × P(i, 10) = $5,000
    b) P(i, 10) = 6.25
    c) Therefore, i must fall between 8% and 10% from examining Table 2.
    d) Interpolation yields i = 9.6%

2. Internal Rate of Return—incorporating cost reimbursement effects
    a) $560 × P(i, 10) = $5,000
    b) P(i, 10) = 8.93
    c) Therefore i must fall below 4% from examining Table 2.
    d) Examining more detailed tables yields i = 1.9%

AN EXAMPLE OF CAPITAL EXPENDITURE PLANNING*

Intermountain Health Care, Inc.'s (IHC) decisions regarding maximum annual levels of capital expenditure are made by balancing what is *wanted* with what is *possible*, both in the short term and long term. In practice, the critical element in this process is the determination of the level of internally generated funds (the major portion of which come from the excess of revenues over expenses) necessary to meet a proposed level of capital expenditure and other cash outflow needs. The necessary level of internally generated funds is, of course, determined in concert with assumptions regarding external funding sources—principally debt. Once the level of internally generated funds necessary to meet a given level of projected cash outflow is determined, it must be compared to operating realities. If the necessary level of internally generated funds is not reasonable, downward adjustments must be made to the amount of projected capital expenditures until the necessary level of internally generated funds is also reasonable.

Reasonable levels of internally generated funds must be defined from a long-term environment-wide perspective. Local, state and national factors relating to the provision of health care services must be considered. The impact of regulation at each of these levels must also be analyzed. While these are difficult, intangible considerations, they are critical to the determination of overall strategic plans and therefore, must be taken into account and updated as new information becomes available. Without consistent environment-related updating of the attainable (reasonable) level of internally generated funds, the long-range strategic planning process loses its value.

After long-term funding levels are determined, decisions must be made regarding the specific projects that should be undertaken in any one year. This involves ranking competing projects to determine the ones that are of the highest overall priority. It should be noted that

---

*Source: Reprinted from William H. Nelson and Stephen D. Nadauld, "An Approach to Capital Expenditure Planning," *Topics in Health Care Financing,* Summer 1981, with permission of Aspen Systems Corporation.

the financial criterion is not the only criterion for the final decision regarding project priorities. Many other factors, including community need, availability of technical expertise and competitive situation, must also be considered.

IHC's Capital Planning Model

What is the appropriate level of annual capital expenditure? IHC developed a capital planning model that could review the results of various capital expenditure and borrowing patterns against required return on assets (internally generated funds). The planning model provided a framework for projecting different long-term capital expenditure plans by hospital (specifically citing major projects and estimates of ongoing capital expenditure needs over the projection period) and for the corporation as a whole. The model compared various borrowing scenarios (amounts and timing) with these different capital expenditure plans, reviewing the impact of different capital expenditure/borrowing scenarios on the required level of internally generated funds, which thus became the dependent variable.

1. Constraints include:
   - maximum ratio of debt to assets; and
   - minimum liquidity.
2. Operating parameters include:
   - the working capital change factor (related to gross revenue);
   - the projected level of contributions;
   - the projected return on liquid reserves (cash and invested funds);
   - yearly depreciation factors;
   - estimated inflation rates; and
   - the ratio of borrowing to investment (i.e., how many dollars of borrowing are necessary to generate one dollar of expendable funds).

After taking all constraints and parameters into consideration, the model functions as a straightforward cash flow projection model. The effects of different capital expenditure and borrowing patterns are assessed with respect to their impact on required levels of internal funding. The numerous iterations force trade-offs between timing and amounts of capital expenditures and borrowing.

Specific Project Evaluation

Once overall annual capital spending maximums are established, the process turns to selecting specific projects. The first step in developing the process was to establish a weighted cost of capital.

(1) The Weighted Cost of Capital

Cost of capital, simply defined, is the required return (cost) on the debt and equity components of capital.

Very simplistically, the debt and equity components of the weighted cost of capital may be defined as follows.

- The cost of debt is the estimated interest rate on an organization's next borrowing.
- The cost of equity is the rate of return on the organization's equity capital required by the owners of an organization.

Once these two factors are determined, they are weighted according to a projected relationship between debt and equity to determine the weighted cost of capital.

(2) The Cost of Debt

In the health care environment, one additional element is added to the determination of the cost of the debt portion. Because Medicare/Medicaid and other cost-based third-party payers reimburse allowable interest expense, this reimbursement factor is reflected in the formula. The interest that an organization receiving cost-based reimbursement must generate is simply defined as equal to that portion of interest expense that is not cost reimbursed.

(3) The Cost of Equity

The specific elements that determine the required return on equity (in addition to historical cost depreciation) will vary with time and economic and technological factors. However, as an example, the summation of these individual factors could result in the following overall cost of equity:

- inflation (related to construction and equipment), 13 percent;
- new technology, 2 percent; and
- contingency and expansion, 2 percent,

for a total of 17 percent.

(4) The Combined Cost of Debt and Equity

Debt and equity elements figure in the formula for deriving the weighted cost of capital (*related to cash flow*) as follows:

$$WCC = (1 - CRR)\, iD + qE$$

where:

WCC = weighted cost of capital
CRR = % third-party cost reimbursement utilization
i = interest rate on next dollar of debt
D = percentage of debt
q = cost of equity
E = percentage of equity

COST FINDING FOR NEW HOSPITAL SERVICES OR EQUIPMENT*

Horizontal Cost Finding

Under the horizontal system the cost for a final product (i.e., the patient treated) is derived by adding charges from each department for units of service the patient consumed from each department. Thus a typical chest X-ray would be charged at the same rate to a pneumonia, lung cancer or heart surgery patient, assuming the procedures required are the same in each case. No accounting is made of the fact that the addition of a heart surgery program may have increased X-ray volume to the point that an additional X-ray machine was purchased. The fixed cost of the additional machine is charged in equal share to all patients having chest X-rays, not simply to the heart surgery patients. This method of cost finding would certainly pose a problem if a hospital must decide whether or not to offer a heart surgery program. That program should bear the cost of the new machine, a cost that would not otherwise have been incurred.

To a physician or hospital administrator, it is logical and natural to think of hospital products in terms of radiology and dietary because they are the traditional "cost centers" of the hospital. However, the physicians and administrators are well aware that they are not attempting to produce X-rays, but rather to treat a patient for an ailment.

Vertical Cost Finding

In contrast to horizontal cost finding, a vertical cost-finding system would lead to a greater focus on the costs for the type of patient treated.

Vertical cost finding can be used for calculating the cost to the hospital of a specific new program or a specialized elective service, such as open-heart surgery.

Stated briefly, the problem is—What costs would a hospital incur if it has a program such as open-heart surgery, which it would not incur if it did not offer that service? In economic terms, what is needed is the marginal cost to the hospital of the entire heart surgery program and the cost for the specific volume of patients expected. Thus vertical cost finding will provide cost information appropriate to the anticipated utilization of heart surgery facilities.

The first step in vertical cost finding is to determine the exact production process for the program under consideration. The costs for a specific volume can be determined once the production process and input requirements are fully understood. It is possible, however, that the hospital will not know the exact volume of heart surgery procedures it will perform each year. It may want to know the costs for a wide range of volumes, in order to see at what level of utilization it becomes economical to offer a service. Governmental regulations, medical standards, experience of administrators and sampling techniques must be used to determine an estimate of input requirements at differing volumes.

To find the resource requirements of a program, the hospital must determine which departments come into direct contact with the program's patients. The flowchart in Figure 21-1 follows the patient through the hospital from admission to discharge. The flowchart serves as a basis to ensure inclusion of all costs. It includes patient movement, patient contact with hospital personnel and indirect inputs such as various overhead cost centers. Note that the latter is referred to as days of hospitalization or "routine care." This category includes a variety of items from heat and light to secretarial pools, recordkeeping and parking lot maintenance.

---

*Source: Reprinted from Steven A. Finkler, "Cost Finding for High-Technology, High-Cost Services: Current Practice and a Possible Alternative," *Health Care Management Review,* Summer 1980, with permission of Aspen Systems Corporation.

336 Hospital Administration Handbook

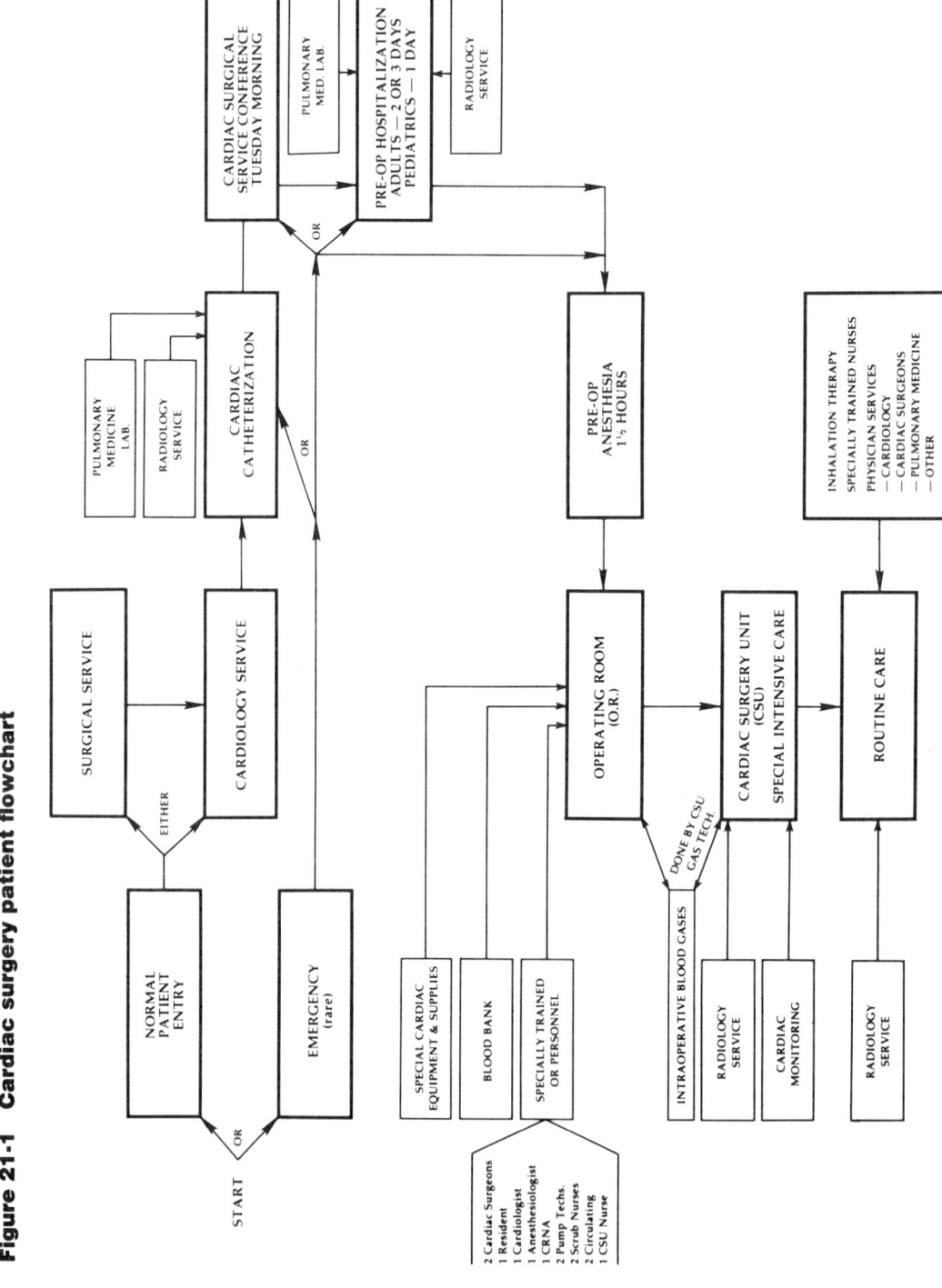

Figure 21-1 Cardiac surgery patient flowchart

All factors of hospital operation must be considered for the effect the program would have on them.

Based on the flowchart, the cost elements of offering heart surgery might be broken down into the following groups: anesthesia, blood processing, cardiac catheterization, cardiac surgery intensive care unit, dietary, ECG, inhalation therapy, laboratory, linens, medications, medical/surgical hospital beds, operating room equipment and supplies, operating room personnel, overhead and radiology.

Identification of Input Factors

Once such groupings are identified for which the addition, deletion or change in volume of the elective program would affect factors of production (resource utilization), all such input factors are identified. This identification of input requirement variation with volume is a crucial phase of the data collection. The input-output relationships for hospital programs are not well known. Ultimately, however, each input is the responsibility of some individual. These individuals should be called upon to identify the inputs that are required for each heart surgery patient and the amount of each input needed at different volumes.

Using the flowchart in Figure 21-1, the hospital administration can break the problem into manageable segments. For each cost element, the administration must determine what input requirements the addition of open-heart surgery places upon it. These input requirements should be divided into fixed, variable, and semifixed resources. The semifixed inputs must be identified for the volumes at which new increments are needed.

When the hospital administration determines input requirements, it is important that a systems approach be taken. That is, the administration should consider all inputs throughout the entire hospital system which might be affected by the program. These are called "relevant" costs. For instance, if offering heart surgery causes the capacity of the hospital's X-ray machine to be exceeded, then heart surgery must bear the entire cost of a new X-ray machine. Similarly, if the heart surgery program uses facilities that would otherwise be unused, there should be no cost associated with that use, since it is not a relevant cost for the analysis.

Cost Concepts

Long Run versus Short Run

A hospital must determine whether long-run costs, short-run costs or those of some intermediate run are appropriate for an analysis of a decision's impact. If the decision is one that is expected to come up for review at frequent short-run intervals, an analysis of short-run costs may be adequate. Thus if a hospital is deciding the hours that a clinic should be open during the next month, the hospital would desire short-run costs. On the other hand, if the decision requires major capital expenditures and is the type that will only be made at long-term intervals, long-run costs are appropriate.

In the case of cost analysis regarding whether to add or delete a program such as heart surgery, major changes within the hospital are required to implement the decision. Once the decision is made, it is unlikely to be changed in the short run; it is intended to be a permanent decision. Thus the hospital considering offering heart surgery is interested in long-run costs.

Historical versus Replacement Costs

The accounting system records costs on a historical purchase price basis. Historical costs are generally used for reporting purposes outside of the hospital industry because such costs are considered to be objective and verifiable.

Replacement cost tells what it would cost today to replace a building or a piece of equipment. If one views a program as a permanent part of the hospital product mix, then it is expected that equipment and buildings will have to be replaced as they wear out. Historical costs do not give information regarding how much it will cost to replace such facilities. While it is true that in the short run the hospital might be interested in only the cost of items to be replaced currently, for a long-run analysis the hospital must consider the cost of all assets utilized by a program since they will all have to be replaced at some time. Replacement costs are therefore more appropriate than historical costs for the open-heart surgery analysis.

Treatment of Joint Overhead Costs

Overhead costs represent a significant measurement problem. It is assumed that there is a basic mix of hospital products that require certain support facilities and personnel. None of these overhead costs should be allocated to open-heart surgery in the sample analysis unless the amount of cost incurred changes because the heart surgery program is offered. This approach, if used for pricing all hospital products, would not allocate all overhead costs and a loss would result. Here, however, the goal is not rate setting, but rather the determination of the incremental cost incurred by the hospital because it offers heart surgery. Thus for purposes of the vertical cost analysis, costs which would be incurred even if the service were not offered should not be considered part of the cost of the service under investigation, no matter how much the service utilizes those resources.

Divisibility of Labor Inputs

In general, personnel—including technicians, assistants and nurses—are cross-trained and can perform a number of functions. They can be shifted between tasks as needed. Labor inputs can generally be added or deleted in continuous increments as volume changes.

In some cases, this is clearly inappropriate. For example, a heart-lung pump technician is a specialist whose duties may very well be clearly specified in a union contract. Such a technician might be idle when not assisting in open-heart surgeries, but will have to be paid during idle hours. In such cases, the technician is a dedicated resource and must be included as a large, discrete increment to costs. The same might be true to some extent for X-ray and medical supervisors, nurses, therapists, orderlies and some maintenance staff, because some of their functions do not change as volume increases.

EQUIPMENT LEASING*

At the present rate of growth, medical equipment leasing is expected to double in just a five-year period. In 1979 despite the recession, one study predicted that the value of new medical equipment placed on lease would surpass an annual level of $1 billion by 1982. Indeed, at present an estimated 20 percent of *all* new equipment accepted for delivery in the United States goes into use through leasing.

Reasons for Leasing

Equipment-Related Reasons

- *Avoid obsolescence:* With today's fast-paced technological change, no one wants to finish paying for a CAT scanner or computer only to find that it has just been outdated by something new.
- *Compensate for temporary or low usage:* Items that may only be needed on a very limited basis, such as an additional fetal monitor, can be efficiently leased short-term or rented as needed.
- *Provide a trial period:* This is an excellent way to give the people who will actually use a piece of equipment "hands on" experience before making a final decision.
- *Take advantage of special manufacturer programs:* Some manufacturers offer generous service programs for leased equipment, or detailed training programs. (These programs may also be available, however, with a purchase.)
- *Obtain limited availability items:* There are still some items of equipment that are introduced to the marketplace only on a lease basis. Certain office copiers have been good examples.

Financial Reasons

- *Improve cash flow:* This may occur over time, depending on the agreement, if reimbursement is accelerated. Many hospitals lease, however, simply because of an immediate cash shortage.
- *Obtain lower financing rates:* This is possible, but certainly not guaranteed. It is very important to assess the actual interest rate, not the quoted rate, and compare it with alternative rates on short-term loans, etc.
- *Conserve existing bank credit lines:* Such credit lines are best reserved for short-term working capital needs, not equipment purchases; but, be careful of borrowing at 15 percent to preserve the right ("some rainy day") to borrow at 11 percent.

---

*Source: Except where noted, this section on "Equipment Leasing" consists of excerpts reprinted from Ned L. Gerber, "A Closer Look at Equipment Leasing," *Hospital Materiel Management Quarterly*, August 1981, with permission of Aspen Systems Corporation.

- *Prevent key financial ratios from being altered:* Operating leases, which are "off-balance-sheet" financing, do not disturb the debt/equity ratio. This may keep a hospital from violating the terms of a bond or other agreement.
- *Obtain flexible payback schedules:* Leasing can be custom tailored in a remarkable variety of ways. The minimal or nonexistent down payment is particularly popular. (However, if a large "balloon payment" is scheduled at the end, budget carefully.)
- *Avoid property taxes:* Nonprofit hospitals in some states can avoid the payment of these taxes if their equipment acquisition is structured as a lease.

Dealing with Inflation*

Leasing a piece of equipment may help offset inflationary costs. For example, assume that a piece of equipment with an estimated life of five years can be purchased for $100,000 or leased for $22,000 for five years. Purchasing this piece of equipment means paying for it with today's dollars. It also means recovering these dollars, through depreciation and possible income-producing capabilities, with tomorrow's dollars—which most likely will be worth less due to the impact of inflation on the purchasing value of future dollars.

Leasing the piece of equipment will cost more in the "number of dollars" but as the five years pass, the "value" of the payments may actually be less because of the decreased purchasing value of the dollars. In other words, you are making the lease payments with cheaper dollars. (For an aid to making the decision to rent, lease or purchase, see Table 21-1.)

Why Not Rent?*

To rent usually refers to a contract for the use of the equipment for a very short period of time relative to its useful life. The rental agreement normally includes a 30-day cancellation clause which allows for the penalty-free return of the equipment.

Rentals normally cost more than either form of leasing because they are usually short term in nature. Rental plans offer maximum protection against obsolescence to the health care facility because of their fast-cancellation clauses.

The rental of equipment may be advantageous to the facility when there is a known short-term need for the piece of equipment (such as when the facility is awaiting expansion or the installation of new equipment). Equipment rental may also be desirable when a facility wants to test it to see how it works and how its professional and technical staff reacts to it on a day-to-day basis.

Evaluating a Lease

Equipment-Related Factors

Below is a list of guidelines for crucial equipment-related factors that should be used to evaluate the serviceability and maintenance aspects of an equipment lease.

Serviceability

- Can the hospital cancel the agreement and return the equipment if the equipment is rendered obsolete by new technology or regulations? Are there penalties involved?
- Can the equipment be "traded up" if the hospital's needs change? How much of an allowance, as a percentage of fair market value, is allowed?
- Will the final acceptance document be signed after delivery, installation, and a trial test?
- How complete is the warranty? Is the manufacturer and/or lessor exempted from all express and implied warranties? Be certain that any assurances that are required in this area are expressed in writing.

Maintenance—labor

- To what extent can the hospital's own personnel service the equipment without voiding the warranty?
- If the manufacturer or lessor services the item, will a comprehensive preventive maintenance program be followed?
- Is the service agreement complete, covering the entire piece of equipment, both parts and labor? If not, what is specifically excluded, and what should the hospital expect in maintenance costs for that portion?

---

*Source: Reprinted from William E. Herber, "To Lease or Not to Lease," *Hospital Materiel Management Quarterly,* November 1979, with permission of Aspen Systems Corporation.

Table 21-1 The Rent/Lease/Purchase Decision

The decision matrix below is printed as a decision-making aid in leasing, renting or purchasing a piece of equipment.

Criteria	Rent (less than one year)	Lease	Purchase
Length of need	Best for short-term use only. Monthly terms usually available.	Best for medium or long-term needs. "Finance" leases usually non-cancellable. "Operating" leases are cancellable and may be thought of as long-term rentals (one year or more).	Best for long-term use only.
Certainty of need	Best solution when need for equipment is uncertain. Good way to test equipment before long-term acquisition.	Less flexible than renting, more than buying. Trade-ups often available if equipment leased through manufacturer. Cancellation options often available to protect lessee.	Not flexible. Trade-ups sometimes possible if purchased with manufacturer's financing.
Initial outlay	None. Monthly rentals include all expenses (including taxes and delivery charge) and are relatively high.	None. Monthly lease payments include all expenses and are lower than rentals.	10% down payment usually required up front, plus delivery fee and taxes. If financed, monthly payments are relatively low.
Equity build-up	None on straight rental. Rent/buy programs are usually available, with some rent credited toward purchase.	None on straight lease. Lease/buy programs usually available.	100%
Effect on budget	Monthly rentals may be treated as operating expense. No special appropriation necessary.	Operating lease payments may be treated as operating expense. No special appropriation necessary.	Large front-end outlay usually requires special budget provision which usually is anticipated and approved in advance.
Effect on credit lines	None, assuming short-term usage.	An additional source of financing if material may effect debit/equity ratio.	None for outright purchase. Time purchase reduces credit availability.
Tax impact of inflation	Rentals are fully tax-deductible.	Operating lease payments are usually tax-deductible. Financial leases may have to be treated as capital assets and depreciated.	Equipment is depreciable. Payments are not tax-deductible. Interest is deductible if equipment financed.
Accounting treatment	Treated as operating expense; usually footnoted if term exceeds more than a couple of months.	Cancellable leases must be footnoted. For non-cancellable leases, consult FASB-13 rulings.	Must be capitalized.
Inflation protection	Nil (assuming short-term contract). Considerable impact as term gets longer because rental charges tend to go up.	Fixed rentals tend to minimize impact of inflation. Payments become progressively less expensive in real dollars.	None if purchased outright; heavy front-end outlay is all in real dollars. If financed, fixed payments are not affected by inflation.

Table 21-1 continued

Criteria	Rent (less than one year)	Lease	Purchase
Apparent cost	Highest per month. Total outlay probably least, depending on length of time used.	Second highest per month. Total outlay on finance lease will be greater than purchase; on operating lease, depends on actual term.	Lowest per month. Total outlay lower than finance lease. Some resale value likely when equipment sold.
Real cost	About the same as apparent cost because of short-term use. Does not tie up cash.	Lower to much lower than apparent cost. Conserves cash, which is free to earn at user's internal rate of return.	May be higher than apparent cost because of cash and/or credit constraints and because it tends to work opposite to the effect of inflation.

Source: Roe, H. E. "The ABCs of Surviving the Information Avalanche: To rent, to buy, to lease . . . that is the question." Reproduced by 3M in a special supplement to *Business Week,* April 1978. Reprinted with permission.

- What is the response time on a service call, i.e., the time until a qualified service representative is actually on site? Check this point carefully with other institutions that have used the same service. Are there surcharges for calls made in the evening or on weekends?
- Does the lease cover shipping, uncrating, and installation? Will local, nonunion employees be permitted to install it?
- How extensive is the training provided for those who will service or use the equipment? Will the sessions be held at the hospital, or some regional or national center?
- Is there any time (especially on Saturdays and Sundays) when a qualified service representative will not be available for emergencies?

Maintenance—components and supplies

- Are all necessary parts stocked locally? If not, how long will it realistically take for them to be shipped to the hospital?
- If "generic" parts are used will the warranty be voided?
- Can supplies produced by another company be used? Be careful here, or a "lease" can turn into an expensive "leash" tying an institution to a manufacturer's product line.
- Are special hookups required, and if so, will the equipment be compatible with the hospital's existing electrical and mechanical services?
- Does the agreement break out the cost of each major component? This is particularly important if part of the equipment is later returned, and a credit memorandum issued.
- Are all applicable federal, state, and local codes met by the equipment without expensive modification?

Disposition

- When the agreement expires, what is the cost for renewal? Can servicing be fixed at a set, annual fee, or must this be renegotiated each year?
- If the equipment is removed and returned, who pays for the labor and shipping? Can the equipment be sent to the nearest local office of the lessor, instead of to the plant where it was manufactured?
- Can the lessor assign the lease to a bank or other secured party? Be careful that you do not end up doing business with a party who knows nothing of your institution, and services it accordingly.

Financial Factors

Below is a list of financial factors to be used in evaluating hospital equipment leases.

Interest rate:

- What is the actual rate being charged, sometimes known as the effective rate? Be sure that this is computed after taking into account all additional payments beyond the

regularly scheduled amounts. For example, the inclusion of security deposits, residual charges, or a month's prepayment will increase the actual interest rate paid.
- How does the actual rate compare to the current prime rate? Remember that prime is set for short-term loans to favored commercial accounts. If an institution locks into a multiyear commitment at a fixed rate with collateral, there should be some compensation.

Additional charges:

- Who pays for insurance? If it comes with the lease, does it include both property and general liability coverage? Be sure that the amounts are consistent with the requirements of the institution's own umbrella policy.
- Are taxes being passed through to the lessee? Who gets the investment tax credit if the hospital is investor-owned?
- Who is paying for shipping and installation? If it is the lessee, try to have these fees paid separately in the beginning, rather than being added to the principal amount owed, where they will accumulate interest far into the future.

General points:

- How long will the bid price be held firm? Does the lessor have the option to increase it if there are delays in shipping and testing the equipment? If so, be sure there is a provision allowing the lessee to reconsider the higher price.
- When do payments start, i.e., when is the crucial final acceptance form actually signed? Will there be charges assessed while partial shipments filter in before the equipment is even assembled?
- Can the hospital buy and resell the equipment at the end of the lease term? Due to inflation, some specialized items have appreciated substantially during lease terms and will have surprisingly high salvage values, even as much as 40 or 50 percent.
- Be sure that costs are not bundled together so that it is impossible to break out what each part or service actually totals.
- Be certain that the footnotes of the lessee's financial statements adequately disclose substantial leasing commitments, including any provision that allows for cancellation.

Leasing and Reimbursement

Today leasing is an umbrella term that covers everything from thinly disguised installment purchases to old-fashioned rentals. As a result, there has been quite some discussion over which leases are "true leases." The Internal Revenue Code, Medicare regulations, and the Financial Accounting Standards Board (FASB) all address the issue.

A "True" Lease*

Most regulatory agencies agree that the decision to purchase or lease remains management's prerogative, that a financial contract arising from outright purchase should be capitalized and that to qualify as an operating expense the lease arrangement must conform to IRS regulations. IRS regulations and the AICPA Opinion #5 are synonymous; most regulatory agencies are using the Opinion #5 to determine conformance. Local Blue Cross and Medicare intermediaries determine what constitutes a true lease; at audit each lease is considered separately. The burden of proof as to period lies with the hospital (lessee). The intent of the two parties is what matters. If the hospital's leasing arrangement meets the criteria in Opinion #5 and is also accepted by the hospital's external auditors, it should be accepted as an operating expense.

A true lease, essentially 1) gives the lessee the right to use the equipment for a specified period for a monthly payment without building up equity in the equipment, either through the monthly payments or through a purchase option; 2) has a term at least two years less than the guideline life of the property; 3) is written with a third party that has no other connection with the lessee (the contract is at "arm's length"), and 4) does not cover property which has an exceedingly high removal cost.

Capital vs. Operating Lease

In the list below, if any or all of the following criteria are met, the agreement is considered to

---

*Source: Reprinted from Stephen W. Smith, "Leasing: An Effective Source of Capital Asset Financing," *Healthcare Financial Management,* with permission of the Healthcare Financial Management Association.

Figure 21-2 The effect of leasing on reimbursement

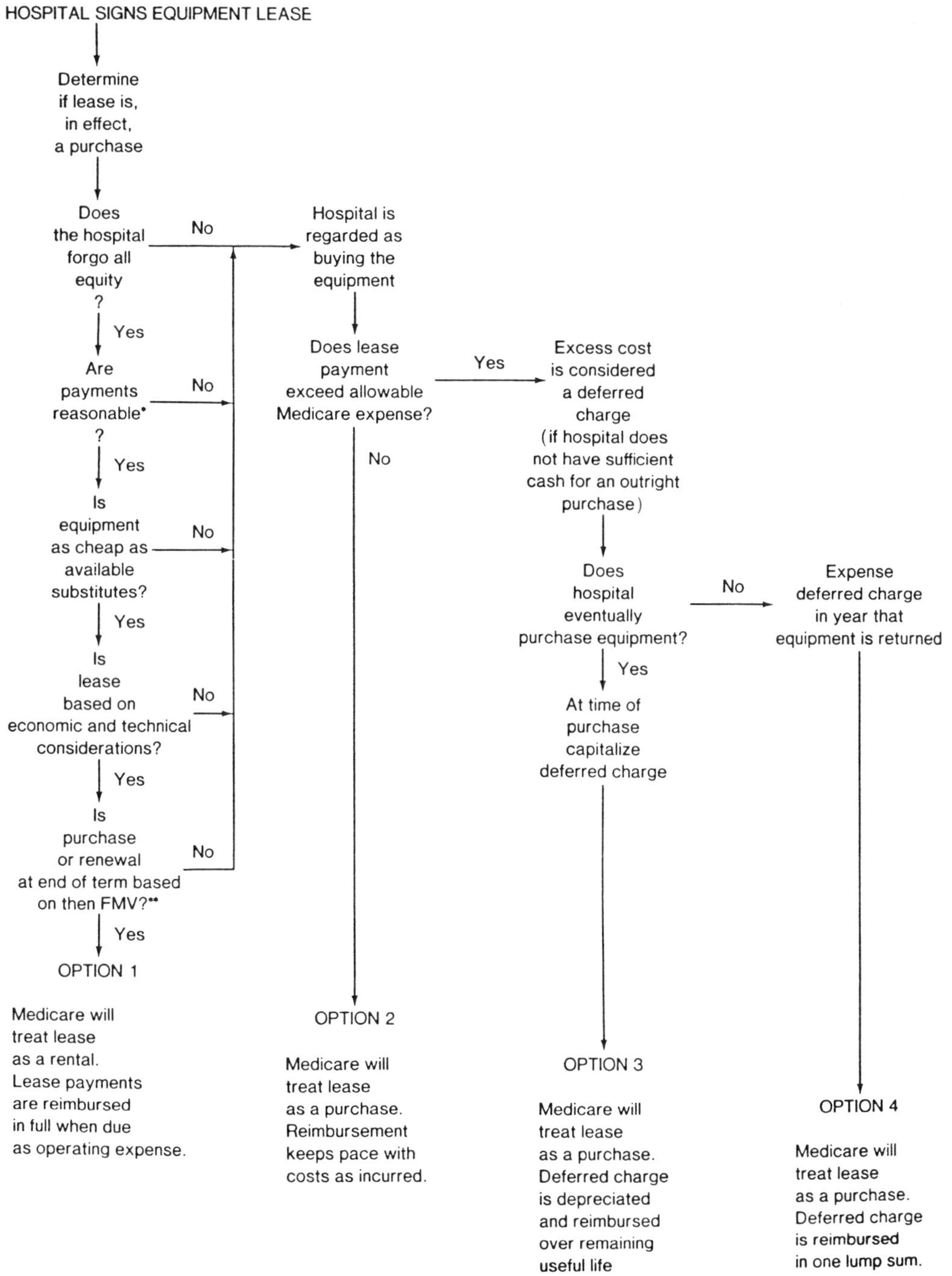

```
HOSPITAL SIGNS EQUIPMENT LEASE
              │
              ▼
     Determine
     if lease is,
     in effect,
     a purchase
              │
              ▼
       Does                        Hospital is
       the hospital    No          regarded as
       forgo all     ─────▶        buying the
       equity                      equipment
       ?                               │
       │ Yes                           ▼
       ▼                         Does lease         Yes      Excess cost
       Are                       payment          ─────▶    is considered
       payments      No          exceed allowable            a deferred
       reasonable*  ─────▶       Medicare expense?           charge
       ?                               │                    (if hospital does
       │ Yes                           │ No                 not have sufficient
       ▼                               │                    cash for an outright
       Is                              │                    purchase)
       equipment     No                │                        │
       as cheap as  ─────▶             │                        ▼
       available                       │                   Does                      Expense
       substitutes?                    │                   hospital        No        deferred charge
       │ Yes                           │                   eventually    ─────▶      in year that
       ▼                               │                   purchase equipment?       equipment is returned
       Is                              │                        │ Yes
       lease                           │                        ▼
       based on      No                │                   At time of
       economic and technical ─────▶   │                   purchase
       considerations?                 │                   capitalize
       │ Yes                           │                   deferred charge
       ▼                               │
       Is                              │
       purchase                        │
       or renewal    No                │
       at end of term based ─────▶     │
       on then FMV?**                  │
       │ Yes                           │
       ▼                               ▼
     OPTION 1                       OPTION 2                OPTION 3                 OPTION 4

Medicare will          Medicare will              Medicare will            Medicare will
treat lease            treat lease                treat lease              treat lease
as a rental.           as a purchase.             as a purchase.           as a purchase.
Lease payments         Reimbursement              Deferred charge          Deferred charge
are reimbursed         keeps pace with            is depreciated           is reimbursed
in full when due       costs as incurred.         and reimbursed           in one lump sum.
as operating expense.                             over remaining
                                                  useful life
```

*Payments are evaluated as reasonable in comparison with charges for comparable items, local market conditions, and the terms of the lease.
**FMV = Fair market value.

be a capital lease; otherwise, it is termed an operating lease. This distinction can quickly become very important, since in practical terms, capital leases are usually regarded as *purchase* agreements—operating leases are not.

- Ownership: The lessee receives most of the benefits of ownership through the provisions of the lease.
- Purchase option: The lease contains an opportunity for the lessee to acquire the equipment at a "bargain" price, i.e., less than current fair market value.
- Term: The lease runs for at least three-fourths of the useful life of the equipment.
- Total cost: At the beginning of the lease, the present value of all required payments is at least equal to 90 percent of the value of the equipment, less any investment tax credit. (This total does not include certain executory costs.)

The Effect of Leasing on Reimbursement

Figure 21-2 gives an outline of the impact of a lease on Medicare reimbursement in flow-chart form. This figure does not include the various implications of local reimbursement procedures in state or Blue Cross plans. However, the effects of these local or regional plans can be crucial especially if there is reimbursement for price-level depreciation. Such an approach can make an installment purchase, for example, much more attractive than leasing in any form.

It is important to note that the actual transfer of title can take place at the *end* of the lease term (for example, through a bargain purchase) and the agreement will still be considered a purchase from the *beginning* for reimbursement purposes. Again, if the lease is structured to run for most of the useful life of the equipment, and the hospital exercises an optional cancellation clause much earlier, reimbursement authorities may still consider the agreement to have been an intended purchase.

The reason for such emphasis on this point is that, if the lease is equivalent to a purchase, the hospital will actually be reimbursed only for the lesser of the lease payment itself, or the applicable portion of interest and depreciation. Furthermore, Medicare can disallow interest on a lease if the hospital had a source of sufficient cash available, such as funded depreciation, to make the purchase outright. However, if such cash is not available and the reimbursement payments are insufficient to cover interest and depreciation, a deferred charge should be recorded for the difference. In any case, if a hospital makes an outright purchase, the depreciation must be computed on the straight-line method for reimbursement purposes. But with a capital lease, the depreciation is often allowed to be computed over the frequently shorter life of the lease itself, which can result in a substantial acceleration of cash flow.

Chapter 22—Construction

The completion of financial plans signifies the start of a new series of decisions and procedural stages—the construction phase. Though administrators may not be implicated in every twist and turn along the way to the completion of a capital project, it is advisable to be aware and knowledgeable about the overall operation. Fortunately the approach to the many facets of the construction phase has been systematic and orderly. The various activities and decision points have been organized sequentially, responsibilities have been carefully defined, and flexible techniques have been devised to allow for individual application and problem modification. These components are presented in this chapter, in addition to numerous informational checklists for decision making and a most important guide to the mandatory approval process for capital projects.

THE MASTER PLAN*

Master planning consists of 12 steps. The Timing Plan of these steps is illustrated in Figure 22-1.

Step 1 of master planning is to define the hospital's role within the area it serves and the programs necessary to meet that role.

*Source: Reprinted from Thomas M. Hechler and John Sweetland, "Minimizing Costs Through Sound Facilities Planning," *Topics in Health Care Financing,* Summer 1977, with permission of Aspen Systems Corporation.

A precise understanding of the hospital's role in inpatient care, ambulatory care, education, research and community service is the basis for any physical development planning. To this end, the programs and service volumes in each area must be appraised.

A thorough understanding of the hospital's current situation is vital for charting its future. The planning team must analyze what's happened annually for the past five to ten years. It must study the trends of growth or decline and determine the factors that caused those changes. The team then forecasts what is likely to happen from the master plan's initial development to its end-point. Projections are made for the period of the master plan. Usually, two points within this time period—a seven- to eight-year horizon and 20 years in the future—serve as benchmarks. These planning projections are based on empirical evidence, not merely speculation.

Step 2 of master planning, concurrent with Step 1, is to analyze the existing site. Is the available acreage limiting or expansive? Is the site topography satisfactory or do unusual factors such as river bed, rock or excessive slope affect the site's suitability? Are the ingresses and egresses affecting traffic circulation satisfactory? Is adjoining land available, and is it suitable for hospital use? Are there zoning requirements that might adversely affect development? Questions of this sort must be addressed before proceeding to **Step 3**—analyzing the existing facilities.

The existing facility analysis focusses on the amount of space each hospital department has

Figure 22-1 Timing of master planning steps

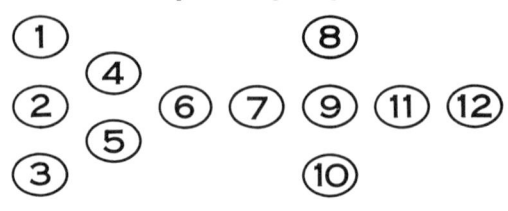

① ⑧
  ④
② ⑥ ⑦ ⑨ ⑪ ⑫
  ⑤
③ ⑩

Table 22-1 Preliminary Building Cost Estimate

Building Gross
Square Footage = Total Net
           Square Footage
           × Net-to-Gross Factor

Base Cost of
Building = Building Gross
           Square Footage
           × Cost/Square Foot

and the department's ability to function properly within that space. Each department's layout and environment are studied, as are interdepartmental relationships.

Besides evaluating the adequacy of the space, the buildings' "life expectancy" and the possible uses to which they can be put during the master plan period are determined. The buildings' exterior and interior conditions and their mechanical and electrical systems are evaluated in this step.

Step 3 culminates in the calculation of each department's required size—the net square footage each department needs—based on its existing programs and levels of activity. This comparison of needed square footage with that available is a measure of the existing facilities' adequacy.

In **Step 4**, the total net square footage of usable departmental space that will be required at the two planning horizons is calculated based on the hospital's proposed role and programs. The usable square footage is then multiplied by a net-to-gross factor to obtain a *building* gross square footage figure.

Unlike a *departmental* total, a *building* gross square footage figure includes everything within a building's perimeter such as stairs, ducts, corridors, wall thicknesses and mechanical areas. This distinction between departmental and building gross square footage is important in obtaining a realistic preliminary cost estimate. (See Table 22-1.)

Step 5 involves outlining basic operational concepts for each department and for the hospital as a whole. What admitting system—centralized or decentralized—will be used? How will materials be distributed and recycled? How will ambulatory programs integrate with the rest of the hospital? What interdepartmental relationships must be established or maintained: Should space be organized on a clinical basis—or instead should space be organized more traditionally on a functional basis?

Analyzing land use is **Step 6;** it overlaps Steps 4 and 5. The planning team must look at the site as a whole. Based on square footage requirements previously determined, it must decide where service elements should be, where inpatient bed elements should be, and where diagnostic and treatment services should be. The team must determine the routing of the different types of traffic and size of parking facilities. This broad evaluation of the site results in a block or land use plan for the two master plan target dates.

Step 7 is determining departmental location. In this step, the team details the land use plan. Based on the concepts developed in Step 5, decisions are made regarding where each department will be in relation to every other department.

Step 8 is to determine the direct project cost. This figure, which has several components, is the meaningful basis for calculating a valid estimated construction cost.

First, all new departmental space is converted to the gross building space to be constructed. A net-to-gross factor is then applied to the net usable space to reach a building gross figure. This figure includes all circulation, mechanical and structural space. It represents an estimate of the total amount of space that will actually be constructed.

The gross building space total is multiplied by a cost factor specific to a point in time and to the city or area in which the hospital will be built. To this figure is applied a factor for escalating construction costs—usually projected to the midpoint of construction, which is the point at which contractors base their bid price.

The expense of remodeling, site acquisition and movable equipment must also be included in the direct project cost. Areas to be remodeled are divided into subgroups on the basis of the complexity or completeness of remodeling required, and then costed separately for each subgroup. The movable equipment cost can be estimated at this stage in either gross or refined terms; generally, it runs from ten to 20 percent of the new construction cost. A working contingency and an owner's contingency are included in the direct project cost, as are fees for architects, consultants and a construction manager. (See Table 22-2.)

The direct project cost does not include interim and long-term financing costs, dedication and start-up costs, and legal fees.

The overall master plan is costed out for the seven-to-eight year period only.

Step 9 is to conduct a preliminary financial capability study, which can be done by the hospital's finance department or let to an outside accounting firm. The study is a quick determination of whether the hospital can sustain the cost of implementing the seven-to-eight-year part of the plan and remain competitive financially in its service area.

Step 10 is to establish priorities on what is to be developed and when. This step often coincides with Steps 8 and 9.

Step 11 is to formalize the entire master planning process in a comprehensive report. This document includes the role and program conclusions; the physical facilities analysis, including space needs and functional requirements; the proposed plan in both pictorial and narrative forms; the cost of the plan; its financial capability, and the suggested phasing of the master plan, if that should become necessary.

The last step of master planning is often the toughest. It climaxes months of meetings, interviews, data collection, calculations and preliminary planning. **Step 12** is decision making.

When the board and administration are presented with a comprehensive master plan, they are faced with everything needed for a simple yes or no response.

If their answer is "no" or "not for a while," the master plan still stands as a living, working document for monitoring the hospital's development. It can and should be reviewed periodically—at least every two years—to check its consistency with what is happening in the service area.

If the answer is yes, the hospital can proceed confidently, knowing that the plan is practical, implementable and affordable. Program changes or physical development can be made with the certainty that they are grounded in an overall, coordinated plan.

The value of this 12-step process lies in the future. When definitive planning begins, whatever action is ultimately taken (construction, demolition, renovation, merger) can be accomplished more quickly and with the prospect of fewer subsequent costly changes or corrections. The increased speed and certainty mean substantial future savings.

HOW TO ORGANIZE FOR THE PLANNING PROCESS*

Organizing for planning requires several actions, most importantly:

- Developing a decision-making mechanism,
- Appointing a director of planning,
- Organizing for internal review of planning documentations,
- Selecting the professional planning team,
- Organizing the planning team and formulating operating procedures.

Each of these actions will be briefly discussed.

Developing a Decision-Making Mechanism

While the governing board represents the ultimate institutional authority, experience has

---

*Source: Reprinted from *Hospitals: The Planning and Design Process* by Owen B. Hardy and Lawrence P. Lammers, with permission of Aspen Systems Corporation, © 1978.

Table 22-2 Direct Project Cost Estimate

Direct Project Cost	=	Base Cost of Building	+	Escalation Factors	+	Fees	+	Remodeling	+	Site Acquisition

shown that only important matters should be routinely decided there. *The planning and design of major building programs impose sufficient additional strain upon the management hierarchy that it is essential to provide a special mechanism to handle issues directly related to these endeavors.*

In major programs, four levels of decision making occur. The first level is usually the *director of planning,* who serves as an arm of hospital administration. The *building committee* is the second level. At the third level, a *special committee* with broad and diverse user representation can be organized to handle significant and controversial matters. Of course, the *governing board,* as the fourth or top level, must retain ultimate authority and responsibility for the entire building program.

The *planning director's* role in decision making may be relatively minor in substantive matters. His functions include scheduling and coordinating the activities of planners, architects, engineers, construction managers, financial advisors and other professional team members; scheduling tasks to be performed by members of the internal hierarchy; formulating appropriate reports; and seeing to it that higher decisions are appropriately channeled.

The *building committee* has traditionally served in a key decision-making role, acting exclusively upon many important matters and reporting directly to the governing board. In such instances, there have usually been only two or three levels in the chain. However, the process can be facilitated by the interjection of the special user committee between the building committee and the governing board. The building committee can consider a variety of highly technical matters and render recommendations and advice.

The *special user committee,* rather than being a working body, has the sole function of decision making, short of the governing board's ultimate authority and responsibilities. Matters should be referred which involve the interests of different disciplines, such as medical vs. administrative, surgery vs. medicine, nursing vs. supply, etc., and broad and diverse representation is critical to the acceptability of its decisions. A physician, for example, will be more inclined to accept a decision made by a committee on which physicians hold membership; nursing administration likewise will be more favorable when nursing has a deciding voice. At the same time, the presence of diverse disciplines will have a compromising influence upon decisions, so that the probability of balance among departmental allocations will become greater.

Appointing a Director of Planning

A major building program warrants a fulltime director, and in some very large programs one or two assistants can be justified.

The job of planning director is highly sensitive, and his ability to coordinate is critical. Managerial skills are more important than technical skills, although knowledge about the basics of design, economics, and/or functional planning is desirable. The person selected should have considerable perceptual ability, and a good appearance and public demeanor. The director's position in the table of organization should be designated and his duties explained to all planning team members, medical staff leaders, and members of the management hierarchy.

Organizing for Internal Review and Planning Documentations

Internal review of planning documents and design drawings can become an extremely tedious and time-consuming process unless handled properly. An appropriate review embraces the decision-making mechanism, but it must be broadened to include certain groups to which no decision-making authority has been delegated. For example, certain user representatives should be asked to review documentations, assess alternatives, and submit recommendations. Decisions, however, would be made by one of four bodies: the planning director, the building committee, the special user committee, or the governing board.

Documentations which should be formally reviewed by medical staff representatives include long-range program plans, master program documents, master site plan, block plan drawings, schematic drawings, and design development drawings on a departmental basis.

Administrative heads of departments should ordinarily review all planning documentations and drawings related to their departments and submit comments in writing to the planning director. He, in turn, should review the comments, hold discussions where necessary, and send written recommendations to the appropriate decision-making body.

In some instances, management has organized user review committees for diagnostic and treatment elements, supporting services, inpatient nursing, administrative services, etc. These committees can well replace department heads for review, but such heads should serve on the committees reviewing documentations related to their departments.

The governing board's finance committee will be charged with important review responsibilities, especially if capital from commercial sources is required. This body will confer frequently with the financial consultant and the investment banker's representative, and from time to time will make recommendations to the governing board.

Selecting the Professional Planning Team

The quality of the professional planning team will determine more than any other single factor the quality and suitability of completed facilities. This team should be selected with care, using judicious criteria. A complete team will possess capabilities in the areas of: (1) financial feasibility consulting, (2) functional planning, (3) architectural and engineering services, and (4) construction management.

On large, complicated projects, each capability should be represented by an independent firm, probably serving as a separate contractor to the owner. In the case of areas (2), (3) and (4), a team of firms can be formed to render services under a single contract. On smaller, less complicated projects, design and construction management can be performed by a single contractor, usually at a savings in fees, or the construction manager can be eliminated.

Financial Feasibility Consultant

This consultant should be independent of all other members of the planning team. While it is true that many competent financial feasibility studies have been done by firms also assigned to tasks of functional planning, the possibility of bias is inherent here and should not be allowed.

Functional Planning Consultant

The American Association of Hospital Consultants requires its members to possess certain minimum qualifications related to past experience and education. The membership roster provides a ready source from which a highly competent functional planner can be selected. Hospital executives are advised to obtain the AAHC's listing, select several firms, and proceed with detailed interviews.

Demonstrated past performance, financial stability, indepth talent of a multidisciplinary nature, current workloads, office proximity, and qualifications of the project manager actually to be assigned to the job are major attributes to be considered in selecting a functional planning consultant.

Architect/Engineer

For selecting an architectural firm, the American Hospital Association has formulated excellent criteria which can be obtained upon request, eliminating the need for detailed discussion here. Hospital management is ill-advised to accept architectural claims of functional planning expertise.

Construction Manager

Construction management offers three primary benefits:

1. It brings detailed knowledge of construction techniques and requirements to the architect early in the design phase so that alternative schemes can be accurately evaluated in terms of cost.

2. It puts the systems which control labor, money and materials to work directly for the owner's interests.

3. It allows overall management to break down the sequential nature of the traditional approach, allowing design and construction to proceed concurrently.

For the selection of a firm it seems logical that experience in constructing hospitals would be highly important.

The construction manager should assume responsibility to some extent for his cost predictions. At the same time he should be given some incentive for cost savings during the course of the construction based on his management skills.

Selection Timing and Methodology

The functional planner, the architect and the construction manager can all make valuable contributions in the early stages of a project and should be contracted at approximately the same time. Because the functional planner has the most intense involvement in the very first stages, he might be hired first, but the other two should closely follow. If an independent financial consultant has been contracted to set initial budgetary limits, he, of course, will have already been selected. In the event that this task has been accomplished internally with or without the advice of a prospective lender, the selection of a financial consultant can possibly be deferred until such time as precise operational parameters and capital cost estimates are in hand. His advice, however, will be desirable at the time workload projections are made.

Rather than merely reviewing brochures and other promotional material which applicants may offer, the hospital, through its director of planning, should submit questionnaires to various interested firms and, on the basis of responses, narrow firms to be interviewed down to a feasible number (usually four to six). The questionnaire should obtain information about the firm's general nature and ascertain its capabilities and experience related directly to the type of proposed project. Client references should be checked.

The interviewing process, which should involve individuals actually to be assigned by a prospective firm to the project, ought to be structured with ample time reserved for mostly predetermined questions.

Some benefit may be gained in holding second interviews when two applicants seemingly have equal capabilities.

Organizing the Team and Formulating Operating Procedures

Organizing the Team

The professional planning team can be organized in a number of ways. One approach employs independent firms, with each reporting separately to the planning director or other officer of the hospital. The other relates the financial planner directly to the hospital, but organizes the remaining three members as a team under one of several possible arrangements.

Where the hospital has a strong planning director whose primary job is to supervise the planning for a major building program, there may be advantages in having all team members report directly to him.

If the planning director is inexperienced or has other major duties, it may be best to contract with a consortium composed of the architect/engineer, functional planner and construction manager. Usually the architect/engineer or construction manager will be assigned a lead role, under terms of the contractual agreement. Of course, the financial feasibility consultant should continue to report directly and independently to the hospital. Communication channels among the team members and the hospital should be clearly outlined and noted in writing at the outset. If this is not done, a strong possibility exists that coordination will deteriorate as the project progresses.

When any formal correspondence is directed from one team member to another, or from a team member to the planning director, copies should be supplied to all. Beyond this, there should be a person in the hospital (other than the planning director) to whom copies of all correspondence should be sent. In most instances, this should be the chairperson of the building committee, preferably also a member of the governing board.

Coordination is best served by regularly scheduled meetings.

A STEP-BY-STEP SCHEDULE OF ACTIVITIES FOR THE PLANNING TEAM*

In their roles as decision makers, hospital officials must carefully analyze specific situations, determine activities to be undertaken, and chart a certain course of action.

Here are the various activities which should usually be performed in the course of a major project. The listing has been arranged in a chronological order of performance, but based in some instances merely upon the need for the output of one activity as input for another, prior

---

*Source: Reprinted from *Hospitals: The Planning and Design Process* by Owen B. Hardy and Lawrence P. Lammers, with permission of Aspen Systems Corporation, © 1978.

to finalization. Where work can be performed concurrently, it has been so stated.

Obviously, the entire flow of work as described can be outlined through the use of either PERT (Program Evaluation and Review Technique) or CPM (Critical Path Method) scheduling techniques. Schedulers frequently utilize one or the other, since the concept of network scheduling was originally developed to speed and order the work of special purpose or "onetime through" projects involving diverse and complex activities.

Figure 22-2 graphically displays an example schedule of the activities described, shows assignments among team members, and relates reviews and approvals by the hospital as the process progresses.

1. Need Survey.

    Primary Responsibility—Hospital Consultant. Often, the firm employed will also have capabilities related to functional planning. However, the need survey should be a stand-alone contract to preclude biased conclusions which might lead to work related to unneeded facility construction.

    Description—May take the form of a regional survey, community survey, or role study for a single hospital.

    Concurrent Activities—Facility planning work should await completion of this study, although portions of the physical and functional evaluation can be undertaken.

2. Feasibility Evaluation.

    Primary Responsibility—Can be accomplished internally if the hospital possesses the capability. May be accomplished by an investment banker or other outside financial advisor.

    Description—Usually, examination of existing financial documentations to determine cash generation capability and net equity for the purpose of estimating borrowing capabilities.

    Concurrent Activities—Portions of the physical and functional evaluations can be performed.

3. Physical Evaluation of Existing Facilities.

    Primary Responsibility—Architect/Engineer or Functional Planner with A/E capabilities.

    Description—This is a study to determine the degree of physical obsolescence of existing facilities, identify major code violations and physical problems, and project future usability.

    Concurrent Activities—Work on the Functional Evaluation can proceed simultaneously and, in most instances, can merely be a part of a single study.

4. Functional Evaluation of Existing Facilities.

    Primary Responsibility—Functional Planner.

    Description—This is a study to define functional problems which detract from operational efficiency, patient care and convenience of building inhabitants; evaluate traffic flows and physical relationships; determine space insufficiencies in terms of current requirements; study need for modernization, alterations and expansion, based upon role survey findings; and make recommendations as to alternative future uses of the structure as a whole, plus various departmental areas.

    Concurrent Activities—Physical Evaluation.

5. Review and Acceptance of Evaluations.

    Primary Responsibility—Hospital Officials.

    Description—The physical and functional evaluations should be read and studied by the planning director and all members of the building committee, as a minimum. The planning director should prepare his comments for the building committee, which should approve, formulate exceptions, or reject the studies. Recommendations should be passed on to the chief executive officer, who will make his personal review and secure action by the governing board.

    Concurrent Activities—Workload projections can be started.

Figure 22-2 Activities of the professional planning team

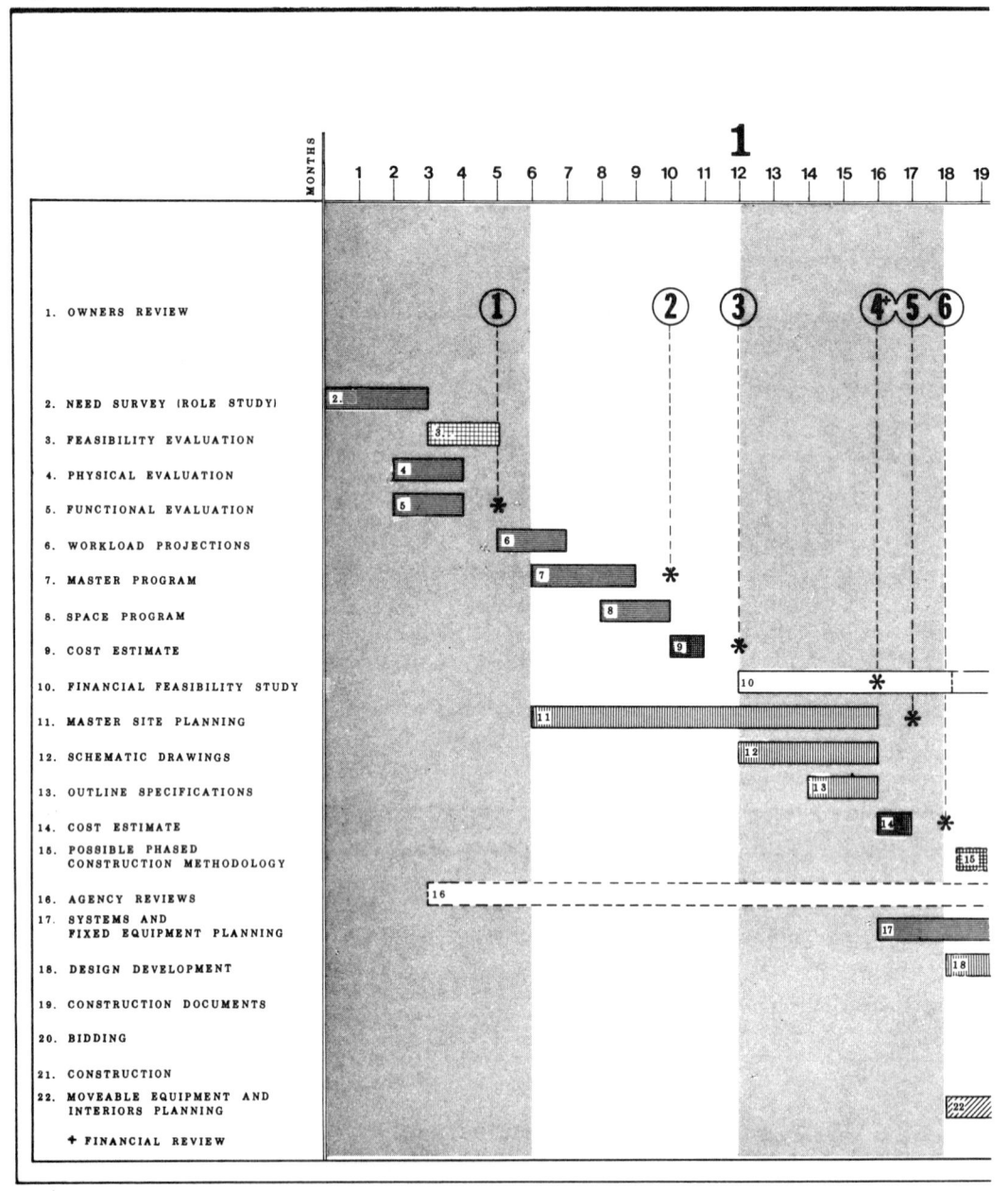

#	Activity
1.	OWNERS REVIEW
2.	NEED SURVEY (ROLE STUDY)
3.	FEASIBILITY EVALUATION
4.	PHYSICAL EVALUATION
5.	FUNCTIONAL EVALUATION
6.	WORKLOAD PROJECTIONS
7.	MASTER PROGRAM
8.	SPACE PROGRAM
9.	COST ESTIMATE
10.	FINANCIAL FEASIBILITY STUDY
11.	MASTER SITE PLANNING
12.	SCHEMATIC DRAWINGS
13.	OUTLINE SPECIFICATIONS
14.	COST ESTIMATE
15.	POSSIBLE PHASED CONSTRUCTION METHODOLOGY
16.	AGENCY REVIEWS
17.	SYSTEMS AND FIXED EQUIPMENT PLANNING
18.	DESIGN DEVELOPMENT
19.	CONSTRUCTION DOCUMENTS
20.	BIDDING
21.	CONSTRUCTION
22.	MOVEABLE EQUIPMENT AND INTERIORS PLANNING
	✦ FINANCIAL REVIEW

(Read Figure 22-2 across two pages.)

Chapter 22—Construction 353

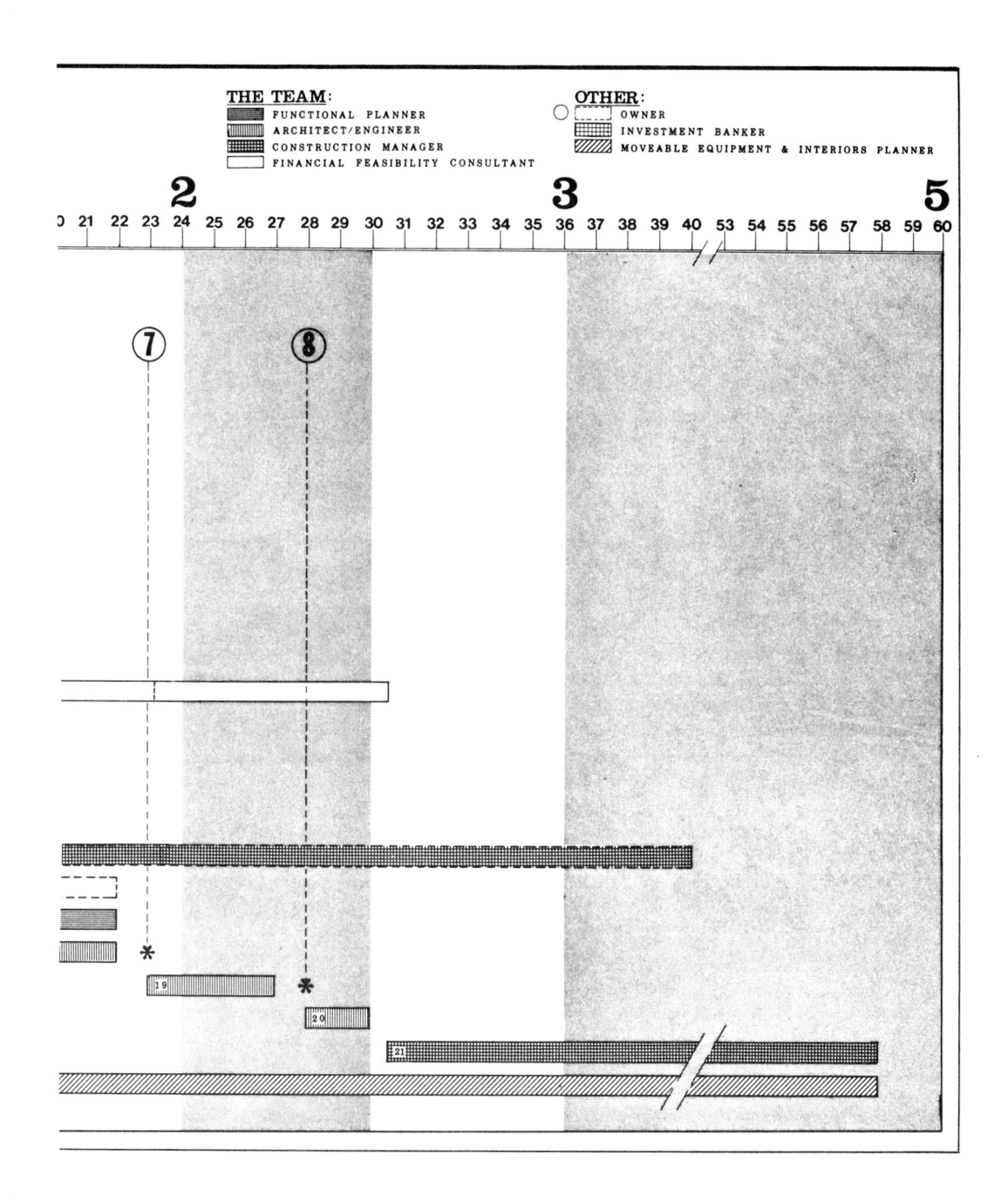

6. Workload Projections.

    Primary Responsibility—Functional Planner, advised by Financial Consultant.

    Description—Historical workloads (laboratory tests, X-ray examinations, operations, etc.) are linked to applicable parameters (outpatient visits, admissions and/or patient days) and a historical pattern in utilization indices established. Both utilization indices and parameters are then extended to desired future years, although the parameters probably will have already been extended in the need survey. Projected indices are applied to forecasted parameters to obtain estimated workloads. All calculations are reviewed with appropriate department heads to identify abnormal deviations in historical data and to ascertain changes in operational methods which could affect the extensions of past trends. These projections form the basis for Master Programming, revenue projections and staffing estimates.

    Concurrent Activities—The functional planner can determine and formulate concepts of operation for the proposed project, based on previous study findings. These concepts will be incorporated in the Master Program.

7. Master Program.

    Primary Responsibility—Functional Planner.

    Description—Based upon findings of the role or need survey study, physical and functional evaluations, and workload projections, the functional planner formulates his recommendations for operational concepts, the detailed room composition of the project, required phasing, alterations, internal and external traffic flows, interdepartmental and intradepartmental relationships, and operating systems. This single document sets the project's basic character and scope.

    Concurrent Activities—Site selection and/or site evaluation can proceed and extend through activity 9 following.

8. Review and Acceptance of Master Program.

    Primary Responsibility—Hospital Officials.

    Description—The planning director, the building committee, the users, the medical staff committees and the governing board (or designated committee) should review workload projections and the master program. The planning director should coordinate the review and submit final recommendations to the chief executive officer, who will also review and then obtain appropriate action from the governing board. The usual output is an approved document with addenda reflecting hospital amendments.

    Concurrent Activities—Assuming that changes will not drastically affect the scope of the project, the functional planner can proceed with net space programming. The architect/engineer can continue site selection or evaluation work.

9. Space Programming.

    Primary Responsibility—Functional Planner and/or Architect/Engineer.

    Description—Based upon the master program, as amended and approved by the hospital, a room-by-room listing is made of all areas in the proposed project. Net square footage is assigned to each space, and totals accumulated for every department and/or functional entity. Conversion factors are applied to the net figures to obtain gross total figures.

    Concurrent Activities—The financial consultant can proceed with expense and income projections, based upon workload projections, and projected staffing patterns. Site planning can proceed.

10. Cost Estimate.

    Primary Responsibility—Construction Manager.

    Description—Based upon the master program, space program and findings of site planning work, plus recorded cost experiences per square foot for similar facility components in the area, an initial cost estimate can be made.

    Concurrent Activities—The financial consultant can proceed with his feasibility study, and master site planning can proceed by the architect/engineer.

11. Review and Acceptance of Space Program and Cost Estimate.

    Primary Responsibility—Hospital Officials.

    Description—The planning director, building committee, users, medical staff committees, and the governing board (or designated committee) should review the space program. The planning director should coordinate the review and submit final recommendations to the chief executive officer, who will then review and obtain appropriate action from the governing board. All reviews should be made in consideration of the cost estimate.

    Concurrent Activities—Block plan drawings can be prepared as site planning continues. Financial feasibility work can proceed.

12. Financial Feasibility Study.

    Primary Responsibility—Financial Consultant.

    Description—Tentative findings of the financial feasibility study should be prepared and reported, based upon the project cost and projected revenue and expenses.

    Concurrent Activities—Master site planning can continue, and early schematic drawings can be started by the architect/engineer. The investment banker can identify the best manner of financing the project if commercial borrowing is required.

13. Review and Acceptance of Financial Feasibility Findings.

    Primary Responsibility—Hospital Officials.

    Description—The finance committee should review findings as submitted by the financial consultant and formulate recommendations to the governing board. The governing board must make relevant decisions and publish instructions based thereon.

    Concurrent Activities—Master site planning, schematic drawings and analyses of financing methods can all move forward.

14. Master Site Planning.

    Primary Responsibility—Architect/Engineer, advised by Functional Planner.

    Description—The preparation of a master site plan can be completed. Four tasks may have been involved; these are: (1) site selection, (2) site evaluation, (3) block plan drawings, and (4) preparing design drawings and specifications for the master plan. Site selection pertains to a quantitative comparison among possible site choices and the selection of one; site evaluation pertains to soil test borings, availability of required utilities, and evaluation of other characteristics of a site already selected. Block plan drawings are single lines of gross areas only, denoting relationships of departments, internal vertical and horizontal traffic flows, external traffic flows (both pedestrian and vehicular), and expansion requirements. A master site plan represents an architectural delineation of programmed facilities situated on the site, usually at $1'' = 40'$ or larger scale. The master site plan should project the ultimate development of the site.

    Concurrent Activities—Schematic drawings and possible financial feasibility study refinements can all proceed. The investment banker can begin preparation of his official statement for bonds to be offered.

15. Review and Acceptance of Master Site Plan.

    Primary Responsibility—Hospital Officials.

    Description—The planning director, building committee, governing board, the chief executive officer, and, in some instances, an appropriate committee of the medical staff should review the work performed under master site planning. Final recommendations, coordinated by the planning director, should be transmitted to the chief executive officer for board approval.

Concurrent Activities—A continuation of work on schematic drawings and matters related to financing is appropriate.

16. Preparation of Schematic Drawings, Elevations, Sections, Details.

    Primary Responsibility—Architect/Engineer, advised by Functional Planner and Construction Manager.

    Description—Schematics should be single line, beginning at $1/16''$ scale and developing into $1/8''$ scale, which reflect all rooms, corridors, and mechanical spaces, level by level. Door openings are shown, but most other details omitted. Planned future additions should be shown. Elevations and other drawings should reflect general disposition of materials and outline typical construction systems.

    Concurrent Activities—Financial work and preparation of outline specifications.

17. Preparation of Outline Specifications.

    Primary Responsibility—Architect/Engineer, guided by Construction Manager.

    Description—The following, and all other items that are significant in determining the design and cost of the project, must be described at a level of detail required for cost estimating: site work; structural system; exterior materials; interior materials; conveying systems; heating, ventilation and air conditioning systems; plumbing and fire protection; electrical systems and requirements; fixtures, furnishings and equipment (all fixed).

    Concurrent Activities—Possible work by the financial consultant and investment banker.

18. Preparation of Cost Estimate.

    Primary Responsibility—Construction Manager.

    Description—With schematic drawings and outline specifications in hand, the construction manager will be able to produce a closely accurate cost estimate. This estimate should be formally prepared and submitted.

    Concurrent Activities—Functional review of schematic drawings can proceed among hospital committees and/or officials, and, possibly, further work by the financial consultant and investment banker.

19. Review and Acceptance of Schematic Drawings, Outline Specifications and Cost Estimate.

    Primary Responsibility—Hospital Officials, advised by the Functional Planner, A/E, and Construction Manager.

    Description—All parties who have review responsibilities should examine the area of their interest on the schematic drawings. The functional planner and the architect should be available for explanations when reviews are accomplished. After necessary changes and compromises at lower echelons, drawings are submitted to the chief executive officer for his review and for governing board consideration and approval. The governing board, with schematic drawings, outline specifications and cost estimate in completed form, can authorize proceeding with design development drawings and preparation of contract drawings and specifications for initial site work and early general contracts if phased construction ("fast tracking") is contemplated.

    Concurrent Activities—Plans for procuring construction funds should be finalized at this point if phased construction is to be undertaken. A guaranteed maximum price (GPM) is sometimes obtained from or by the construction manager. If a GPM is obtained, the financial feasibility study can be completed based upon it. The functional planner can start the preparation of environmental data sheets.

20. Agency Review.

    Primary Responsibility—Appropriate Governmental Agencies.

    Description—Necessary agency reviews vary from state to state, and requirements in this regard must be determined by hospital officials during early planning. However, the completion of schematic drawings and outline specifications represents a certain point of review. We have not described any other review, but have merely made this notation as a reminder that such reviews must be met as required by individual state regulations.

Concurrent Activities—Systems and fixed equipment planning, design development drawings and preparations for marketing of bonds. Environmental data sheets can be finalized.

21. Systems and Fixed Equipment Planning.

    Primary Responsibility—Architect/Engineer advised and assisted by Functional Planner and Construction Manager.

    Description—Planning of systems and/or fixed equipment to include medical gases, housekeeping vacuum, pneumatic tube systems, other transport systems, diagnostic and therapeutic X-ray equipment, supply processing and distribution systems, data processing, trash disposal, laundry, major specialized lighting, dietary system, casework, specialized plumbing fixtures and communication systems may be carried out largely by the functional planner, advised by the architect/engineer and construction manager. Preparation of formal documents is the responsibility of the architect/engineer.

    Concurrent Activities—Full-scale design development work can proceed, and construction documents for initial bid packages can be prepared, in the case of a phased construction program.

22. Design Development.

    Primary Responsibility—Architect/Engineer, advised by Functional Planner and Construction Manager.

    Description—Drawings at 1/8" or 1/4" scale are prepared of all areas to be constructed. Fixed equipment, major movable equipment and items of furniture are shown, together with interior elevations of all specialized rooms.

    Concurrent Activities—Preparation of construction documents can proceed, and first bid packages readied in phased construction methodology. Most guaranteed maximum prices are obtained at this point under phased construction if the owner must have complete assurance of total cost. In these instances, the financial feasibility study is completed, and final plans for funding the construction must be prepared. Movable equipment and interiors planning should begin.

23. Review and Acceptance of Design Development Drawings.

    Primary Responsibility—Hospital Officials.

    Description—Again, all categories of persons with review responsibilities should carefully audit these drawings in sessions with the functional planner, the architect/engineer, and the construction manager. Where exceptions cannot be compromised, they should be referred to the special user committee for decision and recommendations to the governing board. The planning director should coordinate all reviews and finally submit drawings, comments and recommended actions to the chief executive officer for his review and for governing board disposition.

    Concurrent Activities—Initial bids can be awarded and construction started under a program of phased construction. Succeeding bid packages can be readied and work on all remaining construction documents started. Movable equipment and interiors planning is carried forward.

24. Construction Documents.

    Primary Responsibility—Architect/Engineer advised by the Construction Manager and Functional Planner.

    Description—Preparation of working drawings, specifications and conditions of the contract. Under phased construction, these three elements are prepared for each separate contract; under conventional construction, they are prepared for every aspect of the total work.

    Concurrent Activities—Bidding requirements and the form of agreement can be prepared. Movable equipment and interiors planning can proceed. Costing and budget refinements by the construction manager can be carried forward.

25. Review and Acceptance of Construction Documents.

Primary Responsibility—Hospital officials, advised by the Architect/Engineer, Construction Manager and Functional Planner.

Description—Hospital officials should carefully examine all construction documents under both phased and traditional construction approaches to ascertain a level of acceptable quality and to see that owner directives have been followed. Acceptance and/or exceptions should be signified in writing.

Concurrent Activities—Preparation for bidding should be finalized. Final cost estimates should be submitted to the hospital. Movable equipment and interiors planning proceeds.

26. Bidding.

    Primary Responsibility—Architect/Engineer (assisted by CM).

    Description—Invitations to bid, instructions to bidders, and the bid form are prepared and pre-bid activities undertaken (evaluating and ascertaining competent bidders). Invitations to bid are mailed to prospective bidders. Contract documents are delivered to interested bidders. Pre-bid conferences are held, and bids prepared by bidders. Bids are opened, reviewed, and a contract awarded. This process is followed under both phased and conventional construction.

    Concurrent Activities—Finalization of plans for funding. Movable equipment and interiors planning proceeds.

27. Construction.

    Primary Responsibility—Construction Manager and/or General Contractor and/or separate specialized contractors. Work is monitored by the Architect/Engineer.

    Description—Pre-construction conferences are held and the construction of the project is undertaken and carried forward to completion. As is implicit in all these descriptions, construction may be implemented either by a phased or traditional methodology.

    Concurrent Activities—Movable equipment and interiors planning is finalized. Hospital officials schedule opening activities, plan for staff, and undertake employee orientations. In employee orientations, the functional planner should play a definite role.

28. Movable Equipment and Interiors Planning.

    Primary Responsibility—Movable Equipment Planner and/or Interior Decorator. May be one or two respective firms on large projects. Movable equipment planning may be accomplished internally on small projects, and the architect may perform interiors planning.

    Description—This planning, started in design development, is finished during construction. Installation of movable equipment, of course, must be planned as a part of opening together with finalization of interiors planning (completion of signage programs, etc.).

    Concurrent Activities—Design development, the review process, preparation of construction documents, bidding and construction are all undertaken and finished during the planning of movable equipment and interiors.

CONTRACTS FOR SERVICES WITH CONSULTANTS AND CONTRACTORS*

One of the most significant elements of cost in a major capital project is the total amount of fees and profits which the owner will pay to these contractors and consultants, during the course of the project. In controlling project cost, it is obviously important to minimize those fees and profits. Even more important than the dollars involved, however, is selection of the fee structures which give incentive to the other parties to use their talents and experience in keeping the total cost of the project to the lowest possible level.

Sums which may be far in excess of the total fees can thus be saved in the design and construction of the project. Incentives must also be

---

*Source: Reprinted from W. Thomas Berriman *et al.*, "Capital Projects," *Topics in Health Care Financing,* Winter 1975, with permission of Aspen Systems Corporation.

provided to professionals and contractors in order to assure the quality of the design, labor and materials which go into the final product.

1. Basic Price Provisions: Fixed Price Contracts

This is the most common contractual arrangement in the everyday world, the payment of a fixed sum for a stipulated product or service. In providing a service as complicated as designing or supervising the construction of a health care facility, especially in present circumstances, it is extremely difficult for the architect, engineer or construction manager to predict with any degree of confidence the amount of time, effort or materials which he will be required to spend on the project.

Modern usage of the fixed price contract is generally limited to minor consulting services and to the awarding of construction contracts on the basis of sealed bids.

Fixed price arrangements create a definite conflict between the owner and the other contracting party, who must weigh the financial risk of underestimating his costs against the possibility of losing the job by naming too high a price. The contracting party is always under the temptation to reduce costs and expenses in order to maximize his profits. Any ambiguities in the specifications of work may well be interpreted against the owner, in order to achieve that goal.

When the work is properly described, however, there are major advantages to the sealed bid and fixed price contract. First, with invitations to bid being sent to only preselected contractors whose reputation for quality is known, the bids can be compared easily and the lowest overall price can readily be determined. The competitive aspect inherent in submission of sealed bids is a major reason that this method is imposed as a requirement on many public or quasipublic works programs. Each bidder is aware that he is engaged in price competition with others and is under significant pressure (depending on how much he wants to do the job) to submit the lowest possible price. Finally, the possibility of corruption of the contract awarding process is significantly reduced by the requirement of sealed bid procedures.

With the project being minutely defined in the fixed price contract, change orders may be required more frequently. Change orders are sometimes contracted on a fixed price basis, although even a fixed price main contract may often provide that change orders shall be handled on a time-and-material or cost-plus basis. During the course of construction, an owner's ability to have change orders executed by anyone other than the contractor already there is severely limited if not altogether nonexistent. Great care must be exercised in negotiating change order prices for that reason.

2. Variable Price Contracts

Variable price contracts are appropriate where the precise quantity or scope of the product or service being purchased cannot be determined in advance. It assures the owner that he will pay only the actual costs involved in his project and will not be penalized because of an overestimation of the amount of work to be required, and it assures the contracting party that unanticipated difficulties, increases in the scope of the work, or a bad guess as to his own costs will not penalize him. Properly implemented, the variable price contract has much to recommend it from the point of view of both contracting parties.

It does, however, carry with it a number of important disadvantages. First, the contracting party's incentive is to maximize the amount of work performed in order to maximize his income. No longer tempted to cut corners, he may now be tempted to perform "busy work." The contracting party is also under no duty to hold down the charges of others involved in the project since his compensation and profit is not related to other expense. This presents a very difficult budgeting problem for the owner. Further, either an immense amount of good faith or detailed cost accounting is required to insure that the costs reported have actually been incurred on the contracted project. Many of the disadvantages in the variable price contract can be avoided by the use of additional contractual limitations.

Percentage Fee Contracts

Traditionally, architects' fees have been fixed as a percentage of the total construction cost of the project. This arrangement may still be the most frequently used compensation arrangement for architects, although it does have the advantage of relating the architect's fees to the final scope of the contract.

A percentage-of-construction-costs fee provides the most negative kind of incentive to the architect in performing one of his most important services to the owner, that is, minimizing the cost of the project. The owner may be penalized if the project's scope has been reduced because of the architect's failure to keep the costs within the predetermined budgetary limitations.

Cost-plus-fixed-fee Contract

This type will provide no incentive to skimp or to waste, except to the extent that there may be an element of profit in the cost reimbursement mechanism. It is most difficult to eliminate this, since the proportion of fixed to variable expenses on the part of the contracting party will decrease as his reimbursable costs increase.

And so, the next variation on the cost-plus-fee contract is introduced, the ceiling limitation on total contract costs. A ceiling neither too high or too low will assure the contracting party that he will earn his full fee and will provide him with incentives neither to increase costs nor to cut corners.

Timecard Projects

A timecard approach is frequently used to determine payment for professional services. It is common with accountants and attorneys to base their fees on a calculation of hours recorded, multiplied by predetermined hourly rates. A similar approach is receiving substantial current acceptance with respect to architectural services as well. Time card rates may be determined in advance, or may be based upon a multiple of personnel expenses. In addition to using timecard rates for professional employees, a contract may include a fixed fee, or even a percentage fee based upon the amount of time recorded.

Timecard contracts may also be subjected to a ceiling on total costs and this ceiling is encountered in two forms. Preferably, from the owner's standpoint, the professional would undertake to perform the entire contract within a specified maximum. The variation is the "drop tools" clause, under which he will stop work on the project when his charges to the client equal the predetermined limit. Unless the project is to be abandoned at that point, this places the owner in an almost impossible negotiating situation, as he must now agree to pay whatever the architect requires in order to have the contract documents finished by the only firm with the background to do so.

It is not unusual to find an architect's contract divided into stages, with different compensation arrangements for each stage. For example, a timecard basis without limitation may be used in the initial stages, for services which are intended basically to define the scope of the project. This may be followed by a fixed fee, or timecard with a ceiling, for services required to complete the project.

Contingent Fees

The contingent fee may be encountered in the financial area. A mortgage broker's fee (a percentage of the loan called "points") is paid only if a commitment is obtained from a lender.

3. Other Provisions

Incentives

These may be positive incentives, or bonuses, or negative incentives, or penalties. The most common bonus would be the sharing of savings below a predetermined amount with a contractor, or even an architect. The most common penalty provision would be the imposition of a fixed dollar charge for each day consumed beyond a predetermined completion date.

Project Description

The description of the project is, as stated above, one of the most significant of all the terms of the contract. In later stages, particularly with sealed bids, the project may be described by reference to the completed plans and specifications. In the early stages, it may be possible to describe the project by reference to the long range plan, to the submission to the planning agency, or to the program prepared for the architect to interpret.

Change Orders

Some change orders are relatively routine, e.g., supplying details omitted from specifications or issuing clarification of the contract documents. There should be no change in the architect's or contractor's fee arrangements as a result of making such changes. On the other hand, change orders may be required if there is to be a redefinition of all or a major portion of the project, perhaps as the result of the intervention of some outside agency. In such a case, it is entirely appropriate for the architect and the contractor to receive upward adjustments in their fees.

Retainages

To provide the owner and the lenders with assurance that the project will be completed and with a security fund to cover any damages, most construction contracts provide that only 90 percent of the value of the work performed and materials installed will be paid on a current basis. In some cases, however, a reduced retainage is provided for the later stages of the job, so that subcontractors whose work is finished early (steel erectors, foundation excavators) can be paid off entirely. Retainages are also found in contracts of architects and engineers but are not usual with most consultants.

Reports and Accounting

Any cost-plus contract should have built into it the submission of periodic reports by the contracting parties, together with the right of the owner to cause those reports to be analyzed and to audit the books through representatives, including outside accountants. All consultants' contracts should provide for the submission of a written report and it is frequently advisable to require periodic written reports from architects or construction managers on the progress of the work. An important document in the construction contract is the architect's certificate approving invoices for payment during the course of construction. The preparation and submission of this certificate should be described in detail in the contract documents and all contracts should be reviewed to see that all procedures are consistent.

PROJECT MANAGEMENT TECHNIQUES*

1. Decision Points

At the beginning and end of each stage of development, and at several times during the implementation stage, decision points are reached.

---

*Source: Reprinted from Thomas Berriman, William G. Essick, Jr., and Peter Bentivegna, "Project Management Techniques," *Topics in Health Care Financing,* Winter 1975, with permission of Aspen Systems Corporation.

Each of these requires careful evaluation of the information about the project which is then available, including examination of earlier data and assumptions to determine their current validity. At each decision point, the feasibility of continuing the project as defined, or of modifying the project definition, should be critically and carefully analyzed and evaluated.

The difficult task is for the hospital administration, and the Building Committee and, if necessary, the full Board to be able to make a clear judgment of the feasibility of the project and to restructure or terminate it if warranted.

2. Project Modification

It is too late to attempt to control costs after the contract has been let and the construction of the project begun. Cost control on a capital project must be exercised at each decision point, when the financial viability of the project is reviewed, and an appropriate decision must be made. It is fatal, in many cases, to be locked into a project by momentum or inertia.

If a Building Committee report to the Board should show a financial problem, then project conditions must be modified to resolve the problem prior to authorizing the project to proceed. This may mean that fund-raising efforts, including financing efforts, must be expanded, that the scope of the project must be reduced, that timing and phasing must be changed, that certain equipment purchases must be deferred or that other alternatives must be investigated and decided upon. It is essential that the project not be allowed to continue until the immediate problem has been solved.

The cost of the project may be held down in three basic ways:

1. Building less space;
2. Building less expensive systems and details; or
3. Building lower quality.

Building lower quality does not mean building something which will not serve its function or will quickly deteriorate. Unfortunately, a mystique has grown up in the hospital industry that everything connected with "our life-saving institutions" must be of exceptional quality, since a patient's life may depend upon it. In certain areas, this attitude is quite correct and necessary. However, when this attitude is applied to all aspects of hospital functions, the result may be a grossly overdesigned facility.

A thorough life-cycle cost analysis of the major components of the project will aid greatly in controlling over-design, with emphasis on probable innovations in medical care. It is senseless to "build for the ages" what next year's technology will make obsolete.

Life cycle analysts estimate that the total operating costs of a hospital will exceed its construction costs within one to three years. With this in mind, it seems appropriate that the design of a facility should place as much emphasis on reducing operating costs as is placed upon holding down construction costs. Thus, during the design phase consideration must be given to the installation of maintenance- and labor-saving devices which could reduce costs over the life of the structure. Consultation with the contract departments of equipment and supply firms at this stage, rather than after the architect has completed drawings, can often contribute valuable means of integrating operating and structural concepts to bring about the most cost effective patient care.

3. Equipment Procurement

Formulation of equipment specifications should begin during preparation of the detailed program, when basic determinations are made on space allocations, staffing levels and operational volumes to be handled. The equipment to be selected, its size, service requirements and functional capabilities enter into this decision making process. As an example, staffing levels and building area requirements can be held down by the use of automated laboratory equipment, if justified by the number of tests to be performed.

Technical Requirements

During the preliminary design phase, a list of major equipment and technical specifications for that equipment must be given to the architect for incorporation into the design of the basic building systems. Much major equipment requires special mechanical, electrical, structural, or spatial considerations. It is also important at this time for the architect to have an indication of the amount of furniture to be used in each space so that the area layouts and traffic patterns can be determined at the outset of the design, eliminating the necessity for later changes in the design phase or during construction. Such decisions should be adhered to once they are made and direction is given to the design team.

Preparing Specifications

To insure that the hospital is furnished with equipment that will perform the intended function, not over-designed or under-designed, and also that maximum value is received for each dollar expended on equipment, it is important that the equipment specifications be carefully prepared. This assignment can often be handled best by an independent specialist with extensive experience in this field. In preparing the equipment lists and specifying individual items of equipment, the specialist would deal with such items as the functional capabilities of each item of equipment, maintenance requirements and service availability, life cycle costs, budget considerations, equipment payback period, special requirements for trained technicians and their availability and the impending technical obsolescence of each item.

4. Fast-Track Development

Almost any development project can be broken down into definitive parcels of work, each representing one facet of the total process.

In an effort to condense the overall project time frame, this process has been sometimes revised to permit some later tasks to be started prior to the completion of earlier ones. The industry term which describes this foreshortening of the project time frame is "fast-tracking".

Since, on most projects, the elements with the longest duration are the final design and construction phases, the greatest advantage can be obtained by starting construction part way through the design phase.

This represents two major cost saving features to the user:

1. The overlapping of the design and construction processes enables the owner to commit to construction purchases at an earlier date than would otherwise be possible. With the continuing effects of inflation, the advantages of buying materials and services today rather than tomorrow are self-evident.
2. The contraction of the project development period means that the finished facility

is put into productive service at an earlier time than would otherwise be possible. This means that capital is tied up unproductively for a shorter period of time and that the generation of revenue from the project begins at an earlier date than normally would be the case.

This approach is not universally applied because of the risks and disadvantages inherent in fast-tracking. These include:

1. The owner becomes fully committed to the project prior to the time all factors and costs are known. The opportunities for change are greatly restricted and those changes that must be made cost more in time and money than they would under normal scheduling.
2. Accelerated design decisions result in some conservative over-design being built into the project and lead to higher costs for individual components.
3. Construction bids for the initial work may be padded to some extent, depending on the condition of the bid documents and the amounts of ambiguity or detail therein. Bids for subsequent items of work to be contracted for may not be as low as could be obtained from others because the contractors know the owner is committed to the project. A strike, material shortage, weather conditions or a break in awarding contracts will usually have a greater negative financial effect, since the time advantage for which a premium was paid initially has been evaporated.
4. Under most circumstances, the process will require additional cash outlays by the institution, since construction will be started prior to the completion of all contract documents and prior to the time most funding would be available.
5. A greater than ordinary coordination effort is required to keep the various components moving ahead in conjunction with each other if chaos is to be prevented.

5. The Change Order

The change order is the formal document issued by the architect or contracting authority to the contractor changing certain conditions of the contract documents. It is perhaps one of the most overused and most often abused documents in the construction industry.

The best way in which to prevent abuse of the change order is to not use it at all. However, due to the complex nature of health care projects and the atmosphere of changing requirements, regulations and needs in which they are designed and constructed, this goal is not achievable in a health care project. The practical approach in this matter, then, is to minimize the use of the change order by adhering to the following standards:

1. Make sure that the plans and specifications as presented to the contractors for bidding are as complete as possible, and have been reviewed and coordinated both with the design team and with all appropriate review agencies so that changes will be kept to an absolute minimum.
2. Insure that equipment selections are made early in the design process so that special building requirements relating to the equipment can be designed into the contract documents at the outset.
3. Evaluate the reason for each change as it is proposed and require that changes be made only for those instances where the plans as presently constituted absolutely will not work, will not conform to code requirements, or will present an operational liability to the hospital. Changes made simply for personal preference should be evaluated with the utmost scrutiny, and instituted only in those instances where rejection of the change would cause a greater hardship upon the facility than its cost.
4. When changes are deemed absolutely necessary, their cost can often be handled most fairly by agreeing to pay for the work on a "cost plus", "time and materials", or "force account" basis. In this manner, it is only the true cost of the change for which the owner pays, and not some of the other costs outlined above.

6. Construction Funds Management

For the facility, the first step in this activity is to organize capital fund availability. These funds will usually come from a variety of sources and be disbursed for various uses. Some will cost less than others, and the project financial manager should use the less expensive funds first.

For instance, contributed funds would be used before drawing on borrowed funds on which interest must be paid. Considerable planning and coordination are necessary to ensure that funds are available when needed, that available funds do not sit idle, and that lowest cost funds are used first.

The control of disbursements is equally important. Progress payments should not be released until necessary inspections and certifications have been received and the amounts verified. Fees should not be paid until due, and funds reserved for specific uses should not be inadvertently disbursed for other uses.

The contractor's progress against the construction schedule should be updated monthly to identify at the earliest possible point any slippage in the estimated completion date, variance in fund receipts and disbursements, and estimates of total project cost.

Change orders (modifications to the original design after construction bids are final) inevitably arise during the construction phase. For this reason, an amount should be budgeted for contingencies. A contingency fund equal to 5 percent of construction costs is common and conservative in the initial stages, with 3 percent considered an absolute minimum provision. When final costs are known, the contingency fund can be reduced.

The administrator, financial officer, and the Building Committee should periodically review construction progress, all variances, and revised estimates of construction cost. Weekly or monthly monitoring of project status in a structured, formal manner at all levels of project responsibility is essential to successful project completion without excessive cost overruns and inadequate construction financing.

KEY FACTORS

Operational Decisions*

Before the detailed planning for new construction can begin, decisions have to be made regarding a number of operational concepts. It is the responsibility of the planner to bring those which are appropriate to the attention of hospital officials.

Some of the concepts which usually require deliberation and decision making follow:

1. All single patient rooms versus some mix of singles and doubles or of singles, doubles and four-bed wards.
2. An integrated, centralized supply processing and distribution system versus the traditional "central supply" concept which, in reality, features multiple processing points and often multiple receiving points.
3. Automation of supply distribution versus manual distribution.
4. No-nursing-station nursing units versus nursing units with nursing stations (each with implications as to size of units).
5. Team or primary nursing care versus functional nursing care.
6. Combined operating and delivery suite versus separate suites.
7. Triple corridored operating units versus single corridored suite (departmental concept only).
8. Ready foods versus convenience foods versus cook-chill versus traditional dietary systems.
9. In-house laundry versus outside processing.
10. Unit-dose drug dispensing system versus variations of the unit-dose system versus traditional systems.
11. Fully automated data processing versus various degrees of automation.
12. Functional bloc layout of emergency-ambulatory care suite versus traditional layout (departmental concept only).
13. Staff corridor concept in radiology versus traditional concept (departmental concept only).
14. Open bay concept in laboratory layout versus segregated service concept (departmental concept only).
15. Nuclear medicine as a separate service versus a division of radiology versus a division of pathology versus imaging as a part of radiology and in vitro assays as a part of pathology.
16. Shared service data processing versus in-house computer.

---

*Source: Reprinted from *Hospitals: The Planning and Design Process* by Owen B. Hardy and Lawrence P. Lammers, with permission of Aspen Systems Corporation, © 1978.

Teaching hospitals require an even greater definition of operational concepts. In addition to those receiving consideration in community-type hospitals, the following are often debated:

1. Complete decentralization of clinical research spaces by department versus centralized clinical research space, flexibly allocated.
2. Floor laboratories versus a centralized teaching laboratory.
3. Flexibly used ambulatory care areas versus completely segregated clinics, by service.
4. Complete decentralization of faculty offices versus centralized grouping of a selected percentage.
5. Floor pharmacies versus a centralized service only.

Financial Feasibility

Major Considerations*

Financial feasibility is more than a paper exercise to be performed by accountants. Financial feasibility means structuring a financial package so that an institution can secure full financing for a proposed project and can then, over the useful life of that project, repay any debt incurred in constructing the project while, at the same time, meeting full operating costs. Financial feasibility must consider both the market environment and the financial details of a proposed project. To determine the demand for services at the institution, "it is necessary to evaluate the demography, utilization rates, patient flows and competing hospitals within the institution's service area. Once this service area demand is established and a market share is estimated for the specific institution, the focus of the study is that of determining whether or not the estimated demand is sufficient to support the required level of debt." The importance of an analysis of the market cannot be overstated. No matter how good the projected financial statements look, if there is no real demand to support the project, it will not be financially feasible.

---

*Source: Mark S. Levitan and Brian P. Lenane, "Financial Feasibility of Health Facility Reuse," *Health Facility Reuse, Retrofit, and Reconfiguration,* National Center for Health Services Research, February 1980, DHEW Pub. No. (PHS)79-3257.

Market Analysis*

An increasing number of health care institutions are using computerized financial planning models in the early planning phase of a proposed construction program to estimate the institution's debt capacity. Through financial modeling, a series of assumptions can be tested and ranges of debt capacity established.

An experienced financial manager or consultant should be able within a few weeks to identify the key factors that could adversely affect the financial feasibility of a project, and zero in on the probable operating results. It would be prudent to review the following key factors that can affect the financial feasibility of a project early in the planning phase.

- Service Area Definition. What geographic areas do inpatients and ambulatory care patients come from and what are the present and future demographic characteristics of these areas?
- Area Population. A review of forecasted population by age and sex can provide direction about the mix of services that will be required in the future.
- Market Share. Has the institution's percentage of total area admissions and patient days been increasing, remaining constant or decreasing?
- Medical Staff Profile. A summary of physician admissions by age and medical specialty can identify specialties that have an insufficient number of physicians or those where a large number of admissions are provided by elderly physicians. A comparison of two or three years' data can be very informative.
- Average Length of Stay. How does it compare to regional, state and national norms by service? How has average length of stay been affected by changes in case mix and Medicare census?
- Plans of Other Area Hospitals. What hospitals in your institution's service area are planning building programs and how could these programs affect your institution?

---

*Source: Reprinted from Ernst & Ernst, "Health Care Notes," *Topics in Health Care Financing,* Winter 1978, with permission of Aspen Systems Corporation.

- Charge Structure. Is the hospital competitive with other area institutions? Can charges be increased to cover the additional costs (both capital and operating) related to the building program?
- Financial Mix of Patients. Has it been fluctuating? Are any third parties who currently pay charges planning to switch to cost-based reimbursement? Are any major area employers planning to switch medical coverage from a charge-paying to a cost-based insurance company?
- Cost Impact. How much additional cost per unit of service will be added by the interest and depreciation expense related to the construction program? How will the project affect operating costs—staffing, utility costs, etc.?
- Personnel Costs. Are existing staffing levels reasonable? Are existing salaries and fringe benefits competitive?
- Depreciation Expense Related to Existing Assets. Will this reimbursable expense decline significantly over the next five to ten years?
- Third Party Ceiling Limitations. How does the present institution compare to existing third party ceilings? Can the increased operating and capital costs related to the construction program be absorbed without exceeding ceilings? If not, how much revenue could be lost? It should be noted that Medicare and some local third party reimbursers do not automatically pass through capital costs for approved projects.
- Equity Required. Does the institution have the required equity readily available? Is a fund-raising program planned?
- Interest Income. How much interest income is generated annually? If equity is provided, how much will interest income decline? Will the third party reimbursers reduce reimbursable interest expenses by unrestricted interest income?
- Contingent Liabilities. Are there any potential liabilities, in malpractice claims in excess of coverage, that could prohibit a lender from providing the required funds?

By reviewing these factors, your institution should be able to identify potential problems early in the planning process, and then develop an action program to address the key issues.

Construction Costs[*]

With this broad framework in mind, the categories of costs that may be part of a major construction project should be examined to understand in what way they are unique in renovation or reuse. A list of such costs should include the following:

1. land costs,
2. planning and programming costs,
3. architectural fees,
4. interior design fees,
5. engineering fees,
6. construction costs—this would be further subdivided by trade breakdown;
7. legal costs,
8. project management costs,
9. financing costs—including commissions, broker's discount, legal and accounting fees and costs associated with securing financing;
10. implicit costs—not normally recorded such as implicit interest on existing capital, time and effort of management and other entrepreneurial costs;
11. equipment and furnishing, and
12. inventory and supplies.

Workload Projections[**]

Workload projections together with admissions and patient days by service, plus categorized outpatient visits form the basic utilization data required for the financial feasibility study. They are also prime determinants of space provisions as programmed by the functional planner. These projections must be objectively and competently accomplished, for in reality they represent commitments by the governing board which go far beyond financial considerations.

Steps for Estimating New Workloads

1. Relate historical workloads to admissions, patient days and/or emergency-ambulatory

---

[*]Source: Mark S. Levitan and Brian P. Lenane, "Financial Feasibility of Health Facility Reuse," *Health Facility Reuse, Retrofit, and Reconfiguration*, National Center for Health Services Research, February 1980, DHEW Pub. No. (PHS)79-3257.

[**]Source: Reprinted from *Hospitals: The Planning and Design Process* by Owen B. Hardy and Lawrence P. Lammers, with permission of Aspen Systems Corporation, © 1978.

care visits, as applicable. In some instances, ratios of historical workloads to admitting physicians are determined.
2. Analyze trends in the utilization indices so formulated.
3. Extend the utilization indices to the same years as the parameter forecasts (admissions, patient days, emergency-ambulatory care visits) and make appropriate qualitative adjustments.
4. Apply the indices as extended to respective parameter forecasts to obtain the estimated workloads.

There are three prime parameters projected in the role and program study which are used in estimating future workloads: admissions, patient days, and outpatient visits. These parameters are treated as independent variables and workloads as dependent variables flowing from them. Trends in the historical relationship between the two are analyzed and projected into the future. The projected relationship is then applied to the appropriate projected independent variable to ascertain the numerical value of the workload or dependent variable.

It should be pointed out that formulating statistical projections is seldom the single action necessary in determining future workloads. For example, the historical relationships between some procedures and admissions may not constitute a valid base for estimations. Cases in point are chest x-rays and certain laboratory tests sometimes performed upon admission. In these instances, by administrative decision alone (dictated, of course, by clinical considerations), future workloads can be altered considerably. Instituting a new service, such as the creation of a primary care center staffed with full-time physicians, can generate additional workloads not possible to predict on the basis of in-house historical activity, because none has existed; thus, the estimator must look to other hospitals which have already undergone similar experiences. Admission to the medical staff of a new specialist will often substantially alter past trends, as can the departure of a key specialist; in these instances the practice volume of a single individual has to be considered.

The most commonly projected workloads in a typical community hospital are listed in Table 22-3 in terms of the department involved, the workload unit usually designated, and the parameter used as the independent variable from which workload units, the dependent variable, flow. In each instance, the projections should be made for a minimum of ten years, and some authorities believe that a fifteen-year period is reasonable.

CAPITAL COST MINIMIZATION*

What are the ways that the cost of facilities may be minimized through a sound planning process? An important starting point is to identify the major components of the total cost in a planned facility.

The greatest single component of construction cost is the total amount of space to be constructed. The total space includes two distinct categories: usable space and nonusable space. (The latter includes circulation space in addition to space for ducts, shafts, stairs, elevators and mechanical systems.) The initial step in the facility planning process, once the program needs have been established, is to determine how much usable square footage is required to meet defined needs. This phase is called functional programming, the keystone of cost determination. If potential savings can be uncovered, functional programming is the most fruitful area to search.

The other major component is the cost per square foot of the structure to be built. The cost of the building varies with the quality and complexity of the square footage to be built, the amount of time it will take to complete the project and the avoidance or reduction of unnecessary changes during construction. Market conditions in the construction industry also have a great bearing on the cost per square foot. In a period of construction cost escalation, compressing the planning process can speed the start of construction and reduce the project cost.

For new, remodeled or expanded physical facilities, capital cost minimization requires monitoring the entire planning process. Planners must ask themselves: Is this the least expensive alternative that still meets the hospital's func-

---

*Source: Reprinted from Thomas M. Heckler and John Sweetland, "Minimizing Costs Through Sound Facilities Planning," *Topics in Health Care Financing,* Summer 1977, with permission of Aspen Systems Corporation.

Table 22-3 Workload Units

Department (Functional Entity)	Workload unit (Dependent Variable)	Parameter of utilization (Independent Variable)
Laboratory	Tests by functional section—hematology, chemistry, bacteriology, etc.	Admissions, outpatient visits
Blood Bank	Tests and transfusions, by type	Admissions, outpatient visits
Respiratory Therapy	Days of treatment and number of treatments, by type	Patient days, outpatient visits
Pulmonary Functions	Procedures or tests, by type	Admissions, outpatient visits
Pharmacy	Prescriptions, requisitions	Admissions, outpatient visits
Physical Therapy	Treatments, by type	Admissions or patient days, outpatient visits
Occupational Therapy	Visits or treatment, by type	Admissions or patient days, outpatient visits
EKG	Tests	Admissions, outpatient visits
EEG	Tests	Admissions, outpatient visits
Nuclear Medicine	Imaging and scan procedures, by type; in vitro assays, by type	Admissions, outpatient visits
Diagnostic Radiology	Examinations, by type, such as G.I. series, colon, gall bladder, I.V.P.s, chests, etc., and sometimes by location, such as main department, emergency suite, and clinics	Admissions, outpatient visits
Therapeutic Radiology	Visits and treatments (deep and superficial)	Admissions, outpatient visits
Surgery	Surgical procedures (urological procedures separately)	Admissions and number of physicians with surgical privileges
Delivery and Labor Progress	Deliveries	Number of FTE obstetricians (also area birthrate and other factors)
Laundry	Pounds	Patient days
Dietary	Meals	Inpatient census, employee complement, students, physicians, and visitors
Social Service	Counseling sessions or visits	Admissions, outpatient visits

Table 22-3 continued

Department	Workload unit	Parameter of utilization
Autopsy Suite		
a. Morgue	Deaths	Admissions, D.O.A.s
b. Autopsy Room	Autopsies	Admissions, D.O.A.s

Table 22-4 Site Investigation Checklist*

Hospital Name:
Address:
New Hospital, Expansion or Existing:
Number of Beds, Existing or Proposed:
Name of Medical Group:
Address:
Contact:
  Address:
  Phone:

Site Condition

  A—Photos taken:
  B—Acreage:
  C—Soil Conditions:
  D—Borings Needed:
    1. Who is recommended:
  E—Status of Topo:
    1. Surveyor on Plan (or recommended):
  F—Deed Description—(where available):
  G—Obstruction (on site or nearby):
    1. Electrical
    2. Power Line
    3. Radar
    4. Buildings
    5. Other
  H—Get City Map:

Zoning Requirements

  A—Classification:
  B—Need Rezoning?
    1. If so, to what classification:
  C—Planning or Zoning Board:
    1. Name:
    2. Address:
    3. Phone:
  D—Contact:
    1. Phone:
  E—Plans (Preliminary):
  F—Meeting:
    1. Date:
    2. Time:
  G—Copy of Code:
  H—Set Backs:
    1. Front:
    2. Rear:
    3. Side yard:

  I—Land Coverage Requirements:
  J—Parking Requirements:
  K—Info By:
    1. Address:
    2. Phone:

Building Permit

  A—Special Requirements:
  B—Applicable Bldg. Code:
  C—Permit Fees:
  D—What Plans Required:
  E—How Many Sets to be Submitted:
  F—Approximate Time for Processing:
  G—Info By:
    1. Address:
    2. Phone:

Signs

  A—Permit Required:
  B—Restriction on Bldg. Sign:
  C—Restriction on Pylon Sign:
  D—Info By:
    1. Address:
    2. Phone:

State Bldg. Permit

  A—State Building Permit Required:
  B—Regional Comprehensive Health Planning
    Council:
    1. Address:
    2. Phone:
    3. Requirements:
    4. Obtain copy of Code:
  C—Department of Institutions & Agencies:
    1. Address:
    2. Phone:
    3. Requirements:
    4. Obtain copy of Code:
  D—Department of Health & Welfare:
    1. Address:
    2. Phone:
    3. Requirements:
    4. Obtain copy of Code:
  E—Preliminary Plans:
    1. Which Agency Submitted to:

Table 22-4 continued

    2. How Many Sets?
    3. Approximate time for Processing:
F—Final Plans & Specs:
    1. Which Agency Submitted to:
    2. How Many Sets?
    3. Approximate time for Processing:

Highway Traffic & Access

A—State Jurisdiction:
    1. Department:
    2. Address:
    3. Phone:
B—Local Jurisdiction:
    1. Department:
    2. Address:
    3. Phone:
C—Deceleration Requirements (if any):
D—Drainage to Highway:
E—Special Permit; cost:
F—Curbs or Islands:
G—Width and number of Access Roads:
H—Future Planning:
I—Distance from road edge to row line:
J—Information By:
    1. Address:
    2. Phone:
K—Brief Description of Traffic Pattern:

Sanitary Sewer

A—Jurisdiction
    1. Name:
    2. Address:
    3. Phone:
B—Location:
C—Size:
D—Depth:
E—Charge for Tap-in:
F—Required to Tie-into:
G—Allow Dual Pumps:
H—Health Department other than Local:
I—Code:
J—Info By:
    1. Department:
    2. Address:
    3. Phone:

Sanitary System (if sewer available, omit)

A—Jurisdiction:
    1. Address:
    2. Phone:
B—Requirements:
C—Type of System used in Area:
D—Percolation Figures:

E—Info By:
    1. Department:
    2. Address:
    3. Phone:

Storm Sewer

A—Jurisdiction:
    1. Name:
    2. Address:
    3. Phone:
B—Sewer Available (?):
C—Size:
D—Location:
E—Depth:
F—Surface Drainage Allowed:
G—Local Requirements:
H—Charge for Tap-in:
I—Info By:
    1. Department:
    2. Address:
    3. Phone:

Water Service

A—Jurisdiction:
    1. Name:
    2. Address:
    3. Phone:
B—Location:
C—Size:
D—Depth:
E—Pressure:
F—Sprinklers Required:
G—Sufficient Pressure for Sprinklers:
H—Separate line for Sprinklers Required:
I—Charge for Tap-in:
J—Location of nearest Fire Hydrant:
K—Additional Fire Hydrants required:
L—Distance to nearest Fire House:
M—Info By:
    1. Name:
    2. Address:
    3. Phone:

Gas Service

A—Jurisdiction:
    1. Name:
    2. Address:
    3. Phone:
B—Size:
C—Location:
D—Depth:
E—Capacity:
F—Charge for Tap-in:
G—Special Rates:

Table 22-4 continued

H—Info By:
1. Name:
2. Address:
3. Phone:

Electric Service

A—Jurisdiction:
1. Name:
2. Address:
3. Phone:
B—Size Available (120/208 or 277/480):
C—Primary Service:
D—Free Transformers:
E—Underground:
F—Location:
1. Pole No.:
G—Charge to bring to Location:
H—Rate Schedule:
1. Any Special Applicable Rates?
I—Info By:
1. Phone:

Trash-Disposal

A—Waste Incinerator permissible?
1. Pollution Laws:
B—Path. Incinerator permissible?
1. Alternate methods:
C—Trash & Garbage Removal Service:
D—Approximate rates:

Hospitals—(In Sphere of Influence)

A—Names:
B—Type:
C—Distance from our Site:
D—No. of Beds:
E—Other Remarks:

Miscellaneous

A—Special Local Taxes:
B—Architect Sealing Requirements:
C—Brief Description of Existing Easements:
D—New Easements Required:
E—Real Estate Taxes:
F—Valuation Formula:
G—Tax Assessor:
1. Address:
2. Phone:

Telephone Service

A—Jurisdiction:
1. Name:
2. Address:
3. Phone:
B—Service Available:
1. Overhead:
2. Underground:
C—Installation Costs & Requirements:
1. To the Site:
2. From Site to Telephone Equipment Room:
3. Interior Provisions and Cabinets:
D—Owners' Responsibilities:
1. Telephone Equipment Room Required:
a—Interior Finishes:
Walls:
Floors:
Ceiling:
Electric:
Air Conditioning:
Ingress/Egress:
E—Type of Equipment Available:
1. Earliest Delivery:
F—Marketing Representative:
Name:
Address:
Telephone:

*Source: Reprinted from *Capital Projects for Health Care Facilities* by W. Thomas Berriman, William J. Essick, Jr., and Peter Bentivegna, with permission of Aspen Systems Corporation, © 1976.

tional and design needs? The word "needs" makes the question complex. How does one differentiate between legitimate needs and unjustifiable desires? At what point should need be determined—today, tomorrow or ten years into the future? Such questions must be answered to provide a sound, workable facility at low cost.

Planning should also provide a solution that "stands the test of time." The solution must be based on one view of the future but also should offer the flexibility to meet unforeseen contingencies without expensive reassignment of existing facilities.

The Operating Cost Factor

All too often, hospitals tend to concentrate on saving monies solely through reduction in capital expenditures. This is but one area for savings. Of equal, or even greater, importance is planning and designing the facility and its com-

Table 22-5 Cost Breakdown Checklist* [for Building Equipment]

Division	Description	Cost of Item	Cost per sq. ft.	% of total	Remarks
0	General Conditions				
1	Special Conditions Cash Allowances				
2	Demolition & Patching Dewatering Earthwork Subdrainage Foundations Parking & Drive Paving Road & Parking Appurt. Chain Link Fence Irrigation Soil Preparation Lawns Ground Covers Tree & Shrub Planting				
3	Concrete Formwork Concrete Reinforcement Concrete & Cement Fin. Cast-in-place Concrete Insul. Concrete				
4	Concrete Block Masonry Brick Masonry				
5	Structural Metals Steel Decking Ornamental Metal Miscellaneous Metal Equip. Support System				
6	Rough Carpentry Finish Carpentry Millwork				
7	Insulation Roofing Sheet Metal Work Expansion Joints Caulking & Sealants Waterproofing				
8	Metal Doors & Frames Wood Doors, Laminate Mineral Core Lbld. Doors Accordion Doors Overhead Roll-up Doors Hatch Doors Finish Hardware Glass & Glazing Window Wall (Storefront)				
9	Stucco Lath & Plas. (inc. framing)				

Table 22-5 continued

Division	Description	Cost of Item	Cost per sq. ft.	% of total	Remarks
	Gyp. Wlbd. (inc. framing)				
	Access Panels				
	Rated Acous. Tile Clg.				
	Non-Rated Acous. Clg.				
	Luminous Ceilings				
	Resilient Flooring				
	Carpet				
	Seamless Flooring				
	Cond. Seamless Flooring				
	Ceramic Tile				
	Hard Surfaced Flooring				
	Textured Coated System				
	Elastomeric Coatings				
	Sprayed Fireproofing				
	Painting				
	Glazed Paint				
	Vinyl-Coated Fabrics				
10	Privacy Curtain Track				
	Toilet Compartments				
	Louvers & Vents				
	Dock Bumpers				
	Flagpole				
	Toilet & Bathroom Access.				
11	Miscellaneous Equipment				
	Parking Equipment				
	Food Service Equipment				
12	Casework				
13	Insulated Rooms				
	Radiation Protection				
	Incinerator or Compactor				
14	Elevators				
15A	Mechanical				
	Piping, Valves & Fittings				
	Equipment & Specialties				
	Sheetmetal Work				
	Insulation—Sheetmetal				
	Insulation—Piping				
	ATC				
15B	Plumbing				
	Medical Gases				
	Insulation				
	Sanitary				
	Site & Utilities				
	Storm				
	Water Supply				
	Fire & Sprinkler				
	Fixtures				
16	Electrical				
	Switchgear & Main Dist.				

Table 22-5 continued

Division	Description	Cost of Item	Cost per sq. ft.	% of total	Remarks
	Emergency Power Systems				
	Branch Wiring				
	Lighting Fixtures				
	Site				
	Fire Alarm				
	Empty Conduit Systems				
	Ungrounded Systems				
	Motor Control Centers				
	Lightning Protection				
	Unipotential Bonding Sys.				
	Contract Total				
	Contractor's Fee				
	Guaranteed Maximum Cost				

*Source: Reprinted from *Capital Projects for Health Care Facilities* by W. Thomas Berriman, William J. Essick, Jr., and Peter Bentivegna, with permission of Aspen Systems Corporation, © 1976.

ponent systems in such a manner that it will reduce operating costs through efficient staffing, energy conservation and maintenance economies.

It is inappropriate to base the accept/reject decision for a project on a simple sum of the initial investment and the resultant savings. One thousand dollars in savings ten years from now is in no way equivalent to one thousand dollars in hand today. The difference reflects the time value of money, or cost of capital, and this difference must be explicitly recognized in the decision-making process applied to cost-saving alternatives. Life cycle costing is one reliable and theoretically sound basis for imputing the cost of capital into the decision-making process.

Life cycle costing uses discounted present value analysis to arrive at the relative costs of two or more alternatives. Typically, this methodology is used to evaluate the cost effectiveness of implementing one or more new systems that require substantial initial capital outlay but yield reduced yearly expenditures, versus the existing, often labor-intensive system. Examples include communications, data processing, energy and materials handling systems.

When evaluating the relative costs for these two alternatives on a consistent basis, the desired standards of service which the two systems must meet should be defined.

Next, the term of the evaluation period must be determined. Ideally, this should be the life of the equipment of systems involved, but routine maintenance and periodic overhaul can extend the life of some mechanical systems indefinitely. In practice, a ten- to fifteen-year useful life is often assumed.

Data should then be gathered on the relative costs of acquiring and operating the alternative systems. Also, a yearly escalation factor to reflect the reality of wage-rate inflation is necessary.

The final step is to choose the appropriate discount rate at which the two alternatives should be evaluated. This discount rate should be the hospital's cost of capital; that is, the implicit "price of money" from both debt and equity (internally generated) sources. This price, or cost, is the minimum that must be earned on the funds to keep the economic value of the institution unchanged.

The final decision between the two alternatives will use the results of this life cycle costing analysis as only one of the inputs; other inputs will include such intangible factors as overall ease of operation, ability to integrate the new system into present hospital operations and possible contingencies that cannot be quantified for inclusion in the life cycle costing evaluation, e.g., the risk of imminent unionization of employees, accompanied by sharply increased labor costs, or the risk of an untested mechanical system.

PART VI
INFORMATION MANAGEMENT: COMPUTERS, HOSPITAL INFORMATION SYSTEMS, WORD PROCESSORS

CUTTING DOWN ON PAPER FLOW*

Health care institutions are certainly not immune from the deluge of information and escalating flow of paper which today seems to pervade all fields of organization. The generation and the reading of proliferating numbers of reports, memoranda, letters, and other written material can, for many employees, become a most frustrating and time-consuming experience, to say nothing about the time required for duplication and distribution.

The following questions should be helpful in establishing guidelines for reducing the size, scope, and frequency of reports and other written materials, particularly those of a recurring nature:

1. Why is the information needed?
2. Who needs the report?
3. Who wants the report? Why?
4. Is it comprehensive enough?
5. Is it too comprehensive?
6. Who receives copies?
7. Can the material be better presented in another form?
8. How frequently is the report prepared?
9. How many copies are distributed?
10. Can the report be combined with another report?
11. If the report were eliminated what would happen?
12. What other reports presently contain this information?
13. Must this information be considered a permanent record?
14. How can the report be improved?
15. Can this information be made available from the computer's data bank?
16. Who receives the report but doesn't really need it?

In appraising the significance, usefulness, and real need for various kinds of written data, i.e., statistical studies, memoranda, evaluations, and projections, special consideration should also be given to the cost, in time, of securing the raw data. This usually involves many people who may spend endless hours (time which may be used for a more important immediate need), searching and arranging material for the person who actually writes the final report.

---

*Source: Reprinted from *Time Management for Health Care Professionals* by Steven H. Appelbaum and Walter F. Rohrs, with permission of Aspen Systems Corporation, © 1981.

Chapter 23—Computers

HOW HOSPITALS USE COMPUTERS

Three Functional Levels*

Computers are used in hospitals at three levels: administrative data processing, clinical data processing and medical information systems (often called hospital information systems).

1. Administrative Data Processing

At the first level, the role of the computer is the same in the hospital as in any business. It is used for billing, accounts receivable, payroll, accounts payable, general ledger and similar functions concerned with cash flow. It is also used for such hospital-specific counting functions as census, data collection and admission records. At this level, too, fall routine uses such as reporting laboratory data; maintaining inventory records on supplies, drugs and equipment; and staff scheduling. Some systems also provide menu planning, operating room scheduling and message services.

2. Clinical Data Processing

At the clinical data processing level, complete patient medical records are maintained during a patient's hospital stay. Such systems may also provide specialized services to the clinical laboratory, radiology, nursing stations and pharmacy. Typically, such systems provide immediate inquiry response by operating in "real time," and they provide "on-line" medical information which can be used in decision making in administering both the individual patient's hospital stay and the overall hospital. (*Real time* refers to computer operations which keep up with the current situation so as to provide immediate response. *On-line* implies the capability of obtaining such real-time information by interrogating the computer through a terminal that provides information in human-readable form.)

3. Medical Information Systems

The third level, a complete medical information system, provides management information that can be used in decision making in administering both the individual patient's hospital stay and the overall hospital.

A Survey on the Use of Computers in Hospitals*

In 1976 the University of Oregon Health Sciences Center conducted a survey of the use of computers in 75 short-term, general acute-care facilities with more than 250 beds. Each of these institutions was the primary teaching hospital af-

---

*Source: Reprinted from Paul Grey, "The Computer and Hospital Productivity," *Topics in Health Care Financing,* Winter 1977, with permission of Aspen Systems Corporation.

*Source: Reprinted from Gary S. Whitted, "What to Expect from Electronic Data Processing in Medical Centers," *Health Care Management Review,* Winter 1978, with permission of Aspen Systems Corporation.

filiated with one of the 113 U.S. medical schools.

The survey results were analyzed to provide guidelines in eight primary areas of interest to hospital administrative personnel:

Source of EDP Support: As Table 23-1 indicates, nearly three-quarters of the hospitals reported access to onsite computing capabilities (either within the hospital or on the adjacent campus area). Only a very small percentage of teaching hospitals use a commercial hospital service bureau for a majority of their EDP support.

EDP Vendor: Seventy percent of the teaching hospitals procure their EDP support from IBM. (This figure approximates IBM's general U.S. market penetration.) No other hardware vendor or service bureau could claim more than four teaching hospital users.

Usage of Available Processing Time: Survey recipients were asked the following question: "If the hospital has access to an onsite computer, what percentage of the total available processing time is used by the hospital?"

75 percent—100 percent: 24 hospitals (44 percent of the total)

50 percent—74 percent: 15 hospitals (27 percent of the total)

25 percent—49 percent: 7 hospitals (13 percent of the total)

0 percent—24 percent: 9 hospitals (16 percent of the total)

EDP Expenditures: Each responding hospital was requested to provide its annual number of patient days, outpatient visits and emergency room visits. A 3:1 ratio of outpatient/emergency room visits to inpatient days was made so that a weighted number of "patient days" could be calculated for each hospital.

Several hypotheses were investigated regarding EDP expenditures:

- The largest hospitals (in terms of weighted patient days) spend the most on EDP.

Table 23-1   Source of EDP Support

Source	Percent of Hospitals
Onsite	71.8
Onsite + Service Bureau	12.5
Service Bureau	9.4
Other	6.3

- Hospitals spending the most for EDP have the greatest number of operational application systems.
- There is a correlation between expenditures and vendor satisfaction.
- There is a correlation between expenditures and whether a hospital shares or totally utilizes a computer.

Since each responding hospital also was to provide its latest EDP budget allocation, it was possible to derive a **cost per patient day.** As Table 23-2 indicates, the average EDP expenditure per patient day was $3.56 for nonservice bureau users; approximately one-half of the responding hospitals were spending between two and four dollars per patient day, with two-thirds spending between two and five dollars.

It should be recognized that the "cost per patient day" figure by itself is relatively meaningless. Greatest among the defects of this calculation is that it does nothing to demonstrate *how much* one is receiving for this expenditure. The survey results indicated many cases where hospitals with greater EDP expenditures also were providing a greater scope of EDP services.

The largest hospitals definitely were not the biggest spenders, as these mean cost per patient day figures demonstrate for several groupings:

- 100,000 to 200,000 weighted patient days: $3.29 (20 hospitals).
- 200,000 to 300,000 weighted patient days: $3.47 (18 hospitals).
- 300,000 to 400,000 weighted patient days: $4.32 (10 hospitals).
- 400,000 to 500,000 weighted patient days: $3.63 (4 hospitals).

Finally, an attempt was made to analyze the proportion of the EDP budget which was spent

Table 23-2   Distribution of EDP Cost per Patient Day

Calculated Cost Per Patient Day (in U.S. dollars)	Percent of Hospitals
$1–2	17.0
2–3	24.5
3–4	26.4
4–5	17.0
5–6	5.7
6–7	7.5
7–8	1.9

on **hardware** support. Again, the range of values was very broad (29 percent to 80 percent), with a mean value of 55.8 percent.

EDP Plans: Exactly one-half of the responding hospitals provided free-text answers to a question asking about future EDP activities. The nature of the most often-mentioned plans is delineated in Table 23-3. Four of the areas concerned the general methodology of EDP operations, while six areas dealt with specific planned applications. Of particular note is the interest evinced in on-line applications.

Prevalence of EDP Systems: Of the 12 primary EDP applications, as Table 23-4 depicts, the "average" hospital indicated it had computerized about eight of the 12 systems, with about three-quarters of the hospitals having between seven and ten of the applications.

EDP System Characteristics: Table 23-5 summarizes three important variables for each of the 12 applications. The following very general results also were noted:

- 78 percent of all applications were developed inhouse; fewer than 6 percent of all applications were obtained from the hardware vendor.
- 15 percent of all applications used DBMS technology.
- 68 percent of all applications were performed in a batch mode.

Furthermore, 56 percent of the responding hospitals had at least one on-line or real-time application, while 36 percent indicated at least one

Table 23-3 Areas of Future EDP Development

Areas of Future Development	Percent of Total
On-Line Processing	37.5
Data Base Management System	34.4
Pharmacy	28.1
Hardware Upgrades	28.1
Outpatient Scheduling	28.1
On-Line Admission/ Discharge/Transfer	25.0
Clinical Laboratory	21.9
Order Entry	21.9
Full HIS Development	18.8
Switch to Minicomputers	15.6
Payroll/Personnel	12.5

Table 23-4 Prevalence of 12 Major EDP Systems

Application	Percent of Total
Accounts Receivable	100.0
Admission/Discharge/ Transfer	95.2
Payroll/Personnel	92.1
Budget	85.7
General Ledger	79.4
Accounts Payable	76.2
Inventory	69.8
Fixed Asset Accounting	57.1
Results Reporting from Ancillary Areas	47.6
Materials Management	42.9
Outpatient Clinic Scheduling	39.7
Order Entry	33.3

DBMS-based application. And 28 percent of the hospitals had acquired *both* on-line and DBMS capabilities.

Table 23-5 depicts some important distinctions between the 12 application systems. Note that all eight of the standard financial/administrative applications are lowest in terms of DBMS usage. This finding is not unexpected, since several hypotheses would support such a result:

- It is logical to assume that these systems are the oldest ones for most institutions. These systems probably were in a development mode before DBMS technology became prevalent.
- Since these systems have been in existence for awhile, many EDP technicians would be reluctant to convert them to DBMS, for fear that their relative stability might be compromised (at least temporarily). Furthermore, several of these systems are likely large and complex (e.g., accounts receivable), making them unlikely candidates for early testing with DBMS. Finally, it might be harder to justify conversion of these large systems, since one of the most important benefits often associated with DBMS is decreased program development time, an advantage which now could not be claimed.
- Even if the above hypotheses were invalid for a particular hospital, hardware and/or management considerations easily may pre-

Table 23-5 Primary Characteristics of Hospital Application Software

Application	Mode of Processing			Use a DBMS?		Source of Software		
	Batch (%)	Real-Time (%)	Other[1] (%)	Yes (%)	No (%)	Inhouse Developed (%)	Hardware Vendor Package (%)	Other[2] (%)
Accounts Payable	87.5	2.1	10.4	4.5	95.5	89.1	2.2	8.7
Budget	85.2	3.7	11.1	9.4	90.6	86.8	1.9	11.3
Fixed Asset Accounting	83.3	0	16.7	6.3	93.8	79.4	2.9	17.6
General Ledger	82.0	2.0	16.0	10.4	89.6	66.7	8.3	25.0
Payroll/Personnel	79.3	6.9	13.8	13.0	87.0	75.9	3.7	20.4
Inventory	70.5	6.8	22.7	12.5	87.5	88.1	0	11.9
Accounts Receivable	63.5	6.4	30.2	16.7	83.3	65.6	9.8	24.6
Materials Management	63.0	14.8	22.2	19.2	80.8	100.0	0	0
Outpatient Scheduling	52.0	36.0	12.0	21.7	78.3	90.5	4.8	4.8
Admission/Discharge/Transfer	43.3	41.7	15.0	22.4	77.6	65.5	15.5	19.0
Order Entry	38.1	33.3	28.6	36.8	63.2	75.0	5.0	20.0
Results Reporting from Ancillary Areas	33.3	20.0	46.7	25.0	75.0	75.9	3.5	20.7

[1] Includes "on-line," "batch and on-line" and "application exists, but mode of processing unknown."
[2] Includes "other purchased software," "inhouse developed and other purchased software" and "inhouse developed and hardware vendor package."

vent EDP personnel from using DBMS, even if a positive attitude prevailed toward it.

It is interesting to note that the same four systems with the highest percentage of on-line capabilities are also the systems with the greatest percentage of DBMS applications.

As Table 23-5 indicates, the prevalence of "packaged" software from the hardware vendor is rather low (5.5 percent). Even the relative newness of comprehensive, high-quality vendor software offerings for hospitals should not be a complete rationale for the low usage of packaged software. It is significant that nearly twice as many applications (11.2 percent of the total) were secured from nonvendor sources as from hardware vendors.

Prevalence of Other EDP Systems: Table 23-6 enumerates the prevalence of systems other than the 12 in Tables 23-4 and 23-5. It was a bit surprising to see "medical records" as the most often-cited system, since much of the literature seems to indicate that computer advances in this area are progressing rather slowly. However, the term "medical records" certainly is not very definitive, and it may well connote systems which are little more than chart tracking/locating or abstracting applications.

Costs and Benefits*

Hospitals are a labor-intensive service industry in which productivity is difficult to measure. The usual approach to increasing productivity is either to invest in equipment or to increase the efficiency of personnel. To earn its keep, the computer must be able to displace cost and earn revenue which in total is larger than the computer investment.

Costs

Determining the cost of computers is relatively straightforward. A typical balance sheet of computer costs, assuming that the computer (or computer time) is rented, is shown in Table 23-7.

---

*Source: Reprinted from Paul Grey, "The Computer and Hospital Productivity," *Topics in Health Care Financing,* Winter 1977, with permission of Aspen Systems Corporation.

Table 23-6 Additional Systems Noted by Hospitals

Application System	Percent of Total
Medical Records	37.8
Accounting/Billing	28.9
Patient Identification	20.0
Clinical Laboratory	20.0
Pharmacy	13.3
Operating Room	11.1
Professional Fee Billing	8.9
On-Line Data Entry	8.9
Radiology	8.9
EKG	8.9
Dietary	8.9

Table 23-7 Balance Sheet of Computer-Based Expenses

Annual Computer Expense:	
Equipment rental	$_____
Computer program	_____
Program development	_____
Operating (including space, power, keypunching, etc.)	_____
Total Cost	$_____

Benefits

A typical balance sheet of benefits is presented in Table 23-8.

Before discussing the nature of the savings, it is important to point out that unless the anticipated savings exceed the anticipated costs (and these figures have been estimated realistically, particularly on the savings side), a computer-based system should not be installed. Personnel savings are assessed in two ways: (1) immediate reductions in personnel because clerical posi-

Table 23-8 Balance Sheet of Computer-Based Savings

Annual Cost Savings:	
Net reduction in personnel	$_____
Increased employee productivity	_____
Recovery of lost charges	_____
Reduction of costs in special forms	_____
Long-term personnel savings (annualized)	_____
Total Savings	$_____

tions are eliminated and (2) elimination of the need for hiring additional clerks in future years to cope with the increasing paperwork required for government, insurance companies and others.

Increases in employee productivity can come from several sources, among them: an increase in the number of revenue-producing services performed by the employee (e.g., in lab work), an increase in the number of patients cared for by an employee (e.g., in nursing), and a reduction in errors and consequent rework of errors such as in executing physicians' orders.

These increases have to be over and above those resulting from the consolidation of work among fewer employees, and they imply that the hospital will have to serve more patients.

Recovery of lost charges implies that the computer will provide more accurate recordkeeping which will result in improved billing and collection, as well as reduced cycle times on accounts receivable. Special forms for recordkeeping can be a major cost item in many operations.

Electronic Data Processing: Internal Audit Checkpoints*

Increased operating complexity often results when hospitals acquire electronic data processing. This requires sound management of the systems in order to gain the benefits they offer, including lower costs. Lack of attention to managing data processing systems can result in increased costs and eventually inferior results in all hospital areas.

Below are ten general checkpoints that must be included in any audit of a data processing system.

1. How is the data processing area staffed? Are the director and staff properly qualified? Are training programs adequate? Has internal auditing planned for effective uses of commercially available computer auditing software packages?
2. Does the data processing function provide the hospital's administration with timely, accurate, and useful information that effectively and efficiently supports the decision-making process—a key performance measure?
3. Do systems that have been implemented actually perform in the manner planned? How do the costs and actual benefits compare with plan? Are differences carefully isolated and evaluated? Are the differences the result of poor planning, poor performance, or both?
4. What is the relationship of the data processing department to the rest of the hospital? Is it independent or does it report to a department such as finance? It is recommended the data processing function report directly to the hospital director.
5. Electronic data processing requires the design of very complicated systems and procedures. Is there adequate documentation that is accurate and up to date? This is a frequent problem area that cannot be neglected without negative consequences.
6. Have clear goals and objectives been established for data processing? Have standards of performance been set and communicated? Are the standards measurable? A function that is this complicated and expensive and has such a broad impact requires a thorough continuing management oversight process.
7. Is there sufficient short-term, intermediate, and long-range planning? Planning covers the entire range of operations from improving schedules and utilization, to preparing for major changes in hospital operations, to implementing new programs, to complete replacement of existing hardware and software as new technology in health care and computers emerges.
8. What reports are prepared routinely for top management on data processing operations? Are they accurate and of use? Do they enable management to evaluate and control the function?
9. Is top management able to communicate effectively with EDP personnel, do the executives understand EDP, and do they contribute actively to planning, design, and evaluation of data processing systems? Does top management appear to be uninformed about computers and their

---

*Source: Reprinted from *Internal Auditing for Hospitals* by Seth Allcorn, with permission of Aspen Systems Corporation, © 1979.

operation and generally avoid dealing with EDP personnel?
10. Has adequate attention been given to the dehumanizing effects of computerization on patients and employees?

Hospitals using computers in any manner regardless whether they are related to patient care, administration, or both must review all EDP applications carefully and completely. Internal auditors are suited ideally to make these reviews as few hospital staff members will have a broader conception of the total institution and the effects of computerization. Hospital administrators must be certain internal auditing is prepared to perform operations evaluations of all data processing.

POINTERS ON PURCHASING

Types of Hardware and Software Purchases*

"Do-It-Yourself" Systems Development

Traditional practice in hospitals has been to identify single limited applications and buy only the equipment required for the initial application. The hospital then hires one or two people to develop and implement the application. Then a second application is suggested. The equipment is augmented, soon followed by augmentation of the staff. Not untypically, hospitals will discover they are expending half a million dollars or more per year for data processing, with relatively limited results and no clear understanding of how they arrived in this position. Even those hospitals who are in the minority among the "do-it-yourselfers" who have ultimately succeeded in developing a workable system have taken much longer and expended much more money than would otherwise be necessary.

Packaged Software

A variation on the "do-it-yourself" approach involves the acquisition of "packaged software," that is, computer programs previously developed elsewhere, requiring only "tailoring" and implementation to fit the hospital in question. There are two principal sources of packaged software. The first source is other hospitals who have developed the software for their own use. It is then "brokered" to other prospective users, typically by computer equipment manufacturers. Computer equipment sales are, of course, facilitated if claims of available software can be made. Any of the major computer equipment manufacturers thus has an inventory of computer programs for almost every hospital application, typically coming from as many hospitals.

While acquisition of software in this manner is less risky than development *de novo*, it is not without difficulties. Software developed by a hospital is invariably tailored to the idiosyncrasies of that hospital. Further, it may be expected to lack the flexibility necessary to be easily transferrable. This flexibility is achieved only when it is an original design objective, and it substantially increases the cost of design and sometimes operations.

The second source of packaged software is the software company. Such a company is committed as its primary business to the development of software packages. Since transferability and application to a variety of institutions is an objective underlying package development in such a firm, it is likely that such a package can be more easily tailored to the needs of the hospital. Also, the reputation of the software firm rests on the performance of its packages, whereas shortcomings in hospital developed packages can be blamed on the developing institution, and little blame accrues to the brokering equipment manufacturer.

Even well designed software packages must, however, be successfully implemented and operated. Further, the acquisition and interfacing of software packages is a difficult task which is rarely completely successful. Only when a system is developed as a coordinated, integrated whole may its individual component software parts be considered to be truly interfaceable.

Vendor Supplied and Installed Systems

Difficulty with the aforementioned approaches has led to increasing emphasis on acquisition of systems where not only the hardware and software is supplied by the vendor, but the vendor is

---
*Source: *Health Planning Review of Medical Information Systems*, National Center for Health Services Research, 1981, Pub. No. (PHS)81-3303.

also given the job of successfully installing the system. Results from this approach then depend on the excellence of the system in question and the performance of the vendor's staff. Experienced firms have emerged, particularly in clinical laboratory systems and level 1 medical information systems, who have compiled a credible performance record. Operations and maintenance remain the responsibility of the hospital.

For certain classes of systems with more limited functions, this approach has proven quite workable. Perhaps its principal limitation is that in its purest form it is static. The vendor comes in, installs the system and leaves. As the need for changes occurs, the hospital is left to its own devices and rarely possesses the capability to make these changes. For that reason many hospitals prefer to establish a continuing relationship with the vendor.

Vendor Supplied, Installed and Operated Systems

Transfer of responsibility to the vendor may, of course, be carried even further to include operations. This may take one of two forms—facilities management or external service. Under a facilities management agreement the vendor's staff carries out software and equipment maintenance and operations functions and may occupy the data processing facility in the hospital. These services may be provided on either a cost plus fee basis or a guaranteed fixed price basis.

Alternatively, the major computer equipment may be located in the vendor's own facility external to the hospital from which service is provided to the hospital via appropriate communication lines interconnected with hospital-based terminals and printers. The resident staff requirement is then minimized and certain economies of scale are achieved by the vendor. This approach, typically called the service approach, is widely used at both ends of the system spectrum. The most successful business office systems are provided in this manner from computer centers supporting hundreds of hospitals, and at the other extreme, sophisticated medical information systems are available on a service basis from vendor centers.

Under the service approach nearly all costs are rendered explicit, as they are now incurred by the vendor rather than by the hospital, and hence must appear in the vendor's charges.

Comparisons will often suggest that an internal operation can perform the same functions at less expense. Careful analysis, however, may reveal that this apparent difference is attributable to implicit, but ignored, costs. Internal costs which are often overlooked in economic analyses include floor space, utilities, equipment insurance, supplies, and fringe benefits. While clearly the vendor's purposes include achieving a profit, it is not likely that this profit level will offset the economies of shared operations and the additional experience and skill that the vendor can provide.

Under facility management or service agreements the vendor assumes operational cost responsibility in addition to installation responsibility. This can typically be tied to a guaranteed level of operational performance so that the vendor, and not the hospital, carries the risk if the system is down or fails to meet other prescribed performance objectives.

A Guide to the Purchase of Computing Equipment*

Prior to undertaking an evaluation of hardware and software, a management advisory (i.e., systems steering) committee comprising top management, and data processing and user personnel should be established. This committee, which could be the same group that reviews and approves all data processing projects, should work closely with the data processing personnel throughout the evaluation and selection process.

Steps

There are seven major steps in the decision cycle to evaluate and select computer hardware and software:

- Define information needs and systems requirements.
- Identify hardware and software choices.
- Develop request for proposal.
- Define criteria.
- Evaluate vendor proposals.
- Conduct formal presentations and site visits.
- Select hardware and software.

---

*Source: Reprinted from H. Glenn Williams and Jay E. Toole, "Evaluating and Selecting a Computer System," *Topics in Health Care Financing,* Summer 1978, with permission of Aspen Systems Corporation.

Defining Information Needs and Systems Requirements

The effort involved in defining information needs and systems requirements will depend on whether a current systems plan exists, and the number and type of systems applications being defined. In any case the results should be a comprehensive definition of systems applications including inputs and outputs, features of each application and general processing requirements. In addition, the potential benefits, both tangible and intangible, of the proposed applications should be identified.

Identifying Hardware and Software Choices

There are four hardware or processing choices available to hospitals:

- **Inhouse System.** There are two types of inhouse systems that are managed and operated by hospital personnel. The first is a general purpose computer system that can be released or purchased from the vendor. Major vendors usually have specialized hospital application software as well as general business application software. The second type of inhouse system is a minicomputer that is usually installed to process a specialized application such as a laboratory information system or an on-line communication order entry system. Vendors of minicomputers may offer specialized hospital software.
- **Shared System.** A shared system is a computer system providing services to a number of hospitals where processing is performed on centrally located computers with which the hospitals communicate via terminals, remote printers and other communication devices. [NOTE: For a full discussion of shared and inhouse systems see pages 395–401.]
- **Managed Facility.** A managed facility is an inhouse computer system, usually a minicomputer with on-line processing capabilities, in which the software and hardware are maintained by the vendor.
- **Facilities Management.** Facilities management is an inhouse computer system which is operated by an outside vendor on a contract basis. Usually, the outside vendor provides systems analysts, programmers and computer operational personnel on site for the hospital.

After reviewing the advantages and disadvantages of each category, the hospital should choose which types of systems will be evaluated, and select computer hardware and software vendors for each type. This can be done by checking with other hospitals, reviewing data processing publications or talking with a data processing consultant.

Developing a Request for Proposal

The next step in the evaluation process is the development of a request for proposal (RFP). There are several advantages of using an RFP. It gives the vendors the data needed to prepare a proposal. It identifies the information the proposal should contain. Most importantly, the RFP itself forms a framework within which the completeness of proposals can be checked and their comparative merits evaluated.

Preparation of the RFP is such an important part of the evaluation process that an outline of an RFP has been included. (See Table 23-9.)

Defining Criteria

The vendor's ability to meet each criterion should be evaluated.

- ability to meet systems application and hardware requirements;
- flexibility to accommodate changes in hospital requirements;
- installation support;
- systems documentation;
- cost;
- vendor experience in the industry;
- financial stability of the vendor;
- software/hardware ongoing maintenance support; and
- ongoing training support.

The most important criterion is the vendor's ability to meet specific systems application and hardware requirements identified in the RFP.

Evaluating Vendor Proposals

A checklist should be used to identify specific requirements met by each vendor. A description of all vendors including their ability to meet all criteria should be developed in some detail.

Table 23-9 Outline for a Request for Proposal for Hardware and Software

I. *Proposal Definition*
   A. Identification of hospital applications (i.e., laboratory information system) on which the respondent should propose.
   B. Restrictions on the respondent's proposals.

II. *Hospital Information*
   A. Description of the hospital. This will include the physical design, number of beds, emergency room and other outpatient services, and ancillary support services.
   B. Unique considerations that must be taken into account for the hospital applications covered by the proposal.
   C. List of hospital services available.
   D. Volume estimates that relate to the applications covered by the proposal.

III. *Systems Application Requirements*
   A. Identify specific systems features by application which are required by the hospital.
   B. Identify other *desirable* systems features by application.
   C. Direct the respondent to provide a brief narrative of all systems features not identified as those needed in RFP. Unique systems features not identified in the RFP should also be described.
   D. Direct the respondent to provide examples of reports generated by the system indicating the frequency of generation and unique features.

IV. *Hardware Specifications*
   A. Identify specific systems hardware requirements including:
      1. Central processing units
      2. Storage devices
      3. Printers
      4. Terminals
      5. Remote devices
   B. Identify timing requirements for each systems component.
   C. Identify systems software requirements.

V. *Vendor, Installation, Ongoing Information*
   A. Vendor Information
      1. Request a summary of applicable job experience of the vendor's representatives who will service and support the hospital's system.
      2. Request a list and description of other available hospital software not covered by the scope of the proposal. This will include software now being developed.
      3. Request a list of current users of the equipment/software that is being proposed.
      4. Request copies of user description (documentation) manuals.
      5. Request copies of respondent's latest financial statements.
   B. Site and Installation Requirements
      1. Request physical requirements of on-site equipment being proposed.
      2. Request estimate of one-time installation and freight charges.
   C. Installation and Training Assistance
      1. Request respondent to identify by task the installation assistance to be provided and cost.
      2. Request training and education assistance to be provided.
      3. Request specific enumeration of installation responsibilities between vendor and hospital.
      4. Request installation work plan and timetable.
   D. Software
      1. Request one-time charges of software being proposed.
      2. Request any additional one-time charges.
   E. Equipment and Supplies: Request cost estimates of equipment and supplies.
   F. Ongoing Applications Information: Request specific costs by year and other definitive data on the following:
      1. Equipment
      2. Software
      3. Processing (shared services only)
      4. Supplies
      5. Estimated processing schedule
      6. Discounts available
      7. Contract terms

Conducting Formal Presentations and Site Visits

Formal presentations should be made and site visits conducted with the two or three selected vendors. The formal presentation will allow vendors an opportunity to present their proposals to the management advisory committee.

Selecting Hardware and Software

After conducting a site visit, the hospital should be in a position to summarize the information on the remaining vendors and make a final decision. The site visit should prove very helpful in determining user satisfaction at other hospitals and in getting a firsthand view of how the hardware or software is operating. The vendors should be asked to submit a list of several sites where the hardware and software have been installed, and the hospital should pick the specific site for the visit. It is helpful to have both user and data processing personnel make the site visits, and again a list of specific points to be discussed or questions to be answered should be prepared in advance.

Regulatory Requirements

In the present environment computer systems for even the smallest hospitals are likely to exceed $100,000. Accordingly, such expenditures must be approved under Section 1122 of the PL 92-603 if the cost of the system is to be allowable for reimbursement purposes.

Review Points on Systems and Procedures*

Expansion and Flexibility

Two important questions should be addressed to the system supplier. The first question is, "How is the system bounded?" That is, what are the limits of expansion? The hospital must avoid installing a system it will later throw out and replace because it cannot cope with hospital expansion. Three kinds of expansion should be considered—in capacity, in number of terminals, and in applications. Capacity needs are determined by both the number of patients that will be handled by the system and the services performed for them. Ask the supplier how he would handle your hospital if it were to double in size. What happens when the capacity of the computer he is proposing for your hospital is exceeded? Can it be easily replaced by a larger model without reprogramming? What are the financial consequences to the hospital of replacement? If you have any doubts about the answer, seek technical assistance.

Ask the same question concerning the number of terminals. As a general rule, a hospitalwide system requires approximately one terminal for every eight beds. Suppose that you decide in the future to place terminals in doctors' offices across the street or merge with a nearby hospital, which would require doubling the number of terminals; could the system handle the increased number? Finally, consider growth in applications. Remember that the "total" hospital information system will never be completed.

Another dimension of expansion and growth is qualitative; that is, to a progressively more comprehensive system. For a medical information system this may involve evolution from a level 1 system toward a level 3 system. It may be expected that any vendor will claim that his system is capable of such growth, and indeed, that he is working on developments which will result in such growth. The prudent hospital, however, will insist that this growth capability be firmly committed in the contract. Nothing will prove more expensive than to rely on the capability for such growth, and then discover it is necessary to throw out the system in question in order to progress to a higher level system. And, in general, technical considerations suggest such growth capability will not normally be present. Terminals which are suitable for level 1 use are simply not suitable for level 3 use. Storage and processing capabilities for level 1 systems will rarely support or be expandable to those required for level 2 or 3 operation.*

The question, "Is it bounded?", is designed to protect you against being wrong in your current estimates of future activities, volumes, or needs. Medical information systems must be amortized over many years, and an early write-off of a system because it cannot grow along with your institution would be a near-fatal management mistake.

The question, "Is it flexible?", must also be explored with the supplier. This consideration relates closely to the previous one but emphasizes somewhat different considerations. How does the system handle routine changes such as adding new drugs or laboratory tests? Can the system meet the needs of different kinds of hospitals? (For example, how does it function when used by medical students or house officers, as

---

*Source: Reprinted from *Medical Information Systems: A New Source For Hospitals* by Melvin H. Hodge, with permission of Aspen Systems Corporation, © 1977.

*Source: *Health Planning Review of Medical Information Systems*, National Center for Health Services Research, 1981, Pub. No. (PHS)81-3303.

opposed to attending physicians?) Recognize that *your* institution might change significantly over time.

The key to flexibility is the generalization of the programming design. You can learn a great deal about flexibility by examining the range of hospitals in which the candidate system is already installed. In general, software developed by and for a specific hospital is rarely transferable without major reprogramming because even a highly qualified hospital developer cannot justify the significantly greater cost of generalized design necessary for multihospital use. Therefore, investigate the original mission of any system you are considering.

Qualifications of Supplier

Several qualifications of the system supplier should also be considered. The first of these is financial responsibility. It is important that the supplier not be undercapitalized, and that there are sufficient assets behind any contract to provide recourse in the event difficulties are encountered. Remember, millions of dollars are involved. Second, the character of the supplier should also be considered. Unlike most purchases, where the relationship with the supplier is transitory, installation of a medical information system will require a continuing relationship between the hospital and the supplier. No contract can contemplate every issue that will arise. Openness, trust, and fairness are important qualities in any relationship. The hospital should carefully consider the likelihood of a successful, long term relationship. Here again, references are important.

On-site Evaluations

It might be desirable to perform an even more extended final on-site evaluation of the system you have tentatively selected. Members of your medical staff should make rounds over a period of several days with physicians using the system. Arrangements might be made for several of your nurses to spend several weeks in the hospital assisting in patient care, utilizing the system in the process. Although these extended evaluation steps are costly, they will provide assurance that you have penetrated any facade and will also establish within your hospital some highly informed individuals who will represent a very useful resource for implementation.

System selection has deliberately not been presented in check-list fashion. The process is not susceptible to mechanical treatment. It cannot be reiterated too often that the maximum number of people should participate in this process so when the selection is made, it is supported by every major group in the hospital. Everyone must be committed to its success.

Contract Precautions

The culminating step in the selection process is negotiation of a satisfactory contract. The supplier will furnish a proposed contract. It is imperative, of course, that competent legal advice be obtained by the hospital.

Certain considerations are essential. Most important of these considerations is that the contract should call for the hospital to pay for *output*, not *input*. This can be achieved by assuring that the contract includes the following:

1. capabilities of the system are defined in detail within each functional area;
2. quantitative standards of performance are established including schedules, response time, reliability, and any limits on number of patients, file sizes, etc.;
3. acceptance procedures are established, including provision for establishing detailed acceptance criteria by mutual agreement followed by witnessing of acceptance tests and acceptance by the hospital;
4. clear definition of the division of effort and responsibility between the supplier and the hospital is provided.

Be wary of any contract that limits itself to providing only the *input* ingredients—computers, terminals, manhours, etc. Such contracts can be fulfilled by the supplier without a satisfactory working system necessarily resulting. Your attorney and management representatives might find it useful to request copies of contracts and solicit advice from other hospitals that have procured the system you have selected. Remember, however, not to confuse the best *system* with the best *contract*. Weaker vendors sometimes promise anything to secure your business. An "ironclad" contract does not change a deficient system into a good system; it merely gives the hospital a better claim on the supplier's assets.

MAIN FRAME VS. MINI-COMPUTER*

Hospital information systems fall generally into three categories. They are the large monolithic system with a single central processor, a network using a medium-size host central processor, and mini-computer networks.

Large Monolithic Systems with One Central Processing Unit

The philosophy of this approach is to build the entire system around one large central processing unit, usually manufactured by one of the major computer companies. The approach of using a single large central processor has been taken by some major hardware manufacturers, as well as by some independent vendors using a major manufacturer's hardware.

As can be observed in Figure 23-1, all parts of the system operate under a single processing unit. In general this includes the clinical applica-

---
*Source: Reprinted from *Hospital Information Systems* by Homer H. Schmitz, with permission of Aspen Systems Corporation, © 1979.

tions. Where it is present, clinical instrumentation is also interfaced with the central processing unit.

Historically, one argument for this approach has been that it allows the use of a consolidated data base. This means that each piece of information is present in the system only once and is not repeated in other files for other subsystems, thus reducing the possibility of errors both of omission and duplication. It has also been felt that the data base approach in a single processor is the most efficient data handling technique available for use in interactive systems. More recently, there have been software developments that allow the use of a single data base in a distributed network with multiple central processors. This has somewhat diluted the original argument in favor of the large single processor system. However, the network data base capability is only in its infancy.

One disadvantage of the single processor approach is that it tends to be more expensive in hardware cost than the two system philosophies that follow. In addition, some have advanced the notion that the single processor approach limits flexibility in the use of clinical modules.

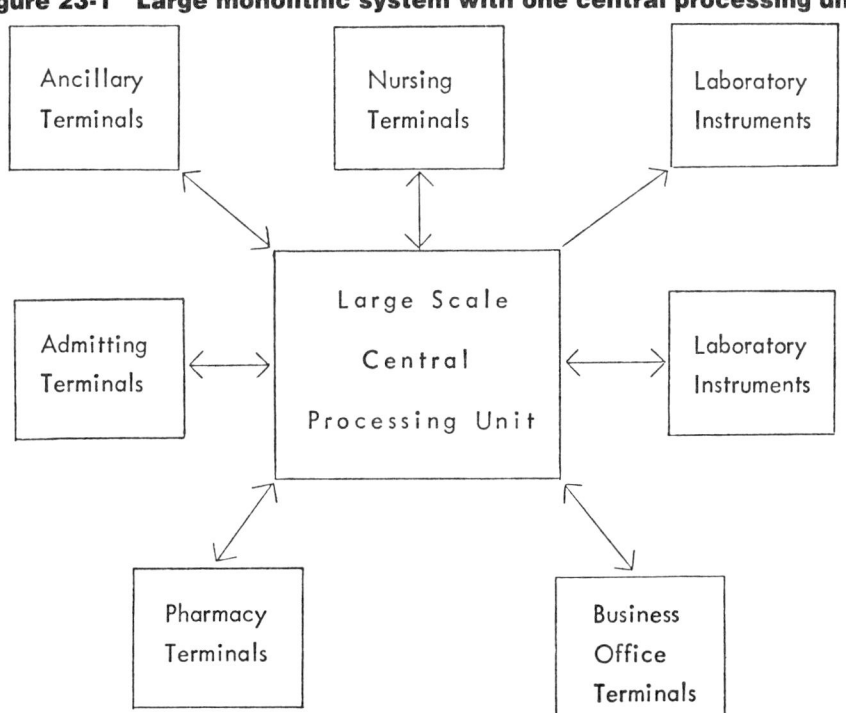

Figure 23-1 Large monolithic system with one central processing unit

That is, the individual hospital is sometimes locked into the use of the clinical module provided by the vendor of the single monolithic processing unit system, thereby losing the flexibility to choose among the various clinical modules available from other vendors.

Network Using Medium-Size Host

This approach uses a medium-size host computer for the communication and data collection function. In addition, it uses individual clinical modules as interfaced subsystems in order to accomplish clinical applications, such as pharmacy profiles and interactions or on-line clinical laboratory instrumentation and reporting.

As can be observed in Figure 23-2, this system is built around a host communication system which has as a central processing unit either a medium-size main frame or a large mini-computer. Clinical applications are accomplished by interfacing separate clinical modules having their own central processing units. Although it is not always the case, these clinical modules are often acquired from a vendor other than the one from whom the hospital acquired the communication system.

The system utilizing this approach usually involves the introduction of clinical modules as they are needed. Using this approach the clinical modules can be introduced and justified by the organization as the need arises. This means that the hospital must have a comprehensive plan from the beginning of its movement into the hospital information system field. If the hospital chooses to use a medium-size communication and data collection network, care must be taken in the selection of the vendor to insure that future system interfaces are viable. Thus, when a system design philosophy specifies several systems tied together into a network, the organization must plan ahead in order to be sure that any clinical modules that may be acquired are compatible. This planning for the future must be done during the early planning stage to assure that the interfaces can be made and that the file

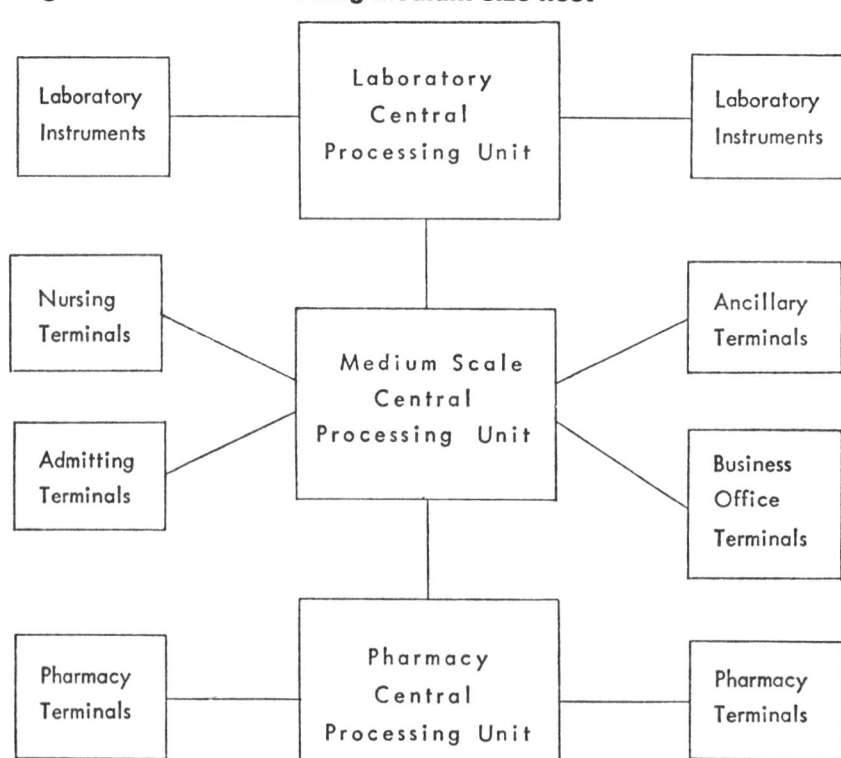

Figure 23-2 Network using medium-size host

structures are appropriate when, at a later date, the hospital decides to go forward with the full-blown plan.

Many people argue that this approach is a good one, in that no hospital can totally assimilate a highly sophisticated system in the clinical modules at the same time that the communication function is being installed. Furthermore, some argue that when this approach is taken, the hospital is free to pick and choose among existing "off the shelf" clinical modules, thereby acquiring the system best suited to the needs of the organization.

This approach has some shortcomings. There may be some fragmentation in a clinical sense; i.e., all of the interactions between subsystems are not necessarily tied together in a single file approach to system development. Moreover, the coordinated planning required to bring the systems together into an integral whole is sometimes lacking.

There is also the problem of controlling multiple files that are shared between modules. However, the state of the art is such that these files can ordinarily be controlled by software. And, as previously noted, recent software developments allow the use of a single data base in a multiple processor environment. However, the potential problem of files in multiple systems is an area of consideration and should be evaluated.

Finally, the modular approach implies that interfaces must be made between foreign systems. Usually these interfaces are the responsibility of the individual user. Alternatively, if either or both of the vendors takes responsibility, responsibility for the various steps in the completion of the interface must be very clearly delineated and should be made a part of the contract.

Mini-Computer Networks

The aim here is not to be highly technical in describing all the sophisticated differences in mini-computer networks. Rather, it is to give the reader a taste of the issues regarding mini-computer networks. Some of the philosophical elements of the large monolithic systems, as well as of the network using a medium-size host, are included in this approach. The major difference in this approach is that it is made up exclusively of mini-computers or micro-computers, and the modules or elements included in the network are always mini-computer based.

Communicating Star Network

Figure 23-3 shows that this approach is much like the network using a medium-size host, except that it uses a mini-computer host to operate the basic communication network. In addition, more of the functions are distributed to other mini-computers. For example, the admitting module is usually based in a separate mini-computer, and is not part of the main communication system. This approach makes use of special purpose mini-computers in the clinical areas. As in the case of the network using a medium-size host, selection of individual clinical modules is an option available to the organization. In this approach the mini-computer host does the message switching, as well as directing appropriate information to and from the various special clinical areas.

Distributed Star

Figure 23-4 shows that this approach is much like the communicating star, except that the central mini-computer controls only other mini-computers and does not have terminals or communicating functions per se. The philosophy of this approach, as contrasted with the communicating star network, is that it is thought to be able to handle a greater terminal load by not degrading the central mini-computer with message switching responsibilities among various terminals. In this approach each module performs its own functions, and switches out into the control mini-computer only when another module has a need to know the information being handled in the first module. For example, the laboratory module would create its draw lists and compile the patient's clinical laboratory profile, and would switch out into the control mini-computer only when there is a need to communicate a result or other information to another terminal outside the laboratory.

Distributed Network

This approach represents the true network system design. As can be observed from Figure 23-5, there are no specialized modules in this network. Each mini-computer can do all of the functions that are performed throughout the network. In this approach the software directs the transactions and "levels" the load within the system. If one mini-computer central processor

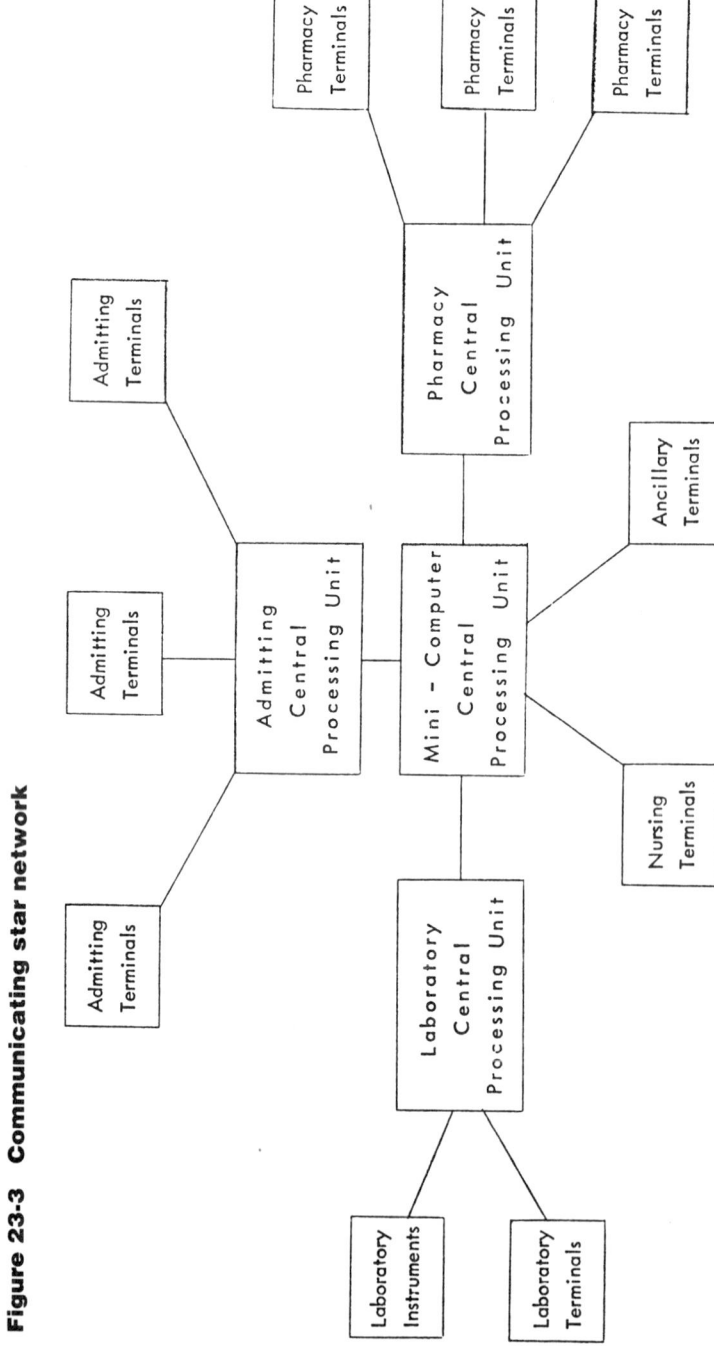

Figure 23-3 Communicating star network

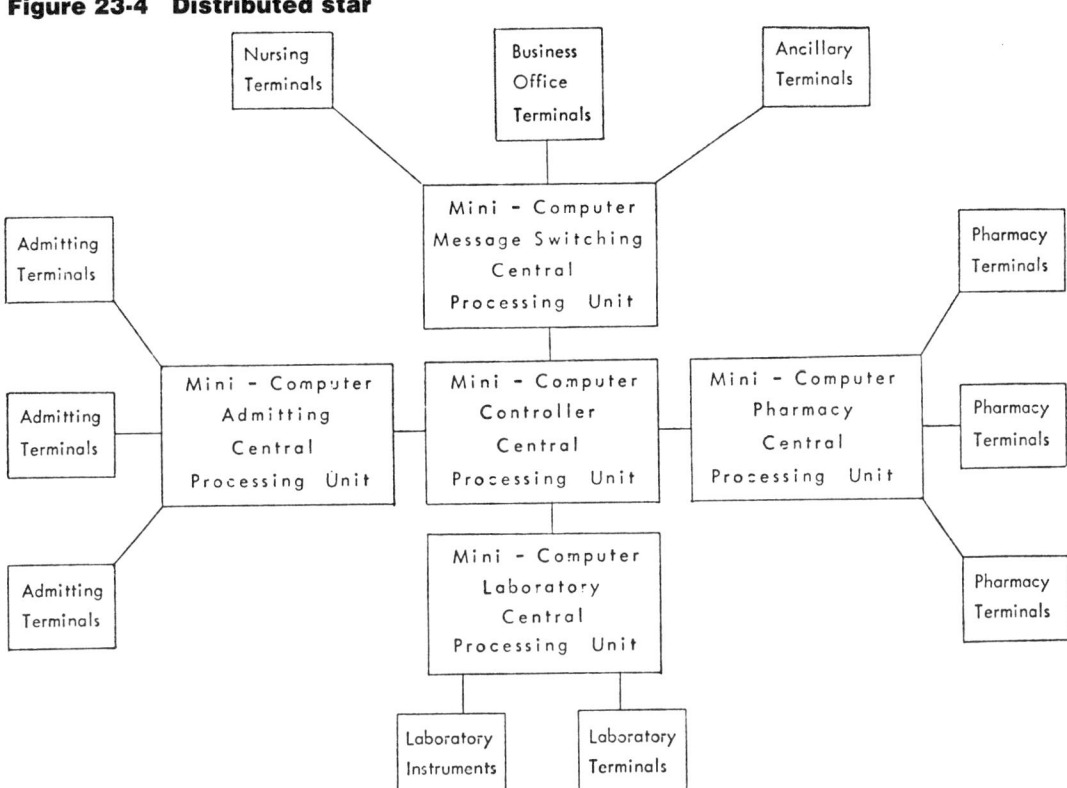

Figure 23-4 Distributed star

```
                    [Nursing      [Business      [Ancillary
                    Terminals]    Office         Terminals]
                                  Terminals]
                            \     |     /
                         [Mini-Computer
                         Message Switching
                         Central
                         Processing Unit]
[Admitting]                                              [Pharmacy
 Terminals]                                               Terminals]
         \                                               /
  [Mini-Computer   —  [Mini-Computer  —  [Mini-Computer
   Admitting           Controller          Pharmacy
   Central             Central             Central
   Processing Unit]    Processing Unit]    Processing Unit]
[Admitting]                                              [Pharmacy
 Terminals]                                               Terminals]
                         [Mini-Computer
                         Laboratory
                         Central
                         Processing Unit]
[Admitting]                                              [Pharmacy
 Terminals]        /           \                          Terminals]
              [Laboratory   [Laboratory
               Instruments] Terminals]
```

fails, the system continues to function, although it continues on a degraded level.

With this kind of approach, the entire network must be designed at the origin of the system, much as the large monolithic system is developed. One advantage is that the central processing hardware required to support the system is somewhat less expensive than the single large main frame. Another advantage is that redundancy and backup, resulting from the multiple mini-computer central processors, give the organization more reason to feel secure about the overall operation of the system.

Issues with Mini-Networks

One problem with the communicating star network and distributed star network is that if a mini-computer central processor malfunctions, that module will be lost. If the central mini-computer in the distributed star malfunctions, the entire system will be lost. By contrast, the loss of a mini-computer central processor in the true distributed network approach only degrades the system.

Most of the mini-computer approaches remain in the developmental stage. Some organizations have done some parts of the networks, but there is not, to my knowledge, any complete network of the type described in this section. In addition, the basic software that controls the distributed network is still largely lacking.

Considerations in Interfacing

In the previous discussion, it becomes obvious that interfaces between systems are a requirement for networks using a medium-size host as well as mini-computer networks. In addition, some large monolithic systems have begun to make use of interfaces in clinical areas.

When one is interfacing two systems from the same hardware manufacturer—which implies that the software of both systems was developed by the same vendor—the problem is reasonably straightforward. In this case, the vendor usually

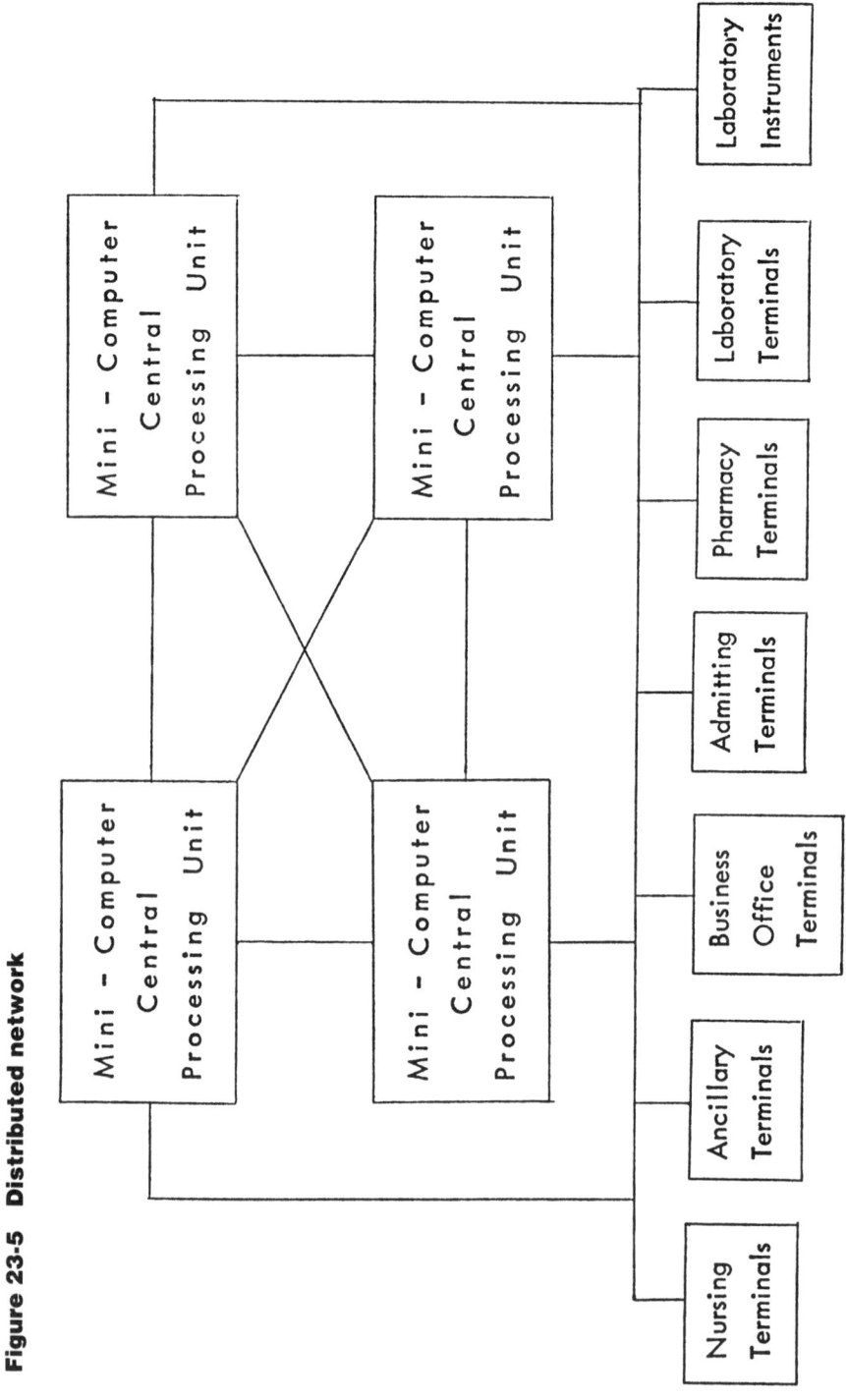

Figure 23-5 Distributed network

takes responsibility for delivering the entire interface package.

However, the various clinical subsystems that a hospital might need in order to solve its problems of appropriate flow of information are not always available from a single vendor. Furthermore, as previously noted, the ability to pick and choose among vendors in the selection of various clinical applications usually means that there is a possibility of producing some economies in the final development of the system, and certainly gives a wide range of choice to the hospital.

The usual situation is that the hospital has to interface systems from two different vendors. Ordinarily there are few technological problems associated with making these interfaces. Rather, the problems are of a more pragmatic nature, and include such issues as (1) compatibility of internal codes between the systems and (2) communication protocols. The internal codes for interrogating the communication system, for example, are likely to differ from the internal codes for interrogating a clinical laboratory system. Furthermore, the communication disciplines within the systems are frequently different; i.e., they are likely to transmit data at different rates or in widely varying formats.

As previously stated, there are few technological barriers to making these interfaces, but it does take time and effort to make the two systems uniform enough to communicate with each other. There is a need for compatibility between the two systems, and there are several ways to approach this problem.

One way is for the hospital to change the coding in one or both of the systems to be interfaced so that they are compatible with each other. This is a time-consuming and expensive approach. In addition, some vendors will withdraw the support of their system if internal coding changes are made to the system's programs.

A second approach is to use a micro-computer between the two systems as a "code converter." As can be observed in Figure 23-6, this approach allows converting the codes from one system to those of the other in the micro-computer without making any changes in the coding of the programs in either of the two primary systems. The technology of micro-computer use, and the attendant cost reductions in the manufacture of these products, makes it practical to use a micro-computer for this kind of application. In general, a very sophisticated micro-computer with ample memory to perform these tasks can be purchased for $4,000 to $5,000.

The interfacing task has become much simpler with the micro-computer technology. It is no longer necessary to make coding changes in the primary systems. In the past, this necessity to change internal coding was a very serious limitation to the interface philosophy. Micro-computer technology is generally felt to be an excellent approach, assuming that the capability to develop the micro-computer software is available to the hospital.

SHARED SYSTEMS VS. IN-HOUSE SYSTEMS*

A hospital's perception of the scope of a management information system can also be a factor in the choice between a shared system and an in-house system. If a hospital views a management information system primarily as a financial reporting system, the shared system approach gains an advantage in the decision process, since most shared systems address primarily the control function of the managerial process. The control function of the managerial process is primarily a financial reporting approach. If, however, a hospital views a management information system as encompassing the operational control function and the planning function of the managerial process, there is a greater likelihood that that hospital will choose an in-house system, since few shared systems address these two functions in a comprehensive way.

Shared Service Approaches

There are at least five different shared service approaches. The distinctions among them are primarily a function of differences in the corporate structures out of which services are delivered, rather than of organic differences in actual system designs.

Religious Order

This approach is as the heading implies: a religious order forms a computer service bureau to

---

*Source: Reprinted from *Hospital Information Systems* by Homer H. Schmitz, with permission of Aspen Systems Corporation, © 1979.

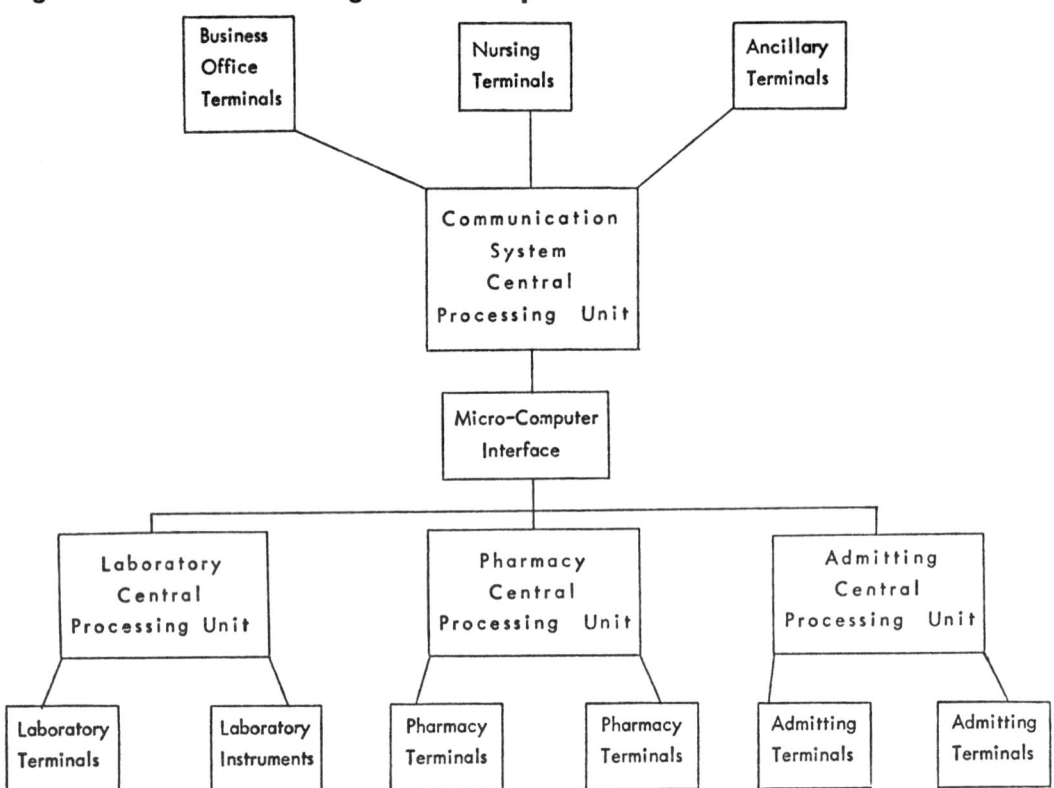

Figure 23-6 Interface using a microcomputer

provide computerized services to the various hospitals that are affiliated with the order. Ordinarily these service bureaus are set up initially to provide services exclusively to the religious order, but sometimes these services are later expanded to hospitals outside of the religious order. In that sense, they become competitive with other shared services.

Cooperating Hospitals

Under this approach, a group of hospitals forms a corporation to provide computer services to member hospitals. Often the groups that formed computer service bureaus have been Metropolitan Hospital Associations, and have provided the organizational framework and support within which the shared service is offered. Such a corporation is usually formed as a nonprofit organization, although this is not always the case. They are usually geographically localized.

The Single Hospital Center

Using this approach, a single hospital (usually a large one) develops a fairly sophisticated system, and then makes it available to other hospitals on a shared basis. Usually the other user hospitals are corporate satellites of a parent hospital, but this is not always the case. This approach is usually quite localized, and rarely goes outside of a single metropolitan area. This type of service is usually operated on a nonprofit basis.

Other Nonprofit Agencies

Under this approach, an agency such as Blue Cross, a municipality, or an academic institution provides shared computer services to a given hospital or set of hospitals. In the case of municipalities and academic institutions, the hospital is usually associated in some way with those institutions. By contrast, when Blue Cross becomes involved in providing computer services to hospitals, it is usually a service offered to all of the hospitals in the region serviced by a particular Blue Cross plan.

For-Profit Vendor

This is now the most widely recognized approach to shared services. Whereas the previous approaches to shared services tend to be largely nonprofit, this approach is for-profit. It is an approach taken by vendors who develop systems and market them commercially to the health care industry. In general, the large shared system corporations operate on a national scale, while the smaller operations tend to be regional.

The In-House Approach

An in-house approach can take either of two major forms. One approach is a pure in-house approach; the second is commonly known as a facilities management approach.

Pure In-House Approach

Under this approach, the hospital elects to have complete control—both organizational and logistical—over the entire data processing operation. This approach includes the selection of the hardware, as well as installation of the systems. The data processing staff is employed by the hospital, and usually has total responsibility for the data processing operation within the organization. (An exception might be a specialized clinical module, where clinical supervisors might have responsibility. Nevertheless, the control of that clinical module remains under the jurisdiction of the hospital where the system resides.) In short, the data processing operation is wholly the responsibility of the hospital, and hardware and software vendors are involved only to the extent of providing the products and services that facilitate successful implementation of the systems.

Facilities Management

This approach is really a hybrid between the pure in-house approach and a shared approach. I classify it as an in-house approach, since the hardware is usually in-house and the vendor tends to be more responsive to the hospital's individual needs than would be the case with a shared system. This approach is distinguished from the pure in-house approach by the fact that the management of the data processing operation is under the jurisdiction of nonhospital personnel. The hospital pays the vendor a fee for this service, and in return the vendor provides personnel to operate the system in the hospital. The hardware is usually in-house, and is operated by essentially permanent vendor personnel on the hospital's property.

Arguments in Favor of Shared Systems

Economies of Scale

A principal argument usually advanced in favor of shared systems is that the shared approach provides economies of scale to the operation of any specific institution. It is felt that it is inherently less expensive for a number of institutions to share a computer facility than for each organization to have its own computer operation. There are several different levels wherein these economies are said to be achieved.

It is argued that a vendor providing a shared service can acquire large computing hardware capable not only of doing very sophisticated operations, but also of handling large transaction loads, and that the vendor can provide these services to a number of individual hospitals, none of which could afford them individually.

As for continuing operational costs, the argument is that these costs—which consist primarily of personnel to program and operate the computer systems—are shared across a larger user base, and therefore produce economies of scale in the overall operation of the system which could not be achieved by an individual hospital. It is argued that several people operating a large-scale system for a group of hospitals is less expensive than one or two persons operating the system in each of a number of hospitals.

Technical Staff

Given the large-scale operation and high level of sophistication of the shared services vendor, some argue that it is easier to recruit qualified technical data processing staff for a shared system than it would be for an individual hospital. It is said that the large shared system's high level of sophistication is more likely to attract highly qualified data processing employees, who are more interested in working on sophisticated systems than on what might be developed in an individual hospital. Furthermore, for the same reasons that economies of scale are effected in operational costs and hardware costs, economies are effected in the technical data processing staff. In addition, because the shared operation is larger and more sophisticated, and because it is said to be able to produce economies of scale, some feel it can pay a higher wage scale than can an individual hospital.

Environment

It is argued that because the central computing facility is not on hospital premises, the hospital escapes both the costs associated with preparation of computer room facilities and the related environmental control costs that are a part of any computer room facility. These costs are counted not only in terms of actual dollars expended, but also in terms of space that is required for computer hardware. The actual cash flows are essentially a one-time cost, and include such things as environmental control facilities, raised floor, and specialized electrical connections.

Entry Level of Sophistication

Another argument advanced in support of the shared system approach is that a hospital is able to begin the use of a computerized management information system at any level of sophistication. That is, it is possible to begin with a straightforward payroll and billing system, and later evolve more sophisticated managerial control systems as the hospital can absorb them and justify them. This advantage is particularly valuable to small institutions that could not otherwise afford shared systems. Because costs are usually calculated on a unit basis (i.e., dollars per bed or dollars per transaction), a small institution can use data processing systems that it could not afford by itself. This argument is less convincing today than it was several years ago because the costs of computer hardware have decreased substantially with the advent of mini-computer and micro-computer technology.

Start-Up Costs

The argument is that a hospital can minimize start-up costs for a shared system because the vendor has all of the knowledge and expertise required to install and implement the system. The individual hospital thus does not need to have personnel skilled in the area of implementation and installation. Nor does it have to spend time achieving those goals. However, the hospital should not ignore the problems associated with abdicating, to the vendor, responsibilities that are rightly its own. These responsibilities include determining the actual needs of the hospital and the methodology by which those needs will be satisfied, which includes evaluation after the system has been installed.

Implementation of Government Regulations

It is argued that shared system vendors—unlike individual hospitals—have sufficient expertise, ability, and resources to quickly and effectively understand, modify, and implement systems that are affected by frequent changes in government regulations governing the hospital industry. Furthermore, shared system vendors are sometimes said to have better access to and knowledge about impending government regulations because of their political contacts, and therefore are able to anticipate these needs and insure that changes are made in a timely and accurate manner.

Data Processing Problems

Another frequently cited advantage of shared systems is that hospitals can avoid the continuing operational problems associated with creating and maintaining a data processing department. Specifically, it is argued that the salary structures required to recruit qualified data processing personnel wreak havoc on the overall salary schedule in a given hospital. Furthermore, it is argued that turnover in an individual hospital setting could be more of a problem than turnover in a shared services setting, simply because an individual hospital has fewer backup capabilities when a key person leaves. However, it should be pointed out that shared systems are not immune to problems in this area: even with large vendors, the departure of one or more key employees has created serious problems for the continuity of the system development effort in those companies.

The Installation

It is maintained that installation of a shared system is quicker because a shared services vendor can bring more experience and personnel to bear on the installation of the system than can an individual hospital. However, the hospital should remember the adage that "haste makes waste." It is not always in the hospital's best interest to install a system as quickly as possible. This is particularly true when quick installation is done at the expense of thorough education of personnel and testing of the system.

Sharing

It has been said that one advantage of a shared system is that ideas of multiple users are shared across the entire user base. This is no doubt true, but it should also be pointed out that in-house computer users have established sharing groups, and thus are able to accomplish the same ends in their own environment.

Arguments against Shared Systems

Less Freedom

While one advantage of a shared system is that ideas can be shared by the entire user base, individual users in a shared system have generally had little ability to influence system design. This is said to lead to less freedom for individual hospitals because the vendors of shared systems are interested in standardizing the system to meet the majority of the needs of the entire user base, as contrasted to an individual hospital's special needs.

Loss of Individuality

Because the shared services vendor is interested in satisfying the basic needs of the entire user group—not the esoteric needs of individual users—there is usually less individuality afforded the individual hospital in terms of report formats and content. Alternatively, if the vendor is able and willing to provide customized reports, it frequently is a very expensive proposition for the individual hospital.

Reaction to Change

It was previously stated that an advantage of shared systems is that they tend to be better able to have their systems react to changes in government regulations. This has many elements of truth, but the changes in systems to meet government regulations affect the entire user group. However, the ability of an individual hospital to implement a substantial change in the system is often a very long-term process because it is generally neither profitable nor desirable for the shared system vendor to make substantial changes to the basic system in order to accommodate an individual hospital.

Vendor's Health Care Expertise

When the shared services vendor is, for example, an academic institution or a municipal government, there can be substantial problems for the user hospital. These problems arise from the fact that the provider of the shared computer services does not have the knowledge or expertise that can be brought to bear on unique problems in the health care industry. Furthermore, this problem is not always limited to academic or municipal providers. Sometimes vendors from outside the health care industry attempt to develop systems without understanding the operation of the health care industry.

Advantages of In-House Systems

The advantages presented in this section are predicated on the assumption that system development and implementation proceed in a systematic and well-informed way. Furthermore, they are based on an assumption that well-trained data processing personnel are operating in an environment conducive to the development of good systems. Unfortunately this is not always the case for in-house systems, and thus the arguments in favor of an in-house system are not inherently true. They are true only when the hospital commits the resources necessary for a successful in-house approach.

Adaptability

One primary argument in favor of in-house systems has always been that this type of approach can better meet the special needs of the individual hospital. Shared system vendors find it neither profitable nor desirable to react to individual hospital needs. In the case of the in-house system, there is only one customer. Therefore, when a need is identified, meeting it requires only that resources be committed to change the system.

Involvement

Ordinarily, system development in an individual hospital involves all personnel who will interact with the system. Involvement of user personnel in system development serves several purposes. First, it substantially increases the probability of identifying most of the hospital's needs for handling information throughout the organization. Second, involving individual members of the hospital in the development of the system creates a commitment on their part to make the system work.

Pace of System Change

In-house system design and implementation takes place at a pace that suits the hospital. A hospital can speed up the process if the need arises, and slow it down when that seems desirable. This is so because there is only one customer. This argument is promoted not only for system design and implementation, but also for modification of existing systems.

Priorities

A hospital can set the priorities for in-house system design, as opposed to having an outside party decide what systems will be designed and when they will be available. Once again, this is the case because the individual hospital is the only customer for the services, and therefore is able to establish its own priorities.

Operational Flexibility

It is argued that there is a distinct advantage for a hospital to be able to adjust operational run times to suit its own needs. When malfunctions occur, or other unavoidable interruptions dictate changes in operational schedules for the computer, the hospital can react immediately to those needs and adjust the computer's operations schedule to meet the most pressing needs. This is in contrast to the usual approach of a shared system, wherein a particular data processing schedule must be met in order to effectively service the entire user base.

Disadvantages of an In-House System

In general, the disadvantages of the in-house system are the converse of the advantages of the shared system.

Qualified Staff

It is generally argued that it is much more difficult for an individual hospital to recruit, train, and retain qualified staff than for a shared service to do so. A shared environment is felt to be more interesting work for the computer professional, owing to the involvement with more sophisticated systems. The shared system also is said to be able to maintain more backup staff.

Environment

It is frequently argued that one clear disadvantage of an in-house system is the required financial commitment for environmental control of computer room facilities and for equipment space. There is no question that these costs can be substantial, but they are not eliminated when using a shared system. The costs of the shared system computer facility are simply transferred, and made a part of the overall fee.

Salaries

Some argue that salaries of qualified data processing personnel often upset hospital wage scales because they are much higher than any other pay category. This argument is not as compelling as it once was. Pharmacists, nurse anesthetists, and surgical assistants have pushed routine wage scales in hospitals to a point where they are comparable, if not in excess of, many of those in the data processing profession.

Hospital Involvement

It is argued that one advantage of the in-house system is that it involves numerous hospital personnel in its development and definition. At the same time, it is felt that this creates some disadvantages. Additional time is required from hospital personnel to help develop the system, and this time expenditure has a clear dollar cost to the hospital. However, if the hospital is willing to commit these time and personnel resources, it can result in having the flexibility to develop those systems that meet the specific operational needs of an individual hospital. In addition, the multiple inputs from individual hospital users make it more likely that the system that is developed will approximate the information needs of the individual hospital.

Administrative Time Requirements

It is argued that hospital administrators must commit additional time to supervise the data processing department during its operations after installation of an in-house system. There is some truth to this argument. However, the administrator who assumes that a shared system vendor needs little or no supervision is surely mistaken, and is likely to encounter far more problems than were originally anticipated.

Computer Terminology*

It is useful to think of a computer system as consisting of input/output devices, a processor, a memory, and a set of programs.

Processing may be done in either a batch mode or a real time mode. "Batch mode" refers to the collection of a large group of similar transactions and then processing them at a given time in a single batch. "Real time processing" involves processing each transaction as it occurs. Each mode of processing has its proper application. For example, computation of the hospital payroll demands batch processing, while transmission of stat X-ray orders from the emergency room to the radiology department requires real time processing.

Another distinction among computer systems is on-line versus off-line processing. "On-line" refers to the direct connection between a user-operated input device and the processor. This may, for example, be a keyboard terminal wired directly into the computer. "Off-line" processing implies use of a document, for example, a payroll time card, which is then physically transported to the computer and translated into computer language by keying at a later time.

The most common off-line input device is the key punch or key tape machine by which manually recorded alpha numeric data is translated into machine-readable form by keystrokes. The keyboard terminal, equipped with a cathode ray tube (CRT) display, performs a similar function, and in addition, is tied on-line to the processor, eliminating any intermediary form of storage such as punched cards or punched paper tape or magnetic tape. Automated document reading is possible by use of mark sense readers or optical character recognition devices.

The light pen, combined with a cathode ray tube, is an extremely powerful input method, permitting selection from among displayed alternatives by simply pointing a pen-like device at the desired word or phrase. This latter device is especially useful for personnel lacking typing skills. Output from a computer may be so-called "hard copy," printed documents which may be produced at either a centralized printer in the computer facility, or on printers located at appropriate work sites throughout the hospital. Or, output may be presented to the user via a cathode ray tube or television-like display when no permanent record is required.

Software is used to describe instructions which control the performance of the "hardware" (the equipment) in a computer system. Computer equipment is analogous to a musical instrument, particularly an automated one such as a player piano, while software is analogous to the musical composition.

Narrowly defined, software consists of computer programs. "Operating system" programs are those which control the machine and its various devices, such as loading programs, running programs, printing, error checking, etc. "Application" programs are those which cause the computer system to perform the function desired by the user. A broader definition of software would also include system analysis; that is, the review of, say, the hospital admitting procedures and recording these procedures in a precise, structured format, including all variations and options, which would then be translated into applications programs by the computer programmer.

EDP Glossary*

Access time. The time required for a processing component of a computer such as the Arithmetic Unit to receive or transmit data to the core storage component.

---

*Source: *Health Planning Review of Medical Information Systems,* National Center for Health Services Research, 1981, Pub. No. (PHS)81-3303.

*Source: Reprinted from *Basic Hospital Financial Management* by Donald F. Beck, with permission of Aspen Systems Corporation, © 1980.

Alphameric. A term used to describe data that contain both alphabetic and numeric characters.

Analog computer. A computer that simulates measurements by electronic means, for example, by varying voltages.

Audit trail. A means of tracing data back to original source data.

Batch totals. The sum of a column of input used later to verify data.

Binary system. A numbering system that has only two digits, 0 and 1. The binary system is used by digital computers.

Buffer. That part of a computer system that temporarily stores information until the computer system processes it.

Bug. An error in the program or in the system.

Central processing unit. That part of the computer that carries out the instructions and solves the programs given to the computer.

Character. One of the digits, letters, or other symbols that are recognized by a computer.

COBOL. Acronym for Common Business Oriented Language. A computer language widely used in business operations.

Coding. Using symbols and abbreviations to give instructions to the computer. Synonymous with writing the program.

Collating. Combining of data from two or more files into sequence in one file.

Compiler. The program that converts the instructions written by the programmer into instructions that can be interpreted by the computer.

Computer operator. The person in a computer system who manually controls the operations of the computer.

Control total. The sum taken on a particular field in a group of records to be used for checking program, machine, or input reliability.

Control unit. A major part of the computer that directs the step-by-step instructions given to a computer and that oversees the scheduling of the operations called for by the program.

Core storage. That component of a computer system in which data or information and program instructions can be stored and from which the computer can obtain at a later time those instructions or data values.

CRT. Acronym for cathode ray tube, which is a television-like device used to display or store data.

Data file. A major unit of information that is stored. Examples of data files include accounts receivable, payroll master file, and general ledger.

Debugging. Identifying and correcting errors in a computer system or program.

Destructive readin. A process of putting new data into a file in which data previously stored are destroyed in the update.

Digital computer. A computer that processes data by combinations of digits.

Direct access. A type of storage in which access can be made directly to any storage location regardless of its position, either absolute or relative to the previously referenced information.

Disk pack. A device that contains a set of magnetized disks.

Editing. The process of deciding what data to accept, examining them for accuracy, and rejecting those that do not meet predetermined parameters.

Electronic data processing. The processing of data and calculating of results by an electronic machine, such as a computer.

Field. A group of consecutive columns of data used for a specific purpose.

File maintenance. The periodic modification of a file to include changes that have occurred.

First generation computer. A class of computers that used vacuum tubes.

Flowchart. A graphic portrayal of a sequence of operations, an accumulation of data, or the steps used to solve a problem.

FORTRAN. Acronym for Formula Translation. A computer language widely used in scientific and engineering applications.

GIGO. Acronym for garbage in, garbage out. A commonly used term meaning that the quality of the computer output cannot be better than the quality of the input.

Hash totals. The sum of numbers of a specific field. Used for verifying purposes.

Input. Data entered into a computer system for processing.

Installation. A particular computer system and its overall process.

Machine language. A system of instructions written in a binary code of electronic impulses that are used to direct the computer.

Magnetic tape. A tape that has been coded with a magnetizable material. Used to record information in the form of polarized spots.

Memory. A device on which data can be stored for retrieval at a later time.

Mnemonic. A contraction or abbreviation used to represent the full expression.

Nondestructive readout. A process in which data are read out of storage repeatedly without being destroyed.

Operation manual. A manual that gives detailed instructions to a computer operator on how to complete a job.

Output. The information transferred from the internal storage of a computer to the outside storage, or to any device outside of the computer.

Peripheral equipment. Equipment that is not under the direct control of the computer, such as a printer, card reader, or cathode ray tube.

Primary storage. Storage in the main storage area of the computer itself.

Procedure. A predetermined way to accomplish a given task.

Programming. The advance preparation of instructions for use by the computer.

Random access. A storage device by which access time in retrieval is made to be independent of the location of data or sequence of input.

Remote access. The ability to obtain data from or place data in a storage device or register directly without serial delay due to other units of data, and usually in a relatively short period of time.

Retrieval. The recovering of desired information or data from a collection of documents or other graphic records.

Second generation computer. A computer that uses transistors and operates in millionths of a second.

Secondary storage. Storage on magnetic tapes, disks, drums, or other devices that are not directly connected to the computer.

Serial access. A data access technique in which the transfer of data elements is successive—that is, in sequence, one after the other.

Simulation. A representation in a computer program of a real model in order to mirror the effects of changes in the model. Used to determine the probable effects of changes in assumptions.

Source document. Original paper from which information regarding a transaction is recorded.

Subsystem. An identifiable portion of a main system.

Terminals. Devices for input and output that are some distance from the computer. They are often connected to the computer by telephone lines.

Third generation computer. A computer characterized by miniaturization and great speed. Operates in billionths of a second.

Time sharing. The use of a computer by two or more processes during the same overall time interval, accomplished by interspersing component actions in time. Usually involves accessing a computer's resources by remote consoles.

Chapter 24—Hospital Information Systems (HIS)

OVERVIEW

The Capability of Systems*

Computers can be used to enable individual hospital departments such as the clinical laboratory or the pharmacy to deal with information that is their sole responsibility—test results, medication orders, or the like. But computers can also provide the foundation for a hospitalwide network to provide direct communications among all departments. In both cases the computer stores data and transmits that information quickly and accurately to those who need it. The computer can deal with medical data, such as doctors' orders and laboratory results, as well as with administrative and fiscal data. It can copy, summarize, sort, and file information; it can review data for abnormal values or prepare bills for services and supplies. These are functions normally performed by a wide variety of hospital personnel, from doctors and nurses to filing clerks.

Purely departmental computer systems have obvious limitations. They cannot communicate with other departments. They might speed up the flow of work within the department, but they do not contribute to the other departments' needs for information as much as a hospitalwide system can. For example, a pharmacy department's computer can print labels for drug orders, but first the orders have to come down from the nursing stations and be entered into the computer one at a time. A hospitalwide system would permit a doctor, nurse, or clerk to enter *all* patient orders at a computer terminal on the nursing floor. The order could include not only medications but also laboratory work, x-rays, diet, physical activity, etc. The computer would store *all* these orders and automatically send the necessary instructions to appropriate departments to carry out each order—drug labels would be printed immediately in the pharmacy, laboratory requisitions in the lab, x-ray orders in radiology, the diet order in dietary, and so on.

In other words, such a computer-based system would be capable of receiving, storing, distributing, and reproducing immediately on demand *all* information pertinent to a hospital. Such systems are called hospital information systems (HIS), but we prefer to use the term *medical information systems* because it emphasizes the patient care component.

Common Benefits*

Although the impact of the medical information system will be seen differently among the various departments, there are generic benefits that affect all users. The relative importance of these benefits will vary, of course, depending on the

---

*Source: Reprinted from *Medical Information Systems: A New Source for Hospitals* by Melvin H. Hodge, with permission of Aspen Systems Corporation, © 1977.

NOTE: HIS (Hospital Information System) and MIS (Medical Information System or Management Information System) are used interchangeably throughout this section.

mission of a given department. Some of these benefits are:

1. *Requisitions.* Service requests are more timely, accurate, and complete. Departments can elect to receive requisitions individually or batched in a convenient fashion or both. For example, the laboratory might elect to receive all STAT requisitions individually when ordered, and all routine blood test requisitions grouped together at 6:00 a.m.
2. *Reports.* Reports from the service department to the requestor are more timely and accurate and are better organized from the viewpoint of the user. For example, laboratory data can be presented in a comparative format.
3. *Status.* Visibility into the status of a service request or resulting report is improved. Status can usually be determined from any terminal, eliminating the need to telephone or visit the performing department.
4. *Workload.* Departments can look ahead at their workload (e.g., scheduled admissions this afternoon, or radiology procedures ordered for tomorrow) and also look back (e.g., procedures done last month).
5. *Clerical Effort.* Most routine clerical work (e.g., charge tickets, patient lists, etc.) is eliminated.
6. *Audit Trails.* Service requisitions can be traced to reports and charges without error or ambiguity (e.g., matching microbiology reports to specimens).
7. *Location Independence.* The relationship between location and information is largely eliminated. Information is now available to authorized personnel at any terminal site in the hospital (e.g., the phlebotomist picking up a STAT specimen on the seventh floor can look in the terminal to ascertain if there are any other specimens to be collected on that floor).

System Types and Functions*

Most hospitals in the United States now use some sort of computer processing. In 1975 an AHA survey showed that more than 80 percent of all hospitals use data processing, with 25 percent having inhouse computers and 56 percent using outside data processing services. Many of the smaller hospitals can now afford automation through the use of either large shared systems or minicomputers and related software packages recently made available. Many of the larger hospitals, as well as the large shared systems, have begun developing medical applications and totally integrated medical/financial systems that operate in the real-time, data base environment.

Three Integrated Information Systems

The late 1960s saw the beginning of integrated information systems. These systems were designed to serve medical functions, with business office functions becoming a byproduct. Three prominent examples of these systems will be described briefly.

In 1965 El Camino Hospital in Mountainview, California, became the development hospital for the TMIS. This was a sophisticated information handling system designed to serve as: an accurate communications device for rapidly sending orders or retrieving current data; a custodian of medical and nonmedical data; and an organizer of the computerized data base, producing useful summary reports.

The Problem-Oriented Medical Information System (PROMIS), based on Lawrence L. Weed's Problem-Oriented Medical Record, was initiated in 1967 at the University of Vermont. PROMIS is unique in that it not only radically restructures the medical record, but also directs the process of patient care. Data are organized by patient problem in such a way that each entry into the system corresponds to a specific problem, with the exception of the initial registration. The major output is a patient status report.

The Computer Stored Ambulatory Record System (COSTAR) was initiated in 1969 by a collaboration between the Harvard Community Health Plan and Massachusetts General Hospital in Boston. Data entry is based on an encounter form, completed by a physician or nurse. Patients' records are stored on computer disks as long as the patient is a plan member.

A decade after their beginning, these three systems are in various phases of development. TMIS is being marketed and is installed in six

---
*Source: Reprinted from Thomas K. Shaffert and Constance E. McDowell, "Hospital Information Systems: An Overview," *Topics in Health Care Financing,* Summer 1978, with permission of Aspen Systems Corporation.

hospitals. Several prototype systems of COSTAR are in the process of implementation.

Functions

There are a great many functions that can be incorporated into a hospital information system. (See Figure 24-1.) These can be categorized into four types or levels of information requirements: transaction systems, control reporting, operational planning and strategic planning.

Transaction systems are developed to handle the day-to-day operational and administrative matters of the hospital. They process the "paper work" necessary to carry on both medical and business functions. This would include such transactions as order entry, results reporting inventory receipts and issues, and patient charges. Transaction systems also produce reports necessary for day-to-day operations, such as treatment scheduling, census, staffing schedules and labor cost distribution reports. As incoming data flow through the transaction systems, master files are built and updated, providing a base of activity which can be used by the other levels.

The operational planning and control reporting systems provide summarized data about the day-to-day operations, giving department managers and health care professionals the necessary information to monitor the various activities for which they are responsible. In addition, these systems will provide executive management with the information necessary to properly plan and control the hospital overall. This information includes operating trends and financial results, as well as data that will improve future decision making. Typically, executive management of a hospital would receive a monthly balance sheet and income statement, key expense summaries, budget variation summaries and occupancy and patient mix reports.

Strategic planning requires the provision of a framework for current decisions with long-range implications, as opposed to operational planning that involves decision making with a short-range impact. Strategic systems have significant influence on operations, and typically offer basic operating and policy alternatives to management for resolution. Some issues in hospital strategic planning are:

- patient care strategy (levels of care, occupancy and service requirements);
- medical staff strategy (recruitment, community needs);
- facilities planning;
- budgeting and rate-setting models;
- personnel policies.

As you can see from Figure 24-1, both medical and business functions are included and are intertwined in a hospital information system. The system is hierarchical, starting with transactions and building to strategic planning. The reporting is decision oriented, and data base management techniques are used.

The MIS Department[*]

The MIS Executive

What type of background and person is necessary for leadership of the MIS department?

Of primary importance to senior management is the MIS executive's knowledge of the total hospital, its objectives, and user department needs and concerns. Senior management expects this person to provide guidance and recommendations concerning the allocation and use of MIS resources. In order to do this, the executive must be fully aware of the hospital's goals and plans.

The chief concern of the executive is the ability to develop a sensitivity to user department operations and concerns. The successful executive realizes that the MIS department can best respond to user needs through a real understanding of these needs and responsibilities.

The executive must be able to design and judge systems. A system must be viewed in perspective of hospital objectives. A user may not have this perspective, and the systems analyst may also not realize the full impact of a given project on organization goals. Often, people, equipment, and interdepartmental problems can be anticipated through the MIS executive's view of the hospital.

An MIS executive's academic background can be business and systems oriented. This provides the proper mix of technical and management skills necessary to communicate effectively with all levels of the hospital.

An MIS executive too technically oriented may lack management perspective, and discussions of hardware and software concerns will frustrate the management team. However, a

---

[*]Source: Reprinted from *Managing Hospital Information Systems* by Stephen L. Priest, with permission of Aspen Systems Corporation, © 1982.

person with only business and management skills may not be able to effectively represent the MIS function and can lose control of MIS development within the organization.

The MIS Department and the Hospital Organization

How should the MIS department fit into the organization?

Until the late 1970s, the DP department usually reported to the financial officer. Computers were first used in the financial area, and financial officers needed the control over computer operations to perform their administrative responsibility effectively. When departments outside of finance requested computer applications, many were prevented from fully utilizing the computer service. The majority of the computer's resources was used on financial applications, and these were given first priority.

An MIS today has to serve all user departments, as seen on the organizational chart in Figure 24-2. An MIS department can serve the special operational needs of each area while providing a common data base for the reports needed by senior and line management for overall control, and then consideration can be given to the merits of individual requests.

The path to the successful MIS department can be realized when the ultimate responsibility for user and DP activities is shared. This means that both the end-user and MIS departments have to be held accountable for the success or failure of an information system. Instead of constant complaints to senior management that the other department is not doing its job, there should be a mutually agreeable approach that allows the MIS and user departments to sit down together and amiably discuss why a problem occurred and how it will be corrected.

SIX CRITICAL ISSUES*

Hospital management should focus initially on six issues:

1. Should the system(s) be departmental, serving departments individually, or should there be one comprehensive system interconnecting all departments throughout the hospital?
2. Should the system only transport information from place to place, or should all information on each patient's care be immediately available for retrieval and ready reference?
3. Should clerks enter information into the system; or should it be used directly by doctors, nurses, laboratory technologists, admitting personnel, etc.?
4. Should the hospital develop its own information system, or should it select one that has already been developed and proven elsewhere?
5. Should the hospital own and operate its own computer center, or should it contract for computer services from an external, shared center?
6. What computer technology should be employed—maxicomputers, minicomputers, or microcomputers?

Departmental or Hospitalwide?

From the vantage point of the hospital administrator, departmental systems appear attractive. First, they tend to fall exclusively within the domain of a single department head, thereby making them appear quite manageable—little need for interdepartmental coordination or consensus exists. Second, the costs are typically in the few hundred thousand dollar range, certainly not an insignificant amount, but probably an amount which, even if spent unsuccessfully, is not fatal from a management point of view. Third, installation of departmental systems in a step-by-step, or so-called modular fashion, is alleged to represent a nontraumatic and orderly way to achieve a comprehensive medical information system when the various previously installed departmental systems are ultimately tied together.

From the vendors' point of view, departmental systems are also attractive. The market for these systems is well defined and focused. The technological difficulties associated with development are limited; hence, the development investment is bounded.

Advocates of departmental systems sometimes claim that the particular system under consideration can later be "interfaced" with other department systems, leading to a comprehensive medical information system. This argu-

---

*Source: Reprinted from *Medical Information Systems: A New Source for Hospitals* by Melvin H. Hodge, with permission of Aspen Systems Corporation, © 1977.

Figure 24-1 Hospital information systems

INFORMATION REQUIREMENTS TYPE	MEDICAL FUNCTIONS				
STRATEGIC PLANNING	**MEDICAL STAFF STRATEGY** Services Offered/Community Needs Physician Recruitment	**PATIENT CARE STRATEGY** Level of Patient Care Occupancy and Service Requirements Forecast Sharing vs. Duplication of Services & Facilities Utilization of Contracted Services Community Services for Continuing Care			
OPERATIONAL PLANNING	**MEDICAL STAFF PLANNING** Medical Staff Education Research Treatment Planning Physician & Treatment Quality Control Administrative Functions	**NURSING SERVICE PLANNING** Flexible Staffing, Pool vs. Part-Time Patient Care Planning Discharge Planning In-Service Education		**OTHER PROFESSIONAL SERVICES PLANNING** Patient Scheduling, Test or Treatment Test/Treatment Equipment New Procedures Research & Development	**GENERAL SERVICES PLANNING** Preventive Maintenance Dietary Planning Purchasing Plans Joint Purchase Arrangements Quality Standards
CONTROL REPORTING	**MEDICAL STAFF CONTROL** Peer Review (PSRO) Concurrent Review Medical Care Evaluation Studies Profile Analysis Medical Audit Utilization Review Intern and Resident Experience	**PATIENT CONTROL** Occupancy Patient Mix	**NURSING CONTROL** Patient Load Staff Level Level (hrs.) of Care Medication/Treatment Scheduling Nursing Audit	**QUALITY CONTROL** QC Procedure Drug Interaction Poison Control Infection Control Personnel/Service Effectiveness	**RECORDS CONTROL** Medical Chart Drug Profile Narcotics Control Medical Audit Incomplete Charts Abstract Reporting	**GENERAL SERVICE REPORTING** Support System Scheduling Inventory Stock Status Equipment Status Trouble Logs Vendor Analysis Personnel/Service Effectiveness Back Orders/Stockouts Quality Control
TRANSACTION SYSTEMS	ORDER ENTRY / TREATMENT SCHEDULING / CENSUS / NURSE STAFFING / NURSE SCHEDULING / PRODUCTIVITY REPORTING / RESULTS REPORTING / MEDICAL INFORMATION / PURCHASING / INVENTORY CONTROL / PRODUCTIVITY REPORTING / WORK ORDERS				

(Read Figure 24-1 across two pages.)

ment, however, seems glib. Although conceptually it can be shown that in certain instances disparate systems can be interfaced, to do so is always difficult, and sometimes impossible.

The hospital is well advised to take the pragmatic view that disparate departmental systems can be successfully interfaced *only* after it has been done successfully in another hospital. In general, only when an integrated, comprehensive system has been developed and demonstrated can the component parts of that system be considered "modular" and, hence, suitable for departmental installation with the intent of integration later into a comprehensive system.

Even when an integrated system consisting of modular departmental system subsystems is obtainable, there are other disadvantages. Although the costs of individual departmental systems appear low, the ultimate cost is likely to be higher because of the inevitable duplication of function among such systems (e.g., each must have admission-transfer-discharge capacity) and because of the lengthy delay in obtaining savings.

Which Level of Sophistication?

Superficially, all hospital information systems appear much the same to the casual observer.

Figure 24-1 continued

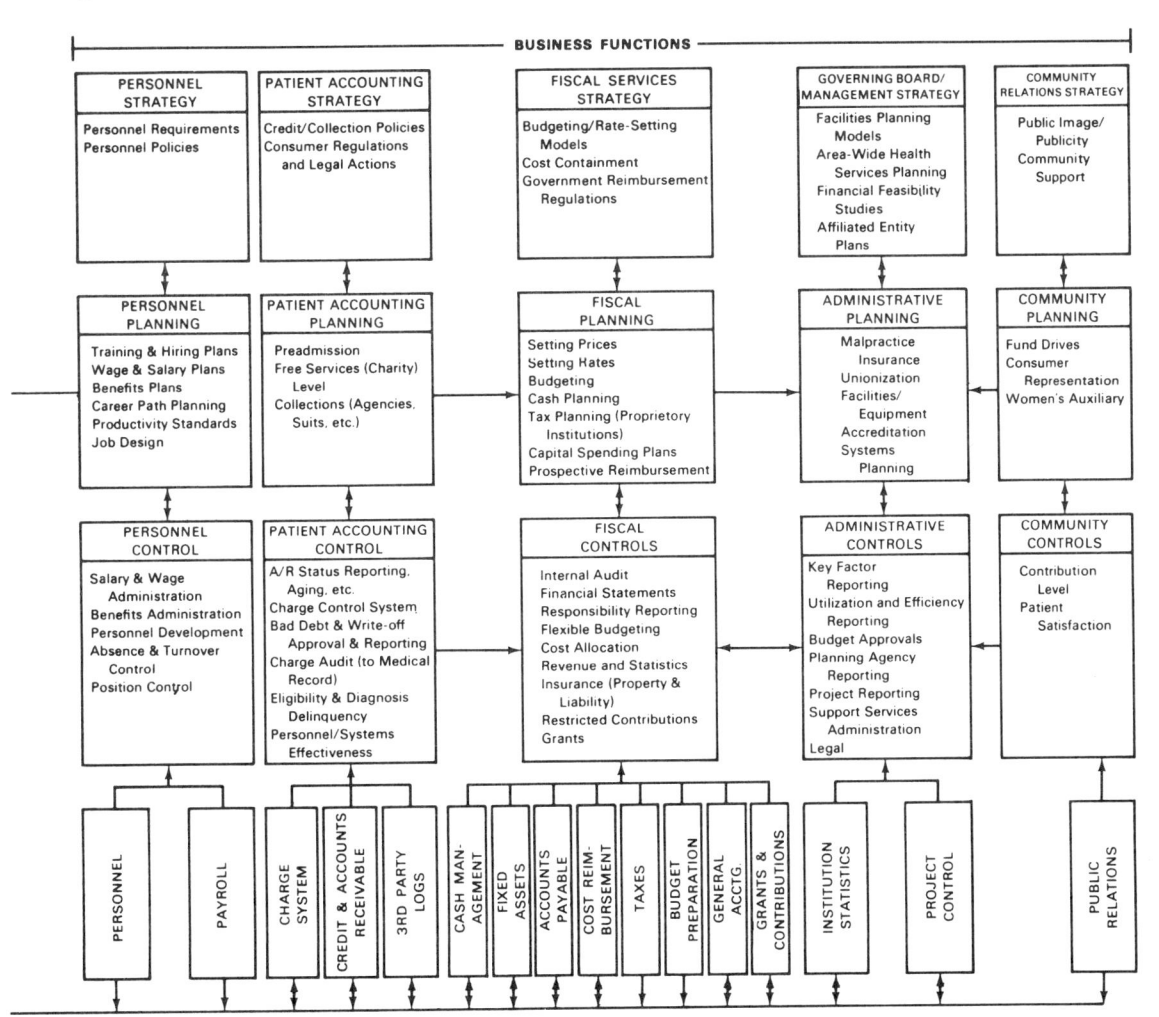

BUSINESS FUNCTIONS

PERSONNEL STRATEGY	PATIENT ACCOUNTING STRATEGY	FISCAL SERVICES STRATEGY	GOVERNING BOARD/ MANAGEMENT STRATEGY	COMMUNITY RELATIONS STRATEGY
Personnel Requirements Personnel Policies	Credit/Collection Policies Consumer Regulations and Legal Actions	Budgeting/Rate-Setting Models Cost Containment Government Reimbursement Regulations	Facilities Planning Models Area-Wide Health Services Planning Financial Feasibility Studies Affiliated Entity Plans	Public Image/Publicity Community Support

PERSONNEL PLANNING	PATIENT ACCOUNTING PLANNING	FISCAL PLANNING	ADMINISTRATIVE PLANNING	COMMUNITY PLANNING
Training & Hiring Plans Wage & Salary Plans Benefits Plans Career Path Planning Productivity Standards Job Design	Preadmission Free Services (Charity) Level Collections (Agencies, Suits, etc.)	Setting Prices Setting Rates Budgeting Cash Planning Tax Planning (Proprietary Institutions) Capital Spending Plans Prospective Reimbursement	Malpractice Insurance Unionization Facilities/Equipment Accreditation Systems Planning	Fund Drives Consumer Representation Women's Auxiliary

PERSONNEL CONTROL	PATIENT ACCOUNTING CONTROL	FISCAL CONTROLS	ADMINISTRATIVE CONTROLS	COMMUNITY CONTROLS
Salary & Wage Administration Benefits Administration Personnel Development Absence & Turnover Control Position Control	A/R Status Reporting, Aging, etc. Charge Control System Bad Debt & Write-off Approval & Reporting Charge Audit (to Medical Record) Eligibility & Diagnosis Delinquency Personnel/Systems Effectiveness	Internal Audit Financial Statements Responsibility Reporting Flexible Budgeting Cost Allocation Revenue and Statistics Insurance (Property & Liability) Restricted Contributions Grants	Key Factor Reporting Utilization and Efficiency Reporting Budget Approvals Planning Agency Reporting Project Reporting Support Services Administration Legal	Contribution Level Patient Satisfaction

PERSONNEL | PAYROLL | CHARGE SYSTEM | CREDIT & ACCOUNTS RECEIVABLE | 3RD PARTY LOGS | CASH MANAGEMENT | FIXED ASSETS | ACCOUNTS PAYABLE | COST REIMBURSEMENT | TAXES | BUDGET PREPARATION | GENERAL ACCTG | GRANTS & CONTRIBUTIONS | INSTITUTION STATISTICS | PROJECT CONTROL | PUBLIC RELATIONS

Television-like terminals are located at many work sites throughout the hospital, and printers are also seen in most busy areas. Differences are, however, profound.

Level 1 systems perform two basic functions. First, they provide the capability for transmission of requisitions and admission-transfer-discharge (ATD) transactions from nursing stations to ancillary departments. Second, they derive associated charge data from the requisitions and ATD transactions, which then is available as computerized input to the patient billing system, thereby eliminating keypunching of charge tickets. A basic characteristic of Level 1 systems is that they do *not* maintain computerized patient records throughout the hospital stay. Rather, each day's transactions are erased once the charges are handed over to the patient billing system. Level 1 systems are sometimes called "Charge Collection" systems.

The danger with Level 1 systems is the difficulty or impossibility of expanding in the future as a hospital's sophistication in harnessing medical information systems technology grows. There can be no greater setback either financially or psychologically than reaching the point where it is necessary to throw out a previously

Figure 24-2 Departments served by MIS

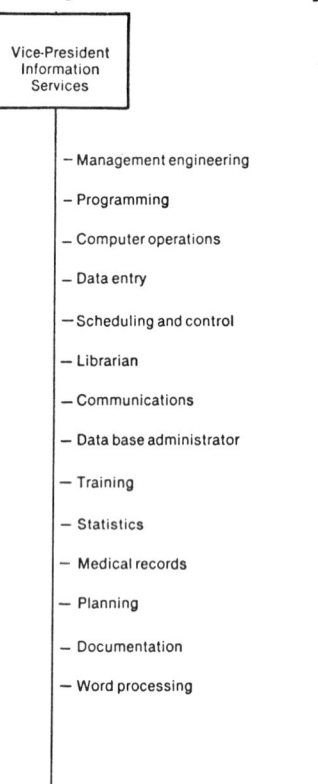

```
Vice-President
Information
Services
    |
    |— Management engineering
    |— Programming
    |— Computer operations
    |— Data entry
    |— Scheduling and control
    |— Librarian
    |— Communications
    |— Data base administrator
    |— Training
    |— Statistics
    |— Medical records
    |— Planning
    |— Documentation
    |— Word processing
```

installed system because its limits have been reached.

Level 2 systems not only perform the function of Level 1 systems, but also create and store a computerized medical record. The paper chart record is also present, although much of it is automatically produced by the medical information system. The chart information is also retrievable from any terminal. Thus, the Level 2 system will typically contain information on all medical orders active on a patient, all medications given the patient since admission, cumulative laboratory test results, x-ray reports, nursing notes, etc.

Level 3 systems are similar to Level 2 systems but differ in that they are designed for direct professional use by doctors, nurses, and other health care professionals.

Clerical or Professional Users?

Perhaps no issue has been more controversial than that concerning the merits of *direct use* of medical information systems by physicians, nurses, technologists, and other health professionals. Opponents have held firmly to two beliefs: first, physician time is too scarce and valuable a resource to require that it be used for a "clerical function;" and second, physicians will refuse to use computers.

It must be the goal of the system designer to invalidate this assumption by fulfilling two requirements. First, the system must operate at a rate that is faster than the physician's thought processes so he is not slowed down or delayed in carrying out his desired activities.

At least two types of modern terminals exist that meet this requirement—the light pen terminal and the touch terminal. The Technicon Video Matrix Terminal™ is a successful example of the former. It is utilized by the physician by simply pointing a light sensing light pen at the desired word or phrase appearing on the screen of a cathode ray tube and pressing a button on the side of the light pen. The Control Data Digiscribe™ terminal is a successful example of the touch terminal, whereby the physician can make this selection by touching the desired word or phrase appearing on the CRT with his fingertip. Other techniques such as the use of buttons located at the periphery of the cathode ray tube or the use of keys to position a cursor to underscore a desired word or phrase have been somewhat less successful.

The second requirement, that of rapid response, has also been met. Experience has shown that the response time to change from one display to the next should not exceed 0.5 seconds and that the time to retrieve data from a patient's record, format it, and present it should not exceed 3.0 seconds. These response times are within the "thinking time" of most physicians; little conscious slowing of activity should occur.

Thus, it has been shown that systems *can* be built that will be used easily by most physicians.

On the other hand, the use of intermediaries requires the communication of medical information through nonmedically trained personnel. Even the most faithful and conscientious data terminal operator lacking understanding of the patient care context will inevitably make errors in transcribing handwritten medical orders, in resolving ambiguous or incomplete communications, or in establishing priorities of instructions contained in a stack of order sheets. This will inevitably lead to errors of commission and omission and to significant delays between the time that orders are written and the time they are executed.

The interposition of a data terminal operator between the physician and the medical information system cuts off potential interaction between the physician and the information contained within the system. The computer is characterized by its ability to store and rapidly present very large quantities of information. The human mind, on the other hand, is characterized by an impressive ability to detect patterns in data—to be reminded by one thing of another. Thus, the computer and the human being can interact synergistically, the capability of one reenforcing the capability of the other. The ability of the physician to rapidly review data on his patient as well as general medical information can enhance his performance.

What becomes of physicians who will not or cannot use the medical information system? Every hospital staff undoubtedly contains a few physicians who, for whatever reasons, will refuse to cooperate in such a venture. Added to this group are the highly infrequent users of the hospital who will probably never gain enough exposure to the system to feel comfortable in its use. The answer is that both groups continue to practice medicine as before by writing their orders on an order sheet. This necessitates transcription of their orders into the system by a nurse or a clerk. This transcription process is, however, now limited to a small minority of patients; the benefits of direct use are obtained for the majority. Information flow throughout the hospital is, however, completely handled by the system for all patients.

Do-It-Yourself or a Developed System?

The hospital that has accepted the merits of medical information systems must address the question of attempting to develop its own system versus acquiring a commercially developed system.

The principal argument used to justify internal systems development is that the needs of the hospital are unique and cannot be well served by an externally developed system. It is true, of course, that no two hospitals are identical. Examination reveals, however, that most differences are superficial, and that the basic functions of admitting patients, writing orders, performing laboratory tests, reporting x-ray results, billing patients, etc. are common to all hospitals.

The question that hospital managements must ask themselves is, "Do we have the financial resources and the *available* technical resources to develop and support our own medical information system successfully?"

Existing commercial systems have required development investments in the range of $10 million to $25 million, as well as three to five years of development time.

In-House Operation or a Computer Service?

Hospitals that elect to utilize a commercially developed system must consider a further question, "Should the hospital acquire the system and install and operate it with its own staff on computers located within the hospital; or, alternatively, should it fulfill its information system needs from computers operated by the vendor outside the hospital?"

Successful examples can be found for both modes. The external computer service concept has been well established over the past decade, particularly for financial processing. Shared Medical Systems, Inc., King of Prussia, Pennsylvania, and McDonnell Douglas Automation Company, St. Louis, Missouri, each provide daily service to more than 300 hospitals. Technicon Medical Information Systems Corp. similarly provides medical information system services to hospitals from centers in Mountain View, California, and Fairfield, New Jersey.

For a full discussion of the advantages and disadvantages of an in-house versus a shared (or external) system see Chapter 23: Computers.

Maxi, Mini, or Micro?

Present successful systems utilize each kind of computer in areas where their applicability has been proven. Large maxicomputers are used for central file management, minicomputers for processing laboratory data from automated instruments prior to transferring it to a central machine, and microcomputers are used in individual terminals to perform so-called "intelligent" terminal functions.

It should also be borne in mind that the cost of the computer utilized does not equate to the cost of the medical information system. In fact, only about 20 percent of the medical information cost system is represented by the central computer; therefore, if the cost of computers suddenly went to zero, a system cost reduction would occur but would be limited to something of the order of 20 percent.

Considerations other than cost also should influence selection. These include:

1. *Ease of capacity expansion.* The need might exist to expand the capacity of the system due to growth in hospital data volumes, or hospital services, or both; therefore, the ability to replace one computer with a compatible but larger one is important.
2. *Financing arrangements.* It is frequently desirable to finance the computers, whether they are provided by a computer services firm or by the hospital itself. The ease of financing can vary from one manufacturer to another.
3. *Computer resale.* Because of the possibility of replacement to satisfy capacity growth, resale value of the computer is also an important consideration. The difference between original cost and resale value amortized over time is, in fact, the real cost of the computer. Therefore, computers with limited resale value should normally be avoided.
4. *Maintenance requirements.* Medical information system reliability is vitally dependent on the availability and quality of computer maintenance services.

PLANNING AN HIS

Using a Steering Committee To Plan and Implement an HIS*

An initial step for the efficient development and operation of hospital information systems is the formation of a systems steering committee. This committee provides an effective means for achieving needed management and user personnel involvement in the data processing systems

*Source: Reprinted from J.F. Lawrence and C. Hunsaker, "Organizing for Systems Development," *Topics in Health Care Financing,* Summer 1978, with permission of Aspen Systems Corporation.

effort. The committee should provide leadership during systems development and review over operations. When fulfilling this function effectively the committee will:

- provide a centralized control area for policy and systems-related decisions with representation for potential user departments;
- provide an effective link between hospital management and the technical electronic data processing (EDP) systems effort;
- protect the data processing manager from unreasonable demands of multiple users who feel that their needs should receive top priority; and
- provide a means for assuring adequate assignment of personnel from user departments to data processing projects.

The systems steering committee should be composed of representatives of executive management and each major functional area in the hospital. It should include representatives from administration, finance, nursing, medical staff, data processing, ancillary departments and any other parties that are required to represent the information systems users.

Planning Role

For the committee to fulfill its role in the planning effort it should:

1. document the business objectives and translate these into long-range systems objectives and policies;
2. define the information needs of the various functional areas of the hospital;
3. determine how, if at all, these information needs are presently being met;
4. document the proposed systems projects for management evaluation and approval; and
5. develop a formal systems plan.

1. Documenting Business Objectives

The first step in the management effort to plan the activities of hospital systems development is to document (and perhaps also define) the overall business objectives of the hospital and then determine their systems implications. Management must define and document its overall business objectives considering the following:

- characteristics of the external environment that significantly affect the hospital, such as a rate review commission or an HSA;
- characteristics of the hospital industry, such as its labor intensity; and
- internal characteristics of the hospital, including organizational structure, long- and short-term goals, policies and information dependencies.

The systems steering committee must further identify a general set of criteria for assigning systems priorities that are consistent with the business objectives. Some criteria more frequently used to set priorities are:

- ability to handle increased volumes;
- flexibility for operational changes;
- reduced operating costs:
- improved information for planning and control;
- improved reliability and control;
- reduced computer requirements; and
- increased prestige of leading edge position.

2. Identifying Information Needs

In this step, the committee must identify the specific information required by hospital personnel to operate the hospital, care for the patients and manage these functions. This step is perhaps the most important of all in the planning effort, because the subsequent specification of systems projects will be based on the defined information needs and related systems features.

Of course, the committee must also recognize information needs that are necessary to meet outside reporting requirements of third parties or to reduce the high volume of paperwork and associated clerical effort connected with existing systems.

3. Determining Present Status

The next step involves documenting the planning and reporting systems that currently exist or are under development in the hospital. The work done here will establish that certain identified requirements have been computerized or that some are operating on a manual or partially mechanized basis, or that some have not previously been identified as systems requirements.

The present systems may meet management's needs. However, they may not be efficient or cost effective; they may be inflexible in terms of data extraction, summarization and reporting capabilities; and they may be difficult to maintain. In evaluating current systems, another important consideration is whether the systems can accommodate the volume levels that are anticipated in the future.

User appraisal of these systems must also be considered. This effort determines not only how effectively users interface with these automated systems, but how effectively they are able to work with the supporting manual procedures that are in place. The impact of future anticipated volume levels must be evaluated with respect to workloads, hardware adequacy, manpower requirements and costs.

4. Documenting Systems Projects

At this point the committee is prepared to define the specific systems that should be part of the hospital's overall management information system.

The definition of projects provides the committee with sufficient criteria for evaluating the projects on an economic feasibility and timing basis, while considering the system objectives.

5. Developing the Systems Plan

After projects are approved for further development, it is necessary for the systems steering committee to determine priorities of the projects in relation to each other. For example, a hospital may choose to order evaluation criteria as follows:

1. maximize reliability and control;
2. increase management information;
3. avoid increasing costs; and
4. provide flexibility for new operations and increased volumes.

Using Task Forces

The systems steering committee provides for direct management leadership and control in systems development. As such, it has the responsibility for providing personnel within the hospital organization to conduct studies and develop information for the committee. A method used for this function is the assigning of personnel to a task force.

The task force composed of user personnel and systems analysts is responsible for developing all information required by the committee, conducting studies and performing the tasks as required in each phase of project development.

Using the skills and knowledge from multiple disciplines, involving user and information systems personnel, and working under the leadership of a competent project manager, the task force helps assure appropriate user involvement and knowledge of the system, clear definition of responsibility for systems projects, and sound coordination and communication between personnel and organization units involved in the project.

At the end of each phase of the development process the task forces should have a formal review with the users. The purpose of the review is to verify that the users' objectives are still being met and that continuing development costs and timing are still reasonable.

Evaluation

As one project is finished and resources are made available to begin another, the systems steering committee must evaluate the progress against the systems plan. This process then closes the circle of the management cycle of planning, performing, controlling and evaluating. This evaluation should cover at least the following:

- the effectiveness of the system in meeting the original objectives;
- the efficiency of the project (how close it came to cost and schedule estimates);
- the level of user satisfaction;
- the level of user understanding and capability to use the system;
- the smoothness of the system's operations; and
- the ongoing accuracy of controls.

It should be noted that the committee's evaluation responsibility should not be limited to individual systems. The committee should also recognize a responsibility for the ongoing evaluation of the production systems support function, i.e., data processing operations and systems maintenance. This review and analysis should:

- identify trouble areas requiring special attention;
- check the adequacy and enforcement of standard systems development and operating practices;
- indicate systems that need to be upgraded because of changes in requirements over time or because of faulty design and installation; and
- evaluate the adequacy of the systems support function.

This overall evaluation of the systems support function should be performed at regular intervals. The reports of these reviews should be presented to management.

Projecting Cost Benefits*

Cost benefits are conveniently segregated into labor saving and nonlabor saving. The latter category can be projected rather easily. This is done by, first, identifying each prospective item of saving (preprinted forms, keypunch machines, accelerated cash flow, etc.), and then determining present volumes (e.g., how many admissions forms are we using now), projecting them forward for the period of study (e.g., adjust current admission form usage for five years by using the hospital's admissions forecast), and finally converting to dollars by applying unit price data and suitable inflation adjustment for future years. The system vendor can usually provide a checklist of prospective saving items.

Projecting labor savings, however, is a little more complicated. It is approached in the following manner:

1. *Task Description.* Each information processing task performed in the hospital that will be affected by the information system is described in detail by actual or narrative flow charting. This is then repeated for the same task using the information system. Perhaps 100 such affected tasks can be identified. It is important to include not only those manual tasks modified or eliminated by the system but also new work tasks created by the system (e.g., removing and filing printouts from the printer) so the overall resulting projection will be a net number.
2. *Task Analysis.* Each task is then analyzed by skill category (e.g., RN, LVN, aide or

---

*Source: Reprinted from *Medical Information Systems: A New Source for Hospitals* by Melvin H. Hodge, with permission of Aspen Systems Corporation, © 1977.

ward clerk), by workshift, and by work motions (e.g., retrieve chart, remove page, retrieve form, enter "discharge time," etc.).

3. *Estimating Task Times.* Using published industrial engineering work standards, estimate time required for each task. These task times must be adjusted to allow for "overhead" such as personal time, rest periods, etc. If 20 percent of total time were considered a reasonable overhead estimate, the task times would be adjusted by dividing them by 0.8.

4. *Estimating Occurrence and Traffic Rates.* The number of times each task occurs for each patient for each day must be estimated. This is conveniently done by analyzing a sample of patients' records and ancillary department records. For example, perhaps it is determined that there are 2.1 laboratory test orders per patient day and that laboratory tests per patient day are increasing at a rate of 12 percent per year. Projected patient days for the five-year period are also estimated.

5. *Estimating Potential Labor Saving.* By combining steps 3 and 4, one can now calculate the savings by subtracting task times with the medical information system from manual task times, and multiplying the result by the appropriate occurrence and traffic factors. Then, aggregate all the tasks for a given work unit (e.g., Nursing Station 6 West) broken down by skill level, shift, and year. This will provide us with the full-time equivalent employees who potentially could be eliminated by introducing the medical information system.

6. *Estimating Realization.* Since the time saved occurs in many small increments, it is rarely possible to aggregate these savings and fully translate them into reduced staff. Realizable savings can be estimated by applying a realization factor to potential savings. Experience has indicated that about 80 percent of potential savings can be realized.

7. *Estimating Dollar Savings.* Now there is an estimate of realizable savings by skill category, by shift, and by year. By applying labor cost factors, which include direct salaries, fringe benefit costs, and future inflation estimates, one can translate labor savings into dollar savings.

Benefit Realization (e.g., in Nursing)

Medical information systems save work, but hospital managers save money. *Potential benefits* refer to saved work. If it is possible to translate the saved work into saved money, that is called a *realizable benefit*. If the necessary action has been taken, one has a *realized benefit*. It must be kept in mind that realized economic benefits occur *only* when the hospital writes fewer paychecks or checks to vendors for products and services *with* a medical information system than without the system.

This section provides an overview of benefit realization in nursing; however, the same approach is equally appropriate to other hospital departments. To carry out this task, the use of one or more teams, each consisting of a management engineer and an RN, should be considered.

Timing of the benefits realization process is important. Most labor savings are not automatic. Work is saved; but if it is not promptly translated into cost savings via staff adjustment, the saved time will be diverted into new activities. In a short time these new activities will come to be regarded as essential, and the opportunity for savings is lost. Of course, it might be desirable to invest some portion of this work savings into new activities rather than into cost savings, but this should be the result of an overt management decision rather than the failure to implement the benefits realization process on a timely basis.

The benefits realization is best carried out in a work unit two to four months after implementation. Sufficient time must be allowed to permit stabilization and for worker proficiency to reach a high level.

The benefits realization team approaches their task on a given work unit (say, a given nursing station) in the following manner:

1. *Observation.* The team observes and documents nursing tasks to understand the pattern of operation of the nursing station. The team is careful to avoid involvement in nursing activities and to extend its observation over each hour of each shift. Focus is on information-related tasks, guided by the cost-benefit projection work done prior to implementation. Documentation

includes task description, performer, reason, and time.
2. *Analysis.* The team then analyzes its observation with the goal of defining an optimum strategy for performing necessary tasks with a minimum labor investment. This process involves asking a series of questions concerning each task:

- Can this task be eliminated? (E.g., the system-produced patient care plan eliminates the need to maintain the Kardex.)
- Can the task be combined with another task resulting in a reduction in combined task time?
- Can the task be shifted from a higher skilled worker to a lower skilled worker without degradation?
- Can the task be shifted in time to a slack period or even to another shift without degradation?
- Can externally imposed policies or rules be modified or eliminated thereby reducing task requirements? (E.g., "Each head nurse will check the census and phone her verification to the nursing office" is no longer necessary.)

3. *Review.* The tentative strategy emerging from the analytical phase should next be reviewed and discussed with the supervisors and the employees on the work unit. Some aspects of the strategy will prove to be impractical because of previously undisclosed constraints. Improvements will also be suggested.

4. *Testing.* Following the review step, arrangements should be made to test the modified strategy on the work unit. Care should be given to assuring that all workers are adequately trained in the new methods. The test should be closely observed by the team to assure that the strategy is being followed and to identify defects or possible improvements. Close collaboration should exist between the team and work unit personnel so the latter feel that they understand and are in control of changes in their methods.

5. *Staff Adjustment and Backup.* The validated strategy will almost certainly permit the work unit to carry out all necessary tasks with a reduced staff. Two considerations are especially important at this point. First, the staff reduction should be *immediately* implemented (by transfer, not by layoff). If reduction is delayed, new tasks will come into existence to fill the vacuum and will rapidly be internalized by the work unit. Second, the work unit supervisor should be given *unqualified authority* to call in temporary workers to assist in the event of an unanticipated increase in workload. This authority will alleviate the fear of giving up slack capacity and the uncertainty the supervisor might feel about the adequacy of the new methods under all circumstances.

6. *Standards.* Particularly in nursing, where multiple work groups performing similar functions are involved, standardization of job duties and methods is desirable to facilitate personnel interchangeability. This is best carried out by establishing a standards committee consisting of affected line supervisors (e.g., head nurses) with staff support by a benefits realization team. Invariably, creative concepts will come from different work groups, and the goal of the committee will be to integrate them into a standardized strategy. By placing this responsibility in the hands of affected supervisors, any threat of imposition of inappropriate methods by administration or "efficiency experts" is removed.

7. *Performance Reporting.* "Earned hours" should be compared with "actual hours" regularly—usually as a byproduct of the payroll system, typically, biweekly. "Earned hours" are computed by applying the task time factors developed by the team to actual work load statistics. In one hospital, the administrator personally met with supervisors for this review, alternating biweekly between nursing supervisors and ancillary department supervisors. The supervisor presented his (or her) performance data along with an analysis of factors affecting performance and recommendations for changes that might allow improved future performance.

8. *Indirect Benefits.* Having implemented (or more accurately, assisted supervisors in implementing) the direct benefits of the medical information system, the team(s) should now work with department heads to

identify and implement indirect benefits. Creativity is required, but two subject areas where further benefits are likely to be found are organization and work schedules. For example, one hospital eliminated their outpatient registration desk and directed outpatients to report directly to the ancillary department from whom they required service for registration. Since both the registration function and checking on prior registration can be done through any terminal, it was no longer necessary to staff a separate desk for a somewhat limited registration volume. Another hospital reduced its admission department hours to the principal admitting periods, referring "off-hour" admissions to the emergency department. Again, the hospital capitalized on the fact that a given function can be performed via any terminal.

HIS Contracts*

During contract negotiations, the user should bear in mind that the standard contract—the one that the vendor will usually advocate—is designed to protect the vendor, not necessarily the user. Accordingly, the user should take as much time as necessary—and spend whatever resources seem appropriate—to determine exactly what is contained in the standard contract. Furthermore, the user should determine whether it feels it can live with the standard contract's conditions and restrictions. If there are items that seem unusual, or that unduly restrict the freedom of the user organization, the user should make every effort to see that these elements of the standard contract are changed.

The complete proposal should be incorporated into the contract. The request for proposal should make it clear that the vendor's proposal will be incorporated into the contract. This tells vendors that they will be held to their proposals and that they must accurately estimate software and hardware requirements as well as associated costs.

Items To Be Included

What follows is an enumeration of some of the items that could prove to be important from the user's point of view. It is not meant to be exhaustive, and represents primarily those items that are likely to affect the operation of the system, as contrasted to the legal technicalities that are usually made a part of any contract.

*Source: Reprinted from *Hospital Information Systems* by Homer H. Schmitz, with permission of Aspen Systems Corporation, © 1979.

Delivery

The delivery date is crucially important to the user. It has implications for the scheduling of education for personnel within the organization, as well as for renovations of physical facilities. As such, the user must know exactly when the equipment will be delivered. The reader should note that hardware and software commonly arrive separately. Furthermore, various pieces of hardware may arrive in sequence, so plans should be made for an orderly flow.

Acceptance of the System

This item spells out the method by which it will be determined when the user will begin paying for the system. The contract should specify the kind of performance test that will be used to determine whether the system meets the user's criteria. Furthermore, a deadline for performing these tests should be specified. If the hardware and/or software arrive at varying times, specific tests for each arrival should be conducted.

Documentation

This section of the contract specifies which items of documentation the vendor will provide to support the continuing operation of the system's hardware and software. Further documentation is often available to help in training personnel; if so, it should be included in the contract.

Rights to the Programs

The primary purpose of this section of the contract is to specify those conditions under which the user may use the programs. Where programs are proprietary (which they usually are), a nondisclosure clause in the contract generally forbids the user's sharing them with other users. If the system being installed is a shared system, the user might want to include nondisclosure provisions to bar the vendor from sharing the user's data files.

Training of Personnel

The purpose of this section is to specify the roles that user and vendor will play in training personnel to use the system. It should state specifically both the amount of time that the vendor will commit to this activity and the price for that service. Furthermore, the contract should specify a minimum level of expertise for the personnel who will conduct the training program.

User Physical Facilities

This section of the contract specifies the physical facilities that the user must make available to accommodate the hardware that the vendor will provide. These facilities include, but are not limited to, environmental controls, space for the hardware, and electrical facilities.

Back-up Equipment

Some vendors specifically disavow any responsibility for providing backup equipment, either on-site or at another user's site. This is a point that can sometimes be negotiated. It should be obvious to the user that it is essential to have a site where processing can take place in the event that the physical facilities of the management information system fail.

Default

This section of the contract outlines those conditions under which default may take place, along with information on the user's and vendor's various remedies in the event of default.

Warranties

This section specifies those warranties that the vendor will honor. Sometimes the vendor will exclude all programs from warranties, but will warrant the operation of the hardware. Again, the user must decide the importance of program warranties, and then negotiate with the vendor if it seems important to pursue the matter.

Insurance

Sometimes there is a section in the contract dealing with those conditions under which the user will assume the risk of loss, and also defining the insurance responsibilities associated with that risk. The user should pay close attention to this section, since it is an area where the user might assume substantial financial risks.

Maintenance

While almost all contracts specify the conditions under which maintenance is provided, particular attention should go to the factor of response time for maintenance personnel. When one is operating an on-line real-time management information system, it is essential that the system be operational as much of the time as possible. Therefore, short response times are mandatory, and should be specified in the contract.

Arbitration

One item that is frequently omitted in a contract is a provision for arbitration. Whether this item should be included in the contract must be determined by the individual user. However, the user should recognize that one important benefit of arbitration is that it allows the user and the vendor to maintain their relationship, and continue to do business, while disputes are being settled. This can be a very important element. Lacking a contractual arbitration clause, arbitration could be used only if both parties agree to do so after a dispute arises. Therefore, if the user feels that arbitration might be advantageous, it should be included in the contract, not left to chance at a later time.

Identifying Total MIS Costs*

A particularly commonplace deficiency in medical information system CONs is failure to consider all elements of cost. While due in some cases to oversight, it is likely that this deficiency is exacerbated by the view that CON review applies only to *capital* costs and not *operating* costs. Yet, it seems clear that if the hospital considers *decreases* in operating costs in its analysis as benefits, it must correspondingly consider *increases* in operating costs as well.

To assist in identifying total costs of a medical information system, Table 24-1 presents a cost checklist. Not every cost element in Table 24-1 will be present in every project; similarly, this table is not necessarily exhaustive, a cost ele-

---

*Source: *Health Planning Review of Medical Information Systems,* National Center for Health Services Research, 1981, Publication No. (PHS)81-3303.

Table 24-1 Cost Checklist

Equipment
  Computers and peripherals
  Terminals and printers
  Communications
  Interface devices
  Shipping
  Storage racks

Facilities
  Floor space
  Site preparation
  Air conditioning
  Electrical
  Cabling
  Sub-flooring
  Controls, monitors, alarms

Software
  Operating systems
    Rental
    Development/conversion
    Maintenance
  Application programs
    Rental
    Development/conversion
    Maintenance

Maintenance (labor, equipment, parts and supplies)
  Computers and peripherals
  Terminals and printers
  Communication equipment
  Facilities (air conditioning, etc.)

Utilities (installation and usage)
  Electrical
  Telephone
  Air conditioning

Taxes and Insurance
  Sales tax
  Property tax
  Casualty insurance

Training
  Initial training and installation support
  Inservice training
  Documentation

Supplies
  Tapes and disks
  Printer paper/ribbons
  Forms and labels
  Punched cards

Management
  Hospital
  Facilities management
  Consultants

Industrial Engineering
  Implementation
  Benefit realization

Table 24-1 continued

Labor Fringe Benefits
  Group insurance
  Retirement
  Payroll taxes
  Vacation and holidays

---

ment not listed might be present in a given project.

In projecting the magnitude of a given cost element, the *marginal* or additional cost should be used, not the average or allocated cost. For example, only the *increase* in the hospital's electric bill should be used, not the average cost per kwh.

Next to omission of cost elements, the next common error in projecting costs is failure to establish a realistic installation and "shakedown" schedule. Many project-related costs are "period costs"; that is, they continue at a certain rate per month once they are started like a running faucet. Equipment rental and data processing personnel salaries are just two examples. If a planned six month installation schedule turns into twelve months in practice, these period installation costs will be doubled.

The best protection against schedule error is to survey several hospitals who have previously installed the system of interest. A realistic installation schedule should emerge from such a survey.

Identifying Total Benefits

Having identified a time-phased estimate of total project costs, the hospital must now similarly identify project financial benefits. Table 24-2, Benefits Checklist, is useful for that purpose.

Realizable Labor Savings will represent as much as 80% of the benefits of level 3 systems. Detailed procedures for estimating them require industrial engineering or hospital management engineering skills; however, the approach is conceptually quite straightforward.

- Identify each hospital function affected by the system (e.g., "admit a patient").
- Flow chart each function using pre-system manual procedures and again, using post-system automated procedures.

Table 24-2 Benefits Checklist

Realizable Labor Savings
  Labor
  Fringe benefits
  Supervision and management
Consumables
  Forms
  Medications and supplies
  Meals
Previous System Costs
  Labor and fringe benefits
  Equipment and maintenance
  Supplies
  Services
Interest Costs
  Accelerated billing
  Reduced receivables aging
  More accurate third party claims
Capital Facility Costs
  Reduced length of stay
  Improved scheduling
  Shared facilities

- Assign standard times to each element by skill category in each flow chart.
- Subtract the times with the automated procedure from those with the manual procedure.
- Estimate the frequency each function will be performed (e.g., "admissions per month").
- Estimate the cost of labor involved (e.g., "admitting clerk monthly wage and fringe").
- Examine fractional savings in a given department (e.g., "Admitting") resulting from different functions and establish a strategy for consolidating these fractional savings into full time positions which can be eliminated (realizable benefits).
- Establish a time phased schedule of positions to be eliminated, identifying *specific positions*.
- Secure written concurrence of the affected manager (e.g., "Admitting Manager") and the hospital administrator.
- Convert eliminated positions into realizable dollar savings by applying the cost of labor to each identified position and aggregating by month.

ESTABLISHING AN HIS[*]

A. Assess Hospital Information Needs

A methodology to identify hospital-wide HIS needs and problems requires key personnel from each department to identify their current information needs and the problems they have in meeting them. These personnel can be selected members of management, department heads, members of the medical staff, and other appropriate personnel as determined by the steering committee. The persons to be interviewed do not need to have an understanding of computer applications, but must know their department's operations and current information needs.

An interview form (see Figure 24-3) to identify information needs is one way to enable data collection in a manner that will identify common hospital information problems and needs.

The form should ask the user to identify any problems with using the information. A problem that makes the information questionable or not usable should be explained. Types of problems will generally fall into the categories of accuracy, timeliness, completeness, and so forth.

Identifying a department's information needs and problems should involve four steps:

Step 1. An analyst explains purpose of study and form. The user has at least a week to complete the problems and needs form.

Step 2. An analyst meets with user a second time to understand the user's information needs and problems.

Step 3. At a third meeting, the analyst presents perceived problems and proposed automation needs for discussion and approval.

Step 4. The perceived problems and proposed automation needs list is given written approval by user.

B. Educate the Staff

The fears that some users have of computerization can often be reduced with an education program directed toward learning the fundamentals

---

[*]Source: Reprinted from *Managing Hospital Information Systems* by Stephen L. Priest, with permission of Aspen Systems Corporation, © 1982.

Figure 24-3 Information needs interview form

PURPOSE: To determine:

- your department's information needs
- the method by which the needs are currently being met
- improvements and deficiencies in meeting these needs

PRESENT INFORMATION NEED:

List the primary information needs of your area. These are the items supplied to you from another area, put together in your area, and/or given by you to another area. They are the data needs that you must have in order to handle your assigned responsibility. You may do work on these needs, make decisions by them, create work for another area. You may also list needs that are not currently being met. THE REMAINING QUESTIONS WILL BE DIRECTED TO THE METHODS THAT ARE USED TO MEET EACH NEED.

MEDIA THAT PROVIDE NEED? LOG, REPORT, TELEPHONE, ETC.:

List all logbooks, reports, documents, telephone, or other media that assist you in meeting the previously mentioned information needs. There may be a number of ways that are used to meet one need.

THE REMAINING QUESTIONS ARE TO BE ANSWERED FOR EACH MEDIUM THAT YOU HAVE JUST LISTED.

WHO USES MEDIA? HOW USED?

For *each* medium listed, state persons who could use medium and how the medium is used in meeting the information need.

WHO ORIGINATES MEDIA?

For *each* medium, state the department that prepares the medium and, if applicable, the department that receives the medium from you.

HOW ARE MEDIA FILED?

Do you keep the media in alphabetical order, by bed, by date, latest copy, etc.?

FREQUENCY OF UPDATE/USE/DELIVERY?

How often do you receive each medium? How often is it used? Do you alter the medium in any way by additions, subtractions, or changes?

DO YOU USE ALL DATA ON THE MEDIA? IF NO, WHAT?

Are you getting more information than you can use? Are you getting a report with a great deal of data and yet using only a small part of it?

ARE THESE MEDIA NECESSARY? ARE THEY TIMELY & RELIABLE?

Now that you have thought about the report, is it necessary? Is it getting to you on time so that the data are current for your needs? Are the data on the medium usually accurate? Can you depend on them?

CAN THEY BE IMPROVED? MANUAL VS AUTOMATION?

This is your chance to give us your thoughts on how your information needs can be improved by changing, adding, deleting, or combining this document either manually or by automation. Can automation assist you?

of computers and MIS services. A user will then understand and be prepared for computerization.

Figure 24-4 is a sample course agenda. Hospital case studies and literature should be freely used to explain and demonstrate the MIS concepts discussed.

Department heads and supervisors with minimum understanding and experience with MIS applications should be the first to attend the sessions. As later sessions are held, persons who have taken the course will promote participation of their subordinates and peers. A 14-hour course offered in 2-hour weekly segments will provide a solid foundation for a team approach to the implementation of a successful MIS. Persons attending the sessions can be given a certificate of achievement to hang in the office or home.

Figure 24-4 Course agenda: introduction to computers

Week 1 Introduction
  Purpose of course
  Basic computer processes
    Input
    Output
    Memory
    Controller
    Logic
  Manual versus computer processes
  Advantages of computerization
  Interaction
  DP vs MIS vs DSS vs IS and other department titles

Week 2 Methods of Input and Output
  Key-to-disk
  Microfiche
  Punch cards
  Magnetic tape
  Punch tape
  OCR
  MCR
  Others
  Sample media and use examples

Week 3 People Requirements
  MIS in the organizational chart
  Steering committee
  Programmer duties
  Systems analyst duties
  Computer operator duties
  MIS executive duties
  Other people

Week 4 MIS and User Controls
  Interaction
  Controls internal to MIS
  Controls internal to user
  Controls between MIS and user departments
  Examples of controls within hospital

Figure 24-4 continued

Week 5 Types of Computer Installations
  Shared
  Service bureau
  Facilities management
  In-house
    Centralized
    Decentralized
    Distributive
    Turnkey

Week 6 Computer Languages (Software)

Week 7 Selecting a Hospital MIS
  Interaction
  Identification of needs
  Priorities
  RFP
  Proposal evaluations
  Selection

C. Promote User and MIS Staff Interaction

Users may frequently complain about the computer, and MIS staff may in turn blame the user for the failure of a project. Users sometimes expect MIS to push a button and have tons of paper come out with the right answers at high speed. Both the user and MIS departments once believed that the user had only to be involved with a project for it to be successful. Involvement means attending committee meetings and approving the numerous MIS memos that define and plan the project. The MIS people were expected to do all the work, with the user department simply overseeing the final product. This approach resulted in users getting reports they could not use or understand.

Such situations could have been avoided through interaction. When a computer report is discussed, interaction means that both the user and MIS staff should be present. If the MIS staff understands how the reports are to be used, they can assist more effectively in the definition of the reports, rather than having to rely on an ability to read between the lines.

The user should provide the first written draft for the design of a new report or system. Instead of explaining to the analyst what the report should be, the user should put it on paper; discussions accompanied by a visual document can be better understood by both parties. In addition, the user may even flow chart the logic for the new report or system.

MIS should offer to sit down with the user and discuss the report before drafts are initiated, but again, the drafts should be made by the user. No programming should be attempted until the reports are formulated and the logic defined.

When it is time to test the programs of the new system, the user should be responsible for supplying all sample data. In addition, the final test calculations should be checked by the user to

Figure 24-5 Techniques promoting interaction between MIS and user departments

The User	The MIS Department
1. Taking the initiative to promote interaction	1. Taking the initiative to promote interaction
2. Attending instruction on basic DP concepts	2. Teaching in-house users basic DP concepts
3. Asking to review the MIS area; inviting MIS to review the user area	3. Asking to review the user area; inviting the user to review the MIS area
4. Inviting MIS to a user committee meeting at which a computer-prepared report is to be presented	4. Asking to attend a committee meeting at which a computer report is to be presented
5. Drafting the design of a new report with MIS assistance; flow charting the logic; designing complete system first on paper	5. Offering to sit down with the users and assisting them in designing the draft; assisting in flow charting the new report; doing no coding until the system is completely designed on paper
6. Providing test data to MIS for new or changed reports; doing manual calculations using test data and comparing with computer report	6. Having the user provide test data and manual calculations
7. Insisting on preparing the systems manual that documents and explains the computer system	7. Having the user prepare the systems manual describing the system
8. Continually controlling data being sent to MIS and monitoring all output reports for accuracy and reasonableness; developing pulse points	8. Balancing to user-supplied control totals
9. Periodically meeting with MIS to review relationships between departments	9. Periodically meeting with the user to show MIS concern and willingness to meet user needs and concerns
10. Making all requests to MIS in writing	10. Requiring report requests and special runs to be in writing
11. Calling MIS and discussing any immediate concern and problem	11. Quickly responding to user problems
12. Checking parallel runs for all system "improvements"	12. Having the user check parallel runs for all system changes
13. Inviting MIS to a meeting with other users	13. Asking to attend user association meetings
14. Sending articles on user systems to MIS for its review and education	14. Sending MIS articles on user systems to the user department for its review and education
15. Having MIS analyst cross-trained in user functions	15. Assigning MIS analyst to user department to learn system workings
16. Writing an article and including MIS as coauthor	16. Writing an article and including the user as coauthor

Figure 24-6 User satisfaction questionnaire

TO: User of MIS Services
FROM: Vice-president, MIS Services

Please indicate your department's degree of satisfaction with the information services that it is receiving. Any additional comments that you would care to make are appreciated.

	Outstanding	Satisfactory	Not Satisfactory	Not Applicable
Time required for new systems development	○	○	○	○
Your participation in establishing MIS priorities	○	○	○	○
Relationship with MIS staff	○	○	○	○
Processing of request to existing systems	○	○	○	○
Timeliness of routine reports	○	○	○	○
Accuracy of reports	○	○	○	○
Response of MIS staff to corrections	○	○	○	○
Degree of training provided by MIS	○	○	○	○
Your understanding of existing systems	○	○	○	○
Formats of existing reports and screens	○	○	○	○
MIS system manuals	○	○	○	○
Uptime of hardware	○	○	○	○
Flexibility of systems	○	○	○	○
Terminal response time	○	○	○	○

Comments:

verify the accuracy of the systems output. If the analyst provides the test data calculations, the analyst will often check only what appears reasonable from his or her perspective. The analyst does not have the user background and specialized knowledge to know all data input possibilities and output reasonableness. Users should be the "experts" in the use of reports and on-line screen displays and therefore should confirm that the test is accurate and reasonable.

The users should prepare all system manuals and documents (other than programming documentation) that explain the computerized system. The MIS analyst can then verify the documentation and reconcile system differences with the user. Differences in opinions and functions can now readily be corrected. With this technique there is at least one person from each department who understands the system's functions.

Likewise, user departments can assign a person to the MIS department. A new internal auditor or even a nursing supervisor can be given a temporary assignment of MIS control clerk. The user can observe computer backup procedures, check computer input and output controls, do data entry at an MIS terminal, and attend meetings with the MIS executive. Users can also view programmers doing on-line development and can begin to appreciate the material and preparation needed for systems development and program changes.

The technique of having the end user sit at the data entry terminal and enter data from source documents he or she previously prepared works wonders in providing the user with a clear understanding of why the documents have to be legible and contain complete data elements. In addition, the need for control totals supplied by the end user now becomes obvious as the user attempts to ensure that all documents are entered into the computer.

Techniques that have been used to promote interaction between MIS and user departments are summarized in Figure 24-5.

D. Monitor User Satisfaction

An MIS department must service users in a timely, accurate, and effective manner. It does that with accurate and timely reports, satisfactory on-line input response times, and by attending to user requests in a responsive and effective manner. The degree to which this responsibility is met should be continually monitored.

Complaints may not be made by a user who has continually been frustrated with MIS services and has turned elsewhere for assistance.

User satisfaction pulse points may be maintained through questionnaires similar to that in Figure 24-6.

Chapter 25—Patient Management: Computerized Information Systems*

Overview

The Data Base

A PMS is a fully integrated approach to maintaining patient care information and provides an opportunity for enhancing communication between members of the health care team. The foundation of a PMS is a set of comprehensive data bases containing various medical, financial, statistical and other pertinent information. The largest of these is the patient data base, which includes all relevant information about each patient registered at the hospital. The data base includes such data as:

- patient identification;
- biographic and financial data;
- patient allergies and other alert data;
- physicians' orders for patient care, medication, therapeutic and diagnostic services;
- test results, interpretations and progress notes;
- drug profile and medication administration records;
- medical activity summaries data; and
- nursing care plans and associated results.

Typically the above patient information would be captured directly during routine operation of a PMS. For example, when a patient is admitted to the hospital, the biographical and financial information normally contained on registration forms would be captured through an on-line admission/registration data entry procedure. Similarly, when pharmacy fills a physician's order for medication, an update of the patient's drug profile and medication administration record would occur automatically.

Case-related data would be used extensively in providing and managing services to the patient and would be maintained in detail during the patient's encounter with the hospital. At the conclusion of the patient's stay, case data would be summarized and stored for future use. Other types of patient data (biographical, financial, etc.) would be maintained in detail for future encounters with the hospital.

In addition to the patient data base, other types of information having dual or multiple functions are normally resident in a PMS. For example, in a pharmacy a PMS would contain extensive pharmaceutical formulary data required to process medication orders. Drug interactions with other medication, I.V.s, dietary or ancillary department procedures would be monitored. The medication data base could also be automatically cross-referenced to vital patient data for administration purposes. Availability of these data would provide the medication nurse with an invaluable information source from which the appropriateness of the drug to be administered could be determined.

The order processing function would permit the entry, control and processing of orders. For example, standard orders for surgical admis-

---

*Source: Reprinted from John J. Sacco, M.D. and Carl G. Longnecker, Jr., "Patient Management Systems," *Topics in Health Care Financing,* Summer 1978, with permission of Aspen Systems Corporation.

sions could be maintained on a PMS and include multiple procedures such as a complete blood count, chest x-ray, routine urinalysis, etc. Each of these procedures could involve different nursing care, specimens, control procedures and results-reporting techniques.

The complex nature of the data interrelationships maintained in a PMS requires the ability to access and update information in a controlled manner. Current data base technology provides the ability to access data quickly in any required sequence without regard to its physical location, and allows unlimited access to common data. This capability sets the stage for multiple authorized use of common data regardless of user location, function or required procedure.

Security and Reliability

The critical and sensitive nature of patient information requires special attention to computer system security and reliability. PMS's would normally be designed to include password protection and selective terminal lockout. For example, through the use of a password, providers' access would be limited to patients under their care. Additionally, all users, including physicians and nurses, would be restricted to the use of only those system features needed to perform their assigned patient care tasks effectively. In life threatening situations, however, these controls could be overridden, and the system would log such usage for subsequent follow-up under established security and control procedures.

Because of the critical nature of the data base information and the system's integration with day-to-day hospital operations, a PMS must be available on a 24-hour, seven-day-a-week basis. To guarantee this availability, hardware configurations for PMS's would normally contain duplicate equipment.

Impact on Departments in the Hospital

A PMS will have a substantial impact on all departments in the hospital, whether they provide direct patient care, diagnostic, therapeutic or general support services. Table 25-1 illustrates those departments that typically receive the most direct benefit from using a PMS.

Admitting

The major function of the admitting department usually includes maintaining an inpatient census and controlling the flow of outpatients and ambulatory surgery patients to service areas in the hospital. To execute these functions, this department performs preadmitting and scheduling, processes all admissions, discharges and transfers, and registers/schedules outpatients.

An on-line PMS would assist in this processing by performing the basic inpatient scheduling, admission, transfer, discharge sequence, and by handling outpatient scheduling and registration. Once entered, the system would contain accurate biographic and financial information for each patient, the current hospital census and other patient care data. This information would then be immediately accessible by all other service areas of the hospital.

In addition to on-line inquiry, a PMS could provide the admitting department with several key hard copy reports such as:

Table 25-1 Departments Most Affected by PMS's

Support	Patient Care	Diagnostic and Therapeutic
Admitting	Clinics	Cardiology
Billing	Emergency medical services	Pathology
Communications	Employee health	Pharmacy
Epidemiology	Hemodialysis	Physical therapy
Food service	Home care	Radiology
Medical records	Inpatient care units	Respiratory technology
Social services	Maternal and child care	
Utilization review	Operating room	
	Psychiatric medicine	

- a patient care unit census report;
- a general census report by patient name, physician or religion;
- an admissions report;
- a discharge report; and
- a transfer report.

The benefits of a PMS to the admitting department occur in four basic areas.

Reduction of Clerical Effort. A PMS would reduce clerical effort by printing medical record face sheets, wristbands and routing slips; automatically notifying medical records of new patient ID numbers; and expediting credit exceptions to the credit department. It would also eliminate manual maintenance of patient census, location, payment, discharge and expiration files.

Accurate and Timely Availability of Patient Data. Information availability would be improved because records could be retrieved quickly, and the data would be the most current entered into the system. Patient records available for inquiry would include scheduled services, patient biographic, financial, insurance, census and payment information.

Faster Order Entry. The order entry capability would allow access and review of standard admitting orders and facilitate the efficient entry of high volume outpatient orders. Conventional hard copy requisition slips would no longer be necessary.

Better Control of Patient Accounts and Records. Improved control of patient accounts and records would be provided through automatic assignment of patient ID numbers and maintenance of active account numbers by the system. All patient information would be tied to a unique patient ID number, and each hospital/patient encounter would have a unique account number to facilitate the accumulation of statistical, financial and case-related data.

Emergency Medical Service (EMS)

A PMS would assist in the coordination of multiple emergent services by providing rapid communication with other hospital service areas, and by expediting order entry–results reporting procedures. In addition, patient registration–discharge procedures and accumulation of statistical EMS activity data would be simplified.

A PMS could provide EMS staff with "condition dependent" flexible registration procedures. A patient in need of immediate treatment would experience an abbreviated initial registration with remaining registration data obtained after the crisis condition subsided. If immediate treatment is not necessary, the complete registration procedure would be used.

In cases where an EMS patient had been treated at the hospital previously, medical and biographical information would be resident in the system data bases, and immediately available for use by EMS personnel. Using the system's order entry and chart review capabilities, EMS personnel could expedite communications with required support services and eliminate initiation of hardcopy requisition slips and transcription of test results. Discharge procedures would be simplified since the system would generate much of the information and paper work normally handled on a manual basis.

Inpatient Care Unit

The major functions of an inpatient care unit include rendering primary care to the inpatient and coordinating the interaction between the patient and other service areas. The inpatient care unit is responsible for initiating the processing of a physician's order, collecting and recording nursing data, transferring patients within the same unit, documenting care-related information and maintaining a complete and accurate medical chart during the patient's stay.

A PMS would provide the following direct benefits to an inpatient care unit:

- improved coordination of ancillary and support services;
- easy access and inquiry into a patient's case-related information;
- reduction of clerical tasks;
- efficient order entry and results reporting; and
- improved control over intra-unit patient transfers.

A PMS has a dramatic impact on the way information is processed at an inpatient care unit. In an on-line environment, the system would accept and process physician's orders, facilitate intra-unit patient transfers, assist in the coordination and performance of nursing care and provide for the ordering and administration of medications. In addition, a care status summary for each patient could be generated daily to replace the manually maintained nursing Kardex, containing a history of the patient care rendered.

With the overall improvement of communications provided by the system, specific functions such as patient scheduling, medication administration and patient care planning would be handled easily and facilitate overall improved patient care. Delays, inconveniences and phone calls, resulting from booking a patient for two different procedures at the same time or failing to provide for the appropriate mode of transportation, such as a wheelchair with an I.V., would be eliminated.

Having terminals at inpatient care units and other areas of the hospital would allow many members of the health care team simultaneously to access a patient's medical chart. Nursing and unit clerk clerical effort would be reduced since the PMS would generate medical summaries and care-related reports previously prepared manually.

The entire order entry and results delivery procedure would be improved by monitoring the order entry, status report sequence on-line. No longer would it be necessary to phone for "stat" requests or for the results of recently completed tests. Clerical effort, on the part of the nursing staff, would be significantly reduced by the system's ability to explode and control patient care orders. When an order is to be repeated for several days, the system would "manage" the order and maintain communications with the patient care team. Nursing would not be required to prepare and release separate requisitions for each day's test. Similarly, the system would generate automatic stop order messages and maintain the medication administration list, if appropriate. Manually updating the Kardex and patient chart, or initiating order requisitions to document these types of activities would be eliminated.

Finally, patient transfers would be automatically communicated to areas such as admissions, pharmacy and the information desk. Any current messages, notifications or results from service departments would be automatically rerouted.

Medical Records

The principal functions of the medical records department include maintaining accurate patient medical records, transcribing key chart documents, and providing authorized persons with statistical and care-related information contained in the patient's medical record. Since the department's entire operation deals with information and documentation handling, a PMS would have a significant impact on its daily operations. It would directly benefit medical records by:

- location monitoring of patient charts;
- automatic assignment of patient ID numbers;
- improved procedures for generating admission, discharge, birth, expiration and other medical records; and
- simplification of chart abstracting functions.

A PMS could be used for many departmental transcription activities. Documents usually typed in the medical records department would be keyed into the system, edited at a computer terminal and printed in patient chart format. If the transcribed document is for a patient currently in the hospital, the chart copy could be printed on-line at the patient's care unit.

Since a PMS could contain data on operating room scheduling, including control indicators on transcribed operative records, a report identifying "tardy" undocumented procedures could be automatically generated.

Another use of the system could include printing the majority of third party requests for chart documents. As a by-product of this request process, the system could generate a daily list of all requests satisfied.

Pathology

The department of pathology provides vital diagnostic services for patients through procedures performed in chemistry, hematology, microbiology, histology, cytology and other clinical areas. These departments are high-volume activity areas often using outdated manual methods to process test requisitions and procedure results.

Installation of a PMS would benefit a pathology department by:

- improving communication with the patient care areas;
- significantly reducing clerical effort;
- effectively controlling specimens;

- improving administrative control of department workflow; and
- enhancing quality control techniques.

Interdepartment communications are heavy and have a tendency to break down more frequently as departmental workloads increase. A PMS would assist these departments by providing all pertinent patient information regarding test requests in a timely and controlled fashion. Results information could be captured through a direct interface with other automated systems such as an SMA 6/60 or Coulter Counter, which handle high-volume laboratory procedures.

Summary reporting reflecting comparative and/or cumulative results throughout the patient's stay would assist physicians and nurses in applying diagnostic evaluation and care planning techniques to each patient case. In some areas, technologists and technicians could work directly at a terminal. For primarily low-volume procedures, results could be recorded on system-generated worksheets and later entered through a terminal. Direct entry of clinical data into a PMS by technicians and technologists, and the availability of patient biographic, schedule and other care data establish the opportunity for significant department, clerical, communication and management improvements.

Clerical effort would be reduced by replacing manual report filing procedures with system-generated daily and weekly report logs. Department workload worksheets would be printed automatically by the system, eliminating manual distribution of test requisitions. In most cases the necessity to key results for quality control analysis would also be eliminated. Secretarial clerical activity would be reduced because the system would generate forms and reports that formerly had to be typed. Also manually maintained specimen logs could be eliminated, and researching past report files would be simplified using the system's terminal inquiry capability.

Communication with patient care areas would be improved through maintenance of order status, a procedure inquiry capability and a more rapid report delivery. The patient care areas would be able to determine the status of any order from their terminal location, thereby eliminating phone communications. Reports, when entered, would be readily available for inquiry by the patient care area and printed immediately if ordered on a "stat" basis.

The system would improve control over specimens, since an accurate and complete specimen label would be available for all specimens obtained from patients. The system would then maintain control of specimens by tracking their status, i.e., collected, received or in process.

The system could provide information that would improve a supervisor's ability to manage the area workflow. At any time, exact status of all work currently in the department could be displayed on a terminal. The system would also provide an opportunity to improve quality control. The availability of computerized test results would simplify delta checking, i.e., comparing old test results with current test results to detect significant trends.

Pharmacy

The pharmacy's primary function is to dispense medication on an inpatient and outpatient basis. An important aspect of this function is to check for potential drug interactions and incompatibility with other ancillary procedures being planned.

A PMS would benefit a hospital pharmacy by:

- facilitating immediate profile checks;
- generating unit dose cart loading lists;
- reducing department clerical routines;
- improving the order entry procedure;
- enhancing chart review capability for pharmacists; and
- producing meaningful statistical data.

Timely communication of data to physicians and nurses is essential to the dispensing of medication. The automated drug checking features of a PMS could be developed to alert pharmacists to situations that call for their professional judgment. In addition, the extensive communications network provided by a PMS would allow the pharmacists' expertise to be readily available over a larger segment of the hospital's health care delivery system.

Physicians, nurses, pharmacists and ultimately the patient would be aided by the system's drug interaction checking capability. Potential deleterious side effects could be averted by automatically identifying inappropriate combinations of medications, dietary, laboratory and other requested care, services or procedures. In addition, normal nurse/pharmacist interaction concerning patient drug profiles would be accomplished on an expedient basis and allow more time for professional discussions than is usually possible when comparing individual manual transcription. Improved patient care would result by using such a medication profile check technique.

A unit dose cart loading list printed on demand would assist pharmacy technicians through improved accuracy and legibility. Systematic organization of drug items would reduce the time needed to load the cart. Clerical effort could be further reduced and pharmacy's response time improved because the system could automatically print notifications of admissions, transfers and discharges including new labels for the unit dose cart.

Clerical effort required to process pharmacy orders would be reduced since the medication nurse's order transcription would be eliminated, and phone calls between nurses and pharmacists would rarely be required. Professional time required to perform an order entry profile check would be reduced, and the extensive time spent providing billing information for both inpatients and outpatients would be eliminated. Initiating pharmaceutical stop orders would be simplified because the system would automatically generate messages when medication orders are about to expire and again upon expiration. These messages would appear in several reports, including a medical administration list and in the message queue for the nursing station.

Physical Therapy

The department of physical medicine and rehabilitation provides a wide range of diagnostic and therapeutic services for patients of the hospital. Physical therapy, usually the largest section in this department, offers services that primarily assist the patient in regaining strength and coordination following an illness. Physical therapy patients include inpatients as well as outpatients, and often home treatment services are required.

A PMS would provide physical therapy with an efficient way to record the patient's treatment plan, including a detailed treatment schedule. Use of hospital-wide scheduling features to control patient movement would provide an opportunity to increase department efficiency by reducing the number of missed appointments and eliminating duplicate "bookings." Patient records would be improved because the therapist could complete on-line the visitation medical record despite the physical location of a patient's chart in medical records. Although progress notes would probably be maintained manually, reports to assist the department in providing scheduled services and documenting treatment could be included in the system. These reports could include a patient treatment summary, daily log of patients treated, weekly department schedule, daily therapists' schedule and a schedule of treatments not performed.

In physical therapy, as in several other areas of the hospital, it is occasionally necessary to review the patient's prior medical history in order to determine patterns or trends that might influence future treatment planning. A PMS would allow inquiry to assist in this type of review. Another approach might include an inquiry and report request for information concerning patients who were treated in physical therapy and who were more than 65 years old with a CVA as a primary diagnosis.

A general benefit provided patient care departments by a PMS is a reduction of clerical effort to process patient orders and related billing information. In physical therapy, for example, patient billing data would be obtained automatically following order acknowledgment by a therapist at a data entry terminal.

Primary Benefits

Primary benefits to be derived from a PMS include improved patient care, realizable cost savings and improved management.

Improved Patient Care

A PMS provides access to a common data base of clinical and biographic information, which is available on a timely basis and in a format that ensures accurate and consistent application among users. The hospital's patient care team members having immediate access to this current information can provide services on an informed and professional basis. Computerized on-line monitoring and communication of order status and clinical results ensure that the most up-to-date information is available at all times for physicians and other members of the health care team to reference. In addition, a PMS could provide access to nursing and clinical area protocols including standard nursing care plans that correspond to physicians' orders.

Through registration and scheduling features provided in a PMS, the physical management of patients would be improved and offer further opportunity for more effective use of hospital facilities. With all members of the health care team cognizant of the latest patient orders and schedules, miscommunication resulting in inconvenience to both the patient and provider would be minimized.

Continuous on-line monitoring of the delivery of patient care ensures that care requested by authorized providers is realized. A PMS would provide exception reports that would identify incomplete results or the nonrendering of prescribed services. Installation of comprehensive quality assurance and drug interaction monitoring techniques would further enhance the quality of care provided by the hospital.

Realizable Cost Savings

Cost reduction can be achieved by minimizing clerical effort in direct patient care areas, by modifying manual procedures to effectively support on-line processing and by improving document processing in admitting, medical records, business office and other nonclinical areas. Several specific opportunities for significant reduction of clerical efforts throughout the hospital are evident. Multiple transcription of orders and results could be eliminated. Typing and filing reports could be reduced since a PMS data base would contain most of the information needed to generate reports either automatically or on demand. This centralized storage of data would also eliminate duplicate maintenance of the same data in multiple departments. Phone inquiry concerning order status or results would be greatly reduced.

Installation of a PMS would provide an opportunity to re-engineer departmental manual procedures throughout the hospital, achieving additional savings through productivity improvements. In addition, procedural improvements, job reassignments and records/document flow within the hospital would require specific attention since cost reduction could be optimized through realization of fractional savings, i.e., 0.8 full time equivalents (FTEs), consolidated functions, redefined job positions and others.

An additional consideration would be to interface a PMS with the order entry, billing and accounts receivable cycle of the hospital to achieve another significant benefit. When this revenue cycle is handled on a manual basis, delayed and inaccurate patient charges often occur. However, since a PMS could capture these charges at the time of order entry, the accuracy and the timeliness of the billing process would be improved. Even the often misunderstood and elusive "lost charge" would be consistently applied to the proper patient account.

Improved Hospital Management

Examining the normal business management cycle we find the functions of planning, execution and control. Installation of a PMS provides an opportunity to respond more effectively to this recurring business environment, whether clinically, administratively or financially based. Data available through a PMS regarding statistical hospital activity and resource utilization would enhance normal decision-making processes regarding staffing, capital requirements, long-range planning and other important aspects of overall hospital operations.

System features facilitating daily scheduling functions, physical movement of patients, census control, order entry, results reporting, records maintenance and document control are only a few of the many functions handled on a more timely and accurate basis by a PMS. The contributions of these improved functions are a more consistent and effective communication and an opportunity to execute and control major management decisions regarding the physical and administrative management of the hospital.

Issues for an Effective System Conversion

Improved patient care, realizable cost savings and more effective management opportunities alone would entice even the most pragmatic and conservative health care industry professional to "hock the family jewels" and invest heavily in this most recent of "do all" phenomena. A word of caution, however, to those who may experience a momentary mirage suggesting PMS's as a means to resolve all hospitals' problems regarding patient care, physician/nurse/patient interaction, routine communications and a host of other problems unique to their respective operations: In its most simplistic format and structure, a hospital information system is not an insignificant consideration in terms of the hardware and software required for a typical installation. Additionally, "total" commitment by physicians, hospital administrators, nurses, professional staff and other PMS users is absolutely essential if an effective and cost-beneficial installation is to be achieved. An important recognition by this group of users is that initially the "total information system" need not be the primary installation objective. Modularity in both design and implementation will afford an opportunity to concentrate on the most cost-beneficial applications and minimize the amount of front-end investment needed.

As an enhanced concept of data collection and communications, the installation of a PMS would provide a catalyst for change to existing procedures that provide and document patient care. To achieve optimum results, a hospital should establish a proper level of industrial engineering support during and after a system conversion. Benefits must be calculated and purposefully established. Additionally, physician and nurse involvement must be absolute and is indispensable to an effective system conversion.

For those institutions with other medical information systems currently in operation (medical records, laboratory or other computer diagnostic type systems), integration of planned patient management applications with these other clinical applications should be a primary conversion objective. This will achieve optimum operating performance and maximize cost-benefit results. In extreme cases this may require redefinition of the hospital's long-range data processing plan and possible retrenchment regarding existing systems.

Some early successes of computerized on-line patient management concepts have been achieved in several different areas of health care information systems. Typically, these projects survived because of the total commitment and many contributions made by members of the medical, nursing, professional, data processing and systems engineering departments.

This little used but innovative concept can be expected to gain momentum as data processing personnel continue to advance the concept of cost-lowering versus cost-raising technology. On-line PMS's can be expected to have a substantial impact on our health care delivery system during the immediate and foreseeable future.

Chapter 26—Word Processing

Word processing is the use of a computer-typewriter interface to prepare documents in such a way that they can be extensively edited, rewritten, combined with other documents, and rearranged internally, all with a minimum of effort. The basic features of any word-processing system are a computer, a terminal with keyboard and cathode ray tube (CRT) for televisionlike display of the text, and a printer to commit the final copy to paper. Documents are generally composed and edited directly on the CRT screen, although they may be produced by the printer as "hard copy" at any point in their preparation. The most important feature of word processors is that no document need ever be retyped in its entirety; only those parts needing changes have to be altered. Whole paragraphs or pages can be moved within the document or added from other documents previously typed into the system and saved on magnetic discs. After extensive editing and reediting on the CRT, the printer may produce a hard copy much more rapidly and accurately than a typist ever could.

As a result, the word processor's most widely recognized utility is with settings in which multiple drafts are required before a final copy is approved and ready for distribution.

Words may be arranged under few if any constraints by a word processor. For example, when a word is added to or a sentence (or paragraph) deleted from a document, the entire page format is automatically modified to compensate—words are moved from line to line, margins are adjusted, and pagination is changed.*

Uses in the Hospital**

Innovative hospital and medical record administrators are discovering that using word processing technology in a centralized transcription center helps solve their mounting paperwork problems. "Boilerplating," text editing, incentive systems, monitoring systems, flexible hours, scrolling ability, camera-ready copy, and message centers are some of the features available through a word processing system that can benefit a medical institution.

"Boilerplating" and Text Editing

Because malpractice has gained more attention from both patients and insurance companies, physicians' dictation for medical records has increased in volume. Using word processing equipment made it possible for secretarial serv-

---

*Source: Reprinted from Lawrence E. Frisch, "Word Processing in Ambulatory Care," *The Journal of Ambulatory Care Management,* February 1982, with permission of Aspen Systems Corporation.

**Source: Reprinted from Glenn H. Johnson, "Centralized Word Processing: A Cost-Containment Measure," *Topics in Health Record Management,* September 1980, with permission of Aspen Systems Corporation.

ices personnel to "boilerplate" much of the repetitive information necessary to document each patient's care. Boilerplating is the recording of normal information in paragraph or chart form that is then used to describe many of the conditions seen by a certain type of physician. When it is appropriate to describe a patient's condition using this method, the physician need only indicate which paragraphs or charts apply, and the typist can then play out all of the descriptive information necessary simply by calling up prerecorded information from submedia, whether it be tape or disk. The information is produced on an automatic typewriter at speeds of approximately 300 words per minute.

The radiology department is a prime example of this application. With word processing, a radiologist need only dictate the patient's name, medical record number, and type of examination. The center can then retrieve stored texts for normal examinations of that type and produce a complete, well-documented report, thus saving both physician and typist time. These stored texts can be universal for the entire X-ray department, or physicians may specify a text tailored to their needs.

Word processing is also efficient in the area of pathology. Autopsies typically take a long time to dictate and an equally long time to transcribe. An autopsy has a specific protocol that must be followed. The final report must be carefully edited to make certain that each physiological system is described accurately. Word processing obviously streamlines this procedure by using the "boilerplating" technique mentioned previously and many of the "text editing" features available on power typing equipment. Text editing features allow for the changing of a letter, word, sentence, or paragraph without causing the retyping of an entire page.

Because many people do not understand aspects of their insurance coverage, hospitals are inundated with questions concerning patients' bills. Many larger hospitals employ a staff of trained people to answer these questions, and word processing has proved invaluable for this purpose.

A centrally supervised and monitored system also allows double or even triple shift use of the same equipment. Because the material to be transcribed is stored on some electronic media, the work is available around the clock. Multiple transcriptionists can use the same desk, typewriter, and transcription equipment to accomplish their work and thereby eliminate the need to purchase additional equipment.

Through the use of stored dictation, it has become evident that a normal eight to five schedule is not mandatory. In one word processing center, flexible scheduling hours are a reality. Many people enjoy the luxury of flexible hours that enable them to meet family needs, and offering employees this option helps in recruiting and retaining quality workers.

Studies conducted by IBM in 1971 revealed that secretaries in a traditional one secretary to one boss situation spend 60 percent of their time in some phase of the transcription process. Because word processing eliminates transcription from the administrative secretary's duties, a talented administrative secretary can support more than one principal. Depending on the nature of the work and the duties of the principal, administrative support secretaries can assist from two to five different people.

Several areas not directly related to patient care also use word processing services; for example, to raise funds through philanthropy. Mass mailings previously processed by computer can be handled at a lower cost with word processing, and each addressee receives a high quality, personalized letter. Word processing equipment can handle small quantities of letters in a cost-effective manner; previously one needed a substantial volume to justify using a computer.

Like the development office, the public relations department at GMC produces numerous documents each month. For years public relations people felt that they had to compose their copy on a typewriter. Many now realize that it is quicker to dictate, have an experienced typist transcribe their thoughts, and then edit the typed document returned to them. Many word processing systems also produce camera-ready copy, thus eliminating the need for typesetting. This means that the public relations department is able to produce professional documents in-house, greatly reducing printing and typesetting costs.

Like any business, hospitals have personnel departments. Applications adaptable to word processing in any personnel department include form letters, advertising, policy and procedure manuals, and employee handbooks. This function is the latest one automated at the medical center.

Accounting Functions

The basic mathematic logic, scrolling ability, and storage capabilities of word processing equipment have made it increasingly useful for accounting functions. Accounting requirements in a hospital are no different than any other business. Reports, documentation and comparisons of previous months and years are needed. The secretary in the accounting department no longer needs to type column after column of numbers to show last month's statistics in comparison with this month's. Current material is stored and during the next reporting period is shifted to the column headed Prior by a command to the machine without the need to retype it. The ability to manipulate information on a screen has allowed accountants to produce necessary reports with ease. This will lead to more informed management in hospitals where word processing is making full use of available technology.

PART VII
HUMAN RESOURCES MANAGEMENT

OVERVIEW*

There are three critical properties in human resource management: development, utilization and engineering:

(1.) Human Resource Development: (Focuses on the human-social system of the organization.) Activities include:

- *Career development* (counseling; career planning; educational and occupational referral services; tuition assistance)
- *Staff development* or continuing education (clinical skill training to either maintain, advance or refresh current skill levels; new product usage; interpersonal skill development; in-house Bachelor and Associate Degree Programs in Nursing)
- *Upward Mobility programs* (GED; secretarial training; medical secretarial training)
- *Orientation processes* (new employee training; new graduate internship; RN refresher training)
- *Pre-Supervisory assessment programs* (assuring an internal supply of competent managerial candidates for promotion whenever vacancies occur)

(2.) Human Resource Utilization (Traditional Personnel Function): (Focuses on the human-social system and the structural system. In large hospitals where so many administrative procedures are computerized, this aspect of human resource management is very affected by the sophistication of the technological system.) Activities include:

- Staffing (assignment, transfer, promotion, separation)
- Rewards (incentive programs, financial rewards, etc.)
- Appraisal (performance review)
- Labor relations
- Grievance systems
- Benefits program
- Wage and salary administration
- Recruitment of new employees
- Payroll administration

(3.) Human Resource Engineering: (Focuses on all the systems, especially goals, structure and tasks.) Activities include:

- Industrial Engineering: (staffing patterns, inventory systems, supply systems, materials management)
- Organizational Development: (a planned process of applying a set of concepts and values, utilizing a definable technology, in order to optimize the attainment of organizational and individual objectives)

OD technology includes interventions such as team-building, process consultation, role clarification, training, management by objectives, etc., and is applied after a period of diagnosis and linkage to organiza-

---

*Source: Reprinted from Jan Margolis, "Cost Effective Human Resource Development in Health Care," *Training and Development Journal,* January 1977, with permission of the American Society for Training and Development Inc.

tional resources available to help solve problems. Most OD technology deals with improving the "processes" by which people relate to one another and work together such as the design of jobs, structure of reporting relationships, communication patterns (formal or informal) and clarity of roles. Its purposes are to encourage growth of people; to foster an open problem-solving work climate; to improve methods of conflict resolution and to develop more effective collaboration among functional groups.

- Manpower Planning (a sophisticated technology for facilitating the effective placement of people within the organization): Manpower planning provides management with the criteria for determining whether particular training or development needs exist; with a way of identifying available manpower supplies and projected shortages; and provides direction for outside recruitment programs. For example, one hospital is developing computerized educational skill inventories for all employee classifications. They are developing many training activities from needs identified by the plan.

Relations with Subordinates: Checklists for 3 Supervisory Levels*

The hospital administrator can use these checklists to alert department heads, intermediate level supervisors and first line supervisors as to their duties and effectiveness in employee relations. Each checklist might serve best as a self-evaluative tool.

Checklist A: For Department-Head Level

This checklist exercise is directed toward key management personnel in health care facilities who are responsible for entire departments and,

---

*Source: Reprinted from *Effective Communication in Health Care* by Harry E. Munn, Jr. and Norman Metzger, with permission of Aspen Systems Corporation, © 1981. Dr. Leslie M. Slote, industrial psychologist, Hartsdale, N.Y., developed many of these suggestions for supervisory practices at the various levels.

therefore, have other levels of supervision reporting to them.

1. Do you as a department head set the pace and attitudes for your people?
2. Do your people share the job of developing goals?
3. Do you share with your people the goals of the institution?
4. Do you give your people a sense of direction, something to strive for and achieve?
5. Does each member of your department understand the relationship and importance of his or her individual job to the department's operations and to the institution's operations?
6. Do the people in your department understand their responsibilities?
7. Do you endorse the management theory that if subordinates are to plan their course intelligently and work efficiently they need to know the where, what, and why of their jobs: where they are going, what they are doing, and why they are doing it?
8. Do your subordinates have a feeling of being "in" on things?
9. Do you share information or do you keep secrets?
10. Are the supervisors who report to you familiar with top management's thinking, the latest institutional-wide developments, and the relative importance of various departmental activities to the institution's short- and long-range plans?
11. Do you recognize and accept that it is your responsibility and a priority obligation to keep everyone in your department informed of institutional policy, day-to-day decisions, and most important, reasons for change that affect them as individuals and as work groups?
12. Do your supervisors understand and accept the institution's goals and know how to motivate their subordinates to achieve those goals?
13. Do you notify your people ahead of time of impending changes?
14. Do your requests to your subordinates include the reasons for the requests?
15. Do you have an accurate feedback mechanism?
16. Do you know how your people react to your decisions?

17. Do you know how your people perceive you and the administration?
18. Are you able to cope with rapidly changing situations?
19. Are you able to replan, reorganize, and take emergency action when indicated?
20. Do you have confidence in the people who work for you?
21. Do you indicate such confidence by delegating responsibility with appropriate authority?
22. Are your actions consistent?
23. Are your actions predictable?
24. Do you recognize effort and good work?
25. Do you recognize poor effort and attempt to correct it promptly?
26. Are you convinced that it is just as easy to be positive as to be negative?
27. Do you realize that praise and encouragement often are more productive than criticism?
28. Do your employees feel free to bring problems to you?
29. Have you established a receptive atmosphere for hearing and acting on employee complaints and suggestions?
30. Are you developing understudies from your immediate management level?
31. Is there someone in the department who can replace you if you leave?
32. Do you have a carefully considered supervisory selection and training program for obtaining and developing the type of supervision you want?
33. Do you hold a good person down in one position because he or she is so indispensable there?
34. Do you take a chance on your people by letting them learn through mistakes, by showing a calm reaction and constructive approach to occasional failure, by encouraging them to stick their necks out without fear of the ax, and by instilling self-confidence?
35. Do you use every opportunity to build up in subordinates a sense of the importance of their work?
36. Are you giving real responsibility to your immediate supervisors and then holding them accountable?
37. Do you interfere with jobs of subordinates or do you allow them to exercise discretion and judgment in making decisions?
38. Are you doing things to discourage your subordinates?
39. Are you interested in and aware of the sources of discontentment, or discouragement, or frustration affecting your supervisors?
40. Do you encourage and listen to the ideas and reactions of your subordinates?
41. Do you give your subordinates credit for their contributions?
42. Do you explain to them why their ideas or suggestions are not acceptable?
43. Do you remember to praise in public but criticize in private?
44. Are you aware that a feeling of belonging builds self-confidence and makes people want to work harder than ever?
45. Do you show your people a future?
46. Are you aware of the fact that maximum self-development always takes place when a person feels, understands, accepts, and exercises the full weight of responsibility for his or her job?

Checklist B: For Intermediate-Level Supervisors

You are in a position where you report to a department head and have first-line supervisors reporting to you. Refer to this checklist throughout the year to gauge your effectiveness.

1. Do you have a thorough understanding of institutional goals, your part in meeting budgets, and do you have full confidence in their attainment?
2. Do you offer suggestions or constructive criticism to your supervisor (the department head) and ask for additional information when necessary?
3. Do you build team spirit and group pride by getting everyone into the act of setting goals and pulling together?
4. Do you deal with emergencies as they come up or do you have scheduled times for meetings with your department head and with your first-line supervisors?
5. Do you encourage each of your supervisors to come up with suggestions on ways to improve things?
6. When you do not accept your supervisors' suggestions, do you explain why?

7. Have you set up an atmosphere that enables your subordinates to approach you with job or personal problems?
8. Do people believe that you listen empathetically and really care about their problems?
9. Do you keep your supervisors informed on how they are doing?
10. Do you give credit where credit is due and offer constructive criticism when necessary?
11. Do your supervisors appear to be too busy with work problems to be concerned about their employees' personal difficulties?
12. Does your example encourage your supervisors to build individual worker confidence and praise good performance?
13. Do your supervisors know that you expect them to communicate to their people how jobs are evaluated and what the job rates and progressions are?
14. Do your supervisors keep their people informed of promotional opportunities?
15. Do your supervisors train their people for better jobs?

Checklist C: For Immediate/First-Line Supervisors

As a first-line supervisor, you should review the following checklist on a regular basis.

1. Do you know that good communication means being available to answer employee questions?
2. Do you accept employees' need to know what is expected of them, how well they are doing their jobs, and how they will be rewarded for good work?
3. Have you permitted your employees freedom and latitude in performing their work, or are you constantly supervising employees?
4. Are you personally interested in the well-being of the people who work for you?
5. Do you recommend good workers for promotions, merit increases, and other forms of recognition?
6. Do you consult with your employees and permit them to share in the decision-making process?
7. Do you realize that pent-up emotions are dangerous and, therefore, do you provide an accessible sounding board for employee complaints and grievances?
8. Do you ever say or do anything that detracts from the sense of personal dignity that each of your people has?
9. When a job is well done do you praise the worker; and when a job is done poorly do you criticize constructively?
10. Do you realize that people want to feel important?
11. Do you realize that people want recognition?
12. Do you realize that people want credit and attention?
13. Do you realize that people have their own self-interest at heart?
14. Do you realize that people want to be better off tomorrow than today?
15. Do you realize that people want prompt action on their questions?
16. Do you realize that people would rather talk than listen?
17. Do you realize that people would rather give advice than take advice?
18. Do you realize that people generally resent too-close supervision?
19. Do you realize that people resent change?
20. Do you realize that people are naturally curious?
21. Do you ask questions instead of giving orders?
22. Do you make suggestions instead of giving orders?
23. Do you keep in mind the employees' self-interest?
24. Do you make your employees feel that their work is useful?
25. Do you make your employees feel that they are trusted members of the work group?
26. Do you represent your employees' interests to the next level of supervision?
27. Do you represent the management to your employees?
28. Are you too busy with work problems to be concerned with employees' personal difficulties?
29. Do you look for and find opportunities to praise and reward a good performance, or are you afraid of being accused of sentimentality and coddling?
30. Are you consistent, or do you play favorites?

31. Are you predictable, or do your employees feel they never know what your next move will be?
32. Do you try to rotate your people and build up skills for individual flexibility within the group?
33. Do you spend enough time training your people?
34. Do you understand the problem with legislating change rather than selling change?
35. Do your employees perceive you as a "people-centered" supervisor?
36. Do your employees trust you?

Evaluation by Subordinates

Would you dare ask your employees to complete this survey rating you as a supervisor? How would you rate yourself?

1. Supervisor's relationship with his/her staff: Well liked and respected ( ), Usually gets along well with others and makes fair impression ( ), Seldom attracts respect from others ( ), Creates antagonism ( ).
2. Work knowledge of supervisor: Excellent ( ), Good ( ), Fair ( ), I know more than him/her ( ).
3. Does he/she set a good example? Always ( ), Sometimes ( ), If I used him/her as an example I'd be fired ( ).
4. Does he/she provide motivation? Yes ( ) No ( )
5. Do you receive respect? Yes ( ) No ( )
6. Are you dealt with honestly? Yes ( ) No ( )
7. Do you receive praise on a job well done? Yes ( ) No ( )
8. Are you criticized when you perform poorly? Yes ( ) No ( ) Is this criticism beneficial? Yes ( ) No ( )
9. Are you encouraged to take initiative? Yes ( ) No ( )
10. Are you encouraged to make suggestions? Yes ( ) No ( )
11. Is your supervisor too demanding? Yes ( ) No ( )
12. Are schedules and job assignments made fairly? Yes ( ) No ( )
13. Do you feel your supervisor plays favorites? Yes ( ) No ( )
14. Do you feel you were adequately oriented to your job? Yes ( ) No ( )
15. Do you feel your supervisor is willing to help with work if your team is shorthanded? Yes ( ) No ( )
16. Do you feel your supervisor has a heavy work load? Yes ( ) No ( )
17. If you want to speak with your supervisor will he/she find the time? Yes ( ) No ( )
18. Do you feel your supervisor will listen with an open mind? Yes ( ) No ( )
19. Does your supervisor accept criticism? Yes ( ) No ( )
20. Do you feel lines of communication are open above your supervisor? Yes ( ) No ( )
21. Do unresolved problems with your supervisor reflect on his/her attitude toward you? Yes ( ) No ( )
22. Are problems usually worked out? Yes ( ) No ( )
23. Do you feel your supervisor will stand behind you when you are right? Yes ( ) No ( )
24. Do you feel your supervisor cares about your personal feelings and problems? Yes ( ) No ( )

Chapter 27—Communications

IMPROVING COMMUNICATIONS

Effective Leadership Communication*

Behind the exchange of information in the communication process are larger concepts which the administrator hopes to convey to his staff: standards of performance, motivation toward effective functioning, and acceptance of innovations. Communication is a force for influencing staff direction. Indirect and direct means can be used. Indirectly, the administrator sends out signals by his own behavior. All the lectures about standards and attitudes will be ineffective if subordinates observe contradictions and lapses in his own actions. Most people learn to communicate through example.

For direct communication, it is important that messages are not only given but heard too. The first step is to promote a responsive communication climate where staff members feel comfortable in expressing their underlying reactions, attitudes and problems. The following steps may help you communicate clearly with your subordinates:

1. Consider your objectives in advance, forming a plan for communication: why, when, how.
2. Express yourself with unmistakable clarity. Be concise and tick off main points by emphasizing them.
3. Formulate messages in a manner which is attuned to the subordinate's self-interest, creating greater acceptance.
4. Be sensitive to differences in needs, experiences and frames of reference among various subordinate levels; adjust messages accordingly.
5. Avoid didactic language. Use conversational language but be aware that words have different shades of meaning, assuming coloration from the type of situation or the background of the listener.
6. Be a listener as well as a talker. Encourage openness and observe accurate criticisms and fresh approaches. Strive for feedback from subordinates to confirm whether the message has been comprehended.
7. Follow-up conversations and meetings with memos or reports to the staff. Let them know that action has resulted from communication or, in the case of individual criticisms, that progress has been noted.
8. Use a variety of communication methods to reinforce an important message or select a single most appropriate method according to the nature of the message: conversations, notes, official memos, meetings, conferences and reports.

Ten Commandments*

Harold Koontz's and Cyril O'Donnell's ten commandments of good communication provide an appropriate summary.

---

*Source: Reprinted from *The Nursing Administration Handbook* by Howard S. Rowland and Beatrice L. Rowland, eds., with permission of Aspen Systems Corporation, © 1980.

*Source: Reprinted from *Management: A Book of Readings* by Harold Koontz and Cyril O'Donnell, with permission of McGraw-Hill Book Co., © 1972.

1. Clarify ideas before communicating—make sure you know and understand what you are going to say and how best you are going to say it.
2. Examine the true purpose of each communication—make sure it is necessary and that you will be accomplishing what you want to.
3. Consider the total physical and human setting—determine the knowledge and experience of the receiver on the subject so that the best presentation can be developed.
4. Consult with others when appropriate—a technique some people find successful is to have colleagues in another discipline read important reports before they are submitted.
5. Be mindful of overtones—your tone of voice and choice of language can affect comprehension.
6. Convey something of value—take into consideration what the receiver wants to hear.
7. Follow up—make certain that every communication has feedback so that complete understanding and appropriate action result.
8. Communicate for the future as well as the present—be consistent with long-range interests and goals.
9. Support communication with action—managers' "do as I say, not as I do" approach has no place in the business world.
10. Seek to understand as well as to be understood—listen carefully to determine the receivers' reaction to the message so that appropriate follow-up can be made.

Get To Know Your Subordinates*

Getting to know your subordinates is not only a primary necessity for effective communications but for good management as well. It is the rare individual who knows his/her employees on a first name basis. Many say they do but in reality don't. You might want to have your department heads and supervisors give themselves the following test:

---

*Source: Reprinted from *The Union Epidemic* by Warren H. Chaney and Thomas R. Beech, with permission of Aspen Systems Corporation, © 1977.

1. What are the first names of all employees that work for you?
2. What is the name of each employee's spouse?
3. How many children does each have, and what grades are they in?
4. What major illnesses have occurred in the employee's family recently?
5. What hobbies does each of your employees have?
6. What educational or vocational courses has each of them taken?
7. Where does each of the employees live? (Not by street address or number, but in what section of town.)
8. How long does it take for each to get to work, and how does each get to work?

They should know the answers to at least 5 questions about each employee under their supervision.

Hospital Communication Objectives*

1. To keep employees informed of current status of operations and conditions of the hospital:

> Maintain program of information to employees regarding patient census, services rendered, areas served; point out changes over past years and evidence of growth:

> Discuss increasing costs, hospital's success in meeting them, changes in methods, and how it keeps up with new developments.

2. To gain acceptance by employees of the following hospital goals:

> Make continuously available to the community the best possible care of the sick and injured;

> Employ a sufficient staff of qualified, satisfied employees to provide the services required;

---

*Source: Reprinted by permission from pages 206–207 in *Personnel Administration in the Health Services Industry*, Second Edition, by Norman Metzger. Copyright 1979, Spectrum Publications, Inc., New York City.

Protect the interests of employees as to salaries, hours, benefits, working conditions, fair treatment, considerate supervision, job security, personal growth, and to do so without regard to race, creed or color;

So manage the hospital that employees will regard it as a good place to work.

3. To develop on the employee's part better understanding of his/her job, and the requirements and standards of performance expected from him/her:

Develop and utilize organization charts, job descriptions, performance standards and performance appraisals, and discuss them with employees.

4. To give employees recognition for good performance:

Assure salary administration based on performance;

"Counsel" employees for good performance as well as to discipline for poor performance;

Arrange public personal recognition where warranted.

5. To give employees advance information on new services, procedures, operations, policies, etc.:

Explain the meaning of and reason for those management actions that affect their job or interests as employees.

6. To obtain reactions, suggestions and viewpoint of subordinate employees; to pinpoint problem areas:

Assure "feedback" of what employees are thinking, proper functioning of grievance procedure, and exit interviews;

Encourage and take appropriate action with respect to employees' comments and suggestions.

7. To demonstrate that the hospital's approach to employees relations problems:

Deal with employees firmly but with fairness;

Seek solutions to problems in terms of maintaining a proper balance of the interests of patients, employees, doctors and the community;

Seek answers from all interests involved so as to assure the continued operation of the hospital on a sound financial basis.

8. To correct, answer or otherwise counteract inaccurate or misleading statements by union leaders, or distortions by them of management's statements or actions:

Monitor, catalog and evaluate misleading statements;

Answer, correct, counteract or, by anticipation, offset the more damaging or significant statements;

Select time (usually immediate), media and tone of communications most appropriate to give employees the facts, and develop understanding of hospital's intentions.

9. To improve communication skills of supervisors, managers and administration:

Define responsibility to communicate;

Train by actual practice.

COMMUNICATION TARGETS*

Effective communications are indispensible to a sound program of employee relations. The goals of such a program can, in fact, only be achieved by means of a continuous and open dialogue between employer and employee. The hospital's attitude toward its employees should be clearly articulated and employees should be encouraged to express their ideas, problems, and aspirations to the hospital.

There are at least two distinct groups of people who are important to the achievement of employee relations goals. They are the professional staff, department heads, and supervisors, on one hand and all remaining employees on the

---

*Source: Reprinted from *Health Care Labor Manual* by Martin E. Skoler, with permission of Aspen Systems Corporation, © 1981.

other. Communicating with each requires a delicate nuance of emphasis, using a broad selection of techniques.

Supervisors

No group communicates the attitude of the hospital to employees more influentially than do department managers and supervisors. Their daily personal contact with employees puts them in an out front position to function as "personnel administrators" in the field. They are usually in a position to confront and respond to problems at the work site before small matters become major issues and at a time when they may best be resolved. They hear of and experience both dilemmas and opportunities that call for policy changes and are in position to make or recommend such changes. To assure their effectiveness in this role requires carefully cultivated channels of communication with supervisory management and the personnel and administrative offices. The methods of communication with supervisory management should reflect the small and manageable size of the group, its relative homogeneity and the continuous need for two-way give-and-take through the spoken and written word.

Communication Vehicles

The Personnel Policy Manual is the basic document reflecting employee relations policies of the hospital. (See "Model Personnel Policy Manual Outline," Table 27-1.) It should contain three types of information:

1. The *policy statement* should reflect the general attitude of the hospital toward a subject. It must necessarily be written in broad terms to allow some discretion and flexibility based on the needs of a situation.
2. A supplemental *administrative procedure* is often added to provide more specific instructions when appropriate for processing information or otherwise handling routine incidents covered by the policy.
3. The *supervisor's guidelines* provide additional information to help them administer the policy (*e.g.*, legal basis for policy, results of violations, decision-making authority, supportive details).

Management Newsletters are an effective means of maintaining communications with supervisors regarding changes or interpretations of policy, about employee relations problems recently resolved, about plans of the hospital affecting supervisors, and for general information about management. Such newsletters should be distributed on a regular basis (often monthly) and may also include supervisory techniques and other developmental literature. As a residual benefit, they serve as a further mark of status to the recipient. Information in this newsletter is generally of permanent value. A section of the Personnel Policy Manual should discuss filing such newsletters.

Periodic management meetings provide a two-way communication with supervisors. Such meetings allow for "comparing notes" between supervisors, discussing common problems, reviewing policies, and making presentations of an instructional or advisory nature by the administrator, personnel director, fiscal director, or others. Management meetings should be hosted by the administrator or personnel director, kept within strict time limits, and managed by the personnel director who is responsible for developing content. Attendance should be strongly encouraged and limited to the supervisory level and up to allow the greatest possible freedom of discussion of management problems.

The Personnel Policy Advisory Committee should be a standing committee of key managers, providing guidance for the continuous review of personnel policies. In this capacity these people can offer substantial insights on the effectiveness of policy from a perspective very close to the employee.

Personalized coaching of supervisors by the professional personnel staff provides guidance to the supervisor in handling specific situations. It is of particular value as a communications link before supervisory mishaps occur in handling disciplinary situations, grievances, and anticipated personnel and job function changes. Its essence is the use of the personnel professional as a somewhat detached counselor in the administration/communication of personnel policy.

Employees

Communication with employees in a health care institution is aimed at those employees who are not yet organized or who are subject to a union organizing campaign. If they are, then the employer is much more limited in his ability to

Table 27-1 A Model Personnel Policy Manual Outline*

SECTION
1. *Introduction*
    Letter from Hospital Director
    Introduction
    Personnel Department Functions
    Administration of Personnel Policies
    Employment Policies
    Organizational Definitions
2. *Employment Policies and Procedures*
    Employment Requirements
    Employment, Status
    Employment Procedures
    New Employee Orientation
    Probationary Period
    Employee Personnel Files and Reference Requests
    Job Opening, Listing and Advertising
    Transfers, In-Hospital
    Termination, Procedure
    Termination, Types and Notice
    Change of Status Form
    Reemployment
    Reinstatement of Permanent Employees
3. *Salary Administration*
    Program, Salary Administration
    Policy, Salary Administration
    Procedures, Salary Administration
    Information to Employees
    Exempt and Non-Exempt Employees
    Overtime Compensation
    Hours of Work
    Time Card, Procedure
4. *Benefits*
    Major Benefits Summary
    Credit Union
    Health Insurance Plan
    Holidays
    Industrial Accidents
    Leave of Absence
    Life Insurance Plan
    Parking Regulations
    Retirement Plan
    Shift and Weekend Differential
    Sick Leave Policy
    Special Absences
    Tax Sheltered Annuity
    Tuition Aid Program
    Unemployment Compensation
    Vacation
5. *Safety and Security*
    Personnel Health Service
    Health Care
    Canvassers and Solicitors
    Credit References
    Lockers
    Purchases through the Hospital
    Smoking
    Fire Regulations
    Lost and Found

Table 27-1 continued

    Safety
    Identification Bag
6. *Employee Relations*
    Absenteeism
    Evaluation
    Performance Rating Form
    Counseling
    Disciplinary Action
    Discipline and Hospital Rules
    Grievances
    Labor Relations Guidelines
    Employment of Relatives
    Personal Appearance
    Uniform Procedure
7. *Working Conditions*
    Dining Facilities
    Bulletin Boards
    Language Manual
    Recreation
    Suggestion Box
    Confidential Information
    Interference with Work
    Press Relations
    Service Awards
    Tours
    Telephone Calls
8. *Blank Forms*
    Employee Accident Investigation and Analysis Report
    Employee's Change of Status
    Employee's Change of Status Special Funds
    Employee Termination Form
    Employment Application Form
    Job Description
    Notice of Resignation
    Paid Sick Leave
    Paid Vacation
    Performance Rating Form
    Personnel Authorization and Requisition Form
    Please Issue
    Report of Employee Accident or Illness
    Report of Unusual Incident
    Time Card
    Warning Notice

*Source: Summary of Personnel Policy Manual, *Health Care Labor Manual*, Aspen Systems Corporation, 1981.

communicate directly and should insure that he will not be subjected to a charge of unfair labor practices. Once the employer becomes aware of a union organizing drive, all such communications must be carefully scrutinized from a legal standpoint to make certain they do not constitute objectionable conduct which could lead to a bargaining order. It cannot be emphasized too strongly the need for a regular pattern of communicating with employees *before* the advent of a union.

The employees as a group are a more complex and diverse audience than the supervisors. Because of the large variety of occupational specialties in a hospital, employee backgrounds tend to be varied. Levels of interest in the hospital and its fortunes also vary substantially based upon the age, sex, pay, and responsibilities of each employee. Traditional communications have thus tended to focus on salaries, benefits, and work rules plus social activities. This trend is changing somewhat as these issues give way to employee demands for more information and participation in both policy and clinical matters. Communication vehicles include a wide variety of written material plus a number of two-way approaches in groups as well as on a person-to-person basis.

Communication Vehicles

Written Communication Vehicles

1. The *Employee Handbook* has traditionally been the primary publication for employees. Versions vary from the very abbreviated handbook to the one which rivals the Personnel Policy Manual in completeness.

    The use of a single comprehensive booklet—a personnel policy manual—for employee information is becoming less common as marketplace competition and government regulations of hospital affairs require more detailed information and often separate publications.

2. *Collective bargaining agreements* are much like the employee handbook mentioned above with at least one important difference. Raymond Fleishman writes, "The collective bargaining agreement is the 'personal manual' for bargaining unit employees and the personnel policy manual is the 'contract' for nonunion employees."

3. *Single subject pamphlets* are being used more frequently with the advent of various insurance benefits. Schedules of in-house training and developmental programs are often in pamphlet form.

4. Many hospitals issue a *quarterly publication,* aimed at both employees and other interested parties (*e.g.,* active medical staff, trustees, benefactors). This provides a broader range of information, but must not be expected to take the place of an internal publication which has a higher concentration of employee-slanted material.

5. *House organs* are published weekly or monthly, and deal strictly with subjects of interest to employees. This publication is particularly well received when it is obviously an unselfish effort by the hospital to communicate with and inform employees. Hence, the important qualities of the house organ are frequency, brevity, content of employee interest, and a lack of propaganda. The quality of presentation is strictly secondary. Often better results are obtained from duplicated typed copy that is simply illustrated than by professionally prepared material that looks like a management presentation.

6. *Letters to employee homes* concerning employee-related topics and employee activities should be periodically sent. These letters update and inform the employee's family about the hospital. Such letters then seem more natural and less inflammatory if they become necessary during a union organizing drive.

7. *Bulletin boards* are used profitably to publicize job openings, one-time letters from the administrator, and pictures of hospital and employee activities.

8. *"I've Got a Question" forms* doubling as an envelope, are part of a program providing direct contact between the employee and the administrator. Response is expedited when anonymous queries are answered on the bulletin board.

9. *The Employee Annual Report* is a modified annual report provided to employees about the hospital's financial and clinical activities.

10. *Fringe Benefit Annual Report* provides an individual annual update on fringe benefits including such items as:

    a. value of employee's pension fund;
    b. vacation accrual;
    c. life and disability insurance coverage;
    d. annual value of hospital paid fringe benefits for the previous year;
    e. summary of other benefits.

Much of written communication is of an informational nature, often publicizing benefits and other programs. Other approaches stress two-way communication which invite employee response in matters of personal interest and in the solving of work-related issues.

Two-Way Communication Vehicles

1. *Employee Discussion Groups* may be scheduled during meal times with luncheon served without charge. Ten to fifteen employees are asked to have lunch (or supper) with the administrator and/or the personnel director. No other members of management are usually present. The objective is to solicit from employees ideas for correcting operations or employee relations problems. It is imperative that the discussion be directed toward issues, not personalities.
2. *Monthly In-service Training* meetings for *all* departments offer problem solving as well as job training opportunity.
3. *"Fact-Fone"* is an approach whereby employees may call a telephone number and (1) hear a prerecorded message about hospital happenings followed by (2) an opportunity to speak onto a tape for an unlimited amount of time to present a problem or idea. Response is either individual or via bulletin board.
4. The *Employee Advocate* is assigned to either the administrator's office or the personnel director's office. His sole responsibility is to represent the employee in problem situations including grievances.
5. An *Employee Committee,* however, formed to recommend or discuss changes in wages, hours, or working conditions on behalf of other employees and themselves, has been found by the NLRB to be a labor organization as defined by Section 2(5) of the Act. Therefore, the health care institution which encourages the formation of such a committee may be subject to Section 8(a)(2) charges of unfair interference with and/or domination of protected concerted activities. A concerted activity does not have to be a union activity to be protected.

Such committee members, when they feel management is unresponsive to their requests, frequently opt to bring in actual unions to reinforce their demands. In many industrial situations, employee committees have been converted into an organizing tool by labor unions.

Additionally, management may discover too late that it has been dealing only with representatives who may not have been truly responsive to the employees' needs, thus lulling the administration into a sense of security which was not realistic.

Therefore, management should communicate with small groups of employees on a rotating basis as well as by those methods outlined above.

COMMUNICATION TECHNIQUES

Listening

Counterproductive Habits*

Developing the art of listening requires in most cases relearning and unlearning bad habits developed over the years. Most of us do not know how to listen. We are often guilty of listening for facts or listening intelligently for the verbal statement alone when the art of listening is the discerning of ideas. Our biases also enter into our listening habits. It is not unusual for certain words—rhetoric—to prejudice our appreciation and understanding. We may well not like the way a speaker "looks" or not like his voice and, therefore, pay little attention to or discount what he has to say.

Some of the prevalent and counterproductive listening habits follow:

1. Talking too much. It is obvious that if one talks too much, one cannot have enough time to listen.

    a. Do you spend too much time explaining or defending your own position, thereby neglecting a careful evaluation of the other individual's position?
    b. Are you so intent on framing the answer to a question which has yet to be fully communicated to you that indeed you stop listening in the midst of someone's communication?
    c. Are you often puzzled about what the other individual really meant?

    All of these actions require a reassessment of our "talking" and "listening" habits. The key to these problems is in disciplining

---

*Source: Reprinted by permission from pages 166 and 167 in *Personnel Administration in the Health Services Industry,* Second Edition, by Norman Metzger. Copyright 1979, Spectrum Publications, Inc., New York City.

oneself to ask questions and wait—remaining silent—for enough time to pass for the other individual to communicate to you. It requires a disciplined approach to listening by appreciating the power of silence.

2. Asking leading questions. One of the most common pitfalls of communication is framing questions in such a way that the "right answer" is obtained.

   a. Are you receiving only the answers you were secretly wishing for?
   b. Are you receiving only limited responses which are guarded?

   In order to obtain the true responses of people to whom you are communicating, it would be best to outline the important areas in which questions should be asked and to frame the questions so that they are "open-ended." This will leave the other individual free to answer in any way and in as elaborate a fashion as he chooses.

3. Selecting the wrong time and the wrong place to communicate.

   a. Is your communication hasty and does it reflect your desire to hurry it?
   b. Do you have one foot out the door and only one ear unlocked when communicating?
   c. Do you communicate in public when the subject cries for a private audience?
   d. Are the phones ringing? Do people come barging in? Are you constantly distracted when in the midst of communication?
   e. Do you communicate too soon or too late?

   It is best to plan your communication time so that a full discussion can be had and the listener and speaker can give full attention to the discussion. It is also best to communicate in an atmosphere without distractions. It is important to be sensitive to the dignity of the listener; therefore, certain communications must be held in private and the listener should not be embarrassed in the presence of his peers.

NOTE: To test yourself as a listener see Table 27-2.

Poor Listener Response[*]

Here are eight examples of poor listener response:

1. *The cliché.* When someone discloses a personal problem, a response with a cliché such as, "Oh, I know how you feel," can be less functional than no response at all. Clichés put distance between people.
2. *The question.* A question can be helpful in probing, that is, in gaining information concerning the sender's problems. But a question can also be perceived as interrogation and place the other person on the defensive. With few exceptions, a question can be rephrased into a declarative statement. The purpose of gaining information is thus still served, but the possibility of defensiveness is avoided.
3. *Inaccuracy.* If your understanding of other people is inaccurate, those people may feel "blocked," that is, they may lose trust in your ability to understand and, as a result, stop the interaction. Perception checking can help the listener avoid inaccuracies.
4. *Feigning understanding.* It isn't always easy to understand what a sender is trying to communicate, even if the listener "attends" well. But if the listener merely pretends to understand, the sender will sense this, and this will create a barrier. Egan says, "If you are confused admit your confusion. . . . Such statements are signs of respect, of the fact that you think it is important to stay with the other."
5. *Parroting.* Mere repetition of what the other person says does little to establish empathy.
6. *Jumping in too quickly or letting the other person ramble.* The good listener will let the other person pace the interaction, unless that person begins to ramble. Listeners should feel free to interrupt if they have something important to say, but generally the senders should be in charge.

---

[*]Source: Adapted from *Interpersonal Living* by G. Egan. Copyright © 1976 by Wadsworth Publishing Company, Inc. Reprinted by permission of the publisher, Brooks/Cole Publishing Company, Monterey, CA.

Table 27-2 How Do You Rate as a Listener?*

Take the following test and see how you rate as a listener. Place an "X" in the appropriate blank. When speaking interpersonally with a patient, nursing supervisor, doctor, coworker, or employee, do you:

Usually	Sometimes	Seldom	
_____	_____	_____	(1) Prepare yourself physically by standing or sitting, facing the speaker, and making sure you can hear?
_____	_____	_____	(2) Watch the speaker for the verbal as well as the nonverbal messages?
_____	_____	_____	(3) Decide from the speaker's appearance and delivery whether or not what he or she has to say is worthwhile?
_____	_____	_____	(4) Listen primarily for ideas and underlying feelings?
_____	_____	_____	(5) Determine your own bias, if any, and try to allow for it?
_____	_____	_____	(6) Keep your mind on what the speaker is saying?
_____	_____	_____	(7) Interrupt immediately if you hear a statement you feel is wrong?
_____	_____	_____	(8) Try to see the situation from the other person's point of view?
_____	_____	_____	(9) Try to have the last word?
_____	_____	_____	(10) Make a conscientious effort to evaluate the logic and credibility of what you hear?

SCORING

This check list, though by no means complete, should help you measure your listening ability. Score yourself as follows: Questions 1, 2, 4, 5, 6, 8, and 10—ten points for *usually,* five points for *sometimes,* and zero points for *seldom.* Questions 3, 7, and 9—zero points for *usually,* five points for *sometimes,* and ten points for *seldom.*

If you scored below 70, your listening skills can be improved because you have developed some undesirable listening habits; 70 to 85, you listen well but can still improve; 90 or above, you are an excellent listener.

*Source: Reprinted from *Effective Communication in Health Care* by Harry E. Munn, Jr. and Norman Metzger, with permission of Aspen Systems Corporation, © 1981.

7. *Discrepancy in language, tone, or manner.* The use of idiosyncratic jargon or behavior by the listener is inappropriate. As far as possible, the listener should follow the cues from the sender so the sender does not feel invaded.

8. *Longwindedness.* The listener's responses should be as succinct as possible. Com-

ments should be to the point, but not too long. Remember, the sender is in control of the interaction.

Other common mistakes in listening include:

- defensive responses
- responses that imply condescension or manipulation
- unsolicited advice giving
- responses that indicate rejection or disrespect
- premature confrontation
- patronizing or placating responses
- responses that ignore what the person said
- use of inappropriate warmth or sympathy
- judgmental remarks

Checklist of Guidelines To Improve Listening Skills*

The following ten guidelines, in conjunction with Table 27-2, should provide a more comprehensive basis to improve your listening skills:

1. *Prepare yourself physically by standing or facing the speaker.* Making sure you can hear physically is essential for good listening. You thereby tell the sender that you are ready to listen and are able to hear the verbal messages and also see the nonverbal messages the speaker is sending. This face-to-face attention also shows that you are interested in what is being said. People tend to avoid and look away from people and things in which they are not interested. Attention and interest are synonymous. You pay attention to the things you are interested in, and you are interested in the things you pay attention to.
2. *Learn to watch for the speaker's nonverbal as well as verbal messages.* Everyone sends two messages. One message is sent verbally, and the other is sent nonverbally through inflection in the voice or through facial expression, bodily action, or gestures. Sixty-eight percent of all messages are sent nonverbally. The nonverbal message conveys the speaker's attitude, sincerity, and genuineness. To miss the nonverbal message is to miss half of what is being said.
3. *Don't decide from the speaker's appearance or delivery that what he or she has to say is worthwhile.* When you start to focus on the speaker's delivery or appearance, you become distracted from the purpose of communication: receiving the speaker's ideas. You should be more interested in what people have to say than how they say it or what they look like.
4. *Listen for ideas and underlying feelings.* Again, the purpose of good communication is to be able to reflect upon and exchange ideas. For example, if I were to meet you on the street and give you a dollar and you gave me a dollar, and you then went your way and I went mine, neither of us would be better off because of the exchange. But if I gave you an idea and you gave me an idea, then both of us would be better off as a result of the exchange.
5. *Try to determine your own biases, if any, and allow for them.* Communication gets blamed for many things. Whenever something doesn't go right, you might say you have a communication breakdown. But many times you don't have a communication breakdown at all. In fact, you might have very good communication; you both know what has been said, and there is a common understanding. But you don't like what you have heard. If the health care supervisor or employee could learn to recognize such differences, better relationships would be formed. You will not always agree with everyone. The trauma in such situations develops when you discover you are no longer talking about the issues, but about each other.
6. *Attempt to keep your mind on what the speaker is saying.* Don't allow yourself to become distracted. Too many times, people fake attention and, like the little dog in the back of the car window, just keep nodding their heads up and down without hearing a word of what is being said.
7. *Don't interrupt immediately if you hear a statement that you feel is wrong.* Indeed, if you listen closely, you many be persuaded that the statement is right. Some-

---

*Source: Reprinted from *Effective Communication in Health Care* by Harry E. Munn, Jr. and Norman Metzger, with permission of Aspen Systems Corporation, © 1981.

times you may fail to listen just because of this fear of something different, of the possibility that you may have to forsake some sacred position you have held for years.

8. *Try to see the situation from the other person's point of view.* This doesn't mean that you always have to agree. However, there is no way that you can change other people's perceptions until you can see how they have formulated those perceptions.
9. *Don't try to have the last word.* Listen to what is being said, and then think about it. This reflection may take some time, but you need time to think before you communicate. Sometimes, in order to solve a problem, you have to walk away from the problem for a while and think about it from different points of view, and about the advantages and disadvantages of possible solutions.
10. *Make a conscientious effort to evaluate the logic and credibility of what you hear.* Our minds function at some 500 words a minute, but we normally speak at 125 words a minute. In other words, we can think four times faster than we can speak. Rather than letting our minds become bored, we can take advantage of this time differential between thinking and speaking. We can attempt to anticipate the speaker's next point, attempt to identify and evaluate supporting material, and mentally summarize what the speaker has said: What has thus far been said that I can use?

Paraphrasing and Parasupporting

Two helpful types of response in listening are paraphrasing and parasupporting. A guideline for paraphrasing would include the following rules:

1. Say in your own words what you heard the other person saying.
2. Try to include some of what you perceive the other person to be feeling.
3. Don't just "word swap." That is, do not merely repeat what the sender has said. Repeating does little to let the sender know that the listener understands. Nor does it really encourage the sender to elaborate.
4. Give the other person a chance to verify your paraphrase.*

Even attentive and active listeners are not always accurate in their interpretations. The purpose of paraphrasing is to determine whether or not the sender's message has been accurately interpreted and understood.

In parasupporting listeners will not only paraphrase what the senders have said but will also carry their own ideas further by providing examples or other data that tend to illustrate, clarify, or support the senders' feelings.

How To Prepare a Speech**

One of the most important elements of successful speaking is the speaker's preparation. Most speech experts agree that preparation for speaking is a simple step-by-step process. The first task that any speaker faces in preparing a speech is to determine and limit the purpose of his speech. He then assembles relevant support materials, plans his organizational pattern, and decides how to begin, develop, and conclude his speech.

Purpose

Every successful speech has a clear and definite purpose designed to achieve a particular audience reaction. This purpose is the goal, or objective for the speech. Like other goals, the purpose serves to guide the speaker in all phases of speech preparation and final delivery.

Within such limitations as the occasion, place, time, speaker's ability, and audience background, all speeches have been traditionally classified according to one of three general purposes: to inform, to persuade, or to entertain.

To inform. The speaker's purpose is to inform when he helps an audience to understand an idea, a concept, a process, or when he broadens the range of the audience's present knowledge. All informative speeches have a clear organization, supporting facts, and illustrative examples and comparisons.

---

*Source: Reprinted from *Together: Communicating Interpersonally* by John Stewart and Gary D'Angelo, with permission of Addison-Wesley, © 1975, p. 195.

**Source: *Principles and Techniques of Instruction,* U.S. Air Force, 1974, (AF 50–62).

To persuade. In the speech to persuade, the speaker wishes to change or reinforce existing beliefs, stimulate activity, or increase emotional involvement. A distinguishing feature of the persuasive speech is its appeal to an audience's emotions in addition to its appeal to their intellectual reasoning.

To entertain. The speech to entertain has as its objective the enjoyment of the audience. This type of speech, then, is characterized by information which is interesting, unusual, or humorous.

Once the general purpose has been selected, the speaker is ready to form the specific purpose by stating the precise response desired from the audience.

When writing the specific purpose, the speaker must conform to the needs of the audience, the limitations of time, and any limitations inherent in the situation.

Research

With his purpose in mind, the speaker now proceeds to the second step—gathering material on his subject. The source of this material is his own experience, or the experience of others gained through conversation, interviews, and written or observed material. The person concerned with giving a good speech will probably draw from all of these sources.

The next step is to evaluate the material gathered. The speaker will probably find that he has enough material for several speeches. The speaker must now combine some ideas, eliminate others and, perhaps, bolster some ideas that appear in his research materials. At this time, the speaker will probably see that the ideas are beginning to form into some type of pattern.

Determining the Pattern

- The *time or chronological pattern* is used when the material is arranged according to the order in which a number of events took place.
- The *spatial or geographical pattern* is very effective in describing things. When using the spatial pattern, the speech material is developed in some directional sequence.
- The *topical pattern* is used when the subject has within itself divisions well known to the speaker and the audience.
- The *cause and effect pattern* is also used in speaking, but does not lend itself to all topics. When using the cause and effect pattern, the speaker may first enumerate specific forces, then point out the results which follow; or he may first describe conditions, then discuss the forces which caused them.
- The *problem-solution pattern* organizes material in terms of problems (needs) and solutions (plans). The problem-solution pattern is particularly effective with a persuasive speech.

The Outline

An effective outline helps to make a good speech. By establishing the structural form of the speech, the outline facilitates evaluation. Is the thinking clear? Is each point treated according to importance? Does the speech need more support material? Are ideas in the proper sequence? Such evaluation questions will insure that the speech has unity, is coherent, and has a smooth progression from beginning to end.

The first step in the rough draft is listing the main points, and arranging them in a systematic sequence. Once this is accomplished, the speaker inserts his subpoints and decides which support material will best verify and/or illustrate each point. Then comes the crucial question. Does the draft cover the subject and fit the purpose? If not, the speaker revises his draft.

Delivery

One object of speech delivery is to achieve a sense of direct communication with the audience. Both the speaker and the listener(s) must feel that they are in touch with each other. The speaker must believe in both the content and the need to communicate the same. This may not be a permanent conviction, but must be the conviction of the moment.

Variety in voice is one secret to effective delivery. The speaker may vary his loudness, pitch, and rate, but variations must be in harmony with meaning, emotional content, and emphasis. One effect of movement is that the audience tends to follow your body as you move across the platform. This effect can be used to gain attention or to aid in the transition from one point to the next. Too much movement becomes distracting while too little movement becomes boring for lack of change.

Gestures should appear natural, definite, and well-timed. They should never draw attention from the point they are emphasizing. Any gesture should be harmonious with the speaker's attitude, conviction, and topic.

Use of Notes

Through the use of notes in delivery, the speaker can remain flexible and responsive to the needs and attitude of his audience.

The use of notes allows the language and phrasing of the speech to remain flexible. The speaker is not restricted to reading a set speech. He can vary the support material collected during his earlier preparation to meet the needs of his audience. Notes used wisely have certain advantages; namely, to stimulate memory; to help with the reporting of complicated information; to help vary the support material to meet the needs of the audience; and, to ensure organizational accuracy during delivery.

DEVELOPING PERSONNEL POLICIES*

Personnel policies deserve particular attention if they are to achieve several important objectives. By thoughtful development and communication such policies can:

- Insure to all employees an equitable level of treatment.
- Insure to the hospital the optimum level of cost efficiency in personnel decisions.
- Provide to managers and supervisors valuable supportive guidelines for management action.
- Insure employee confidence in the hospital, minimizing the potential for union organization.
- Insure that the hospital complies with governmental laws and regulations.

In terms of categories, there are several broad subjects that are generally defined as personnel policy.

1. *Salary Programs and Economic Benefits* involving direct payment to the employee or direct cost to the hospital (policies of salary grades and ranges, shift premium pay, vacation leave, benefits and life insurance).
2. *Noneconomic Benefits and Employee Services* including those whose cost to the hospital is not as visible (employee health services, credit unions, arrangements for tax-deferred annuities or preretirement counseling).
3. *Employee Relations Practices* encompassing hospital-wide work rules and employee rights (grievance and disciplinary procedures, meal and rest break provisions, attendance/absenteeism policies).
4. *Major Noneconomic Personnel Programs* which are both hospital and employee oriented (performance appraisal, the employee communications system, employee training and development, and the retirement policy).
5. *Management Oriented Personnel Policies and Procedures* involving control over personnel utilization or expense (centralized employment, authorizing new positions, employment of relatives) and; finally,
6. *Statements of Support and Compliance* with laws and regulations involving either the required or voluntary statement of policy in areas such as Equal Employment Opportunity, Affirmative Action, and the Employee Retirement Income Security Act disclosure provisions.

Approaches to Policy Development

Two premises have been accepted by many trustees and administrators.

First, many policies have become so complex that they require management specialists including personnel people, fiscal professionals and legal and actuarial consultants, to draft and advise on policy.

The second premise recognizes that a policy's success is as dependent on its acceptability as it is on its technical excellence. Personnel policies particularly have a very personal impact on employees whose response and support (or acquiescence) can significantly influence their long-range success.

Also important to the implementation of a new policy is its degree of acceptability to managers and supervisors. As the first-level interpreters and administrators of policy they influ-

---

*Source: Reprinted from *Health Care Labor Manual* by Martin E. Skoler, with permission of Aspen Systems Corporation, © 1981.

ence its success by their own degree of commitment. They are in a position to accurately gauge its strengths and weaknesses and potential for acceptance by employees. Both supervisors and employees should be sold a new policy. More important, both groups can contribute valuable suggestions for improving personnel policy.

Employee participation is probably the least utilized and most underestimated necessity. Though the opportunities for *formal* participation are limited if actual collective bargaining is to be avoided, contacts with employees should be continuous and ongoing. Small group meetings between employees and personnel professionals, *with and without* supervisors present, effectively indicate that the hospital is seriously interested in the employees' viewpoint on personnel policy.

Manager and supervisor participation in policy development should be more formalized and extensive. By establishing a standing Personnel Policy Advisory Committee of representative managers and supervisors, this group can be involved in several levels of policy development. By its continuing dialogue with the personnel director it provides a two-way conduit for information and ideas, a "sensing" device to anticipate needed change.

In its role in reviewing and advising on draft policies, it improves their overall quality and provides an indication of the reception they will receive if adopted.

Technical/Managerial participation in policy development usually focuses on the personnel director and his staff. As the "floor manager" as well as the staff professional he is responsible for the process from the original draft policy to the presentation of the recommendation for administrative approval. It is essential that operating managers at the associate/assistant director level be involved in the most appropriate way that the nature of the policy suggests. Ideally, this should be a one-on-one review with the personnel director. Although associates may not have formal responsibility for such policy, they are keystone to its effective implementation. Their support is essential to its success.

Finally, there is sometimes a need in policy development for *consultant participation*. The hospital must function within the law, and its policy commitments must be prudent. Though the trained personnel professional should be competent in legal and actuarial subjects, he should also be aware when outside support is needed.

The Personnel Policy Manual will be used principally by supervisors, managers, and administrators, including the personnel department staff, although it is designed for employees as well as employers. Thus, management should be expected to be fully acquainted with it. It should be the subject of management meetings, and everyone at management levels should be responsible for understanding it.

Additionally, employees should be aware of it and it should be available to them. All new policies should be posted on bulletin boards and distributed to all new employees at their orientation.

Employees usually receive a *Hospital Employee Handbook* for their own use.

Strategy of Policy Communication

The strategy of introducing new policy includes not only critical timing but also a selection of media based on the size and nature of the audience. Though they will usually be of interest to all supervisors, some policies may interest only a select involved employee group (*e.g.*, management employee salary administration or authorization of new positions). Some will be important to employees' families (*e.g.*, salary and economic benefits), whereas other policies will be of interest principally to employees only (*e.g.*, meals breaks).

Communication to management should precede other publicity and be as comprehensive as possible. Senior associates should receive copies of new policies prior to others and at that time comment or question the director of personnel. A management meeting (with supervisors) should also precede a general announcement at which time a descriptive presentation should be made. Policies and policy summaries should be distributed together with the communication that will be sent to employees. This meeting should precede notice to employees by a day or two to enable managers to resolve any questions they may have.

If it is a major policy change, managers and supervisors should be requested to discuss it with employees in a group setting directly after the employee notification. On major policy matters the administrator should initially notify the employees. For minor policies the personnel director re-enforced by managers informs the employees. The initial contact may take the form of an internal letter, letter in the employee house organ, or a letter to the home if the subject matter is appropriate. An alternative approach for lesser matters is to provide an enclosure to the pay envelope.

In addition, bulletin boards should carry a copy of the new policy and all communication should include two or more telephone numbers to call for further information. These telephones, in the personnel department, should be staffed for a period to accommodate evening and night shift employees.

The above sequence will, of course, vary with the circumstances and the magnitude of the policy involved. It is, however, important to consider these as basic components in most situations: notification to management on a personalized basis followed by employee notification by both administrators and supervisors.

Chapter 28—Recruitment, Interviewing, and Orientation

RECRUITMENT

Sources*

Hospitals often form recruitment committees for the purpose of establishing recruitment policies and procedures and developing an action program to recruit qualified nursing staff.

Among the sources and techniques used for recruitment are: public employment agencies, private employment agencies, advertising in newspapers, professional journals, and magazines. Schools and colleges can be informed of job opportunities. The American Nurses' Association Professional Credentials and Placement Service supplies nationwide personnel services. State professional counseling and placement service offices, while offering nationwide services, tend to encourage filling of vacancies in their respective states.

Management consulting firms or executive recruiters are best used for top positions in administration or management only. Also of growing importance are the annual conferences or meetings of professional associations, where you or your representative can meet job-seeking members of the association and discuss job opportunities. And, of course, there is internal recruitment. Vacant positions can be posted on bulletin boards or announced at departmental meetings and employees who feel qualified can be invited to apply. If the hospital has an official publication, it too could be used to announce job openings.

Executive Recruiters*

From the administrator's point of view, when it comes to filling management-level positions, the traditional employment agency is often felt to be inadequate and inept, neglecting to screen applicants or verify qualifications and references. The applicant too may be in distress when inappropriately matched with an organization that doesn't meet personal requirements—or presented with a fat fee.

This gap of dissatisfaction has given rise to the executive search firm or the executive recruiter. The executive recruiter provides a specialized pool of talent and an awareness of market needs. He emphasizes validation of references, accurate candidate assessment and confidentiality for all parties.

Confidentiality plays an important role for the executive researcher works for the hiring organization, literally searching out appropriate managerial candidates who are employed happily—or unhappily—elsewhere. The solicited candidate may be flattered or enticed by new possibilities where none existed before and may wish to explore them without jeopardizing her existing position. Confidentiality is welcomed. So too, the client organization doesn't wish to publicly broadcast this bit of executive "stealing."

---

*Source: Reprinted from *The Nursing Administration Handbook* by Howard S. Rowland and Beatrice L. Rowland, eds., with permission of Aspen Systems Corporation, © 1980.

Before the executive searcher starts approaching qualified managers, he spends considerable time in consultation with the client organization. (After all, the hiring organization assumes total responsibility for the search firm's fee, paid on a retainer or per diem arrangement.) Meetings are set up with top and middle level executives, future peers and subordinates in order to ascertain the exact demands and specifications required in the available position by the client organization. Once this picture is developed, the executive recruiter depends on a resource file and personal contact to ferret out potential candidates who are then thoroughly interviewed and investigated before presentation to the client.

Since much effort is expended in the search process, the executive search firm deals with higher levels of management. In nursing this would include directors and assistant directors in charge of the nursing service or patient care.

One last comment for nurse executives who may eventually wish to change in work environment. Though executive recruiters do not locate employment for individual job-seekers, they do require pools of manpower resources to meet client demand. Unsolicited resumes form a valuable file of potential candidates for future recruitment.

The Search Committee*

The search committee is becoming a popular ritual in virtually all but the smallest organizations. Usually, the search committee is put together for the purpose of filling a vacancy created by firing, resignation, or the development of a new position. The committee itself is not normally empowered to hire anyone, but rather is asked to recommend a person or several people to the next higher level where the decision will be made. Thus, the committee has the chore of recruiting and sifting but not the responsibility for the final decision. On the other hand, through its sifting process and recruitment strategy, it has a tremendous influence on the selection.

There is also a cynical interpretation of the function of search committees. They often buy time for management while it considers what to do about filling a position; they provide an image of a democratic process, which is certainly significant when an organization must comply with various government regulations on affirmative action; and a committee process assuages hostile constituencies. As with other committee structures, it also relieves managers of the responsibility for unpleasant decisions and gives them the clout to make the decisions they want to make.

However, if management is to utilize search committees effectively, then certain principles must be followed. First, the committee must have adequate staff support so that its recruiting strategy can be properly implemented. For example, the committee should be able to develop an advertisement for the *New York Times* health care opportunity section and not have to place the ad personally and sort through the couple of hundred replies likely to be engendered. Later on in the process, the committee should be able to have letters prepared asking for references. Finally, committee members should know that their recommendations will be given the most serious consideration; and, if rejected, they will be given adequate explanations.

Part of their brief as they begin deliberations should be an investigation into the job itself. Does the organization really need the position? As part of this investigation, the search committee should conduct an exit interview with the person leaving so that the committee members can understand the nature of the job better. In certain instances, particularly when the job to be filled is a senior one or a very sensitive one, the committee should have access to consultants outside of the organization in order to get a better understanding of the position.

Checklist for Recruitment Procedures*

1. Advertising: does it say what you want it to? Is it timely? Does it produce the response you need in relation to cost? Are the media used still drawing the applicants you need?
2. Are recruiting handouts and other materials current? Do they still sound bright and fresh?

---

*Source: Reprinted from *Health Care Management* by Seth B. Goldsmith, with permission of Aspen Systems Corporation, © 1981.

*Source: Reprinted from *Health Care Labor Manual* by Martin E. Skoler, with permission of Aspen Systems Corporation, © 1981.

3. Is your receptionist sensitive to the institution's recruiting objectives? Do all recruitment staff members know your posture regarding equal opportunity and affirmative action?
4. Are interviewers projecting the kind of image you want—neat appearance, clean offices, avoidance of personal telephone calls, friendly helpful manner to all, positive approach to problem solving?
5. Do interviewers use good judgment? Do they exercise care and not recommend applicants who are not qualified? Do they call just to make appointments for candidates to see department heads or do they follow-up and facilitate decision making? Do they check references carefully?
6. Do department heads trust your interviewers and have an understanding of their problems?
7. Is your employment staff considered both competent and discreet?

INTERVIEWING TECHNIQUES*

Ordinarily you can expect to look to the personnel department for locating a number of candidates who generally fit the requirements of a position; that is, the personnel staff find people who have the appropriate academic credentials and minimum required experience and who otherwise fit the hiring criteria you established. In most cases the personnel staff will screen applicants to locate generally qualified candidates and will arrange personal interviews for the administrator or supervisor.

Preparing for the Interview

Your first step in preparing for a selection interview should consist of careful review of the individual's employment application (or résumé, or both). You need the application in advance of the interview; do not allow yourself to be put in a position in which you must read the application for the first time while the applicant sits before you. Should this ever occur, do what you can to discourage the employment office from sending you applicants with applications in hand. You need at least a few minutes, and preferably longer, to familiarize yourself with information about the job applicant. Oherwise you may make the applicant uncomfortable by reading when you should be speaking or listening, or you may miss something important and ask questions that have already been answered on paper.

Have a definite plan in mind when you approach an interview. Know all you can about the job you are trying to fill, and back up this knowledge with a copy of the job description or at least with a fairly complete list of the duties of the job. Be especially aware of any unique aspects of the job or any unusual requirements the applicant should be made aware of, and be prepared to tell the applicant precisely where the job fits in the total operation of the institution.

It may also be useful to have a few sample questions prepared in advance of the interview. You are likely to discover that the most valuable questions emerge while you are in conversation with the applicant, but you may well need some starter questions to enable you to get the conversation going. Prepare yourself to guide the applicant and listen, never losing sight of your basic purpose: to learn as much as possible about the applicant.

Make sure the interview takes place in private and in relatively comfortable surroundings. Your ability to learn about the applicant is severely impaired by interruptions, and interruptions can be unsettling to the applicant.

Psychological Barriers at Interviews*

Unequal Power

The emotional state of each party in an interview is likely to be entirely different. The interviewer can afford to be relaxed and comfortable—perhaps even blasé. The interviewee cannot enter into this relationship in such a relaxed manner, however; it is far too important.

---

*Source: Except where noted this section on "Interviewing" consists of excerpts reprinted from *The Effective Health Care Supervisor* by Charles R. McConnell, with permission of Aspen Systems Corporation, © 1982.

*Source: Reprinted from "Psychological Barriers to Effective Employment Interviewing" by Richard G. Nehrbass, February 1977, with permission of *Personnel Journal,* Costa Mesa, California; all rights reserved.

Given this situation, it is perhaps even naive to expect that the typical applicant can be at ease during the interview. On the contrary, we should expect in many cases to see an applicant who is ill at ease, uncomfortable and nervous. This is certainly a very "natural" way to react to a stressful situation. If we convince ourselves that the seemingly comfortable, self-assured applicant is somehow "better" than the uncomfortable and nervous applicant we run the risk not only of basing our decision on largely superficial personality traits but also of potentially succumbing to the second psychological barrier: "phoney" behavior.

"Phoney" Behavior

Related to the power imbalance inherent in job interviews is what can best be termed "phoney" behavior. Phoney behavior is familiar to anyone who has done extensive job interviewing—the feeling that the applicant is attempting to project an "image," to convey an impression of being a certain type of person. To get a job, many applicants seem to feel, one must be perceived as sociable, highly intelligent, considerate, and so on. They love to "work with people," never have problems with superiors, and are universally liked; they are seeking a job with challenge, responsibility and an opportunity to prove themselves. The clichés runneth over.

Questions without Answers

The third psychological barrier to effective employment interviewing is the tendency of some interviewers to ask questions that do not really have answers. Some examples of such questions are: "Tell me something about yourself," "How would you describe yourself?" and "Where would you like to be 10 years from now?"

Given the power imbalance inherent in the situation and the emphasis on phoney behavior, there is little reason to believe that answers to these questions are completely honest anyway. This puts the interviewer in the position of providing a probably incorrect analysis of a dishonest answer from a tense and uncomfortable applicant.

Overcoming the Barriers

Awareness of these three barriers can aid an interviewer. Awareness, by itself, won't solve the problem but it can emphasize to the interviewer the need to create (to the extent possible) a psychologically safe and supportive atmosphere for the interview. The interviewer can show by behavior and active attention to the applicant that he/she considers the interview to be as important as the applicant does.

A short introductory statement to the effect that the organization is looking for the best person to fit the position, rather than any particular personality type, can also partially alleviate the applicant's felt need to project a certain image.

Perhaps, most importantly, the interviewer can ensure that the interview stresses facts and not opinions or feelings. Through his/her emphasis on questions that require the applicant to relate factual events from the past, the interviewer can steer the conversation away from projecting an image and towards reality.

A number of these factually-oriented questions exist and have been used by some interviewers for years. It is usually a good idea to pair a "positive" with a "negative" question to further reduce the uneasiness of the applicant. Some examples of such questions are: "There are always some things about our jobs we like and some we dislike. Tell me a couple of things about your last job that you particularly liked and a couple of things you particularly disliked." This question can also be asked about the applicant's previous superiors. Another such question is, "What were some of the things about your last job that you felt were particularly difficult to do? What were some of the things you did best?"

Questions To Ask

The questions you ask should be broad and in many instances open ended. Remember, you are interested in learning as much as you can about the applicant in a limited amount of time and the way to do this is to listen to the person talk. Try these in conversation with the applicant:

- What are your career goals? What would you like to be doing five or ten years from now? How would you like to spend the rest of your career?
- Who have been your prior employers, and why did you leave your previous positions?
- What did you like or dislike about the work in your previous positions?

- Who recommended you to our institution? How did you hear about this job opening?
- What is your educational background? What lines of study did you pursue? (Be careful, however, of attempting to delve into specifics as cautioned in the list of questions to avoid.)
- What do you believe are your strong points? What do you see as your weaknesses?
- Will you grant permission for us to check references with former employers?

The Actual Interview

Put the Applicant at Ease

At the beginning of the conversation you need to put the individual at ease and instill a degree of confidence. You might want to try several different topics at the start of the interview—for instance, the weather, the ease with which the person may have found your office, or an invitation to enjoy a cup of coffee—to get the person talking and take you a step toward conversational rapport. Whatever opener you employ—and usually it need be only brief—it will get you off to a far better start than the shock of something like: "Good morning. Why do you want to work here?"

During these first few critical minutes try to avoid making judgments and freezing a picture of the applicant in your mind. First impressions are often difficult to shed, and when formed while the person is not yet at ease they can be unfair.

Avoid Short-Answer Questions

Avoid asking questions in such a way that they can be answered in one or two words, and especially avoid questions that can be answered simply "yes" or "no." For instance, a question such as: "How long did you work for County General Hospital?" might simply be answered: "Three years." This gives you very little information. Rather, a request on the order of: "Please tell me about the work you did at County General Hospital," requires the person to use more than just a couple of words in response. Your purpose is to learn about the applicant, and you can do so only by getting the person to talk.

However, you should avoid permitting the applicant to wander off the subject for minutes at a time. When this occurs, interrupt (as politely as possible) with another question or a request for clarification intended to draw the conversation back to the focus of the interview.

Avoid Leading or "Loaded" Questions

Avoid questions that lead the applicant toward some predetermined response. For instance, if you ask: "You left County General because the pay raises weren't coming along, is that right?", you are channeling the applicant toward a response that you may have already decided is correct. It is far better to ask, "Why did you leave County General?"

Leading questions can be a particular hazard when you are talking with someone who is shaping up favorably in your eyes. In the process of unconsciously deciding you like this person, you may begin to bend the rest of your questions in a fashion that calls for the answers you would like to hear. Most people are sensitive to leading questions and, depending on the nature of the questions, will feel either forced or encouraged to deliver the answers that seem to be wanted.

Ask One Question at a Time

Avoid hitting the applicant with something like: "What kind of work did you do there and why did you leave?" This is in fact two questions, and although they may well be properly asked one after the other the person should be given the opportunity to deal with them individually. Combining or pyramiding questions tends to throw some people off balance; a person prepared to deal with a single question is suddenly confronted with two or three at once. It is always preferable to limit your questioning to one clear, concise question at a time.

Keep Your Writing to a Minimum

Try not to take voluminous notes while the prospective employee is talking. This can be disconcerting to the individual, creating the impression that everything that is said is being taken down in writing. Also, it is distracting to you. Writing and listening are both communication skills subject to their own particular ground rules and neither can be done with maximum effectiveness if you are trying to do the other at the same time. The more note-taking you attempt, the more it detracts from your listening capacity. Take down a few key words if you must, but focus most of your attention on listening to the applicant. If you need or desire a written report of the interview, generate this report immediately after the applicant leaves and the conversation is still fresh in your mind.

Use Appropriate Language

At all times deliver your questions and comments in language appropriate to the apparent level of education, knowledge, and understanding of the prospective employee.

Always assume a reasonable degree of intelligence—you wish to avoid "talking down" to the person—but do not dazzle or confuse the applicant with unfamiliar terminology.

Do More Listening Than Talking

Throughout the interview be interested and attentive, never impatient or critical. Avoid talking too much about yourself or the institution. Remember, you are not selling yourself to the applicant—it is supposed to be the other way around. Also, you are not necessarily selling the institution to the applicant, although if the interview moves far enough in constructive directions you may wish to answer the applicant's questions about the institution. However, even on this score there are precautions to note: specifics of certain features of employment like insurance, retirement, and other benefits for which you may not have all the details should be left to the personnel department and broached only when you have extended an offer of employment and the individual needs this information to aid in making the decision.

Indicate Some Type of Follow-up

Conclude the interview with a reasonable statement of what the applicant may expect to happen next. It is true you generally cannot (and probably should not) make a definite statement at this time, but you should suggest what may be expected and when it might occur. For instance, you can always say something like: "We'll let you know our decision after we've finished all scheduled interviews, say within a week or 10 days," or, "You should be getting a letter from us next week," or simply "We'll call you by Friday." In any case, conclude the interview with some simple indication of impending follow-up. Never let the applicant go away with the feeling of "Don't call us—we'll call you."

Follow-Up

Follow-up is no problem when you decide to extend a job offer to an applicant—you will extend the offer and the person will either accept or decline the job. In either case the interview process has been taken full cycle.

However, even in instances when you do not wish to extend a job offer you should nevertheless follow-up and complete the interview cycle. Follow-up by the institution is a simple but deserved courtesy; although the applicant was looking for a job, you were also looking for an employee, and this particular individual traveled to meet you and gave you a certain amount of time.

Appropriate follow-up takes very little time. Once you have decided you do not wish to extend a job offer, a short, polite letter to that effect is appropriate. Also, you can use this same approach to let individuals know that although you cannot extend a job offer at the present time you would like to keep their applications on file for future consideration. In any case, and even for the most clearly unqualified of applicants, you should conclude the interview process with an answer. It is a courtesy due the applicant, and it serves to protect the image of the institution as an employer in the community.

ORIENTATION*

A sound orientation is the institution's best opportunity to insure a positive employee relations climate while developing productive and knowledgeable workers. The new employee should be accurately informed about the hospital's policies and the programs that affect him and his individual status there. He should be properly introduced to his duties and to the assignments of others. Finally, the hospital should insure a good first impression. It must show its concern with the quality of services provided and indi-

---

*Source: Reprinted from *Health Care Labor Manual* by Martin E. Skoler, with permission of Aspen Systems Corporation, © 1981.

cate that the hospital will be demanding of him, yet at the same time be demanding *for* him in such matters as salaries, benefits and fair treatment and will encourage him to grow in his work.

The First Orientation

Orientation is of great importance once a person has been hired, yet it begins while he is still a candidate for employment. As a candidate, he should receive the courtesies of a visitor. A member of the personnel department should coordinate appointments and make certain that the applicant is escorted and properly introduced to his interviewers. The personnel officer should insure that the candidate has a clear understanding of what the job is and is not, together with information on supervisory relationships, promotional opportunities, and salary potential. This is important so as to avoid an employee being surprised at the conditions of the job. Such misunderstandings can seriously impair a working relationship and injure an otherwise well-conceived employee relations program.

When a job offer has been made and accepted, the new employee should be referred back to the personnel department to review and confirm conditions of employment. These include the agreed starting salary and salary review dates, major benefits for which the employee is eligible, his starting date and time, the location and the person to whom he should report, working hours, and workdays. To avoid broken promises, whether real or imagined, that can impair future relationships, all such information should be in writing with copies to the department head and for the employee's file. Finally, employee handbooks and written information on benefits should be given to the new employee at this time. This will allow the new employee to learn about the hospital even before he begins working.

Orientation to the Department

The orientation to the department varies with the specific nature of the work environment but usually includes an introduction to five general areas:

1. the *role and function* of the department;
2. its *organization,* including various supervisors; fellow employees and a brief look at their functions;
3. *departmental policies,* rules and procedures;
4. the *various facilities* in and around the department;
5. the *general job functions* the new employee will be performing.

To properly introduce the new employee to this often bewildering information, the department head should meet with him immediately upon arrival. A supervisor or senior employee should be responsible for completing the orientation and should be available to answer questions.

The new employee should be introduced to fellow employees and their functions and should be informed of such things as hours of work, workdays, meal and rest breaks, time-clock and payroll procedures, calling-in requirements when absent, accident reporting procedures, and other department rules. It is imperative that each new piece of information support rather than contradict what the employee may have already been told during the hiring process.

He should also be made familiar with the location of various facilities. The employee will be more effective when he has learned where he must go for personal or job needs.

Orientation to the Hospital

The hospital-wide orientation is designed to familiarize a new employee with hospital goals, history and development, organization and facilities, and with the policies, programs and benefits that affect the employee. It should also introduce him to the administrator, to the personnel department staff and to others in leadership positions. Orientation is also designed to reflect the employee relations posture of the hospital. It should set the tone for future relationships with employees as useful and respected members of the health care team.

The design and management of this program will usually be the responsibility of the personnel director, in cooperation with the administrator and senior operating management. They will, in fact, be integrating the hospital-wide program with their own department orientation activities.

A model for this orientation program provides for a 75 to 90 minute meeting followed by a 30 to 40 minute tour of major areas of the hospital, with emphasis on areas an employee may not see in the course of his work.

This orientation should be scheduled on the least busy day of the week. Groups of new employees should be invited within two weeks of their first day of work. Departments should be advised that the release of employees for the full two hours is required. Success of the program will depend on its regularity, on the priority it is given by departments, and, of course, on the quality of the presentation.

The program itself should include the following subjects:

- Introduction of the program and participants;
- A welcome by the administrator;
- A review of hospital roles, objectives, history, and development;
- A pictorial tour of the hospital (slide or movie presentation);
- A discussion in summary form of:
  - Hospital-wide policies and procedures (flip chart presentation);
  - Fire prevention and safety rules (fire extinguisher and alarm procedure demonstration);
  - Employee relations policies and programs (flip chart presentation);
  - Employee benefits, services, and activities (slide presentation);
- A general question and answer period and review of previous handouts (employee handbook, benefit booklets, etc.);
- A tour of major hospital areas.

The tenor of this meeting should be relaxed with an informal seating arrangement and refreshments (at least coffee). It should radiate a concern for each employee and suggest that there are many who wish to help him succeed.

Participants in the meeting should include the administrator (or his assistant if his schedule will allow more regular attendance), the director of personnel, and his specialists who are responsible for salary and benefits administration. The group should be welcomed by the administrator who then discusses the hospital generally, its activities, the services it provides, its place in the community, its growth and development, trends that will have an impact on it, and the employees' roles in achieving the hospital's goals.

The staff of the personnel department should be responsible for the other topics with each member discussing his specialty (*e.g.,* salary administrator on salary administration, payroll, premiums). The personnel director will host the program and be responsible for presentations on policies, rules, and procedures.

The use of several participants is an important factor in the program's success. A variety of voices keeps the group alert and this method also introduces employees to those people they may approach for assistance.

Visual aids and handouts are other ways of stimulating interest in the program. Films, film strips, tapes, and slide presentations have been used effectively to insure consistency in the presentation and to provide a professional program. A less professional but more personal approach can be achieved with artistically designed color slides, overhead transparencies, or flip charts narrated by a person using outline notes. In any event, it is important to keep up with changes in policies and benefits.

The tour of the hospital will be a particularly memorable part of the program for many, particularly for those in nonclinical jobs, who will rarely have another opportunity to see areas such as the radiology department, laboratories, operating rooms and other patient-related facilities. This will be especially effective if a representative from each major area can be introduced and discuss the operation of his department.

Hospital-wide orientation completes an employee's introduction to his new employer. However, if the program has succeeded it will not end at this point. There should be a follow-up contact by the employing personnel officer in the first few weeks of work to reinforce the relationship developed during the hiring process. The new employee's supervisor will also be involved in follow-up in the course of job instruction training.

Chapter 29—Troubled and Troublesome Employees

TROUBLED EMPLOYEES

Alcoholism, drug abuse, emotional illness, and family crisis are employees' personal problems that spill over into the environment of the health care organization and ultimately affect the individuals' job performance. A personal crisis situation involving marital, family, financial, or legal troubles is considered the most prevalent problem among all employee groups.

How To Help*

There is a way of approaching troubled employees who may be in need of help through early diagnosis and intervention.

What may be most important is that the managers are aware of available resources and can encourage the employees to make an appointment. It is advisable for managers to follow up with the identified employees to ensure that they are obtaining the help needed. Organizations should make available for their managers lists of referrals and alternatives needed in dealing with problem employees.

If employees do not want this help, it should be made clear that their continued employment will depend on effective performance and the elimination of the problem, which is affecting the workers, the managers and the organization milieu.

*Source: Reprinted from *Stress Management for Health Care Professionals* by Steven H. Appelbaum, with permission of Aspen Systems Corporation, © 1980.

Adopting the Proper Manner*

Employees with personal problems—those that people cannot help but bring to work with them—are rarely able to do their best work. An administrator should be interested in the employee as a whole person, but the employee's private life and personal problems are none of your business; they represent an area you cannot enter without specific invitation.

In dealing with the apparently troubled employee, do not prod and do not push. Make yourself available to the employee, and make known your willingness to listen. You may have to go as far as to provide the time, the place, and the opportunity for the employee to talk with you, without specifically asking the employee to "open-up." Quite often, if your openness is evident the troubled employee will turn to you.

In relating to the troubled employee:

- *Listen*—but be aware at all times of the temptation to give advice. Some of the most useless statements you can make begin with, "If I were you. . . ." Also, although many troubled employees could use advice, it is usually advice that you are unqualified to deliver. The best you can do under most circumstances is gently to suggest that the employee seek help from qualified professionals.

*Source: Reprinted from *The Effective Health Care Supervisor* by Charles R. McConnell, with permission of Aspen Systems Corporation, © 1982.

- *Be patient*—and show your concern for the employee as an individual. Although you should naturally be concerned with an individual's impairment as a productive employee, do not parade this before the troubled person. Rather, be patient and understanding. Perhaps, when possible, you can even be patient to the extent of easing off on tight deadlines and extra work requirements until the person is able to work through a problem.
- *Do not argue*—and do not criticize an employee for holding certain feelings or reflecting certain attitudes. Avoid passing judgment on the employee based on what you are seeing and hearing.
- *Be discreet*—let nothing a troubled employee tells you go beyond you. Be extra cautious if an employee tends toward opening up to the extent of revealing much that is extremely personal and private. While it often does good for someone to be able to simply talk to someone else about a problem, a person often runs the risk of saying too much and might afterward feel extremely uncomfortable about having done so. If you can, try to demonstrate that you sympathize and understand without allowing the employee to go too far. Always provide assurance that what you have heard in such an exchange is safe with you.
- *Reassure*—when you are honestly able to do so, provide the employee with reasonable assurance of things of importance such as the security of the employee's job, the absence of undue pressure while problems get worked out, and the presence of a friendly and sympathetic ear when needed. You need not even know the nature of the employee's outside problem to supply very real assistance by reducing the job-related pressures on the individual.

In dealing with the troubled employee in general, listen honestly and sympathetically and do what can be done to reduce pressure on the employee but leave the giving of specific advice related to the problem to persons qualified to deal with such matters.

Alcoholism Programs

Early identification and referral of alcoholics is important because the prognosis for successful treatment becomes less favorable toward the latter stages of the disease. However, early identification often is delayed because employees are able to conceal the problem or perhaps supervisors do not want to become involved. In other cases, the supervisors may be drinking with the individuals and do not wish to expose their own personal problems. Rather than looking for a drug or alcohol problem, it is suggested that managers be concerned with identifying employees who are not performing.

Some of the symptoms of alcoholism are absenteeism, tardiness, increase in physical symptoms, irritability, changes in motor activity, smell of alcohol on breath, repeated arrests for drunk driving, excuses for absence, and a decrease in job performance.

*Approaches**

Several important approaches that organizations should use in developing counselling policies and programs for employees with problems include:

- Policy statements or written suggestions and lists of outside referral sources are the most common techniques for helping supervisors deal with troubled employees. Training sessions to assist supervisors are conducted in approximately one-fourth of the organizations responding, somewhat more frequently for alcoholism than for drug abuse, emotional illness, or personal problems.
- Supervisory consultation and referral to an outside agency is the most common approach and nearly half of the organizations noted that this action was recorded on the employees' personnel records.
- Some type of in-house counselling, usually informal, is provided by nearly half the organizations that respond to employees' problems involving alcoholism, emotional illness, or personal crisis.
- Less than half of the respondents developed any type of organizational program to alert employees to problems associated

---

*Source: Reprinted from *Counseling policies and programs for employees with problems* by American Society of Personnel Administrators–Bureau of National Affairs, with permission of the Bureau of National Affairs, © 1978.

with alcohol. Educational programs focusing on drug abuse and emotional or family problems were even more uncommon.
- The overwhelming majority of companies rated the effectiveness of their current programs or methods for dealing with troubled employees as only fair or poor.

PROBLEM EMPLOYEES

Guidelines for Dealing with Problem Employees*

1. Listen. Make it clear that you are always available to hear what is bothering your employees. Display an open attitude, conscientiously avoiding the tendency to shut out possible unpleasantries because you "don't want to hear them." Many employees' doubts, fears, and complaints are created or magnified by a closed attitude on the part of the supervisor, so your obvious willingness to listen will go a long way toward putting some troubles to rest.
2. Always be patient, fair, and consistent, but retain sufficient latitude in your behavior to allow for individual differences among people. Use the rules of the organization as they were intended, stressing corrective aspects rather than punishment. Apply disciplinary action when truly deserved, but do not use the threat of such action to attempt to force change by employees.
3. Recognize and respect individual feelings. Further, recognize that a feeling as such is neither right or wrong—it is simply there. What a person *does* with a feeling may be right or wrong, but the feeling itself cannot be helped. Do not ever say, "You shouldn't feel that way." Respect people's feelings, and restrict your supervisory interest to what each employee does with those feelings.
4. Avoid arguments. Problem employees are frequently ready and willing to argue in defense of their feelings or beliefs. However, by arguing with an employee you simply solidify that person in a defensive position and reduce the chances of effective communication of any kind.
5. If possible, let your supposedly stubborn or resistant employees try something their own way. As a supervisor you are interested first in results and only secondarily in how those results are achieved (as long as they are achieved by reasonable methods). There is no better way to clear the air with the employee who "knows better" than to provide the flexibility for that person to try it that way and either succeed or fail. In other words, the employee who appears stubborn or resistant may not be so by nature but may rather be reacting to authoritarian leadership. More participative leadership might be the answer.
6. Pay special attention to the chronic complainers, those employees who seem to grouch and grumble all through the day and spread their gloom and doom to anyone who will listen. Chronic complaining is, of course, a sign of several potential problems and also breeds new problems of its own. The chronic complainer can affect departmental morale and drag down the entire work group. You should make every effort to find out what is behind the complaining, and perhaps even consider altering assignments such that a complainer is semi-isolated or at least limited in the opportunity to spread complaints.
7. Give each employee some special attention. The supervisor-employee relationship remains at the heart of the supervisor's job, and each employee deserves to be recognized as an individual as well as a producer of output. Honest recognition as individuals is all that some of our so-called problem employees really need to enable them to stop being problems.

Types of Problem Employees*

Here are some of the more common types of problem workers and some ways in which you might be able to turn the very thing that makes them hard to get along with into productive assets.

---

*Source: Reprinted from *The Effective Health Care Supervisor* by Charles R. McConnell, with permission of Aspen Systems Corporation, © 1982.

*Source: Reprinted from *The NFI Standard Manual for Supervisors* with permission of the Bureau of Business Practice, © 1977.

Some of the problem types may have traits that can't be converted to positive action. There is the fellow who believes that odd behavior or nonconformist dress is merely a way to assert his independence, and he thinks that being a "character" somehow makes him superior. Your best bet is to show him that his striving to be different is actually a hindrance to advancement. It's doubtful if punishment will bring any improvement, so you'll have to depend on your power of persuasion. Probably the worst thing you can do is ridicule or make an example of a nonconformist employee.

If you are unable to correct a problem worker through persuasion or other nondisciplinary tactics, it may be necessary to apply some kind of penalty. It is usually best to do it in a gradual manner.

1. The Nit-Picker

This is the fellow who's always finding fault. He tells you what's wrong with the job, he criticizes policy and he tells others how to do their jobs . . . making him a potential source of trouble. If you can give him a job that is particularly painstaking, he might meet the challenge and have too much to do to get into other people's hair. This type also frequently makes a first-class inspector.

2. The Mule

One of the more common problems is the fellow who is unreasonably stubborn. Caution: Don't let him make you bullheaded in return. Give him a chance to tell his side of the story and let him prove its validity. If you have a dispute over how to do a job, for instance, let him do it both ways, his and yours. This will give you a direct comparison of the results. If there is little difference in the outcome or in the time expended, try to let him do it his way. Of course, if there is an important difference favoring your instructions, you have to insist that he follow them. And once you let him prove it to himself, even the most stubborn man will cooperate.

3. The Know-It-All

Tone down the worker who knows so much you can't tell him a thing. One way is to give him enough rope so he gets all tangled up, then you can quietly demonstrate—in private—just how far off the track he really is. If he is bright, this fellow could make a good instructor or assistant supervisor, once you have brought him into line.

4. The Cross-Examiner

The person who asks too many questions can also give you problems. It's hard to know when people are asking questions to better understand the job (which they should do) or whether they are just trying to be annoying or pass a buck. If you suspect that a worker is just asking questions to give you a bad time or because he's the curious sort who wants to know the inside of things even when they are of no direct concern, try to find a way to get some good from this inquisitiveness. You may be able to fill a job that requires research or digging for facts.

5. The Chatterer

A common problem worker is the yacker—the guy who talks on and on about little or nothing to anyone he can corner. He's a real bottleneck because while he's chatting neither he nor his audience is producing. You might be able to turn this readiness to converse into constructive channels by having him give instructions or handle other jobs requiring considerable talking. If nothing like this is available, the solution might be to load him down with work and put him on deadlines so that he just doesn't have time to chat.

6. The Wise Guy

This type of employee is often quite competent. But you will find some who use a rather officious, know-it-all attitude to cover up lack of ability, aptitude, or training. The wise guy usually tends to argue at the drop of a hat, has a quick comeback for everything that's said, often disrupts meetings by getting off the beam and trying to stay off the beam. Usually he talks well, expresses himself well. In this fact alone, he has certain qualities that can sometimes be used in developing a really good member of your department and company.

Frequently he's likable. Sometimes, however, he tends to be sarcastic and antagonizes other people in the department. He can help a supervisor build competitive spirit and enthusiasm, though he may decide to buck some well-laid plan, and succeed in confusing others in the group. How can a supervisor hope to make a good all-around employee, and possibly develop supervisory material, from this wise-guy type? Here are some suggestions:

- Keep him on his toes
- Avoid arguments
- Be firm
- Give him more responsibility
- Expect more
- Let him hang himself now and then
- Try to bring out the best of his good qualities

7. The Chronic Grouch

Sometimes the chronic grouch is mad at the world. More often he's simply mad at himself. Keep this in mind when you try to find the reasons for his being grouchy to his associates and to you. Get to know him well; talk to him. Probably the most obvious place to start in finding out about a man of this type is in his relations in the company:

What is his record? Does it show steady progress or a series of ups and downs and failures? Is he able to keep up with other people? Or does he lack ability and aptitudes that others in the group usually have? Is his surliness confined to you and the immediate members of your group? Or is it evident he has this attitude toward everyone? Did something occur in his relation to the company that causes him to feel he has been treated unfairly?

It's also a good idea to find out about his life outside the plant. Is he happy with his family? Does he associate with other people, and join with them in hobbies or sports? Is he living beyond his means? Is his family extravagant, causing him to have financial worries? It takes patience and investigation to determine the underlying cause of a grouchy person's attitude. But if you intend to keep him on the job, you must find the reason before he lowers morale in the department.

Two of the most important things you can do for a person of this type are to keep him occupied and help him succeed. If he has enough work to do and knows how to do it, he's less likely to think about his misfortunes, real or imaginary injustices that have been done to him, and troubles that do not exist.

Help him to achieve things; show friendly interest in his development. If you handle this diplomatically, you very likely will be able to change his viewpoint.

8. The Complainer

The chronic grouch may do a lot of complaining. Here, however, we're thinking of the person who, though not necessarily grouchy, is antagonistic toward you, the company, his associates, or things in general. He may be one who is naturally pessimistic. He may be looking for trouble and if no trouble exists, he may imagine it. The complainer can be very irritating to you and to your subordinates. Often his complaints breed dissatisfaction among other workers and lead to general discontent.

The complainer is frequently an introvert. He thinks about himself too much and is overly conscious of any little aches or pains he may have. He's particularly sensitive to attitudes and remarks by other people. Often he feels he is being persecuted. About the only way to overcome this attitude is to direct his interest into other things. Get him interested in his work and, if possible, in study, a special training course or outside activities and hobbies.

Sometimes it's possible to "kid" the complainer out of his antagonistic attitude. If you can carry his complaint through to a ridiculous or absurd conclusion, his latent sense of humor may come to the surface and help him overcome the trouble himself. *Note:* Make sure you don't offend his dignity, or cause him to feel he is a subject of ridicule. Otherwise he might be worse off than before.

If a man complains about something that doesn't exist, give him something to really worry about. Present a problem that your group faces, and assign to him the job of working out the answer. This may not only produce valuable results but also may show that the man is a valuable member of your department. And, increased pride in his work will take the place of complaints.

9. The Meddlesome Do-Gooder

Here's the fellow who goes around trying to improve things and helping people whether he's needed or not. He's the reformer. Often he's so busy taking care of other people's troubles that he has little or no time for his own work. In handling this problem you'll have to be objective. The man may be so earnest that at times his suggestions will be offered with the best intentions.

One of the first things to do for a man of this type is to give him plenty of work to do. Insist that he complete it in the shortest possible time. In other words, keep him so busy that he has no time to interfere with other people. *Caution:* The "do-gooder" has a tendency to spend as much time as possible with his boss, and so may give other employees the impression that he's a favorite. This must be avoided. Any appearance of favoritism toward a person who is generally unpopular will breed dissension and distrust.

10. The Weakling

Now and then there are employees who have real aptitude and ability. Yet they're unable to do a really good job due to lack of self-confidence, fearful personality, or a combination of physical weakness and emotional instability. Usually they depend upon others for detailed instructions. They hesitate to take the initiative, are sensitive to ridicule or criticism, and may be quite shy. Often a person is like this only because he has not come under the proper influence of supervisors who understand him and can help him gain self-confidence.

Let's assume a man wants to do a good job and can do it, but is kept back through his own fear and mistrust of himself. What can you do? Your first step is to keep him on jobs that he can do at least fairly well, and which he has shown he can do to his own satisfaction as well as yours. At the same time, avoid making other people in the group carry the load that should be his.

Whatever the assignment, make sure he carries it through to successful completion. That's how you can help him avoid a feeling of frustration. Every time he fails, he becomes weaker. By helping him realize that he can succeed, even if success is in small or simple jobs, you build his self-reliance. Eventually he may come to cooperate freely and willingly with others in your department.

11. The Noncooperator

We're not dealing here with the man who doesn't want to work, doesn't want to do a good job, or is insubordinate. In this case, the noncooperator is one who feels he's superior to his fellow workers and to his job; or is bashful and does not mix well with people; does not cooperate freely and willingly with others.

Try to team him up with men who are friendly and have natural ability in getting along with people. This may slowly help break down his noncooperative attitude, particularly if it is due to bashfulness or a feeling of not belonging to the group. You can help build team spirit in him by showing how he participates in successful achievements of the group. Be sure to include him in any praise of the group, or group discussions. If you can help him share in cooperative success, he may come to like it and be willing to cooperate without special attention.

Caution: Sometimes when a supervisor is aware of a noncooperative attitude, he begins to expect noncooperation. Guard against this attitude in yourself. Expect people to cooperate as the natural, normal attitude. When you assume that people want to cooperate, they are likely to do so as a matter of course. On the other hand, if you expect opposition, that is what you may possibly get.

12. The Nonconformist

This type of employee can always think of a different way of doing things. But his ways are based on the desire to do something differently rather than to do it better. Frequently this is simply an expression of a deep desire to stand out and be an individualist. To stand out is not necessarily a bad trait. But if it interferes with production, it can become annoying.

A nonconformist, when he comes into a new group, is sometimes encouraged because at first he gives the impression that he is "just full of good suggestions." Sometimes his desire to be different leads to personal idiosyncrasies and habits that irritate. When this occurs, something must be done.

In dealing with a nonconformist, you will want to avoid encouraging him in his efforts to be different from the group. But, at the same time, you will not want to discourage any ability he may have of creative and individual thinking that may be put to good use.

Assign him to jobs that he can do best. Be patient and fair with him. However, if you can put him on jobs that will represent a real challenge to him—and possibly present problems with which he's not too familiar and will, therefore, have to follow standard practice—you may be able to keep him in line. Sometimes you can bring him to understand that others can be right, also, and that their opinions are worth just as much as his.

It may be that you can find a place for him in which there is real opportunity for individual achievement. If he can make good on such a job, it's likely he will be highly successful and very valuable to both the company and to himself.

13. The Playboy

This fellow is a first cousin to the "wise guy." He manages to give the impression that he is not particularly interested in working; that he prefers to enjoy life and have a good time.

Sometimes, in spite of the surface attitude of people of this sort, they seem to manage to accomplish a great deal. At times they just don't feel it's necessary to "look busy" yet they manage to get work out right and on time. But regardless of whether they get their work out or not, they are often a disturbing influence for other employees. Sometimes they indulge in horseplay that can be dangerous. Usually, their absenteeism and tardiness is above average.

Frequently they are likable people who by their very pleasant manner make it difficult for a supervisor to "crack down." Nevertheless this is often necessary. What can the supervisor do about the playboy?

The first thing to do is to give him enough work so he just doesn't have time for foolishness. Attempts to keep him from exerting a bad influence on a department as a whole will be a problem. But, knowing that he probably will exert his influence one way or another, you may be able to turn his high spirits into useful channels.

He is probably enthusiastic and inclined to get along well with other people. This means he has certain qualities of leadership that you can put to good use. If you can get him sufficiently interested in important problems on which the group is working, he will help by spreading his enthusiasm to others.

Here's one hint that may at times come in handy. The playboy usually has a sense of humor, like the "wise guy." He probably enjoys confusing or irritating other people at times. If you let him confuse or even irritate you, you might feel he has the upper hand. Don't take him too seriously; don't let him "get under your skin."

As a rule, the playboy does not endanger group morale—unless he's really malicious in his attitude. He's more likely to be irritating to his supervisor than his fellow workers. Remember this in all your dealings with him and avoid being unfair or unreasonable. The man with this type of personality is naturally friendly. He likes to have the good esteem and respect of those around him. Very likely he wants your respect, too. If he can earn it and knows he earns it through good work and sincere accomplishment, you will gain a loyal and helpful friend.

14. The Busybody

He is what might be termed a professional meddler. He thinks he knows everything—and he's almost always wrong.

The supervisor may depend on this fellow to put him on the griddle from time to time, demanding that he face up to something Busybody feels needs facing up to.

The supervisor should get him alone in a corner somewhere, then ask him to be specific about his accusation. But he should not act like a prosecuting attorney dealing with a hostile witness. The idea is not to *prove* the meddler wrong, but to help him see *why* he's wrong—and how these whispered charges hurt the department, and himself. Until the supervisor can get *him* to see this, he's not going to stop his meddling.

15. The "Blameless" One

Whenever something goes wrong, and there is the slightest chance that this worker will be blamed, he just wasn't there.

Of course, the supervisor may *know* he was there—but just try to prove it. The employee is a veteran at this kind of infighting. Attempt to pin him down, and he'll insist in an aggrieved tone: "I wasn't within a mile of the place."

The most disturbing aspect of his buck passing, however, is that it is contagious. Moreover, it tends to demoralize the other workers—for he hints, but never quite accuses *them* of making the mistake.

The supervisor should take pains to spell out the exact scope of this worker's duties. Then make it clear he is responsible for anything that goes wrong within that area; if the "blameless" one wasn't there—or says he wasn't—he still will be responsible.

16. The Indifferent Man

Although he never breaks a rule or causes trouble overtly, this type makes it clear he is completely indifferent to his job and the department.

He does only what is required, rejects all efforts to arouse his enthusiasm, and passively resists change. In short, this man is just not "with" it.

The supervisor must keep probing until he discovers something that really interests the worker. There has to be *something* he likes. Once he discovers what it is he should display an interest in it; ask questions; offer opinions.

As the supervisor gets closer to this indifferent man, he should try to induce him to see his point of view about the department. At some point in this process, the supervisor should place him in a group of highly motivated workers. After a while, he will begin to understand why they are enthusiastic and willing. Their job interest should prove contagious.

17. The "Lawyer"

This employee is a legal "expert," a so-called curbstone lawyer who relishes putting it "right on the line" for the supervisor—and he's no joy to have around.

"According to the contract," he is forever reminding the supervisor in a dogmatic tone, "you can't make us do this. If you do . . . etc."

He is his own lawyer and, in his own eyes, the departmental defender of right. He is frequently wrong, of course, but on the other hand manages to arouse so much suspicion and confusion among the men that the supervisor can't afford to ignore him.

The first rule is for the supervisor to be absolutely sure of his ground before going into "court" with this worker. If he isn't he should simply say that he will look it up and give his answer later.

If the supervisor knows the worker is in error, he must be tactful when he puts him down. He should quote chapter and verse from the contract; and, whenever possible, cite a few actual cases involving the same question. But no innuendos on the "lawyer's" knowledge; no signs of hostility about his raising the point.

His obstructionist attitude may be a subconscious bid for recognition. He may be bitter because he feels his job is beneath his abilities, or because he feels no one appreciates his work. The supervisor should call on him for opinions from time to time. He should try giving him more opportunity to exercise judgment and make decisions.

More Nuisances

- *The self-centered, insecure fellow* who demands praise and preference. He goes out of his way to be sure that he gets "everything to which I'm entitled." He's afraid someone might be getting preferred treatment. More often than not he feels unappreciated. He stirs up trouble by working in spurts that make normal achievement appear piddling. Other employees resent his efforts to "show them up."

   The supervisor can build his confidence by making him realize he can do a good job without showing off. He should tell him he wants good, steady performance, and voice appreciation when the worker delivers.

- *The noisy, boastful type* who has to dominate the scene. Beneath his brash facade, he feels inadequate. He is resentful and complains about discrimination whenever he is not accorded preferential treatment. He wants better assignments, lavish praise, overnight promotions.

   The supervisor should treat this man fairly, but make sure he earns everything he gets—and let his co-workers handle his loudness and complaints. He may not last long; if he does, it's because he has good qualities which were there all along.

- A more subtle type—and difficult to spot— is *the man with superior ability* and leadership potential. Because the job fails to offer him the proper challenge, he's apt to try going his own way—looking for holes in operation sheets and bypassing procedures in favor of his own work methods. His way may be as good as, or sometimes even better than, the prescribed procedures, but his example is a bad one for group morale.

   Once the supervisor has pinned this man down, he can put his ability to work by assigning him to the more challenging jobs, and by calling on him for suggestions.

- *The "morning glory."* At first, this fellow is a bundle of enthusiasm and energy as he tries to make a reputation as a genius. By the end of the third day, however, he's sick of the job and grumbling about how far beneath his talents it is. The supervisor should not waste any time with this type. He'll probably quit before the end of the month; if he doesn't the supervisor should try to get rid of him. He's a chronic nonperformer and troublemaker. Nobody wants his type around.

DEAD-END EMPLOYEES*

The dead-end employee is that employee who can go no further in the organization. Promotion to supervision may not be possible because basic qualifications are lacking; promotion into a higher level is not possible because the employee is already at the top of grade; pay raises are infrequent because the employee has reached the top of the scale and can move only when the scale itself is moved. In short, the dead-end employee is blocked from growth and advancement in all channels. This employee is a special problem in motivation because there are no more material rewards left with which to prevent creeping dissatisfaction from setting in and other rewards, the true motivators that should be inherent in the job, are limited.

It is unfortunate that many dead-end employees become problems because these employees very often have the most to offer to the organization. It falls to the supervisor to deal with the problem by appealing to the individual through true motivating forces that stress job factors rather than environmental factors.

In dealing with the dead-end employee:

- *Consult* the employee on various problems and aspects of the department's work. Ask for advice. It is possible that an employee with years of experience in the same capacity has a great deal to offer and will react favorably to the opportunity to offer it.
- Give the employee a bit of additional *responsibility* when possible, and let the person earn the opportunity to be more responsible. Some freedom and flexibility may be seen as recognition of a sort for the employee's past experience and contributions.
- *Delegate* special one-time assignments. Again, years of experience may have prepared the employee to handle special jobs above and beyond ordinary assignments.
- Use the dead-end employee as a *teacher*. The experienced employee may be quite valuable in one-on-one situations, helping to orient new employees or teaching present employees new and different tasks.
- Point the dead-end employee toward certain *prestige* assignments such as committee assignments, attendance at an occasional seminar or educational program, or the coordination of a social activity such as a retirement party or other gathering.

Note that all of the foregoing suggestions deal with ways of putting interest, challenge, variety, and responsibility into the work itself. In dealing with the dead-end employee, special attention must be given to true motivating forces because the potential dissatisfiers, that is, the environmental factors such as wages and fringe benefits and working conditions, are present in force.

There are other potential solutions to the problem of the dead-end employee, conditions permitting. Maybe it is possible to transfer the person to a completely different assignment or perhaps set up a rotational scheme in which several employees trade assignments on a regular basis. Also, the dead-end employee may be cross-trained on several other jobs within the department and thus be given a chance to do a variety of work and become more valuable to the department.

---

*Source: Reprinted from *The Effective Health Care Supervisor* by Charles R. McConnell, with permission of Aspen Systems Corporation, © 1982.

Chapter 30—Motivation and Job Enrichment

MOTIVATION

How Not To Motivate*

Incompetent workers are often made, not born. With a little effort, you can squelch an enthusiastic worker's initiative and cut his efficiency in half.

You can actually demolish his common sense so that he will apply your instructions to obviously inappropriate situations. The quality of his work will decline while his errors increase. Then, when his confidence plummets, you can let him go.

You can even get his replacement to follow the same path. If any of your workers retain their capabilities, you can make sure that they find better jobs elsewhere or are promoted out of your department.

As a result, you will become busier and busier, buried under a burden of work, completing tasks that your subordinates should have completed and reinstructing them in procedures that they should have learned long ago.

How can you accomplish this unfortunate situation? How can you destroy your subordinates' confidence and watch it crumble? The answer lies in your attitude toward them and the way you treat them.

---

*Source: Reprinted from "Sure Fire Ways to Wreck Employee Competence," *Hospital Topics*, November–December, 1975, with permission of the publisher.

Sure-fire Techniques

1. *Be so vague about what you want your subordinate to do that he cannot pinpoint precisely what you want.* In other words, don't mention any specific cases or show any examples to which he can refer. Give your instructions matter-of-factly, as if you had no doubt that anyone of minimum intelligence would understand them. Give criticism in the same way so that he won't know what he can do to correct his performance.

2. *Give an audible sigh of resignation if he asks you to clarify something you have explained.* Imply that no one has ever asked you to clarify such simple instructions. Remember to avoid giving him any examples that would clear up the problem.

3. *If he asks the same questions more than once, point out that you have already answered that question.* Sometimes you can do this even when he asks the question the first time—especially if his confidence has already been shaken. You may be able to convince him that his memory is failing—which should make him feel guilty for having unnecessarily taken up so much of your valuable time.

4. *Make an obvious effort to contain your impatience if he still doesn't understand what you mean.* This time, instruct him so slowly—in minute detail, with very sim-

ple words—that you underscore your low opinion of his intelligence. Continue to give him this kind of explanation and impression on other occasions—even when he insists that he understands.
5. *Be sure to criticize specific acts—even where the error is minor and would have been corrected in the normal course of events with no harm done.* You can, in fact, make a game out of trying to catch him in "errors" of procedure. Monitor his work closely and point out minor details that he could have accomplished "better" some other way.
6. *Always give him step-by-step instructions, but leave out an explanation of the purpose or expected results.* This makes it impossible for him to claim that another procedure would better serve the purpose. Be specific enough to prevent him from exercising his initiative.
7. *Change your instructions from time to time as he proceeds with a project.* It may help sometimes to deny having given the earlier instructions—particularly if the results do not seem to be turning out too well.
8. *If unforeseen problems arise from following your instructions, insist that he always return to you for the solution.* Don't let him solve the problem himself even if he claims he knows how to do so. If he challenges this restriction, tell him that there are many details you cannot give him because of lack of time.
9. *Give him a deadline that you know he cannot meet.* When he fails to meet it, as expected, you can blame it on his lack of efficiency.
10. *Improve on everything he does.* Tell him that you do this only to make his work acceptable. Then if he starts taking two or three times as long to complete tasks in a futile attempt to meet your "rigorous" standards, point again to his lack of efficiency. Or, if he gives up and does each task carelessly, point out how slovenly he is.

Following these guidelines will ensure two things: (1) Your subordinates will be totally demoralized, and (2) you need not worry about being promoted to a position that you cannot fill.

Motivating Physicians*

Central to management's concerns about motivation of the physician is an understanding of their professional value system, which in a major way, it can be argued, determines their likely behavior. What was learned during those early years of training very much shapes the motivation and attitudes toward their own practice and the activities of other health providers that they must interact with in the health system.

The role of physicians is functionally specific; their work relates only to medicine, and technical competence is the keystone of status. In effect, that physicians should always strive to remain technically competent. A second attribute is that of neutrality, meaning that the physician should behave in an objective, evaluative, and, in a sense, unemotional manner.

The third variable is collective orientation. "The ideology of the profession lays great emphasis on the obligation of the physician to put the welfare of the patient above his personal interest." The final attribute is universalism; physicians must abide by the overall rules of the profession as approved in the specific relationships between them and their patients.

It can be seen that the motivation of professionals requires skills in negotiation and politics, not simply directing. For example, appeals to generalized notions of quality, technical competence, professional standards, and the general well-being of a class of patients are likely to produce more action than economic or political threats (overt or masked).

Motivating Semiprofessionals and Emerging Professionals*

Large numbers of people working in health organizations should be classified as semiprofessionals or emerging professionals. In many respects, what they do has some of the flavor of a profession: the work is cerebral in nature, the training takes several years after high school, and, in many respects, it is difficult for someone not in the particular field to judge the quality of a person's output. The way our system has been structured, however, these people are not autonomous and must function as part of an organization.

---

*Source: Reprinted from *Health Care Management* by Seth B. Goldsmith, with permission of Aspen Systems Corporation, © 1981.

A cynic could make a convincing argument that the health system teases people with the notion of professionalism. In fact, it may be a way of keeping people in line when, because of the tight structure of the system, there is no way for an individual to advance. Physician's assistants are a case in point.

The professional and emerging professional groups are composed of individuals who, for the most part, have trained in and around the health system and whose jobs, for the most part, are restricted to the health system. For example, the jobs outside of the health system for a nurse, physician, or x-ray technician are quite limited. Others who work in the health system, such as an accountant or housekeeper, could just as easily be working in other parts of the public or private sector. Since their interest and commitment to the health system may be somewhat different from those whose careers are dependent on the system, what interests or motivates them may also be different.

Motivating Employees at Top Salary Grades*

A good recognition program will enable you to retain an employee who has reached a temporary dead end. Here are six ways you can help an employee at the top of his grade to maintain an active interest in doing a superior job.

1. Seek his advice regularly.
2. Give him decision-making responsibility.
3. Ask for suggestions.
4. Assign him to train new employees.
5. Appoint him to direct one-shot tasks.
6. Award him prestige symbols and assignments.
7. Consider a lateral transfer or special assignment.
8. Appeal to his social motives.
9. Stay alert for symptoms of discontent.

How To Assess Motivation**

Too many times our perceptions of another's needs are false perceptions.

---

*Source: Reprinted from *The NFI Standard Manual for Supervisors* with permission of the Bureau of Business Practice, © 1977.

**Source: Reprinted from *Effective Communication in Health Care* by Harry E. Munn, Jr. and Norman Metzger, with permission of Aspen Systems Corporation, © 1981.

Many different types of instruments are used in an attempt to determine organizational and employee needs. The feedback information from such instruments can be used to implement new policies or, if need be, to change existing ones.

The Motivation Feedback Questionnaire (see Table 30-1) will tell you what motivates. Try it on yourself first. However, remember that, just because some of these items motivate you, that does not mean they will motivate everyone else.

MOTIVATION THEORY*

Management's Task: The Conventional View

The conventional conception of management's task in harnessing human energy to organizational requirements can be stated broadly in terms of three propositions. In order to avoid the complications introduced by a label, let us call this set of propositions "Theory X":

1. Management is responsible for organizing the elements of productive enterprise—money, materials, equipment, people—in the interest of economic ends.
2. With respect to people, this is a process of directing their efforts, motivating them, controlling their actions, modifying their behavior to fit the needs of the organization.
3. Without this active intervention by management, people would be passive—even resistant—to organizational needs. They must therefore be persuaded, rewarded, punished, controlled—their activities must be directed. This is management's task. We often sum it up by saying that management consists of getting things done through other people.
4. The average man is by nature indolent—he works as little as possible.
5. He lacks ambition, dislikes responsibility, prefers to be led.
6. He is inherently self-centered, indifferent to organizational needs.
7. He is by nature resistant to change.

---

*Source: Reprinted, by permission of the publisher, from "The Human Side of Enterprise," Douglas M. McGregor, *Management Review,* November, 1957, © 1957 by American Management Association, Inc. All rights reserved.

Table 30-1 Motivation Feedback Questionnaire

Motivation Feedback Questionnaire
Part I

Directions:
The following statements have seven possible responses.

Strongly agree	Agree	Slightly agree	Don't know	Slightly disagree	Disagree	Strongly disagree
+3	+2	+1	0	−1	−2	−3

Please score each statement by circling the number that corresponds to your response. For example, if you "strongly agree," circle the number +3.

1. Special salary increases should be given to employees who do their jobs well.   +3 +2 +1 0 −1 −2 −3
2. Better job descriptions would be helpful so that employees know exactly what is expected of them.   +3 +2 +1 0 −1 −2 −3
3. Employees need to be reminded that their jobs are dependent upon the group's ability to meet its objective.   +3 +2 +1 0 −1 −2 −3
4. Supervisors should give a great deal of attention to the physical working conditions of their employees.   +3 +2 +1 0 −1 −2 −3
5. Supervisors ought to work hard to develop a friendly working atmosphere among their employees.   +3 +2 +1 0 −1 −2 −3
6. Individual recognition for above-standard performance means a lot to employees.   +3 +2 +1 0 −1 −2 −3
7. Indifferent supervision can often bruise feelings.   +3 +2 +1 0 −1 −2 −3
8. Employees want to feel that their real skills and capacities are put to use on their jobs.   +3 +2 +1 0 −1 −2 −3
9. The group's retirement benefits and medical insurance programs are important factors in keeping employees on their jobs.   +3 +2 +1 0 −1 −2 −3
10. Almost every job can be made more stimulating and challenging.   +3 +2 +1 0 −1 −2 −3
11. Many employees want to give their best in everything they do.   +3 +2 +1 0 −1 −2 −3
12. Management could show more interest in the employees by sponsoring social events after hours.   +3 +2 +1 0 −1 −2 −3
13. Pride in one's work is actually an important reward.   +3 +2 +1 0 −1 −2 −3
14. Employees want to think of themselves as the "best" at their jobs.   +3 +2 +1 0 −1 −2 −3
15. The quality of the relationship in the informal work group is quite important.   +3 +2 +1 0 −1 −2 −3
16. Individual merit raises would improve the performance of employees.   +3 +2 +1 0 −1 −2 −3
17. Visibility with upper management is important to employees.   +3 +2 +1 0 −1 −2 −3

Table 30-1 continued

18. Employees generally like to schedule their own work and make job-related decisions with a minimum of supervision. +3 +2 +1 0 −1 −2 −3
19. Job security is important to employees. +3 +2 +1 0 −1 −2 −3
20. Having good equipment to work with is important to employees. +3 +2 +1 0 −1 −2 −3

Part II

Scoring:

1. Enter the numbers you circled in Part I in the blanks below after the appropriate statement number.

Statement No.	Score	Statement No.	Score
10	___	2	___
11	___	3	___
13	___	9	___
18	___	19	___
Self-Actualization ___ Total		Safety ___ Total	
Statement No.	Score	Statement No.	Score
6	___	1	___
8	___	4	___
14	___	16	___
17	___	20	___
Esteem ___ Total		Basic ___ Total	
Statement No.	Score		
5	___		
7	___		
12	___		
15	___		
Belongingness ___ Total			

2. Record your scores in the chart by putting an "X" in each row under the number of your total score for that area of need-motivation. After you have completed this chart, you can see the relative strength of your response in each area of "need-motivation." There is of course no "right" answer. What motivates you might not motivate someone else. In general, however, most motivational theorists believe that most employees are motivated by managers who stress the belongingness and esteem needs of their employees.

DEGREE OF EMPHASIS	−12	−10	−8	−6	−4	−2	0	+2	+4	+6	+8	+10	+12
Self-Actualization													
Esteem													
Belongingness													
Safety													
Basic													

LOW USE   HIGH USE

8. He is gullible, not very bright, the ready dupe of the charlatan and the demagogue.

The human side of economic enterprise today is fashioned from propositions and beliefs such as these. Conventional organization structures and managerial policies, practices, and programs reflect these assumptions.

In accomplishing its task—with these assumptions as guides—management has conceived of a range of possibilities.

At one extreme, management can be "hard" or "strong." The methods for directing behavior involve coercion and threat (usually disguised), close supervision, tight controls over behavior. At the other extreme, management can be "soft" or "weak." The methods for directing behavior involve being permissive, satisfying people's demands, achieving harmony. Then they will be tractable, accept direction.

This range has been fairly completely explored during the past half century, and management has learned some things from the exploration. There are difficulties in the "hard" approach. Force breeds counterforces; restriction of output, antagonism, militant unionism, subtle but effective sabotage of management objectives. This "hard" approach is especially difficult during times of full employment.

There are also difficulties in the "soft" approach. It leads frequently to the abdication of management—to harmony, perhaps, but to indifferent performance. People take advantage of the soft approach. They continually expect more, but they give less and less.

Currently, the popular theme is "firm but fair." This is an attempt to gain the advantages of both the hard and the soft approaches. It is reminiscent of Teddy Roosevelt's "speak softly and carry a big stick."

Is the Conventional View Correct?

The findings which are beginning to emerge from the social sciences challenge this whole set of beliefs about man and human nature and about the task of management.

Perhaps the best way to indicate why the conventional approach of management is inadequate is to consider the subject of motivation.

Physiological Needs

Man is a wanting animal—as soon as one of his needs is satisfied, another appears in its place. This process is unending. It continues from birth to death.

Man's needs are organized in a series of levels—a hierarchy of importance. At the lowest level, but preeminent in importance when they are thwarted, are his *physiological needs*. Man lives for bread alone, when there is no bread. Unless the circumstances are unusual, his needs for love, for status, for recognition are inoperative when his stomach has been empty for a while. But when he eats regularly and adequately, hunger ceases to be an important motivation. The same is true of the other physiological needs of man—for rest, exercise, shelter, protection from the elements.

A satisfied need is not a motivator of behavior! This is a fact of profound significance that is regularly ignored in the conventional approach to the management of people. Consider your own need for air: Except as you are deprived of it, it has no appreciable motivating effect upon your behavior.

Safety Needs

When the physiological needs are reasonably satisfied, needs at the next higher level begin to dominate man's behavior—to motivate him. These are called *safety needs*. They are needs for protection against danger, threat, deprivation. Some people mistakenly refer to these as needs for security. However, unless man is in a dependent relationship where he fears arbitrary deprivation, he does not demand security. The need is for the "fairest possible break." When he is confident of this, he is more than willing to take risks. But when he feels threatened or dependent, his greatest need is for guarantees, for protection, for security.

The fact needs little emphasis that, since every employee is in a dependent relationship, safety needs may assume considerable importance. Arbitrary management actions, behavior which arouses uncertainty with respect to continued employment or which reflects favoritism or discrimination, unpredictable administration of policy—these can be powerful motivators of the safety needs in the employment relationship *at every level*.

Social Needs

When man's physiological needs are satisfied and he is no longer fearful about his physical welfare, his *social needs* become important motivators of his behavior—needs for belonging, for association, for acceptance by his fellows, for giving and receiving friendship and love.

Management knows today of the existence of these needs, but it often assumes quite wrongly that they represent a threat to the organization. Many studies have demonstrated that the tightly knit, cohesive work group may, under proper conditions, be far more effective than an equal number of separate individuals in achieving organizational goals.

Yet management, fearing group hostility to its own objectives, often goes to considerable lengths to control and direct human efforts in ways that are inimical to the natural "groupiness" of human beings. When man's social needs—and perhaps his safety needs, too—are thus thwarted, he behaves in ways which tend to defeat organizational objectives. He becomes resistant, antagonistic, uncooperative. But this behavior is a consequence, not a cause.

Ego Needs

Above the social needs—in the sense that they do not become motivators until lower needs are reasonably satisfied—are the needs of greatest significance to management and to man himself. They are the *egoistic needs,* and they are two kinds:

1. Those needs that relate to one's self-esteem—needs for self-confidence, for independence, for achievement, for competence, for knowledge.
2. Those needs that relate to one's reputation—needs for status, for recognition, for appreciation, for the deserved respect of one's fellows.

Unlike the lower needs, these are rarely satisfied; man seeks indefinitely for more satisfaction of these needs once they become important to him. But they do not appear in any significant way until physiological, safety, and social needs are all reasonably satisfied.

The typical organization offers few opportunities for the satisfaction of these egoistic needs to people at lower levels in the hierarchy.

Self-Fulfillment Needs

Finally—a capstone, as it were, on the hierarchy of man's needs—there are what we may call the *needs for self-fulfillment*. These are the needs for realizing one's own potentialities, for continued self-development, for being creative in the broadest sense of that term.

It is clear that the conditions of modern life give only limited opportunity for these relatively weak needs to obtain expression. The deprivation most people experience with respect to other lower-level needs diverts their energies into the struggle to satisfy *those* needs, and the needs for self-fulfillment remain dormant.

Management and Motivation

The man whose lower-level needs are satisfied is not motivated to satisfy those needs any longer. For practical purposes they exist no longer. Management often asks, "Why aren't people more productive? We pay good wages, provide good working conditions, have excellent fringe benefits and steady employment. Yet people do not seem to be willing to put forth more than minimum effort."

The fact that management has provided for these physiological and safety needs has shifted the motivational emphasis to the social and perhaps to the egoistic needs. Unless there are opportunities at *work* to satisfy these higher-level needs, people will be deprived; and their behavior will reflect this deprivation. Under such conditions, if management continues to focus its attention on physiological needs, its efforts are bound to be ineffective.

People *will* make insistent demands for more money under these conditions. It becomes more important than ever to buy the material goods and services which can provide limited satisfaction of the thwarted needs. Although money has only limited value in satisfying many higher-level needs, it can become the focus of interest if it is the *only* means available.

The Carrot-and-Stick Approach

The carrot-and-stick theory of motivation (like Newtonian physical theory) works reasonably well under certain circumstances. The *means* for satisfying man's physiological and (within limits) his safety needs can be provided or withheld by management. Employment itself is such a means, and so are wages, working conditions, and benefits. By these means the individual can be controlled so long as he is struggling for subsistence.

But the carrot-and-stick theory does not work at all once man has reached an adequate subsistence level and is motivated primarily by higher needs. Management cannot provide a man with self-respect, or with the respect of his fellows, or with the satisfaction of needs for self-fulfillment. It can create such conditions that he is encouraged and enabled to seek such satisfactions for *himself,* or it can thwart him by failing to create those conditions.

But this creation of conditions is not "control." It is not a good device for directing behavior. And so management finds itself in an odd position. The high standard of living created by our modern technological know-how provides quite adequately for the satisfaction of physiological and safety needs. But by making possible the satisfaction of low-level needs, management has deprived itself of the ability to use as motivators the devices on which conventional theory has taught it to rely—rewards, promises, incentives, or threats and other coercive devices.

The philosophy of management by direction and control is essentially useless in motivating people whose important needs are social and egoistic. Both the hard and the soft approach fail today because they are simply irrelevant to the situation.

People, deprived of opportunities to satisfy at work the needs which are now important to them, behave exactly as we might predict—with indolence, passivity, resistance to change, lack of responsibility, willingness to follow the demagogue, unreasonable demands for economic benefits. It would seem that we are caught in a web of our own weaving.

A New Theory of Management

For these and many other reasons, we require a different theory of the task of managing people based on more adequate assumptions about human nature and human motivation. Call it "Theory Y," if you will.

1. Management is responsible for organizing the elements of productive enterprise—money, materials, equipment, people—in the interest of economic ends.
2. People are *not* by nature passive or resistant to organizational needs. They have become so as a result of experience in organizations.
3. The motivation, the potential for development, the capacity for assuming responsibility, the readiness to direct behavior toward organizational goals are all present in people. Management does not put them there. It is a responsibility of management to make it possible for people to recognize and develop these human characteristics for themselves.
4. The essential task of management is to arrange organizational conditions and methods of operation so that people can achieve their own goals *best* by directing *their own* efforts toward organizational objectives.

This is a process primarily of creating opportunities, releasing potential, removing obstacles, encouraging growth, providing guidance. It is what Peter Drucker has called "management by objectives" in contrast to "management by control." It does *not* involve the abdication of management, the absence of leadership, the lowering of standards, or the other characteristics usually associated with the "soft" approach under Theory X.

Some Difficulties

People today are accustomed to being directed, manipulated, controlled in organizations and to finding satisfaction for their social, egoistic, and self-fulfillment needs away from the job. This is true of much of management as well as of workers.

Another way of saying this is that Theory X places exclusive reliance upon external control of human behavior, while Theory Y relies heavily on self-control and self-direction. It is worth noting that this difference is the difference between treating people as children and treating them as mature adults. After generations of the former, we cannot expect to shift to the latter overnight.

Steps in the Right Direction

Decentralization and Delegation. These are ways of freeing people from the too-close control of conventional organization, giving them a degree of freedom to direct their own activities, to assume responsibility, and, importantly, to satisfy their egoistic needs.

Participation and Consultative Management. Under proper conditions, participation and consultative management provide encouragement to people to direct their creative energies toward organizational objectives, give them some voice in decisions that affect them, provide significant opportunities for the satisfaction of social and egoistic needs.

Performance Appraisal. Even a cursory examination of conventional programs of performance appraisal within the ranks of management will reveal how completely consistent they are with Theory X. In fact, most such programs tend to treat the individual as though he were a product under inspection on the assembly line.

A few hospitals have been experimenting with approaches which involve the individual in setting "targets" or objectives *for himself* and in a *self*-evaluation of performance semiannually or annually. Of course, the superior plays an important leadership role in this process—one, in fact, which demands substantially more competence than the conventional approach. The role is, however, considerably more congenial to many managers than the role of "judge" or "inspector" which is usually forced upon them. Above all, the individual is encouraged to take a greater responsibility for planning and appraising his own contribution to organizational objectives; and the accompanying effects on egoistic and self-fulfillment needs are substantial.

Applying the Ideas

The not infrequent failure of such ideas as these to work as well as expected is often attributable to the fact that a management has "bought the idea" but applied it within the framework of Theory X and its assumptions.

Delegation is not an effective way of exercising management by control. Participation becomes a farce when it is applied as a gimmick or a device for kidding people into thinking they are important. Only the management that has confidence in human capacities and is itself directed toward organizational objectives rather than toward the preservation of personal power can grasp the implications of this emerging theory. Such management will find and apply successfully other innovative ideas as we move slowly toward the full implementation of a theory like Y.

Herzberg's Theory

The usual personnel practices used to instill motivation are:

1. Reducing time spent at work.
2. Spiraling wages.
3. Fringe benefits.
4. Human relations training.
5. Sensitivity training.
6. Communications.
7. Two-way communication.
8. Job participation.
9. Employee counseling.

However, as Frederick Herzberg (*The Motivation to Work,* Wiley) points out, the factors involved in producing job satisfaction (and motivation) may be quite different from the factors that lead to job dissatisfaction. (See Figure 30-1.)

Herzberg first categorized specific job aspects into major job factors. Reporting on various studies totaling several thousand employees in nonhospital occupations, he found the job factors, in order of importance to the employees, to be

1. Security
2. Opportunity for advancement
3. Company and management
4. Wages
5. Intrinsic aspects of job
6. Supervision
7. Social aspects of job
8. Communication
9. Working conditions
10. Benefits

However a different perspective was provided when he then sought to isolate those factors that caused job satisfaction from those that caused job dissatisfaction.

JOB ENRICHMENT

Establishing a Job Enrichment Program*

Effective Procedures

1. Get the support of subordinate supervisory personnel.

---

*Source: Reprinted with permission from *Industrial Management* magazine, May/June 1977. Copyright Institute of Industrial Engineers, Inc., 25 Technology Park, Atlanta, Norcross, GA 30092.

484 HOSPITAL ADMINISTRATION HANDBOOK

Figure 30-1 Comparison of satisfier and dissatisfier

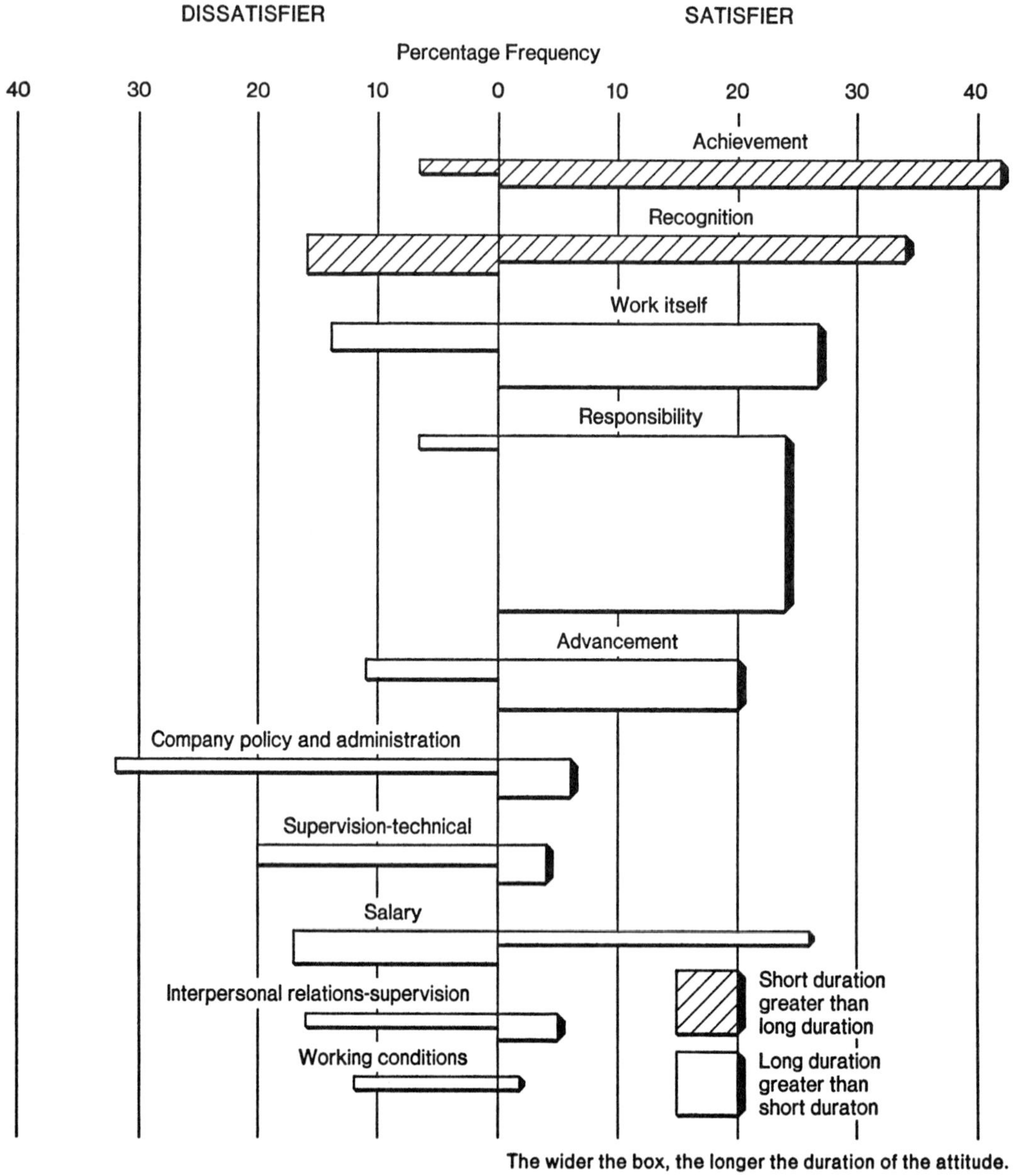

[Figure: Horizontal bar chart comparing dissatisfier and satisfier percentage frequencies for factors: Achievement, Recognition, Work itself, Responsibility, Advancement, Company policy and administration, Supervision-technical, Salary, Interpersonal relations-supervision, Working conditions. Hatched bars indicate short duration greater than long duration; open bars indicate long duration greater than short duration. The wider the box, the longer the duration of the attitude.]

Source: Reprinted from *The Motivation to Work* by Frederick Herzberg et al. with permission of John Wiley & Sons, Inc., © 1959.

2. Train or acquire personnel with knowledge of job design and job enrichment theory to work as consultants.
3. Identify the jobs that need to be enriched by using questionnaires, opinion and attitude surveys, observation, and the reports of supervisors.
4. Define specifically what supervisors are responsible for doing in the job enrichment program and spell out how they should do it.
5. Redesign the jobs selected for enrichment by:
    a. Performing job and work flow analysis.

b. Selecting a group of people who represent instructors and training-support personnel to generate ideas for enriching the job.
  c. Brainstorming the job.
  d. Screening and selecting ideas for implementation on a trial basis.
6. Redesign the job and implement the changes on a time-phased basis.
7. Establish a means of interchanging ideas and experiences.
8. Evaluate results based on feedback and analysis and redesign the job as needed.

Obstacles to Implementation

1. Misunderstandings about the nature of jobs and the job enrichment process, such as the belief that:
   a. Job fragmentation and rigid controls are essential to efficiency.
   b. Job enrichment is just another type of human relations program.
   c. Technological considerations make job changes either trivial or impossible.
   d. Employees are disinterested in or incapable of dealing with enriched jobs.
   e. Job enrichment is just good management.
2. Resistance to change, as exemplified by:
   a. Rejection by a manager on the basis that his organization is unique.
   b. Statements to the effect that work pressures, personnel turnover, and competition doom the program to failure.
3. Lack of knowledge and skills, such as:
   a. Lack of knowledge of job design and enrichment theory.
   b. Lack of skill in job and work flow analysis.
   c. Failure to use systematic analysis to determine when job enrichment is needed.
4. Costs, in terms of:
   a. Managerial, supervisory, and employee time.
   b. Consultants to assist in developing the program.

Misconceptions and Limitations of Job Enrichment*

Among the common misconceptions and limitations in many job enrichment programs is the belief that if a man is given more to do, he is motivated. This has not proven to be the case. Recently, some interesting experiments were conducted at General Motors, wherein the scope of a number of jobs was increased. The result was *not* that the workers were motivated but that they complained that they had less break time. Another misconception is that addition of the planning, goal setting, and decision-making responsibilities to a job takes care of the situation automatically. It is not necessarily so, because the worker gets more frustrated if he is not given the skills to carry out these responsibilities. Focusing the attention on the worker and redesigning his job while the supervisor is being completely forgotten is another misconception. By giving the worker the opportunity to plan all aspects for conducting his work, the supervisor has such a little part left in the problem solving, decision making and goal setting that he can easily become a source of failure in job enrichment programs.

Another misconception lies in the fact that the job enrichment program is utilized for jobs other than those for which it was designed (where job content is the root of problems such as those in which attitudes are poor). It can't be assumed that job enrichment solves all ills.

In addition to previous misconceptions, there are many limitations experienced in the job enrichment approach. It is very difficult, for example, to convince all workers to take part in job enrichment programs because some of them have fear stemming from the lack of knowhow.

New managers fear that any changes that prove unsuccessful will be assessed as their failure whether it is true or not, while they feel it would be safer if something goes wrong when it is done the way it has always been done. Because of the time consumption of many weeks needed to plan, develop, and implement job enrichment, some managers lose their enthusiasm before job enrichment program has a chance to work.

When a change in the current method is recommended, the feeling often is that there was fault with that method. Overcoming this kind of management problem is difficult as it means admitting that there was some error.

Increased responsibility is not always seen by the worker as an opportunity for advancement, achievement and recognition. He often regards it as an overburden. Workers must be able to

---
*Source: K. S. Bagadia and M. M. Baker, *op. cit.*

voice their opinion concerning job enrichment of their jobs. Excluding such representation may jeopardize the success of any job enrichment efforts. The scope of job enrichment is often not clear to workers. Rotation through a succession of boring jobs, and/or adding more of the same boring tasks have been called job enrichment. Job enrichment has become a source of confusion and uncertainty to them.

Employee Career Planning*

Planning for replacement of key people is an important management responsibility. If possible the internal supply of personnel should be considered and trained for responsibilities. Manpower inventories can indicate the present capabilities of the staff. Management's responsibility to change present capabilities to those needed, thus providing paths or career ladders and training programs to acquire needed skills, is of particular importance in planning for management replacements. By providing job satisfaction, employee performance will improve as well as health care delivery.

To work with and assist the employee in developing his or her potential, management must know about the employee's capabilities, needs and aspirations. Counseling and motivation go hand in hand.

---

*Source: Reprinted from Joan Holland, "Workshop: Manpower Planning to Meet Needs," *Health Care Management Review*, Fall 1976, with permission of Aspen Systems Corporation.

Inventory of Skills Form

The form should contain sections for entering nine major types of information. (To discover both the potential and aspirations of employees, a form for inventorying skills might be devised.)

- formal education
- training
- skills/work experience
- memberships/licenses/committees
- emergency skills/languages
- civic activities/public
- speaking/volunteer work
- special achievements
- career interests

The information the employee places in the inventory skills file could be used to develop a master career plan for each individual. Once the career plan has delineated job requirements and perimeters, the employee can be told of job opportunities, and the training and education needed to achieve his or her career goals, as well as how and where to secure these skills and knowledge. The continued use of this system will provide the personnel department with an intelligent means of identifying individuals with needed skills. Once they have been identified, their availability for promotional opportunities can be checked as openings occur. Thus selection can be less time consuming and less expensive.

Chapter 31—Absenteeism and Turnover

How do administrators go about the job of combatting the drain on manpower caused by excessive turnover and absenteeism? Those administrators who have been most successful in meeting these problems preplan their work and allow for absences. They keep accurate and complete records of attendance. They provide for exit interviews and analyze separations to find the real reasons for discharges, voluntary quits, and absences from the job. They carefully select new workers; make use of training, safety, and health programs; and cooperate with community agencies to provide child-care, shopping, banking, transportation, and recreational facilities. They make careful analyses and evaluations of the facts and take steps to identify and relieve or eliminate the causes of employee dissatisfaction because they are aware that management cannot afford to ignore either excessive rates of turnover or unrealistic reasons for absenteeism or lateness.

Excessive turnover and absenteeism are expensive to both employer and worker in terms of money, morale, and wasted manpower. Some turnover and absenteeism must be expected, but excessive rates can be reduced by sound personnel policies in which management and labor work closely together.

OVERVIEW*

Relationship between Absenteeism and Turnover

Absenteeism and turnover are generally seen as forms of employee alienation or withdrawal from an organization. The nature of the relationship between absenteeism and turnover consists of three parts. In the first case, absenteeism is a form of withdrawal behavior that represents an alternative to turnover. Here the employee does not desire termination nor does he believe his employer will terminate him for his behavior. Some condition related either to the job or to the employee personally seems to justify the absence and restores the individual or the employment relationship to equilibrium. The second position identifies a continuum of withdrawal with absenteeism preceding turnover. The individual's decision to absent himself from his job is just a miniature version of the more important decision he makes when he quits his job. In the third case, there is no consistent relationship be-

---

*Source: Reprinted from "Absenteeism and Turnover," by Donald L. Hawk, with permission of *Personnel Journal,* June 1976.

tween absenteeism and turnover. An individual's decision to terminate will depend upon: a) the relative importance of a particular job to other factors in the individual's life; or, b) his perception of alternative employment opportunities which are superior to his current job.

Factors in Absenteeism

1. Demographic factors. Female workers have a higher absolute absenteeism rate and it is rising faster than that of males. Age is inversely related to absenteeism while the highest rates are in the 18–25 year old age group and the lowest in the 40–65 group. Both unmarried males and females have a lower absenteeism rate than the married group.

2. Personal life. Traumatic experiences or abnormal pressure levels in one's personal life can result in higher absenteeism rates as the individual takes the time required to restore some semblance of psychological equilibrium.

3. Need state. If an individual is obtaining most or all of his need satisfaction off the job, he will subordinate both his job and the time spent on it to his outside projects.

4. Organization policy. Salary continuance or sick pay plans may contribute to absenteeism in two ways. First, if an employee feels his peers are contributing less to the organization than he is, the existence of a liberal sick pay program will help that employee make up his mind to stay home. Although a sick leave policy does not necessarily encourage absenteeism, it does seem to authorize it. Secondly, in a case where the sick pay program provides no payment for the first two or three days of absence an employee is enticed to remain off the job until he becomes eligible for sick pay for his total absence.

5. Work planning and scheduling. The natural work cycle (e.g. a monthly accounting period) which creates substantial differences in an employee's workload may result in absenteeism immediately following the peak level. Employees feel that this absenteeism is justified because it represents a return to equilibrium, that is, the job requires intensive work during a period of time and thus the employee rests to return to normal prior to the next peak.

Factors in Turnover

1. General economic conditions. Historically studies have shown that turnover follows directly (with practically no lag time) the peaks and troughs of the general economy.

2. Local labor market conditions. The concept of a local labor market refers not only to a limited geographic area but also to the supply-demand ratio for a particular occupation or profession.

3. Personal mobility. In addition, the individual's own skill or background will greatly influence his mobility and thus be a potential cause of attribution.

4. Job security. The number of involuntary transfers and terminations in a department directly affect an individual's perception of job security and impact on his feelings about the fairness or equity of policy. If he perceives the work environment to be volatile, that is, unstable or unpredictable, then his tenure may well be affected.

5. Demographic factors. Females have a much higher turnover rate than males. Married males and middle aged married females have the longest average tenure while unmarried young females have the shortest tenure.

Factors in Absenteeism Leading to Turnover

The level of job dissatisfaction will directly influence both the rate of absenteeism and turnover.

1. Supervisory style. Supervisory style can affect job satisfaction in several ways. First when work planning and scheduling are perceived as arbitrary and/or inefficient, employees react to the "punishing" supervisory incompetence by withdrawing. Second, role ambiguity created by unclear performance expectations can cause high levels of psychological stress. Third, the lack of feedback on performance and the perceived inequity of performance appraisal can often reduce job satisfaction.

2. Interpersonal relationships. An organization structure which creates and/or reinforces destructive competition, reduces team spirit, group pride, or group cohesiveness and causes job dissatisfaction.

3. Working conditions. A working environment which is unsafe or interferes with efficient, productive work contributes to job dissatisfaction.

4. Salary. There are two elements related to salary that can affect the individual's satisfaction level. The first of these and perhaps the most obvious is wage rate. If an individual's wage rate is substantially below that of the area average he will be dissatisfied. The second case and perhaps the more important is the intraorganization dimension of salaries, that of wage level. If there are substantial differentials in wage levels, employees may perceive the wage structure to be arbitrary and inequitable when compared to the work required.

5. Job expectations. From interviews, orientation training and perhaps job descriptions individuals develop preconceptions of what a job will be like. If an individual's job expectations are a great deal different from what he finds his job is really like, he is apt to be dissatisfied with his decision to join the company.

6. Job fit. When through selection, placement, and/or promotional practice, an individual's capabilities are systematically under-utilized and/or there is no career path available to him he becomes dissatisfied. The contrary is also true. Should the job require more ability than the individual has, the individual will feel incompetent and be dissatisfied.

7. Job design. Jobs with low motivating potential (i.e. low skill variety, low task identity, low task significance, little autonomy, and little or no feedback from the job itself) produce employee dissatisfaction.

Developing an Absenteeism/Turnover Reduction Strategy

After discovery of an absenteeism or turnover problem most organizations react one of three ways:

1. They develop an elaborate "control" program;
2. They adopt a current fad;
3. They implement a program that worked well for some other organization.

Since the causes or the circumstances surrounding absenteeism or turnover problems are not necessarily the same, these programs inevitably have less than the desired effect or fail outright.

It is for this reason that careful diagnosis of management's absenteeism/turnover position must precede the formulation of any plans to deal with the problem. The first step in this diagnosis should be a detailed analysis of both absenteeism and turnover data.

Next, the costs of the problem should be identified. If the cost is significant enough to merit an investment in change, the next step is to identify which of the major variables listed are contributing most to the absenteeism/turnover problem.

In determining which are the most significant causal variables, valuable information can be obtained from:

1. a review of exit interview data especially where similar reasons for termination occur frequently.
2. an analysis of current performance problems (e.g. substandard work output).
3. the administration and analysis of an appropriate attitude survey.

Implementation of the most appropriate and direct solution will then provide the best return (i.e. maximum results for minimum investment).

ABSENTEEISM

Rate and Cause[*]

The rate of unscheduled absenteeism last reported for all hospitals was an average of 3.2 days per year per employee. Almost 40 percent of hospitals indicated their rate as less than 1 day per employee (0 and no response). On the other end of the scale, 2 percent of hospitals reported a rate of 12 or more days of unscheduled absences per year per employee.

Small hospitals (25–99 beds) had a rate of 2.8 days, slightly lower than the 3.2 rate for all hospitals. Medium-sized hospitals (100–299 beds) had a rate of 3.5 days, while large hospitals (300+ beds) reported a rate of 3.9 days per year per employee. (See Table 31-1.) Illness was clearly the most frequent cause of absence listed

---

[*]Source: NIOSH *Hospital Occupational Health Services Study*, U.S., 1972. [Survey of 5,298 Hospitals] Pub. No. (NIOSH 75-154).

Table 31-1 Unscheduled Absenteeism

Days per year per employee	Number Total	Percent All hospitals	Hospital size[1] Small	Medium	Large
Total	5,298	100.0	100.0	100.0	100.0
0 & Blank	2,091	39.5	38.8	39.3	42.3
1	539	10.2	15.0	6.4	2.2
2-3	957	18.1	22.0	15.4	10.5
4-7	1,338	25.3	19.9	30.4	31.9
8-11	264	5.0	2.8	5.8	10.9
12-15	81	1.5	1.0	2.4	1.3
16-19	5	0.1	0.2	—	—
20+	23	0.4	0.4	0.3	0.9

[1]Hospital Size based upon number of beds: (Small: 25-99) (Medium: 100-299) (Large: 300+)

by all hospitals, regardless of size or geographical region. (See Table 31-2.)

Control Methods

Supervisors must assume the bulk of responsibility for reducing absenteeism. Often supervisors are aware that certain employees are chronic absentees, but the personnel department must make sure that supervisors have adequate training in handling problems of this kind. The personnel department should provide the supervisor with statistical information reflecting absenteeism patterns in this department.

The one-day absence, the worker's "inalienable right" to use up allotted sick days one by one, is the scourge of an efficient nursing service. Supervisors who reason with staff members about the department budget problems caused by recurrent absences offer them scant cause for changing their habits.

Conversations with habitual offenders in which the supervisor warns of an inverse relationship between absences and advancement on the other hand are considered too heavy-handed. Appeals to team loyalty, and some nasty comments from those forced to work harder that day, may have some impact. But most effective, many supervisors have found, is the careful recording of absences and the documentation of absence patterns. In this way personnel know that supervisors know what's going on.

Many hospital administrators handle these short term absences in a more systematic fashion using select rewards, penalties and surveillance devices. The following control methods are used.

Bonus for health. Employees receive full pay for any of the allotted sick days they don't take. Another method gives one day's pay for accruing x amount of sick days.

Check-up and surveillance. This method takes the one-day sickness excuse at face-value and sends the returned absentee down to the em-

Table 31-2 "Scores" and Rank of Causes of Absenteeism

Cause of absenteeism	All hospitals Rank	"Score"	Small Rank	"Score"	Medium Rank	"Score"	Large Rank	"Score"
Illness	1	3.63	1	3.56	1	3.73	1	3.66
Family health	2	1.56	2	1.41	2	1.74	2	1.65
Other problems	3	1.34	3	1.17	3	1.53	3	1.51
Injuries	4	0.92	4	0.78	4	1.02	4	1.18
Total	—	7.45	—	6.92	—	8.02	—	8.00

[1]Hospital Size based upon number of beds: (Small: 25-99) (Medium: 100-299) (Large: 300+)

ployee health clinic to explain the causes (symptoms?) to the doctor. A more concerned attitude is seemingly displayed in a variation of this method where a nurse hired for this purpose actually visits the absentee worker's home to find out how they feel or if medical help is needed. This solicitude fools no one, nor is it meant to. In one hospital, substantial reductions in sick leave time have been achieved since the method was instituted.

Penalties. Many hospitals deduct the first day of illness but some use a system of make-up work. For example, absences unaccompanied by doctor's notes on scheduled weekends must be made up by work on the employee's next off-weekend. This type of program helps to curb one-day or two-day absences that are abuses. However, it can have a negative effect on conscientious employees. This problem could be alleviated by converting the unpaid days to paid days only for employees who have accumulated at least 15 sick leave days or whatever other limit seems appropriate.

Supervisors' Guidelines for Reducing Absenteeism*

For control of absenteeism, department heads should be encouraged to consider the following eight guidelines:

1. In dealings with employees, stress that employment is a two-way street. Sick leave is an employee benefit with an associated cost, provided for use when needed. It is more privilege than right and as such should not be abused. Let your employees know that absence should not be taken for granted, and let them know what it does to your department in terms of added cost and lost output.
2. Let your employees know that their attendance is important to the operation of the department. Openly publicize your concern for absenteeism and its effects on department performance.
3. Start new employees the right way, including in their orientation your expectation of regular attendance. Make sure they clearly understand all the rules governing absenteeism and the use of sick leave benefits.
4. Keep accurate attendance records, and do so with the knowledge of each employee. Do not put yourself in the position of having to have another department (for instance, personnel or payroll) research an employee's attendance record when a question arises.
5. Have absentees report to you when returning to work. This generally will not bother legitimate absentees, but it puts a certain amount of pressure on the healthy "stay aways." In any case, even assuming that a particular absence may indeed be legitimate, you should be sufficiently interested in your employees' well-being to briefly check with someone returning from a day or two of absence.
6. Do not allow your system to reward for absenteeism. For instance, in some departments in which employees rotate to provide weekend coverage there may be people who seem to experience "illness" only when scheduled to work on Saturday or Sunday. Arrange your scheduling such that a person who calls in sick on a scheduled Saturday or Sunday will be rescheduled to work that day on the following weekend so the employee cannot avoid the fair share of weekend duty through the use of sick leave.
7. Discuss unusual patterns of absence with the employees involved. If someone's supposed illness or personal problem always creates a long weekend or stretches a holiday into two days, at least make it known that you are aware of the pattern and feel perhaps it would be more than coincidence should this pattern continue.
8. Use incentives available to you as a supervisor to discourage absenteeism. For instance, it would make sense to delegate a special assignment or a particularly interesting or appealing task to someone you can reasonably count on to show up regularly for work and to make it known that this measure of dependability is one of your reasons for selecting the person you chose. Also, make appropriate use of employee's attendance records at performance appraisal time. While attendance is not likely to weigh heaviest in a perform-

---

*Source: Reprinted from *The Effective Health Care Supervisor* by Charles R. McConnell, with permission of Aspen Systems Corporation, © 1982.

ance appraisal, unless, of course, it is exceptionally poor, you can certainly apply attendance in its proper relationship with other appraisal factors in either extending or withholding praise and reward.

A Model Absenteeism Control Program*

At St. Thomas Psychiatric Hospital, Ontario, an absentee reduction program in one department in the first year achieved a reduction of 40 per cent and will probably exceed 50 per cent in the second year.

The step by step procedure (see Figure 31-1) is only a guide to control absenteeism, and is primarily aimed at the correction or eventual dismissal of the "chronic abuser" of sick credits.

TURNOVER

Costs of Turnover

Turnover is expensive to an institution because the costs of turnover include recruiting and selecting a replacement, socializing the replacement with regard to hospital norms, overpayment of the replacement during the period of learning when she or he cannot produce at full capacity, overtime work performed by others during the period between the turnover and the replacement's achievement of full capacity, and achieving social adjustment between the nursing unit and its new members. (See Table 31-3.)

That is why administrators require up-to-date records of turnover rate in order to estimate more accurately their total budget. It also allows them to identify areas of weakness as well as opportunities for cost reduction.**

Cost Components**

Three distinct cost components are usually examined: recruitment, on-the-job training, and termination. By estimating the appropriate wage rate for the amount of time spent by hospital personnel in each of these phases of employment, managers can determine hospital costs for turnover.

1. Recruitment

Interviewing. Time is spent by personnel staff in handling applications, holding preliminary interviews and processing initial forms.

Physical examination. Time is spent by medical personnel in conducting routine health examination.

Clerical staff. Time is spent completing records and payroll forms.

Orientation. Time is spent off regular job duties (non-operational) by one or more staff members and the new employee, based proportionately on the wage rate for each person involved.

2. On-The-Job Training

Time to reach proficiency. The complexity of duties and the difference in worker backgrounds vary the amount of time needed to reach proficiency. However, the supervisor should be able to provide an average time estimate.

Excess wages paid for duties performed. Until the new staff member learns the job requirements, she can not be working at full capacity.

Estimated costs of supervision during training. Wages of supervisors during instruction periods are based upon the amount of time spent in direct contact and the number of trainees involved during the training period.

3. Termination

Payment of wages. A departing employee is paid for non-productive time, i.e. salary is received through checkout and exit interview periods.

Exit interview expenses. Depending on how elaborate the hospital's system is, costs vary but are essentially based on salary time for the interviewee.

Clerical staff. Again, time is spent for completion of records and payroll forms.

When all these factors are calculated to arrive at a turnover cost, expenses can be quite high.

---

*Source: Romeo Cercone, "Controlling Sick Leave Abuse," *Dimensions in Health Service,* Journal of the Canadian Hospital Association, April 1978.

**Source: Reprinted from *The Nursing Administration Handbook,* eds. Howard S. Rowland and Beatrice L. Rowland, with permission of Aspen Systems Corporation, © 1980.

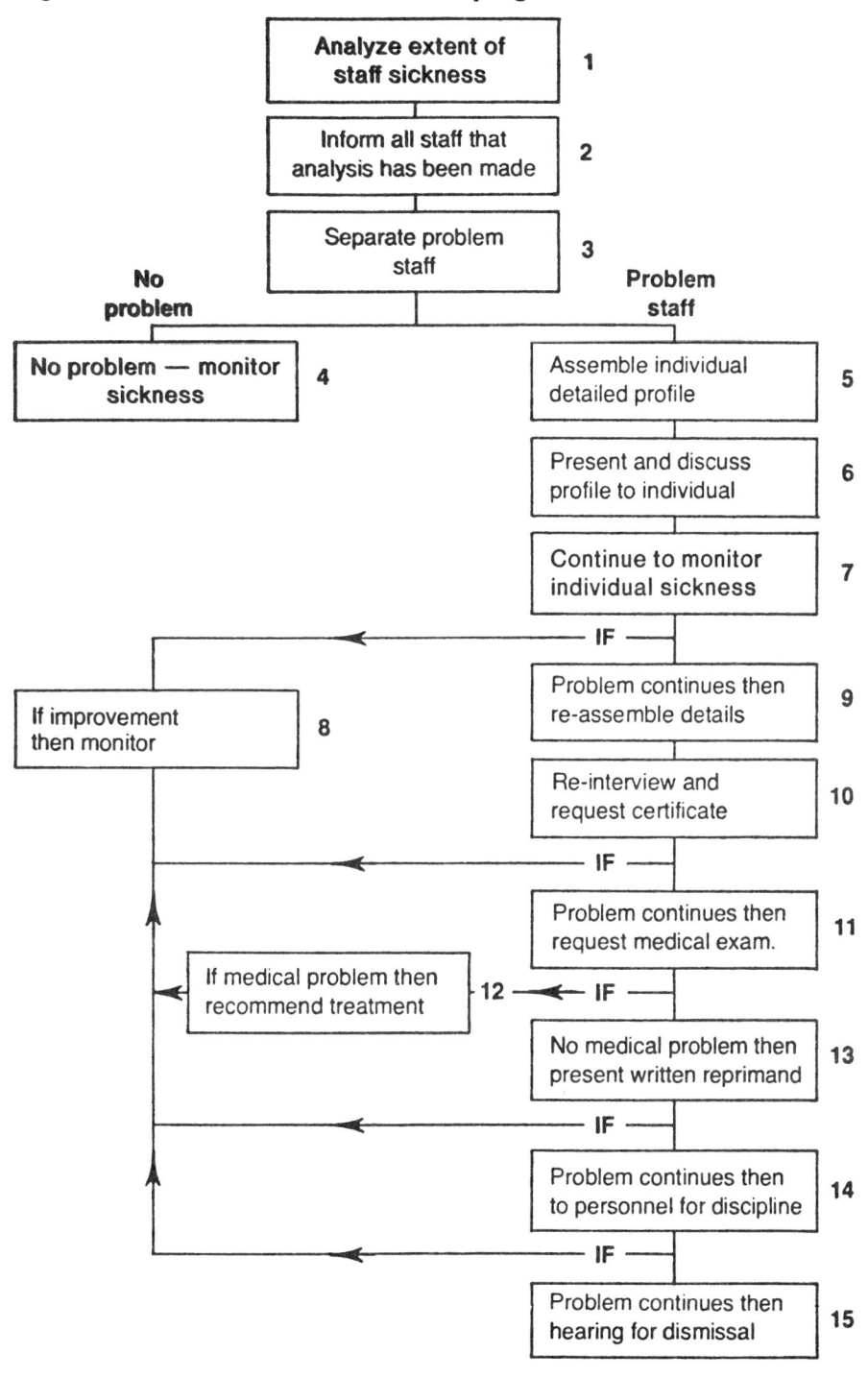

Figure 31-1 An absenteeism control program*

```
                    ┌─────────────────────┐
                    │  Analyze extent of  │  1
                    │   staff sickness    │
                    └──────────┬──────────┘
                               │
                    ┌──────────┴──────────┐
                    │ Inform all staff that│  2
                    │ analysis has been made│
                    └──────────┬──────────┘
                               │
                    ┌──────────┴──────────┐
       No           │  Separate problem   │  3   Problem
     problem        │       staff         │       staff
                    └──────────┬──────────┘
    ┌───────────────┐          │          ┌──────────────────┐
    │ No problem —  │  4       │          │ Assemble individual│ 5
    │monitor sickness│                     │ detailed profile  │
    └───────────────┘                     └─────────┬────────┘
                                                    │
                                          ┌─────────┴────────┐
                                          │ Present and discuss│ 6
                                          │ profile to individual│
                                          └─────────┬────────┘
                                                    │
                                          ┌─────────┴────────┐
                                          │ Continue to monitor│ 7
                                          │ individual sickness│
                                          └─────────┬────────┘
                                          ◄──── IF ────
                                          ┌─────────┴────────┐
    ┌───────────────┐                     │ Problem continues then│ 9
    │ If improvement │ 8                   │ re-assemble details  │
    │  then monitor  │                    └─────────┬────────┘
    └───────────────┘                               │
                                          ┌─────────┴────────┐
                                          │  Re-interview and │ 10
                                          │ request certificate│
                                          └─────────┬────────┘
                                          ◄──── IF ────
                                          ┌─────────┴────────┐
                                          │ Problem continues then│ 11
                                          │ request medical exam.│
                  ┌──────────────────┐    └─────────┬────────┘
                  │If medical problem then│ 12 ◄── IF ──
                  │ recommend treatment │   ┌─────────┴────────┐
                  └──────────────────┘    │ No medical problem then│ 13
                                          │present written reprimand│
                                          └─────────┬────────┘
                                          ◄──── IF ────
                                          ┌─────────┴────────┐
                                          │ Problem continues then│ 14
                                          │to personnel for discipline│
                                          └─────────┬────────┘
                                          ◄──── IF ────
                                          ┌─────────┴────────┐
                                          │ Problem continues then│ 15
                                          │ hearing for dismissal│
                                          └──────────────────┘
```

*Source: Romeo Cercone, "Controlling Sick Leave Abuse," *Dimensions in Health Service*, Journal of the Canadian Hospital Association, April 1978.

Table 31-3 Relevant Turnover Cost Components

Recruitment	Selection and Placement	On-the-Job Activities	Separation
1) Advertising	1) Letter of application	1) Putting person on the job	1) Exit interview
2) College recruiting	2) Application blanks	2) Safety or working equipment	2) Severance pay
3) Employment agency fees	3) Interviewing ■ Personnel department ■ Line managers	3) Indoctrination and on-the-job training	3) Extra Social Security
4) Literature ■ Brochures ■ Pamphlets	4) Medical examinations	4) Formal training programs ■ Waste of materials	4) Extra U.I.C. (unemployment)
5) Employee prizes and awards	5) Reference checking	5) Break-in ■ Increased production ■ Increased supervision ■ Increased maintenance ■ Increased accidents	5) Reduced productivity ■ Increased waste of materials ■ Increased maintenance ■ Loss in productivity of exiting employee ■ Loss in productivity of colleagues ■ Increased accidents
6) Public relations activities	6) Psychological testing		
	7) Applicant's travel expenses ■ Actual travel ■ Reservations ■ Conducted tours		
	8) Personnel department overhead		

*A Formula for Determining Turnover**

Hospitals may use the formulas of the Bureau of Labor Statistics* for compiling, computing, and recording turnover. They are as follows:

Separation rate: The number of separations (includes all persons who left for any reason—resignation, dismissal, layoff) during the month is divided by the total number of workers on the payroll in the pay period ending nearest the 15th of the same month, and the result is multiplied by 100.

$$\frac{S \text{ (number of separations)}}{M \text{ (midmonth employment)}} \times 100$$
$$= T \text{ (separation rate)}$$

Example:

$$\frac{20 \text{ separations}}{100 \text{ employees}} \times 100 = 20\% \text{ separation rate}$$

Quit rate: The number of quits or resignations during the month is divided by the total number of workers on the payroll in the pay period ending nearest the 15th of the same month, and the result is multiplied by 100.

---

*Source: U.S. Dept. of Labor, *Suggestions for Control of Turnover & Absenteeism*, 1972.

$$\frac{Q \text{ (number of quits)}}{M \text{ (midmonth employment)}} \times 100$$
$$= R \text{ (resignation rate)}$$

Example:

$$\frac{10 \text{ resignations}}{100 \text{ employees}} \times 100 = 10\% \text{ resignation rate}$$

In addition, the American Hospital Association encourages hospitals to consider calculating the stability factor, which reflects the number of positions with no changes in staffing, related to total authorized positions, for a given month. This figure counteracts distortion caused by the turnover of one position several times. When one position turns over three times, this is reflected in the turnover rate, tending to make the staff appear unstable.

Costs: Measurement and Control*

The Determination of Measurable and Unmeasurable Turnover

Some costs are extremely clear-cut and easy to measure, such as costs for advertising specific management positions and for administration of psychological or skill tests. Other costs are not so obvious (e.g., the cost of management time used in interviewing prospective candidates). The cost of things such as the level of productivity of the individual is even more difficult to measure. Is it acceptable to simply assume the salary as the cost, or should attempts be made to measure the cost of lost production during the learning period?

In many cases, it is possible and valuable to calculate "standard costs" of turnover. This figure, if accepted by management, provides an average figure of the normal cost per turnover, as well as a quick and easy way of estimating possible savings that might result from reductions in the turnover rate. These standard cost figures should be updated periodically.

Clearly, management cannot and would not want to eliminate all turnover within the firm. Like it or not, many turnovers are unavoidable: people retire, people become ill, people leave for family and personal reasons which are beyond the control of those in the firm. However, some categories of turnover are more controllable than others. For example, management has some control over the nature of the work, the working conditions, supervision and wages.

In calculating turnover costs and making related decisions, it is important to consider only the turnover that results from controllable factors. Table 31-4 outlines some of the reasons for turnover and classifies them as controllable or uncontrollable.

Monitoring Turnover*

The sample turnover control form (see Figure 31-2) demonstrates how monthly control information can be summarized. The information in

Table 31-4 Controllable and Uncontrollable Turnover Categories

Controllable Categories‡
Secured other job
Returned to school
Nature of work
Working conditions
Wages
Uncontrollable Categories‡‡
Pension
Health
Deceased
Family reasons
Not Classified
Discharge
Personal reasons
Housing conditions

‡Controllable here means that the hospital could have a major influence over whether the individual leaves. Thus, "returned to school" is controllable in that the hospital might entice the employee to stay. "Pension" is uncontrollable in that once the company has an established plan, people will leave the hospital according to that schedule.

‡‡These classifications have been derived from exit interviews.

---

*Source: Reprinted from Thomas F. Cawsey and William C. Wedley, "Labor Turnover Costs: Measurement & Control," *Personnel Journal*, February 1979, with permission of the publisher.

*Source: Reprinted from Thomas F. Cawsey and William C. Wedley, "Labor Turnover Costs: Measurement and Control," *Personnel Journal*, February 1979, with permission of the publisher.

Figure 31-2 Monthly labor turnover control form

LABOR TURNOVER CONTROL												

Responsibility: T.P. Bettison
Average Work Force — 310
Current T.O. Rate — 6.3/mos.; 75.6/yr.
Current T.O. Cost — $44,372/mos.; $532,465/yr.

Job Classification — Plant Operators

Cost Components:
(1) Separation $ 80
(2) Hiring   427
(3) Training   438
(4) Adjustment   123
(5) Lost Production   432
(6) Lost Productivity   272
Total $2,272

Month	Current Projection		Budget		Actual Number				Actual Cost		Comments
	No.	Cost	No.	Cost	Quits	Dismissal	Layoff	Other	Total	Amount	% of Budget	
Jan.	23	52,256	18	40,896	14	2			16	36,352	88.8	
Feb.	14	31,808	10	22,720	7	1			8	18,176	80.0	
March	18	40,896	16	36,352	13			2	15	34,080	93.7	
April	15	34,080	11	24,992	11	1		1	13	29,536	118.2	
May	20	45,440	16	36,352	13	1	20		34	33,408	91.9	Only separation costs occur for the 20 layoffs.
June	15	34,080	11	24,992	5	2			7	15,904	63.6	
July	13	29,536	10	22,720	5				5	11,360	50.0	
Aug.	29	65,888	24	54,528	13	2		2	17	38,624	70.8	
Sept.	26	59,072	21	47,712								
Oct.	22	49,984	18	40,896								
Nov.	20	45,440	17	38,624								
Dec.	18	40,896	15	34,080								
TOTAL	233	529,376	187	424,864								

496   Hospital Administration Handbook

this format serves several functions. Its first is to impress upon the responsible person the costs associated with labor turnover and the need to lower these costs. The direct association of the costs to a department or division induces further pressure to do something about them. Of course, the responsible managers do not have complete control over the variables which affect labor turnover.

The second function of the control form is to specify and document an agreed-upon budget. The current projections are then used as a framework for establishing some kind of target which must be reasonable and attainable for the budget to have true meaning.

The final function is the actual monitoring. Each month, the number of departures should be recorded according to the reason for termination, and the associated actual costs are calculated. The actual costs can then be compared to the budget. The responsible manager can easily record this information, thereby monitoring his or her own progress. This monitoring can subsequently lead to actions to reduce turnover levels to some optimum. This optimal level is a delicate balance at which turnover costs are minimized while still allowing a sufficient flow of new employees with fresh skills, talents and creativity.

Reducing Turnover

Computerized accounting systems can develop turnover data into useful management tools by correlating them with personnel and job characteristics. Detailed data collection can result in recommendations for hiring and allocation of personnel.

Sometimes "exit interviews" will provide significant insight on how to reduce turnover.

Rewards*

In one investigation the influence of specific safety, social and psychological rewards and incentives on the rate of nursing staff turnover was studied. Results indicated that 59 percent of the RNs who left their staff positions could have been influenced to stay on the job by rewards and incentives—of which 34 percent

---

*Source: Joanne McCloskey, "Influence of Rewards and Incentives on Staff Nurse Turnover," *Nursing Research*, May–June 1974.

could have been easily held on the job. The remaining 41 percent could not have been influenced to stay on the job.

The Exit Interview*

The exit interview can be a valuable source of information concerning reasons for labor turnover. A few factors contributing to turnover, for example—death or retirement, are not controllable. However, numerous factors which give workers cause for leaving an organization are controllable, and a carefully conducted exit interview will help bring these to light. The exit interview is not intended to absolve the supervisor of her responsibility for maintaining conditions that keep turnover low. It is intended to provide additional assistance after the supervisor has done her utmost toward retaining a desirable worker.

Exit interviews offer opportunities to:

- Determine the real reasons employees wish to resign.
- Retain competent employees by exploring the causes of the dissatisfaction and trying to find a solution for their grievances or problems.
- Clarify complaints against employees who are separated involuntarily.
- Promote good relations with employees who separate voluntarily or involuntarily.
- Obtain reliable data on problem areas which will enable management to set up corrective measures.

A person of mature and sympathetic outlook should be selected to conduct the interview. A friendly atmosphere is important. The interviewer's purpose is to get information, not to argue with the employee over her reasons for leaving. With understanding and tact, valuable information concerning causes of separation may be obtained. Even though the employee leaves she may leave with friendly feelings and a better understanding of the hospital and with assurance that the exit interview will not be detrimental to her references.

In order to offset the reluctance of employees who have not given frank and candid statements during the exit interview, a questionnaire may

---

*Source: *Suggestions for Control of Turnover and Absenteeism*, U.S. Department of Labor, 1972.

be sent to the employee 30 to 60 days after her termination. (It should be accompanied by an explanatory letter and a self-addressed, stamped envelope.) The questionnaire should contain questions concerning the employee's feelings about the hospital, her job, and her supervisor.

If the employee has become established in a new job, she may feel freer to give candid, objective answers. These answers can be checked against information given in the exit interview and discrepancies noted. These additional comments can supplement the information gathered in the exit interview. Analysis of information gathered in this manner over a period of time will pinpoint areas in which corrective action may be taken.

Exit interviews should be held in a private office where the employee will feel at ease and may speak without fear of being overheard. Where this situation is impossible, conditions of maximum privacy should be arranged.

Conducting the Interview

Interviews with employees, for the most part, follow a general pattern by progressing through the following stages:

(1) Informal conversation of general interest. Every effort should be made to establish rapport with the worker. An atmosphere of "quizzing" will illicit little useful information. A chat about something of general interest can be steered around to the principal reason for the interview in a pleasant and informal manner.

(2) The employee's own statement. The employee should be given every opportunity to tell why she wishes to resign, if that is the reason for the interview. Interrupting her to influence her statements should be avoided. Attention to all of her remarks is important for subsequently directing the interview to an effective conclusion.

(3) Questioning by the interviewer. When the employee finishes her statement, the interviewer should ask appropriate questions in an attempt to determine, in the case of an employee who plans to resign, the true reasons for the worker's dissatisfaction—her attitudes, feelings, and motivations. The interviewer should:

a. Ask for specific information about the situation she describes and evaluate it in view of statements made by the supervisor.
b. Ask the employee if she has explored the possibilities of taking training to obtain greater satisfaction in her present position, or to prepare herself for promotion, or if she has explored the possibility of transfer to another unit in the nursing department.
c. Suggest ways in which the present situation might be improved to the worker's satisfaction, or state what arrangements might be made to transfer her to another job, paying careful attention to the employee's reaction to all suggestions.
d. Attempt to restate in specific terms the problems she may encounter in leaving the organization, and encourage her to try to adjust to the present situation with whatever changes or improvements are suggested. Sometimes, stimulating interest in the importance of her job to the completed product or services of the company, or pointing out her loss in seniority resulting from her separation, will be effective in retaining a worker.

(4) Final stage of informal conversation. Closing stages of the interview are important to insure a mutual understanding of any arrangements agreed upon and to plan for any followup required. The interview should close on a friendly basis, even if the employee persists in her decision to leave. She should be made to feel that she will be given every consideration if she cares to return.

Since so many eventualities are considered in an outline for an exit interview, the process may appear rather complicated and time consuming. An experienced interviewer can usually conduct a satisfactory interview in from 15 to 30 minutes.

Chapter 32—Criticizing, Disciplining, and Handling Grievances

CRITICIZING

Criticism in its highest sense means trying to learn the best that is known and thought and measuring things by that standard.

Criticism can be used and met constructively or destructively. It can be the means by which people receiving it climb, or it can be used to bolster the critic's vanity. Captious criticism takes note of trivial faults; its author is usually unduly exacting or perversely hard to please. Carping criticism is a perverse picking of flaws. Cavilling criticism stresses the habit of raising petty objections. Censorious criticism means a tendency to be severely condemnatory of that which one does not like.

Ordinary faultfinding seems to indicate less background and experience than the art of criticism requires. It is wholly concerned with tearing down and scolding, whereas criticism is the art of analyzing and judging the quality of something.

Silence is sometimes the severest criticism.*

What Is Fair Criticism?*

Fair criticism does not judge without factual information. It considers the event on which it is to pass judgment in the light of these factors: What was said or done? What did the person mean to say or do? What was his reason for saying or doing it? What is the effect of what he said or did? Why do I object to it?

Fair criticism does not exaggerate. All but a few careful and considerate persons seem to be urged either to overstate things by 100 percent, or to understate them by 50 percent, in order to criticize them with greater enjoyment.

Fair criticism does not include common gossip. Gossip may be merely friendly talking or useless chatter, but it too often degenerates into mischievous comment on neighbors or business associates.

The Ideal Critic*

The ideal critic would know the topic, he would be dispassionate in weighing the evidence, he would have ability to see clearly what follows from the facts, he would be willing to reconsider the facts if that seemed advisable, and he would have courage to follow his thoughts through to the bitter end. He would not, in all this process, brush aside the help of advisors. He would retain a keen and lively consciousness of truth.

In making his criticism known, the ideal critic would have regard for the feelings of the other fellow. Courtesy is easily the best single quality to raise one—even a critic—above the crowd.

Charming ways are quick winners. When an end is sought, why browbeat and shout and storm if one can persuade?

The good critic will not force the person he criticizes too far. It is always good strategy to let the other fellow save face.

---

*Source: Reprinted from John R. Heron, "On Criticism," *Monthly Letter*, November 1977, with permission of Royal Bank of Canada.

Correcting Errors*

The *purpose* of correcting errors is to help the employee improve his work performance.

Correction must be focused on helping the employee identify and understand his error and learn how to avoid repeating it. He must know what the supervisor expects and feel confident that he can live up to these expectations.

There are three steps in correcting errors: (1) review the standards by which the job was to be done; (2) point out the error; (3) indicate what must be done to correct it. These steps should be followed in sequence. Unfortunately, most supervisors start by pointing out the error. This usually results in defensiveness, excuses or an attempt to focus on the things that the employee does do right. He tries to justify his poor performance rather than to correct it.

Reviewing Standards

The importance of reviewing standards as the first step in correcting errors cannot be overemphasized, even though it is seldom done.

When an employee ignores step-by-step procedures for accomplishing a particular task, the supervisor should review the procedures with the employee and insure that the latter understands the standards. But what about standards that govern certain behavior or practices but are not in writing? Often hospitals have no written policies, procedures, or rules about gossiping, passing along rumors, arguing with other employees, improper personal appearance, and so on.

Here one must fall back on broad policies of the organization, some of which may only be implied, not available in writing. The supervisor may even point out that management does not tolerate gossip and rumor because they waste time, affect morale and reduce the quality and quantity of work.

Step by Step Guidelines

Effective guidelines have been developed for carrying out the three steps of correcting errors. Supervisors who follow these guidelines can make corrections far more objectively and are less likely to become involved in personalities and personal problems.

1. *Correct the first error.* No employee should be allowed to get by with a work error, even once. If he does, other employees will be encouraged to put forth less than their best effort.
2. *Choose the proper time and place.* Corrections should be made as soon after the error as feasible. Waiting a few days lessens the effectiveness of the correction. Correction interviews should be in private, never before fellow employees.
3. *Be objective.* To be objective, the supervisor must correct errors when he is not angry or irritated. Being objective means correcting the *situation*, not a personality. It is important not to criticize the employee as a person. Correction should be made to help him improve his work.
4. *Be specific.* Never make general statements. General statements make the employee defensive. He responds by pointout the things he does correctly and believes can defend. Focus on a specific error.
5. *Stick to the facts.* Never base a correction on hearsay. Get all sides of a story before acting.
6. *Do not react to excuses.* Employees often try to justify their errors, to explain that errors were not their fault. Never let the listener divert attention from the specific work error under discussion, but stick to the three steps, saying, "These are the standards you agreed to follow, this is what you did wrong, and this is what must be done."
7. *Be serious.* Avoid joking or teasing. If a work error is serious enough to call to an employee's attention, it is worthy of a serious approach.
8. *Spell out the remedy.* Be as specific about the remedy as about the error. Don't leave the employee uncertain of what is expected.
9. *Allow employee questions.* Let the employee ask questions, if he desires. This gives immediate feedback on whether he understands the standards, the error and the remedy.

---

*Source: Reprinted from Winborn E. Davis, "Correcting Errors in Work Performance," *Hospital Topics,* August 1973, with permission of the publisher.

10. *Don't make excuses yourself.* Supervisors often lessen the value of correction by being apologetic. Supervisors are paid to deal openly with errors in work performance. It is part of the job.
11. *Individualize the employee.* Sensitivities vary; approach employees differently, yet follow the same steps and guidelines.
12. *Tie up loose ends.* Get immediate feedback on whether the employee truly understands what went wrong and what is expected.

DISCIPLINING

Nature and Importance of Discipline*

Over the years, discipline has had at least two meanings. Discipline first meant complete and total obedience to rules and regulations and to the directives and orders of superiors. Failure to comply resulted in punitive actions. Closer examination of discipline reveals that the most constructive and effective forms of discipline involve something more than mere obedience to authority. The second and higher discipline, then, involves self-control and a sense of personal responsibility for behavior and performance.

Traditional discipline is achieved through the authority of the individual in a supervisory capacity. The self-control form is achieved through the influence of a systematic frame of reference that is held in common by all individuals in the organization and that guides their actions.

Factors Influencing Discipline*

There are several factors that influence the learning of self-discipline. They can be considered to be conditions that must be satisfied if discipline is to be developed and maintained within an organization.

Understanding of requirements. Good discipline rests upon the security of understanding. Each individual in an organization must know and understand the ground rules, the limits, and the actions and behavior that are approved and disapproved. And those requirements must remain relatively consistent if subordinates are to learn them.

Atmosphere of confidence. Good discipline rests on a foundation of mutual trust and confidence. That confidence includes the confidence of managers in their subordinates, of subordinates in the decisions and actions of their supervisors, and of everyone in the organization in his own ability to perform effectively.

Informal sanctions. Good discipline is the result of the operation of informal sanctions—social pressures generated within a group or organization to enforce informal norms of performance and conduct. The extent to which norms allow a group to accept or resist organizational rules and principles plays an important part in the development and maintenance of discipline. The concept of group norm is comparable with such concepts as codes, customs, and traditions.

Formal sanctions. When authority is used to enforce discipline, formal sanctions must play an important part in the process. But it is not just the sanctions themselves that exert an influence upon the development and maintenance of discipline. The way in which they are used to enforce compliance with decisions, rules, and principles is even more important. Two principles apply: first, justice and fairness to all concerned must be assured and, second, the sanctions must be applied consistently. Subordinates must be confident that they will be treated fairly, and they must know that punishments come to them because of what they *do* and not because of how someone in authority *feels*.

Goals, cohesion, and morale. When an individual develops strong commitment to the objectives of an organization, he is more likely to be highly motivated. Such motivation leads to acceptance of organizationally approved standards of conduct. Cohesion is related to identification with the organization and to the capacity of the unit to exert influence without the use of punitive measures. In general, cohesion results in greater conformity with the norms of conduct of the organization. Morale influences discipline because attitudes affect behavior. Poor morale

---
*Source: Reprinted, by permission of the publisher, from *Managing Training and Developing Systems*, William Tracey, © 1974 by AMACOM, a division of American Management Associations. All rights reserved.

and poor discipline are often partners in the disintegration of an organization.

Discipline Approaches*

Key Ingredients for an Effective Discipline Program

The two most widespread problems in the administration of discipline are 1) a broad managerial failure to act promptly in dealing with discipline problems as they occur; or 2) over-reaction when a long-overdue action is finally taken. The basic foundation of any sound disciplinary program must be a set of procedures which are tailored to achieve the particular objectives of a given organization.

However, a well-written discipline policy is only as effective as its enforcement. And this is where most organizational efforts at effective discipline administration break down or are less than fully successful. Implementation is only successful when discipline is characterized by: 1) promptness; 2) impartiality; 3) consistency; 4) non-punitiveness; 5) fairness; 6) advance warning; and 7) followthrough.

The single efforts of a supervisor acting alone are quite insufficient to make an organizational discipline program effective. Any successful program must include the following elements: 1) an organizational set of discipline policies and procedures; 2) a uniform application of discipline rules; 3) supervisors who are trained in the knowledge and skills related to implementing a discipline policy; 4) an orientation program which informs all new employees about management's expectations of appropriate performance and behavior; 5) a continuous management effort which communicates to employees all changes and revisions in personnel and discipline policies—*before* changes are actually put into effect.

Key Factors in Analyzing Discipline Problems

1. *Seriousness of problem.* How severe is the problem or infraction?
2. *Time span.* Have there been other discipline problems in the past, and over how long a time span?
3. *Frequency and nature of problems.* Is the current problem part of an emerging or continuing pattern of discipline infractions?
4. *Employee's work history.* How long has the employee worked for the organization, and what was the quality of performance?
5. *Extenuating factors.* Are there extenuating circumstances related to the problem? For example, if there was a fight, was the employee provoked?
6. *Degree of orientation.* To what extent has management made an earlier effort to educate the person causing the problem about the existing discipline rules and procedures and the consequences of violations?
7. *History of organization's discipline practices.* How have similar infractions been dealt with in the past within the department? Within the entire organization? Has there been consistency in the application of discipline procedures?
8. *Implications for other employees.* What impact will your decision have on other workers in the unit?
9. *Management backing.* If employees decide to take their case to higher management, do you have reasonable evidence to justify your decision?

Problem Solving

A basic idea in contemporary management practice is that discipline should not be used as a substitute for effective supervision. The first approach to most employee-caused problems should be characterized by problem solving. Supervisors are expected to aid their employees in analyzing work problems, obtaining information not readily available to the employee, and in some cases serving as a counselor on personal problems affecting the employee's work problems.

In other words, the supervisor has an obligation to attempt to deal with the root cause of the employee's discipline problem. This approach does not preclude expressing management's concern over the employee's infraction; therefore, a problem-solving effort by the supervisor should be part of an oral warning discussion. In

---

*Source: Reprinted from "Effective Discipline in Employee Relations" by Wallace Wohlking, September 1975, with permission of *Personnel Journal*, Costa Mesa, California; all rights reserved.

other cases, depending on the judgment of the supervisor, he or she may want to try a counseling problem-solving interview without resorting to a disciplinary action.

Disciplinary Action

While problem-solving efforts can eliminate or significantly minimize future employee discipline infractions, problem-solving will not always work. At this point, a disciplinary action should be taken. The typical sequence of steps under "progressive" or "corrective" discipline is as follows:

1. Oral warning
2. Written warning
3. Suspension
4. Dismissal

Oral Warning

As a rule, the oral warning should be conducted in an informal atmosphere. The purpose of this informality is to encourage employees to relate their view of the problem with an opportunity for a reasonably complete statement of the facts as they see them. The supervisor may expect to question the employee during the discussion, but normally the supervisor should avoid interrupting the employee. It is important to obtain all relevant facts.

After the supervisor knows the relevant facts, and after these facts have been analyzed and evaluated against the employee's past record, the employee should be informed of the supervisor's determination. This includes:

- Any expected improvement in future behavior
- Assistance, if appropriate, that the supervisor plans to give to the employee in correcting the problem
- The disciplinary penalty being imposed (assuming there is one)
- Any follow-up action which will be taken.

Written Warning

The written warning is the second step. It is preceded by an interview similar to the oral warning-type discussion. Employees are told at the conclusion of the interview that a written warning will be issued. The key points that should be included in a written warning are:

- A statement of the problem
- Identification of the rule which was violated
- Consequences of continued deviant behavior
- The employee's commitment to make correction (if any)
- Follow-up action to be taken (if any)

Suspension

Suspensions can only occur for minor discipline violations after there has been a record of oral and written warnings established. Suspension, of course, can be applied without such a record if a major discipline infraction has occurred. Suspension rather than dismissal is used by management when it feels that there is still some hope for "rehabilitating" the employee. Or, because of a union presence, management may feel that it cannot sustain a discharge if that discharge was taken to arbitration.

Suspension may be for a period of one day to several weeks. Disciplinary layoffs in excess of thirty days are rare.

Dismissal

The move to discharge a person should only be invoked when all other problem-solving and disciplinary efforts have failed. A word of warning. There should be an accurate documented record of the oral and written warnings, and suspension, if any, received by the employee. If the employee primarily is being discharged for one violation, the supervisor should be very sure that the reason for the discharge conforms to the organization's criteria of a major discipline violation and that she can effectively support the case if it is reviewed by higher levels of management, or if the case should go to arbitration or before governmental agencies, such as The Human Rights and Equal Employment Opportunity Commissions.

Other Kinds of Steps

Though the sequence of oral and written warnings, suspension and dismissal are considered to be the standard steps in the discipline process, some organizations have developed embellishments of the process by adding other elements to that sequence. For example, there is the "corrective" interview. This step is designed to precede any formal disciplining act. The corrective interview is used to instigate an improvement in behavior without having the interview necessarily go on the employee's personnel record.

Another device which is occasionally used in a progressive discipline policy is the "final warning." The final warning is a step inserted between the written warning and suspension. The effect of this extra step is to allow the employee additional and more gradual notification that he or she is approaching a point where severe punishment (suspension and/or dismissal) is about to be imposed.

The "Slide Rule" Approach to Discipline

Some organizations attempt to eliminate judgments that a supervisor is required to exercise in disciplinary cases by developing a "slide rule" set of discipline policies.

For example, discipline policy based on this concept might state, "the second time an employee is found smoking in the work area, he will be suspended for three days."

Slide rule policies remove much of the traditional considerations which must go into analyzing and assessing a determination in discipline cases. Factors normally considered in evaluating most discipline cases are ignored for a mechanistic, formularized approach.

HANDLING GRIEVANCES*

Minimizing Grievances

Although there is no way to completely eliminate grievances, there are commonsense guidelines that will reduce the number and the cost of grievances. Here are some suggestions:

1. Be alert for common causes of irritation within your area of responsibility. Correct minor irritations promptly before they explode into major problems.
2. Do not knowingly violate established policy, procedure, or practice. This, of course, requires you to be completely familiar with all policies and contractual clauses that affect the supervisor-employee relationship.
3. Keep promises. Do not make commitments you cannot keep. Many grievances are over the nonfulfillment of a commitment made by a supervisor.
4. Let your employees know how they are getting along. Don't wait for the formal performance review to keep an employee informed of progress or problems. This will minimize the number of grievances that develop when employees are warned about poor performance after having received positive performance reviews earlier in the year.
5. If an employee doesn't measure up, let that employee know. Find out why there is a problem and provide direction and coaching.
6. Encourage constructive suggestions; act on these suggestions where feasible and give proper recognition to the originators. Participation will go a long way to minimize grievances that may develop because of policy changes.
7. Assign and schedule work impartially; avoid favoritism in respect to working conditions or employee benefits.
8. Be sure your employees understand the meaning of and reasons for your orders and instructions. Use language that is meaningful from their point of view.
9. Be consistent in your words and actions unless there are important reasons for deviation. Where deviation is justified, clearly communicate those reasons to the employees. Explain changes in or deviations from policy, procedure, or established practice.
10. Act promptly on reasonable requests from your employees. Don't keep employees waiting for answers to their questions. Nothing is more destructive than a grievance allowed to grow because of lack of prompt response on the part of a superior. Remember, you may have to say "no," but a constructive and sympathetic "no" can do less damage than a harsh "yes."
11. If corrective action must be taken, take it promptly; but do not discipline an employee in public.

---

*Source: Reprinted from *The Health Care Supervisor's Handbook* by Norman Metzger, with permission of Aspen Systems Corporation, © 1978.

12. It is essential that you maintain and preserve the dignity of the employee. This may be difficult when dealing with grievances, but it is at the heart of a sound supervisor-employee relationship.
13. Remember that employees want to be appreciated; they want to know that you recognize their meritorious performance. Give credit where it is due. This will minimize many grievances which spring from a lack of recognition.
14. Look to your employees for suggestions and advice. Give them the feeling that they are in on things. Many grievances arise because the employee is not prepared for change.
15. "A stitch in time. . . ." This old adage is most appropriate in effective grievance handling. Look around and try to anticipate areas and actions that may cause irritation. By anticipating problems you will minimize them.
16. Employees who are properly trained are less likely to have grievances. Employees who know what they are doing and, therefore, do it well, are less frustrated. This is of particular relevance when dealing with the new employee.
17. Unclear, unexplained orders or instructions can lead to grievances. Make certain that you communicate clearly and back up orders and instructions with a "why."
18. When you must administer discipline, be objective, equitable, and consistent. The majority of grievances stem from real or perceived inequality of treatment.
19. Don't belittle employees or underestimate them. If they have a grievance, it does not really matter whether it falls under the personnel policy manual or the labor contract. It is real to the employee and you must deal with it.
20. Remember—The people who work for you are just that, people. Treat them as individuals.

Tips for Handling Grievances

The principal requirements for handling grievances effectively are:
- a strong desire to make the personnel policy manual and/or labor contract work, to resolve dissatisfactions and conflicts, and to supervise more effectively;
- a strong effort on the part of first-line supervisors to settle grievances at the very first step in the grievance procedure;
- a sound working knowledge of the personnel policy manual and the labor contract, including new interpretations and precedents;
- a consistent approach to carrying out provisions of the personnel policy manual and/or labor contract.

Key Points

1. Employees deserve a complete and empathetic hearing of all grievances they present.
2. The most important job in the handling of grievances is getting at the facts. Therefore, listen attentively, encourage a full discussion, and defer judgment.
3. Look for the hidden agenda. Look beyond the selected incident, judge the grievance in context.
4. Hasty decisions often backfire. On the other hand, the employee deserves a speedy reply. In order to determine the proper disposition of a grievance, ask yourself the following questions.
   a. What actually happened?
   b. Where did it happen?
   c. What should have happened?
   d. When did it happen?
   e. Who was involved?
   f. Were there any witnesses?
   g. Why did the problem develop?[*]
5. While you are investigating the grievance, try to separate fact from opinion or impressions. Consult others when appropriate. Most important, check with your personnel people.
6. After you have come to your decision, promptly communicate that decision to the employee. Remember, a sympathetic "no" is far more effective than a harsh "yes." Therefore, give the reason for the decision and inform the employee of the right to appeal.

---

[*]Source: J. Brad Chapman, "Constructive Grievance Handling," included in M. Gene Newport, ed., *Supervisory Management: Tools and Techniques* (New York: West Publishing Company, 1976), p. 268.

7. Remember that you have to sell your decision. The decision is yours, don't pass the buck by placing the blame on your superiors.
8. There is no substitute for common sense in arriving at a decision.
9. Written records are most important, they serve as a review for the supervisor to ensure consistency.
10. Followup is essential. Even if the employee does not appeal your decision, you should check back to see if the decision "took" or was upheld. There is no better way to win employee respect than to give due recognition to employee problems. A little bit of followup goes a long way.

A Grievance Procedure*

In many hospitals the grievance procedure is essentially a set of appeal steps to higher and higher levels of management. Labor relations experts generally agree that prompt settlement of grievances is the preferred method. Delays in processing grievances may result in employee frustration and can lead to a breakdown in union-management relations or even to a wildcat strike. A smooth-functioning grievance procedure, on the other hand, can lower employee frustration and improve the general morale. Of course, it takes the cooperation of both parties to resolve grievances promptly and efficiently.

Obviously, the number of steps in a grievance procedure influences the amount of time it takes to process a grievance. According to a recent study of a large national sample of hospital contracts, a four-step grievance procedure is most common in the industry.

Note that the grievance procedure outlined here specifies that in Step 1 the aggrieved employee attempts to adjust the complaint with his or her immediate supervisor. The employee may or may not, under the HELP contract cited above, request that the union steward be present. Discussion with the complainant's supervisor may result in the resolution of the grievance, thus eliminating the need to go through the entire procedure. Moreover, settling the problem at this level in the procedure may be most satisfying to the grievant. In the first place, he or she perceives that the problem is being handled promptly. There is also a closer identification with his or her own supervisor than with higher hospital personnel or with an arbitrator. Notice that in the HELP contract cited above, the second-step hospital representative is the unit head, while at the third step this representative is the hospital administrator.

A Model Grievance Procedure*

While the exact wording of the grievance procedure may vary from contract to contract, it is instructive to reproduce here a procedure found in a number of Hospital Employees Labor Program (HELP) contracts:

Step 1. The employee involved shall orally discuss the grievance with his immediate supervisor. The employee or the supervisor may request that the area steward be present during such discussion. The supervisor shall reply to the grievance within four (4) calendar days.

Step 2. If the matter is not satisfactorily adjusted in Step 1, or an answer is not given within the time specified, the employee and/or the area steward shall orally discuss the grievance with the unit head and/or his designee within ten (10) calendar days after the initial discussion with the immediate supervisor. The union staff representative shall be permitted to meet with the department head before the grievance is reduced to writing in order to assist in adjusting the grievance. The reply to the grievance shall be given within four (4) calendar days.

Step 3. If the matter is not satisfactorily adjusted in Step 2 or an answer is not given within the time specified, the grievance shall be reduced to writing on a standard grievance form, signed by the employee involved and the area steward, dated and submitted to

---

*Source: Reprinted from *Arbitration in Health Care* by Donald J. Petersen, Julius Rezler, and Keith A. Reed, with permission of Aspen Systems Corporation, © 1981.

*Source: Reprinted from *Chicago Hospital Council: Analysis of Collective Bargaining Agreements in Chicago Area Hospitals, 1975–1976,* with permission of Chicago Hospital Council, © 1975.

the hospital administrator within seven (7) calendar days after the Step 2 answer or the time specified for such answer. The written grievance shall contain a brief statement of the nature of the grievance and shall state the relief sought. The grievance shall be taken up in a meeting between the chief steward and/or staff representative and with the hospital administrator or his designee. Any area stewards involved in the grievance may be present at the meeting and participate in discussing the grievance. The hospital administrator or his designee shall reply to the grievance in writing within ten (10) calendar days after the meeting.

Step 4. If the matter is not adjusted in Step 3 or an answer is not given by the hospital administrator or his designee within the time specified, the union may, by written notice to the hospital within ten (10) calendar days after the Step 3 answer or the time specified for such answer, request that the grievance be referred to an impartial arbitrator selected in the manner hereinafter stated. The parties will attempt to select an arbitrator and if they fail to agree upon an arbitrator within seven (7) calendar days, the union shall, within fourteen calendar days from the date of its notice to the hospital, request the American Arbitration Association to furnish each party with an identical panel of seven arbitrators. In the event that either party is dissatisfied with the names appearing on such panel, such party may request a second panel, from which an impartial arbitrator must be chosen. Following the selection of the arbitrator, the parties shall make arrangements with him to hear and decide the grievance without unreasonable delay. The arbitrator selected shall have authority only to interpret and apply the provisions of this agreement to the extent necessary to decide the submitted grievance and shall not have authority to add to, detract from or alter in any way the provisions of the agreement. His award shall be final and binding upon the hospital, the union and all employees. The fees and expenses of the arbitration shall be borne equally by the hospital and the union.

Chapter 33—Employee Salaries

SALARY POLICIES*

The salary ranges and levels are key ingredients to a successful salary program. They must be substantial enough to attract and retain the most able employee yet modest enough not to waste the hospital's resources. The ranges and levels are primarily the responsibility of the personnel director and justifiably are scrutinized carefully by the hospital since they represent such a substantial impact on its funds. (See Figure 33-1 for a sample outline of "Salary and Wage Guidelines," and Table 33-1 for a sample listing of "Hospital Positions by Grade.")

The salary ranges provide for a minimum, a midpoint and a maximum. The minimum must be high enough for 80 to 90 percent of the candidates to accept it as a starting salary. It must be competitive. The midpoint must be enough to retain the employee once he has become thoroughly skilled and contributing to the job. The maximum must be sufficient to retain the best employees, avoiding their loss by piracy or disenchantment.

To achieve these objectives the salary range will usually be narrower at entry-level positions, broadening out either on a dollar or percentage basis at higher grades. A common variance in salary ranges is from 20 percent (minimum to maximum) at entry-level positions to 35 to 40 percent at the senior positions (department head). This reflects a greater need at senior levels for salary flexibility to reward a greater variety of skills and to minimize turnover, the impact of which increases dramatically at high levels. Such differences in the breadth of ranges and salary levels introduce a great emphasis on market requirements as opposed to equity requirements.

The salary levels within a system are the "moment of truth" to that program and are the most important factor to both employer and employee. Determining optimum salary levels depends most on management judgments rather than on a system. In arriving at these judgments many questions must be resolved by the hospital, only some of which can be answered in objective terms.

What is the hospital's philosophy toward salaries? Should it be the highest paying employer? Should it be competitive or slightly over or under the competition? Also, do cost of living changes play a role in salary level determination?

What are the present market forces? Are neighboring hospitals and other employers raising salaries, or do they expect to? Is there a labor shortage or a surplus?

What are the prevailing union salaries? If you are a nonunion hospital, what levels will be necessary to discourage collective bargaining?

What have been the cost of living changes? Are they fully represented by the market forces?

---

*Source: Reprinted from *Health Care Labor Manual* by Martin E. Skoler, with permission of Aspen Systems Corporation, © 1981.

Figure 33-1 Salary and wage guidelines: sample form

FROM:	Administrator
TO:	Distribution List
SUBJECT	SALARY AND WAGE GUIDELINES
PURPOSE	To provide for a sound, fair and equitable system of compensating hospital employees by paying the best possible wages based on job evaluation, area wages, effect on hospital costs and employee performance.
PAY PERIOD AND WORK WEEK	*Pay Period*—will begin Sunday morning, at one (1) minute after Saturday midnight and end fourteen (14) days later at midnight Saturday. *Work Week*—will begin at one (1) minute after Saturday midnight and end Saturday midnight seven (7) days later.
OVERTIME	Authorized overtime will be paid at 1 ½ times the employee's regular rate for all hours *worked* in excess of forty (40) hours per work week. Exemptions to the time and one-half provision will be based on the revised Federal Wage and Hour Laws and hospital policy. All overtime must be approved prior to the hours of actual overtime work, by the Department Head and counter-signed by Administration.
LEAVE	Leave paid hours are hours not actually worked and *will not* be included in the computation of overtime.
GRADES & STEPS	All non-department head positions have been assigned a grade of 1-20. Each grade has a minimum step and 8 other steps. Employees may progress within their grade by receiving step increases.
WAITING PERIOD	Is the length of time an employee must wait before proceeding to the next step in grade. New waiting periods begin with promotions and/or step increases. Merit increases do *not* change the waiting period. The minimum time (waiting period) required to advance from the minimum step to step 1 is six (6) months; from step 1 to step 2, step 2 to step 3, step 3 to step 4, etc. is one (1) year.
EXCEPTION-MERIT INCREASE	The exception to the above waiting period is the employee who is recommended for, and received a merit increase (1 step). A merit increase recommendation, however, must be based on at least six (6) months of observed performance.
PROMOTIONS	Promotions will normally result in an approximate 10% increase in salary.
MAXIMUM ADVANCEMENT	Employees will not normally be advanced more than two (2) steps in any twelve (12) continuous months.
WITHHOLDING INCREASES	Step increases may be withheld with proper justification for a period not to exceed forty-five (45) days. If not granted then, a *new* waiting period will begin.
HIRING RATES	New employees will normally be hired at the minimum step of the position they are filling. New employees may be hired at step 1 or step 2 of the appropriate grade provided the Department Head and the Personnel Director agree. Hiring at above minimum will be guided by the following: 1. Applicants with from two (2) to five (5) years of directly related recent experience or an additional education degree deemed appropriate without experience may be hired at step 1. 2. Applicants with over five (5) years of directly related recent experience may be hired at step 2. 3. Applicants with from two (2) to five (5) years experience as in 1, and an additional education degree deemed appropriate may be hired at step 2. 4. The above guidelines apply to applicants who the department head feels will be outstanding employees.
TRAINEES	New employees hired as bonafide trainees will normally be paid at 90% of the minimum step established for the position. The trainee will receive an increase to the

Figure 33-1 continued

	minimum step when satisfactorily completing the training period. A new waiting period will begin with that increase.
SHIFT DIFFERENTIAL	Additional compensation will be paid to employees in specific job classifications who work either an evening or night shift. They are as follows:

	Evening	Night
1. R.N.s, Lab Technologist, Respiratory Therapist (Reg.)	$.25 ph	$.30 ph
2. LPN, X-Ray Tech., Lab Technicians, Respiratory Therapy Technician	$.15 ph	$.10 ph
3. All Others	$.15 ph	$.10 ph

SPECIALTY DIFFERENTIAL	Additional Compensation will be paid to the following Nursing Personnel who work in ICU, CCU, PCU, OR, RR and ER:

Staff Nurses	$.15 ph
LPN	$.10 ph
Nursing Assistant	$.10 ph
Unit Secretary	$.10 ph

CALL PAY	Employees subject to call will be paid at a rate of $1.00 per hour of call. Employees on call who are called in to work will be paid at their normal base rate for no less than one (1) hour for the first hour and any time beyond for actual time worked. Call pay stops when the normal shift begins and/or the employee comes to the hospital in response to being called in.
EFFECTIVE DATES	Salary changes will be effective *only* at the beginning of a pay period.
RESPONSIBILITY AND AUTHORITY	The Administrator or his designee will approve any salary increases. The Personnel Director will be responsible for staff supervision of the Salary and Wage Program.

Submitted by: Approved by:

_____ _____

Director of Personnel Administrator

Distribution List

All Departments

Source: Reprinted from *Health Care Labor Manual* by Martin E. Skoler, with permission of Aspen Systems Corporation, © 1981.

Do they suggest even higher salaries than the market might dictate?

Finally, what about the hospital's ability to pay? If it is limited does this ability result in adjustments only in areas of most critical need within budget limitations?

The answers to many of these questions will modify the answer to the basic question: what salary levels will be demanded on us by the market place if we are to attract and retain competent staff?

Salary surveys can be particularly valuable in answering this question, although they are only part of the answer. Most hospital associations have reliable salary information, particularly about jobs involving large numbers of employees or for which there is a labor shortage. Additionally, survey information from nonclinical sources should be reviewed for managerial, business, craft and service positions. A common mistake made by hospitals is to ignore the fact that many employees can sell their abilities to nonhospital employers.

Table 33-1 Hospital Positions by Grade

1
Transportation Aide
Food Serv. Ass't. I
Housekeeping Ass't. I
Laboratory Aide

2
Nursing Ass't.
Food Service Ass't. II
Housekeeping Ass't. II

3
Medical Records Clerk
Receiving & Stock Clerk
Physical Therapy Aide
Phlebotomist
File Clerk—Cashier
File Clerk—X-Ray
X-Ray Assistant

4
Clerk Typist (Pool)
Statistic Clerk (M.R.)
Keypunch Operator
PBX Operator
Answering Service Operator
Personnel Clerk
Food Service Clerk
Lab Clerk
Assistant Cook

5
Insurance Verification
Cashier—Medicare Log
Insurance Clerk
Admitting Clerk
Credit Clerk
Payroll Clerk
Accounts Receivable & Payroll Clerk
Cook
EKG Tech.
Purchasing—Inventory Clerk
Unit Secretary

6
Medical Transcriptionist
Food Service Supervisor
Housekeeping Supervisor
Watchman
PBX Operator, Chief
Receiving & Stock Supervisor
Admitting—Reservation

7
Secretary (Dept. Head)
LPN
Answering Service, Chief
Medical Transcriptionist—Utilization Clerk—(M.D.)

8
Personnel Assistant
EKG, Chief
LPN (Meds.)
O.R. Tech.
EMT
Office Manager—X-Ray
Office Manager—Surgery

9
Admitting Supervisor
Patient Finance Counselor (Supervisor)
Insurance Supervisor
Executive Secretary (Medical Staff)
Respiratory Tech. (not certified)
State Tech. (Laboratory)

10
Executive Secretary (Administration)
Grounds Keeper
Respiratory Tech. (certified)

11
Ass't. Director—Food Service
Ass't. Director—Housekeeping
X-Ray Tech. (Gen.)
Med. Tech (CLA)
Bookkeeper
Maintenance Engineers

12
Computer Operator
EEG Tech.
Respiratory Therapist (Registered or eligible)

Table 33-1 continued

13 Maintenance Foreman X-Ray Tech. (Special Procedures) Medical Tech. (AMT)	*14* Chef
15 Staff Nurse	*16* Inservice Instructor, R.N. Discharge Co-ordinator, R.N. Nurse Clinician Programmer Nuclear Medicine Tech. Medical Tech. (ASCP) Team Leader, R.N.
17 Dietitian Employee Health Nurse Accountant Charge Nurse, R.N.	*18* Epidemiologist Head Nurse Supervisor, R.N.
19 Assistant Director, R.N.	*20* Therapy Tech.

Merit vs. Longevity

What will be the basis for individual salary determination and salary increment? There are two major alternatives for consideration: the merit system and the longevity system.

The Merit Approach

This system is characterized by the ranges of salary increase that an employee may receive, based on relative achievement reflected by his supervisor's recommendation at predetermined review times.

Also common to this approach are the concepts of salary minimum, midpoint, and maximum. The salary minimum is the starting rate for employees not having exceptional experience. The employee then moves to the midpoint by 2 to 3 increases, often occurring at, let us say, six month intervals. The midpoint of the range is also the competitive rate for similar work being done in the community. The spread between minimum and midpoint reflects the learning period necessary to become job competent. Once an employee arrives at the midpoint of the range, salary review periods are longer (at least 12 months), and the basis for any change is exceptional, rather than competent performance. The maximum salary is the highest that can be received by a person in a particular salary grade.

To many, the merit system has a very logical theoretical base. Should not the hard-working employee be rewarded for his superior effort and ability? Should not the resources of the organization be directed primarily to substantial contributors, rather than to the indolent and mediocre?

Some administrators have taken exception to the merit system and its salary range concept based on problems they have experienced in its operation. For instance:

- If the midpoint is the competitive salary in the community, and particularly if many employees in the area are on a single rate (union) system, how can employees be recruited at less than that midpoint rate?
- If the range between minimum and midpoint is the learning period, does not the learning period differ from job to job and person to person? Can there be an arbitrary time between minimum and midpoint?
- Can the hospital remain competitive and deny employees some annual increase after

they arrive at midpoint? It not, the notion of exceptional performance is in jeopardy.
- Finally, the most common criticism of the merit system is management's imprecise ability to determine degrees of merit, and the resulting small differences in salary between employees. In practice, can management effectively measure the differences in contribution? Is it possible that the employee who is less of a rival to the supervisor and is more deferential, receive the larger increase?

This latter criticism is particularly common at entry level positions where degrees of merit are more difficult to determine.

These challenges to the basic merit system have resulted in conversion by some hospitals to other systems such as longevity.

However, many who retain a belief in the efficacy of rewarding merit have developed modifications to meet the weaknesses in the merit program. These include:

- Establishment of step increments rather than a range of possible increase and a "go-no-go" decision by the supervisor as to whether a raise is merited or is to be delayed to another specified review date. This decision often must be approved at the next level of supervision.
- Establishment of quantitative bases for evaluation wherever possible (*e.g.*, attendance, typing production speed, etc.).
- Development of participating approaches to performance evaluation, including self-appraisal, objectives-related appraisal, or appraisal by several supervisors.
- Moving to a longevity approach for entry level positions, where differences in performance are difficult to assess.

Under this program, employees would receive modest longevity increases to midpoint, then be reviewed on the merit system. Other employees, in positions whose achievements are more measurable, would be eligible for merit increases from the minimum.

The Longevity Approach

Much of the structure described under the merit system also applies to any pay increase program based upon longevity. There is still the minimum, midpoint, maximum concept, with a person eligible for salary reviews at stated intervals. The principal difference is that increases are based upon length of service only, irrespective of achievement. The employee's supervisor has no significant say in determining the amount or appropriateness of the increase.

An interesting factor about longevity is its recent growth and application with various groups. Historically, there has been an emphasis on longevity for nonprofessional groups. Presently, there is a tendency toward a longevity base also among many professional groups.

The growth of the longevity system suggests some important advantages that should be noted here.

- It eliminates a source of real stress between employer and employee, to the extent that employees have been dissatisfied with the supervisor's salary recommendations.
- It effectively counteracts union organizing claims of arbitrary management, by adopting the salary increase approach espoused by unions.
- Finally, it demands that supervisors concentrate on other ways of motivating employees.

There are also disadvantages attributed to any longevity program including the following.

- There is no tangible way to reward excellence within a particular job.
- There is no way to encourage the resignation of marginal employees by withholding increases.
- Longevity foregoes any leverage provided by the merit program for a continuous, formalized performance appraisal program. This could also lead to a breakdown in the informal day-to-day performance appraisal process. Without this, employees who have taken their jobs for granted may be terminated, without what they feel is adequate warning.
- A supervisor has little opportunity to assume responsibility and authority in a highly judgmental area.
- Finally, longevity creates the tendency to have narrow salary ranges (minimum to maximum) to avoid overpaying the modest performer. The regrettable effect of this decision is that exceptional performers are also limited. The exceptional people may

leave for a better paying opportunity, whereas the less capable will tend to remain.

Who Decides Starting Salaries?

A common approach is that the department head, with prior notice to the personnel department, may authorize salaries up to one-half of the midpoint of the salary range. Salaries beyond that point are authorized individually by the personnel director.

Job Changes

Changes in position also require salary administration policies. These can include promotions, lateral transfers, demotions, and re-evaluation of positions.

Promotions, by implication, usually involve a higher salary. Frequently, however, due to salary range overlap, an employee already is within the salary range for the new position. Nevertheless, most programs will provide an increase unless the employee is higher than the midpoint of the new salary range, which is a rare situation.

Lateral transfers demand salary review and thorough communications. Usually the employee will transfer to the new position at the same salary, assuming that the same skills are used in the new position. If, however, he is using a new set of skills, the salary should be negotiable. It may even be less than before, in fairness to the co-workers in the new department.

An employee may be *demoted* for cause or because of personal preference; the difference is important. Commonly, health care institutions may employ a senior employee who is no longer able to perform his old job, whether due to personal disability or a change in the demands of the position. Under these circumstances, many programs allow the employee to transfer, retaining his previous salary level, but exclude him from merit review raises until the new salary range catches up to his salary level.

When an employee requests a change to a lower graded position (*e.g.,* the RN who wishes to treat patients rather than supervise), the salary should be adjusted to a level no higher than the maximum of the grade for the new position. This is a negotiated process and may result in a salary level lower than the maximum.

Finally, when a job is *re-evaluated,* employees should be treated as though promoted. They should be brought at least to the new minimum. To provide a proper spread, increases should also be allowed within the new range up to midpoint.

Job Evaluation

In an effort to create an even-handed, cost effective, yet equitable approach to measuring the financial worth of jobs, an increasing number of hospitals are turning to the mechanism of job evaluation. There are several approaches: ranking, grading, the point system, and factor comparison.

The point system is by far the most common and is used both in hospitals and industry. This is a quantitative approach by which job factors (*e.g.,* education, experience, responsibility, working conditions) are established, numerical point values are assigned to each factor, and all jobs are evaluated based upon the sum of the points. A detailed description and set of specifications is developed for each job. The description is then evaluated in relation to the predetermined job factors, which are assigned the point values. The salary grade is based upon the total point value; thus, salary ranges are systematically determined for each salary grade.

Developing a New Job Evaluation Program

Managers will ordinarily see the advantages of a formal program providing some guidance for difficult salary decisions where inequities within their own and other departments may be resolved by some central authority.

Employees also can be reassured successfully and will be inclined to support the program since they recognize the same inequities, once they are convinced that no employee's salary will be reduced after such a program has begun.

The writing of job descriptions is a time consuming yet important task. A standard format is normally used and information input by managers and employees is required. Since job descriptions are the foundation for a sound program, it may be worthwhile to temporarily assign a junior manager as a full time job analyst or possibly hire a person on a project basis who is skilled in interviewing and writing, and who may have knowledge of hospital personnel. A consultant could provide technical training and guidance but would ordinarily not be responsible for the detailed preparation of individual job descriptions.

The next major task is to select the person who will evaluate the job descriptions and determine the salary grade. Various approaches may be suggested. One alternative is to establish a broadly-based committee within the institution. Such a group is usually chaired initially by the consultant and later by the personnel director or his representative. The committee usually includes 8 to 10 managers and senior supervisors from various hospital departments. Its function is to decide on point values for each factor in each position being evaluated. This precedes the determination of what point totals will relate to which salary grades. The committee should retain the same members throughout the initial evaluation of hospital positions (4 to 8 months). Committee members will gradually develop expertise with the point system and provide a consistency of judgment that is important. Given the proper leadership the committee will also be able to expand on and improve upon the description content by the members' knowledge of hospital functions and interrelationships.

Once the descriptions and evaluation are complete it is possible by using the point totals, the existing average salaries for each job, and salary survey information to develop appropriate point and salary ranges for each grade.

The final stage in job evaluation is fixing of grades, inaugurating salary change policies, and assigning individual employees to a schedule for merit review. This often results in a substantial one-time expenditure for the hospital.

A useful approach may include the following sequence:

1. A general pay increase coincident with initiation of the salary system, replacing any increase previously planned for the near future;
2. Raising the salary of any employees below the new minimum to that minimum;
3. Allowing spread adjustments on an exceptional basis only;
4. Initiating merit review increases effective within 6 months or longer from the date of the adjustments.

Communication to supervisors and employees must be extensive prior to the date the program is initiated. The following sequence is suggested.

1. Department heads should receive lists of their employees indicating the new grades, salary ranges, and the new salaries before the effective date of the program. There should then be discussion between the personnel department and department heads to create a mechanism for appeals and to reinforce the department heads' understanding of the program.
2. A comprehensive briefing for all managers and supervisors should be held a week before the effective date of the program. Policies and other general information should be distributed.
3. A brochure should be distributed to employees describing in full the program, its immediate impact on salaries, and provisions for future salary reviews. Each employee should also be advised of his salary grade and salary range.

ADMINISTERING SALARIES OF HOSPITAL MANAGERS*

Salary programs designed for managers, principally from the level of department head up, are replacing the casual approaches of the past or reliance on the salary systems designed for nonexempt employees. It used to be possible to administer the salaries of a small group of management decision-makers on an informal basis. Now, the demands for improved hospital administration have increased the number of management professionals and have involved department heads in more management decision-making than before. The increased numbers and more demanding roles suggest the need for a systematic approach to determine appropriate salary levels when recruiting individuals and for providing optimum rewards and incentives.

Basic to a management salary program is a structure that will answer several primary questions:

1. What are the levels and areas of responsibility for each management position?
2. What is the relative value of each management position compared to that of other such positions, hospital-wide?

---

*Source: Reprinted from *Health Care Labor Manual* by Martin E. Skoler, with permission of Aspen Systems Corporation, © 1981.

3. What is a reasonable grouping based on position value, generally at the same salary level?
4. Finally, what is the least and most that the hospital should pay for various management services?

These questions are not unlike those answered by other salary programs. The structure, too, will be similar and will include position descriptions, position evaluation, salary grading, and salary ranges.

Yet the similarity ends with this basic structure. The content and administration of the program differ by their dominant concentration on the hospital's goals and objectives.

The Position Description

For evaluation purposes, the management position description emphasizes the professional and managerial responsibilities of the position as well as the background normally demanded by the position. There is a noticeably greater emphasis on the processes and functions in the manager's area of responsibility than in the nonexempt job descriptions.

Position Evaluation

The evaluation and grading of management positions may be accomplished in a variety of ways, dependent on the size and inclinations of the institution. For a small management group of 15 to 20 (beginning with the senior supervisor or department head) the grading objective may be achieved by an informal ranking, using the position description as a general guide. The ranked positions are grouped (graded) based on a system provided by the consultant, and salary ranges are then established.

However, when large numbers are involved, or where sensitivities dictate a more objective approach, then a more systematic ranking or modified point system will be appropriate. Such systems are available from professional consultants who evaluate criteria from the position description.

Evaluation criteria include:

- The level of managerial and professional expertise required;
- The level of impact that the incumbent has on the quality goals of the hospital;
- The potential that the incumbent has for influencing hospital-wide policies and practices;
- The level of budget (or facilities) responsibility; and,
- The level of responsibility for personnel (in numbers, in variety of positions, and in skills).

Additionally, standards of performance are built into the position descriptions for purposes of manager evaluation and development. They should include such quantitative measures as: (1) budget efficiency; (2) staffing level efficiency; (3) controllable turnover; and (4) quality control measures. Of the four, quality control measures are least used, yet often available, and may include such measures as the following:

- *For the Nursing Service:* The extent and effectiveness of patient care planning, the continuity of patient care, the reported level of patient or physician satisfaction (or dissatisfaction) with nursing services, the extent of staff technical improvement (via in-service training, etc.), the efficiency of staff schedule, and the level of staff absenteeism.
- *For the Medical Records Department:* The transcription lead time and record availability lead time.
- *For the Housekeeping Department:* The bacteria count in critical areas of the hospital, the housekeeping manhours per square foot of space, and the level of employee grievances.
- *For the Business Department:* Billing lead time and level of accounts receivable.

The process of developing the management position description is the keystone to the management salary program.

The process of evaluation and grading of department heads is usually conducted by a senior management committee, including or reporting to the administrator. By so doing, many of the status relationships can be worked out and functions clarified by consensus of senior management rather than by the action of a remote consultant or by a single administrator. This should lead to a greater acceptance of the grading system by those affected. Grading recommendations for immediate associates of the administrator are usually worked out by him with his consultant and submitted with all salary ranges to the trustees for approval.

The salary ranges for management positions deserve particular comment. They are particularly broad, with department heads commonly at the 35–40% level from minimum to maximum, extending to 55–60% for the administrator. This reflects the needs for flexibility when determining salaries for managers using a merit-based approach and the varied levels of contribution that can be made even by managers in a single salary grade. It also acknowledges the need for flexibility to attract the most talented candidates to a position.

Administration of the Management Salary Program

The most notable variations from the nonexempt program occur in the administration of the management salary program. With regard to beginning salaries, it is customary for the administrator and his associates, when filling a position, to exercise salary discretion up to midpoint of the salary range, or 20% of minimum for a department head (*e.g.*, from $15,000 to $18,000 for a range of $15,000 to $21,000.00). Discretion beyond the midpoint is discouraged to avoid damaging the basic program.

Chapter 34—Employee Benefits (Pension, Disability, Medical, and Death Benefits)

OVERVIEW*

An employer has a number of goals which its benefit program should meet.

- An ideal retirement program, including Social Security benefits, should permit the career employee to retire at normal retirement age and maintain a standard of living equal to the preretirement standard of living.
- Life and health insurance benefits, Social Security and a reasonable amount of individual coverage should permit dependents to maintain their standard of living after the premature death of the breadwinner.
- Disability benefits should permit a disabled employee to maintain a somewhat lower standard of living during the period of disability. The level of disability benefits should be such as to provide an incentive to return to work upon recovery.
- Medical care reimbursement programs should protect the employee from unusual and catastrophic health care costs.

Setting objectives for an employee benefit plan is a three step process. *First,* determine the needs of your employees; *second,* determine the extent to which those needs are being met through Medicare, Social Security, Workmen's Compensation and State Disability benefits, if any; *third,* decide upon the specific benefits and the benefit levels to be provided through your plan.

Determining Employee Needs

An employer must consider the needs of different groups of employees in selecting desired benefits and in setting priorities. The hospital work force consists of a mixture of full-time and part-time employees. Long-term workers may change their work schedules from time to time. The staff will include a wide variety of skill levels ranging from highly paid professionals to low-paid unskilled workers. Some of the workers will be planning a career in health care, and others will be temporary with high rates of termination.

A benefit program should be able to accommodate workers in different circumstances and at different times in their life cycles.

The traditional approach to benefit design has been to develop a single pattern of benefits, with some completely paid for by the employer, some cost shared and some paid for solely by the employee. The working husband, dependent wife and minor children model has served as the family prototype around which this pattern was built. The employee's only choice has been whether to participate in contributory coverages. This benefit pattern was chosen to represent a compromise which would best meet the needs of a majority of the work force.

Table 34-1 shows different family types and their need for benefits.

---

*Source: Reprinted from Anna M. Rappaport, "Benefits Plan Design Issues Today and Through the 1980s," *Topics in Health Care Financing,* Spring 1980, with permission of Aspen Systems Corporation.

Table 34-1 Household Types and Benefits Needed

| | Does Household Have Income and Benefits Source Other Than Worker? | Medical Benefits Needed For ||| Death Benefits Needed For |||| Disability Benefits Needed | Retirement Benefits Needed |
| | | Worker | Spouse | Children | Final Expenses | Support of Dependents || | |
						Spouse	Children		
Two-worker couple—no dependent children	Yes	Yes*	*	No	Yes	No†	No	Yes	Yes
Two-worker couple—with dependent children	Yes	Yes*	*	Yes*	Yes	No†	Yes	Yes	Yes
One-worker couple—no dependent children	No	Yes	Yes	No	Yes	Yes	No	Yes	Yes
One-worker couple—with dependent children	No	Yes	Yes	Yes	Yes	Yes	Yes	Yes	Yes
Single—no dependent children	No	Yes	No	No	Yes	No	No	Yes	Yes
Single—with dependent children	No	Yes	No	Yes	Yes	No	Yes	Yes	Yes

*Coverage needed only once. Both can be covered under one spouse's plan, or each can be covered as worker. If both have coverage, there is overlapping coverage and duplication so that couple could be better off if one spouse could choose other coverage.

†Either or both spouses may wish to provide some income to survivor in order to supplement the survivor's earnings. Living expenses for one person are more than 50% of the living expenses of two. Needs vary depending on the income mix of the spouses.

Note: "Spouse" is used here to refer to either partner in a couple maintaining a household involving a sharing of income and expenses.

The factors which will determine the pattern of benefits that best fits a particular employee are:

- family situation
- availability of other sources of benefits
- willingness to assume risks
- priorities of the individuals
- general financial situation

Flexible Benefits

A new approach to benefit plan design is currently developing in the United States. This approach provides for flexible benefits and permits individual employees to tailor a benefit package that best fits individual needs. This new approach is in the experimental stage.

Such programs involve a core of benefits provided by the employer for all employees, together with numerical credits which allow employees to select additional benefits beyond the core. Whether this method will work out well over the long term remains to be seen.

Sample Hospital Benefit Program

Table 34-2 shows a sample of the type of benefit program that might be provided by a hospital. The program provides coverage for a variety of risks, and is complex and expensive.

Nearly all larger employers provide some protection to cover loss of income at death, disability and retirement, and for payment of medical expenses. However, there is considerable variation in the level and design of the benefits and in the split between employer versus employee contributions. Some employers pay for all benefits whereas others expect their employees to make a significant contribution.

Alternative Funding Methods for Employee Benefit Programs*

There are a number of alternative funding methods currently available today that replace the traditional "insured" approach to the funding of Employee Benefit programs. These alternatives take a number of forms:

---

*Source: Reprinted from William P. Davis III et al., "Your Employee Benefit Plan," *Topics in Health Care Financing,* Summer 1975, with permission of Aspen Systems Corporation.

1. A minimum premium plan
2. A fully self-insured plan
3. Self-insurance plus excess insurance
4. Self-insurance via high deductibles

Minimum Premium Plan

By definition, a minimum premium plan is one under which an employer contracts with an insurance company and agrees to self-insure all claims up to some predetermined level and then purchases insurance coverage, from that company, in the event total claims exceed the agreed-upon level. The predetermined self-insurance level could be set at 90 to 98 percent of the total amount that would normally be expected to be paid out in benefit payments. The insurance company actually has full legal liability for the payment of all benefits covered in the policy.

The primary—and perhaps only—advantage of this type of plan is in the savings of the premium taxes that would otherwise have to be paid.

Fully Self-Insured Plan

This is a plan under which an employer self-assumes or self-insures all claims incurred under a benefit contract. The mechanics of such an arrangement are as follows:

1. A non-taxable–interest earning trust fund would be established, according to IRS regulations (Section 501(c)(9)). The money that would otherwise have been paid to the insurance company in the form of premiums would instead be paid to the trust.
2. Trustees would be appointed to oversee the fund's operation.
3. A self-insurance agreement, proof of coverage, certificates, claim forms, etc. would be provided by the employer.
4. Claims incurred under a self-insurance agreement would be paid by the employer, or a separate third party administrator could be employed.
5. Periodic actuarial evaluations of the funds assets would be made, to determine their adequacy.

The purpose of this self-insurance agreement, with its corresponding interest-earning trust fund, would be to maximize the value of each dollar being spent for the Employee Benefit Pro-

Table 34-2 Sample Benefit Program

Risk	Primary Protection	Other Protection Paid for by Employer Dollars	How Dependents Covered
Death in active service	Group life insurance—one times salary plus survivor benefit targeted to produce total income of 20%–60% of predeath salary depending on circumstances	Social Security survivor benefit Social Security lump-sum benefit Pension plan preretirement death benefits Accidental death and dismemberment Tax sheltered annuity account balance	As beneficiaries Survivor income paid to stated dependents
Disability	*Short-Term* 75% of pay up to 90 days 60% of pay between 90 and 180 days *Long-Term* 60% of pay to age 65 offset by benefits from Social Security and Worker's Compensation	Social Security disability benefits Worker's Compensation Waiver of premium in group life Continued medical care coverage during disability Continued pension plan accrual (State short-term disability program in certain states)	Indirectly—disabled worker shares income
Medical care	Medical expenses paid subject to deductible, coinsurance and certain inside limits	Dental Vision care	Directly—via dependent coverage
Retirement	Pension payable at 65—annual accrual is 1½% of pay to taxable wage base plus 2½% of excess	Tax sheltered annuity program (nonprofit hospitals only) Postretirement life insurance of $2,000/year Postretirement Medicare supplement	Indirectly—via income shared with dependents
Other benefits	Educational assistance Thrift or savings plan Prepaid legal coverage		

gram. After the fund has been in operation for a period of two or three years, it could reasonably be expected that the earned interest could be enough to pay for the administrative expenses involved with the fund's operations.

The intent of such an arrangement should never be to avoid the establishment of necessary reserves, but rather to receive the full interest that such necessary reserves could earn.

The major disadvantage of this type of an arrangement is the unlimited risk that an employer could be confronted with in any given year. The number of catastrophic Major Medical claims incurred during one year could seriously deplete the fund's reserves.

Self-Insurance Plus Excess Insurance

This arrangement is simply a plan that utilizes the best qualities of a minimum premium plan and the fully insured plan. It is, in fact, the same self-insurance arrangement just described with the addition of insurance protection. It would differ from the minimum premium plan in that the insurance company is contractually liable only for those expenses that exceed some predetermined amount.

For example, assume that the self-insurance plan plus the excess insurance arrangement with an excess insurance provision become operative after $100,000 of claims are paid during a year.

As soon as that dollar level is reached no additional claims will be paid from the trust funds; instead, they will be paid from the insurance company's funds, through the excess insurance arrangement.

Table 34-3 shows the financial advantages that can be realized through a self-insurance plus excess insurance arrangement. It depicts four years (1972-1975) of employee growth, premium payments, claim payments, retention charges and dividends under an insured plan. It also shows what the employer might realize in terms of dollar savings if, during 1975, a self-insurance plus excess insurance arrangement is initiated.

The assumed result of this arrangement is an actual savings of $34,500, compared to the $1,000 dividend the employer would have received through the insured plan at the end of 1975. The $34,500 savings is realized, of course, only if the assumed claim payment figure of $63,000 proves to be accurate. It is important to note, however, that even if this assumed figure proves to be too low, this employer could not be out-of-pocket more than $109,000 (the $103,000, he would have paid, in premium, to the insurance company, plus the $6,000 incurred in establishing and administering the self-insurance plan).

Self-Insurance via High Deductibles

In its most elementary form, the employer would simply maintain the existing medical benefits program (whatever that may be) with the exception that a deductible of $2,000 or any other acceptable amount would be applicable to all hospital expense claims and a separate deductible of $2,000 (or any other acceptable amount) would be applied to the physicians, surgeons, and x-ray and laboratory claims. This deductible would be paid by the employer to the provider of the service. If you assume an average hospital confinement of 7.8 days, and an average per diem charge of $175.00, a $2,000 hospital deductible would result in self-assuming the entire bill.

This particular arrangement of self-insurance via high deductibles is particularly applicable to a hospital employer when a large number of the hospital's employees are confined to the hospital itself when they need medical care. In other words, it is very possible for a hospital-employer to reduce the cost of providing hospital benefits to its employees by deciding to mark the hospital bills, incurred by their employees and the dependents of their employees, "paid in full." This eliminates entirely the "swapping of dollars" that results when an insurance company or Blue Cross is employed as a hospital benefit underwriter.

Communicating Benefits*

It is absolutely essential that your employees be fully aware of their life, disability, medical and retirement benefits and of the attendant costs, since those benefits represent part of their total compensation.

Beyond what is now required by law in the pension area, the problem of communicating benefits generally should be addressed on a number of successively detailed levels and specific questions should be encouraged from those employees who wish more information. You may wish to consider the following:

Level 1:

1. Required ERISA summary to each employee's home with cover letter from the personnel department or hospital administrator inviting questions.
2. Bulletin boards calling attention to specific benefits and costs but avoiding detailed explanations. Feature name and telephone extension of the benefits manager. Invite questions.
3. A brief list and description of benefits in institution's newsletter.
4. Letters home (no more than one per month), devoting several each year to brief explanation of benefits. Invite questions.
5. Employee handbook. Keep it up to date and restrict benefit explanations to a few lines for each.
6. Personal visits (by department head invitation) to meetings of employees. Personnel director accompanied by administrator or benefit manager should briefly describe major benefits, answer questions, seek directions for the future.

---

*Source: Reprinted from *Health Care Labor Manual* by Martin E. Skoler, with permission of Aspen Systems Corporation, © 1981.

Table 34-3 Fully Insured Plan vs. Self-Assumption with Excess Insurance

Fully Insured Plan

Year	Monthly Prem. Per Employee	Number of Employees	Annual Premium	Paid Claims	Incurred Reserves	Total Incur. Claims	Retention	Total Incur. Claims Plus Retention	Dividend (Deficit)
1972	$25.00	200	$ 60,000	$36,000 +	$15,000 =	$51,000	$ 9,000	$60,000	-0-
1973	$27.50(A)	200	$ 66,000	$52,800 +	$ 1,500 =	$54,300	$ 9,900	$64,200	$1,800
1974	$30.00(B)	250	$ 90,000	$72,000 +	$ 6,000 =	$78,000	$13,500	$91,500	($1,500)
1975	$31.50(C)	250	$103,000	$78,000 +	$ 7,000 =	$85,000	$14,000	$99,000	$1,000
(Assumed)									

(A) Rates increased 10% over 1972, because of claim experience.
(B) Rates increased 9.1% over 1973, because of claim experience.
(C) Rates increased 15% over 1974, because of claim experience.

Self-assumption Plan

In place of insured plan, during 1975, employer self-insures the expected liability and purchases Excess insurance. The result could be as follows:

1- Total Benefits Paid		$78,000
2- Expenses		
Start up Costs	$1,500	
Administration	$3,500	
Excess Insurance	$1,000	
Total Expense	$6,000	$ 6,000
3- Total Expenditures		$84,000
4- Total Savings		$15,000 ($103,000 premiums minus $84,000 minus $1,000 dividend)

This example insures "Run-Out Claims"—claims that would have been paid by the prior carrier from its incurred claim reserve. If these claims were considered savings would be larger.

Level 2:

1. Personnel Policy Manual summary of each benefit. The manual normally goes only to department heads because of frequent changes. Each benefit should be sufficiently explained to enable department heads to discuss it intelligently. Employees should know of manual's existence and their privilege to examine it at reasonable times.
2. Meetings with department heads to brief them on benefits, inform them that original insurance policies may be studied by them, and the personnel benefits manager will be available to answer more questions. Inform them that following your explanation and answers to questions, future communications to employees will suggest that they consult their department heads first on all personnel policies including benefits.
3. By letters and meetings (if necessary), inform department heads first of any new benefits or major changes in existing benefits. They will never forgive you for being told of changes or additions after everyone in the cafeteria already knows.

Level 3:

1. The administrator is preoccupied with many concerns other than benefits. Yet the cost may be high and the return difficult to measure as each new benefit is suggested or an existing one improved. Be prepared to offer considerable detail if requested—including which employees could be affected, probable cost over a 2-5 year period, expected improvements in productivity (or morale or competitive stance), major provision of the benefit, proposed beginning date, etc. Be prepared to discuss with board of trustees if requested.
2. Establish working file of all blanket insurance policies, riders, changes, correspondence, notes of telephone calls, etc. that occurred during negotiations with outside vendors. Key policies and documents should be kept in institution safes. Maintain files of claims forms, procedural instructions and signed beneficiary cards for all insurance benefits.

Evaluation & Feedback*

The following are some considerations that may be helpful in establishing an evaluation or feedback program on communicating benefits:

1. Is a response system in place
   - for channeling and answering questions, complaints, and comments correctly and positively?
   - for obtaining feedback on specific communication efforts and materials?
2. If not, can and should one be established?
3. What will indicate that the hospital's efforts are successfully meeting its goals?
4. What changes does the hospital expect in the employees' actions or attitudes as a result of its efforts to communicate?
5. What actions will indicate these changes? What will be the evidence of a successful effort or campaign?
6. When should a meeting be held to review projects and, if necessary, implement additional strategies to attain the hospital's goals?
7. When will it be appropriate for implementation of the next benefit communication effort?

Employee communications and benefit communications must be frequent if the effort is to prosper and succeed. It is vital that new information be pumped through the system regularly, continually and with a purpose.

RETIREMENT BENEFITS**

A retirement program is nothing more than a formalized method of accumulating funds for the future benefit of your employees when they leave your employ at retirement. Once put into effect, a retirement plan is a financial organization entirely separate from the hospital. The

---

*Source: Reprinted from James D. Hawthorne, "Employee Benefits Communication," *Topics in Health Care Financing,* Spring 1980, with permission of Aspen Systems Corporation.

**Source: Reprinted from William P. Davis III et al., "Your Employee Benefit Plan," *Topics in Health Care Financing,* Summer 1975, with permission of Aspen Systems Corporation.

plan may allow employees to make contributions in the form of individual savings, or the full cost can be paid by the hospital. In either event, the funds that are contributed will be invested and as a result earn interest with all gains being used for the benefit of your employees.

The items shown below represent major questions pertaining to all retirement programs:

1. Should the employee be required to contribute to the plan? If yes, to what extent?
2. Should the plan be funded through an insurance company or a trust arrangement?
3. What is the definition of eligible employees?
4. Retirement dates?
5. The benefit formula?
6. Death benefits, before retirement and after retirement?
7. Vesting?

Employee Contributions

The following summary lists the principal arguments for and against employee contributions to a pension plan:

Advantages

1. Employee contributions will on occasion allow the implementation of a plan that provides more liberal benefits, consequently making the plan more effective;
2. Contributions to a retirement plan are actually a means of savings, which can be valuable to the employee;
3. Employee–Employer relations can be improved by cooperation in providing Retirement Income benefits;
4. Employees are usually more appreciative of and have more confidence in a plan for which they contribute.

Disadvantages

1. Without employee contributions, all employees are automatically in the plan and no employee will reach retirement age without some form of a retirement benefit;
2. A non-contributory plan is simpler and more economical to administer;
3. In a unionized or potential unionized group of employees, there are no grounds for union participation in the management of the plan;
4. Because of the reduced take-home pay, the demands for wage increases will sometimes be made sooner with a contributory plan.

An employee contribution, if made, does not necessarily have to have a logical or consistent relationship to the total cost of the plan, nor to the amount of benefits that are being provided by the plan. The relationship can be purely arbitrary. It can be as large as may reasonably be expected to be accepted by the members of the plan, in order to increase the benefits of the plan or to decrease the employer costs. It may be as small as to represent merely a token contribution. In this situation, however, it needs to be on the order of two percent of salary or more per year. Any amount smaller than two percent would hardly justify the additional administrative work involved in collecting and recording employee contributions.

Other Concerns

Insurance Company or a Trust

The arguments in favor of one method over another are far from conclusive. (See "Alternative Funding Methods for Employee Benefit Programs," discussed earlier.)

Eligible Employees

Generally, you cannot exclude from participation an individual who has attained the age of 25 and has been employed for a period of one year. Restrictions concerning minimum age and minimum service requirements, before an individual is eligible for membership in the plan, are intended to result in the elimination from participation those employees who are most likely to terminate their employment.

Retirement Dates

The pension plan must define the dates as of which each participant in the plan will become qualified for a pension benefit.

1. The normal retirement date
2. An early retirement date
3. Late, delayed or deferred retirement date
4. Disability retirement date

Capital Accumulation Programs*

Defined benefit pension plans are designed to provide stipulated benefits payable as regular income, and income is the key reason for establishing these plans. Defined contribution plans are designed around capital accumulation, whereby the accumulation may or may not be converted to income.

Various forms of defined contribution programs can be used in conjunction with defined benefit pension plans to provide a means of capital accumulation on an advantageous basis. The funds accumulated may be used either for additional periodic retirement income, for other retirement needs or, in the case of thrift plans, for needs before retirement. An employer may offer a capital accumulation facility to its employees without participating directly, or may offer to match a portion of the employee's contribution.

The most popular forms of capital accumulation programs are tax-sheltered annuities, where available, and thrift plans. These programs offer the employee the chance for automatic savings through payroll deduction. Many of these plans offer investment vehicles more attractive than available elsewhere, particularly when the taxation of the programs is considered. A program may offer a choice of investment in one or more equity funds, and in a fixed income fund with interest guaranteed.

Many insurance carriers offer special contracts designed for investment of the funds generated by these programs, and tailored to the needs of these programs. Nonprofit hospitals operating under Section 501(c)(3) of the Internal Revenue Code can sponsor tax-sheltered annuity programs. Under these programs, the employee can generally contribute up to 16 2/3 percent of income on a before-tax basis into the tax-sheltered annuity. The money accumulates on a tax-free basis until the annuity income is received. At that point the employee pays tax on both the amount put into the annuity and the investment income. A special use of this type of program is to provide supplemental retirement income for higher-paid employees.

These programs, since the benefits are immediately vested, offer a benefit with immediate value to the younger employee for whom retirement is remote. Even though the benefit may not be payable for many years, the employee can see the dollar amount of an accumulation account. An employer contribution to a capital accumulation program is often an alternative to an improvement in a pension plan.

DEATH BENEFITS*

There are two commonly accepted methods of implementing a replacement income objective—Group Term Life insurance, and Survivor's Income benefits. The extent to which an individual's income will be replaced (the plan's objective) will dictate the method to be used.

If a portion of the individual's income is to be replaced for a limited period of time, say one to four years, Group Term Life insurance is the most effective and economical method. Income replacement objectives extending beyond four years dictate the use of a Survivor Income benefit, by itself, or in combination with Group Term Life insurance.

Assuming 50 percent of an individual's annual compensation is to be replaced, for maximum of four years, a Group Term life insurance benefit equal to two times annual earnings will be the death benefit provided by your plan. Increasing the percentage of income to be replaced and/or extending the period of time during which it will be replaced, will obviously require that the life insurance benefit be increased to some higher amount.

Beyond the two-times-annual-earnings level, however, costs will increase to the extent that a survivor benefit plan will become more economical than term insurance and, in addition, will guarantee to management that the "income to dependents" objective will be met.

In principle, a Survivor Income benefit is the same as a widow's benefit in a pension program; a stipulated benefit is paid to a designated individual (spouse and/or children) for a pre-determined period of time. The specific benefit can be

---

*Source: Reprinted from Anna M. Rappaport, "Benefits Plan Design Issues, Today and Through the 1980s," *Topics in Health Care Financing,* Spring 1980, with permission of Aspen Systems Corporation.

*Source: Reprinted from William P. Davis III et al., "Your Employee Benefit Plan," *Topics in Health Care Financing,* Summer 1975, with permission of Aspen Systems Corporation.

any amount between 10 and 50 percent of the employee's income at the time of death. The spouse's benefit can be paid for a specified number of years, or until a certain age is attained, or for the life of the spouse. In any event, the benefit payable is designed to cease at the spouse's remarriage.

Contractually, a Survivor's Income benefit is available only to individuals actually dependent upon the employee for financial support. This is further refined to specifically include only the employee's spouse and the employee's children. Consequently, "friend" or "distant relative" is excluded from eligibility (unlike group term life insurance).

The agreed-upon percentage of the individual's income to be replaced through a Survivor Income benefit is an aggregate benefit that is always integrated with the benefits the surviving spouse is eligible to receive through Social Security. Table 34-4 depicts several different death benefits, each implementing a different employer objective. Group Term life insurance would seem the most economical and efficient method of funding an employer-provided death benefit.

Self-Insurance

For three reasons, Death benefits should *not* be funded through a self-insurance arrangement.

1. The wide fluctuations that will occur in the number of deaths each year make it impossible for the average employer to adequately pre-fund this benefit;
2. Death benefits paid from an insurance policy are subject to more favorable taxation than benefits paid by an employer;
3. Under a self-insurance death benefit, the individual cannot convert his Group benefit to an individual policy.

DISABILITY BENEFITS*

A short term disability is usually a period of disability that exists for six months or less, since it coincides with the Social Security Disability benefit payment provisions. A long term disability will then be a period of disability that exceeds six months, lasting as long as the employee is unable to perform any work for income, or until he or she is eligible for Retirement benefits.

Short term disability is a temporary interruption of an employee's continuing employment. During that period of time, a realistic level of benefits will help an employee meet his financial requirements and at the same time discourage malingering.

---

*Source: Reprinted from William P. Davis III *et al.*, "Your Employee Benefit Plan," *Topics in Health Care Financing,* Summer 1975, with permission of Aspen Systems Corporation.

Table 34-4 Alternate Death Benefit Plans

Plan Objective	Implementation of Objective
Provide a benefit of $5,000 for each employee.	Group Term Life insurance
Provide a benefit equal to 30% of the individual's income, payable for the life of the employee's spouse or until remarried.	Survivor's Income benefit that is integrated with any Social Security and Workmen's Compensation benefits the spouse may be eligible to receive.
Provide a benefit equal to 50% of the individual's income, for a period of four years after the individual's death.	Group Term Life insurance equal to 2 times annual income. Benefit paid through the optional Installment method, included in the contract, rather than a lump sum.
Provide a benefit of $5,000, paid in a lump sum and a benefit equal to 15% of the individual's income for the life of the spouse or until remarriage.	Group Term Life insurance for the $5,000, payment and a Survivor's Income benefit for the 15% of income benefit.

A Sick Leave benefit providing some number of days each year, at 100 percent of salary, should be the first level of benefits. At the employer's option, the sick leave benefit can be extended to apply to absences due to personal reasons, such as a death in the family, etc. For absences beyond the period of time covered by the sick leave benefit, the benefit could be reduced from 100 percent of salary to approximately 65 percent of the individual's gross salary. A benefit equal to 65 percent of an employee's gross income is within 10 to 15 percent of the amount he would normally earn after taxes.

This 65 percent of income benefit ideally should continue until the six month period has expired. At the six month point, the benefit could be reduced to 60 percent of salary and from that point on would continue at that rate, until the individual is able to return to work or becomes eligible for a retirement benefit.

Because the sick leave benefit would be paid directly from payroll, it is obviously a self-assumed and a self-funded liability. There is also frequently a great deal of merit for an employer to self-assume the 65 percent of salary benefit—or whatever the agreed upon percentage of salary benefit may be—that would be continued from the date the sick leave benefit expires until the six month point. When insured, this type of benefit is to a large degree an exchange of dollars between an employer and the insurance company.

Hints for Disability Programs

Some of the areas to build into short-term programs are:

- use of employer-paid physicians for review of medical status of claimants;
- benefit levels that encourage return to work;
- review of claims procedures to see that appropriate and complete information is developed for each type of disability.

Source: Reprinted from Anna M. Rappaport, "Benefits Plan Design Issues . . . , *Topics in Health Care Financing*, Spring 1980, with permission of Aspen Systems Corporation.

Long Term Disability

During the first two-year period of disability, an employee might be considered totally disabled and therefore eligible for benefits if he is unable to perform the duties of his *own* occupation. Thereafter, the definition could change to one that states an employee is totally disabled if he is unable to engage in *any* occupation for which he is or may become qualified by education, training or experience. There has been a recent trend among insurance companies to restrict the "his own occupation" definition to one year instead of two.

A provision for the rehabilitation of a disabled employee is an important one that should be included in all Long Term Disability programs. To demonstrate the need for such a provision, consider the situation of an individual age 35 who becomes totally disabled and eligible for a monthly income of $1,000 until he attains the age of 65. The potential liability produced by this benefit is $360,000. To a small extent this might be reduced by Social Security and perhaps Workmen's Compensation benefits, but the extent of the liability clearly illustrates the catastrophic nature of this type of risk. While the ability to rehabilitate an employee will depend on many factors, such as his age, nature of the disability and his educational level, such a provision should be included in all contracts.

The Social Security Disability benefit offset should be one that allows increases in Social Security benefits, after an individual has become disabled, to be passed directly to that individual without being used to further reduce the benefit paid from the plan. When this is done, (referred to as a "Social Security Freeze provision") any subsequent increases in the Social Security benefit will serve as a direct cost-of-living increase to the disabled employee.

The inclusion of a rehabilitation provision will frequently allow the employee to return to some type of gainful employment, without the complete termination of the benefits payable under the Long Term Disability plan. Table 34-5 suggests an outline of a realistic disability income benefits program.

MEDICAL BENEFITS*

The usual or customary method of designing a medical program is to have a basic benefit and a

---

*Source: Reprinted from William P. Davis III *et al.*, "Your Employee Benefit Plan," *Topics in Health Care Financing*, Summer 1975, with permission of Aspen Systems Corporation.

Table 34-5 A Model Disability Benefits Program

Plan Objective	Implementation of Objective
1-Provide 100% of income for first 10 days of disability each year.	Self-assumed and paid directly from payroll.
2-Provide 65% of income from 11th day of disability to the 26th week (170 days).	Self-assumed and paid from a reserve account, established for this benefit.
3-Provide 60% of income from the 26th week (180th day) of disability, until age 65.	Insured, non-experience rated Long Term Disability plan.

All benefits provided by the Plan are fully integrated with Social Security, Workmen's Compensation and any other Group Disability Income benefits the individual is eligible to receive including any State Disability Benefits.

SUGGESTED LONG TERM DISABILITY PLAN

Amount of Benefits

60% of an individual's gross salary to a maximum of $1,500 per month. The amount of the monthly benefit will include benefits received from:

    A. Workmen's Compensation
    B. The individual's full Social Security Disability benefit.
    C. Any disability or early retirement benefits.
    D. Any other Group Disability benefits.

These deductions are made on a dollar for dollar offset basis.

Benefit Period

Benefits will be paid to age 65 for disabilities due to an accident or a sickness.

Elimination Period

Disability benefits will commence with the first day of disability following the completion of 180 calendar days of continuous disability.

Definition of Disability

During the first two years of the benefit period, benefits shall be payable if the individual, because of mental or physical disability, is unable to perform any or all duties of his own occupation. Thereafter, benefits are payable if the individual is unable to engage in any gainful occupation for which he is reasonably fitted by education, training or background.

Social Security Freeze

The contract should include a "Social Security Freeze" provision as of the date an employee becomes eligible for Disability benefits.

---

supplemental Major Medical benefit. The basic benefit will provide first-dollar coverage (no deductible, no coinsurance) for hospital, surgical and certain types of physician's medical expenses. The individual must then satisfy a deductible which is usually $100, before the Major Medical portion of the plan will pay 75 to 80 percent of the expenses not covered by the basic program. This rate of reimbursement would continue up to some overall maximum such as $25,000 or $50,000. Most plans also provide a stipulated maternity benefit for a normal delivery, miscarriage and a cesarean section.

First-dollar reimbursement under a Group Medical plan is the most expensive aspect of that plan, simply because each and every dollar that is incurred is reimbursed at a cost of approximately $1.10 (assuming the plan is administered with maximum efficiency). Because each expense is reimbursed, there is little if any incentive on the part of the individual to control or minimize expense. Medical reimbursement programs should provide adequate benefits to meet expenses and at the same time maintain a degree of employee participation in the cost to prevent over-utilization of benefits. What is an "adequate" benefit and what the "degree of employee participation in the cost" should be are two key questions that, when answered, establish the objective of a Medical Reimbursement program.

First dollar, or basic benefits, should be limited to:

1. Hospital expense (both in-patient and out-patient);
2. Surgical expense;
3. In-hospital medical expense, incurred by the physician;
4. Diagnostic x-ray and laboratory expense;
5. Maternity expense.

There is little logical reason for providing a first-dollar benefit, specifically for accidents, that exceeds the benefits paid for sicknesses. A well-designed plan provides adequate levels of benefits regardless of the cause of the expense.

The basic portion of the plan should include an extremely comprehensive x-ray and laboratory benefit that will allow a substantial level of reimbursement for diagnostic x-ray and laboratory expense, without requiring an individual to be hospital-confined. By including such a benefit in the plan, you are:

1. Reducing expense on the part of the employee;
2. Reducing expenses paid under your plan and consequently helping to maintain a lower level of premiums.

Major Medical plans are designed to reimburse an individual for expenses that are incurred as a result of a catastrophic accident or sickness. The cash deductible provision included in the Major Medical plan is the method used to define a catastrophic occurrence. If the individual incurs charges in excess of the deductible amount, benefits are payable; if charges are less, it is not a catastrophic occurrence and benefits therefore are not payable.

Because the definition of a catastrophic occurrence is a monetary one, the deductible should correctly vary with an individual's income. For example, a person earning $15,000 per year should be able to meet a $150 deductible as "easily" as an individual earning $5,000 per year could meet a $50 deductible. Once the Major Medical deductible has been met, benefits are paid on the coinsurance reimbursement basis, up to some overall maximum. During a prolonged illness or a serious accident, the coinsurance reimbursement required on the part of the individual can result in a substantial financial burden for him and his family.

Hints for Medical Benefits

There are three directions which can be pursued in order to contain the cost of medical benefits:

1. increase the portion of the medical expenses paid by the individual through the use of higher deductibles or more coinsurance;
2. decrease the employer's share of the cost through a higher employee contribution;
3. design the benefit structure so as to create a favorable climate for change in the patterns of care.

The trend in the recent past has been to reduce the amount the employee has to pay, but this may reverse over the next few years as cost pressures grow. The greatest opportunity lies in the area of encouraging changes in the pattern of care. Second-opinion programs can reduce surgery and are beneficial for all concerned. Benefit schedules can be designed to encourage maximum use of outpatient facilities whenever medically sound. In the past, benefit structures often had the reverse effect. Hospitals, as medical care experts, are in a position to play a leadership role in promoting benefit design which encourages efficient use of health care facilities.

Source: Reprinted from Anna M. Rappaport, "Benefits Plan Design Issues . . . ," *Topics in Health Care Financing,* Spring 1980, with permission of Aspen Systems Corporation.

CURRENT PRACTICES AND TRENDS

Hospital Practices in Supplementary Benefits*

A U.S. Dept. of Labor survey of hospital practices regarding supplementary benefits, con-

---

*Source: *Industry Wage Survey: Hospitals and Nursing Homes, September 1978,* Bureau of Labor Statistics, November 1980, Bulletin 2069.

ducted in 22 major metropolitan areas in 1978 (see Table 34-6), disclosed the following findings:

Paid holidays. Paid holidays were provided to virtually all private and government hospital workers. In most southern and western areas, the majority of professional and nonprofessional employees received from 7 to 8 paid holidays annually. In most of the north central areas, 8 to 9 paid holidays were the most common provisions; and in the northeastern areas, 10 to 11 holidays. Among the most liberal areas for holidays were New York and San Francisco, where a majority of employees received 11 to 12 paid holidays per year. Generally, provisions for government hospital workers were slightly more generous than those for private workers.

Paid vacations. All hospital workers were provided paid vacations after qualifying periods of service. Typical provisions called for 2 weeks of vacation pay after 1 year of service; 3 weeks after 5 years; and at least 4 weeks after 15 years. In most of the areas studied, vacation provisions for professional employees were identical to those for nonprofessional workers. Where differences existed, provisions tended to be more liberal for professionals.

Vacation provisions for up to 20 years of service were approximately the same for both government and private hospital employees, but maximum vacation provisions beyond this point tended to be higher for government workers. In New York, for example, just under seven-tenths of all nonprofessionals in government hospitals received at least 5 weeks of vacation pay after 25 years of service compared to about one-eighth of their private hospital counterparts.

Health, insurance, and retirement plans. Life insurance, hospitalization, basic medical, major medical, and surgical insurance coverage applied almost universally to hospital employees in most of the areas studied. Sick leave provisions, usually full pay with no waiting period, also were widespread. Although typically the same proportion of both government and nongovernment workers in each area were covered by these provisions, the source of funding varied considerably. In Boston, for example, hospitalization insurance paid for entirely by the employer applied to about nine-tenths of the private hospital work force, while in non-Federal government hospitals all workers were required to contribute at least part of the cost. Accidental death and dismemberment insurance coverage was much more prevalent among private hospitals than among government hospitals in most of the areas studied.

Dental insurance plans applied to one-third or less of the private hospital work force in 12 areas; to between one-half and seven-eighths of the workers in 4 areas; and to all or virtually all employees in Portland, San Francisco, and Seattle. Dental insurance for government hospital employees was reported in fewer areas—12 areas compared to 19 areas for private hospitals.

Some form of maternity benefit plan, as part of the hospital's health insurance package, was widespread in the majority of areas studied. While maternity policies providing additional paid leave were rare, nearly all hospitals allowed their employees to use either sick leave and/or vacation time during a pregnancy.

Some form of retirement plan applied to the entire work force covered by the survey. A combination of private pensions and social security was the most prevalent type of coverage—usually applying to at least nine-tenths of all private and non-Federal government hospital workers. In Cleveland, Denver, Houston, Miami, and Washington, however, pension plans for government workers typically did not include social security.

Perquisites. Earnings data presented for hospital workers did not include the value of room, board, or other perquisites, although the incidence of such benefits was obtained for six occupations: General duty nurse; licensed practical nurse; hospital cleaner; nursing aide; flatwork finisher; and food service helper.

Free meals were not prevalent; they applied to no more than one-fifth of the food service helpers and to smaller proportions of the other job groups. Similarly, meals offered at a reduced cost were typically available to one-fifth or less of the workers in the six jobs. Provisions for free lodging were almost nonexistent. Provisions for free uniforms, laundering of uniforms, or both, or monetary allowance in lieu of these perquisites were widespread among the areas. Free uniforms and laundering services were more commonly provided to nonprofessionals—cleaners, nursing aids, flatwork finishers, and food service helpers—than to either general duty or licensed practical nurses.

Table 34-6 Employee Benefits in Private Hospitals by Region

(Percent of full-time professional and nonprofessional employees in hospitals with specified health, insurance, and retirement plans, 22 selected areas, September 1978)

See footnotes at end of table.

Table 34-6 continued

(Percent of full-time professional and nonprofessional employees in hospitals with specified health, insurance, and retirement plans,[1] 22 selected areas, September 1978)

Type of benefit	Cleveland Prof.	Cleveland Non-prof.	Detroit Prof.	Detroit Non-prof.	Kansas City Prof.	Kansas City Non-prof.	Milwaukee Prof.	Milwaukee Non-prof.	Minneapolis-St.Paul Prof.	Minneapolis-St.Paul Non-prof.	St. Louis Prof.	St. Louis Non-prof.	Denver-Boulder Prof.	Denver-Boulder Non-prof.	Los Angeles-Long Beach Prof.	Los Angeles-Long Beach Non-prof.	Portland Prof.	Portland Non-prof.	San Francisco-Oakland Prof.	San Francisco-Oakland Non-prof.	Seattle-Everett Prof.	Seattle-Everett Non-prof.
All employees	100	100	100	100	100	100	100	100	100	100	100	100	100	100	100	100	100	100	100	100	100	100
Employees in hospitals providing:																						
Life insurance	100	100	100	100	82	82	100	100	71	90	89	88	82	81	97	95	100	100	100	100	83	92
Noncontributory plans	100	100	94	96	82	82	100	100	71	90	76	77	66	66	97	95	100	100	100	100	63	73
Accidental death and dismemberment insurance	100	100	93	89	78	76	90	96	40	37	64	65	69	69	75	64	94	95	87	85	83	92
Noncontributory plans	100	100	80	79	78	76	90	96	40	37	59	60	54	54	71	59	94	95	87	85	63	73
Sickness and accident insurance or sick leave or both[2]	100	100	100	100	100	100	100	100	100	100	94	100	100	100	98	99	100	100	100	100	100	100
Sickness and accident insurance	37	30	79	65	4	6	29	35	52	73	36	42	6	5	16	26	40	42	-	-	-	-
Noncontributory plans	33	27	62	52	4	6	24	31	52	73	36	42	6	5	16	26	40	42	-	-	-	-
Sick leave (full pay, no waiting period)	81	75	88	82	54	52	65	64	100	100	79	97	95	96	92	81	100	100	100	100	100	100
Sick leave (partial pay or waiting period)	19	25	1	4	43	42	33	35	-	-	6	3	5	4	3	13	22	10	-	-	-	-
Long-term disability insurance	48	46	19	19	47	50	46	47	45	32	39	38	56	57	24	21	35	47	16	21	-	-
Hospitalization	100	100	100	100	98	98	100	100	100	100	76	95	100	100	98	99	100	100	100	100	100	100
Insurance	74	80	100	100	99	98	100	100	72	100	76	80	100	100	98	99	100	100	100	100	100	100
Noncontributory plans	66	69	100	100	55	42	45	45	72	100	32	32	25	24	72	77	35	22	100	100	94	95
Care provided outside of insurance	-	-	-	-	-	-	-	-	-	-	2	2	-	-	-	-	-	-	-	-	-	-
Combination of insurance and care provided outside of insurance	26	20	-	-	-	-	-	-	-	-	16	13	-	-	-	-	-	-	-	-	-	-
Surgical	100	100	100	100	99	98	100	100	100	100	95	95	100	100	98	99	100	100	100	100	100	100
Insurance	52	61	100	100	99	98	100	100	72	100	85	87	100	100	98	99	100	100	100	100	100	100
Noncontributory plans	44	50	100	100	55	42	45	45	72	100	41	38	25	24	72	77	35	22	100	100	94	95
Care provided outside of insurance	-	-	-	-	-	-	-	-	-	-	2	2	-	-	-	-	-	-	-	-	-	-
Combination of insurance and care provided outside of insurance	48	39	-	-	-	-	-	-	-	-	7	6	-	-	-	-	-	-	-	-	-	-
Medical	100	100	95	97	99	98	100	100	100	100	95	95	100	100	98	99	100	100	100	100	100	100
Insurance	52	61	95	97	99	98	100	100	100	100	85	87	100	100	98	99	100	100	100	100	100	100
Noncontributory plans	44	50	95	97	55	42	45	45	72	100	41	38	25	24	72	77	35	22	100	100	94	95
Care provided outside of insurance	-	-	-	-	-	-	-	-	-	-	2	2	-	-	-	-	-	-	-	-	-	-
Combination of insurance and care provided outside of insurance	48	39	-	-	-	-	-	-	-	-	7	6	-	-	-	-	-	-	-	-	-	-
Major medical	79	73	74	71	99	98	100	100	100	100	95	95	100	100	98	98	100	100	100	100	100	100
Insurance	31	34	74	71	99	98	100	100	100	100	85	87	100	100	98	88	100	100	100	100	100	100
Noncontributory plans	23	23	74	71	55	42	45	45	72	100	41	38	25	24	71	68	35	22	100	100	94	95
Care provided outside of insurance	7	3	-	-	-	-	-	-	-	-	2	2	-	-	-	-	-	-	-	-	-	-
Combination of insurance and care provided outside of insurance	41	36	-	-	-	-	-	-	-	-	7	6	-	-	2	7	-	-	-	-	-	-
Dental insurance	12	10	77	79	15	17	13	11	3	3	15	11	26	29	61	62	96	98	100	100	94	95
Noncontributory plans	12	10	59	67	15	17	-	-	3	3	15	11	26	29	59	60	22	10	100	100	94	95
Retirement plans:																						
Retirement pension, social security or both	100	100	100	100	100	100	100	100	100	100	100	100	100	100	100	100	100	100	100	100	100	100
Pension (other than Social Security)	11	19	14	15	-	-	-	-	-	-	-	-	-	-	24	27	-	-	18	19	-	-
Noncontributory plans	11	19	14	15	-	-	-	-	-	-	-	-	-	-	19	25	-	-	18	19	-	-
Combination of pension and Social Security	89	81	79	72	85	83	100	98	100	100	98	98	91	91	58	52	94	95	82	81	94	95
Noncontributory plans	57	56	73	72	79	73	65	66	75	83	98	98	91	91	49	41	89	93	79	77	55	51
Severance pay	-	-	-	-	-	-	6	9	19	27	2	17	5	7	1	-	-	-	-	-	-	-

[1] Includes those plans for which the employer pays at least part of the cost and excludes legally required plans such as workers' compensation and social security; however, plans required by State temporary disability laws are included if the employer contributes more than is legally required or the employees receive benefits in excess of legal requirements. "Noncontributory plans" include only those plans financed entirely by the employer.
[2] Unduplicated total of workers receiving sickness and accident insurance and sick leave shown separately.
[3] Less than 0.5 percent.

NOTE: Because of rounding, sums of individual items may not equal totals.

Source: *Industry Wage Survey: Hospitals and Nursing Homes, September 1978*, Bureau of Labor Statistics, November 1980, Bulletin 2069.

Trends in Benefit Programs*

A U.S. Chamber of Commerce survey stated that in 1977 total employee benefits were costing hospitals an additional 25.7 percent beyond salary expenditures.

Listed below are some of the benefits that will appear on the scene, be expanded, or receive increased attention by labor unions and other employee groups in the near future.

1. Old Age
    a. Social Security—increased benefits; equalized male survivor benefits
    b. Medex—increased benefits
    c. National Health Insurance
    d. Retirement Programs—trend toward noncontributing plans; increased regulations under ERISA; broader coverage, earlier vesting, trend toward full portability, early retirement, cost of living escalators, tie-in with life insurance and deferred annuity programs
    e. Life Insurance—full coverage
    f. Sick Leave—use of unused accrued sick leave
    g. Vacation—increased allotment in years before retirement
2. Loss of Income
    a. Health Insurance—trend toward full payment by employer; psychiatric, maternity, diagnostic, "health maintenance," dental, optical coverage, increased dollar maximums, catastrophic illness coverage
    b. Employee Clinics—expanded on-premises health facilities, captive HMOs, routine health care including immunizations for family members, discounts for prescription drugs and professional services
    c. Long and Short-Term Disability—employer paid, shorter waiting periods (180 to 90 to 30 days for LTD), increased benefits including inflation hedge and some payment to surviving spouse
    d. Life Insurance—increased coverage from flat $2,000 to $5,000 toward multiples of annual salary, privilege of conversion from term to straight life, shorter, waiting period for coverage
    e. Unemployment Compensation—continuation of group health insurance, life insurance, sick pay, strike benefits
    f. Workmen's Compensation—increased individual and family allowances
    g. Business Travel Accident—24-hour coverage during a business trip
    h. Sick Leave—unlimited accrual or tie-in with long or short term disability and Social Security disability, payment for unused sick leave
    i. Miscellaneous Leave—marriage, birthday, maternity, paternity, divorce, educational, relocation, sabbatical, etc., all with full or partial employer payment
    j. Severance Pay—informal program based upon salary level and length of employment
3. Miscellaneous Benefits
    a. Expansion of "Pursuit of Happiness" Benefits previously listed
    b. Group Purchasing—personal and household articles
    c. Free or Low Cost Legal Services
    d. Group Auto & Homeowner's Insurance
    e. Day Care Centers
    f. Automatic Bank Deposit of Pay Checks
    g. Traveler's Checks
    h. Foreign Travel Immunizations
    i. Vocational Counseling
    j. Subsidized Parking and Public Transportation
    k. Suggestion Programs with suitably attractive awards
    l. Pre-Retirement Counseling
    m. Flexible Work Schedules—outgrowth of the 3 day/40 hour work week
    n. Social/Recreational Activities—expanded programs with increased financial support by employer
    o. Relocation Expense Reimbursement
    p. Sabbatical Leave—partly or fully paid
    q. Educational and Management Training Leave on work time
    r. Business Travel Expenses—increased mileage, meal, hotel, public transportation reimbursement

---

*Source: Reprinted from *Heath Care Labor Manual* by Martin E. Skoler, with permission of Aspen Systems Corporation, © 1981.

s. Cafeteria or Supermarket Benefit Plans
t. Employee Store—partially subsidized
u. Tax Deferred Annuities—increased flexibility and broader investment vehicles
v. Blood—available as needed by employee and family
w. On-premises banking

Chapter 35—Employee Performance Appraisal

The primary objectives of performance appraisal should be:

- to encourage improved performance in the job each employee presently holds
- to provide growth opportunity for those employees who wish to pursue possibilities for promotion, and, conversely, provide the organization with people qualified for promotion to more responsible positions.

In general, the true objectives of appraisal are not well served. An appalling number of appraisal systems are oriented almost entirely toward criticism and faultfinding. Certainly these systems were not intended to be used in this fashion, but their weaknesses, primarily their focus on the past, have brought about their general misuse. Rather than simply looking at the past and stopping there, an effective performance appraisal system should seek to utilize the past only as a starting point from which to move into the future.*

APPRAISAL METHODS*

The major approaches to performance appraisal are:

---

*Source: Reprinted from *The Effective Health Care Supervisor* by Charles R. McConnell, with permission of Aspen Systems Corporation, © 1982.

Rating Scales

Rating scales, the oldest and most widely used appraisal procedures, are of two general types.

In *continuous scales*, in reference to a particular evaluation characteristic, the evaluator places a mark somewhere along a continuous scale (Figure 35-1). There is usually a numerical scale involved, so the evaluator is actually assigning a certain number of "points" to the individual for that particular characteristic. Generally, the evaluator is aware of some position on the scale that constitutes "average" or "satisfactory" performance.

In *discrete scales*, each characteristic is associated with a number of descriptions covering the possible range of employee performance. The evaluator simply checks the box, or perhaps the column, accompanying the most appropriate description (Figure 35-2).

Rating scale methods are easy to understand and easy to use, at least in a superficial manner. They permit numerical tabulation of scores in terms of measures of average tendency, skewness (the tendency of a group of employees to cluster on either side of a so-called average), and dispersion.

Rating scales are relatively easy to construct, and they permit ready comparison of scores among employees. However, rating scales have several severe disadvantages. Do total scores of 78 for Jane and 83 for Harriet *really* mean anything significant? These systems are also subject

Figure 35-1 One characteristic from a continuous-type rating scale appraisal
ATTITUDE:

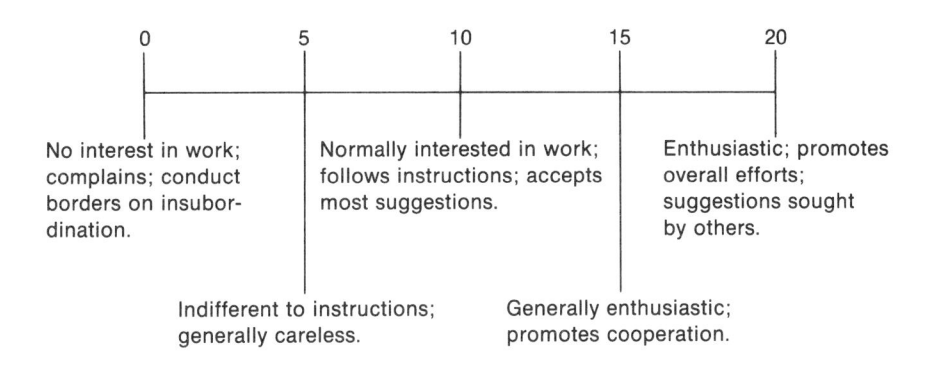

```
     0            5            10           15           20
     |------------|------------|------------|------------|

No interest in work;     Normally interested in work;     Enthusiastic; promotes
complains; conduct       follows instructions; accepts    overall efforts;
borders on insubor-      most suggestions.                suggestions sought
dination.                                                 by others.

        Indifferent to instructions;     Generally enthusiastic;
        generally careless.              promotes cooperation.
```

Figure 35-2 One characteristic from a discrete-type rating scale appraisal
JOB KNOWLEDGE:

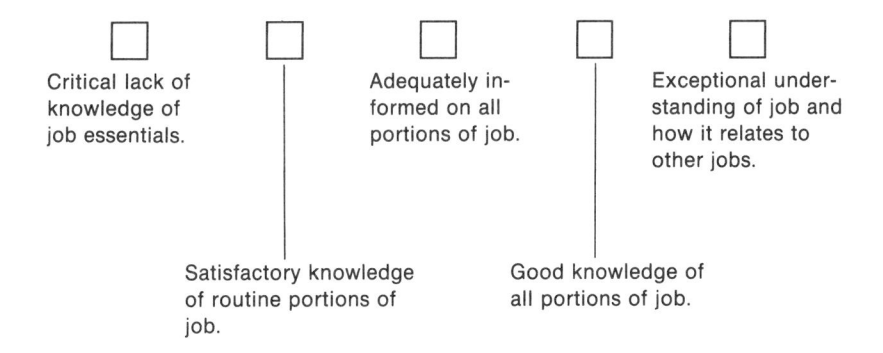

```
   □            □            □            □            □

Critical lack of         Adequately in-              Exceptional under-
knowledge of             formed on all               standing of job and
job essentials.          portions of job.            how it relates to
                                                     other jobs.

        Satisfactory knowledge        Good knowledge of
        of routine portions of        all portions of job.
        job.
```

to assumptions of the ability of a high score on one characteristic to compensate for a low score on another. For instance, if an employee scores low relative to quantity of work produced, can this really be counterbalanced by high scores for attendance, attitude, and job knowledge?

Ratings frequently tend to cluster on the high side when rating scales are used. Supervisors may tend to rate their employees high because they want them to receive their fair share of pay raises and feel good about themselves, and also because it is easier to praise than it is to leave oneself open to the appearance of being critical. Also, different supervisors tend to rate differently. Some consider *average* as precisely that—average acceptable work, nothing to be ashamed of. However, other supervisors seem to think of *average* as something of a dirty word and thus tend to rate most employees on the high side of the scale.

Employee Comparison

Employee comparison methods were developed to overcome certain disadvantages of the rating scale approaches. Employee comparison may involve the ranking method or the forced distribution method.

Ranking

The ranking method forces the supervisor to rate all employees on an overall basis according to their job performance and value to the institution. One approach is to simply look at your work group and decide initially who is the best and who is the poorest performer and then to pick the second and next-to-last persons in your rank order by applying the same judgment to the remaining employees. This is simple enough to accomplish, but the process is highly judgmental and strongly influenced by personality factors. Also, some employee must end up as "low person on the totem pole," and this may not be a fair assessment overall.

Forced Distribution

The forced distribution method prevents the supervisor from clustering all employees in any particular part of the scale. It requires the evaluator to distribute the ratings in a pattern conforming with a normal frequency distribution. The supervisor must place, for instance, 10% of the employees in the top category, 20% in the next higher category, 40% in the middle bracket, and so on. The objective of this technique is to spread out the evaluations. However, while it is true that the general population may be distributed according to a normal curve, in an organization we are dealing with a select group of persons. If employees have been properly trained and probationary periods correctly used to eliminate the genuine misfits, then the true distribution of abilities and performance in the work group should be decidedly skewed. That is, your group's "average" should be better than the general average assumed by the so-called normal distribution.

Checklists

Weighted Checklist

The weighted checklist consists of a number of statements that describe various modes and levels of behavior for a particular job or category of jobs. Every statement has a weight or scale value associated with it, and when rating an employee the supervisor checks those statements that most closely describe the behavior exhibited by the individual. The completed rating sheet is then scored by averaging the weights of all the descriptive statements checked by the rater. This is much like the rating scale approach except for the application of the weights. Some evaluation characteristics are worth more or less than others. Often in checklist evaluation systems the weights are intentionally kept secret from the supervisor. This is done supposedly to avoid deliberate bias on the part of the supervisor; it is not possible to "slant" a rating to make the final score come out in some predetermined manner.

Forced Choice

Like the pure checklist approach, the forced choice method requires the development of a significant number of statements describing various types of behavior for a particular job or family of jobs. These statements are arranged in groups of four or five each, and within each group the evaluator must check the one statement that is most descriptive of the performance of the employee and the one statement that is least descriptive of the employee's performance. The groups are so designed that each will contain two statements that appear favorable and two that appear unfavorable. A set of five statements from among which the supervisor must make the choice just described is shown in Table 35-1. While statements A and B both appear favorable, only statement B actually differentiates between high and low performance employees. Statement C is actually descriptive of low performance employees. Although E also appears to be unfavorable, it is inconsequential in this set because of the presence of C. Statement D is neutral. Once again,

Table 35-1 Illustrative Group of Statements from a Forced-Choice Appraisal

Circle the letter for the statement that is *most* descriptive of the employee's performance and the letter for the statement that is *least* descriptive of the employee's performance:

Most	Least	
A	A	Makes mistakes only infrequently
B	B	Is respected by fellow employees
C	C	Fails to follow instructions completely
D	D	Feels own job is more important than other jobs
E	E	Does not exhibit self-reliance when expressing own views

the actual value or weight of the statements is kept secret from the supervisor.

Critical Incident

The critical incident method requires a supervisor to adopt the practice of recording in a notebook all those significant incidents in each employee's behavior that indicate either effective or successful action or ineffective action or poor behavior. The notebook itself is designed to provide reminders of performance characteristics under which various incidents can be recorded. For instance, if an employee saved the day by spotting an urgent problem and taking bold and imaginative action, you might want to record the incident under "initiative."

There is a severe hazard in the use of the critical incident method. Supervisors are busy people, and often everything that should be recorded does not reach the notebook. However, negative incidents, because of their "seriousness," are more likely to reach the pages of the book than are many occasions of positive performance. Also, this approach can lead to overly close supervision, with the employees feeling that the supervisor is watching over their shoulders and that everything they do will be written down in the "little black book."

Field Review

Under the field review appraisal method the supervisor has no forms to fill out. Rather, the supervisor is interviewed by a representative of the personnel department who asks questions about the performance of each employee. The interviewer writes up the results of the interview in narrative form and reviews them with the supervisor for suggestions, modifications, and approval. No rating forms or factors or degrees or weights are involved; rather, simple overall ratings are obtained.

The field review approach relieves the supervisor of paperwork. It also assures a greater likelihood that supervisors will give adequate and timely attention to appraisals because the personnel department largely controls the process. However, the process takes the valuable time of two management representatives (the supervisor and the personnel interviewer), and it requires the presence of far more personnel department manpower than most institutions feel they can afford.

Free-Form Essay

This method simply requires the supervisor to write down impressions about the employee in essay fashion. If desired by the organization, comments can be grouped under headings such as: job performance, job knowledge, and goals for future consideration, for example. To do a creditable job under this method, the supervisor must devote considerable time and thought to the evaluation. On the plus side, this process encourages the supervisor to become more observant and analytical. On the other hand, the free-form essay approach generally demands more time than the average supervisor is willing or able to spend. Also, appraisals generated by this method are often more reflective of the skill and effort of the writer than of the true performance of the employees.

Group Appraisal

Under this approach an employee is evaluated at the same time by the immediate supervisor plus three or four other supervisors who have knowledge of that employee's work performance. The virtue of this method is its thoroughness. It is also possible for multiple evaluators to modify or cancel out bias displayed by the immediate supervisor. However, the drawbacks of this approach are such that it is rarely used: it is extremely time consuming, tying up perhaps four or five members of management to evaluate a single employee, and it is often inapplicable because there may be few managers beyond the immediate supervisor who are sufficiently familiar with the employee's performance.

Behaviorally Anchored Rating Scales (BARS)*

The BARS system measures employee effectiveness through specific behaviors anchored to a scale that ranges from ineffective to effective performance. The development of BARS is a time-consuming process requiring, as a prerequisite, a large number of employees who perform reasonably similar tasks. It has received some use in nursing departments—an applica-

---

*Source: Reprinted from Howard L. Smith and Norbert F. Elbert, "An Integrated Approach to Performance Evaluation in the Health Care Field," *Health Care Management Review,* Winter 1980, with permission of Aspen Systems Corporation.

tion that is aided by the size of nursing departments and the ability to identify nursing skills.

A sample of the employees, along with their supervisors, generates a list of task dimensions and associated critical behaviors. A second sample of employees and supervisors then proceeds to "retranslate" the critical behaviors by matching them to the task dimensions. The result is a thorough job analysis that reveals specific items of effective behavior as judged by the personnel and supervisors most familiar with the task itself.

The BARS system of evaluation has proven to be more acceptable than either traditional trait ratings or single global ratings in the areas of acceptability by supervisor and subordinate, counseling and clarification of the nature of the job. The only negative drawback to BARS is the requirement of similar job tasks, but this is not a problem in large health care organizations.

Objectives-Oriented Methods*

Management by objectives (MBO) typically involves administrator-employee development of specific objectives and agreement on how these objectives are to be measured. For example, a medical records supervisor may discuss with a medical records clerk the goals (more readable entries and more correct filing) that the clerk will seek to achieve in the next six months. The primary advantage of MBO lies in eliciting employee participation which may ultimately produce greater commitment for the attainment of specific goals. Objectives-oriented techniques are particularly attractive in overcoming the weaknesses of the BARS approach.

The basic weakness of the MBO system is encountered in jobs that do not consist of easily measurable attributes that are therefore difficult to appraise objectively. Even so, many hospitals and medical centers are implementing MBO programs with apparent success.

A memorandum of an employee evaluating himself should include:[1]

1. The objectives agreed upon at the beginning of the year
2. The results achieved for each objective
3. A list of personal growth as seen by the individual for his/her own improvement on the job and by way of preparation for future assignments in his/her career

BARS and MBO*

An ideal solution to the problem of developing a good individual performance evaluation system in the health care field might be the simultaneous implementation of BARS and MBO systems. Behaviorally anchored rating scales can provide performance measures for largely behaviorally oriented positions that are difficult to objectify (health social work or special needs education). Behaviorally anchored rating scales can also be used to determine the suitability of objectives for each individual. The MBO system would act as an effective deterrent to the problems of lack of developmental feedback. The integration of BARS and MBO in an evaluation system would also offer the following advantages: (1) it would allow the employee's fullest level of participation in the evaluation process, (2) it should facilitate the development of objective measures and (3) it can assist administrators and personnel when setting moderately difficult goals.

The above solution represents an ideal model that many health care administrators should strive to achieve. However, as so often occurs, the ideal is never realized. An alternative would be the operation of two somewhat separate appraisal systems: one to handle extrinsic rewards such as pay and bonuses, the other for development training and intrinsic motivation purposes. When separated by time, and when the developmental sessions are held after the reward decisions have been made, constructive employee development can take place without pay and promotion considerations lurking in the background.

---

*Source: Reprinted from Howard L. Smith and Norbert F. Elbert, "An Integrated Approach to Performance Evaluation in the Health Care Field," *Health Care Management Review,* Winter 1980, with permission of Aspen Systems Corporation.

[1] Reprinted from *Management by Objectives for Hospitals* by Arthur X. Deegan II, with permission of Aspen Systems Corporation, © 1977.

---

*Source: Reprinted from Howard L. Smith and Norbert F. Elbert, "An Integrated Approach to Performance Evaluation in the Health Care Field," *Health Care Management Review,* Winter 1980, with permission of Aspen Systems Corporation.

COMMON APPRAISAL PROBLEMS*

A common problem encountered in performance evaluation is the "halo effect." This refers to the tendency of an evaluator to allow the rating assigned to one or more characteristics to excessively influence the rating on other performance characteristics. The rating scale methods are particularly susceptible to the halo effect. For instance, if you have declared an employee to be excellent in terms of "initiative" and "dependability," so might you be inclined to rate high relative to "judgment" and "adaptability." Since it is extremely difficult to force oneself to completely separate the consideration of each performance factor from the others (many performance characteristics actually include shades of others), there is no guaranteed way of eliminating the halo effect.

Another common problem in most rating systems is the tendency of many supervisors to be liberal in their evaluations, that is, to give their employees consistently high ratings. Most approaches to rating are partially based on the assumption that the majority of the work force will be "average" performers. However, many people (supervisors included) do not like to be considered "only average."

Central tendency or clustering is another problem, one that some of the rating methods have attempted to overcome. Some supervisors are reluctant to evaluate people in terms of the outer ends of the scale. To many supervisors it is "safest" to evaluate all employees consistently. This often leads to a situation in which "everyone is average," contrary to the likelihood that in a work group of any considerable size there are, in fact, performers who are both better and worse than the so-called average.

Interpersonal relationships pose a considerable problem in performance evaluation. The supervisor cannot help but be influenced, even if only unconsciously, by personal likes and dislikes. Often a significant part of an evaluation will be based on how well the supervisor likes the employee rather than how well the employee actually performs.

When the administrator is writing an evaluation of a worker's past performance, it is important to omit details about the individual's personality. Rather, it should include:*

1. Results accomplished compared with desired results
2. Summary judgment about the overall worth of the individual to the organization

STANDARDS FOR EVALUATING EMPLOYEES

1. Kaiser-Permanente Medical Group**

The ten principal factors shown for performance evaluation (see Table 35-2) may only be relative in varying degrees and some may not be appropriate in every case. These factors are *not* what the employee is being measured on. He or she is being measured against the requirements, responsibilities, and accountabilities shown on the position description.

These ten factors are primarily useful in *discussing* poor, acceptable, or outstanding performance. It may be, other, unlisted factors are important elements in the position and should, therefore, be included in the narrative section of the evaluation.

The following questions may be asked in preparing an evaluation of these factors:

1. *Job Knowledge.* What has this individual done to actually demonstrate depth, currency, or breadth of job knowledge in the performance of duties?
2. *Judgment and Decisions.* Does this person think clearly and develop correct and logical conclusions? Report on how this person grasps, analyzes, and presents workable solutions to problems.
3. *Plan and Organize Work.* Does this person look beyond immediate job requirements? How well does he/she anticipate critical events?
4. *Management of Resources.* Does this individual "manage" to achieve optimum

---

*Source: Reprinted from *The Effective Health Care Supervisor* by Charles R. McConnell, with permission of Aspen Systems Corporation, © 1982.

*Source: Reprinted from *Management by Objectives for Hospitals* by Arthur X. Deegan, with permission of Aspen Systems Corporation, © 1977.

**Source: Reprinted from Ralph A. Anthenien, "Performance Salary Increase Program," *Handbook of Health Care Human Resources Management,* Norman Metzger, ed., with permission of Aspen Systems Corporation, © 1981.

Table 35-2 Standards for Evaluating Employees

SALARIED PERFORMANCE STANDARDS
(To be used with Performance Evaluation Form # 94366)

Performance Factors	(5) Unsatisfactory	(4) Meets Minimum Requirements (Needs Improvement)	(3) Meets Requirements	(2) Exceeds Requirements	(1) Outstanding
1. Job Knowledge (Depth, currency, breadth)	Standards: • Has serious gaps in technical and professional knowledge • Knows only most rudimentary phase of job • Lack of knowledge affects productivity • Requires abnormal amount of checking	Standards: • Technical and professional knowledge is inadequate for the job • Must be assigned only routine duties and monitored regularly • Requires close supervision	Standards: • Demonstrates adequate technical and professional knowledge required for the job • Searches out facts and arrives at sound solutions to problems • Broad knowledge of related jobs and functions • Conversant with significant job-related developments	Standards: • Possesses keen insight and the ability to evolve it into practical solutions • Keeps informed of important developments in related fields • Can handle difficult situations effectively • Broad knowledge of related missions • Rarely requires guidance or assistance	Standards: • Possesses superb technical and professional knowledge • Sufficiently well versed in his/her job to discuss and implement improved methods resulting in savings in manpower or material • Maintains and increases professional and technical knowledge • Actively pursues new ideas and developments and their relation to the overall mission • Recognized authority in his or her field
2. Judgement and Decisions (Consistent, accurate, effective)	• Reluctant to make decisions on his or her own • Decisions are usually not reliable • Declines to accept responsibility for decisions	• Usually makes sound routine decisions • Tends to procrastinate on necessary decisions • Reluctant to evaluate factors before arriving at decisions	• Seeks out all available data before arriving at decisions • Consistently provides accurate decisions • Accepts responsibility for decisions and learns from incorrect judgements • Provides effective decisions by clear and logical thinking	• An exceptionally sound, logical thinker • Does not hesitate to make required decisions • Decisions are consistently correct • Opinions and judgements are often solicited by others	• Keen, analytical thinker • Makes accurate decisions under intense pressure • Extremely effective in exercising logic in broad areas of responsibility
3. Plan and Organize Work (Timely and creative)	• Fails to plan ahead • Disorganized and usually unprepared • Objectives are not met on time	• Scheduling and organizational efforts normally fail • Encounters difficulty with tasks other than routine • Finished products are usually behind schedule	• Careful, effective planner • Anticipates and solves problems • Effectively balances resources • Finished products are consistently submitted on time	• Plans beyond requirements of present job • Plans coincide with related activities • Is flexible and able to adjust priorities • Frequently called on to organize complex tasks	• Able to anticipate critical events and makes prior provisions to deal with them • Plans encompass all feasible contingencies • Extremely effective in utilization of resources
4. Management of Resources: (Manpower and material)	• Wastes or misuses resources • No system established for accounting of material • Causes delay for others by mismanagement	• Accomplishes conservation of material on a sporadic basis • Squanders resources to get job done	• Uses minimum material with good results • Establishes controls to ensure that manpower and material are accounted for and conserved • Develops and uses cost-effective methods	• Excellent results accomplished at minimum cost • Consistently suggests methods of conserving resources • Skillfully uses cost-effectiveness studies	• Extremely effective in use of material • Consistently seeks and projects ways of using existing equipment • Is often assigned to difficult and important projects where limited resources are a significant factor
5. Adaptability to Stress (Stable, dependable) flexible	• Panics in new situation • Tendency to shirk difficult situations • Reaction is unpredictable	• Prefers to work on routine tasks • Jumps to erroneous conclusions in new situations • Hesitates to become involved in new situations	• Flexible and open to new ideas • Willingly seeks assistance in difficult situations • Provides reliable decisions under pressure • Consistently displays calm and controlled behavior	• Readily adapts to fluctuations and changing priorities • Consistently performs well in difficult situations • Anticipates changes and is prepared to react accordingly	• Responds quickly and effectively to crises • Systematically succeeds where others fail • Consistently provides outstanding leadership and guidance under difficult and stressful conditions

Table 35-2 continued

Performance Factors	(5) Unsatisfactory	(4) Meets Minimum Requirements (Needs Improvement)	(3) Meets Requirements	(2) Exceeds Requirements	(1) Outstanding
6. Oral Communication (Clear, concise, confident)	Standards: • Does not convey ideas clearly and concisely • Has limited vocabulary • Cannot express thoughts in a logical sequence	Standards: • Only occasionally able to verbally convey useful information • Briefings and discussions frequently exhibit a lack of confidence	Standards: • Gives direct and understandable responses to questions • Gives briefings which are organized and well presented	Standards: • Very articulate in a wide range of difficult communications situations • Puts extra effort into conversing well • Capable of persuading an audience	Standards: • Delivers concise, well-organized presentations • Is often called on to present and explain difficult and complex subjects • Can sway a hostile audience to his or her point of view
7. Written Communication (Clear, concise, organized)	• Written communications are inadequate due to errors in vocabulary, spelling and grammar • Communications often raise doubt as to exact meaning • Others must continually seek clarification or correct errors	• Clarity of written communications is inconsistent • Only occasionally able to convey a cogent idea • Extensive editing and correcting is usually required before communications can be dispatched	• Writing is clear and concise • Written instructions and reports are readily understandable • Written communications are consistently well organized and grammatically correct	• Written reports can be easily followed by all readers • Communications are succinct and concise, containing only those words necessary to express an idea	• Able to describe complex or technical concepts so well that even the casual reader can readily comprehend the idea • Is consistently chosen for the most important and difficult writing assignments • Is frequently asked to edit the written correspondence of others
8. Human Relations	• Openly and knowingly practices discrimination • Uses racial epithets or sexual slurs maliciously • Is deliberately hostile to minorities or members of the opposite sex • Does not show any consideration or concern for others	• Displays very limited sensitivity to equal opportunity policies • Treats minorities or members of the opposite sex markedly different than other personnel • Employs inflammatory or derogatory terms toward minorities or members of the opposite sex • Tends to lack concern for peers and subordinates	• Treats all personnel fairly and equitably • Voluntarily participates in activities in support of equal opportunity • Shows concern and is sensitive to needs of others	• Demonstrates exceptional skill working with others and eliciting their cooperation • Establishes and enthusiastically maintains standards of equal opportunity • Encourages practice of equal opportunity and treatment in all activities • Displays a high degree of sensitivity and concern for others	• Demonstrates clearly superior ability to work with others and to elicit their cooperation • Displays extreme sensitivity and a deep concern in all dealings with peers and subordinates • Is extremely effective in solving human relations problems . solutions always reflect fair and equal treatment
9. Quantity	• Assignments and tasks are often not completed on a timely basis • Completes assignments in a sporadic basis and overall completion rate is unsatisfactory • Often wastes time in completion of nonessential tasks or duties while higher priority items await attention • Does not meet time limits or expectations on a frequent basis • Does not adjust pace to meet work demands	• Does not complete all required work in a timely basis • Does not always anticipate work flow or adjust to peak and slack periods of work • Works sporadically, and at times unable to adjust work level to demand • Often does not establish or meet deadlines in completion of long projects. Therefore, is not often able to take corrective action in order to meet deadlines	• Completes all required work assignments on time • Able to anticipate work flow and accommodate for peak periods and slack periods • Works at a steady pace generating a normal amount of output in a satisfactory manner • Establishes time targets to insure work is progressing as planned and takes necessary corrective action to meet deadlines	• Completes all required, in addition to "extra" work assignments, in a most timely manner • Assists others frequently in completion of their assignments • Frequently volunteers and completes additional work projects • Able to forecast work peak loads and arrange and adjust pace to easily accommodate extra assignments as necessary • Consistently meets all deadlines while often completing more than expected or required	• All work is completed at a fast pace and is consistently completed early • Continually assists others in the completion of their assignments • Continually volunteers for additional assignments and projects and meets deadlines with ease • Easily adjusts to changing workloads and completes all assignments as required
10. Quality	• Frequent errors are made and validity of completed work must be frequently checked for accuracy • Completed work does not often meet expectations or does not meet standards, policies or procedures • Other staff members must frequently assist employee in the adequate completion of work assignments • Completed work must often be redone, or reassigned in order to meet acceptable standards	• Most work completed is accurate, but mistakes or inaccuracies are discovered • Some work completed does not meet expectations or does not adhere to policies • Employee does not always spot check work in order to discover and take corrective action on errors or problems • Work needs frequent follow-up to insure accuracy, objectives and expectations are met	• Work completed is accurate, adheres to policies and procedures and is acceptable in all respects • Employee conducts periodic spot audits to insure that work meets standards • Maintains expectations work assignments. Work is completed and rarely needs follow-up	• Work completed is always accurate and thoroughly checked for completeness. Needs little, if any, supervisory review for accuracy • Work produced exceeds normal expectation and adheres to all standards of quality, policies and procedures. • Work is extremely presentable and exhibits those qualities of professionalism and is clearly superior to the "normal" work expected	• Regardless of situation, always completes work assignments with clearly exceptional accuracy, and serves as a "model" for high quality work • Acts as a resource person for others in the completion of accurate work • Work always exceeds standards, meeting policies, procedures and expectations and is thoroughly checked prior to submission. Needs no follow-up or checking for accuracy • Works consistently brings praise as to the degree of accuracy, understandability and remark results

Source: Kaiser-Permanente Medical Care Program.

economy through effective utilization of personnel and material? Consider the balance between minimum cost and false economy to the ultimate expense of the project or objective.
5. *Adaptability to Stress.* What is the effect of stress on this person's performance? Does he/she work as well or better under adverse conditions? In difficult situations, heavy workloads and pressures, does his/her work deteriorate?
6. *Oral Communication.* How well has this person been able to present ideas orally?
7. *Written Communication.* How well has this person been able to present ideas in writing?
8. *Human Relations.* How does this person work with and relate to others? How does this person demonstrate his/her support of the company's Equal Opportunities and Affirmative Action programs?
9. *Quantity.* How does the volume of work compare to your expectations of all things such as interruptions, special projects, etc. considered? You must, of course, balance quantity of work with quality of work considered next. Standard output will vary for different kinds and levels of positions, and in each instance the supervisor should refer to the position description in determining a reasonable standard.
10. *Quality.* How accurate, presentable, or reliable is the work of this individual? Does it need more or less checking? Does it meet organizational standards, policies, and procedures? How consistent was the quality of his work under varying conditions? Is the work complete and thorough? Again, this factor must be balanced with quantity.

There are many factors, however, which are *not* job related, are extraneous and should not be used, considered, or referred to in the evaluation process. They include:

1. Time in position/time in company
2. Time before retirement
3. Age
4. Race
5. Color
6. Sex
7. National origin
8. Handicap
9. Veteran status
10. Religion
11. Physical appearance
12. Marital status
13. Relationship to others (Relatives, associations, etc.)

2. Rating Scale Elements

The most common elements in a rating scale can be described as follows:

- Job knowledge: measures how well the employee understands his work assignment; whether he has the necessary skills and the ability to recognize work errors. It attempts to gauge the employee's ability to execute the job tasks whether or not he acts accordingly.
- Productivity: relates to the quantity or amount of work produced by the employee over a given period of time. Yardsticks of output vary, depending upon the nature of the job; for example, tallying the number of forms filled, tests assessed or orders delivered.
- Quality: refers to the relative merit of the employee's work, whether it is "good" or "bad," whether it is accurate and thorough, neat and non-wasteful of equipment and finally, whether it meets specified standards.
- Dependability: evaluates the consistency with which a worker applies himself to the job at hand. It refers to attendance, punctuality, and the continuity of his work effort. Does he stay at the task or wander off, work sporadically, loaf or generally waste time?
- Versatility: assesses whether the employee demonstrates the ability to perform a number of tasks. It refers to whether shifts in tasks are accomplished satisfactorily, both in performance and in ease of adjustment.
- Initiative: estimates the worker's willingness and ability to initiate tasks, to identify the best method, and to follow up on a job independently, with minimal supervision.
- Appearance: evaluates the employee's attention to grooming and attire, keeping in mind the nature and standards of his work.
- Cooperation with Management: refers to the active willingness of a worker to do the job as opposed to a passive acceptance of

orders. It measures the employee's attitude in accepting assignment and suggestions, desiring to work with the supervisor as a team member or resisting instructions.
- Personal Relationships: evaluates how well the employee gets along with his peers. The review of a worker's social conduct can be highly subjective and consequently should be treated with caution.

THE APPRAISAL INTERVIEW*

The objective of a personal interview is to evaluate past, present, and future potential of an individual. The following points are offered as a general guide:

1. Establish a friendly atmosphere by selecting the right time and place for the interview. Be sure the interview will be free of interruptions.
2. Let the employee talk first, discussing the summary memo prepared. Be alert to this discussion for opportunities that might help you inject two or three main points you have on your mind.
3. Be sure to cover priorities so sufficient groundwork has been laid for preparing a list of objectives for the next operational period.
4. Make a final overall judgment about the individual, progress to date worth to the hospital, as well as any recommendations (of a personal nature) you might be expected to make on the written instrument. Get a signature and explain that the signature does not necessarily signify that the person agrees with your judgment, but understands your position.

The Personality Function

Some useful hints for evaluating employees follow.

1. Criticism has a negative effect on achievement goals.
2. Praise in the employee evaluation has little effect one way or the other.
3. Performance improves most when specific goals are established.
4. Defensiveness produces inferior performance. Employees reacted defensively to criticism 54% of the time—blamed others, made excuses, etc.
5. Coaching should be made day-to-day, not once-a-year activity.
6. Mutual goal setting, not criticism, improves performance.
7. Interviews designed primarily to improve performance should not be held at the same time you weigh salary or promotion in balance.
8. Participation by the employee in goal setting helps produce favorable results—greater mutual understanding between supervisor and employee, greater acceptance of job goals, and a feeling of greater self-realization.

Mutual Goal Setting

Employees felt the following things were accomplished when mutual goal setting was used by their supervisors:

1. The amount of help the supervisor was giving them through day-to-day coaching was improving their job performance.
2. The supervisor appeared to be more receptive to new ideas and suggestions.
3. The supervisor's ability to plan appeared to improve.
4. The supervisor made greater use of their abilities and experience.
5. Employees felt the goals they were working for were what they should be.
6. The supervisor helped them plan for future job opportunities.
7. Employees valued discussions with their supervisors because these discussions opened communication and provided an exchange of information.

Dealing with Employee Attitudes*

One task that every supervisor faces reluctantly is rating his workers on their job performance. It takes skill, practice, and judgment to evaluate

---

*Source: Reprinted from *Management by Objectives for Hospitals* by Arthur X. Deegan II, with permission of Aspen Systems Corporation, © 1977.

*Source: Reprinted from *The NFI Standard Manual for Supervisors,* with permission of the Bureau of Business Practice, © 1977.

Figure 35-3 Sample form: employee performance appraisal*

THE _____ HOSPITAL MEDICAL CENTER

PLEASE PRINT - DO NOT USE TYPEWRITER

EMPLOYEE INFORMATION

NAME				DATE
DEPARTMENT	AREA	SECTION	JOB TITLE	
REASON FOR REVIEW	☐ MERIT INCREASE ☐ END OF THREE MONTH TRIAL ☐ TRANSFER/PROMOTION	☐ ANNUAL REVIEW ☐ OTHER	JOB CODE AND GRADE	

INSTRUCTIONS:
- SELECT THE APPROPRIATE DESCRIPTION AND POINTS FOR EACH CATEGORY.
- DESCRIPTIVE COMMENTS ARE MEANT AS GUIDES, AND NEED NOT BE STRICTLY INTERPRETED. YOUR RATING SHOULD ALLOW FOR THE LENGTH OF JOB EXPERIENCE OF THE EMPLOYEE BEING RATED.
- INCLUDE EXPLANATORY REMARKS WHEREVER POSSIBLE.
- REVIEW APPRAISAL WITH THE EMPLOYEE, PARTICULARLY COMMENTS ON IMPROVEMENT.

QUALITY OF WORK (1 to 10 points)

WORK DONE CARELESSLY. ALMOST CONSTANT CHECKING REQUIRED. ERRORS FREQUENT. **1-2**	WORK IS SOMETIMES INADEQUATE. MORE OFTEN IS SATISFACTORY BUT SUBJECT TO CHECKING. ERRORS MAY BE A PROBLEM. **3-5**	POINTS: REMARKS:
WORK IS DONE WELL AND IS NEAT AND ORDERLY. ONLY OCCASIONAL CORRECTION REQUIRED. ERRORS ARE FEW. **6-8**	WORK IS CONSISTENTLY VERY WELL DONE AND IS NEAT AND ORDERLY. SELDOM REQUIRES CHECKING AND CORRECTION. ERRORS ARE RARE. **9-10**	

QUANTITY OF WORK (1 to 10 points)

EMPLOYEE RATING

VERY SLOW EMPLOYEE. USUALLY TAKES FAR TOO LONG TO PERFORM WORK. OUTPUT IS LOW. **1-2**	SLOW IN PERFORMING WORK. SOMETIMES DOES NOT COMPLETE ASSIGNMENTS. TENDS TO BE INFLEXIBLE IN METHODS. OUTPUT IS AVERAGE. **3-5**	POINTS: REMARKS:
COMPLETES ASSIGNMENTS IN A REASONABLE TIME. USUALLY USES EFFICIENT METHODS AND ROUTINES. OUTPUT IS GOOD. **6-8**	STARTS PROMPTLY. COMPLETES ASSIGNMENTS IN A VERY SHORT TIME. CONSISTENTLY USES EFFICIENT METHODS. OUTPUT IS HIGH. **9-10**	

INITIATIVE (1 to 14 points)

LEARNS NEW TASKS SLOWLY. MUST BE TOLD WHAT TO DO FREQUENTLY. IS INDIFFERENT. DOES NOT DO OTHER RELATED JOBS. **1-3**	DOES ROUTINE WORK WITHOUT WAITING FOR DIRECTIONS. ABLE TO LEARN NEW TASKS. WILL DO SOME RELATED JOBS. **4-7**	POINTS: REMARKS:
ALERT TO OPPORTUNITIES FOR IMPROVING WORK FUNCTIONS. IS USUALLY RESOURCEFUL. PERFORMS WELL ON UNRELATED JOBS. **8-11**	SEEKS OUT ADDITIONAL TASKS. USES INITIATIVE. HIGHLY INGENIOUS AND RESOURCEFUL. EXCELLENT IN PLANNING WORK. SKILLED ON SEVERAL UNRELATED JOBS. **12-14**	

*Source: Reprinted from *Health Care Labor Manual* by Martin E. Skoler, with permission of Aspen Systems Corporation, © 1981.

Figure 35-3 continued

ATTITUDE (1 to 14 points)

EMPLOYEE RATING

DOES NOT GET ALONG WELL WITH OTHERS. SOMETIMES UNWILLING TO COOPERATE. DIFFICULT TO HANDLE. **1-3**	MODERATELY MOTIVATED TOWARD WORK AND ORGANIZATION. COMPLIES WITH ORDERS, AT TIMES NOT TOO PROMPTLY. GETS ALONG WITH ASSOCIATES **4-7**	POINTS: _____ REMARKS:
GENERALLY WELL MOTIVATED TOWARD WORK AND ORGANIZATION. WORKS WELL WITH AND ASSISTS OTHERS. IS WELL-LIKED BY ASSOCIATES. **8-11**	IS HIGHLY MOTIVATED TOWARD WORK AND THE ORGANIZATION. GOES OUT OF WAY TO BE HELPFUL. IS VERY WELL LIKED. INSPIRES TEAMWORK. **12-14**	

JOB KNOWLEDGE (1 to 10 points)

LACKS DESIRE OR ABILITY TO GAIN JOB KNOWLEDGE. IS INDIFFERENT TO TRAINING. RESPONDS POORLY. **1-2**	HAS MODERATE KNOWLEDGE OF THE WORK. TRIES FOR BETTER PERFORMANCE. SOMETIMES RESPONDS SLOWLY TO TRAINING. **3-5**	POINTS: _____ REMARKS:
GOOD KNOWLEDGE OF THE JOB AND EQUIPMENT. SHOWS INTEREST IN DOING A BETTER JOB. RESPONDS TO TRAINING AND SUGGESTIONS. **6-8**	THOROUGH KNOWLEDGE OF ALL PHASES OF WORK. TAKES EVERY OPPORTUNITY TO IMPROVE SELF. ASSUMES RESPONSIBILITY. **9-10**	

DEPENDABILITY (1 to 14 points)

WORK HAS TO BE FOLLOWED UP CONSTANTLY. DOES NOT APPLY SELF. NEEDS TO BE REMINDED ABOUT DETAILS. NEEDS EXCESSIVE SUPERVISION. **1-3**	USUALLY DESERVES CONFIDENCE. FAIRLY STEADY WORKER. COULD WORK SOMEWHAT HARDER. NEEDS AND RESPONDS TO NORMAL SUPERVISION. **4-7**	POINTS: _____ REMARKS:
CAN BE RELIED UPON FOR SUCCESSFUL COMPLETION OF WORK. FOLLOWS INSTRUCTIONS. WORKS HARD WITHOUT DRIVING. NEEDS LITTLE SUPERVISON. **8-11**	ALWAYS JUSTIFIES IMPLICIT CONFIDENCE. CAN BE RELIED UPON TO COMPLETE ALL TASKS WITH LITTLE IF ANY SUPERVISION. **12-14**	

EVALUATE (ON 1-4 POINT SCALE:)	(4) ALMOST ALWAYS	(2-3) USUALLY	(1) SELDOM	POINTS: (to 28)
APPEARANCE SUITABLE TO JOB?				REMARKS:
TACTFUL?				
SUFFICIENTCY HEALTHY FOR JOB?				
OBSERVES GOOD SAFETY HABITS?				
PUNCTUAL & AVAILABLE DURING WORKING DAYS?				
GOOD ATTENDANCE?				
SHOWS LEADERSHIP QUALITIES?				

SIGNATURE OF SUPERVISOR	☐ 31-40 UNSATISFACTORY	TOTAL POINTS:
SIGNATURE OF DEPARTMENT HEAD	☐ 41-55 BELOW AVERAGE ☐ 56-75 SATISFACTORY	
SIGNATURE OF EMPLOYEE	☐ 76-90 GOOD ☐ 91-100 OUTSTANDING	RESULT OF RATING:

EXPLAIN WHERE AND HOW EMPLOYEE CAN IMPROVE; IF FURTHER SPACE NEEDED, USE SEPARATE SHEET.

Figure 35-4 Sample form: a hospital employee evaluation and counseling record*

EMPLOYEE NAME _____ TITLE _____

DEPARTMENT _____ JOB CODE/GRADE _____

EVALUATED BY _____ DATE REVIEWED BY _____ DATE

REASON FOR EVALUATION ☐ INITIAL ☐ PERIODIC ☐ OTHER (SPECIFY) _____

SECTION I EVALUATION COMMENTS

SECTION II EVALUATION RATING
(INDICATE "X" FROM UNSATISFACTORY TO OUTSTANDING)

1. QUANTITY OF WORK

2. QUALITY OF WORK

3. JOB KNOWLEDGE (EDUCATION, EXPERIENCE AND UNDERSTANDING OF DUTIES AND RESPONSIBILITIES)

4. DEPENDABILITY (RELIABILITY IN MEETING COMMITMENTS)

5. COOPERATION (WILLINGNESS AND ABILITY TO WORK WITH ASSOCIATES, SUPERVISORS, PATIENTS AND PARENTS):

*Source: Reprinted from *Health Care Labor Manual* by Martin E. Skoler, with permission of Aspen Systems Corporation, © 1981.

Figure 35-4 continued

6. INITIATIVE (TAKING ACTION TO SOLVE PROBLEMS AND TO SEEK INCREASED RESPONSIBILITY):

_____
_____
_____
_____

U |_|_|_|_|_| O

7. ADAPTABILITY (WILLINGNESS TO ACCEPT AND GRASP NEW APPROACHES AND CHANGES IN WORKING CONDITIONS):

_____
_____
_____
_____

U |_|_|_|_|_| O

8. ATTENDANCE: (BE SPECIFIC IF ATTENDANCE OR PUNCTUALITY IS A CONCERN)

_____
_____
_____
_____

U |_|_|_|_|_| O

9. SUMMARY EVALUATION (WHAT IS YOUR OVERALL APPRAISAL OF THE EMPLOYEE'S PERFORMANCE?):

_____
_____
_____
_____

U |_|_|_|_|_| O

SECTION III
IN YOUR JUDGEMENT, IS THE EMPLOYEE'S OVERALL PERFORMANCE IMPROVING ☐, REMAINING THE SAME ☐, REGRESSING ☐ ?

NOTE: THE EMPLOYEE SHOULD BE COUNSELED CONCERNING THIS EVALUATION. IF ANY SIGNIFICANT PROBLEMS ARE NOTED IN THIS EVALUATION, PLEASE INDICATE BELOW WHAT ACTION IS BEING TAKEN TO RESOLVE THEM.

_____
_____
_____

APPRAISAL REVIEWED WITH EMPLOYEE ON _____ EMPLOYEE'S SIGNATURE _____

NOTE: EMPLOYEE'S COMMENTS CAN BE ATTACHED

and counsel employees to assure improvement rather than resentment. To get the information and results you want, you must develop a suitable approach.

The Approach

Appraisal interviewing can take many forms—from the rigid formula approach to the free discussion interview. One advantage of the formula method is that you're using time-tested questions geared specifically to your operation. But, on the negative side, it leaves little room for adjusting to individual people or situations.

With the free discussion interview you can cover a wide range of subjects but, unless you're extremely skillful, the discussion can get out of hand. A likely result will be a frustrated employee who has nothing but unsatisfying generalities to tell him how he's progressing or what his chances for advancement are.

In practice you'll probably find that your best bet will be somewhere in between the extremes mentioned. For one thing, in most hospitals a standardized form is used to provide the essential information for personnel records. To get a more meaningful and individual appraisal, though, it is usually a good idea to prepare an outline of questions for the particular individual being evaluated. Because each person and each situation differs in some way, the middle-ground approach provides certain safeguards to assure that you'll cover the required points. It also gives you enough leeway to adjust to the individual situation.

Employee Attitudes

Just as different individuals have different problems, they also react differently to an appraisal interview. You probably consider the people who become emotional or argumentative to be your biggest problems. But, in the long run, it may be just as troublesome if the employee has no reaction or merely pretends to agree. How you deal with the various reactions you encounter will make the difference between a productive or a futile appraisal program. Here are some of the typical reactions you can expect and a few suggestions on the best way to handle each:

1. *The employee who refuses to agree.* He maintains stubbornly that your evaluation and criticism are unfair. He controls his emotions during the interview but remains adamant. When this happens, don't push for agreement in the first session. You may need several discussions. The primary objective is to make your position clear. It may take him some time to accept it, but you can make it easier for him by remaining calm.

   It will help if you can figure out whether his disagreement is a result of his personality, his experience in his work, or other people. Try to get him to talk. A stubborn, silent disagreement is much more difficult to deal with. Listen . . . listen carefully to find out WHY he disagrees. Then suggest that you both think it over for a few days so you can review the situation in a later interview. *CAUTION: Don't be stubborn yourself. If later information or a change in attitude indicates that you should change your evaluation . . . do it. And let the man know of the change.*

2. *The employee who agrees too quickly.* Some people will agree to anything you say, even when you criticize. They figure that by doing so they can avoid harsher criticism. When this happens, first, find out if his agreement is sincere. If it is, ask him for suggestions on how he can improve and get his agreement on a realistic goal. But, should you find that he's agreeing just to get the interview over with quickly, you'll have to make a direct suggestion yourself. Tell him exactly what steps he'll have to take to improve and let him know you'll be following up to see that he's working toward improvement.

3. *The employee who expects instant promotion or an on-the-spot raise.* Every once in a while you'll run across a person who gets a little praise and expects that it will result in an immediate promotion or raise. When this happens, remind him that raises are given for real merit and for excellent performance over a period of time. As far as promotions are concerned you should explain that jobs are not created for purposes of promotions.

   Warning: If you find many of your employees are expecting advancement, try to recall your past discussions. Have you been stressing promotions and money too much? Remember, the purpose of evaluation is to first improve the employee's performance in his present job. And, if advancement is not justified, a successful appraisal interview should make it clear to the worker.

4. *The employee who wants to quit.* During an appraisal interview, the employee surprises you by saying he's dissatisfied and wants to quit. When this happens, if the employee has been a good worker, the first thing to do is find out why. This may take a little time because he may not be sure himself. Maybe all he wants to do is get something off his chest, or maybe he's insecure and wants to know that he's appreciated. If you find that he has a genuine gripe about working conditions or personalities, try to correct the situation.

Whatever the reason, don't be afraid to tell him that you want him to stay. If he is going to another job for a temporary advancement, explain the opportunities for growth in your hospital . . . without committing yourself.

5. *The employee who loses his temper.* Some people just cannot take criticism, even if it's constructive. As soon as they hear an adverse word, they fly off the handle and make all sorts of charges about unfair treatment and being picked on. When this happens, LISTEN . . . in silence until he talks himself out. Don't add fuel to the fire by arguing with him. When he calms down, assure him that there's no permanent black mark against him. Let him know that there's no resentment on your part by being cordial when you see him again.

Set up another interview in a few days. Usually the employee will be willing to talk reasonably the second time around. If he isn't, listen again without arguing. But this time you should explain your position and request action for improvement.

6. *The employee who is completely passive.* Sometimes in trying to discuss an employee's performance, you draw a complete blank—no comments, no questions, nothing. When this happens, first ask yourself a couple of questions. Is this behavior normal for this man? Is he trying a wait-and-see policy? Is he setting up a protective shield?

You naturally expect some silence and frequently a delayed reaction, especially if you've just made a critical statement. Be alert for any sign of interest and try to develop it. Ask as many questions as you can. If you get nothing but a minimum response, it is better to schedule another interview than to push too hard.

Beware Being Transparent

You've probably been told many times that you shouldn't criticize a worker without first finding something you can praise. While it's true that an all-negative interview can completely destroy a worker's incentive and morale, it's also true that many supervisors develop a technique that becomes completely transparent to the perceptive employee. When the worker comes in for an appraisal interview, the first item is usually on the positive side; then comes the criticism, probably taking up most of the time. Finally, in an attempt to keep the worker from being entirely deflated, the supervisor ends up on a cheery note. He finds something else to praise or makes an extravagant prediction about how well the worker can do if he'll only "shape up."

Chapter 36—Productivity

OVERVIEW

Trends*

Health care productivity levels in recent years have increased for a variety of reasons, including:

- Rapidly increasing technological improvements, particularly in the areas of diagnostic and treatment equipment and procedures. In most cases, service output level and quality are increased significantly with less than a corresponding increase in output costs.
- Replacement of outdated structures with modern facilities designed to provide for more efficient delivery of patient care services. Such changes often improve the quality of patient service, making the productivity increase difficult to measure objectively.
- Upgrading of management and supervisory capabilities of hospital administrative personnel through more intensive in-service programs. This is an excellent example of improving input quality (e.g., supervisory ability of department head) and thereby increasing output level and/or quality.
- Implementation on a local or regional basis of shared and contract services programs in areas such as purchasing, patient billing, laundry, laboratory and other support and ancillary services. Productivity improvements usually occur through a shift in the mix of the input resources from hospital personnel to purchased services. Output quality may also improve.

Despite these trends, the reality of day-to-day operations indicates that there are often as many factors tending to decrease productivity level as there are steps being taken to increase them. For example:

- Inflation in salary, supply and other operating costs that are not fixed obligations continues to raise input costs. Annual cost increases in excess of 12 percent are being experienced in many of these hospital cost components.
- More sophisticated and complex medical practices have resulted in greater intensity of services being required for a given diagnosis or patient stay. Also, the number of diagnostic procedures required per case has been increased to minimize the potential for malpractice claims. Because these increases generally work to the hospital's economic benefit (revenues increase in proportion to the additional services provided) they are not generally considered unfavorable trends from an overall viewpoint.
- Fringe benefit levels are increasing dramatically in response to outside pressures, new government regulations and other factors,

---

*Source: Reprinted from Thomas F. Kelly and Terrill F. Ellis, "Toward More Effective Management of Hospital Productivity," *Health Care Horizons*, 1976, pp. 9–12, with permission of the publisher.

boosting inputs with no proportionate rise in outputs.
- Patients themselves are demanding more services, resulting in increased input resources relative to the output levels achieved. Again, because the quality of the output is affected, objective measurement becomes more difficult.

Comparison: Productivity Indexes*

The hospital industry (see Table 36-1) has apparently achieved some modest improvements in labor productivity. This is especially remarkable in the ancillary areas where quality improvements and complexity of output mix make the productivity gains doubly impressive. The only major sorepoint is in the administration area where costs have skyrocketed. A variety of explanations are possible; certainly increased regulation is a major one.

---

*Source: Reprinted from William O. Cleverley, "Cost Containment in Health Care Industry," *Topics in Health Care Financing,* Spring 1977, with permission of Aspen Systems Corporation.

Checklist for Increasing Productivity

It has been said that people produce more when they know the following things about their work:
1. What they are supposed to do.
2. What authority they have.
3. What their relationships are to other people in the organization.
4. What constitutes a job well done in terms of specific results.
5. What they are doing exceptionally well.
6. Where they are falling short.
7. What they can do to improve unsatisfactory results.
8. That there are appropriate rewards for work done exceptionally well.
9. That what they are doing and thinking is of value.
10. That the supervisor has a deep interest in and concern for them.
11. That the supervisor truly wishes them to succeed and progress.*

---

*Source: Max B. Skousen, "Increasing Individual Productivity Through Motivation Controls," *Meeting the Productivity Challenge,* American Management Association, 1960.

Table 36-1 Departmental Productivity Indexes (Hospitals with Bed Size 200–299)

Department	Indicator	12/31/75	12/31/70	Percentage Change	in Productivity
Obstetrics	MH/Patient Day	6.59	5.37	22.7	D
Delivery	MH/Delivery	16.65	14.32	16.3	D
Nursery	MH/Newborn Day	5.95	4.53	31.3	D
Medical-Surgical	MH/Patient Day	6.11	6.01	1.7	D
Operating Room	MH/Visit	10.56	10.35	2.0	D
Central Service	Line Items/MH	4.99	3.53	41.4	I
Emergency Service	MN/Visit	1.51	1.39	8.6	D
Laboratory	Tests/MH	5.59	4.38	27.6	I
Blood Bank	MH/Unit Drawn	2.73	2.61	4.6	D
Radiology	MH/Procedure	1.17	1.18	0.1	I
Pharmacy	Line Items/MH	11.23	11.00	2.1	I
Physical Therapy	Treatments/MH	1.50	1.34	11.2	I
Social Service	MH/Case Accepted	4.48	4.86	7.8	I
Medical Records	MH/Discharge	2.70	2.41	12.0	D
Dietary	Meals Served/MH	3.18	3.15	1.0	I
Cafeteria	Cafeteria Meals/MH	7.82	6.86	14.0	I
Plant Engineering	MH/1000 Feet	17.97	18.82	4.5	I
Housekeeping	MH/1000 Feet	41.95	48.52	13.5	I
Laundry	Pounds/MH	39.75	34.93	13.8	I

Source: Hospital Administrative Services: MH = Manhours, D = Decrease, I = Increase.

In more formal studies* researchers have identified ten primary factors that need to be taken into account if an organization is to achieve the system-wide changes that are essential to raising its productivity and improving its performance. Paraphrased, these are:

1. Employee compensation tied to performance and to sharing in productivity gains.
2. Participation of workers in decisions affecting their own and related jobs.
3. Job enlargement, including challenge, variety, wholeness, and self-regulation.
4. Employees' sense of involvement in the total organization.
5. Adequate safety conditions, pay, fringe benefits, and working conditions.
6. Simplification of channels of communication and authority.
7. Resources at workers' disposal to facilitate work effectiveness and reduce frustration associated with getting the job done.
8. Improved work methods that have involved workers in their planning and work.
9. Opportunities for greater employee "stewardship," that is, direct care of and attention to co-worker needs.
10. Allowance for flexibility in relation to type of incentive and authority patterns.

Using the foregoing list of ten critical factors, the administrator should attempt to diagnose the hospital's strengths and weaknesses in order to set priorities and assess the potential for improvement in each area, so that decisions can be made as to which areas are most promising of favorable results.

DEVELOPING WORK STANDARDS

In order to achieve staff savings and to monitor labor productivity on a continuing basis, labor standards are essential. Their development requires not only technical expertise, but also the exercise of managerial judgment.

The techniques available for developing standards are varied, ranging from the simple utilization of historical data to highly refined, predetermined time systems.

In developing work standards certain basic principles and precautions should be borne in mind. The standard should be:*

- Meaningful to all hospital management, adaptable to future plans, and applicable to existing conditions and mix of procedures.
- Simple and understandable by all personnel, and it must be relevant (i.e., based on units of work as now organized and activity data presently in existence).
- Reproducible in other departments or possibly other hospitals.
- Achievable with the skills available to the hospital.
- Acceptable, lead to action, and encourage and facilitate cost reduction and control.
- Implemented and used.
- Maintainable economically and practically.
- Viewed favorably throughout the hospital.

The selection of an appropriate technique for measuring work depends on a number of factors, such as:

- the nature of the work being measured
- the degree of precision desired
- employee and supervisory attitudes
- the availability of trained management engineering resources
- the availability of hospital staff to assist in work measurement

Work Standard Techniques**

A number of methodologies for formulating work standards have been developed. Three are adaptable for hospital use: (1) estimating the time required to perform a given task; (2) classi-

---

*Source: Reprinted, by permission of the publisher, from *Productivity: The Measure and the Myth* by Mildred E. Katzel, pp. 34–36, © 1975 by AMACOM, a division of American Management Associations. All rights reserved.

*Source: Reprinted from Stephen Melesko, "Developing Work Standards for Hospitals," *Management Controls,* November 1974, pp. 239–245, with permission of Peat, Marwick, Mitchell & Co.

**Source: Reprinted from William E. Young, "An Overview of Productivity-Monitoring Systems for Hospitals," *Topics in Health Care Financing,* Summer 1980, with permission of Aspen Systems Corporation.

cal time and monitor study approach; and (3) historical data evaluation approach.

(1) Estimating the time required to perform a given task is difficult at best. The process is very subjective and is not accurate. Work standards developed using this technique are not precise measurements useful in improving employee productivity or reducing health care cost. Using estimated time standards will have little or no positive impact on a hospital's productivity.

(2) The time-motion study approach for setting productivity standards is the classical technique developed by Galbreth. The technique, using a series of timed observations, has been utilized in production-related industries traditionally. The process of developing standards using this method is complex and requires personnel with specialized training. There are three basic steps required in developing a productivity standard using this classical approach. Because of the nature of this process, each of these steps must be completed for each task performed by workers. These steps are:

1. Observe and measure the actual time required to perform a given work task or activity by several employees with various skill levels, e.g., time to give an injection or prepare medications for a patient.
2. Develop a normal time for the observed task by adjusting the actual time to reflect any observed variance. In doing this, the observer is able to eliminate the effects of unusual occurrences like location of supplies or distances between work locations.
3. Develop an adjusted normal time that allows for unavoidable personal delays. This adjusted normal time becomes the time standard for all employees performing the same work task.

Once adjusted normal times have been developed for each work task, the engineer must determine the expected occurrence or frequency that each work task will be performed during a given work shift. When this frequency analysis is complete, the work observer can set an aggregate work standard that will be used to staff the work unit with individuals of varying skills.

The time study standards can be very precise and statistically supportable. However, the process involves time of individual work tasks; therefore employee anxieties can be increased during the study. Because the process is so detailed, several months may be required to collect and adjust data before setting standards.

(3) Although not as precise as the classical time study, the evaluation of historical productivity data as a means of setting work standards may be the most desirable approach for hospitals. The process for setting standards using this approach involves several steps.

1. Develop a data base of historical productivity results from an individual cost center. The data base should include the total hours worked, i.e., during a given period, either a payroll period or monthly, divided by the total production units for the same period. If during January a total of 1,700 paid hours were reported in the labor and delivery cost center, and 200 deliveries were performed, the productivity index for that month would be 8.5 hours per delivery.
2. Repeat the process until productivity indexes have been developed for 18 or more months.
3. Array the historical productivity index and analyze variations between the months studied.
4. Determine a degree within the range of data that shows improvement over the least productive month (i.e., the month with the most time spent per work output unit).
5. Through negotiations with the responsible manager, set a productivity standard that shows an improvement over the department's past productivity.

Some management engineers have found setting the actual productivity standard at a given percentile within the historical data array to be helpful. Once the standard is set, department managers must agree that the standard is achievable and that they are responsible for staffing their department against this standard. This standard-setting approach is much less sophisticated than the more classical approaches; however, setting standards in this manner should prevent employee anxiety. In addition, because department heads are included in this standard-setting process, their acceptance level should be higher.

Accountability

Regardless of the method used to develop standards, if the standards are to be effective in improving productivity and reducing cost, hospital managers must be held accountable for performance against these standards. Depending on the size of the institution and the sophistication of the hospital's management team, several different accountability/measurement methods may be considered.

In a small hospital, a handwritten report like the one shown in Figures 36-1 and 36-2 can be completed at the end of each payroll period. This report shows actual performance for each department and compares this performance with the desired or standard performance. By dividing the actual performance by standard or desired performance, the department head can determine a percentage of achievement against his or her agreed-upon standard. In more sophisticated hospitals with substantial MIS capabilities, the same type of report can be produced by integrating data from several sources.

Self-Logging (A Step-by-Step Procedure)*

In self-logging standards are developed from the actual times recorded on the individual work activity records (self-logging forms) of each employee. There are three major procedures that should be developed prior to starting: defining the units of measure (tasks); the logging techniques; and the statistical data to be collected during the logging period.

- *Units of measure* (*tasks*). We should first determine the breakdown among classifications of employees to be used for the work being performed within a department (i.e., technician, orderly, clerk, etc.). Once the classifications are established, we identify the tasks that will normally be performed by each group and decide which will be used for logging time. The tasks should be easily definable, and there should be logical breaks between tasks. The times for these individual tasks will be used to develop

standard times and then labor standards for specified department reporting units. These reporting units selected should be based on current available activity statistics so that the application of the standards will be meaningful and updating will be easy. Reporting units could be patients, exams, minutes, tests, weeks, etc. Exhibit 1 is an example of tasks and employee classifications that could be used for the operating room. The illustrated tasks include productive time (both fixed and variable), delay, personal and standby time.
- *Logging techniques.* When designing the forms for self-logging, we should keep in mind the time that will be required to record the data so that the form will be simple to use. (See Table 36-2 and Figure 36-3.) Once the data are recorded, review and summary should be easy.
- *Statistical profile.* Figure 36-4 is an example of the type of statistical data that would be recorded by the department head during the logging period. The data would indicate the mixture of patients, types of tests or exams, and case load, and would serve as the basic department profile.

The foregoing procedures should be completely understood by all participants prior to commencement of the actual time logging. The logging period should be long enough to include normal fluctuations in activity volume, type and mix, but not too long or employees will lose interest and generate inaccurate data.

Development of Standards

During the self-logging period, a qualified observer should monitor and sample the employee forms to ensure that the data are being recorded correctly. Corrections should be made quickly to avoid collecting unusable information.

After the time logging has been completed, the raw task times should be summarized by employee classification and separated into productive, personal and delay times. At this point, the task times should be purged of any non-representative times caused by training, student activities, problems or abnormal values. After purging, the normal time should be calculated for each task.

As stated previously, these task times will be used to develop a standard time for a depart-

---

*Source: Reprinted from Stephen Melesko, "Developing Work Standards for Hospitals," *Management Controls,* November 1974, pp. 239–245, with permission of Peat, Marwick, Mitchell & Co.

Figure 36-1 Example report: standard data methodology approach—department head's personnel productivity report

Constant Units: _____

Variable Units: _____

Reporting Period	Reported Work Load		Standard Required Hours	Actual Hours Worked	Utilization Index-%		Employee (F.T.E.)		Employee Variance	
From-To	Constant Units	Variable Units			Target	This Period	3 Period Average	Target	Actual	This Period	3 Period Average

Figure 36-2 Administrator's personnel productivity report

Report From _____ Up To and Including _____

Department	Variable Work Load		Standard Hours Required	Actual Hours Worked	Utilization Index-%		Employee (F.T.E.)		Employee Variance	
	Units	Count			Target	This Period	3 Period Average	Target	Actual	This Period	3 Period Average

Table 36-2 Operating Room Task List

Task no.	Task	Task unit
1	**Personal**	
	A. Dress in OR attire	Occ.
	B. Rest periods	Occ.
	C. Meals	Occ.
	D. Miscellaneous	Occ.
2	**Preparation**	
	A. Scrubbing — gown and glove	Patient
	B. Set up — major) scrub or	Patient
	C. Set up — minor) circulate	Patient
	D. Prepare patient (wash, paint, drape)	Patient
	E. Prepare instruments, packs & supplies (specify)	Patient
	F. Restocking and rotating, room set up	Occ.
	G. Getting patients	Patient
	H. Miscellaneous (specify)	Occ.
3	**Surgical procedure** (list procedure)	
	A. Scrub	Patient
	B. Circulate	Patient
	C. Assist (1st or 2nd)	Patient
	D. Other departments (specify)	Occ.
	E. Miscellaneous (specify)	Occ.
4	**Clean-up**	
	A. OR room after case — infected	Occ.
	B. OR room after case — non-infected	Occ.
	C. OR room end of day	Occ.
	D. Other areas	Occ.
	E. Cleaning and/or sterilizing instruments	Occ.
	F. Miscellaneous (specify)	Occ.
5	**Delays**	
	A. Equipment	Occ.
	B. Patient	Occ.
	C. Doctor	Occ.
	D. Miscellaneous (specify)	Occ.
6	**Clerical**	
	A. Phone	Occ.
	B. Log — statistics	Occ.
	C. Scheduling	Occ.
	D. Secretary and clerical duties	Occ.
	E. Requisitions (ordering)	Occ.
	F. Billing	Occ.
	G. Messengers	Occ.
	H. Miscellaneous (specify)	Occ.
7	**Orderly or aide**	
	A. Transport patient (specify dept.)	Patient
	B. Lab, x-ray, etc. (specify)	Occ.
	C. Miscellaneous (specify)	Occ.
	D. Preps (shave)	Patient
	E. Assisting nurses	Occ.
8	**Education — supervision**	
	A. Assigns, directs, coordinates	Occ.
	B. Reviews statistics	Occ.
	C. Orientation and in-service (students)	Occ.
	D. Evaluates and counsels	Occ.
	E. Scheduling and staffing	Occ.
	F. Planning (specify)	Occ.
	G. Helps when necessary	Occ.
	H. Attends classes or meetings	Occ.
	I. Miscellaneous (specify)	Occ.

Table 36-2 continued

9	Stand-by	
	A. Call (from hospital)	Occ.
	B. Call (from home)	Occ.
	C. Call in	Occ.
	D. Stand-by	Occ.
	E. Miscellaneous (specify)	Occ.

mental reporting unit, so a frequency (occurrence ratio of each task within the total reporting unit) must be calculated that will indicate the number of times a task is performed per reporting unit. When we apply this factor to each normal task time, we obtain the normal task time per reporting unit, and the sum of the task times is the normal reporting unit time. We can also calculate a personal allowance for each classification of employee, using the actual time logged for the personal time tasks. The personal allowance, expressed as a percentage, is applied to the normal reporting unit time to obtain the standard time per reporting unit. This procedure is then repeated for each reporting unit and each classification of employee.

It is seldom possible to keep the employees busy 100 percent of the available time in these departments because of delays inherent in the type of work, standby time, waiting time and unavoidable interruptions. Also, no employee performs at the level of 100 percent. In order to develop accurate budgets and staffing levels, this must be taken into consideration and the standards adjusted accordingly. We can either calculate the actual performance level of the department employees from the logged time and apply this to our standard time, or we can select a higher performance level to allow for future improvement.

The standard reporting unit time multiplied by the actual or forecast volume of the reporting unit is the standard hours produced or required. If these standard hours are adjusted for the projected performance level and the hours required for evening, night and weekend shifts and call-time added, the result will be the expectancy level hours required for each classification of employee in each department. This is the number of hours that a department should require (or did require) to perform a given volume of work over a specified period of time. Figure 36-5 is an illustration of a budget calculation worksheet.

An example of the computation required for an OR nursing budget follows:

Total normal task times = 1.38 hrs/surgical case
Personal allowance = 8%
Standard hours per case = 1.50
Forecast Volume = 5,200 cases

5,200 cases × 1.50 std. hrs./case
= 7,800 standard hours required

Projected Productivity = 90%

Adjusted standard hours required
$$= \frac{7,800}{.90} = 8,677 \text{ hours}$$

Adjusted standard hours required:
Normal shift (8 a.m.–4 p.m.)	8,677
Evening shift (4 p.m.–12 p.m.)	2,080
Weekends (8 a.m.–12 p.m.)	1,664
On-call hours (12 p.m.–8 a.m.)	2,920
Expectancy level hours	15,341

Even after standards have been developed, they may never be used because of internal politics, poor salesmanship or other reasons. If the standards are too technical and not easily understood by the personnel responsible for their implementation, they will not be used. They should be simple and easy to understand.

Another problem that may be encountered is reluctance to use standards because of the feeling that all costs are fixed anyway. This statement, however, is not accurate. Both schedules and workloads are variable, and the so-called fixed costs vary accordingly, but they can be controlled by sharing services and by careful utilization of personnel.

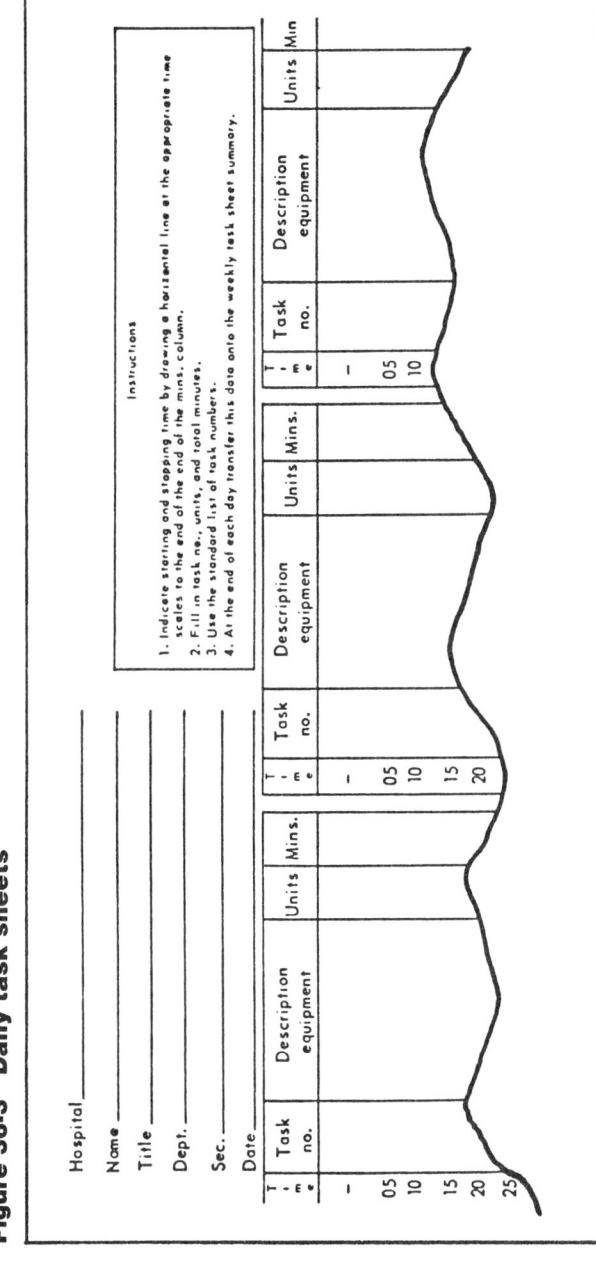

Figure 36-3 Daily task sheets

Figure 36-4 Sample department weekly summary sheet

Sample department weekly summary sheet

Operating room _____

Hospital _____ Operating room no. _____

For Week ending Sunday _____, 1974

Day	No. of operations*1 7am to 12 noon	12 noon to 3:30pm	3:30pm to 7am	Daily total	O.R. minutes*2 7am to 12 noon A	12 noon to 3:30pm B	3:30 pm to 7am C	Daily total D	O.R. mins. available*3 7am to 12 noon E	12 noon to 3:30pm F	3:30pm to 7am G	Daily total H	Percent utilization*4 7am to 12 noon A-E	12 noon to 3:30pm B-F	3:30pm to 7am C-G	Daily total D-H
Monday									300	210	930	1,440				
Tuesday									300	210	930	1,440				
Wednesday									300	210	930	1,440				
Thursday									300	210	930	1,440				
Friday									300	210	930	1,440				
Mon-Fri subtot.									1,500	1,050	4,650	7,200				
Saturday									300	210	930	1,440				
Sunday									300	210	930	1,440				
Sat-Sun subtot.									600	420	1,860	2,880				
Weekly total									2,100	1,470	6,510	10,080				

*1 – If operation starts in one time period and runs into next period, indicate number only in time period in which it starts.
*2 – Time from patient's entry into O.R. to exit.
– If operation starts in one time period and runs into next period, break total O.R. minutes into respective time periods.
*3 – Indicates maximum availability of room.
– Do not enter anything in these columns.
*4 – Indicates ratio of O.R. minutes to O.R. time available for each time category.

WORK SIMPLIFICATION

Five Questions To Ask*

The ideal design of any work operation should aim to make the procedure productive, smooth-flowing and simple.

Work simplification is the organized application of common sense to find easier and better ways of doing work. This organized and systematic approach to improvement and problem solving is a step-by-step procedure. It provides a guide to thinking that not only makes improvement easier, but it also is a desirable and continuous way of performing everyday work. Making use of the pattern helps one organize and "sell" his ideas for improvement. . . .

---

*Source: From Sloane, Robert M., and Sloane, Beverly LeBov: *A guide to health facilities*, ed. 2, St. Louis, 1977, The C. V. Mosby Co., pp. 119–121.

The following questions concerning work simplification should be addressed.

Can we eliminate? In far too many instances we devote much time to studying various activities for possibilities of improvement without asking the most important question, "Why do we perform this activity?" If we succeed in eliminating the operation or even part of it, the ultimate in work simplification is achieved.

Can we combine? This opportunity for improvement is one that should not be overlooked. Whenever two activities can be combined, they are often performed for a little more than the cost of one activity, and the make-ready and put-away details of one of the operations are eliminated.

Can we change the sequence? The flow diagram or template layout of the area often helps here. By changing the sequence of an activity, we may be able to eliminate the backtracking.

Figure 36-5 Staffing budget calculation worksheet

Item	Reporting unit (specify) (1)	Standard hours per reporting unit (2)	Forecast performance factor (3)	Adjusted standard hours per reporting unit (4) (2) · (3)	Forecast volume (5)	Forecast hours (6) (4) × (5)	Average hourly rate (7)	Salary budget (8) (6) × (7)
Measured work								
Sub-total							$	$
Unmeasured paid work On-call - not worked On-call - worked Special shifts (specify)								
Sub-total							$	$
Fringe benefits Vacation Holiday Illness, absence Others (specify)								
Sub-total							$	$
Total budget hours and salaries							–	$

Although much of the order in which the details are performed is necessary as a part of the process, in many instances a change of sequence can be made with consequent saving.

Can we improve or simplify? Unfortunately, many attempts to make improvements in the past have started without the benefits of an organized approach to this question. Failure to find improvements has resulted in stifling creativity, accepting things as they are, and taking no steps to improve them. We should question everything.

Can we change the place? Naturally, the question "where?" challenges the place where the operation is performed. Why is it done there? Too many times work is done in one place or department mainly because it has always been done there. Can we change the person? Challenging the detail with the question "who?" often results in the discovery that it could be done better by some other person. The questions "how?" and "why?" challenge the method of doing a particular activity. A part of the philosophy of work simplification is, "It is not *what* we do, but the *way* we do it." Often we can more than double productivity by improving the method. Improvement generally means a study of the motions used in the performance of the job. Simplification of these motions is accomplished by utilizing the principles of motion economy. (See Table 36-3.)

A Six-Step Job Improvement Plan*

The proper method of work simplification is a logical, orderly approach to the solution of a problem, frequently referred to as the job improvement plan, which includes the following six steps:

_____
*Source: Sloane & Sloane, 1977.

Table 36-3 Analytical Techniques for Work Simplification

The Analytical Technique	When It Should Be Used
1. The flow process chart	A work study situation in which it appears desirable to follow the actions pertaining to a *single* person, a *single* material or a *single* form. This would include: (a) the activities of a *person* who is involved in a straight sequence of events, with some movement from place to place; (b) the handling of any single *material* that flows through a connected series of events; (c) the flow of a single-copy or single-part *form*. (See Figure 36-6.) (Although this vertical type chart may be ideal for gathering and recording facts relating to a single item, involving process, the procedure flow chart (a horizontal type chart) is more adaptable to work procedures of a more complex nature.)
2. The flow diagram	A work study situation in which it appears desirable to examine the *paths* of movement of people, paperwork or materials. This form of analysis is particularly useful in work where: (a) distance traveled is excessive; (b) flow is complicated; (c) work area is congested; (d) backtracking is evidenced. The flow diagram in its simplest form is used to supplement the flow process chart.
3. The organization chart	A work study situation in which it appears desirable to analyze and evaluate the present organizational structure of a department or unit. This chart can be helpful in providing a broad over-all view of the department or unit as it now exists.
4. The work distribution chart	A work study situation in which it appears desirable to examine in greater detail the work being done in a department or unit. This chart will present clearly in one place: (a) the work activities performed by the department, and the total time it takes to perform them; (b) the individuals who are working on each of these activities and (c) the amount of time spent by each person on each activity.
5. The procedure flow chart	A work study situation involving the performance of many different work routines by individuals in different capacities and, perhaps, in different departments. It is also recommended for charting the details of procedures which involve the flow of multicopy or multipart forms.
6. Work sampling	Work study situations in which the functions being investigated are nonrepetitive in nature. This technique makes it possible to gather detailed information that would be difficult to obtain by means of continuous observation.

Source: Addison C. Bennet, *Methods Improvement in Hospitals*, J. B. Lippincott Company, 1964.

1. *Select a job to improve*
   - Ask what needs improvement most.
   - Make the best use of your time by selecting the right job.

2. *Get the facts*
   - [Select the appropriate analytical technique]
   - Look at each detail of the job.

3. *Challenge the job*
   - Challenge each detail of the job.
   - List the improvement possibilities.

4. *Develop the improvement*
   - Evaluate all possible solutions.
   - Chart the new method.

5. *Install the improvement*
   - Sell your idea to all concerned.
   - Get approval, and then get your idea installed.

6. *Follow up*
   - Follow through to be certain that the improved process is fully operating so that the full gains are being realized.

Several of these techniques and the forms used are demonstrated in the following material. (*Note:* The technique of work sampling is discussed under "Productivity.")

Work Distribution Chart*

For a technique that permits a further step in the analyzing of the functions performed in a department or unit, we must turn to the work distribution chart. When properly prepared, it enables us to see clearly in one place:

- The work activities performed and the time it takes to perform them,
- The individuals who are working on these activities,
- The amount of time spent by each person on each activity.

Some ways in which the work distribution charting technique can help in developing improvements in the way things are being done:

1. It tells us what activities take the most time.
2. It points out the unnecessary work that is being performed.
3. It indicates whether or not skills are used properly.
4. It indicates whether or not any employees are doing too many unrelated tasks.
5. It points out tasks that may be spread too thinly throughout the department or unit.
6. It shows whether or not work in the unit is distributed evenly.

Preparing a Work Distribution Chart

To begin with, the preparation of a work distribution chart is made possible through the use of a *Task List,* and an *Activity List.* The information that is entered on these records is assembled subsequently onto a work distribution chart.

Step 1. Making the Task List

The task list is used to develop a listing of the duties actually being performed by each employee in the department or the unit, indicating the estimated number of hours spent per week on each duty. This listing of tasks should be made out for each position presently occupied in the organizational unit, including the department head and supervisory positions.

The task list is intended to reflect what each person actually does, not what he should be doing. Therefore, it is recommended that each employee prepare his own task list, since he knows best the activities which he actually performs.

Also, it is important that the supervisor review and verify the accuracy of the recorded information with each employee following his completion of the task list. If difficulty is encountered in estimating time spent on each task, it may be necessary for the employee to maintain a record of hours spent on each activity over a period of one or two weeks so as to establish a proper allocation of time. Here are some simple guide rules for making out a task list:

1. At least a 5-day period of observation should be made in preparing the listing.
2. Statements of duties performed should be brief and specific. The job description should not be referred to when preparing the list.
3. The duties should be listed in the order of their importance, with the task considered to be most important shown first.

Step 2. Making the Activity List

The activity list is used to record the major activities that are performed or that should be performed to fulfill the objectives of the department or the unit. The list should be prepared by the supervisor of the organizational unit.

When the list is completed, it should be possible to classify each task shown on the employees' task lists under one of the activities indicated on the supervisor's activity list.

Here are some simple guide rules to remember when preparing an activity list:

1. The listing should not be too detailed. Only general activities should be shown.
2. Reference should be made to organization manuals, administrative memorandums etc. in developing a listing of those activities considered to be the responsibility of the unit.
3. The listing normally should contain no more than about 10 major activities.
4. The activities should be listed in the order of their importance, with the most important activity shown first.

---

*Source: Addison C. Bennet. *Methods Improvement in Hospitals,* J. B. Lippincott Company, 1964.

Figure 36-6 Flow process chart

PRESENT METHOD ☑ PROPOSED METHOD ☐

FLOW PROCESS CHART

PAGE 1 OF 1

SUMMARY

1 TRIP:	PRESENT	PROPOSED	DIFFERENCE
○ OPERATIONS	7		
⇨ TRANSPORTATIONS	8		
□ INSPECTIONS	1		
D DELAYS	3		
▽ STORAGES	2		
DISTANCE TRAVELLED	740 FT.	FT	FT
TIME MIN.	45		

JOB HANDLING VALUABLES OF PRIVATE AND SEMI-PRIVATE PATIENTS

Subject Charted NURSE

CHART BEGINS AT NURSES' STATION

CHART ENDS AT NURSES' STATION

CHARTED BY L. WEEKS DATE 10/25/61

	DESCRIPTION OF EVENT	Symbols (Operation, Transport, Inspection, Delay, Storage)	Quantity	Distance in Feet	Time (MIN.)	NOTES
1	AT NURSES' STATION	○⇨□D▽				3rd FLOOR
2	GETS ENVELOPE AND FORM	○⇨□D▽			1	
3	FILLS IN NECESSARY DATA	○⇨□D▽			2	
4	WALKS TO PATIENT'S ROOM	○⇨□D▽		30	1/2	
5	CHECKS VALUABLES WITH PATIENT	○⇨□D▽			5	
6	RECORDS AMOUNT + KIND OF VALUABLES ON ENVELOPE + FORM	○⇨□D▽			2	
7	SIGNS TEMPORARY RECEIPT	○⇨□D▽			1/2	
8	DETACHES TEMPORARY RECEIPT AND GIVES TO PATIENT	○⇨□D▽			1/2	
9	WALKS TO ELEVATOR	○⇨□D▽		180	3	
10	WAITS FOR ELEVATOR	○⇨□D▽			5	AVERAGE OF 6 TRIPS
11	RIDES TO MAIN FLOOR	○⇨□D▽		35	1	PER DAY
12	WALKS TO CASHIER	○⇨□D▽		125	2	
13	GIVES VALUABLES TO CASHIER	○⇨□D▽				
14	WAITS WHILE VALUABLES ARE CHECKED + PERMANENT RECEIPT OBTAINED	○⇨□D▽			10	
15	WALKS TO ELEVATOR	○⇨□D▽		125	2	
16	WAITS FOR ELEVATOR	○⇨□D▽			5	
17	RIDES TO NURSING FLOOR	○⇨□D▽		35	1	3rd FLOOR
18	WALKS TO PATIENT'S ROOM	○⇨□D▽		180	3	
19	GIVES PERMANENT RECEIPT TO PATIENT	○⇨□D▽			1	
20	RETURNS TO NURSES' STATION	○⇨□D▽		30	1/2	
21	AT NURSES STATION	○⇨□D▽				
22		○⇨□D▽				
23		○⇨□D▽				
24		○⇨□D▽				

5. The completeness of the listing should be checked by correlating each task on the task lists with an activity on the activity list.

Step 3. Preparing the Work Distribution Chart

With the completion of both the task lists and the activity list, practically all of the essential information required for the work distribution study has been compiled. The next step is to assemble the data in such a way as to be able to analyze conveniently. This is accomplished by transferring the information found on the activity list and the task lists onto a work distribution chart, which may be prepared in the following manner:

1. Select a blank sheet of paper of adequate size. Sizes 11 × 17 or 17 × 22 usually prove to be most convenient. At the top of the sheet, identify the chart as a work distribution study, indicating the name of the department or the unit, the method which the chart represents ("present" or "proposed"), the date on which the chart was prepared and the name of the person who prepared it.
2. Starting at the extreme left of the sheet, rule a column for activities, followed by a column for each employee in the unit. On the right side of each of these columns, allow space for the entry of hours per week.
3. Assign a column to each employee, entering the employee's name and job title at the top of the column. Starting at the left with the department head or supervisor, the columns should be assigned in order of responsibility.
4. Transfer the first activity shown on the activity list to the activity column at the extreme left of the chart.
5. Review all task lists for the purpose of identifying each entry with an activity number appearing on the activity list.
6. Enter in each appropriate employee column all the tasks that have been classified as number 1. At the same time, record the number of hours spent on activity 1 by each employee.
7. When all tasks and hours have been entered for the first activity, total the time spent on the activity by all employees and enter this figure under "hours per week" in the activity column as well as in the appropriate column on the activity list.
8. Transfer the second activity shown on the activity list to the activity column on the chart. Follow the above procedure for this activity and for all remaining activities on the activity list.
9. When all information has been entered on the chart, total the time entries for all employees as well as for all activities. Both of these totals should be the same.

A work distribution chart that provides us with an over-all view of the work presently being done in the medical information department is depicted in Figure 36-7 with notations for improvement already made.

In challenging the data appearing on the work distribution chart, it is convenient to enter ideas and suggestions for improvement directly on the chart itself.

NOTE: Table 36-4 offers a three-step procedure for analyzing a work distribution chart.

PRODUCTIVITY IMPROVEMENT PROGRAMS

1. Ernst and Whinney*

Successful implementation of a productivity improvement program requires that management have a thorough understanding of what productivity levels mean in various hospital departments and how productivity measures can be derived.

Analyzing productivity levels is only one step in an overall productivity improvement and monitoring process that should include:

- Assessing current productivity levels to determine the potential for improvement. This encompasses forecasting productivity levels and their financial impact, at least to the end of the current fiscal year, if not through the next year.
- Developing productivity objectives and standards for each department, using a weighting system to measure work force requirements accurately. This may involve using more than one unit of output for a department or cost center.
- Developing management action plans to improve productivity to the desired levels.

---

*Source: Reprinted from Mark L. Andersen, "Productivity Monitoring: A Key Element of Productivity," *Cost Containment in Hospitals,* ed. Efraim Turban, Aspen Systems Corporation. © 1980, pp. 157–164, with permission of Ernst & Whinney, © 1979.

568 Hospital Administration Handbook

Figure 36-7 Work distribution chart

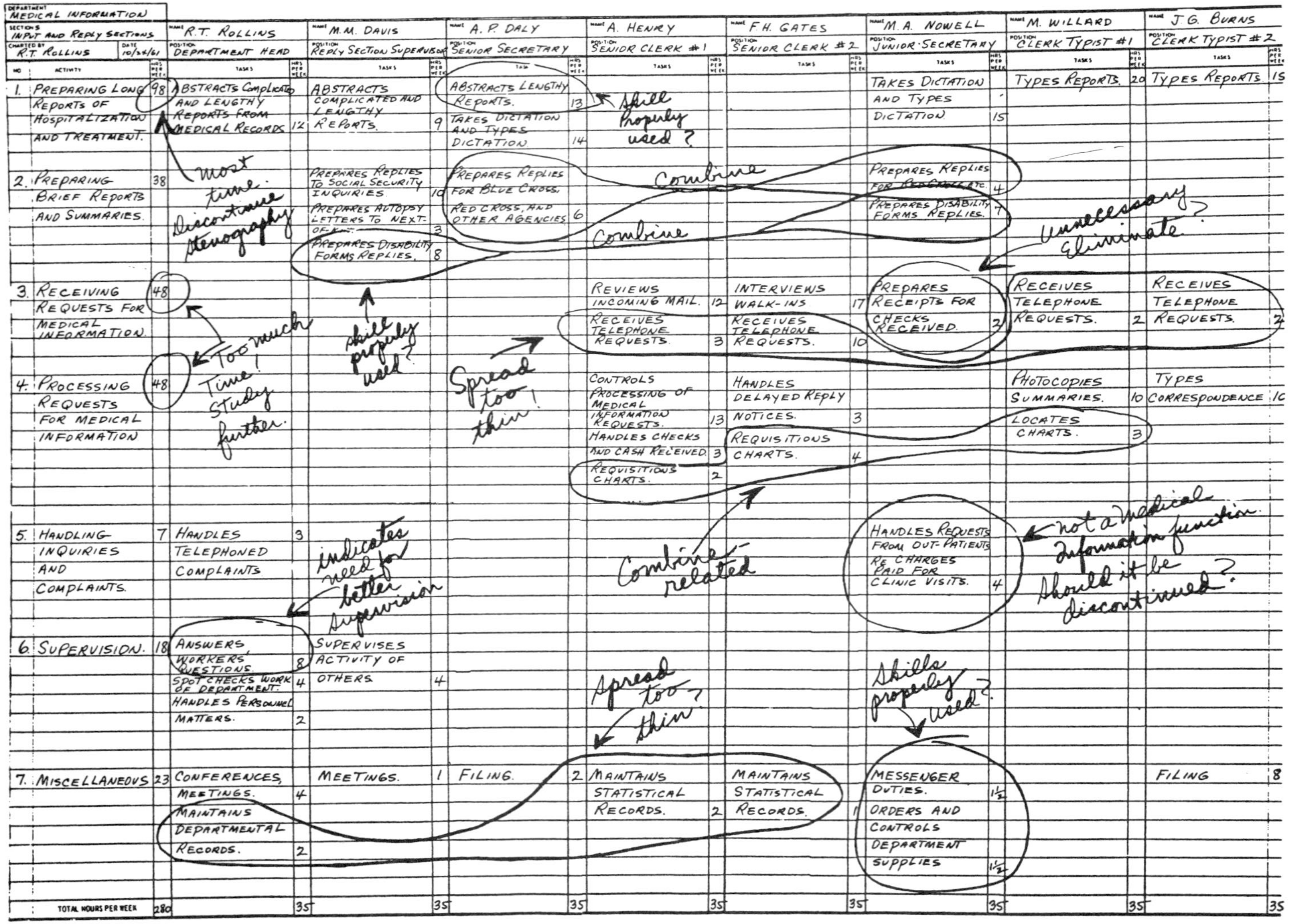

Table 36-4 Analyzing the Work Distribution Chart

Step 1. Analyzing All Activities

Take each activity listed vertically in the column at the extreme left of the chart.	*What* is the purpose of the activity? *Why* is it necessary? *Why* is this activity a function of this department? *What* activities take the most time? *Why*? *What* is a reasonable time for each activity? etc.	These questions will help to determine the importance of each activity and whether any activity can be eliminated.

Step 2. Analyzing Each Task of Each Activity

Taking one activity at a time, read horizontally across the chart and ask these questions about each task assigned to it.	*What* is the purpose of the task? *Why* is it necessary? *Where* should the task be done? *When* should the task be done? *Who* should perform the task? *Who* duplicates or overlaps in performing the task? etc.	These questions will help to determine whether each task is being done in the right place, at the right time, by the right person and in the right way.

Step 3. Analyzing Each Person's Tasks and Activities

Taking one person at a time, ask these questions concerning each duty or task listed vertically in the assigned column.	*How* closely related are the duties? *How* are skills utilized? *How* heavy is the workload? *How* repetitive are the tasks? etc.	These questions will help to uncover unrelated tasks, misuse of skills, uneven distribution of work and tasks spread too thin.

- Monitoring the action plans and providing feedback to management and department personnel to track changes and adjust action plans as necessary. (See Figure 36-8.)

Management must express interest in and commitment to improving productivity throughout this process to develop department head support for such a program. Working with department heads throughout the implementation and operation of the process, management should seek advice and recommendations from them and other personnel (including physicians) about the program and ways in which productivity could be improved. Care must be taken to overcome the typical response to productivity improvement—resistance, fear of job loss, loss by a department head of part of a "domain."

Productivity monitoring, a key element of any productivity improvement process, should be initiated only if the hospital is willing to dedicate adequate resources to the effort. The overall goals of this process are to identify out-of-line departments for immediate action, and initiate periodic monitoring for long-term control and improvement.

Productivity Assessment

The first phase of a productivity monitoring program is an assessment of the hospital's productivity, department by department, against appropriate operating indicators. Initially, the hospital should develop indicators based on historical data to determine whether staffing changes—warranted or not—have occurred compared to the time period used to develop the operating indicators. After this is done, the hospital may also wish to use operating indicators based on a survey of a peer group of hospitals to develop a gross indicator for comparative purposes. It must be remembered that such comparisons provide "gross" comparisons as no two hospitals are alike and the comparisons are useful only as a means of identifying wide variations in productivity. Nonetheless, the comparisons serve as a starting point for identifying areas for potential productivity improvement programs. Further, the hospital may also wish to

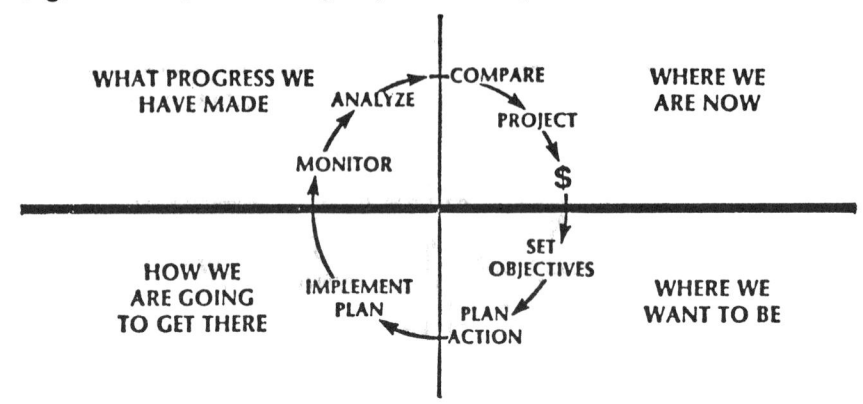

Figure 36-8 Productivity improvement process

```
WHAT PROGRESS WE      COMPARE         WHERE WE
   HAVE MADE    ANALYZE               ARE NOW
                      PROJECT
              MONITOR        $
                      SET
                   OBJECTIVES
  HOW WE                              WHERE WE
ARE GOING   IMPLEMENT  PLAN           WANT TO BE
TO GET THERE   PLAN   ACTION
```

compare itself to regional, state or national industry averages. Again, the objective of this phase is to identify departments that may be operating at inappropriate productivity levels or appearing to be staffed inappropriately, offering potential savings through productivity improvement. (See Table 36-5.)

The findings of this assessment should report year-to-date figures as well as projected results to the end of the current year, incorporating trends and seasonal fluctuations in utilization. Personnel cost variances accounting for the variations in departmental wages should be reported to management. Knowing only that a department is overstaffed or understaffed does not provide sufficient information upon which to make a management decision regarding the importance of potential changes in staffing; the cost impact of the overstaffing should also be identified.

Hospitals using this approach should repeat the comparative process at regular intervals, e.g., quarterly or semi-annually, for adequate management control and decision-making. Departments reporting improvement should receive appropriate recognition; those reporting no improvement should be reviewed, and new approaches to improve their productivity should

Table 36-5 Productivity Monitor Report I

COMPARATIVE OPERATING INDICATORS USING SURVEY COMPARISON WITH GROSS IMPACT
COMMUNITY MEMORIAL HOSPITAL
AS OF OCT 31, 1979

Department Cost Center	Hours/UOS Work	Hours/UOS Comp	FTE Work	FTE Comp	FTE Variance	Avg Cost Per FTE	Gross $	Rank
70 Special Service Summary								
9973 Labor/Delivery			Delivery					
Year-to-date:	14.72	10.40	8.8	6.2	2.6	4,094		
Fiscal yr projection:	14.42	10.40	8.5	6.1	2.4	16,379	39,312	5
9972 Intensive Care			ICU PT. DAYS					
Year-to-date:	16.14	16.50	37.7	38.5	(0.8)	3,802		
Fiscal yr projection:	17.89	16.50	40.9	37.7	3.2	15,209	48,672	2
9970 Special Services			TOTAL PT. DAYS					
Year-to-date:	0.07	0.06	1.4	1.3	0.1	4,312		
Fiscal yr projection:	0.06	0.06	1.2	1.2	0.0	17,249		10
70 Special Service Summary—Total Pt. Days								
Year-to-date:			47.9	46.0	1.9			
Fiscal yr projection:			50.6	45.0	5.6		87,984	

be discussed. This first step—productivity assessment—helps management to identify areas with the greatest potential for productivity improvement, and allows management to measure the impact of productivity improvement action plans.

Productivity Performance Monitoring

Performance monitoring, the second phase of a productivity monitoring program, focuses on departments identified in the first phase in which monthly monitoring based on detailed standards is cost-justified. Departments not requiring detailed performance monitoring because they are relatively efficient or are too small should continue using as a measure of productivity performance the comparative indicators developed in the first step. These departments should be monitored monthly as well, allowing action to be taken as soon as it is deemed necessary.

Detailed time standards should be developed for each major departmental procedure or activity. Productivity measurement should not be attempted using a single measure and a weighted standard. For example, as a measure of output, nursing units should use patient days by acuity level, not merely total patient days. This allows management to document the volumes of individual procedures produced, apply to those volumes a time standard tailored for each procedure, and thereby pinpoint changes in service intensity and staffing requirements.

To make allowances for hospital policies or operating constraints which require the provision of services that may reduce productivity—such as 24 hour coverage in the emergency room or specific turn-around times in the laboratory—the hospital should also establish target productivity levels. Use of these administrative "allowances" enables the hospital to track actual productivity levels. It also equips the hospital to monitor performance based on targeted productivity levels, and to document changes in service intensity (hence, required costs). For an example of this type of report see Table 36-6.

Because this process should be performed at least monthly, forecasts of staffing requirements for coming periods should be presented for use by department heads in determining the most appropriate times to make staffing changes. These forecasts should be based on expected volume and must incorporate seasonal variations to be of use to the hospital.

Table 36-6 Productivity Monitor Report II

PRODUCTIVITY & IMPACT USING PSU STANDARD WITH GROSS IMPACT
COMMUNITY MEMORIAL HOSPITAL
AS OF OCT 31, 1979

Department Cost Center	FTE Work	FTE Target	FTE Variance	Pct Prod	Pct Tgt	Avg Cost Per FTE	Gross Impact	GI Rank	Prod Rank
70 Special Service Summary									
9973 Labor/Delivery									
Current month:	8.7	6.7	2.0	57.7	77.0	1,365	2,730		
Year-to-date:	8.8	6.2	2.6	52.9	70.5	4,095	10,647		
Fiscal yr projection:	8.5	5.6	2.9	49.4	65.9	16,380	47,502	8	16
9972 Intensive Care									
Current Month:	38.0	36.2	1.8	81.0	95.3	1,267	2,281		
Year-to-date:	37.7	34.3	3.4	77.3	91.0	3,802	12,927		
Fiscal yr projection:	40.9	35.5	5.4	73.8	86.8	15,210	82,134	5	3
9970 Special Services									
Current month:	1.5	1.3	0.2	82.4	86.7	1,437	287		
Year-to-date:	1.4	1.3	0.1	88.3	92.9	4,312	431		
Fiscal yr projection:	1.2	1.2	0.0	95.0	100.0	17,250		17	1
70 Special Service Summary									
Current month:	48.2	44.2	4.0	76.9	91.7		5,298		
Year-to-date:	47.9	41.8	6.1	73.3	87.3		24,005		
Fiscal yr projection:	50.6	42.3	8.3	70.3	83.6		129,636		

Standards Development

A key element of productivity monitoring is the development of meaningful comparative indicators in Phase 1, and accurate, detailed standards in Phase 2. Each phase requires a different type of productivity measure, developed through different methods. The first phase provides the hospital a measure of productivity against relatively fixed standards without knowing whether or not the standards are really comparable or productivity can be improved. The second phase provides management a tool to monitor internal productivity.

Standards, more appropriately called operating indicators, used in the first phase can be developed from a number of sources. Most easily, historical data may be used to produce indicators which will provide information describing current performance compared to that of the last year or a combination of several previous years without accounting for changes in service intensity. Also, budget data may be used to compare year-to-date performance to budgeted performance. Another source of operating indicators is the industry norm, an average based on the performance of other institutions in the hospital service area or throughout the country. As mentioned earlier, truly comparable interhospital data are not available because of the inherent differences among hospitals. Any figures developed in this manner should only be used as guides for further investigation, not as definitions of staffing requirements. These data are available through such sources as local or state hospital associations, or independent survey of hospitals selected according to specific operating characteristics. If the latter approach is taken, it is suggested that department heads be involved in selecting comparable hospitals, because they are likely to be aware of specific similarities or differences among them.

Several work measurement techniques may be used to develop performance standards for the second phase, productivity performance monitoring. The applicability of these techniques depends on the nature of the work being measured and the availability of trained personnel to do the measuring. The techniques discussed here are stopwatch timing and self-logging.

Stopwatch timing is particularly suited to short-cycle activities or repetitive work. In this process, the operation under consideration is divided into elements about thirty seconds long, each of which is timed. Stopwatch timing provides a very accurate measure of time requirements but is not well suited to many hospital activities beyond routine housekeeping and service functions. Because of the wide variances among patients, stopwatch techniques do not lend themselves to use with direct patient care activities. Stopwatch timing has been used in developing nursing time standards to devise detailed standards for each nursing activity (e.g., application of bandage) but the record-keeping required can be extremely burdensome—even if nursing personnel accept this approach to staffing.

Self-logging is a work measurement technique in which employees record their own activities. Each employee maintains an activity log or series of activity log-in/log-outs. Each activity to be measured must be determined and described in advance. The table of activities to be analyzed should include the major activities of the department or personnel involved, and may include both clinical and non-clinical tasks. After the logs have been maintained for a specified period (anywhere from one week to several months), the data must be summarized and average time requirements calculated to determine the time requirements for each activity. Self-logging is easy to install and understand but requires close attention, particularly in the early stages, to ensure accurate data collection.

Reporting

Ideally, any productivity monitoring system will have the ability to produce reports using several different sets of comparative indicators or standards, allowing management to examine performance relative to each set of performance measures. With this type of information available, management can analyze staffing variances according to the different standards and discuss the reasons for the variances with department heads to understand and improve operations.

As with any other management information system, reports must be timely, readable, and understandable. To facilitate timeliness, the system should be able to use data as they become available. For example, the labor input (hours worked and/or paid) should be accrued by the system, rather than by hospital personnel, saving time and improving data accuracy.

Additionally, the reports should be presented in a manner consistent with the reporting hierarchy of the hospital, allowing various levels of summarization. For example, each nursing unit should be able to monitor the utilization of nursing personnel by job category (e.g., R.N., L.P.N., etc.) as well as report accumulative results to the Director of Nursing.

The reports should include this information:

- number of FTEs that actually worked
- number of FTEs that should have worked (i.e., a target figure based on performance standards, output and administrative allowances)
- actual productivity
- productivity incorporating administrative allowances
- average cost per FTE
- staffing and cost variances highlighting both excess staffing and excess costs

Summary

A properly installed and maintained productivity monitoring system as part of an overall productivity improvement process can help management control manpower utilization. Defining target levels of staffing based upon actual operating practices and levels of output provides the information necessary for labor control utilization.

A productivity monitoring system can also provide a number of valuable by-product benefits such as:

- improving the balancing of work load/work force relationships
- identifying areas in which excess capacity exists (although staffing reductions may not be feasible)
- developing and maintaining meaningful staffing standards related to the provision of quality patient care
- justifying cost increases based on documented increases in the service intensity
- developing the data base necessary for future planning and control of resources through budgeting and rate setting.

2. CHI Systems*

According to CHI Systems, Inc., improvement of productivity of ongoing operations should strive for a minimal goal of five percent, an expected goal of ten percent, and in many instances, a realizable goal of 15 percent.

Their approach to improving productivity in ongoing operations has seven steps:

1. Management Orientation
2. Overview Studies
3. Productivity Reporting
4. In-depth Studies
5. Quality Control
6. Performance/Reward Systems
7. Monitoring, Review and Change

Management Orientation

First, a philosophical framework must be established, which in turn should establish why productivity efforts are necessary and what benefits are expected.

A set of objectives must next be stated. These objectives should relate to expected benefits within a certain period of time.

The objectives must also state the responsibility of top management and middle management and the kind of commitment and support they will contribute.

Finally, the program costs must be a consideration, so return on investment will be included in the objectives. Obviously, one should not want to expend more dollars on a productivity improvement program than it can return in additional service and in reduced costs.

The Overview Study

The overview provides a profile of manpower productivity and the initial baseline for a productivity reporting system.

The application of an overview study requires the skills of a person trained in the use of such a technique. If a staff person with these qualifications is not available, consultants from shared management engineering programs or management consulting firms should be retained.

---

*Source: Reprinted from Karl G. Bartscht and Richard J. Coffey, "Management Engineering—A Method to Improve Productivity," *Topics in Health Care Financing,* Spring 1977, with permission of Aspen Systems Corporation.

The overview study should provide three outputs:

The *staffing analysis* utilizes gross workload data and predetermined time standards to determine total staffing needs in comparison with existing staff.

The *quality survey* measures performance relative to quality. This is particularly crucial to ensure that increased productivity does not have a negative impact on quality. Quality surveys are conducted by random sampling involving observations and work counts.

System and management review. Management structure analysis looks at organization, skills, and work assignments. Systems analysis looks for duplication of effort, unnecessary steps, and imbalance of work stations.

Productivity Reporting

An effective productivity reporting system should provide the following information:

1. A continuous (at least monthly) timely report on productivity of each department.
2. A comparison of productivity over time to show trends. Examples are:
   - This month compared to last month
   - This month compared to same month last year
   - Year to date compared to last year to date
3. Actual productivity measured in manhours per output. These outputs are specific for each department.
4. Actual productivity (manhours per output) compared to a performance goal of manhours per actual output. The performance goal is based on a manhour/procedure standard. For example, in a physical medicine and rehabilitation, the following may be outputs of the department (these outputs may also be referred to as procedures or as workload units):

Workload Unit

Therapeutic Exercise	Whirlpool-all
Gait Training	Exercise-others
Hot Packs	Massage-all
Ultra Sound	Diathermy-all
Room Visit	P.T. Levels-all
Hubbard-unassisted	Other Modalities
Hubbard-w/therapist	Traction

For each of these workload units a manhour per procedure time is established. This is referred to as a "time standard." These time standards may be developed in various ways. A detailed industrial engineering approach may be used. Predetermined time standards are available through most consulting firms and shared management engineering services.

They are less costly, rapidly developed, and provide sufficient precision to effectively measure departmental productivity. From there, one proceeds to define major work activities. Time standards are applied to these major work activities. These are modified to take into account fluctuations in workloads such as different degrees of patients, peak and valley demands, delays, and approved time off.

In some cases, the department managers may not accept the predetermined times. Since the first objective is to establish a productivity reporting system, an interim time standard may be established as an initial goal. This "negotiated" time standard would then be used at the initial reporting phase.

The establishment of a system to report productivity is beneficial in itself. This provides a regular focus for the department manager to review the performance of his or her department. As a result of this report, the department manager starts initiating studies and changes to increase productivity. Most good managers want to do a better job, and now they have a way of measuring improvement.

5. Written reports to all management levels: hospital, divisions within the hospital, departments within each division, and sections within each department. The reports should cover the level of detail necessary at each level for effective management control.

Tables 36-7 and 36-8 illustrate monthly reports for two different levels within the sample organization.

The reports must be continuously updated. This is necessary for two reasons. First, the procedures being performed (the output) change over time. New procedures are added, others are deleted. Second, as more data are developed

Table 36-7 Sample of Hospital Report

```
CHI SYSTEMS          21-Apr-76           22:35              REPHOS.L38    PAGE
                                                                           1
HOSPITAL                                            ········ CHIMIS ········
                                                    ··· HOSPITAL  REPORT ···
                                                    ····MARCH        1976····

                          EARNED          PAID
DIVISION                  MAN-HOURS       MAN-HOURS     % PROD

HOSP ADMINISTRATION         519.000         528.000       98.3
EMPLOYEE SERVICES         14746.417       13528.000      109.0
ALLIED SERVICES           21135.314       21784.000       97.0
FISCAL SERVICES           21410.943       21834.000       98.1
SUPPORTIVE SERVICES       35482.832       32818.000      108.1
NURSING SERVICES          66734.731       68158.000       97.9
DEVELOPMENT                 173.000         177.000       97.7
PLANNING                    519.000         531.000       97.7

          TOTALS         160721.238      159358.000      100.9

--- HISTORICAL ---    * INDICATES CURRENT MONTH

JAN     FEB     MAR     APR     MAY     JUN     JUL     AUG     SEP     OCT     NOV     DEC

PERCENT PRODUCTIVITY
90.5   102.7   100.9*   0.0     0.0     0.0    86.2    86.0    91.9    92.0    92.3    85.6

THIS MONTH EARNED FTE   929.0
THIS MONTH PAID FTE     921.1

PAST 12 MONTHS PRODUCTIVITY   91.9

Source: Chi Systems Inc. CHIMIS, A Management Information System (Chi Systems, Inc., May, 1976) Pg. 22.
```

Source: Reprinted from Chi Systems Inc. *CHIMIS, A Management Information System* (Chi Systems, Inc., May, 1976) Pg. 22, with permission of the publisher.

for each department, more refined time standards can be developed. This may be accomplished by dividing certain gross procedures into more specific procedures. In addition, negotiated time standards, set as initial goals, should be reviewed and revised as necessary.

In-Depth Studies

The in-depth study is exactly what it says. This is a detailed study of a function or department directed at either the entire operation or a specific problem identified by the overview study. An indepth study is warranted when the overview study provides the following results:

- Significant staffing differences between existing and required.
- Significant quality control problems creating safety, health, and/or public relations problems.
- Interaction with other departments and functions is ineffective creating problems for the other departments.

Specific Problems

The in-depth study is usually directed at a specific problem. Examples of such problems are:

- Organization
- Scheduling

Table 36-8 Sample of Section Report

```
CHI SYSTEMS              21-Apr-76              22:34              REPSEC.L38    PAGE 7

HOSPITAL       —                                          ........  CHIMIS    ........
DIVISION       — ALLIED SERVICES                          ***  SECTION        REPORT  ***
DEPARTMENT     — P.M. & R.                                ***  MARCH          1976    ***
SECTION        — PHYSICAL THERAPY
```

WORKLOAD UNIT	VOLUME	M-H/PROC STANDARD	EARNED MAN-HOURS	PAID MAN-HOURS	% PROD
THERAPEUTIC EXERCISE	780	0.601	468.780		
GAIT TRAINING	569	0.694	394.886		
HOT PACKS	340	0.432	146.880		
ULTRA SOUND	281	0.555	155.955		
ROOM VISIT	503	0.324	162.972		
TRACTION	128	0.447	57.216		
HUBBARD-UNASSISTED	4	0.863	3.452		
HUBBARD-W/THERAPIST	7	1.202	8.414		
WHIRLPOOL-ALL	76	0.478	36.328		
EXERCISE-OTHERS	267	0.554	147.918		
MASSAGE-ALL	314	0.516	162.024		
DIATHERMY-ALL	119	0.468	55.692		
P.T. LEVELS-ALL	11	0.678	7.458		
OTHER MODALITIES	66	0.615	40.590		
FIXED			221.000		
EPI			0.000		
SECTION TOTALS			2069.565	1799.000	115.0

--- HISTORICAL ---   *INDICATES CURRENT MONTH

JAN	FEB	MAR	APR	MAY	JUN	JUL	AUG	SEP	OCT	NOV	DEC
PERCENT PRODUCTIVITY											
95.5	116.8	115.0*	0.0	0.0	0.0	95.6	95.5	106.1	153.3	112.8	94.8

THIS MONTH EARNED FTE   12.0
THIS MONTH PAID FTE   10.4

PAST 12 MONTHS PRODUCTIVITY   108.7

Source: Chi Systems Inc. *CHIMIS, A Management Information System* (Chi Systems, Inc., May, 1976) Pg. 23.

Source: Reprinted from Chi Systems Inc. *CHIMIS, A Management Information System* (Chi Systems, Inc., May, 1976) Pg. 23, with permission of the publisher.

- Information flow and handling
- Methods Improvement
- Patient/Materials Movement
- Layout and Equipment

Organization

Organization studies are directed at achieving the correct balance between span of control and delegation of responsibility with related authority. Too large a span of control may result in poor supervision, and in turn, low productivity. The number of persons supervised is further complicated by their location of work. In a hospital, they may be on different floors and in different departments (e.g., housekeeping personnel). Conversely, too small a span of control may result in additional levels of hierarchy. Such levels may be established to ensure growth positions. In a nursing department, one may find several levels of supervision before one finds a nurse totally committed to patient care (e.g., nursing director, associate nursing director, assistant nursing director, nursing supervisor, head nurse, assistant head nurse, team leader, nurse).

Scheduling Systems

The biggest payoff in achieving cost containment and improvement in operations is through the installation of effective scheduling systems. This very broad area involves patients, employees, and available facilities.

Scheduling of patients may be difficult because of the random arrival of certain types of patients. However, statistically they follow certain patterns, and upon further analysis, one finds that a majority of inpatients and outpatients can be scheduled. The biggest fault in scheduling is the peak load syndrome. In too many cases, patients are scheduled "en masse" for a block time. Examples are 8:00 a.m. surgery, admissions from 1:00 p.m. to 3:00 p.m., and the noon meal from 11:00 a.m. to 12:00 p.m. When one realizes that the processing of ten patients in one hour takes twice as many personnel as five patients per hour for two hours, the peak load scheduling problem should be obvious. The usual case is that the number of required employees is determined by the peak load, with the rest of their eight hours being used with fill-in operations. Usually, reduction of the peak load requirements (spreading out the patient schedule) results in reduction of staff.

The biggest inefficiency in scheduling employees is in the seven day operations (nursing, dietary, housekeeping) which involve the majority of employees. Since most employees work only five days, coverage is required for the other two. The actual requirements for a seven-day position is 1.4 Full-Time Equivalents (FTE). It is not uncommon to see scheduling of three employees for every two positions. This results in an excess of 0.2 FTEs for every 3.0 FTEs. This may not seem like much, but in a 300-bed hospital with 450 nursing, 90 housekeeping, and 75 dietary personnel, this would represent over 40 extra personnel.

Peak load requirements must be smoothed as much as possible and traditional hours (i.e., 7:00 a.m. to 3:30 p.m., 8:00 a.m. to 5:00 p.m.) must be examined as to whether they are the times necessary to the tasks.

Information Flow

Management cannot function without a proper flow of information, both historical reporting and projecting for the future. Departments cannot effectively interact with and serve other departments without the timely receipt of adequate requirements of others' needs. Some studies have suggested that up to 25 percent of all activities in a hospital are involved with information handling. A reduction in this activity must have an effect on improved productivity. The major problem is that most of the effort is spread over all employees. Therefore, an improvement in information handling may decrease an employee's workload by 30 minutes.

Methods Improvement

Methods improvement is the study of how work is performed and looks to reducing human motion (walking, handling, reaching, etc.).

Patient/Materials Movement

Too often one hears from a department manager that department members are doing the best they can, but they never have the patients or materials on time.

The important step in this analysis is the recognition that movement problems can not be solved by individual departments because they involve all those departments that must interact with each other. System benefits come from smoothing the workload in the individual departments.

A related activity is material management studies, the analysis of the purchase, storage, handling, movement, and use of supplies and other purchased materials.

Layout and Equipment

Layout and equipment studies should be geared to reduction of walking and total manpower input. For existing operations, it is rare that significant manpower savings can be achieved through layout changes. The major benefit is usually a more effective use of space resulting in the availability of more space, which in most hospitals, is a real benefit.

Manpower savings are being achieved through replacement of certain activities by automation. Earlier effects have been seen in departments such as dietary (automated dishwashing, tray preparation) and housekeeping (floor washers). More recently, the clinical laboratory is benefiting from highly automated processing of procedures. Limited examples are occurring in the radiology department. A major question is whether the labor replacement results in real cost reduction.

When an analysis of the cost benefits of an equipment investment is made, objectives must be clearly understood. For example, is the investment for increased service, labor reduction, or both? If the objective is labor reduction, this is a savings that must be realized; saving one hour per day for each of eight persons is not a cost reduction unless work can be reassigned to achieve a reduction in one staff position. Another weakness in equipment studies is in the basis for comparison. Most comparisons are with the existing operations. Despite the review of many reports able to justify a large investment in automated material handling systems, one is hard pressed to justify such systems when looking at how the existing system can be improved without (or with very little) capital investment. In other words, justification for equipment should be made based on comparison with the most effective manual system.

Implementation of In-Depth Studies

The responsible operating manager must understand how the new systems and procedures are to work, and what the expected benefits are. Many times, all of the recommendations may not be acceptable to the manager. This may mean partial implementation with further development by the analyst and the manager on the remaining recommendations.

The next step in implementation is to establish with the manager a timetable of activities and expected results. This should then be followed with an orientation of all employees involved in any changes. They in turn must be informed of the desired goals and the timetable.

If a change in procedures, methods, or use of equipment is proposed, instructions must be formalized and training must take place. If new schedules are developed, then assignment of tasks must be developed to be consistent with new schedules.

The actual change to new schedules and/or procedures necessitates close monitoring and continuous support in the form of directions and encouragement. Included in the implementation plan must be a periodic review (e.g., monthly) to ensure that everything is going as expected.

Quality Control

There is significant indication that increased quality can be consistent with increased productivity. Common sense tells us that if something is done correctly the first time, there is no need to repeat the effort.

Quality of services can be measured from three perspectives: input, process, and output. Input measurement involves the quality of inputs to provide the departmental services. The inputs are labor, facilities, equipment, and supplies. Input quality measurements include staff educational requirements, types of linen purchased, type of lighting installed in the operating room, and the physical characteristics of the building.

Process measurement involves the quality of the organization and the methods it uses to provide services. Assessment of process answers the question, "Is the process proper or performed correctly?" It involves comparison with standard procedures and determination of relative values when standards do not exist or are not applicable. Sample process quality measurements are written procedures for the care of isolation patients, identification procedures for patients going to surgery, staffing schedules being posted, sterile technique maintained in the operating room, and contaminated linen tagged appropriately.

Output measurement involves the quality of the services provided by a department. Examples include timely delivery of drugs by the pharmacy, cleanliness of a patient's room after discharge cleaning, timely and courteous answering of telephones, and nursing care objectives achieved.

The following specific examples demonstrate both increased productivity (decreasing cost) and increased quality.

Example 1—Pharmacy ordering. In many hospitals, physicians write pharmacy orders on the patients' charts. These orders are then transcribed by a ward clerk, checked by the head nurse, then sent to the pharmacy to be filled. Changing the system to where a carbon copy of the physician's order is sent directly to the pharmacy:

- Decreases errors interpreting the physician's order. This increases quality.
- Reduces staff time to transcribe and verify the physician's order, which can increase productivity or decrease cost.

Example 2—Coordinated admission and surgery scheduling. Close coordination of admission scheduling and surgery scheduling is very important for surgery patients. This can be done several different ways but the advantages are similar:

- Quality is improved by fewer schedule changes and cancellations which results in less patient and physician disruption.
- Productivity is improved by reducing the personnel time to schedule and reschedule both admissions and surgery. The probability of unused surgical time due to last minute cancellations is also reduced.

Example 3—Paging system. Although widely used, many institutions still do not take advantage of paging systems for their communication needs:

- Quality is improved by reducing response time of services required by patients. Physicians, nurses, and others can be reached in emergencies or other situations.
- Productivity is improved by reducing walking time and delays.

Problems with Quality and Productivity Controls

Key problems encountered with the implementation and use of productivity and quality control programs have been:

a. Complexity and subsequent difficulty in implementation resulting in only partial use.
b. Reports produced are not:
   - used at all.
   - integrated into the management process or into the review of managers' performance.
c. The systems have not been comprehensive nor specific enough resulting in the common and easy practice of blaming lack of productivity and/or quality on another department. Interactive effects between departments have been largely ignored.

Performance Reward Systems

Underlying the entire process of managing productivity gains is the realization that some reward should ultimately result from the improved performance. These rewards may range from bonuses to "getting to keep your job." The nature and extent of the reward mechanism will certainly be dependent upon the level of employee considered. The range, however, should encompass cost reduction participation, incentives, perquisites, improved reimbursement formulas with third party payers, alternative uses of funds, compensatory time off, etc. In no case, can it be expected or warranted that improved results will be obtained without some form of recognition of an individual's contribution to these results.

Monitoring, Review and Change

Productivity improvement for on-going operations must be a continuous activity. Productivity and quality control reporting systems provide regular feedback. These must be monitored on an exception basis, that is, to detect when productivity and quality deviate from an expected range including both high and low deviations. In the case where productivity and/or quality is below performance expectations, it should be investigated. The same is true of above expected performance. In this case, it may be due to new procedures, services, or equipment. This would then require updating the productivity and/or quality control program.

This continuous reporting system has several by-products. Evaluation of new equipment purchases may be based on their effect on productivity. Personnel budgets can be developed based on existing utilization of personnel. The justification for new positions should have a very reliable basis. Performance objectives for management can target on increased productivity or quality level goals that can be quantified. Performance reward systems must also be reviewed and updated.

3. MEDCO Programs*

The Productivity Trend-Management System

The Productivity Trend-Management System has been installed by MEDCO, a professional health care consulting organization, in approximately 70 hospitals, many having less than 100 beds. It can be implemented in just two to three months.

The hospital then has the option of maintaining the system in-house, or monthly updates can be processed on one of MEDCO's mini computers. Multi-hospital summaries are also provided periodically for those who wish to compare their departments with those in hospitals of similar size. The elements of this program include:

- A man-hour/workload reporting system for each labor center.
- Long-term trend charting of departmental productivity data.
- Participative goal setting by department heads.
- Exception reporting (department head accountability to administration).

Data Inputs. The system is usually implemented by gathering two years of monthly historical data relating to hours worked and relevant workload statistics for each of the hospital cost centers or departments. The Monthly Input Sheet used to record this information is shown as Figure 36-9. This sheet is customized to meet the needs of each individual hospital. The chart of accounts is typed on the left-hand side of the page and the appropriate workload indicator for each department is typed on the right-hand side by MEDCO who provides the forms for data collection.

---

*Source: Reprinted by permission of MEDCO, Inc., Langhorne, PA. Courtesy of Ronald L. Ellingson, Vice-President, Western Region.

[The "preferred" and "alternate" units of production or service for various hospital departments are shown in Table 36-9.] Once the left and right-hand columns have been typed and copies have been run, the four columns of data may be filled in by hospital personnel for each month as follows:

From the payroll records:

1. Regular hours worked
2. Overtime hours worked
3. Total hours paid, including vacation, sick, holiday, etc.

From the official hospital records:

4. Number of units of product or service provided by each of the departments each month (patient days, procedures, meals served, etc.). As can be seen, up to two workload indicators can be used, as appropriate, to increase accuracy.

The same forms and types of information are used after the initial two-year historical data have been processed and reported. New data are then provided on a routine basis, normally before the 8th day of each month, for updating the system.

Man-Hour Management Reporting. The data supplied by the hospital are processed on MEDCO's computer to produce a month-by-month statistical report for each department or cost center. Once the initial two-year period has been processed, the second year is moved to the top of the page and a new year is begun, adding one line of information each month as it occurs (see Figure 36-10).

This report not only shows the hours, workloads and productivity ratios, but the dollar impact of productivity variances is also calculated. When the hours per unit productivity ratio increases or decreases are converted to dollars saved or lost, it is more meaningful for those using the reports. It also ties the productivity variances directly to budget expectations for month-by-month controls.

Because many people have difficulty seeing long-term trends in a set of statistical reports, four columns of the data are plotted on a graph that provides for monthly trend analyses over a four-year period. These long-term trends, as shown in Figure 36-11, are being used to forecast future workloads and manpower requirements for budgeting, for labor position controls,

Chapter 36—Productivity 581

Figure 36-9 Monthly input sheet

ACC'T NO	DEPARTMENT	REG. HRS. WK'D	O.T. HRS. WK'D	TOTAL HOURS PAID	#1	#2	DESCRIPTION
	MONTHLY INPUT DATA	HOSPITAL COMMUNITY				MONTH OF: October	FISCAL MO. 0 4 FISCAL YR. 8 3
601	Nursing Admin.	346	0	346	1438	–	Total Patient Days
610	Surgical Unit	3662	24	4127	606	–	Patient Days
611	Medical Unit	3053	12	3318	596	–	Patient Days
620	Coronary Care U	889	8	936	98	–	Patient Days
630	Intensive Care	1049	16	1092	78	–	Patient Days
660	Surgery&Recovery	1689	32	1835	260	–	Operating Hours
678	Emergency Room	545	4	580	685	–	ER Visits
702	Laboratory	1763	28	1856	8654	–	Tests
721	Radiology	928	64	1087	928	–	Procedures
730	Pharmacy	248	10	266	1438	–	Total Patient Days
	With the hospital's specific chart of accounts						
999	TOTAL HOSPITAL	25884	776	28760	1438		TOTAL PATIENT DAYS

Note: Please complete a separate sheet for each month.
Total hours paid include hours worked plus vacation, sick, holiday&call
Total Patient Days exclude newborn pt. days

Table 36-9 Units of Service: Productivity Trend-Management System
(To obtain the best peer comparisons)

Department	Unit of Service*	Alternate Unit
Administration	Total Patient Days	Calendar Days
Admitting	Admissions	—
Ambulance	Service Occasions	—
Anesthesiology	Operating Hours	Surgery Cases
Blood Bank	Units of Blood	—
Business Office	IP Admits + 1/3 OP Admits	Discharges or Total Patient Days
Cafeteria	Equivalent Meals	—
Central Service	Line Items Sold	Total Patient Days
Central Transportation	Transports	Calendar Days
Chaplaincy Services	Total Patient Days	—
Clinics	Visits	—
Communications	Total Patient Days	—
Dialysis	Hours of Treatment	Treatments
Dietary	Patient Meals	Total Patient Days
EEG	Procedures	—
EKG	Procedures	—
Emergency	ER Visits	—
Employee Health Service	Total Patient Days	—
Home Health Services	Home Contacts	—
Housekeeping	Sq. Ft. Served	Calendar Days
Inservice Education	Total Patient Days	—
Intravenous Therapy	Fluids Infused	Line Items Sold Total Patient Days
Labor and Delivery	Deliveries	—
Laboratory	CAP Workload Units	Number of Tests
Laundry and Linen	Pounds Processed	—
Maintenance & Plant	Gross Sq. Ft.	Calendar Days
Management Engineering	Total Patient Days	—
Medical Records	IP Admits + 1/3 OP Admits	Discharges or Total Patient Days
Nursing Administration	Total Patient Days	Calendar Days
Nursing Care Units	Patient Days	—
Occupational Therapy	Treatments	—
Personnel	Total Patient Days	Patient Days
Pharmacy	Total Patient Days	Doses/Line Items
Physical Therapy	Treatments	Modalities
Purchasing & Stores	Purchase Orders	Calendar Days
Radiology	Procedures	—
Recovery Room	Patients Recovered	Surgery Cases
Recreational Therapy	Treatments	—
Respiratory Therapy	Treatments	—
Social Services	Personal Contacts	Total Patient Days
Surgery	Operating Hours	Surgery Cases
Volunteer Services	Total Patient Days	—

*Excluding Relative Value Units that are available through MEDCO's National Productivity Management System.

and to assist in making day-to-day operating decisions. The combined reports (trend charts and statistical sheets) are also of significant value in providing objective data for department head and supervisory performance evaluations. The graph section at the top of the trend chart page may be used either to report percent overtime or, if the department has a quality assurance

Figure 36-10 Productivity management system monthly departmental data record

COMMUNITY HOSPITAL　　　　　　　　　　　　　　　　　　　　　　　　　　　　　　　　　　　DEPT. NO. 610　SURGICAL FLR

	WORKLOAD				ACTUAL - PRODUCTIVE				YEAR-TO-DATE	DOLLAR DIFFERENCE		PAID		PER-CENT
MONTH	#1 NO. OF PAT DAYS	#2 NO. OF PATNT DAYS	TOTAL PATNT DAYS	AVERAGE DAILY WRKLOAD	HOURS WORKED	FULL-TIME EQUIV	PERCNT OVER-TIME	HOURS PER PATIENT DAY	HOURS PER PATIENT DAY	THIS MONTH	YEAR-TO-DATE	TOTAL HOURS	FULL-TIME EQUIV	PRODUC-TIVE HOURS
YEAR: 1982			THIS YEAR'S GOAL:			6.58 HOURS PER PATIENT		DAY			DEPT. LABOR COST: $ 8.20 PER HOUR			
JULY	657.00	0.00	657.0	21.19	3,792	21.4	3.1%	5.77	5.77	$4,355	$4,355	4,804	27.1	78.9%
AUGUST	724.00	0.00	724.0	23.35	4,285	24.2	2.7%	5.92	5.85	$3,927	$8,282	4,717	26.6	90.8%
SEPTEMBER	696.00	0.00	696.0	23.20	4,225	24.9	5.5%	6.07	5.92	$2,908	$11,190	4,826	28.4	87.5%
OCTOBER	594.00	0.00	594.0	19.16	3,895	22.0	2.2%	6.56	6.06	$111	$11,301	4,357	24.6	89.4%
NOVEMBER	601.00	0.00	601.0	20.03	3,901	22.9	7.4%	6.49	6.14	$439	$11,740	4,377	25.7	89.1%
DECEMBER	539.00	0.00	539.0	17.39	3,784	21.4	4.4%	7.02	6.27	-$1,947	$9,794	4,583	25.9	82.6%
JANUARY	614.00	0.00	614.0	19.81	4,180	23.6	4.4%	6.81	6.34	-$1,147	$8,647	4,694	26.5	89.0%
FEBRUARY	536.00	0.00	536.0	19.14	3,671	22.9	1.0%	6.85	6.40	-$1,182	$7,465	3,960	24.8	92.7%
MARCH	510.00	0.00	510.0	16.45	3,529	19.9	1.1%	6.92	6.45	-$1,420	$6,045	4,170	23.6	84.6%
APRIL	670.00	0.00	670.0	22.33	3,776	22.2	1.0%	5.64	6.36	$5,187	$11,232	4,363	25.7	86.5%
MAY	661.00	0.00	661.0	21.32	3,836	21.7	2.3%	5.80	6.30	$4,210	$15,442	4,371	24.7	87.8%
JUNE	717.00	0.00	717.0	23.90	4,345	25.6	1.6%	6.06	6.28	$3,057	$18,499	4,785	28.1	90.8%
YEAR TOTALS			7,519.0	20.54	47,219	22.6	3.1%					54,007	25.9	87.4%
YEAR: 1983			THIS YEAR'S GOAL:			5.80 HOURS PER PATIENT		DAY			DEPT. LABOR COST: $ 8.77 PER HOUR			
JULY	660.00	0.00	660.0	21.29	3,601	20.3	4.4%	5.46	5.46	$1,991	$1,991	4,533	25.6	79.4%
AUGUST	749.00	0.00	749.0	24.16	4,206	23.8	0.9%	5.62	5.54	$1,212	$3,203	4,818	27.2	87.3%
SEPTEMBER	732.00	0.00	732.0	24.40	4,331	25.5	3.3%	5.92	5.67	-$749	$2,454	4,843	28.5	89.4%
OCTOBER	606.00	0.00	606.0	19.55	3,662	20.7	0.8%	6.04	5.75	-$1,291	$1,163	4,127	23.3	88.7%
YEAR-TO-DATE - THIS YEAR			2,747	22.33	15,800	22.5	2.3%		5.75			18,321	26.1	86.2%
SAME MONTHS - LAST YEAR			2,671	21.72	16,197	23.1	3.4%		6.06			18,704	26.7	86.6%
PERCENT CHANGE			2.8%		-2.5%				5.1%			-2.0%		

Note: Increase in Pt. Days　　Decrease in Hours Worked　　Improvement in Productivity　　Dollar Savings

program, the monthly quality index can be effectively related to labor productivity performance. This helps hospital management to meet its overall responsibility of providing quality services at reasonable costs.

Goal Setting. To assist in this process, MEDCO provides a sheet that contains, for each labor center, the two-year hour and statistical summary and a suggested long-range goal toward which the group should work. This long-range goal is determined from a combination of engineering studies done in the department and peer comparative data from other participating hospitals.

After overall hospital department head orientation sessions so that everyone is familiar with the system and how it works, the goal setting sheet is used to obtain a commitment (a short-term goal) from each department head for the coming year.

Exception Reporting. Figure 36-12 shows the form used for holding department heads accountable to administration for productivity goals that they, themselves, have set. It is required only for those months the department fails to reach its goal. It causes the responsible manager to ponder the reasons for the defi-

Figure 36-11 Long term trend
DEPARTMENTAL SUMMARY

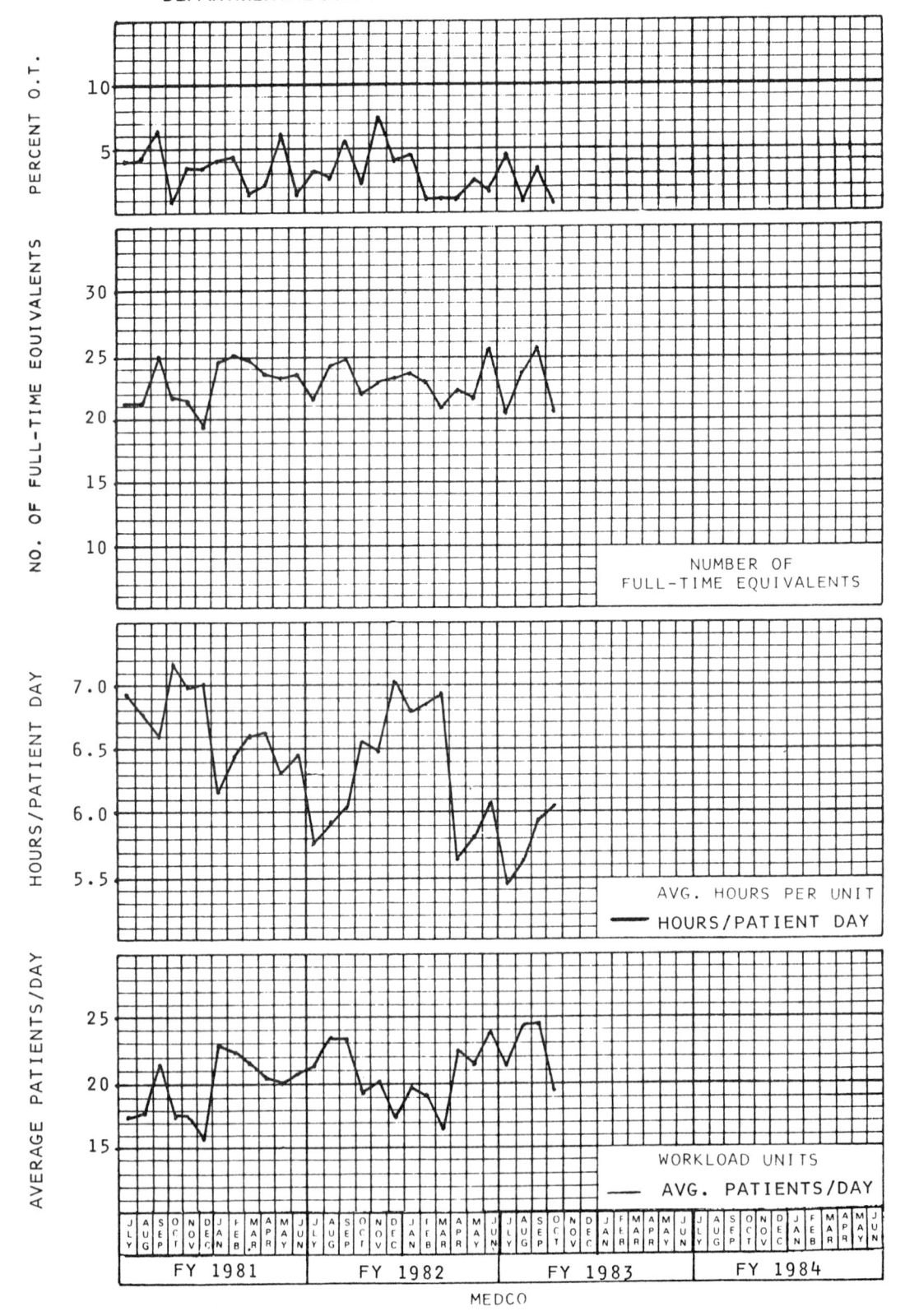

Figure 36-12 Exception report

EXCEPTION REPORT PRODUCTIVITY MANAGEMENT SYSTEM	**Report For Month of:** September 19_82_ **Department Or Unit:** Surgical Nursing
Date Exception Report Issued: October 8, 1982	**Date Due Back To Administration:** October 13, 1982
Productivity Performance: Unit of Measure Is Hours Per _Patient Day_	**Goal:** 5.80 **Actual For Month** 5.92

1. **The Primary Reason For The Difference Between Our Goal And Our Actual Performance Is:**

   We started procedures for adding help to meet the census increase that started in August and didn't get them turned off in time.

2. **Our Plan For Action To Affect An Improvement In The Problem Defined In No. 1 Above Is As Follows:**

   Develop our part-time staff component to be a larger percentage of the total so we will have more flexibility to respond both to increases and decreases in census. We also need to keep working on methods improvements so the staff will be more comfortable operating at our new goal level.

3. **Additional Department Comments:**

   We will bring up the subject of flexible staffing at our October 21 management meeting.

Submitted By: Sue Morrison	**Date:** October 12, 1982

4. **Administration Comments:**

   Your plans look good. Please have the department contact me if help is needed with policy changes.

By: Fred Martin	**Date:** October 18, 1982

ciency and asks for a plan of action to get back on target.

National Productivity and Cost Management System

A second system has been devised by MEDCO which assists hospitals with "per case" and prospective reimbursement programs, in addition to giving needed consideration to the *intensity* of services being provided in each of the hospital departments. It uses Relative Value Units (RVU's) as its productivity measurement base.

One of the primary concepts of MEDCO's RVU system is to link productivity data to the hospital's own billing and financial data system. This eliminates a major credibility gap that exists in older systems where productivity data are reported separately, and are quite different, from official hospital statistics and standard financial data. The system is best explained by looking at revenue and non-revenue departments separately.

Revenue Departments. Each procedure, test, etc., performed by a department has a unit value established for the labor expended. These values are entered in a standing data bank in a similar manner to the charge file that exists in any automated billing system. Whenever a charge is made in the billing system for the department's work, the unit counts (RVU's) for labor productivity are made at the same time. So, a Radiology department, or any of the other revenue departments, will automatically receive additional Earned Units when more complex procedures are performed. This means that, if the hours worked remain constant, the department will score more "RVU's per hour" for their *performance* measure. At the same time, more "RVU's per procedure" are recorded for the department's *service intensity* level for that period. Conversely, if more simple procedures are done during a reporting period, a lower intensity level will be recorded and the RVU's per hour would drop, unless a corresponding reduction is made in the hours worked.

Since a uniform, hospital-wide time value is placed upon the Relative Value Unit, it can be determined both what the impact is on the staffing levels, and also in terms of per unit labor costs for variances occurring during each reporting period.

Non-Revenue Departments. These departments are similar in concept to Revenue Departments except for the nature of the work activities counted and the method of counting. Whenever possible, counts are based on standard statistical measures that are normally counted, permanently recorded and subject to easy audit and verification (such as Admissions, Patient Days, Discharges, etc.).

Of course, in most areas, additional activity volume counts will be needed to provide the same volume "mix" accuracy that is built into the Revenue Departments.

In some areas, a "selected value" and "add-on" approach is used to customize the values to the equipment and systems in use in each hospital.

In other areas, component parts to a standard statistical count will be used (i.e., type of patient day, etc.). Other count and audit techniques will be fully explained to assure accuracy and validity.

In all cases, the volumes reported for all of the required items are multiplied by the RVU labor units to yield the total Earned Units which are summed for the department for that period. These units are then divided by the hours worked and the workload indicators to obtain the productivity performance and service intensity ratios. As can be seen on the sample report (Table 36-10) the current year's ratios are compared with base year averages. Some hospitals are also charting the key ratios and data on long-term trend charts similar to those used with MEDCO's Productivity Trend-Management System.

All participating hospitals submit their monthly statistics for input to MEDCO's national data bank where it is processed and reported back in total by department with the high-low-mean and median averages for both the performance (RVU's per hour) and intensity (RVU's per unit) ratios.

FLEXIBLE STAFFING APPROACHES

The heart of a productivity project is in placing the people where the work is. The two basic approaches are to adjust the staffing or to manipulate the workload.

One obvious technique is the use of part-time and casual staff, bringing them in when the work

Table 36-10 Performance Report: Radiology Department

Month	(1) Procedures	(2) Rel. Val. Units-RVU	(3) RVU/ Proc.	(4) Paid Hours	(5) Worked Hours	(6) RVU/ Pd. Hr.	(7) RVU/ Wkd. Hr.
Base*	59,339	4,424,201	74.6	85,708	77,170	51.6	57.3
July	4,897	363,309	74.3	8,211	7,402	44.3	49.1
August	4,547	353,990	77.9	7,959	7,114	44.5	49.8
Sept.	4,483	341,034	76.1	7,351	6,601	46.4	51.7
Total	13,927	1,058,833	76.0	23,521	21,118	45.0	50.1

*Last year's (baseline) data and ratios

is at its peak. Maintaining a staff of trained people who will work part-time or who are available on a few hours notice may pose a problem, however.

Another approach is the use of float staff or pool staff. Float staff are specially designated employees who move from one section of the department to another as the need arises. This is most useful if different areas have their workload peaks occurring at different times of the day. Pool staff are similar to float staff except that they have no "home section" and are a separately identified group who are assigned on an "as needed" basis.

Cross-training of employees is another approach that allows for more flexibility in work assignments. Employees should be trained to perform all or most of the positions required in the department.

Staggering the times at which various groups start and finish their work day may also provide a better distribution between employees and responsibilities required during the day.*

Variable Staffing**

It is imperative for hospital managers to monitor the appropriateness of staffing levels so that action can be taken when indicated. Although matching personnel availability to variations in hospital and departmental demands can be tedious and time-consuming, the financial rewards are great.

Traditionally, definitions of variable staffing have centered around the utilization of part-time employees to support the hospital's work force during peak demand periods. Functionally, the utilization of variable staffing has meant substantially reducing your full-time work force and recruiting and maintaining a large part-time work force to be used on an "as needed" basis to meet unexpected upward fluctuations in patient census, to replace personnel during peak holiday and vacation periods or to bolster a staff when many of its members are absent due to illness.

Greater utilization of part-time agency personnel who work on a contingency or an on-call basis has many advantages and can assist the administrator in solving otherwise difficult scheduling problems. Not only does variable staffing, via greater utilization of part-time personnel, afford hospital administrators greater scheduling flexibility but the fiscal advantages can also be substantial. Aside from the obvious monetary advantages resulting from improved manpower scheduling—only paying an employee when the work load is sufficient to warrant those expenditures—the total labor cost of part-time personnel is generally substantially less than for their full-time counterparts. For example, part-time employees are usually not extended a full complement of benefits such as holiday, vacations, sick pay or employer contributions toward health insurance. Furthermore, the hospital can accrue substantial savings by increasing the hours worked by part-time personnel and reducing overtime payments to full-time employees.

---

*Source: Reprinted from *Cost Effective Quality Food Service: An Institutional Guide* by Judy Ford Stokes, with permission of Aspen Systems Corporation, © 1979.

**Source: Submission, Texas Voluntary Cost Containment Review Committee, *Issues Affecting the Financing and Operation of Hospitals*, House Committee on Ways and Means, Oct. 16, 1980, Serial 96-128, pp. 172–173.

Problems with Part-Time Personnel

Although the utilization of part-time personnel to meet specific demands can generate substantial personnel savings, some mention of the potential pitfalls associated with a greater utilization of part-time personnel must be considered. Whereas the potential advantages of having an extensive part-time employee pool are impressive, administrators must be sure that they are not needlessly utilizing part-time personnel just because they are available. Identifying your hospital's fixed and variable workloads is a vital part of matching available personnel to fluctuating demand. Because the level of most hospital manpower requirements is essentially variable—changing in direct proportion to changes in such workload measures as patient census, outpatient volume, number of tests performed and other similar work units—trends in workload levels should be carefully observed from month to month to determine if the manpower requirements are changing significantly. Only by continually reviewing departmental needs can appropriate utilization of part-time personnel be made.

Another possible pitfall of extensive utilization of part-time personnel rests in the amount of Social Security payments made by the hospital. In some situations, it is possible to cease Social Security payments after an employee has received the maximum taxable income (for Social Security purposes). However, if the hospital pays two part-time employees the same amount of money the institution would have to contribute additional monies to the Social Security Fund. Similarly, additional supervision and record keeping should be considered as part of the costs associated with the utilization of part-time employees. Each administrator must carefully weigh the advantages and pitfalls associated with the utilization of part-time personnel.

Benefits of Variable Staffing

Several other aspects of variable staffing are worthy of note, not only because they are potentially cost reducing but also because they do not have the disadvantages associated with large part-time labor pools. Every hospital can carefully monitor historical fluctuations in workload, not only for the hospital at large but also for individual departments. Familiarity with trends in workload can suggest possible manipulations in staffing patterns that will be economically advantageous to the hospital.

By matching staffing needs with vacation and holiday leave the hospital can improve productivity and save extra dollars in both personnel expenses that would be spent on staffing replacements and in the monies spent on paying holiday pay or shift differential.

For example, a hospital's lowest occupancy rate may be experienced in July and December; these months traditionally produce low occupancy. If the administrator encouraged his employees to plan their vacations around the Fourth of July and/or the Christmas–New Year's periods there should be minimum need to hire vacation replacements.

Like matching personnel availability to seasonal variations in workload, matching personnel availability to hourly variations in workload can produce substantial monetary savings. That is why most hospital administrators schedule the largest work force during the day shift when the heaviest workloads occur. Although the need for differential staffing patterns are usually apparent, few hospital administrators vary staffing patterns within an 8-hour shift even though hourly fluctuations in workload are marked and predictable. Figure 36-13 illustrates some traditional hourly fluctuations in workload on an average nursing unit during a single 24-hour period.

By employing permanent part-time employees (permanent part-time employees are part of the hospital's regular work force but only work a few hours a day) to meet this workload demand, the hospital administrator might reduce his day shift personnel and still provide ample personnel for this high demand period.

Another possible utilization of variable staffing includes internal personnel manipulations that don't demand any additional work force. Cross-training of employees can provide a great deal of flexibility for interdepartmental staffing. For example, if a floor nurse is sufficiently familiar with the emergency room procedures and has the appropriate training she could be used as additional support for the emergency room staff in crisis situations.

The applications of this technique are numerous and only limited by imagination and ingenuity. Again, the monetary savings for this type of procedure accrue by not hiring additional per-

Figure 36-13 Average workload distribution during the day

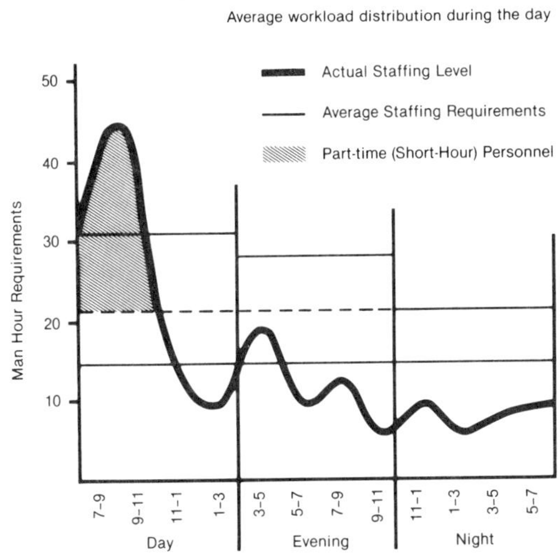
Average workload distribution during the day
Actual Staffing Level
Average Staffing Requirements
Part-time (Short-Hour) Personnel
Man Hour Requirements
50
40
30
20
10
7-9
9-11
11-1
1-3
3-5
5-7
7-9
9-11
11-1
1-3
3-5
5-7
Day
Evening
Night

sonnel to handle peaks in departmental or hospital workloads.

EMPLOYEE INCENTIVES

Using Employee Initiative*

If the abilities and potentialities of employees are recognized, encouraged and developed, organizations will be in a better position to fully utilize their lower-level management personnel. Behavior is greatly determined by the attitudes of employees themselves, and management. If employees believe that the organization is concerned with the full development and realization of employee potential, then employee attitudes toward the company, supervision and the job will significantly improve and be reflected in behavior that is in the best interests of both the organization and the individual.

Too rigid observance of the formal organizational concepts and requirements may lead to stagnation and frustration of employees. The need for revisions and changes in organizational programs and relationships should be given more consideration. Particularly, the typical authority and responsibility system needs to be challenged. Recognition should be given to the fact that people frequently can and do operate beyond the authority-responsibility system, and that the results obtained are often superior to the formal method in terms of efficiency, saving of time and effects on people.

It is frequently found that lower-level employees who operate outside of the formal authority-responsibility system are superior employees with a high degree of creativity, initiative and resourcefulness. But these qualities are frequently not recognized or tapped by management. So these people look for other outlets for their ingenuity and initiative, and use them to get things done outside of the authority-responsibility structure. This creativity, without a legitimate outlet, may be directed by the individual at things other than organizational goals.

The creativity, initiative and resourcefulness of employees may be used to help realize the goals of management by "getting things done" outside of the authority-responsibility structure. People with a high degree of creativity see many alternatives, and are able to go over, around or under obstacles in attaining their goals. Frequently, however, these creative individuals are looked upon as mavericks, and attempts are made to hold them in check.

Employee Incentive Plans*

The employee incentive plan is a system of financial rewards to workers, usually bonuses or profit-shares, based upon measured increments in productivity as reflected in higher savings and operational capacity for the organization.

A hospital facility that administers an efficiently designed incentive system benefits in a number of ways:

1. Enables the hospital to provide higher income for employees without increasing the salary budget
2. Motivates workers to higher levels of efficiency
3. Reduces costs yet maintains, possibly improves, the quality of patient care

*Source: "The Encouragement of Employee Creativity and Initiative," by Alfred H. Jantz. Reprinted with permission of *Personnel Journal,* Costa Mesa, California; all rights reserved, © 1975.

*Source: Reprinted from *The Nursing Administration Handbook* by Howard S. Rowland and Beatrice L. Rowland, eds., with permission of Aspen Systems Corporation, © 1980.

4. Releases funds for other forms of utilization, purchase of new equipment, etc.

To institute an incentive plan and have it function effectively, the various administrative levels involved must understand the concept and the manner in which it can be applied to departmental functions. Objectives must be spelled out, as well as the ongoing progress made in meeting those objectives. All employees should be motivated to participate, with particular attention paid to their suggestions and special skills.

The employee incentive plan can work on a departmental basis or a hospital-wide basis. The departmental program tends to unite each department in a tighter cooperative effort though the smaller "teams" may lose sight of the larger organizational needs. The hospital-wide approach has the reverse effect: cooperation between departments is maximized but the impact of teamwork is diffused.

Note: Caution should be exercised in the use of employee incentive plans. Despite some well-publicized successes, an extensive review of these programs indicated that some hospitals had dropped their incentive plans. Investigators discovered the primary difficulties stemmed from insufficient objective measures of output, opposition by employee groups, and inadequate guidelines for Internal Revenue Service approval of the shared savings system which could possibly alter the hospital's nonprofit status.

*General Characteristics**

Wage incentive systems contain two essential elements: 1. The establishment of performance standards for jobs and tasks carried out in an organization; and 2. variation of employe earnings based upon individual or group performance measured against pre-established standards. *Individual incentive* systems measure the productivity of each worker and vary his earnings accordingly. *Group incentive* plans measure the output of operating units within the organization (or the entire organization itself), and all employes in the group share equally in the savings or additional profits that result from their efforts. Compensation from incentive systems may be paid immediately, as a supplement to employes' regular earnings, or may be placed in trust for subsequent bonus payments or savings plans (deferred incentive systems).

For the successful application of wage incentives, the following steps must be taken:

1. Management must be convinced of the value of the incentive plan and support it vigorously.
2. The details of the plan must be established in close reference to organizational goals. If goals are not clearly defined, their establishment becomes the single, most important step in the entire process.
3. Once the plan has been developed, it must be carefully explained and "sold" to employes.
4. Sound standards must be determined, established, and maintained. Undoubtedly, this step is the most difficult task. Some of the problems connected with the establishment of performance and/or cost reduction standards are discussed below.
5. After all the preliminary work has been completed, the system must be initiated and tested. Since the initial standards for measurement and determination of incentive pay are based upon a considerable amount of intuition, it should be made clear to all concerned that the initial period of operation will be a test period for evaluation and subsequent adjustment of standards and procedures.

*Wage Incentive Plans in Hospitals**

1. Baptist Hospital, Pensacola, Fla. The Baptist Hospital group incentive plan is operated on a departmental basis, with each productivity-share-plan tailored to the department in which it is used. Departmental productivity-share-plans and formulae are developed jointly by management, department heads, and key employes. Once the plan is developed, a meeting is held with all employes of the department to initiate the plan, and periodic follow-up meetings are held to review progress. Following publication of a monthly report, each department head computes the incentive amount for the month and forwards it to the payroll department. A supplemental but separate paycheck is prepared for

――――――
*Source: Reprinted from Charles J. Austin, "Wage Incentive Systems: A Review," *Hospital Progress,* April 1970, with permission of the Catholic Health Association.

each employe and distributed at a special monthly departmental meeting for this purpose.

2. Memorial Hospital, Long Beach, Calif. The Long Beach plan, called MERIT (Memorial Employes Retirement Incentive Trust), is a group incentive plan applied on an over-all basis to all employes in the hospital. The plan is designed to combine financial incentive with work simplification. The basic measurement of productivity is a formula which relates expense to income.

The MERIT system is an example of a deferred incentive plan, since the incentive pay is placed in trust and invested. Employes become vested in the plan on a straight line percentage basis over a 10-year time span. After 10 years in the plan, an employe is fully vested and would receive both his contribution and the full hospital contribution plus interest and dividends accumulated should he retire or leave the hospital.

3. East End Memorial Hospital, Birmingham, Ala. This proprietary hospital operates a group incentive system on a departmental basis, similar to the one operated by Baptist Hospital in Pensacola. Monthly bonus pay is awarded on the basis of cost reductions obtained through increased productivity and lower usage of supplies and materials.

Productivity incentives have been applied to personnel in nursing service, operating room, recovery room, emergency room, dietary, and housekeeping. Nursing service incentives are computed on the basis of two factors: reduced man-hours per patient-day and reduced supply costs per patient-day.

4. Montana Deaconess Hospital, Great Falls, Mont. Montana Deaconess Hospital established a departmental group incentive system in 1966. Average cost per productivity unit (patient-day, surgical operation, laboratory procedure, etc.) was computed for a three-month period for each department participating in the plan. Subsequent monthly savings in reduced unit costs are divided two ways: one-half reverting to the operating budget and one-half distributed as additional pay to departmental employes. Base-line unit costs are recomputed for the same three-month period each year.

Chapter 37—Unions

WHY EMPLOYEES JOIN UNIONS

Checklist for Employee Satisfaction*

The most important questions that health care executives should ask in appraising the overall level of employee satisfaction or dissatisfaction are these:

1. Does the employee *believe* that he is regularly treated with courtesy, respect and dignity?
2. Does the employee *believe* that he is treated as an individual with unique needs, skills and aspirations?
3. Does the employee *believe* that management makes personnel decisions fairly, without regard to race, sex, age, religion, nationality or the like?
4. Does the employee *believe* that his supervisors are careful to avoid favoritism in directing work, imposing discipline and dispensing rewards?
5. Does the employee *believe* that his efforts and loyalty are known and appreciated by his immediate supervisors and by higher management?
6. Does the employee *believe* that management has and will *voluntarily* grant reasonable, competitive wage increases and improve fringe benefits?
7. Does the employee *believe* that day-to-day working relations are friendly and relaxed?
8. Does the employee *believe* that his workplace is attractive, healthy and safe?
9. Does the employee *believe* that his job is secure from unwarranted discharge or layoff?
10. Does the employee *believe* that his work is genuinely important to the welfare of patients and the community?
11. Does the employee *believe* that he has received adequate training to enable him to perform his job well?
12. Does the employee *believe* that the institution itself is managed in a highly professional manner so that he can be proud to identify with it?
13. Does the employee *believe* that his job holds promise for a better future, that he will be offered opportunities to upgrade his skills, enjoy greater responsibility and achieve higher earnings?

If these questions can be answered affirmatively, employees will have little interest in union representation. But note that each question is framed in terms of employee perceptions, not objective reality. Health care executives often have an unrealistic sense of their employees' true feelings. Not uncommonly an institution that believes it has been a model employer learns to its dismay that employees have a distinctly negative opinion of it.

---

*Source: Reprinted from *Health Care Labor Manual* by Martin E. Skoler, with permission of Aspen Systems Corporation, © 1981.

Analyzing Vulnerability to Unions[*]

The AFL-CIO, in its *Guidebook for Union Organizers,* cautions that before contacting any employees, a union should first do a full-scale study of the employer. One such study lists 45 separate areas of employer analysis from location of facility through wages, male-female rates, hours, starting and quitting time, benefits, layoff practices, recall procedures, disciplinary procedures, financial condition of the facility to whether it has bowling leagues and house magazines.

A similar profile should be prepared by management. Such an analysis identifies where an institution is strong, and where it is vulnerable and susceptible to attack. It points up the areas that should be remedied long before a union appears on the scene. It reveals areas of weakness which may be the source of employee discontent and therefore points out where a union may attack. It is a continuing reference source for the preparation of responses to union communications to employees. It can help in preparing for hearings before the NLRB if any are necessary. It serves as a guideline for the institution's putting forward its position and meeting hostile propaganda during a union campaign.

The following are areas which should be covered in a full-length self-study and analysis undertaken by management.

Personnel Administration

- Staffing, organization and structure of the personnel office
- Training of personnel department employees
- Sources of labor supply: professional, semiprofessional, technical, non-professional, clerical, service and maintenance
- Interview procedures, pre-employment and post-employment
- Testing
- Probationary periods
- Job specifications
- Reference checks
- Maintenance and up-dating of employee files
- Orientation of new employees

- Employee transfers
- Length of Service considerations—layoffs and recall
- Incentive plans (policy and practice)
- Merit reviews—by whom, frequency, policy and actual practice
- Overtime or premium pay, daily, weekly, Saturdays, Sundays, Holidays
- Overtime distribution procedures
- Shift differentials
- Reporting and call-in pay for time lost due to weather or other external acts
- Deductions for absences and tardiness
- Paid rest periods and wash up times
- Cost of living escalators
- Applicability of federal and state wages, wage and hour laws

Benefits

- Holidays
- Vacations
- Insurance
- Pensions
- Rest periods
- Jury duty
- Sick pay
- Maternity leave
- Uniform allowances
- Leave of absence
- Tuition allowances
- Bereavement leave
- Medical care
- Prescription and Medication discounts
- Internal promotions (both policy and practice)
- Turnover rate of personnel, identifying the areas and departments
- Rules regarding solicitation and distribution of notices and handbills
- Suggestion systems
- Equal employment opportunity—policies and practices
- Affirmative action program

Employee Facilities

- Lockers
- Lunchroom/Cafeteria vending machines
- Rest rooms
- Equipment
- Parking
- Drinking fountains

---

[*]Source: Louis Jackson, "Preventive Labor Relations," *American Health Care Association Journal,* July 1976.

Wages and Hours

- Work Week and Work Day
- Wage chart showing rates for all job classifications
- History of general wage increase
- Method and frequency of payment (cash or check, weekly or bi-weekly)
- Wage and benefit surveys (comparison with other institutions and with related local, regional and national wage trends)
- Job evaluation and wage progression systems policy and practice

Physical Working Conditions

- Physical plant and equipment
- Housekeeping and sanitation of employee areas
- Maintenance and refurbishing cycles and standards
- Employee distribution—level of work and work load
- Safety provisions and safety committee

Career Enhancement

- Opportunities for advancement
- Notification of job opportunities
- Internal opportunities for promotion
- Professional training and upgrading
- Opportunities for professional to take part in policy making
- Exercise of initiative by professionals or semiprofessionals in the care of patients or other matters
- Paid tuition

Training Programs

- For supervisors
- For technical staffs
- Induction to task assignments

Supervision

- Source of past problems
- Level of loyalty
- Belief in institution's philosophy
- Degree of rapport with employees
- Understanding of institution policy
- Ability to lead
- Ability to communicate

Union and Union Activities

- Prior attempts to organize
- Extent of current unionization
- Present activity—handbilling, calls at home, letters, in-house activity, other
- Union status of other local healthcare institutions
- Union climate in the community
- Professional association influence and employee involvement
- Current collective bargaining agreements—units involved, physical locations if more than one

THE ORGANIZING CAMPAIGN*

The Union Organizer and His Strategies

The organizer is a specialist in identifying sources of employee dissatisfaction. If he finds no legitimate complaints among employees, he will magnify minor ones. He is usually well-informed about personnel problems of the health care field and can quickly identify low morale, uncompetitive wages, high-handed supervision and other sources of employee dissatisfaction.

Typically, he poses as all things to all employees. To the black worker, he denounces "racism" and promises "equality" under a union contract. To the kitchen worker, he criticizes poor ventilation and unpleasant working conditions and promises that the union contract will make things better. To aides and orderlies, he emphasizes wages and job security, making promises about how the union will improve both. To nurses he stresses professionalism, while to non-professionals he stresses "solidarity." His job is to convince employees that they should be dissatisfied with the status quo—regardless of the objective situation.

Steps in Organizing**

Union organizing attempts primarily incorporate one or more of three steps.

---

*Source: Except where noted, this section on "The Organizing Campaign" consists of excerpts reprinted from *Health Care Labor Manual* by Martin E. Skoler, with permission of Aspen Systems Corporation, © 1981.

**Source: Reprinted from *The Union Epidemic* by Warren H. Chaney and Thomas R. Beech, with permission of Aspen Systems Corporation, © 1977.

Step 1: The Hospital Survey—Background information is a necessary part of any campaign. Unless the organizer has a thorough understanding of the hospital, its policies, its key people, its problems, etc., a formalized strategy cannot be developed. Consequently, the first step is to do a "target" survey.

Initially, the organizer spends several hours simply observing the facility, talking to cafeteria employees, workers in housekeeping, nurses, and so on. From such conversations the organizer attempts to determine the number of employees per shift; employee breakdown by sex, age, race, etc.; what eating and drinking facilities are nearby; available transportation facilities for the employees; and special problems the facility might face.

The second part of a survey involves establishing contact with the existing labor movement in the community. Here the organizer determines the labor position of the mass media; the labor history of the organization; names of employees who are active in community work such as churches, civic groups, and politics (these persons often make good initial contacts); names of former employees who belonged to a union; a general idea of wages, conditions, and problems; community relations with the target facility; community reaction to organized labor; and meeting dates and places for local union groups.

Step 2: Selecting the Employee Leaders—Having completed his initial survey of the facility, the organizer is now ready to make his first contact with the employees of the health care facility. Most union organizers are primarily interested in finding the employee who is respected by his/her fellow workers and who has informal influence within the health care facility. These are the workers that the organizer will depend on for "internal leadership" and information about the specific problems and complaints of the employees.

The labor organizers court potential internal leaders. The benefits of the union are explained, and an attempt is made to build up the trust of the leaders. The organizers try to get leaders for every faction within the organization; for the women, the men, the minority groups, etc. They create committees and encourage mass participation.

Step 3: Showing the Union Presence—In Step 3 the union will begin actively to distribute handbills and/or begin seeking authorization card signatures for the purpose of forcing an election. The purpose of this first handout distribution is little more than to show union presence. Such leaflets tend to be general in nature and are usually prepared by the union's international or national office.

Once the "internal leaders" begin bringing the organizer the signed union authorization cards, the organizer dramatically steps up the campaign by seeking the trouble spots, evaluating internal leadership, determining the area in which to build additional support and determining the best areas for the key supporters within the health care facility.

Employee Organizing Committees

An organizing committee can play a vital role in the campaign because its members (if they are chosen with care) enjoy a trusted relationship with their fellow employees. The professional organizer, on the other hand, is an outsider whose motives are unknown and credibility is untested.

An organizing committee customarily meets several times a week throughout the campaign. It supports the organizer in these major respects: identifying other employees who might favor the union; supplying information about potential campaign issues and about grievances, problems, and changing sentiments within the institution; evaluating the effectiveness of the union's and management's strategies; and performing the "leg work" of the campaign, such as soliciting union authorization cards and distributing handbills.

Union Authorization Card*

The typical union authorization card simply authorizes the union to act as an employee's agent for purposes of collective bargaining with the hospital.

In addition, the card serves four other important purposes. The first one is to satisfy the NLRB's 30% showing of interest requirement. In other words, the union must obtain a 30% show of interest by signed authorization cards or employees' signatures on a petition to file with

---

*Source: Reprinted from *The Union Epidemic* by Warren H. Chaney and Thomas R. Beech, with permission of Aspen Systems Corporation, © 1977.

the NLRB to hold a secret ballot election (conducted by the NLRB).

Second, the authorization cards are usually a reliable barometer of the employee sentiment within the hospital. Third, authorization cards are useful as a check on an overzealous union organizer who might forge or persuade employees to sign cards without regard to the employees' real interest in the union.

Fourth, a hospital can be ordered by the NLRB to bargain with the union, even if the union lost the election. This can happen if 50% or more of the employees have signed authorization cards *and* the employer/hospital commits serious unfair labor practices, which tend to preclude the possibility of conducting a second election.

Union Persuasion Techniques

Handbills

A familiar technique of the union organizer at an early stage of the campaign is handbill distribution. One morning, without any prior notice, the organizer will simply appear at the main employee entrance of the institution with a stack of handbills.

The typical union handbill recites the advantages of union membership and criticizes management for its insensitivity and arbitrariness. Most unions in the health care field have several standard handbills that they use in one campaign after another, but they also draft handbills to serve their needs at particular institutions. Recent studies indicate that employees are rarely persuaded by any printed propaganda. Union organizers have a right under the Federal Constitution and under Section 7 of the Taft-Hartley Act to distribute handbills peacefully on public property. But whether organizers may enter privately-owned premises without permission is a more complex issue. Generally speaking, however, a health care institution may lawfully exclude *non-employee* organizers from its parking lots and buildings; like other property owners, health care institutions are entitled to protection from trespassers. But *employees*—as distinguished from outsiders—have a statutory right to distribute handbills and engage in other forms of union solicitation on the employer's premises *on their own time*, provided that they do not interfere with the work of other employees and provided further that they restrict their activities to non-public areas of the institution.

Home Calls

A familiar tactic of the professional union organizer is the so-called "home call," a visit by the organizer to an employee's home. Many unions believe that they can express their message to an employee most convincingly in the comfort and security of his own living room. The law permits unions to engage in home call as a form of protected activity under Section 7. Although there is room for some doubt, the law appears to prohibit such home calls by management on the theory that a visit by a supervisor to an employee's home to urge him to vote against a union would be coercive, especially in the context of other anti-union conduct.

Parties and Other Entertainment

It is common for unions to woo employees with various kinds of entertainment, usually of a modest type. Employee organizing committees typically meet at restaurants and bars where the union organizer pays the bill. Beer-and-pizza parties are a familiar entertainment provided by unions for prospective members, especially young ones.

Such kinds of entertainment are lawful forms of concerted activity. When unions exceed the bounds of reasonableness, however, by making expensive gifts or offering free life insurance, the NLRB will set aside an election that the union wins on the ground that employees have been unduly influenced or even bribed to vote for the union.

Mass Meetings

The mass meeting is another old-fashioned union tactic. The meeting might be advertised through handbill distribution or by word of mouth. Typically, the program of the meeting consists of speeches by union organizers and union leaders in the community exhorting employees to join the union. It is also typical at such meetings to hear strong denunciation of the health care *institution* and its employment policies, but not of the administrators. Sophisticated union organizers are careful not to attack health care administrators by name because employees often become defensive when their supervisors are attacked as individuals.

Attendance at such meetings often, but not invariably, indicates whether the union's campaign is meeting with success. Of course, such meetings are lawful, and management must be extremely careful not to engage in surveillance of union meetings or even to give the impression that union meetings are under surveillance.

One purpose of the mass meeting is to encourage employees to sign the union's authorization card.

Demand for Recognition*

Early in a campaign the union usually will send a telegram, letter, or even the organizer in person demanding recognition as the official bargaining unit for the health care employees. This demand for recognition usually asserts that:

1. the union has been officially designated as the exclusive bargaining agent by the majority of employees in the bargaining unit,
2. the union is prepared to begin immediate bargaining with management,
3. the union is prepared to present its authorization cards to management or to a third party to validate its claim of majority representation, and
4. the employer should beware of violating its "employees" statutory rights guaranteed under the National Labor Relations Act.

The purpose in sending this demand is to seek voluntary recognition without an election. Failing that, the demand is reflected in the official petition for an election filed to initiate the National Labor Relations Board's election procedures. Usually, the hospital's labor counsel will send a standard letter to the union stating that the hospital doubts that the union represents an uncoerced majority of employees; the hospital believes that the best method for determining the true wishes of the employees is through the secret ballot; the hospital has no knowledge of the method by which the union solicited authorization cards and, thus, cannot accept their validity; and the hospital recommends that the union file an election petition with the NLRB, which has jurisdiction over such activities.

The Election*

Having failed to get management to agree voluntarily to collective bargaining, it now becomes necessary to carry the campaign toward an election. The majority of effort is spent on encouraging those that signed the cards to actually vote for the union. Inside the health care facility the prounion employees try to persuade the other employees to support the effort. Participation is the key word in a union organizing attempt. The organizers create all types of committees:

1. membership (accumulate potential members, names, groups):
2. publicity (to discuss union information within the facility);
3. distribution (mimeographing, handing out pamphlets, maintaining mailing lists, etc.);
4. strategy (works with organizer in developing tactics and strategies for the campaign effort); and
5. community (to explain the need for the union to the community and to try to get its support).

Another primary purpose for getting as many inside workers as possible on committees is to prevent management from claiming that the union activity is the result of "outside agitation," or to protect from the attack that it is the work of "a minority of disgruntled employees."

Collective Bargaining Representation

See Figure 37-1 for an outline of collective bargaining representation procedures.

Strikes and Job Actions during the Organizing Stage

Section 8(b)(7) of the Taft-Hartley Act, the so-called organizational picketing provision, is designed to provide protection to employers who are picketed by a union for the purpose of either organizing employees or demanding recognition from the employer.

Generally speaking, Section 8(b)(7) permits unions to engage in such picketing for only a short period of time (not to exceed 30 days) without filing an election petition. The employer can bring a halt to such picketing by filing an unfair labor practice charge with the NLRB, which will, in most instances, lead the NLRB to seek a federal court injunction against the picketing. Moreover, when an employer is being picketed for organizational or recognition purposes, it may also file an election petition of its own with the NLRB (a so-called "RM" petition), which—because of the picketing—will

---

*Source: Reprinted from *The Union Epidemic* by Warren H. Chaney and Thomas R. Beech, with permission of Aspen Systems Corporation, © 1977.

598 Hospital Administration Handbook

Figure 37-1 Outline of collective bargaining representation procedures

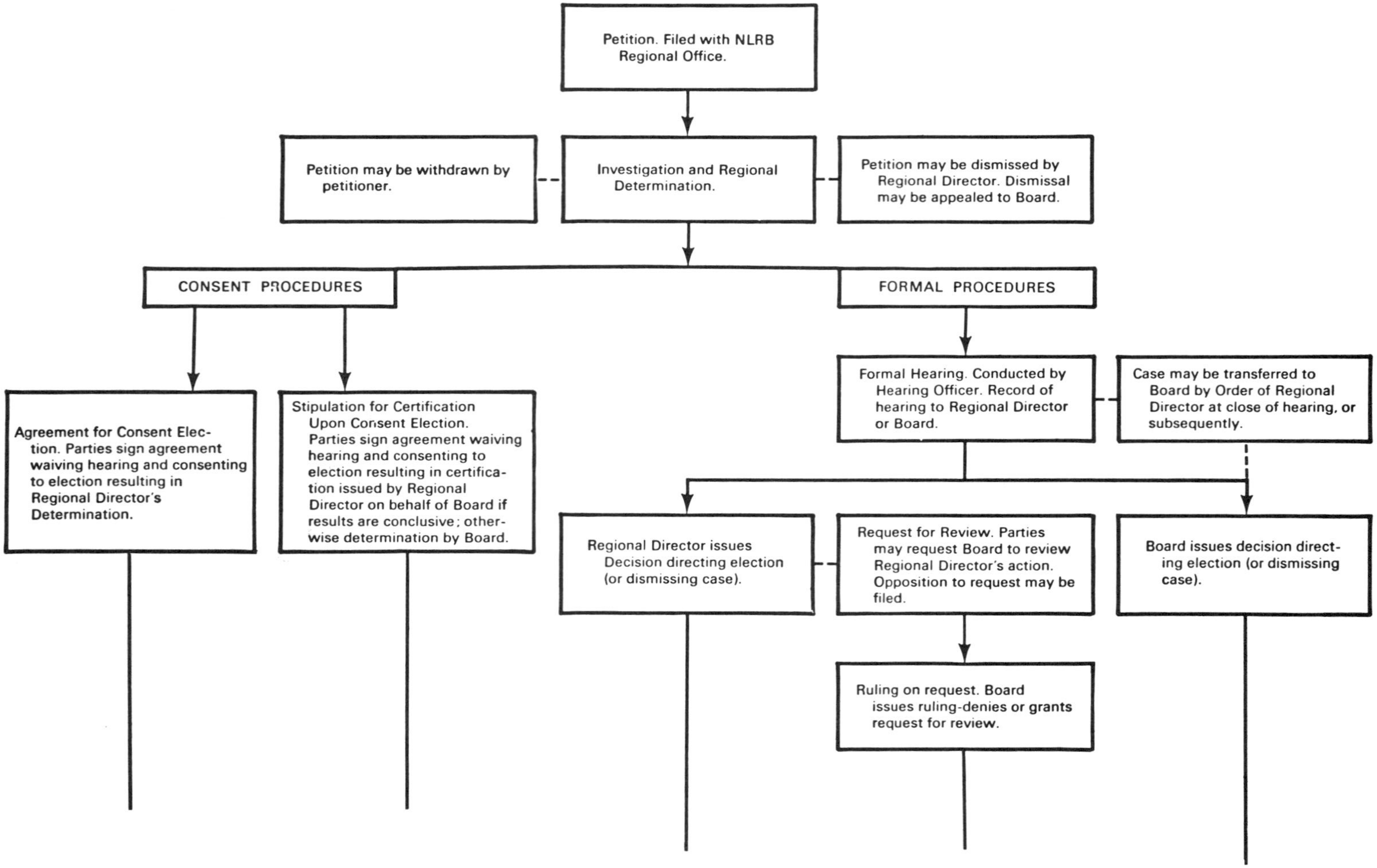

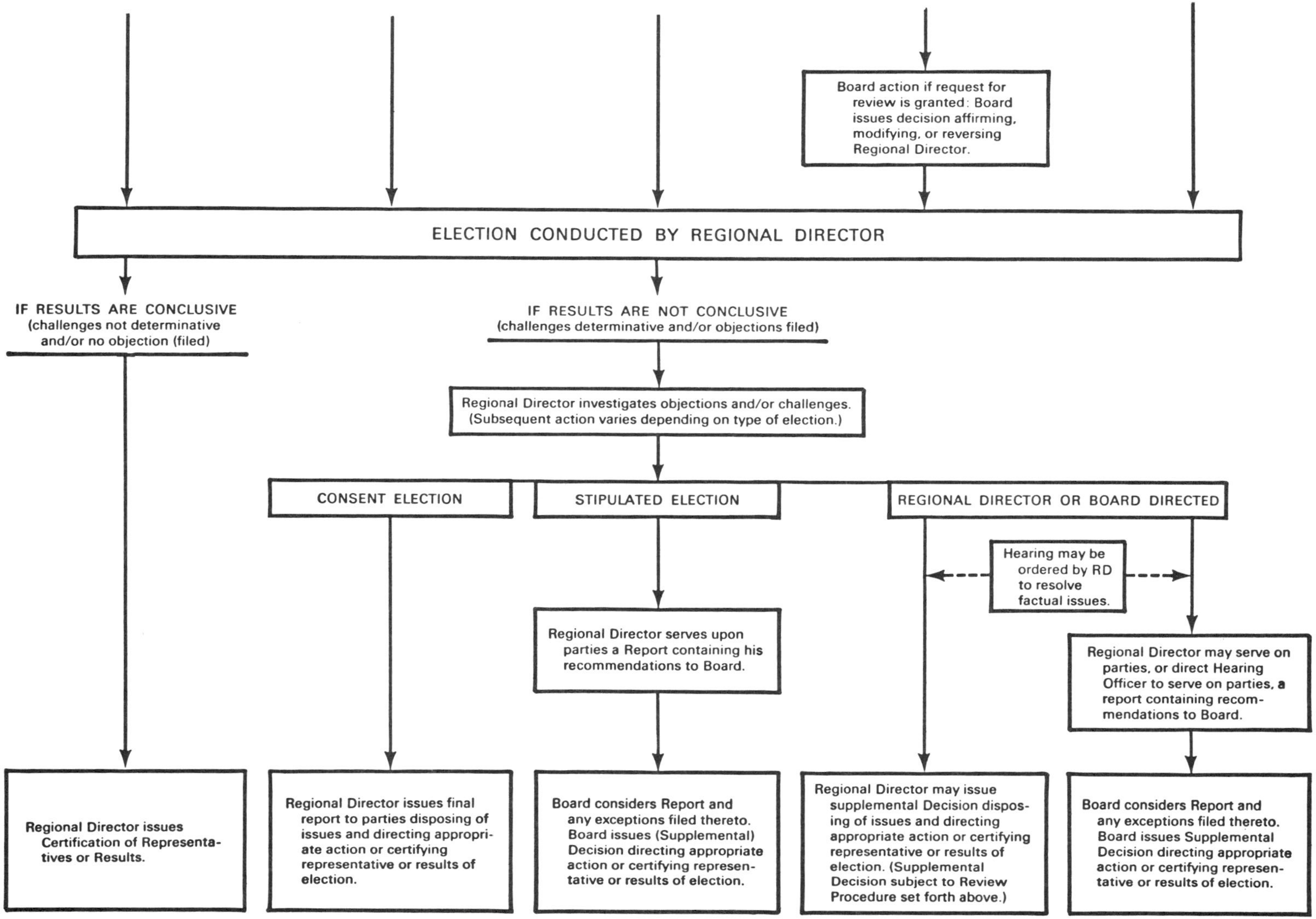

Chapter 37—Unions 599

Source: Reprinted from *The Union Epidemic* by Chaney and Beech, with permission of Aspen Systems Corporation, © 1977.

result in a "quickie" or expedited election. If a union loses such an expedited election, further picketing is strictly prohibited by Section 8(b)(7)(B).

The health care institution is legally entitled to discipline or discharge employees who engage in *misconduct* during an organizing campaign. For example, no employee—during an organizing campaign or at any other time—is immune from discipline if he physically attacks or verbally abuses a health care administrator, or persistently blocks the patients' entrance to the lobby of the institution, or disobeys orders to carry out his assignments, or the like. While discipline of union leaders during an organizing campaign will be examined by the National Labor Relations Board with particular care, employees gain no immunity from discipline by virtue of the fact that they have become active union adherents.

The distinction between "misconduct," for which employees may be disciplined during an organizing campaign, and lawful "concerted activities," for which employees may not be disciplined, is a crucial one.

Employees are entitled to engage in a work stoppage to present grievances to management. Section 7 of Taft-Hartley expressly protects the right to engage in "concerted activities," and employees may not be disciplined or discharged for exercising this statutory right. However, the federal law does not permit health service employees to conduct a protracted sit-in or sit-down demonstration or to abandon their assignments in such manner as actually to endanger the welfare of their patients.

The Union Hit List for the 1980s

Those hospitals most likely to face the greatest organizing pressure include the following:*

- federal hospitals (five times more likely to be unionized than nonfederal hospitals)
- hospitals with 500 or more beds (three times more likely to be unionized than those with less than 100 beds)
- hospitals in metropolitan areas (one-third more likely than those located in nonmetropolitan areas)

---
*Source: Paul D. Frenzen, "Survey Update: Unionization Activities." Reprinted, with permission, from *Hospitals*, published by the American Hospital Association, copyright August 1, 1978, Vol. 52, No. 15.

- hospitals in the Middle Atlantic census division (15 times more likely to be unionized than those in the East South Central States)
- hospitals in the nongovernment, not-for-profit category (since 1973 these have become unionized faster than those in the state and local government categories)
- hospitals where some union contracts already have been successfully negotiated (33 percent of union hospitals reported labor union organizing activity, as opposed to only 15 percent of the hospitals without contracts).

MANAGEMENT STRATEGIES TO OPPOSE UNIONS*

Viewpoints**

Employer's Entitlement and Strength

An employer is entitled to actively oppose unionization and may conduct a vigorous, yet lawful, campaign against the union. The employer should seize the opportunity, take the initiative and explain to the employees why they have no need for union representation.

The employer cannot threaten employees, promise and/or grant benefits or inducements, interrogate employees, discriminatorily discipline employees or engage in surveillance during the election period. Management should consult legal counsel on any such personnel policies during the campaign period.

The employer's campaign can take numerous channels. The employer may choose to communicate its views in a group meeting of employees or by a series of letters to employees regarding the employer's position.

A "straight from the shoulder" presentation is often the best approach. The employer's representative should clearly state his or her position regarding the union. This is the time to highlight such inherent union problems as dues

---
*Source: Except where noted, this section on "Management Strategies to Oppose Unions" consists of excerpts reprinted from *Health Care Labor Manual* by Martin E. Skoler, with permission of Aspen Systems Corporation, © 1981.

**Source: Reprinted from Robert W. Mulcahy and Dennis W. Rader, "Trends in Hospital Labor Relations," *Topics in Health Care Financing,* Spring 1980, with permission of Aspen Systems Corporation.

deduction, pension slush-fund reports or their constitution.

The general areas most vulnerable to employer attack are:

1. Possibility of mandatory dues deduction or fair share checkoff from employees' paychecks.
2. The purpose of the authorization cards or sheet that the union is circulating because the union may be planning to utilize these cards to establish a majority for voluntary recognition or for a bargaining order as opposed to merely signing a card to get an election.
3. Employer and its employees have always gotten along without a union, and there is no need for one now. All the union does is cost the employees money.
4. Collective bargaining will be from scratch, and the union cannot guarantee the employees anything in terms of wages, fringe benefits or contractual language items.
5. If there is a problem in the future and the employee files a grievance, the union under current law can choose which, if any, cases it processes to arbitration. The U.S. Supreme Court standard affords the union a "wide range of reasonableness" in processing grievances and in representing its members.

What Employees Want

Research findings have been remarkably consistent in identifying the employees' priorities and needs, which include:

1. fair treatment on complaints and discipline;
2. reasonable job security;
3. praise and credit for worthwhile suggestions and performance;
4. corrections and suggestions made in a constructive way;
5. merit pay increases;
6. promotion of the best-qualified workers; and
7. pay and fringe benefits equal to at least the area standard in the industry.

There are provisions in hospital contracts that are of paramount importance to employees, including employer-funded training and education to allow employees to achieve higher occupational status. Employers should take the time to enlighten themselves as to the sensitive needs of employees and should conduct in-depth studies of present personnel policies and procedures.

Unfair Labor Practices

Contrary to popular misconception, federal labor relations statutes provide wide latitude for management to oppose unions vigorously and effectively, without committing unfair labor practices or violating the integrity of the election process. Whether a health care institution wishes to oppose the unionization of its employees is a sensitive policy decision that should be made in the light of relevant considerations.

The four management unfair labor practices that pertain to the organizing stage are:

1. Interference, restraint and coercion—There are seven major types of management conduct that are proscribed: 1. violence, 2. espionage, 3. surveillance, 4. threats, 5. promises of benefit, 6. interrogation, and 7. interference with the right of employees to communicate with each other.

2. Assistance to or domination of a labor organization—To protect the integrity of unions management may not assist a union's organizing efforts by giving it money, free office space, free legal counsel, information about employees or the like. It may not permit professional organizers of one union to enjoy ready access to the institution's premises, while barring a second union's organizers.

3. Discrimination to discourage or encourage union membership—The classic example of "discrimination to discourage" union membership is the discharge of a leading union adherent shortly after management becomes aware of his role in an organizing campaign. Equally illegal types of discrimination to discourage union activity are: closing a facility to avoid union activity; blacklisting union adherents; demoting union adherents; reducing wages or fringe benefits; withdrawing traditional overtime opportunities; supervising employees more strictly than has been customary; increasing the severity of penalties for minor employment offenses; and withholding wage increases that had been promised before the organizing campaign began.

It is equally illegal to discriminate against employees *to encourage* union membership by tak-

What Can a Hospital Do during a Union Election Campaign?

DO	DON'T
State your opposition to a union.	Promise wage increases, better jobs or other benefits if employees vote against a union. Neither can you threaten loss of benefits if the union wins.
List existing benefits given to employees without payment of union dues so long as there is no expressed or implied promise or threat.	Say that the hospital won't recognize or bargain with the union even if it wins.
Note financial obligations imposed by unions (dues, initiation fees, etc.).	Make statements whose general tone constitutes a threat to the economic welfare of the employees.
Answer union's charges.	Make "captive-audience" speeches to employees less than 24 hours before the election.
Detail risks (strikes, loss of wages, etc.) involved in being represented by a union so long as you do not appear to say that a strike is inevitable if the union wins.	Say that the hospital will close or that a strike is inevitable if the union wins.
Say that national union decisions affecting employees are not made by local employees but by higher officials far removed from the local area.	Show movies depicting strikes, crime, and violence where such a movie is part of a general campaign suggesting that these occurrences are the necessary result of unionism.
Point out that employees who signed union representation cards may vote against the union because the election is by secret vote.	Make statements involving a substantial departure from the truth so late in the campaign that the union won't be able to answer them.
Say that the hospital has the right to hire replacements in case of a strike (provided that you do not suggest the inevitability of a strike).	Call employees into a supervisor's or foreman's office or away from their usual place of work to talk to them about a union.
Call attention to employees' right to ignore a union.	Question employees about their union activity.

ing hostile action against employees who decline to support a union favored by the employer or by granting benefits to employees who agree to support the union favored by management. It is illegal, for example, for management to deny a promotion because an employee failed to join a union favored by management in an organizing campaign.

4. Discrimination against an employee because he filed charges or gave testimony under the Labor Act—This is a rarely used prohibition, intended to protect employee *access* to the NLRB. An employer may not retaliate against an employee who has either filed unfair labor practice charges or given testimony which the employer does not like by engaging in any form of discrimination in the terms or conditions of employment.

Management Communications

Most employees make up their minds in a campaign on the basis of factors that predispose them to favor or oppose unions and, moreover, that most employees pay only scant attention to literature circulated by either labor or management. Notwithstanding these data, employers (as well as unions) traditionally circulate letters and other communications to influence the voters.

Other tactics, especially informal small group discussions led by immediate supervisors, are probably far more effective. However, it would be a mistake for health service managers to overlook the potential value of literature and speeches to achieve three specific, tactical objectives: 1. to make known management's attitude toward unionization; 2. to educate workers about the mechanics of the election process and the realities of the collective bargaining process; and 3. to inform workers about the negative facets of the union and its record, which would otherwise never surface.

(1.) The Opening Letter

Management's first communication to employees usually occurs shortly after it is convinced that the union is to be taken seriously, and this may occur long before the union files an election petition with the NLRB. The purpose of an opening letter is to let employees know that management is opposed to unionization, to urge employees to be extremely cautious about signing a union authorization card, and to assure employees that federal law protects them from the coercion and harassment of union organizers.

(2.) The Pre-election Speech or Question and Answer Session

Several days before the election, but *not* within 24 hours of the scheduled commencement of the election, management typically calls a meeting of employees eligible to vote in order to make a final plea for them to vote "NO." Commonly this meeting, which is held on the institution's premises, is billed as a "Question and Answer Session," for it is important that the institution deal forthrightly and accurately with questions invariably arising during a campaign.

(3.) The Final Letter

Near the end of the campaign, it may be advisable to send a letter to each employee. In the case of a married employee, it may be especially significant to send this letter home so that his or her spouse may also read it. Often the employee's husband or wife may manage the family finances and have strong feelings about the impact any potential work stoppages may have on the family's well-being.

The final letter should be short enough so that it can be quickly read and understood, but long enough and strong enough in tone to leave no doubt whatever about where management stands and why.

Script for Question and Answer Session with Employees during an Organizing Campaign

I have asked you to come to this meeting today so that I might answer several questions which employees have been asking about the election that is going to be held very soon. We hope that when you vote, you will be very well informed:

1. Q. *When will the election be held?*
   A. _____ (day), _____ (hours), _____ (place).

2. Q. *Who will be allowed to vote?*
   A. The National Labor Relations Board has ruled that the following employees are eligible to vote:
   _____

3. Q. *What will the election actually be like?*
   A. The election will be conducted by an agent of the National Labor Relations Board, which is a federal agency. He will hand you a secret ballot. Then, in complete secrecy and privacy, you can mark your ballot "yes" or "no." No one will know how you have voted—*not* the union, *not* your fellow employees, *not* your employer and *not* the government.

4. Q. *If I have signed a union card, do I have an obligation to vote for the union?*
   A. Absolutely no. You are perfectly free to vote against the union even if you signed a union authorization card. No one will ever know how you cast your secret ballot. Even if you have told a union organizer that you would vote for the union, it is your legal right to vote "NO."

5. Q. *How does the hospital (or nursing home, medical center, etc.) feel about the union?*
   A. Frankly, we hope you will vote against the union. Now we know that the union organizer has made big promises to you. But union organizers are like used car salesmen: they are very good at making promises, but whether the promises are any good is something you'll have to decide for yourself.

   We believe that you will have greater freedom, more job security and more personal dignity without a union. The union is an outsider that does not really know you, and it does not really care about you or your family or your job.

   But the hospital *does* care. We hired each of you because we believed in you. We believed that you would do your work with a lot of skill and a lot of pride, and we have faith in you. We have tried to make this a good place for you to work. And we want it to become better. We don't need outsiders—strangers—to help make this an even better place to work and to make your job more rewarding.

   It is your right under the law to be represented by a union or *not* to be represented by

Question and Answer Session   continued

a union. I think you will be better off without a union, and I urge you to vote "NO."

6. Q. *Will things change a lot if employees vote the union in?*

   A. Yes, things could change in many ways if the union comes in. A big change would be that the hospital could no longer deal with you on an individual basis. You should still come to us as an individual, but if we decided to make changes we would have to check with the union first. We would have to go through the union in order to make any changes in your wages, hours and working conditions. At other hospitals, experience shows that things become much more formal when a union comes in. We just wouldn't be free to work things out between us. Many things would be regulated by the contract.

7. Q. *What will the employees get if they vote for the union? Will they get more money and better benefits?*

   A. I know the union has made promises, but remember that promises are cheap. What can the union actually deliver?

   No matter what it promises, *the truth is that the union can't guarantee you anything.* No one knows what the outcome of collective bargaining negotiations will be. You may get more than you now enjoy, but you may get less. No one knows.

   The law does *not* require the hospital to agree to any of the union's proposals. And the hospital will not agree to any proposal which is unwise or contrary to the best interests of our employees and patients.

   What we do know is this: the union does not pay your wages. The hospital does. The union does not pay for your vacations, your health insurance, your holidays or for the other benefits that you have now. The hospital does.

8. Q. *If the union comes in, will I have to join the union and pay dues?*

   A. That depends on the contract which the hospital and the union agree on. Unions usually want something called a "union shop" agreement. Under such an agreement, every employee would have to join the union and pay dues to it every single month. If an employee doesn't pay his dues or other union fees, the hospital would have to fire him.

   Frankly, we don't think that anyone ought to be compelled to pay dues and fees to a union in order to work here. But, if the union comes in, that may be one of the things we'll all have to live with. Furthermore, under a union shop contract, the union itself decides how much its monthly dues will be. And there is nothing the hospital can do about it, regardless of the rate that the union sets.

9. Q. *What about strikes? Will we have to go on strike if we vote for the union?*

   A. I hope that none of you will ever go on strike against the hospital. But you must be realistic. The fact is that unions have called strikes against hospitals and nursing homes. When that happens, it's not like a strike against a factory. In a hospital strike, the patients always suffer. It is sometimes necessary to evacuate them to other institutions during a strike and to close the hospital down.

   Strikes are not inevitable. But they occur. There have been a number of long, bitter hospital strikes around the country.

10. Q. *If I go on strike, will I get paid by the hospital? Will I lose my job?*

    A. No one gets paid to strike. Your income from the hospital, of course, would come to an end if you engage in a strike.

    You do not normally lose your job because you go on strike, if it is a lawful strike. But the hospital has the legal right to maintain its operations during a strike, and it also has the right to hire permanent replacements to fill the jobs of the strikers. If that occurs, the strikers who have been replaced are not entitled to their old jobs back automatically when the strike finally ends.

11. Q. *What will happen if we vote against the union? Will our wages go up and will we get improved benefits?*

    A. Here are the facts. It is illegal for the hospital to make any promises during a union organizing campaign to raise wages and improve benefits. But this hospital for many years has had a policy of improving wages and benefits on a regular basis. This policy will continue. We want you to enjoy your work at the hospital, to take pride in what you do, to feel secure in your job. We want to make this a really good place for you to work. I think we can do that *together*, without an outside organization.

    Let me conclude by urging each of you to vote in the election. It is your right to decide this matter by secret ballot. I urge you to vote, and to vote "NO."

The Significant Role of Supervisors

What can higher level supervisors effectively do? Administrators who have not had regular contact with employees should not drastically change their pattern of behavior during an organizing campaign. To do so would arouse employee suspicions. Administrators should gradually increase their contacts with employees, especially those with whom they enjoy a positive relationship.

In such contacts administrators would be well-advised not to talk about union issues. Instead, it is usually more effective, and legally safer, to talk about general matters with the objective of creating a friendly and supportive mood in the institution.

It is a good tactic for a respected, credible administrator to hold a question-and-answer session devoted solely to the election near the end of the campaign.

A *fundamental* strategy followed by most management professionals at the outset of a campaign is to enlist first-level supervisors in the effort to oppose the union. They have not only the most frequent contact with employees, but probably the most influence over employees' attitudes toward unionism.

What can first-level supervisors effectively do? They are permitted by the law to discuss the possible impact of unionism on the institution *informally* and in noncoercive ways with employees at their work stations.

In addition to engaging on management's behalf in "soft voiced," informal campaigning in small group discussions, supervisors can also engage in *surveys* of employee sentiment. Without undertaking illegal interrogation or polling, first-level supervisors can usually make an accurate estimate of employee sentiment toward the union.

Key Points for Supervisors in a Union Organizing Drive*

1. More employees vote for or against their immediate supervisor than for or against top management, the board of trustees, or consultants.
2. Unions rarely organize employees; rather, it is administration's poor record in employee relations that drives employees into unions.
3. Institutions that provide all the benefits and conditions of the union shop will not become unionized.
4. There is a marked relationship between worker morale and the extent to which employees feel their boss is interested in discussing work problems with their work group. If the boss—*that's you!*—is not interested, workers will discuss those problems with outside groups—*in some cases, unions.*
5. Employees who feel group loyalty and pride do not look outside to unions for need fulfillment.
6. Improved managerial practices and the supervisor's attention to the best utilization of people and technology can increase job satisfaction and productivity. *Satisfied and fulfilled employees do not look to unions.*
7. Unions are looking for bona fide issues to use in the organizing drive. Although they will latch on to petty gripes and perceived injustices, they often look for supervisors who are vulnerable. Such supervisors are usually not employee-centered, have not built up group loyalty, and are not interested in employee needs.
8. Labor unions capitalize on management mistakes.
9. You should not threaten employees or promise them any reward for staying out of the union. Do not interrogate them about their preferences during a union organizing drive. These are unfair labor practices.
10. You can tell employees how the institution feels about unionization. You can share with them the employee disadvantages of belonging to a union.
11. You cannot call employees away from their work areas into your office in order to urge them to vote against the union.
12. You should tell employees that they do not have to sign union authorization cards or speak to union organizers if they do not so desire.
13. You should inform employees that even though they have signed a union authori-

---

*Source: Reprinted from *The Health Care Supervisor's Handbook* by Norman Metzger, with permission of Aspen Systems Corporation, © 1978.

zation card, *they can change their mind and vote any way they wish at the time of an election.*
14. You should encourage each member of your department who is in the bargaining unit (those employees eligible to vote) to actually cast a ballot in the election.
15. You should continue to enforce all rules and regulations in effect prior to the union's request for recognition.
16. You should keep top management apprised of day-to-day developments during the union organizing campaign. You will be the person closest to the employees at that time. Your perception of trends is critical to administration planning.
17. Recent statistics indicate that unions win only 47 percent of elections in the health care industry. This is a reversal of earlier statistics obtained during the first year of the industry's coverage under the Taft-Hartley Act. The reversal indicates a more sophisticated and concerned management approach toward employee needs.

A Model Management Proposal for a Union Agreement

Management Rights

The Union recognizes that the Hospital has the obligation of serving the public with the highest quality efficient and economical medical care and in meeting medical emergencies.

The Hospital and the Union further agree that the provisions of this Agreement shall be expressly limited to wages, hours and working conditions of Employees, and no provisions shall be construed to restrain the Hospital from the management of its operations. The Hospital retains the sole right to manage the Hospital, which right shall include, but shall not be limited to, the right to determine the size and composition of the work force, the right to determine medical and patient care standards and methods, the staffing pattern or patterns, the areas to be worked, the quantity and type of equipment to be used, the operation of such equipment, the manning requirements and speed of such equipment on any job; to determine the time for work, the work to be performed, the method and place of performing work, including the right to determine that the Hospital's workforce shall not perform certain work, the schedules of work and of work breaks; to fix, alter, modify or change standards of quality and/or quantity of work to be done; to determine whether any part or the whole of its operations shall continue to operate; to alter, combine, or abolish any job classification or service; to contract out work, to maintain order and efficiency; to determine the duties of employees; to discharge probationary employees for any reason whatsoever; to hire, to lay off, to assign, to transfer, to demote, to discharge Employees, to determine the qualifications of Employees; to promote Employees; to determine the starting and quitting time, overtime, and the number of hours to be worked; and the Hospital also retains all other rights and prerogatives including those exercised unilaterally in the past, subject only to such regulations and restrictions governing the exercise of these rights as are expressly provided in this Agreement. All matters covered by this particular paragraph shall not be subject to the grievance and arbitration provisions of this Agreement.

The Hospital also retains the right to promulgate, enforce and periodically modify written rules and regulations, not in conflict with the expressed provisions of this Agreement, as it may from time-to-time deem best for the purposes of maintaining order, discipline, safety, and/or effective operation of the Hospital and, after advance notice thereof to the Union and the Employees, to require compliance therewith by Employees. It is recognized that the Union reserves the right to question the reasonableness of these rules or regulations issued pursuant to this particular paragraph through the grievance procedure within the time limits set forth in such procedure after receipt of a copy of such rules and regulations, but the effectuation of such written Hospital rules and regulations shall not be stayed pending grievance or arbitration procedures.

The Hospital also retains the right to discipline and/or discharge Employees for insubordination, absenteeism or tardiness, violations of Hospital rules and regulations, and for just cause; provided that, in the exercise of this right, the Hospital will not act in violation of the expressed terms of this Agreement. Complaints that the Hospital has violated this paragraph may be taken up through the grievance procedure.

No Strike, No Lockouts

The Hospital agrees that so long as this Agreement is in effect there shall be no lockouts. The Union agrees that there shall be no strikes, sit-downs, slowdowns, stoppages of work, boycotts, mass sick days, or any similar interference with the operation of the Hospital or any other unlawful acts that interfere with the Hospital's operations. In the event there is a breach of this Article, the Hospital need not resort to the grievance and arbitration provisions of this Agreement, but may pursue any legal remedy. Furthermore, if there is any violation of this Article, the Hospital may take disciplinary action, including discharge.

Grievance Procedure

In the event of any controversy concerning the meaning, application or alleged violation of any provision of this Agreement, not expressly excluded from grievance procedures, such controversy shall be treated as a grievance and shall be settled, if at all possible, by the following procedure. No grievance shall be filed or processed based upon facts or events which have occurred more than three (3) working days before the grievance is filed. Failure of the Hospital to respond to a grievance within the time limits prescribed shall automatically refer the grievance to the next step in the grievance procedure. Any grievance not carried to the next step by the Union or Employee within the prescribed time limits shall be automatically closed on the basis of the last disposition. Grievances shall be settled in the following manner:

STEP 1. Between the Employee and the Supervisor, with the Employee being accompanied by his delegate, if he so desires. If the grievance is not disposed of within three (3) working days, it shall be reduced to writing in duplicate by the Employee and one copy shall be given to the Hospital and one copy to the union.

STEP 2. Within forty-eight (48) hours after the response by the Hospital or the end of the three (3) day response period provided in STEP 1, the written grievance (which shall state the date of the original complaint) shall be taken up by the Personnel Director and the Union's Business Agent. If the complaint is not disposed of within three (3) working days, then, within forty-eight (48) hours the Union shall have the option of taking the matter to arbitration.

No grievance or grievance processing shall interfere with the work of the Hospital.

Arbitration

In the event any grievance has not been adjusted or resolved by the end of STEP 2 above, then the Union may refer the matter to arbitration pursuant to the rules of the Federal Mediation and Conciliation Service. Any grievance not so referred within five (5) days after the end of STEP 2 shall be deemed abandoned and nonarbitrable. The parties agree that the only remedy for breach of this Agreement, unless specifically provided elsewhere, is through the instant grievance and arbitration provisions, and that the decision of the arbitrator, meeting the requirements of this Article, is final and binding on all of the parties. The expense of the Arbitrator shall be shared equally between the Union and the Hospital. Each party shall be fully responsible for all other expenses it incurs for such arbitration. The powers of the Arbitrator shall be limited as follows:

1. The Arbitrator shall have no power to add to, delete from, or modify any of the terms of this Agreement nor to rule on any matter except while this Agreement is in full force and effect.
2. The Arbitrator shall have no power to establish language for this Agreement, wage scale rates on new or changed jobs, or to change any wage rates or fringe benefits.
3. The Arbitrator shall have no authority to impose any obligation upon the Hospital unless clearly required by an express provision of this Agreement.
4. The Hospital in no event shall be required to pay back wages for more than three (3) working days prior to the date a written grievance is filed. In the case of a pay shortage which the Employee could not have been aware of before receiving his or her pay, any adjustment shall be retroactive to the beginning of the pay period covered by such pay, if the Employee files his or her grievance within three (3) working days after receipt of such pay.
5. All claims for back wages shall be limited to the amount of wages the Employee otherwise would have earned less any unem-

ployment compensation or compensation for personal services that he may have received or could with diligent effort have received from any source during the period in question.

COLLECTIVE BARGAINING

Management Roles*

The Labor Relations or Personnel Director

It is essential that one person in the institution be fixed with the responsibility to supervise, guide, and monitor overall policy and strategy in relations with the union, especially with respect to the labor agreement.

This person—whether he is the personnel director, labor relations director, or other administrator—should know the background and current status of each pending grievance. He should also have detailed knowledge of the contract's history. In other words, he should know as much as possible about the entire contract. It is he to whom the first-level supervisor should turn for advice, and it is he who should have responsibility for reporting to higher management serious problems.

The Administrator or Top Management

Except in unusual circumstances, the institution's top management should not be directly involved in labor contract administration. While top management should be fully informed of the status of grievances, arbitration cases, and other labor matters, the conduct of day-to-day labor relations should be left to the institution's labor relations professionals.

It may be tempting for the chief administrator to intervene in a particularly important grievance case by using his personal prestige to effect a settlement with the union, but this temptation should be resisted. The risks of such interventions are twofold: first, the union will instantly assume that the personnel director or labor relations director has been by-passed and found wanting; and, second, in the future the union will itself attempt to ignore the grievance procedure in favor of trying to reach an agreement directly with top management.

If the institution has chosen its personnel or labor relations representatives with care, it should give them wide discretion and flexibility to act on the institution's behalf.

Supervisors

Management should act promptly after a contract becomes effective to ensure that its own representatives—especially first and second line supervisors—understand its significant aspects.

Good training is the most sensible way to ensure that supervisors will know when to act independently and when to seek guidance.

Training of the supervisor, at a minimum, should include instructions about how to respond to grievances filed with him. Under the typical collective bargaining agreement, all grievances by the union are first filed with him. He must be careful to note whether the union has observed the contract's time limits, and he must respond to the union within the contract's time limitations. His training should also prepare him to reply to a grievance with such clarity that there can be no doubt about the institution's position. Any defect in the union's handling of the grievance should be expressly noted because, if the grievance is carried to arbitration, the institution's defenses may be limited to those set forth by the first-level supervisor in his initial response to the grievance.

Impasse Resolution Procedures*

Presently, there are three basic procedures used in the health care industry to peacefully resolve impasses that occur in bargaining situations: (1) mediation; (2) factfinding; and (3) binding interest arbitration.

Mediation

Mediation is the first possible step leading toward the resolution of an impasse reached during collective bargaining. It is also the mildest form of third-party intervention in the bargaining process. Mediation is generally welcomed and accepted by the disputing parties because

---

*Source: Reprinted from *Health Care Labor Manual* by Martin E. Skoler, with permission of Aspen Systems Corporation, © 1981.

*Source: Reprinted from *Arbitration in Health Care* by Donald J. Petersen, Julius Rezler, and Keith A. Reed, with permission of Aspen Systems Corporation, © 1981.

the resulting settlement, if any, is reached by the parties themselves (through the help of the mediator) and is not forced upon them by an outside neutral party.

Although, at least in principle, mediation may be performed by any person selected and trusted by the parties, in practice this function usually is performed by commissioners of the Federal Mediation and Conciliation Service (FMCS) Independent federal agency of considerable reputation.

Under the 1974 health care amendments, whenever a bargaining dispute involves health care employees, mediation becomes mandatory. Parties to a dispute in the health care industry must notify FMCS and the state mediation agency 60 days prior to the expiration date of their contract. During this 60-day period, mediation becomes *mandatory,* in contrast to other industries covered by the NLRA where mediation is *voluntary*. In an initial bargaining situation, the union that became the bargaining agent must give to FMCS and the appropriate state mediation agency a 30-day notice of the existence of a dispute. During this 60-day or 30-day period, the parties must participate in the mediation process, or be subject to charges of unfair labor practice.

The following were conditions under which mediation proved to be most effective in resolving impasses:

(1) the negotiators—especially the union negotiators—lacked experience; (2) the negotiations process broke down because one of the parties was overcommitted to a particular position; (3) a dispute was below average in intensity or difficulty, that is, the magnitude and number of sources of impasse were relatively small; (4) the parties were motivated to reach a settlement; and (5) an aggressive, experienced and high-quality (as perceived by the parties) mediator was involved. On the other hand, mediation was least successful in situations (1) where the underlying dispute arose because of an employer's inability to pay; (2) where the parties had a history of going to impasse and to the later stages of the dispute-resolution procedure; and (3) where the jurisdiction was among the largest.

Managers and union officers in the health care industry may promote successful mediation by furnishing the following vital information to the mediator: (1) the history of relations between the parties; (2) the stress-points existing in their present relationship; (3) the priority of the issues at impasse; and (4) the identity of each party's spokesperson(s).

Obviously mediation will be short and successful primarily in those situations where mediation was preceded by hard bargaining and, as a result, the positions of the parties became narrow enough to be reconciled through the efforts of a skillful and sensitive mediator.

Factfinding

Factfinding is a second method of impasse resolution in collective bargaining. In this method the alleged facts surrounding a dispute over the terms and conditions of employment are presented by the negotiators to a neutral third party for investigation and possible recommendations.

Before the passage of the 1974 Amendments, factfinding had been used in the nongovernment sector of the health care industry on a voluntary basis. However, the Amendments made factfinding mandatory, at the discretion of the FMCS director. First, the parties are required to give FMCS timely notice (60 days prior to the expiration date of their contract) of a potential dispute. Second, the Director of FMCS is empowered to appoint an impartial Board of Inquiry (BOI) if, in his or her opinion, "a threatened or actual strike or lockout affecting a health care institution will, if permitted to occur or continue, substantially interrupt the delivery of health care in the locality concerned." Such a BOI must be appointed not more than 30 days from the date of the notice filed by the parties.

If and when a BOI is selected, it is required to investigate the issues involved in the dispute and make a written report containing the finding of facts and its recommendations for settling the dispute—all within 15 days after its appointment. However, the recommendations of a BOI are not binding on either party.

Presently, the Director of the FMCS relies on two criteria in determining whether or not to appoint a BOI: (1) threat or existence of a strike that would cause a health care crisis in the community; and (2) the status of the collective bargaining involved.

Under new regulations, FMCS may defer to the parties' own factfinding or interest arbitration procedure, rather than appoint a BOI. This new FMCS policy is based on the fact that in a number of bargaining situations the parties have long established their own private factfinding or interest arbitration procedures, usually in their pre-election agreement. The new regulations allow FMCS to establish a written policy of deferral so long as such private impasse resolution procedures meet the following conditions:

1. The factfinding procedure must be invoked automatically at a specified time (for example, at contract expiration if no agreement is reached).
2. It must provide a fixed and determinate method for selecting the impartial factfinder.
3. It must provide that there can be no strike or lockout and no charges in conditions of employment (except by mutual agreement) prior to and during the factfinding procedure and for a period of at least seven days after the factfinding is completed.
4. It must provide that the factfinder(s) will make a written report to the parties, containing the findings of fact and any recommendations for settling the dispute, a copy of which is sent to FMCS.

In case of a deferral to interest arbitration, an additional condition is set by FMCS: that the award must be final and binding on both parties. In both private factfinding and interest arbitration, both parties should jointly submit a copy of their agreed-upon private procedure to the appropriate regional office of FMCS as early as possible.

Thus far, less than three percent of all bargaining situations required the appointment of a BOI or factfinder under stipulation.

Interest Arbitration

Interest arbitration is potentially the final phase of the bargaining process in the health care industry. Furthermore, it is the impasse resolution procedure through which a third party exerts the greatest impact on the contractual relationship of the negotiating parties. Obviously in only a small fraction of the bargaining situations will the parties submit their dispute to interest arbitration, as it allows a third party to make a binding determination of those contract terms over which the parties reached an impasse. Thus, interest arbitration constitutes a "court of last resort" for the bargaining parties.

The only major similarity between interest arbitration and grievance arbitration is the binding nature of the award delivered by a neutral third party. There are, however, numerous differences between these two:

1. Grievance arbitration and interest arbitration differ in their functional role. While grievance arbitration performs a quasi-judicial function, interest arbitration is held to legislate the terms of employment.
2. An interest arbitration case is more important to the parties than a grievance arbitration case. The outcome of the former will affect the relationship between the parties for the duration of their contract—that is, for two or three years. On the other hand, in a grievance case, particularly a discipline case, the award will have only a rather isolated effect on industrial relations between the parties.
3. Arbitrators called on to decide interest arbitration cases should have qualifications that are different from those required in grievance arbitration. Interest arbitrators should be able to deal effectively with economic and financial matters. Grievance arbitrators are usually trained in the law and are equipped for contract interpretations.
4. Hearing an interest arbitration case may take longer than a typical grievance case; therefore, the former are more time-consuming and costly.

Arbitration*

Why Arbitration Is Used So Widely

Arbitration has proved to be enormously acceptable to both hospital administrators and unions. According to a recent national survey of 817 hospital collective bargaining agreements, 87.9 percent provided for binding arbitration of at least some issues, and an additional 4.4 percent had provisions for advisory arbitration. (See Table 37-1 for ranked listing of the most frequently arbitrated issues.)

---

*Source: Reprinted from *Arbitration in Health Care* by Donald J. Petersen, Julius Rezler, and Keith A. Reed, with permission of Aspen Systems Corporation, © 1981.

Table 37-1 Most Frequently Arbitrated Issues (1978)

Rank	Issue	Rank	Issue
1	Discipline and discharge	12	Scheduling of work
2	Seniority	13	Job posting and bidding
3	Arbitrability	14	Job evaluation
4	Overtime	15	Health and welfare
5	Work assignment	16	Reporting, call-in and call-back pay
6	Job classification		
7	Pay	17	Wage issues
8	Scope of agreement	18	Working conditions, including safety
9	Management's rights		
10	Holidays and holiday pay	19	Incentive rate or standards
11	Vacations and vacation pay	20	Discrimination

Source: The Federal Mediation and Conciliation Service (FMCS).

There are several very good reasons why arbitration clauses appear in so many contracts, both within and outside the health care area.

1. *Arbitration is a voluntary process.* In most instances, arbitration is not a compulsory process. This means that the parties have control over whether and how often they resort to arbitration. No law states that arbitration must be in a collective agreement. Such clauses are included in these agreements because the parties think they will be mutually beneficial. If arbitration does not meet the parties' expectations, they can always negotiate it out.

2. *Arbitration is a substitute for a strike.* The inclusion of an arbitration clause in a collective agreement may persuade a union to refrain from work stoppages during the term of the bargaining agreement. A national survey of hospital contracts revealed that three-quarters of these contracts had some type of no-strike (no lockout) provision. A no-strike agreement assures a hospital of relative labor peace for the duration of the contract. For a union it means that the hospital will submit to binding arbitration all grievances that cannot be resolved at lower steps in the grievance procedure.

3. *Arbitration is a less costly and less time-consuming process than its alternatives.* Essentially there are three basic ways to resolve a grievance over which the parties are deadlocked: (a) the union can resort to a strike; (b) the matter can be submitted to the courts; or (c) the grievance can be settled through arbitration. Imagine having to face the possibility of a strike for each grievance that came along!

Strategic Aspects of Arbitration

The decision to arbitrate is initially a union decision. This is because a hospital has the option of denying a grievance at the last grievance step before arbitration. This gives the union three choices: (1) do nothing, which can and often is interpreted by the contract to bar the grievant/union from contesting the claim further; (2) agree to the hospital's position, which settles the grievance; or (3) appeal the grievance to arbitration. Of course, the hospital can forestall arbitration by capitulating to the union's position by compromise, or by challenging the arbitrability of the grievance.

In a study of 400 arbitration awards it was found that almost one arbitration case in four (23.5 percent) was brought to arbitration by unions primarily for political or strategic reasons. Some of the most important reasons for arbitration were:

- to maintain union membership and improve morale
- to support the position and status of the union steward
- to harass supervision for strategic reasons
- impact of the Taft-Hartley Act (NLRA)
- to avoid the issue of race and/or religion
- to use the arbitrator as a scapegoat
- reaction to intraunion factional rivalries

Criteria Used in Selecting Arbitrators

Although parties prefer to appoint arbitrators with whom they are familiar, the limited availability of such persons requires that parties consider arbitrators who have not handled cases for them previously. On the basis of a study of 26 labor and management representatives regularly involved in the task of selecting arbitrators the relative importance of selection criteria ranked as follows: 1) experience; 2) issue in the case; 3) the party's familiarity with the arbitrator; 4) arbitrator's legal background; 5) arbitrator's early availability; 6) arbitrator's nonlegal background; 7) arbitrator's geographic proximity to the dispute; and 8) arbitrator's fee.

Arbitrators come primarily from the professions of law, labor economics, industrial engineering, and the clergy. Approximately 60 percent of all arbitrators are lawyers. There is a tendency for lawyers to be chosen for quasilegal issues such as arbitrability, subcontracting, and admissibility of evidence. Economists are often preferred for interest disputes, and industrial engineers are preferred for job evaluation, time study, and wage incentive cases. Employers usually look with favor on an arbitrator with industrial labor relations experience, whereas union advocates tend to prefer professors and members of the clergy. Both sides agree, however, that background is perhaps not as important as integrity, wisdom, and ability to reason through to a justifiable result.

Factors Influencing Arbitrator Decisions

Two primary factors ultimately affect the arbitrator's decision: (1) subjective factors such as values, biases, and predilections; and (2) objective factors such as the basic rules of contract interpretation. Normally the subjective factors are subordinated to the objective ones, but when there is a conflict in objective standards of contract interpretation, arbitrators' values may determine which arbitration standards they prefer over others.

The standards by which arbitrators interpret collective agreements provide the reader with most of the objective criteria arbitrators use in making decisions. These criteria are summarized below:

1. Specific language prevails over general language.
2. Clear and unambiguous language prevails over past practice or any other standards.
3. Role of past practice.
4. Role of precedent.
5. Role of precontract negotiations.
6. The *de minimis* rule.

1. Specific Language Prevails Over General Language

In most hospital agreements arbitrators normally are bound to limit themselves to consideration of the contract language. If the contract speaks to a particular issue, the arbitrator will look first to determine whether there is *specific* language covering the problem—that is, language that is "clear, unambiguous, or exact." If such language exists in the contract, the arbitrator must go no further. Of course, sometimes specific language can be ambiguous. In situations where this occurs, the arbitrator must look for other standards of contract interpretation.

2. Clear and Unambiguous Language Prevails Over Any Interpretation of a Standard

This standard of contract interpretation is undoubtedly the most persuasive of the six. It is so compelling that violation of it constitutes the primary reason for vacating arbitration awards. Arbitrators owe their fidelity to the collective agreement. They must not change the existing language, or alter or modify it in any way. To do so risks having their awards set aside by the courts.

3. Role of Past Practice

The importance of past practice must be kept in proper perspective. In contract interpretation, past practice should never supersede clear and unambiguous language.

It is a proper standard when: (1) the language in the agreement is too general, vague, or ambiguous to be applied to a specific issue, or (2) there is no language in the agreement covering the situation.

In the latter case, hospital management often will assert it has an unfettered right to make the final decision. This contention may not be persuasive, however, where the benefit is a relatively important one and the union can demonstrate that a practice exists.

Of course, it is one thing to assert that a past practice exists and another thing to prove it. Some of the criteria for determining whether a practice is binding include the following:

- Does the practice concern a major condition of employment?
- Was it established unilaterally?
- Was it administered unilaterally?
- Did either of the parties seek to incorporate it into the body of the written agreement?
- What is the frequency of repetition of the "practice"?
- Is the "practice" a longstanding one?
- Is it specific and detailed?
- Do the employees rely on it?

4. Role of Precedent

In arbitration precedent may be defined as the "force or weight given to prior arbitration decisions." As a practical matter, arbitrators have no obligation to give any weight at all to prior arbitration decisions, because an arbitrator owes fidelity only to the collective bargaining agreements presently under interpretation. Thus, other cases involving *different* language and *different* circumstances are not persuasive.

It would, however, be a mistake to assume that precedent is never persuasive. Precedent can be given a great deal of weight if a prior arbitration case exists involving the *same* company, the *same* issue, and the *same* contract language. To hold otherwise would be very disruptive to the stability of the hospital-union collective bargaining relationship. The parties have a right to expect that arbitration awards settle particular issues, and unless language changes are made through contract negotiations, prior arbitration decisions should be given considerable importance.

5. Role of Precontract Negotiations

When contract language is unclear or ambiguous, arbitrators will sometimes look to the history of the parties' negotiations. This standard can be very persuasive if the parties have kept careful notes of their negotiations.

6. De Minimis Rule

Occasionally an arbitrator may invoke a principle of contract interpretation called the "*de minimis* rule." Actually the complete term is "*De minimis non curat lex*," which means the "law does not concern itself with trifles." This does not mean that arbitration issues do not involve trifling sums of money. Indeed, major principles may be at stake, though monetary damages may be miniscule.

Arbitrators must be judicious when invoking the *de minimis* rule. Work assignment disputes, in particular, may seem trifling to the uninitiated, and seem to beg for the invocation of the *de minimis* rule. An arbitrator may wish to follow this guideline: if neither of the parties mention the rule, the arbitrator should not invoke it.

Management Check List for Negotiation of Collective Bargaining Agreements*

This is a check list of questions management must ask itself concerning each clause in a collective bargaining contract. Although many contracts will not follow the order of the clauses set forth here, the check list is arranged by grouping clauses related by subject matter together.

Agreement Clause

- Does this clause accurately spell out the names of the parties as certified by the Labor Board?
- Does the clause bind successors?
- Should the Local as well as the International be covered?
- Does the clause sufficiently limit the scope of the agreement so that no confusion arises as to it being applicable to other geographic locations?

---

*Source: Reprinted from *Health Care Labor Manual* by Martin E. Skoler, with permission of Aspen Systems Corporation, © 1981.

- Is the clause too vague or does it imply undesirable restrictions on management?
- Does the clause cede to the union decisions normally considered management rights?
- Does the clause pledge both parties to mutual cooperation?
- Does the clause pledge the union to peaceful and uninterrupted operation of the institution?

Recognition of the Union

- Does the unit description cover the Labor Board certified unit?
- Does the clause provide the exact language for the exclusion of:
    - Employees not covered by the certification?
    - Part-time employees—is there an hourly requirement for inclusion or exclusion?
    - Temporary employees?
    - Seasonal employees?
    - Supervisors?
    - Guards and watchmen?
- Does the unit description cover other locations affiliated with the institution?
- If part-time employees are covered, is there a provision as to whether or not they receive fringe benefits and on what basis—pro rata or otherwise?

Union Security

- Does the union security clause cover only employees covered by the agreement; and at what location?
- Have you considered the open shop agreement permitting employees to have the freedom whether or not to join the union?
- Have you considered the maintenance of membership clause?
- Have you considered a modified clause requiring all members to remain members and all new employees to become members; however, all present employees need not become members?
- Have you considered an agency shop agreement?
- Does the clause prohibit use of coercion in getting employees to join?
- Does the clause clearly indicate what the requirements of union membership are?
- Must employees pay dues?
- Must employees pay initiation fees, fines, and assessments?
- Does the clause have an escape period?
- Can you modify the thirty-day period?
- What must an employee do to remain a member in good standing and should the clause merely require the tendering of normal periodic dues to remain a member in good standing?
- What happens in the event of a strike?
- Does the clause establish a well-defined procedure which the union must comply with if it makes a demand for discharge under the clause?
- Does the clause comply with the Section 19 Religious Exemption provided for in the new health care amendments?
- Is there a listing of at least three charitable organizations from which an employee exercising his/her rights under Section 19 may choose one?

Check-Off

- Is the institution's obligation to check-off conditioned on the voluntary submission by the employee to the institution of a signed written authorization card?
- Does the clause contemplate only normal periodic dues or some arbitrary sum?
- Does the clause specify when the money must be checked off, and when it should be remitted to the union?
- Is the check-off authorization a legal check-off provision?
- Can provisions be made to permit employees to escape from the check-off provisions?
- Does the clause provide that the union will "indemnify and save harmless" the institution if the institution adheres to the provisions of the check-off?
- Does the clause state that the union agrees to reimburse the institution for any costs it incurs from claims arising out of the check-off procedure?
- Does the clause provide for circumstances when check-off need not be made such as (a) termination of employment, (b) transfer out of the unit, (c) layoff from work, (d) leaves of absence, (e) earnings not covering the amount of the check-off?

- Is a procedure for revocation of check-off authorization established?

Management Rights

- Does the clause reserve to management the right to determine the size and composition of the workforce?
- Does the clause reserve to management the right to determine medical and nursing care standards?
- Does the clause reserve to management the right to determine the number and location of facilities?
- Does the clause reserve to management the right to determine the quantity, type, and speed of equipment?
- Does the clause reserve to management the right to determine the manning requirements of any equipment or job?
- Does the clause reserve to management the right to set hours of shifts and the time for work?
- Does the clause reserve to management the right to determine the staffing pattern and areas to be worked?
- Does the clause reserve to management the right to determine the methods and places of performing work?
- Does the clause reserve to management the right to decide that certain work will not be performed by employees?
- Does the clause reserve to management the right to subcontract out bargaining unit work?
- Does the clause reserve to management the right to schedule work and work breaks?
- Does the clause reserve to management the right to control the method of performing work and the quality of work?
- Does the clause reserve to management the sole right to introduce procedures, methods, and facilities?
- Does the clause reserve to management the right to determine whether all or any part of its facility will continue to operate?
- Does the clause give management the authority to establish, change, or abolish any job classification of service?
- Does the clause give management the authority to determine the duties of employees and to discharge probationary employees for any reason whatsoever?
- Does the clause give management the authority to hire, lay off, assign, transfer, demote, promote, and determine the qualifications of employees?
- Does the clause give management the authority to set starting and quitting times, hours to be worked, and overtime?

No Strike or Lockout

- Does the clause prohibit employees from engaging in strikes, sit-downs, sit-ins, slow-downs, cessations, or stoppages of work, boycotts or other activities which interfere with the operation of the institution during the term of the agreement?
- Does the clause prohibit the union, its officers, agents, representatives, and members from, directly or indirectly, authorizing, encouraging, participating in, sanctioning, ratifying, condoning, or supporting such conduct?
- Does the clause reserve to management the right to discipline (including discharge) employees who violate the no strike clause?
- Does the clause restrict arbitration of discharges to the issue of employee participation?
- Does the clause allow selective discipline where all participants cannot be discharged?
- Does the clause require the union to take positive action to publicly disavow violations by employees and to notify employees of its disapproval?
- Does the clause require the union to instruct employees to return to work immediately?
- Does the clause ban employee refusals to cross picket lines?
- Does the clause's prohibition of a "lockout" prevent the closing of all or part of the institution for business reasons?
- Does the clause make provision that in the event of a violation of same, neither party shall negotiate concerning the matter until such time as all work activities have returned to normal?

Grievance Procedure

- Does the clause define the word "grievance" as a dispute arising out of the inter-

pretation or application of the collective bargaining agreement?
- Are all the provisions of the agreement subject to the grievance procedure?
- Does the clause require the grievant to reduce his or her grievance to writing and to sign and date it before submitting it to Step 2?
- Does the clause state that grievances must be filed within a stated period of time after it arises or it will be invalid?
- Does the clause clearly specify whether work days or calendar days are involved in the time limitations? Must separate grievances be filed by each individual employee where the grievances all arise from the same event?
- Is the clause clear whether the grievant must personally sign the grievance?
- Does the clause provide for several working days before management is required to respond in any step?
- Does the clause provide strict time limits within which the grievance must be appealed or considered abandoned?
- Does the clause make it clear that grievance meetings are to be held at mutually agreeable times so that the union cannot call them at will?
- Does the clause make it clear that a failure of management to respond does not constitute acceptance by management of the grievant's position but merely allows the grievant to go to the next step?
- Does the clause provide that any settlement made in Steps 1 or 2 is not precedent for other grievances or interpretations of the contract?
- Does the clause specifically state that the institution should be able to use the grievance procedure?
- Does the clause make it clear that an employee may process his own grievance without the union?
- Does the clause make it clear what the employer's obligation is with respect to paying representatives for time spent?
- Does the clause fix a time for appealing to arbitration?
- Does the clause require that the grievance procedure be exhausted before going to arbitration, except by mutual consent?
- Does the clause make it clear that the employer cannot file a grievance or move a case to arbitration?

Arbitration

- Does the clause specifically define what grievances may be submitted to arbitration?
- Does the clause provide a time limit within which grievances must be referred to arbitration or abandoned?
- Does the clause permit both the institution and the union to refer grievances to arbitration?
- Does the clause state how arbitrators will be selected and under what rules arbitrations will be conducted?
- Does the clause provide that fees and expenses will be borne equally by the parties?
- Does the clause provide that the decision of the arbitrator will be final and binding on the employer, the union, and the employees?
- Does the clause limit the arbitrator's authority so he cannot modify, detract from, add to, or alter the provisions of the contract, nor substitute his discretion for management's discretion?
- Does the clause prevent the arbitrator from deciding questions of arbitrability of an issue?
- Does the clause provide for a submission agreement?
- Does the clause limit the number of grievances which may be heard by the arbitrator at one time?
- Does the clause describe and/or limit the kind of relief the arbitrator may grant?
- Does the clause require the arbitrator to reduce his award to writing?
- Does the clause prohibit the arbitrator from mediating the dispute and require that he restrict himself to hearing the case and deciding the issues?
- Does the clause prevent the arbitrator from modifying discipline, allowing him only to sustain or overrule it?
- Does the clause eliminate rates for new jobs from arbitration?
- Does the clause prevent the arbitrator from changing wage rates?
- Does the clause prevent use of the decision as precedent in later cases?

- Does the clause specify which party pays the expenses of the arbitrator?
- Does the probationary employee have access to the grievance and arbitration process?

Discipline and Discharge

- Does the clause provide for progressive discipline in the form of a specified number of warnings before an employee may be disciplined/discharged?
- What form must such warnings take, written or oral?
- Does the clause provide for a specified period of time after which written warnings will cease to be effective?
- Does the clause clearly specify what acts of employees will lead to immediate discharge without warning?
- Does the clause provide that the union must be notified prior to any disciplinary actions by the employer?

Union Visitation

- Does the union visitation clause prohibit interference with work and the operations of the institution?
- Does the clause provide for visitation only at reasonable times such as day shift?
- Does the clause provide for permission to enter particular work areas?
- Does the clause limit such visits or delegate activity to matters arising under the agreement?
- Does the clause provide that delegates will not be paid while engaged in such activities?
- Does the clause prohibit union activity, including the distribution of literature which could interfere with the performance of work during working time?

Bulletin Boards

- Does the clause indicate how many boards and where they are to be located?
- Does the clause restrict the material to legitimate union material?
- Does the clause give management the right to inspect and approve all material which the union proposes to post?
- Does the clause restrict such material to notices of union meetings, elections, and recreational and social activities?
- Does the clause specifically exclude the posting of political or inflammatory material?

No Discrimination

- Does the discrimination clause broadly outlaw all forms of discrimination even if the employee or applicant can't conceivably perform the job, or in some manner is unsuited?
- If so, should it be modified to bar only discrimination under applicable state and federal law?
- Does it apply to union and employer alike?
- Does it cover:
  - Age?
  - Sex?
  - Marital Status?
  - Religion?
  - Nationality?
  - Race?

Seniority

- Do the definitions provide that seniority is from the last date of hire?
- Do the definitions provide for continuous work?
- Do the applications of seniority provide circumstances under which seniority would not accrue, *i.e.*, leaves of absence or other absences such as sickness?
- Does the application clause indicate that probationary or part-time employees are to be treated differently, and should they?
- Does the application provision take into consideration the relative abilities of employees, their mere capability, or is ability not even an issue?
- Must the application provision provide for bumping and can it be avoided? What kind of bumping—upwards or downwards or jobs previously held?
- Does the application provision permit temporary layoffs with recourse to seniority?
- Does the seniority provision provide for the accrual of seniority during layoffs?
- Does the clause sufficiently define "layoff" so that there will be no confusion as to

bumping rights, etc. during brief periods, *e.g.* partial days, of unemployment?
- Is the institution's duty to recall conditioned on the employee's supplying it with a current address and/or telephone number?
- Does the termination of seniority provision provide for failure:
    - to return from a leave of absence on time?
    - to report for work without notifying the Hospital?
    - to report for work for any reason, including sickness, for extended periods of time?
    - to give a truthful reason for a leave of absence?
- Is there provision for a specific form of recall notice?
- Is an employee subject to discharge if he/she refuses recall to a suitable job?
- Must the institution notify the union in advance of a layoff?
- Does the termination provision provide for a settlement of a Workmen's Compensation case for total disability?
- Does the clause make provision for the seniority of two employees hired the same day?
- Who prepares the list of seniority? What about revisions?
- Is there a super-seniority provision covering union officers, delegates, or stewards at the institution?
- Is it restricted to layoff situations?

Promotions

- Does the clause provide for the employee having either sufficient ability or being the most capable in addition to taking into consideration seniority?
- What kind of seniority is contemplated—departmental, classification, or institution-wide seniority?
- Does the clause provide for trial period, and what occurs if the employee does not qualify?

Probationary Employees

- Does the clause provide for continuous work during the probationary period from the last date of hire?
- Does the clause provide the Employer with the right to discharge the employee during or at the end of the period even if the employee's performance has been satisfactory or for any reason whatsoever, without recourse to the grievance procedures?
- Does the clause indicate whether or not the probationee receives fringe benefits during the period?
- Does the clause provide that seniority shall run from date of hire once the probationary period is completed?
- Does the clause provide a different period for part-time employees?

Wages and Minimums

- Does the clause reserve to management the right to fix rates of new jobs and job classifications?
- Does the clause reserve to management the right to combine jobs and eliminate classification unilaterally?
- Does the clause make raises dependent upon merit or something else other than straight seniority?
- Does the clause clearly spell out the rates for each classification?
- Does the clause spell out what happens if employees temporarily work in a higher paid or lower paid classification?
- Does the clause specify when payday will be and under what circumstances management may change it?
- Does the clause specify what shift premiums (if any) will be paid?
- What rights as to severance pay, etc. are afforded employees upon discharge?
- Does the clause make special provision for employees who train other employees?

Hours

- Does the clause provide for a normal, regular workday and workweek?
- Does the clause distinguish between full-time and part-time employees?
- Does the clause state or imply that the workday or workweek is guaranteed?
- Does the clause reserve to management the right to alter, increase, or reduce hours?
- Does the clause provide for scheduling of days off?

- Does the clause assure adequate weekend coverage?
- Does the clause set specific penalties for unexcused absences or tardiness?
- Does the clause define precisely the hours of work for each shift?
- Does the clause properly define when call-in pay is available and how it will be computed?
- Does the clause establish the numbers, length, and scheduling of breaks?
- Does the clause reserve to management the right to schedule overtime?
- Does the clause contain language which clearly states that shift premiums are only paid to employees assigned to a particular shift and not to persons working overtime or called in during the hours of that shift?
- Does the clause provide for the usual, normal amount of overtime pay?
- Does the clause differentiate between full-time and part-time employees?
- Does the clause provide for pay only for authorized overtime?
- Does the clause prevent pyramiding of overtime?
- Does the clause define overtime to be hours in excess of forty (40) a week or eight (8) a day?
- Does the clause allow management to require employees to work overtime?
- Does the clause describe how overtime will be distributed?
- Does the clause make any differentiation between the daily distribution of overtime and weekend or call-in overtime?
- Does the clause state whether shift premiums (if any) will be included in overtime pay calculations?
- Are there recordkeeping requirements as to overtime imposed on management?
- Does an employee who is working on a temporary transfer have any rights to overtime in that job classification?

Shifts

- Does the clause reserve to management the initial assignment of shifts?
- Does the clause reserve to management the right to reassign personnel from shift to shift?
- Does the clause provide management control over the filling of shift vacancies?
- Does the clause limit the number of shift changes an employee may request during a period of time?
- If bidding on shifts is allowed, does the clause reserve to management the final decision based upon factors other than straight seniority?
- Does the clause allow rotation of shifts for training purposes?
- Does the clause limit shift changes to those within the same job classification?

Holidays

- Does the clause clearly specify which holidays are granted?
- Does the clause state who is eligible for holiday pay?
  - Probationary employees?
  - Part-time employees?
- Does the clause require that, to be eligible for holiday pay, the employee must have worked his full scheduled shift before the holiday and his full scheduled shift after the holiday?
- Does the clause require that, to be eligible for holiday pay, the employee must have performed some work in the calendar week in which the holiday falls?
- Does the clause deal with holidays which fall during leaves of absence, vacations, or layoffs?
- Does the clause deal with the amount of holiday pay and when it will be paid?
- Does the clause allow management to require an employee to work on a holiday?
- Does the clause provide for a usual number of holidays?
- Does the clause provide a method for determining who will be off on a holiday?
- If an employee scheduled to work on a holiday calls in sick, must he/she produce a doctor's written verification of inability to work?

Vacations

- Does the clause define eligibility in terms of the employee's accrued working time, seniority, etc.?
- Does the clause differentiate between full-time and part-time employees?

- Does the clause make it clear whether time lost due to illness, accident, layoff, etc., is counted as hours worked?
- Does the clause cover what happens if an employee quits?
- Does the clause reserve to management the right to schedule vacations, unhindered by union consent or individual preference?
- Does the clause provide that vacations are not accruable and must be taken in the year earned or waived?
- Does the clause define vacation pay as based upon the employee's regular hourly rate?
- Are the base periods for determining eligibility and amount of pay clearly delineated?
- May an employee elect to take vacation pay rather than time off?

Sick Leave

- Does the clause specify how sick leave is to be accumulated?
- Does the clause state the requirements of length of service before an employee is eligible?
- Does the clause distinguish between fulltime and part-time employees?
- Does the clause provide that sick leave will be eight (8) hours per day at the employee's regular hourly rate?
- Does the clause clearly state whether sick leave is cumulative or what happens to unused sick leave?
- Does the clause allow management to require satisfactory proof of illness?
- Does the clause require employees to report their inability to work within a reasonable time?
- Does the clause allow management to require an examination by a physician of management's choice?

Funeral Leave

- Does the clause limit eligibility by length of service and hours per week of work?
- Does the clause limit availability of funeral leave to the sole purpose of attending a funeral?
- Does the clause provide specifically that three (3) days are a maximum and include only regularly scheduled workdays?
- Does the clause define precisely what is meant by "immediate family"?
- Does the clause require the days to be consecutive?
- Does the clause require that three (3) days must include the day of the funeral?
- Does the clause state whether funeral leave will be counted in computing overtime?
- Does the clause state that funeral leave will be compensated at the regular straight-time hourly rate?

Unpaid Leave

- Does the maternity leave clause meet the requirements of state and federal rules against sex discrimination?
  (1) Does it provide for a leave of sufficient duration?
  (2) Does it allow the retention of seniority?
  (3) Does it provide for reinstatement?
  (4) Is the leave at least as long as that provided for other temporary disabilities?
- Does the clause insist that, except for maternity leave, the granting of personal leave is entirely within the discretion of the institution?
- Does the clause state that personal leave for illness will be considered only if a doctor's certificate identifies the illness, explains why the leave is needed, and estimates how long the disability will continue?
- Does the clause restrict leaves available for the purpose of carrying on union business?
- Does the clause require written application for all leaves and extensions of leaves?
- Does the clause provide for a maximum limit on number of leave days?
- Does the clause provide that employees will retain, but not accrue, seniority during leaves?
- Does the clause provide that all leaves are without pay?
- Does the clause explain what happens to fringe benefits during a leave?
- Does the clause cover issues of whether the leave is counted as time worked in computing vacation benefits?
- Does the clause prohibit employees from working at other jobs during leaves of absence?

- Does the clause state that failure to report to work at the end of a leave will be considered a voluntary resignation?
- Does the clause make provision for a leave of absence for political office?

Jury Duty

- Does the clause apply to probationary employees?
- Does the clause specify that the employee must serve advance notice upon the institution or submit proof of having actually served on a jury upon return to work?
- Does the clause provide for the return to work by the employee when the jury service fills only a part of the work day?
- Does the clause make specific provision for employees who work on a second or third shift?
- Does the clause exclude overtime or holiday pay?
- Does the clause limit the amount of time for which the employee will be reimbursed?

Work by Supervision

- Does the clause specify that it only applies to work usually performed by employees?
- Does the clause apply only to "substantial" work performed by supervisors?
- Does the clause allow supervisors to perform bargaining unit work in a strike or emergency situation?
- Does the clause interfere with the training duties of the supervisors?

Job Posting

- Does the clause specify exactly when an employee may bid on a job?
- Does management have complete control over whether a position will be posted and subsequently filled?
- Does management have the right to temporarily fill a posted position until the bidding process is completed?
- Do employees on leave of absence, layoff, or sick leave have to be notified of a job posting?
- Does management have the right to consider factors such as relative ability and prior performance in addition to seniority?
- Does the clause restrict the number of bids an employee may submit in a given period of time?
- Does the clause specify which jobs are subject to bidding and which are not?
- Does the clause specify a trial period of limited duration during which management will judge the employee's performance?
- Is such a performance evaluation solely in the hands of management?
- Does the clause make provision for the future disqualification of an employee who refuses to accept the bid?

Safety

- Does the clause provide for a safety committee composed of representatives of both management and the employees?
- Does the clause specify that the institution will adhere to all OSHA and/or local safety requirements?
- Does the clause impose on the employees the duty to adhere to all safety requirements subject to discipline?

Duration

- Does the clause specify the exact term of the agreement?
- Does the clause provide for automatic extension or renewal?
- Does the clause provide for written notification of a desire or termination of the agreement by either party at least 90 days before its expiration?

THE STRIKE*

Evaluating the Institution's Ability To "Take" a Strike

From the perspective of a health care administrator, the decision whether to "take" a strike in order to resist a union's demands may be one of the most sensitive he may ever be called upon to make. If the administrator decides to "take" a strike, he must then make another decision; should the facility operate or close down during

---

*Source: Reprinted from *Health Care Labor Manual* by Martin E. Skoler, with permission of Aspen Systems Corporation, © 1981.

the strike. The following is a generalized checklist of factors that should be thoughtfully reviewed by management in making this strategic decision:

1. The institution's ability to maintain a satisfactory level of services for patients and other users.
2. The institution's ability to receive necessary supplies of all types, even though there may be pickets stationed at all of its entrances.
3. The institution's ability to maintain the services and support of nonstriking employees, especially the medical staff.
4. The institution's ability to elicit community support for its decision either to operate or to close down for the duration of a strike.
5. The institution's ability to maintain the support of its governing board and its volunteers.
6. The institution's ability to enlist cooperation, as needed, from sister institutions in the community.
7. The institution's ability to hire personnel replacements with satisfactory skills.
8. The institution's ability to provide comprehensive personal security for its patients and nonstriking employees as well as security for its buildings, grounds and equipment.
9. The union's ability to persuade all, or most, of the employees whom it represents to strike.
10. The union's ability to provide strike benefits to strikers from its own treasury or with assistance from its parent organization.
11. The availability under state law of unemployment compensation, welfare benefits or food stamps to strikers and their families.
12. The likelihood that local labor or civil rights groups will provide moral and financial support to the strikers.

Strike Contingency Plans

Preparing for a strike requires careful planning to assure continued services which the union will—in pursuit of its strike or job action—attempt to interrupt. While each institution's problems are unique, some aspects of pre-strike planning are common to most health care institutions.

1. Alternative Plans for Patient Care

Because the institution's foremost consideration must be to protect the health and safety of its patients, substantial attention should be given to whether a threatened strike might, either at the onset or later, require evacuation of some or all patients. If there is any realistic likelihood that the institution might be required to move its patients, plans should be made with neighboring health care facilities to transport, receive and care for them. Careful advanced planning by major health care institutions in a community might produce a reciprocal agreement to come to each other's aid in a variety of grave circumstances.

Understandably, the patients and family of patients who are in an institution which has been struck will be extremely apprehensive. They will need reassurance that the institution is fully capable of maintaining a high level of patient care. There are many ways to provide such assurance, and at a minimum the institution should write to families of patients as soon as possible. Similarly, prospective patients, who have been scheduled for admission, should be informed as soon as possible of any difficulties that might be occasioned by a threatened strike.

Needless to say, the institution's ability to maintain a satisfactory level of patient care will depend in no small measure on the employee group. A doctor's strike, for example, is likely to be far more damaging to the institution than a strike by groundskeepers. On the other hand, a strike by large numbers of housekeeping employees might so impede the institution's operating efficiency as to require a sharply reduced level of services. Often, one cannot predict with full accuracy the potential impact of a strike, however carefully one plans. The health care administrator who has never experienced a strike, but who is threatened by one, might usefully visit an institution which has experienced such a strike to learn first hand the consequences of a strike and the lessons that "battle scarred" administrators can pass on.

2. Security Planning during a Strike

Security at health care institutions may present a major problem during a strike, for many health care institutions tend to be open and less than totally secure under the best and most normal circumstances. During a strike the problems of personal security and protection of property are compounded.

If an institution's security guards strike or refuse to cross another union's picket line, it may be necessary to hire a private security organization for the length of the strike. It might also be useful to schedule security patrols by supervisory personnel. Off-duty local police may often be hired at an hourly rate for patrolling.

Local and state police should be alerted to the strike possibility as soon as a union's Section 8(g) strike notice is received.

Security and maintenance of an institution's power plant should be given particular attention in prestrike preparations. Loss of power could quickly bring an institution to its knees. Security at the power plant should be directed at preventing sabotage.

To assure that deliveries will continue and that nonstriking personnel will have access to the institution, picket lines should be monitored and tested periodically by management personnel. If they are unable to gain access, they should promptly request police assistance, while exercising care to avoid engaging in self-help. Any violence directed towards managerial personnel or others should be carefully and fully recorded.

Observers should be assigned to monitor each picket line. They should make a record of misconduct by strikers and others and seek police help if needed.

Security guards must be instructed to avoid conflict with pickets. They should lock all doors and windows from the inside and even change locks where necessary. Strikers are not legally entitled to enter the institution's premises during a strike, and security guards should be carefully instructed on this subject. Strikers who insist upon entering a facility when they have been instructed to leave are trespassers.

Special attention should be given to protecting nonstriking personnel. They should be informed of their legal right to cross a picket line in order to work. It is sometimes necessary to engage a special bus to transport them to and from work. Nonstriking employees also should be instructed that name-calling, threats, verbal abuse or any other form of harassment should be immediately reported to management.

To protect computer operations, particularly computer-based payrolls, second copies of cards, tapes, or discs including the program should be stored in a secured area.

3. Planning for Essential Deliveries

Another major problem during a strike is to assure that the institution will receive deliveries or essential supplies. Organized drivers for common carriers or suppliers may be unwilling to cross a picket line. It is advisable to contact regular common carriers and major suppliers as early as possible of the strike threat and to make alternative arrangements.

4. Other Planning Needs for a Strike

An inventory of available, necessary skills among supervisors may be useful. Contingent work schedules for supervisory and administrative personnel should be planned.

Possibly, local church groups and other charitable service organizations might be approached to determine whether they will help out with volunteers.

The institution should designate one spokesman for the purpose of communication with the media. Ideally, this person should be fully acquainted with the substantive issues in dispute and should be able to articulate the institution's positions convincingly.

A common tactic of unions is to bypass the management bargaining committee and to approach the institution's governing board directly. Before the strike, the directors should be warned and prepared for this tactic. It is often useful to maintain close liaison between the bargaining committee and directors during this period to avoid confusion.

A strategic office or "command post" should be established to which questions may be directed, and from which decisions may be made and orders given. Staffing such an office will, of course, depend on the institution's size and need.

If strike replacements are to be sought, it is necessary to observe local laws. Many states regulate advertisements for such replacements. Generally, word of mouth may be a more desirable method of seeking strike replacements.

PART VIII
QUALITY ASSURANCE AND SAFETY

Chapter 38—Quality Assurance

OVERVIEW

Management-oriented administrators can be as responsible for the quality of hospital care as they are for financial matters. While administrators do not have the personal skills and knowledge to perform many specialized activities, they can, through the development of measuring instruments and reporting systems, ensure that programs receive the support they deserve from both medical and nonmedical professionals.[*]

There are a number of different strategies for assessing the quality of medical care. Quality assessment methods differ, for example, in time frame for review (prospective, concurrent, and retrospective), in data-gathering methods (record review, abstract, encounter form, observation, and interview), and in categories of criteria (structure, process, and outcome).

Types of Audit Administration[*]

Type 1. *One Central Audit Committee.* This type of organization was usually composed of representatives from the various departments and sometimes included representation from the nursing staff, the medical records office, and the governing board of the hospital.

Type 2. *One Central Committee with Distributed Responsibility.* This type of organization was similar in construction to the Type 1 committee, but distributed the responsibility for the actual conduct of patient care evaluation to separate departmental committees.

Type 3. *Decentralized Departmental Audit Committees.* This type of organization consisted of *separate departmental audit committees* with coordination of activities in the hands of an administrator.

Audits and the Process of Change[*]

The process of institutional change involves three major steps:

1. Recognition of the problem. This includes a focused review of the experience of the hospital with the identification of those elements that are representative of trends and major problems. Both the Professional Standards Review Organization (PSRO) and the Joint Commission on the Accreditation of Hospitals (JCAH) have stressed the importance of identifying major problems in the audit process.
2. Preparation of appropriate corrective action, including the development of a plan for improving performance. The nature of the action required depends on the results of medical care evaluation studies and re-

---

[*]Source: Reprinted from *Continuing Education in the Health Professions* by Robert Boissoneau, with permission of Aspen Systems Corporation, © 1980.

[*]Source: Reprinted from Howard Weinberg, "Effecting Change in Hospital Performance: Issues and Realities," *Quality Assurance in Hospitals: Strategies for Assessment and Implementation,* ed. Nancy O. Graham, with permission of Aspen Systems Corporation, © 1982.

audits, chart reviews, preadmission studies, PSRO reports, etc.
3. Implementation. A scheduled and structured process is required to assure compliance with the plan of corrective action and measurement of the results. A logical outgrowth of this process is the practitioners' acceptance of the need for the change and its adoption in practice.

The first two steps can usually be accomplished. A review of hospital organization can explain why the third step frequently is not achieved and why hospitals usually establish quality assessment rather than quality assurance programs.

The Hospital Administrator

The administrator has limited authority to deal with medical care problems, although care cannot be upgraded without the cooperation of the medical staff. Frequently, the administrator must rely predominantly upon informal methods for influencing staff, which involve persuasion and bargaining. Many administrators achieve results by these processes, but these tactics are no substitute for the single authority that is enjoyed by presidents of large corporations.

Although generally recognized as the expediter in motivating change, the administrator does not always command sufficient authority to be effective in this role. This is directly related to the administrator's inability to control the factors that can lead to changes in the organization. For example, the administrator requires the full support of the governing body when medical staff controversies or conflicts with individual practitioners arise. Unfortunately, the dependence of the hospital upon physicians to maintain full occupancy frequently inhibits the use of sanctions to ensure correction of recognized deficiencies. This is one basic conflict in hospital structure. Moreover, allegiances between the medical staff and governing body may obstruct change. Many an administrator has been defeated at this juncture, and the potential for the coalition of medical staff and governing body should never be underestimated.

The Medical Staff

Within each hospital, the medical staff organization provides the framework for regulating the conduct of its members and the level of care. In hospitals that have highly structured departments and full-time staff, supervisory activities may be relatively effective. In most cases, however, it is difficult for the medical board to control the activities of the staff. This difficulty is manifested by delinquent, inadequate entries into medical records and poor attendance at committee meetings. In order to deal with these problems, an administrator usually requires medical board cooperation, which may be withheld because of the traditional reluctance of a medical staff to enforce sanctions against colleagues. This reluctance is a major contributor to institutional failure to take corrective action against professional deficiencies. The absence of formal employment contracts between a voluntary medical staff and the governing body also reduces accountability.

The result of conflicts among the governing body, administrator, and medical staff is confusion over responsibility and authority for actions and changes in policy. Hospital organization is therefore distinguished by the lack of a single operating authority and the sharing of power among several centers of authority which inhibits change.

External Pressure

Changes in the policies of hospitals are usually brought about by external rather than internal pressures. The most compelling motive is reimbursement.

Recently, quality assurance has become a concern of third party payers; their reviews have extended beyond utilization. Some Blue Cross plans have begun to review the quality of the medical care provided to patients and have denied payment to hospitals that do not perform a sufficient number of specialized procedures or have substandard programs.

Several state health departments have instituted cost control mechanisms that affect payment for substandard care. In addition, by virtue of its authority to monitor PSRO reviews, the state health department can focus on unresolved issues and problems. This process can set into motion corrective actions that the hospital could have implemented earlier after having conducted appropriate medical care evaluation studies.

Regulations adopted by the Health Care Financing Administration (HCFA) clearly establish procedures under which the HCFA may invoke sanctions against a provider who furnishes services that "are not medically necessary, *do not meet professionally recognized standards* or are not properly documented as to the medical necessity or quality of the services." The regulation further stipulates that "in addition to any other sanction provided under law, a practitioner may be excluded from Medicare and Medicaid or required as a condition for continued participation in those programs to pay an amount not in excess of the cost of the improper or unnecessary services that were furnished or ordered."

JCAH is another major influence on hospital behavior. A new quality assurance standard developed by JCAH requires hospitals to identify major problems and to take action to correct these problems through an integrated quality assurance program. Since most hospitals seek accreditation and are responsive to JCAH standards, this new standard has potential value in motivating change.

Another major influence on hospital policies has been the substantial amounts awarded to plaintiffs in malpractice actions. Court-backed liability acts as a tangible deterrent to poor practices and has resulted in the adoption of cooperative risk management programs. As hospitals and physicians are exposed to the threat of unfavorable publicity in addition to economic losses, there are increasing incentives for effecting change. The administrator is more than likely to use the existence of any or all of these processes with caveats to the staff such as "If we don't change, they will compel us."

Terms and Definitions*

A consensus has emerged that quality of care measurement involves two basic concepts: the quality of the technical care, and the quality of the art-of-care. Technical care refers to the adequacy of the diagnostic and therapeutic processes; and art-of-care relates to the milieu,

---

*Source: Reprinted from Robert H. Brook, Kathleen N. Williams, and Allyson D. Avery, "Quality Assurance in the 20th Century," *Quality Assurance in Health Care,* ed. Richard Egdahl and Paul Gertman, with permission of Aspen Systems Corporation, © 1976.

manner, and behavior of the provider in delivering care to and communicating with the patient.

Seven terms recur frequently in the discussion of quality of care: quality assessment, quality assurance, structure, process, outcome, efficacy, and effectiveness. *Quality assessment* involves measuring the level of quality provided at some point in time; it connotes no effort to change or improve that level of care. *Quality assurance* has been used in the literature to mean both measuring the level of care provided *and*, when necessary, improving it. Thus, quality assessment is the first step in quality assurance.

Structure, process, and outcome refer to three different variables that can be used to assess or measure quality of care. *Structural measurements* are concerned with the descriptive, innate characteristics of facilities or providers (e.g., the soundness of a building, whether a poison chart is posted in an emergency room, or the age and board certification status of the physician). *Process measures* are, in a sense, simply those measures that evaluate what a provider does to and for a patient (e.g., ordering a cardiogram for a patient with chest pain). They can also mean how well a person is moved through the medical care system, either in a "macro" sense (e.g., from first symptom to seeking care to obtaining care) or in a "micro" sense (e.g., from arrival to departure at an emergency room or outpatient clinic). *Outcomes* reflect what happened to the patient, in terms of palliation, treatment, cure or rehabilitation. Obviously, the definitions of structure, process, and outcome are not sufficiently precise to prevent the unreliable labeling of some measures which are used to assess quality. Nevertheless, the conceptual distinction among these three measures is important to maintain, since in essence they measure three different things: the resources necessary to solve a problem, the way the problem was solved, and the results of the problem solving, respectively.

Efficacy and effectiveness are two additional words defined differently within the medical care literature. *Efficacy* relates to the benefit or lack of benefit a procedure or treatment has when performed under ideal circumstances. *Effectiveness* relates to the average benefit of a procedure or program when used by the average provider in the average community. A procedure clearly can be both efficacious and effective. It can also be efficacious and ineffective, but the reverse cannot occur. A kidney transplant program at a university hospital may be efficacious but, when done in the average hospital by the average surgeon, may be ineffective in improving the health of patients in renal failure.

The literature is replete with comments about how quality should be defined. From these comments, a consensus has emerged that quality of care measurement involves two basic concepts: the quality of the technical care, and the quality of the art-of-care. Technical care refers to the adequacy of the diagnostic and therapeutic processes; and art-of-care relates to the milieu, manner, and behavior of the provider in delivering care to and communicating with the patient. A provider who delivers a higher level of the art-of-care should promote the following behaviors in his patients: willingness to discuss sensitive problems; utilization of medical services in a manner which would maximize the chance of these services benefiting the patient's health; increased compliance with regimens directed at controlling or alleviating chronic diseases (many of which at the time of diagnosis may be only mildly symptomatic or asymptomatic); and adoption of lifestyles and health habits conducive to longevity and decreased morbidity. Virtually all quality assessment studies have evaluated the technical aspects of quality; measurement of the art-of-care is just now beginning.

ORGANIZING FOR QUALITY ASSURANCE (QA)

QA Support Strategies*

Centralized Strategies

Larger hospitals with a number of fulltime positions allocated to QA programs' needs should consider a centralized approach either through organizing a QA department or centralizing QA functions in an existing department. Considerations in organizing a separate QA department include the following:

---

*Source: Reprinted from Linda L. Pfeffer-Kloss, "Managing Quality Assurance Information," *Topics in Health Record Management,* December 1980, with permission of Aspen Systems Corporation.

- The director should report to or be at an administrative level such as associate, assistant administrator, vice president, or medical director. The QA support function involves work at all levels of the organization including work with various medical staff committees, department heads, chiefs of service, and members of the hospital management team. The department needs the latitude to initiate communication and cannot function well if relegated to an inappropriate level in the organization.
- Since complete centralization of individuals who directly and indirectly support the goals of the QA program is seldom possible, the department's placement should facilitate communication with other departments that contribute QA data.
- Personnel who staff the centralized QA department should include those who are most directly involved in information gathering and management efforts such as medical records professionals, health data analysts, infection surveillance personnel, utilization review (UR) coordinators, and clerical support personnel.

Not all centralization requires creating a totally new department. The same results can be accomplished by supplementing and expanding the role of an existing department. Two strategies are seen most often, one that builds on the QA program support provided by the medical records department and another based on an existing utilization review department. Steps must be taken to ensure that the QA support function is autonomous if centralized in the medical records department.

Decentralized Strategies

In smaller hospitals in which fulltime assignment of more than one employee to coordinate QA support functions is neither possible nor necessary, autonomy of the support function may be preserved by

- Appointing an overall QA director/coordinator;
- Formalizing the role and functions of other personnel who contribute to the QA program goals on a parttime basis, including their relationship to the QA director/coordinator; and

- Defining in writing the relationships of the QA director/coordinator with the various departments that contribute to the accomplishment of the support functions.

Whether a centralized or decentralized structure is adopted, nearly every hospital will need a fulltime QA director/coordinator. The demands of the program are too expansive to expect that they can be met by someone in an *ad hoc* fashion on a time-available basis.

QA Staffing Organization

Table 38-1 provides a sample inventory of QA staffing patterns in a 400+-bed hospital. The current QA program requires approximately 9.4 fulltime equivalents engaged directly in gathering and managing data and working with committees. This calculation excludes indirect support such as that provided by the medical staff secretary and other clerical support personnel who prepare and maintain committee minutes. It also excludes administrative time and services provided by various ancillary departments.

The Quality Coordinating Council*

In most hospitals, the QCC is a relatively small council, composed of one to three representatives of the medical staff (one usually serves as chairperson), one or two representatives of the hospital administration, one to three representatives of nursing, one or two representatives from patient care departments, a hospital trustee, and the quality care coordinator.

There is no need to appoint a council and have monthly meetings unless the council has real purpose. A major key to productive results is to assign specific functions to the QCC. These functions of the QCC should include, but need not be limited to:

- *coordination*

    collection information
    consider activities that should be related, e.g., quality appraisal and continuing education

---

*Source: Reprinted from Richard E. Thompson, "Organizational Considerations," *Quality Assurance in Hospitals: Strategies for Assessment and Implementation,* ed. Nancy O. Graham, with permission of Aspen Systems Corporation, © 1982.

   communicate across patient care disciplines
   coordinate actions of hospital authority groups

- *information*

    provide a centralized source of reports to board
    suggest need for intervention to hospital authority groups

- *planning*

    establish priorities

- *prodding*

    insist on effective, productive quality appraisal efforts from all hospital components

- *consultation*

    provide specific assistance, usually through the coordinator

- *response*

    internally, acknowledge issues of importance to individuals and departments when suggesting high-priority areas for immediate attention
    externally, provide the organizational home for responding to quality requirements of external agencies, e.g., JCAH and the Professional Standards Review Organization (PSRO)

- *search for expertise*

    operate openly, not behind closed doors
    seek out the specific clinical and/or management expertise necessary to reach sound conclusions

- *follow-up*

    insist on reports of the impact of implemented changes

The orientation of council members is crucial in view of the subtle approach that must be used if quality assurance is to be effective rather than threatening, controversial, and counterproductive. Council members must recognize that their major functions are:

- to coordinate, not to control
- to inform, not to scold

Table 38-1 Inventory of QA Program Staffing

Current Departmental Assignment	Position	Description of QA Program Contribution	Hours per Week	Full-Time Equivalent
Utilization Review	Department head	Coordinates and supervises UR staff Member UR committee Performs UR duties Liaison with PSRO	40	1
	Utilization review coordinators	Admission, continued stay review Abstract preparation Other tasks as assigned	60	1.5
	Clerk-typist	Report preparation General secretarial, clerical functions	40	1
Medical Records	Director	Providing liaison with departments doing audits, UR, or other studies Reviewing questionable records for referral to various committees Meeting with medical records and audit committee	8	.20
	Health data analyst	Data retrieval for audit, including PSRO areawide studies Special studies on request Coordinating record retrieval for tissue committee, medical records committee, mortality review Meeting with audit committee	60	1.5
	Clerk-typist	Pulling records and fulfilling other info. request from UR, nursing, other departments doing audits	8	.20
Discharge Planning	Department head	Supervises personnel Provides liaison with UR dept., social services, and other dept. as needed Carries out discharge planning functions Member UR committee	40	1
	Discharge planner	Provides discharge planning services for automatic and special referral Prepares reports and documentation of activities	40	1
Nursing	Infection surveillance nurse	Carries out surveillance efforts through record review and other procedures Prepares statistics and reports Reviews policies and recommends change Staffs the infection control committee	40	1
	Quality assurance supervisor	Coordinates department QA efforts and studies Meets with nursing, evaluation, nursing practice, and nursing standards committees Liaison to medical audit committee	40	1
		Total	376	9.4

Source: Reprinted from L. L. Pfeffer-Kloss, "Managing Quality Assurance Information," *Topics in Health Record Management,* December 1980, with permission of Aspen Systems Corporation.

- to plan, prod, and suggest priorities, not to do detailed studies "in committee"
- to recommend and report, not to intervene directly

The council receives reports, passes on recommendations, makes reports to the governing body, and prepares information for outside agencies with the proper blend of firmness, fairness, compliance, and respect for confidentiality. Most of the recommendations of the committee—since they go to authority figures or groups for final action—are by consensus rather than by vote. With this approach, the council need not be feared as interfering with or threatening established authority, such as that of the board of trustees, administrator, medical staff executive committee, or administrator of nursing services.

With respect to the position of the QCC in the hospital structure, several options have been suggested.

Option A

Rather than "Quality Coordinating Council," the multidisciplinary group is called something like the "Quality Assurance Board" and is awarded superpower status. This "Big Brother" approach obviously raises two difficulties:

1. It immediately establishes an adversary relationship between the council and the existing hospital authority, which is hardly in line with the intended functions of sharing information, increasing communication among health care disciplines, and finding cooperative solutions to common problems.
2. "Quality assurance" activities tend to become procedural and legalistic, rather than substantive and patient care-related.

Option B (a Variant of A)

A "Quality Assurance Board" is established on a par with existing authority (administrator, clinical and patient care department heads, medical staff executive committee, and the board of trustees). This option implies a division of authority, with the new Quality Assurance Board assuming some areas of authority traditionally controlled by other authority structures. However, it also creates an adversary relationship rather than a cooperative one, since hardly any authority group in any organization is anxious to deliver part of its authority into the hands of a new structural component. Again, the result is more likely to be procedural distraction than substantive accomplishment.

Option C

The "Quality Assurance Department" is created and placed on a par with existing hospital departments, usually reporting directly to an assistant or associate administrator. This model raises the question of whether or not others will respond to the suggestions of the quality assurance department.

Example: A nurse in a large, complex urban hospital is the Vice-President for Nursing Quality Assurance, on a par with four other vice-presidents, all of whom report directly to the administrator of nursing services. After only a few months on the job, she is frustrated because, unless the other vice-presidents of nursing respond to her suggestions, she cannot achieve her goals. However, the other vice-presidents of nursing consider her suggestions to be (a) intervention with their rightful areas of authority and (b) accusations of inappropriate management.

Although a large, complex hospital often has a "Quality Assurance Department," its assigned functions are usually to support the activities of authority groups and the QCC.

Option D

The existing authority structure is left intact, and recommendations of the council—often framed by consensus rather than formal votes—are conveyed to the proper authority group in the hospital for consideration and implementation. This model seems to reflect best the intended function of coordination/integration.

At first glance, the main problem with this model appears to be inadequate clout for the QCC. There is a subtlety that can be recognized and implemented, however; the clout of the quality QCC can come, not from a bylaws provision, but from the fact that the council is well appointed. The clout of the QCC then comes from the positions of its members in the traditional authority structure of the hospital. Thus, since the council is usually composed of the chief executive officer or a representative, the chief of the medical staff plus a physician department head or two, the administrator of nursing services plus one or two nursing supervisors, a hospital trustee, and the heads of one or two patient care departments, the recommendations of this group are not to be taken lightly; when a recommendation is discussed by the proper hospital authority group, important voices will be urging its adoption and implementation. Hospitals organized in this way are reporting substantive results, accomplished without threatening existing authority.

The QCC need not be an additional layer of internal bureaucracy. It is not necessary to appoint another committee or hire another person to implement this function. The key is to put existing groups and individuals to work in new ways.

Example: Hospital A combined two existing medical staff committees, added a nurse, an administrator, and a trustee, renamed the group the QCC, and proceeded with the functions as stated earlier.

Streamlining Medical Functions in Quality Assurance*

Physicians have long (and rightfully, it now appears) complained about the profusion of medical staff committees, both from the standpoint of efficiency (waste of time in the procedural sense) and effectiveness (waste of time in the lack of substantive accomplishment). One major reason medical staffs have had too many committees and too many meetings is that JCAH requirements *formerly* mandated a committee for every function, although the main purpose of the committee was described as meeting monthly and keeping minutes. Since JCAH requirements now emphasize accomplishing medical staff functions, medical staff leaders are free to consider alternative organizational approaches.

Traditionally, for example, the medical staff has a tissue and transfusion committee that meets monthly in order to monitor the use of blood and blood products. This committee provides regular reports to the medical staff executive committee. The following steps illustrate one possible alternative:

1. The QCC and medical staff executive committee, with input from department heads (e.g., medicine, surgery, obstetrics-gynecology, pathology, blood bank, and nursing) state what information is to be collected each month.
2. It is the responsibility of the quality care coordinator, working with medical records, blood bank personnel, and personnel from any other departments in which the information may be located, to design/adapt a format for displaying this information and to prepare this information monthly.
3. One physician accepts the role of transfusion monitor, whose assigned functions include:
    - analyzing the information initially
    - obtaining more detailed information from individuals or departments if necessary
    - solving minor and/or noncontroversial problems on an informal basis
    - reporting his or her activities to the QCC and/or the medical staff executive committee (a) for group discussion of a controversial issue, (b) whenever formal authority structure may be needed to assist with solution of a problem, and (c) routinely at least quarterly.
4. Needed changes are implemented by the individual/department with authority/responsibility to do so.
5. The QCC assumes responsibility for insisting on follow-up reports of impact (or lack of impact) of implemented changes.
6. A brief, summary report of this activity is included in the QCC's regular reports to the governing body.
7. Brief, summary reports of this activity are included in the file of material to be supplied to the JCAH and other agencies seeking evidence of compliance with their requirements.

---

*Source: Reprinted from Richard E. Thompson, "Organizational Considerations," *Quality Assurance in Hospitals: Strategies for Assessment and Implementation,* ed. Nancy O. Graham, Aspen Systems Corporation, © 1982.

Applying this approach to medical staff functions allows medical staffs to eliminate several meetings per year without eliminating medical staff functions. In fact, as experience is gained with this mechanism, participation of physicians with the needed clinical expertise is more likely, and the activity actually will become more effective because of its improved efficiency.

IDENTIFYING ISSUES/CONCERNS/PROBLEMS IN QA INVESTIGATION*

A quality assurance topic list that is likely to result in effective activity will reflect a combination of three sources of topics: (1) what health care practitioners and institutional managers want to study and improve; (2) what they know they ought to study, but do not really want to study; and (3) what others think they should study.

Health care practitioners and institutional managers are most interested in the issues that are causing blocks and frustrations to the individual or department suggesting the topic. For example:

- Why does it take so long to make an inpatient bed ready to receive a patient?
  —Emergency room physicians/nurses

- Why do the physicians insist on discharging diabetic patients before completion of the patient's "education program"?
  —Nursing in-service educator

- Why can't laboratory results be returned faster?
  —Physicians

- Why can't patients scheduled for cardiac catheterization be sent to the cath lab on time?
  —Head nurse, cardiac catheterization lab

- Why can't the doctors write complete and legible oxygen orders?
  —Respiratory therapist

---

*Source: Reprinted from Richard E. Thompson, "A Method for Identifying Quality Assurance Issues/Problems," *Quality Assurance in Hospitals: Strategies for Assessment and Implementation*, ed. Nancy O. Graham, with permission of Aspen Systems Corporation, © 1982.

- Why don't internists call a surgical consult faster and more often?
  —General surgeons

- Why don't surgeons allow a trial of medical therapy instead of resorting to surgery so fast?
  —Internists

- Why do physicians insist on routine use of this dangerous antibiotic when an equally effective yet safer alternative is available?
  —Hospital risk manager

It is readily apparent that resolving these problems would have several beneficial effects; it would relieve frustration of the people suggesting them, improve patient care, please third party payers, and assist with liability and loss control.

Examples of situations that are often studied without enthusiasm include:

- Members of the department of surgery, as well as the operating room nurses, know that about three of five appendixes removed by Dr. Y are normal, whereas the more clinically acceptable rate is one of five.

- Special radiological procedures are overused by the physician who contributes heavily to the hospital's income by admitting about one-third of its total patients.

- The nursing errors can clearly be traced to one unit, one shift, and one nurse. The one nurse has served the hospital well for 29 years and is close to retirement; no one wants to hurt her feelings.

- Reasons for "long" length of stay are not really of great interest to health care practitioners, but the study must be done to prevent accusations of arbitrary overutilization by the local PSRO.

This can be a most productive topic area, and it will be even more productive when explanation and persuasion are used so that individuals change by choice. The adversary, threatening, punitive approaches that were more common in the 1970s often increased resistance to change.

- Someone always believes length of stay should be studied.

- Hospitals will be pressured to examine politically expedient issues such as "unnecessary surgery" and total cost figures.

- JCAH's requirements for the medical staff include review of blood use, tissue, medical records, and antibiotics.

This is the least productive method of topic selection. Even if data reveal a problem, an external demand usually transfers attention from the patient care problem to the issue of resisting external interference.

In these present early days of evolving quality assurance methods, most productive results come from examination of problems/issues suggested by practitioners.

The Key Question

The key question now becomes: How can valuable perceptions of health care practitioners be collected and used as a primary source of productive topics? There are two traditional methods:

1. Questionnaire. Through a memo, the quality assurance committee asks, "What do you suggest we study?"
2. Suggestion box type activity. Quality assurance coordinators, administration, medical staff leaders, nursing leaders, and patient care department heads make a topic request form available.

A third method to consider is the "focus group" method. A focus group is an informal discussion convened for the specific purpose of identifying issues and attitudes. The procedure involves a free and open discussion by a small group (no more than 10 or 12 individuals) led by a moderator whose function is to focus discussion on essential topic areas. The typical focus group discussion session lasts one to two hours.

The purpose of focus groups is not usually to codify data; while codifying the information can provide insights, the base is almost always too small to make quantifiable projections to the total population. When quantifiable projections are desired, the focus group sample, as well as the questions to which they are asked to respond, must be carefully selected. Such attention to detail is not necessary for most focus groups, *the purpose of which is to initiate, isolate, and verbalize specific areas to be submitted to further study and action.*

Discussions among practitioners, administrators, and department heads can become a systematic part of the problem identification portion of the hospital's quality appraisal/action plan. Such focus groups, purposely constructed and convened by the quality assurance coordinator or other suitable person for the express purpose of identifying issues for study, provide an effective and inexpensive problem identification method that can be instituted by a hospital of any size.

Examples of Topics Identified in Focus Groups

The following productive topics did not come from data, but from interaction among health care professionals convened expressly for the purpose of identifying issues to be addressed through the quality appraisal mechanism:

- length of time for pharmacy to respond to new medication orders.
- suspicion that results of sputum cultures are not valid.
- physician/nurse resistance to isolation procedures.
- preoperative stays over 2 days. In this instance, this topic suggestion did *not* come from a third party payer. The physicians in this focus group discussed the fact that they could not obtain beds for their elective admissions because a few physicians kept the hospital's occupancy rate high by ordering prolonged workups in the hospital prior to elective surgery.
- questionable pediatric admissions. This topic was not suggested by Blue Cross, but by pediatricians who felt that emergency room physicians should have better instruction in handling infants with such problems as high fever.
- a high incidence of repeat gallbladder x-rays.
- indications for IPPB.
- the number of units of blood ordered crossmatched or screened related to the number actually used, to be displayed by surgical procedure and by physician.
- use of arterial blood gas measurements in asthma patients. The new respiratory disease specialist on the staff insisted that such determinations be made in all patients and accused other members of the staff of "practicing medicine by the seat of their pants." This is an excellent example of an

issue that must be resolved objectively, rather than emotionally.

QUALITY ASSESSMENT TECHNIQUES*

In quality assessment the underlying values of the patients, providers, or institutions must be made explicit. The purpose of the assessment, whether it be improvement in patient care, cost containment, accreditation, or some combination of these, must also be made explicit.

When the problem to be studied has been identified, a number of decisions must be made before a specific assessment strategy is chosen:

1. the purpose of the assessment
2. the scope: general or specific (statistical profiles of an organization or a symptom, a diagnosis, patient behavior)
3. setting/service: one/several/many
4. aspect of quality: one/several/many and technical versus art of care aspects
5. approach: structure, process, outcome, or some combination
6. patient focus: individual, group, or population
7. time frame: retrospective, concurrent, prospective
8. criteria/standards: explicit, implicit, or some combination
9. sources of information: one/few/many (billing forms; discharge abstract; charts; profiles; incidence reports; malpractice claims; committee reports, e.g., tissue, mortality, or infection; length of stay data)
10. obtaining information: direct observation, interview, encounter form
11. samples: random, nonrandom, population
12. timing: one shot, periodic, continuous

In general a good methodological approach should (1) measure what happens to the patient, i.e., it should be directly or indirectly related to outcome; (2) be relatively simple, practical, timely, and inexpensive (in terms of both money and provider time); (3) not disrupt the medical system; (4) be consistent and objective so that it can be applied repeatedly, using the same set of ground rules; and (5) be widely acceptable to the medical community.

During the last few years, several improvements have been made in *process assessment*. One is *criteria mapping,* in which "laundry lists" of criteria have been replaced by branching, weighted, contingent criteria. This method attempts to reflect the decision-making process of physicians as it is applied to individual patients. The development of criteria and of branched abstracting guidelines required by this method is complex, but only those criteria items that are relevant to a given diagnosis are applied. Results from this method may correlate better with outcome because they reflect differences among patients.

Two of the newer strategies are based on *outcomes*: the use of the staging concept and the use of sentinel health events. The basic premise underlying the *staging concept* is that the seriousness of a patient's condition at a point in the treatment process is a good indicator of the quality of prior care. If, therefore, a large proportion of patients admitted to hospitals with disease X are in an advanced stage of that disease, it may indicate a failure of prehospitalization ambulatory care for disease X. With this method, inpatient records are used to assess ambulatory care, an advantage because ambulatory care records are often less reliable than inpatient records. It may be limited in its usefulness to a fairly small number of diseases and to large patient samples, however.

Sentinel health events, the other outcome-based approach, utilizes the occurrence of preventable diseases, avoidable complications, and untimely deaths as warning signs of suboptimal care. It is of most value when used by an institution or agency that can foster improvements in any of the multiple settings where problems may have contributed to such outcomes (e.g., clinics, hospitals, and private practitioners).

The process of care can be examined in terms of intermediate or short-run outcomes, i.e., those outcomes discernible from the medical record. In the *comprehensive quality assurance system,* practitioners review a small number of charts to identify problems (microsampling). Based on identified problems, standards are set and a chart audit is done to compare the charts

---

*Source: Reprinted from Nancy Graham and Stephen N. Rosenburg, "Overview of Newer Strategies," *Quality Assurance in Hospitals: Strategies for Assessment and Implementation,* ed. Nancy O. Graham, with permission of Aspen Systems Corporation, © 1982.

with the standard. Charts that do not meet the standard are subject to peer review, corrective action, and reaudit. This is a method for assessing care and assuring it.

Profile analysis is a form of retrospective review in which aggregated patient care data undergo pattern analysis. A profile is defined as the presentation of aggregated data in formats that display patterns of health care services over a defined period of time. Three types of profiles may be reviewed: (1) patient profile, (2) physician profile, and (3) institutional profile. Profiles of patterns of practice can assist not only in the utilization review process, but also in the general planning process, specifically for staff allocations, budget justification, and quality assessment and assurance.

Two other methods that can be used to examine the process of care and a wider range of outcome criteria are the use of *tracers* and health accounting. *Tracers* are health problems that, when combined into sets (three or more conditions), supposedly shed light on the quality of all care and components of care. At least one tracer condition in the set should involve each age and sex group in the population served, and at least one should test each aspect of care (e.g., diagnostic problems, patient management, or follow-up). An explicit review is then made of process and outcome for each condition in the set. *Health accounting* is a five-step cyclical process in which priorities are set and expected outcomes are estimated for a group of patients and then compared with actual outcomes. If they differ, the process of care is assessed to determine the reason; corrective actions are taken; and outcomes are reassessed. The cycle continues until expected and observed outcomes match.

Medical audits are retrospective chart reviews of patient care. The most commonly used chart audit is the one developed by the Joint Commission on Accreditation of Hospitals. The medical audit is a method of assessing care, but it does not assure the quality of patient care.

Each of these methods has strengths that make it most appropriate in some situations and limitations that make it inappropriate in others. Table 38-2 presents the pros and cons for these methods.

With a little ingenuity, most of these strategies can be adapted and improved to overcome the specific limitations listed on the table.

Some of the table's columns require comment. For each of the seven strategies, a focus on process and/or outcome is indicated. Those strategies that measure outcome alone need to be coupled with other techniques if specific defects in process are to be identified and corrected. Under Time Frame, it has been indicated whether a strategy provides concurrent information that can be used improving the care of the patients under review or retrospective information for the benefit of future patients only.

Some of the strategies can easily be used to assess the care of patients with certain presenting symptoms, regardless of their diagnoses. Other strategies depend on a prior diagnosis and, therefore, may exclude from evaluation those patients for whom the diagnosis was missed.

SETTING CRITERIA FOR QUALITY OF CARE*

A criterion should answer the question: What does a physician, nurse, or patient have to do or demonstrate in order to achieve satisfactory care or status? Written criteria should start with action verbs that describe the specific desired behavior or clinical status, e.g., assess, teach, observe, monitor, or record. The action verb should be followed with the content involved, e.g., assess character, depth, and rate of respiration; observe dressing for evidence of bright red blood; or monitor amount of urinary output per hour.

The California Medical Association and California Hospital Association developed a guide for criteria formation. They ask the question: Can the criterion RUMBA?

Relevant. Each criterion must be specifically related to the objective of the study. It should be the most efficient or effective indicator of good care for this particular group of patients. It should not represent a routine test or standing order.

Examples: Does this criterion apply to this phase or would it more appropriately be

---

*Source: Reprinted from Nancy Graham, "Criteria Development," *Quality Assurance in Hospitals: Strategies for Assessment and Implementation,* ed. Nancy O. Graham, with permission of Aspen Systems Corporation, © 1982.

Table 38-2 Advantages and Disadvantages of Seven Newer Strategies of Health Care Assessment

	Focus of Approach		Most Appropriate Setting		Source of Data			Time Frame	
	Process	Outcome	Inpatient	OPD or Group	Patient Charts	Patient Exam or Interview	Other	Concurrent	Retrospective
Criteria mapping	x		x	x	x				x
Staging		x	x	x	x				x
Sentinel health events		x	x	x	x		x		x
Comprehensive quality assurance	x	x Short-run	x	x	x	x		x	x
Profile analysis	x	x Short-run	x	x	x		x		x
Tracers	x	x	x	x	x	x			x
Health accounting	x	x	x	x	x	x		x	x

	Care Assessed of			Comparison		Criteria		Considerable Preparation Required	Many Tasks Delegatable to Nonprofessionals	Applicable to Symptoms	Built-in Corrective Phase
	Individual Patients	Patients Groups	Populations	Individual Clinicians	Institutions	Explicit	Implicit				
Criteria mapping	x			x	x	x		x	x	x	
Staging		x	x		x	x		x	x		
Sentinel health events		x	x		x	x					
Comprehensive quality assurance		x		x	x	x	x		x	x	x
Profile analysis		x	x	x	x	x			x		
Tracers		x	x		x	x		x	x	x	x
Health accounting	x			x		x		x	x	x	x

part of another audit of this topic with a different objective? Could this criterion also be applicable to another diagnosis/procedure? Is it routine care (such as pre-op chest x-rays) for all surgical patients or specific to cholecystectomy patients (such as operative cholangiograms)?

Understandable. Each criterion may be written in specific medical terminology, but must be worded explicitly as a complete statement to eliminate any possibility of misinterpretation.

Examples: Are there any other words which should be added to this criterion? Does "chest x-ray" mean "chest x-ray ordered" or "post-op chest x-ray shows no atelectasis?" Does "fever" mean 90° or 100° orally or rectally?

Measurable. Each criterion should include the time frame of the activity, the frequency of the activity and/or the specific range of test data expected.

Example: "Temperature recorded every four hours during first 24 hours post-op"; "hematocrit not less than 33% prior to surgery."

Behavioral. Each criterion should be indicator of the activity of a specific group of practitioners or patients in order to identify what or whose behavior should be changed.

Example: "Nurse's notes during first 24 hours post-op will document presence or absence of vaginal discharge."

Achievable. Each criterion should be realistic given the present state of the art, the local patient population, and the hospital staff's capabilities.

Example: Mortality from pneumonia may be expected to be higher in a small rural facility serving a population consisting largely of elderly patients.

DATA COLLECTION

Multi-Purpose Reviews*

Once the organizational structure is in place, data gathering tasks can be assigned on the basis of source of the information rather than by specific QA function. The goal should be to collect data to serve more than one QA function on each review of the record. Rather than reviewing a cohort of records sampled for a single study, all records or a random sample should be screened for the information needed for a variety of QA activities. For example, a single record of a postsurgical patient might be looked at for all the following information:

- Need for continued stay based on UR criteria;
- If transfused, the indications for transfusion;
- Indications and course of treatment with prophylactic antibiotics;
- Presence of postoperative morbidity;
- Documented tissue findings and agreement between the postoperative pathologic diagnosis and, if necessary, the documented preoperative indications for surgery;
- Completeness and adequacy of record documentation;
- Presence of any unexpected occurrences that should be reported to risk management; and
- Data to support any special studies such as monitoring aspects of therapy.

All of the above information should be documented 48–72 hours after surgery and could be collected concurrently.

Certain other data must be collected after discharge, including the most diagnosis-specific data, since final diagnoses are not available until after discharge, and data on readmissions, discharge status, and other post-discharge events or follow-up.

---

*Source: Reprinted from Linda F. Pfeffer-Kloss, "Managing Quality Assurance Information," *Topics in Health Record Management,* December 1980, with permission of Aspen Systems Corporation.

Data Sources*

To assess adequately priorities for problem-solving, one emphasis of the 1980 Joint Commission on the Accreditation of Hospitals (JCAH) quality assurance standard, hospitals will need valid information upon which to base their focus. This information must be derived from an array of data sources supplied by all areas involved in quality assurance activities and transformed into a tool for decision making. The challenge will undoubtedly be to integrate data collection activity in such a way as to avoid duplication and maximize the probability that problems will be identified.

The Incident Report

The role that quality assurance plays in the prevention of risk makes the hospital incident report mechanism a major source of untapped information for identifying problems. The systematic aggregation of problem-related information from incident reporting once centralized, integrated, and analyzed can assist in problem identification and correction before harm occurs.

Correspondence Logs

Medical record departments can contribute greatly to control of liability in the area of claims prevention by the collection of data from routinely received attorneys' requests for medical records. Correspondence logs that keep track of dates that requests are received and information is mailed can be redesigned to capture events that may have initiated a patient's seeking an attorney. Incidents that are not reported by hospital staff can be identified by this mechanism.

Use of Claims Runs

Many hospitals insured under corporate liability programs receive quarterly claims runs that can be used as a tool for quality assurance activity. These reports are usually divided into general and professional liability categories that summarize all claims by type of liability, type of

---

*Source: Reprinted from Jacquelin G. Diener, "Data Collection—New Tools for Quality Assurance," *Topics in Health Record Management,* December 1980, with permission of Aspen Systems Corporation.

expense (indemnity cost, attorney fees, investigating fees, court costs) and claim status. Problems identified by an analysis of claims can then be corrected by quality assurance personnel if sufficient communication exists between risk management and quality assurance.

Questionnaire Data

Patient questionnaires and employee questionnaires can provide valuable information with which to assess the quality of services offered.

Committee Review Findings

A method for gathering data that can facilitate analysis and draw attention to emerging patterns uses a simple grid that lists provider numbers along one axis and all review committees by name along the other axis. Whenever a review committee such as blood utilization or tissue review refers a provider for disciplinary action, that provider is entered on the grid for that review committee. The medical record number can also be entered so that an individual record that is referred to more than one committee will stand out. Monthly summaries should be reported to the quality assurance committee.

The grid can be expanded to include physicians whose privileges have been suspended due to failure to complete medical records and who were responsible for denial of hospital reimbursement by third party payers. The dollar amount of each denial can be accumulated by a physician for administrative information and fed back to the physician as part of an ongoing attempt to modify behavior. An annual report can be used for the credentialing process as well as providing information necessary for the reporting to the Quality Assurance Committee any physician whose privileges have been suspended for more than a specific number of days in the calendar year.

Concurrent Monitoring Data*

Another technique for data collection that has recently gained attention and has wide potential for problem identification and early resolution is concurrent monitoring.

Use of Utilization Review Personnel

An excellent vehicle for concurrent monitoring is utilization review personnel. In addition to the traditional review of indications for admission, length of stay, and appropriateness and necessity of ancillary services delivered, explicit criteria can be abstracted by the utilization review coordinators. At the time of admission review a preselected list of screens is checked to see if the patient should be entered into the study. If so, a data collection form is used to record conformance to the criteria. This approach offers an ongoing compilation of data that contributes to speedy problem identification, rapid correction, and instant monitoring of effectiveness of action taken to eliminate the problem.

Generic Screens

Concurrent review using generic screens can be useful to both quality assurance and risk management programs. The generic criteria concept, developed by the California Hospital Association-California Medical Association Medical Insurance Feasibility Study, was originally designed to assist in the identification of potentially compensable events (PCEs). Twenty nondiagnostic-specific screening criteria that can be easily applied to any medical episode have been published as a result of the study. Examples of criteria that can be adopted or adapted to be used as screens for problems in hospital quality assurance programs are transfers to special care units, returns to the operating room during the current admission, and transfers to another acute care hospital. In-depth peer review of cases identified by generic screens may reveal evidence of a problem in the making. This information would not easily be obtained by a retrospective review of a particular diagnosis. Thus concurrent data collection may provide a clue that might not be available once the patient's medical record is stored in the medical record department. There is no easy way to retrieve such information on routine discharge abstracts by medical record personnel without time-consuming review of every entire medical record to find possible events.

Concurrent monitoring of antibiotic use can illuminate patterns of misuse and overutiliza-

---

*Source: Reprinted from J. G. Diener, "Data Collection—New Tools for Quality Assurance," *Topics in Health Record Management*, December 1980, with permission of Aspen Systems Corporation.

tion. A minireview of the ordering of cultures and sensitivities might reveal some interesting information; a simple telephone call to a physician who has failed to order one might be much more effective than the accumulation of statistics on the lack of physician compliance with standards for use of antibiotics.

Discharge Analysis Data

The discharge analysis function carried out in the medical record department may be more useful if moved to the floor and incorporated into the ongoing concurrent review process. Failure to verify verbal orders by physicians is often the source of problems such as medication administration errors and the ordering of duplicate laboratory tests. These could be monitored by the discharge analyst. The analysis of records immediately after discharge can prove fruitful in obtaining the final diagnosis from the physician before the record arrives in the medical record department. This can assist in providing accuracy of information in the medical record itself, the most frequently used data source in the hospital. The discharge analyst can perform small studies on records of surgical patients to ensure that histories and physicals as well as other vital information are recorded before the patient goes to surgery. Also, studies on the adequacy of documentation of pre- and postanesthetic evaluations can be done concurrently. These small studies can easily be compiled manually on abstracts and submitted for tabulation and display for the quality assurance committee.

Index Data

Hospitals that subscribe to discharge abstract systems that provide reports based upon coding of diagnoses and procedures may find these methods of limited usefulness to quality assurance activities. However, more creative use of these reports is now called for. The comparative analysis of data summarized in the reports may indicate changes in behavior patterns of providers, changes in patient population, utilization of services, etc. The *ICD-9-CM* provides misadventure codes which, if carefully interpreted, can offer red flags for further investigation. The abstract services frequently provide some flexibility in data collection at relatively low cost, allowing hospitals to tailor reports to facilitate monitoring of selected aspects of care.

THREE SPECIFIC TECHNIQUES

1. A Comprehensive Quality Assurance System (CQAS)[*]

The Comprehensive Quality Assurance System (CQAS), an approach based on audits of single criteria related to problems with a high index of suspicion, began to evolve in 1968. By 1973, it existed as a formal program used in the Northern California Kaiser Permanente Medical Centers.

CQAS rejects the traditional approach of "demonstrating good care" as a primary objective of the audit and substitutes "finding what's wrong and fixing it." If objective audit measurement does not corroborate suspicions about a problem, good care in regard to that element has inadvertently been shown. Aiming toward the demonstration of good care, however, tends to maintain the status quo, develop large data banks of relatively useless information, and expend large sums of money; in the end it can convince no one that all care is good. Total quality literally has an infinite number of elements and it is impossible to assess them all. All we can demonstrate is improvement in suboptimally performed elements of care, tracking each of these elements (expressed as audit criteria) separately through action and remeasurement.

According to an analysis by the Institute of Medicine, CQAS (for both hospital and ambulatory care) costs 25 cents per member per year for Northern California Kaiser's 1.3 million members. This is considerably less expensive than most other systems.

CQAS needs only short lead times to improve care. The system can literally be started the day after a problem has been identified. The measurement can be done the next day and the results returned in a week. It is not necessary to develop lists of criteria, stages of disease, new forms, data bases, etc. Coded diagnoses of procedures are never used in the ambulatory sector, and are rarely used in the hospital sector. Errors most often occur across diagnostic lines and,

---

[*]Source: Reprinted from Leonard Rubin and Meg A. Kellogg, "The Comprehensive Quality Assurance System," in *Quality Assurance in Hospitals: Strategies for Assessment and Implementation*, ed. Nancy O. Graham, with permission of Aspen Systems Corporation, © 1982.

more important, a missed diagnosis is often the worst error. Even when a problem confined to one disease entity is studied, ways to pull charts other than by codes are usually found to be more satisfactory. "Shoe box files" are often used to select chart numbers. Examples of such "files" are recent X-ray logs, operating room logs, emergency room logs, requisition slips or result logs kept by the laboratory, and prescription slips kept in the pharmacy.

CQAS Characteristics

1. Does *not* depend on: abstract, coding, chart format (3" × 5" cards okay), computer, electronic data processing, *any* data base, style of practice (fee-for-service or prepaid) or disease orientation (missed diagnosis problem)
2. Primarily addresses problems
3. Based on improvement (evaluation built in)
4. Comprehensive
   A. Setting—ambulatory, hospital, long-term care, etc.
   B. Performance improvement of: physician, nurse, patient, ancillary services, etc.
   C. Timing: concurrent or retrospective
5. Addresses many (not all) kinds of problems
   A. Quality (process or outcome)
   B. Utilization (over or under)
   C. Medicolegal hazards
6. Economical operation
7. Short lead time to improvement
8. *Locally* determined standards or criteria
9. Minimizes practitioner (physician, nurse, etc.) time, expense

The CQAS Process

Figure 38-1 presents a flow chart of the CQAS process. Note that the standard is not set until the problem has been identified and is found to be one that can be objectively measured. (The words "criterion" and "standard" are used interchangeably.) The objective of the process is eradicating the problem.

Regarding Medical Care Evaluation (MCE), criterion setting is *not* the first step. The ten essential MCE study steps required by PSRO are numbered in circles in Figure 38-1. The six essential steps of a "patient care evaluation" by the Joint Commission on Accreditation of Hospitals are numbered without circles. The diagram shows the interdepartmental or interdisciplinary activity in quality assurance as well as the departmental activity. Each department goes through a problem identification and standard setting process and submits audit standards to the central audit committee for priority setting and measurement. Some standards are also adopted for measurement across departmental lines.

The first step then—the "input" into the audit cycle—is the identification of problems. Note that suggestions for problems to be studied can come from any source: complaints from staff or patients, medicolegal review, statistical reports, chart audit, etc. The problem identification method of chart audit or "microsampling" consists of having practitioners review charts without preconceived, explicit criteria. This method is a very effective and enjoyable way to discover large numbers of significant problems but it is not an indispensable component of CQAS.

The process of microsampling is quite simple. A small number of charts (5 to 20) are picked by index visit about six weeks prior to the meeting. This interval allows time for any follow-up to have taken place or for laboratory tests to be filed. By selecting hospital and clinic charts of patients, more problems are discovered. These problems sometimes involve the hospital-ambulatory interface, but just as often are unrelated to the reason for hospitalization. Two practitioners in turn look for problems in each chart and the agreed-upon results are presented to the group. The group or committee then selects by unanimity elements agreed to be problems. This procedure takes the old "one-on-one" review and converts it to a more objective process without losing its virtues. Figure 38-2 shows a free format data collection sheet for chart review which avoids the "tunnel vision" imposed by fixed forms. The range of potential problems found is totally unconstrained. Record identification is coded to decrease the chance of someone using the data in malpractice actions, but does not preclude tracing the patient in a case where the patient is still at risk and intervention can be helpful (one concurrent aspect of CQAS). Such intervention is entered under "Refer for Action."

It is important to note that it is essential to achieve unanimity in regard to the observation being an error in the particular chart under re-

Comprehensive quality assurance system flowchart

view but it is not essential to have unanimity in regard to the standard or criterion. Requiring unanimity here may stop all progress because of differing views about the purpose of the standard. The standard is written so that a measurement can be made to determine if the agreed-upon error was just a fluke, and if not, its frequency. In addition, if its frequency is not zero, the measurement will reveal the distribution (i.e., just on night shift, only among some physicians, only among physicians in one department, just on weekends, etc.). The purpose for setting standards is not to create performance standards or directives for proper practice. Standards in quality assurance result *from* professional decisions; they do not result *in* professional decisions or actions. The criterion should be based on what action peers consider preferable in similar circumstances (not limited to identical situations). Generalization is neces-

Figure 38-2 Comprehensive quality assurance system microsample data sheet

```
CODE_____INDEX DATE_____HOSPITAL CLINIC FACILITY_____
REVIEWER #1_____REVIEWER #2_____TODAY'S DATE_____
AGE_____ SEX_____ REASON FOR INDEX CONTACT_____
REFER FOR ACTION_____
NOTE:  ENTER JUST "WHAT'S WRONG"
       NOT "WHO'S WRONG"
       NOT "WHAT'S RIGHT"
       LOOK FOR PROBLEMS IN QUALITY, WASTE, MEDICOLEGAL AREA
```

sary in writing a standard or criterion, because the agent responsible for the problem is unlikely to limit the error to a particular circumstance (e.g., if a significant gastrointestinal X-ray finding is overlooked, the likelihood that other types of X-ray findings will be overlooked is probably the same) and the likelihood of finding an identical circumstance is quite low. Thus, if a preoperative procedure is omitted in one instance of major surgery, it is likely to be omitted in others, and the likelihood of determining the frequency and distribution of the error is increased by widening the base of surveillance.

2. Profile Analysis: Retrospective Review*

Profile Analysis is a form of retrospective review in which aggregated patient care data are subjected to pattern analysis. Abstracting services such as the Professional Activity Study (PAS) and the Utilization Information Service (UIS) have been generating computerized displays of inpatient care patterns for many years.

The PSRO legislation specifically identifies three types of profiles that must be reviewed: (1) patient profiles, (2) practitioner profiles, and (3) institutional profiles. However, there is no reason why the techniques of profile analysis should be limited to the PSRO setting.

---
*Source: Reprinted from Elaine Remmlinger, "Profile Analysis," *Quality Assurance in Hospitals: Strategies for Assessment and Implementation,* ed. Nancy O. Graham, with permission of Aspen Systems Corporation, © 1982.

It is important that the hospital administrator understand the techniques of profile analysis and how this method can be applied to day-to-day operations. Profiles of practice patterns can not only assist in the utilization review process, but also can be used in the planning process, e.g., for staff allocations and budget justifications. Specifically, patient origin data (i.e., by ZIP code or area of residence) are utilized in studying services needed as compared with services available by area.

Patient Profiles

Patient profiles can be generated about individual patients or about a group of patients. One example of an individual patient profile is the study of a patient's readmissions both to the same and to other hospitals in the PSRO area. Once PSRO review is in use at all levels of care, profiles can be generated on the multiple encounters of a single patient traveling through the health care delivery system. An individual can be followed from the outpatient department, to the emergency room, to inpatient hospitalization, and, lastly, to a nursing home to determine if the care provided at all of these levels has met professionally recognized standards.

Patient profiles can also be generated for a group of patients according to any dependent variable (e.g., by diagnosis, procedure, or payment source).

Practitioner Profiles

Profiles are also to be prepared for each health care practitioner who provides inpatient health care services to federal beneficiaries, such as those whose care is paid for by Medicare, Medicaid, and Maternal Child and Health Programs. Since the PSRO data set requires the collection of unique identifiers for each physician, this type of profiling is feasible both within hospitals and among several hospitals.

Such analyses may be performed according to any number of dependent variables including total length of stay (LOS), preoperative LOS, or mortality rates. Table 38-3 is a simple example of a physician profile at Hospital 123. It displays for the top ten surgeons performing unilateral inguinal herniorraphies the number of cases, average preoperative LOS, and average (total) LOS. The wide range of values for these variables should be noted. This display presents many more questions than it answers; however, it is a place to begin further inquiry.

Physician profiles are also performed in the area of quality review. High mortality and/or complication rates among an individual physician's patients might indicate a problem in that practitioner's mode of practice. Profile analysis is one technique to study the extent of a potential problem. Table 38-4 is an example of a physician profile that includes patients in all hospitals where Physician No. 123456 practiced during the first six months of 1980. Each line represents the record of an individual patient treated by this physician during this time period. The single most striking fact in this display is the high mortality rate. Follow-up study, including chart reviews and meetings with the physician, would be required to determine whether a quality problem exists and what action is necessary. Continuing medical education may be indicated.

Institutional Profiles

Institutional profiles serve as the basis for decision making regarding delegation status, identification of problem areas, modification of review programs, selection of Medical Care Evaluation (MCE) study topics, and documentation of impact. Institutions can be compared to one another and to the PSRO area as a whole with respect to a number of variables.

Table 38-5 is one example of an institutional profile that would be studied in order to modify Hospital 456's review program. It shows the top 20 elective surgical procedures for this hospital during calendar year 1978. The mean preoperative and total LOS for each of these procedures would be compared with the experience of similar hospitals, the PSRO area as a whole, and the PAS norms to determine where review could be eliminated and where intensified review is required.

The Process of Profile Analysis

Once profiles are generated, a number of techniques can be utilized to analyze the results.

Table 38-3 Profile of Top Ten Operating Physicians Performing Unilateral Inguinal Herniorraphy [Elective Federal Admissions, 1980, Hospital 123]

Physician	No. Cases	Average Preoperative LOS	Average LOS
1	30	1.20	5.47
2	22	1.77	8.64
3	20	2.40	7.75
4	19	1.05	2.11
5	13	1.31	4.69
6	13	1.15	6.08
7	12	1.67	8.33
8	9	1.33	9.89
9	8	3.00	10.75
10	8	1.63	8.63
PSRO Areawide Experience		2.20	7.90

Table 38-4 Attending Physician Profile by Patient Record [No. 123456, January–June, 1980]*

Surgeon	Hosp. ID	Med Rec No.	Admit Date	Dis-charge Date	Dis-charge Status		Diag-nosis 1	Proce-dure 1	Diag-nosis 2	Diag-nosis 3		Admit Type
034567	123	1330173	2/13/79	3/03/79	1	(home)	5715	9904	57420	5789	1	(elective)
123456	123	1261268	2/27/79	3/17/79	1		7243		7292	359	1	
123456	123	1261291	3/29/79	3/31/79	8	(died)	4280	5794	514	7991	3	(emergency)
123456	123	1261295	3/06/79	4/01/79	1		1749	9202	1970	V163	1	
123456	123	1354184	3/19/79	4/10/79	1		1541	4869	1534	1532	1	
123456	456	1330103	3/21/79	4/16/79	1		4439		7079	2859	1	
123456	456	1354187	4/10/79	4/21/79	1		1985		1970	7823	1	
123456	456	1330148	2/27/79	4/22/79	1		7071	9202	7078	4439	1	
123456	789	1265370	4/16/79	4/26/79	8	(died)	4280		4151	42731	1	
123456	789	1354159	4/10/79	4/28/79	1		4111		4118	42789	1	
123456	789	1330166	4/29/79	5/02/79	1		5609		25000	4019	1	
123456	789	1354120	4/30/79	5/08/79	1		2859	4131	4519	7892	1	
123456	789	1354119	5/22/79	6/01/79	8	(died)	4111	5794	4409	4149	1	
123456	789	1354137	5/21/79	6/01/79	1		25000		4019	4101	1	
123456	012	1403454	6/04/79	6/08/79	1		55092		4556	71590	1	
123456	012	1348532	6/04/79	6/23/79	8	(died)	4538	9215	4409		1	
123456	012	1348548	6/18/79	6/30/79	1		4019	8721	2397	7883	2	(urgent)
123456	012	1348562	7/02/79	7/09/79	1		8472	8773	6180	56211	2	
123456	012	1348570	7/09/79	7/13/79	8	(died)	585	8773	25000	4019	1	
					1		3501	8752	53390	2639	2	

*All diagnoses and procedures are coded in the ICD-9-CM coding system.

Table 38-5 Top Elective Surgical Procedures [January–December, 1978 Hospital 456]

ICDA-8 Code	Procedure Name	No. of Cases	Mean Pre-Operative LOS	Mean LOS
14.5	Extraction of lens, intracapsular	92	2.33	8.70
70.3	Dilatation and curettage of uterus	80	1.67	4.83
74.0	Amniocentesis	64	0.43	2.00
58.2	Prostatectomy, transurethral	59	4.67	15.18
38.2	Repair of inguinal hernia, except recurrent	55	2.07	9.02
92.1	Local excision of lesion of skin and subcutaneous tissue	43	1.53	8.93
29.8	Cardiac revascularization	43	5.53	18.37
68.5	Ligation and division of fallopian tubes, bilateral	36	0.50	3.05
A4.6	Cystoscopy and urethroscopy without effect upon tissue	35	3.31	9.83
65.2	Mastectomy, partial	34	1.91	6.59
A4.5	Endoscopy of colon and rectum without effect upon tissue	32	3.33	10.33
75.9	Episiotomy	23	0.26	3.57
A4.4	Esophagoscopy and gastroscopy without effect upon tissue	22	4.77	15.36
47.5	Resection of colon, partial or subtotal	19	7.47	27.47
43.5	Cholecystectomy	18	4.17	16.78
A1.8	Biopsy of stomach and intestines	17	5.00	16.06
69.2	Abdominal hysterectomy, complete or total	17	1.81	11.38
61.2	Circumcision	16	1.07	2.47
A1.6	Biopsy of thorax	15	6.53	17.00
30.2	Cardiac catheterization, right or left heart	15	3.93	7.87

Generally, institutions and practitioners are compared with peer groups to determine aberrant patterns.

A second type of comparison is known as trend analysis. In this case, data are displayed over time to determine if changes (in LOS, for example) can be linked to specific events (e.g., PSRO binding review and withdrawal of delegation).

A third comparison utilizes existing norms, standards, or criteria.

The basic steps in profile analysis are as follows:

1. *Define the purpose of the analysis.* It is important that the purpose of the analysis be clearly defined, e.g., (a) to focus review activities, (b) to assess impact in preadmis-

sion review programs, (c) to review practice patterns of selected physicians for potential quality problems, or (d) to respond to outside requests for information.
2. *Identify the report formats appropriate for the defined purpose.* Many reports already available can be adapted for the purposes of the current study. Where necessary, additional information should be generated through the automated data system.
3. *Establish agreement on statistical patterns meriting further action.* Agreement on what constitutes an outlier requiring further inquiry should be preestablished when possible.
4. *Analyze profiles generated.* The team should analyze the profiles generated and request additional data when necessary.
5. *Determine findings.*
6. *Recommend appropriate corrective action and follow-up.* Follow-up can run the gamut from making decisions on focus review programs to initiating sanction reports.
7. *Monitor corrective action plan.* Monitoring must be conducted periodically to determine if improvements have been realized.

3. The Nursing Audit Approach*

Three audit approaches are commonly used today. They are the *organizational audit,* where staffing, facilities, and procedures are examined; the *outcome audit,* where the state of health of the discharged patient is deemed the significant criterion; and the *process audit,* where the quality of care being given patients in the hospital is the focus of inquiry. In this audit quality is evaluated from the viewpoint of the patient as well as the professional.

Requirements common to all such quality control programs are:

- the creation of a meaningful grading and recording unit questionnaire or instrument;
- a set of procedures for processing and analyzing the questionnaires to produce useful numerical measures of the quality of care when several dimensions of quality are simultaneously being monitored;
- an efficient mechanism of reporting quality measures generated over time by the audit system.

The Joint Commission on Hospital Accreditation (JCAH) has opted for an outcome audit based on the charts of discharged patients for both its medical and nursing audits. In effect, the Commission is assuming that professional standards have been employed by the medical and nursing staffs during a patient's stay if the end result and chart adhere to certain standards.

The Professional Activity Study—Medical Audit Programs (PAS-MAP) Information System is the most popular discharge abstract system, with 21 percent of the 7000 hospitals in the United States as subscribers. Although care elements deemed generally necessary for specific diagnoses are specified, as well as a "passing" percentage of patients who should receive each care element, the check is done after the patient has been discharged. This does not provide the kind of in-depth current audit of patient care plans as does, say, a peer review of a doctor's problem-oriented record. The latter system provides review while the patient is still present.

The Audit Committee

The primary responsibility for developing the audit instrument rests with the audit committee. The chairman, as well as other members of the committee, must possess broad clinical experience and expertise. He should know the procedures and policies of the hospital and should have well-developed communication skills. Ex-officio members might be medical directors, medical records officers, in-service and out-service coordinators, directors of nursing, and others. All members should have an active interest in the development of the audit system and should have the time necessary for the task.

The committee should first establish their objectives and outline the philosophy that will guide them through their endeavors. By review of these stated purposes, they may reassure themselves and others that their actions are consistent with their objectives and basic concepts.

The work of the committee should be directed toward specific end products, such as:

- The selection of the elements of the health care delivery process that are to be audited;

---

*Source: Reprinted from *Evaluating Quality of Care* by M. Clinton Miller, III and Rebecca Grant Knapp, with permission of Aspen Systems Corporation, © 1979.

- The development of a set of expectations and performance standards for these elements;
- The development of a valid, reliable, efficient audit instrument;
- The development of a reliable data collection process;
- The development of an analytic system;
- The development of a feedback system.

Audit Systems

There are several popular audit systems for audit committees to choose among, and as might be expected, each has its proponents.

1. Closed Audit Systems

Maria C. Phaneuf Nursing Audit Procedure

The Phaneuf procedure is a "closed" monthly audit based upon randomly selected charts of about 5 percent of the patients discharged since the last such audit. Each clinical area has a representative on the audit committee who works on approximately ten charts for up to three weeks. Chart scores are based upon 50 questions with different point weightings divided among the following seven nursing functions:

1. application and execution of physician's legal orders (6 questions)
2. observation of symptoms and reactions (6 questions)
3. supervision of the patient (7 questions)
4. supervision of those participating in care (except the physician) (4 questions)
5. reporting and recording (5 questions)
6. application and execution of nursing procedures and techniques (16 questions)
7. promotion of total health by direction and teaching (6 questions)

Questions may be answered "yes," "uncertain," or "no." The first two responses are assigned points; a "no" answer always earns zero. Total chart scores are obtained and the nursing service graded: unsafe, poor, incomplete, good, or excellent. The committee maintains graphs of the running averages of overall chart scores and of the scores in each of the seven categories.

Critics point out that due to the closed nature of the Phaneuf procedure many aspects of nursing care quality are never recorded on a patient's record.

2. Open Audit Systems

Commission on Administrative Services in Hospital (CASH) Scale

This audit instrument has 105 questions spread over nine categories. Each item has its own importance weight. The ten or so questions in a category are answered yes, no, or not applicable. It is estimated that it takes a trained observer 45 minutes to apply the questionnaire to a single patient. A difficulty with this instrument is that each question is to be answered with reference to a supplied list of auxiliary criteria that are not individually graded. As a consequence, in practice, auditors have variously interpreted the required number of passing criteria to give a positive answer to a particular question, thus making for unreliability.

The Slater Nursing Competencies Rating Scale

The purpose of most auditing instruments is to grade the quality of care being given by the nursing staff of a hospital unit. Corrective actions by an audit committee usually take the form of group lectures or general directives. The Slater scale, however, is designed to grade the individual practitioner. Typically, the auditing is done by instructors and head nurses. The ideal standard of performance for a first level staff nurse is postulated. The auditor creates an individual frame-of-reference card by listing the names of five staff nurses in the order best to poorest. There are 84 questions per form divided into the following six groups:

1. psycho-social-individual
2. psycho-social-group
3. physical
4. general
5. communication
6. professional

A question is graded from 1 to 13 depending on a comparison with the auditor's frame of reference, which includes categories of best staff nurse, average staff nurse, poorest staff nurse (as well as intermediate levels of functioning), not observed, and not applicable.

The subject's score is the total score divided by the number of items scored. The nurse is observed for specific question-related patient interactions. About 2½ to 3 hours is allowed per audit so that the auditor can observe well over the suggested minimum of 60 items. A "cue sheet" of criteria to back up the questions is provided. As in the case of the CASH instrument, this presumably contributes to unreliability when the same subjects are studied by different observers.

Quality Patient Care Scale (QualPaCS)

QualPaCS is a development of the Slater Nursing Competencies Rating Scale in which the salient innovations are reduction in the number of questions from 84 to 68, and advocacy of two auditors rating a single question. A mean score is obtained for each question answered. These means are averaged to get a questionnaire score. A cue list is still used as in the Slater scale.

MEDICUS Corporation Nurses Audit

The system developed at MEDICUS Corporation utilizes different questionnaires for different classes of patients. Any given class does not have a specific questionnaire but a set, which taken together constitutes a full questionnaire. Any given audit uses one of these partial questionnaires, chosen at random. The results of many such questionnaires are then pooled for a hospital unit. The motivation for this approach is a concern that nurses will learn in time to "look good" on a particular set of audit questions they are always exposed to. This is a proper concern for a noncomprehensive series of questions. However, since the audit questionnaires were developed as a comprehensive instrument for use throughout the hospital, most nurses' audit committees welcome the possibility that the nurses will learn how to score well on this instrument.

JCAH QUALITY ASSURANCE STANDARD*

Principle

The hospital shall demonstrate a consistent endeavor to deliver patient care that is optimal within available resources and consistent with achievable goals. A major component in the application of this principle is the operation of a quality assurance program.

Standard

There shall be evidence of a well-defined, organized program designed to enhance patient care through the ongoing objective assessment of important aspects of patient care and the correction of identified problems.

Interpretation

It is the governing body's responsibility to establish, maintain, and support, through the hospital's administration and medical staff, an ongoing quality assurance program that includes effective mechanisms for reviewing and evaluating patient care, as well as an appropriate response to findings. The plan for assuring the comprehensiveness and integration of the overall quality assurance program and for delegating responsibility for the various activities that contribute to quality assurance must be defined in writing. The mechanisms for assuring the accountability of the medical and other professional staffs for the care they provide should be described in the plan. The quality assurance program should be comprehensive, and it should be flexible enough to permit innovation and variation in assessment approaches. This does not imply that a totally new system should replace existing committees or functions concerned with quality assurance. To obtain maximal benefit, any approach to quality assurance must focus on the resolution of known or suspected problems (that impact directly or indirectly on patients) or, when indicated, on areas with potential for substantial improvements in patient care. It is incumbent on a hospital to document evidence of an effective quality assurance program.

The essential components of a sound quality assurance program-in-the-aggregate shall include:

- Identification of important or potential problems, or related concerns, in the care of patients.
- Objective assessment of the cause and scope of problems or concerns, including the determination of priorities for both investigating and resolving problems. Ordinarily, priorities shall be related to the degree of impact on patient care that can be

---

*Source: Reprinted from Joint Commission on Accreditation of Hospitals, *Accreditation Manual for Hospitals,* 1983 ed. (Chicago, 1982), with permission of the publisher.

expected if the problem remains unresolved.
- Implementation, by appropriate individuals or through designated mechanisms, of decisions or actions that are designed to eliminate, insofar as possible, identified problems.
- Monitoring activities designed to assure that the desired result has been achieved and sustained.
- Documentation that reasonably substantiates the effectiveness of the overall program to enhance patient care and to assure sound clinical performance.

The mechanisms for assuring that the components of the quality assurance program are used *as indicated* in specific studies or other quality assessment activities should be described in the plan.

The medical record remains an important data source in the identification of problems. However, other potentially useful sources include morbidity/mortality review; monitoring activities of the medical and other professional staffs; findings of hospital committee activities (for example, safety, infection control); review of prescriptions; profile analysis, including PSRO and other regional data; specific process-oriented/outcome-oriented studies; incident reports relating to both individual safety and clinical care; review of laboratory, radiologic, and other diagnostic clinical reports of services rendered; financial data (for example, hospital charge data on services rendered, liability claims resolutions); utilization review findings; data obtained from staff interviews and observation of hospital activities; patient surveys or comments; and data originating from third party payers/fiscal intermediaries.

Once an actual or potential problem is identified, it may be assessed prospectively, concurrently, or retrospectively. Whatever time frames for review and whatever quality assessment activities are used, representative care (that is, adequate sampling) provided by all clinical departments/disciplines and individual practitioners must be evaluated. While the evaluation of physician-directed care must be performed by physician members of the medical staff, nonphysician health care professionals should assess those aspects of care that they provide. However, the participation of both physicians and other health care professionals in the same quality assessment activities, when appropriate, is strongly encouraged.

Written criteria that relate to essential or critical aspects of patient care and that are generally acceptable to the clinical staffs shall be used to assess problems and measure compliance with achievable goals. These criteria should be clinically valid in that, when applied to actual practice, they can be expected to result in improved patient care/clinical performance. Structure, process, or outcome criteria; standards of practice of professional organizations; or criteria developed within the hospital or in cooperation with local hospitals may be utilized as appropriate. Although the use of criteria is required, there is no requirement to employ any specific method in the review or evaluation of patient care, nor is it implied that a specific number of criteria shall be employed.

Appropriate action must be implemented to eliminate or reduce the identified problem. Such action may include, but is not limited to, educational/training programs, new or revised policies or procedures, staffing changes, equipment or facility change, or adjustments in clinical privileges. Periodic monitoring of the results of the corrective action taken must be conducted to assure that the identified problem has been eliminated or satisfactorily reduced.

Pertinent findings of quality assurance activities throughout the hospital shall be reported to one, two, or all of the following, as appropriate, through their designated mechanisms: the medical staff, the chief executive officer, and the governing body. Findings related to the quality of care provided by a clinical unit that is not represented in a specific assessment activity shall be made available to the director of the unit.

Although each clinical discipline is responsible for identifying and resolving problems related to patient care, administering or coordinating the overall quality assurance program may be performed through a committee, group, or individual. The role of the patient care monitoring activities of the medical and other professional staffs that are already in effect, for example, the medical staff and clinical department rules and regulations relating to patient care requirements, must be identified within the quality assurance program.

Quality assurance activities proven to be effective should be integrated/coordinated to the degree possible. To the extent that such integration/coordination preserves any productive interrelationships, minimizes duplication, and assimilates information gathered, communication should be greatly enhanced and, in addition, there may be a potential for cost savings. Although some overlap between two or more activities is frequently desirable, any unnecessary or nonproductive duplication should be avoided. In the interest of consistency, terminology used to describe studies performed or methods employed in quality assessment activities should be defined.

As appropriate, the administration and medical staff shall determine the extent, if any, to which outside aid (consultants, voluntary or mandatory review bodies, and so forth) is used in the performance of quality assessment activities to identify and assess problems. However, attaining a suitable solution to problems is a function and responsibility, as appropriate, of the governing body, medical staff, or hospital administration.

In the coordination/integration of a hospital's quality assessment and control activities, related requirements specified in the following sections of the *JCAH Manual* should be considered: Anesthesia Services, Dietetic Services, Emergency Services, Functional Safety and Sanitation, Governing Body, Home Care Services, Hospital-Sponsored Ambulatory Care Services, Infection Control, Medical Record Services, Medical Staff, Nuclear Medicine Services, Nursing Services, Pathology and Medical Laboratory Services, Pharmaceutical Services, Radiology Services, Rehabilitation Programs/Services, Respiratory Care Services, Social Work Services, Special Care Units, and Utilization Review.

The quality assurance program shall be reappraised through a designated mechanism at least annually. The reappraisal should identify components of the quality assurance program that need to be instituted, altered, or deleted. Resultant recommendations, when instituted, should assure that the program is ongoing, comprehensive, effective in improving patient care/clinical performance, and conducted with cost-efficiency.

The effectiveness of a hospital's quality assurance program shall be emphasized in determining a hospital's accreditation status.

MEDICAL AUDIT

Medical audit is a general term for a method of peer review to assess the quality of care through a retrospective examination of certain key elements (critical criteria) in given diagnostic categories. Audits are conducted by groups of physicians who examine either the "process" (methods) or "outcomes" (results) of treatment, with an emphasis on uncovering overall patterns of patient care. Process medical audit examines whether specified procedures thought necessary for the patient are in fact being done. Outcome audit, on the other hand, assesses medical care by looking at the condition of patients during and after treatment and comparing the findings with hospital, regional, or national standards.

Medical audit could be expanded to areas other than quality review, becoming a tool to evaluate physician behavior in determining hospital privileges or to uncover administrative problems. Many methodologies for medical audit are inadequate and have been subject to widespread criticism, although few alternative systems have been developed. Besides methodology weakness, a fundamental problem is the lack of understanding of medical audit in general by health professionals.[*]

The Medical Audit Process[**]

While the methods used in medical audits vary, audit can be basically understood as a series of steps: selection of the study topic, selection of a time frame, development of criteria, chart review, committee analysis, and implementation of a corrective action plan.

In selecting a topic to be studied, the audit committee focuses on discharge diagnoses that are most frequently encountered or that present the most severe treatment problems. Randomly selecting discharge diagnoses for audit subject matter is not an accurate way of pinpointing problem areas; a method of topic selection more likely to reveal areas in which care can be improved is to obtain a medical staff or audit committee consensus on what diagnostic areas present the most problems. Topic selection should involve consideration of the severity of the illness, the extent to which adequate care can prevent injury to the patient, and an analysis

---

[*]Source: Reprinted from *PSROs and the Law* by John D. Blum, Paul Gertman, and Jean Rabinow, with permission of Aspen Systems Corporation, © 1977.

[**]Source: C. E. Lewis, "The State of the Art of Quality Assessment 1973," *Medical Care* 12, no. 10 (1974): 803.

of whether an audit can cause positive change. Topic selection may dictate the time period within which the audit will be conducted and the number of charts that must be included, although in some instances these can be left to committee discretion.

The next major stage in audit is the development by the audit committee of appropriate criteria for evaluation. Criteria having been broken down into four major types: "(a) indications for admissions; (b) hospital services recommended for optimal care; (c) range of length of stay and indications for discharge and; (d) complications for additional diagnoses." A delineation of criteria can also be broken down into therapeutic process criteria and outcome-at-discharge criteria. "Process" criteria can be developed by a method like the following; first, the indications for admissions are discussed and agreed upon, considering diagnosis and possible care. Some, but not all, admissions are clearly necessary by the time a diagnosis is suspected or, in surgical cases, by the time an operation is planned. Some admissions are discretionary; some may be contraindicated. Criteria must at least distinguish between the groups and may distinguish between "good" and "bad" discretionary decisions.

Second, the hospital services recommended for optimum care are discussed and agreed upon—the diagnostic procedure and then the optimum therapeutic procedures themselves. Significant "negative" values are also recorded here, such as the avoidance of morphine in bronchial asthma, or the avoidance of anticoagulants in peptic ulcer and other bleeding states.

Third, the optimum length of stay, or range of stay, is recorded. It may be easier to choose a fairly narrow range of stay rather than a single date because of conflicting experience of panel members, different therapeutic approaches, and, most important, the unknown in the equation—the patient himself.

Finally, complications or additional diagnoses requiring additional care and days of stay are considered, and recorded in as much detail as seems appropriate. The criteria are ready for use.

In the development of criteria, a committee generally attempts to reach some consensus as to what criteria should be adopted. Failure to reach a consensus may indicate that the criterion involved should not be used. Some audit committees do not develop their own criteria, but may borrow all or part of already-existing sets such as the diagnostic criteria established by the AMA or length of stay guidelines created by PAS.

Once criteria have been agreed upon, the actual review begins, following a three-stage process: screening, data review, and medical evaluation. A record analyst (e.g., medical record librarian, nurse) screens patients' charts in the diagnostic category being studied. The initial screener compares information in the patients' charts with the committee's criteria; results of the screening process are recorded on special worksheets. Generally, the completed worksheets contain information sufficient to enable the committee to act. In some instances, where the screening isolates problems, the committee may need one or more medical records in addition to the worksheets in order to perform adequate review.

It is the audit committee's task to evaluate whether or not the variations from the criteria were clinically justified. Deficiencies are documented and analyzed to determine to what or whom they can be attributed, i.e., the institution, the individual physician, the nursing staff, etc. The data analyzed by the committee for a given audit are compiled by committee aides (or by machine) according to key medical variables.

After the audit, the committee reports its findings, the types of evaluations made, and the criteria used. The report should be sent to the audit committee's parent organization (PSRO, hospital, or whatever) as well as to the reviewed physicians, nurses, etc.

The medical audit must also result in recommendations for corrective action whenever deficiencies are uncovered. Corrective action can take the form of suggested or required continuing education, individual counseling, reduction in staff privileges, alteration of institutional procedures, etc., depending upon the type of deficiency uncovered. Corrective action recommendations are passed to the appropriate person in the institution (whoever has the authority either to implement the recommendation or to initiate further studies). Serious deficiencies in institutional care may result in the implementation of concurrent monitoring for a specific problem area, to continue until a positive change has occurred.

A Survey of Hospitals' Use of Medical Audit*

In one study of 17 hospitals it was found that all of the hospitals were currently conducting medical audit. In addition, all of these hospitals were utilizing the system of quality assurance which had been developed and promoted by the Joint Commission on Accreditation of Hospitals. Several hospitals had used different audit systems prior to the introduction of the JCAH system but *all had switched to the JCAH system*. Three different types of organization of medical audit were identified with the larger hospitals tending to have more decentralized systems for distributing responsibility. In general, the quality of the criteria used to evaluate patient care varied between hospitals but was generally fair to poor. The few criteria sets which were judged to be good or very good by the raters tended not to be reflected in the quality of other criteria sets submitted by the same hospital.

Examination of the end product of medical audit at the hospitals revealed several problems. Audit directors frequently demonstrated problems in discriminating between "variations" and "deficiencies" in patient care. This resulted in a tendency not to explore the reasons for variations from the criteria and significant hesitation in labeling any variation as a deficiency. Feedback on either variations or deficiencies was handled on an informal basis, such as in conversation between audit director or department chairman and staff members. The use of formal continuing education programs based on audit findings was very infrequent. The fact that many of these hospitals had received delegated status from their local PSROs raises questions about the criteria used by PSROs to evaluate hospital medical audit processes.

The fact that all of the hospitals were using the JCAH quality assurance system probably reflects three factors. First, the JCAH has developed a system which appears to be useful to most of the people involved in medical audit. Second, there is a tendency for hospitals to use the system recommended by the accrediting agency. Third, and of greatest importance the use of the JCAH quality assurance system probably reflects the fact that the Joint Commission made an intensive effort to educate physicians and other health workers in the use of the system between 1972 and 1976. There were many workshops around the country which were well received and created intensive interest. These workshops focused primarily on explanation of the system and the development of criteria.

UTILIZATION REVIEW

Overview*

Utilization review is designed to aid in making the medical treatment process cost-effective, mainly through analyzing institutional length-of-stay and hospital bed utilization.

The Medicare Law made hospital-based utilization review committees a requirement for participation in Medicare reimbursement. Title XVIII of the Social Security Act required that participating hospitals and extended care facilities establish a plan for utilization review and that a standing UR committee be maintained:

1. for the review, on a sample or other basis, of admissions to the institution, the duration of stays therein, and the professional services (including drugs and biologicals) furnished (A) in respect to medical needs of the service; and (B) the purpose of promoting the most efficient use of available health facilities and services;
2. for such review to be made by either: (A) a staff committee of the institution composed of two or more physicians, with or without participation of other professional personnel; or (B) a group outside the institution which is similarly composed and (i) which is established by the local medical society and some or all of the hospitals and extended care facilities in the locality, or (ii) if (and for as long as) there has not been established such a group which serves such institution, which is established in such other manner as may be approved by the Secretary;

---

*Source: Gerald H. Escovitz, G. Burkett, Joan Kuhn, Carter Zeleznik, and Joseph Gonella, "The Effects of Mandatory Quality Assurance: A Review of Hospital Medical Audit Processes," *Medical Care* 16 (1978): 941–949.

*Source: Reprinted from *PSROs and the Law* by John D. Blum, Paul Gertman, and Jean Rabinow, with permission of Aspen Systems Corporation, © 1977.

3. for such review, in each case of inpatient hospital services or extended care services furnished to such an individual during a continuous period of extended duration, as of such days of such period (which may differ for different classes of cases) as may be specified in regulations, with such review to be made as promptly as possible, after each day so specified, and in no event later than one week following such day; and
4. for prompt notification to the institution, the individual, and his attending physician of any finding (made after opportunity for consultation to such attending physician) by the physician members of such committee or group that any further stay in the institution is not medically necessary.

While Utilization Review under Title XVIII (and later XIX) was designed to be a useful tool to gain medical information and to act as a means of continuing physician education, its main thrust was cost control. Sample retrospective review was to be adopted as an effective method to identify abuses in institutional missions, services, and patterns of care, without placing undue pressure on providers or practitioners. Extended stay review, on the other hand, was designed to prevent lengthy hospital stays that represented the greatest cost strain on the system. Thus the federal government attempted to build into a costly system a method to economize in the area of greatest abuse, which was felt to be extended stay.

After 1965, the JCAH took on the function of hospital certification. Under the then-new Medicare law, a JCAH-accredited facility with an acceptable utilization review plan was eligible to receive payment under Title XVIII. The JCAH, by virtue of the Medicare law, had in effect become a quasi-public licensing authority.

The function of a hospital utilization review committee is "to minimize the cost of patient care by monitoring the use of the hospital and its resources, primarily so that excess usage (and cost) is prevented," according to the American Hospital Association. If review is to be cost-effective, inappropriate admissions, unnecessary hospital stay, and overutilization of hospital ancillary services must all be considered.

Utilization review can take place at any of three times in relation to the service provided: it can be *prospective, concurrent,* or *retrospective.*

Prospective Review

Prospective review involves preadmission certification for elective hospital admissions. The purpose of preadmission certification is to insure that the hospital is the proper setting for providing the treatment a patient requires. This is accomplished in two ways: (1) By reviewing admissions against implicit or explicit admission criteria for the most common diseases; (2) by prospective authorization for a length-of-stay based on empiric, average regional or national experience for that specific disease. A length-of-stay range is assigned to each admission based upon experience within the hospital or data derived from the area.

Concurrent Review

Concurrent review is ordinarily used to monitor the appropriateness of the utilization of hospital beds and/or other facilities, and is applied to any admission, whether emergency or elective, within a certain number of hours after the patient has entered the institution. The number and types of cases reviewed will depend on the specific review program. Although concurrent review can be limited to "problem" cases, federal regulations appear to require more extensive (total) review. In concurrent review, a specific time period, based upon the admitting diagnostic category, is assigned to the patient's hospital stay. Length-of-stay determinations were originally based upon an arbitrarily fixed period, but now a certified length-of-stay for a given diagnosis usually represents an average (often the 50th percentile) stay, based on regional or national statistics. When the initial length-of-stay period is about to expire, if a request for additional days is made, an extension may be granted. Prior to an extension's approval, the case will be re-reviewed (continued-stay review) to determine whether or not there is medical necessity for continued hospitalization.

Retrospective Review

Utilization review programs also frequently use the technique of *retrospective review*, which begins after a patient has been discharged. Retrospective UR is usually used to determine medical necessity and appropriateness of care by examining the collected patient data. The patient's record, selected on the basis of criteria and standards set by the UR Committee, is "pulled" and certain data abstracted. The collected data are assessed for evidence of the need for treatment, length-of-stay, type of services, level of medical practice, etc. On the basis of data analysis, the UR Committee may draft certain reports (e.g., admission and discharge analysis, length-of-stay comparison, surgical procedure index) that are helpful in illustrating institutional care.

CLTR (A Retrospective Utilization Review)*

A key purpose of utilization review is to reduce "currently avoidable hospitalization"—the unnecessary admissions and excessive lengths of stay occurring within the context of commonly accepted medical practice and existing service availability. Avoiding admissions by treating people on an outpatient basis can save $75 to $100 per inpatient day if hospital beds and staffing levels can be reduced in line with a declining patient load over the medium term. Cutting average length of stay through timely provision of care reduces "hotel" costs by about $30 if the freed bed capacity is not immediately filled by new admissions.

Current techniques for utilization review focus on determining the extent of inappropriate utilization but do little to help the hospital manager identify its causes. What a manager needs to know is that limited operating room capacity or suboptimal scheduling procedures delay the timely delivery of surgical services, and that this extends length of stay for surgery cases by a specific amount—not just that average length of stay is one day longer than it is at broadly comparable institutions. Similarly, the knowledge that admissions are up because certain physicians consistently avoid outpatient treatment is far more useful to a manager than the mere fact that X percent of the hospital's admissions in a given year were unnecessary.

---

*Source: Reprinted from Arch B. Edwards, "Care Level and Timeliness Review—An Approach to Curbing Inappropriate Hospital Utilization," *Topics in Health Care Financing,* Spring 1981, with permission of Aspen Systems Corporation.

One technique developed by McKinsey & Company, Care Level and Timeliness Review (CLTR), was tested and refined in eight American hospitals. The technique enables hospital managers to answer two critical questions:

1. Do unexacting admissions procedures result in the hospitalization of patients who could be treated more appropriately in a clinic or other outpatient setting?
2. Once a patient is admitted, are delays in the provision of care extending stays unnecessarily, and where are these delays occurring?

The process is based on a retrospective review of a random sample of medical records that is conducted by a three- to four-person team within the hospital. Their work can be completed in two weeks if necessary, but more typically is carried out in about three months to minimize diversion of team members from their normal responsibilities. The review is divided into three major phases: (1) getting started, (2) conducting the records review and (3) developing corrective action programs.

Phase I—Getting Started

The first month of a typical three-month review effort is devoted to organization. Before this preliminary work begins it is critical that the hospital's physicians are assured that the review respects the delicate balance between the shared responsibilities of the physicians who make the admitting and discharge decisions and the hospital managers who must provide timely support services for patient care. The physicians' judgment will be needed in making difficult and primarily medical decisions about the appropriateness of admissions and discharges. Physicians' assistance will be necessary in evaluating the timeliness with which support services are provided—a responsibility shared with hospital administrators. The physicians must understand the project and be enthusiastic about it, for their cooperation and collaboration are critical to its success.

Select CLTR Steering Committee

The first step is selecting a steering committee to organize the review effort. This will be a functioning group with responsibility for approving the review plans, schedule and key elements such as performance standards to be used in assessing the timeliness of care. The committee should also review progress and results from the CLTR, and should advise on and approve action programs and their implementation schedule. The committee should be made up of five to seven people in total, and certainly should include the administrator and one or more representatives of the medical and nursing staffs. The heads of one or more of the functional departments might be included also. This diversity of membership will help ensure balanced action based on the results of CLTR.

Organize CLTR Team

The second step is organizing a three- or four-member CLTR team to carry out the review and make recommendations. The project manager, typically a senior member of the administrative staff or an outside consultant, will lead the team's effort and assume responsibility for its recommendations. The physician adviser is usually a senior member of the hospital's medical staff; his or her role is primarily the important and sensitive one of assisting the records analyst in applying criteria and standards for admissions and care timeliness in difficult-to-interpret cases. The records analyst may be a medical student, resident or utilization review coordinator, all of whom have proven to be effective in this role with the support of the medical adviser.

Establish Review Criteria

Admissions criteria may be developed from existing sources. The hospital's own utilization review committee may have already decided upon such standards, and these may merely need to be updated and verified. A number of PSROs in the United States have developed admissions criteria that can be readily modified for each hospital situation.

Timeliness of care and discharge can be measured against performance standards like those shown in Table 38-6. These standards are developed by working with department heads responsible for key diagnostic and therapeutic services. The aim is to first determine which diagnostic or therapeutic actions and procedures extend length of stay if not performed in a timely fashion. Performance criteria reflecting the hospital's accepted standards or target turnaround times are then set for these procedures.

Specify Patient Record Sample Structure

Once the review criteria are established, the CLTR team specifies a random sample of medical records that provides a representative cross-section of cases necessary to draw meaningful conclusions about the pattern of overall hospital utilization and operations.

Since about 200 representative cases will be ultimately required to give reasonable assurance of accuracy in gauging the number of available days incurred, the initial sample should be around 300 to allow for the culling out of statistically invalid cases.

Select Sample Cases

Cases whose length of stay is substantially fixed by considerations other than physician or hospital management action should be excluded from the final sample. Admissions that terminate in discharge against medical advice or death should be excluded, as should admissions with closely prescribed lengths of stay such as for dialysis and alcoholism programs.

Phase II—Conducting the Records Review

The second phase of CLTR is the analysis of the medical records selected in phase I. This review usually takes six to eight weeks to complete and is conducted by the records analyst with the help of the physician adviser. There are six steps in this phase.

Analyze Patient Histories

Each patient record is reviewed in detail to determine exactly what happened and when—from admission, through the course of care, to discharge. All diagnostic and therapeutic procedures and tests from admissions on are recorded chronologically to provide the basis for subsequent evaluation of the timeliness of the care program.

Assess Appropriateness of Admissions

Using the data from the previous step and the admissions criteria defined in phase I, the records analyst determines whether each patient's indications support admission. If one of these criteria is satisfied by indications recorded in the

Table 38-6 Performance Standards (CLTR)

Medical and surgical	Neuro/Psychiatric
1. **Physician ordering** a test, procedure, consultation, or referral as soon as clinically indicated: same day, or first weekday after last diagnostic decision or test result	1. **First medical evaluation:** within 24 hours of admission
2. **Laboratory tests, diagnostic X-ray, EKG, EEG return** a. Routine lab tests and X-ray: same day if ordered in a.m. or next weekday if ordered in p.m. b. Special X-ray, EKG, and EEG: same or next weekday c. Special lab tests (cultures, Australian Antigen): 1 week, or as indicated	2. **Final diagnosis made:** within 3 to 14 days following admission 3. **Consultations and referrals:** same day as ordered or next weekday 4. **Outplacement:** delay, if any, is counted from the day after disposition request is noted except where unusual arrangements involved
3. **Consultations and referrals:** same or next weekday	5. **Discharge, medical:** as soon as final diagnosis is made, patient is physically/mentally stabilized, and medication is on maintenance dose
4. **Operative procedures:** delay, if any, is counted from next operating room day available to service following decision to perform surgery unless patient situation (e.g., delay in signing consent form, medical complication) interferes	6. **Discharge, administrative:** 1 day after discharge order is written
5. **Outplacement:** delay, if any, is counted from the day after disposition request is noted except where unusual arrangements involved	
6. **Discharge, medical:** as soon as final diagnosis is made, patient is physically/mentally stabilized, and medication is on maintenance dose	
7. **Discharge, administrative:** 1 day after discharge order is written	

chart, the records analyst judges the admission necessary and proceeds with review of the timeliness of care. If neither of the criteria is found, the chart is referred to the physician adviser for judgment on the necessity of admission. If the physician adviser deems the admission appropriate, the care timeliness review is undertaken; if the admission is judged inappropriate, the entire stay is categorized as avoidable for that reason.

Assess Care Performance Times for Reasonableness

The reviewer next evaluates timeliness of care using the target turnaround times established in phase I. Using those standards the actual performance is compared and delays are identified.

Evaluate Delays for Impact on Length of Stay

The following questions help establish whether delays in the care process did prolong length of stay:

- Were delayed test results critical to the next step or to continuation of the patient's active treatment?
- If there were delays in completing specific procedures, did the necessity for ongoing therapy or treatment to alleviate the patient's illness during this period offset any impact the delays might otherwise have had on length of stay?

Identify the Major Causes of Avoidable Days

Identification of the specific causes for avoidable days of hospitalization is the starting point for developing corrective programs. Critical delays in the course of care should be broadly categorized as either medical or administrative, and then subcategorized as shown in Table 38-7.

Estimate Total Avoidable Hospital Inpatient Days

Avoidable inpatient days are summarized from the analyses of individual patient records in total and by major causes. The results are then extrapolated from the sample base to provide an estimate of the avoidable days of hospitalization incurred overall during the sample period.

During phase II, the CLTR project team would meet at least twice with the CLTR steering committee to discuss the progress of the review. When the analysis is complete, the team should present and possibly reach agreement on (1) the extent of potentially avoidable hospitalization, (2) the causes of problems identified, (3) the relative priority of these problems and (4) the major areas requiring further study.

Phase III—Developing Corrective Action Programs

The final phase of CLTR typically takes 8 to 12 weeks to complete.

Table 38-7 Summary of Causes of Avoidable Hospital Days

MEDICAL

1. Physician management
   a. Delays in ordering something on the critical path
   b. Delayed discharge

2. Part or all of treatment could have been on outpatient basis

3. Consultation delays on the critical path

4. Inadequate pre-admission scheduling
   a. Of diagnostic workup
   b. Of operating room time

5. Other

ADMINISTRATIVE

1. Diagnostic radiology

2. Nuclear medicine

3. Clinical laboratory/pathology

4. Surgery delays
   a. Operating room scheduling preferences
   b. Operating room capacity constraints
   c. Cause not known

5. Outplacement

6. Administrative discharge delay

7. Other (EKG, EEG, etc.)

OTHER

1. Patient/family pressure

2. Teaching

3. Research

Analyze Underlying Causes

Appropriate and feasible actions to remove major causes of unnecessary hospitalization may be clear from the results of the records review alone. It is more likely that follow-up studies will be required to identify the specific causes of each problem area. For example, it will be important to know whether physician management problems (discharge delays, delayed orders, etc.) are concentrated among certain services and individual practitioners.

In this first step of phase III, the CLTR team carves out the necessary follow-up studies to determine the underlying causes of avoidable days attributed to general problem areas. (For

Figure 38-3 Results of record analysis in three hospitals

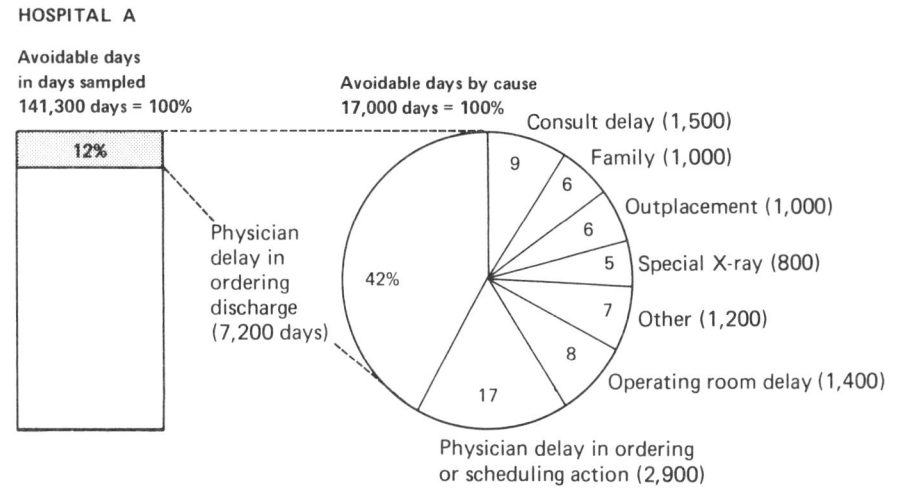

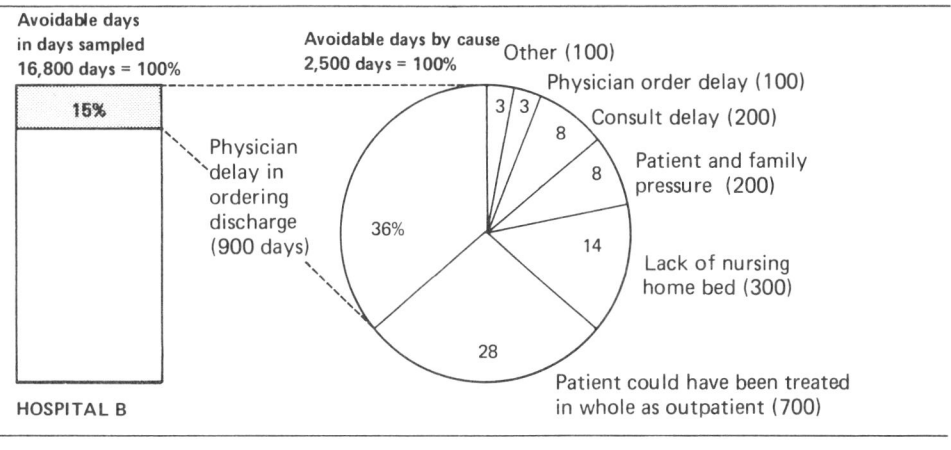

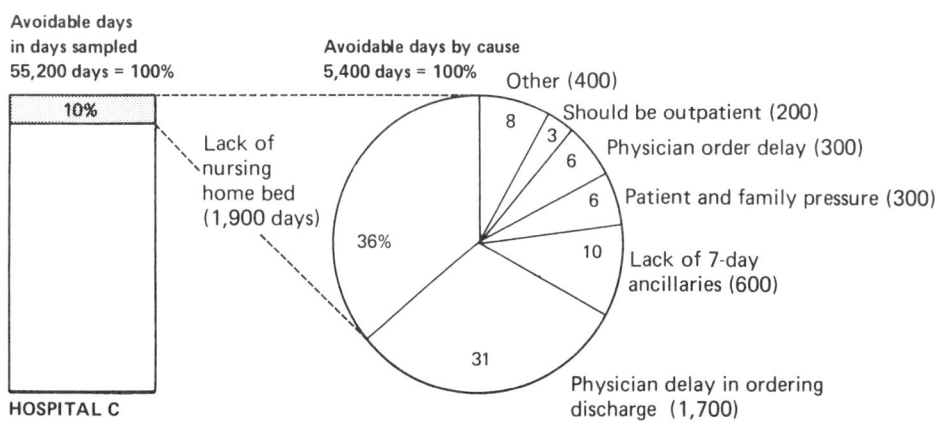

HOSPITAL A

Avoidable days in days sampled 141,300 days = 100%

12%

Avoidable days by cause 17,000 days = 100%

- Consult delay (1,500) — 9
- Family (1,000) — 6
- Outplacement (1,000) — 6
- Special X-ray (800) — 5
- Other (1,200) — 7
- Operating room delay (1,400) — 8
- Physician delay in ordering or scheduling action (2,900) — 17
- Physician delay in ordering discharge (7,200 days) — 42%

HOSPITAL B

Avoidable days in days sampled 16,800 days = 100%

15%

Avoidable days by cause 2,500 days = 100%

- Other (100) — 3
- Physician order delay (100) — 3
- Consult delay (200) — 8
- Patient and family pressure (200) — 8
- Lack of nursing home bed (300) — 14
- Patient could have been treated in whole as outpatient (700) — 28
- Physician delay in ordering discharge (900 days) — 36%

HOSPITAL C

Avoidable days in days sampled 55,200 days = 100%

10%

Avoidable days by cause 5,400 days = 100%

- Other (400) — 8
- Should be outpatient (200) — 3
- Physician order delay (300) — 6
- Patient and family pressure (300) — 6
- Lack of 7-day ancillaries (600) — 10
- Physician delay in ordering discharge (1,700) — 31
- Lack of nursing home bed (1,900 days) — 36%

Table 38-8 Summary Action Plan for Hospital A

Apparent cause of delay	Annual potentially avoidable days (% of all days) for year beginning January 1976	Planned hospital, PSRO, or third party actions to correct problems	Agreed improvement in avoidable days (% of all days) for year beginning June 1978
1. Physician management delay • Discharge • Orders on critical path	10,100 days (5.9%)	a. PSRO staff member and second physician advisor will re-examine all cases in sample to confirm findings b. If unnecessary hospitalization is found but attributed to causes other than physician management, they will be addressed c. If physician management problems largely are confirmed, the profile analysis data will be re-examined to determine what physicians, diagnoses, or age categories are focus of problem; then staff education program will be focused accordingly	7,000 days (4.1%)
2. Operating room delay	1,400 days (0.8%)	a. The cystoscopy room will be equipped and scheduled for other types of surgery b. The Chief of Surgery will monitor emergency surgery cases to ensure that these major interruptions to operating room scheduling are indeed unavoidable c. Policies to ensure full pre-operative patient preparation and prompt arrival of surgical personnel will be developed and stringently enforced d. A pre-operative holding area will be opened in which the patient will be checked for missing pre-operative test and anesthetists can begin their work e. Complete data on workflow through the OR, utilization levels, and staff time will be collected on an on-going basis to assist management in assessing improvement and pinpointing continuing problems	1,400 days (0.8%)

illustrations of record analysis in three hospitals see Figure 38-3.)

Establish Improvement Objectives

Not all of the days found to be potentially avoidable from a record sample analysis and follow-up studies can be eliminated through direct hospital action; some of the causes will be outside hospital control. Other causes may require corrective actions that would cost more than could be saved, or that simply cannot be acted on by the hospital.

For example, if CLTR analysis found "avoidable" days of care resulted from the area's only neurologist visiting the hospital only twice a week for consultations, the cost of having him come every day might well outweigh the "hotel" costs saved by eliminating an extra day or two from the stay of patients requiring neurology consultations.

Develop Corrective Action Programs

Developed by the hospital's management staff, the proposed actions are aimed specifically at the causes of avoidable inpatient days as identified in the review of the patient records sample. As shown in Table 38-8 Hospital A's management chose to first tackle apparent physician delays in treating and discharging their patients, and operating room delays. In the former case, the plan calls for more intensive analysis to confirm the problem and focus on improvement efforts. The actions needed to lessen operating room delays were apparent at the conclusion of the review, and were specified and implemented without further study.

Chapter 39—Disaster, Fire, Infection, and Occupational Health

HANDLING DISASTERS

Overview*

It is necessary for hospitals to have a written document that outlines procedures to be followed by hospital staff in the event of a community catastrophe or disaster, such as a train wreck, airplane crash, large industrial accident, major fire, or natural disasters. The JCAH requires each hospital to have a written disaster plan and to rehearse the plan at least twice annually.

Hospitals should be prepared for three kinds of disasters. The first is an internal hospital disaster, such as an explosion or major fire. The second is an external disaster, such as a hurricane, tornado, flood, or transportation accident. The third is a forewarned disaster, such as the receipt of a large number of patients from a neighboring hospital that has had to evacuate.

Key areas in a disaster plan include the reception area and the triage area, usually near the emergency department. Triage comes from the French word meaning to sort out. It is common for emergency departments to sort out (screen) patients upon their arrival. They may be sorted out to a walk-in clinic or a trauma treatment area, or be admitted directly to the hospital. There also must be a room for families and the press. There must be a plan for the evacuation of patients who are able to leave and give up their beds for more seriously ill patients. There should be a temporary morgue if it is not already located in the hospital's present morgue. There must be an understanding of how communications will flow during the disaster. In addition, a labor pool with assignments for physicians should be ready to set in motion. External traffic control and police protection must be considered. Finally, places to secure additional medical supplies and food for the duration must be known.

JCAH Standards*

The hospital shall have written plans for the timely care of casualties arising from both external and internal disasters, and shall document the rehearsal of these plans.

External Disaster Plan

To meet its responsibilities for the care of emergency casualties at the time of disaster, the hospital shall develop a disaster plan based on its capabilities. A hospital's capabilities may range from providing simple first aid or preparing casualties for transfer elsewhere to administering definitive care.

---

*Source: Reprinted from *Medical Records in Health Information* by Kathleen A. Waters and Gretchen F. Murphy, with permission of Aspen Systems Corporation, © 1979.

*Source: Reprinted from Joint Commission on Accreditation of Hospitals, *Accreditation Manual for Hospitals,* 1983 ed. (Chicago, 1982), with permission of the publisher.

The disaster plan should be developed in conjunction with other emergency facilities in the community so that adequate logistical provisions are made for the expansion of the hospital's activities in coordination with the activities of these facilities. Planning should include consultation with local civil authorities and with representatives of other medical agencies in order to establish an effective chain of command and to make appropriate jurisdictional provisions. Such planning should result in disaster-site triage and distribution of patients that assures the most efficient use of available facilities and services. The hospital has the responsibility for informing the community of its capabilities and its limitations in handling a disaster in the community. The extent of each hospital's capability or resources should be clearly identified for use by local police, rescue squads, and ambulance teams. The plan shall include coordination with law enforcement agencies, as required, to provide a mechanism for physician identification as well as route access and entrance to the hospital when such are compromised by a disaster situation.

The external disaster plan shall be rehearsed at least twice a year. There should be evidence that a concerted effort has been made to use the plan in a coordinated exercise in which other community emergency service agencies participate. Drills should be realistic, and they shall involve the medical staff, as well as administrative, nursing, and other hospital personnel. Actual evacuation of patients during drills is optional. There shall be a written report and evaluation of all drills.

The disaster plan should make provision, within the hospital, for:

- an efficient system of notifying and assigning personnel.
- unified medical command.
- availability of adequate basic utilities and supplies, as well as essential medical and supportive materials. The hospital should be essentially self-sustaining in these areas for a minimum of one week. This may include preestablished mechanisms for immediate supply of certain major critical items such as water, food, and fuel.
- a method of identifying patients who are immediately dischargeable or transferable, and that includes provision for their expeditious transportation. A manual method of identification is acceptable.
- conversion of all usable space to provide triage, observation, and treatment areas. In a small hospital, the emergency services area is usually not best suited for this, and the size of the disaster may dictate that an area outside the hospital is more realistic, particularly for secondary triage and for accessibility to large numbers of patients simultaneously.
- prompt transfer of patients, when necessary, to the facility most appropriate for rendering definitive care, in accordance with any regional plan in operation.
- the use of a special disaster medical record or medical tag that accompanies the patient at all times and contains specific required information.
- establishment of a centralized public information center with a designated spokesman.
- security, to minimize the presence of unauthorized individuals and vehicles in or near the triage, observation, and immediate care areas. Additional security measures may be required when the casualties have resulted from riots and civil disobedience.
- a preestablished radio communication system for use when telephone communications are out or overtaxed.
- instructions on the use of elevators.

Internal Disaster Plan

The hospital shall assure that it has fire protection services either from the local fire department or by providing its own.

Internal disaster plans shall be developed with the assistance of qualified fire, explosion, safety, and other experts as required. These plans should provide for at least:

- notification of emergency department/service and other designated personnel;
- assignment of specific responsibilities to all personnel;
- instructions relative to the use of alarm systems and signals;
- instruction concerning the location and use of fire-fighting equipment, and methods of fire containment;
- an operational plan in case of threat of explosion by bomb or other device, including

notification of designated authorities, search procedures, and evacuation of patients and personnel;
- specification of evacuation routes and procedures; and
- management of casualties when the resources of the hospital remain functionally intact.

Internal disaster plans shall be made available to all hospital personnel and should be posted on appropriate bulletin boards at nurses' stations and in other areas of the hospital that assure maximum exposure.

Effective internal disaster, fire, and evacuation drills shall be held at least quarterly for each work shift of hospital personnel (totaling not less than 12 drills per year) in each separate patient-occupied hospital building, and shall be designed to:

- assure that all personnel are trained to perform assigned tasks;
- assure that all personnel are familiar with the location, use, and operation of the firefighting equipment; and
- evaluate the effectiveness of the internal disaster plan.

To be realistic, the drills shall be held at varied times, and not at the time of change of work shifts. The actual evacuation of patients to designated safe areas during a drill is optional. There shall be a written report documenting the evaluation of each drill and the corrective action recommended or taken for any deficiencies found.

At the Scene*

Development of efficient communications, on-site response by medical personnel, rapid field triage and stabilization and ambulance dispatch are components of a planned process to manage mass casualties most efficiently.

However, hospitals require a lead time to organize and transport the medical teams and to prepare their facilities to receive inordinate numbers of patients.

To notify hospitals of a disaster, Chicago uses a unique system based on the Mobile Intensive Care Unit (MICU) system, which employs advanced life-support vehicles staffed by paramedics. Hospital medical staff are trained in triage and field stabilization, and are transported to the disaster site with appropriate medical equipment, protective gear and identification.

A green hard hat marked "Emergency Medical Team" is the official identification permitting access to the disaster site. The advantage of this identification is that it is protective and immediately visible, facilitating ready field identification of medical teams at the disaster site, even though the geographical area of the site may be quite large.

Rapid Field Triage

Rapid field triage, coupled with stabilization by paramedics, must be directed from a Medical Command Post (MCP) at the disaster site. All paramedics and hospital-based medical teams must report to the MCP before going into the actual disaster site. The MCP coordinates medical operations, establishes triage, decides on the appropriateness and location of field hospitals and the site and operation of the ambulance dispatch area. Personnel at the MCP are also responsible for the allocation of material resources, and must have a direct communications link with the resource hospital, which coordinates the hospital-based aspects of these operations.

The first priority is to obtain an overview of the severity of the disaster and the resources available. Only then can clinical triage begin. Triage personnel should not spend an inordinate amount of time on any single patient before determination of the priorities of care for all of the patients at the disaster site. Medical teams can later return to the most critical patients and begin field stabilization.

A four-color, coded triage system and standard triage tag should be used, since it is the easiest method to use and remember. One triage tag, designed by the *Journal of Civil Defense* located in Starke, Florida, is ideal in that it allows for identification of the patient, as well as the listing of critical information such as the pa-

---

*Source: Reprinted from Frank J. Baker, II, "The Management of Mass Casualty Disasters," *Topics in Emergency Medicine,* Fall 1980, with permission of Aspen Systems Corporation.

tient's injuries and the medications received. In addition, it is clearly color-coded and extremely easy to use. Category 0 (or black) indicates an expired victim. Category 1 (or red) is used for the critical patient whose survival is dependent on immediate stabilization of a life threat. Category 2 (or yellow) indicates an urgently or seriously injured patient who requires some medical stabilization in the field prior to transportation, but whose life is not immediately threatened. Category 3 (or green) is applied to the ambulatory or walking wounded patient who does not require any medical attention at the disaster site prior to transportation to a hospital. Providing the maximum care for the greatest number of patients, aimed at maximum survival, must always be kept in mind. The operational plan must allow medical personnel the flexibility to make these judgments.

Field Stabilization

After assessment and categorization, medical personnel should move into the next phase of the disaster plan, stabilization prior to transport.

The size of the disaster and the location and the availability of resources will determine whether the patients should be stabilized where they lie in the field or whether field hospitals should be established. It is conceivable that in a major disaster at a remote locale, with large numbers of victims and few medical facilities nearby, the patients may remain for up to 24 hours in field hospitals prior to transport to a hospital for more definitive care.

Ambulance Dispatch and Transport

The priority for removing patients from the site is as follows: critical patients (red) first; followed by the urgent patients (yellow); next the walking wounded (green); and finally the expired patients (black). In addition, the ability of hospitals to care for the patients they will receive must be a prime factor in determining the numbers, triage categories and destinations of the patients. Ambulance dispatch must take into account information from the resource hospital about the capabilities of its receiving institutions to care for the various types of patients.

Patients arriving at individual institutions will need retriage since some unfortunately will have deteriorated.

Disaster Planning*

"First Responder" Concept

The concept of "first responder" could be used in creating a new section of the Disaster Manual, called "First Response" (see boxed material). A brief list of instructions for the various protocols contained in the manual would be placed in it, including where to transfer a call or whom to notify. This section would be the first to appear in the manual and it would make the process of putting a disaster plan into effect more orderly and efficient.

The basis for the "First Response" is brevity and conciseness. This concept could be expanded to include the style of the rest of the manual.

Two steps should be taken to deal with this: rewriting the plan in a concise, directive style and finding a way to remove the individual departmental plans from the general manual. The first can be accomplished by identifying the key individuals in the operation of the plan and graphically mapping out their functions so that a sequence could be established and the interrelationships that existed could be shown. Having done this on a variation of a PERT or Gantt flowchart, each individual's functions could then be listed in order, under their titles, in simple, direct terms. For the external event, the plan would then contain the necessary instructions for putting the plan into effect, notifying the proper people, and setting the apparatus in motion to accept victims into the hospital. A brief example is shown in the boxed material labeled "Departmental Instructions."

At the same time each of the identified departments should submit a disaster plan, in similar format, to the disaster committee. The committee should review each plan, make suggestions for revisions where they are needed, and ask the departments to include these instructions in their own work station's copies of the disaster manual. Where departments are interrelated, this relationship can be reflected in both the in-

---

*Source: Reprinted from Howard M. Henze, Denise C. Harrison, and Carolyn W. Cady, "Disaster Planning: Planning a First Response," *The Journal of Ambulatory Care Management*, May 1981, with permission of Aspen Systems Corporation.

> *First Response Instructions*
>
> This section will give you the initial steps if you become aware of any of the following situations.
>
> *External Disaster*
> Major fire, accident, etc.
> Transfer call to *Emergency Department Charge Nurse—3131*
>
> *VIP*
> Arrival or potential arrival of a person of major local or national importance
> Notify Administration—3585
>   or
> Administrator On Call
> If arrival will be in the Emergency Department, also notify the *Emergency Department Charge Nurse—3131*
>
> *Radiation Accident*
> Emergency arrival of patient(s) even remotely exposed to or contaminated with radioactive material.
> Transfer call to *Emergency Department Charge Nurse—3131*
>
> Water Emergency ⎱ Temporary disruption of water
> Power Emergency ⎰ or power service to hospital
> Transfer call to or notify Assistant Director, General Services—*3595*
>   or
> Administrator On Call
>
> *Helicopter Transfers*
> Monday—Friday, 8:30 a.m.—5:00 p.m.
> Transfer call to Assistant Director, General Services—*3595*
> All other times—Administrator On Call

stitution's plan and in the individual department's plans.

A "Super Disaster Manual"

As a final step, all of these plans need to be available to certain groups, namely the disaster committee and administrators who would be called on to coordinate functions during disasters. To accomplish this, a second manual should be created, a "Super Disaster Manual," and stationed with the chairman of the disaster committee. A copy should be placed in the emergency department, where many of these events would converge. This manual should contain several of the individual protocols, all of the departmental plans, a master list of key physicians with their phone numbers, and a master list of all of the designated departmental command posts, along with several checklists as aids during the event. This will eliminate unnecessary information from the manuals and provide necessary information to those needing it. It also will create a "moveable command post" for the administrator on the scene. The administrator will have all of the information easily at hand and could more reasonably direct operations.

> *Departmental Instructions*
>
> *The Nursing Supervisor N.S. #3* will:
> 1. Go to the Emergency Department and assist charge nurse.
> 2. Assist charge nurse in assessing staffing needs and in gathering staff.
> 3. Coordinate staffing from floor staff.
>
> *Emergency Department Business Office* will:
> 1. Follow all internal departmental procedures.
> 2. Set up intake procedures and prepare for intake of patients at the designated triage point.
>
> *Floor House Staff* will:
> 1. Report to their counterpart on emergency department house staff (or Emergency Department Attending).
> 2. Aid in providing care.
> 3. Remain in Emergency Department or return to normal duties as the situation warrants.
>
> *Emergency Department House Staff* will:
> 1. Notify senior resident of service that a disaster is underway and that extra staff will be needed.
> 2. Aid senior resident in arranging for additional medical staff (interns, residents, and attendings).
>
> *Emergency Department Attending Staff* will:
> 1. Set up triage area.
> 2. Provide direction to medical treatment in the emergency department.
> 3. Coordinate with administrator in calling in additional members of the medical staff (attendings) as needed.
>
> THE IDEAL IS TO ACHIEVE ONE-TO-ONE PHYSICIAN TO PATIENT COVERAGE IN THIS SITUATION.

FIRE*

Fire is the most frequent of all major emergencies. Your emergency team must therefore be fully trained by a local fire department on all aspects of fire fighting and methods of fire prevention. Such training should be relatively extensive, not a mere overview; it will pay for itself if you are ever faced with a fire problem. The knowledge and training of your inhouse emergency team, led by your security department, will eventually save you many times the payroll cost of the training program. By obtaining this protection, you also will be conforming to OSHA requirements.

Every facility, regardless of size, must have a workable *and working* fire-prevention program. Management must recognize the program's importance by accepting and backing its policies and procedures, and by agreeing to enforce disciplinary measures against any and all violators. Conversely, a "bonus" type of reward for individuals and/or departments who show extra effort in aiding the program should be established and publicized. Without such managerial support, the program of fire prevention will grow lax and ultimately fail.

Each employee must be made aware of the following:

1. Safe methods of handling any hazards within the immediate work area.
2. Proper disposal methods of flammable wastes such as rags, paper, and combustible fluids.
3. The advantages of good housekeeping principles.
4. The importance of strict compliance with the rules concerning the facility's specific fire precautions.
5. Proper use of fire extinguishers.
6. The principles involved in the automatic sprinkler system. No obstructions must be placed in a way that may make the system inoperable or inefficient.
7. Locations and accompanying hazards of vulnerable fire areas.
8. Correct operation methods for all alarm systems.
9. Proper conduct in the event of fire.
10. Location of all fire equipment, exits, and evacuation routes.

In addition to the time set aside for drills, management must also set aside time, and provide monetary incentive, for the education of the fire team.

MANAGEMENT OF INFECTION CONTROL*

Because infections acquired in the hospital or brought into the hospital from the community are potential hazards for all persons having contact with the hospital, effective measures must be developed to prevent and to identify and control such infections.

The Joint Commission on the Accreditation of Hospitals recommends the establishment of a program through a hospital committee made up of representatives of the medical staff, the administration, the nursing service and, when available, the microbiology section of the laboratory.

The basic elements of the program shall include the following:

- Definitions of nosocomial infections, for surveillance purposes, to provide for early uniform identification and reporting of infections and to determine pertinent infection rates.
- A practical system for reporting, evaluating, and maintaining records of infections among patients and personnel. This must include assignment of responsibility for the ongoing collection and analytic review of such data, as well as for required follow-up action.
- Ongoing review and evaluation of all aseptic, isolation, and sanitation techniques employed in the hospital. Such technqiues shall be defined in written policies and procedures.
- Written policies defining the specific indications for isolation requirements in relation to the medical condition involved. There

---

*Source: Reprinted from *Hospital Security and Safety* by A. Michael Pascal, with permission of Aspen Systems Corporation, © 1977.

*Source: Reprinted from Joint Commission on Accreditation of Hospitals, *Accreditation Manual for Hospitals,* 1983 ed. (Chicago, 1982), with permission of the publisher.

must be provisions to assure that the quality of care, including nursing care and the use of monitoring and other special equipment, is not compromised for any patient whose condition requires isolation.
- Preventive, surveillance, and control procedures relating to the inanimate hospital environment, including sterilization and disinfection practices, central service, housekeeping, laundry, engineering and maintenance, food sanitation, and waste management. Such procedures shall be evaluated on a continuing basis and revised as necessary.
- Provision for all necessary laboratory support, particularly microbiological and serological.
- Input into the content and scope of the employee health program.
- Orientation of all new employees as to the importance of infection control, personal hygiene, and their responsibility in the program, and documented in-service education for all departments and services relative to infection prevention and control.
- Coordination with the medical staff on action relative to the findings from the regular review of the clinical use of antibiotics. The ongoing monitoring of antibiotic usage in the hospital is a medical staff responsibility.

An effective hospital infection control program should also include other elements that may be implemented to varying degrees depending on the hospital and the services provided. These elements include, but are not limited to:

- control of traffic in all areas, including the monitoring of visiting policies.
- the development and revision of all forms used for collection and collation of data relative to the program.
- a mechanism for the initiation, the approval, and the review of results of all special studies relative to infection control.
- the institution of antibiotic susceptibility/resistance trend studies as appropriate.
- consultation relative to the purchase of all equipment and supplies used for sterilization, disinfection, and decontamination purposes.
- the periodic review of cleaning procedures, agents, and schedules in use throughout the hospital, and consultation relative to any major change in cleaning products or techniques.
- the monitoring of all findings from any patient care quality assessment activities that relate to infection control.
- the review of necropsy reports for the presence of any undiagnosed antemortem infections.
- the evaluation of hospital disposal systems for all liquid and solid wastes.
- compliance with ventilation patterns and air exchange rates for operating rooms and isolation rooms of all types, as established by the authority having jurisdiction. This includes the provision of a room with a negative pressure system, to prevent potential airborne pathogens from being distributed to other patients and personnel from designated isolation cases, as well as the maintenance of a room at positive pressure relative to other areas of the hospital, as in the case of protective (reverse) isolation, when either of these facilities is required by the condition of the patient.

Written policies and procedures pertaining to the elements of the infection control program shall be reviewed at least annually and revised as necessary.

Responsibility for Monitoring*

The JCAH proposes the following standard with regard to monitoring infection control in the hospital:

> Responsibility for monitoring the infection control program shall be vested in a multidisciplinary committee. The committee shall recommend corrective action based on records and reports of infections and infection potentials among patients and hospital personnel.

Interpretation

The infection control committee should be a hospital committee. However, the infection control committee function may be performed

---

*Source: Reprinted from Joint Commission on Accreditation of Hospitals, *Accreditation Manual for Hospitals,* 1983 ed. (Chicago, 1982), with permission of the publisher.

by a medical staff committee if representatives of other professional disciplines and the administration participate, and if an effective hospital-wide infection control program is evident. Membership on the infection control committee shall include representation from the medical staff, administration, nursing department/service, and, when available, the microbiology section of the laboratory. Any individual employed in a surveillance or epidemiological capacity shall be a member of the committee. If the medical staff is departmentalized, it is recommended that the committee include representatives from surgery, medicine, obstetrics/gynecology, pediatrics, and pathology. Representation from the house staff, where applicable, is encouraged. Representation from housekeeping, central services, the laundry, the dietetic department/service, the engineering and maintenance department/service, the pharmacy, and the operating suite is recommended on at least a consultative basis. An effort should be made to include a liaison member from the local or state health department.

The chairman of the committee shall be an individual whose credentials document knowledge of, and special interest or experience in, infection control. It is recommended but not required that the committee chairman be a physician. The role of physicians on the committee should be to provide direction and strengthen the clinical aspects of the program. Policies and clinical decisions shall be made by the committee only when an appropriate physician member is present.

The infection control committee shall determine the type of surveillance and reporting programs to be used. The committee shall provide standard criteria for reporting all types of infections, including respiratory, gastrointestinal, surgical wound, skin, urinary tract, septicemias, and those related to the use of intravascular catheters. Recorded data on all infections should include the identification and location of the patient, the date of admission and onset of infection, the type of infection, the cultures taken and the results when known, any antibiotics administered, and the identity of the practitioner responsible for the care of the patient.

The use of full-time or part-time surveillance personnel who are qualified by training and/or experience is strongly recommended. When there is a hospital epidemiologist, this individual should direct the surveillance activities, provide consultation on infectious diseases as required, and help moderate the infection control policies, procedures, and practices in the hospital. In addition to the required routine data, surveillance personnel shall also be involved in the investigation of clusters of infection above expected levels, the investigation of single cases of unusual nosocomial infections, the development and implementation of improved patient care procedures, the employee health activity and in-service education on infection control, and the verification of required reporting to public health authorities. In the interest of accurate reporting, nosocomial infections identified postdischarge should be included when determining the infection rate of the hospital, departments/services, or individual staff members.

In the absence of qualified surveillance personnel, infection data usually originate in nursing care units. When an individual patient report form or a daily work sheet form is used in the nursing care unit, it shall contain the basic information stated on the preceding page. The data should be forwarded immediately to the individual charged with their collation and initial evaluation.

In the interest of early and complete reporting, authority may be given by the medical staff to the epidemiologist, surveillance personnel, or the registered nurse responsible for the care unit to report any actual or suspect infection, to initiate a culture and sensitivity testing, and to institute any appropriate isolation procedures. When any of these actions are taken, the medical staff member responsible for the patient shall be notified.

Medical records must accurately reflect in the final diagnosis or list of complications all infections occurring during hospitalization. However, the medical staff should determine whether or not infection control report forms are to be subsequently filed in the patient's medical record.

The infection control committee shall meet not less than every two months, and should review at least the following in assessing the effectiveness of the hospital infection control program:

- Infections within the hospital, particularly with regard to their proper management and to their epidemic potential. A determination should be made as to whether an infection is nosocomial, and, if so, what action the committee recommends be taken to minimize other such occurrences. Review may be directed to surveillance data, when available, looking particularly for unusual epidemics, clusters of infections, infections due to unusual pathogens, or any occurrence of nosocomial infection that exceeds the usual baseline levels.

- Any cultures of personnel or the environment required by the hospital, the medical staff, or local, state, or federal agencies or regulations. Except for local, state, or federal requirements, such sampling activities shall be originated, supervised, reviewed, and acted upon by the infection control committee. In addition, the sampling should ordinarily be reserved for specific situations when the outcome can be expected to have a potential beneficial effect on standards of care, or to support change in maintenance practices, personnel practices, or equipment. Occasionally, routine sampling may be used as a quality control mechanism or as an educational or training exercise, as, for example, in demonstrating to patient-care personnel the reduction of microbial contamination by hand washing, or to housekeeping personnel a reduction in surface bacteria after the use of instituted cleaning practices.

- The results of any antimicrobial susceptibility/resistance trend studies.
- Proposals and protocols for all special infection control studies to be conducted throughout the hospital, and any subsequent findings.
- Medical records reflecting the presence of infections that were not reported in the final diagnosis. This requires the cooperation of the medical record department and the use of preestablished criteria.
- Pertinent related findings from other hospital committees.

The infection control committee shall report its findings and recommendations to the medical staff (through the executive committee), to the chief executive officer, and to the director of the nursing department/service.

OCCUPATIONAL HEALTH AND SAFETY IN HOSPITALS

Overview*

Hospitals are now the third largest employer in the United States, with approximately three million employees working full and part-time.

*Source: National Institute of Occupational Safety and Health, 1976.

Table 39-1 Nosocomial Infections Summary by Hospital Category, 1979

	Community	Community—Teaching	Federal	Municipal or County	University	All Hospitals
Number of Hospitals	35	23	4	5	15	82
Number of Discharges	454,359	443,619	31,495	119,348	313,521	1,362,342
Number of Infections	11,203	13,755	1,169	4,893	13,765	44,785
Infection Rate/100 Discharges	2.5	3.1	3.7	4.1	4.4	3.3
Percent Infections Cultured	90.9	91.7	90.0	90.6	91.6	91.3
Percent Infections Causing Death	0.6	0.7	0.4	3.4	2.0	0.9
Percent Infections Contributing to Death	3.0	2.7	3.3	5.9	2.0	2.9
Median Infection Rate/100 Discharges	2.3	3.1	3.8	4.4	4.5	3.0
Range of Infection Rates: Low	0.8	2.0	2.5	3.0	1.3	0.8
High	5.1	5.2	5.3	4.6	8.9	8.9

Table 39-2 Nosocomial Infection Rates* by Site of Infection and Service, 1979

	Medicine	Surgery	Obstetrics	Gynecology	Pediatrics	Nursery	All Services
Primary Bacteremia	24.3	19.2	3.1	3.4	17.8	12.3	17.0
Surgical Wound	7.7	137.4	104.1	105.5	17.0	4.5	70.7
Upper Respiratory	5.8	4.3	1.3	2.1	13.2	1.6	4.5
Lower Respiratory	65.9	72.5	4.3	13.9	21.6	11.7	49.1
Cardiovascular	7.4	6.6	0.8	1.4	5.4	3.0	5.4
Gastrointestinal	0.4	0.4	0.0	0.0	11.9	3.3	1.4
Intra-abdominal	5.2	3.8	0.1	0.5	1.7	1.5	3.2
Urinary Tract	182.6	174.5	43.7	150.2	21.4	6.2	132.7
Gynecologic	1.6	1.6	43.8	7.4	0.1	0.1	6.7
Central Nervous System	0.8	2.0	0.1	0.0	3.2	3.1	1.5
Cutaneous	21.2	18.3	5.3	5.3	28.3	45.4	20.3
Burn Wound	0.2	3.7	0.0	0.0	0.6	0.1	1.4
Other Sites	20.1	13.0	0.6	2.7	19.3	26.6	14.8
ALL SITES	343.4	457.2	207.3	292.4	161.6	119.4	328.7
Secondary Bacteremia	21.1	25.2	12.0	6.4	11.1	7.9	18.5

*Per 10,000 patients discharged.
Source: Centers for Disease Control: *National Nosocomial Infections Study Report, Annual Summary 1979*, Issued March 1982.

Because the accident frequency rate for hospitals was increasing alarmingly, the National Institute for Occupational Safety and Health conceived and implemented the Hospital Occupational Health Services Study in 1972—the first such major study ever conducted.

Among its findings were the following:

- Most hospitals provide some form of general occupational health and safety orientation for new employees.
- About half of the hospitals reported having a formally organized program for employee safety and health education. Again, analyzed results showed that more of the large hospitals (70%), about half of the medium, and only one-third of the small had formally organized programs.
- Routine in-service training programs on radiation exposure were *not* provided to employees in about 90% of the small hospitals, 75% of the medium and 60% of the large hospitals. While this topic shows the highest percentage with no training, other topics are almost as high. For all hospitals, 55% have *no* training for chemical exposures, 50% have *no* training programs for infectious disease exposure, 60% have *no* training for safe use of equipment, 50% have *no* training for use of personal protective equipment, and 70% have *no* training for teaching proper lifting and body mechanics. As expected, small hospitals had higher percentages and large hospitals lower.
- Upon inquiry most hospitals indicated that their safety committee had been assigned the responsibility for managing their hospital's health and safety program.
- Respiratory problems ranked first as the most frequent occupational health problem, exclusive of injuries. Other infections ranked second and dermatitis ranked third.
- Strains and sprains were the most frequently reported types of occupational injuries listed by the total of all hospitals. Puncture wounds were the second ranking type of injury reported. Abrasions and contusions took third place.
- In 80% of the hospitals, injuries and illnesses of employees on the job were treated in the Emergency Room. About 10% of all hospitals reported using an Employee Health Unit, and these were predominantly among large hospitals. Only a third of those hospitals which had separate facilities for employee health care reported use of the Emergency Room in addition to an employee health unit for treatment of employee illness or injury.

- In general, the findings reveal that nearly 50% of all hospitals stated that the Emergency Room Staff provided the day-to-day health care services for hospital workers. About 10% named the Occupational Health Nurse or the Floor Nurse. In 40% of the large hospitals, an Occupational Health Nurse was specified as the primary source of employee health care.

An Occupational Health and Safety Program*

An effective hospital occupational health program should provide but is not limited to the following services:

A. Pre-placement Physical Examinations
B. Periodic Health Appraisal Examinations
C. Health and Safety Education
D. Immunizations
E. Care for Illness and Injury at Work
F. Health Counseling
G. Environmental Control and Surveillance
H. Health and Safety Records System
I. Coordinated Planning with Hospital Departments and Services

Established Guidelines

A. *Pre-placement Physical Examinations*
   1. Physical examinations should be done on all new full-time employees to include:
      a. Routine blood tests
         (1) Complete Blood Count
         (2) Fasting Blood Sugar or 2 Hour Postprandial
         (3) Renal Function Tests
         (4) Creatinine
         (5) SGOT
         (6) SGPT
         (7) Serology for Syphilis
      b. Urinalysis, routine
      c. Electrocardiogram, for employees over age 35, or for special indications
      d. Chest X-ray, P.A., and lateral
      e. Skin testing for TB, other as indicated

      f. Vision tests, near and far, with and without correction, and tonometry
      g. Audiogram, speech range
      h. Cervical cytology (Pap smear) for females

B. *Periodic Health Appraisal Examinations for:*
   1. Employees who are exposed to hazardous environments to include blood tests and other laboratory procedures, as appropriate.
   2. Employees who are returning from an illness/absence.
   3. Employees who are being transferred to another department or service.
   4. Employees who are retiring.

C. *Health and Safety Education*
   A program, directed by a knowledgeable person, to provide health, safety and environmental information for all employees, on a consistent, continuing basis. The instruction must include job orientation, safe working habits, relevant health information, and use of the occupational health unit for reporting injury and illness.

D. *Immunizations*
   1. Suggested immunizations for hospital workers:
      a. Smallpox
      b. Tetanus
      c. Polio
      d. Diphtheria
   2. Elective immunizations for:
      a. Special situations, as epidemics or unusual laboratory conditions.
   3. A suspense system for up-dating immunizations shall be maintained.

E. *Care for Illness and Injury at Work*
   1. A specific site should be available for employees to receive medical, psychological, and other consultative services on a 24-hour basis.
   2. An adequate facility should be provided to give medical, surgical, psychological and rehabilitative services to all employees.
   3. A competent consulting staff shall be maintained.
   4. A formalized procedure to contact a family or a private physician is advisable.

---
*Source: *NIOSH Guidelines,* 1981.

5. Adequate follow-up measures to facilitate continuity of care shall be maintained for all employees.
6. Treatment and reporting of occupational injuries and illnesses must conform to the State Workmen's Compensation Law, and to OSHA standards.

F. *Health Counseling*
1. A health counseling program should be made accessible and available to provide services for medical, psychological and social counseling, including help for employees with various addictive problems, as tobacco, drugs, food and alcohol.
2. A formalized system for referral and review should be provided for employees having problems which need professional intervention unavailable in the facility.
3. Where a social service or psychiatric department is not available, persons with special interests or training should be designated to assist in counseling sessions.

G. *Environmental Control and Surveillance*
1. An environmental control and surveillance program, as a part of the occupational health program, should be directed by an individual or consultant capable of managing harmful exposures in the hospital.
2. An individual shall be responsible for nuclear medicine and radiological activities.
3. Conformance to State rules and regulations pertaining to radiation and safety hazards must be maintained.

H. *Health and Safety Records System*
1. Each employee shall have a health record maintained in the health unit, to include: all examinations, reports of injury and illnesses, reports to and from physicians, and all other safety and health matters.
2. Reports shall be kept on a monthly and yearly basis to indicate injury and illness rates, accident facts, and reports on the monitoring and on the control of environmental hazards.
3. Records shall be handled with confidentiality and available only to appropriate personnel.

I. *Coordinated Planning with Hospital Departments and Services*
1. A committee representative of all hospital departments and services shall function to advise on the policy, on the direction and in support of the occupational health program.
2. A Safety Committee and the Infection Control Committee shall consider the health of all employees in their planning.
3. A member of the Hospital Occupational Health Program shall be on the Safety Committee and on the Infection Control Committee.

OSHA Standards*

The health care administrator should be sensitive to OSHA's three mandates:

1. to furnish employment conditions free from recognized hazards
2. recordkeeping
3. training employees to meet particular standards under the regulations.

The list that follows sets forth only a few of the more familiar and important OSHA standards.

Housekeeping

1. The floor of every workroom must be kept as clean and dry as possible. Where wet processes are used, some form of drainage is required; false floors, platforms, mats and other dry standing places should be provided.
2. To facilitate cleaning, every floor, working place, and passageway should be kept free from protruding nails, splinters, holes or loose boards.

Aisles and Passageways

1. Where mechanical equipment is used for handling materials, sufficient safe clearance must be allowed in aisles, at loading docks, through doorways, and wherever turns must be made. Aisles and passage-

---

*Source: Reprinted from *Health Care Labor Manual* by Martin E. Skoler, with permission of Aspen Systems Corporation, © 1981.

ways should be kept clear, in good repair, and free from obstruction across or in aisles that could create a hazard.
2. Permanent aisles and passageways must be appropriately marked.

Floor Loading Protection

1. In every building or other structure used for storage purposes, approved load limits must be marked on plates of approved design in a conspicuous place to which they relate.
2. It is unlawful to place upon a floor a load greater than that approved by the building official.

Means of Egress

1. Exits and access to them must be readily accessible at all times.
2. A door from a room to an exit or to a way of an exit access must be of the side-hinged, swinging type. It must swing with exit travel when the room is occupied by more than 50 persons or used for a high hazard occupancy.
3. In no case may access to an exit be through a bathroom or other room subject to being locked, except where the exit is designed to serve only the room subject to locking.
4. Exit access must be arranged so that it is not necessary for employees to travel through or near areas of "high hazard occupancy"—*e.g.* storage area for highly flammable chemicals—unless the path of travel is effectively shielded from such areas by a physical barrier or partition.
5. The minimum width of any way of exit access may not be less than 28 inches. Where a single access leads to an exit, its width must be at least equal to the required capacity of the exit to which it leads. Where more than one access leads to an exit, each must have a width adequate for the number of persons it is designed to accommodate.
6. All exits must discharge directly to a street, yard, court, or other open space that affords safe access to a public way.
7. Exits must be marked by readily visible signs. Access to exits must also be marked by readily visible signs where the exit is not immediately visible to the occupants.
8. Any door, passage, or stairway—which is neither an exit nor an exit access which is likely to be mistaken for an exit—must be identified by a sign reading "Not an Exit" or some similar designation or by a sign indicating its actual character, such as "To Basement."
9. Every exit sign must be suitably illuminated by a reliable light source giving a value of not less than 5 foot-candles on the illuminated surface. Artificial lights giving illumination to exit signs other than the internally illuminated types must have screens, discs, or lenses of not less than 25 square inches area made of translucent material to show red or other specified designating color on the side of the approach.
10. Every exit sign must use the word "exit" in plainly legible letters at least 6 inches high, with the principal strokes or letters not less than three-fourths-inch wide.

Fire Protection

1. Automatic sprinkler systems must be continuously maintained in reliable operating conditions.
2. Alarm and fire protection systems must be under the supervision of a responsible person who is required to conduct proper tests at weekly intervals and who will have general charge of the systems.
3. Fire retardant points or solutions must be renewed at intervals necessary to maintain their flame retardant properties.
4. Portable fire extinguishers must be fully charged and in operable condition and kept in their designated places at all times when not in use. They must also be conspicuously located so as to be readily accessible and immediately available in the event of fire.
5. If extinguishers are intended for different classes of fire, their intended use should be marked conspicuously to insure choice of the proper extinguisher at the time of a fire.
6. The selection of extinguishers for a given situation depends upon the character of the fires anticipated, the construction and occupancy of the individual property, the ve-

hicle or hazards to be protected, and other factors.

Sanitation

1. Every enclosed workplace should be constructed, equipped, and maintained to prevent—as far as possible—the existence of rodents, insects, and other vermin.
2. Each facility must provide adequate toilet facilities which are separate for each sex. The number of such facilities is dependent upon the number of employees for whom the facilities are furnished.
3. Each water closet shall occupy a separate compartment with a door and walls or partitions between fixtures sufficiently high to assure privacy.
4. Food may not be stored or eaten in any area where the presence of toxic materials or other substances might be injurious to health.

Electrical

OSHA has adopted the National Electrical Code, which contains the basic minimum provisions as a national consensus standard.

Protective Equipment for Personnel

1. Whenever danger of injury to the eyes and face exists, protective equipment must be worn.
2. Where necessary to protect the health of employees, respirators must be provided.

Accident Prevention Signs and Tags

1. Danger signs should be used only where an immediate hazard exists. There shall be no variation in the type of design for signs posted to warn of specific dangers and radiation hazards.
2. Employees should be instructed that danger signs indicate immediate danger and that special precautions are necessary.

Laundry Machinery and Operations

1. Each clothes drying tumbler must be equipped with an interlocking device that will prevent the inside cylinder from moving when the outer door is open.
2. Each washing machine must be equipped with an interlocking device that will prevent the inside cylinder from moving when the outer door is open.

Other standards especially relevant to the health care field include: guarding floor and wall openings and holes, air contaminants, vinyl chloride, cancer producing substances, ventilation, noise exposure, radiation, compressed gasses, flammable and combustible liquids, eye and face protection, medical services and first aid, and materials handling and storage. The following two areas of coverage are particularly important if an institution has its own maintenance department: hand and portable powered tools and other hand-held equipment, and welding, cutting, and brazing.

PART IX
THE HOSPITAL AND THE LAW

Chapter 40—Hospital Liability*

OVERVIEW

Historically, the hospital was rarely held liable for damages arising from negligent medical treatment rendered by physicians using its facilities. The courts perceived the hospital much like an innkeeper who was providing quarters in which patients could receive care and treatment from a privately selected physician. Moreover, the courts emphasized that hospitals, unlike physicians, were not licensed to practice medicine and, therefore, could not be held liable for the deficiencies in the medical treatment rendered to their patients. The sole measure of the hospital's conduct under the traditional analysis involved the maintenance of an appropriate physical environment and adequate support staff for the attending physician. Determination of the hospital's liability was limited to an evaluation of the adequacy of the facilities and support staff and did not extend to the quality of the medical care rendered.

However, the limited concepts of liability historically applied to hospitals have been eroded in recent years, as courts have held the hospital more directly responsible for the quality of medical care provided by its independent staff physicians. The courts have recognized a public expectancy that the hospital owes a duty to its patients that transcends the rigid line previously drawn between the hospital administration and the medical staff and which increasingly involves the hospital in the adequacy and quality of care provided to its patients.

Negligence*

Negligence is the omission or commission of an act which a reasonably prudent person would or would not do under given circumstances. It is a form of conduct caused by heedlessness or carelessness, which constitutes a departure from the "standard of care" generally imposed upon members of our society.

Forms of Negligence

The basic forms of negligence are as follows:

1. Malfeasance—execution of an unlawful or improper act.
2. Misfeasance—the improper performance of an act.
3. Nonfeasance—the failure to act when there is a duty to act.
4. Malpractice—negligence or carelessness of a professional person, such as a nurse, pharmacist, physician, accountant, etc.
5. Criminal negligence—reckless disregard for the safety of another. It is the willful indifference to an injury which could follow an act.

---

*Source: Except where noted, all material in this section consists of excerpts reprinted from *Hospital Law Manual*, Vol. IB by Martin E. Skoler, with permission of Aspen Systems Corporation, © 1981.

*Source: Reprinted from *Legal Aspects of Health Care Administration* by George D. Pozgar, with permission of Aspen Systems Corporation, © 1979.

681

Most Frequent Negligence Categories

(By area of occurrence or nature of injury)

Entrances, exits and grounds	X-ray
Hospital bed and table falls	Blood transfusion
Stairways and elevators	Bed accidents
Burns: hot water bottles and bags	Injections
Burns: x-ray	Lost personal property
Burns: other	Improper diagnosis
Wheel chairs	Equipment failure
Lack of attention: Mental patients	Non-consensual touchings
Lack of attention: Other patients	Condition of floors
Infections	Obstructions in halls and floors
Anesthesia	Autopsies
Leaving foreign substances in patient	Pharmacy, drugs, solutions
Negligence in operating room	Accidents on premises

AREAS OF HIGH LIABILITY RISK

Defective or Improper Equipment

A hospital has an obligation to furnish reasonably adequate equipment and appliances for use in the diagnosis and treatment of patients. A hospital that lacks proper equipment may be held liable for consequent injuries to a patient. The hospital is not required, however, to provide the latest equipment.

The hospital impliedly warrants that its equipment and appliances are reasonably fit for their intended use. It therefore assumes the responsibility for periodic tests and inspection of its instruments and equipment for defects. A hospital's obligation to make reasonable inspections of equipment and to remedy all defects discoverable by such inspections does not, however, constitute a guarantee by the hospital that such equipment will function properly during customary use.

One method of reducing the hospital's liability exposure for equipment defects is through the use of well-drafted contracts with hospital-based physicians. The greatest degree of protection is obtained when the hospital contracts with an independent contractor physician, such as a radiologist, who agrees under the written agreement to assume all responsibility for the inspection and repair of x-ray equipment and other appropriate equipment. In addition, contracts with the seller or manufacturer of equipment should include a seller/manufacturer agreement to maintain and repair equipment. Such contractual provisions, however, may not completely absolve the hospital of all responsibility toward patients. Some courts have held that this duty is nondelegable and that the hospital retains the ultimate responsibility even when an independent contractor has failed to fulfill a contractual obligation to inspect and repair equipment.

Negligent Drug Handling

The hospital assumes a dual responsibility with respect to the medication received by its patients. The hospital is responsible both for the systematic organization of the process by which drugs are ordered and stored, and also for the safe and responsible administration of these various medications to patients.

Liability can arise from the improper labeling of medication in either bulk or patient dosage form. Further, the hospital is charged with the duty to store, prepare, and dispense medication in a manner that prevents deterioration or contamination of the drug.

Hospital liability may also arise from the improper administration of drugs that are otherwise safe and appropriate for a particular patient. The hospital is responsible for the failure of an employee to follow standard procedures when administering a drug.

When the manner and rate of administration of a prescription drug have been detailed by the attending physician, the hospital faces numerous responsibilities. If the physician's instructions appear to be appropriate, the hospital is responsible for administering the medication in the manner and at the rate prescribed.

Conversely, if the physician's directions are unclear or unorthodox, or if the prescription contravenes the drug manufacturer's instructions, the hospital, through its employees, has an obligation to challenge or demand clarification of the physician's orders.

Finally, the hospital may be held liable for any adverse effects caused by the unnecessary use of experimental drugs. In addition, the hospital may have an affirmative duty to warn the recipients of an otherwise appropriate experimental drug if unforeseen, treatable dangers are discovered following termination of the treatment.

Failure To Warn Regarding the Risks of Treatment

The hospital's duty to warn a patient of the risks of treatment arises in two contexts: (1) the duty to detail risks as a necessary prerequisite to obtaining the patient's consent to certain treatment and (2) the duty to warn of risks that are discovered subsequent to the time of treatment.

The general rule established by prescription drug cases is that the duty to warn a patient about a drug's risks rests with the prescribing physician. That duty has been imposed on prescribing physicians because they know the drug and its effects on patients, and because it is impossible for the manufacturer to contact and warn each patient directly about a drug's hazards.

Finally, the hospital should be sensitive to emerging areas of liability for failure to warn. As the adverse side effects of radiation and other types of advanced medical treatment are discovered, the hospital should incorporate into its procedures a mechanism for ensuring appropriate pretreatment and posttreatment warnings for the recipients of such therapy.

Negligent Monitoring of a Patient's Condition

A hospital is under a general obligation to monitor all patients periodically. This duty is distinct from the hospital's obligation to monitor the competence of its medical staff and the quality of care rendered to patients within the institution. Hospital liability for the negligent monitoring of a patient's condition by its employees, such as nursing personnel, is typically imposed on a vicarious basis. Liability may arise where a hospital fails to monitor properly a postoperative patient when such monitoring would have resulted in the detection and treatment of a deterioration in the patient's condition, such as an adverse blood transfusion reaction that in one case was readily apparent for approximately 36 hours. This general standard of care also applies to the detection and prevention of infection.

Although it is not obligated to monitor each patient 24 hours a day, a hospital is required to check a patient continually if close surveillance is warranted. Circumstances requiring such surveillance arise most frequently with respect to postoperative patients, patients in the intensive care and cardiac care units, patients with known or apparent self-destructive tendencies, and patients who have received drugs with potentially severe side effects.

A hospital obviously may incur liability for the negligence of its nursing personnel in failing to follow a physician's orders.

The requisite degree of patient monitoring may also require the hospital and its nursing staff to recognize developing complications and to take action to supplement the care given by the attending physician if such care fails to abate the seriousness of the patient's condition.

Courts rely heavily on hospital records when determining an issue such as proper monitoring.

Negligent Supervision of a Patient

The duty of patient supervision is generally defined by the patient's ability to take responsibility for self-care. For example, where a mentally competent patient disregards warnings and instructions, such as those against smoking or leaving bed without assistance, the hospital may have no liability for any injury resulting from the patient's failure to follow these instructions. By contrast, where the hospital is aware that a patient is extremely hostile or otherwise unwilling to comply with regulations, it may be expected to provide a greater degree of surveillance.

The hospital is also obligated to provide devices, such as bedrails and siderails, designed to prevent injury to patients who are in a weakened condition. This duty includes the responsibility to install lavatory supports and to provide necessary nursing assistance.

Protecting the Mentally Ill Patient

A primary area of hospital liability in the treatment of the mentally ill involves situations in which the hospital either knows or should have known that patients are likely to cause harm to themselves or others. In such circumstances, the hospital has a duty to take certain steps to prevent harm to anyone. In the case of the mentally ill patient with a propensity for self-inflicted harm, the hospital is responsible for exercising reasonable care to prevent such an injury.

A hospital's responsibility to protect patients from reasonably foreseeable self-inflicted harm may require use of such preventive measures as close monitoring of patients or placing bars on their windows. It must be shown, however, that the hospital should have reasoned from the patient's actions or condition that suicide or self-inflicted harm was foreseeable. In other words, the hospital is under a duty to protect the patient from self-inflicted harm where the patient's propensity for such conduct is known or reasonably should be known by the hospital.

Under this standard, the hospital may be found negligent if it fails to relay complete information to the attending physician or fails to solicit available information regarding the patient's proclivities for self-inflicted harm from the patient's relatives.

A hospital may also be responsible for the negligent release or elopement of patients who are mentally ill.

Physical Condition of the Premises

It is clear that a patient is entitled to the hospital's exercise of reasonable care in maintaining its premises in a reasonably safe condition. The unique population of infirm and disabled persons using hospital facilities dictates a higher standard of care for hospitals in the design and maintenance of hospital premises since the hospital's physical plant must meet the special needs of its patients. Thus, depending on the nature and cause of the particular injury sustained by the patient, it may be insufficient for the hospital to argue in its defense that its facilities were safe for people of ordinary physical condition. This standard of care translates into the hospital's obligation to provide handrails in lavatories, siderails in corridors, etc., where appropriate to maintain the safety of its patients.

The hospital may also be liable for injuries sustained by visitors and other business invitees, because the hospital must exercise the same reasonable care as any other commercial establishment that regularly invites the public onto its premises. Accordingly, the hospital is liable for injuries caused by wet or slippery floors, broken or cracked stairs, ripped carpets, unsafe accumulation of snow and ice, or even balconies or large windows not designed to prevent falls.

Infection

The duty to protect patients from injury due to infections is another obligation imposed on hospitals. Because a primary purpose of the hospital is to provide facilities for the care and treatment of the sick, the hospital has an obligation to keep the environment clean and sanitary with the aim of preventing infection.

Typically, where injury as a result of infection has been alleged, proof of general unsanitary conditions such as dirty floors, improperly sterilized instruments and cold, dusty rooms, has been enough to impose hospital liability. More recent cases, however, have reflected a shift in emphasis from proof of mere existence of unsanitary conditions to proof of a causal relationship between those conditions and the alleged injury.

Virtually every state has standards and regulations with respect to infection control. These standards vary widely from state to state, and each hospital must consult the requirements of the state in which it is located.

Available as a source for establishing the standard of care respecting infection are the numerous JCAH requirements that deal with infection control.

If sterilization procedures are under the control of hospital personnel, infections caused by contaminated equipment, appliances, or instruments may also result in liability. Such liability has been imposed where the nurse failed to sterilize a needle used in giving a patient an injection. Further, in addition to its general duty to protect against use of contaminated equipment, a hospital must exert a greater degree of care regarding sterilization when it knows of a patient's unique susceptibility to certain infections.

Liability may also be imposed on a hospital for its failure to isolate patients with communicable diseases or its failure to guard adequately against cross-infection. However, the hospital must have notice of the contagious infection and may avoid liability where a physician fails to inform hospital personnel that a patient may have an infectious or contagious disease. There are provisions requiring isolation facilities for patients with communicable disease in every state's hospital-licensing regulations.

The hospital may also be required to screen its own personnel for infectious disease by testing new employees and periodically screening existing employees.

In addition, the hospital may be negligent for failing to recognize obvious symptoms of an employee's poor health and removing any employee suspected of carrying disease or infection from duty.

Nonphysical Injuries

In addition to its liability for physical injuries caused by a failure to exercise due care, a hospital may be held liable for emotional injuries as well. Tort law presently recognizes causes of action for both the intentional and the negligent infliction of emotional distress. Further, the plaintiff in such actions can be either the hospitalized patient or a third party, such as the spouse or parent of an injured patient.

It is generally recognized that the hospital is liable for emotional injuries accompanying a physical injury for which there is legal responsibility. In such cases, the mental pain and anxiety are inseparable from the physical injury to the plaintiff, and the defendant's liability encompasses both aspects of the claim.

In some instances, a determination of the hospital's liability with respect to claims that do not allege corresponding physical injury may be based upon the characterization of the hospital's conduct as either intentional or negligent. A claim for emotional injury is cognizable if the injury resulted from the willful or outrageous conduct of the defendant. Thus, if the hospital or its agent has intentionally subjected the plaintiff to severe emotional distress, it may be held liable for resulting emotional injuries. The hospital's liability in such cases may also extend to third parties, especially if the third party is a family member present at the time of the outrageous conduct. Hospital liability for this tort frequently arises in situations involving the abandonment of a patient, or the refusal to diagnose or treat a patient in obvious need of medical care.

In most states, a hospital is not liable if the plaintiff's emotional injury is unaccompanied by a corresponding physical injury and if the conduct of the defendant hospital has been merely negligent rather than intentional and outrageous.

Blood Services*

Providing blood services, one of the vital activities in which hospitals engage, is an activity that contains both a high risk of injury to the patient and a high risk of legal liability for the hospital.

The principle of *respondeat superior* is the means by which liability is imposed on a hospital. Liability can also be based upon a corporate negligence theory when the hospital fails to provide the necessary facilities for the processing and administration of blood as required by statutes, regulations or standards of practice followed by other hospitals in the community.

Blood services that take place in a hospital may include the solicitation and acceptance of a donor, the extraction of a donor's blood and its processing, storage, delivery to and transfusion into the body of a recipient. All such services can lead to liability if not performed in accordance with acceptable standards. When the hospital receives prepared blood from community blood banks, it is not responsible for any negligence of the agency unless it knew or had reason to know that the blood bank had been negligent in the past.

In a number of states regulations regarding the storage of blood have been enacted. These regulate maximum temperatures at which the blood may be stored as well as other aspects of blood services. If injury occurs from a failure to meet the standard of care as set out in these regulations, a court may find negligence on the part of the hospital. In addition, where plasma irradiation has become accepted practice to purify blood, failure to employ it to eliminate pathogenic organisms may be considered negligence.

---

*Source: Reprinted from *Problems in Hospitals Law* by the Health Law Center, with permission of Aspen Systems Corporation, © 1974.

Imputed Negligence

There are a number of situations in which the negligent act of an individual or group of individuals is imputed to the hospital. In these situations, the hospital is held vicariously liable even though it is otherwise without fault. The most common doctrine imposing vicarious liability is known as *respondeat superior,* in which the wrongful acts of an employee resulting in injury to a third party are imputed to the employer, who is otherwise without fault, simply because of the existence of the employment relationship. In order for this theory to apply, however, the employee must have been acting within the scope of employment.

This doctrine is based upon the theory that an employer has the right to control and direct the conduct of its employee. Therefore, the hospital is said to be responsible along with the employee who negligently performs an act. The employee is not relieved of liability, nor is the employer held liable for any direct act of negligence; rather, both have liability for the employee's negligent conduct.

There are times, however, when a hospital is said to have relinquished its rights to direct and control the activities of its employees and to have transferred these rights to another person, such as a staff physician. In such circumstances, the employee is said to be a "borrowed servant" of the physician, and the doctrine of *respondeat superior* does not apply to the hospital (though it may apply to the physician).

Hospital Liability for Medical Staff

As a general principle, a hospital is not liable for the negligent acts of independent staff physicians. Independent staff physicians are those who have been granted the right to use hospital facilities for their own patients, as distinguished from the hospital's full-time, salaried employees, such as residents and certain hospital-based physicians. Historically, the negligence of an independent staff physician has not been imputed to the hospital because of the implied existence of a contract between the physician and the patient. According to this implied contract, the physician, not the hospital, assumed the duty to render care. In this situation, the hospital was not held vicariously liable for the physician's conduct, because it had no duty to render care and no right to control the manner in which the physician's work was performed, unless the physician was performing on the hospital's behalf a nondelegable corporate duty. The physician in this situation may be termed an independent contractor.

Conversely, where there is a bona fide employer/employee relationship between the hospital and the physician, the hospital is vicariously liable for the physician's negligent acts occurring within the scope of employment. Thus, where the plaintiff does not allege any dereliction on the part of hospital personnel in caring for the patient or the hospital in the discharge of some direct obligation owed the patient, the characterization of the relationship between the hospital and the physician becomes critical. Generally, the physician's status as either an independent contractor or an employee of the hospital is a question of fact for the jury's determination. The criteria applied in making this determination typically focus on the hospital's right, under an oral or written contract, to control the time, manner, and method of the work that the physician performs. Indications of such control include the right to hire and fire; the right to determine working schedules, salary, and maximum permissible absences; and the right to select the patients to be treated by the physician.

While it is clear that, for purposes of tort liability, many courts will not defer to contractual provisions proclaiming a physician to be an independent contractor, such provisions may have some legal effect in other situations. Thus, a contract between a physician and hospital that declares the physician to be an independent contractor may be relevant in determining the hospital's right to obtain indemnification from the physician or the scope of coverage of the hospital's professional liability insurance policy.

Further, there is a distinction between the hospital's vicarious liability for a physician's medical activities and its vicarious liability for any administrative functions performed by the physician, for example, as a member of the board of directors or as head of a department. Even when the hospital is not liable for negligence in rendering treatment because of the physician's status as an independent contractor or staff physician, there may be grounds for hospital liability when negligent patient care results from the physician's administrative decisions. In this latter context, the physician administrator is acting as a corporate officer or agent of the hospital, and his or her negligence may be imputed to the hospital on that basis.

Hospital Liability for Its Employed Physicians, Residents, and Graduate Medical Trainees

As discussed in the previous section, a hospital will be vicariously liable for the negligence of a physician if a bona fide employer/employee or agency relationship exists. Where hospital-based physicians are treating private patients, however, and thus rendering treatment as private physicians, their negligence may not be imputed to the hospital.

By permitting residents and graduate medical trainees to perform services in its facility pursuant to an established training program, a hospital faces yet another liability exposure. A resident is a licensed physician who pursues medical studies under the direction of the hospital staff and is paid a salary by the hospital for the performance of certain patient care duties. A graduate medical trainee, or intern, is usually unlicensed, and is employed by the hospital on a salaried basis to perform services while obtaining the experience necessary for licensure. Generally, residents and graduate medical trainees are considered employees, rather than independent contractors, because they are salaried by the hospital and generally do not have private patients. Both categories of medical personnel may subject the hospital to liability under the doctrine of *respondeat superior,* because there is no contractual relationship between patients and these salaried employees, and because there is an employment relationship.

Permitting a graduate medical trainee to care for a patient without the patient's consent may result in hospital liability, at least for technical battery or assault. Furthermore, when unlicensed, graduate medical trainees who perform medical acts requiring licensure as a physician may be presumed to have acted negligently or may at least be held to a physician's standard of care, if injury results. Finally, the hospital may incur direct liability for failing to discharge its independent obligation to safeguard patients if it allows graduate medical trainees to participate in the care of patients without adequate supervision. Hospital licensing acts and regulations almost uniformly require that the care and treatment of all patients must be under the direct control and responsibility of a member of the medical staff.

Hospital Liability for Nurses

Like graduate medical trainees and residents, nurses are generally considered to be employees of the hospital. Therefore, the negligence of nurses, whether registered or practical, may be imputed to the hospital for acts or omissions within the scope of employment. If the nurse is acting under the direct control of an independent staff physician, however, the hospital may avoid liability under the "borrowed servant" doctrine.

The conduct of nursing personnel is to be measured against the standard of care generally observed by other members of the nursing profession in the community.

Based on the standard of care requiring a nurse to exercise that degree of learning, skill, and care possessed by a prudent and competent nurse, nurses may be held negligent for a failure to follow a physician's orders.

Although a nurse's faithful execution of the physician's orders will in many situations insulate the nurse, and hence the hospital, from liability, it is by now well established that blind conformity to a physician's orders will not satisfy the requisite standard of nursing care where those orders are unclear.

Even though a special nurse is employed by the patient, there are certain circumstances in which the hospital may be held liable where a special nurse is negligent in the performance of administrative duties required by the hospital. Moreover, use of the designation "special nurse" does not preclude the nurse from being held an employee or agent of the hospital under certain circumstances. Where the facts of the situation indicate that a master/servant relationship exists between the hospital and the special nurse, the usual doctrine of *respondeat superior* may impose liability upon the hospital for the nurse's wrongful conduct. (See Table 40-1 for some guidelines on nurse negligence.)

Table 40-1 Guidelines on Nurse Negligence*

ELEMENTS OF LIABILITY	EXPLANATION	EXAMPLE GIVING MEDICATION
1. Duty to use due care (defined by the standard of care)	The care which should be given under the circumstances (what the reasonably prudent nurse would have done)	A nurse should give medications: • accurately and • completely and • on time
2. Failure to meet standard of care (breach of duty)	Not giving the care which should be given under the circumstances	A nurse fails to give medications: • accurately or • completely or • on time
3. Foreseeability of harm	Knowledge that not meeting the standard of care will cause harm to the patient	Giving the wrong medication or the wrong dosage or not on schedule will probably cause harm to the patient
4. Failure to meet standard of care (breach) *causes* injury	Patient is harmed because proper care is not given	Wrong medication causes patient to have a convulsion
5. Strict Liability	Liability imposed by statute based on public policy although no one may be negligent	Some courts have upheld and others rejected a strict liability theory in administration of blood transfusions
6. Injury	Actual harm results to patient	Convulsion or other serious complication

*Source: Reprinted from *Nursing and the Law,* ed. Mary Williams Cazalas, with permission of Aspen Systems Corporation, © 1978.

Checklist for Potential Liability Problems*

General

- Does an effective system exist to identify problem situations?
- Is there a process of screening and determining the seriousness of each problem?
- Do review, analysis, and resolution take place as part of the system?
- Do follow-up procedures correct or eliminate incident/accident causes?
- Is there a consciousness of possible litigation resulting from problems and necessary means of preparation for that possible eventuality?

*Source: Reprinted from *Risk Management for Hospitals: A Practical Approach* by Bernard L. Brown, Jr., with permission of Aspen Systems Corporation, © 1979.

Identification of problems

- Are appropriate means established and understood for reporting problems by members of the hospital's staff?
- Does adequate documentation occur when a problem is identified?

Incidents and accidents

- Does a clear definition of problems (incidents) involving patients, visitors, and the general public exist?
- Does a clear definition of problems (accidents) involving employees exist?
- Are incident and accident report forms available and used properly?
- Are comprehensive policies and procedures relative to the handling of incidents and accidents formulated and followed?
- Do these policies and procedures incorporate definitions of responsibility and authority?

Centralization of information

- Does the hospital have a systematic method of centrally recording and maintaining incidents and accidents?
- Does the risk manager administer this program?
- Do basic logging systems for incidents and accidents exist?

Screening process

- Are incident/accident reports separated in major and minor categories?
- Do major incidents/accidents receive priority in terms of review and follow-up?
- Does the hospital attorney receive copies of all major incident/accident reports and support information?
- Is a determination made as to the attitude of those effected by the incident/accident?
- Are strategy and judgment used in choosing the hospital's representative to contact those involved?
- Are these persons versed in ways of best handling the contact?

Review, analysis, and recommendations

- Are adequate special purpose forms available to assist in the review and analysis of problem situations?
- Are the choices of action in the resolution of individual problems understood and considered?
- Are good investigative techniques and judgment used to determine the best course of action?
- When settlements are made, are release forms generally signed?
- Are general problems in terms of trends and patterns identified, addressed, and resolved?
- Does an adequate system of review and analysis exist within the committee structure?

Litigation preparation

- Does factual comprehensive documentation that can be used in litigation preparation generally exist in most risk situations?
- Are review and analysis reports available for use by the hospital's legal counsel?
- Is the hospital attorney thoroughly oriented in the technical and operational aspects of problem situations that must be litigated?
- Do the governing body and administration participate in judgmental and strategic decision making?
- Is a position of flexibility maintained throughout the litigation process?

TORTS[*]

Assault and Battery

An assault is the deliberate threat, coupled with the apparent present ability, to do physical harm to another. It is the deliberate threat and/or attempt to injure another or the attempt by one to make bodily contact with another without consent. An assault may be permissible if proper consent has been given (i.e., invasion of the body through surgery) or if it is in defense of oneself or of a third party.

In the health context, the principle of law concerning battery and the requirement of consent to medical and surgical procedures is critically important. Liability of hospitals, physicians, and nurses for acts of battery is most common in

---

[*]Source: Reprinted from *Legal Aspects of Health Care Administration* by George D. Pozgar, with permission of Aspen Systems Corporation, © 1979.

situations involving lack of or improper patient consent to medical and surgical procedures. It is inevitable that a patient in a hospital will be touched by many persons for many reasons. Procedures ranging from bathing to surgery involve some touching of a patient. Even the administration of medications may entail touching. Therefore, medical and surgical procedures must be authorized by the patient. If they are not authorized, the person performing the procedure could be subject to an action for battery.

It is of no legal importance that a procedure constituting a battery has improved a patient's health. If the patient did not consent to the touching, the patient may be entitled to such damages as can be proven to have resulted from commission of the battery.

False Imprisonment

False imprisonment is the unlawful restraint of an individual's personal liberty or the unlawful detention of an individual. Actual physical force is not necessary to constitute a false imprisonment.

In certain cases, preventing a patient from leaving a hospital may constitute false imprisonment. For example, detaining a patient until the bills are paid would qualify as false imprisonment. However, hospitals or their employees are not liable for false imprisonment if they compel a patient with a contagious disease to remain in the hospital. In addition, as is governed by statute in many states, mentally ill patients may also be kept in the hospital if there is a danger that they will take their own lives or jeopardize the lives or property of others. Those who are mentally ill, however, can be restrained only to the degree necessary to protect themselves from self-harm or harming others. A patient's insistence on leaving should be noted on the medical record. The patient should also be informed of the possible harm in leaving against medical advice. The patient should be requested to sign a discharge against advice and release of responsibility form, if the individual insists upon leaving the hospital against medical advice.

Defamation of Character

Defamation of character is the oral or written communication to someone, other than the person defamed, which tends to injure that person's reputation. By tradition, libel is the written form and slander the spoken form of defamation. Libel can be presented in the form of signs, photographs, letters, etc. To be an actionable wrong, defamation must be communicated to a third person. Defamatory statements communicated only to the injured party are not grounds for an action.

No proof of actual damage is needed in order for libel to be actionable. With slander, on the other hand, actual damage must be proved by the person bringing suit. There are four generally recognized exceptions where no proof of actual harm to reputation is required in order to recover damages: (1) accusing someone of a crime; (2) accusing someone of having a loathsome disease; (3) using words which affect a person's profession or business; and (4) calling a woman unchaste.

When any allegedly defamatory words refer to a person in a professional capacity, the professional need not show that the words caused damage. It is presumed that any slanderous reference to someone's professional capacity is damaging; the plaintiff therefore has no need to prove damage.

Each professional is legally protected against libel when complying with a law requiring a report of venereal or other diseases which might be considered loathsome. There are very few defamation of character lawsuits because of the difficulty in proving such cases, the small awards, and the high legal fees. Professionals who are called incompetent in front of others have a right to sue to defend their reputations. However, it is difficult to prove an individual comment injurious. If the person making an injurious comment cannot prove it, that person can be sued. A nurse should not complain about a physician to a patient or family. The patient's condition should not be discussed with anyone not directly involved in the case.

Fraud

Fraud is defined as willful and intended misrepresentation that could cause harm or loss to a person or property. Intentional misrepresentation in many states gives rise to an action for deceit. Physicians who know they have no foundation for believing a statement to be true and make it anyway, can be held liable for misrepresentation (for example, a physician who claims that a certain surgical operation will cure a patient's ailment, when the physician knows it is not so).

Invasion of Privacy

Invasion of privacy is a wrong that invades the right of a person to personal privacy. Absolute privacy has to be tempered with reality in the medical or nursing care of any patient. This fact is recognized by the courts. Negligent disregard for the individual patient's right of privacy is intolerable and legally actionable, particularly when patients are unable to adequately protect themselves because of unconsciousness or immobility.

Hospitals, physicians, and nurses may become liable for invasion of privacy if they divulge information from a patient's medical record to improper sources, or if they commit unwarranted intrusions into the patient's personal affairs.

Hospitals could be held liable under this principle if they were responsible for the unwarranted intrusion into the private affairs of a patient. A hospital could be sued for allowing pictures to be taken of a malformed, dead child. A doctor who takes pictures of a patient's disfigured face while the patient is in extreme pain and semiconscious could be legally restrained from developing or making prints of the negatives.

The information on a patient's chart is confidential and cannot be disclosed without the patient's permission. Those who come into possession of the most intimate, personal information about patients have both a legal and an ethical duty not to reveal confidential communications.

There are occasions when there is a legal obligation or duty to disclose information. The reporting of communicable diseases, gunshot wounds, child abuse, and other matters is required by law. There are also certain exceptions to the right of privacy. Virtually all the doings of a person who is a public figure are of legitimate interest to the public.

Representatives of reputable news media should be accommodated within the limitations placed upon such communications by the administration of the hospital and applicable statutes and/or regulations pertaining to the release of information. In any event, the patient's right of privacy must be protected. Public relations officers, physicians and nurses should restrict their interviews and releases to avoid any injury to the reputation of the patient.

Chapter 41—Informed Consent*

OVERVIEW

A large proportion of the medical and surgical procedures that give rise to lawsuits alleging a lack of consent are performed in a hospital setting.

The accreditation standards of the Joint Commission on Accreditation of Hospitals (JCAH) contain several requirements regarding patient consent, noting prominently in the introductory section on "Rights and Responsibilities of Patients":

Consent:

The patient has the right to reasonably informed participation in decisions involving his health care. To the degree possible, this should be based on a clear, concise explanation of his condition and of all proposed technical procedures, including the possibilities of any risk of mortality or serious side effects, problems not related to recuperation, and probability of success. The patient should not be subjected to any procedure without his voluntary, competent and understanding consent, or that of his legally authorized representative. Where medically significant alternatives for care or treatment exist, the patient shall be so informed.

The patient has the right to know who is responsible for authorizing and performing the procedures or treatment.

Where a procedure is performed on a patient by hospital employees, it is the hospital's responsibility to assure that the consent obtained from the patient is adequately informed. No court has yet held, however, that the hospital has an affirmative obligation to monitor the content of disclosures given by nonemployed health care practitioners to patients being treated within the hospital's facilities to assure that consent is "informed."

Express or Implied Consent

"Express consent" is that which a patient gives by direct words. These words may be spoken or written; in theory, there is no difference. Practically, however, the problems involved in proving an effective oral consent may be substantial. When possible, the health care provider should always secure a written consent from the patient (or, in certain cases, from another person authorized to act in the patient's behalf). On the other hand, a formal, written consent is not always sufficient; numerous cases can be found in which it was claimed that extenuating circumstances invalidated the consent formally given by the patient.

"Implied consent" is that which arises by reasonable inference from the conduct of the patient. Its underlying basis is the health care provider's reliance on the patient's actions to conclude that the procedure is authorized. If a

---

*Source: Reprinted from *Informed Consent: A Guide for Health Care Providers* by Arnold J. Rosoff, with permission of Aspen Systems Corporation, © 1981.

patient voluntarily submits to a procedure with actual or apparent knowledge of what is about to transpire, this submission will constitute implied consent even though there was no explicit oral or written expression of consent.

Emergency Treatment

A medical emergency may obviate the need for consent. When immediate treatment is required to preserve life or prevent a serious impairment to health, *and* it is impossible to obtain the patient's consent or that of someone authorized to consent on the patient's behalf, the physician may undertake the required procedure without liability for battery.

The attempt to locate next of kin frequently falls to the hospital's administrative officials, which explains in part the significance of the so-called administrative consent to emergency care. Properly handled, the administration's approval serves three basic purposes: (1) It helps to document that the fullest possible attempt was made to secure a proxy consent. (2) It shows that someone with experience in emergency health care situations concurred with the physician's judgment that immediate care was needed; in fact, it might be used to provide additional proof that the hospital took all reasonable steps to assure adequate medical consultation. (3) It prevents the hospital from later instituting any disciplinary action against the physician who proceeded without consent. Thus, it protects both the institution and the practitioner. It must be recognized, however, that the administration of a hospital has no special power to grant a legally effective consent; that must come from the patient, a duly empowered representative, or from the circumstances.

Some hospital administrations have set up channels for seeking court orders authorizing the provision of treatment when consent cannot be obtained in the regular manner. The court's power in this regard may be set forth by statute. Such procedures are often used with respect to the treatment of minors when their parents cannot be located to give consent or, more rarely, when the parents are available but refuse consent.

Tests Performed upon Police Order

From time to time, the police may call upon medical personnel, particularly those based in hospitals, to perform test procedures upon criminal suspects. Such tests range from simple examination, through analysis of breath, urine, or blood samples to more invasive procedures, such as removal of a bullet for ballistics analysis or the pumping of a suspect's stomach to recover swallowed items.

In theory, a hospital or health care professional might be held liable for performing a nonconsensual procedure even when there was a police request or order, but no reported decisions of this nature could be found.

MEDICAL EXPERIMENTATION AND RESEARCH

While the states have the power to restrict medical experimentation, regulation has largely been left to the federal government, which has focused its attention on research performed in hospitals or other health care institutions. Regulations of the Department of Health and Human Services (HHS), and its subagency the FDA, require prior approval of all research involving human subjects by institutional review boards (IRBs) established in institutions receiving federal research funding. However, all hospitals, however funded, have a common law responsibility to assure that their patients and facilities are not improperly used for research or experimentation. Thus, even institutions that do not engage in federally funded research should look to the HHS regulations as a guide for setting up their own institutional review systems to safeguard patient welfare.

Institutional Review Boards

HHS regulations require each institution to have an IRB, composed of no less than five persons whose background and experience enable them to assess research applications and proposals in terms of institutional commitments and regulations, applicable law, standards of professional conduct and practice, and community attitudes. No IRB may consist entirely of persons employed by or affiliated with the institution, nor may it consist entirely of members of a single professional group. No IRB member may participate in the review of an activity in which he or she has a conflicting interest.

The function of the IRB is to review in advance all proposed research activities that involve the institution's patients to determine whether any research subjects will be placed at risk and, if risk is involved, whether:

1. The risks to the subject are so outweighed by the sum of the benefit to the subject and the importance of the knowledge to be gained as to warrant a decision to allow the subject to accept these risks;
2. The rights and welfare of any such subjects will be adequately protected; and
3. Legally effective informed consent will be obtained by adequate and appropriate methods.

No application to HHS for funding of research involving human subjects will be considered unless the individual submitting it is affiliated with or sponsored by an institution that not only can and does assume responsibility for the subjects involved but also submits a certification of its review and approval of the proposed research. Proposals involving investigational new drugs and devices must also satisfy the requirements imposed by FDA under the Federal Food, Drug and Cosmetic Act.

Obtaining and Documenting Informed Consent to Research

Assuming that the proposed research is deemed justifiable by the IRB, approval still cannot be given unless the research protocol provides for the securing of adequate informed consent from all subjects. The basic elements of information necessary to such consent include:

1. A fair explanation of the procedures to be followed, and their purposes, including identification of any procedures which are experimental;
2. A description of any attendant discomforts and risks reasonably to be expected;
3. A description of any benefits reasonably to be expected;
4. A disclosure of any appropriate alternative procedures that might be advantageous for the subject;
5. An offer to answer any inquiries concerning the procedures; and
6. An instruction that the person is free to withdraw his consent and discontinue participation in the project or activity at any time without prejudice to the subject.

Under this definition, it is essential to legally effective consent that the person consenting, either the subject or someone legally authorized to act on the subject's behalf, be competent to do so and that the consent be wholly voluntary. Promises of compensation or special favors in return for participation must be carefully scrutinized to see that they do not overbear the will of the proposed subject.

CONSENT FORMS

For medical and surgical care rendered in a hospital, the most satisfactory way to prove that the patient has consented is by the integrated use of two consent forms. A general admission consent form should be signed when the patient is admitted to the hospital. Such a form is presently used by many hospitals. It provides a record of consent to routine hospital services, diagnostic procedures, and medical treatment. The only significant danger regarding its use is the possible reliance upon it as authorization for specific procedures, such as surgery, for which it is not designed and is largely ineffective.

The written general consent form serves as evidence of the patient's voluntary submission to treatment, which is generally self-evident, but in no way does it demonstrate that the patient understood the specifics of the treatment that was to be undertaken.

A signed special consent form should be procured prior to every substantial medical or surgical procedure beyond routine treatment. Proper use of such a form should satisfy the requirements of an informed consent. The special and admission consent forms, used together, will protect the hospital, its employees, and members of the medical staff by reducing the likelihood that a court will find a particular medical or surgical procedure not to have been authorized.

Specialized forms required for given procedures and circumstances can be created by adapting the special consent form. Such an adapted form may be useful when a defined procedure is performed frequently in the course of the hospital's care of its patients. Legal counsel should be consulted to ensure that forms used comply with any special requirements of the relevant state law or the provider's situation. Counsel's advice should also be obtained regarding any modifications of these forms needed to serve specialized purposes.

Elements of a Valid, Informed Consent

- the diagnosis
- the nature and purpose of the procedure(s) for which consent is sought
- all material risks and consequences of the procedure(s)
- an assessment of the likelihood that the procedure(s) will accomplish the desired objective(s)
- any reasonably feasible alternatives for treatment, with the same supporting information as is required regarding the proposed procedure(s)
- the prognosis if no treatment is provided

It must be signed by the patient or, if the patient is incompetent, by someone who is legally authorized to consent on the patient's behalf.

Admission Consent Form

The admission consent form should be executed by the patient, or the patient's legally recognized representative, as part of the hospital's regular admission procedure. Admitting office personnel should expressly inform each patient that he or she is being asked to sign a consent form, and the purpose of the form should be explained. For a suggested admission consent form see Figure 41-1.

Special Consent Form

The special consent form should not be completed in the admitting office of the hospital. It is meant to serve as a record of a full and complete discussion between the patient and physician, or in some cases between the patient and another member of the health care team, and should not be completed in advance of such discussion. If a procedure that normally calls for the use of a special consent form is to be performed very soon after admission, it may be advisable for the physician to provide the necessary information and procure the patient's written consent before the admission.

Generally, the attending physician will take responsibility for completing the special consent form and having it executed by the patient. However, some hospitals have adopted administrative procedures to assure that such a form is completed and placed on file before any significant medical or surgical procedure may be performed. While the hospital makes no check on the substance of the information disclosure to the patient, such a check upon the physician's apparent satisfaction of the obligation to obtain informed consent is a prudent practice.

A special consent form should be executed by the patient or a representative of the patient before any of the following types of procedures are performed:

- major or minor surgery involving an entry into the body, either through an incision or through a natural body opening
- all procedures in which anesthesia is used, regardless of whether an entry into the body is involved
- nonsurgical procedures, including the administration of medicines, that involve more than a slight risk of harm to the patient, or that may cause a change in the patient's body structure. Such procedures would include, but are not limited to, chemotherapy for cancer, hormone treatments, and diagnostic procedures such as myelograms, arteriograms, and pyelograms
- all forms of radiological therapy
- electroconvulsive therapy
- all experimental procedures
- all other procedures that the medical staff determines require a specific explanation to the patient. Any doubts as to the necessity of obtaining a special consent from the patient for a procedure should be resolved in favor of procuring the consent.

Consent Forms Tailored to Specific Procedures

Although the special consent form can be adapted to various uses, forms designed for specialized applications may be most useful. Certain procedures may be performed so often and be so straightforward, e.g., a blood transfusion, that it is more convenient to have a specially tailored form prepared for this particular procedure. In addition, there are procedures sufficiently complex and sensitive, such as electroconvulsive therapy (ECT) or an intravenous pyelogram (IVP), that it is both safer and more economical of time to use a tailored form than to attempt adaptation of a general purpose form.

Figure 41-1 Admission consent form

[NAME OF HOSPITAL]
CONSENT TO HOSPITAL ADMISSION AND
MEDICAL TREATMENT

Name of Patient: _____

Name of Attending Physician(s): _____

Date of Admission: _____ Time: _____ (AM) (PM)

    1. I, (or [NAME OF AUTHORIZED REPRESENTATIVE] acting on behalf of) [NAME OF PATIENT], suffering from a condition requiring hospital care, hereby consent to the rendering of such care, which may include routine diagnostic procedures and such medical treatment as the named attending physician(s) or others of the hospital's medical staff consider to be necessary.

    2. I understand that the practice of medicine and surgery is not an exact science and that diagnosis and treatment may involve risks of injury, or even death. I acknowledge that no guarantees have been made to me as to the result of examination or treatment in this hospital.

    3. I understand that:

        (A) It is customary, absent emergency or extraordinary circumstances, that no substantial procedures are performed upon a patient unless and until he or she has had an opportunity to discuss them with the physician or other health professional to the patient's satisfaction;

        (B) Each patient has the right to consent, or to refuse consent, to any proposed procedure or therapeutic course; and

        (C) No patient will be involved in any research or experimental procedure without his or her full knowledge and consent.

    4. I understand that many of the physicians on the staff of this hospital, including the attending physician(s) named above, are not employees or agents of the hospital but, rather, are independent contractors who have been granted the privilege of using its facilities for the care and treatment of their patients. Further, I realize that among those who attend patients at this hospital are medical, nursing, and other health care personnel in training who, unless requested otherwise, may be present during patient care as a part of their education. Still or motion pictures and closed circuit television monitoring of patient care also may be used for educational purposes, unless a patient expressly requests otherwise.

    5. This form has been fully explained to me, and I am satisfied that I understand its content and significance.

Date of Execution: _____

_____   _____
[SIGNATURE OF PATIENT]   [SIGNATURE OF WITNESS]

    (If patient is unable to consent or is a minor, complete the following:) Patient [is a minor _____ years of age] [is unable to consent because]: _____

_____   _____
[SIGNATURE OF LEGAL GUARDIAN OR   [SIGNATURE OF WITNESS]
CLOSEST AVAILABLE RELATIVE]

The mix of services offered at each individual hospital, the volume and frequency of such services, . . . number of staff members, and the degree of their cooperation will all need to be considered in deciding whether to develop special forms for given procedures.

REFUSAL OF CONSENT

An adult patient who is conscious and mentally competent has the right to refuse to permit any medical or surgical procedure. A competent patient's refusal must be honored whether the refusal is grounded upon a doubt that the contemplated procedure will be successful, a concern about the probable or possible results of the procedure, a lack of confidence in the surgeon who recommends it, a religious belief, or a mere whim.

The attempt to save a patient's life in the face of the patient's express prohibition is a humanitarian gesture that may not be supported by law. Even if the procedure is skillfully performed, the patient's right to be secure in his or her person has been violated, and damages may be sought for the unauthorized treatment. A sizable award seems unlikely, however, in a case where the patient's life was saved by treatment rendered in disregard of his or her rights.

Refusal of Artificial Life-Prolonging Measures

A hospital should not be liable if it refrains from using "heroic" measures or withdraws artificial life support from a patient whose death is imminent, so long as it can be proved that this was the patient's wish, formulated and declared at a time when the patient was competent to make such a decision. In states that have natural death acts it is, of course, essential that their procedural requirements be followed to the letter. Such safeguards typically include waiting periods before a patient's directive to cease life-sustaining care becomes effective, witness requirements, and other protections against forgery, overbearing, or misinterpretation of the patient's intent. Even in states without specific statutes on the subject, a so-called living will executed by a competent patient should go far toward immunizing any hospital or physician who honors the patient's wishes regarding discontinuance of extraordinary treatment. On the other hand, without such direction from the patient, the law presumes that a patient wishes to be kept alive whenever there is reasonable hope for recovery or significant prolongation of life. The obligation of the health care provider to the patient incorporates the patient's implicit expectation that care will be rendered accordingly.

With regard to health care generally, when the patient is unconscious or is otherwise not competent to declare his or her wishes, the hospital can look to the next of kin for direction. Where cessation of life-sustaining care is involved, however, the right of the patient's close relative(s) to make such a decision is unclear. Still, when hope for the patient's recovery or the significant extension of the patient's life has been exhausted, and particularly when the patient is suffering, it may be appropriate for the hospital to discontinue artificial life support. In such case, concurrence of the patient's next of kin should be obtained and documented, serving more as a release of liability, i.e., a promise not to sue, than as a direct authorization. While not a perfect safeguard, such documented concurrence offers substantial practical assurance that no litigation or liability will result. The focus should be on what is in the patient's best interest and, insofar as it is ascertainable, what the patient would desire. The documentation of the decision should reflect this focus.

Before the hospital ceases life-sustaining measures upon such direction, it should make certain that the person concurring in the decision to discontinue extraordinary life support measures is the closest kin to the patient reasonably available and that no other person has better claim to speak on the patient's behalf. Where there is any doubt of this, or of the motives of the next of kin, or where there is reason to believe that other family members are in substantial disagreement with this course, the hospital should not discontinue life support without a court order authorizing this.

Health care administrators are urged to familiarize themselves with the relevant law and, after consultation with legal counsel, to adopt and communicate appropriate procedures to all involved professional and support staff. Hospitals should devise adequate mechanisms for recording the patient's instructions and noting them prominently on the patient's chart. For many hospitals, this will require little change from

Figure 41-2 Form for patient's refusal of treatment

PATIENT'S RELEASE UPON
REFUSAL OF TREATMENT

For the reason(s) stated below, I, [NAME OF PATIENT], direct that the following procedure(s) not be performed upon me.

PROCEDURE(S) REFUSED: _____

_____

The REASON FOR MY REFUSAL to consent to such procedure(s) is: _____

_____

I understand that it is the considered opinion of the qualified health professional(s) attending me, whose signature(s) appears below, that I will likely need the above-described procedure(s) and that the possible/probable consequence of my refusal is: _____

Despite the chance that my health may be negatively affected and my life possibly endangered, I request that my refusal be honored, and I hereby release [NAME OF INSTITUTION] and all health care personnel directly or indirectly involved in my care from all liability that might otherwise be asserted as a result of not providing the described care.

I attest that I am of full age (AGE: _____) and am mentally competent to make such a determination and direction.

TIME: _____ DATE: _____ SIGNED: _____

SIGNATURE OF WITNESS(ES):
[CLOSE RELATIVE(S):
IF AVAILABLE]:

SIGNATURE(S) OF HEALTH CARE
PERSONNEL ATTENDING PATIENT:

present procedures for handling orders not to resuscitate. Some institutions have ethics committees that can be called upon to assist in the making of difficult decisions regarding termination of life support.

Hospital Liability

A hospital will be liable if it fails to prevent a health professional from treating a patient in the face of the patient's clear refusal to consent to

Figure 41-3 Form for discontinuance of extraordinary life support measures

REQUEST FOR DISCONTINUANCE OF EXTRAORDINARY LIFE SUPPORT MEASURES FOR TERMINAL PATIENT

("LIVING WILL")

I, [NAME OF PATIENT], being of sound mind and full age, record the following request, recognizing that the time may come when I can no longer actively take part in decisions regarding my medical care and other treatment.

If I am so afflicted by illness or injury that, in the opinion of qualified medical practitioners, there is no reasonable expectation of my recovery to a conscious, cognitive state, I request that I be allowed to die and not be kept alive by artificial means or heroic measures. If necessary to relieve terminal suffering, I request also that pain-suppressing drugs be administered to me, even though this may hasten my death. I ask not that my life be directly taken but only that my dying not be unreasonably prolonged nor the dignity of my remaining life sacrificed.

With full realization of what I am asking, I sincerely request that any person(s) having responsibility for my care or for my estate will respect my wishes recorded here and will hold harmless any provider of health services who abides by them.

DATE:_____ SIGNED:_____
[PATIENT'S SIGNATURE]

WITNESS:_____

CERTIFICATION BY PATIENT'S RELATIVE

I, _____, am related to the above-named patient as follows: _____.
As the person of closest relationship to the patient who is available for consultation at this time, I certify my sincere belief that the above directive represents the sentiment of the patient and [that he/she is competent to make such a decision] [is what he/she would request if able to express himself/herself] at this time. I hereby request the medical personnel caring for the patient to act in accordance with the above directive.

DATE:_____ SIGNED:_____

WITNESS:_____

Figure 41-4 Form for relative of patient refusing treatment

RELEASE BY RELATIVE UPON
PATIENT'S REFUSAL OF TREATMENT

I, [NAME OF RELATIVE], am the [WIFE, FATHER, ETC.] of [NAME OF PATIENT], a patient at the [NAME OF INSTITUTION]. My [HUSBAND, DAUGHTER, ETC.] has refused to consent to the following procedure(s), [NAME OF PROCEDURE(S)] _____
because [STATE PATIENT'S REASON FOR REFUSAL] _____
_____.

The qualified health professional attending the patient, whose signature appears below, had explained to my [HUSBAND, DAUGHTER, ETC.] the serious need for the above-described procedure and that the possible/probable consequence for his/her refusal is _____
_____.

I fully understand that refusal of this treatment may jeopardize my [HUSBAND'S, DAUGHTER'S, ETC.] health and/or life, but it is my wish that his/her refusal be honored. I hereby release the named institution and the health personnel attending the patient from any liability that I might assert against them for not providing the treatment described herein. I attest that I am of full age, am mentally competent to execute this release, and am the patient's closest relative reasonably available at the present time for consultation as to the patient's need for care.

TIME: _____ DATE: _____ SIGNED: _____

SIGNATURE(S) OF HEALTH CARE _____
PERSONNEL ATTENDING PATIENT: _____

---

such treatment. The hospital has a duty to use reasonable care to protect its patients from procedures to which they have expressly refused consent. If a patient refuses to sign a consent form for the contemplated procedure or communicates a refusal of consent to hospital employees, the hospital can be found to have notice of such refusal and, thus, to have the duty to prevent the procedure from taking place on its premises.

It is recommended that no medical or surgical procedures be performed within the hospital in the face of a patient's refusal. In order to avoid liability for not providing appropriate treatment, however, the hospital should first ascertain that the patient is competent at the time of the refusal. Any question regarding competence should be considered by the attending physician in consultation with at least one other physician, and their determination should be documented. The refusal should be noted in the medical record, and the physician should render the best care possible within the limits imposed by the patient's refusal. If possible, a written release should be secured from the patient acknowledging that appropriate treatment would have been rendered if the patient had not refused. It is advisable that the hospital administrator, with the aid of legal counsel, formulate a policy regarding treatment in those rare and serious cases where the hospital feels it necessary to proceed with treatment despite the patient's refusal. An ad-

Figure 41-5 Form for patient discharge from hospital against medical advice

---

DISCHARGE OF PATIENT FROM HOSPITAL
AGAINST MEDICAL ADVICE

Being about to leave [take [NAME OF PATIENT] from] [NAME OF INSTITUTION], I acknowledge that I understand this action to be against the advice of the attending physician(s) and/or hospital authorities.

1. I have been informed of the possible/probable dangers to my [Wife's, Son's, Etc.] health that may result from [his/her] leaving the hospital at this time, including:
[NAME SPECIFIC RISKS OF DEPARTING]
_____
_____
_____
_____.

2. [Cross out if inappropriate.] I recognize that the above listing of dangers may not be complete and that a fuller explanation of the consequences is available upon my request. However, I do not wish any further explanation.

3. I assume the risk and accept the consequences of my/the patient's departure from [NAME OF INSTITUTION] at this time and hereby release all health care providers, including the hospital and its staff, from any liability for ill effects that may result from discontinuance of treatment.

4. I have read and fully understand this document. All blank spaces were filled in and/or sections crossed out prior to my signing below.

DATE:_____
SIGNED:_____
[PATIENT OR AUTHORIZED PERSON TAKING
RESPONSIBILITY FOR PATIENT]

WITNESS: _____

---

ministrative procedure should be established to facilitate applying for a court order when one is needed so that all unnecessary delay can be avoided.

Qualified Consent

A patient may, before treatment is begun, specifically prohibit a procedure or technique that might become necessary during treatment. In the event of such refusal before the fact, two alternate courses are possible. (1) The hospital can refuse to admit the patient on the grounds that proper care cannot be rendered because of the patient's refusal to allow procedures that the hospital believes may be necessary for the preservation of life or health. No legal liability will result from denying admission in such a case. (2) The hospital can admit the patient and provide only such services and procedures as are within the limits stated by the patient. If this approach is used, procedures should be developed for adequately communicating to hospital staff the agreed limitations upon the patient's care. What the hospital cannot do is admit the patient and, unless circumstances change unexpectedly, disregard the limitations upon which the hospital-patient relationship was established.

A patient who imposes such limits by refusing consent to certain procedures should be required to execute a release, stating that he or she understands and voluntarily assumes the risk(s) incident to the refusal. This release will protect both the physician and the hospital from liability if it is later asserted that proper medical care was not rendered to the patient. Having a corresponding release executed by the patient's spouse or closest available relative will provide additional evidence.

Sample forms for dealing with the situations discussed are provided in Figures 41-2, 41-3, 41-4 and 41-5. All blanks should be fully filled in before a form is signed. Since some states have specific requirements for documentation of informed consent, the state-by-state analysis of informed consent laws should be consulted. In all cases, legal counsel should review forms before they are put into use to ensure that they are appropriate to the particular provider's situation.

Chapter 42—Medical Records and the Law*

MAINTAINING RECORDS

Retention Requirements

The length of time a medical record is retained will be determined by federal or state law, by regulations, or by sound hospital administrative policy and medical practice.

In the absence of regulatory requirements, each hospital should establish its own policy governing medical records retention. It is clear that hospitals should retain medical records for as long as there is a medical or administrative need for them, e.g., subsequent patient care, medical research, review and evaluation of professional and hospital services, or defense of professional or other liability actions.

There are several factors that the hospital should consider in establishing a retention policy: statutory and regulatory requirements, statutes of limitations and future litigation, extent of medical research, storage capabilities, microfilming and other processes, and recommendations of hospital associations.

The American Hospital Association (AHA) and the American Medical Record Association (AMRA) have adopted a policy on record retention that recommends retaining records for a period of ten years after the most recent patient care usage and retaining certain parts of the record permanently. In addition, some state hospital associations have issued record retention guidelines that may be useful in developing a hospital record retention policy.

Hospitals that destroy their records must establish procedures to protect confidentiality of record information and ensure that records are completely destroyed.

Medical Record Entries

Legible and Complete

Hospital medical, nursing, and other professional personnel, as well as students and others who write in patient records must understand the importance of creating legible, complete, and accurate records. Court decisions have shown that a hospital's exposure to negligence liability increases if it permits its staff to make improper entries. Moreover, federal regulations and some state laws require certain record entries to be made within a specified period following the patient's discharge. Corrections to records, while perfectly permissible, can create serious problems for hospitals, especially those involved in negligence litigation, if appropriate changes are made in an improper manner. Significant alterations made simply to improve the defense of a lawsuit or to defraud reimbursement agencies can have serious adverse consequences for the hospital, including the imposition of criminal sanctions.

The medical record is often the single most important document available to a hospital in

---

*Source: Except where noted, the material in this section consists of excerpts reprinted from *Hospital Law Manual,* Vol. IA by Health Law Center, with permission of Aspen Systems Corporation, © 1981.

the defense of a negligence action and ordinarily is admissible as evidence of what transpired in the care of the patient. Without a legible and complete medical record, the hospital may be unable to defend itself successfully against allegations of improper care. Therefore, hospitals must take great care to establish policies that will ensure that entries made in its medical records are thorough and proper.

Who Can Make Entries?

When undergraduate medical students and unlicensed house staff make chart entries that show the application of medical judgment, medical diagnosis, the prescription of treatment or any other act defined by applicable state law to be the practice of medicine, these entries should be countersigned by a licensed physician, who may be an attending or a resident physician.

Similarly the entries of undergraduate nursing students should be countersigned by a licensed professional nurse. Without evidence of proper supervision, a nursing student practicing professional nursing could be held in violation of the state's nursing licensure act, unless the act specifically authorizes nursing students to practice nursing in the course of their studies. Entries by social service staff should be limited to relevant factual observations or to data and judgments that such staff are competent to make; highly subjective or unfounded remarks should be avoided.

Verbal Orders

A physician's verbal orders and other instructions generally considered by the medical staff to be associated with any potential hazard to the patient must be transcribed in the medical record and signed by the physician within 24 hours. JCAH accreditation standards and hospital-licensing regulations in some states require all physician orders to be written in the patient's medical record. A physician's signature on a transcribed verbal order authenticates the order and indicates that it is correct. Who may receive and transcribe a physician's verbal order is a matter of hospital policy, usually set forth in the medical staff rules and regulations. Only personnel who are qualified to understand physicians' orders should be authorized to receive and transcribe verbal orders.

In view of the increased potential for error in verbal orders, hospitals should discourage all verbal orders except those issued by telephone. Physicians giving orders on the patient care unit should be able to write their orders in the patient charts. If circumstances require other personnel to transcribe a physician's orders, they should ask the physician to authenticate the orders before leaving the unit. Nursing or house staff in most hospitals receive and transcribe telephone orders from attending physicians. Although not practicable in all cases, having a second person at the hospital on the telephone to witness the conversation reduces error and controversy concerning the order given. For especially sensitive orders, such as do-not-resuscitate orders, hospitals should require a witness to the order.

Corrections and Alterations

As medical record entry errors are inevitable, hospitals should give some attention to the method by which their staffs correct errors in patient charts. Generally, there are two kinds of errors made in charts: (1) minor errors in transcription, spelling, and the like and (2) more significant errors involving important test data, physician medication orders, inadvertently omitted progress notes, and similar substantive entries. Any person authorized by hospital policy to make record entries may correct minor errors, but only a physician or an administrative or nursing staff supervisor should correct substantive errors and errors that are discovered some time after the original, incorrect entry was made.

The person correcting a charting error should line out the incorrect entry, enter the correct information, initial the correction, and enter the time and date the correction was made (if not otherwise shown in the entry). Mistakes in the chart should not be erased or obliterated, since erasures and obliterations may create suspicion in the mind of a jury concerning the original entry. A single line through incorrect entries leaves no doubt as to what has been corrected.

After a claim has been made or a lawsuit has been threatened or filed against the hospital or a practitioner on its staff, hospital personnel and medical staff should make no changes in the complainant's medical record without first consulting their defense counsel.

Deliberately altering a medical record or writing an incorrect record may subject the practitioner and the hospital to statutory sanctions. In some states, a practitioner who improperly alters a medical record is subject to a license revocation action for unprofessional conduct.

ACCESS TO MEDICAL RECORD INFORMATION

The hospital owns the physical medical record subject to the patient's interest in the information in it. It is generally accepted that the record is a confidential document and that access to it should be limited to the patient, to the patient's authorized representative and attending physician, and to hospital staff members who have a legitimate interest in the record. There are several exceptions to this general rule, however, each of which permits individuals other than those listed to review the medical record. The exceptions include disclosures that are made pursuant to the federal Freedom of Information Act (FOIA); those required by the federal and state reimbursement regulations; those necessary to meet Professional Standards Review Organization (PSRO) requirements, as well as other review and state statutory reporting requirements; and those made to law enforcement agencies or other government agencies for appropriate purposes. Furthermore, access to certain records is more restricted than the general rule would allow. For example, alcohol and drug abuse patient records may not be disclosed except as specifically authorized by the applicable federal regulations, and access to the records of mental health patients is severely limited in some states. Regardless of the applicable access rules in the state, hospitals must devise effective record security procedures that will protect patient confidentiality and preserve the hospital's physical record. Hospitals that have converted all or part of their medical records to computer media should be especially careful to establish adequate record security measures.

Most hospitals receive numerous legal requests to provide patient record information. Medical records departments should be prepared to manage subpoenas, court orders, and other process served upon the institution in connection with medical records.

Hospitals have been held liable to their patients for the improper or unauthorized disclosure of medical record information. Aside from statutory penalties established in some jurisdictions, hospitals and practitioners may be liable for defamation, invasion of privacy, betrayal of professional secrets, and breach of contract for such disclosures.

Disclosures with Patient's Consent*

A patient's consent must be in writing and must contain the following:

1. The name of the program that is to make the disclosure;
2. The name or title of the person or organization to which disclosure is to be made;
3. The name of the patient;
4. The purpose or need for the disclosure;
5. The extent or nature of information to be disclosed;
6. A statement that the consent is subject to revocation at any time except to the extent that action has been taken in reliance thereon, and a specification of the date, event, or condition upon which it will expire without express revocation;
7. The date on which the consent is signed; and
8. The signature of the patient or other person authorized to sign under the regulations.

Disclosure is prohibited if a consent is nonconforming on its face or if program personnel know, or in the exercise of reasonable care should know, that the consent is materially false in any way. A sample consent form is shown in Figure 42-1.

Liability for Improper Disclosure of Medical Records

A release of medical records information that has not been authorized by the patient or that has not been made pursuant to statutory, regulatory, or other legal authority may subject the hospital and its staff to civil and criminal liability. Three possible civil liability actions are available to patients who show injury as a result of a disclosure of information in their medical records by hospitals or physicians: defamation, invasion of privacy and breach of contract.

---

*Source: Reprinted from William H. Roach, Jr. and Lisa M. Harms, "Legal Review," *Topics in Health Record Management,* March 1981, with permission of Aspen Systems Corporation.

Figure 42-1 Patient consent form for disclosures

AUTHORIZATION FOR RELEASE OF INFORMATION

TO: _____ Hospital
          (Address)

THIS WILL AUTHORIZE YOU TO RELEASE TO:

_____
(Name) of Person and/or Agency

_____
(Address)

_____
(City & State)

THE FOLLOWING INFORMATION:

Discharge Summary _____	X-Ray Report _____
Operative Report _____	X-Ray Films _____
Pathology Report _____	
Other (specify)	_____

from the medical records of _____
                                                  (Patient)

hospitalized from _____, 19___, to _____, 19___, under the care of
_____, M.D. The purpose of this authorization is _____.

I understand that I have the right to inspect and copy the information to be disclosed and I may withdraw this authorization at any time, except to the extent that action has been taken based on this authorization.

If I refuse to authorize disclosure of this information, the following consequences may result: _____.

I understand that this authorization shall expire, without my express revocation, 90 days from the date written below.

DATE: _____   _____
                                                                  Signature of Patient

Witness (Someone who can attest to the identity
of the person signing this form):   If the consenting party is other than patient:

_____   _____
Signature of Witness   Signature of Consenting Party

_____   _____
Witness' Name (Please Print)   Name—Please Print

_____   _____
Witness' Address   Relation to Patient

This authorization must be signed by the patient. In the case of a minor patient, this authorization must be signed by a parent or guardian. In the case of a patient who is physically unable to sign this authorization, he/she should place an "X" on the signature line and have his/her assent witnessed. In the case of a patient who has been declared mentally incompetent, this authorization may only be signed by a legally appointed guardian. In the case of a deceased patient, this authorization must be signed by the executor/administrator of the estate.

Figure 42-1 continued

NOTICE
[TO ACCOMPANY RELEASE OF ALCOHOL AND DRUG ABUSE RECORDS]
This information has been disclosed to you from records whose confidentiality is protected by Federal law. Federal regulations (42.F.R. Part 2) prohibit you from making any further disclosure of it without the specific written consent of the person to whom it pertains, or as otherwise permitted by such regulations. A general authorization for the release of medical or other information is NOT sufficient for this purpose.

Defamation

Defamation may be defined as a written or oral communication to someone other than the person defamed of matters that concern a living person and tend to injure that person's reputation. Traditionally libel is a written form of defamation, while slander is oral, and libel is actionable without proof of actual damages. Certain types of slander, such as the imputation of crime or a loathsome disease, are also actionable without proof of actual damages, although special damages would ordinarily have to be shown in order for oral publications to be actionable. Medical records may contain information that is inaccurate and, if published, would tend to affect a person's reputation in the community adversely. Thus, conceivably, disclosure by a hospital to an unauthorized person would result in an action for defamation.

However, the possibility of a patient's obtaining a recovery against the hospital for defamation for release of medical record information is slight.

A qualified privilege exists as to

> ... communications made in good faith, without actual malice, with reasonable or probable grounds for believing them to be true, on a subject matter in which the author of the communication has an interest, or in respect to which he has a duty, public, personal or private, either legal, judicial, political, moral, or social, made to a person having a corresponding interest or duty. [*Libel & Slander* 53 C.J.S. §89, p. 143 (1948).]

Insurance companies, litigating parties, newspapers, and the like may request permission to examine or obtain information from the hospital records. It is conceivable that, in answering a private and confidential inquiry, depending upon the facts of the situation, the hospital is acting in the discharge of a legal, moral, or social duty, and its answer may thus be privileged.

The hospital is well advised to take the conservative approach and withhold medical record information unless it finds an exceptionally good reason to disclose it. Should it do so under the circumstances described earlier, the theories of qualified privilege may provide a defense to an action by the patient in defamation. The existence of qualified privilege should not in itself justify disclosure of medical record information, however.

Invasion of Privacy

To be actionable, this invasion, exploitation, or intrusion must be done in such a manner as to cause outrage or mental suffering, shame, or humiliation to a person of ordinary sensibilities.

The plaintiff's right of privacy is a personal one. It does not extend to family members, is not assignable, does not arise from a publication concerning one who has died (unless the state's statutes establish such a cause of action), and does not exist for corporations or partnerships. Economic loss need not be proved, but monetary and other damages can be recovered if it can be proved that they resulted from the invasion.

Invasion of privacy has been divided into four categories: (1) appropriation of plaintiff's name or likeness for the defendant's benefit, (2) intrusion upon the plaintiff's solitude or private concerns, (3) public disclosure of embarrassing private facts, and (4) publicity that places the plaintiff in a false light in the public eye. Given the highly personal quality of medical records, improper disclosure of patient information can easily constitute invasion of privacy, as the court decisions illustrate.

Intrusion upon a patient's solitude or private concerns has been found unwarranted where the hospital has bugged the patient's telephone or bedroom, invaded the patient's house, or in other ways has intruded in an objectionable manner into the patient's private concerns. Monitoring a patient's telephone conversations from the hospital may subject the institution not only to liability for invasion of privacy, but also to liability under federal statutes prohibiting the interception of private communications. Allowing nonmedical personnel to witness medical procedures or to examine the patient without the patient's authorization may constitute an unlawful invasion of the patient's privacy by the hospital.

Publication of private facts that causes embarrassment to a patient or that places the patient in a false light in the public eye is actionable if the publication exceeds generally accepted standards of decent conduct, but may not be actionable if such disclosures are in the community's interest or are required to protect the publisher's freedom of speech.

However, the right of privacy is not an absolute right. The distinguishing characteristic of the right is that it protects the citizen from mass dissemination of information concerning private, personal concerns. It has also been said that oral publication cannot constitute an invasion of privacy nor can the publication of data to an extent reasonably calculated to serve the legitimate interests of the publisher constitute such an invasion. Thus, the release or disclosure of information in the medical record to private individuals, such as attorneys, insurance company representatives, or family members, for purposes of reimbursement, litigation, and the like, would not ordinarily constitute an invasion of the right of privacy. It must be further remembered that the release, disclosure, or publication must be of such a nature as to outrage or cause mental suffering, shame, or humiliation to a person of ordinary sensibilities.

Where the patient expressly consents to disclosure of private information, the patient cannot later be heard to complain that the disclosure was an invasion of privacy, provided the patient wanted the information disclosed for his or her benefit and the hospital disclosed the information in the manner authorized. Therefore, hospitals should endeavor to obtain the patient's written consent to the disclosure of information about the patient that might fall into the categories discussed.

Teaching hospitals, especially, should be certain their patients understand that they will be participating in the education and training of medical, nursing, and other students who may observe or assist in the patients' treatment. Hospitals should establish and enforce strict rules against permitting lay persons to observe patient treatment without express patient consent. Hospital policy should include safeguards against the use of patient-authorized photographs or videotape in an unauthorized manner or for an unauthorized purpose.

Disclosure to News Media

Perhaps the hospital practice most likely to give rise to questions of the invasion of privacy is the release of information concerning patients to news agencies. A hospital has no legal obligation whatsoever to disclose medical record information to news media. However, hospitals may, as a matter of local policy, release such information in certain circumstances. While the right of privacy does not prohibit publications that are of public or general interest, the extent of publication is still a matter to be weighed carefully by the hospital in each case. Announcements simply of patient admissions, discharges, or births ordinarily pose no problem. However, the situation may be different if the hospital specializes in the care of patients with specific diseases that are considered shameful in the popular mind. To publicize the fact that Mrs. Jones gave birth to a normal, healthy boy could not ordinarily be considered overstepping the bounds of propriety, but to publicize the fact that Mrs. Jones gave birth to a stillborn monstrosity or that Miss Brown had a child might be actionable.

The patient may be a public figure; this prominence, in itself, makes virtually all of the patient's doings of interest to the public. Relatively obscure people may voluntarily take certain actions that bring them before the public, or they may be victims of occurrences that are newsworthy, such as accidents, crimes, and the like, thus making them of interest to the public. The latitude extended to the publication of personal matters, names, photographs, and the like varies in these situations. Public figures may not complain if their lives are given some publicity, and this may be true long after they have ceased to be in the public eye. Ordinary citizens who voluntarily adopt a course of action that is newsworthy cannot be heard to complain if the activity is reported along with their names and pictures. However, as time passes, the identity of the participant loses importance and action for invasion of the right of privacy may then be allowable.

Patient Access to Medical Records

Several of the statutes that authorize the patient or the patient's representative to inspect records do not permit inspection of records until after the patient has been discharged from the hospital. The question is frequently raised as to whether the hospital must allow patients to examine their records while they are still hospitalized. In the absence of a statutory or common law right of access during hospitalization, the hospital is not obligated to permit its patients to inspect their records on the hospital's patient care units. However, hospitals should consider whether a refusal to permit such an inspection will create unnecessary problems for the institution and its staff. A patient who is not allowed to examine his or her chart in the hospital may become hostile and more difficult to treat and may file a claim against the hospital if treatment ends in a poor result. Therefore, unless the patient's attending physician can establish a reasonable basis for an opinion that disclosure of the inpatient medical record would be harmful to the patient, the hospital should allow the patient to review the record.

Minors

The generally accepted rule is that a hospital may disclose the medical record of a minor patient only upon the authorization of one of the patient's parents, unless a legal guardian has been appointed for the minor, and that a minor's parents must be allowed access to such records upon request.

Security Precautions

It is essential that hospitals establish effective procedures for safeguarding medical records, not only to protect patient confidentiality, but also to prevent intentional alteration or falsification of records by individuals who wish to file a personal injury claim against a practitioner or the hospital, or otherwise to use the records for an unlawful purpose.

To protect their medical records from such abuse, hospitals should adopt at least the following security precautions:

1. Competent medical records or risk management personnel should review a record before it is examined by the patient or the patient's representative and should notify the appropriate hospital manager if the record is incomplete or otherwise defective, or if the record reveals a problem that could give rise to negligence liability in the hospital or its staff.
2. An original medical record should not be permitted to be taken from the hospital's premises except pursuant to legal process.
3. Neither the patient, the patient's representative, nor any other person who is not an authorized hospital employee or staff member should ever be allowed to examine a medical record alone. The hospital should provide accommodations for people to inspect records in its medical records department or other location where proper surveillance by hospital personnel is possible.

Hospital Staff Access

Hospitals should specify in their medical records policies which members of the hospitals' staffs may review records and for what reasons. The policies should also include the procedures staff members should follow to obtain access to medical records. Hospitals may incorporate these policies in their medical staff rules and regulations, as well as in hospital administrative policy statements.

Disclosures for Medical Research

In most hospitals, medical and nursing staff members may examine medical records for any of the purposes established by the hospitals' medical records policies. One legitimate purpose for staff inspection of patient records is medical research. Typically, a medical study involves the inspection of past patient records to determine relationships between the administration of a medication and certain treatment complications or between population characteristics and incidence of illness, or to obtain statistical information important to the development of more efficient treatment protocols.

If the hospital permits its staff to conduct medical research, it should establish an *Institutional Review Board* to determine the appropriateness of proposed research projects.

The criteria by which an IRB or other committee evaluates proposed medical records studies should be established as hospital policy. The IRB or research committee should require that the following safeguards are in place before authorizing disclosure of medical records information to medical investigators:

1. The information will be treated as confidential.
2. The information will be communicated only to qualified investigators pursuing an approved research program designed for the benefit of the health of the community.
3. The results of the investigation will be presented in a way that prevents identification of individual subjects.

Statutory Reporting and Other Disclosure Requirements

Many state statutes and regulations and a few federal regulations require hospitals to disclose confidential medical record information without the patient's authorization. Disclosure of medical record information made pursuant to such a statutory or regulatory requirement does not subject a hospital or practitioner to liability, even if the disclosure is made against the patient's express wishes.

Child Abuse

The child abuse reporting laws of most jurisdictions require hospitals and practitioners to report cases of actual or suspected child abuse. The statutes also protect persons making such reports in good faith from liability for improper disclosure of confidential information.

These reports frequently require the disclosure of information from hospital medical records, and such disclosures do not subject the hospital to liability. *Failure* to make a report of child abuse by those required to do so can lead to liability in negligence for any additional injuries the child later sustains when discharged to a hostile home environment.

Abortion

Several states require hospitals and practitioners to report abortions they perform and any complications that may develop. Other states require hospitals to report fetal deaths, including those resulting from abortions.

Cancer

A few states require disclosure of information from the records of cancer patients to central state or regional tumor registries. These registries usually contain information about patients who suffer from the same or similar disease and are designed to provide raw data for studies concerning incidence of a disease in the population; long-term prognosis of the disease; type, duration, and frequency of treatment rendered to patients with the disease; and other indicators of the health care industry's ability to manage the disease. Usually operated by state-wide tax-exempt organizations funded by federal grants, the registries rely to a large extent upon the cooperation of individual hospital registries and obtain patient information directly from participating hospitals pursuant to agreements between the hospitals and the registry.

Communicable Diseases

Communicable disease reporting laws that require hospitals and practitioners to inform public health authorities of infectious disease cases are among the oldest compulsory reporting statutes in many states. The statute or regulation usually lists diseases that should be reported and directs practitioners to give local public health officials the patient's name, age, sex, address, and identifying information, as well as the details of the patient's illness. Hospitals should disclose only the information required by the statute.

Misadministration of Radioactive Materials and Blood Transfusion Reactions

Federal regulations require hospitals to report to the Nuclear Regulatory Commission any misadministration of radioactive materials. "Misadministration" is defined as the administration of a radiopharmaceutical or radiation other than the one intended; and of a radiopharmaceutical or radiation given to the wrong patient or administered to the right patient by a route other than that prescribed by the physician. Regulations also require hospitals to report to the director of the Bureau of Biologics of the federal Food and Drug Administration all fatalities resulting from collection or transfusion of blood.

Poison and Industrial Accidents

A few states require physicians to report illness or disease that they believe was contracted in connection with employment. The reports are made to the state's department of public health and usually include the name, address, occupation, and illness of the patient and the name and address of the patient's employer. The purpose of these statutes is to enable public health officials to investigate occupational diseases and to recommend methods for eliminating or preventing them.

PSRO Utilization Review and Quality Assurance Activities

A PSRO may examine records pertinent to health care services provided to federal reimbursement program patients in any hospital in the PSRO's area.

However, a PSRO may examine the medical records of patients whose care is not federally funded only if the hospital authorizes access to such records. The extent to which the PSRO may examine medical records is limited by federal regulation.

The JCAH and other regulatory bodies require hospitals to conduct utilization review and other quality assurance activities that are based upon review of medical records.

Government Agencies

As a general rule, a hospital should not permit a government agency to examine or receive confidential medical records information unless the agency has specific statutory authority to do so or is acting pursuant to a valid court order, warrant, or other legal process.

Although an agency may be authorized by statute or regulation to inspect hospital records kept in accordance with a regulatory scheme, it is by no means clear in the law that the agency may, without a warrant, inspect patients' medical records, other than those "required to be kept."

Other State Statutes and Regulations

Several states have enacted statutes that authorize or require the release or disclosure of medical records without the patient's consent, such as when a patient is transferred to another health care facility, when they are required by the state's board of medical examiners, or when state health department inspectors or county medical examiners request them. As these statutory provisions authorizing release of medical records vary from state to state, hospitals should be aware of the special disclosure rules applicable in their jurisdictions.

Law Enforcement Agencies

As a general rule, hospitals should not release medical records or other patient information to law enforcement personnel without the patient's authorization. In the absence of statutory authority or legal process, a police agency has no authority to examine a medical record.

There are several exceptions to the rule, however. The law enforcement agency may be authorized by a specific statute to inspect medical records without patient consent. Law enforcement personnel also may be authorized to obtain medical record information in connection with child abuse reports or investigations. A law enforcement agency may compel disclosure of records pursuant to a subpoena or court order.

Finally, the hospital, with the advice of its attorney, may determine that it would be in the community's best interest to release medical record information to law enforcement personnel. In such cases, the hospital may rely upon the doctrine of qualified privilege. When there is no specific statutory prohibition, this doctrine permits communications made in good faith. The doctrine of qualified privilege protects the hospital only if the law enforcement officer who receives the medical record information is acting in an official capacity.

Certain types of cases, such as those involving rape or other crime victims, create routine police inquiries. When possible in these cases, hospitals should seek, preferably during the admitting process, the patient's consent to release of information to law enforcement agencies. Where a report to police is required by statute or ordinance, as in cases involving gunshot wounds, patient consent is not required. Consultation with the hospital's attorney to establish policies for responding to requests for information from law enforcement agencies, and for specific responses in certain instances, is highly recommended.

Alcohol and Drug Abuse Patient Records

Access to the records of alcohol and drug abuse patients is severely limited and strictly controlled by regulations. Unless the patient consents in writing to the release of information concerning his or her treatment, all inquiries must be met with noncommittal replies. Moreover, the ordinary consent-to-treatment form that is signed upon admission to a health care facility is considered insufficient to authorize release of information concerning alcohol or drug abuse treatment. The health care provider may even be held liable for complying with a court-issued subpoena for record information, unless the validity of the subpoena has been upheld. The regulations provide that records of the identity, diagnosis, prognosis, or treatment of any patient connected with any drug or alcohol abuse prevention program shall be disclosed only upon the specific written authorization of the patient or under the following circumstances: (1) to medical personnel to the extent necessary to meet a bona fide medical emergency; (2) to qualified research personnel, providing that the patient's identity remains anonymous; or (3) upon an appropriate court order after a hearing has been held.

A patient's legal counsel may have access to records upon the patient's written authorization; however, family members, third party payors, and even the criminal justice system must obtain full written consent for disclosure from the patient.

Some states require physicians and others to identify patients who obtain drugs that are subject to abuse so that patient names and addresses can be entered into a state registry.

How To Respond to Subpoenas and Court Orders

Hospitals generally are concerned with two types of legal process: the subpoena and the court order.

Subpoenas

Hospitals customarily receive two types of subpoenas: (1) a subpoena *ad testificandum*, which is a written order commanding a person to appear and give testimony at a trial or other judicial or investigative proceeding; and (2) a subpoena *duces tecum*, which is a written order commanding a person to appear, give testimony, and bring all documents, papers, books, or records described in the subpoena. In some states, a subpoena may require the hospital to present a medical record at a photocopy service to be photocopied for a party to a proceeding. These devices are used to obtain documents during pretrial discovery and to obtain testimony during trial. By statute in most states, clerks of the courts, and various boards and commissions are given the power to issue a subpoena. In federal courts, the clerks of the courts may issue subpoenas.

In most jurisdictions, a valid subpoena includes the following information:

- name of the court (or other official body in which the proceeding is being held)
- names of the plaintiff and the defendant
- docket number of the case
- date, time, and place of the requested appearance
- specific documents sought (if subpoena is a subpoena duces tecum)
- name and telephone number of the attorney who caused the subpoena to be issued
- signature or stamp and seal of the official empowered to issue the subpoena
- proper witness and mileage fees

The hospital staff member most frequently served with subpoenas is the person with custody of the medical records, who, in most cases, is the director of the medical records department. The director of medical records or the person in the medical records department assigned to process subpoenas should respond in accordance with a procedure established by the hospital and reviewed by the hospital's attorney. The procedure should include at least the following provisions:

- Examine the record subject to subpoena to make certain it is complete, that signatures and initials are legible, and that each page identifies the patient and the patient's hospital number.
- Read the record to determine whether the case forms the basis for a possible negligence action against the hospital and, if so,

notify the appropriate administrator. (In some hospitals, the medical records department performs this function in coordination with the risk management or legal department.)
- Remove any material that may not properly be obtained in the jurisdiction by subpoena, such as, in some states, notes referring to psychiatric care.
- Number each page of the medical record, and write the total number of pages on the record jacket.
- Prepare a list of the medical record contents to be used as a receipt for the record if the record must be left with the court or an attorney. (Most medical records departments use a standard form for this purpose.)
- Whenever possible, use a photocopy of the record rather than the original in responding to the legal process.

Rather than send original medical records to a court or an attorney through the mail, hospitals should designate a person to deliver records in person. Hospitals lose all control over their records once they are placed in the mail, and the loss of an original medical record may be a serious problem for a hospital defendant in a negligence action or for a patient who may require future hospitalization.

Court Orders

Occasionally, a state or federal court, or a state commission, orders a hospital to release medical records or other confidential patient information or to produce patient records in court. Written court orders are usually served upon hospitals in a manner similar to that of subpoenas. Provided the court order does not violate a statute or regulation, the hospital should make every effort to comply with it. A hospital can contest a court order and present its case to the court before any sanctions for failure to comply are imposed. Failure to comply with a final, valid court order subjects the person ordered to act or hospital corporate officers, if the corporation has been ordered to act, to a contempt-of-court citation.

Using Medical Records as Evidence

Most modern judicial decisions have held medical records to be admissible. Whether medical records are admissible is of primary importance to the hospital in its own defense, since medical records may contain information damaging to the defendant. The admission of records in proceedings in which the hospital is not a party should be of less concern, provided the hospital properly discloses the medical records sought in such proceedings.

The introduction of medical records may still be objected to on the ground that the information contained therein is subject to a physician-patient confidential communication statute. Although confidential communications statutes have been held to apply to confidential matters appearing in medical records, they affect the hospital directly only in those cases in which the hospital is a litigant. In suits between the patient and others, it is not the hospital's concern or right to assert the privilege, or to attempt to destroy it when the records are subpoenaed. Whether the privilege should be asserted or applies is a problem for the courts and parties litigant.

In suits in which the hospital is a party but neither the patient nor the physician is a party, the hospital should consider asserting the physician-patient privilege on behalf of the patient. A hospital that asserts the privilege under these circumstances is acting consistent with its interest in protecting its patient's confidentiality, and the court will decide whether the privilege applies.

Committee Records

Hospitals are required by a variety of authorities to establish and maintain programs to monitor and improve the quality of patient care they provide. Included in these quality assurance programs are certain committees of the medical staff, each of which may collect data and generate records concerning the performance of individual physicians practicing in the hospital or the treatment provided to particular patients in the hospital.

Counsel representing plaintiffs in professional negligence actions against practitioners and hospitals have shown an increasing interest in the proceedings, records, and reports of these committees as a source of important evidence. The potential value of such records to the plaintiff in a negligence action is clear, and the demand for access to them has created a substantial body of law. A hospital should be familiar with the applicable statutory provisions and relevant court decisions in its state before it establishes procedures for creating and maintaining hospital and medical staff committee records.

Computerized Medical Records

Although the mechanics of storage and access in an automated records system may differ from those in a manual one, the rules governing confidentiality of information in a computerized system are the same as those in a traditional record system. The unauthorized release of patient information, whether by means of a photocopied medical record or a printout at a remote computer terminal, is actionable.

Hospitals with automated record systems should have a records confidentiality policy encompassing both manual and computerized records. Hospitals should include security devices in their computer programs to prevent unauthorized access to stored data. One problem hospitals with automated systems face is their lack of control over computer access codes given to hospital personnel. The hospital's medical records policy, employment policy, and medical staff bylaws should establish severe sanctions for the disclosure by hospital medical, nursing, and other staff members of their computer access codes. Some hospitals require staff members to sign a statement acknowledging that disclosure of their computer access codes is justification for immediate termination of employment or medical staff privileges. Hospital computer data banks and storage media should be secure from unauthorized access through other computer or electronic facilities, and the hospital should conduct periodic systems security checks to determine whether record confidentiality can be breached. Hospitals that contract with outside computer service bureaus for automated record storage should include in their service contracts carefully drawn provisions governing confidentiality of patient data, storage security, and indemnification of the hospital by the bureau for costs and judgments arising from the unauthorized disclosure of confidential information by the bureau.

Chapter 43—Licensure and Permits*

Hospitalwide

Hospital licensure regulations usually require the governing body and medical staff to operate under written bylaws, and the regulations may specify in some detail what the bylaws must contain relative to the procedures that must be followed in processing the applications of practitioners for medical staff membership or clinical privileges.

As might be expected from the public health nature of hospital licensing, regulations generally emphasize the hospital's duty to conduct its operations in a safe and sanitary manner. Safety and disaster plans and drills are mandated, and the hospital's dietary department, housekeeping department, and infection control and waste disposal operations are closely regulated.

Services

The hospital licensure authority may require that general hospitals provide certain basic services, including some degree of emergency service; that laboratory, x-ray, and pharmacy services be available; and that adequate nursing personnel be available at all times. The statutes or agency rules may also establish standards for facilities, equipment, and personnel relative to specialized services, if the hospital elects to establish surgical, obstetrical, pediatric, psychiatric, or other specialized components.

Physical Plant

Approval of the integrity of hospital buildings is a major part of hospital-licensing regulation. Not only must the structures be sound, but there are numerous special requirements as to corridor widths and lengths, door widths, interior finishes, electrical systems, fireproofing, and other matters—all based on the special nature of hospitals. State licensing agencies frequently have a division dedicated exclusively to the regulation of hospital physical plants.

Waivers, Exceptions, and Variances

The licensing agency often has provided by rule for the granting of waivers of rule requirements, exceptions to rules, and variances from standards because it recognizes that undue hardship may result from unbending applications.

Certificate of Need and Cost Containment

A fairly recent development in the licensure of hospitals is the linking of licensure to certificate-of-need requirements so that facilities built or changed without a certificate of need may be denied a license. Even more recent is the initiation of hospital cost containment activities at the state level, often tied to the licensing process.

---

*Source: Except where noted, the material in this section consists of excerpts reprinted from *Hospital Law Manual,* Vol. IA by Health Law Center, with permission of Aspen Systems Corporation, © 1981.

Departmental

While the hospital as a health care facility may be licensed under one agency's authority, other agencies of state government more and more often are requiring licensure of individual hospital departments and services together with permits for the performance of specialized hospital functions.

The failure of individual components of the hospital's operations to hold required separate licenses or permits may jeopardize the hospital's institutional license, and the trend seems to be toward increased separate regulation of individual departments, in addition to general hospital licensure.

Pharmacy

Pharmacies must be licensed in all states; hospital pharmacies must be separately licensed in a number of jurisdictions. The state pharmacy act establishes standards for hospital pharmacies relative to equipment, staffing, and handling of medication, usually with some modification from those standards imposed on community pharmacies. Narcotics and alcohol permits are customarily a function of the hospital's pharmaceutical service and may depend on state licensure of the pharmacy.

Laboratory

State laws requiring licensure of clinical laboratories may also apply to hospital laboratories. Even if hospital laboratories per se are exempt, licensure may be required if the hospital seeks to perform clinical laboratory services for other hospitals or for physicians' office patients. Standards for equipment, personnel qualifications, reporting of results, and recordkeeping may be imposed by the state clinical laboratory law.

Radiology

State involvement in licensure as it relates to radiology has customarily been directed at certification of the safety of x-ray equipment under the state radiation hazards law. In some jurisdictions, regulation has been expanded to include setting standards for personnel qualifications, reporting, recordkeeping, and exposure monitoring.

Renal Dialysis

Recently, some jurisdictions have begun to require the licensure of renal dialysis units. Standards are set for equipment, qualifications of personnel, recordkeeping, and reporting. The fact that renal dialysis programs are funded by state and federal programs may give further impetus to the specific licensing of dialysis units.

Other Types of Permits

A number of hospital functions may be subject to regulation by authorities other than the state hospital-licensing agency.

If the local granting of permits conflicts with state licensure statutes, state law prevails. However, when no conflict results, or when local units of government have been authorized to perform all or part of the hospital-licensing function, the hospital must comply with local ordinances.

One area in which a local permit is commonly required is the hospital's dietary department, where food service establishment rules may require sanitation inspections and health screening of dietary personnel. It is not uncommon for the state hospital-licensing statute or rules and regulations to demand compliance with local or state food service ordinances as a condition of hospital licensure.

Local authorities may also require occupational licenses, vending machine permits, and other licenses that are designed to regulate business within the community. Where the purpose of requiring a local permit is to raise revenue, it is unlikely that such a requirement will conflict with the hospital licensure act, although there may be some question as to whether charitable hospitals are exempt from such revenue-raising measures. Where the granting of permits is intended simply to regulate business, it is not uncommon to find that state licensing laws exempt licensed hospitals from some or all local requirements.

Environmental concerns have prompted the federal, state, and local governments to take a number of measures to regulate the disposal of wastes and the generation of air pollutants. It may be necessary to obtain an environmental permit for certain hospital activities, e.g., operation of an incinerator, disposal of liquefied chemicals and laboratory wastes into the sewerage system, disposal of garbage and noninfectious solid wastes, and disposal of contaminated, infectious materials and body parts. The possession of appropriate environmental permits may be a prerequisite to licensing of the hospital.

Personnel Licensure

All members of the hospital's medical staff, as well as many hospital employees, must be individually licensed to practice their professions. The hospital may find its own licensure in jeopardy if it knowingly permits unlicensed employees or physicians to practice within its walls in violation of law.

Individuals or hospitals who aid or abet the ... subject to licen... s imposed under ... and the profes-

for Limited ...itioners

...d advances in the ... restorative tech-
... the importance of
...nter for specialized
...ners. Unlike physi-
...e been held compe-
...ng a general supervi-
...atient, limited health
...n restricted by law or
...ecialized area of the
...cular type of medical
...some specialized care
...rvision of a physician.
...gly assumed responsi-
...ntials to limited health
...actice on the hospital

...on of credentials to lim-
...tioners is the consider-
... such practitioners are
the extent to which they
...d professionally, of prac-
...ng without physician supervision. Certain limited health care practitioners may also be called upon by physicians to provide specialized treatment that they are particularly trained to provide. In such cases, the physician maintains general medical supervision and responsibility but defers in part to the professional judgment of the limited practitioner. For purposes of discussion, limited health care practitioners may be conveniently divided into two categories: independent and dependent.

Independent

Those practitioners who are permitted by state law to provide specialized health care services to patients without physician direction or supervision are independent practitioners. These practitioners may carry on an independent office practice, even though the scope of their practice may be limited by the state licensure act and regulations. The three most commonly encountered professions in this category are

1. podiatrists, whose practice encompasses the diagnosis and treatment of diseases of the foot, as well as many types of foot surgery
2. psychologists, who, when engaged in clinical practice, provide services such as psychological testing, counseling, psychotherapy, and hypnosis
3. chiropractors, who treat various conditions by adjusting the spinal column through manipulation, without the use of prescription drugs or surgery

Dependent

The scope of the services dependent practitioners may provide is also limited by licensure laws. In addition, they are subject to the general supervision and direction of a physician, and their performance of at least some of the functions permitted them under licensure laws is dependent on a link or association with a physician. The number of dependent limited health care practitioners has grown rapidly in recent years, and most jurisdictions have adopted laws regulating their practice. The institutional granting of credentials for these rather new types of health care professionals is a matter that has been and should continue to be of growing concern. The following are principal types of dependent limited health care practitioners:

1. Physician assistants, an outgrowth of military medicine, assist physicians in a wide range of diagnostic and therapeutic activities, from taking patient histories to assisting at surgery.
2. Nurse practitioners are licensed registered nurses with additional training and experience that enables them to provide a range

of physician-supervised diagnostic and therapeutic services involving significant independent judgment to a degree not customary in the traditional practice of nursing.
3. Nurse-anesthetists, also licensed registered nurses with additional training, provide surgical anesthesia services, including intubation, induction, and intrasurgical and postsurgical monitoring of patients. Their practice is subject to the supervision of a physician qualified in anesthesiology.
4. Nurse-midwives are licensed registered nurses who not only deliver babies, but also provide prenatal monitoring, counseling, and education, as well as postpartum care and follow-up. Services are generally provided under the direction of a physician, who may or may not be an obstetrician.

Hospitals that grant clinical privileges to dependent limited health care practitioners must be aware of any limitations on the scope of practice of particular classes of practitioners explicitly imposed by state law so as not to be exposed to sanctions. Furthermore, they may be required to delineate in their own rules the scope of practice for dependent limited health care practitioners in such areas as writing orders on the clinical chart, performing therapeutic or diagnostic procedures without immediate physician supervision, and securing physician assistance or advice. JCAH requires accredited hospitals that elect to grant clinical privileges to dependent limited health care practitioners to define their scope of practice in the medical staff bylaws.

Since dependent limited health care practitioners are necessarily employees of or sponsored by a physician member of the medical staff when they are not hospital employees, the employing or sponsoring physician is subject to liability for the dependent practitioner's malpractice under the doctrine of respondeat superior.

In general, the JCAH standards and government regulations seem to require that hospital bylaws contain certain minimum elements regarding the granting of credentials to health care practitioners:

1. a definition of those classes of practitioners that will be granted privileges, with specific reference to their education, training, and professional licensure
2. a delineation of the types of services that the practitioner will be permitted to perform or is barred from performing
3. if applicable, a statement regarding the admission and discharge of patients by the practitioner and a statement providing that a physician member of the medical staff must have responsibility for the general medical needs of the patient
4. the fixing of responsibility upon a particular medical staff department for supervising and monitoring the practitioner's performance, both for purposes of initial appointment and ongoing evaluation
5. the establishment of procedures for application, evaluation of competence, and the granting of privileges
6. the establishment of procedures for providing an appropriate level of continuing physician supervision of practitioners

Institutional Liability

The liability of hospitals for the malpractice of independent limited health care practitioners might be predicated on failure to:

1. establish adequate standards of education, training, and experience for the granting of clinical privileges to the limited health care practitioner
2. apply such standards in a reasonable manner in granting clinical privileges
3. monitor performance adequately after privileges are granted and take corrective action when deficiencies are noted

Licensing Boards*

The common pattern of licensing authorities has been to establish a separate board, organized and operated within the guidelines of specific legislation, to license each of the health occupation categories. Among board duties are the determination of eligibility for initial licensing and relicensure, enforcement of licensing statutes including suspension, revocation, and restoration of licenses, and the regulation of advertising.

---

*Source: Reprinted from *Hospital Law Manual,* Vol. IA by Health Law Center, with permission of Aspen Systems Corporation, © 1980.

Figure 43-1 Health professions required to be licensed

	1 ADMINISTRATOR (Health Dept.)	2 ADMINISTRATOR (Hospital)	3 ADMINISTRATOR (Nursing Home)	4 ACUPUNCTURIST	5 CHIROPRACTOR	6 CLINICAL LAB. PERSONNEL	7 DENTAL HYGIENIST	8 DENTAL LABORATORY PERSONNEL	9 DENTIST	10 EMERGENCY PERSONNEL	11 ENVIRONMENTAL HEALTH ENGINEER	12 MASSEUR	13 MIDWIFE	14 OPTICIAN	15 OPTICAL TECHNICIAN	16 OPTOMETRIST	17 PHARMACIST	18 PHYSICAL THERAPIST	19 PHYSICAL THERAPIST ASS'T	20 PHYSICIAN (M.D.)	21 PHYSICIAN (D.O.)	22 PHYSICIAN'S ASS'T	23 PODIATRIST	24 PRACTICAL NURSE	25 PSYCHIATRIC AIDE	26 PSYCHOLOGIST	27 RADIOLOGIC TECHNOLOGIST	28 REGISTERED NURSE	29 RESPIRATORY THERAPIST	30 SANITARIAN	31 SANITARIAN TECHNICIAN	32 SOCIAL WORKER	33 SPEECH PATHOLOGIST & AUDIOLOGIST
Alabama		X	X		X		X	X	X							X	X	X	X	X	X	X	X	X		X		X		X			
Alaska					X		X		X							X	X	X		X	X	X	X	X		X		X		X			
Arizona					X		X		X				X	X[1]	X	X	X	X	X	X	X		X	X		X		X		X			
Arkansas		X			X		X		X							X	X	X		X	X	X	X	X		X		X		X	X	X	
California			X		X	X	X	X	X	X		X	X[1]			X	X	X	X	X	X	X	X	X	X	X	X	X	X	X		X	
Colorado			X		X	X	X		X	X			X[1]			X	X	X	X	X	X		X	X		X		X		X			
Connecticut			X		X	X	X		X	X			X[1]	X	X	X	X	X	X	X	X		X	X		X		X		X			
Delaware			X		X		X		X							X	X	X		X	X		X	X		X		X		X			
District of Columbia			X		X		X		X			X				X	X	X	X	X	X		X	X		X		X		X			
Florida		X	X		X	X	X		X							X	X	X	X	X	X	X	X	X	X	X		X		X			X
Georgia		X	X	X	X		X		X				X	X		X	X	X	X	X	X		X	X		X		X		X			
Hawaii		X	X		X		X		X	X			X	X		X	X	X		X	X		X	X		X		X		X			
Idaho		X	X		X		X		X		X					X	X	X		X	X		X	X		X		X		X			
Illinois		X	X	X	X		X	X	X				X[1]			X	X	X		X	X	X	X	X		X		X		X		X	
Indiana		X	X		X		X		X				X			X	X	X	X	X	X		X	X		X		X		X			
Iowa		X	X		X		X		X							X	X	X	X	X	X	X	X	X		X		X		X			
Kansas		X			X	X	X		X							X	X	X		X	X		X	X		X		X		X			
Kentucky		X	X		X	X	X		X					X	X	X	X	X	X	X	X		X	X		X		X		X			X
Louisiana		X			X		X		X					X		X	X	X		X	X		X	X		X		X		X		X	X
Maine		X	X		X		X		X						X	X	X	X		X	X		X	X		X		X		X		X	
Maryland		X	X		X	X	X		X			X	X			X	X	X	X	X	X		X	X		X		X		X		X	X
Massachusetts		X	X		X		X	X	X	X				X		X	X	X		X	X		X	X		X		X		X			
Michigan		X	X	X	X		X		X				X			X	X	X		X	X	X	X	X	X	X		X		X			
Minnesota	X	X	X		X	X	X	X	X			X				X	X	X		X	X		X	X		X		X		X			
Mississippi		X	X		X		X		X							X	X	X		X	X		X	X		X		X		X			
Missouri		X		X	X	X	X		X							X	X	X	X	X	X	X	X	X		X		X		X			
Montana		X			X		X		X							X	X	X		X	X	X	X	X		X		X		X	X		
Nebraska		X			X		X		X							X	X	X	X	X	X	X	X	X		X		X		X			
Nevada		X	X	X	X	X		X	X		X		X			X	X	X	X	X	X	X	X	X	X	X		X		X			
New Hampshire		X	X		X		X		X							X	X	X		X	X		X	X		X		X		X			
New Jersey	X	X	X	X	X		X		X				X	X	X	X	X	X		X	X		X	X		X	X	X	X	X			
New Mexico		X	X		X		X		X				X			X	X	X		X	X		X	X		X		X		X			
New York		X	X	X	X	X	X	X	X							X	X	X		X	X		X	X		X	X	X		X	X		
North Carolina		X	X		X		X		X				X	X		X	X	X		X	X	X	X	X		X		X		X			
North Dakota		X	X		X		X		X							X	X	X		X	X		X	X		X		X		X			
Ohio		X	X		X		X		X			X				X	X	X		X	X		X	X		X		X		X			
Oklahoma		X	X		X	X	X	X	X							X	X	X	X	X	X	X	X	X		X		X		X		X	X
Oregon		X	X		X		X		X							X	X	X		X	X		X	X		X		X		X			
Pennsylvania		X	X		X	X	X		X							X	X	X		X	X		X	X		X		X		X			
Rhode Island		X			X		X		X				X			X	X	X		X	X		X	X		X		X		X			
South Carolina		X		X	X		X	X	X	X	X		X			X	X	X		X	X	X	X	X		X		X		X	X	X	X
South Dakota		X	X		X		X		X							X	X	X		X	X		X	X		X		X		X			
Tennessee		X	X	X	X	X	X		X	X			X			X	X	X		X	X		X	X		X		X		X			X
Texas		X			X		X	X	X				X			X	X	X	X	X	X	X	X	X		X	X	X		X			
Utah		X	X		X		X		X				X			X	X	X		X	X		X	X		X		X		X			
Vermont		X	X		X		X		X							X	X	X		X	X		X	X		X		X		X			
Virginia		X	X		X		X		X				X	X		X	X	X	X	X[1]	X		X	X		X		X		X		X	X
Washington		X	X		X	X	X	X	X	X		X				X	X	X		X	X		X	X		X		X		X			
West Virginia		X	X		X	X	X		X							X	X	X		X	X		X	X		X		X		X			
Wisconsin		X	X	X	X	X	X		X							X	X	X	X	X	X		X	X		X		X		X	X		
Wyoming		X	X		X		X		X				X	X		X	X	X		X	X		X	X		X		X		X			
Total States Licensing Profession	1	2	48	1	50	13	51	9	51	16	2	7	24	22	2	51	51	51	14	51	51	35	51	51	2	48	4	51	2	40	1	13	10

Sources: National Center for Health Statistics: *Health Resource Statistics 1972–73*. DHEW Pub. No. (HSM) 73-1509. Public Health Service, U.S. Department of Health, Education and Welfare. Washington, U.S.G.P.O., 1973. Health Law Center, *Analysis of 1973 State Health Manpower Licensure Legislation*, Appendix B. DHEW Contract No. HSM 100-73-510, 1974. March 1980, © 1980 Aspen Systems Corporation.

While many state licensing boards establish and maintain their own standards for accreditation, an increasing number of boards now accept standards established by professional associations and national accrediting agencies. This trend toward application of a national standard within the various occupations has tended to standardize the programs of instruction at schools training health personnel.

Because each state has its own licensing statutes, boards have had to deal with the problem of licensing qualified practitioners from

Table 43-1 The Health Care Team

Profession	Total length of professional training beyond H.S.	Basic curriculum structure	Indicator of academic achievement	Certifying bodies	Geographical location of training	Basic skills
Dietitian	5 yr	4 yr academic training; 1 yr dietetic internship	B.S.—Foods and nutrition certificate for internship completion	American Dietetic Assn. (ADA)—registry exam (trend toward state licensure)	University setting; Hospital, nursing homes, etc.	1. Determination of appropriate diet content for treatment of specific diseases 2. Source of information and advice to physicians
Inhalation therapy or respiratory therapy	Usually 2 yr, one summer	1st yr: 70-80% didactic training; 20-30% clinical training. 2nd yr: 70-80% clinical training; 20-30% didactic training	Associate degree, inhalation therapy	American Assn. of Inhalation Therapists (AAIT)—registry board AMA-AAIT—review and approval of schools, state and local educational rules and regulations	Vocational technical school; Hospital	1. Performs selected tests used in diagnosis of pulmonary diseases 2. Performs selected treatments for patients having pulmonary diseases
Laboratory assistant	12 mo	20% didactic training 80% clinical experience in affiliated lab	Diploma and certification	Amer. Society of Clinical Pathologists (ASCP) Amer. Medical Tech. Assoc. State and local educational rules and regulations	Vocational technical school; Hospital	1. ECG techniques 2. Hematology 3. Urinalysis 4. Bacteriology 5. Serology 6. Chemistry
Medical technologist	4 yr	3 yr (90 credits) (basic sciences, liberal arts, etc.) 1 yr: 60% didactic training, 40% clinical experience in lab. (includes 3 mo. internship)	B.S. in med. technology Certificate upon completion of internship	AMA ASCP University approval	University setting; Hospital affiliated lab.	Laboratory practice and theory Chemistry Immunology Bacteriology Hematology
Occupational therapy	4 yr 10 mo	4 yr academic (liberal arts and professional subjects)—some "preclinical" experience, 10 mo. clinical experience	B.S. occupational therapy Certificate for completion of clinical experience (trend toward master's degree in O.T.)	Americ. Occ. Therapy Assn. AMA—university approval	University setting; Hospital	Manual arts and crafts, practice in functional prevocational and homemaking skills and activities of daily living. Sensorimotor, educational, recreational and social activities for patients
Pharmacy technician	1 mo	On-the-job training under supervision of trained technician and pharmacist	None	None	Hospital	1. Drug dispensation 2. Preparation of selected drugs 3. Maintenance of records
Pharmacist-B.S.	5 yr plus usually 1 yr internship	1st 2 yr: liberal arts; 3rd thru 5th yr: professional courses & basic sciences	B.S. pharmacy	University standards & state licensure	University setting	1. Knowledge of drug action & human physiology 2. Responsibility for drug dispensing 3. Source of information to physician, nurse, patient
Doctor of Pharmacy (Referred to as Pharm D.)	6 yr plus 1 yr internship	3rd thru 6th yr: professional courses	Doctor of Pharmacy	University standards and state licensure	University setting	Same as B.S. but more depth
Pharmacist-M.S. hospital pharmacy or Pharm. D.	2-3 yr beyond B.S.	1 yr academic 1 yr residency or combination of the above in 2-3 yrs.	M.S. hospital pharmacy or Doctor of Pharmacy	University standards and state licensure	University setting; Hospital	1. More highly developed understanding of clinical implication of drug use or 2. Improved development of management skills in hospital pharmacy
Physical therapist	4-6 yr; 4 mo. internship	4 yr academic 4 mo clinical experience	B.S., physical therapy	University standards Amer. Registry of Physical Therapists (certification) AMA	University setting Certificate for completion of clinical experience	Therapy programs for patients involving physical means, e.g., exercise, heat, massage

Table 43-1 continued

Profession	Total length of professional training beyond H.S.	Basic curriculum structure	Indicator of academic achievement	Certifying bodies	Geographical location of training	Basic skills
Radiological (x-ray) technician	24 concurrent months 1. New trends: 4 yr programs leading to B.S. in radiological technology 2. 2 yr training programs in vocational technical schools	Combinations of didactic training (physics, electronics, etc.) and clinical experience; 1/8 didactic training; 7/8 clinical experience	Certificate from hospital	Amer. Registry of Radiological Technologists (ARRT) AMA Amer. College of Radiologists	Hospital	Performance of radiographic examination
Social worker, B.S.	4 yr	4 yr didactic training—small amount of "field" experience	B.S., social work	University standards	University Selected agencies	1. Knowledge of human behavior (small groups and organizational life) 2. Structure and function of community agencies 3. Understanding of development of social policy 4. Planning and evaluation of treatment using above knowledge (casework, group work, and community organizations)
Social worker, M.S.	1 to 2 yr beyond B.S.	Didactic training 50%; clinical experience 50%	M.S., social work	University standards	University hospital or health agency	1. More depth knowledge practitioners 2. Supervisor of social work practitioners

Source: *Medical Care Chart Book,* 5th ed., Department of Medical Care Organization, School of Public Health, University of Michigan, Ann Arbor, 1972.

other states. Generally there are four methods by which boards license out-of-state licentiates: reciprocity, endorsement, examination or waiver.

Reciprocity may be a formal or informal agreement between states whereby a licensing board in one state will recognize licensees of another state if the board of that state will extend reciprocal recognition to licensees from the first state. To have reciprocity the initial licensing requirements of the two states must be essentially equivalent. In licensing by endorsement, boards determine whether the out-of-state practitioner's qualifications were equivalent to their state's requirements at the time of initial licensure. Refusal to recognize the validity of a national examination for endorsement purposes is within the discretion of state officials.

Where applicants do not meet all of the requirements for licensure, but have other equivalent qualifications the specific educational, experience or examination prerequisites may be waived. Some states will not recognize out-of-state licentiates and require that all applicants must pass the regular examination as well as fulfill the other requirements for initial licensure.

A majority of the states grant temporary licenses for some health occupations (the most common are nurses and doctors). These licenses may be given pending a decision by the board on permanent licensure or to out-of-state practitioners who intend to be in a jurisdiction for only a limited time. (For a comprehensive breakdown of all health personnel required to be licensed by each state, see Figure 43-1. For the characteristics of representative members of the health care team see Table 43-1.)

Unprofessional Conduct

Unprofessional conduct constitutes grounds for the suspension or revocation of a license and covers a wide spectrum of actions. It encompasses fraud by the intentional submission of erroneous billings for reimbursement by state or federal governments or private insurance companies, the misuse of controlled drugs and repeated acts of excessive drug prescription; the excessive administration of diagnostic procedures; and engaging in physical intimacies with patients. The failure to inventory, securely store and properly record the receipt of controlled drugs and the maintaining of inadequate medical records can be the basis of a board's decision to revoke or suspend. Also included within the scope of unprofessional conduct are the intentional inhaling of nitrous oxide gas during office hours; the aiding and abetting of an unlicensed individual to practice medicine; the representation to a patient that a manifestly incurable disease could be cured; and misconduct during surgery.

Revocation or Suspension of License

An important power possessed by most licensing boards is the authority to suspend or revoke the license of a practitioner who is found in violation of specified norms of conduct. Such violations include the procurement of a license by fraud; malpractice; the unlawful practice of acupuncture by a chiropractor; the revocation of an out-of-state license; and the conviction of a crime constituting unprofessional conduct.

Chapter 44—Trustees/Administrators and the Law*

TRUSTEES

The duty to supervise and manage is applicable to the trustees of a hospital as well as any other business corporation. In both instances there is a duty to act as a reasonably prudent person would act under similar circumstances. The hospital board must act prudently in administering the affairs of the hospital and exercise its powers in good faith.

The basic management functions of the governing board are: (1) the selection of corporate officers and agents; (2) general control of the compensation of such agents; (3) delegation of authority to the administrator and the administrator's subordinates for administrative action; (4) establishment of policies; and (5) supervision and vigilance over the welfare of the whole corporation.

Specific management duties peculiar to hospitals include: (1) determining the policies of the hospital in connection with community health needs; (2) maintaining proper professional standards in the hospital; (3) assuming a general responsibility for adequate patient care throughout the institution; and (4) providing adequate financing of patient care and assuming businesslike control of expenditures.

The authority of the board to fix policies for the hospital may be exercised by the board through the promulgation of rules and regulations for the conduct of the hospital or, like other authority of the board, may be delegated.

Responsibilities and Liability

Provide Satisfactory Patient Care

The most important aspect of the governing board's duty to operate the hospital with due care and diligence is its responsibility to provide satisfactory patient care. It is only through the fulfillment of this duty that the basic purpose of the hospital will be accomplished; this duty includes the maintenance of a satisfactory standard of medical care through supervision of the medical staff, nursing and ancillary staffs of the hospital.

Select a Competent Administrator

The members of the governing board are responsible for selecting an administrator to act as their agent in the management of the hospital. The individual selected must show the competence and character to set and maintain satisfactory standards of patient care within the institution. Minimum qualifications for administrators are contained in several hospital licensing statutes, or the rules and regulations promulgated under them. However, the governing board may, in its discretion, decide that these minimum requirements are insufficient and demand that its administrator meet this higher level of competency.

The general duty of the governing board to exercise due care and diligence in supervising

---

*Source: Reprinted from *Legal Aspects of Health Care Administration* by George D. Pozgar, with permission of Aspen Systems Corporation, © 1979.

and managing the hospital, in order to provide satisfactory patient care, does not cease upon the selection of a competent administrator. The governing board will be liable if the level of patient care becomes inadequate because of the board's failure to supervise properly the administrator's management of the hospital. Failure to remove an incompetent administrator or agent is as much a breach of the duty of due care and diligence as the failure to appoint a competent one.

Select Competent Physicians

The granting of staff privileges should be done only after the appropriate committees of the medical staff have made an effective and thorough investigation of an applicant. Hospital trustees have a duty and obligation to protect patients from physicians who they know, or should have known, were unqualified to practice medicine at their hospitals.

A license from the state to practice medicine does not establish a physician's right to membership on a hospital's staff. If the hospital is to be responsible for each physician's conduct, it must be permitted to determine the nature and extent of the privileges granted physicians to practice in the institution. However, in light of the importance of staff appointments to physicians, the courts have prohibited hospital governing boards from acting unreasonably or capriciously in rejecting physicians for staff appointments or in limiting their privileges.

Self-Dealing/Conflict of Interests

There should be full disclosure to the board of each board member's dealings with the hospital. Transactions between a board member and the hospital must be just and reasonable; board members must refrain from self-dealing and conflict of interest situations.

Generally, a contract between a hospital and a trustee financially interested in the transaction is at the most voidable; it would be upheld if the interested trustee abstained from speaking or voting in favor of the contract, or did not fully disclose the material facts respecting his interest. This resolution of the self-dealing problem is based on the belief that if an interested board member does not participate in the board's action, and makes full disclosure of interest, the disinterested remaining members of the board are able to protect the hospital's interests. If the transaction's fairness is questioned, the burden of establishing fairness falls upon the trustee involved.

Require Competitive Bidding

Many states have statutes requiring competitive bidding for work and materials commissioned by public hospitals. The fundamental purpose of this requirement is to eliminate, or at least reduce, the possibility that abuses such as fraud, favoritism, improvidence or extravagance will intrude into the institution's business practices. Governing board members must be aware of such statutory requirements because any contracts made in violation of such statutes would be void; in such cases personal liability might be imposed upon the individual governing board members if they were aware of the true nature of the transaction.

Provide a Safe Working Environment

The hospital is liable for work-related injuries to its employees provided such employee was not negligent in sustaining the injury. The hospital must provide its employees with safe working conditions and safe equipment. Employees must be warned of any unusual hazards attached to the job.

The hospital is not liable for unavoidable accidents; it cannot guard against the unforeseeable. However, it is liable for injuries resulting from dangers that the hospital knowingly failed to guard against appropriately or those which it should have known about and failed to guard against.

Respondeat Superior

Respondeat superior is a legal doctrine holding hospitals liable for the negligent acts of their employees that are committed within the scope of the employee's duties and obligations. The question of liability frequently rests on whether or not persons treating a patient are independent agents (responsible for their own acts) or employees of the hospital. The answer to this depends on whether or not the hospital can exercise control over the particular act which was the proximate cause of the injury.

Since the law holds negligent persons responsible for their negligent acts, employees are not absolved from liability when the hospital is held liable through the application of *respondeat superior*. Not only may the injured party sue the employee directly, the employer, if sued, may also seek indemnification from the employee, that is, compensation for the financial loss occasioned by the employee's act.

The doctrine of *respondeat superior* may impose liability upon a hospital for a nurse's acts or omissions that result in injury to a hospital patient. Whether such liability attaches depends on whether the conduct of the nurse was wrongful, and whether the nurse was subject to the control of the hospital at the time the act in question was performed. Determination of whether the nurse's conduct was wrongful in a given situation depends on the standard of conduct to which the nurse is expected to adhere. In liability deliberations, the nurse who is subject to the control of the hospital at the time of the negligent conduct is considered a hospital employee and is not the "borrowed servant" of a staff physician or surgeon.

Provide Adequate Insurance

The duty of the hospital board is to purchase insurance against various risks. Hospitals in states which do not follow the doctrine of charitable immunity face as much risk of losing their tangible and intangible assets through judgments for negligence as through fires or other disasters. Where this is true, the duty to insure against the risks of negligence is as great as to insure against fire. The amount of insurance must be adequate for the circumstances.

THE HOSPITAL ADMINISTRATOR[*]

Authority and Liability

The primary source of the administrator's authority is the governing board. The board normally delegates the duty, responsibility and authority to manage the hospital to the administrator. Resolutions of the board may, from time to time, enlarge the administrator's authority or give him special authority to deal with certain problems. Certain aspects of the administrator's authority may also be provided for in organizational documents, such as the hospital's articles of incorporation or association, or in the hospital's bylaws. In addition, other aspects of the administrator's authority may be covered in his contract of employment. Finally, state statutes or regulations may provide for certain administrative powers.

Torts

Any person who either voluntarily or negligently acts in such a way that harm results to another will be liable for that injury. This principle is applicable to administrators as well as to all others. If, in the performance of his duties, the administrator wrongfully injures another, he will be liable to that person. The hospital may also be liable for his act, depending upon the type of hospital and the state in which it is located.

However, the administrator will not be held liable in every case involving injuries in the hospital. In the case of a negligent injury, for example, there must be a showing that his personal acts were the proximate cause of the injury.

The administrator may also be held liable for injuries which are willful rather than negligent. Thus, a hospital manager was held liable for false imprisonment when he told a patient that she could not leave the hospital unless she paid her bill.

As a general rule, whether or not the hospital is found to be liable, the administrator will not be held liable unless he is found to have been the cause of the alleged injury. Conversely, the administrator will be liable if it can be shown that he caused the injury, irrespective of whether the hospital is found to be liable.

The administrator is liable for the negligence of other hospital employees only if he personally takes part in the commission of the negligent act or is negligent in selecting or directing the person committing the injury.

Respondeat Superior

Under the doctrine of *respondeat superior* an employer can be held liable for the negligent acts of an employee if those acts cause injury to other persons. The doctrine is applied when the employee's negligent act has occurred while he is within the "scope of employment." Generally, the courts have defined "scope of employment" as that period of time in which the em-

---

[*]Source: Reprinted from *Hospital Law Manual*, Vol. I by Health Law Center, with permission of Aspen Systems Corporation, © 1979.

ployee is actually performing his duties. However, *respondeat superior* does not create liability for the administrator because the hospital, and not the administrator, is the employer of the hospital's personnel.

Contracts

The administrator is not personally liable on contracts made by him within the scope of his authority on behalf of the hospital. However, if the administrator exceeds his authority, the hospital is not bound and the administrator may be liable civilly for damages occurring to the other contracting party and may incur criminal liability as well. Liability to the other party to the contract will accrue unless it can be shown that the third party was justified in believing the administrator had apparent authority or that there was ratification of the originally unauthorized contract.

Statutory Liability

The administrator may be liable civilly or criminally for the breach of duties imposed by statute. For example, where the law requires that a license or permit be obtained before certain acts are performed, failure to obtain the requisite certificate may lead to a fine or imprisonment. However, the courts generally hold that an agent, such as administrator, will not be personally liable for the penalties imposed by statute on persons or institutions conducting activities without the requisite license.

ADMINISTRATOR'S PREPARATION FOR LITIGATION*

General Guidelines

The following principles relating to the litigation process primarily reflect an administrative viewpoint.

1. *Insure that factual comprehensive documentation is accomplished.* One of the primary tools that a hospital's legal counsel needs in preparation for a courtroom battle is a file full of well-documented facts. The confidential and privileged nature of the attorney–client relationship can be used in the accumulation process.

    Incident/accident reports with supporting information should be forwarded immediately to the hospital attorney. The timeliness of information gathering is directly related to the accuracy and caliber of facts obtained. When any incident/accident occurs, the process of preparing for a potential day in court should start.

2. *Remember that subsequent review and analysis can also provide insight from a legal standpoint.* The activities of committees in regard to evaluation of both individual and general risk problems can be most helpful to legal counsel. The deviation from recognized standards of any incident is generally discovered during the review and analysis stage. This is significant, since one of the main criteria used in establishing the liability of a hospital is often the prevailing standard in the professional community. The practical expertise of those involved in committee work can be very helpful in establishing and evaluating the hospital's position on and approach to a given problem situation.

3. *Thorough orientation and education of the attorney relative to the technical and operational aspects of the problem situation are necessary.* Most attorneys are members of the laity relative to hospital activities. In this regard, it is important that the hospital's legal counsel be given a quick course in the technical aspects of the incident/accident. This is not only important from the standpoint of preparation but also necessary in the course of the proceedings within the courtroom.

4. *Active participation by the hospital's governing body and administration in judgmental and strategic decisions is desirable.* At times, there may be a tendency to have the hospital attorney shoulder the entire burden when decisions need to be made in the course of litigation activities. This can be very unfair to the counsel; more important, an excellent intellectual resource may go untapped. The viewpoint of the hospital's governing and operational representatives needs to be incorporated in the deci-

---

*Source: Reprinted from *Risk Management for Hospitals: A Practical Approach* by Bernard L. Brown, Jr., with permission of Aspen Systems Corporation, © 1979.

sion-making process. For example, the selection of witnesses who will take the stand for the institution needs to be made carefully. The knowledge of administrators, who work daily with hospital personnel, concerning potential witnesses' abilities to handle pressure situations, their temperament, and their other capabilities can be very helpful in the final selection of witnesses.

5. *Flexibility should be maintained throughout the entire litigation process.* In the course of battle, particularly a legal one, emotions usually rise and positions often harden. Despite these tendencies, an attitude of equitable compromise should always be maintained. The high principles and integrity of the institution should always be protected; of course, these may from time to time need to be flavored a bit by reality and practicality. Decisions should always be influenced by what will be best for the hospital.

On the Witness Stand*

The following are some helpful guidelines for a witness undergoing examination in a trial or a court hearing:

1. Do not be antagonistic towards the plaintiff's counsel. The jury may already be somewhat sympathetic toward the injured party; your antagonism may only serve to reinforce such an impression.

2. Be organized in your thinking and recollection of the facts regarding the incident.
3. Do not use the witness box to show how knowledgeable you are. What you think is harmless may be the downfall of the case.
4. Explain your testimony in simple, succinct terminology.
5. Do not overdramatize the facts you are relating. The witness box is not the place to make your stage debut.
6. Do not allow yourself to become overpowered by the crossexaminer.
7. Be polite, sincere and courteous at all times.
8. Dress appropriately and be neatly groomed.
9. Pay close attention to any objections your attorney may have as to the line of questioning being conducted by the opposing counsel.
10. Never deny discussing the case with your attorney when questioned about such practice.
11. Be sure to have reviewed any oral deposition which you may have participated in during examination before trial.
12. Be straightforward with the examiner. Any answers designed to cover up or cloud an issue or fact will, if discovered, serve only to discredit any previous testimony you may have given.
13. Do not show any visible signs of displeasure regarding any testimony with which you are in disagreement.
14. Be sure to have questions that you did not hear repeated, and questions which you did not understand rephrased.

---

*Source: Reprinted from *Legal Aspects of Health Care Administration* by George D. Pozgar, with permission of Aspen Systems Corporation, © 1979.

INDEX

A

Abortion, statutory reporting of, 710
Abrasive managers, 60-61, 67
Absences, 467, 487-491
   unscheduled, 490. *See also* Absenteeism
Absenteeism, 71, 487-491
   control, 490-491
   control program, 492, *493*
   factors, 488
   rate and cause, 489-490
   reduction, 489
   supervisor guidelines, 491-492
   and turnover, 487-488. *See also* Absences
Academics, as consultants, 95
Acceptability:
   in supervisory personnel, *63*
Accessibility, manager, 85
Accidents, 677, 689
Accommodation, and problem solving, 76
Accountability:
   administrator, 4
   and marketing, *180*
   restrictive, 18
   and work standards, 556
Accounting:
   and automation, 271-272
   construction project, 361
   health, 638
   in management control, 208
   by word processor, 436
Accounts payable, 227, 229
Accounts receivable, 229-230
Accrued expenses, as short term financing, 325
ACHA. *See* American College of Hospital Administrators
Achievement, 60, 67
   and criticism, 545
   measures, 83
Acquisitions, 144
   as horizontal integration, 150
Activity list, 565-566
Adaptability, 399-400
Adaptation method (problem solving), 72
Administration manual, 56
Administrative:
   burnout, 69-70
   data processing, 377
   department heads, 4
Administrators, 3-20
   authority and liability, 725-726
   competent, 723-724
   and hospital surveys, 97-98
   jobs for, 127-128
   and the law, 725-727
   legal responsibilities, 725
   as owners, 3
   personnel productivity report, *558*
   as power brokers, 23-25
   and quality assurance, 628
   quitting time, 70
   role in collective bargaining, 608
   specific duties, 3-5
   statutory liability, 726
   on witness stand, 727. *See also* Hospital Administrators
Admissions, 4
   computer, 427-428
   consent form, 695, *696*
   and marketing image, 186
   sources for, *164*
   from staff, 159-160
   and surgery scheduling, coordinated, 579
Advancement, employee, 550
Advertising, 158, 184-185
   and public relations, 204-205
AFL-CIO, 593
Age, as patient demographic factor, 199
Agencies:
   lobbying, 150
Agency review, 356-357
Agendas, 23
Agreements:
   collective bargaining, 613-621
   employee, 550
Air pollution, 677
   local regulation, 716
Aisles, 675
Alcohol, 68
Alcoholism, 25, 139, 712
   programs, 467-468
   treatment, 174

Note: Page numbers in italics indicate entry wll be found in a figure or table. Page numbers ending in n indicate entry will be found in a note.

Allcorn, Seth, 47n, 227n, 382n
Ambiguity, 12
Ambulances, dispatch and transport, 667
Ambulatory care services, 139
American Association of Hospital Consultants, 349
American College of Hospital Administrators, list of chief executive duties, 5
American Hospital Association (AHA), criteria for architects/engineers, 349
American Medical Association (AMA), 199, 654
American Nurses' Association Professional Credentials and Placement Service, 458
Analysis, 93
  in management control, 208
  as supervisory trait, 63
Ancillary services, 552
  reimbursement for, 295
Anderson, Mark L., 567n
Annuity trust, charitable, 309
Antitrust:
  and hospital systems, 132-133
Anxiety, 67
  and internal analysis, 148
Appearance, employee, 544
Applebaum, Steven H., 60n, 67n, 71n, 84n, 85n, 90n, 91n, 375n, 466n
Applications, computer, 387
Appraisal, 513, 536-551
  checklist, weighted, 538-539
  common problems, 541
  employee, 10, 60-67, 437
  interview, 545-551
  methods, 536-541
  rating scale, elements, 544-545
  rating scales, 536-537
Appropriateness, of control, 46
Appropriateness review, for conversion, 178
Arbitration, 121, 607-608, 610-613, 616-617
  in HIS purchasing, 418
  and suspension, 503
Architects, 349
Artificial life-prolonging measures, 697-698
Art-of-care, 629
Assault, 689-690
Assessment:
  of competition, 147
  of executive strengths and weaknesses, 20

management skills, 15-16
organizational, 148
productivity, 569-571
programs, pre-supervisory, 437
Asset expansion, 126
Athenian, Ralph A., 541n
A. T. Kearney, Inc. (Chicago), 20
Attitudes:
  approaches, 549-550
  employee, 545, 549-551, 550
Attitude scale, continuous, 537
Attorneys, 203
Audit administration, 627
Audit committee, 649-650
Auditing:
  control system, 47
  internal, 47-49
Auditor, internal, 47-48
Audits, and change, 627-629
Audit systems, 650-651
Audit trails, 405
Austin, Charles J., 590n
Authority, 101-102
  delegation, 102
  flexibility in, 554
  line and staff, 103
  parameters, 10
  simplified channels, 554
  subordinate leader, 59
Authorization card, union, 595
Automated records systems, 714
Automatic sprinkler systems, 676
Automation, 271-272. See also Computers; Electronic Data Processing
Avery, Allyson D., 629n

B

Backward vertical integration, 149
Bagadia, K. S., 485n
Baker, Frank J., II, 666n
Baker, M. M., 485n
Banking, 535
Bank loans, 325
Baptist Hospital (Pensacola, Fl.), 590
Barrett, Diana, 120n
Bartscht, Karl G., 573n
Batch mode, 401
Battery, 689-690
Beck, Donald F., 236n, 247n, 248n, 401n
Beds:
  capacity, 174
  in multihospital systems, 134
  swing, 174

Beech, Thomas R., 443n, 594n, 595n, 597n, 599n
Behavior:
  as market analysis variable, 171
  in marketing audit, 199-200
Behaviorally anchored rating scales (BARS), 539-540
  and MBO, 540
Behavior modification programs, 165
Benchmarks, 148
Benefit program:
  alternative funding, 520-522
  communicating, 522-524
  in personnel policy manuals, 524
  sample, 520, 521
  traditional approach, 518, 519
Benefits:
  employee, 518-535
  flexible, 520
  total MIS, 419-420
Bennet, Addison C., 564n, 565n
Bennett, A. C., 71n
Bentivegna, Peter, 319n, 358n, 361n, 371n
Besse, Ralph, 75
Better Business Bureau, 203
Bidding, 358
  competitive, required, 724
Big 8 public accounting firms, 20
Billing, 232, 516, 552
Birthing centers, 166
Blanket insurance policies, 524
Blanton, Wyndham B., 158n
Blood:
  as employee benefit, 535
  services, 685
  transfusion, 695, 710-711
Blue Cross, 220
  as hospital benefit underwriter, 522
  negotiated budgets by, 281
  periodic interim payments (PIP), 224
  prospective rate setting, 304
  quality assurance requirements, 628
  shared computer services, 396
Blue sky discussion, 143
Blum, John D., 653n
Blume, Frederick R., 319n, 327n
Board:
  corporate, 132
  planning committee, 138
Board of directors, 119
Board of governors, 119. See also Governing board
Boilerplating, 434-435
Boissoneau, Robert, 16n, 627n

Bond credit rating agencies, 330
Bonds:
  participants, *328*
  public taxable, 320-321
  refunding, 323
  tax-exempt revenue, 315, 320, *322*
Borrowing:
  full cost of, 327-329
  intangible costs, 328-329
  points, 327
  strategy, 143
Bradford, Charles K., 292n
Brainstorming method (problem solving), 72-73
Brazing, 677
Break-even analysis, 259-261, 301-302
  graphic computation, *260*
Brewsterm, Agnes W., 255n
Brook, Robert H., 629n
Brown, Bernard L., Jr., 688n, 726n
Brown, David, 82
Brown, Montague, 116n, 119n, 122n, 123n
Broyles, Robert W., 214n, 224n, 240n, 262n, 263n
Budget:
  assumptions, 238
  cash, 246-247, 255, 277
  as control tool, 47
  cost centers, 227
  and decision making, 78
  documents, 246-247
  expense and revenue, 241
  Gantt chart as, 89
  glossary, 263-264
  hearings, 239
  integration, *247*
  manual, 236
  master, 239-240
  model of computer financial planning, 217
  operating, 246
  process, 236-240
  reports, 247-253
  timetable, *237, 238*
  variance analysis, 250-253
Budget glossary, 263-264
Budgeting, 80, 235-264
  approaches, 240-246
  basic program, 235-236
  financial requirements, 235-236
  forecast vs flexible, *245*
  internal audit checklist, 261, 264
  in management control, 208
Budget reports, 247-253
Building:
  committee, 348
  cost estimate, *346*
  equipment cost breakdown, *372-374*. *See also* Capital projects; Construction
Bulletin boards, 448, 617
Burger, Eugene, 73n
Burkett, G., 655n
Burnout, 69-70
Business:
  accident expenses, 534
  department, 516
  diversification, 147
  gaining more, 158-160
  health care as, *181*
  objectives, 412-413
  office manual, 56
  transactions, written, 5
  travel expenses, 534

C

Cady, Carolyn W., 667n
Cain, Daniel M., 321n, 326n
Cancer, 165, 710
Capability, 79
  of hospital information systems, 404
Capacity, 174
Capital:
  budget, 246
  cost, 367-374
  erosion, 160
  investment, 329-330
  vs operating lease, 342-344
  planning model (IHC), 334-335
  for satellite primary care, 168
  weighted cost of, 334
Capital accumulation programs, 526
Capital cost, 367-374
Capital expenditures, 331-344
  planning, 333-335
  requests, 331-333
Capital financing, 123
  alternatives, 315
Capital formation, 147, 219-220, 315-330
  federal intervention, 316-319
  financing/investment model, *221*
  sources, 316
Cardiac surgery, *336*
Care, criteria for, 638-640. *See also* Patient care; Quality of care
Career development, 128, 437
  employee, 486
Care level and timeliness review (CLTR), 657-663
Carrot and stick motivation, 481-482
Case:
  -based incentives, 306-307
  -based payment, 305-307
  discussion, 74
Cash:
  collection, 224
  flow, 150
  receipts, 231
Cash budget, *225, 227, 228,* 246-247
Cash management, 223-227
Categorically needy, *283*
Cathode ray tube (CRT), 402, 434
Cawsey, Thomas S., 495n
Cazalas, Mary Williams, 688n
Census, 159
Central staff, *105*
Centralization, 128
CEO. *See* Chief executive officer
Cercone, Romeo, 492n, 493n
Ceremony, 7
Certificate of need (CON), 133, 315
  and cost containment, 715
  state, 318
Certified public accountant, 209
Chain of command, 7, 8
Chains, hospital, 125-128
Chairman:
  committee, 110-111
  department, 103
Chaney, Warren H., 443n, 594n, 595n, 597n, 599n
Change, 71-78
  and audits, 627-629
  job, 514
  monitoring, review, and, 579-580
Change orders, 360-361, 363
Chapman, J. Brad, 505n
Character defamation, 690
Charge collection systems, 409
Charges, 300-302
Charitable gift annuity, 311
Charitable hospital, 3
Charitable lead trusts, 310-311
Charitable remainder annuity trust, 309
Charitable remainder unitrust, 309
Check off, 614-615
Chief executive officer (CEO), 3-5
  assistant to, 138
  and chief financial officer, 208
  lobbying by, 150
  management style, 130
  marketing function assignment, 188
  MBO training for, 34
Chief financial officer (CFO), 208
Chief operations officer, 208
Chief of service, 103

Chief of staff, 103
Child abuse, 710
CHI systems, 573-580
CHI Systems, Inc., 573
Claims runs, 640-641
Classification method (problem solving), 72
Clayton Act, 133
Clerical MIS users, 410
Cleverley, William O., 207n, 214n, 218n, 222n, 243n, 246n, 265n, 325n, 332n, 553n
Clinical data processing, 377
Clinics, 165
Coinsurance, 282
Collective bargaining, 608-621
  management roles, 608
  representation, 597, *598-599*
Command, 101
Commercial businesses, 161
Committees, 5, 109-115
  audit, 649-650
  board planning, 138
  building, 348
  CEO use, 18
  chairman, 110-111
  checklist, 109-110
  employee organizing, 595
  medical staff, 111
  members of, 110
  planning, *140*, 138
  records, 713-714
  recruitment, 458
  roles members play, 114-115
  running, 111-114
  types in hospitals, 111
Communicable diseases, 4, 5, 710
Communication(s), 9, 442-457
  benefits, 522-524
  consumer, 184
  in FVA, 278
  improving, 442-444
  leadership, 442
  management, and unions, 602-603
  physician, 159
  as PMS user department, *427*
  in rate setting, 305
  targets of, 444-449
  techniques, 449-455
  vehicles, 448-449
Community:
  characteristics surveyed, 137
  gaps in service, 137
  groups, 138-139
  health education, 173
  health needs, 153
  low use, 270
  maldistribution of resources, 175

patient demographics, 197
planners, 176
served, 153
service gaps, 153
Community hospitals, *117*, 134, 238
Competition:
  analysis, 201
  assessment, 147
  and diversification, 160
  in hospital industry, 268
  information, *192*
  in marketing, 185
  in marketing audit, *196-197*
  nonprice, 149
  primary care, 169
  researching, 201-204
Competitive assessment, 147
Competitive bidding, 724
Complaints, 71
Complexity, 12
Compliance, 214
Comprehensive Quality Assurance System (CQAS), 642-645
Computerized information systems: patient management, 426-433
Computerized medical records, 714
Computers, 377-403
  costs and benefits, 381-382
  course agenda for, 422
  gaming with, 94
  in hospital information systems, 411
  hospital uses, 376-383
  main frame vs mini-computers, 389-395
  models for financial planning, 216-218
  purchasing, 383-389
  request for proposal (RFP), 385-386
  shared systems vs in-house systems, 395-401
  systems and procedures, 387-388
  terminology, 401-403. See also Computerized information systems; Computerized medical systems; Data processing; Electronic data processing; Hospital information systems (HIS)
Concurrent review, 656
Conditions of Participation, 4
Condominium hospitals, 118
Conduct, 721
Conduit financing, 327
Confidentiality, 458
Conflict, 47
Conflict of interest, 25, 724

Connor, Robert A., 305n
Consent:
  disclosure with patient, 705
  express/implied, 692-693
  forms, 694-697
  informed, 692-702
  qualified, 701-702
  refusal of, 697-698, 700-702
Consortia, 117-118
Construction, 345-374
  cost estimate, 354
  costs, 366, *372-374*
  director, 348
  documents, 357-358
  feasibility, 351, 355
  funds management, 363-364
  management techniques, 361-364
  manager, 349-350
  master program, 354
  need survey, 351
  planning team, 349-358
  site, 355
  workload projections, 354, 366-367
Consultants, 95-96
  building, 358-361
  functional planning, 349
  market research, 194
  outside marketing, 189
Consulting firms:
  individual entrepreneur, 95
  large national, 96
  specialty, 95
Consultive leadership, 22
Consumable supplies, 216
Consumer:
  choice of hospitals, 205
  defined, 182
  health education, 182, 186
  needs, demands, preferences, 147
Contingency funds, 331
Contingent fees, 360
Continuing education, 16, *17*
Continuous rating scales, 536
Contract management, 123-125
Contractors, construction, 359-361
Contracts, 6, 762
  construction, 359-361
  HIS, 417-418
Contribution margin, 259
Contributions, 308-309
  employee benefit, 525
Control, 9, 46, 47
  of absenteeism, 490-491, *493*
  comprehensive, 46
  defined, 46
  and delegation, 79, 81
  and Gantt charts, 85
  infection, 669-672

internal, 48, 229
management, 9, 46-56
phases, management, 207-208
positive, 46
quality, 272
tools, 47
of turnover, *496*
Controller, 208
Conventional mortgage financing, 324
Conversion:
  health facilities, 174-178
  PMS, 432-433
Cooper, Philip D., 181n, 190n
Cooperation, 9
  in computer systems, 396
Cooperative attempts, defined, 113
Coordination, 9
Coordinator:
  for hospital manual, 53
  MBO, 39
Corporate board of directors, 119, 132
Corporate management, 120, 131
Corporate services, 131-132
Cost analysis, 243, 245
Cost benefit analysis, 253, 254-255
  departmental, 258-261
  HIS, 414-417
Cost concept glossary, 262-263
Cost containment, 188, 265-280
  case study, 271-275
  and certificate of need, 715
  proposals, *266*
  and reimbursement, 306
  strategies, 269-271
Cost effectiveness analyses, 255-256
Cost evaluation, *256-257*
Cost finding, 220-223
  horizontal/vertical, 335, 337
  for services/equipment, 335-337
  step down, *298*
Cost influencing variables (CIVs), 267, 268
Cost-plus-fixed-fee contract, 360
Cost reduction, 188, 255
Cost reimbursement, 144. *See also* Reimbursement
Cost reimbursement (computer) model, 217
Cost report, 288
  medicare, 288, *289*
Costs:
  behavior, *252*
  building, preliminary, 346
  computers, 381-382
  concepts, 337
  consumable supplies, 216

of debt, 334
of equity, 334
financial decisions about, 214, 216
glossary, 262-263
HIS checklist, *419*
indirect, 222
intangible, 328-329
joint overhead, 337-338
labor, 216
opportunity, 6, 258-259
as problem indicator, 71
replacement, 337
tangible, 327-328
turnover, *494,* 492
Cost saving investment, 329, 330
Counseling, *548-549. See also* Human resources management
Courtesy discharge, 186
Court orders, 712-713
Creativity, 11-14
Credentials, 717-718
Credit:
  balances, 230
  rating, 319
  trade, 325
Criminal activities, 25
Crisis management, *86*
Critical factor method (problem solving), 72
Critical incident, 539
Critic, ideal, 499
Criticism, 11, 499-501
Current giving, 308-309
Custom (computer) model, 218

D

D'Angelo, Gary, 453n
Data:
  base, patient, 426-427
  collection, 640-642
  disaggregate, 147
  evaluation, 555
  gathering techniques, 48
  sources, 640-641
Data processing, 48, 377-403
  problems, 398-399
Davis, William P., III, 520n, 527n
Davis, Winborn E., 500n
Day care centers, 534
Deadlines, 476
Death benefits, 526-527
  self-insurance for, 527
Debt financing:
  alternatives, 319-320
  for construction funds, 316
  factors affecting, *321*

long term, 319-324
and rate regulation, 330
sources, 320
Debts:
  capacity, 143
  cost of, 334
  long term, 316, 321-323
  refunding, 321-323
  short and immediate term, 325-329
Decentralization, 482
Decision making, *64*
  centralization, 18
  and change, 75-78
  constraints, 78
  in construction projects, 347-348
  financial information for, 214-216
  FVA, 280
  group, and change, 74
  in hospital manual, 51
  as managerial role, 7-9
  in managers, 58-59
  in multiunit organizations, 126
  process, creative, 76-78
  to rent, lease, or purchase, *340-341*
  riskless, 19
  withdrawal, and stress, 18
  by workers, 554. *See also* Decisions
Decisions, 71-78
  considered, 76
  in construction management, 361
  financial, 214, *215,* 216
  operational, in construction, 364-365
  origination and finalization, 126
  sour, 75
  types of, 76-78, *77*
Decision tree (conversion), *177*
Deegan, Arthur X., 34n, 541n
Defamation, 690, 707
Defensiveness, 545
Deferred borrowing, 143
Deferred giving, 309
Deferred incentive plan, 591
Deferred revenue, 325
Deisenroth, J. Keith, 235n, 241n, 243n, 246n
Delegation, 9, 74-75, *86*
  of authority, 80, 101-103
  barriers to, 82
  and decentralization, 482
  guide to, 80-82
  stress and, 18
  tasks for, 79-82
  and time management, 79-94
Deliberation, 76
Delphi technique, 155
  advantages, 40

process, 45
questionnaire, 40, *42-44*
Demand:
consumer, 147
employee, 157
forecasting, 154-155
health care service, 160
Democratic leadership, 22
Demography, 146
and absenteeism, 488
Demonstration, 56
Dental insurance, 531
Department(s), 8
administrators, 4
audit, 49
budgeting control, 103
chairmen of, 103
cost analyses applicable, 258-261
and decision making constraints, 78
disaster planning, 668
of fiscal services, *210*
function, 106
goals determination, 35, 580
human resources development in, 438-439
indirect costs to, 222
and institutional objectives, 141-143
licensure and permits, 716
long-term productivity data, 580
long term trends, *584*
MBO method in, 34, 36-38
misuse of surveys, 97
movement problems in, 577
participative goal setting by, 580
patient management systems in, 427-431
productivity indexes, *553*
productivity report, *557*
service intensity, 586
weekly summary sheet, *562*
and work standard development, 555
Dependability, 544
Design:
construction, 357
documents, 144
job, 489
Diagnosis, 148
Diagnosis Related Group (DRG)
rate setting, 307
Diagnostic equipment, 552
Dickie, Kenneth J., 258n
Diener, Jacquelin G., 640n, 641n
Diet and nutrition programs, 165
Dietary department, 716

Direction:
and leadership, 9
as management function, 8-9
and motivation, 482
proportion of management time to, *10*
Directory of Investor-Owned Hospitals and Hospital Management Companies 1975, 125
Disability, 534
benefits for, 528
Disability benefits, 518, 527-528
model program, *529*
program, 528
and rehabilitation, 528
Disabled patients, 172
Disaster, 664-669
emergency operations, 6
handling, 664-669
plan, 664-666
planning, 667-668
Discharge, 4, 617
against medical advice, *701*
analysis data, 642
courtesy, 186
Disciplinary action, 4, 503
Discipline, 501-504, 601, 617
approaches, 502-504
slide rule approach, 504
as substitute for supervision, 502
Disclosure:
of medical records, 705
patient consent form, *706-707*
requirements, 710
Discounting, 254
Discrete scales:
for appraisal, 536
sample characteristic, *537*
Discrimination, 617
Dismissal, 503
Distributed (mini-computer) network, 391, 393, *394*
Distribution chart, 47
Distrust, 9
Disturbance, *8*
Disunity, 9
Dittman, David A., 329n
Diversification, 147, 160, 161
Division of labor, 7-8
Divisions, 8
Doctrine of qualified privilege, 711
Documentation:
for construction planning, 348
HIS, 417
hospital manual as, 51
Dolan, Richard C., 19n, 208n
Double apportionment cost finding, 223

Double distribution cost finding, 223
Dowling, William L., 303
Dress code, 6
Drucker, Peter, 36, 262, 482
Drug abuse, 25, 139, 174, 467
patient records, 712
Drugs, 68
negligent handling, 682-683

E

East End Memorial Hospital (Birmingham, Ala.), 591
Economic myths, hospital, 209, 211-213
Economies of scale, 122
and horizontal integration, 150
in shared computer systems, 397
Economy, adequate control, 46
Education:
AHA defined, *296*
cost containment, 270-271
as demographic data, 199
hospital administrator, 16
hospital information systems, 420-422
on worktime benefit, 534
Edwards, Arch B., 657n
Effectiveness:
defined, 629-630
evaluation, *257-258*
financial, 214
Efficacy, 629
Efficiency:
financial, 214
production, 269-270
variance, productivity, 252-253
Egan, G., 450n
Egdahl, Richard, 629n
Ego needs, 481
Egress, means of, 676
Elbert, Norbert F., 539n
Election, union, 597
Electro-convulsive therapy (ECT), 695
Electronic Data Processing (EDP), 377-403
cost per patient day, 378
glossary, 401-403
internal audit checkpoints, 382-383
major systems, *379. See also* Computers; Data processing; Management information systems
Ellingson, Ronald L., 580n
Ellis, Terrill F., 552n

Emergency ambulance service (EAS), computerized, 428
Emergency operations, hospital, 6
Emergency room services, 139
Emergency treatment, 693
Emergicare centers, 172-174
Emotional stability, 21
Employee annual report, 448
Employee benefits, 518-535
  costs beyond salary expenditures for, 534
  current practices and trends, 530-535
  facilities, 593
  overview, 518-524
  in private hospitals, *532-533*
  trends in programs, 534-535
  and unionization, 593. *See also* Benefits
Employee clinics, 534
Employee Handbook, 448
Employee performance appraisal, 10, 536-551
Employees:
  absenteeism, 487-491
  advocate, 449
  audit, 49
  benefits, 518-535
  benefits program, 437
  bonus for health, 490
  career planning, 486
  committee, 449
  communication, 10, 448-449
  as communications target, 445-449
  comparison, and appraisal, 573-538
  as consumers, 183
  cross-training, 588
  dead-end, 474
  delegation to, 79-82
  demand, 157
  discussion groups, 449
  eligible for retirement benefits, 525
  evaluation, 46
  evaluation form, *548-549*
  exit interviews, 497-498
  health services, 188
  human resources management, 437-441
  incentive plan, 589-591
  long-term, and problem solving, 73
  as market segment, 197
  motivation, 22
  new, and hospital manual, 51
  organization committees, 595
  participation in appraisal, 545
  performance, 47
  performance appraisal, 536-551
  personnel handbook for, 55
  preferences in managers, *32-33*
  present and forecasted, 156
  priorities and needs, 601
  probationary, 618
  problem, 468-474
  question forms for, 448
  questionnaires, 641
  recruitment, 437
  recruitment and interviewing, 458-463
  retraining, 46
  rewards, 10
  salaries, 508-517
  satisfaction, checklist, 593
  sense of involvement, 554
  standards for evaluation, *542-543*, 541-545
  store, 535
  troubled, 466-468
  turnover, 71, 487-489, 492-498
  union election information for, 603-604
  See also Personnel; Subordinates; Workers
Employers:
  as consumers, 182, 187-188
  entitlement and strength, 600-601
Employment:
  agencies, 458
  as demographic data, 199
Emrich, James S., 220n, 221n
Endorsement, 153
Engineering:
  human resource, 437-438
  systems, 151-152
Engineers, 349
  health systems, 151-152
Entrepreneur:
  consulting, 95
  manager as, *8*
Environment:
  computer, 398
  health services, changing, 183
Environmental permits, 716
Equipment:
  building, cost breakdown, *372-374*
  computing, 384-387, 418
  defective or improper, 682
  financial information, 216
  fixed, 357
  in-depth study of, 576
  installation, 274
  leasing, 338-344
  movable, in construction, 358
  procurement for building, 362
  servicing, 273-274
  sharing, 273
Equity, *297*
  costs, 334, 336
Equivalent Annual Cost method, 333
Ernst and Ernst, 237n
Ernst and Whinney, 567, 569-573
Errors:
  correction, 500-501
  and criticism, 500
Escovitz, Gerald H., 655n
Essick, William J., Jr., 319n, 361n, 371n
Ethical issues, 254
Evaluation:
  of capital expenditures, 332-333
  of construction feasibility, 351
  cost, *256-257*
  of current facilities, 351
  effectiveness, *257-258*
  of employee benefits communication, 524
  of facilities, 154
  formal and informal, 49-50
  hospital, 96-98
  of hospital information systems, 414
  internal vs external, 50
  job, 514-515
  MBO, 39
  in planning, 138
  standards for employees, 541-545
  by subordinates, 441
  subordinate self-, 60
  and systems engineering, 151-152
Evaluators, 96-98
Evidence, medical records as, 713
Exception report, 583, *585,* 587
Executive:
  burnout, 69
  creative, 11-14
  health physicals, 188
  quitting of, 70
  recruitment firms, 19-20
  self-evaluation, 14-16
Executive committee, 111
Executive officer, state government list of duties for, 5-6
Executive recruiting firms, 19-20
Executives:
  high-risk, 67-68, 70
  MIS, 405-406, 406-407
  neurotic, 68
  planning, 138
  recruitment, 458-459
  search for, 458, 459
  state list of duties for, 5-6. *See also* Chief executive officer
Executive vice president, as planner,

138
Exercise programs:
  corrective, 165
  promotion, 165
Exit interview, 497
Expansion, 150
  in computer systems, 387-388
  projects, 137-138
Expenditures:
  capital, 331-344
  increasing, 267-269
Expense budget, 241-242
Expenses:
  accrued, 325
  forecasting, 225, 227
Explosion, emergency operations, 6
External analyses:
  in strategic planning, 146-148
Extinguishers, 676
Eye and face protection, 667

F

Facilitation, 51
Facilities, 147
  audit, 49
  conversion, 174-178
  employee, 593
  evaluation, 154, 351
  inventory, 148
  management computer system, 385, 397
Factfinding, in impasse resolution, 609
Fact-fone, 449
Factor comparison system (job evaluation), 514
Failure, 12
Fairview Hospital system, 130
False imprisonment, 690
Family practitioners, 166
Farm, as gift, 310
Farmers Home Administration (FmHA), 318
Fast-track development, 362-363
Fatigue, 71
Feasibility:
  of construction projects, 349, 351
  of conversion, 175-176
  study, 319, 641
Federal:
  financing, 315
  interventions in capital formation, 316-319
Federal hospital, 3
Federal Housing Administration (FHA), 318, 320, *323, 324*

Federal reimbursement, 281-307. *See also* Medicaid; Medicare; Reimbursement
Federal tax law, 133
Federation of American Hospitals, 125
Feedback, 96
  committee, 110
  of employee benefit communication, 524
Feeder hospitals, 144
Fees:
  contingent, 360
  loan, 327-329
Fiedler, Fred, 59n, 61n
Field review, appraisal method, 539
Field stabilization, 667
FIFO supplies valuation method, 127
Final letter, in unionization process, 603
Finances:
  corporate, 131-132
  evaluation, 154
Financial analysis, 161-162
Financial auditing, internal, 227-233
Financial condition, 214
Financial feasibility:
  construction, defined, 365-367
  consultant, 349
  study, 96, 355
Financial information, 214-216
Financial management, 207-344
  budgeting, 235-264
  cost containment, 265-280
  of operations, 214-234
  overview, 207-213
Financial performance, 148
Financial planning, 214-218
  computer models for, 216-218
  revised, 306
Financial reports, 248-250
Financial reserves, 328
Financial statements, budgeted, 247
Financial transactions, 216
Financing:
  organizational sharing, 123
  short and intermediate term, 325-329
  tax exempt, 326. *See also* Capital formation
Finkler, Steven A., 335n
Fire, 669
  emergency operations for, 6
  protection, 676-677
First aid, 677
First responder concept, 667
Fiscal services, 305
  department, 305

FitzGerald, Ardra F., 152n
FitzGerald, John M., 152n
Fixed price contracts, 359
Fleishman, Raymond, 448
Flexibility:
  in computer systems, 387-388
  conditioning, 165
Flexible budgeting, 243-246
  process, *244*
Flexible work schedules, 534
Flexner, William A., 197n, 204n
Flight behavior, 68
Floor loading protection, 676
Floor and wall openings, 677
Flow chart, 47, *336, 644*
Flow diagram, *564*
Flow process chart, *564, 566*
  as control tool, 47
Followership:
  continuum, *29*
  and leadership, 29-32
  profile, *32-33*
Follow up:
  fund raising, 319
  interview, 463
  on planning decisions, 137
Food service, 716
Forced distribution, 538
Ford, Paula J., 267n
Forecast budgeting, 242-243
Forecasting, 7, 154-157
  cash budget, 225, 227
  community needs, 153
  demand, 154-155
  demographic, 146-147
  manpower, 156-157
  periodical, 157
  utilization, 155-156
  work volume, 560
Foreign travel immunization, 534
Forward vertical integration, 149
Foundations, 311-312
Fox, Leonard B., III, 266n
Fragmentation, 6
Frank, C.W., 287n
Fraud, 690-691
Freedom of Information Act, 203
Free-form essays, 539
Freeman, John R., 151n
Free rein leadership, 23
Free-standing birth centers, 166
Free-standing hospitals, 128
Frenzen, Paul D., 600n
Fringe benefits, 448, 552-553, 554
  industry standard, 601
Frisch, Lawrence E., 434n
Fully insured plan, *523*
Fully self-insured plan, 520

Functional planning consultant, 349-350
Functional value analysis (FVA) program, 277-280
 function tree, *278*
 resource allocation worksheet, *279*
 team, *277*
Fund raising, 319
Funds, 96-97
 and evaluation results, 97-98
Funeral leave, 620
FVA. *See* Functional value analysis program

G

Galbreth time-motion studies, 555
Gaming, as time management technique, 94
Gantt chart, 87
 checklist, 89
 as control tool, 47
 as time management technique, 85, 87, *88,* 89
Garber, A. Brent, 72n
Gate keeping, 115
General internists, 166
General model of computer financial planning, 217
Generic screens, 641
Geography, as market analysis variable, 170
Gerber, Ned L., 338n
Gertman, Paul, 629n, 653
Gifts, 308-312
 qualified, 308
 unrestricted, 219
Gilbert, R. Neal, 261n, 321n, 326n
Ginsburg, Sigmund G., 58n
Giving, 308-309
Glossaries, 262-264
 EDP, 401-403
Goals:
 audit, 49
 departmental, 36-38
 department head determining, 35
 development in strategic planning, 148
 and discipline, 501
 of the institution, 5
 MBO long and medium range, 34, *35*
 mutual setting, 545
 pyramid of, 39
 sample annual hospital, *37*

setting interviews, 38
supervisors determining (MBO), 38-39
time schedule, 5
Goal setting:
 interviews, 38
 participative, 580
 in productivity trend management system, 580
Goldsmith, Seth B., 95n, 459n, 476n
Golightly, Cecelia K., 73n, 78n
Gonella, Joseph, 655n
Good-will bank, 70
Gossip, 6, 499
Gotcher, J. William, 331n
Governing board, 3-4
 confrontations with medical staff, 25
 executive power brokering with, 24
Government, as consumer, 182-183, 188
Government agencies, medical records disclosure to, 711
Government hospital, 3
Government National Mortgage Association (GNMA), 320, *323*
Graham, Nancy O., 627n, 631n, 634n, 635n, 637n, 638n, 642n, 645n
Greenville Hospital System, 130
Greiner, L.E., 74n
Grey, Paul, 377n, 381n
Grievances, 504-507, 607, 615-616
 minimizing, 504-505
 model procedure, 506-507
 systems, 437
Griffith, John R., 269n
Gross revenues, 219
Group:
 appraisal, 539
 decision making, 74
 dynamics, 16
 problem solving, 74
Group auto and homeowner's insurance, 534
Group incentive program, 591
Groups:
 blocking roles in, 114
 building roles, 114-115
 maintenance roles, 114-115
Group term life insurance, 526
Groupthink, 111-114
Growth:
 planning strategies for, 158-178
 through acquisition, 144
Grubb, Reba Douglass, 51n
Guidebook for Union Organizers (AFL-CIO), 593

Gunshot wounds, medical information release and, 4, 711

H

Haley, Michael J., 307
Handbills, 596
Hansen, R.C., 45n
Hard copy, computer, 401
Hardware:
 purchases, 383-385
 selecting, 386-387
Hardy, Owen B., 347n, 350n, 364n, 366n
Harms, Lisa M., 705n
Harrison, Denise C., 667n
Hawk, Donald L., 487n
Hawthorne, James D., 524-526, 524n
HBV, 6
Health accounting, 638
Health appraisal examinations, 674
Health benefit plans, 531
Health care:
 demand for, 160
 leadership, 21-33
 productivity, 552-591
 reimbursement, 4
 team, 720-721
 trends, 78
 utilization, 153-154
Health care assessment, *639*
Health care consulting firm, 95
Health care facilities, conversion, 174-178
Health Care Financing Administration (HCFA), 292, 294, 628-629
Health Care Index, 225
Health care institutions:
 planning overview, 137-143
 structure and change, 116-123
 studies, 96
Health care marketing, 179-205
 issues, *181*
 reasons for interest in, *180-181*
Health and Education Facilities Authority (CN), 326
Health insurance, 534
 benefits, 518
Health maintenance organizations (HMOs), 182
 and cost containment, 270
Health planning, 318. *See also* Planning
Health Planning and Resources Development Act of 1974 (PL 93-641), 132, 133, 317, 318

Health professionals, *171.* See also
  Administrators; Chief executive
  officer (CEO); Chief financial
  officer (CFO); Employees; Medical
  staff
Health regulation, 318. See also
  Regulation; Regulatory agency;
  Regulatory mapping
Health Systems Agency (HSA), 132
  and conversion, 176, 178
Health systems engineers, 151-152
Hearings, budget, 239
Hearsay, 6
Hechler, Thomas M., 345n, 367n
Heidrick & Struggles, Inc. (Chicago), 20
Helner, Olaf, 40
Hemodialysis units, 6, 174
Hennepin County Medical Center, 118
Henze, Howard M., 667n
Hepatitis B virus, 6
Herber, William E., 339n
Herkimer, Allen G., Jr., 220n, 222n, 300n, 301n
Herman, Albert W., 308n
Heron, John R., 499n
Herzberg, Frederick, 483
Herzberg's theory, 483
Hierarchy, 101
  pyramidal, *102*
Hill-Burton free care provisions, 219
Hodge, Melvin H., 387n, 404n, 407n, 414n
Holding company model, 130
Holidays, 619
  paid, 531
Holland, Joan, 156n, 486n
Home:
  call, organizing, 596
  stress at, 69
Horizontal condominium, 125
Horizontal diversification, 161
Horizontal integration, 150
Hospital:
  administrators, 130-131
  chains, 125-128
  charitable, 3
  committees, 109-115
  financial studies, 96
  goals, 37
  government, 3
  history, 54
  long range plan-model outline, 152-154
  nonprofit, 162
  proprietary, 3
  systems, 116-134. See also

Hospitals
Hospital administration professional
  organizations, 20
Hospital administrators, 3-20, 130-131
  authority and liability, 725-726
  duties under Conditions of Participation, 4
  educational needs, 16
  job changing by, 19-20
  managing by, 6-11
  planning role, 137
  and quality assurance, 628
  strength and weakness assessment, 20
  training, 119. See also
    Administrators
Hospital committees, 109-115
  types, 111-114
Hospital Employees Labor Program (HELP), 506-507
Hospital evaluation, 96-98. See also
  Evaluation
Hospital information systems (HIS), 305-306, 404-425
  acceptance, 417
  benefits, 404-405
  contracts, 417-418
  costs checklist, *419*
  critical issues, 407-412
  delivery, 417
  departmental vs hospitalwide, 407-408
  diagram, *408-409*
  do-it-yourself vs developed, 411
  establishing, 420-425
  in-house, 411
  integrated, 405-406
  maintenance, 418
  planning, 412-420
  sophistication, 408-410
  systems steering committee, 413
Hospital insurance program (HIP), 282
Hospital liability, 680-691
  for malpractice suits, 718
Hospital licensure, 715, 716
Hospital managers, 515-517. See
  also Administrators; Hospital administrators; Management; Managers
Hospital manual:
  committee, guidelines, 53-54
  content, 54
  control by, 51-57
  coordinator for, 53
  developing, 52-53
  distribution lists, 55-56

uses for, 52
Hospital mission statement, 5
  and objectives, 140-141
  questions to determine, 139-140
  in strategic planning, 145, 148. See
    also Mission statement
Hospitals:
  charges, 300-302
  checklist of potential liability, 688-689
  computer use, 377-403. See also
    Computers; Hospital
    information systems (HIS)
  condominium, 118
  consortia, 117-118
  economic myths, 209, 211-213
  expenditure increases, 267-269
  failure rate, low, 315
  feeder, 144
  financially troubled, 233-234
  financial requirements of, *296-297*
  high liability risks by, 682-689
  information needs, 420
  as labor-intensive industry, 381
  and law, 679-727
  management, and PMS, 432
  in multihospital systems, *134*
  multiunit organizations, 118-119
  occupancy rates, 315
  occupational health and safety in, 672-677
  positions, 511-512
  premises, physical condition, 684
  private, employee benefits, *532-533*
  profitability for, 218-219
  rate setting, 281, 295-307
  reports, sample, *575*
  software applications, *379, 380*
  use of computers, 376-383
  wage incentive plans, 590-591
  word processing use, 434-435. See
    also Hospital
Hospital safety committee, 5
Hospital surveys, 96-97
Hospital systems, 116-134
  antitrust complaints, 132-133
  assets, 119-120
  cooperative attempts, 133
  governance and management structure, 119-120
  integration, 116-119
Hours, 618-619
  flexible, and word processing, 434
  studied, 594
Housekeeping department, 675
  position evaluations, 516
Human resources, 5

development, 437
engineering, 437-438
management, 437-441
utilization, 437
Human resources management, 437-441
Humor, 16
Hunsaker, C., 412n
Hydrotherapy, 165

I

Identification, 59
I-factor test, 58-59
Illinois Masonic Medical Center (Chicago), 271
Illness, personal, 5-6
Illumination, and problem solving, 76
Immunizations, 5, 674
Impasse resolution procedures, 608-610
Implementation:
 as administrator evaluation role, 51
 of discipline, 502
 of hospital manuals, 56
 of in-depth studies, 578
 as manager skill, 59
 MBO, 35-39
 of modeling in time management, 93
 in strategic planning, 154
Incentives:
 in construction projects, 360
 employee, 589-591
 flexibility, 554
 plan, deferred, 591
 program, insurance, 188
 systems, 434
Incident reports, 640, 689
Income:
 as demographic data, 199
 loss benefits, 534
 personal, rising, 269
 target population, 170
Incubation, problem solving, 13-14, 76
In-depth studies, 575, 578
Index data, 642
Indirect costs, 222
Individual entrepreneur, as consultant, 95
Induction training, 5
Industrial accidents, reporting, 689, 711
Industrial engineering, 437

Industrial engineers, 151
Industrial health, 166
Industry model, of computer financial planning, 217
Infection committee, 111
Infections, 669-672, 684-685
 monitoring responsibility, 670-672
 records for, 669-672
Inflation, 339, 552
Information:
 centralization, 689
 controlling, 24
 controlling and power brokering, 23
 financial, 214-216
 flow, 576-577
 in-depth study, 576
 management, 48-49
 needs interview form, *421*
 transfer, 7-9
 withholding, 24
Information systems, 5
 computerized, patient management, 426-433
 hospital, 404-425
 total, 433
Informed consent, 692-702
Inhouse computer systems, 385, 399-401
Initiation, 50-51
Initiative, 544
 employee, 589-591
Injury, 674, 685
Innovation, 59
 method of problem solving, 72
Inpatient care unit, computerized, 428-429
Inpatient services, acute/nonacute, 150
Input quality, 552
In-service training, 449, 552
 MBO method, 37
Installation, data processing, 399
Institutional profiles, 638, 646
Institutional review boards, 693-694
Insurance:
 coverage, 199
 HIS, 418
 hospitals providing adequate, 725
Insurance benefit plans, 531. *See also* Benefit; Employee benefits
Integration, 149-150
 geographic, 150
 horizontal, 150
 of hospital systems, 116-119
 vertical, 149
Integrity, 59
Intelligence, 58

network, 185
Intensity, 59
Intensive care, 174
Interest arbitration, 610
Interest rates, 327
Interfacing, between computer systems, 393, 395
Interiors planning, 358
Intermediate term financing, 326
Intermountain Health Care, Inc., 130, 333-335
Internal analyses, 148
Internal auditing, 47-49
Internal auditors, 47-49
Internal financial auditing, 227-233
Internal rate of return, 333
Internal review, construction, 348
Interpersonal relations, 59
 and managerial role, 7-9
Interviewing techniques, 460-463
Interviews, 460, 462-463
 appraisal, 545-551
 exit, 497
 job, 20
 psychological barriers, 460-461
Intravenous pyelogram (IVP), 695
Invasion of privacy, 691, 707-708
Investment:
 cost savings, 329, *330*
 income, 219
 strategy, 143-144
 yields, maximizing, 219
Issue analysis, 148

J

Jackson, Louis, 593n
Jackson Memorial Hospital (Miami), 270
Jantz, Alfred H., 589n
Jargon, 40
Jobs:
 actions, 597, 600
 changes, 19-20, 514
 descriptions, 514-515
 design, 489
 emphasis, and delegation
 enlargement, 554
 enrichment, 483-486
 evaluation, 514-515
 expectations, 489
 fit, 489
 graded, *511-512*
 growth, subordinate, 82
 hopper, 20
 improvement plan, 563-565
 interview, 20

knowledge, *537,* 544
posting, 621
re-evaluated, 514
security, 488, 601
titles, 106, 108. *See also*
    Employees; Positions
Johannides, David F., 151n
Johnson, Everett A., 16n
Johnson, Glenn H., 434n
Johnson, Richard L., 16n, 23n, 209n
Joint Commission on Accreditation of Hospitals (JCAH), 36, 51, 627, 649, 692
Joint conference committee, 111
Joint management model, of contract management, 125
Joint overhead costs, 337-338
Jones, Kenneth M., 143n
Journal of Civil Defense, 666
Judgment, 24
Jury duty, 621

K

Kaiser-Permanente Medical Center (Northern California), 642
Kaiser-Permanente Medical Group, 541
Katzel, Mildred E., 554n
Kellogg, Meg A., 642n
Kelly, Thomas F., 552n
Kessler, Theodore W., 82n
Key punch machine, 401
Key results areas:
    departmental, 38
    MBO, 36
Key tape machine, 401
Kirby, Peter G., 76n, 77n
Kirk, R.J., 112n
Knapp, Rebecca Grant, 40n, 649n
Koontz, Harold, 442n
Korngold, Aaron, 72n
Krasny, Jacques, 276n
Kuhn, Joan, 655n

L

Labor:
    analysis, in cost management, 586
    costs, 216, 495
    division of, 7-8, 338
    market, 488
    practices, unfair, 601-602
    productivity, 553
    relations, 437. *See also* Unions
    turnover, control form, *496. See also* Turnover
    use, 216
Laboratory:
    licensure and permits, 716
    services, 552
    tests, personnel, 5
Labor relations, 437
    director, 608. *See also* Unions
Labor unions, 592-623
    as consumers, 182
Laissez-faire leadership, 23
Lammers, Lawrence P., 347n, 350n, 364n, 366n
Lang, Gerald S., 258n
Lateral transfers, 514
Laundry, 552
    machinery and operations, 677
Law:
    and hospitals, 679-727
    and medical records, 703-714
    and trustees and administrators, 723-727
Law enforcement agencies, 693, 711-712
Law office partnership model (contract management), 125
Lawrence, J.F., 412
Layout (building), 576
Leader decision-making authority, 21
    continuum, *22*
Leaders, 8
    subordinate, 59-60
Leadership, 21-33, *63-64*
    autocratic, 21-22
    committee, 110
    communication, 442
    consultive, 22
    continuum, *29*
    democratic, 22-23
    and direction, 9
    emphasis, 25-27
    employee-centered, 21
    and followership, 29-33
    knowledge, 27
    laissez-faire, 23
    manager style of, 9
    participative, 22
    questionnaire, 25-29
    styles of, 21-23
    in successful strategic planning, 150
    tests, 25-29
    training, 60
    work-centered, 21
Leadership profile, 28
    structural, *30-31*
Leasing:
    equipment, 338-344
    evaluation, 339
    and reimbursement, 342-344
Legal services, 534
Lemer, Robert S., 295n, 298n, 301n
Lenane, Brian P., 365n, 366n
Length of stay (LOS), 646
Letters, to employees, 448
Levenstein, Aaron, 72
Levinson, Harry, 60n
Levitan, Mark S., 365n, 366n
Lewis, C.E., 653n
Liability:
    current, 225
    high risk, hospital, 682-689
    hospital, 680-691
Licensing:
    boards, 718-721
    inspection, 96
    revocation or suspension, 722
Licensure, 715-722
    health professional requiring, *719*
    personnel, 717
    requirements and exceptions, 715
    suspension or revocation, 721
Liebler, Joan Gratto, 46n, 101n
Life cycle costing, 374
Life insurance, 518, 534
Line authority, 103
Line manager, 138
Line-staff relationships, *104-105*
Linking process, 140-141
Liquidation, 175
Listeners, 450-452
Listening, 449-453
    skills, 452-453
Litigation, 726-727
    preparation, 689
Living will, 697, 699
Loans, 320, 327. *See also* Debt financing
Lobbying, 150
Location independence, 405
Lock box service, 227
Lockouts, 607, 615
Long, Dane M., 145n
Longest, B., 21n
Longevity vs merit, 512-514
Longnecker, Carl G., Jr., 426n
Long range (MBO) goals, 34, *35*
Long range plans, model outline, 152-154
Long term debts, 321-324
Long term disability, 528
Lusk, Edward J., 224n, 319n, 320n
Lusk, Janice Gannon, 224n, 319n, 320n

M

MacDonald, Dan, 188n
Mackenzie, R. Alec, 82n, 87n, 111n
MacStravic, Robin E. Scott, 154n, 155n, 162n, 166n, 167n, 168n, 179n, 195n, 198n
Mail, 6
Main frame computer, 389-395
Major medical insurance plans, 529-530
Malfeasance, 681
Malloy, James W., 294n
Malpractice, 681
Management, 9-11
 appraisal, *62*
 bad, 9-11
 by objectives, 482
 cash, 223-227
 centralization, and expansion, 150
 and CHI systems, 573
 communications, 602. *See also* Communications
 construction funds, 363-364
 construction project, 361-364
 contract, 123-125
 control, 46-56
 cost, 586
 and cost containment, 271-272
 decisions, information for, *215*
 development, 10
 financial, 207-212
 functions, 9, 10
 general functions of, 7-9, 96
 human resources, 437-441
 improved, 160, 432
 information, 48-49
 ladder, 9
 MBO training for, 34
 and motivation, 477-482
 multiunit organizations, 119
 newsletters, 445
 new theory of, 482-483
 organizational sharing, 122
 participatory, 22, 34-35
 patient, 426-433
 performance appraisal, *66*
 periodic meetings, 445
 position changes by, 19-20
 promotions to, 58-59
 review, 574
 rights, 606, 615
 salaries, 517
 skills, 14-16
 span, 102-103
 and strategic planning, 145-146
 strategies to oppose unions, 600-608

 stress, 16-19
 of subordinates, 58-70
 task, 480
 time, 79-94
 tools, 34, 271
 training, 10, 534
 and type of work, 102
 upgraded, 552. *See also* Administrators; Hospital administrators; Misadministration
Management by objective (MBO) program, 34-40, 482
 and behaviorally anchored rating scales, 540
 as control tool, *47*
 employee appraisal, 540
 summary, *41*
Management consulting firms, 458
Management control, 46-56
 internal auditing, 47-49
 phases, 207-208
 program evaluation, 49-50
Management corporations, 127-128, *129*
Management engineers, 151, 555
Management information systems (MIS), 404-425
Managers, 6-11, 95-98
 abrasive, 60-61, 67
 accessibility, 85
 authority, 101-108
 burned-out, 69-70
 neurotic, 60, 67, 67-68
 overmotivated, 12
 preferred, *32-33*
 problem, 60-61, 67-70
 quitting of, 70
 roles, 7-9
 salaries, 515-517
 style of leadership, 9. *See also* Leadership
 traits for successful, 58-59
 transparency, 551
 work, 6-7
Manpower:
 evaluation, 154
 forecasting, 156-157
 planning, 438
 productivity, 573
Manuals, 51-57
 budget, 236
 departmental, 432
 model personnel policy, *446-447*
 personnel policy, 445
 super disaster, 668
Mapping, 147
Margin of safety, 261, 301

Margolis, Jan, 437n
Maria C. Phaneuf nursing audit procedure, 650
Market:
 "basket," 267
 changing, 155
 defined, 146
 efficiency, 270
 negative, 169
 primary medical care, 167-171
Market analysis, 365-366
Marketing, 179-205
 activities, hospital, *190*
 and case-based incentives, 306-307
 consultants, 189-190
 elements, 179
 organizing for, 188-204
 and research, 183-184
 in strategic planning, 145
 targets, 186-188
 team, in house, 190
Marketing audit, 195-201
 elements, *196-197*
 market segments in, 195, 197, 199-201
 procedure, *198*
 results, 201
Marketing information, 190-191, *192*
 general, *192-193*
Market profile, 183-184
Market research, 183-184, 190, 193-195
 consultants, 194-195
 questions, 193-194
Market segments, 195, 197, 199-201
Market survey, 194. *See also* Surveys
Martin, Morgan D., 96n
Maryland Health Care System (Baltimore), 130
Mass meetings, 596-597
Master budget, 239-240
Master construction site, 355
Master organization chart, 106-108
Master plan:
 construction, 345-347, 354
 timing, *346*
Material management studies, 577
Materials handling and storage, 576, 577-578, 677
Maternal Child and Health Programs, 646
Maternity benefit plan, 531
Maxicomputers, 411-412
McCloskey, Joanne, 497n
McConnell, Charles R., 80, 80n, 460n, 466n, 468n, 474n, 491n, 536n
McDonnell Douglas Automation

Company (St. Louis), 411
McDowell, Constance E., 405
McGregor, Douglas M., 477n
McIver, Brian, A., 45n
McKinsey & Company, 657
McLaughlin, Curtis R., 45n
McNeil, Melissa Craig, 125n
Meals, free, 531
Meares, Larry B., 9n
MEDCO programs, 580-586
Medex, 534
Mediation, 51, 608-609
Medicaid, 4, 281-282, 646
  as capital formation source, 316
  coverage under AFDC, 281, *284-285*
  eligibility, *283*
  services, *286-287*
Medical audit, 638, 643-655
  hospital use, 655
  process, 653-654
Medical benefits, 528-530
  cost containment, 520
Medical care reimbursement programs, 518. *See also* Medicaid; Medicare; Reimbursement
Medical command post (MCP), 666
Medical director, 103
Medical experimentation and research, 693-694
Medical information systems (MIS), 377, 404-425
  department, 405-407
  departments served by, *410*
  executive, 405-407
  total benefits, 419-420
  total costs, 418-419
  user-staff interaction, 422-425
  and work standard development, 556
Medical records, 305, 306
  access to information, 705-714
  committee, 111
  computerized, 429, 714
  corrections and alterations, 704-705
  department, 516
  disclosures, 705, 709
  entries, 703-705
  as evidence, 713
  improper disclosure, 705
  maintaining, 703-705
  patient access to, 709
  patient disclosure consent form, *706-707*
  retention requirements, 703
  security precautions, 709
  state statutes and regulations, 711

statutory reporting, 710
Medical research, *693-694*, 709-710
Medical schools, 139
Medical services, sharing, 122
Medical staff:
  and administrator, 3-4
  CEO relationship with, 18
  committees, 111
  corporate, 120
  and dual pyramid organizations, 103
  graduate, and hospital liability, 687
  hospital liability for, 686-687
  and hospital mission, 139
  in hospital systems, 131
  marketing workshops and discussions, 187
  MBO training for, 34
  in multiunit organizations, 120
  organizational sharing, 122
  power brokering with, 24-25
  president, 103-104
  prospective case-based payment and, 305
  quality assurance and, 628. *See also* Physicians Medical trainees
Medicare, 4, 646
  benefits, 518
  as capital formation source, 316
  cost finding and, 220
  cost report information, *289*
  cost report planning, 288-289
  hospital insurance, 282-292
  hospital manual requirement, 51
  law, 655
  limit on operating cost reimbursement, 134
  maximizing reimbursement from 287-292
  periodic interim payments (PIP), 224
  and prospective rate setting, 304
  reimbursement in hospital systems, 133-134, 655
  step down cost finding, 222
MEDICUS Corporation nurses audit, 651
Medium range (MBO) goals, 34, *35*
Meetings, 4, 6, 24, 87, 445
Melesko, Stephen, 554n, 556n
Memel, Sherwin L., 292n, 294n
Memorial Employees Retirement Incentives Trust (MERIT), 591
Memorial Hospital (Long Beach, Cal.), 591
Memory, 13
Mentally ill patient, 139, 684

Mental retardation, 174
Mergers, 118, 150
Merit pay, 601
Merit rating, *65*
Message centers, 434
Message strategies, 204
Methods improvement, 576, 577
Metropolitan Medical Center (Minneapolis), 118
Metzger, Norman, 25n, 82n, 438n, 443n, 449n, 452n, 477n, 504n, 541n, 605n
Michnich, Marie E., 49n
Microcomputers, 411-412
Miller, M. Clinton, III, 40n, 649n
Minicomputers, 391, 411-412
Minimum premium plan, 520
Minors, 709
Mintz, Howard, 266n
Mintzberg, Henry, 7n
Misadministration, 710-711
Misfeasance, 681
Mission, statement, 78, 153
  development in strategic planning, 148
  and institutional role, 153
  linking objectives to, *141*, 140-141
  proposals for, 5
  questions to determine, 139-140
  strategic planning and, 145
Mobility, 488
Modeling:
  in time management, 93
Modernization projects, 137-138
Money, William H., 123n
Monitoring, 8
  productivity, 569, 571
  and quality care, 641-642
  by word processing, 434
Montana Deaconess Hospital (Great Falls, Montana), 591
Moody's Bond Survey, 330
Mooney, Dr. Ross L., 14
Morale, 19, 501
Mortality rates, 646
Mortgage loans, 320, *323, 324*
Motivation, 9, 12, 81, 82, 475-483, 486
Motivation Feedback Questionnaire, *477, 478-479*
Motivation to Work (Herzberg), 483
Mount Sinai Hospital (New York), 130
Mulcahy, Robert W., 600n
Multihospital systems, 128-134
  investor-owned, 162
  marketing, 188
  mergers and acquisitions, 162

Index 743

progressive nonprofit, 162
variations, 128, 130. *See also*
  Multiunit organizations
Multiple regression, 156
Multiunit organizations:
  developmental stages, 120-121
  management, 119
  operational characteristics, 120.
    See also Multihospital systems
Multivariate quantitative techniques, 156
Municipal ordinances, 4
Munn, Harry E., Jr., 25n, 438n, 452n, 477n
Murphy, Gretchen, F., 242n, 664n
Mutual goal setting, 545

N

Nadauld, Stephen D., 333n
National consulting firms, 95, 96
National Electrical Code, 667
National health insurance, 534
National Health Planning Resources and Development Act. *See* Health Planning Resources and Development Act of 1974 (PL 93-641)
National Housing Act, 318
National Labor Relations Board (NLRB), 593, 595, 596, 597, 600, 602, 603
National productivity, 586
Natural death acts, 697
Needs:
  and absenteeism, 488
  for committees, 109
  consumer, 147
  determining employee, 518-520
  and marketing, *180*
  and motivation, 480-481
  survey, construction, 351
Needs analysis tool, 36
Negligence, 681-682, 686
Negotiation, 7, *8,* 613
Nehrbass, Richard G., 460n
Nelson, William H., 333n
Net present value, 333
Neurotic managers, 67-68
Newman, W.H., 76n
Newport, M. Gene, 7, 7n, 10n, 505n
Newsletters, 445
News media, 708-709
Noise exposure, 677
Nonfeasance, 681
Nonprice competition, 149
Non-revenue departments, 586

Nonsalary worksheet, 238-239
Nosocomial infections, 669, *672, 673*
Note issue, 326
Notice of Program Reimbursement (NPR), 292
Nuclear medicine manual, 56
Nuclear Regulatory Commission, 710
Nurse practitioners, 717-718
Nurses:
  as anesthetists, 718
  hospital liability for, 687
  as midwives, 718
  negligence, 688
  private duty, 4
  professional organization, 458
  uniform perquisites, 531
Nursing:
  audit approach to quality assurance, 649-651
  HIS benefit realization, 415-417
  position evaluations, 516
  service manual, 56
Nutrition, 165

O

Objectives:
  audit, 49
  communication, 443-444
  development in strategic planning, 148
  and hospital mission, 140, *141*
  oriented appraisal methods, 540
  responsibility chart, *142*
  yearly cycle for, 142-143
Objectives system. *See* Management by Objectives (MBO); MBO Method
Observational tours, 6
Obsolescence, 338
Obstetrics, 144
Occupational disease, 166
Occupational health and safety, 672-677
Occupational licenses, 716
O'Donnell, Cyril, 442
O'Donovan, T., 21n
Ofer, Aharon R., 329n
Off-line, 401
Old age benefits, 534
Oltvedt, Gregory T., 172n
One-institution person, 20
On-line, 377, 401
On-the-job training:
  as turnover cost, 492
Open audit systems, 650
Opening letter, 602-603

Openness, 11
Operating budget, 246
Operating cost factor (construction), 371, 374
Operating division model (contract management), 124-125
Operating expenses, 219, *298*
  in multihospital systems, 134
Operating lease, 342, 344
Operating margin and requirements (AHA), *296*
Operating revenues, 218-219
Operating room, 559-560
Operating system (computer) programs, 401
Operational decisions, 76-77
  for construction, 364-365
Operations, 214-234
  evaluation, 154
Operations analysis, 151
Opportunity costs, 6, 258-259
Optimism, 16
Optimization model, 93
Options, strategic, 148
Oral warning, 503
Order, 12
Organization, 99-134
  audited, 48
  charts, 106-108, *564*
  of committees, 109-110
  development, 437-438
  dual pyramid, 103, 106
  flexible formats, 173-174
  hospital systems, 116-134
  in-depth study, 575
  inter-institutional 120-121
  as market segment, 197
  primer, 101-108
  section 501(c)(3), 133
  section 501(e), 133
  structure and manpower forecasting, 156
  as supervisor trait, *64*
  using committees in, 109-115. *See also* Hospital; Hospitals
Organizational development, 437-438
Organization chart, 106-108, *564*
Organizing, 7-8, 10. *See also* Unions
Orientation, 437, 463-465
  departmental, 464
  and discipline, 502
  hospital, 464-465
  program, 465
Originality, 11
OSHA Standards, 675-677
Outcomes, 629, 637
Outline specifications (construction), 356

Outpatient clinic, *249*
Outpatient surgery, 163-164
Output, 14
Outreach programs, 172
Outsiders, managing, 95-98
Outside services, 272-273
Overbudgeting, 239
Overdelegation, 80
Overlapping institutional board membership model, 130
Overmotivation, 12
Overstaffing, 570
Overstress, 18
Overtime, 11
Overview study, 573-574

P

Pacenka, Joseph O., 276n
Paging system, 579
Pamphlets, employee, 448
Panoramic method (problem solving), 72
Paperwork, *86, 375*
Paraphrasing, 453
Parasupporting, 453
Participation management, 34-45, 482-483
Participative leadership, 22
Participatory management, 34-45, 482-483
  Delphi technique as, 40-45
  MBO method as, 34-40
Part-time personnel, 587
  problems, 588
Pascal, A. Michael, 669n
Passageways, 675
Passivity, 551
Password protection, 427
Pathology, 429-430
Patient. *See* Patients
Patient care, 4, 5, 139, 296.
  PMS improved, 431-432
  in strikes, 622
  trustees' responsibilities and liabilities for, 723-725. *See also* Patients
Patient management system (PMS), 426-433. *See also* Patients
Patients:
  accounts, uncollectable, 231-232
  and administrator, 3-4
  billing, 232
  care. *See* Patient care
  computerized management, 426-433
  condition, and reimbursement policies, 295
  consent to disclose records, 705, *706-707*
  as consumers, 182
  demographic factors, 199
  discharge, against medical advice, *701*
  hospital preferences, 205
  long-term, 139
  management, 426-433
  as marketing targets, 186-187
  as market segment, 197
  medical records, computerized, 429
  movement, 576, 577
  negligent monitoring, 683
  negligent supervision, 683
  and physician relationship, changing, *180*
  profiles, 638, 645
  questionnaires, 641
  refusal of treatment, *698, 700*
  rights and responsibilities, 692
  satisfaction, 159
  services, 5
  treatment refusal and physician's disregard, 698, 700-701
  volume, and troubled hospitals, 233. *See also* Patient care; Patient management systems
Payback period, 332
Payroll, 230-231, 437
Pension vesting, 10
Percentage fee contracts, 359-360
Perfectionism, 60
Performance, 14-16
  appraisal, management, *66*
  employee, 437, 467-468, 536-551, 554
  managerial, 14-16
  measurement, 9
  report, 587
  reporting, by HIS, 416
  review checklist, *67*
  reward systems, 579
  subordinate personnel, 9
Periodic interim payments (PIP), 224
Perlin, Martin S., 137n, 140n, 152n
Permits, 715-722
Perquisites, 531
Personality, 545
Personal relationships, 545
Personnel:
  assessing, 60-67
  development plans, *65*
  dress code, 6
  handbook, 55
  HIS, training, 418
  hospital, and administrator, 3-4
  hospital, follow-up training, 5
  hospital, induction training, 5
  illness, 5-6
  licensure, 717
  manual, 56, 445
  physical examinations for, 5
  policies, developing, 455-457
  policy advisory committee, 445
  productivity report, *558*
  programs, 278
  protective equipment for, 677
  recruiting and retaining, 140
  requirements worksheet, 239. *See also* Administrators, Employees, Hospital administrators, Medical staff
Personnel handbook, 55
Personnel manual, 56, 445
Persuasion, 23
PERT network, 47. *See also* Program evaluation review technique (PERT)
Peters, Joseph P., 139n
Petersen, Donald J., 506n, 608n, 610n
Pfeffer-Kloss, Linda L., 630n, 632n, 640n
Pharmacy, 426, 430-431, 579, 716
Philanthropy, 178, 219, 308-312, 435
Phobia clinics, 165
Physical examinations, 5, 166, 674
Physical facilities, 102, 122, 154, 216, 715
Physical therapy, 165, 274, 431
Physicians, 16-17
  admitting patterns, 148
  assistants, 717
  autocratic leadership, 21-22
  competent, 724
  computer use, 410
  as consumers, 182
  control of CIVs, *268*
  cost containment and, 270-271
  disregard of patients' refusal of care, 698, 700-701
  employed, hospital liability for, 687
  fees, reimbursement for, 295
  habits, and census increase, 159
  and limited health care practitioners, 717-718
  as marketing targets, 187
  as market segment, 199
  motivating, 476
  needs, 187
  non-staff, 139
  operating, profiles, *646*

and patient relationship, changing, *180*
  power brokering with, 24-25
  profiles, 638, 645-646, *647*
  referring, preferences of, 159
  sponsoring recruitment, 158
  verbal orders, 704. *See also* Medical staff
Physiological needs, 480
PL 93-641, 132, 133, 317, 318
Place:
  defined, 200
  as marketing element, 179
Placement, 60
Planning, 135-205
  approaches, 137-138
  capital expenditure, 333-335
  committees, 138-139, *140,* 150
  construction, 347-358
  construction director, 348
  disaster, 667-668
  executive and staff, 138
  financial, 214-218
  health, 318
  hospital information system, 412-420
  and hospital mission, 139-140
  internal audit checklist, 261, 264
  lack, as time waster, 86
  as management function, 7
  marketing and, 179-205
  master site for construction, 355
  organizing for, 137-157
  participants, 153
  as political exercise, 145
  process, 150, 153
  proportion of management effort to, *10*
  strategies for growth, 158-178
  team, 349-358
  work, 82-83
Planning team, construction, 349-358
Plant, 102, 122, 154, 216, 715
Podiatrists, 717
Poison, 711
Police, 693, 711-712
Political arbitration, 121
Pooled income fund, 310
Population, service, 156, 167, 169-171
Position control system, 239
Positions:
  descriptions, 10, 516
  elimination, and cost containment, 271
  evaluation, 516-517
  hospital, by grade, 511-512. *See also* Employees; Job

Positive control, 46
Potentially compensable events (PCEs), 641
Power, 74-75, 260-261
Power broker, 23-25
Pozgar, George D., 681n, 723n, 727n
Practice of Management, The (Drucker), 36
Practitioners:
  dependent, 717-718
  dependent, credentials for, 717
  independent, 717
  limited health care, credentials for, 717
  profiles, 645-646
Praise, 601
Predictability, 12
Preferences:
  of employees for managers, *32-33*
President, 138
Prevention:
  diagnostic services, 188
  disease, *180*
Price:
  defined, 200
  as marketing element, 179
  of primary care satellite services, 171-172
  variances, 251, 252. *See also* Prices; Pricing
Prices:
  decisions on, 126
  fixed, in construction, 359
  input, reductions, 269
  market basket, 267
  reduction, and cost containment, 265-266
  variable, in construction, 359. *See also* Price; Pricing
Pricing, 144, 184
Priest, Stephen L., 406n, 420n
Primary care, 166-172
Primary care satellite, 168-172
  checklist, 168-169
  market analysis, 169-171
  need and demand for, 171
  service design, 171
  site, 172
Processing, 401
Product, 179, 200
Production, 9, 269-270
Productivity, 544, 552-591
  actual, 574
  analysis, 157
  assessment, 569-571
  checklist for increasing, 553-554
  controls, 579
  data, and work standards

development, 555
  improvement process, *570*
  improvement programs, 567, 569-586
  indexes, 553
  management systems, *583*
  measurement, 571
  monitoring, 569, *570, 571,* 572, *579-580*
  overview, 552-554
  and quality control, 578-579
  reporting, 574, *577, 578*
  trends, 552-553
Productivity trend-management system, *580-586*
Professional Activity Study—Medical Audit Programs (PAS-MAP), 649
Professionalism, *180,* 476-477
Professional Standards Review Organization (PSRO), 627
  reviews, 628
  utilization review, 711
Profile analysis, 638, 645-649
  process, 646, 648-649
Program budgeting, 240
Program delivery trends, 147-148
Program evaluation, 49-51, 89-92
Program Evaluation and Review Technique (PERT), activity chart, *91*
Program Evaluation Review Technique (PERT), 89-92
Programming, 207
Progress reports, 142-143
Project descriptions (construction), 360
Projections, 147
Promotions, 68, 179, 514, 550, 601, 618
  to management, 58-59
  procedure, 10
Proprietary health care services, 3, *180*
Prospective case-based payment, 305-307
Prospective rate-setting (PRS), 303-307
Provider Reimbursement Review Board (PRRB), 292-294
Prussin, Jeffrey A., 295n
Psychiatric services, 165, 174
Psychographic information, 200
Psychologists, 295, 717
Public accounting firms, 95, 96
Public relations, 120, 204-205
Public taxable bonds, 320-321, 324
Purchasing, 552

and cost containment, 274-275
delay, 269
plan-ahead, 275
Pursuit of happiness benefits, 534
Pyramidal hierarchy, 101, *102*

Q

Quadrangle Hospitals (Detroit), 130
Qualified consent, 701-702
Quality:
  assessment techniques, 629, 637-638
  assurance. See Quality assurance of care. See Quality of care
  control, 272, 578-579
  employee performance, 544
  services, 159
  and value analysis, 275-276
Quality assurance, 305, 627-663
  board, 633
  defined, 629
  department, 633
  director/coordinator, 630-631
  issues, 635-637
  program, 630, 637
  and PSRO utilization review, 711
  staffing, 631
  terms and definitions, 629-630
Quality of care, 24
  criteria, 638-640
  data collection for, 640
  organizational sharing, 122
Quality control, 272, 578-579
Quality coordinating council, 631, 633-634
Quality patient care scale (QualPaCS), 651
Quarterly publications, 448
Questionnaires, 25-29, 40, 42-44
Quitting, 19-20, 550

R

Rabinow, Jean, 653n
Rader, Dennis W., 600n
Radiation, 677
Radioactive materials, 710-711
Radiology, 716
Railhall, Denis T., 331
Rakich, J., 21n
Rand Corporation, 40
Ranking system:
  employee appraisal, 537-538
Rape, 25, 711
Rapid field triage, 666-667

Rappaport, Anna M., 518n, 526n, 528n
Rate setting, 281-307
  diagnosis related group (DRG), 307
  mechanics, 295-299
  methods, 300-302
  prospective, 303-307
  rooms, *301*
  state systems, 302-303
  time rate method of, *300*
  variance, 251-252
Rating scales (employee), 536-537
Raudsepp, Eugene, 11n
Real time processing, 377, 401
Receivables, 216
Recognition, 57, 89-91
  PERT chart in, 89-91
Record analysis, *661*
Recordkeeping, 14
Recruitment, 437, 458-460
  interviewing techniques, 460-463
  as turnover cost, 492
Redemption privileges, 328
Reductions, 265, 269
Reed, Keith A., 506n, 608n, 610n
Referring agencies, 199
Refunding, 321-323
Regional multiunit health care organization, 117
Regulation:
  of computer systems, 387, 398
  health, 318
  rate, and debt financing, 330
  state, 4. See also Reimbursement
Regulatory agency, 182-183
Regulatory mapping, 147
Rehabilitation, 165, 527
Reimbursement, 281-307
  for allied professionals, 295
  as capital formation, 316, 317-318
  capital investment and, 329-330
  for computer purchases, 387
  constraints on hospital systems, 133-134
  cost, computer model for, 217
  first-dollar, medical benefits, 529
  formula, Medicare, 288
  and leasing, 342-344
  mechanism, planning for, 144
  and organizational sharing, 122-123
  services covered, 295
Relative value units (RVUs), 586
Reliability (patient record), 427
Religion, 199
Religious order shared services, 395-396

Relocation expense reimbursement, 534
Remedial action, 46
Remmlinger, Elaine, 645n
Renal dialysis, 716
Renting, 339, *340-341*
Replacement costs, 337
Reports:
  construction project, 361
  HIS benefits, 405
  in management control, 208
  monthly departmental, 249
  monthly MBO, 39
  productivity monitoring, 570-573, *557, 558*
  quarterly progress, 142-143
  special problem, 248-250
Requalification principle, 47
Request for proposal (RFP), computer, 385, *386*
Research:
  market, 190, 193-195
  and marketing, 183-184
  medical experimentation and, 693-694
Residence, 199, 310
Residents, 687
Resource allocation, *8, 178*
Resource utilization, 123, 265-266
Respondeat superior, 685, 724-725, 726
Responsibility, 46-47, *64,* 101, 142-143, 216
Responsibility center budgeting, 241-242
Retainages, 361
Retirement, 518, 524, 525
Retirement benefits, 524-526, 531, 534
  capital accumulation for, 526
Revenue budget, 242
Revenues, 216, 218-219
  deferred, 325
  departmental, 586
  forecasting, 225, 227
  non-operating, 219
  patient-related, 218-219
Revocation of license, 722
Revolving credit agreement, 325-326
Rewards, 10, 437, 497, 579
Reynolds, James, 128n
Rezler, Julius, 506n, 608n, 610n
Rice, James A., 172n
Richardson, William C., 49n
Rifai, Ahmed, 276n
Rights, patient, 692
Risk, 12, 162, 170
Roach, William H., Jr., 705n

Robinson, Larry M., 181n, 190n
Rohrs, Walter F., 71n, 85n, 91n, 375n
Roseman, Cyril, 174n
Rosoff, Arnold J., 692n
Rowland, Beatrice L., 422n, 458n, 492n, 589n
Rowland, Howard S., 442n, 458n, 492n, 589n
Rubin, Leonard, 642n
Rubright, Robert, 188n, 201n
Run out claims, 523
Rural areas, 122, 167, 174

S

Sabbatical leave, 534
Sacco, John J., M.D., 426n
Safety, 5, 554, 621
 needs, 480
 occupational, 672-677, 724
Salaries, 4, 437, 508-517
 and absenteeism/turnover, 489
 continuances, 488
 guidelines, *509-510*
 merit vs longevity, 512-514
 policies, 508-515
 as short term financing, 325
 starting, 514
Sanctions, 501
Sanitation, 677, 716
Saturation (problem solving), 76
Scheduling, 575, 577
Schlien, Dr. A., 13
Schmitz, Homer H., 389n, 395n, 417n
Schwartz, E. B., 85n
Scioto Valley Convalescent Center, 332
Scott, Terence, 164n
Screening services, 164-165, 689
Section, 8, *576*
Security, 427, 614, 622-623, 709
Seifert, Vernon D., 142n
Self-assessment, 82
Self-confidence, 11-12, 21, 58
Self-dealing, 724
Self-evaluation, 14-16, 60
Self-fulfillment needs, 481
Self-insurance, 520, 521-522
Self-knowledge, 58
Self-logging, 556, 560, 572
Semiprofessionals, 476-477
Seniority, 10, 617-618
Senior managers, 6-11
Sensitivity sessions, 74
Sentinel health events, 637

Service:
 delivery trends, 147-148
 populations, 156
Services, 137, 216
 ancillary, 295
 centralization, 120, 132
 community gaps in, 137, 153
 cost finding for new, 335
 decisions, 126
 design, for primary care, 171
 duplication, *180*
 extending, 158-160
 integrated, 139
 intensity, 552
 need and demand, 147
 new, 158, 162-166, 335
 outside, 272-273
 required by licensure, 715
 sharing, 273
Severance pay, 534
Sex, 199
Shaffert, Thomas K., 405n
Shared computer systems, 385, 397-399
Shared management model (contract management), 125
Shared Medical Systems, Inc. (King of Prussia, Pa.), 411
Shared power, 74
Shared service (computer) approaches,, 395-397
Shared services, 117, 552
 data processing, 273, 385, 395-399
 opportunities for, 122-123
 as system integration, 116
Sheldon, Alan, 45n, 120n
Sherman Act, 133
Shifts, 619
Shortell, Stephen, 49n
Short term financing, 325-326
Shyavitz, Linda, 191n
Sick leave, 488, 490, 528, 531, 534, 620
Side:
 construction, 355, *369-370*
 visits, 386
Simon, James D., 179n
Simulation, 94, 156, 302
Sisters of Mercy Health Care Corporation, 130
Skilled nursing facility-intermediate care facility (SNF-ICF), 174
Skills, *15*
Skoler, Martin E., 62n, 444n, 455n, 459n, 463n, 508n, 510n, 515n, 522n, 534n, 546n, 548n, 592n, 594n, 600n, 608n, 613n, 621n, 675n, 681n

Skousen, Max B., 553n
Slater Nursing Competencies Rating Scale, 650-651
Slide rule policies, 504
Sloane, Beverly LeBov, 562n, 563n
Sloane, Robert M., 562n, 563n
Slote, Leslie M., Dr., 438n
Small Business Administration, 318
Smalley, Harold E., 151n
Smith, Howard L., 539n, 540n
Smith, Stephen W., 432n
Social maladjustment, 25
Social marketing, 188
Social needs, 480-481
Social Security, 281, 294, 518, 528, 588
Software, 383, 401
 hospital applications, *380*
 purchases, 383-387
 rights to, 417
 selecting, 386
Solicitation, 319
Space programming, 354
Sparks, Leroy, 72n
Specialty consulting firms, 95-96
Special user committee (construction), 348
Specificity of control, 46
Speculation, 6
Speeches, 453-455, 603
Spencer, Stewart and Associates (Chicago), 20
Sports medicine, 165
Springate, David D., 125n
Stability, organizational, 102
Staff:
 audit, 49
 authority, 103
 development, 437
 professionalism, *180*
 scheduling, 80
 specialists, 102
 support, 150-151
Staffing, 437, 586-589
 analysis, 574
 budget calculation worksheet, *563*
 quality assurance, 631
 variable, 587-589
Staging concept, 637
Standard hours, defined, 560
Standard and Poor's Register, 330
Standards
 control by, 9
 as operating indicators, 572
 review, 500
 work, 554
Standby time, 560
State government:

capital financing, 315
conversion approval, 176
disability benefits, 518
health authorities, 4, 628
hospital, 3
laws, 4
list of CEO duties, 5-6
Statistical budget reports, 250
Statutory reports, 710
Step down cost finding, 222, 223, *298-299*
Stewardship, 214
   employee, 554
Stewart, John, 453n
Stokes, Judy Ford, 587n
Stop-smoking clinics, 165
Strategic planning, 7, 143-151
   approach, 146-148
   characteristics, 145
   financial, 143-144
   vs master planning, 145
   process, *146*
   successful, 150-151
Stress, 16-19, 67, 69, 166
Stretch target, 277
Strikes, 597, 600, 615, 621-623, 697
Structural:
   followership profile, *32-33*
   leadership profile, *30-31*
   measurements, 629
Stunden, Ann E., 128n
Subcontractors, 95
Subordinate:
   leaders, 59-60, *61*
   management, 58-70. *See also* Managers; Subordinates
Subordinates, 438-441
   managing, 58-70
   supervisors relations with, 439-440. *See also* Employees; Worker
Subpoenas, 712-713
Success, 12, 83
Suggestion programs, 534
Summer, C. E., 76n
Super disaster manual, 668
Supervision, 106, 594
Supervisors:
   and absenteeism, 491-492
   appraising, 60, *62*
   capabilities upgraded, 552
   coaching, 445
   as communication target, 445
   goal setting interviews, 39
   qualifications, 102
   relations with subordinates, 439-440, 440-441

style, and absenteeism, 488-489
   with unions, 605, 608
Supplemental Security Income (SSI), 281
Supplementary benefits, 530-531
Supplementary organizational charts, 106, 108
Surgery, 579, *648*
Surgical centers, 182
Surveys, 96-97, 351
Survivor's income benefits, 526-527
Suspension, 503
   of license, 722
Sweetland, John, 345n, 367n
Swing beds, 174
System review, 574
Systems analysis, 152
Systems engineering, 151-152

T

Taft-Hartley Act, 597
Task:
   forces (HIS), 413-414
   list, 565
   operating room, *559-560*
   sheets, daily, *561*
   timed, and work standard development, 554
Tax deferred annuities, 535
Taxes, 308-312, 339
Tax-exempt financing, 326, *327*
Tax-exempt revenue bonds, 315, 320, *322*
Tax-exempt status, 162
Tax law, 133
Tax Reform Act of 1969, 310
Taylor, Elworth, 117n
Taylor, Robert B., 246n, 247n, 251n
Technicon Medical Information Systems Corporation, 411
Technicon video matrix terminal, 410
Technology, 147, 268-269, 552
Telephone, 6, *87*
Temper, 551
Terminal:
   diseases, 25
   patients, *699*
Terminals:
   computer, 387-441
   selective lockout, 427
Termination, 492
Texas Children's Hospital, 118
Texas Heart Institute, 118
Texas Medical Center (TMC), 118
Thieme, Carl W., 145n

Third party insurance carriers, 188
Third party payors, 188, 281, 295. *See also* Reimbursement
Thompson, Richard E., 631n, 634n, 635n
Tichon, Michael J., 292n, 294n
Time, 6, 84-94, 554-555
Timecard projects, 360
Time logging, 556
Time management, 46, 84-94
Time-motion studies, 554-555
Time standards, 574
Timetable, budget, *237,* 238
Timing, 23, 78, *346*
Tissue committee, 111
Titles, 10
Toole, Jay E., 348n
Tools, 677
Top management, MBO training for, 34
Torts, 689-691, 725
Tours, 6
Tracers, 638
Tracey, William, 501
Trade credit, 325
Training, 5, 9, 102
   in-service employee, 449
   leadership, 60
   programs, 594
Transfer procedure, 10
Transfers, lateral, 514
Transfusion, 695. *See also* Blood transfusions
Trauma, 488
Treatment:
   emergency, 693
   equipment and procedures, 552
   failure to warn of risks in, 683
   patient's refusal of, *698*
Trends:
   in institutional data, 148
   in productivity, 552-553
Troubled hospital syndrome, 233-234
Trustees, 723-725. *See also* Board of directors
Trusts, 308-312, 520
Tuberculosis, 6
Turban, Efraim, 567n
Turnover, 71, 487-489, 494-495
   costs of, *292,* 492

U

Ultra sound equipment, 274
Unanimity, 113-114
Underdelegation, 80
Understaffing, 570

Unemployment compensation, 534
Uniforms, 531
Unions, 592-632
 agreement model (management proposal), 606-608
 authorization card, 595-596
 hit list, 600
 organizing campaign, 594-600
 and personnel administration studies, 593
 recognition, 597, 614
 security and, 614
 studied, 594
 visitation, 617
 vulnerability to, 593-594
 why employees join, 592-594
Unitrust, 309
Units, 8
University of Oregon Health Sciences Center, 377
Unpaid leave, 620-621
Upward mobility programs, 437
Urban areas, 122
Uris, Auren, 14n, 60n, 75n, 79n
User satisfaction (MIS), *424,* 425
Use Your Head (Levenstein), 72
Utilization, 268
 forecasting, 155-156
 of hospital services, 148
 human resource, 437
 of programs and services, 153-154
 projected, 154
 resource, 123
 trends, 570
Utilization review, 655-663
 committee, 111
 personnel, 641

V

Vacations, 10, 531, 534, 619-620
Value:
 analysis, 275-276
 net present, 333
 system, 102
Variable price contracts, 359
Variable staffing, 587-589
 and part-time personnel, 587
Variance analysis, budget, 250-253
Variances, in licensure requirements, 715
Vending machine permits, 716
Vendors:
 computer, 383-389, 397
 health care expertise, 399
Veninga, Robert, 110n
Ventilation, 677
Verbal contact, 6
Verbal physicians' orders, 704

Versatility, 544
Vertical condominium, 125
Vertical diversification, 161
Vertical integration, 149
Videotape training, 57
Visitors, 4, *87*
Vocational counseling, 534
Volume:
 mix, 586
 patient, 233
 reduction, 270
 variance, patient revenue, 253
Von Bergen, C. W., Jr., 112n
Vraciu, Robert A., 132n, 269n

W

Wages, 4, 437
 automatic deposit benefit, 534
 guidelines, *509-510*
 incentive plans, 590
 industry standard, 601
 minimums, 618
 as short term financing, 325
 studies, 594
 variations reported, 570
Waiting time, 560
Waivers, 715
Warnings, 503
Warranties (HIS), 418
Waters, Kathleen A., 242n, 664n
Wedgwood, Hensleigh C., 110n, 114n
Wedley, William C., 495n
Weed, Lawrence L., 405
Wegmiller, Donald C., 119n
Weinberg, Howard, 627n
Welding, 677
Whitney, John J., 311n
Whitted, Gary S., 377n
Whittington, F. Brown, 181n, 190n
Wholly owned subsidiary model (contract management), 125
Williams, H. Glenn, 384n
Williams, Kathleen N., 629n
Willman, David D., 295n, 298n, 301n
Wilson, Thomas E., 145n
Witt & Dolan Associates, Inc. (Oak Brook, Ill.), 19
Wohlking, Wallace, 502n
Wolford, G. Rodney, 160n
Wood, Jack C., 207n, 236n, 295n
Word processing, 434-436
Work:
 area, 71
 backlog, 71
 conditions, 488, 489, 594
 delays, 560

 flow, 102
 location, 102
 methods, 554
 planning, 82-83, 488
 success criteria for, 621
 and type of management, 102
 volume, 560. *See also* Workload
Workaholics, 67, 69
Workday, 618-619
Work distribution chart, *564, 565-566, 568, 569*
Worker:
 absenteeism, 487-491
 job enrichment, 483-486
 long-term, benefits, 518
 resources, 554
 satisfaction, 483, 484
 turnover, 487-489, 492-498
Work force, forecasting, 156
Working capital requirements (AHA), *296*
Workload, 577
 and census, 588
 distribution, average, *589*
 HIS benefits, 405
 man/hour, 580
 projections, construction, 354, 366-367
 units, *368-369*
Workmen's Compensation, 220, 518, 528
Work sampling, 47, *564*
Work simplification, 562-567
Worksheets:
 budget, 238-239
 FVA resource allocation, *279*
 staffing budget calculation, 563
Work standards, developing, 554-562
Workweek, 618-619
Written warning, 503

X

X-rays, 272
 personnel, 5

Y

Young, William E., 554n

Z

Zeleznik, Carter, 655n
Zero-base budgeting, 240-241
Zuckerman, Howard S., 132n